PHILIP'S

STREET A
Staffordshire

C000296790

www.philips-maps.co.uk
First published in 1995 by
Philip's, a division of
Octopus Publishing Group Ltd
www.octopusbooks.co.uk
Endeavour House
189 Shaftesbury Avenue
London WC2H 8JY
An Hachette UK Company
www.hachette.co.uk

Third colour edition 2005
Third impression 2012

STACB

ISBN 978-1-84907-248-9 (spiral)

© Philip's 2007

Ordnance Survey®

This product includes mapping data licensed
from Ordnance Survey® with the permission
of the Controller of Her Majesty's Stationery
Office. © Crown copyright 2007. All rights
reserved. Licence number 100011710.

Contents

III **Key to map symbols**

IV **Key to map pages**

VI **Route planning**

X Administrative and Postcode boundaries

1 **Street maps** at 3½ inches to 1 mile

282 **Street maps** of centres of Hanley, Newcastle-under-
Lyme, Longton and Stafford at 7 inches to 1 mile

286 **Index** of towns and villages

289 **Index** of streets, hospitals, industrial estates, railway
stations, schools, shopping centres, universities and
places of interest

Digital Data

The exceptionally high-quality mapping found in this atlas is available as digital data in TIFF format,
which is easily convertible to other bitmapped (raster) image formats.

The index is also available in digital form as a standard database table. It contains all the details
found in the printed index together with the National Grid reference for the map square in which each
entry is named.

For further information and to discuss your requirements, please contact
philips@mapsinternational.co.uk

PHILIP'S MAPS
the Gold Standard for drivers

◆ **Philip's street atlases cover all of England, Wales, Northern Ireland and much of Scotland**

- ◆ Every named street is shown, including alleys, lanes and walkways
- ◆ Thousands of additional features marked: stations, public buildings, car parks, places of interest
- ◆ Route-planning maps to get you close to your destination
- ◆ Postcodes on the maps and in the index
- ◆ Widely used by the emergency services, transport companies and local authorities

For national mapping, choose **Philip's Navigator Britain** the most detailed road atlas available of England, Wales and Scotland. Hailed by Auto Express as 'the ultimate road atlas', Navigator shows every road and lane in Britain.

Street atlases currently available

England

Bedfordshire and Luton	Surrey
Berkshire	East Sussex
Birmingham and West Midlands	West Sussex
Bristol and Bath	Tyne and Wear
Buckinghamshire and Milton Keynes	Warwickshire and Coventry
Cambridgeshire and Peterborough	Wiltshire and Swindon
Cheshire	Worcestershire
Cornwall	East Yorkshire Northern Lincolnshire
Cumbria	North Yorkshire
Derbyshire	South Yorkshire
Devon	West Yorkshire
Dorset	
County Durham and Teesside	**Wales**
Essex	Anglesey, Conwy and Gwynedd
North Essex	Cardiff, Swansea and The Valleys
South Essex	Carmarthenshire, Pembrokeshire and Swansea
Gloucestershire and Bristol	Ceredigion and South Gwynedd
Hampshire	
North Hampshire	Denbighshire, Flintshire, Wrexham
South Hampshire	Herefordshire Monmouthshire
Herefordshire Monmouthshire	Powys
Hertfordshire	
Isle of Wight	**Scotland**
Kent	Aberdeenshire
East Kent	Ayrshire
West Kent	Dumfries and Galloway
Lancashire	Edinburgh and East Central Scotland
Leicestershire and Rutland	Fife and Tayside
Lincolnshire	Glasgow and West Central Scotland
Liverpool and Merseyside	Inverness and Moray
London	Lanarkshire
Greater Manchester	Scottish Borders
Norfolk	
Northamptonshire	**Northern Ireland**
Northumberland	County Antrim and County Londonderry
Nottinghamshire	County Armagh and County Down
Oxfordshire	Belfast
Shropshire	County Tyrone and County Fermanagh
Somerset	
Staffordshire	
Suffolk	

Philip's maps and atlases are available from bookshops, motorway services and petrol statio

For further details visit
www.philips-maps.co.uk

Key to map symbols

Motorway with junction number	
Primary route – dual/single carriageway	
A road – dual/single carriageway	
B road – dual/single carriageway	
Minor road – dual/single carriageway	
Other minor road – dual/single carriageway	
Road under construction	
Tunnel, covered road	
Speed cameras – single, multiple	
Rural track, private road or narrow road in urban area	
Gate or obstruction to traffic – may not apply at all times or to all vehicles	
Path, bridleway, byway open to all traffic, restricted byway	
Pedestrianised area	
Postcode boundaries	
County and unitary authority boundaries	
Railway with station	
Tunnel	
Railway under construction	
Metro station	
Private railway station	
Miniature railway	
Tramway, tramway under construction	
Tram stop, tram stop under construction	
Bus, coach station	

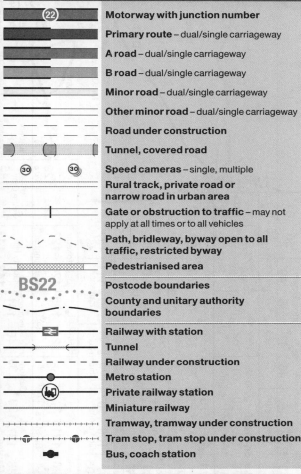

BS22

Ambulance station	
Coastguard station	
Fire station	
Police station	
Accident and Emergency entrance to hospital	
Hospital	H
Place of worship	+
Information centre – open all year	i
Shopping centre	
Parking	P
Park and Ride	P&R
Post Office	PO
Camping site	
Caravan site	
Golf course	
Picnic site	
Non-Roman antiquity	
Roman antiquity	ROMAN FORT
Important buildings, schools, colleges, universities and hospitals	Univ
Built-up area	
Woods	
Water name	River Medway
River, weir	
Stream	
Canal, lock, tunnel	
Water	
Tidal water	

Adjoining page indicators

112   58   87

The small numbers around the edges of the maps identify the 1-kilometre National Grid lines

The dark grey border on the inside edge of some pages indicates that the mapping does not continue onto the adjacent page

Enlarged maps only

Railway or bus station building	
Place of interest	
Parkland	

Abbreviations

Acad	Academy	Meml	Memorial
Allot Gdns	Allotments	Mon	Monument
Cemy	Cemetery	Mus	Museum
C Ctr	Civic centre	Obsy	Observatory
CH	Club house	Pal	Royal palace
Coll	College	PH	Public house
Crem	Crematorium	Recn Gd	Recreation ground
Ent	Enterprise	Resr	Reservoir
Ex H	Exhibition hall	Ret Pk	Retail park
Ind Est	Industrial Estate	Sch	School
IRB Sta	Inshore rescue boat station	Sh Ctr	Shopping centre
Inst	Institute	TH	Town hall / house
Ct	Law court	Trad Est	Trading estate
L Ctr	Leisure centre	Univ	University
LC	Level crossing	W Twr	Water tower
Liby	Library	Wks	Works
Mkt	Market	YH	Youth hostel

The map scale on the pages numbered in blue is 3½ inches to 1 mile
5.52 cm to 1 km • 1: 18 103

| 0 | ¼ mile | ½ mile | ¾ mile | 1 mile |
| 0 | 250m | 500m | 750m | 1km |

The map scale on the pages numbered in red is 7 inches to 1 mile
11.04 cm to 1 km • 1: 9051

| 0 | 220yds | 440yds | 660yds | ½ mile |
| 0 | 125m | 250m | 375m | 500m |

Key to map pages

| 114 | Map pages at 3½ inches to 1 mile |
| 284 | Map pages at 7 inches to 1 mile |

Leicestershire STREET ATLAS

Warwickshire STREET ATLAS

Birmingham & West Midlands STREET ATLAS

Worcestershire STREET ATLAS

Shropshire STREET ATLAS

Melbourne • Ibstock • Measham • Newton Regis • Bedworth • Kenilworth

Newton Solney • Ashby-de-la-Zouch • Shuttington • Atherstone • Nuneaton • Coleshill • Dorridge

Swadlincote • Clifton Campville • Wood End • Castle Bromwich • Solihull

Ahlow 166 167 Burton upon Trent • Netherseal 218 219 • Thorpe Constantine 234 235 236 • Wigginton 251 Tamworth • Fazeley 262

165 186 • 217 219 Edingale 216 • Harlaston • 250 261 Middleton 260

164 185 Barton-under-Needwood • Elford 215 • Whittington 232 233 • Hints 248 249 Hopwas 259

163 184 • Yoxall 202 • Orgreave 200 201 • Alrewas 214 • Wall A51 230 231 • Shenstone 246 247 • Roughley 258

162 183 Hamstall Ridware 181 • King's Bromley 199 • Handsacre 198 • Farewell 213 • Lichfield Little Hay 245 • Sutton Coldfield 257

161 182 Colton 180 • Rugeley 179 • Armitage 197 • Longdon Green 212 • Elmhurst • Hammerwich 229 • Stonnall 244 • Aldridge Little Aston 256

160 Admaston • 178 Colwich • Slitting Mill 196 • Chorley • Longdon Green 211 • Burntwood 228 • Brownhills 243 • Walsall

159 Great Haywood 177 Brocton 195 • Pye Green 210 • Hednesford • Little Wyrley 242 • Willenhall

158 157 Stafford 176 • Bednall 194 • Huntington 209 • Cannock 227 226 • Shareshill 241 • Essington

156 Ingestre 175 Coppenhall 193 192 Penkridge • Gailey Hatherton 208 • Norton Canes 225 • Featherstone 240 • M6

155 285 174 Acton Trussell • Lapley 207 • Stretton 206 • Brewood 224 • Coven 223 • Codsall 239 Oaken 238 • Perton 255 • Wolverhampton • Sedgley 266 Dudley 271

154 Doxey 173 172 Haughton • Apeton 191 • Church Eaton 190 • Kiddemore Green 222 • Tettenhall 254 • Lower Penn 265 • Himley 270 • Wordsley 275

153 152 Derrington 171 Gnosall 170 • Outwoods 189 • High Onn 188 Orslow • Bishops Wood 221 220 • Bobbington 253 • Albrighton 237 • Wombourne 269 • Swindon 268 • Kingswinford 274 • Stourton 279 Stourbridge

151 150 Norbury 169 • Edgmond 168 • Chetwynd Aston 187 • Weston-under-Lizard • Boningale • Pattingham 252 • Claverley 267 • Enville 273 • Kinver 277 • Blakedown 281

149 Sutton 149 Forton 168 Newport • Donnington • Shifnal • Rudge 263 • Trysull 264 • Seisdon • Six Ashes 272 • Romsley 276 • Cookley 280

Pickstock • Telford • Dawley • Madeley • Much Wenlock • Bridgnorth • Kinver • Bewdley • Stourport on Severn

Shawbury • Wellington • Tenbury Wells • Kidderminster

Motorways and A-roads shown include: A42, A511, A444, A5, A513, A515, A519, A460, A460, A449, A41, A5, A518, A464, A454, A458, A442, A456, A469, A449, A450, A451, A117, M6, M42, M6 Toll, M54, M69, M40, M5, M45, A452, A446, A4091, A51, A38, A452, A41, A34, A40, A4041, A4123, A4036, A491, A461, A34, A4040

Route planning

X

Cheshire

CW12

SK11

Flash
Wincle

Longnor
SK17

Hartington

ST8
Biddulph

Leek

Warslow

Alstonefield

ST13

Staffordshire
Moorlands

DE6

Derbyshire

Kidsgrove

CW1

ST7

ST6

ST9

Cheddleton

Weston
CW2

Stoke-on-
Trent

ST2

Werrington

Kingsley

CW5

Betley

ST1

City of
Stoke-
on-Trent

Cheadle

Mayfield

Newcastle-
under-Lyme

CW3

Newcastle-
under-Lyme

ST4

ST3

ST10

Alton

Woore

ST5

Baldwin's
Gate

ST11

Rocester

Norton in
Hales

Ashley

ST12

Barlaston

Church Leigh

ST14

TF9

Swynnerton

Yarnfield

ST15

Stone

Uttoxeter

DE6

Sudbury

Marchington

Market
Drayton

Shropshire

ST21

Eccleshall

S t a f f o r d s h i r e

Stafford

ST18

Weston

Abbots
Bromley

East
Staffordshire

DE65

Tutbury

Egginton

Burton upon
Trent

DE15

ST16

Stafford

DE13

DE14

ST20

Gnosall

Haughton

Brocton

ST17

WS15

Yoxall

DE11

TF10

Newport

Rugeley

Longdon

Alrewas

DE12

Telford and
Wrekin

Cannock
Chase

WS12

WS13

Fradley

Netherseal

Weston under
Lizard

TF11

Wheaton
Aston

Penkridge

ST19

Cannock

WS11

Lichfield

WS14

Lichfield

B79

Newton
Regis

South
Staffordshire

Burntwood

WS7

Shenstone

Albrighton

WV10

WV8

WV9

Featherstone

WS6

WS8

WV7

Codsall

WV11

WS3

Brownhills

Tamworth

B78

Tamworth

Drayton
Bassett

B77

SJ
SO

Shropshire

WV6

Pattingham

WV3

WV2

Walsall

WS9

Aldridge

B74

B75

SK
SP

Warwickshire

WV4

Sandwell

WV5

Wombourne

Claverley

Sedgley

DY3

DY1

WV15

DY6

Dudley

DY7

Kinver

DY8

SO
SP

DY12

DY11

DY10

Blakedown

Worcestershire

Major administrative and Postcode boundaries

County and unitary authority boundaries
District boundaries
Postcode boundaries
Area covered by this atlas

Scale
0   5   10   15 km
0   5   10 miles

Birmingham
City of Wolverhampton

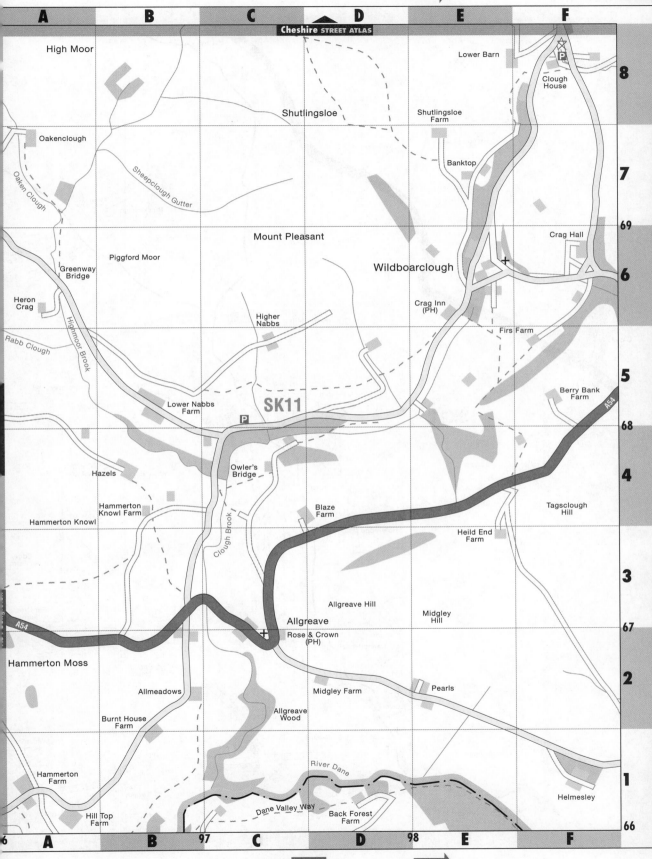

Cheshire STREET ATLAS

A   B   C   D   E   F

High Moor

Oakenclough

Oaken Clough

Sheepclough Gutter

Shutlingsloe

Lower Barn

Clough House

Shutlingsloe Farm

Banktop

Mount Pleasant

Greenway Bridge

Piggford Moor

Wildboarclough

Crag Hall

Heron Crag

Rabb Clough

Highmoor Brook

Higher Nabbs

Crag Inn (PH)

Firs Farm

SK11

Berry Bank Farm

A54

Lower Nabbs Farm

Owler's Bridge

Hazels

Hammerton Knowl Farm

Hammerton Knowl

Clough Brook

Blaze Farm

Heild End Farm

Tagsclough Hill

Allgreave Hill

Midgley Hill

A54

Allgreave

Rose & Crown (PH)

Hammerton Moss

Allmeadows

Midgley Farm

Pearls

Burnt House Farm

Allgreave Wood

Hammerton Farm

River Dane

Helmesley

Hill Top Farm

Dane Valley Way

Back Forest Farm

A   B   C   D   E   F

6   97   98

8   7   69   6   5   68   4   3   67   2   1   66

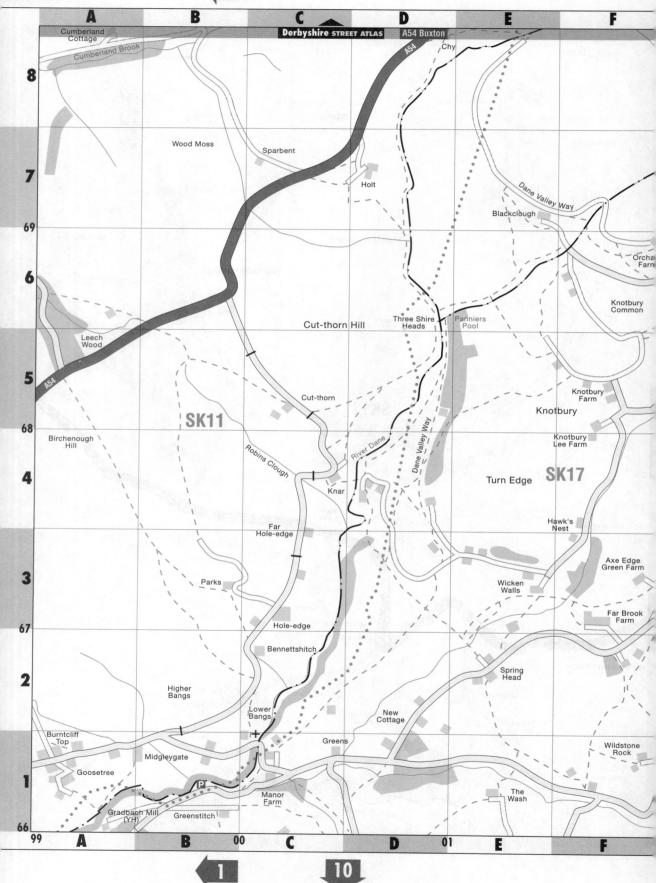

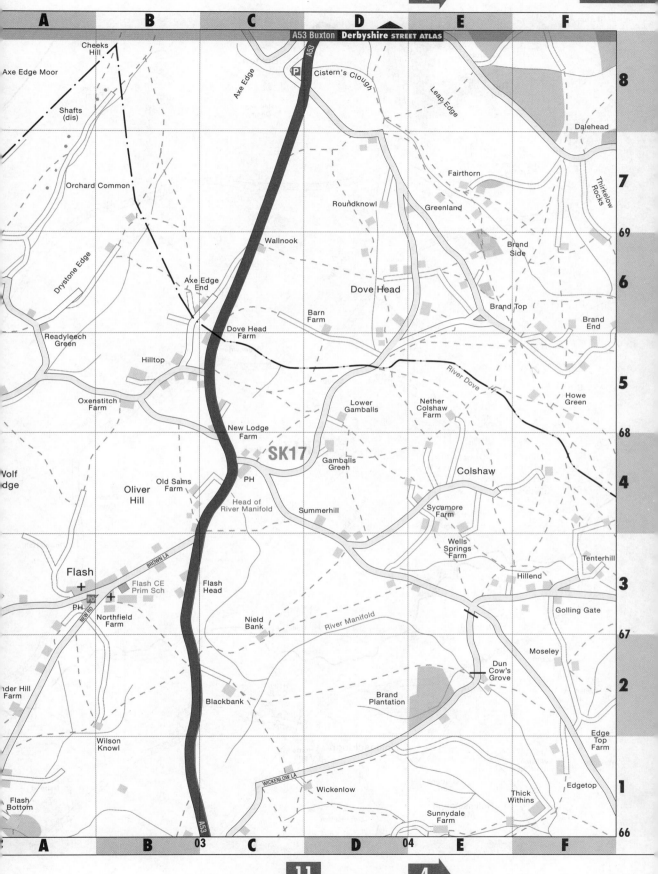

A B C D E F

8
7
69
6
5
68
4
3
67
2
1
66

A53 Buxton **Derbyshire** STREET ATLAS

Cheeks Hill
Axe Edge Moor
Shafts (dis)
Orchard Common
Drystone Edge
Readyleech Green
Hilltop
Oxenstitch Farm
Wolf Edge
Oliver Hill
Old Sams Farm
Flash
Flash CE Prim Sch
PH
PO
Northfield Farm
NEW RD
der Hill Farm
Wilson Knowl
Flash Bottom

Axe Edge
Axe Edge End
Axe Edge End
Dove Head Farm
Wallnook
New Lodge Farm
SK17
PH
Head of River Manifold
BROWN LA
Flash Head
Blackbank
WICKENLOW LA
A53

Cistern's Clough
Leap Edge
Roundknowl
Dove Head
Barn Farm
Lower Gamballs
Gamballs Green
Summerhill
Nield Bank
River Manifold
Wickenlow

Fairthorn
Greenland
Brand Side
Brand Top
Nether Colshaw Farm
Colshaw
Sycamore Farm
Wells Springs Farm
Hillend
Brand Plantation
Dun Cow's Grove
Sunnydale Farm

Dalehead
Thirkelow Rocks
Brand End
Howe Green
Tenterhill
Golling Gate
Moseley
Edge Top Farm
Edgetop
Thick Withins

River Dove

P

03
04

11
4

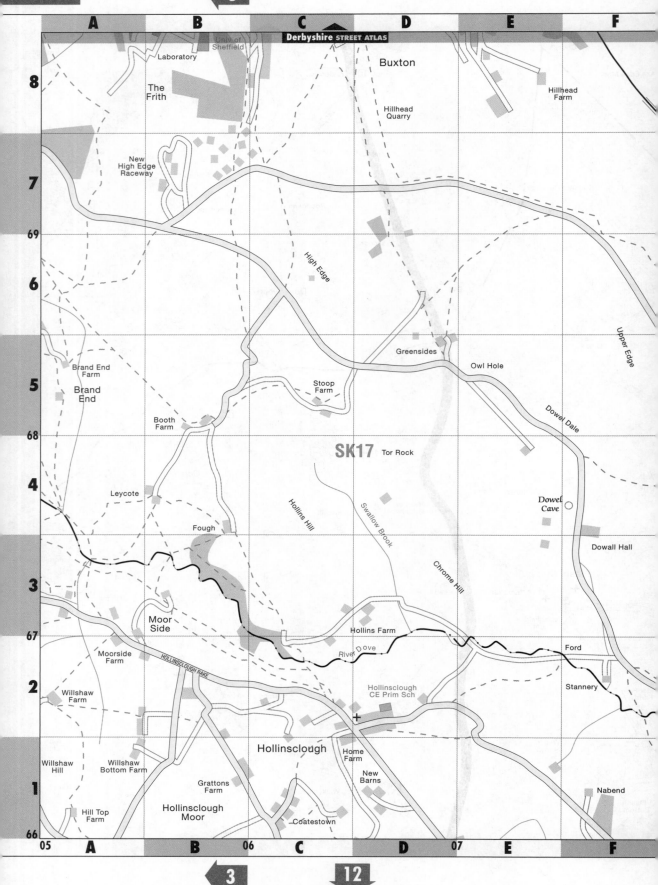

Derbyshire STREET ATLAS

A515 Buxton

A5270 Bakewell (A6)

A515

B5053

BRIERLOW BAR

A5270

Brierlow Bar Farm

Chelmorton

A5270

OLD COALPIT LA

Farditch Farm

THE DITCH

DITCH COTTS

Netherlow Farm

Morland

Red Hurst

Hindlow

Brierlow Grange

Nether Low

Buxton Quarry

Hindlow Tunnel

Hind Low

69

STERNDALE MOOR

Blindlow Hollow

6

Brier Low

Derbyshire STREET ATLAS

Great Low

5

68

Harley Grange

SK17

Greatlow

A515 Ashbourne

A515

Dowlow Farm

4

Jericho Farm

Hindlow Quarry

Hatch-a-Way

Dowlow Works

Glutton Dale

Fernydale

3

Glutton Farm

DALE VIEW

Earl Sterndale CE Prim Sch

Earl Sterndale

67

Parkhouse Hill

Quiet Woman (PH)

Hall Farm

Home Farm

HOME FARM COTTS

PO

Braemar House

2

Hitter

Underhill Farm

Mast

Aldery Cliff

Abbotside Farm

Glutton Bridge

River Dove

Fox Hole Cave

High Wheeldon

Wheeldon Trees

1

B5053

Underhill

Green La

66

8

A

B

09

C

D

10

E

F

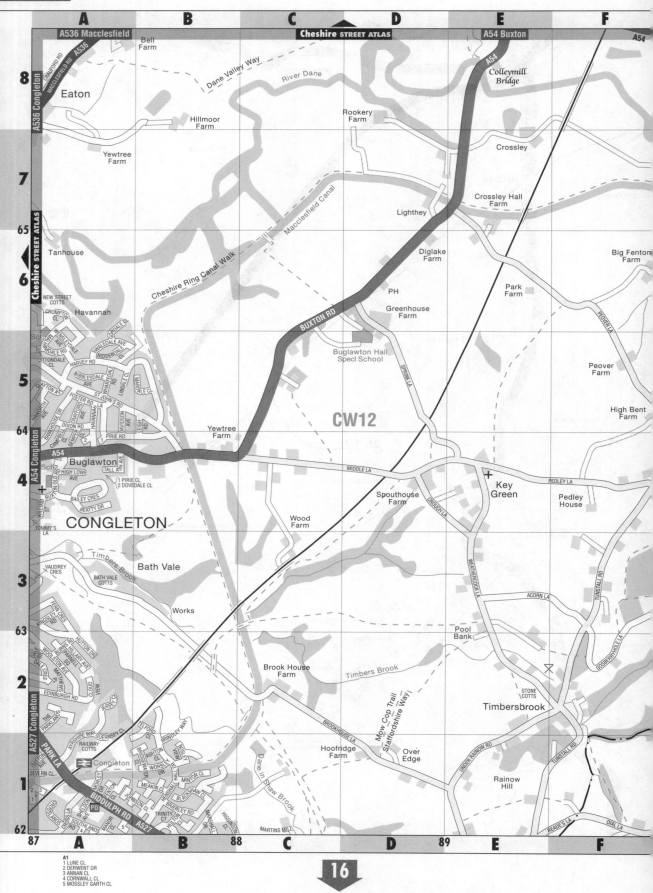

A536 Macclesfield

A54 Buxton

A54

Cheshire STREET ATLAS

Bell Farm

Dane Valley Way

River Dane

Colleymill Bridge

Eaton

Hillmoor Farm

Rookery Farm

Crossley

Yewtree Farm

Crossley Hall Farm

Macclesfield Canal

Lighthey

Big Fenton Farm

Tanhouse

Cheshire Ring Canal Walk

Diglake Farm

Park Farm

PEOVER LA

NEW STREET COTTS

PH

Havannah

BUXTON RD

Greenhouse Farm

Peover Farm

SPINK LA

Buglawton Hall Specl School

High Bent Farm

CW12

Yewtree Farm

Buglawton

MIDDLE LA

Key Green

REDLEY LA

Pedley House

1 PIRIE CL
2 DOVEDALE CL

Spouthouse Farm

CROUCH LA

CONGLETON

Wood Farm

WEATHERBROOK LA

ACORN LA

TUNSTALL RD

Timbers Brook

Bath Vale

BATH VALE COTTS

Pool Bank

GOSBERRYHOLE LA

Works

Timbers Brook

STONE COTTS

Brook House Farm

Timbersbrook

BROOKHOUSE LA

Mow Cop Trail

Staffordshire Way

Over Edge

Hoofridge Farm

UNDER RAINOW RD

TUNSTALL RD

Congleton

Dane in Shaw Brook

Rainow Hill

REANE'S LA

PARK LA

A527 Congleton

BIDDULPH RD

A527

PO

Martins Mill

DIAL LA

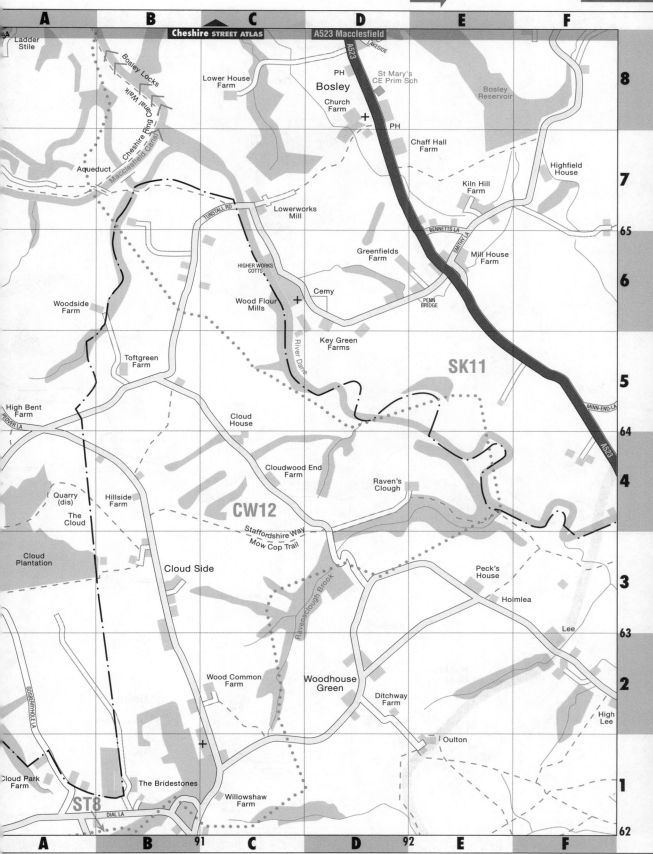

Cheshire STREET ATLAS

A523 Macclesfield

A B C D E F

8

7

65

6

5

64

4

3

63

2

1

62

Ladder
Stile

Bosley Locks

LAKESIDE

St Mary's
CE Prim Sch

Bosley
Reservoir

PH

Bosley

Church
Farm

PH

Chaff Hall
Farm

Highfield
House

Lower House
Farm

Kiln Hill
Farm

Aqueduct

Cheshire Ring (Macclesfield Canal) Canal Walk

BENNETTS LA

SMITHY LA

Mill House
Farm

TUNSTALE RD

Lowerworks
Mill

Greenfields
Farm

Woodside
Farm

HIGHER WORKS
COTTS

Cemy

PENN
BRIDGE

Wood Flour
Mills

Key Green
Farms

SK11

River Dane

Toftgreen
Farm

High Bent
Farm

PECOVER LA

Cloud
House

MINN-END-LA

A523

Cloudwood End
Farm

Raven's
Clough

Quarry
(dis)

Hillside
Farm

CW12

Peck's
House

The
Cloud

Staffordshire Way
Mow Cop Trail

Cloud
Plantation

Cloud Side

Ravensclough Brook

Holmlea

Lee

Wood Common
Farm

Woodhouse
Green

Ditchway
Farm

High
Lee

GOSBERRYHOLE LA

Oulton

Cloud Park
Farm

ST8

The Bridestones

DIAL LA

Willowshaw
Farm

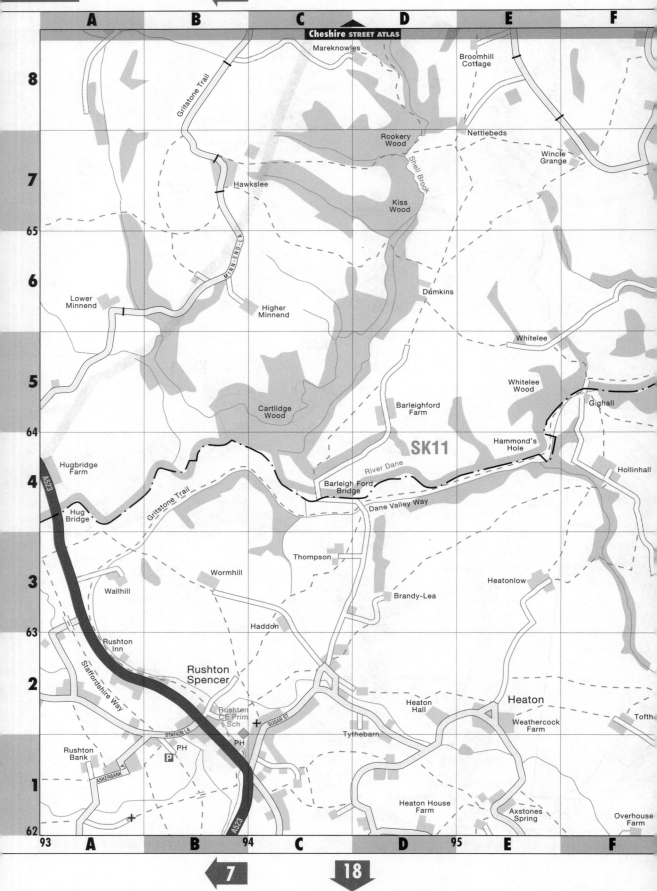

A   B   C   D   E   F

8

Mareknowles

Broomhill
Cottage

Gritstone Trail

7

Hawkslee

Rookery
Wood

Nettlebeds

Shell Brook

Wincle
Grange

65

Kiss
Wood

MINN-END-LA

6

Lower
Minnend

Higher
Minnend

Dumkins

Whitelee

Whitelee
Wood

5

Gighall

Cartlidge
Wood

Barleighford
Farm

SK11

Hammond's
Hole

64

Hollinhall

Hugbridge
Farm

Gritstone Trail

River Dane

Barleigh Ford
Bridge

Dane Valley Way

A523

Hug
Bridge

4

Thompson

Heatonlow

3

Wormhill

Wallhill

Brandy-Lea

Haddon

63

Rushton Inn

Staffordshire Way

**Rushton
Spencer**

2

Rushton
CE Prim
Sch

Heaton
Hall

Heaton

SUGAR ST

Weathercock
Farm

Tofth

STATION LA

PH

Rushton
Bank

PH

P

Tythebarn

ASKERBANK

1

Heaton House
Farm

Axstones
Spring

Overhouse
Farm

62

A523

93   A   B   94   C   D   E   95   F

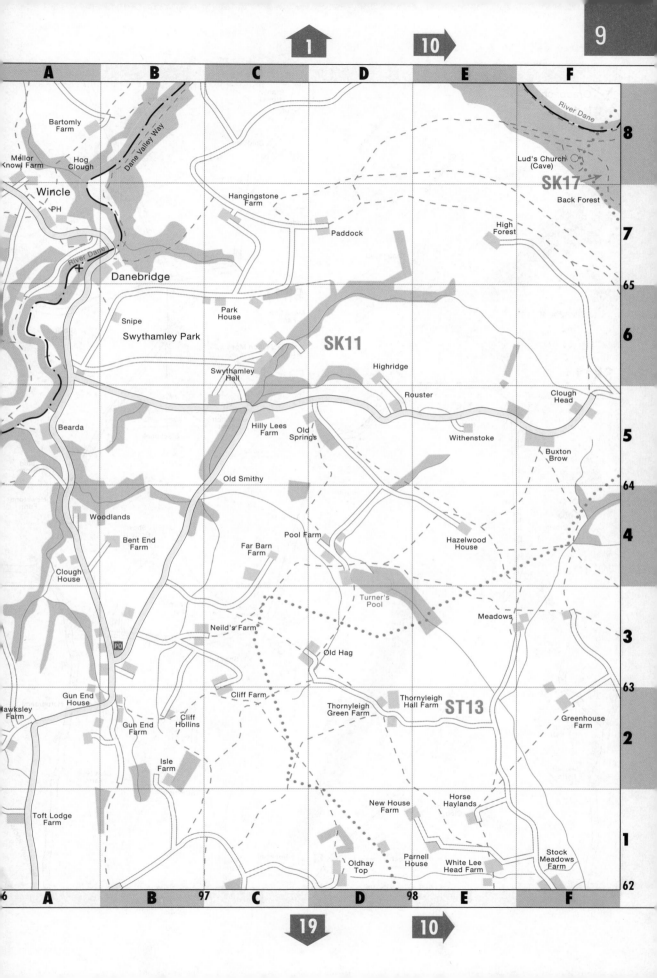

9
2
A
B
C
D
E
F
8
7
65
6
5
64
4
3
63
2
1
62
99
00
01
Gradbach
SK11
Bradley
Howel
Green Gutter
Head
Middle Edge
Sniddles
Gradbach Hill
Little
Hillend
Gradbach Wood
Sniddles Head
Farm
Cloughead
SK17
Moss
Top
Black Brook
Back Forest
Moss End
Farm
Gib Torr
Rocks
Goldsitch Moss
SK11
Roach
End
Goldsitch
House
Blackbank
Bald
Stone
Newstone
Farm
Brownsett
Shaw
Bottom
Hazel
Barrow
Shawside
Shafts
(dis)
Shaw
House
Roche
Grange
ST13
Shawtop
The Roaches
Harpersend
Roach Side
Farm
Five Clouds
Newsett
Farm
Blue Hills
Farm
Summerhill
Pheasants
Clough
Ramshaw Rocks
Rockhall
P
Well
Farm
Roach
House
9
20

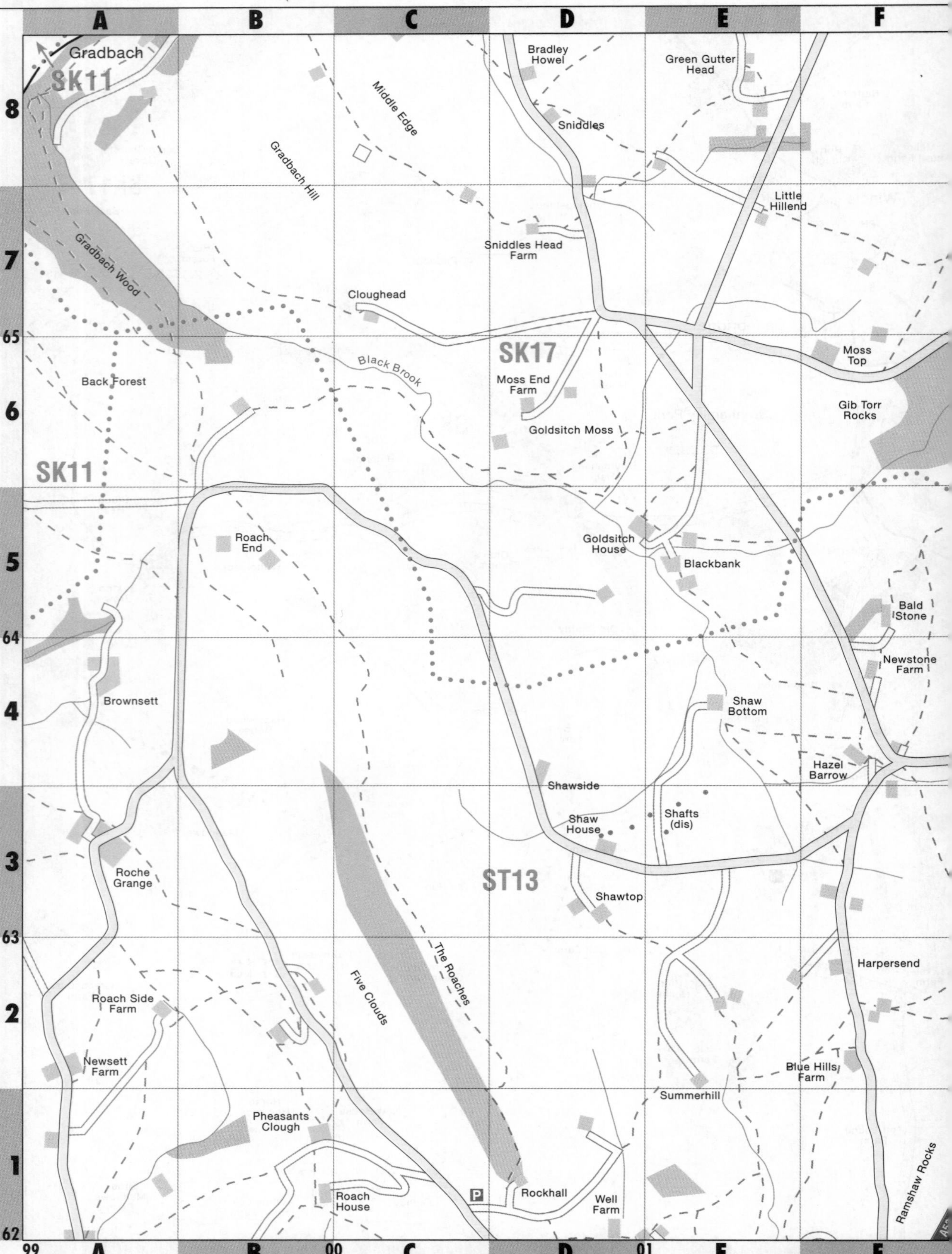

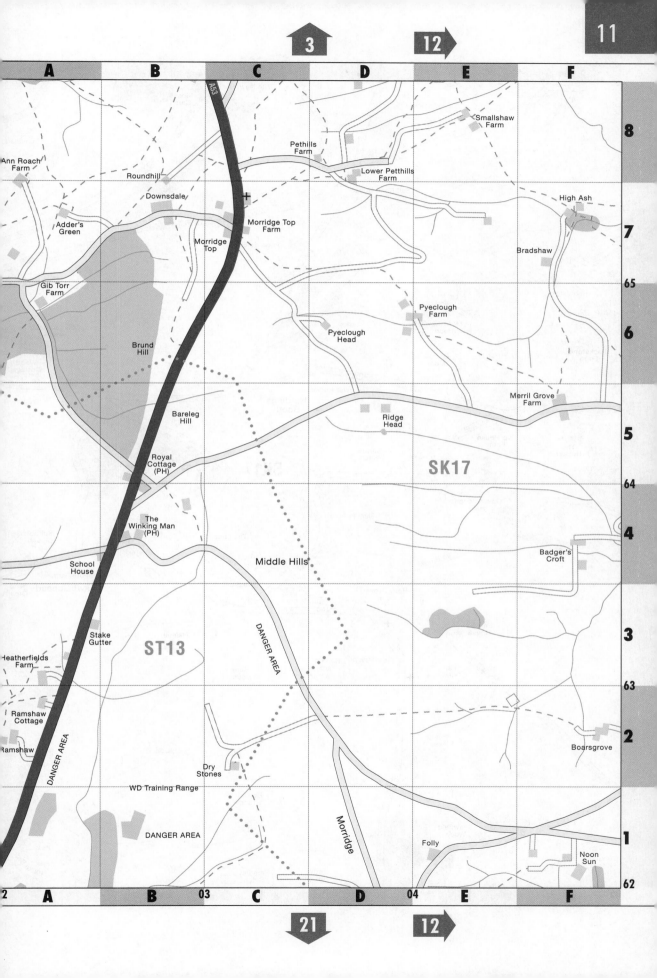

A · B · C · D · E · F

8

Smallshaw
Farm

Pethills
Farm

Ann Roach
Farm

Roundhill

Lower Petthills
Farm

High Ash

7

Downsdale

Adder's
Green

Morridge Top
Farm

Bradshaw

Morridge
Top

Gib Torr
Farm

65

Pyeclough
Farm

6

Brund
Hill

Pyeclough
Head

Bareleg
Hill

Merril Grove
Farm

Ridge
Head

5

Royal
Cottage
(PH)

SK17

64

The
Winking Man
(PH)

4

Badger's
Croft

School
House

Middle Hills

Stake
Gutter

3

Heatherfields
Farm

ST13

DANGER AREA

63

Ramshaw
Cottage

2

Ramshaw

DANGER AREA

Boarsgrove

Dry
Stones

WD Training Range

Morridge

DANGER AREA

Folly

1

Noon
Sun

62

2 · A · B · 03 · C · D · 04 · E · F

11
4

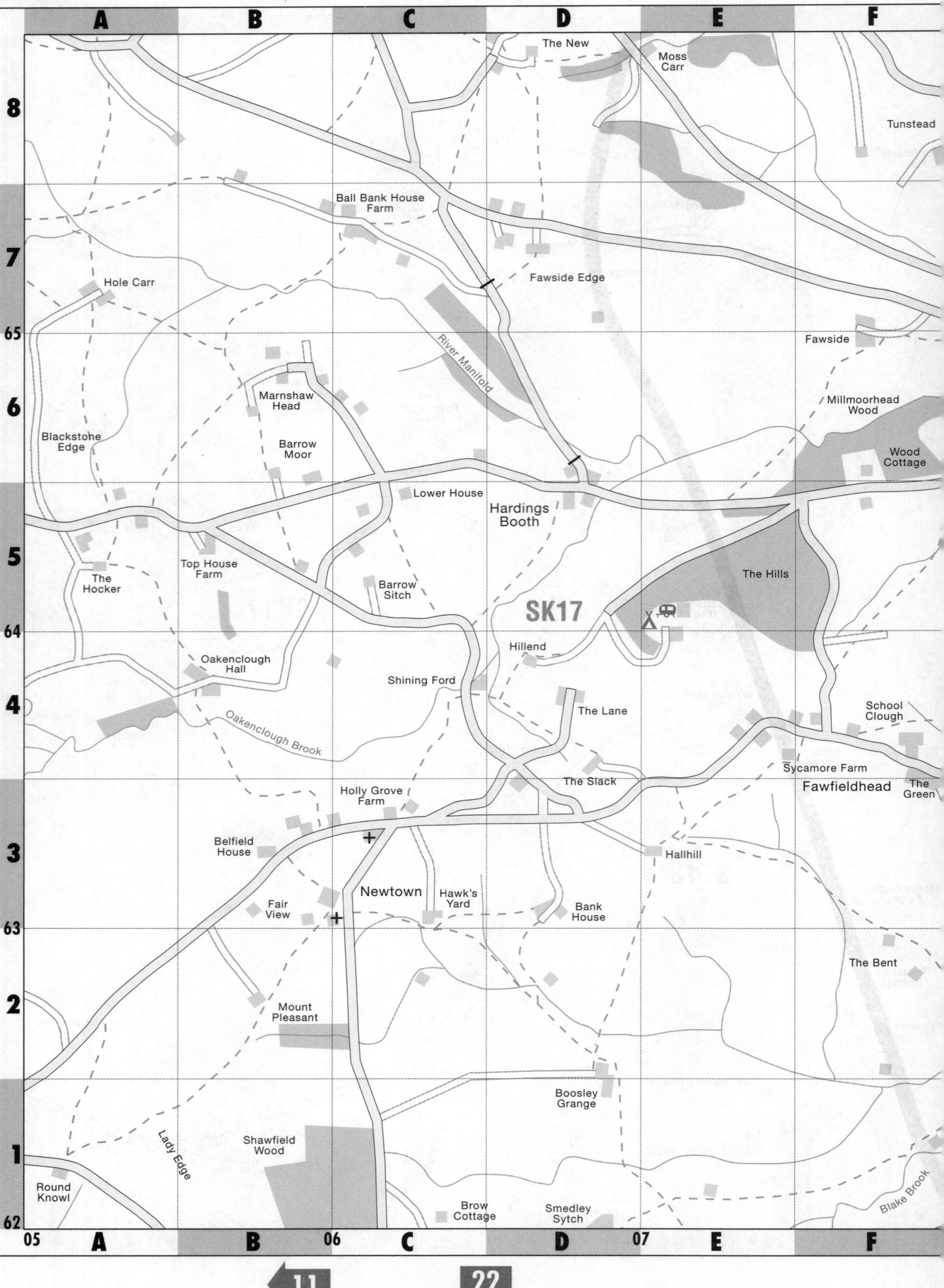

A B C D E F

8

7

65

6

5

64

4

3

63

2

1

62

The New

Moss Carr

Tunstead

Ball Bank House Farm

Fawside Edge

Fawside

Hole Carr

River Manifold

Millmoorhead Wood

Wood Cottage

Marnshaw Head

Barrow Moor

Blackstone Edge

Lower House

Hardings Booth

The Hills

The Hocker

Top House Farm

Barrow Sitch

SK17

Oakenclough Hall

Hillend

School Clough

Shining Ford

The Lane

Oakenclough Brook

Sycamore Farm

Fawfieldhead

The Green

Holly Grove Farm

The Slack

Belfield House

Hallhill

Newtown

Hawk's Yard

Bank House

Fair View

The Bent

Mount Pleasant

Boosley Grange

Shawfield Wood

Lady Edge

Round Knowl

Brow Cottage

Smedley Sytch

Blake Brook

05 A B 06 C D 07 E F

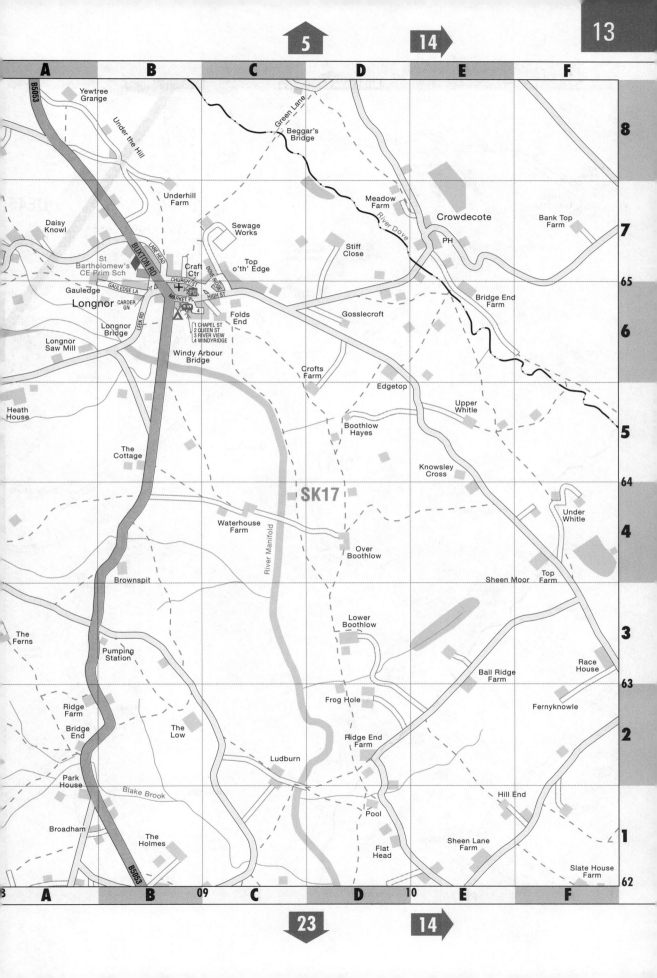

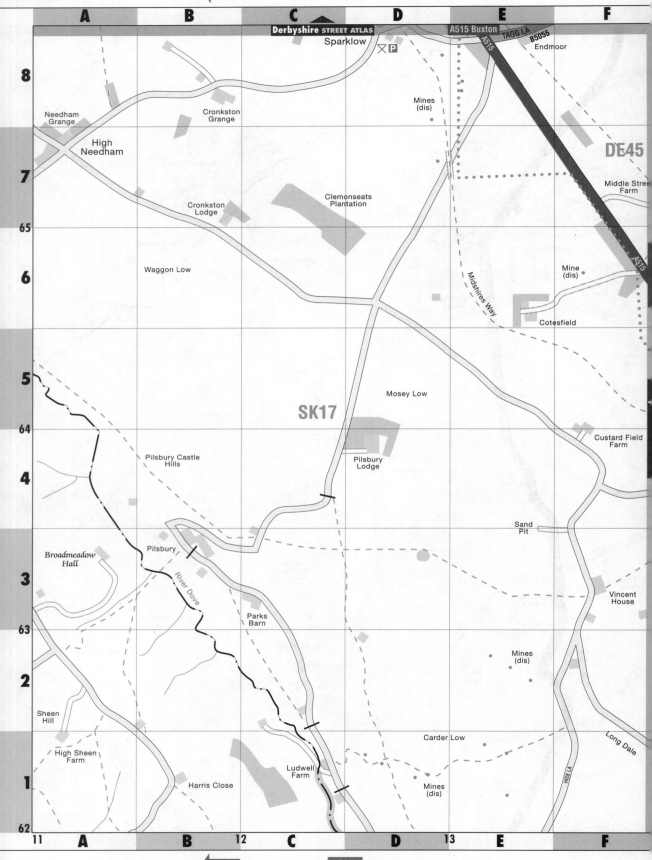

Derbyshire STREET ATLAS

Sparklow

A515 Buxton

TAGG LA

B5055

Endmoor

Mines
(dis)

DE45

Needham
Grange

High
Needham

Cronkston
Grange

Middle Stree
Farm

Cronkston
Lodge

Clemonseats
Plantation

Waggon Low

Midshires Way

Mine
(dis)

Cotesfield

Mosey Low

SK17

Custard Field
Farm

Pilsbury Castle
Hills

Pilsbury
Lodge

Sand
Pit

Broadmeadow
Hall

Pilsbury

River Dove

Vincent
House

Parks
Barn

Mines
(dis)

Sheen
Hill

Carder Low

Long Dale

High Sheen
Farm

Harris Close

Ludwell
Farm

Mines
(dis)

HIDE LA

16

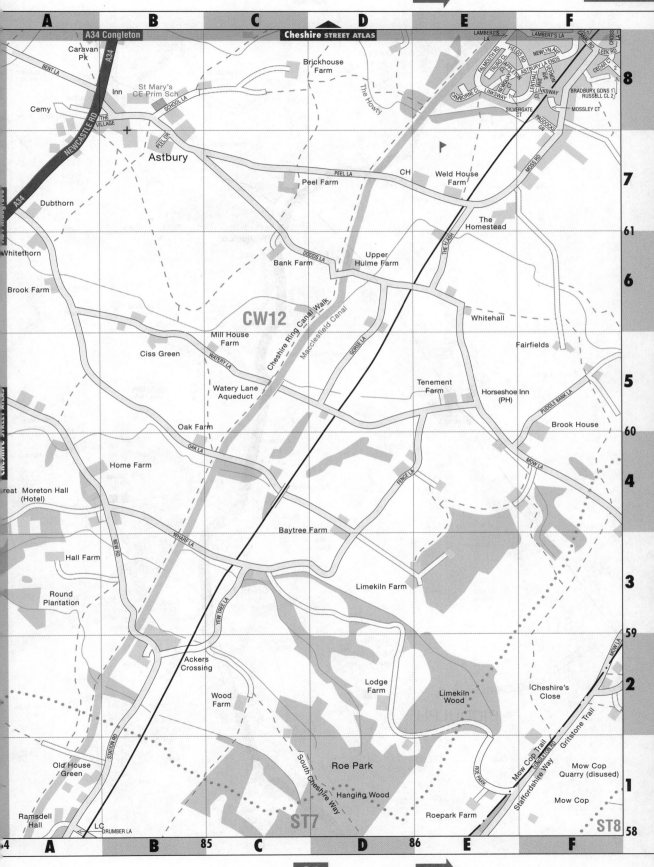

Cheshire STREET ATLAS

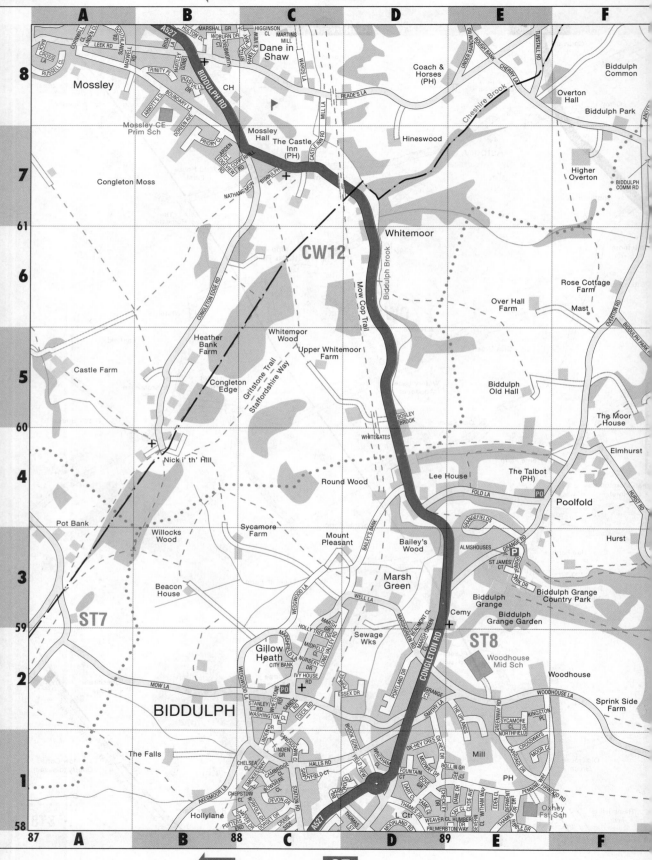

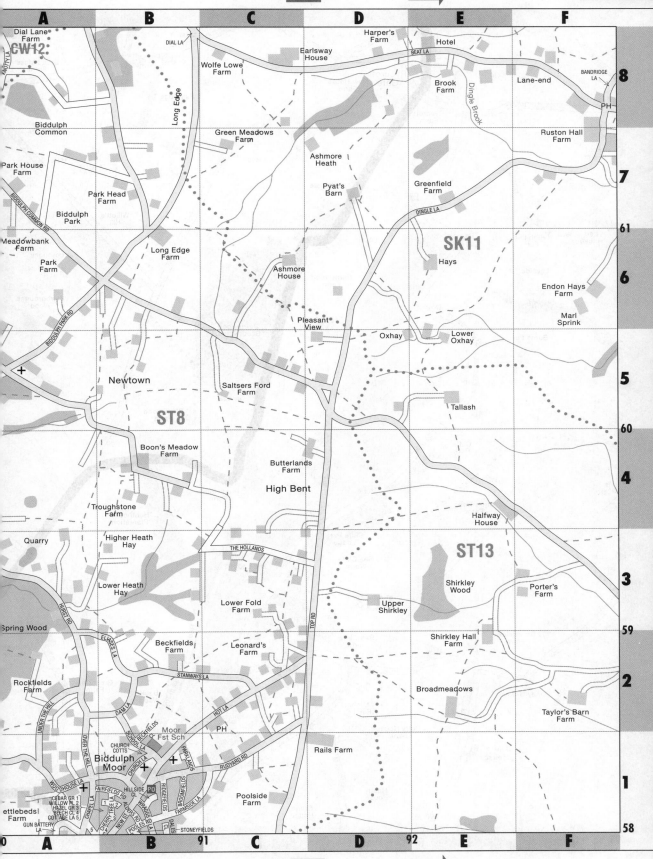

A B C D E F

ASKERBANK LA

BANDRIDGE LA

8

BEAT LA

Ryecroft Gate

New House Farm

Mast

Fair Edge Hill

Overhous Farm

Broad Moss Farm

Ryecroft Farm

Fold Farm

Dingle Brook

Rad Brook

Intakes

Moss Cottage

Rotten Hole

7

P

Wolf-Dale

Willott's Hill

Fairboroughs

61

Lee House

High Lee Farm

Oldhill

6

Leeside

Barnswood Farm

SK11

Fairboroughs Wood

Staffordshire Way

Barns Lee

Barnswood Scout Camp

5

Garage

Blackwood Farm

60

REACLIFFE RD

Cliffe Park

Rudyard Resr

Hunt House Farm

Hunthouse Plantation

4

Birch Trees Farm

Cliffe Park Lodge

3

Rea Cliffe Wood

The Lady of the Lake

ST13

59

Brownslow Farm

Rea Cliffe Farm

Rudyar Manor

Rudyard Lake Steam Rly

2

Horton Brook

Coney Greave

St Michael's CE Fst Sch

Horton Lodge Com Specl Sch

RUDYARD VALE CVN PK

Back Wood

Greentree Farm

GREEN LA

Dairy House Bank

THE CRESCENT

Dairy House

Heath House

Rudyard Lake Visitors Ctr

Willgate Farm

1

HEATH HOUSE LA

Stone House

LAKE RD

Hotel

B5331 RUDYARD RD

B533

58

93 A B 94 C D 95 E F

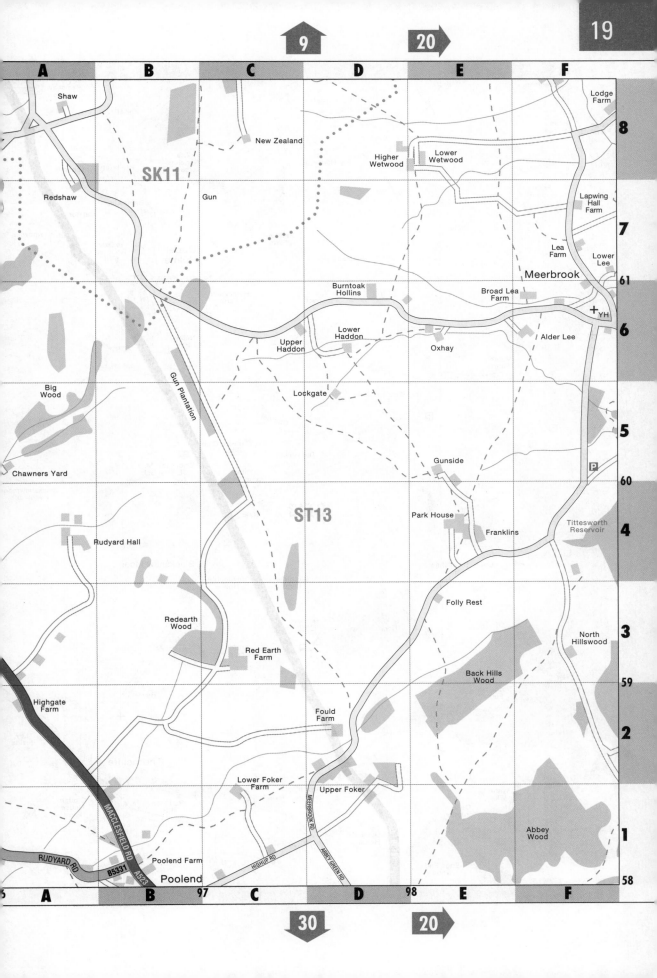

A   B   C   D   E   F

Shaw

Lodge Farm

8

New Zealand

Higher Wetwood   Lower Wetwood

SK11

Gun

Lapwing Hall Farm

Redshaw

7

Lea Farm   Lower Lee

Meerbrook

61

Burntoak Hollins

Broad Lea Farm

+ YH

6

Upper Haddon   Lower Haddon   Oxhay   Alder Lee

Big Wood

Lockgate

Gun Plantation

5

Chawners Yard

Gunside

P

60

ST13

Park House   Franklins   Tittesworth Reservoir

4

Rudyard Hall

Folly Rest

North Hillswood

3

Redearth Wood   Red Earth Farm   Back Hills Wood

59

Highgate Farm

Fould Farm

2

Lower Foker Farm   Upper Foker

MEERBROOK RD

Abbey Wood

1

RUDYARD RD   MACCLESFIELD RD   Poolend Farm   HIGHUP RD   ABBEY GREEN RD

B5331   A523   Poolend

58

A   B   97   C   D   98   E   F

A   B   C   D   E   F

Greenlane

8 Lodge   Rose
   Farm   Cottage

   Frith
   Bottom

7

         Benthead

61

         The
         Prospect

   PH
6 IVY
   COTTS

   Marsh
   Farm   WHITTY LA

         Middle Hulme
         Farm

5   New
         Cottage

         The Hollies

   Visitor
   Ctr

60

4 Tittesworth
   Reservoir

         Lower Blackshaw
         Farm

         The
         Coppice

3

59

         Troutsdale
         Farm

2

         Water
         Wks   Oaks
                    Plantation

   South
1 Hillswood
   Farm

         Edge End
         Wood

58
   99   A   00   B   C

Windygates

Far House

Hen Cloud

The Roaches
House

Paddock
Farm

Ferny
Khowl

Ramshaw
Rocks

Naychurch

Dains Mill

Cat Tor

Knowles

Upper
Hulme

Ye Olde
Rock Inn
(PH)

Wks

Homestead
Farm   WHITTY LA

Nether
Hay

BRIDGE TERR

River Churnet

Stoney
Cliffe

The Caravan Club
Site

Blackshaw Moor
CE Prim Sch

Three
Horse Shoes
Inn

ST13

Blackshawmoo
Reservoirs

Resr

Blackshaw Moor

Birchtree
Farm

Hawthorne
House

BLACKSHAW
GRANGE
CVN PK

Anzio
Camp

Resr

Underbank
Farm

Ley
Fields

Thorncliffe

Upper
Tittesworth

Red Lion
(PH)

Clough
House
Farm

Lower
Farm

Grove
Bank
Farm

Solomon's
Hollow

A53 BUXTON RD

C   D   01   E   F

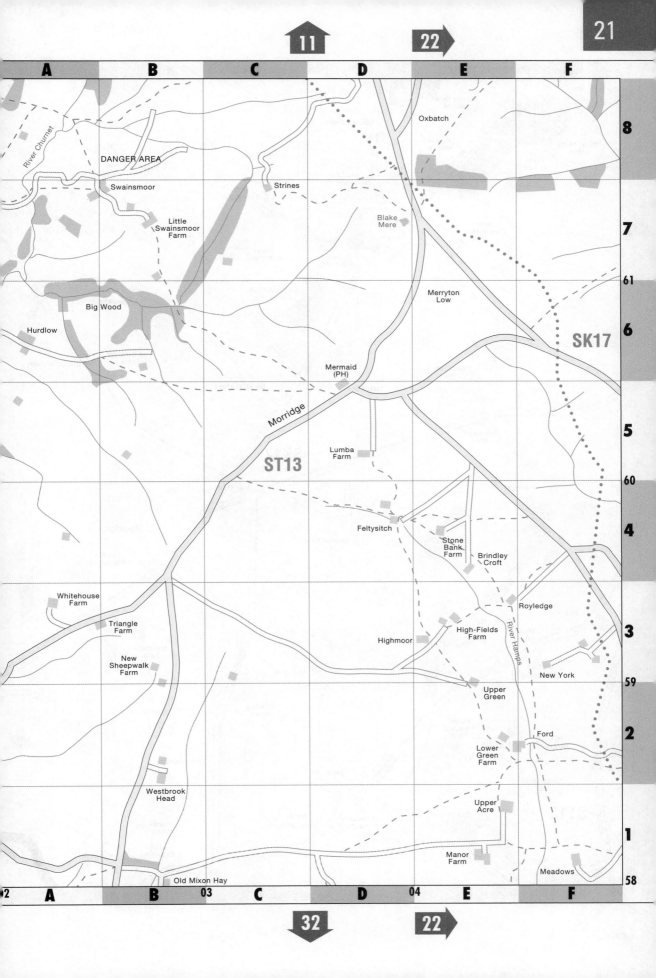

A   B   C   D   E   F

8

Oxbatch

River Churnet

DANGER AREA

Swainsmoor

Strines

7

Little
Swainsmoor
Farm

Blake
Mere

61

Merryton
Low

SK17

Big Wood

6

Hurdlow

Mermaid
(PH)

Morridge

5

Lumba
Farm

ST13

60

Feltysitch

4

Stone
Bank
Farm

Brindley
Croft

Whitehouse
Farm

Royledge

Triangle
Farm

High-Fields
Farm

River Hamps

3

Highmoor

New
Sheepwalk
Farm

New York

Upper
Green

59

Ford

2

Lower
Green
Farm

Westbrook
Head

Upper
Acre

1

Manor
Farm

Meadows

58

Old Mixon Hay

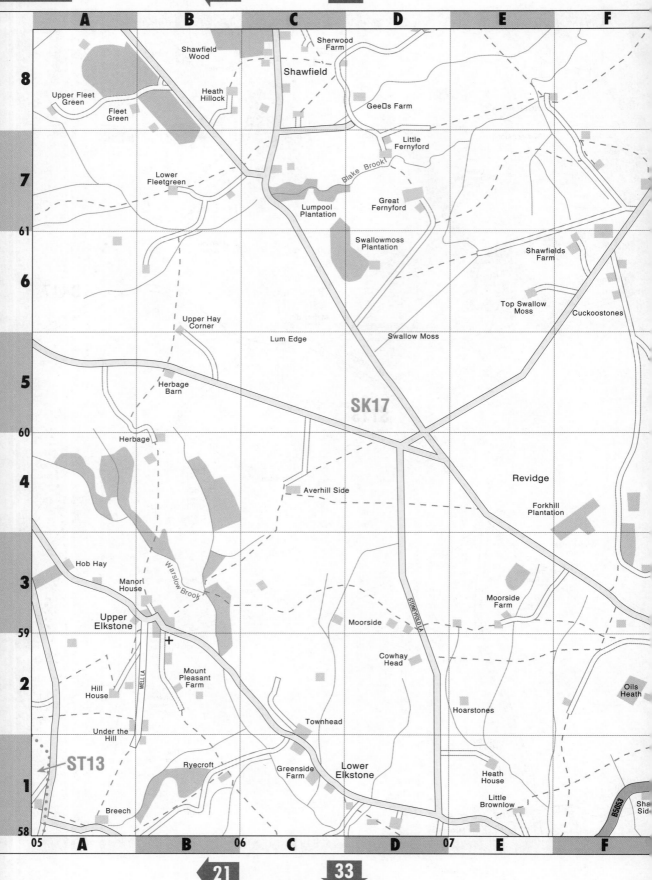

A **B** **C** **D** **E** **F**

8

Shawfield Wood

Sherwood Farm

Shawfield

Upper Fleet Green

Fleet Green

Heath Hillock

Gee□s Farm

Little Fernyford

7

Lower Fleetgreen

Blake Brook

Great Fernyford

Lumpool Plantation

61

Swallowmoss Plantation

Shawfields Farm

6

Upper Hay Corner

Top Swallow Moss

Cuckoostones

Lum Edge

Swallow Moss

5

Herbage Barn

SK17

60

Herbage

Revidge

4

Averhill Side

Forkhill Plantation

Hob Hay

Warslow Brook

Manor House

Moorside Farm

3

Upper Elkstone

Moorside

STONEYFIELD LA

59

+

Cowhay Head

2

Hill House

WELL LA

Mount Pleasant Farm

Hoarstones

Oils Heath

Under the Hill

Townhead

ST13

Ryecroft

Greenside Farm

Lower Elkstone

Heath House

1

Breech

Little Brownlow

B5053

Sha Side

58

05 **A** **B** 06 **C** **D** 07 **E** **F**

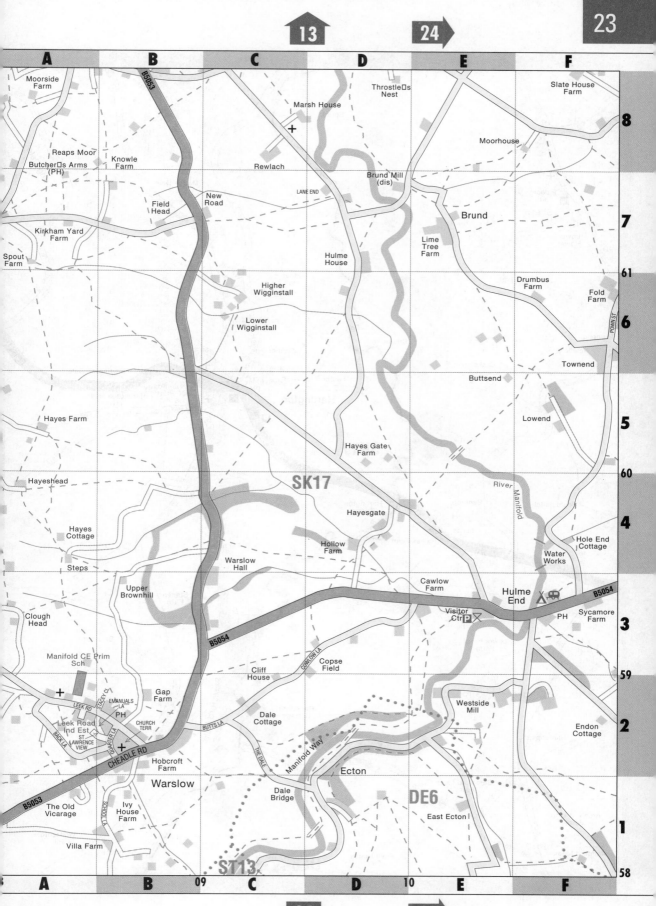

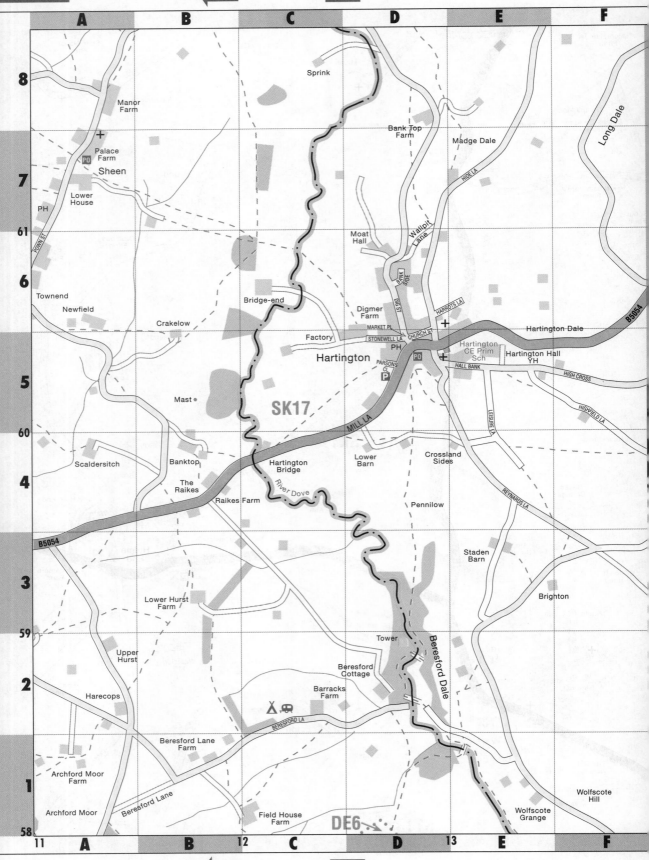

A B C D E F

8

Manor Farm

Sprink

Bank Top Farm

Madge Dale

Long Dale

Palace Farm

Sheen

HIDE LA

Wallpit Lane

7

Lower House

PH

61

Moat Hall

POWN ST

BANK SIDE

DIG ST

HARROTS LA

6

Townend

Newfield

Crakelow

Bridge-end

Digmer Farm

B5054

MARKET PL

Hartington Dale

Factory

STONEWELL LA

CHURCH ST

PH

Hartington CE Prim Sch

Hartington Hall YH

Hartington

PARSONS CL

PO

HALL BANK

HIGH CROSS

5

Mast

SK17

HIGHFIELD LA

60

Scaldersitch

Banktop

Hartington Bridge

Lower Barn

Crossland Sides

LEISURE LA

The Raikes

MILL LA

4

Raikes Farm

River Dove

Pennilow

REYNARDS LA

B5054

Staden Barn

3

Lower Hurst Farm

Brighton

59

Tower

Beresford Dale

Upper Hurst

2

Harecops

Beresford Cottage

Barracks Farm

Beresford Lane Farm

BERESFORD LA

1

Archford Moor Farm

Beresford Lane

Wolfscote Hill

Archford Moor

Field House Farm

DE6

Wolfscote Grange

58

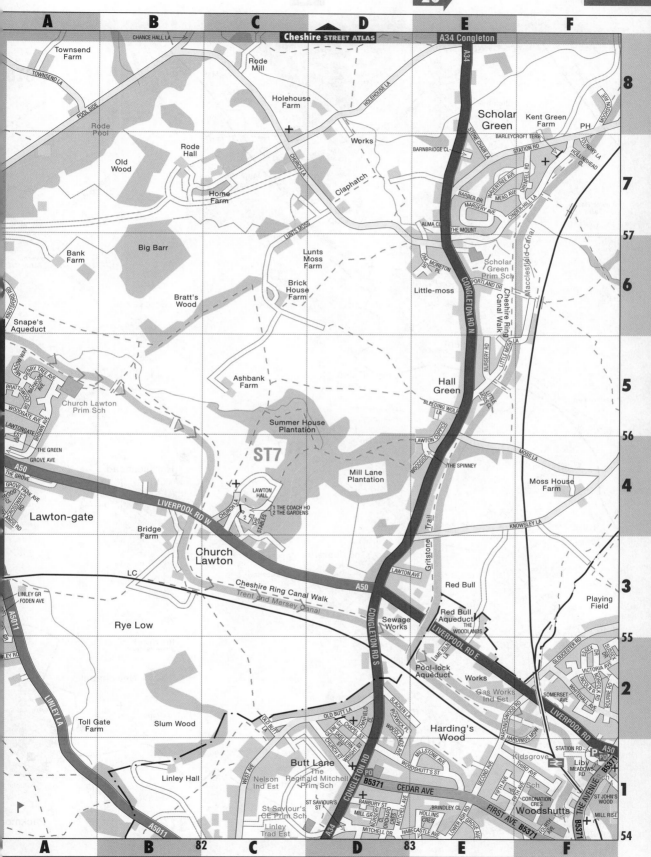

Cheshire STREET ATLAS

ST8

The Bank

Lower Bank Farm

Birch Tree Farm

Close Farm

Quarry Wood

Old Man of Mow

Mow Cop Castle

Mainwairing Farm

Mast

Mow Cop

Mus

Perseverance Mill

Towerhill Farm

Woodcocks' Well CE Prim Sch

Castle Prim Sch

Mount Pleasant

Dales Green

Hall o' Lee

Brieryhurst

Blue Pot Farm

ST7

Holly Farm

Hollin House Farm

Stone Trough

Harriseahead

Wa Le

Playing Field

Maryhill High & Prim Schs

Thursfield Ave 1
Priory Pl 2

The Rookery

3 Castle Ho
4 Dove Ho

Trubshaw Edge Farm

Trubshaw Farm

Thursfield Prim Sch

Bullocks House Farm

Thursfield Lodge

Dove Bank

White Hill

Newchapel Observatory

Newchapel

1 Sparrowbutts Gr
2 Sandpiper Ct
3 Phoenix Cl

KIDSGROVE

The Grapes (PH)

1 Jasmin Way 1
Harebell Gr 2
Woodruff Cl 3

Packmo

Packmore Prim Sch

LIVERPOOL RD

A50

CURLEW RD 1
LINET GR 2
WOODPECKER DR 3

ST6

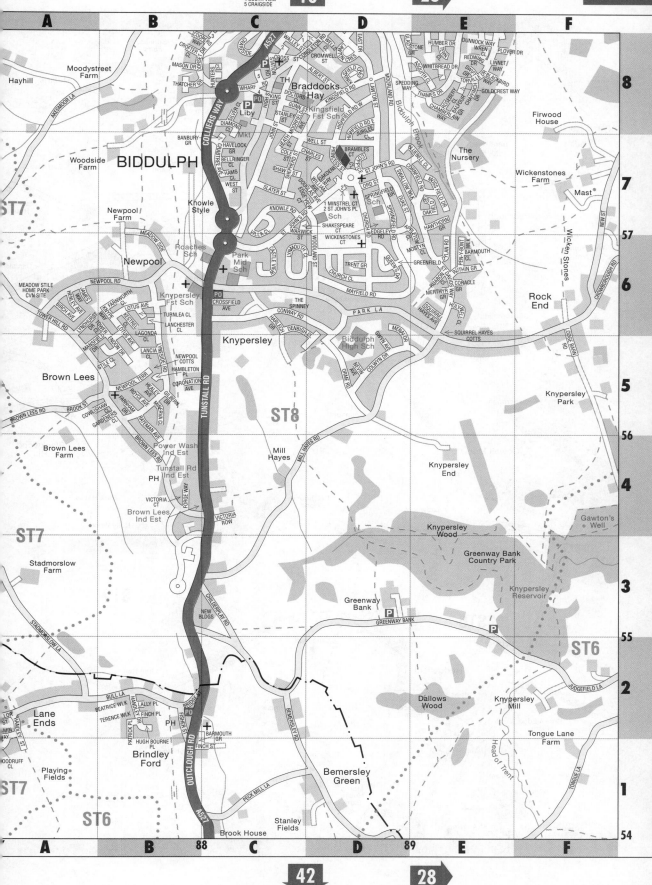

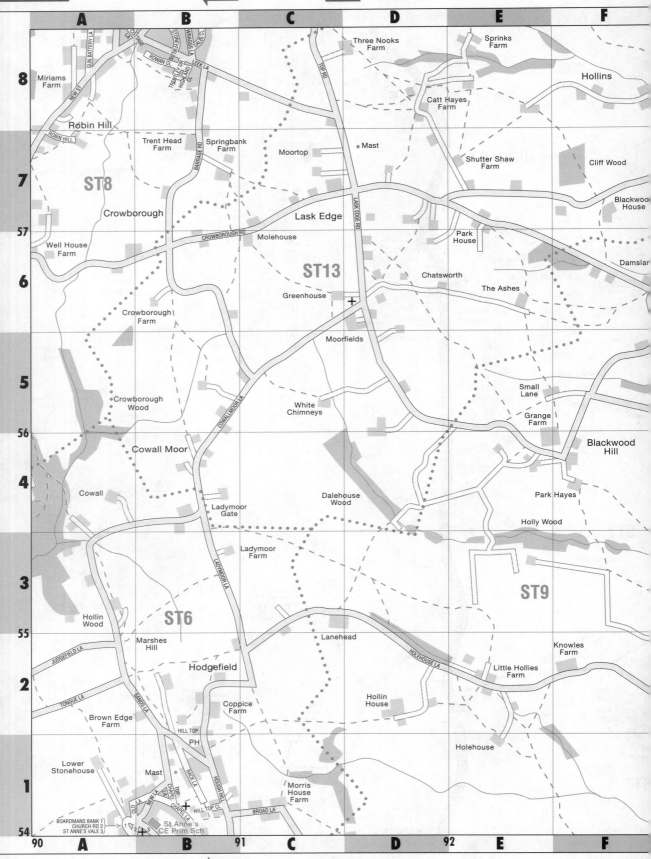

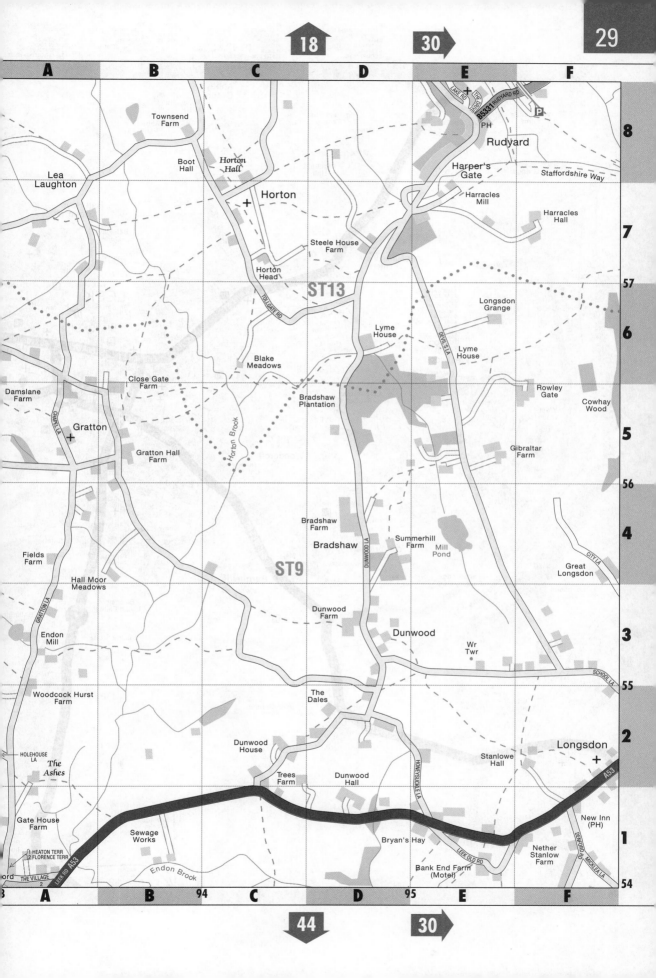

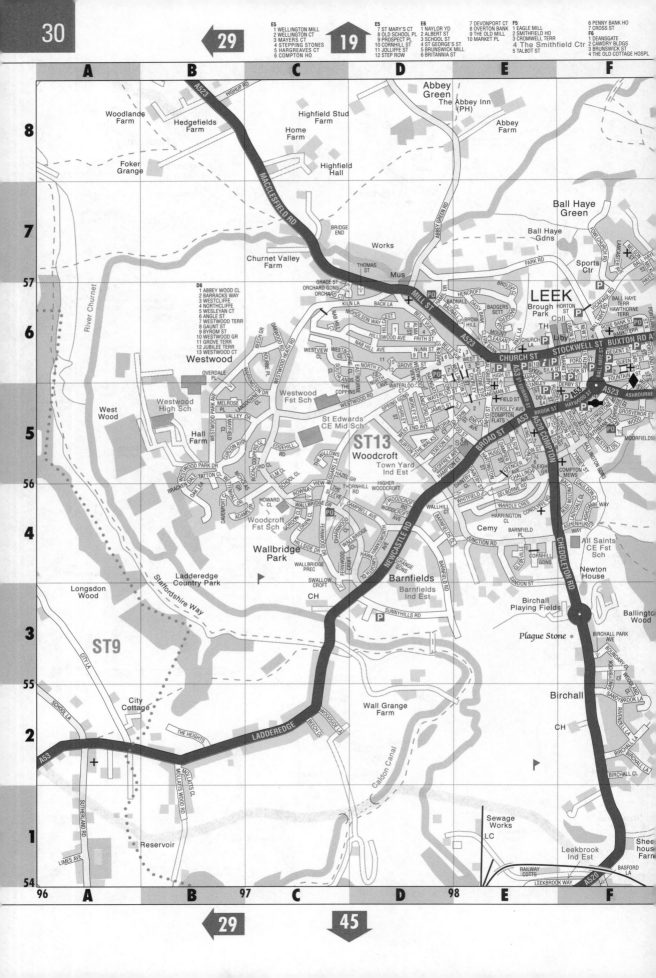

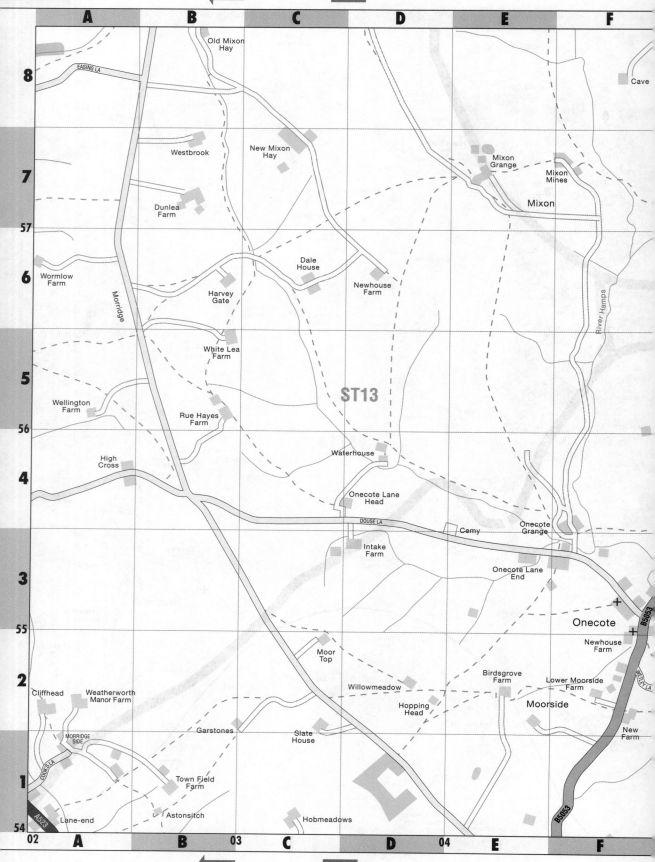

A   B   C   D   E   F

8

Old Mixon
Hay

EASING LA

Cave

Westbrook

New Mixon
Hay

Mixon
Grange

Mixon
Mines

7

Dunlea
Farm

Mixon

57

Wormlow
Farm

Morridge

Dale
House

6

Harvey
Gate

Newhouse
Farm

River Hamps

White Lea
Farm

5

Wellington
Farm

Rue Hayes
Farm

ST13

56

High
Cross

Waterhouse

4

Onecote Lane
Head

DOUSE LA

Cemy

Onecote
Grange

Intake
Farm

Onecote Lane
End

3

Onecote

B5053

55

Moor
Top

Newhouse
Farm

Cliffhead

Weatherworth
Manor Farm

Willowmeadow

Birdsgrove
Farm

Lower Moorside
Farm

WETLEY LA

2

Hopping
Head

Moorside

MORRIDGE
SIDE

Garstones

Slate
House

New
Farm

COOK'S LA

Town Field
Farm

1

A523

Lane-end

Astonsitch

Hobmeadows

B5053

54

02   A   B   03   C   D   04   E   F

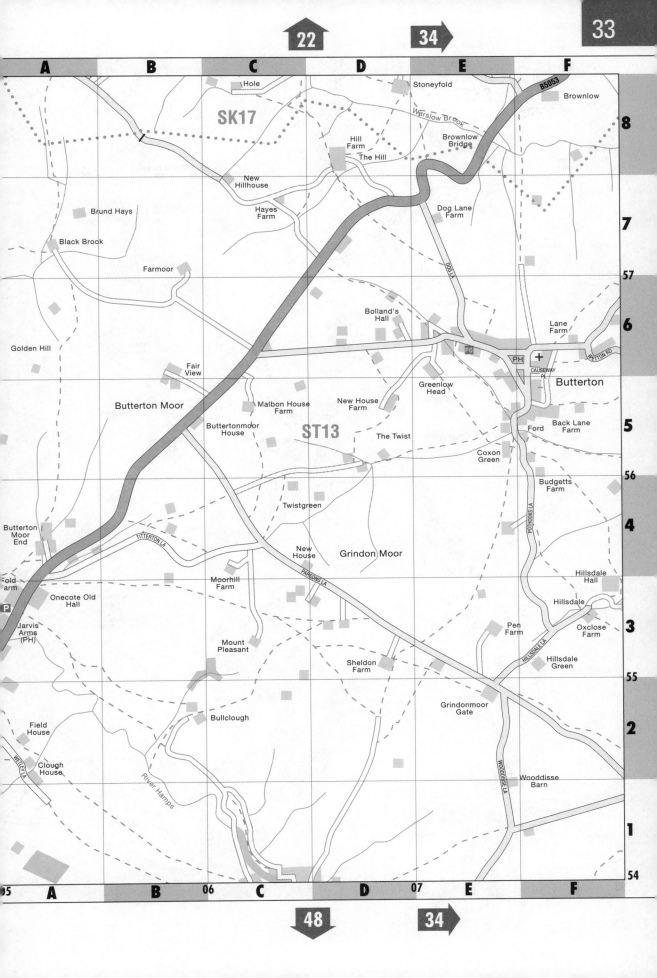

A B C D E F

SK17

The Lee

Ecton Bridge

Ecton Hill

Back of Ecton

8

Warslow Brook

Swainsley

Tunnel

Mines (dis)

Paddock House Farm

Heathy Roods

Top of Ecton

Broad Ecton Farm

Back of Ecton

Swainsley Head

Clayton House

Summerhill Farm

Cantrell's House

7

Ivy House

57

Lees Farm

Kirksteads

6

Fenns House

Sugarloaf

Manor House

Lanehouse Farm

Wallacre

Wetton Hill

5

WETTON RD

River Manifold

Dale Farm

Waterslacks

Wettonmill Cave

DE6

56

Broadmeadow

Ford

Hoo Brook

Cave

4

Darfar Bridge

Ossoms Hill

ST13

Wetton

BUXTO RD

Hillsdale

Ossoms Hill

Hallfields Farm

Ye Olde Royal Oak (PH)

3

Big Hillsdale

Ladyside Wood

LEEK RD

Thor's Lane

Ladyside

55

Caves

Thors Cave

CARR LA

2

Grindon

CHURCH AVE

Newclose Farm

Crown Farm

LARKSTONE LA

1

The Cavalier Inn (PH)

FLEETS LA

Buckfurlong Farm

Weag's Bridge

Beeston Tor

Caves

54

08 A B 09 C D 10 E F

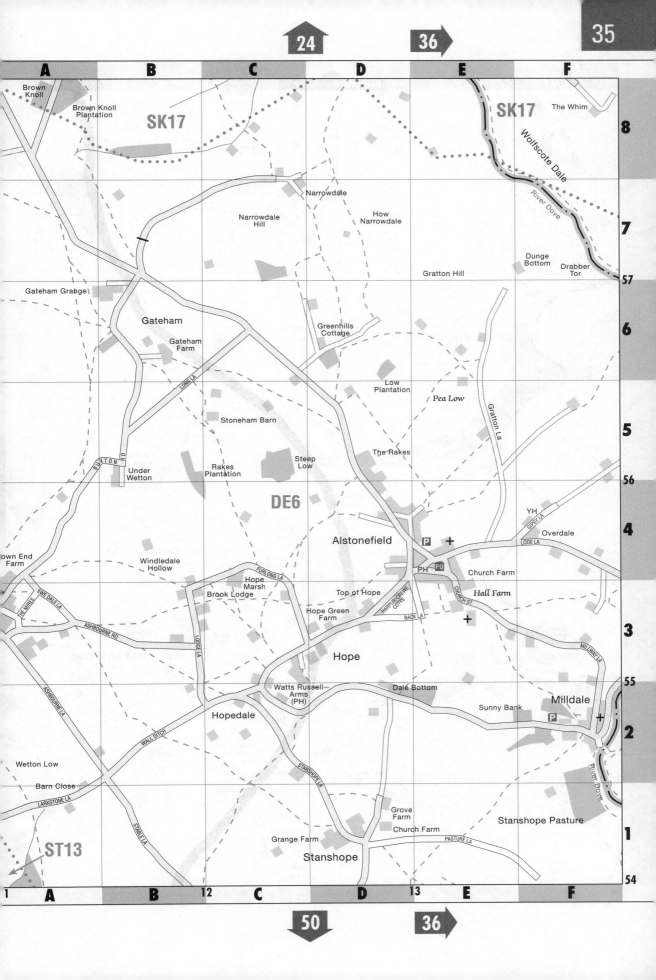

A · B · C · D · E · F

Brown Knoll

Brown Knoll Plantation

SK17

The Whim

SK17

Wolfscote Dale

River Dove

8

Narrowdale

Narrowdale Hill

How Narrowdale

7

Gratton Hill

Dunge Bottom

Drabber Tor

57

Gateham Grange

Gateham

Gateham Farm

Greenhills Cottage

6

Low Plantation

Pea Low

LONG LA

Gratton La

Stoneham Barn

5

BUXTON RD

Rakes Plantation

Steep Low

The Rakes

56

Under Wetton

DE6

YH

Overdale

GIPSY LA

LODE LA

own End Farm

Windledale Hollow

FURLONG LA

Alstonefield

P

+

Church Farm

4

Hope Marsh

Brook Lodge

Top of Hope

PH

PO

Hall Farm

CHURCH ST

THE MIRES

EWE DALE LA

ASHBOURNE RD

LODGE LA

Hope Green Farm

HARPUR-CREWE COTTS

BACK LA

+

3

MILLWAY LA

Hope

ASHBOURNE LA

55

Watts Russell Arms (PH)

Dale Bottom

Milldale

Hopedale

Sunny Bank

P

+

2

WALL DITCH

STABLE LA

STANSHOPE LA

River Dove

Wetton Low

Barn Close

Grove Farm

Stanshope Pasture

LARKSTONE LA

Church Farm

1

ST13

Grange Farm

Stanshope

PASTURE LA

54

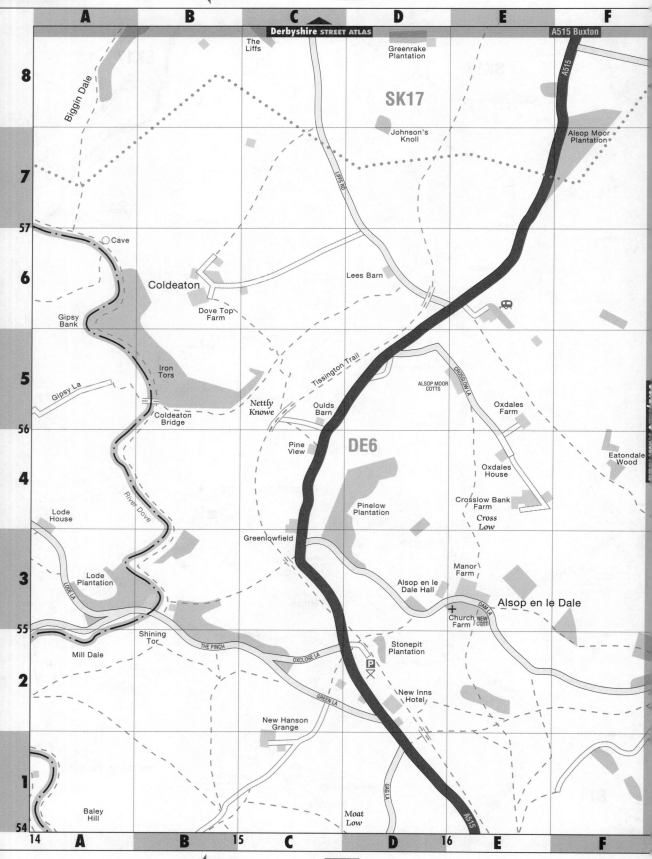

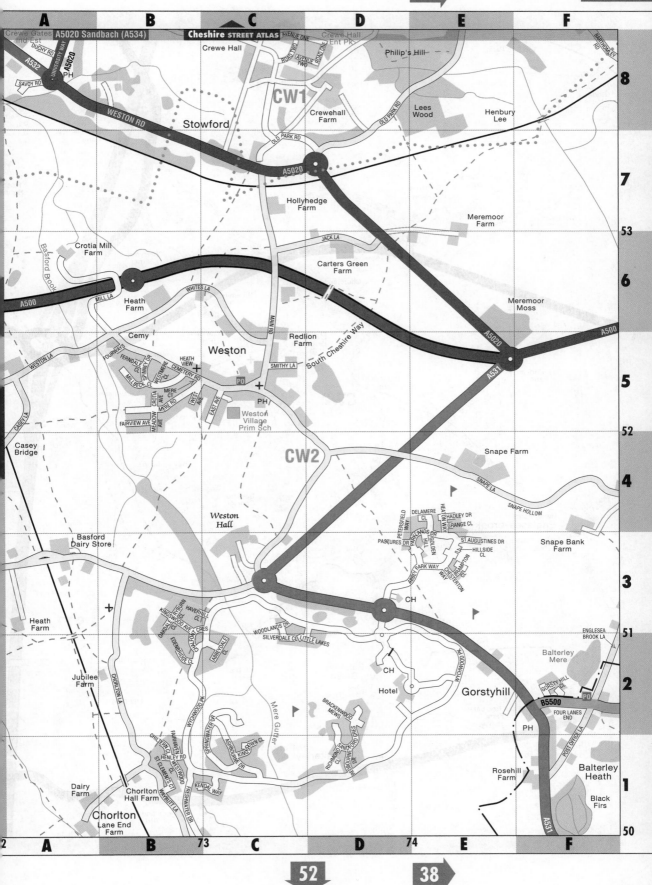

38
52
38

Cheshire STREET ATLAS

A5020 Sandbach (A534)

Crewe Gates Ind Est
Crewe Hall
Crewe Hall Ent Pk
Philip's Hill

CW1
Crewehall Farm
Lees Wood
Henbury Lee

Stowford

Old Park Rd

Savoy Rd
University Way
A5020
PH
Duchy Rd

Weston Rd

Meremoor Farm

Hollyhedge Farm

A5020

Jack La

Carters Green Farm

Meremoor Moss

Crotia Mill Farm

Basford Brook

A500
Mill La
Heath Farm
Whites La

Cemy

Weston

Redlion Farm

Main Rd

South Cheshire Way

A5020

A531

A500

Weston La
Fourways
Ferndale Cl
Westmere Cl
Spinney Dr
Millbeck Cl
Heath View
Cemetery Rd
PO
Smithy La

Mere Ct
Crotia Ave
Meadow Ave
West Ave
Mere Rd
East Ave
Fairview Ave

Casey La

PH

Weston Village Prim Sch

CW2

Snape Farm

Snape La

Snape Hollow

Casey Bridge

Weston Hall

Delamere Cl
Hadley Dr
Heaton Way
Grange Cl
Petersfield Way
Pastures Dr
Parklands Dr
The Golden
Abbey Park Way
St Augustines Dr
Hillside Cl
Frampton Cl
Chesterton Way

Snape Bank Farm

Basford Dairy Store

CH

Heath Farm

Haverhill Cl
Kingswood Ave
Cres
Oandale
Welburn
Edgbridge Cl

Abbeydale

Woodlands Dr
Silverdale Cl Little Lakes

CH

Englesea Brook La

Balterley Mere

Jubilee Farm

Chorlton La

Wychwood Pk

Springwater Dr
Fairhaven
Westwood
St Clements Ct
Henley Rd
Ashchurch Dr
Kings
Crown Cl
Richmond Cl
Sandford Dr

Mere Gutter

Brackenwood Mews

Hotel

Wychwood Dr

Gorstyhill

Gorsty Mill Cl
PO

B5500
Four Lanes End
PH

Post Office La

Chilfern Cl
Freshwater Dr
Waybutt La
Kendal Way

Dairy Farm

Chorlton Hall Farm

Rosehill Farm

Balterley Heath

Chorlton Lane End Farm

Black Firs

A531

Cheshire STREET ATLAS

A | B | C | D | E | F

8

Bank Top

CW2

7

Lower Foxley

Foxley

Mosshouse

53

Foxley Drumble

Foxley Gorse

Foxley Farm

EARDLEYEND RD

6

Brockwood Hill Farm

High Foxley Farm

Eardleyend

Wrench's Coppice

Park Manor Farm

ALSAGER RD

5

Brockwood Hill

The Fields

Millend

MILLEND LA

HULLOCK'S POOL RD

CROSS LA

A500

Eardley Hall

52

Cross Farm

ST7

Poole House

Hullock's Pool

Great Oak Farm

4

Brook Farm

Sewage Wks

New Farm

GREATOAK RD

Park Lane Farm

Yewtree Farm

PARK LA

Park End

Townhouse

Park Farm

BIGNALL END RD

3

Moat Farm

Pear Tree Farm

Ravensmead Com Prim Sch

PUMP CT

EDWARD ST

WOOD ST

RAVENS CL

Bignall End

TIBB ST

MOR LA

Firs Farm

Community Ctr

OLD RD

CHAPEL ST

ALBERT ST

DIGLAKE ST

PO

51

New Peel Farm

NEW RD

RAVEN'S LA

B5500

BARTHOMLEY RD

Kent Hill Farm

WILBRAHAM'S WLK

P

ST JAMES CT

Liby

WATLANDS RD

McKELLIN CL

GEORGES WAY

RILEYS WAY

BENJAMINS WAY

KINS DR

Audley

BOYLES HALL RD

GRESLEY WAY

WESTLANDS

AARONS CR

BRIDGETT RD

MONUMENT WAY

2

NANTWICH RD

The Quarry

WESTFIELD AVE

MEADOWSIDE AVE

VERNON AVE

VERNON CL

CHESTER RD

DEAN HOLLOW

CHAPEL LA

HALL ST

CHURCH ST

P

PO

Wereton

KELSALL CL

BOOTH ST

DURBER CL

KING ST

MELLARD ST

MADDOCK ST

GEORGE ST

HEIGHER WALL RD

GRASSYGREEN LA

CHERRY TREE RD 1
CEDAR CRES 2
WEDGEWOOD AVE 3

BOON HILL RD

ELM TREE DR

PEAR TREE RD

1

B5367

PEEL HOLLOW

CARR LA

Old Peel Farm

NEW KING ST

QUEEN ST

PRINCESS AVE

DEAN VIEW

Quarry New Farm

WERETON RD

Ryehill Farm

RYEHILLS

Rye Hills

Grange Farm

Boon Hill

HAWTHORNE AVE

TOM FIELDS

Wood Lane Prim Sch

50

Shraleybrook

Greenbutts House

A | B | 79 | C | D | 80 | E | F

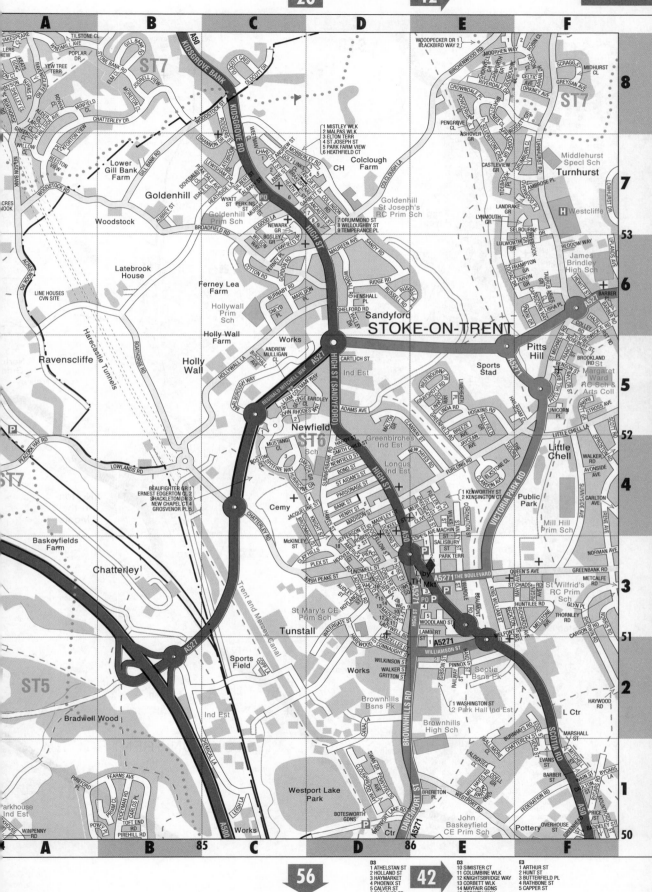

ST7

Woodpecker Dr 1
Blackbird Way 2

ST7

8

1 MISTLEY WLK
2 MALPAS WLK
3 ELTON TERR
4 ST JOSEPH ST
5 PARK FARM VIEW
6 HEATHFIELD CT

Colclough
Farm

Middlehurst
Specl Sch

Turnhurst

7

Lower
Gill Bank
Farm

Goldenhill

Woodstock

Goldenhill
Prim Sch

Goldenhill
St Joseph's
RC Prim Sch

7 DRUMMOND ST
8 WILLOUGHBY ST
9 TEMPERANCE PL

Westcliffe

53

Latebrook
House

LINE HOUSES
CVN SITE

Ferney Lea
Farm

Hollywall
Prim
Sch

James
Brindley
High Sch

6

Harecastle Tunnels

Ravenscliffe

Holly Wall
Farm

Holly
Wall

Works

Sandyford

STOKE-ON-TRENT

Pitts
Hill

5

P

Newfield

ST6
Sch

Cartlich St

Ind Est

Sports
Stad

St
Margaret
Ward
RC Sch &
Arts Coll

Greenbirches
Ind Est

BEAUFIGHTER GR 1
ERNEST EDGERTON CL 2
SHACKLETON DR 3
NEW CHAPEL CT 4
GROSVENOR PL 5

Cemy

Longus
Ind Est

Little
Chell

52

4

1 KENWORTHY ST
2 KENSINGTON CT

Public
Park

Mill Hill
Prim Sch

Baskeyfields
Farm

New Hayes Rd

Chatterley

Greenbank Rd

3

St Mary's CE
Prim Sch

Tunstall

TH MKT

A5271 THE BOULEVARD

St Wilfrid's
RC Prim
Sch

51

ST5

Sports
Field

Works

1 WASHINGTON ST
2 PARK HALL IND EST

L Ctr

2

Bradwell Wood

Ind Est

Brownhills
Bsns Pk

Brownhills
High Sch

Westport Lake
Park

Works

BOTESWORTH
GDNS

John
Baskeyfield
CE Prim Sch

Pottery

1

arkhouse
Ind Est

WINPENNY
RD

Works

L
Ctr

50

D3		E3
1 ATHELSTAN ST	10 SIMISTER CT	1 ARTHUR ST
2 HOLLAND ST	11 COLUMBINE WLK	2 HUNT ST
3 HAYMARKET	12 KNIGHTSBRIDGE WAY	3 MARKET ST
4 PHOENIX ST	13 CORBETT WLK	4 BUTTERFIELD PL
5 CALVER ST	14 MAYFAIR GDNS	5 RATHBONE ST
6 PARADISE ST	15 CORINTH WAY	5 CAPPER ST
7 PICCADILLY ST	16 PERSIA WLK	
8 McGOUGH ST	17 STRINGER CT	
9 FARNDALE ST	18 COOLIDGE ST	

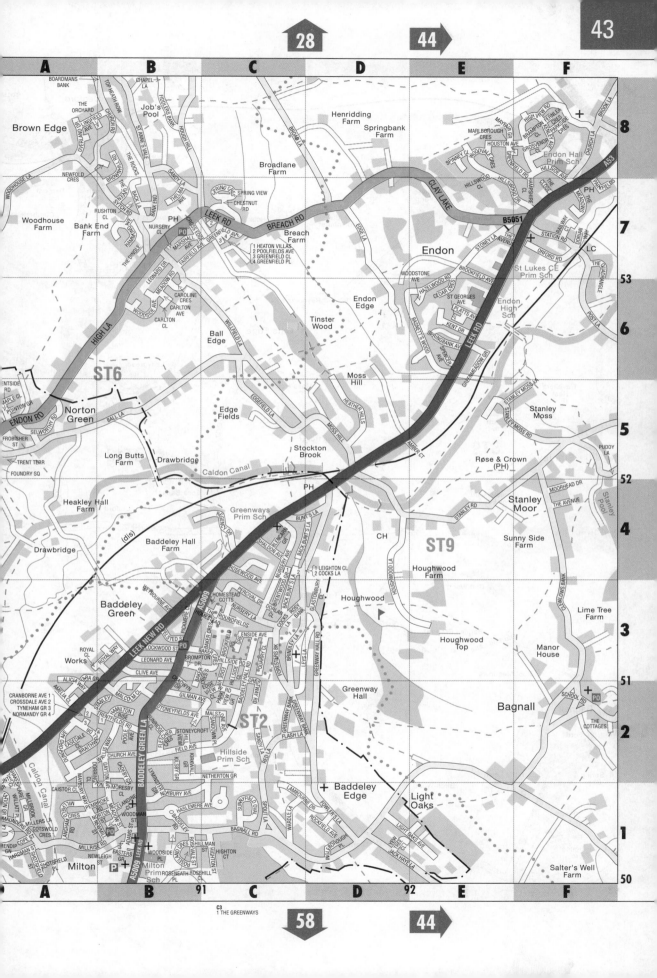

43
29

| | A | B | C | D | E | F |

8

BROOKSIDE DR
1 BROOK CL
2 FORGE SIDE
3 EMBERS WAY
4 THE PRIORY

BROOK LA

LEEK RD

A53

(dis)

Denford

MICKLEA LA

DENFORD RD

Caldon Canal

SANDY LA

Manor Farm

Hazelhurst Aqueduct

HOLLY BUSH COTTAGES

Holly Bush (PH)

Denford Farm

7

Hayes Farm

PARK LA

Lawn Farm

Little Hollinhurst

Hollinhurst

Hazelhurst

HUNTLEY RD

Cumberledge Park

53

Park Farm

Reynolds Hay Farm

6

Cats Edge

Ladygreen

POST LA

Moss House

STANLEY BANK

Travellers Rest (PH)

Acres Barn

Lee House

5

PUDD LA

Dogcroft Farm

Newhouse Farm

Clough House

BLACK BANK RD

ST13

Stanley

ST9

Whistonshaw

52

Rose Bank Farm

P

Stanley Head Outdoor Education Centre

TOMPKIN RD

Colford Farm

4

Stanley Pool

COALPITFORD LA

Wood Lane Farm

Ford Farm

BRUND LA

Cliff Wood

Tompkin

KNOWSLEY RD

Bigwood

Big Susan's Wood

3

Old Mill Lane

Bagnall Grange Farm

OLD MILL LA

P

Knowsley Farm

51

OLD MILL LA

Pool Meadows

Moor Hall

Bagnall

SPRINGS BANK

2

Ford

THORNYEDGE RD

Far Rownall Farm

Cicely Haughton Sch

Spring Bank

Little Lawn Farm

Birch Wood

Rownall Cottage Farm

1

Newhouse Farm

THORNYEDGE RD

Thornyedge

Rownall Farm

Bramhous Farm

50

| 93 | A | B | 94 | C | D | 95 | E | F |

43
59

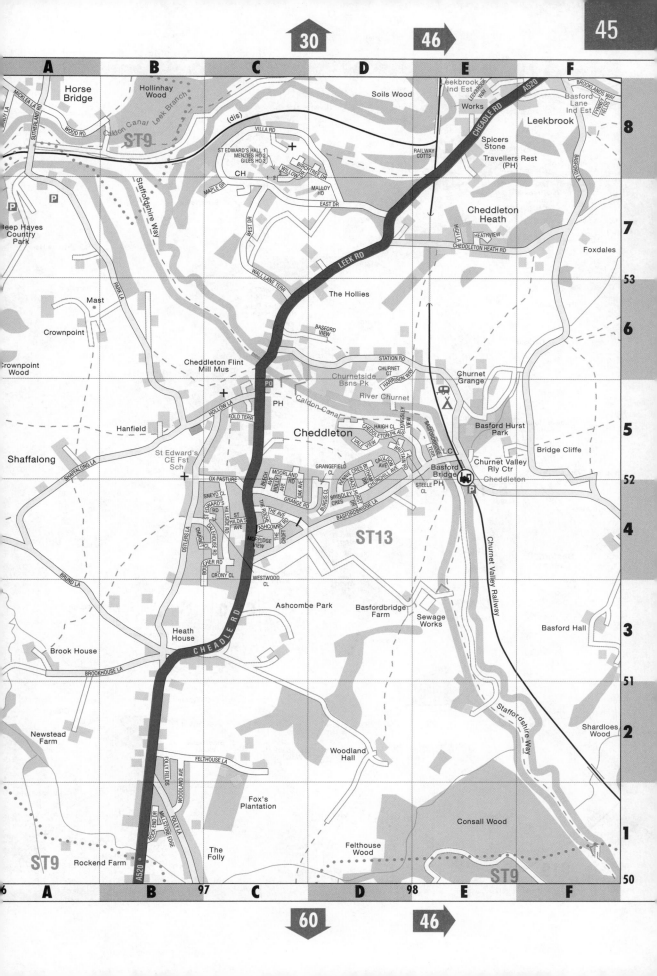

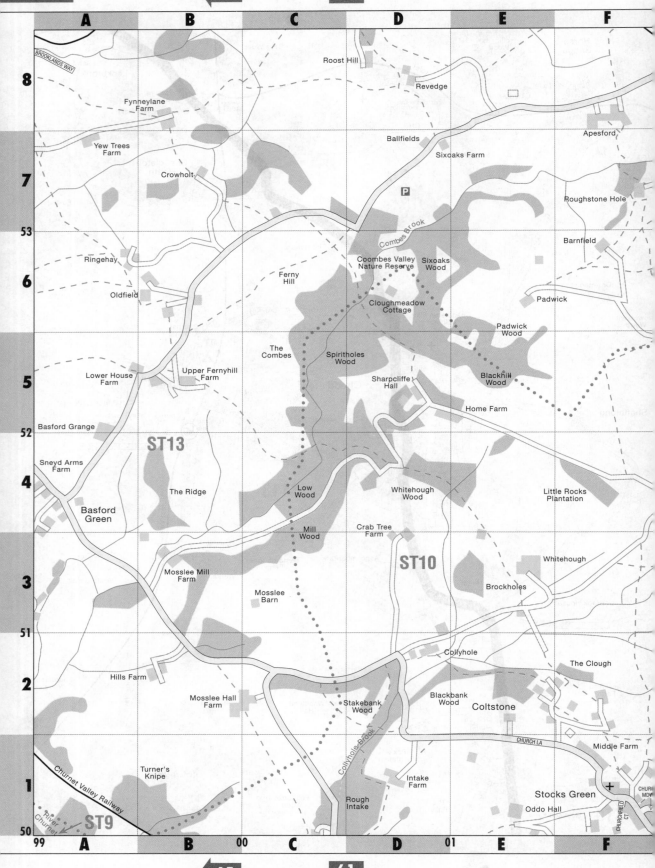

A **B** **C** **D** **E** **F**

BROOKLANDS WAY

8

Fynneylane Farm

Yew Trees Farm

Crowholt

7

Roost Hill

Revedge

Ballfields

Sixoaks Farm

Apesford

P

Roughstone Hole

53

Ringehay

Oldfield

Combes Brook

Barnfield

6

Ferny Hill

Coombes Valley Nature Reserve

Sixoaks Wood

Cloughmeadow Cottage

Padwick

Padwick Wood

The Combes

Spiritholes Wood

Blackhill Wood

Lower House Farm

Upper Fernyhill Farm

5

Sharpcliffe Hall

Home Farm

52

Basford Grange

ST13

Sneyd Arms Farm

The Ridge

4

Low Wood

Whitehough Wood

Little Rocks Plantation

Basford Green

Mill Wood

Crab Tree Farm

ST10

Whitehough

Mosslee Mill Farm

Brockholes

3

Mosslee Barn

51

Collyhole

The Clough

Hills Farm

2

Mosslee Hall Farm

Stakebank Wood

Blackbank Wood

Coltstone

Middle Farm

CHURCH LA

Turner's Knipe

Churnet Valley Railway

River Churnet

ST9

1

Collyhole Brook

Rough Intake

Intake Farm

Stocks Green

Oddo Hall

CHURI MDV

CHURCHFIELD CT

50

99 **A** **B** 00 **C** **D** 01 **E** **F**

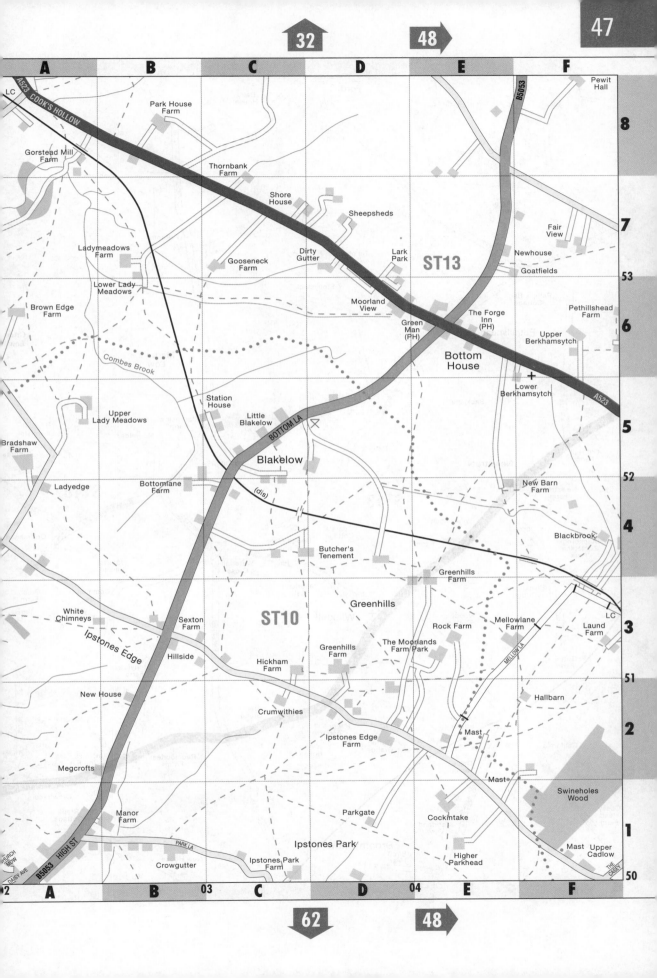

47
33

A B C D E F

8

Ford

Dairy House

Ford Wetley

Ford Farm

Ryebrook

7

Ten Acre Barn

Ford Grange

Sycamore Lodge

Felthouse

53

Bingham

Stonyslack

Pethills Bank Cottage

6

Pethillshead

Martin's Low

Grub Low

Backlane

Martinslow Farm

Moorside

Lawnfield

5

A523

Pethills

Ironpits

Gibgree

Old Hall Farm

Newstreet

ST10

52

Newstreet Farm

MARTINSLOW LA

HAYS LA

TOWNEND

4

Winkhillbank

Bank Farm

River Hamps

Coate's Cottage

Bridge Flats Farm

Croftshead

Blackbrook Zoological Park

BROMLEYHEDGE LA

Waterfall Cross

Waterfall Common

WATERWORLD LA

Black Brook

Moorland View

Common Side

Green Farm

Blackbrook Bridge

WATERFALL LA

LIME GR

3

LC's

Woodbine Cottage

Winkhill

BENTYGRANGE LA

Stonylow Farm

CROSS LA

BREECH CL

Gutter Farm

51

Benty Grange

Waterhouses CE Prim Sch

2

Station House

Paper Mill Farm

WATERFALL HA

ONE WAY

PORTLAN PL

California

(dis)

Cotton Grange

Willow House

Redmoorlee Farm

Crowtrees Farm Ind Est

HAMPS VALLEY RD

MANIFOLD C

Dulce Domun

ELLASTONE RD

THE CASEY

DUKE'S LA

A523

Swineholes Wood

Crowtrees

1

Moorland View

Steps Cottage

Casey Head Farm

Broomyshaw

New House Farm

Lee Brook

Birch Head

50

05 A B 06 C D 07 E F

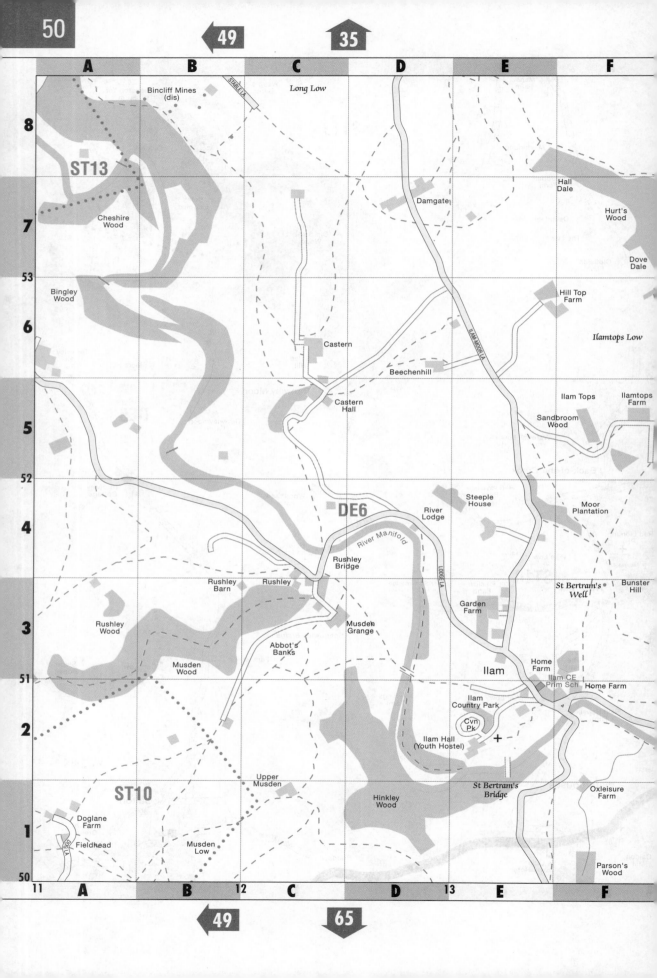

Bincliff Mines (dis)

STABLE LA

Long Low

ST13

Cheshire Wood

Damgate

Hall Dale

Hurt's Wood

Dove Dale

Bingley Wood

Hill Top Farm

Castern

ILAMMOOR LA

Ilamtops Low

Beechenhill

Castern Hall

Ilam Tops

Ilamtops Farm

Sandbroom Wood

DE6

Steeple House

River Lodge

Moor Plantation

River Manifold

Rushley Bridge

Rushley Barn   Rushley

LODGE LA

Garden Farm

St Bertram's Well

Bunster Hill

Rushley Wood

Musden Grange

Abbot's Banks

Musden Wood

Ilam

Home Farm

Ilam CE Prim Sch   Home Farm

Ilam Country Park

Cvn Pk

Upper Musden

Ilam Hall (Youth Hostel)

+

ST10

Hinkley Wood

St Bertram's Bridge

Oxleisure Farm

Doglane Farm

LANE

Fieldhead

Musden Low

Parson's Wood

A B C D E F

8

Hanson Grange

Moatlow Farm

A515

The Tissington Trail

Hillside

Hall Dale

The Nabs

Stand Low

Newton Grange

Dove Holes

Upper Taylor's Wood

Standlow

7

53

Pickering Cave

Bostern Grange Farm

Gaglane Barn

Broadclose

Ilam Rock

Pickering Tor

Bose Low

6

Dovedale Wood

Reynard's Cave

Dove Dale

Sharplow Farm

RAKES LA

Air Cottage

Sharplow Dale

Hollington Barn

A515

5

52

Jacob's Ladder

Tissington Spires

Moor Barn

DE6

A515 Ashbourne

Twelve Apostles

Lover's Leap

Derbyshire STREET ATLAS

4

River Dove

WASHBROOK LA

Dovedale Castle

Stepping Stones

Thorpe Pasture

Hollington End Farm

Wash Brook

Cave

Lin Dale

Limestone Way

Highfields Farm

51

Thorpe Cloud

Pike House

SPINDLA

MARLOW LA

3

Izaak Walton Hotel

P

Rifle Range

Hamston Hill

2

River Manifold

Peveril of the Peak Hotel

WINTERCROFT LA

The Narlows

St Mary's Bridge

Thorpe Mill Farm

DIGMIRE LA

Dog and Partridge Hotel (PH)

P

Station House

P

1

Fishpond Wood

WOODLANDS CL

CHURCH LA

The Firs

50

Thorpe

Broadlowash

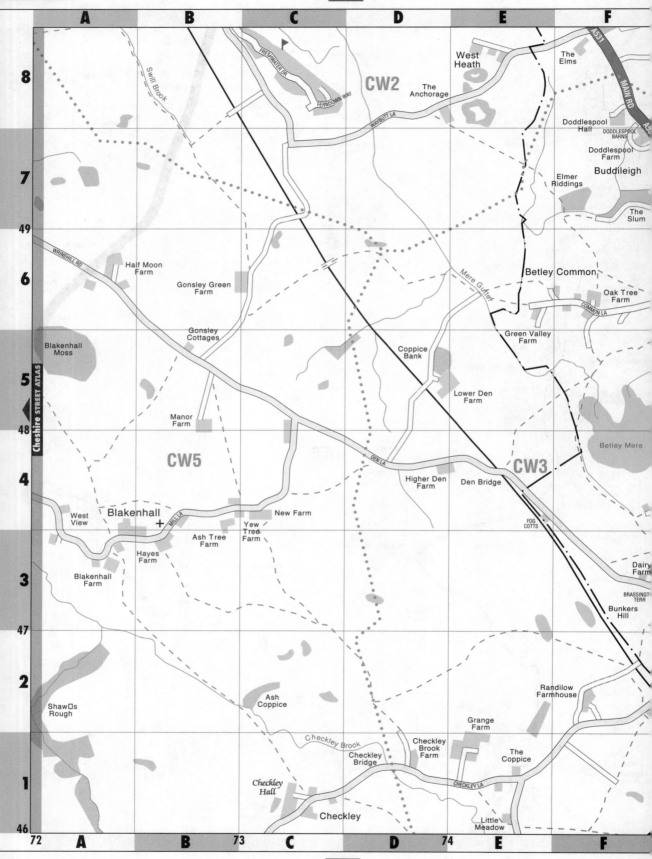

| | A | B | C | D | E | F |

8

Swill Brook

FRESHWATER DR

FERNDOWN WAY

CW2

WAYBUTT LA

West Heath

The Anchorage

The Elms

MAIN RD A531

Doddlespool Hall

DODDLESPOOL BARNS

Doddlespool Farm

7

Buddileigh

Elmer Riddings

The Slum

49

WRINEHILL RD

Half Moon Farm

Gonsley Green Farm

Mere Gutter

Betley Common

6

Oak Tree Farm

COMMON LA

Gonsley Cottages

Green Valley Farm

Blakenhall Moss

Coppice Bank

Cheshire STREET ATLAS

5

Manor Farm

Lower Den Farm

CW5

Betley Mere

48

DEN LA

Higher Den Farm

CW3

Den Bridge

4

West View

Blakenhall

MILL LA

New Farm

Ash Tree Farm

Yew Tree Farm

FOG COTTS

Dairy Farm

Hayes Farm

BRASSINGTON TERR

Blakenhall Farm

Bunkers Hill

47

Randilow Farmhouse

2

Shaw□s Rough

Ash Coppice

Grange Farm

The Coppice

Checkley Brook

Checkley Brook Farm

Checkley Bridge

CHECKLEY LA

1

Checkley Hall

Checkley

Little Meadow

46

| 72 | A | B | 73 | C | D | 74 | E | F |

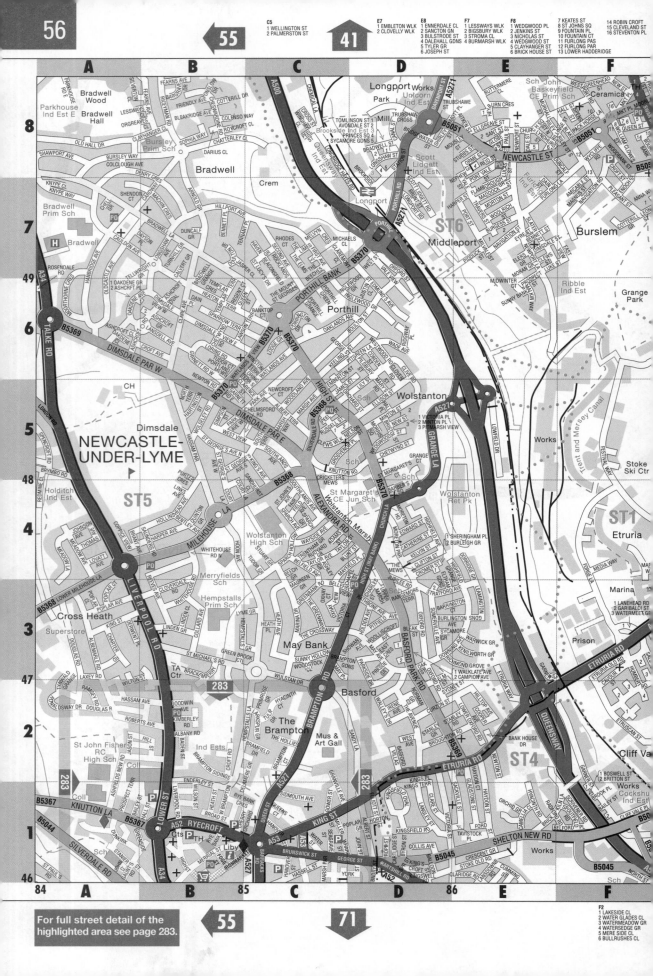

A B C D E F

8

Barns Farm

ST13

Park House

Consall Wood

A520

Rock View Farm

Powys Arms (PH)

CHEADLE RD

FOLLY LA

St John's CE Prim Sch

Smithy Pool

7

MILL LA

Wetley Rocks

Smit Sprir

Spout House

Old Hall Farm

THE BUNTING

MAIN RD

A522

PLOUGH BANK

49

Plough Inn (PH)

PO

Long Meadows

MEADOW AVE

Knowle Bank Farm

Consall Hall

OAKLANDS CL

Platt Newhouse Farm

RANDLES LA

ABBEY RD

CONSALL LA

Consall

6

LEEK RD

Park House

Consall

Middle Farm

A520

Darleyshire

Tunnel Farm

New Farm

Upper Farm

Keeper's Lodge Farm

Highfields Farm

Blackbank Plantation

ST9

Lodge Spinney

5

Wetley Abbey

CONSALL LA

Wetley Abbey Farm

Ivy House Farm

48

Upper Ladypark Woo

Consall Wood

4

Gate House Cottage

Mast

Windyhouse Wood

Out Wood

Broadoak Wood

Rangemoor Farm

New Park Farm

Little Broadoak Farm

Broadoak Farm

3

A52

KINGSLEY RD

LEEK RD

A522

New Farm

Blakeley Farm

Youngsgreen Farm

Brough's Wood

Overmoor

Richmoorhill Farm

Blakeley Lane

47

MARSH LA

ST10

Aboverpark Farm

Greenhead Farm

Greenhead

2

WINDYCOTE LA

Mount Pleasant

Little Aboverpark

Moor Farm

DAIRYHOUSE LA

Bank Top Farm

Waggon and Horses Inn (PH)

1

Little Bank Top Farm

Dairy House Farm

Kingsley Moor

A52

TICKHILL LA

DAIRYHOUSE LA

Lower Above Park

46

96 A B 97 C D 98 E F

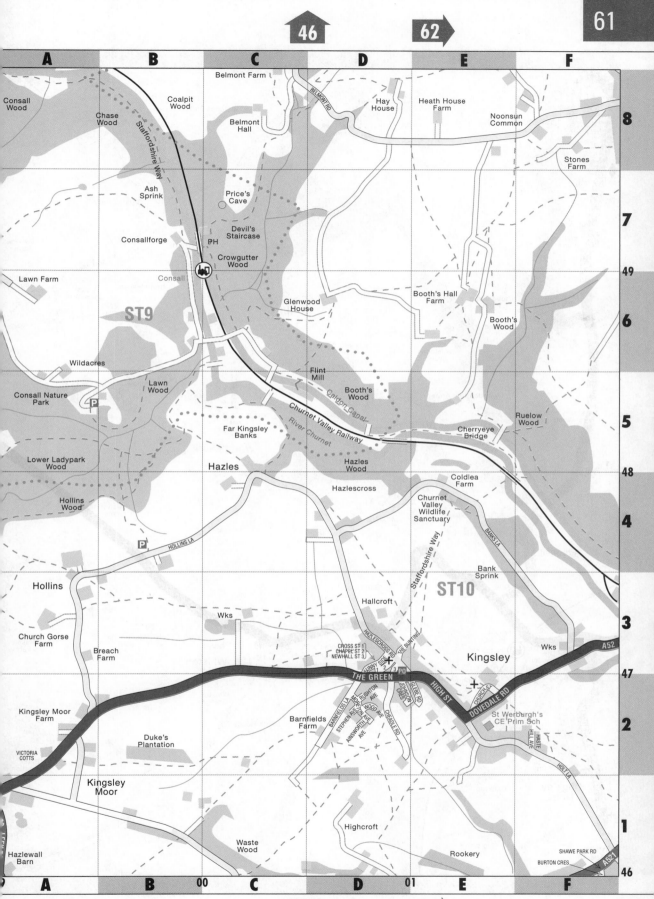

A   B   C   D   E   F

Consall
Wood

Belmont Farm

Chase
Wood

Coalpit
Wood

Belmont
Hall

Hay
House

Heath House
Farm

Noonsun
Common

8

Ash
Sprink

Price's
Cave

Stones
Farm

Consallforge

PH

Devil's
Staircase

7

Crowgutter
Wood

Consall

49

Lawn Farm

Glenwood
House

Booth's Hall
Farm

ST9

Booth's
Wood

6

Wildacres

Lawn
Wood

Flint
Mill

Booth's
Wood

Caldon Canal

Ruelow
Wood

Consall Nature
Park

P

Churnet Valley Railway

River Churnet

Cherryeye
Bridge

5

Far Kingsley
Banks

Hazles
Wood

48

Lower Ladypark
Wood

Hazles

Hazlescross

Coldlea
Farm

Hollins
Wood

Churnet
Valley
Wildlife
Sanctuary

4

P

HOLLINS LA

Staffordshire Way

Bank
Sprink

BANKS LA

Hollins

ST10

Church Gorse
Farm

Breach
Farm

Wks

Hallcroft

Kingsley

Wks

A52

CROSS ST 1
CHAPEL ST 2
NEWHALL ST 3

RYE BUNTING

3

SUNNY SIDE

PO

47

THE GREEN

HIGH ST

Kingsley Moor
Farm

Barnfields
Farm

BARNFIELDS LA

STEPHEN AVE

AINSWORTH
AVE

MORETON
AVE

WOOD AVE

CHEADLE RD

RUSHTON
AVE

JOHNSON
CRES

GLEBE RD

CHURCH
St

DOVEDALE RD

St Werburgh's
CE Prim Sch

HASTE
HILL AVE

HOLT LA

2

Duke's
Plantation

VICTORIA
COTTS

Kingsley
Moor

Highcroft

Waste
Wood

Rookery

SHAWE PARK RD

BURTON CRES

A521

1

Hazlewall
Barn

46

A   B   00   C   01   D   E   F

A B C D E F

8

7

49

6

48

5

4

47

3

2

46

02 A B 03 C D 04 E F

St Leonard's CE Fst Sch
PO
B5053
MAYFAIR AVE
MOUNT PLEASANT
BROOKFIELDS RD
Ipstones
St LEONARD'S AVE
BARLEY RD
REGENT CT
BIRLOW
Far Lane Ind Est
Paddock Farm
FROGHALL RD
Massey's Wood
Cloughhead Farm
Cloughhead Wood
Moseymoor Wood
Hermitage
Froghall
Froghall Wharf
P
Caldon Canal
B5053
RAILWAY TERR
BANK VIEW
RAILWAY
BROOKSIDE
A52
A521
The Railway Inn (PH)
Froghall Bridge
Kingsley & Froghall
HILLCREST AVE
HILLCREST CT
HILLCREST RD
SNEYD CT
CHURNET VALLEY RD
PO
Bank Top
Kingsley Holt
Staffordshire Way
A521
CHAPEL LA
LOCKWOOD CL
LOCKWOOD RD
Whiston Bridge
Churnet Valley Railway
River Churnet
Ochre Wood
Banktop Woods
Hag Wood
Well Wood
Eavesford Farm
Ross La
Ipstones Park
Lower Park Farm
Blackbank Wood
Whieldon's Wood
Foxt Wood
Woodcutters Arms (PH)
THE VILLAS
NEW COTTS
Fox and Goose (PH)
Foxt
PO
SHAY LA
Shirley Brook
ST10
Harston Wood
Gimmershill
Leys
St Mildred's CE Prim Sch
Whistonbrook
Heath House Farm
Littleheath Houses
Hopestone Farm
Ipstones Park Farm
PARK LA
Town Head
Newfields
SHAW-WALL LA
Shirley Hollow
Shirley Farm
Oldridge
Mount Pleasant Farm
The Sneyd Arms (PH)
PO
BROOKFIELD CL
ROSS RD
Whiston
THE SQUARE
BLACK LA
JUBILEE DR
Whiston Grange
WHISTON EAVES LA
Whiston Eaves
Parkhead
Parknook
Gorsty Croft Farm
Shaw Walls Farm
Lower Shaw-Wall
Shaw Wall Cottage
Shirley Common
A5
Whiston Common
BLAKELEY LA
Whiston Hall (CH)
Blakeley Farm
Whiston Barn
Black Plantation
Moneystone Quarry
EAVES LA
ST1

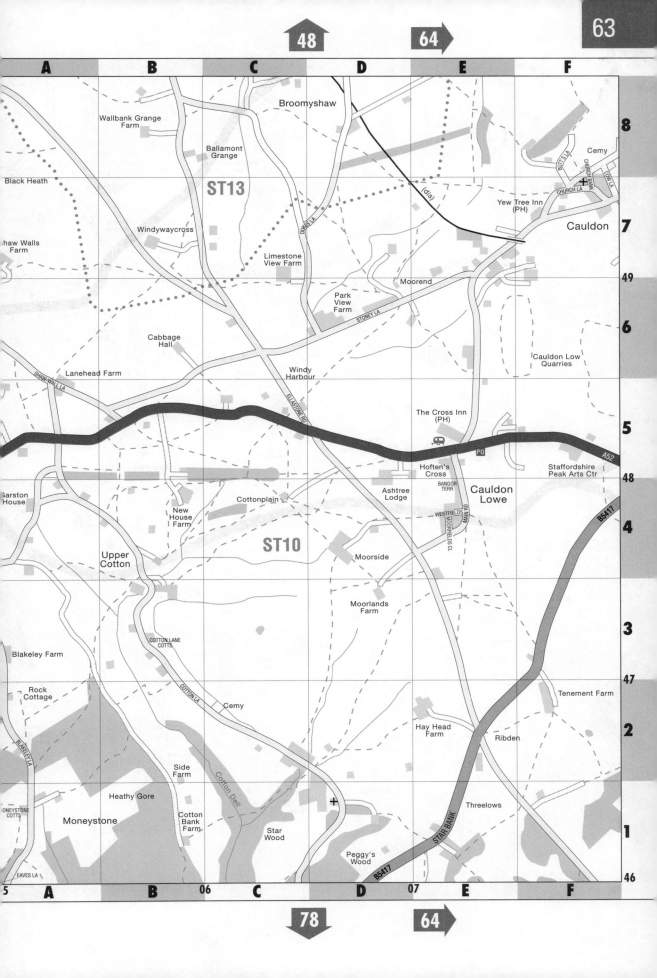

48
64

A **B** **C** **D** **E** **F**

8

Broomyshaw

Wallbank Grange Farm

Cemy

Ballamont Grange

BUTTS LA

CHURCH BANK

COW LA

ST13

Black Heath

CHURCH LA

Yew Tree Inn (PH)

Cauldon 7

Windywaycross

DUKES LA

(dis)

haw Walls Farm

Limestone View Farm

49

Moorend

Park View Farm

STONEY LA

6

Cabbage Hall

Cauldon Low Quarries

Lanehead Farm

SHAW WALL LA

Windy Harbour

ELLASTONE RD

The Cross Inn (PH)

5

PO

A52

Staffordshire Peak Arts Ctr

48

Garston House

Cottonplain

Ashtree Lodge

BANGOR TERR

Cauldon Lowe

B5417

New House Farm

WESTFIELDS

MOORFIELDS CL

ST10

Hoften's Cross

NEW RD

4

Upper Cotton

Moorside

Moorlands Farm

3

Blakeley Farm

COTTON LANE COTTS

47

Rock Cottage

COTTON LA

Tenement Farm

Cemy

Hay Head Farm

Ribden 2

BLAKELEY LA

Side Farm

COTTON DELL

Threelows

ONEYSTONE COTTS

Heathy Gore

Moneystone

Cotton Bank Farm

Star Wood

STAR BANK

1

Peggy's Wood

B5417

EAVES LA

46

A 06 **B** **C** **D** 07 **E** **F**

78
64

A **B** **C** **D** **E** **F**

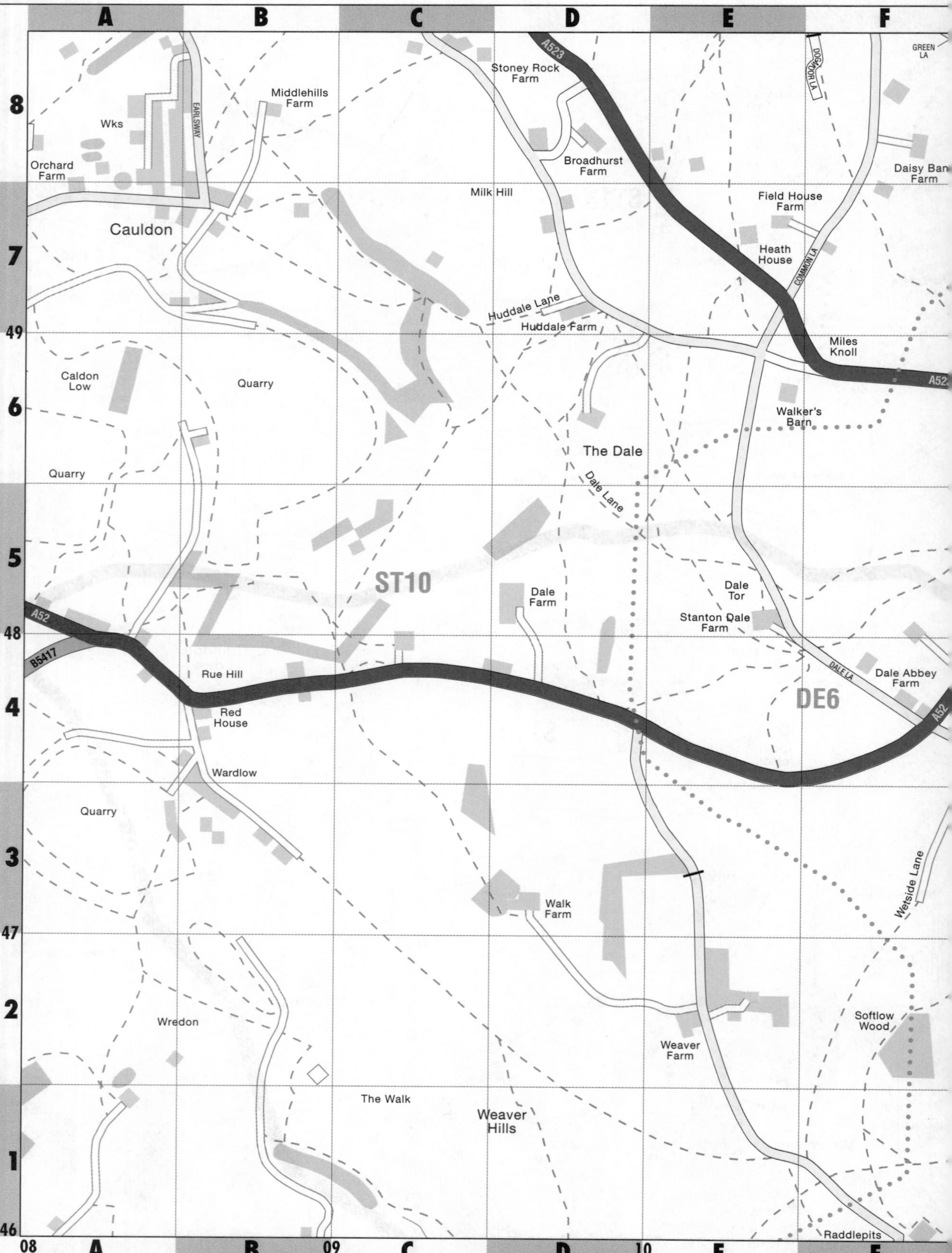

A523

8
Wks
Orchard Farm
Middlehills Farm
Stoney Rock Farm
EARLSWAY
Broadhurst Farm
Milk Hill
Field House Farm
DOG LOW LA
GREEN LA
Daisy Ban Farm

7
Cauldon
Heath House
COMMON LA

49
Huddale Lane
Huddale Farm
Miles Knoll
A52

6
Caldon Low
Quarry
Walker's Barn

Quarry
The Dale
Dale Lane

5
ST10
Dale Farm
Dale Tor
Stanton Dale Farm

48
A52
Stanton Dale Farm
DALE LA
Dale Abbey Farm

4
B5417
Rue Hill
Red House
DE6
A52

Wardlow

3
Quarry
Walk Farm
Wetside Lane

47

2
Wredon
Weaver Farm
Softlow Wood

The Walk
Weaver Hills

1

46
Raddlepits

08 **A** **B** **09** **C** **D** **10** **E** **F**

A **B** **C** **D** **E** **F**

8

Coldwall
Bridge

Limestone Way

Little Peg's
Wood

Tissington Trail

Spendlane
Farm

SPEND LA

7

Coldwall
Farm

49

Littlepark

6

Lees House
Farm

Yerley
Farm

YERLEY HILL

Kendar
Wood

Hinchley
Wood

Hinchleywood

5

Martin
Hill

Cowclose
Wood

Okeover
Hall

DE6

Mill
Okeover
Bridge

Bank
Farm

48

Marten
Hill

Okeover
Park

Okeover
Arms
(PH)

Mapleton

4

A52

Limestone Way

Lower
Grounds
Farm

Smythe's
Plantation

River Dove

Callowend
Farm

3

Cornpark

The
Orchards

BIRDSGROVE LA

Manor
House

Callow
Hall

47

Snelsdale

Snelsdale
Wood

2

SWINSCOE HILL

Throstle
Nest

Birdsgrove
Farm

Butler's
Holme

Bentley Brook

Limestone Way

Lordspiece

STANTON LA

The
Cliffs

1

Harlow
Farm

Big
Quarry
Wood

Birdsgrove
House

Sewage
Wks

**Upper
Mayfield**

PICCADILLY LA

GALLOWSTREE LA

SLACK LA

HOLLOW LA

A52

Buckholme

Cemy
WATERY LA

46

14   **A**   **B**   15   **C**   **D**   16   **E**   **F**

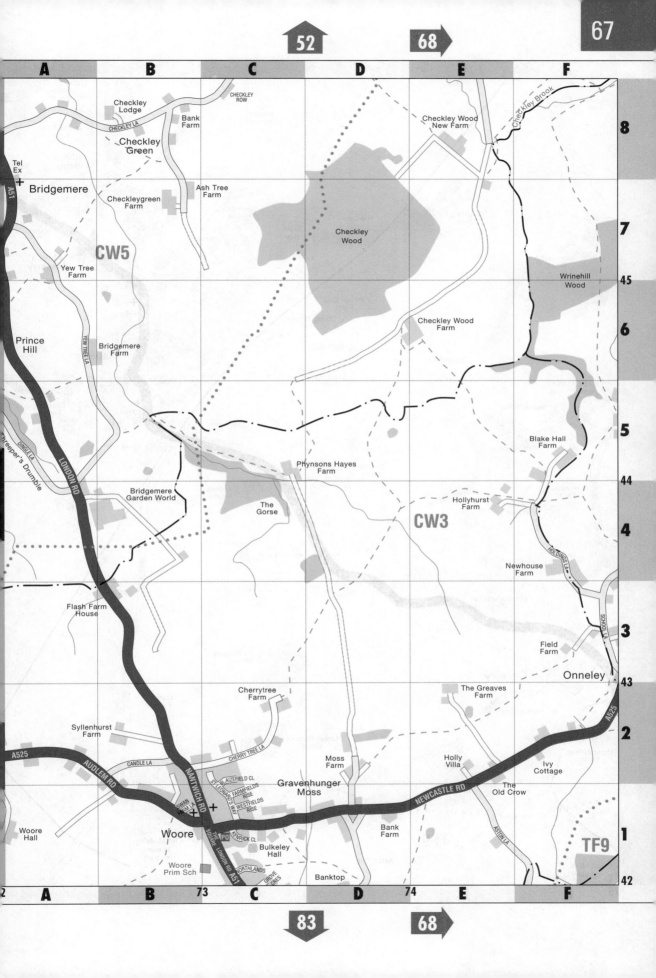

A B C D E F

8
7
45
6
5
44
4
3
43
2
1
42

Checkley Lodge
CHECKLEY LA
Bank Farm
CHECKLEY ROW
Checkley Wood New Farm
Checkley Brook

Checkley Green

Tel Ex
Bridgemere
Checkleygreen Farm
Ash Tree Farm

CW5

Checkley Wood

Wrinehill Wood

Yew Tree Farm

Checkley Wood Farm

Prince Hill
YEW TREE LA
Bridgemere Farm

DINGLE LA
Creeper's Drumble
LONDON RD

Blake Hall Farm

Phynsons Hayes Farm

Bridgemere Garden World

The Gorse
CW3
Hollyhurst Farm

HOLDINGS LA

Newhouse Farm

Flash Farm House

SCHOOL LA

Field Farm

Onneley

A525

Cherrytree Farm
The Greaves Farm

Syllenhurst Farm

A525
AUDLEM RD
CANDLE LA
NANTWICH RD
CHERRY TREE LA
BLAIZEFIELD CL
ST LEONARD'S WAY
FARMFIELDS RISE
WESTFIELDS RISE
Moss Farm
Gravenhunger Moss
Holly Villa
NEWCASTLE RD
Ivy Cottage
The Old Crow

Woore Hall

SWAN
THE SQUARE
PRIM LA
Woore
PO
KEVRICK CL
Bank Farm
ASTON LA
TF9

Woore Prim Sch
NORTHLANDS
LONDON RD
A51
Bulkeley Hall
GROVE CRES
Banktop

A
B 73
C
D 74
E
F

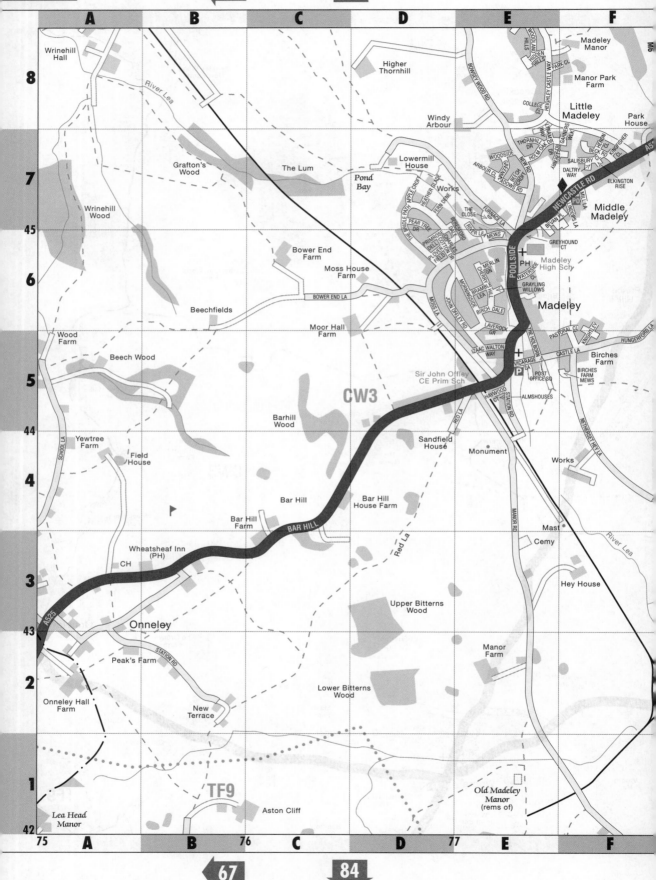

A   B   C   D   E   F

8   Hulme

Stonehouse Farm

HULME LA

THE DOTTS

The Candlesticks (PH)

Hall Farm

HULME RD

MALTHOUSE LA

Malthouse Farm

ST9

Creswell's Piece

ST10

Winterfield Farm

WINTERFIELD LA

SALTERS LA

A520

7

Blythe Lea

Smallbrook Farm

LEEK RD

Captain's Barn

Ford

Sheepwash Farm

Sheepwash

Ward H Farm

45

6

Visitor Ctr

Parkhall Ctry Pk

Boltongate Farm

Roughcote

Tickhill Farm

COALVILLE PL

ASTER CL

CARNATION CL

DAHLIA CL

EAST ST

LYNN ST

Caverswall Common

Hardiwick Farm

FERN LEA GR

COUPE DR

SELBY ST

IRIS CL

LILAC CL

LIME CL

LAVENDER CL

River Blithe

5

Weston Coyney

HORTON DR

ENGLESEA AVE

OSWALD AVE

PARK AVE

BATH ST

CROSS ST

FLINT ST

DIMMELOW CL

WEST ST

MAIN ST

SITE ST

FOXGLOVE CL

THE CLOSE

Sch

ROUGHCOTE LA

Cocking Farm

44

PARK HALL RD

A5272

ST3

HEATHCOTE RISE

HEYSHAM CL

WELDON AVE

STRANRAER CL

HOLYHEAD CRES

Intakes Farm

ST11

ST10

4

KENDAL GR

MINARD GR

ROSS CL

TAME WLK

Sch

IBSEN RD

GEOFFREY ST

WESTON DR

PARK HALL CRES

THE MOAT

HALL GR

FITZGERALD CL

HAYNER GR

PALADIN AVE

COLIN CRES

CAVERSWALL RD

Green Farm

Yewtree Farm

CARBERRY WAY

TRAITORS DR

PARKHEAD GR

WESTON COYNEY RD

NEW KINGSWAY

QUEENS WLK

PRINCESS DR

FIELD VIEW

AXON CRES

DALE VIEW

YORK RD

VALLEY VIEW

QUEENS CT

THE GREEN

THE LONG ROW

HALLDEARN AVE

HADLEY BANKS

Parkhead

COPPICE GR

PADWORTH PL

DAWN VIEW

TERRY CL

NATHAN CL

TREVOR DR

Cookshill Hall

3

Weston Sprink

COYNEY GR

SPRINGWOOD GR

WESTON RD

TILLET GM

MICHAEL CL

BRINDON CL

MYRTLE AVE

Cookshill

MILL LA

VICARAGE RD

HIGH ST

THE CROCKETT

Tunstall Sytch

43

WHITCOMBE RD

LANSBURY GR

CLIVES ST

GLANVILLE

BURY PL

WEBB ST

MAIN ST

BEVERIDGE CL

Weston Coyney Jun Sch

MACDONALD CRES

BIRD ST

GOODWIN RD

BROOKHOUSE

WESTWOOD RD

CODSER

SNOWDEN WAY

BURNS WAY

BONDFIELD ROW

MAXTON WAY

TWINEY CRES

DEVANS CL

FELL ST

St Peter's CE Prim Sch

THE DAMS

PO

The Red House PH

Caverswall

DILHORNE LA

2

BROADWAY

OAK PL

CHERRY HILL AVE

ELLIS ST

YARNFIELD PL

BROWNFIELD RD

WOODVILLE RD

HARVEY ST

WOOD RD

BLATCHFORD ST

MAPLE PL

STANSMORE RD

MONTGOMERY CL

PENNINGTON CL

THE WOOD

Castle

St Filumena's RC Prim Sch

GABLE COTTS

BLYTHE BRIDGE RD

STOKE-ON-TRENT

1

Meir

LOMBARDY GR

BROADWAY

BRIGHT ST

EAST GR

PENLEET AVE

STANTON RD

ROWNALL RD

NORTH WLK

SOUTH WLK

TIPPING AVE

RAM WOOD CL

BECKETT AVE

DENEWOOD PL

BRIARWOOD PL

MEADOW

Crescent Prim Sch

Wood House Farm

Caverswall Park

PO

Meir Prim Sch

LYME RD

GEORGE AVE

WILLOWOOD GR

CAVERSWALL LA

Caverswall Road

Mast

Foxfield Steam Rly

42

Elby

A50

SANDON RD

GRANGEWOOD RD

HARTWELL RD

HARBROOK RD

MOLLISON RD

EDNAM

UTTOXETER RD

APPLEWOOD CRES

EDENHURST AVE

LC

93   A   94   B   C   95   D   E   F

← 73

↓ 90

A1
1 DENEHURST CL
2 ROWNHALL PL
3 CORNELIOUS ST
4 SMITHS BLDGS
5 REDWOOD PL
6 BROADWAY CT
7 QUEENSWAY CT
8 PICKFORD PL
9 CHATSWORTH PL
10 SARACEN WAY
11 CROSSLAND PL W
12 COBHAM PL

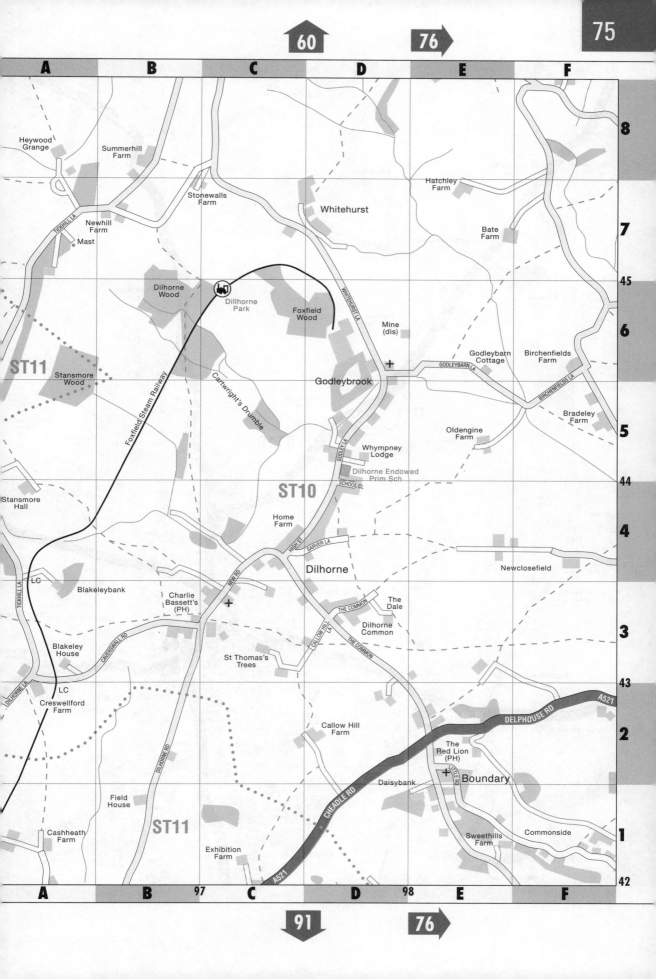

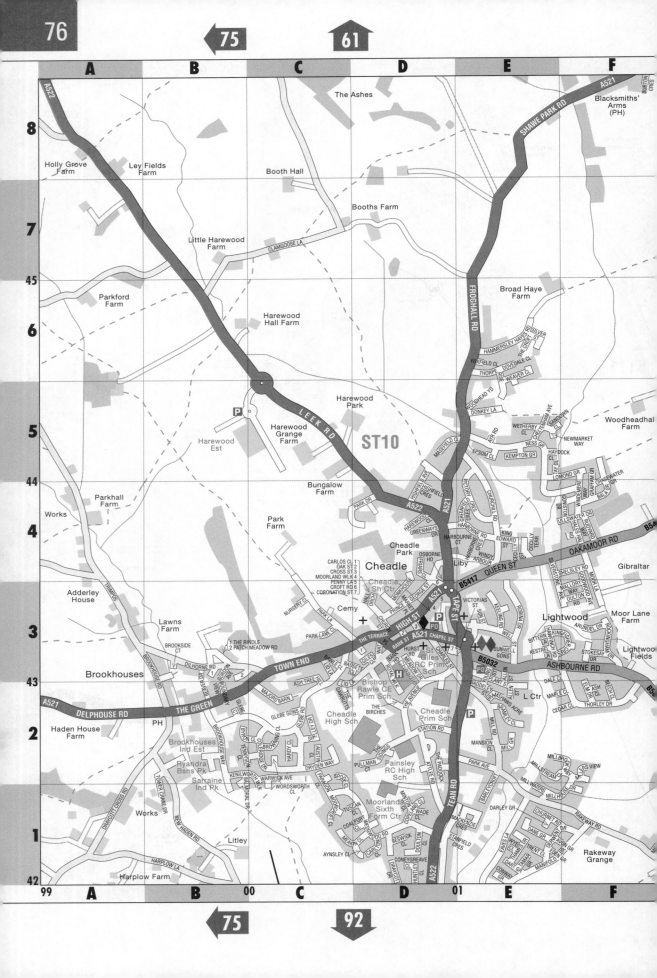

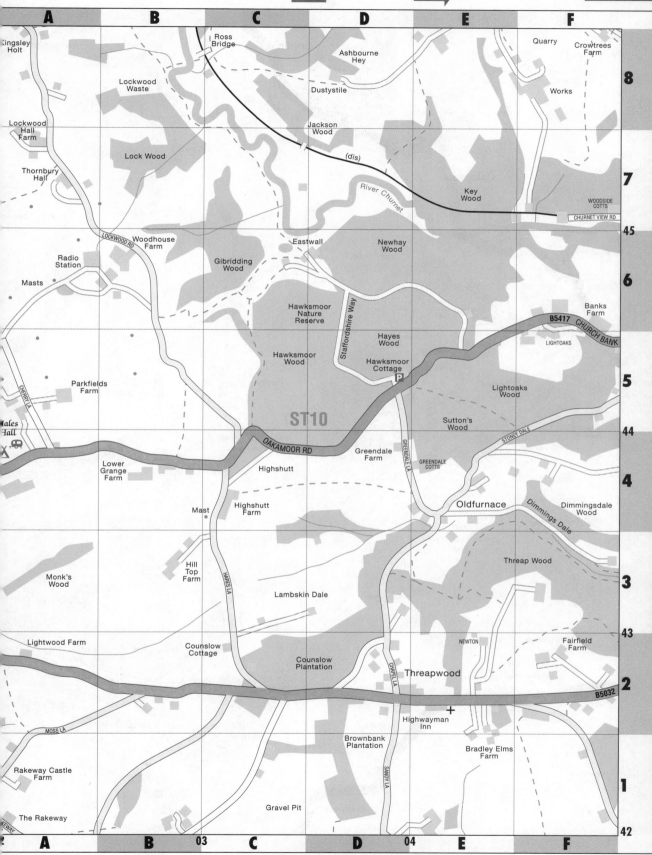

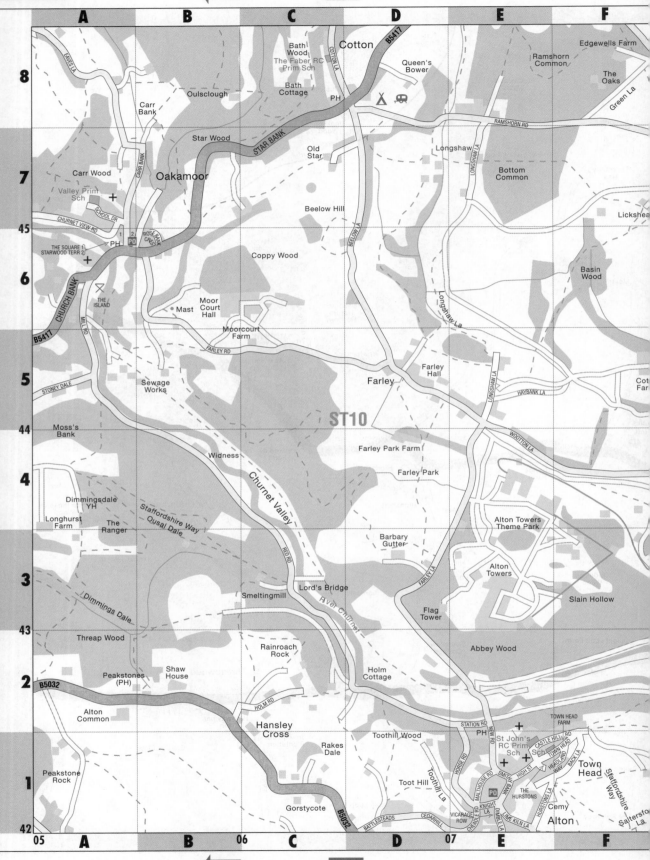

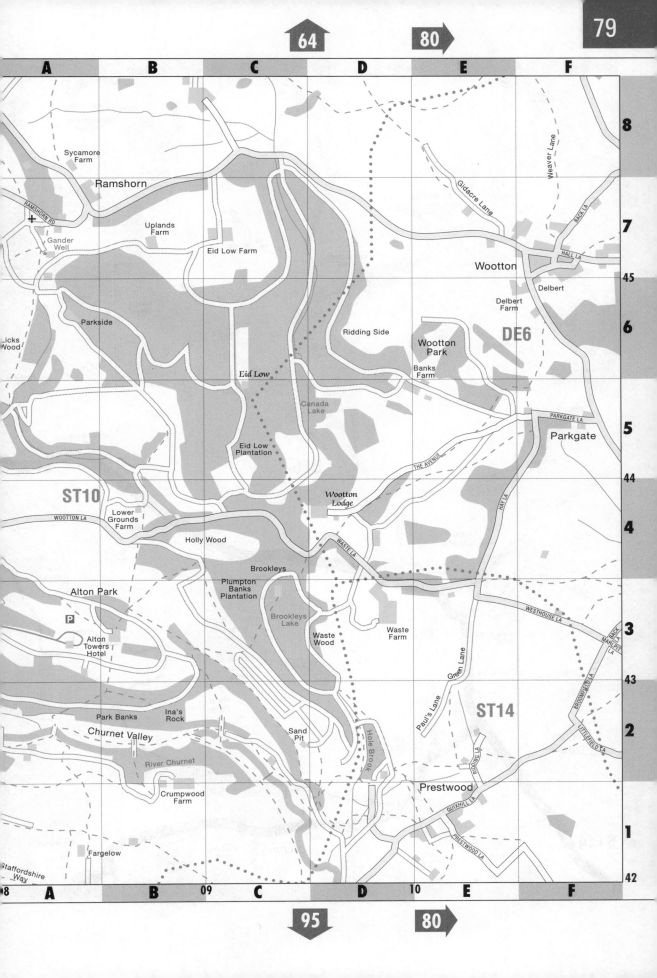

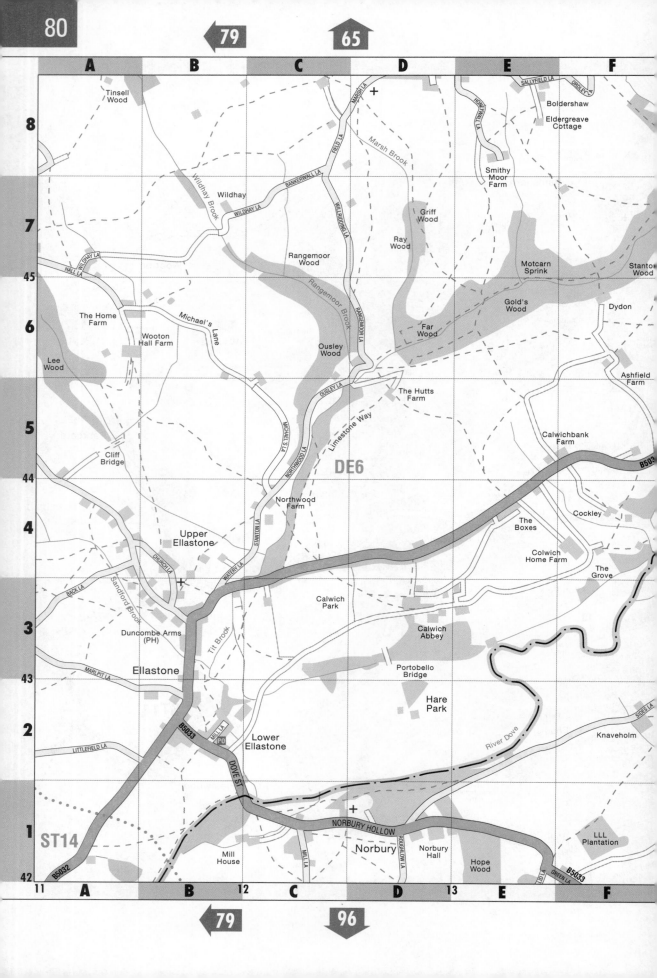

A B C D E F

8

WATERY LA

Woodside Farm

A52

PH

OLD BANK

BRIDGE VIEW

Hanging Bridge

MAYFIELD RD A52

A52 Derby

Harlow Wood

SLACK LA

GALLOWSTREE LA

Mayfield

THE PARK

TOLLGATE COTTS

STONE COTTS

DIAMOND JUBILEE COTTS

Hangingbridge

A515 Ashbourne

CHURNET CL 1
KINVER CL 2
SUNNYBANK 3
HOLME BANK 4
DOVESIDE 5
OXMEAD 6
SYCAMORE RD 7
EAST VIEW 8

Slack Lane

ASHBOURNE RD

MAIN RD B5032

PO

Alrewas Mill

Holme Farm

GREEN LA

Ford

DOLES LA

7

Holme Farm

SLACK LA

HERMITAGE LA

WALLASH

ASHLEY

JUBILEE DR

THE CRESCENT

CONYGREE LA

WEIRSIDE

MEADOWSIDE

WATERY LA

Doles Farm

DOLES LA

THE GREENACRE

CLIFTON RD

A515 Ashbourne

45

THE FAIRWAYS

CROSS SIDE

Clifton CE Prim Sch

Middle Mayfield

PH

Factory

1 2 3

Clifton Bridge

CLIFTON RD

PO

Henmore Brook

CHURCH VIEW

COCK HILL

CH

6

CHURCH LA

River Dove

1 MAYFIELD TERR
2 WEST VIEW
3 SOUTH VIEW

Church Mayfield

PH

Clifton

HOLLIES CL

CHAPEL LA

Cliff Bank Cottage

SPRINKSWOODS LA

Cemy

A515

DOBBINHORSE LA

5

SIDES LA

Sides Plantation

Mountpleasant Farm

Derbyshire STREET ATLAS

44

Toadhole Foot Bridge

DE6

Collycroft

4

PARKFIELD LA

Gravelpit Covert

LITTLEFIELD LA

Snelston Park

Lower Dumble

Collycroft Farm

3

Snelston

BROOKSIDE COTTS

CHURCH RD

Snelston Hall

Windmill Farm

Upper Dumble

OLDFIELD LA

CACKLE HILL LA

Cackle Hill

BETLINGSPRING LA

WINDMILL LA

43

DEEPDALE LA

Old Slade La

Overton Farm

SNAPES LA

Thornyhill Farm

VIRGINSALLEY LA

Brook Farm

Gorse Covert

A515

2

Deepdale

Ashton Close

Virginsalley

Lower Brookfarm Dumble

Headlow Fields

High Grounds

Snelston Firs

Anacrehill

1

Rose Cottage

A515 Lichfield

42

CW3

Long
Wood

College
Fields

College
Fields

College Field
Cottages

Hankins
Heys

Poplars
Farm

Square
Plantation

Mere
Cottage

Mere
Farm

Bellaport
Home Farm

Bellaport
Old Hall

New
Cottages

Norton
Wood
Farm

The
Grove

Bellaport
Wood

Ladies
Wood

Wet Butts
Plantation

Greenacre

TF9

THE
CROFT

Bellaport
Lodge
Farm

Brand Hall
Farm

Cemy

River Tern

Napley
Farm

CHURCH
FIELDS

CHURCH
WLKS

ST CHAD'S
WAY

Brook
Farm

Napley
Lodge

PH

Norton in Hales
CE Prim Sch

Norton in
Hales

Marlpit
Plantation

Brand
Hall

83
68

A B C D E F

8

Radwood Copse

CW3

Rock House Farm

7

ASTON LA

SCHOOL LA

Aston

Lunts Farm

Radwood Hall Farm

41

Yew Tree Farm

HOLLOWAY LA

6

Minnbank

Bank Farm

Holloway Pit Holes

Holloway Farm

Holloway Lane Farm

Radwood Farm

Minnbank Farm

MAERWAY LA

Maerway Lane Farm

Mast

5

Greenfields

Willoughbridge

Camp Wood

40

A51

The Dorothy Clive Garden

ST5

4

TF9

Sidway Hall Farm

Maer Hills

Sidway

BADGER LA

3

Willoughbridge Bogs

Sidway Mill Farm

WOOD LA

A5

River Tern

THE CROFT

39

Blackbrook

White Farm

A53

Swan with Two Necks (PH)

A5

2

Park House

Lower Bogs Plantation

A53

The Bogs

WHARMADINE LA

MOSS LA

Maer Moss Farm

Workings

Hungersheath Farm

NEWCASTLE RD

1

PARK LA

A53

ROCK LA

The Wellings

38

75 A B 76 C D 77 E F

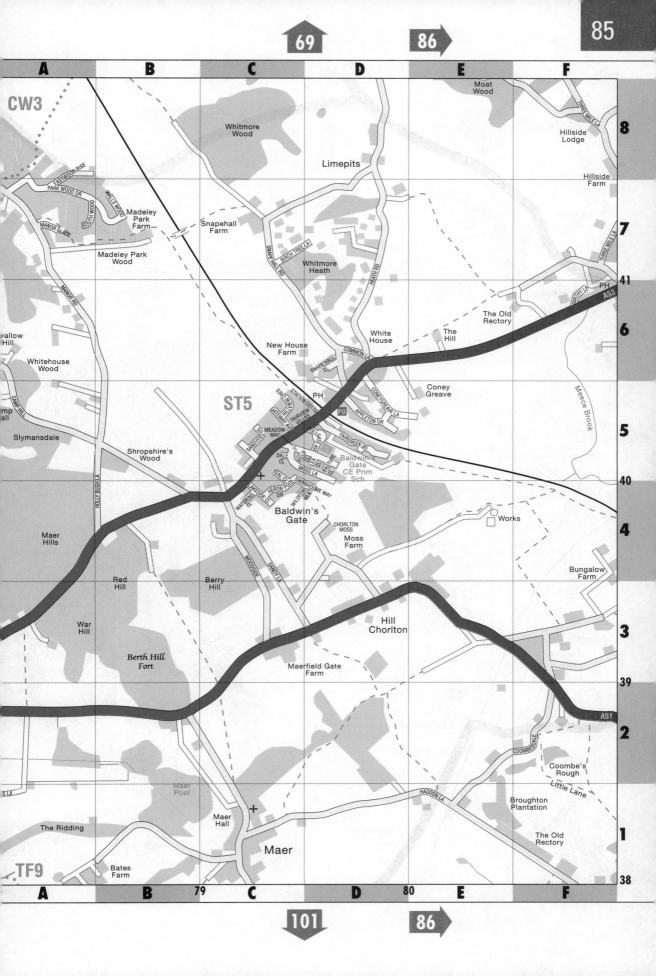

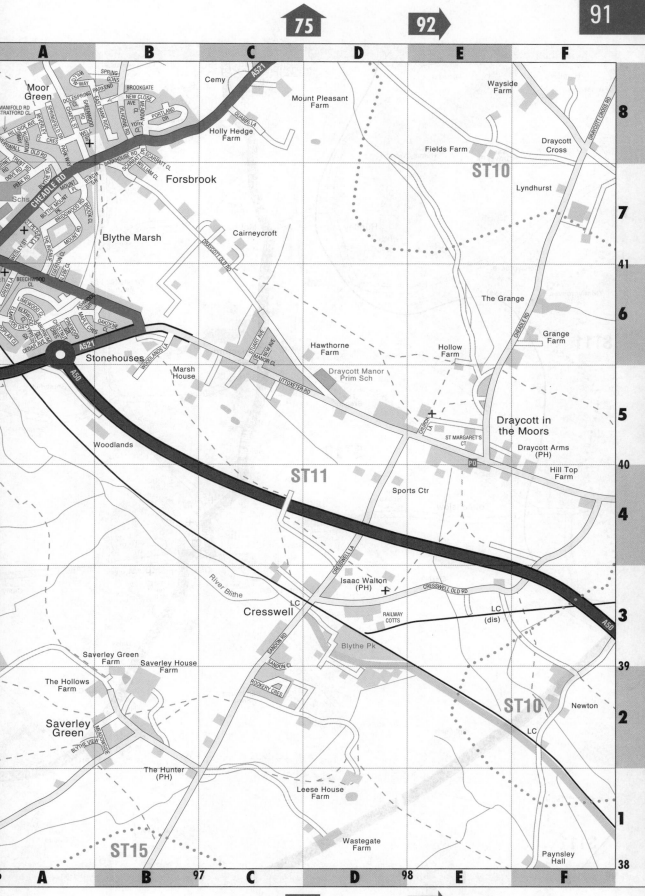

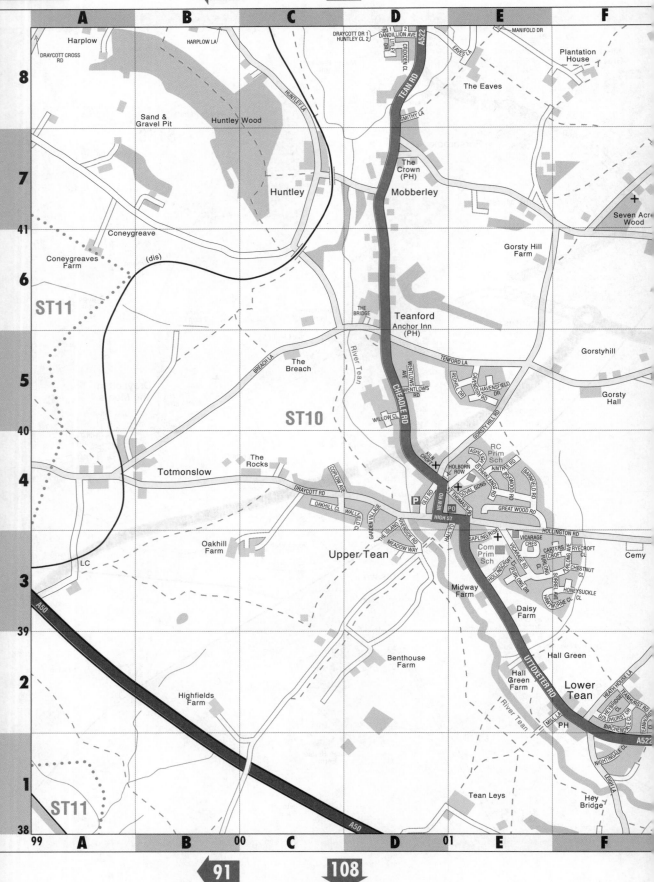

Harplow

Draycott Cross RD

HARPLOW LA

Sand & Gravel Pit

Huntley Wood

HUNTLEY LA

DRAYCOTT DR 1
HUNTLEY CL 2

DANDILLION AVE
LITLEY DR
CROXDEN CL

MANIFOLD DR

Plantation House

8

TEAN RD

The Eaves

A522

SMITHY LA

EAVES LA

7

Huntley

The Crown (PH)

Mobberley

Seven Acre Wood

41

Coneygreave

Gorsty Hill Farm

ST11

Coneygreaves Farm

(dis)

THE BRIDGE

Teanford

Anchor Inn (PH)

Gorstyhill

6

TENFORD LA

WENTLOWS AVE

WENTLOWS RD

5

BREACH LA

The Breach

River Tean

CHEADLE RD

REDHILL DR

CAVENDISH RD

HAVENSFIELD DR

GORSTY HILL RD

Gorsty Hall

ST10

WILLOW CL

40

The Rocks

KILN CROFT

RC Prim Sch

4

Totmonslow

COPLOW AVE

DRAYCOTT RD

OAKHILL CL

WALLE CL

GARDEN VILLAGE

OLD RD

NEW RD

HOLBORN ROW

ST THOMAS'S RD

OVAL GDNS

ASH LEA

ORCHARD LANE

AINTREE

HEYWOOD RD

BARNFIELD RD

GREAT WOOD RD

HOLLINGTON RD

CARTERS CROFT

CHESTNUT CL

RYECROFT CL

Cemy

Oakhill Farm

THE ISLAND

RIVERSIDE RD

MEADOW WAY

Upper Tean

HIGH ST

HALL LTD

SAPLING RISE

Com Prim Sch

VICARAGE CRES

VICARAGE RD

HOLLINSCROFT

FURLONG DR

FURLONG CL

SORREL AVE

HONEYSUCKLE CL

LC

Midway Farm

HAWTHORNE CL

Daisy Farm

3

39

A50

Highfields Farm

Benthouse Farm

Hall Green

UTTOXETER RD

2

Hall Green Farm

Lower Tean

HEATH HOUSE LA

TEANHURST RD

GOLDHURST CL

TEANFORD RD

BIRCHENDALE LA

MILL LA

PH

A522

1

ST11

Tean Leys

NIGHTINGALE CL

LEIGH LA

Hey Bridge

38

99 A B 00 C D 01 E F

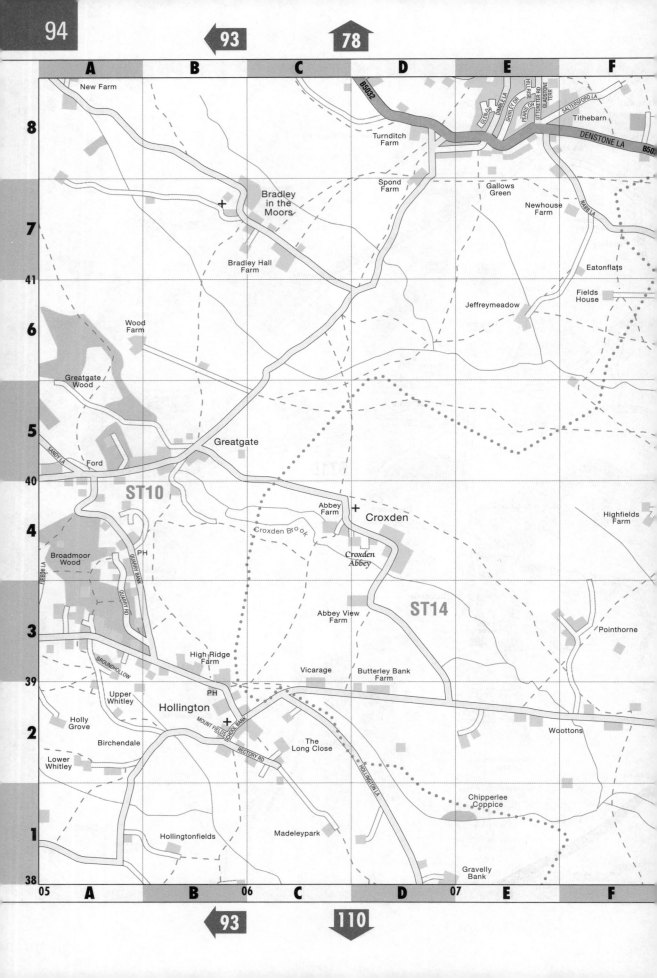
New Farm

B5032

Turnditch Farm

GLEN DR
DIMBLE LA
PEARS DR
SHIRLEY DR
BSMITH
UTTOXETER RD
GLADSTONE TERR
SALTERSFORD LA

Tithebarn

DENSTONE LA

B50..

8

Bradley in the Moors

Spond Farm

Gallows Green

Newhouse Farm

NABB LA

Eatonflats

Fields House

41

Bradley Hall Farm

Jeffreymeadow

7

Wood Farm

6

Greatgate Wood

SANDY LA

Ford

Greatgate

5

ST10

40

Croxden Brook

Abbey Farm

Croxden

Highfields Farm

4

Broadmoor Wood

PH

QUARRY BANK

QUARRY RD

FARRM LA

Croxden Abbey

ST14

Pointhorne

Abbey View Farm

3

GROUNDHOLLOW

High Ridge Farm

Vicarage

Butterley Bank Farm

39

Upper Whitley

PH

Holly Grove

Hollington

MOUNT FIELDS
SCHOOL BANK

Woottons

2

Birchendale

RECTORY RD

The Long Close

Lower Whitley

HOLLINGTON LA

Chipperlee Coppice

1

Hollingtonfields

Madeleypark

Gravelly Bank

38

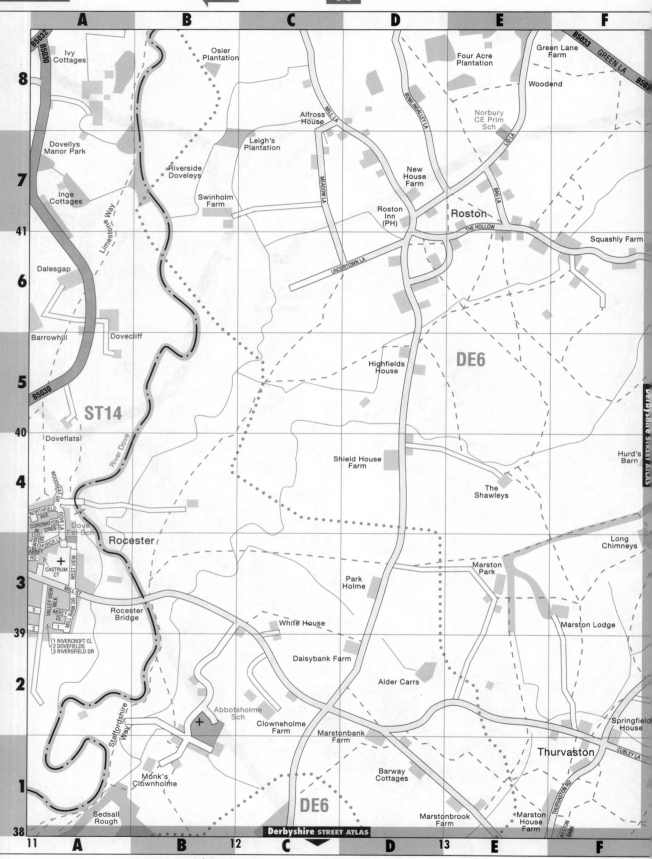

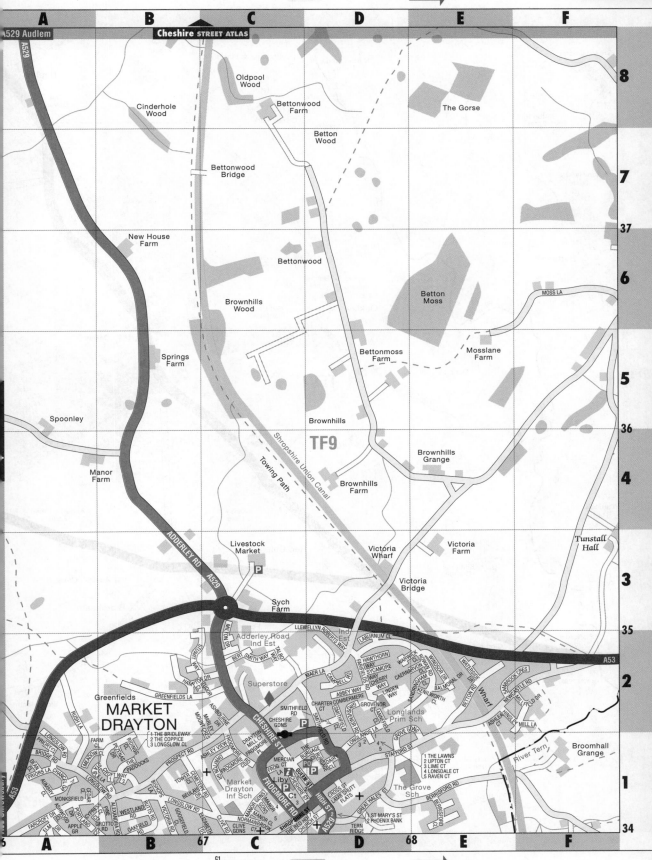

A529 Audlem

Cheshire STREET ATLAS

TF9

MARKET DRAYTON

C1
1 WILKINSON WLK
1 THE BRIDLEWAY
2 THE COPPICE
3 LONGSLOW CL
C1
1 WILKINSON WLK
2 THE BUTTERCROSS
3 RODENHURST HOUSE FLATS
4 CORBET CT
5 WARREN CT

A   B   C   D   E   F

Greenhill Farm

FORGE LA

The Arbour

NAPLEY RD

8

Norton Forge
Farm

Devil's Ring & Finger

Napley

Betton Hall
Farm

Oakley Park

The Haven

7

Betton Hall

Park
House

37

OAKLEY LA

Betton

Oakley Hall

6

Betton
Farm

Oakley
Park
Farm

Bache
Pool

Oakley

Old Pool
Plantation

MOSS RD

River Tern

Oakley
Folly

5

Marlpit Wood

TF9

The
Folly

36

Drayton
Spinney

Oakley
Lodges

4

Tunstall
Hall

The
Rough

Daisy
Lake

Audley's Cross
Farm

A

3

Shiffords
Grange

Red Bull

Audley's Cross

The
Park

B5415

SANDY LA

Bloreheath

35

Shifford's
Bridge

Clod Hall

Bloreheath
Farm

A53

PINFOLD LA

2

NEWCASTLE RD

NEW
COUNCIL HOS

Almington

Sand Pit

Blore Heath
Farm

BLORE RD

Upper House
Farm

Little Heath
Green

Almington
Hall

1

Coal Brook

Sand Pit

Hales Farm

FLASH LA

34

Hales

69   A   B   70   C   D   71   E   F

99
84

A **B** **C** **D** **E** **F**

8

Birch House
Rough

Manor
House
Farm

Castle Hill

Manor
Hill

Fields
Farm

Oak
Wood

7

LORDSLEY LA

NEWCASTLE RD

A53

PARK LA

SANDY LA

Holly Croft
Farm

Rock
House

WHARMADINE LA

Sniggle
Pits

37

6

A53

The
Oaks

WESLEYAN RD

SCHOOL LA

CHAPEL LA

ELDERTREE LA

ELDERTREE LA

CHURCH RD

ROCK LA

Akesworth
Coppice

Peel
Arms
(PH)

GRAVELLY HILL

THE DALE

BACK LA

ST JOHNS RD

ST
JOHNS
WAY

DOCTOR'S BANK

CHURCH
FARM

GERARDS WAY

GREEN LA

Middle Coppice

5

Ashley

Ashley
Dale

ORCHARD
CL

SOVEREIGN LA

CHAINES RD

WOODROW
WAY

THE CRESCENT

BELL ORCH

36

TIMKERS LA

LARKHILL LA

CHARLESFORD LA

NORRIS CL

ESSELIE AVE

TF9

Greenlane
Coppice

4

The
Robin Hood
(PH)

LOWER RD

JUG BANK

Jugbank

Podmo
Pool

RUDGE DALE RD

3

35

The
Rudge

2

B5026

Broughton
Birches

New
Wood

Bromley
Hall

Ashley Road
Plantation

1

Broughton
Folly

B5026

ST21

Broughton Wood

34

75 **A** **B** **76** **C** **D** **77** **E** **F**

85

102

A B C D E F

8

New Pool

7

TF9

ST5

Western Meres
Farm

Swinchurch
Rough

Swinchurch Brook

Swinchurch
Farm

37

6

CLAYALDERS BANK

Shortwood
Cottages

Weston
Hall

WESTON LA

Weston House
Farm

Weston House
Cottages

Burley
Cottage

Shortwood
Farm

BARHILL A

5

MAER LA

36

Gorse View

Podmore House
Farm

Podmore

Shortwood
Barn

ST21

Standon Hall
Wood

Standon Old
Hall

STANDON
CT

4

Pear Tree
Farm

Chatcull Brook

3

Bromley Mill
Farm

35

Bromley Brook

Ford

Gerrard□s
Bromley

2

Chatcull
House

Chatcull

Green
Farm

CHATCULL LA

The Alders

The Green

Applegate
Cottage

1

Chatcull
Wood

34

A B C D E F

79 80

116

102

A B C D E F

8

7

37

6

5

36

4

35

2

1

34

New Waste Plantation

A519

ST4

Green Lane

Beech House Farm

TOP LA

The Greathills

M6

BEECHDALE LA

BLUEBELL CL

FIELD RISE RD

Groundslow Fields

ST12

WINGHOUSE LA

CHASE LA

Swynnerton Heath Farm

BOTTOM LA

The Stretters

Cash's Pit

Calloway Pit

Wing House Farm

Green Birch Farm

Sandyford

Eastwood

Long Compton Farm

Whitehouse

Closepit Plantation

Sandyford Farm

Wood Cottage Farm

A51

ST15

Lodge Covert

ST21

Swynnerton

FITZHERBERT CL 1
THE ORCHARD 2
BERNARD CHEADLE CL 3

Fitzherbert Arms (PH)

Kennels Cottages

PO

Flash Pit

FAIRBANKS WLK
THE HAY BARNS
LAWRENCE DR
MILL WAY
MONKS WAY
FITZHERBERT DR
EARLY LA
WILLIAMS WLK
WEAVERS WLK

PARK VIEW

Our Lady's RC Prim Sch

Swynnerton Hall

HALL LA

Blakelow

M6

Swynnerton Park

The Dixons

Grange Cottages

Cotes

COTES LA

The Crossash

Swynnerton Grange

Cotes House Farm

BIRCH HOUSE LA

COATES AVE

The Doles

BLACKFLATS RD

PILSTONES RD

CENTRAL AVE

PILSTONES WAY

Withy Bed

Highlowbank

HORSLEY RD

BIRCH HOUSE RD

A B C D E F

85 86

A B C D E F

8

Barton Land

Heyfields

TITTENSOR RD

HEYFIELDS COTTS

Heyfields Farm

ST12

RIDGE CL

DIAMOND RIDGE

DIAMOND CL

PARK DR

SILVER RIDGE

BOATYARD COTTS

Downs Banks

7

CHASE LA

Inn

CH

Tittensor Chase

Spring Vale

37

Tittensor Chase

Warren House Farm

MEAFORD RD

6

Saxon's Lowe

Hilltop

Turnover Bridge

Ford

5

A51

Firs Cottage

Meaford Farm

WASH DALE LA

36

Bury Bank Farm

Bury Bank

BANKSIDE

River Trent

Siddall's Bridge

4

Marlpit House

Burybank

The Darlaston (PH)

A34

A51

P

ST15

Meaford Hall

ST VINCENT MEWS

Meaford

Meaford Old Hall Farm

Outlanes Mill Farm

M6

JERVIS LA

3

Darlastonwood Farm

The Drumble

George and Dragon (PH)

Turnover Bridge

KNOWLES DR

BARNTON EDGE

Trent and Mersey Canal

1 CRESSY CL
2 CALDON WAY
3 HARECASTLE BANK
4 SALTERSFORD RISE
5 RANGELEY VIEW
6 DARWIN CL
7 DIXON CL

Edge Hill

Common Plot

35

ANDERTON VIEW

BENTLEY CL

REMDER GR

BRINDLEY CL

RUDYARD CL

NEW MILLENNIUM WAY

STATION RD

LC

Works

Stonefield

Mount Ind Est

KENT GR

MOUNT AVE

2

Darlaston Wood

WHITEBRIDGE

CHANNEL RD

CENTRE RD

CANAL SIDE

WHITEBRIDGE WAY

CHESTNUT GR

Whitebridge Ind Est

Stone

Mount Rd

FIELD HOUSE CT

MOUNT CRES

BERKELEY ST

VICTORY ST

B5375

1

Darlaston Park

Home Farm

THE FILLYBROOKS

B5027

NEWCASTLE RD

STATION APP

LC

TRINITY ST

REGENT ST

ALMA ST

TUNLEY ST

STATION RD

B5375

B5379

34

M6

Darlaston Grange

YARNFIELD LA

A34

TRENT RD

HARTLEY RD

NEWCASTLE ST

CAMERON ST

St Dominic's Priory Sch

87 A B 88 C D 89 E F

F1
1 EDWARD ST
2 ALEXANDRA ST
3 KING'S AVE
4 NORTHESK ST
5 DOMINIC ST
6 MARGARET ST
7 RIVERSIDE GR
8 LIMEDALE CT

F2
1 CHESTNUT CT
2 STONEFIELD CT

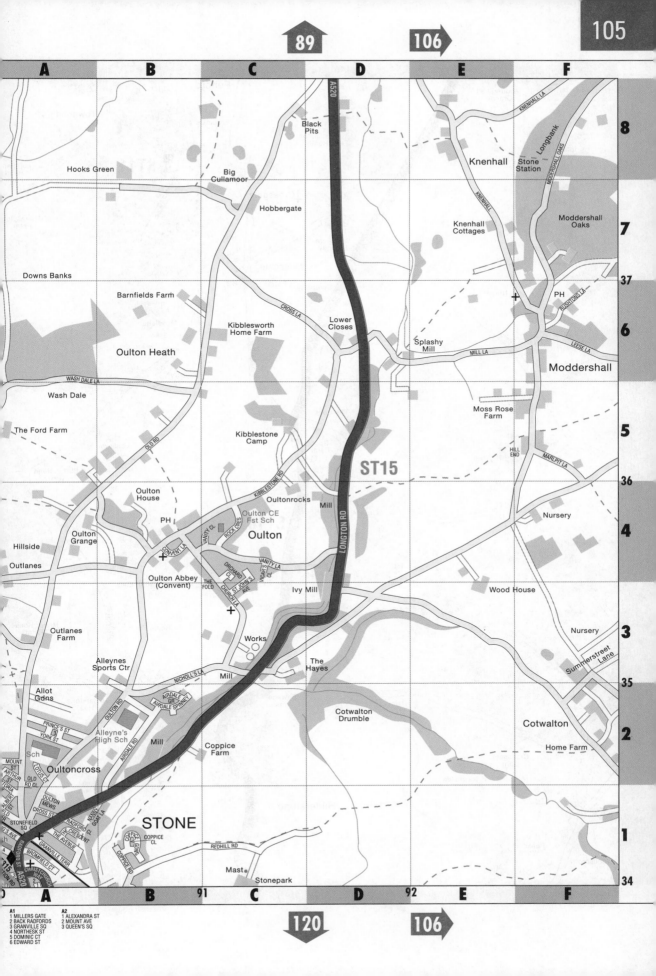

105
90

A B C D E F

8

Moddershall
Grange

B5066

Fulford

CHERRY CL
TOWNEND
HILLSIDE
CL LA
MEADOW
SAVERLEY GREEN RD

Townend

Broom□s
Farm

KINGSFISHER CRES
BAULK LA
HIGH MEADOW RD

Idlerocks
Farm

Stallington
Heath

FULFORD RD
Fulford
Prim
Sch
PO
ST11

Longlan
Head
Farm

Idlerocks

Crossgate

7

Idlerocks

Spot Acre
Spinney

Greensytch
Farm

Spot
Acre

Mossgate

Nurseries

Flats
Farm

37

Spotgate
Inn
(PH)

Mosslane

6

Nursery

Rushlade

BALAM'S LA

MOSS LA

HILDERSTONE RD

The Spot

5

Spot
Farm

The
Leasows

Farthings

36

Bird in Hand
(PH)

Spot
Grange

4

ST15

LEGE LA

The
Hurstage

High Elms

CRESSWELL RD

3

Home Farm

Manor House
Farm

HALL LA

35

Sewage
Works

Hilderstone
Hall

2

Crossgate
Barn

DINGLE LA

BREAMSCROFT

BREAMPTON CROFT
ROEBUCK CT
TEA FARM VIEW
THE MEADOWS

Hall
Wood

Newfields

SANDON RD

Roebuck
Inn
(PH)

Hilderstone

Hall
Farm

1

Peakshill
Wood

EASTHOLME

STONE

Wooliscroft

WHITESYTCH LA

B5066

34

93 A B 94 C D 95 E F

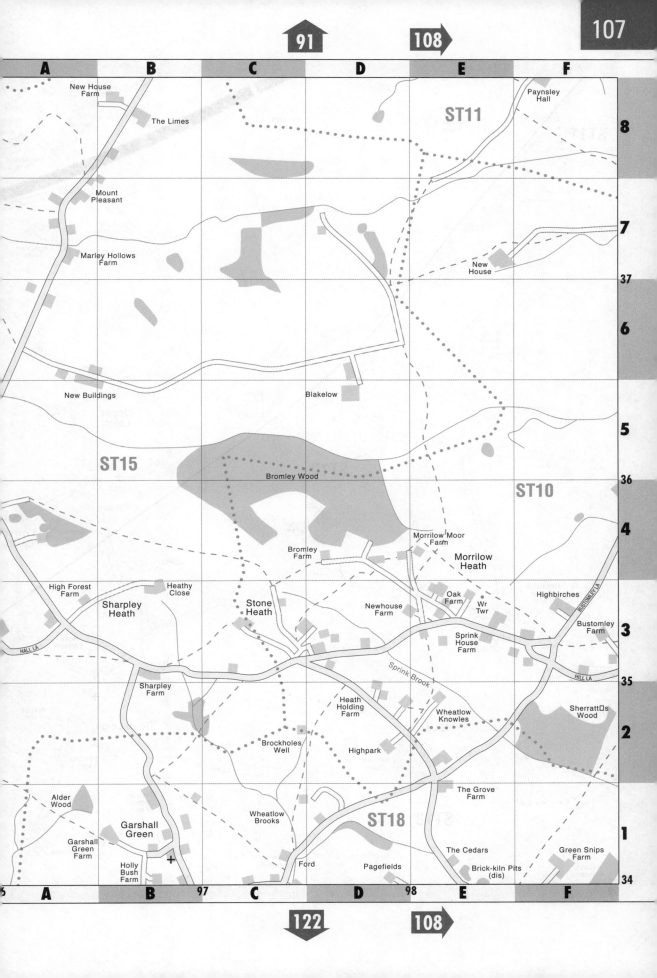

A B C D E F

8
7
37
6
5
36
4
35
2
1
34

New House Farm
The Limes
Mount Pleasant
Marley Hollows Farm
New Buildings
ST15
High Forest Farm
Sharpley Heath
Heathy Close
Sharpley Farm
HALL LA
Alder Wood
Garshall Green
Garshall Green Farm
Holly Bush Farm

ST11
Paynsley Hall
New House
Blakelow
Bromley Wood
ST10
Morrilow Moor Farm
Bromley Farm
Morrilow Heath
Stone Heath
Newhouse Farm
Oak Farm
Wr Twr
Highbirches
BUSTOMLEY LA
Bustomley Farm
Sprink House Farm
Sprink Brook
HILL LA
Heath Holding Farm
Wheatlow Knowles
Sherratt's Wood
Brockholes Well
Highpark
The Grove Farm
Wheatlow Brooks
ST18
The Cedars
Green Snips Farm
Ford
Pagefields
Brick-kiln Pits (dis)

A B C D E F

107
92
107
123

ST11

ST10

ST18

A50

Far
Teanleys

Shortwoods

The
Wing
Drumble

LEIGH BANK

Leighbank
Farm

Blythe
House

Leigh
Lane
Farm

Leighbank
Gorse

Dairy
House
Farm

Blythe
Gate
Farm

HEN LA

Blythe
House

Yew Tree
Farm

Moor
Farm

Upper
Leigh

Manor
House

BROOK LA

Bitternsdale

LEIGH LA

LC

Bridge
Farm

Ivy
House

RUSTOMLEY LA

MOOR LA

Brook
Farm

Lower
Leigh

Heempit
Gorse

Fields
Farm

LC

INTAKES LA

Middleton
Green
Farm

HILL LA

Wood
Leasow
Farm

Rose
Cottage

Dodsley
Fields

Windy
Fields

Middleton
Green

Manor
Farm

Dods Leigh

LEES LA

White's
Wood

Lees La

Top House
Farm

Sprink Brook

Dodsley
Cottage
Farm

Bear's Brook

Birchwood
Park

New
Plantation

Godstone

Black
Plantation

River Blithe

A B C D E F

8

Hutchinson Meml
CE Fst Sch

A522

New Broom
(PH)

CHURCH LA

NEW RD

ST MARY'S CL

Green
Farm

Green
PK

BADGERS HOLLOW

CRANBERRY AVE

PH

Checkley

Checkleybank
Farmhouse

Rectory
Farm

Broadgatehall Brook

FOLE LA

Folebank
Farm

FOLEBANK
BARNS

OLD LA

DEADMAN'S
GN

UTTOXETER RD

7

Sewage
Works

River Tean

Dairy

THE SQUARE

Fole

A522

Fole
Bridge

BROOK LA

37

Fole
Farm

6

Park Hall
Farm

Hell
Clough

Fole
Hall

ST14

5

Parkhall
Cottage

Amesbury

A50

New
Farm

High
Farm

36

RECTORY CL

LANE DK

PARKHALL LA

All Saints CE
Fst Sch

PH

Church
Leigh

ST10

Crossways
Farm

Nobut
Hall

Upper
Nobut

4

PH

BAGOTS
VIEW

COUNCIL
HOS

Brook House
Farm

Heath
Cottage

BENTS LA

Wellcroft
Cottage

CONHOUSE LA

Withington
Green

Nobut
Farm

3

Withington

HOLLY
MOW

Farmers Arms
(PH)

35

The Bents
Farm

Cuckoo
Lane
Farm

Cuckoo Lane

Benter
Farm

Manorhouse
Farm

2

River Blithe

The Bents

FIELD LA

HOTHILL LA

Lower
Nobut

ST14

34

ST14

Hothill
Farm

Headlands

Hayes
House

ST14

1

2 A B 03 C D 04 E F

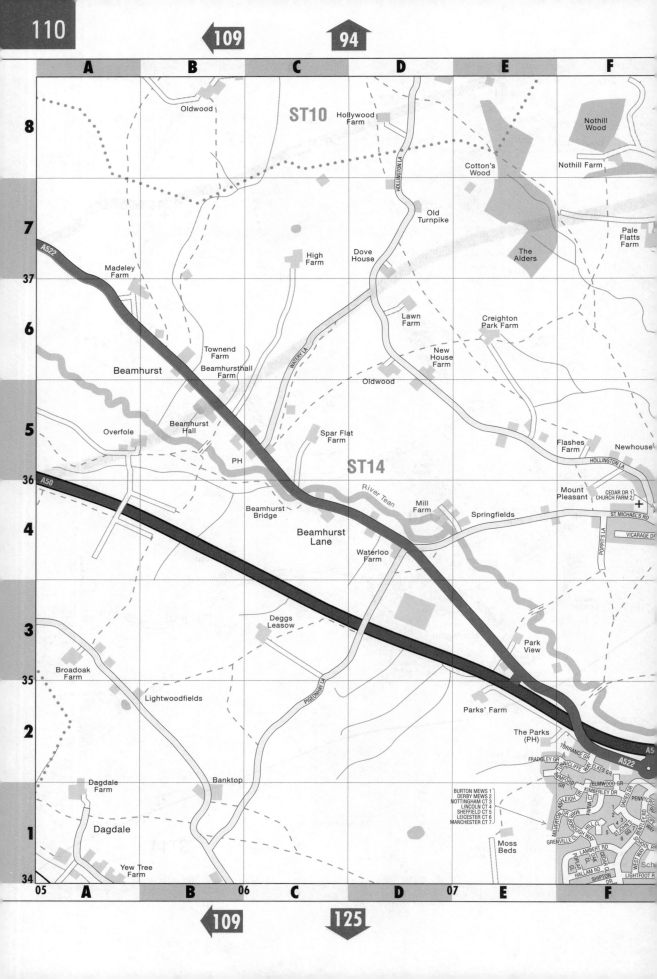

ST10

Oldwood

Hollywood Farm

Nothill Wood

Cotton's Wood

Nothill Farm

Old Turnpike

Pale Flatts Farm

HOLLINGTON LA

Dove House

The Alders

High Farm

A522

Madeley Farm

Lawn Farm

Creighton Park Farm

Townend Farm

New House Farm

Beamhurst

Beamhursthall Farm

WATERY LA

Oldwood

Overfole

Beamhurst Hall

Spar Flat Farm

ST14

Flashes Farm

Newhouse

HOLLINGTON LA

PH

River Tean

Mount Pleasant

CEDAR DR 1
CHURCH FARM 2

A50

Beamhurst Bridge

Mill Farm

Springfields

ST MICHAEL'S RD

Beamhurst Lane

Waterloo Farm

POPPIT'S LA

VICARAGE DR

Deggs Leasow

Park View

Broadoak Farm

Parks' Farm

Lightwoodfields

PIGEONHA LA

The Parks (PH)

TORRANCE GR

A522

A5

FRADGLEY GR

NICLIFFE GR

ELKES GR

Dagdale Farm

Banktop

BURTON MEWS 1
DERBY MEWS 2
NOTTINGHAM CT 3
LINCOLN CT 4
SHEFFIELD CT 5
LEICESTER CT 6
MANCHESTER CT 7

BAMFORD
SLEIGH

KIMBERLEY DR

ELMWOOD GR

PENNY CRE

Dagdale

Moss Beds

MILVERTON DR

ARGYLE

PARVA CT

DAVIES DR

DIXEY WAY

HILL CL

ST JOHN'S SQ

WEST WAY

BENTLEY DR

GRENVILLE

LAMBERT RD

HALLAM RD

CEDAR CL

SHIPTON

WEST WAY

Sch

Yew Tree Farm

LIGHTFOOT R

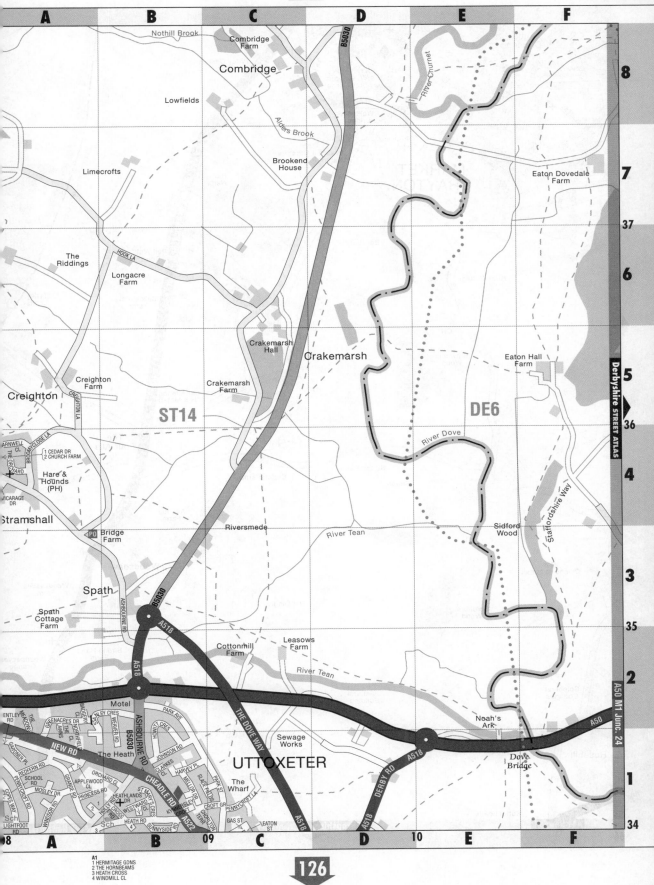

95

A B C D E F

8

Nothill Brook

Combridge Farm

Combridge

Lowfields

Alders Brook

7

Limecrofts

Brookend House

37

The Riddings

HOOK LA

6

Longacre Farm

Crakemarsh Hall

Crakemarsh

Eaton Dovedale Farm

River Churnet

Creighton Farm

Crakemarsh Farm

Eaton Hall Farm

5

Creighton

1 CEDAR DR
2 CHURCH FARM

ST14

DE6

36

ARNWELL CL
THE ORCHARD
BADGCLOSE LA
BROOM

Hare & Hounds (PH)

River Dove

Staffordshire Way

4

VICARAGE DR

Stramshall

Bridge Farm

Riversmede

River Tean

Sidford Wood

3

Spath

Spath Cottage Farm

ASHBOURNE RD

B5030

A518

Leasows Farm

35

A518

Cottonmill Farm

River Tean

2

Motel

PARK AVE

THE DOVE WAY

Sewage Works

Noah's Ark

A518

A50

NEW RD

B5030

CHEADLE RD

UTTOXETER

Derby RD

Dove Bridge

1

The Wharf

A522

GAS ST

A518

A518

34

A B 09 C D 10 E F

126

A1
1 HERMITAGE GDNS
2 THE HORNBEAMS
3 HEATH CROSS
4 WINDMILL CL

A50 M1 Junc. 24

ST21

8

Park Springs

Burnt Wood

Burntwood
Farm

Lloyd
Drumble

Keeper's
Lodge

Smith's Rough

7

Park
Springs
Farm

Knowleswood

Bishop's Wood

The
Lloyd
Farm

33

The
Nook
Farm

Goldenhill
Farm

Glass
Houses

6

Coal Brook

Dales
Wood

The
Lees

Chipnall Lees

5

Chipnall Lees

Heatherdale
Farm

32

Chipnall
Mill
Farm

TF9

4

Lipley
Heath
Farm

Chipnallhall
Farm

Chipnall Farm

Rushymoss
Wood

Lipley
Farm

3

TAG LA

Chipnall

MOSS LA

Lipley

Bishop's Wood

Moss
Lane
Farm

31

THE
BUNGALOWS

2

Cheswardine Hall

Sycamore
Cottage

1

Lipley Hall
Farm

Lipley
Cottages

Lipley
Villa

Greaves
Plantation

Marsh
House

30

ST20

ST20

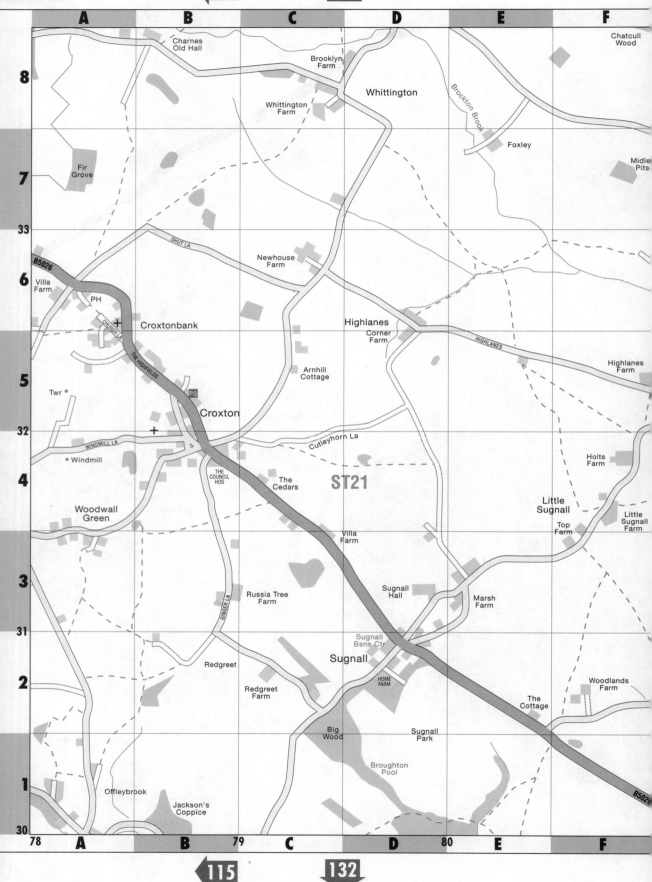

115
101

A   B   C   D   E   F

8

Charnes
Old Hall

Brooklyn
Farm

Whittington

Chatcull
Wood

Whittington
Farm

Brockton Brook

Foxley

7

Fir
Grove

Midle
Pits

33

SHUT LA

Newhouse
Farm

B5026

6

Villa
Farm

PH

Croxtonbank

CHURCH LA

Highlanes

HIGHLANES

Corner
Farm

Highlanes
Farm

THE HIGHFIELDS

5

Twr

PO

Arnhill
Cottage

Croxton

32

Windmill

WINDMILL LA

Cutleyhorn La

Holts
Farm

4

THE
COUNCIL
HOS

The
Cedars

ST21

Little
Sugnall

Woodwall
Green

Villa
Farm

Top
Farm

Little
Sugnall
Farm

3

GINGER LA

Russia Tree
Farm

Sugnall
Hall

Marsh
Farm

31

Redgreet

Sugnall
Bsns Ctr

Sugnall

Woodlands
Farm

2

Redgreet
Farm

HOME
FARM

Sugnall
Park

The
Cottage

Big
Wood

1

Broughton
Pool

B502

Offleybrook

Jackson's
Coppice

30

78   A   B   79   C   D   80   E   F

115
132

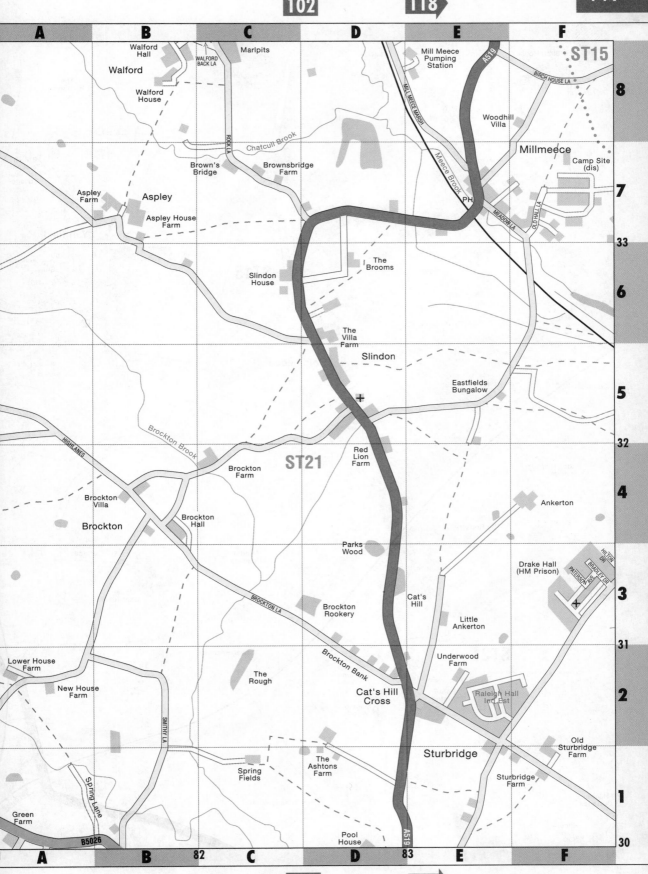

ST15

A B C D E F

8

Walford Hall
Marlpits
WALFORD BACK LA
Walford
Mill Meece Pumping Station
A519
BIRCH HOUSE LA

Walford House
Woodhill Villa

Chatcull Brook
Millmeece
Camp Site (dis)

7

33

Aspley Farm
Brown's Bridge
Brownsbridge Farm
Meece Brook
PH
MEADOW LA
OLD HALL LA

Aspley
Aspley House Farm

The Brooms
6

Slindon House

The Villa Farm

5

Slindon
Eastfields Bungalow

32

Brockton Brook
ST21
Red Lion Farm

Brockton Farm

Ankerton

4

HIGHLANES
Brockton Villa
Brockton Hall

Brockton

Parks Wood

Drake Hall (HM Prison)
HILTON DR
BRADLEY DR
PATTERSON AV

3

Cat's Hill
Little Ankerton

BROCKTON LA
Brockton Rookery

31

Lower House Farm
Brockton Bank
Underwood Farm

New House Farm
The Rough
Cat's Hill Cross
Raleigh Hall Ind Est

2

SMITHY LA
Sturbridge
Old Sturbridge Farm

Spring Fields
The Ashtons Farm
Sturbridge Farm

Spring Lane
1

Green Farm
B5026
Pool House
A519

30

A B 82 C D 83 E F

121
107

A **B** **C** **D** **E** **F**

FOUR LANE ENDS

Garshall Green

8

Summerhill

Garshall House

Castle Farm

Birch Rough

Withysitch Lane

7

Dayhills Farm

Oulton House

Withysitch Farm

Wheatlow Brook

Calloway Farm

Grange Farm

33

ST15

Coton Hayes

6

B5027

Grimblebrook Farm

Potsmans La

Darley Lane

Coton Hill

B504

PO

Burleypool Bridge

Salt's Bridge

THE ALLWAYS

ALLWAYS

ALLWAYS

Milwich

Coton Hill

CROSSHILL BANK

Burley Pool Farm

UTTOXETER RD

5

The Green Man (PH)

Coton Cottage

32

SANDON LA

Milwich Hall

Coton

Wheatsheaf Inn (PH)

ST18

Park Farm

+

Shaw Wood

Coton Green Farm

4

MILL LA

Green Lea Fst Sch

WALLBROOK RD

Fradswell H Farm

3

Cromer Hill

Coton Mill Farm

Oxclose Wood

Beacon Bank Farm

Mill Lane

Model Farm

HAWKINS LA

31

Lander's Wood Farm

Lander's Wood

Beacon Bank

Old Gayton Gorse

2

Fox's Wood Farm

Kendrick's Barn Farm

Sandon Wood Farm

The Doglan

Gayton Brook

1

Kendrick's Wood

DOGLA

30

96 **A** **B** 97 **C** **D** 98 **E** **F**

121
138

ST10

HOTHILL LA

FIELD LA

Painleyhill
Farm

Painleyhill

The
Gorse

Longleys

Bank
Farm

Hobbhill

Field
Farm

Fieldmill
Farm

Spring
Farm

B502

B5027

Field

Moor House

Carry
Coppice

Carry
Coppice

Carry Lane

ST14

Round
Wood

River Blithe

Church
Farm

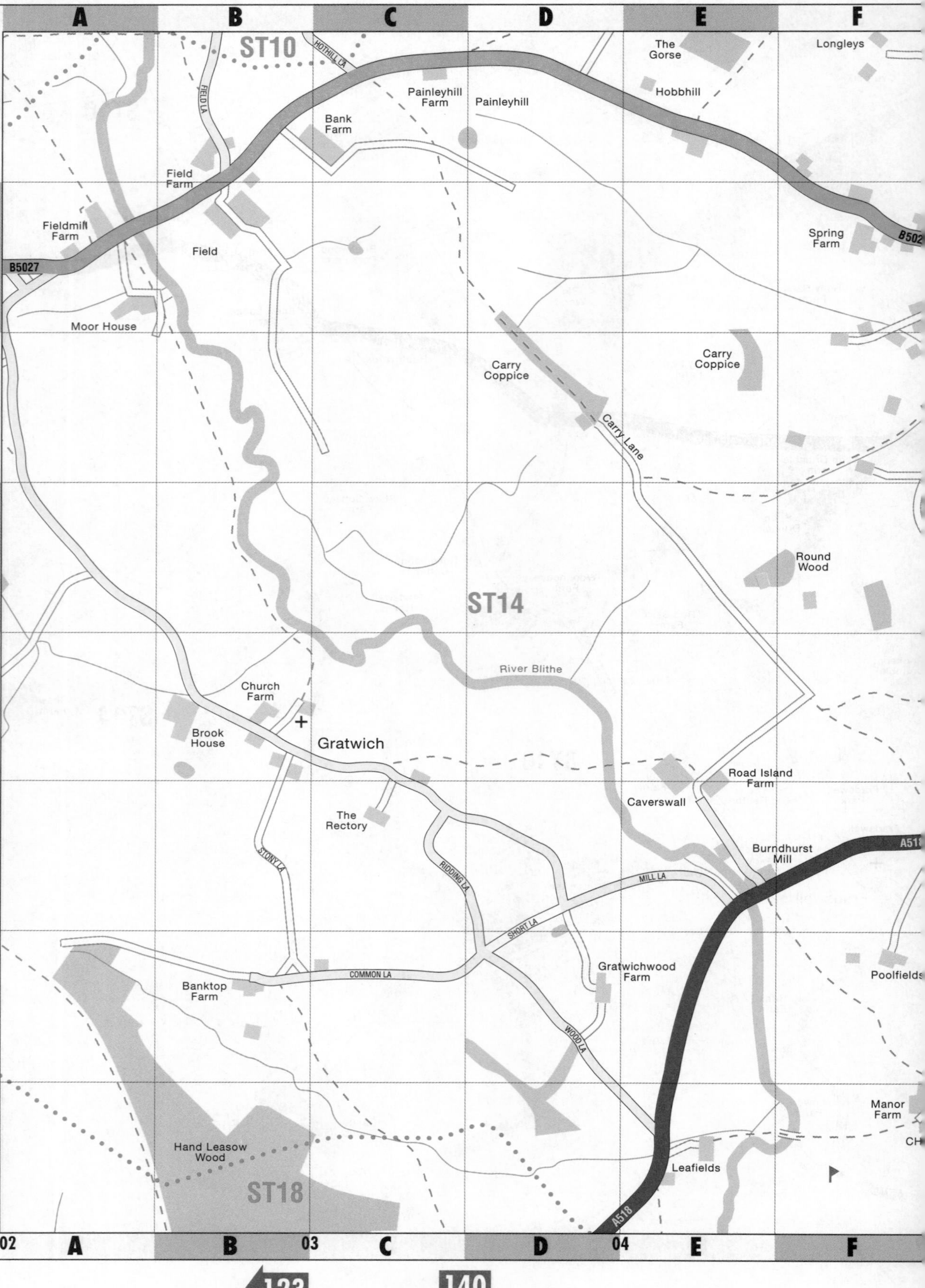

Brook
House

Gratwich

Road Island
Farm

Caverswall

Burndhurst
Mill

A51

The
Rectory

STONY LA

RIDDING LA

SHORT LA

MILL LA

Gratwichwood
Farm

Poolfields

Banktop
Farm

COMMON LA

WOOD LA

Manor
Farm

CH

Hand Leasow
Wood

Leafields

ST18

A518

A   B   C   D   E   F

Springfield Farm
PH
The Old Rectory
Bramshall
WEST VIEW
Stock's Farm
1 DUROSE CT
2 FRADGLEY CT
3 COUNCIL HOS
STOCKS LA
LEIGH LA
WILLOUGHBY CT
OVERCROFT
VERNEY CL
MALLENS CRS
LEE BUCKLEY CL
THORNE CL
CHURCH LA
CHURCH CROFT
HALL ORCH
PH
PO
Park Fields
BRAMSHALL RD
SCAMORE CL
PINE WLK
BYRD'S CL
BYRD'S LA
LAMBERT RD
SHIPTON DR
HAWTHORNDEN AVE
B5027
8
Hawthornden Gdns
Ryecroft Lodge
Park Farm
Park Place
The Elms Farm

Crossings Farm
LC
Bramshall Ind Est
Dagdale Brook
7
33

LC
LC
Bakers Pit Plantation
Green Farm
6
The Dearndales
Blounts Green
A518

Wellbank Plantation
LOXLEY LA
Eastfield Plantation
Lower Leasow
STAFFORD RD
Popinjay
B5013
5
Lower Loxley
Loxley Hall Sch
Highfields Hall
32
ST14
Long Walk
Gibbs Leasow Farm
Longclose Farm
4
Park View
Alder Carr
Grove Farm
B5013
Park Covert
Willslock
3
Aldery Bank Farm
Park Belt
Loxley Bank
Grey Cottage
31
Upper Loxley Farm
2
eese Hill
Leese Hill Farm
WATERY LA
The Oaklands
Loxley Green
Wallheath Farm
QUEE LA
PH
Holly Dene
Rose Cottage
Holly Hayes Farm
HOLLY LA
Ashencroft Farm
1
Hitchcock's Rough
COUNCIL HOS
B5013
West Lodge
30

A   B   06   C   07   D   E   F

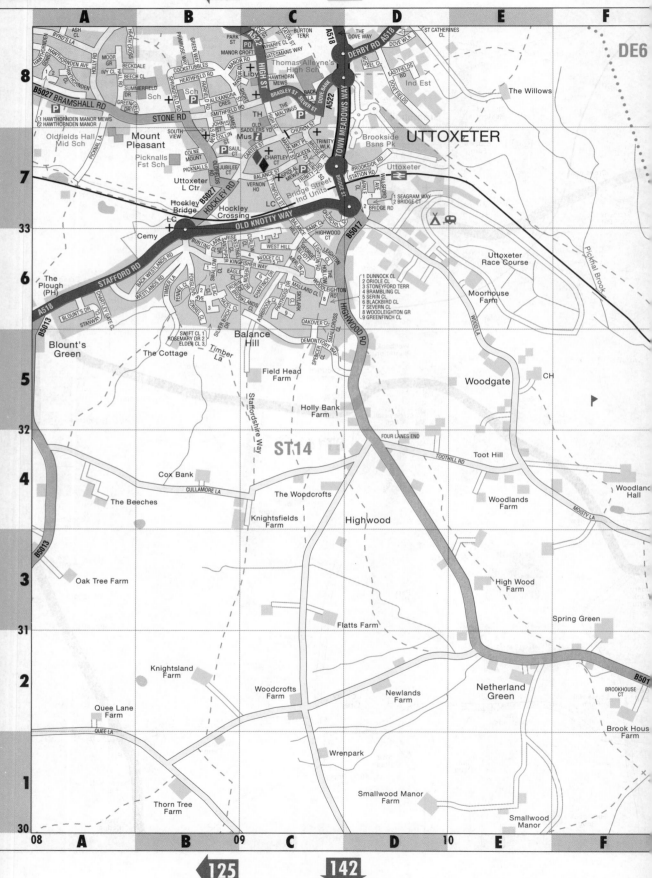

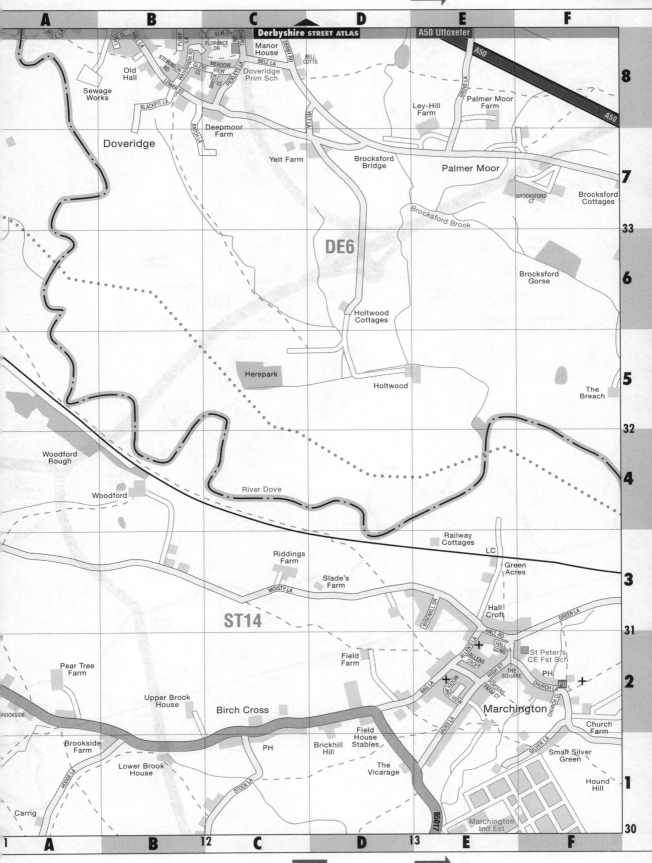

Derbyshire STREET ATLAS

A50 Uttoxeter

A **B** **C** **D** **E** **F**

8

BIRCH LA
LILAC CL
HALL LA
STEVENSON RD
LOWER ST
WATERPARK
GLEBE CL
PUMP LA
ELM CL
FLORENCE DR
CHAPEL GR
MEADOW VIEW
PICKLEY LA
BROOK CL
Manor House
Bell Cotts
BELL LA
DERBY RD
A50

Sewage Works

Old Hall

Doveridge Prim Sch

Ley-Hill Farm

Palmer Moor Farm

Deepmoor Farm

BATCH LA

Doveridge

Yelt Farm

Brocksford Bridge

Palmer Moor

7

PELL LA

BROCKSFORD CT

Brocksford Cottages

33

Brocksford Brook

DE6

6

Brocksford Gorse

Holtwood Cottages

Herepark

Holtwood

5

The Breach

32

Woodford Rough

4

River Dove

Woodford

Railway Cottages

LC

Green Acres

3

Riddings Farm

MOISTY LA

Slade's Farm

ST14

WINDMILL DR

Hall Croft

HALL RD

31

Pear Tree Farm

Field Farm

ALLENS LA
ALLENS CROFT
HALL GDNS
St Peter's CE Fst Sch
PH
HIGH ST
THE SQUARE
CHURCH LA
PO

Upper Brook House

Birch Cross

BAG LA
LAND VIEW
PORTERS
PARK CT
CHURCH CL

2

BROOKSIDE

Brookside Farm

Field House Stables

Marchington

Church Farm

PH

Brickhill Hill

SILVER LA

Small Silver Green

Lower Brook House

HOUSE LA

STOCK LA

The Vicarage

B5017

Hound Hill

1

Carrig

Marchington Ind Est

30

A **B** **C** **D** **E** **F**

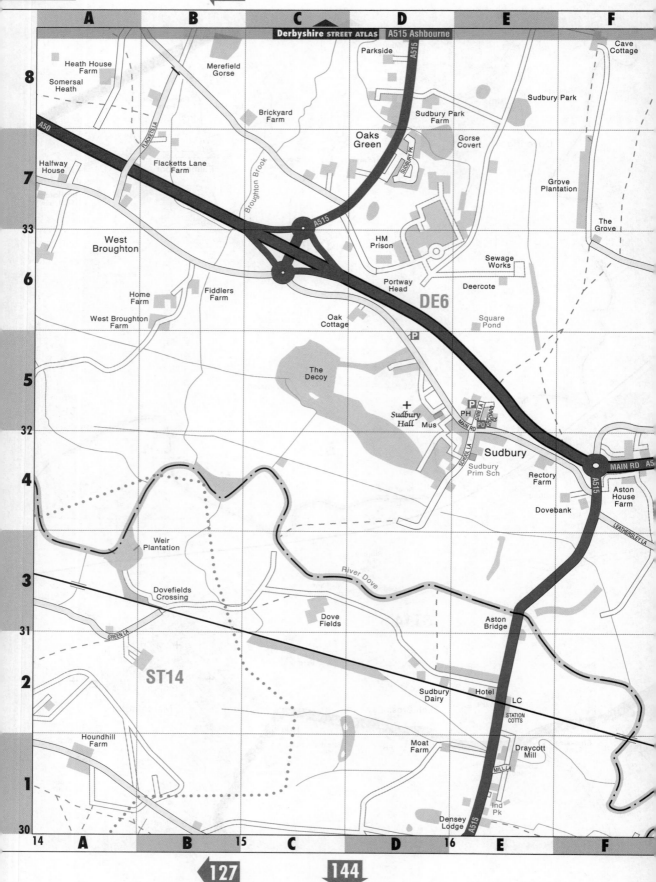

Derbyshire STREET ATLAS | A515 Ashbourne

Cave
Cottage

Heath House
Farm

Somersal
Heath

Parkside

A515

Sudbury Park

Merefield
Gorse

Brickyard
Farm

Sudbury Park
Farm

Gorse
Covert

Oaks
Green

Grove
Plantation

Halfway
House

Flacketts Lane
Farm

A50

FLACKETTS LA

Broughton Brook

A515

The
Grove

West
Broughton

HM
Prison

Sewage
Works

Home
Farm

Fiddlers
Farm

Portway
Head

Deercote

DE6

West Broughton
Farm

Oak
Cottage

Square
Pond

P

The
Decoy

Sudbury
Hall

Mus

P

PH

BIRB LA

P.O

ORCHARD CL

MAIN RD

SCHOOL LA

Sudbury

Rectory
Farm

MAIN RD A5

Sudbury
Prim Sch

Dovebank

Aston
House
Farm

Weir
Plantation

River Dove

A515

LEATHERSLEY LA

Dovefields
Crossing

GREEN LA

Dove
Fields

Aston
Bridge

ST14

Sudbury
Dairy

Hotel

LC

STATION
COTTS

Houndhill
Farm

Moat
Farm

Draycott
Mill

MILL LA

Ind
Pk

Densey
Lodge

A515

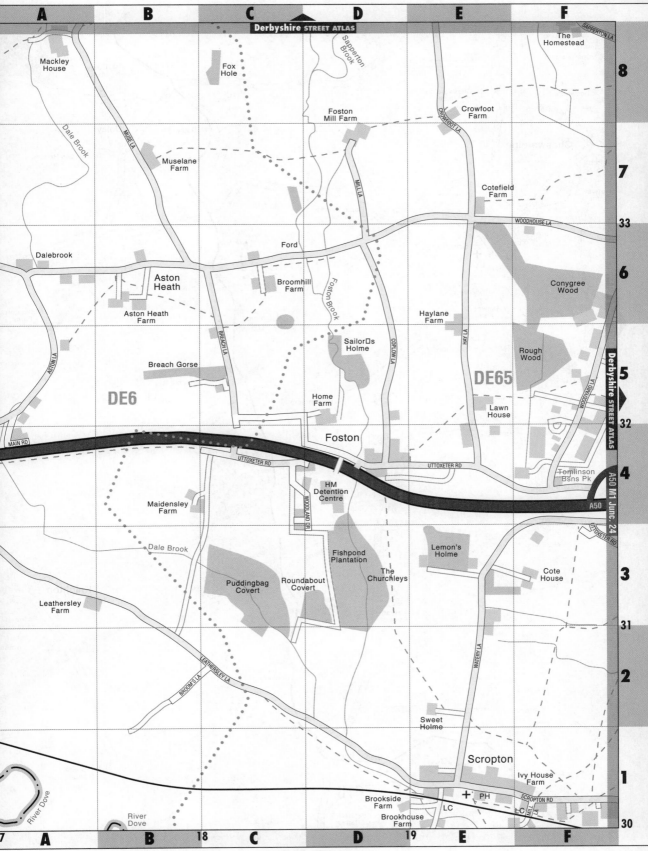

Mackley House

Fox Hole

The Homestead

Foston Mill Farm

Crowfoot Farm

8

Muselane Farm

Cotefield Farm

7

33

Dalebrook

Ford

Conygree Wood

6

Aston Heath

Broomhill Farm

Aston Heath Farm

Haylane Farm

Rough Wood

DE65

5

Breach Gorse

Sailor's Holme

32

DE6

Home Farm

Lawn House

Foston

4

Maidensley Farm

HM Detention Centre

Tomlinson Bsns Pk

UTTOXETER RD

UTTOXETER RD

A50

A50 M1 Junc. 24

Dale Brook

Fishpond Plantation

Lemon's Holme

Cote House

3

Leathersley Farm

Puddingbag Covert

Roundabout Covert

The Churchleys

31

2

Sweet Holme

Scropton

Ivy House Farm

River Dove

River Dove

Brookside Farm

Brookhouse Farm

PH

LC

SCROPTON RD

LC

1

30

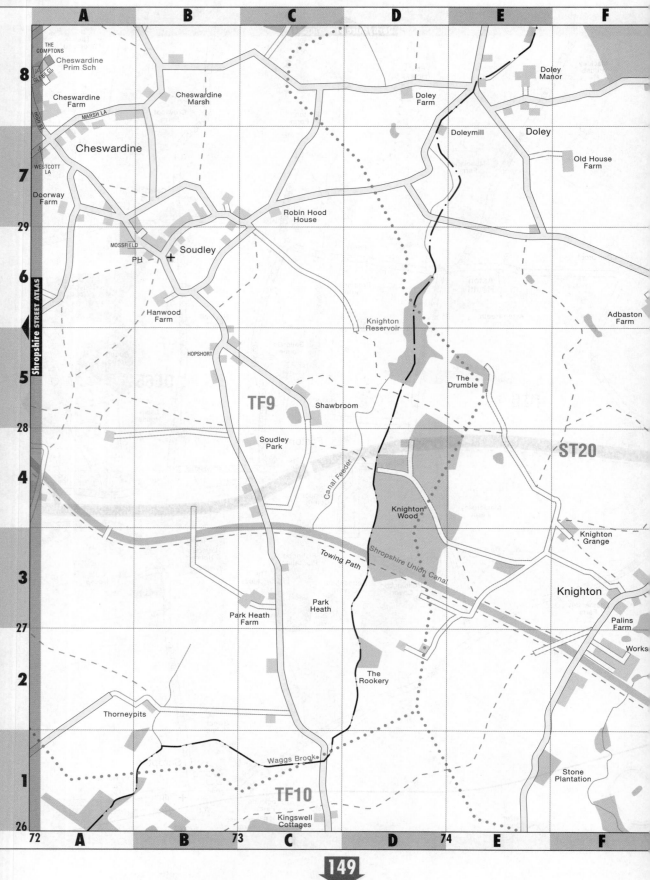

A B C D E F

8

THE COMPTONS

Cheswardine Prim Sch

Cheswardine Farm

GLEBE CL

Cheswardine Marsh

Doley Manor

Doley Farm

Doleymill

Doley

MARSH LA

Cheswardine

Old House Farm

7

HIGH ST

WESTCOTT LA

29

Doorway Farm

Robin Hood House

MOSSFIELD

PH

Soudley

6

Shropshire STREET ATLAS

Hanwood Farm

Knighton Reservoir

Adbaston Farm

HOPSHORT

The Drumble

5

TF9

Shawbroom

ST20

28

Soudley Park

Canal Feeder

Knighton Wood

4

Knighton Grange

Towing Path

Shropshire Union Canal

Knighton

3

Park Heath Farm

Park Heath

Palins Farm

27

Works

2

The Rookery

Thorneypits

Stone Plantation

1

Waggs Brook

TF10

Kingswell Cottages

26

72 A 73 B C 73 D 74 E F

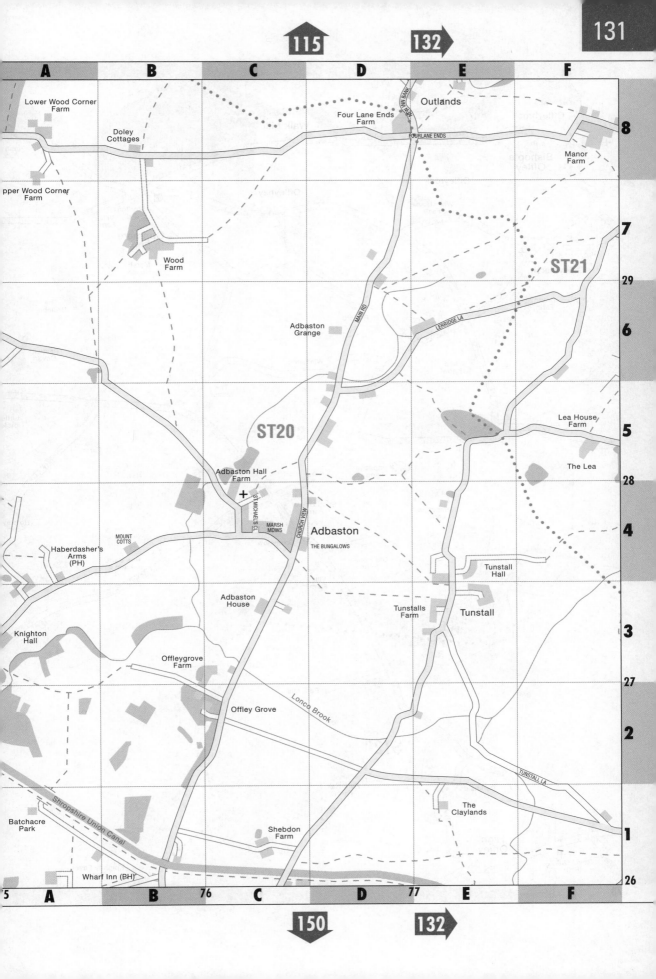

A B C D E F

8 Offleybrook Walk Mill Walk Mill Cop Mere Persha Pool

Bishop's Offley Offleyrock

White House Farm Offleyhay MERE RISE PO Star Inn (PH) Villa Farm

7 Offleymarsh Copmere End

Marsh House

29 Brann Farm The Drumble

Rufford Peafield Covert

6 Lea Knowl Windsend

The Manor Little Horsle

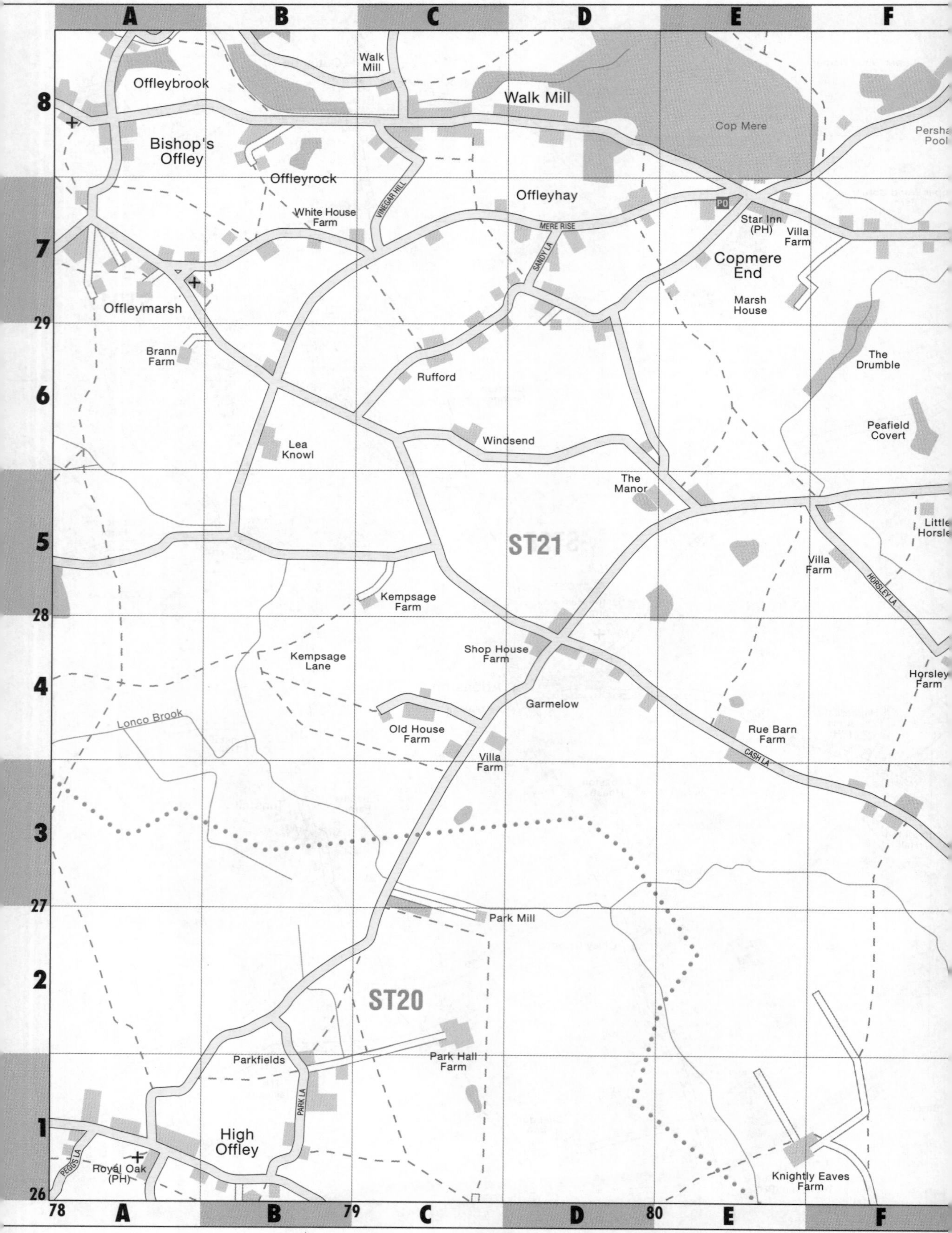

5 ST21 Villa Farm HORSLEY LA

28 Kempsage Farm

Kempsage Lane Shop House Farm Horsley Farm

4 Garmelow Rue Barn Farm CASH LA

Old House Farm

Villa Farm

3

27 Park Mill

2 ST20

Parkfields Park Hall Farm PARK LA

1 High Offley Knightly Eaves Farm

26 Royal Oak (PH) PEBBS LA

78 A B 79 C D 80 E F

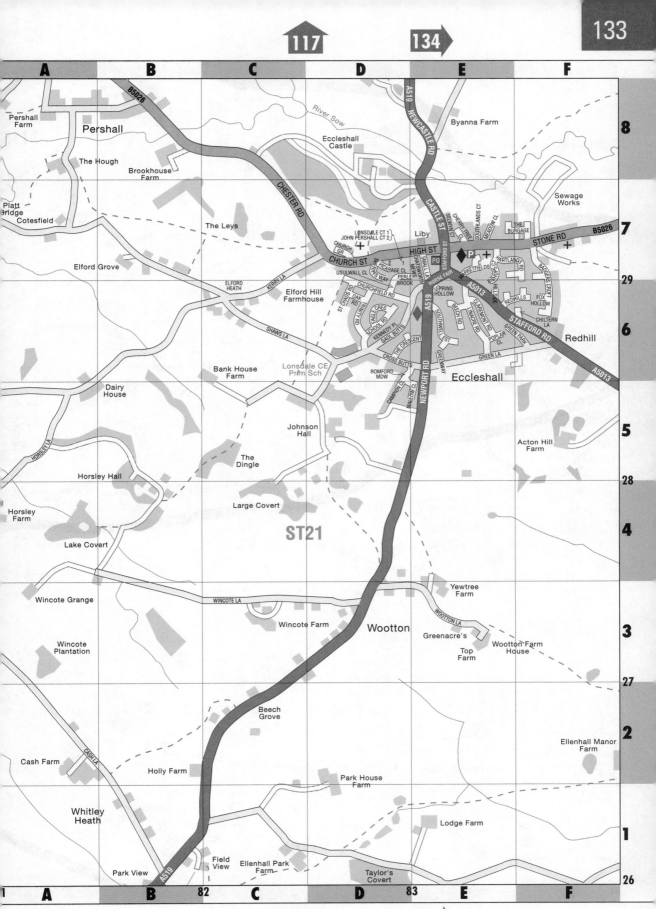

A   B   C   D   E   F

8

7

29

6

5

28

4

3

27

2

1

26

Pershall
Farm

Pershall

The Hough

Brookhouse
Farm

Platt
Bridge
Cotesfield

The Leys

Elford Grove

ELFORD
HEATH

Elford Hill
Farmhouse

KERRY LA

Elford
Heath

SHAWS LA

Bank House
Farm

Dairy
House

Horsley Hall

Horsley
Farm

Lake Covert

HORSLEY LA

Large Covert

The
Dingle

Johnson
Hall

Lonsdale CE
Prim Sch

Wincote Grange

Wincote
Plantation

WINCOTE LA

Wincote Farm

Wootton

WOOTTON LA

Beech
Grove

Cash Farm

CASH LA

Holly Farm

Whitley
Heath

Park View

A519

Field
View

Ellenhall Park
Farm

Park House
Farm

Taylor's
Covert

Lodge Farm

Ellenhall Manor
Farm

River Sow

Eccleshall
Castle

CHESTER RD

Byanna Farm

NEWCASTLE RD

A519

CASTLE ST

Sewage
Works

THE
BURGAGE

Liby

STONE RD

B5026

LONSDALE CT 1
JOHN PERSHALL CT 2

CHURCH
GR

CHURCH ST

HIGH ST

STAFFORD ST

SELWYN CL

CHERRY TREE

SOUTHLANDS CT

MEADOW CL

HARTLANDS CT

USULWALL CL

VICARAGE CL

SHERRY'S WAY

CHATSWORTH
MEWS

SMALL LA

PERLES
BROOK

PO

P

MARKETFIELDS

BIRCH HILLSIDE

REDHILLS

BADGERS CROFT

CHURCHFIELD RD

ST CHADS RD

OAK
RD

KENNEDY PL

EAGLE CRES

SCHOOL RD

GAOL BUTTS

HORSE FAIR

A519

SPRING
HOLLOW

A5013

CLAREMONT RD

BEECH RD

TINACRE RD

POPLAR
CL

GREEN PARK

FOX
HOLLOW

CHILTERN
LA

STAFFORD RD

Redhill

A5013

THE CRESCENT

CROSS BUTTS

ROMFORD
MDW

SOUTHWELL CT

GREENWAY

NEWPORT RD

GREEN LA

Eccleshall

CAMPION CL

MALLOW CL

Acton Hill
Farm

ST21

Yewtree
Farm

Greenacre's

Top
Farm

Wootton Farm
House

A   82   B   C   D   83   E   F

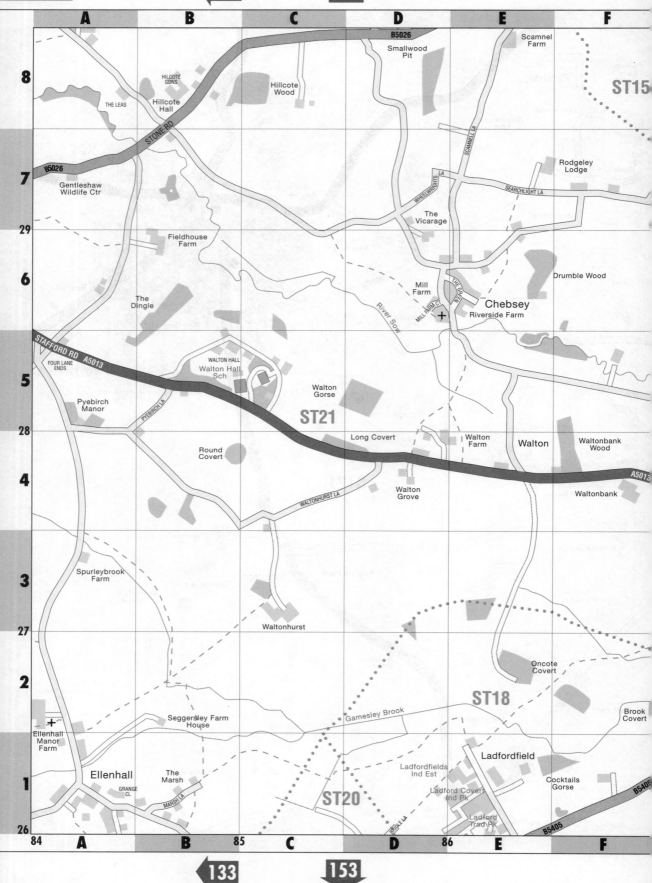

Peasley Bank

Elmhurst

New Plantation

Newhouse Farm

Spring Farm

Far Enson Farm

ENSON LA

Yarlet Bank Farm

Yarlet Hall (Yarlet Sch)

Yarlet Hall Farm

Yarlet Hill

New Ensonmoor Farm

Meadow Farm

Greenwood

GREEN LA

Grove Farm

Yarlet

Greyhound Inn (PH)

Black Plantation

Whitgreave

Top Farm

Park Farm

YARLET LA

New Farm

Manor Farm

WHITGREAVE LA

Upper Farm

ST18

Grange Farm

Woodhill Farm

Marston

Church Farm

Whitgreave Manor

Marston Farm

MARSTON LA

Brook Far

Newbuildings Cottage

Redhill Farm

STONE RD

Newbuildings Farm

Little Gorse

Marstongate Farm

Marston Brook

M6

ST16

RAF Stafford

New Plantation

Creswell Grove

M6

CHAULDEN RD 1
BUCKLAND RD 2
ASHRIDGE WLK 3
MARSWORTH WAY 4

BEACONSIDE

SHACKLETON WAY

HURRICANE CL

MUSTANG DR

OSPREY

CL

A34

A513

ALDERSHAW AVE

PARKSIDE AVE

LAWNSFIELD WLK

AMBLEFIELD WAY

ALDBURY CL

FELDEN CL

PARKSIDE AVE

PITSTONE CL

Stafford Common

COMMON RD

A513

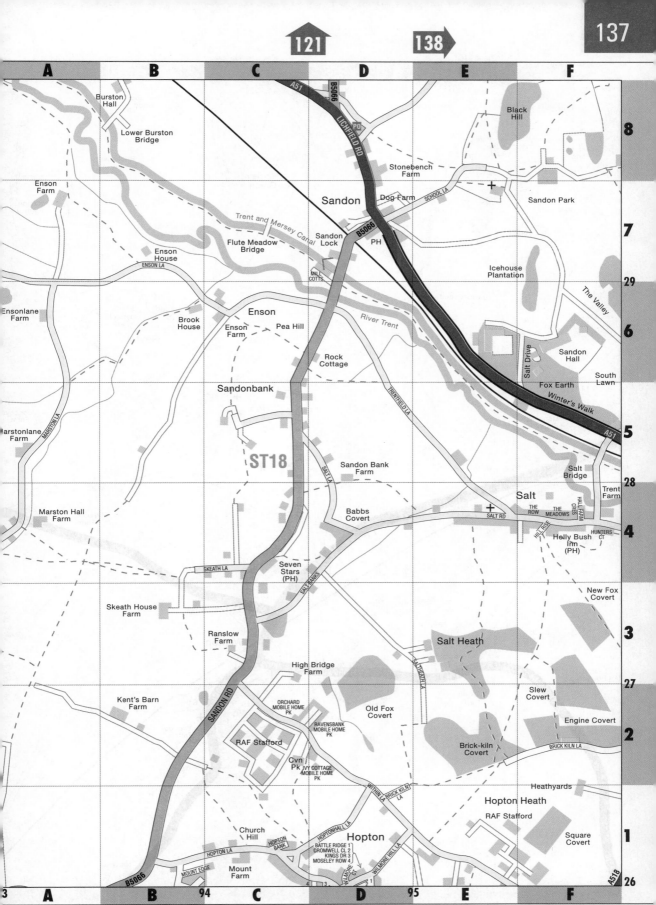

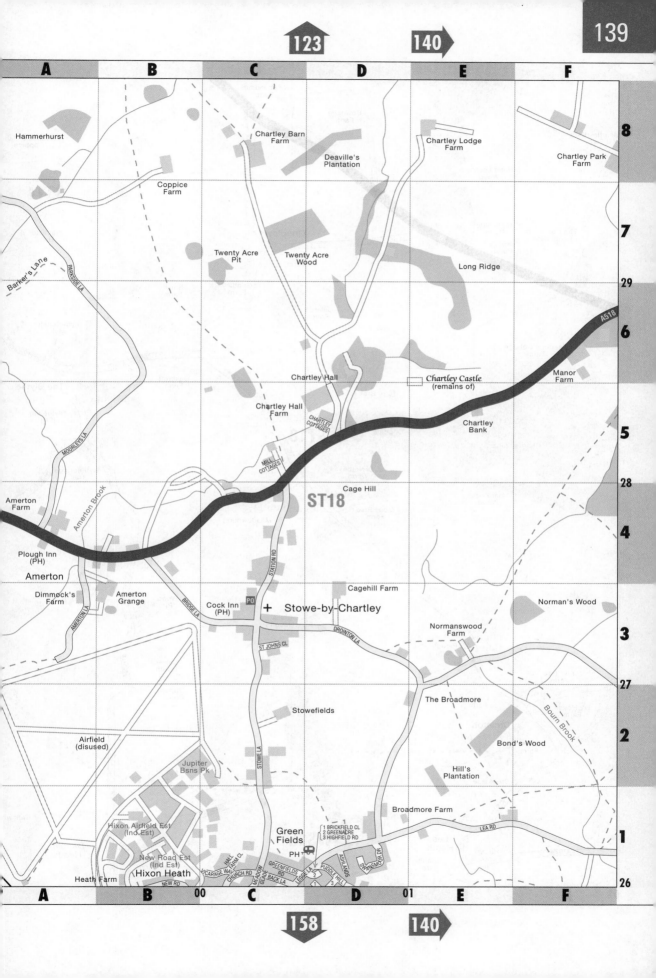

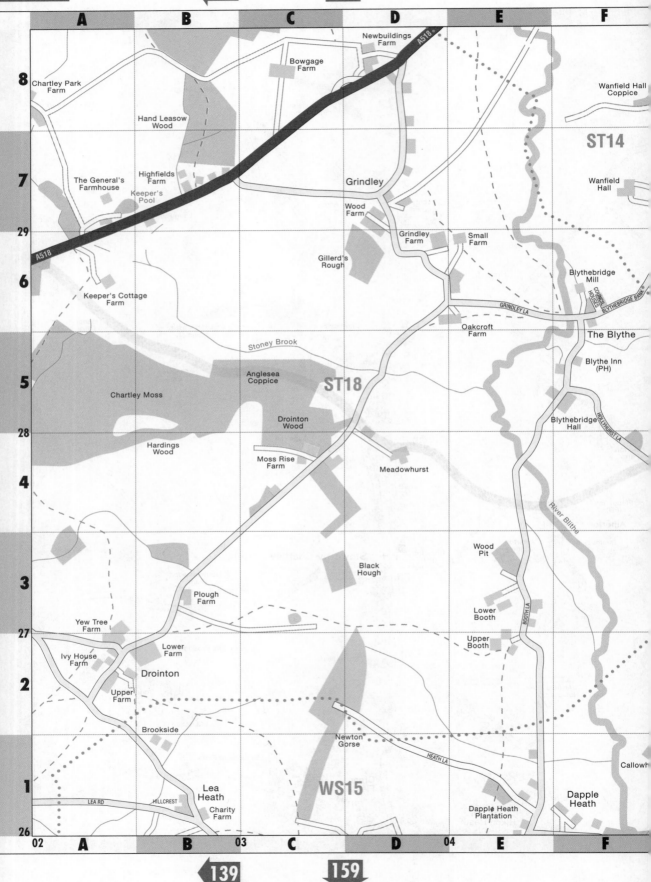

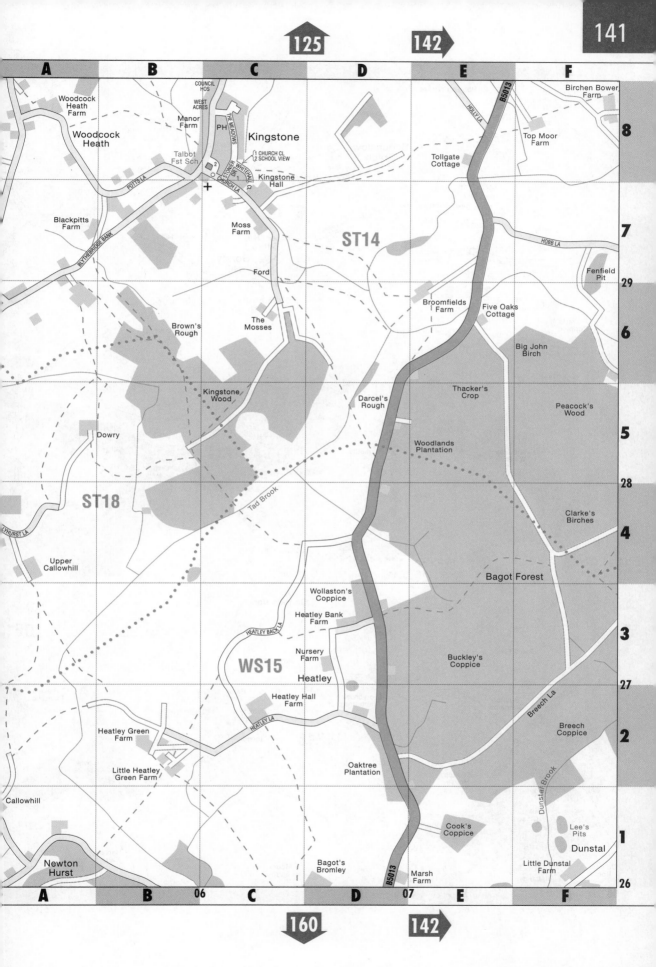

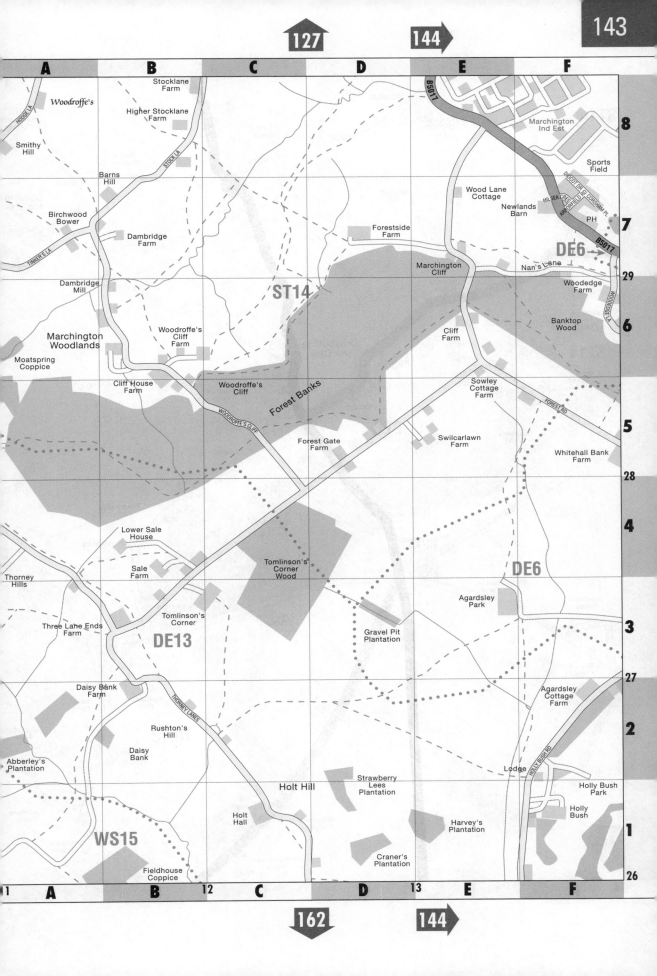

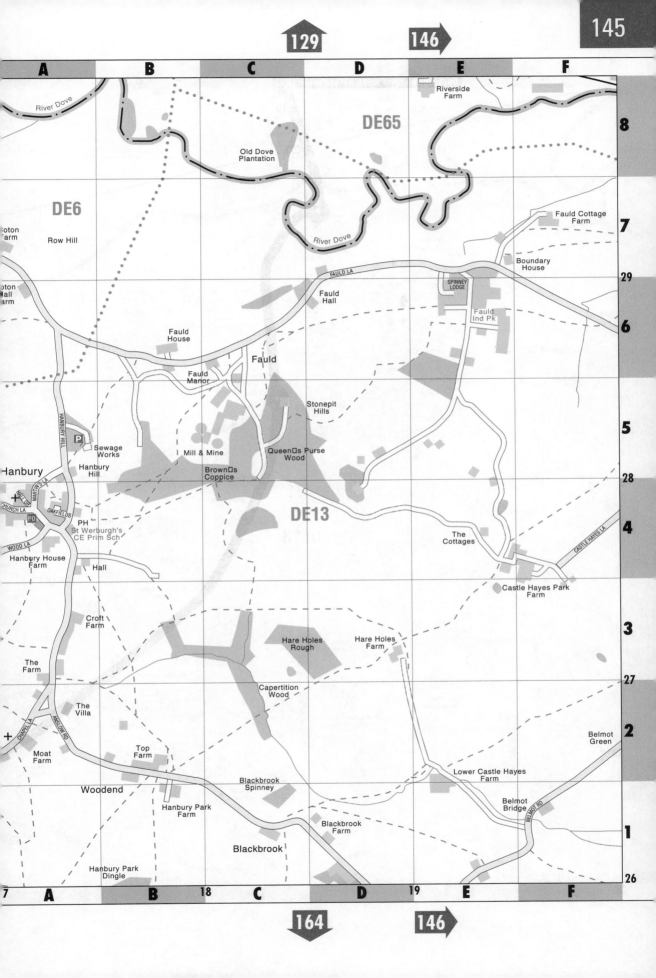

129
146

A   B   C   D   E   F

8

DE65

Riverside Farm

DE6

Row Hill

Fauld Cottage Farm

7

coton arm

Boundary House

29

coton all arm

FAULD LA

Fauld Hall

SPINNEY LODGE

6

Fauld House

Fauld Ind Pk

Fauld

Fauld Manor

Stonepit Hills

HANBURY HILL

P

Sewage Works

Mill & Mine

Queen□s Purse Wood

5

Hanbury

Hanbury Hill

Brown□s Coppice

28

MARTIN□S LA

WHITE LOW

OAKFIELDS

DE13

CHURCH LA

PO

PH

St Werburgh's CE Prim Sch

The Cottages

4

WOOD LA

Hanbury House Farm

Hall

Castle Hayes Park Farm

CASTLE HAYES LA

Croft Farm

Hare Holes Rough

Hare Holes Farm

3

The Farm

CRAPEL LA

ANSLOW RD

Capertition Wood

27

The Villa

Belmot Green

2

Moat Farm

Top Farm

Lower Castle Hayes Farm

Woodend

Blackbrook Spinney

Belmot Bridge

BELMOT RD

Hanbury Park Farm

Blackbrook Farm

1

Blackbrook

Hanbury Park Dingle

26

7   A   B   18   C   D   19   E   F

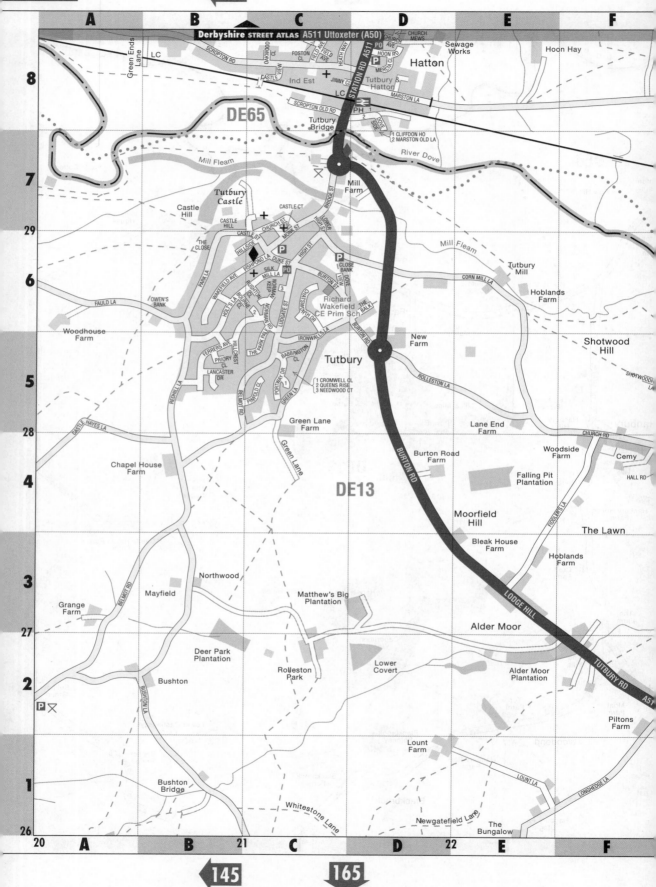

148

148

E1
1 PRINCESS WAY
2 CARISBROOKE DR

F1
1 ALDERHOLME DR
2 MANTON CL

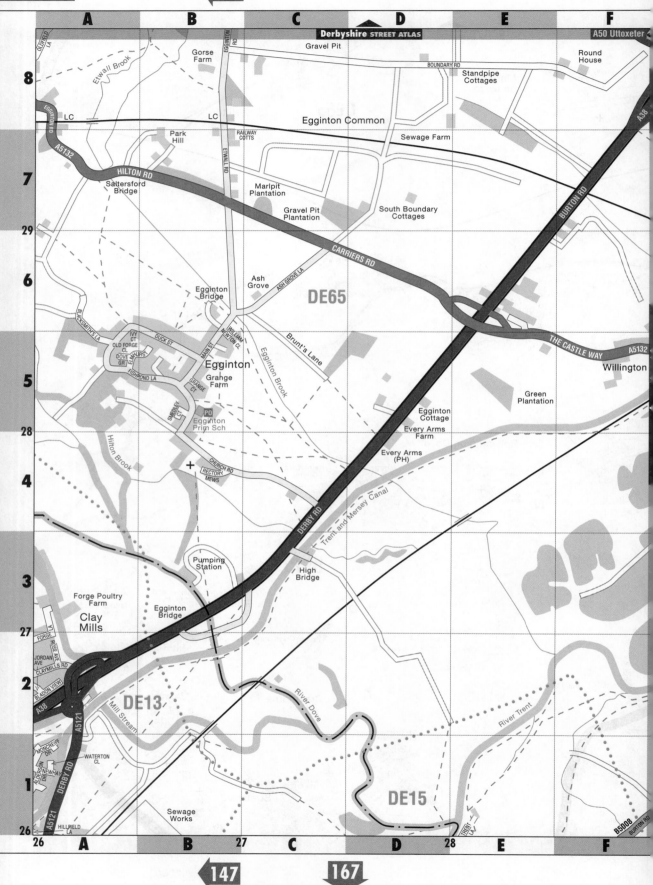

Derbyshire STREET ATLAS

A50 Uttoxeter

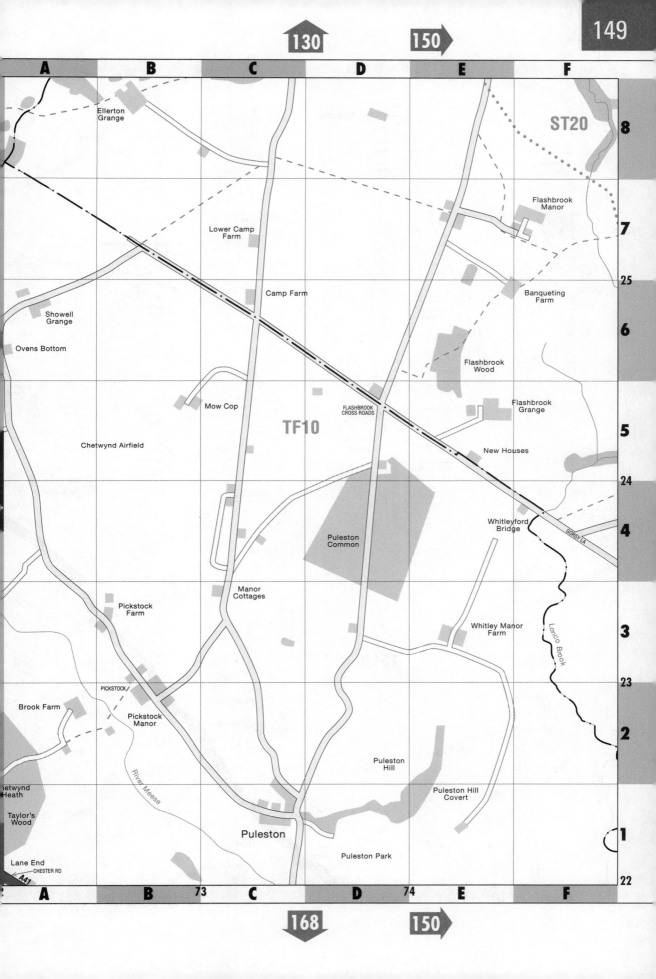

130

150

ST20

A B C D E F

8

Ellerton
Grange

Flashbrook
Manor

7

Lower Camp
Farm

25

Camp Farm

Banqueting
Farm

Showell
Grange

6

Ovens Bottom

Flashbrook
Wood

Mow Cop

Flashbrook
Grange

TF10

5

Chetwynd Airfield

FLASHBROOK
CROSS ROADS

New Houses

24

Puleston
Common

Whitleyford
Bridge

GORSY LA

4

Manor
Cottages

Pickstock
Farm

Whitley Manor
Farm

3

Lonco Brook

PICKSTOCK

23

Brook Farm

Pickstock
Manor

2

Puleston
Hill

Chetwynd
Heath

River Meese

Puleston Hill
Covert

Taylor's
Wood

1

Puleston

Lane End
CHESTER RD

A41

Puleston Park

22

A B 73 C D 74 E F

168

150

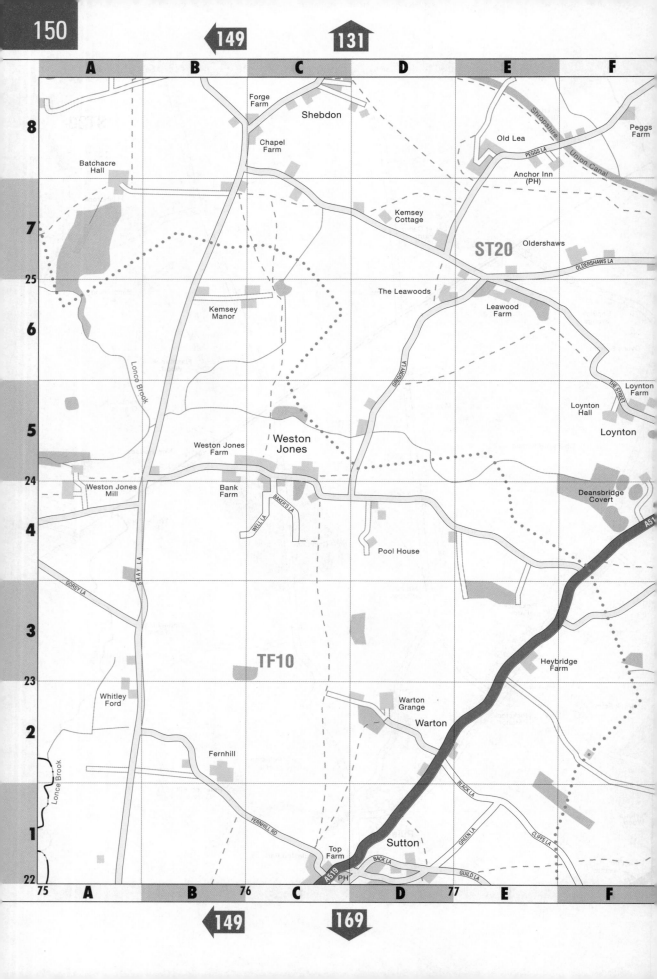

149
131

A   B   C   D   E   F

8

Forge
Farm

Shebdon

Chapel
Farm

Old Lea

PEGGS LA

Peggs
Farm

Shropshire

Union Canal

Batchacre
Hall

Anchor Inn
(PH)

7

Kemsey
Cottage

ST20

Oldershaws

25

OLDERSHAWS LA

The Leawoods

Kemsey
Manor

Leawood
Farm

6

Lonco Brook

GREGORY LA

THE STREET

Loynton
Farm

Loynton
Hall

Loynton

5

Weston Jones
Farm

Weston
Jones

24

Weston Jones
Mill

Bank
Farm

BAKER'S LA

Deansbridge
Covert

WELL LA

A51

4

Pool House

SHAY LA

GORSY LA

3

TF10

Heybridge
Farm

23

Whitley
Ford

Warton
Grange

Warton

2

Fernhill

Lonco Brook

BACK LA

GREEN LA

CLIFFS LA

1

FERNHILL RD

Top
Farm

Sutton

A519

BACK LA

GUILD LA

PH

22

75   A   B   76   C   D   77   E   F

A   B   C   D   E   F

8

A519

ST21

Old Hall
Farm

Hollow
Farm

Home
Farm

Back La

High Offley Rd

The Green

Woodseaves

Moss La

Grub
Street

Dershaws La

Newport Rd

Blackberry Way

Newport Rd

Dicky's La

Woodhaven

PO

B5405

New
Farm

Woodseaves
CE Prim Sch

WILLOWCROFT

7

B5405

Moss
Farm

Grub St

Littleworth

Moscow La

Bridge Ct

PH

Birchtree
Farm

Riley La

Bleak
House
Farm

25

Lodge La

Knightley Park
Farm

6

Rue Hill

Knightley
House

Blakemere
Pool

Hob Hill

Grange Rd

5

Weston
Wood

24

ST20

Coneygreave
Haft

Knightley
Grange

Gibraltar

Boggy
Rough

Yeld Bank

4

Pinfold La

The Roundabout

Big
Campions

Spring
Leasow

St Peter's Ct

High Meadow

3

Norbury

Shropshire Union Canal

Norbury
Manor

23

Blakemore
House

Junction Inn
(PH)

Canal
Cotts

Norbury
Junction

Wood Brook

2

Mill Haft

Oulton
House

Oulton

Norbury Rd

1

Oulton
Farm

Oulton La

Shelmore
Wood

Norbury
Park

22

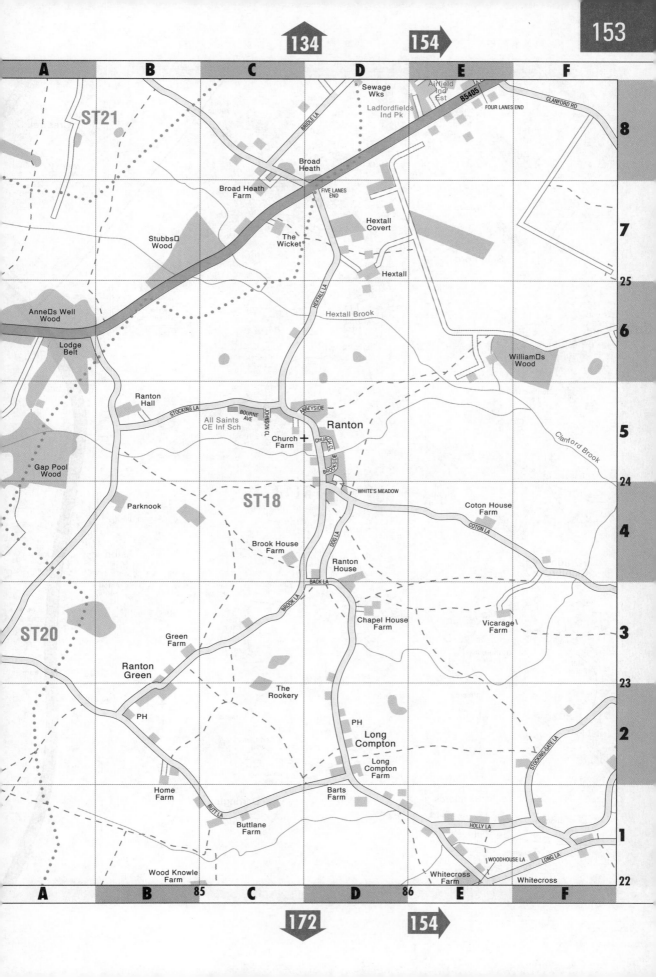

or full street detail of the
highlighted area see page 285.

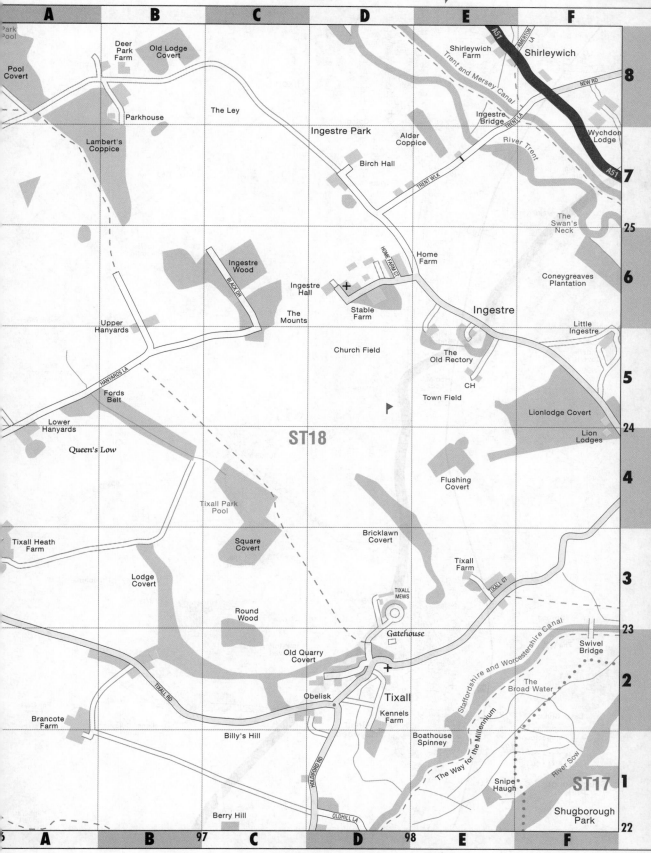

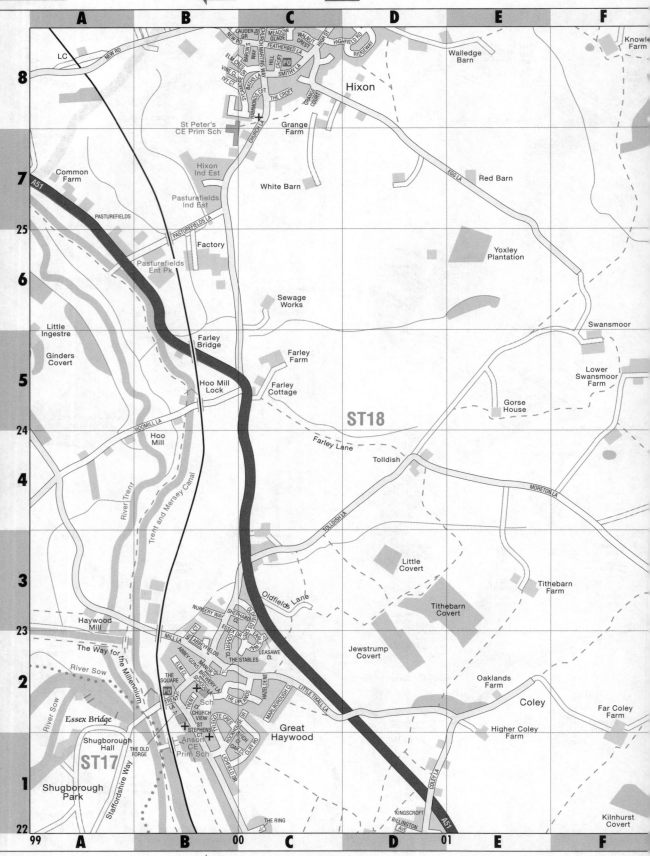

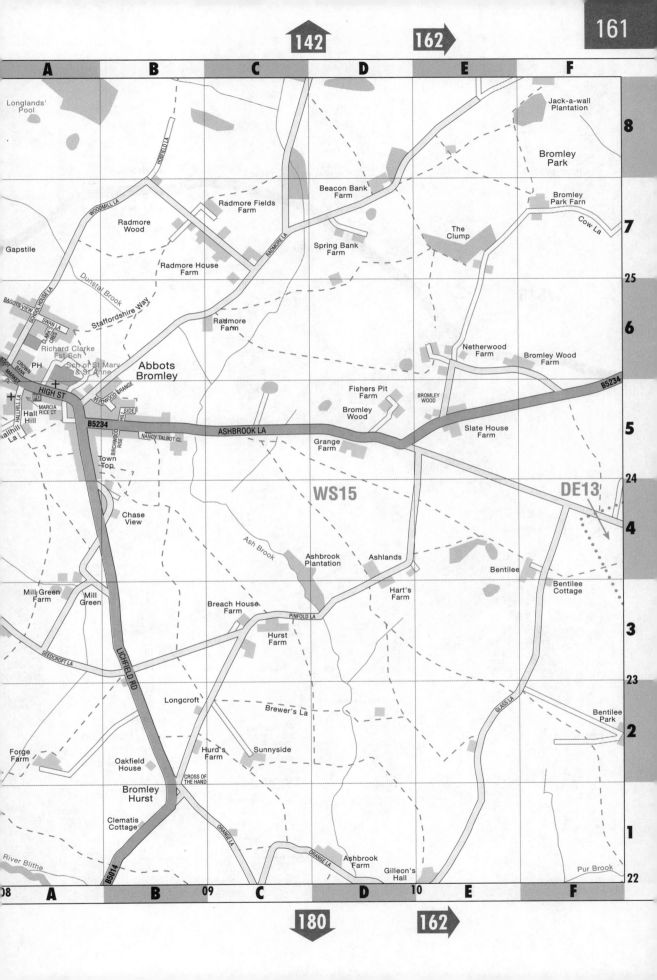

161
143

A **B** **C** **D** **E** **F**

8

Fieldhouse Farm

Briary Hill Plantation

Newborough Hall Farm

Briary Hill Farm

HOLLY BUSH RD

ELTON LA

Bromley Park

Child's Plantation

MILL MDW

Pound Farm

Newborough

PO

7

Cow La

Parkgate

Noah's Ark Farm

Needwood CE Prim Sch

ELTON CL

CHAPEL LA

DUFFIELD LA B523

SQUIRREL RD

The Red Lion (PH)

Newborough House Farm

25

WS15

DARK LA

YOXALL RD

Poplars Farm

Eason's Coppice

Newhall Farm

Thorntree Hall Farm

6

B5234

THORNEY LANES

Chantry Wood

River Swarbourn

Moat Hill

MOAT LA

Moat Hall

Birch Wood

Roosthill Wood

Newborough End Farm

5

Roost Hill

Newborough End

Dolefoot Farm

24

Barn Farm

Birch Wood Cottage

Chantry Farm

DE13

DOLEFOOT LA

Birchwood Farm

Locker's Rough

4

Netherwood Farm

BLUNT'S HOLLOW

Poole's Coppice

Mare Brook

Pur Brook

ABBOTS BROMLEY RD

Home Farm

Brackenhurst Wood

3

Paddock Rough

St Michael's House

Hoar Cross

Meynell Ingram Arms (PH)

Bath Wood

Hoar Cross Hall

Vicarage

23

Church Flatts

Beck's Bank

2

Bentilee Park

Lawnpit Covert

Yew Tree Farm

MAKER LA

Far Hoarcross

BECK'S LA

Far Hoar Cross Farm

Makerlane Farm

Park Hollow

Ford

1

Ladysmith Farm

Round Hill

Cross Hayes Farm

The Deer Park

22

11 **A** **B** 12 **C** **D** 13 **E** **F**

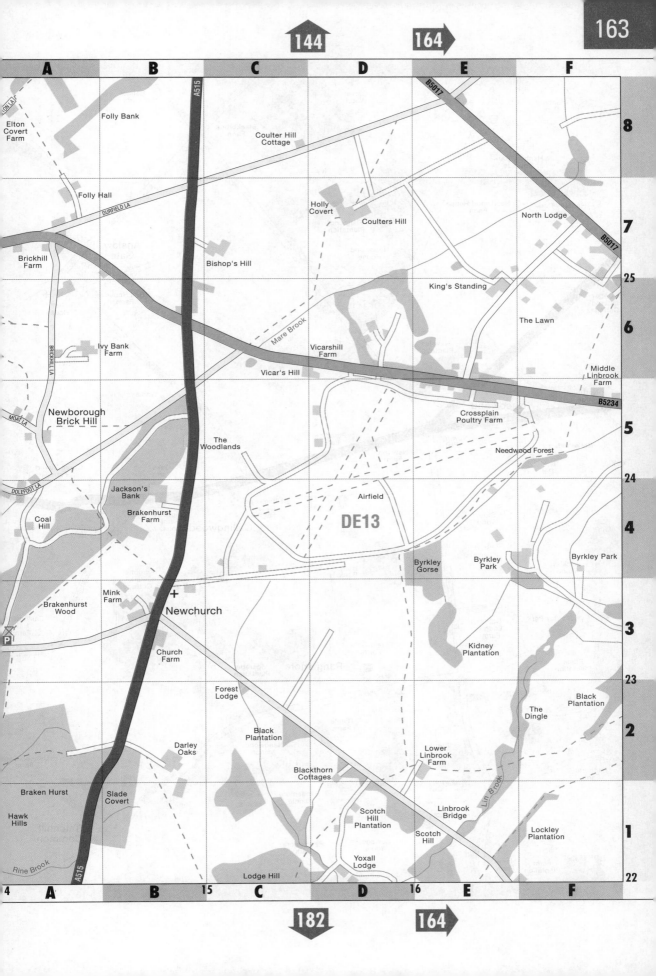

◀ 163 145 ▲

◀ 163 183 ▼

A   B   C   D   E   F

Stockley Park
Stockley Plantation
Whitestone Lane
Newgatefield Lane
Hill Top Farm
Upper Outwoods
8
BUSHTON LA
Poplars Farm
Mount Pleasant Farm
Anslow Park Farm
Upper Outwoods Farm
LONGHEDGE LA   PH
BEAMHILL RD
MAIN RD
Mosley Prim Sch
Mill Hill Farm
Anslow
7
OUTWOODS LA
Bell Inn (PH)
OUTWOODS LA
LEYFIELDS FARM MEWS
FIELD LA
25
Riddings Farm
Outwoods Lane
Bungalow Farm
Mayfields Farm
Mast
MANVERS LA
Anslow Common
Henhurst Field
Lower Outwoods
6
LOWER OUTWOODS RD
ST GEORGE'S RD
ST MARGARETS
HOPLEY RD
Henhurst Wood
Snobnall Brook
Redhouse Farm
CHAPEL LA
5
PH
Henhurst Wood Farm
RESERVOIR RD
24
Leys Farm
Henhurst Farm
Shobnall Dingle
Nursery
FOREST RD
DINGLE DR
FRED BREWER WAY
Oaks Wood
HENHURST HILL
DE13
Shobnall Brook
Shobnall Prim Sch
4
PO
HENHURST RIDGE
AVIATION LA
PO
HIGHCROFT DR
SHOBNALL RD
A38
Rough Hay Farm
Rough Hay
Depot
LONGSWELL RD
SINAI CL
PRIDE CT
POSTERN RD
Sandyford Dingle
Shobnall Grange
B5017
DE14
Brewery
3
Postern House Farm
ANGLESEY ST
CALLISTER WAY
Shobnall
HANDLEY RD
23
Glenfield
Sinai Park
Lord's Well
CALLINGWOOD LA
The Rough
Trent and Mersey Canal
2
Pool Green Bridge
Pool Green Farm
The Thorns
The Way for the Millennium
WATERSIDE LA
THIRD AVE
Pool Green Bridge
Prince's Covert
The Bungalows
PARKWAY
Tatenhill
School Bridge
Battlestead Hill
Lawns Farm
1
NEW ROW
MAIN ST
Towing Path
A38
SECOND AVE
WELLINGTON RD
A5121
DARK LA
22

A   B   21   C   D   22   E   F

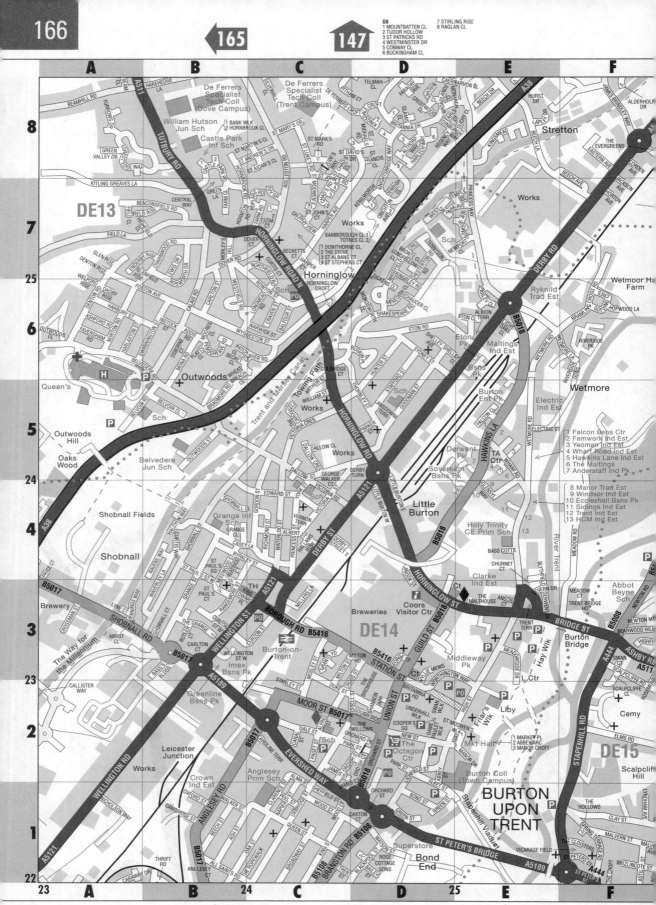

D8
1 MOUNTBATTEN CL
2 TUDOR HOLLOW
3 ST PATRICKS RD
4 WESTMINSTER DR
5 CONWAY CL
6 BUCKINGHAM CL
7 STIRLING RISE
8 RAGLAN CL

A B C D E F

DE13

DE14

Sewage
Works

Castle
Wood

Newton
Park

Bladon
Castle

Home
Wood

Bladon
Hill

The
Ridge

THE
CLOSE

Bladon House
Sch

Meadows
Farm

Bladon
Paddocks

Dale Brook

BROOKSIDE

Bladon Farm
Cotts

DE15

Burton
Mill

River Trent

NEWTON RD

Wranglands
Plantation

Victory
Plantation

Bladon
Farm

1 ELIZABETH CT
2 RHODES HO
3 CLIVE HO
4 JUBILEE RISE
5 BUCKINGHAM CT
6 STAMPS CL
7 BLENHEIM CL

Newton
Solney

DE65

Trent
Farm

Grange
Farm

The Hill
Farm

MAIN ST

Newton Solney
CE Inf Sch

Hotel

Newton
Park Farm

Beaconhill
Plantation

Grafton
Smallholdings

REPTON RD

B5008

BURTON RD

Derbyshire STREET ATLAS

Nursery

Abbot Beyne Sch
(Evershed Bldg)

Abbot Beyne Sch
(Linnell Bldg)

Holy
Rosary
RC Prim
Sch

1 BALMORAL RD
2 OSBOURNE GDNS
3 KENSINGTON RD

Winshill

Tower
View Prim
Sch

Common
Farm

HAWFIELD LA

Oldicote
Farm

Crem

Crem

BRETBY LA

Scalpcliffe Rd

Water
Tower

ASHBY RD

Bretby
Fairways

Geary
House

Stanhope
Bretby

1 HOPMEADOW WAY
2 HERITAGE WAY
3 BARLEYCORN CL

Blue Cedars
Dr

Stockings
Plantation

CH

ASHBY RD E

STANHOPE
GN

A511

Clay St

Malvern Ave

Woods La

Redwood
Dr

Dunstall
Brook

The Maltings

1 GRIZEDALE CL
2 DALESIDE
3 CAMERON CL
4 WEDGEWOOD CL

Brizlincote
Hall Farm

PH

A 27 B C D 28 E F

8 7 25 6 5 24 4 3 23 2 1 22

ST20

A B C D E F

Forton
Forton
Monument

SUTTON CT
Sutton Bank
Farm

Sheepeley La

A519

Windswell
Pool

8

Swan Inn
(PH)

River Meese

Thistleyfield
Covert

7

New
Guild

21

6

Meretown

Meretown
Farm

Moss
Pool

PLOUGH LA

KESTREL CL

BEECHFIELDS WAY

Clark's
Plantation

Aqualate
Mere

5

TF10

20

Broom
Hill

WALKLEY BANK

Roundabouts

Boathouse
Wood

The
Spectacles

Aqualate
Hall

4

Canal (dis)

BEN JONES AVE

NORBROOM DR

NORBROOM CT

DROVERS WAY

PLOUGHMANS
CROFT

DANIELS CROSS

SHEPHERDS
CT

FARRERS

1 TOMKINSON CL
2 AQUALATE CL
3 HENLEY DR
4 FISHERS LOCK
5 SUMMERHOUSE GR
6 THE OVAL BGLWS

Aqualate
Castle

Castle
Wood

Aqualate Park
(Deer Park)

The
Shrubbery

Gardener's
Wood

HARCOURT
DR

HAMPTON DR

HAMPTON
CL

HAMPTON
WAY

LAPWORTH
WAY

STAFFORD RD

HIGH
MDWS

MEADOW CL

SCHOOL
GROUND LA

MEADOW RD

BROADWAY

MEADOW VIEW RD

BARNMEADOW
RD

BARNMEADOW
CT

BARNMEADOW RD

A518

Parson's
Barn

3

19

AUDLEY HOUSE
MEWS

AUDLEY
HO

Cemy

Park
Wood

2

The Burton
Borough Sch

AUDLEY AVE

Audley
Avenue
Ind Est

Bsns
Pk

Park
Farm

Park
Bank

QUEEN'S DR

PRINCESS GDNS

STATION CT

Lime Tree
Cottage

A518

A518

A41

1

18

A B 76 C D 77 E F

169
151

A B C D E F

8

Shropshire Union Canal

Shelmore Wood

Brook
Covert

NORBURY RD

Ryland's
Covert

Shelmore
House

RADMORE LA

Shelmore
Valley
Farm

Spring
Coppice

7

Wood Brook

Hatchwell's
Covert

Radmore
Lane Farm

Barn
Bridge

21

GUILD LA

Humesford Brook

Guild
of
Monks

Cotonwood

6

Pollymoor
Farm

ST20

A5

Weavers Hill

Swanpit
Farm

5

David's Pits
Covert

Broadhill

TF10

Windmill
(dis)

Coley
Brook

20

4

The Way for the Millennium

Lindore
Wood

Broadhill

A518

Coley Mill

Lindore
Farm

Beffcote
Farm

3

Polesworth

BEFFCOTE RD

Beffcot

19

Back Brook

Beffcote
Manor

Beffcot

2

Back Brook

Windmill Bank

Wilbrighton
Hall

GNOSALL RD

Tinwood
Bank

Manor Farm

Bromstead
Common

1

Euxley Farm

Outwoodsbank
Farm

HEATH RD

Outwoods

Tavern
Cottage

18

78 A B 79 C D 80 E F

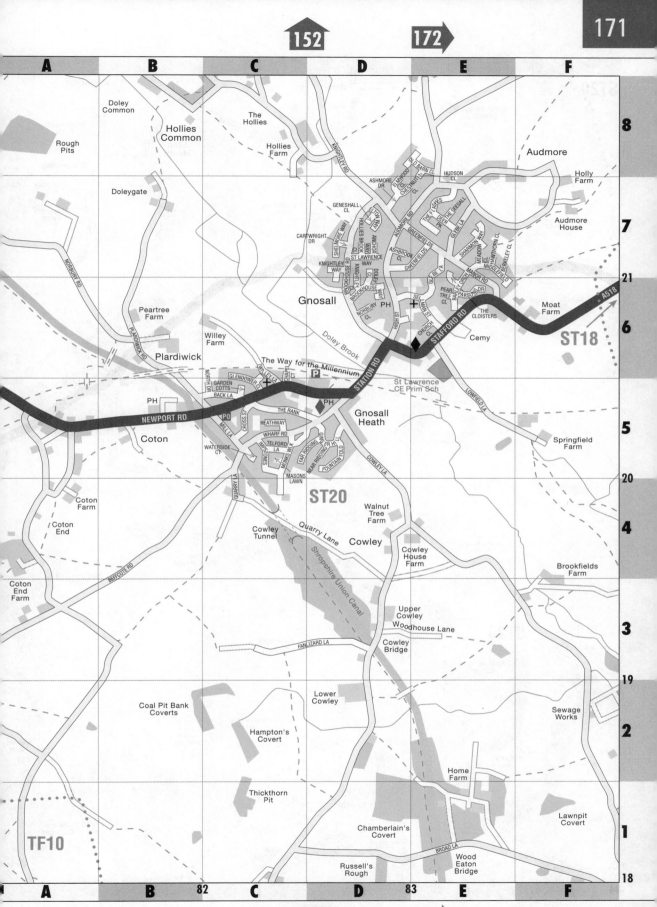

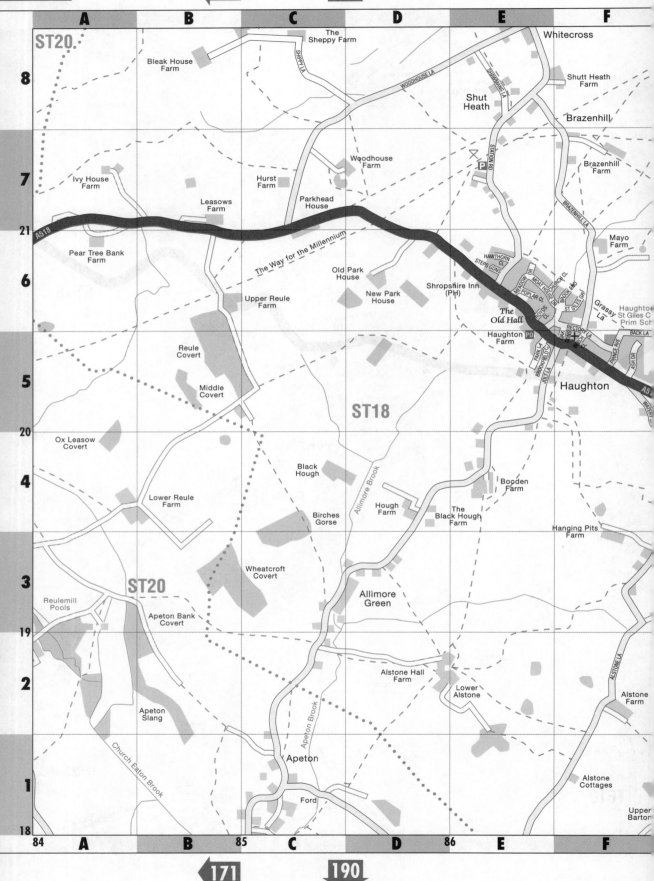

ST20.

8

Bleak House Farm

The Sheppy Farm

Whitecross

SHIPPY LA

WOODHOUSE LA

Shut Heath Farm

SEABANKS LA

Shut Heath

Brazenhill

7

Ivy House Farm

Hurst Farm

Woodhouse Farm

STATION RD

P

Brazenhill Farm

BRAZENHILL LA

Leasows Farm

Parkhead House

Mayo Farm

21

A518

The Way for the Millennium

HAWTHORN CL

STEP'S GDNS

MEADOW DR

CHURCH CL

BROOK END

ST GYLES GRN

6

Pear Tree Bank Farm

Old Park House

New Park House

Shropshire Inn (PH)

POPLAR CL

MOAT HOUSE DR

LOTUS

The Old Hall

Haughton Farm

PO

RECTORY LA

Grassy La

Haughto St Giles C Prim Sch

Upper Reule Farm

PARK LA

BROWNFIELD CT

JOLT LA

Haughton

BACK LA

PRINCE AVE

ASH DR

5

Reule Covert

Middle Covert

ST18

A5

WATERI

20

Ox Leasow Covert

Lower Reule Farm

Black Hough

Allimore Brook

Hough Farm

Booden Farm

Hanging Pits Farm

4

Birches Gorse

The Black Hough Farm

3

Reulemill Pools

ST20

Wheatcroft Covert

Allimore Green

ALSTONE LA

Apeton Bank Covert

19

Alstone Hall Farm

Alstone Farm

2

Apeton Slang

Lower Alstone

Apeton Brook

Church Eaton Brook

Apeton

Alstone Cottages

1

Ford

Upper Bartor

18

84

85

86

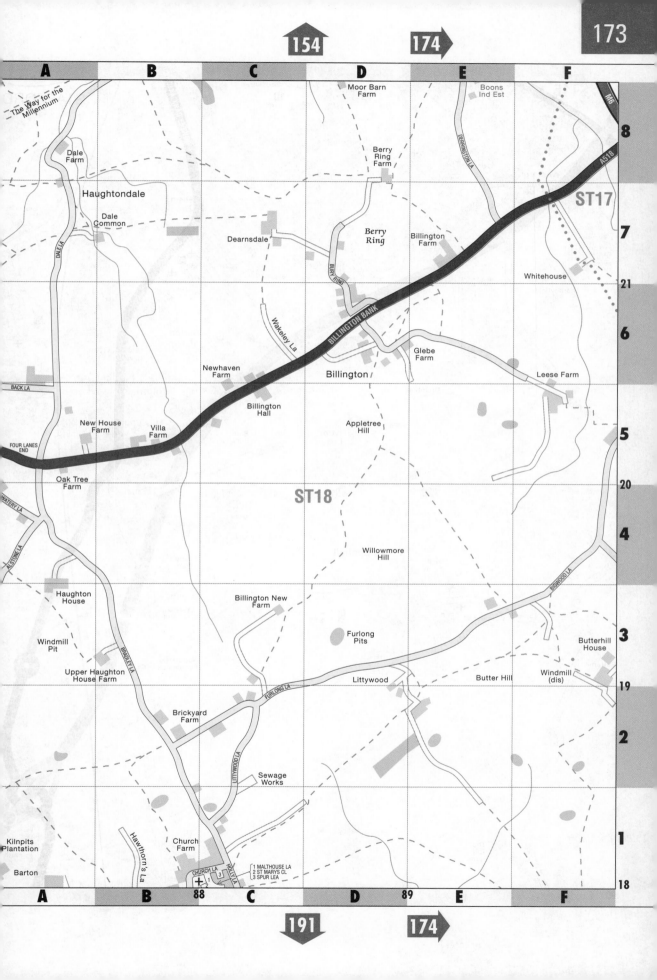

154
174

A B C D E F

The Way for the Millennium

Moor Barn Farm

Boons Ind Est

M6

Dale Farm

8

Berry Ring Farm

DERRINGTON LA

A518

Haughtondale

ST17

Dale Common

Berry Ring

Billington Farm

7

DALE LA

Dearnsdale

Whitehouse

BURY RING

21

BILLINGTON BANK

6

Wakeley La

Glebe Farm

Leese Farm

BACK LA

Newhaven Farm

Billington

Billington Hall

Appletree Hill

5

New House Farm

Villa Farm

FOUR LANES END

Oak Tree Farm

ST18

20

WATERY LA

Willowmore Hill

4

ALSTONE LA

Haughton House

BIGWOOD LA

Butterhill House

3

Windmill Pit

Billington New Farm

Furlong Pits

Butter Hill

Windmill (dis)

Upper Haughton House Farm

BRADLEY LA

Littywood

19

FURLONG LA

Brickyard Farm

2

LITTYWOOD LA

Sewage Works

HALL LA

Kilnpits Plantation

Church Farm

1 MALTHOUSE LA
2 ST MARYS CL
3 SPUR LEA

1

Barton

Hawthorn's La

CHURCH LA

18

A B C D E F
88 89

191
174

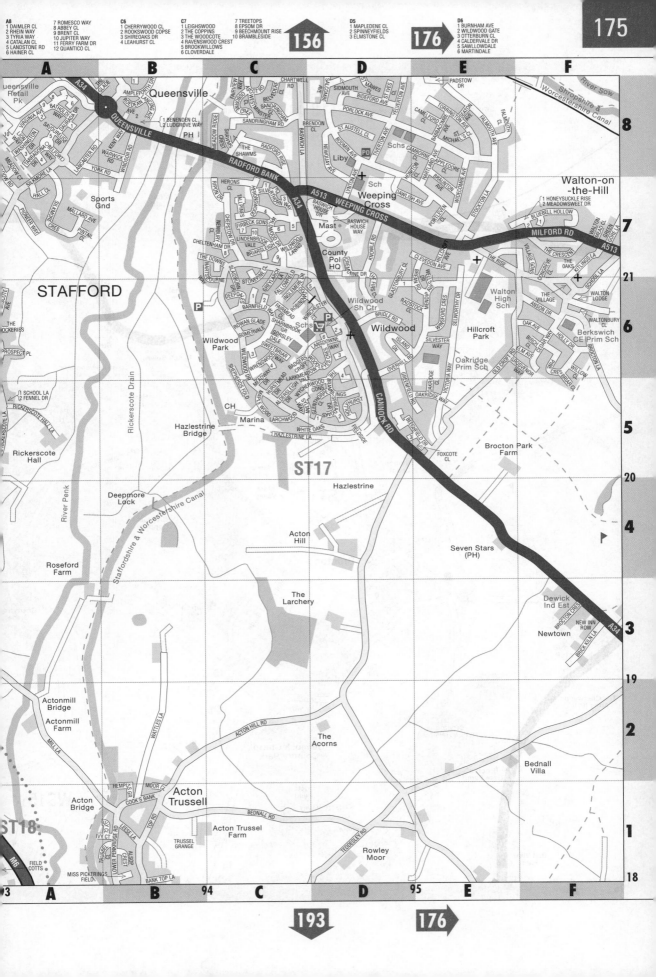

175
157

A B C D E F

8

Walton Bridge

The Swimmings

Black Covert

ST18

Oldhill Bridge

OLDHILL LA

Tixall Bridge

Tixall Lock

The Dark Lantern

Aqueduct Covert

Staffordshire and Worcestershire Canal

HOLLIFORD RD

River Sow

Mon

Shugborough Park

White Bar Farm

7

A513

Milford Lodge

MAIN RD

PO

PH

RAILWAY TERR

THE GREEN

Stafford Plantation

A513

Milford

Milford Hall

21

P

Milford Common

Satnall Hills

P

Sher Brook

Milford Covert

Spring Hill

P

6

Moor Covert

LYSAR LA

P

The Punch Bowl

Alder Carr

P

Haywoodpark Covert

Cressel Wood

Cressel Pool

BROCTON RD

P

Harts Hill

Berry Hill

5

BROCTON LA

WALTON LA

Brocton Lodge

The Hole

Broc Hill

Oat Hill

Staffordshire Way

20

CH

ST17

Mere Pits

Mere Valley

Heart of England Way

Brocton Coppice

Devil's Dumble

4

DEER THE

POOL LA

BROOK LA

OLD COACH LA

Brocton

BROOK LA

Sherbrook Valley

Cherrytree Slade

PARK LA

PO

NEATHER HEATHER CL

COPPICE BROOK

BRAGGEN HILL

HEATHER VIEW

BROCTON PITS

Hollywood Slade

Coppice Hill

P

3

A34

SHERBROOK CL

SANDPIT LA

CHASE CRES

THE GREEN

OLDACRE LA

Oldacre

Tar Hill

P

CHASE RD

P

19

CANNOCK RD

The Chetwynd Arms (PH)

Oldacre Brook

P

2

Brocton Nature Reserve

Cannock Chase Country Park

Dry Pits

Sherbrook Banks

WS15

Brocton Gate Farm

Brocton Field

Oldacre Valley

1

Sycamore Hill

CAMP RD

Belt View Farm

A34

18

175
194

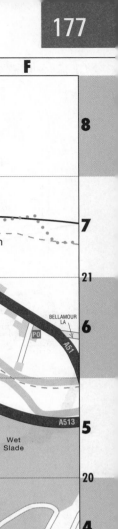

A B C D E F

8

ST18

Bishton Farm

Moreton Lane

Lount Farm

Hamley Cottage Farm

Hamleyheath

B5013

Bishton Lane Farm

MOOR LA

7

Bellamour

21

Wilmour Farm

Boughey Hall Farm

BISHTON LA

6

Bishton
Bishton Hall
St Bede's Sch

The Taft

Taft Bridge

BELLAMOUR LA

St Mary's CE Prim Sch

SCHOOL LA

BELLAMOUR WAY

A51

Wolseley Garden Park
The Wolseley Ctr

ST17

Trent and Mersey Canal

Staffordshire Way

Colwich Lodge

Bellamour Lodge Farm

COACHMAN WLK

WS15

A513
PH

5

A51

Wharf Cottage

River Trent

COLTON RD

20

Rydal Est

4

Chapel Hill

Sewage Works

A51

A460

Pumping Station

RUGELEY

FOG COTTS

Rugeley Trent Valley

BLITHBUR

Long Covert

Stafford Brook

The Way for the Millennium

Trent Valley Trad Est

COLTON

3

Bower House

WOLSELEY RD

19

HORSESHOE DR 1
HUTCHINSON CL 2
DAFFODIL WLK 3
LANSDOWNE WAY 4
HURSTBOURNE CL 5
REDMOND CL 6

2

Playing Field

STATION RD

Power

Bosto Ind Es

Etchinghill

WESTERN SPRINGS RD

1 LOWER BROOK ST
2 MARKET SQ
3 PENNY BANK CT
4 SHREWSBURY MALL
5 BALLAM MEWS

1

Aelfgar Ctr

ANSON ST

B5013

Liby

Ct

Sneydlands

Cvn Power STATIO Site

18

02 A 03 B C 04 D E F

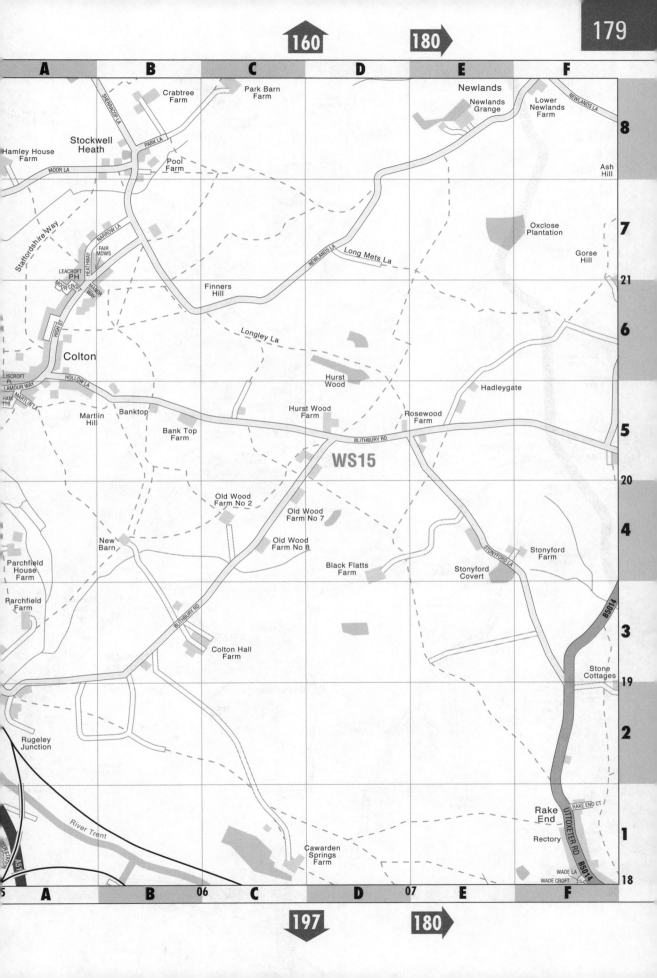

A B C D E F

Newlands

Newlands Grange

Lower Newlands Farm

8

Crabtree Farm

Park Barn Farm

Stockwell Heath

Hamley House Farm

Pool Farm

Ash Hill

SHERACOP LA

PARK LA

MOOR LA

Staffordshire Way

NARROW LA

FAIR MDWS

HEATHWAY

LEACROFT PH

MOOR CROFT

MANOR WAY

HIGH ST

Colton

LISCROFT PL

LAMOUR WAY

MARTLIN LA

HAM TTS

HOLLOW LA

Martlin Hill

Banktop

Bank Top Farm

New Barn

Parchfield House Farm

Parchfield Farm

Rugeley Junction

River Trent

Oxclose Plantation

7

Gorse Hill

21

NEWLANDS LA

Long Mets La

Finners Hill

6

Longley La

Hurst Wood

Hadleygate

Hurst Wood Farm

Rosewood Farm

BLITHBURY RD

5

WS15

20

Old Wood Farm No 2

Old Wood Farm No 7

Stonyford Farm

4

Old Wood Farm No 8

Black Flatts Farm

Stonyford Covert

STONYFORD LA

BLITHBURY RD

Colton Hall Farm

Stone Cottages

3

19

2

B5014

Rake End

Rectory

RAKE END CT

UTTOXETER RD

B5014

1

Cawarden Springs Farm

WADE LA

WADE CROFT

18

A51

A B 06 C D 07 E F

179
161

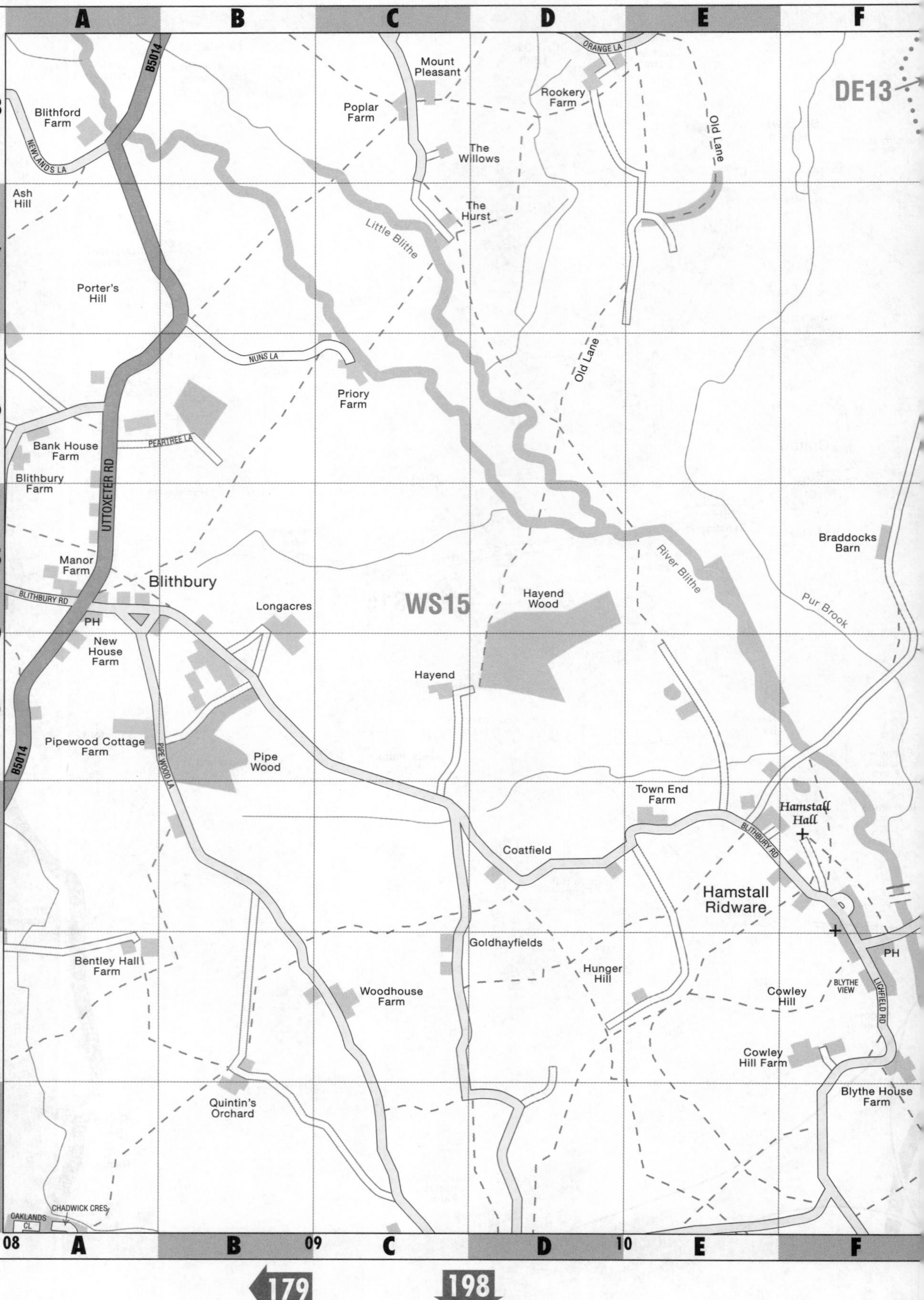

A **B** **C** **D** **E** **F**

DE13

8

B5014

Blithford
Farm

Newland's La

Mount
Pleasant

Poplar
Farm

Rookery
Farm

Orange La

The
Willows

Old Lane

Ash
Hill

Little Blithe

The Hurst

7

Porter's
Hill

Old Lane

21

NUNS LA

Priory
Farm

6

Bank House
Farm

PEARTREE LA

Uttoxeter Rd

Blithbury
Farm

River Blithe

Braddocks
Barn

5

Manor
Farm

Blithbury

Pur Brook

BLITHBURY RD

Longacres

WS15

Hayend
Wood

PH

20

New
House
Farm

Hayend

Town End
Farm

Hamstall
Hall

4

B5014

Pipewood Cottage
Farm

Pipe Wood La

Pipe
Wood

BLITHBURY RD

Coatfield

Hamstall
Ridware

3

19

Bentley Hall
Farm

Goldhayfields

Hunger
Hill

PH

BLYTHE
VIEW

LICHFIELD RD

Cowley
Hill

2

Woodhouse
Farm

Cowley
Hill Farm

Blythe House
Farm

1

Quintin's
Orchard

18

OAKLANDS
CL

CHADWICK CRES

08 **A** **B** 09 **C** **D** 10 **E** **F**

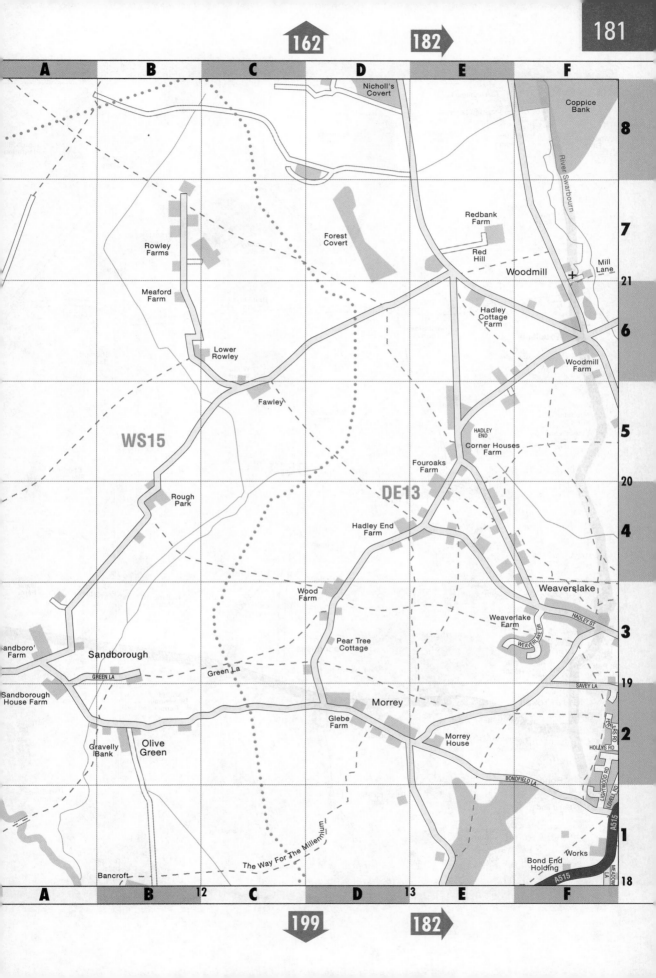

A   B   C   D   E   F

8

Highfields Farm
LODGE LA
Woodside Farm
Whitemere Farm
Lodgehill Farm
Foxholes Covert
Yoxall Park
Brankley Lodge
Scotch Hill Plantation

7

Forest Farm
Mill La
THATCHMOOR LA
Lin Brook
Brankley House
Brankley Covert

21

Brankley Farm
Sherholt Lodge

6

PH
Woodlane
Stonyford Brook
Forest Side Farm
White Wood

Woodlane Bridge
Wood Lane Bridge Farm
Sales Farm
Whitewood Farm
Sherholt Lodge

5

Longcroft Farm
DE13
Sherholt Plantation

20

SUDBURY RD
LONGCROFT LA
Wall House

4

Lucepool
Hollyhurst House
Hilltop Plantation
Holly Bank Farm

Thistledown
LUCEPOOL LA
SICH LA
B501

3

PO
ALEXANDRA DR
GISBORNE CL
VICTORIA ST
KING ST
Yoxall Farm
HADLEY ST
PH
The Rough
River Swarbourn
Woodhouses
Hollybank Farm
Upper Blakenhall Farm

19

St Peter's CE Prim Sch
SAVEY LA
MAIN ST
Yoxall
STRINGER'S LA

2

CHURCHFIELDS
RAVEN RD
FERRERS
HOLLYS RD
LOVELL RD
ALWYN RD
B5016
TOWN HILL
BROWN'S LA
1 SWAINSFIELD RD
2 ROOKERY CL
3 SWARBOURN CL
Bank House
MEADOW LA

A515
Bond
High-hall-hill Farm
Park Piece Plantation

1

Bond End Farm
The Way For The Millennium
Mason's Barn
Twichills
The Coppice

18

Sewage Works

14   A   B   15   C   D   16   E   F

A B C D E F

8 7 21 6 5 20 4 3 19 2 1 18

Home Farm
Deanery Plantation
Deanery Farm
Fernhill Farm
RANGEMORE HILL
Dunstall Cross
Dunstall Hill
Dunstall Cross
Yew Tree Farm
FOREST RD
Forest Thorn
Forest Barn
Needwood Rise
Brick Kiln Lane
The Bell (PH)
Barton Gate
Silver Hill
BARTON GATE
BAR LA
Blakenhall
Gorsey Hill Farm

Bannister's Hollies
The Exchange
Sprinks Barn Farm
The Larches
Dunstall
Old Hall
Mill Pond
Saw Mill
Smith Hills Cottages
DE13
Smith Hills
Woodside Farm
The Knoll
Barton-under-Needwood
MAIN ST
Barton Park
PARK RD
THE GREEN
CAPTAIN'S
ASH TREE RD
OAK RD
WILLOW RD
HOLLY
LINDEN RD
CEDAR RD
SHORT LA
BEECH RD

Highlands Park
Rockets Oak
TATENHILL COMM
MOORS HILL COTTS
TATENHILL LA
The Oaks
Hobholes Dingle
The Caves
Bikersdale Wood
The Hills
Dunstall Home Farm
Dunstall Hall
The Park
Greenlane Plantation
Gravel Pits
Lower Farm
The Pool
ARMITAGE HILL
DUNSTALL RD
Small Meadows
SMALL MDWS
Barton Hall
MANOR CT
Liby
John Taylor High Sch
Telephone Exchange
STATION RD
B5016
BARTON TURN
PALMER RD
HOLLAND PARK
Thomas Russell Inf Sch
PH
MEADOW RISE
NEEDWOOD PK
EFFLINCH LA
GILMOUR LA
Thomas Russell Jun Sch
Sewage Works
Marina

P
PO
CROWBERRY LA
ST JAMES CT
BELL LA
RADRHUST LA
WALES LA
COLINSON RD
CHURCH LA
ST JAMES RD
ST LUKE'S RD
BARTON LODGE
Barton Cottage
H
TILMINGTON
FALLOW DR
RISE
PARK RD
SAFFRON CL
THE ALDERS
BROOKSIDE RD
WESTMEAD RD

183
165

A **B** **C** **D** **E** **F**

8

DARK LA
Tatenhill
MAIN ST
PH
Manor
Farm
CORONATION
COTTS
MANOR
CROFT
TATENHILL LA
THE
WOODLANDS
Lawns Farm
Cottage
Yews
Bridge
BRANSTON RD
Branston
Lock

7

DUNSTALL RD
Robinson□s
Plantation
THE DRIVE
Brookfields
Farm
Branston
Bridge
PH
TATENHILL LA
Branston
Water Park
A5121
SECOND AVE
WELLINGTON RD
A5121
Ref
Pk
OEIGHTH AVE
SPRINGIT
RD
CLEVELEY RD
WARWICK
CL
HARCOURT
RD
MERLIN CRES
HARWOOD AVE
CLAY'S LA
COTSWOLD RD
MAPLE WAY
FIRST AVE
FARADAY
CT
LYNWOOD RD
LYNWOOD
CL
FESTIVAL
BRIDGFORD RD
Branston
Rykneld
Prim Sch
B5108
LEAMINGTON
RD
BLENHEIM HO 1
CHATSWORTH HO 2
REGENTS HO 3
FONTWELL RD
LINGFI
RD
WETHERBY
CL
1
2
3
PO
COURT
FARM LA
MAIN ST
OLD RD
CHURCH
RD
HOLLYHOCK WAY
WOODBINE CL
CLOVER
CT
BRAMELL
CL
MAIN ST
WARREN LA
LANSDOWNE
RD
RIVERSIDE DR
B51
Hotel
Bean
Cove
Branston

21

Visitor
Ctr
P

6

DE14
Nature
Reserve

5

Black Meadow
Wood
Tatenhill
Lock
The Way for the Millennium
Trent & Mersey Canal
Works
Gallow
Bridge
LC
Ppg Sta

20

Works
LICHFIELD RD
Works
Drakelow
Power Station

4

DE13
Gorsehall
Plantation
Works
River Trent
DE15

3

Newbold Manor
Farm
Tucklesholme
Farm
LC
Sewage
Works

19

2

Warren
Farm
Warren
Hill

1

B5016
WHARF
HOS
STATION RD
B5016
Motel
Graycar
Bsns
Pk
Rylance
Farm
Barton
Turn
Walton
Bridge
STATION LA
RIVERSIDE
MEWIES CL
PH
P
MAIN ST
PO
CASTLE END
CATON RD
LA
ORCHARD
CL
BELLS END RD
LEEDHAMS
CROFT
HARBIN
RD
DE12
Barr
Hall
Walton-on-Trent

18

BARTON TURN
A38

20 **A** **B** **21** **C** **D** **22** **E** **F**

A **B** **C** **D** **E** **F**

Nature Trail

Ferry Bridge

BURTON UPON TRENT

DE14

Stapenhill

Paulet High Sch

Upper Mills Farm

Waterside Com Jun Sch

Edge Hill Jun Sch

Heathlands Grange

BURTON RD

Paget High Sch

The Rookery

CH

River Trent

Heath Farm

The Wilderness

Factory

SYCAMORE CL

LC

Drakelowe House

Home Farm

LC

WALTON RD

Stapenhill Fields Farm

Drakelow Power Station

DE15

Flint Mill

Barn Farm

Royle Farm

Grove Wood

Grove Farm

DE12

Hill Covert

Morris Croft

Ashleigh House Farm

DE12

A **B** **C** **D** **E** **F**

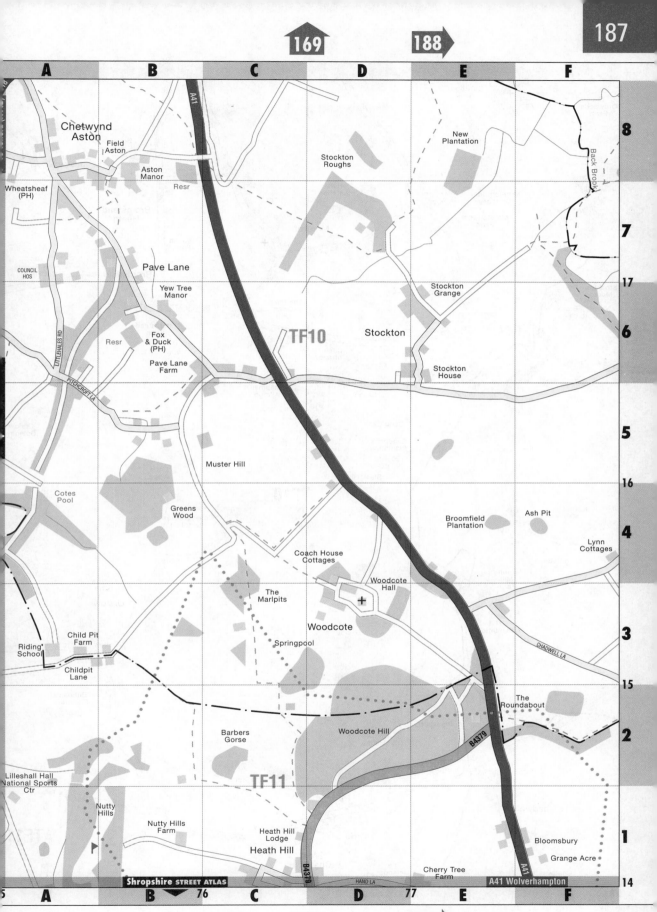

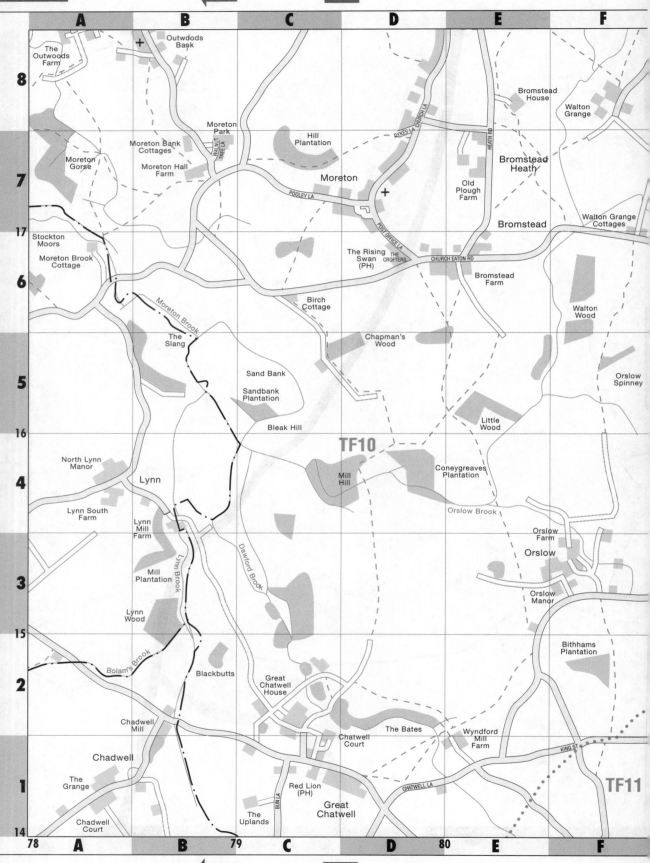

A **B** **C** **D** **E** **F**

8

BROAD LA

The Hall
Farm

Barlands La

Oscotte La

Goosemoor

INTAKE LA

Daisybank
Plantation

Intake
Plantation

7

Bank
Cottage

Turnover Bridge
Plantation

Homers
Farm

Shropshire Union Canal

JOAN EATON'S
CROSS

17

CHURCH EATON RD

Walton
Fields

Taylor's
Plantation

High Onn
Wharf Farm

High Onn
Bridge

6

Stoney
Plantation

St Edith's
Well

TF10

High Onn
Wood

High
Onn

5

High
Onn Manor

Hollowdine
Pits

16

ST20

The Home
Farm

Little
Onn

4

Rail Pit
Plantation

The Uplands

Little Onn
Hall

Tinker
Pits

Keeper's
Cottage

Calvescroft
Plantation

Gorse
Covert

3

15

Airfield
(dis)

SWEETPLACE LA

2

Marston Brook

KING ST

TF11

BIRCHMOOR LA

1

New House
Farm

Marston
Farm

Elm Tree
Farm

Aquamoor

Burnt
Witheys

Fox Inn
(PH)

14

A **B** 82 **C** **D** 83 **E** **F**

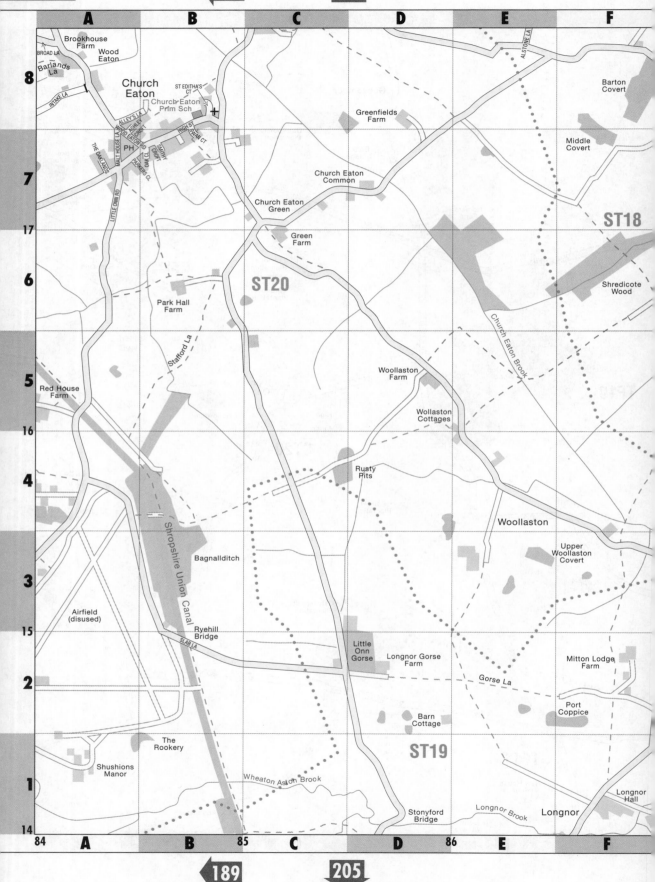

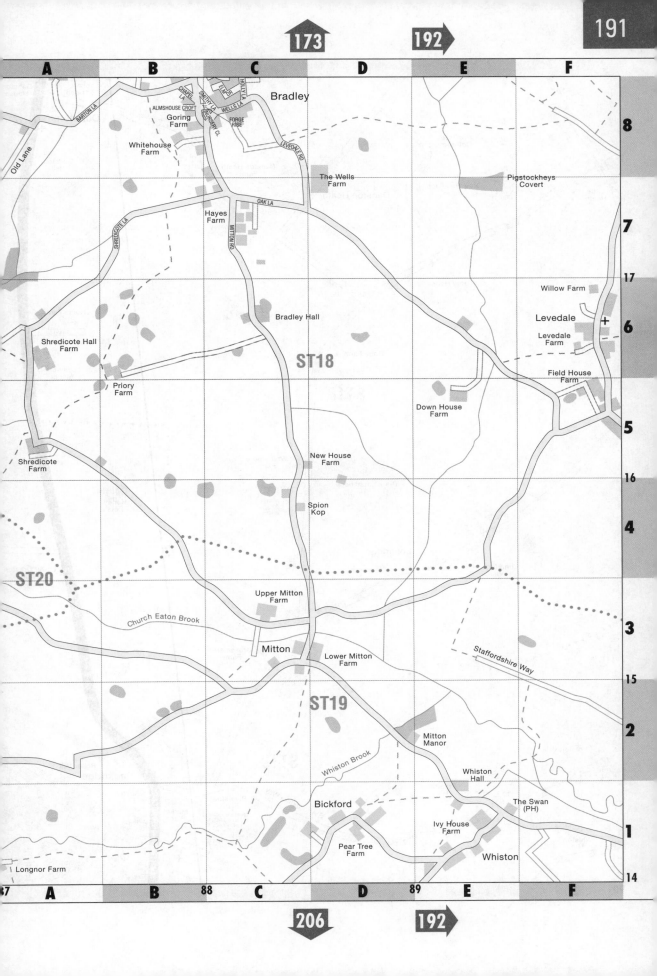

A B C D E F

8

Bradley

CHAPEL LA
SMITHY LA
ELM DR
HOLLY LA
WELLS LA
ALMSHOUSE CROFT
NURSERY CL
Goring Farm
FORGE RISE

Whitehouse Farm

LEVEDALE RD

The Wells Farm

Pigstockheys Covert

OAK LA

Hayes Farm

SHREDICOTE LA
MITTON RD

7

17

Willow Farm

Levedale

Bradley Hall

Levedale Farm

6

Shredicote Hall Farm

ST18

Field House Farm

Priory Farm

Down House Farm

5

Shredicote Farm

New House Farm

16

Spion Kop

4

ST20

Upper Mitton Farm

Church Eaton Brook

Staffordshire Way

3

15

Mitton

Lower Mitton Farm

ST19

Mitton Manor

2

Whiston Hall

Whiston Brook

The Swan (PH)

Bickford

Ivy House Farm

1

Pear Tree Farm

Whiston

Longnor Farm

14

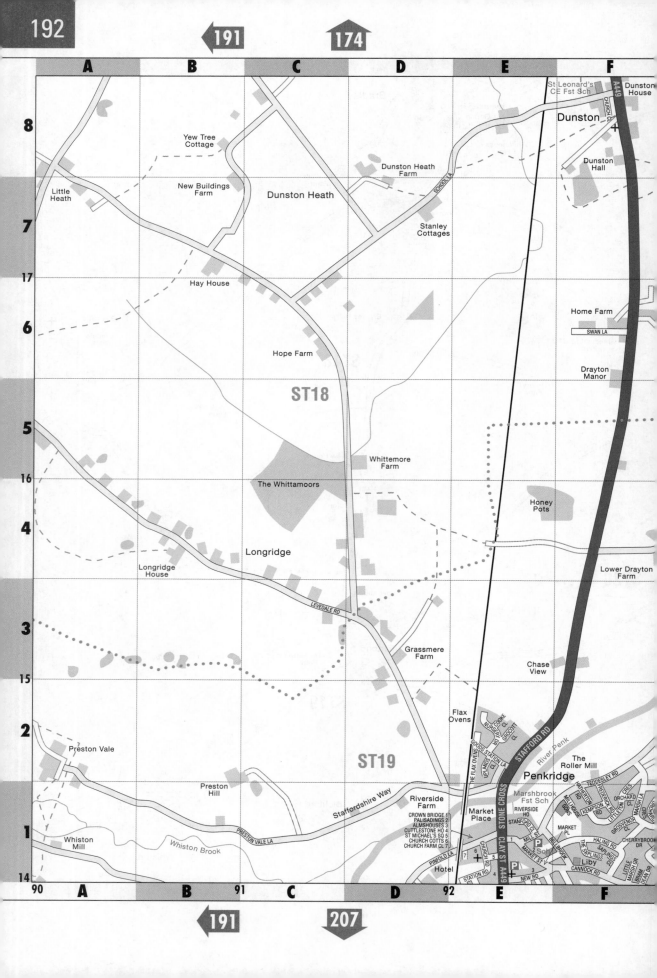

197
180

A B C D E F

8

OAKLANDS CL
B5014
Hill Ridware
Henry Chadwick Prim Sch
CHADWICK CREST
SCHOOL LA
UTTOXETER RD
SANDFORD CL
CHURCH LA
MAVESYN CL

PIPE LA
Bentley Brook
RIDWARE RD

Littleton House Farm
Pipe Ridware
Hall Farm
Upper Nethertown Farm
YEAR'S LA
BANCR
Nethertown
The Way for the Millennium

7

Eastfields
Sitch Covert
River Trent
Penk Holme

17

Gate House
Old Hall
Mavesyn Ridware
High Bridge
B5014
Willow Cottage
Bromley Lane Farm
KING'S BROMLEY LA
Glebe Farm
Football Gnd
RUGELEY RD
A51

6

Pipe Place Farm
WS15

Old Road Farm
Sewage Works
Marsh Barn Farm
Ketchithayes Plantation
New Plantation
DE13
Echills

5

BOAT HOUSE LA
OLD RD
ROOKERY
PINFOLD DR
Ford Way
ORCHARD COTTS
THE GREEN
WATERS EDGE
GLEBE RD
ST BARBARA'S
LAKESIDE AVE
Handsacre
Tuppenhurst

16

RUGELEY RD
A513
NEW RD
PO
P
STATION DR
B5014
UTTOXETER RD
LINFORD CL
THE CROFT
POPLARS RD
HARVEY RD
WOODSHOT CL
BRIDGE RD
PIKE LA
RECTORY GDNS
GREENFIELD AVE
MILLMOOR AVE
YEOMAN WAY
CHASE
MEADOW WAY
REEVE CL
LAKESIDE VIEW
Armitage
SHELLEY CL
DYKE RD
LEET CT
SPODE AVE
WOODLANDS
WOODLANDS

4

HOOD LA
Brick Kiln Farm
WORDSWORTH
ELIOT CL
SHROPSHIRE
BROOK RD
PEAK CL
HAZEL
WINCHESTER CL
MOAT WAY
MAJOR COURT DR
MILLCROFT WAY
FOX LEIGH
MDWS
FAIR VIEW
CTORS RD
4 3 2 1
5
6
Hayes Meadow Prim Sch
1 ST LUKE'S WLK
2 BROOME WLK
3 ARDEN WLK
4 HIGHFIELDS AVE
5 BEECH CL
6 JOHN'S AVE
7 ALANDALE AVE
8 THE ORCHARDS
TUPPENHURST LA
Westview Cottages

3

Hood Lane Farm
HANDSACRE CRES
HILL TOP VIEW
WARREN CROFT
BOXER CL
ROYAL
BARN RD
CHESTNUT CL
Trent and Mersey Canal
Shaw Barn

15

LICHFIELD RD
Ashton Hays
Shaw Lane Farm
WS13

2

HAWCROFT
Brook End
St James CE Prim Sch
PH
FORD LA
MILL WAY
BROMLEY WAY
BEECH WLK
Newtown
Barn Farm
SHAW LA

1

ST JAMES CL
BROOK END
CHURCH LA
Longdon
A51
Hill Top
OLD BARN HOUSE MEWS
Hill Top Farm
LYSWAYS LA
B5014
Bourne Bro
A51

14

08 A 09 B C 10 D E F

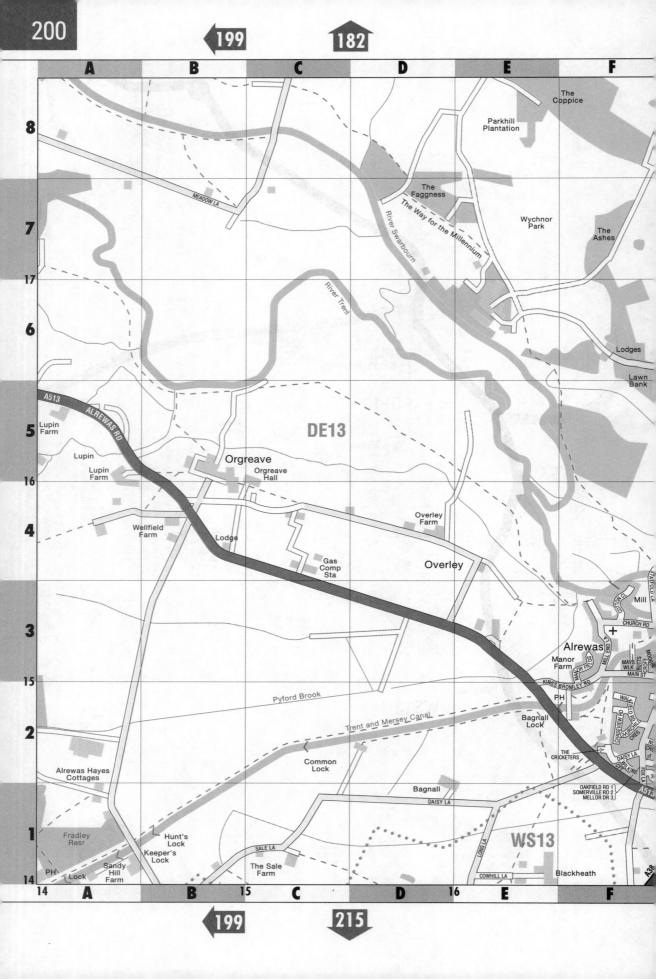

199
182

The Coppice

Parkhill Plantation

The Faggness

The Way for the Millennium

Wychnor Park

The Ashes

River Swarbourn

MEADOW LA

River Trent

Lodges

Lawn Bank

A513

ALREWAS RD

DE13

Lupin Farm

Lupin

Lupin Farm

Orgreave

Orgreave Hall

Overley Farm

Overley

Wellfield Farm

Lodge

Gas Comp Sta

Mill

CHURCH RD

COTTON LT

Alrewas

Manor Farm

MILL END LA

MAYS WLK

BUTTS CROFT

MODEL VILLAGE

MAIN ST

PH

STATFULLA LA

Pyford Brook

KINGS BROMLEY RD

Trent and Mersey Canal

Bagnall Lock

THE CRICKETERS

CHASEVIEW RD

WALK FIELD RD

MIRCHILL CRES

DAISY LA

WILKINS

FOX LA

Alrewas Hayes Cottages

Common Lock

Bagnall

DAISY LA

OAKFIELD RD 1
SOMERVILLE RD 2
MELLOR DR 3

A513

Fradley Resr

Hunt's Lock

Keeper's Lock

SALE LA

The Sale Farm

LONG LA

COWHILL LA

WS13

Blackheath

A38

PH

Sandy Hill Farm

Lock

199
215

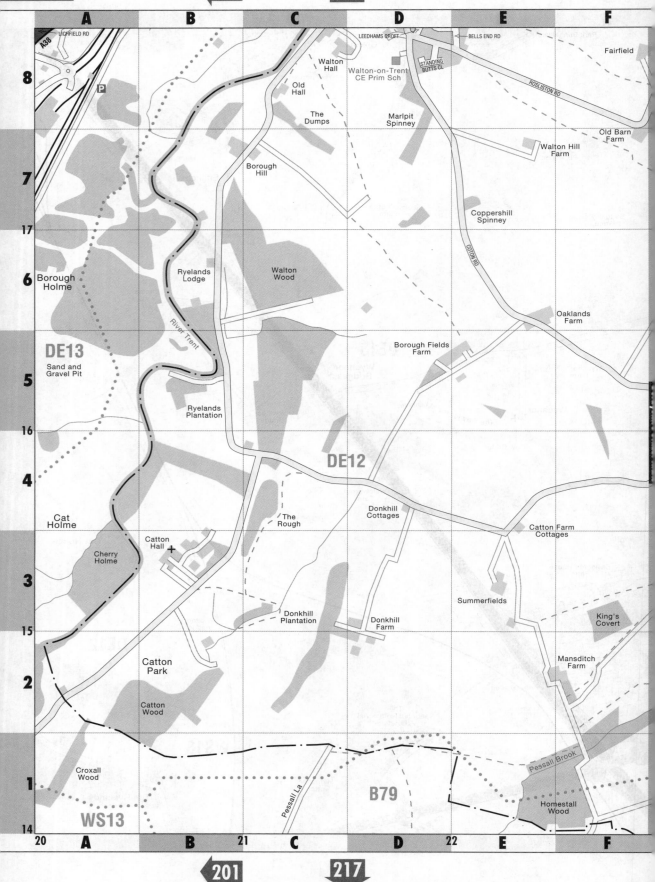

A   B   C   D   E   F

8

A38 LICHFIELD RD
P

7

17

6 Borough
Holme

Ryelands
Lodge

Walton Hall

Old Hall

The
Dumps

Walton
Hall

Leedhams Croft

Walton-on-Trent
CE Prim Sch

STANDING
BUTTS CL

← BELLS END RD

Fairfield

ROSLISTON RD

Old Barn
Farm

Walton Hill
Farm

Marlpit
Spinney

Borough
Hill

Walton
Wood

Coppershill
Spinney

COTON RD

River Trent

DE13

Sand and
Gravel Pit

5

16

4

Cat
Holme

Cherry
Holme

3

15

Catton
Park

2

Catton
Wood

Croxall
Wood

1

WS13

14

Ryelands
Plantation

DE12

The
Rough

Catton
Hall

Donkhill
Plantation

Donkhill
Cottages

Donkhill
Farm

Borough Fields
Farm

Oaklands
Farm

Catton Farm
Cottages

Summerfields

King's
Covert

Mansditch
Farm

Pessall La

B79

Pessall Brook

Homestall
Wood

20   A   B   21   C   D   22   E   F

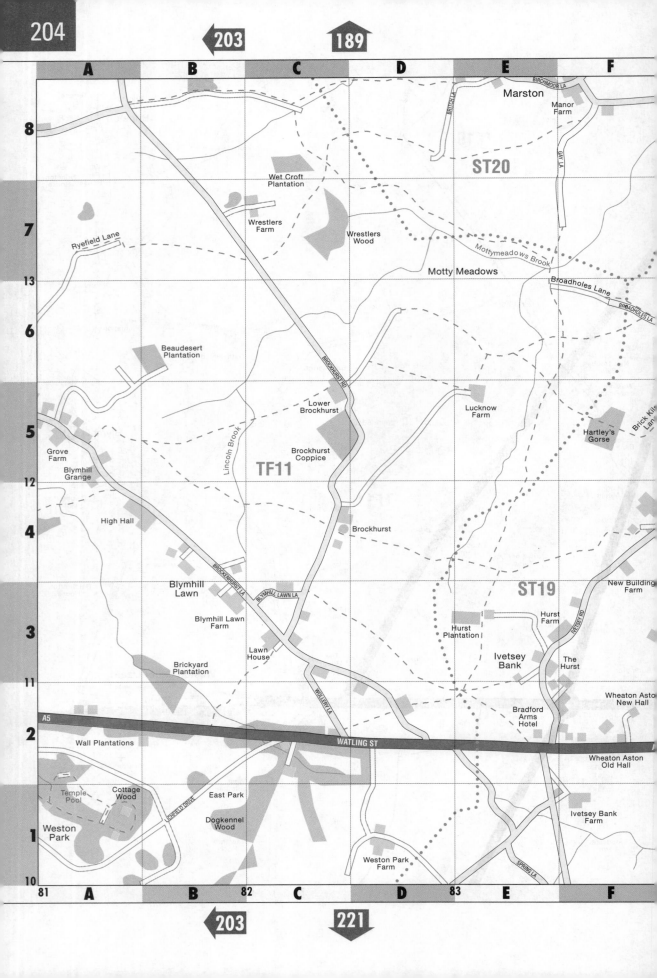

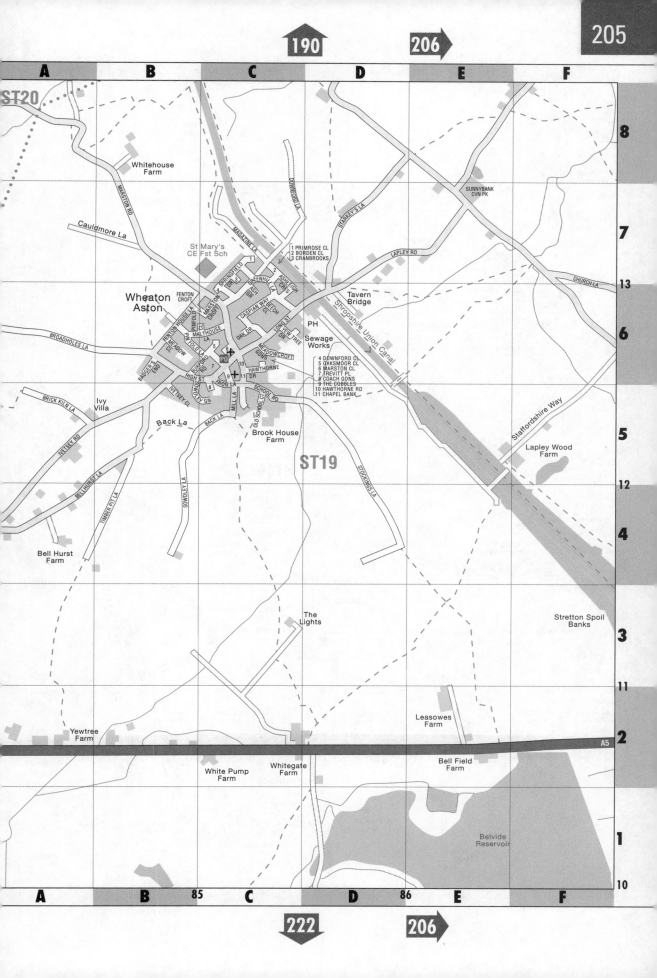

ST20

A B C D E F

8

Whitehouse
Farm

Cauldmore La

MARSTON RD

DOWNFORD LA

MAGAZINE LA

SUNNYBANK
CVN PK

7

STARKEY'S LA

LAPLEY RD

St Mary's
CE Fst Sch

1 PRIMROSE CL
2 BORDEN CL
3 CRANBROOKS

13

SPRINGFIELD
GREENHILL LA
ASHLEIGH CRES

Wheaton
Aston

FENTON
CROFT

MARSTON
CROFT

CASPIAN WAY

BEECH CL

LONG ST

FEW TREE

Tavern
Bridge

PH

Shropshire Union Canal

CHURCH LA

BROADHOLES LA

FENTON HOUSE LA

PINFOLD

MALTHOUSE

OAK DR

MEADOWCROFT
GDNS

Sewage
Works

4 DOWNFORD CL
5 OAKSMOOR CL
6 MARSTON CL
7 TREVITT PL
8 COACH GDNS
9 THE COBBLES
10 HAWTHORNE RD
11 CHAPEL BANK

6

BADGER'S END

MEADOW CL

COLD LA

BURFORD RD

HIGH RD

HAWTHORNE
DR

SCHOOL RD

13

BRICK KILN LA

IVETSEY RD

Ivy
Villa

IVETSEY CL

LOMSEY GN

Back La

MILL LA

BACK LA

OLD SCHOOL CT

STOCKINGS LA

Brook House
Farm

ST19

Staffordshire Way

Lapley Wood
Farm

5

BELLHURST LA

SOWDLEY LA

12

TIMBER PIT LA

Bell Hurst
Farm

4

The
Lights

Stretton Spoil
Banks

3

11

Leasowes
Farm

Yewtree
Farm

A5

2

White Pump
Farm

Whitegate
Farm

Bell Field
Farm

Belvide
Reservoir

1

10

A B C D E F

85 86

A   **B**   **C**   **D**   **E**   **F**

8

Pool Plantation

Staffordshire Way

Bickford Grange Farm

Bickford Grange

7

BICKFORD RD

MERCIAN WAY

QUEENS COTTAGES

Beacon Hill

13

CHURCH LA

PH

Lapley

PRIORS CL

BICKFORD CL

PARK LA

LAPLEY HALL MEWS

STRETTON RD

Lapley Hall

6

Lapley Gorse

Stretton Wood

5

Keeper's Cottage

ST19

Rabbit Slack

12

The Wilderness

Home Farm

Twenty Acre Pit

LAPLEY LA

WOOD LA

ROWLEYHILL DR

4

The Stubblers

Wood Farm

Stretton Hall

Stretton Park

Rowleyhill Plantation

SLING LA

GARDEN LA

Stretton

STONEY LA

Upper Pool

The Pool

3

Stretton Spoil Banks

SCHOOL LA

Vernon Lodge Prep Sch

PO

School Farm

Lodge Plantation

THE AVENUE

11

Stretton Mill

Aquaduct House

Stretton Wharf

Road Farm

Crown Farm

The Ivy House

2

A5

A5

Shropshire Union Canal Main Line

Staffordshire Way

The Bell Inn (PH)

River Penk

Horsebrook

Horsebrook Hall

HORSEBROOK HALL LA

IVY HOUSE LA

Bungalow Farm

1

Bell View Farm

HORSEBROOK LA

Horse Brook

Broom Hall Farm

Horsebrook Farm

Engleton Hall

10

87   **A**   **B**   88   **C**   **D**   89   **E**   **F**

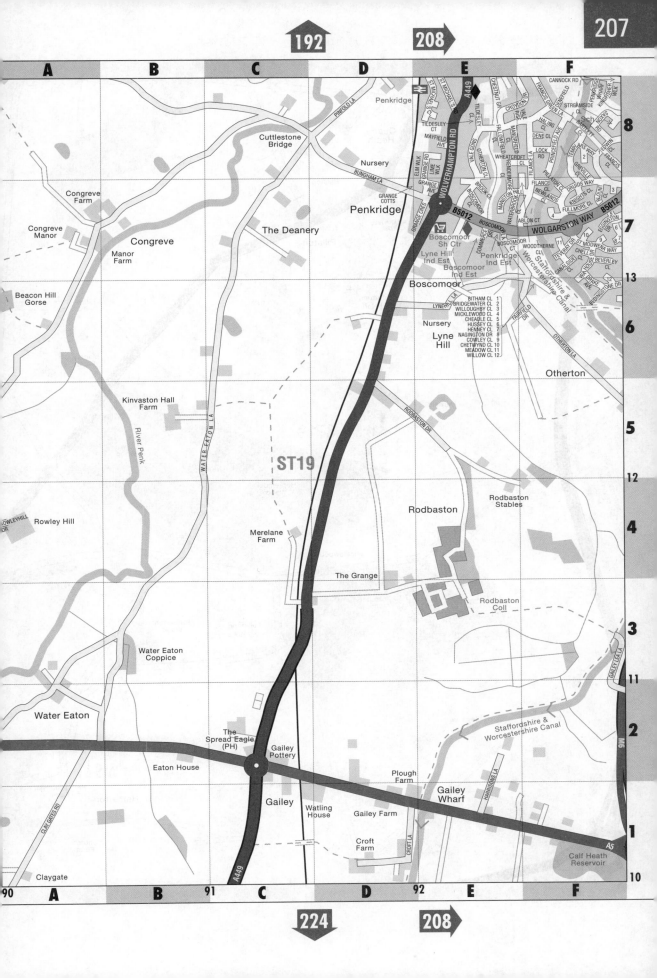

A   B   C   D   E   F

8

Penkridge

Cuttlestone
Bridge

Nursery

Congreve
Farm

BUNGHAM LA

Penkridge

Grange
Cotts

B5012

Boscomoor
Sh Ctr

Congreve
Manor

The Deanery

Lyne Hill
Ind Est

Boscomoor
Ind Est

Penkridge
Ind Est

7

Congreve

Manor
Farm

Boscomoor

13

Beacon Hill
Gorse

Boscomoor

LYNE HILL

Nursery

Lyne
Hill

BITHAM CL   1
BRIDGEWATER CL 2
WILLOUGHBY CL   3
MICKLEWOOD CL   4
CHEADLE CL   5
HUSSEY CL   6
HENNEY CL   7
NAGINGTON DR   8
COWLEY CL   9
CHETWYND CL   10
MEADOW CL   11
WILLOW CL   12

6

Otherton

River Penk

WATER EATON LA

Kinvaston Hall
Farm

ST19

RODBASTON DR

5

12

Rodbaston
Stables

Rowley Hill

Rodbaston

4

Merelane
Farm

Rodbaston
Coll

The Grange

3

Water Eaton
Coppice

GAILEY LEA LA

11

Staffordshire &
Worcestershire Canal

2

Water Eaton

The Spread Eagle
(PH)

Gailey Pottery

Eaton House

Plough
Farm

Gailey
Wharf

M6

HARRISONS LA

Gailey

Watling
House

Gailey Farm

CROFT LA

1

A5

Croft
Farm

Calf Heath
Reservoir

10

CLAY GATES RD

Claygate

A449

90   A   B   91   C   D   92   E   F

207
193

A B C D E F

8

B5012
CANNOCK RD
GREENWAYS
PRIDE CL
SAXON RD
ATHELSTAN CL
L Ctr
Wolgarston High Sch
BROOM... CL
EL MOOR
NORMAN RD
KENILWORTH CL
M6
WOLGARSTON WAY

Quarry Heath

Newlands Wood

7

B5012
FRANCIS CL
DRUIDS WAY
OVERDON CL
PAGET CL
KILDWENA WAY
ASTON CL
BOYDEN CL
BENTLEY
MOOR HALL LA
NAGINGTON DR
Moor Hall Cottages

Pillaton Farm

PILLATON HALL FARM

Pillaton

13

BECKINGHAM
SCON DR
MALLARD WAY

Pillaton Old Hall +

6

Marina

Mansty Farm

5

OTHERTON LA
Staffordshire & Worcestershire Canal

Airfield

ST19

Mansty Wood

B5012

12

MICKLEWOOD LA

Horsemoor Wood

4

Micklewood

Fullmoor Wood

Fullmoor Lodge

Hatherton Wood

3

11

2

Gailey Lea Farm

GAILEY LEA LA

WS11

Hatherton

Hatherton Hall Farm

1

A5
12
M6
A5

Gailey Upper Reservoir

Gailey Lower Reservoir

Church Farm

CHURCH LA

10

93 A B 94 C D 95 E F

A5

207
225

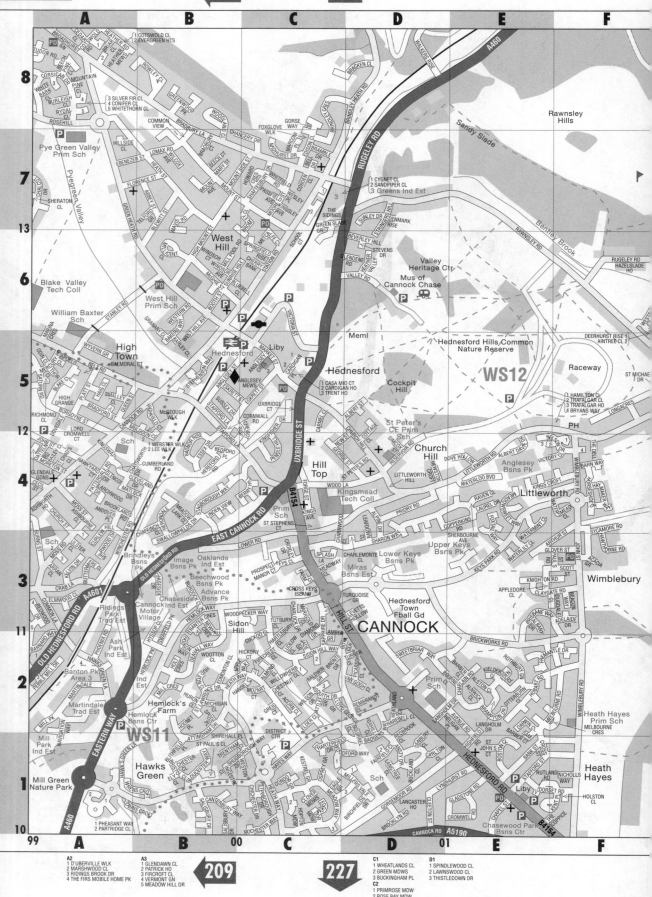

A2
1 D'UBERVILLE WLK
2 MARSHWOOD CL
3 RIDINGS BROOK DR
4 THE FIRS MOBILE HOME PK

A3
1 GLENDAWN CL
2 PATRICK HO
3 FIRCROFT CL
4 VERMONT GN
5 MEADOW HILL DR

C1
1 WHEATLANDS CL
2 GREEN MDWS
3 BUCKINGHAM PL

C2
1 PRIMROSE MDW
2 ROSE BAY MDW
3 CALLAGHAN GR

D1
1 SPINDLEWOOD CL
2 LAWNSWOOD CL
3 THISTLEDOWN DR

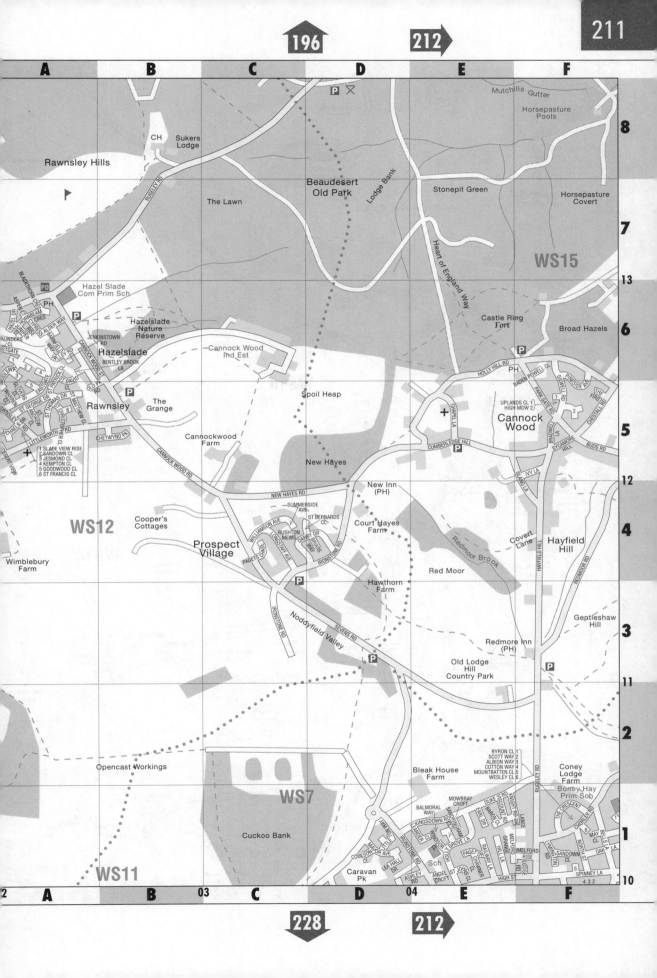

211
197

A B C D E F

8

Stonyflats
Covert

Horseylane
Farm

Shropshire Brook

Coppice Hills

HORSEY LA

George's
Hayes

Churchfield
Cottage

BOROUGH LA

SMITHY LA

Beaudesert Hall
(remains of)

Beaudesert New Park

Grand
Lodge

7

Darklane
Farm

13

DARK LA

Piggot's
Bottom

Cross Ash

Gorton
Green

Alfred's
Coppice

THORLEY'S HILL

Gorton
Lodge
Farm

Longdon
Old Hall

Gorton
Green

STONYWELL LA

STONEYWELL
LA

6

Chestall
Farm

WS15

Gorton
Lodge

Stonywell
Farm

Mast

MALT HOUSE RD

Darling's Hayes

Tithe
Barn

5

SCHOOL LA

Windmill Bank

TITHE BARN LA

Farewell
Gorse

1 BUDS RD
2 REDMOOR RD

Gentleshaw
Prim Sch

WINDMILL BANK

Cold
Well

DARLING'S LA

12

CHAPEL LA

Windmill
Inn
(PH)

Gentleshaw

BRIERLEY HILL LA

Goosemoor Green

4

WINDMILL LA

SHAW LA

Green Lane

Ivy
House
Farm

WS13

Summer
House

The
Hollows
Farm

Watery Lane

Chorley
Hall

Summerhouse
Lane

3

Gentleshaw
Hill

Brook
Farm

DODDS LA

Dodds
Place
Farm

Chorley

COMMONSIDE

Heart of England Way

GREEN LA

Green
Lane
Farm

Malt Shovel
Inn (PH)

LODGE LA

GREENWAYS

Shute
Hill

11

LOWER LA

Chorley Place
Farm

MOOR
VIEW

Lower Lane
Farm

FORD LA

2

CHORLEY RD

Maple Brook

SQUIRREL'S HOLLOW

Hillside
Farm

PADBURY LA

Nelson Inn
(PH)

Littl
Pipe
Far

HEATH VIEW

Sch

COMMON
VIEW

UGLEY HAY RD

RUGELEY RD

1 BYRON CL
2 CHAUCER DR
3 KIPLING AVE
4 MASEFIELD CL
5 SUNNYMEAD RD
6 WORDSWORTH RD

WS7

Creswell
Green

HOBSTONE HILL LA

SHAW DR

BEAUDE

1 LONGFELLOW RD

OAK LA

BIRCH

Nag's Hill
Farm

Heart of England Way

COULTER LA

1

SPINNEY

TENNYSON
AVE

TERR

SHELFIELD RD

MEG LA

Drill Inn
(PH)

Green Lane
Farm

GREEN LA

SPINNEY LA

Boney
Hay

RAKE HILL

Nether Lane
Farm

LITTLE PIPE LA 1
THE ROCHE 2

CAMSEY LA

10

5

6

4

Castle Farm

SPRINGLE STYCHE LA

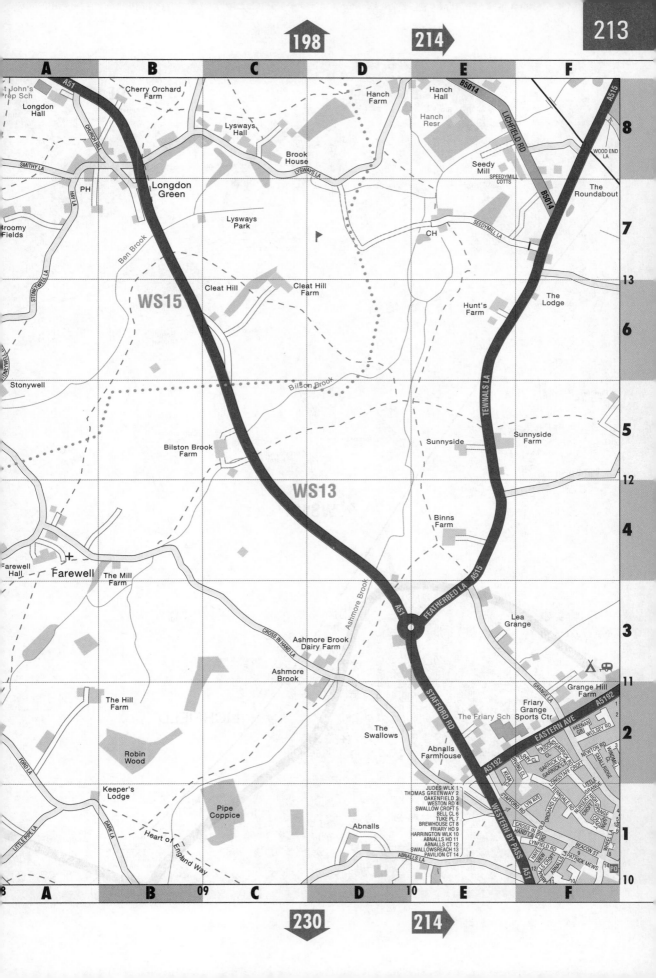

DE13

Cranberry

Shade House Lock

Midd Loc

Vicar's Coppice

Black Slough

Ravenshaw Wood

Woodend Lock

Trent and Mersey Canal

Fradley Wood

WOOD END LA

Woods Farm

Black Slough Farm

Tomhay Wood

Wood End Farm

13

New Farm

Full Brook

Big Lyntus

GORSE LA

Fullbrook Farm

Sewage Works

Sprint Course

Little Lyntus

Elmhurst Hall Farm

NASH LA

Curborough Brook

Corporation Farm

Curborough

Curborough Farm

Elmhurst

FOX LA

Apsley House

Curborough Hall Farm

Curborough House

WS13

WATERY LA

1 AUGUSTINES WLK
2 PAULS WLK
3 CHRISTOPHER WLK
4 MATTHEWS WLK
5 STEPHENS WLK
6 MARKS WLK
7 PETERS WLK
8 THOMAS GREENWAY
9 JAMES GREENWAY
10 LUKES WLK

Ringway Ind Est

Brownfield Cottage

A5192

SALISBURY CL

WINCHESTER CL

Nether Stowe

Brownsfields Farm

Charnwood Prim Sch

David Willows Prim Sch

LICHFIELD

PURCELL AVE

SAMUEL CL

Handel Wlk

EASTERN AVE

Sullivan Wlk

WALKERS CROFT

Winter CL

VULCAN RD

Lichfield Bsns Ctr

Nether Stowe High Sch

STOWECROFT

HAYWORTH RD

FECKNAM WAY

HERMES RD

Chadsmead Prim Sch

CRANE FIELD

DIMBLES HILL

Sch

PO

Scotch Orchard Prim Sch

Streethay Lodge

BURTON RD

Stowe

1 ARMITAGE HO
2 WHITTINGTON HO
3 SHENSTONE HO
4 RIDWARE HO
5 PENNYS CROFT

A5127 BURTON RD

BEACON GDNS

Stowe Pool

ST CHAD S RD

ST MICHAEL RD

WISSAGE RD

A5192

Trent Valley Cotts 1
Bailye Cl 2

10

DE13

Roddige

RIDGET LA
BARLEY GREEN LA

Whitemoor
Haye

RODDIGE LA

Chetwynd or
Salter's Bridge

Brown's
Island

A513

Croxall

CROXALL RD

Dovecote

The
Hall

WS13

Broadfields

Oakley
Farm

River Mease

Croxall
Mill

13

6

Sittles

River Tame

Lady
Walk

Elford
Park

New Buildings
Farm

A5

5

12

Sand & Gravel
Pit

Park
Farm

The Bungalow

4

Bisphill
Plantation

B79

11

STOCKFORD LA

Greendales
Farm

A513

Home
Farm

BRICKHOUSE LA

3

Elford

Howard
Prim Sch

2

OLD HALL DR

THE GARDENS

THE SQUARE

CRAFT CL

THE BECK

CHURCH RD

PH
PO

EDDYS LA

Raddle
Farm

The
Hill

Old
Orangery

THE SHRUBBERY

BURTON RD

A513

1

10

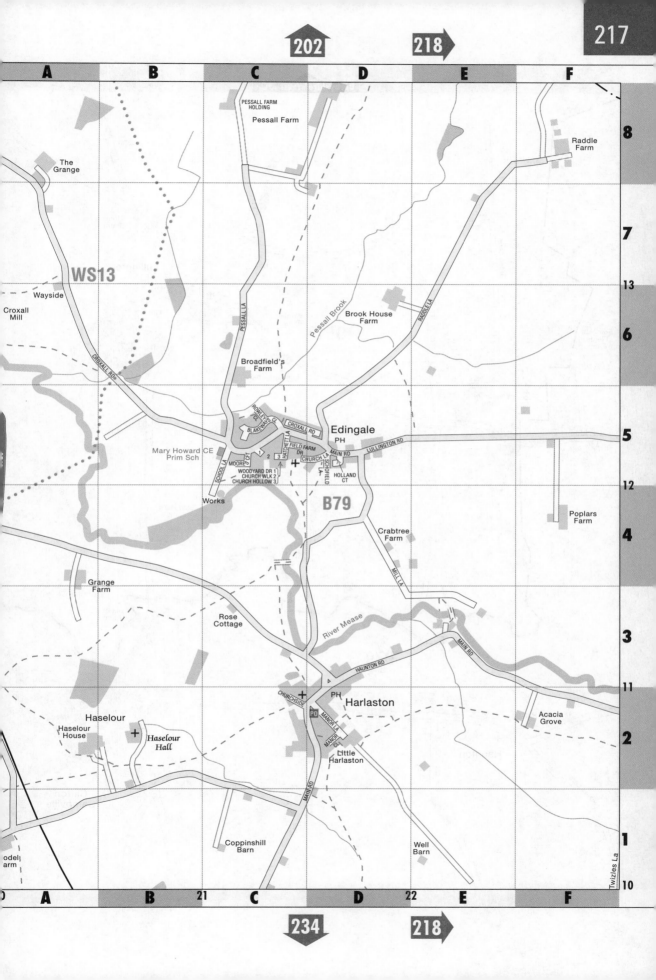

217

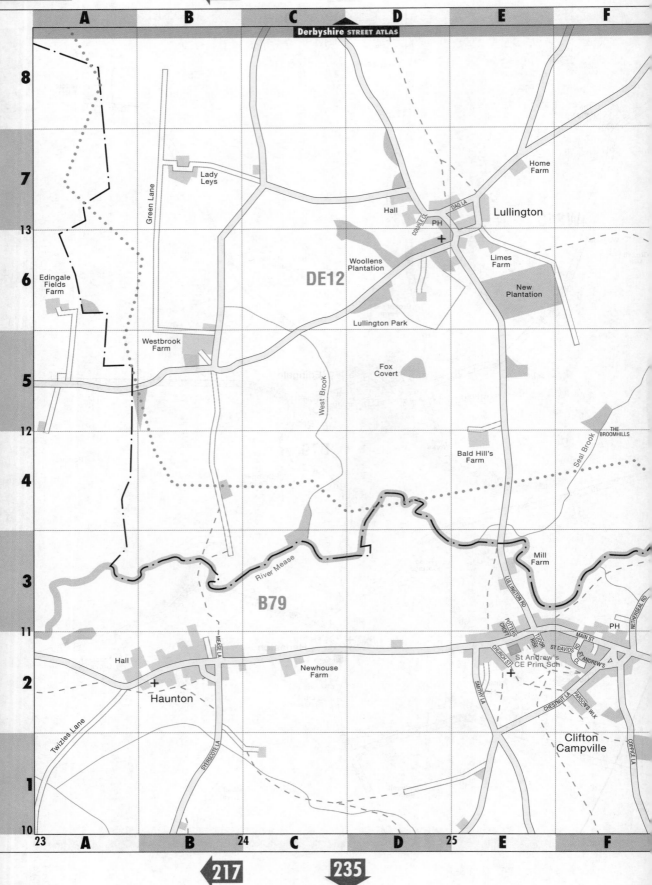

Derbyshire STREET ATLAS

DE12

Lullington

Home Farm

Lady Leys

Green Lane

Hall

PH

DAG LA

COW LE CT

Limes Farm

New Plantation

Woollens Plantation

Edingale Fields Farm

Lullington Park

Westbrook Farm

Fox Covert

West Brook

Bald Hill's Farm

THE BROOMHILLS

Seal Brook

River Mease

B79

Mill Farm

LULLINGTON RD

NETHERSEAL RD

POTTERS CROFT

TUDOR RISE

MAIN ST

PH

ST DAVIDS

ST ANDREW'S

ST ANDREW'S CL

CHURCH ST

St Andrew's CE Prim Sch

Hall

Haunton

MEASE LA

Newhouse Farm

SMITH'S LA

CHESTNUT LA

PARSON'S WLK

Clifton Campville

COPPICE LA

Twizles Lane

SYERSCOTE LA

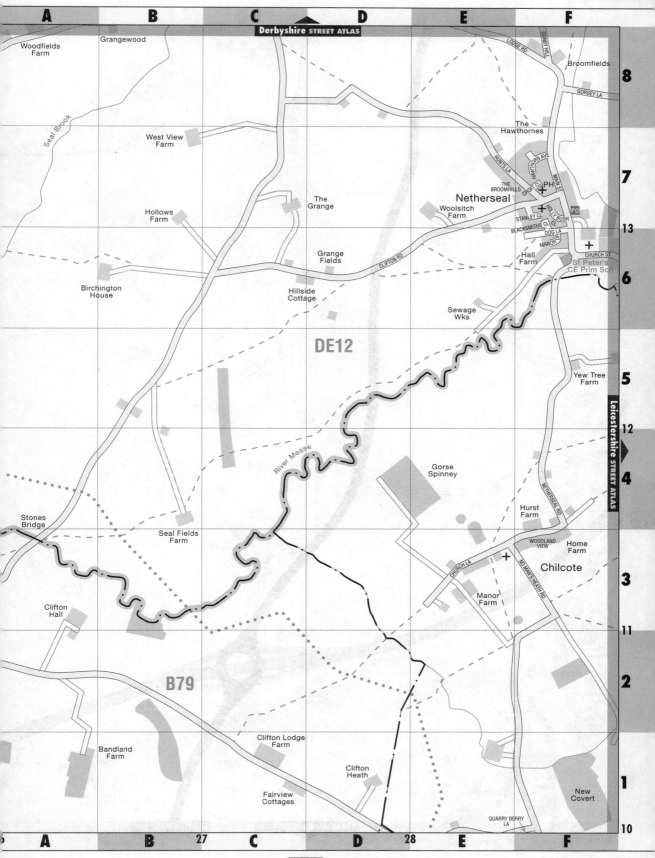

A B C D E F

Woodfields Farm

Grangewood

Broomfields

LODGE RD

GUNBY HILL

GORSEY LA

8

Seal Brook

West View Farm

The Hawthornes

HUNTS LA

HAWTHORN AVE

MAIN ST

THE BROOMHILLS

CROFT CL

PH

7

Hollows Farm

The Grange

Netherseal

Woolsitch Farm

HOLLY BUSH

PO

STANLEY CL

BLACKSMITHS CL LA

DOG LA

MANOR DR

13

Grange Fields

CLIFTON RD

Hall Farm

CHURCH ST

St Peter's CE Prim Sch

6

Birchington House

Hillside Cottage

Sewage Wks

DE12

Yew Tree Farm

5

12

River Mease

Gorse Spinney

NETHERSEAL RD

4

Stones Bridge

Seal Fields Farm

Hurst Farm

WOODLAND VIEW

Home Farm

Chilcote

Clifton Hall

CHURCH LA

Manor Farm

NO MAN'S HEATH RD

3

11

B79

Bandland Farm

Clifton Lodge Farm

Clifton Heath

New Covert

2

Fairview Cottages

QUARRY BERRY LA

1

10

A B 27 C D 28 E F

Leicestershire STREET ATLAS

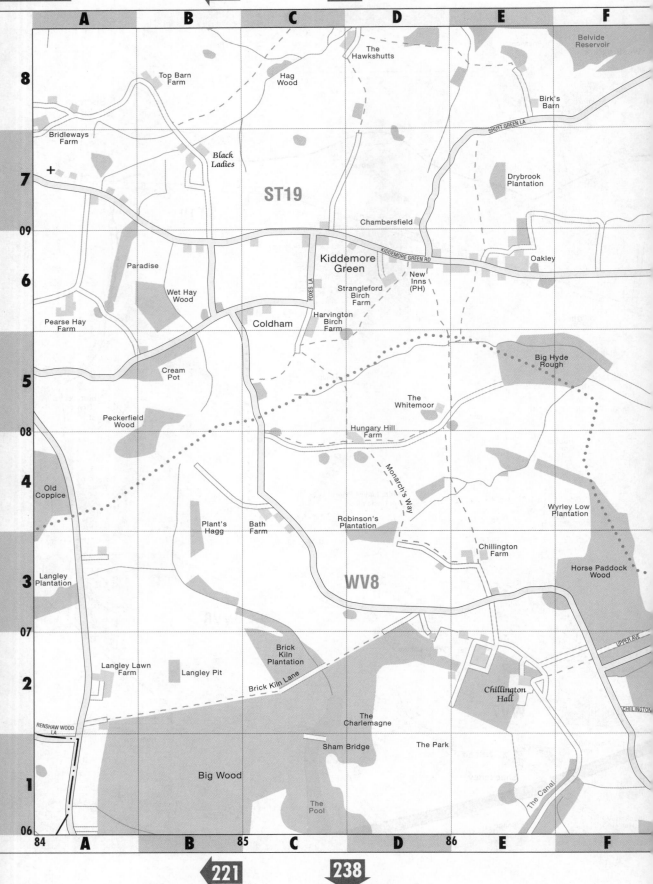

221
205
221
238

Belvide Reservoir

The Hawkshutts

Top Barn Farm

Hag Wood

Birk's Barn

Bridleways Farm

SHUTT GREEN LA

Black Ladies

ST19

Drybrook Plantation

Chambersfield

KIDDEMORE GREEN RD

Oakley

Paradise

Kiddemore Green

New Inns (PH)

Wet Hay Wood

Strangleford Birch Farm

FOXES LA

Pearse Hay Farm

Coldham

Harvington Birch Farm

Big Hyde Rough

Cream Pot

The Whitemoor

Peckerfield Wood

Hungary Hill Farm

Old Coppice

Monarch's Way

Wyrley Low Plantation

Plant's Hagg

Bath Farm

Robinson's Plantation

Langley Plantation

Chillington Farm

Horse Paddock Wood

WV8

UPPER AVE

Langley Lawn Farm

Langley Pit

Brick Kiln Plantation

Brick Kiln Lane

Chillington Hall

CHILLINGTON

RENSHAW WOOD LA

The Charlemagne

Sham Bridge

The Park

The Canal

Big Wood

The Pool

84   85   86

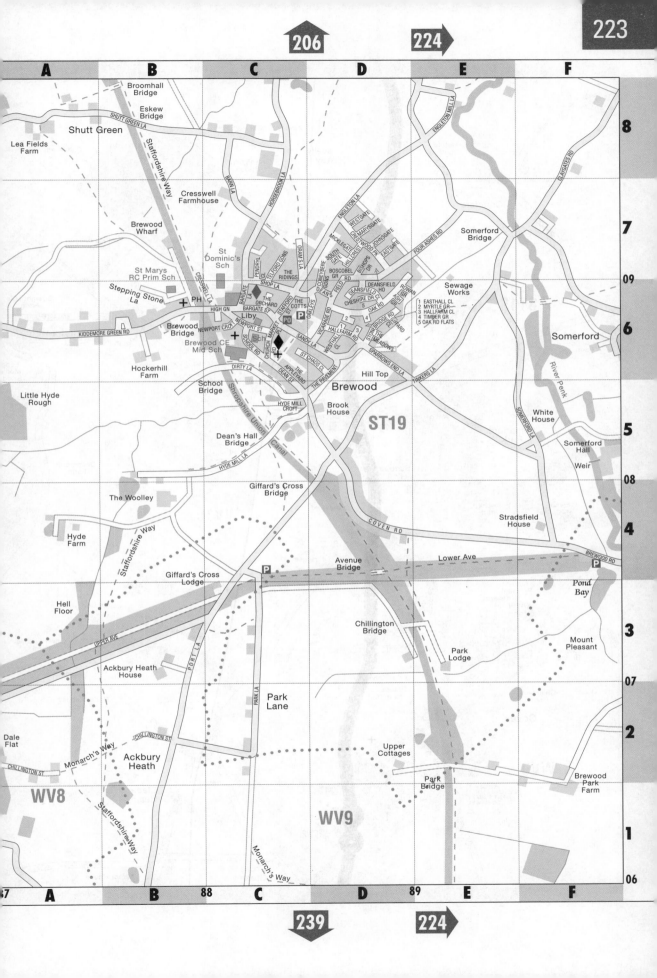

223
207
223
240

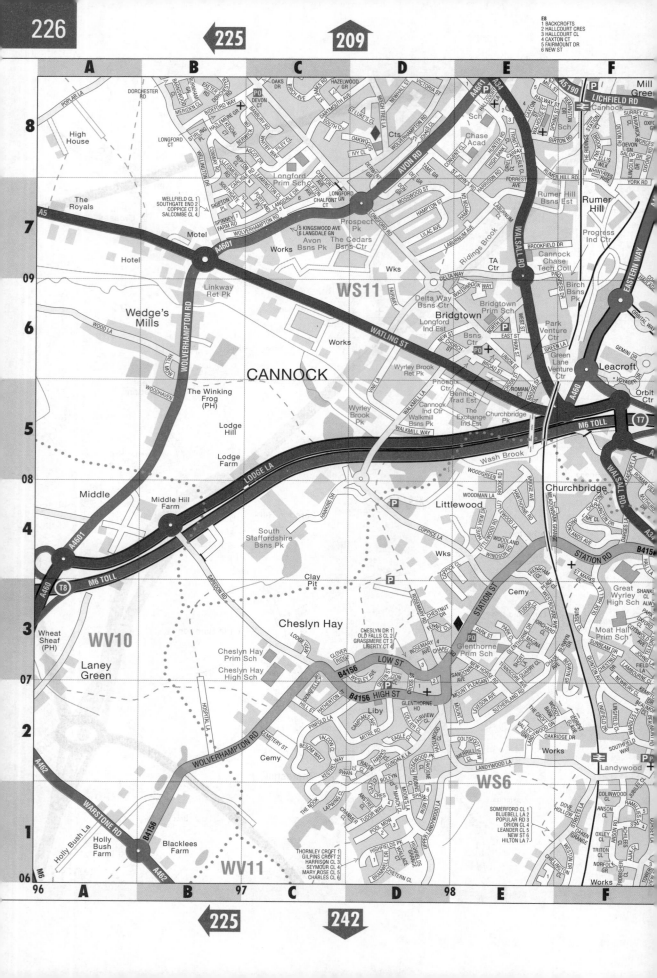

229
213

F6
1 BROADBENT CL
2 CATERBANCK WAY
3 COLLINS DR
4 MADDOCKE WLK
5 ALLINGTON AVE

THE ROCHE

ABNALLS LA

Spade
Green

Pipe Hall Farm
Nature Reserve

Pipe
Hall

Jubilee
Wood

The Dell

HARRINGTON WLK

Wor

Heart of England Way

The Park

Maple Hayes Hall Sch

Pipe
Green

Leamonsley Brook

A51 WESTERN BY PASS

Parker's
Plantin

Maple
Hayes

Christ Church
CE Prim Sch

Woodhouses

The
Roundabouts

Leamonsley

ST MATTHEW'S RD

WOODHOUSES RD

Woodhouses
Farm

Edial
Farm

Grange La

Herbert's
Spinney

WS13

LEOMANSLEY CT

LEOMANSLEY RD

THE RISE

CHRISTCHURCH LA

SAXON DR

ROOKERY CT

Sloppy
Wood

SORREL CL

WALSALL RD

BARDELL RD

ORMOND'S CL

ALESMORE MDW

HARMAN DR

VICTORIA GDNS

09

A5190

Fearn's
Farm

LICHFIELD RD

Lower
Hilltop
Farm

Pipe
Grange

Sandyway

Three Tuns
(PH)

Sandyway
Farm

C-NUT WLK

WHITEHOUSE CL

LAWRENCE LA

THE WITHENS

6

The
Meadows

PETER'S LA

Pipe Grange
Farm

Pipehill

A5190

Mickle
Hills

WALSALL RD

Sandyway
Farm

A461

ST FOY AVE

WS7

Broad La

DENMARK
VILLAS

5

Sewage
Works

Pipehill Wharf
(dis)

Pipehill
Farm

Pipe Hill
Manor

Fosseway
Court

FOSSEWAY LA

LC

Aldershawe
Hall

The
Lodge

CLAY PIT LA

08

4

Coppice
Lane
Farm

COPPICE LA

Pipe Place
Farm

WALL LA

3

Bridge
Farm

Muckley Corner
Bridge

Wall
Farm

MARKET LA

07

Muckley
Corner

HALL LA

A461

HOTEL BLDGS

PH

Moat Bank
House

Wall
Lane

WS14

The Butts

Wall Roman Site
(Letocetvm) Mus

Wall

THE BUTTS

ROMAN WLK

GREEN LA

Wall (Letocetvm)
Roman Site (Town)

MANOR COTTS

Manor
Farm

2

A5

A461

Wall
Butts

Wall Lane
Farm

LETOCETVM
ROMAN TOWN

PH

ASHCROFT LA

1

BOAT LA

CRANEBROOK LA

BULLMOOR LA

Hilton
House

M6 TOLL

BULLMOOR LA

M6 TOLL

06

08   09   10

229
246

WS13

Huddlesford

Fulfen Wood

Plough Inn (PH)

BROAD LA

PARK LA

Holly Cottage

Huddlesford Bridge

Potter's Thatch

Watery Lane Bridge

CAPPER'S LA

Fulfen Farm

Mill Farm

Huddlesford Grange

Bowman's Bridge

Coventry Canal

HUDDLESFORD LA

Bridge Farm

BURTON RD

Fisherwick Dairy Farm

Fisherwick Brook

09

NOVINGTON LA

SWAN COTTAGES

6

SWAN RD

NODDINGTON LA

NODDINGTON AVE

NEAL CROFT

ROCK FARM RD

DYOTT AVE

BAYTREE WK

PASS AVE

DARBY AVE

MIDDLETON RD

FISHERWICK

SPRING LA

Marsh Farm

DARNFORD LA

Hill Farm

BACK LA

BLACKSMITH

LANGTON CRES

CHAPEL LA

MAIN RD

BARLEY RD

THE GREEN

PEEL

PEEL

GRINE CL

MARSH LA

Ellfield House

PAMLEY WAY

CHURCH ST

Church Farm

PH

CLOISTER WK

FALCON

KESTREL WY

EY CL

KESTREL

CL

MEY

Whittington Bridge

5

Ellfield Lodge

Whittington

BABBINGTON CL

FISHERWICK RD

08

WHITTINGTON COMMON RD

BEECHWOOD

WINDMILL HILL LA

Vicarage Lane

Peel Farm

Birmingham Fazeley Can

A51

WS14

Whittington Prim Sch

Coton House

4

Brewery Farm

SANDY LA

COMMON LA

Windmill Hill

Bailey's Beating

Whittington Heath

HEATH AVE

Rifle Range

Hopwas Hays Lane

DANGER AREA

3

Lochranza

CH

TAMWORTH RD

WORCESTER RD

STAFFORD CRES

Rifle Ranges

STAFFORD CRES

DERBY RD

Hopwas Hays Lane

DANGER AREA

Freeford Home Farm

CHESTER RD

NOTTINGHAM RD

Hopwas Hays Lane

07

The Staffordshire Regiment Mus

NOTTINGHAM RD

2

Ingleyhill Farm

Heart of England Way

Whittington Barracks

Horsley Brook Farm

The Bungalow

Botany Bay

LEVETT RD

Ice House Covert

1

JERRY'S LA

A51

Packington Hall Farm

Packington Hall Works

06

14   A   15   B   C   15   D   16   E   F

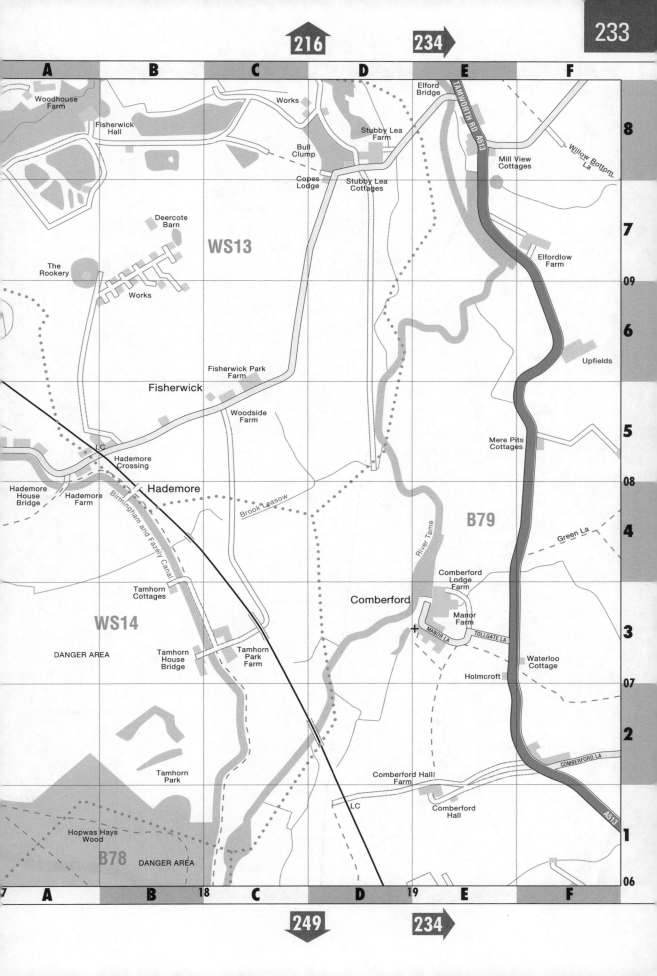

A | B | C | D | E | F

Woodhouse Farm

Fisherwick Hall

Elford Bridge

TAMWORTH RD A513

8

Stubby Lea Farm

Bull Clump

Mill View Cottages

Willow Bottom La

Copes Lodge

Works

Stubby Lea Cottages

Deercote Barn

WS13

7

09

The Rookery

Elfordlow Farm

Works

6

Upfields

Fisherwick Park Farm

Fisherwick

Woodside Farm

Mere Pits Cottages

5

LC

Hademore Crossing

08

Hademore House Bridge

Hademore

Hademore Farm

Brook Leasow

B79

River Tame

Green La

4

Birmingham and Fazely Canal

Comberford Lodge Farm

Comberford

Manor Farm

Tamhorn Cottages

WS14

MANOR LA

TOLLGATE LA

3

DANGER AREA

Tamhorn House Bridge

Tamhorn Park Farm

Waterloo Cottage

Holmcroft

07

2

Tamhorn Park

Comberford La

Comberford Hall Farm

LC

Comberford Hall

A513

1

Hopwas Hays Wood

B78

DANGER AREA

06

233
217

A **B** **C** **D** **E** **F**

8

PORTWAY LA

Fishpits
Barn

Dunimere
Farm

7

Hogs Hill

Portway

WILLOW BOTTOM LA

09

6

Winterdyne
Farm

Cherryfield
Cottages

Green La

Birdsley
Farm

5

Mere Pits

08

Wiggington
Fields
Farm

B79

4

Hanging Hill

Syerscote
Manor

3

Watergate
Cottage

07

Wigginton
Manor

SYERSCOTE LA

Syerscote Barn

2

COMBERFORD LA

PH

Wigginton

St Leonard's CE
Prim Sch

Bridge Cottages

World's End
Cottages

MAIN RD

WALRAND
CL

Arkall Farm

Amington
Hall
Cottages

1

A513

SILL
GREEN

Rawlett
Sch

ASHBY RD

B5493

06

20 **A** **B** **21** **C** **D** **22** **E** **F**

Twi...
La

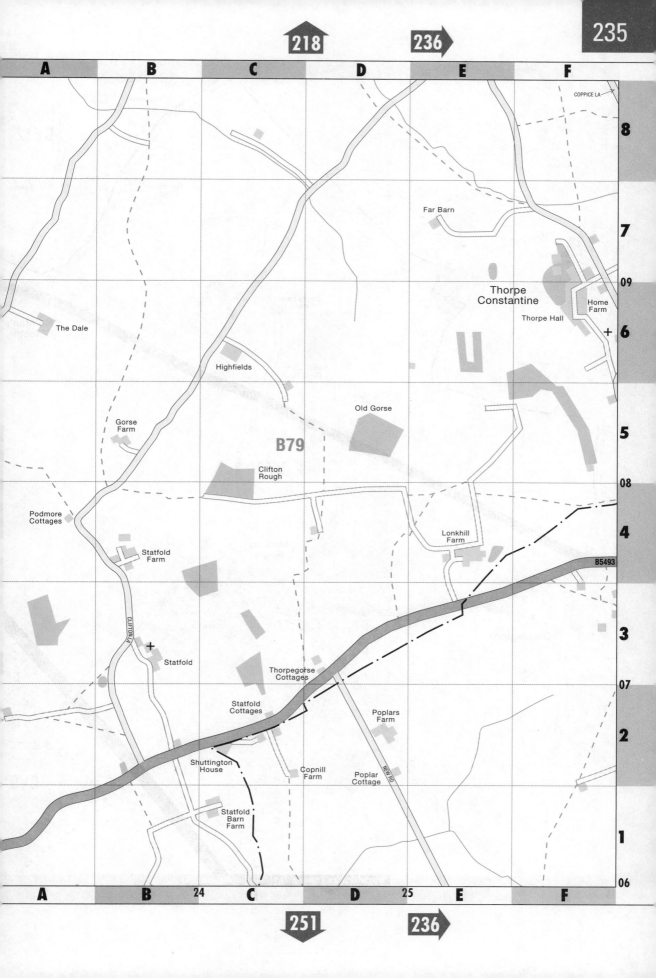

A B C D E F

8

7

09

6

5

08

4

B5493

3

07

2

1

06

COPPICE LA

Far Barn

Thorpe Constantine

Home Farm

Thorpe Hall

The Dale

Highfields

Old Gorse

B79

Gorse Farm

Clifton Rough

Podmore Cottages

Lonkhill Farm

Statfold Farm

CLIFTON LA

Statfold

Thorpegorse Cottages

Statfold Cottages

Poplars Farm

Shuttington House

Copnill Farm

Poplar Cottage

NEW RD

Statfold Barn Farm

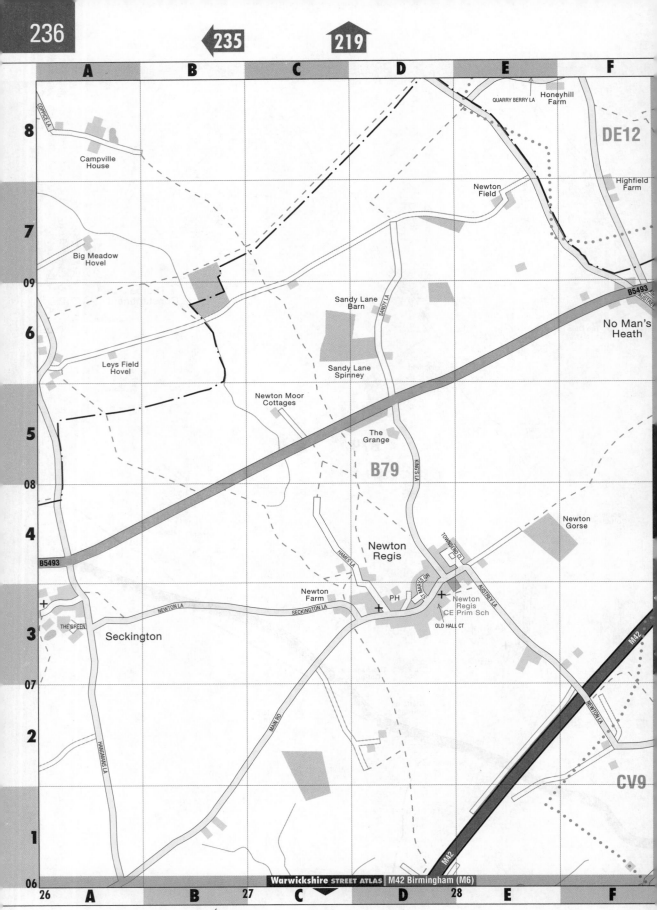

A B C D E F

8

7

09

6

08

5

4

3

07

2

1

06

DE12

QUARRY BERRY LA

Honeyhill Farm

Newton Field

Highfield Farm

B5493

No Man's Heath

Sandy Lane Barn

Sandy Lane Spinney

Newton Moor Cottages

The Grange

B79

Newton Gorse

KING'S LA

SANDY LA

TOWNSEND CL

Newton Regis

HAMES LA

Newton Farm

Newton Regis CE Prim Sch

OLD HALL CT

PH

ST MARY'S GR

AUSTREY LA

Campville House

Big Meadow Hovel

Leys Field Hovel

COPPICE LA

B5493

Seckington

THE GREEN

NEWTON LA

SECKINGTON LA

HANGMANS LA

MAIN RD

M42

NEWTON LA

CV9

26 A B 27 C D 28 E F

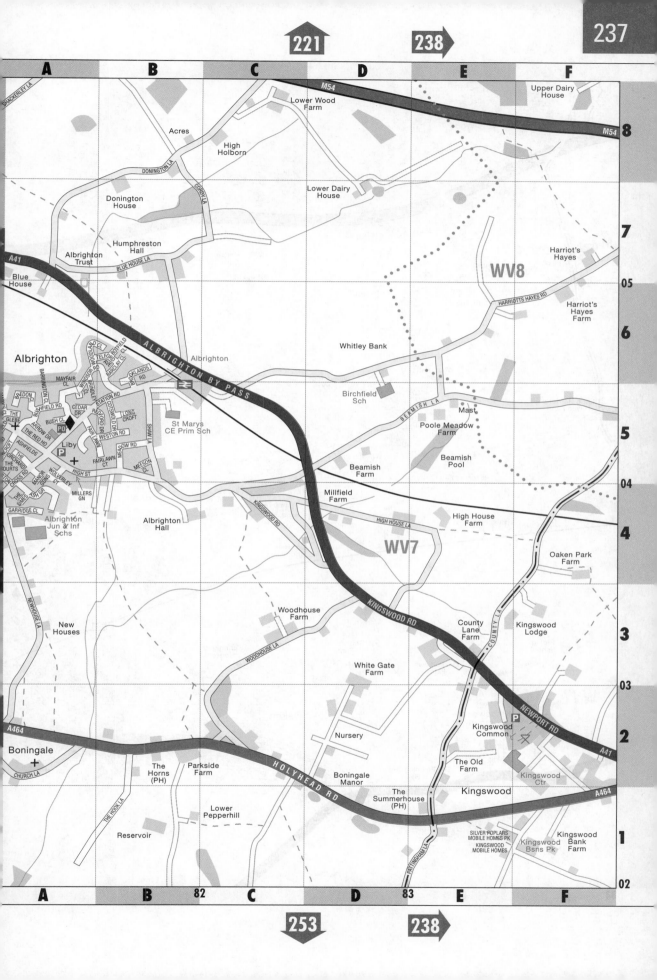

245
230
245
257

M6 TOLL

A B C D E F

8

Barn Farm
Hilton
Hilton Farm

Bullmoor Lane Covert

Chesterfield Farm
Chesterfield
Lawton Grange

M6 TOLL

Crane Brook

Chesterfield Lodge

ASHCROFT LA

7

Cranebrook Farm

Raikes Covert

RAIKES LA

Poultry Houses

Ashcroft Farm

ESSINGTON CL

THORNYHURST LA

Gayley Cottage

Keeper's Cottage

Malkin's Coppice

ROSEN CL
MILLBROOK DR
GROSVENOR
PINFOLD HILL

05

Ppg Sta

6

Lynn Lane House

LYNN LA

Dairy Farm

BIRCH BROOK LA

Shenstone

Birchbrook Ind Pk

Station RD
ASTON
MAIN ST

The Bungalow

Owlett Hall Farm

Footherley Rough

RICHARD COOPER RD
FOOTHERLEY RD
ST JOHN'S HILL
CHURCH

Lynn

The Nurseries

WS14

HOLLY HILL RD
THE FARTHINGS

5

04

Laurels Farm

Keeper's Cottage

HOLLYHILL LA

CHESTNUT DR
ST JOHN'S

Swan Farm

Footherley Hall

COURT DR

Shenstone Court

4

Lower Stonnall

MILL LA

Spinney Farm

FOOTHERLEY LA

Home Farm

FOOTHERLEY LA

Footherley

GRAVELLY LA

New Barns Farm

NEW BARNS LA

HOOK LA

Footherley Brook

Griffin's Covert

3

WS9

03

Cockheath Coppice

WOOD LA

Footherley Farm

Crof Farm

2

White's Farm

MOOR LA

Bagot's Barn

Biddle's Field Wood

Bosses

BACK LA

1

02

08 A B 09 C D 10 E F

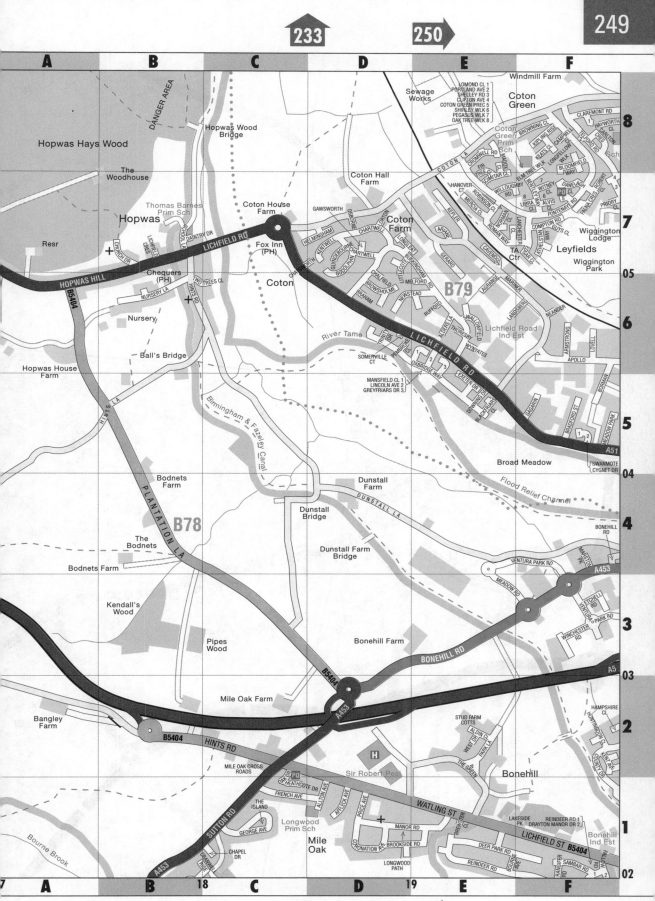

TF11

WV7

Bishton
Cottages

Bishton
Manor

RUSHEY LA

Shropshire
Lodge

Albrighton
Lodge

Home
Farm

Patshull
Park

Wildicote

FARM RD

Rous's
Covert

HOME FARM RD

Monkey
Bridge

Wilderness
Hill

Patshull
Hall

Snowdon
Pool

Bennetts
Wood

Monkeybridge
Plantation

Old Park

Burnhill
Green

SNOWDON RD

Decoy
Wood

Church
Pool

Lower
Snowdon

Dartmouth
Arms (PH)

Middle
Ley

Old Park
Plantation

Half Moon
Plantation

Shepherds
Buildings

Cut
Spinney

The
Great Pool

Shepherds
Plantation

WV6

Plant's
Neck

Green's
Coppice

Far Ley

Oulton
Garden

Jubilee
Plantation

Mill
Pond

Hotel
CH

Bridgenorth
Plantation

Pasford
Farm

Stanlow
Farm

Pasford

Kingslow
Cottages

Kingslow

Kingslow
Farm

Kingslow
Hall

Pasford
House

Nun Brook

WV15

Chesterton
Cottage

Birchley
Farm

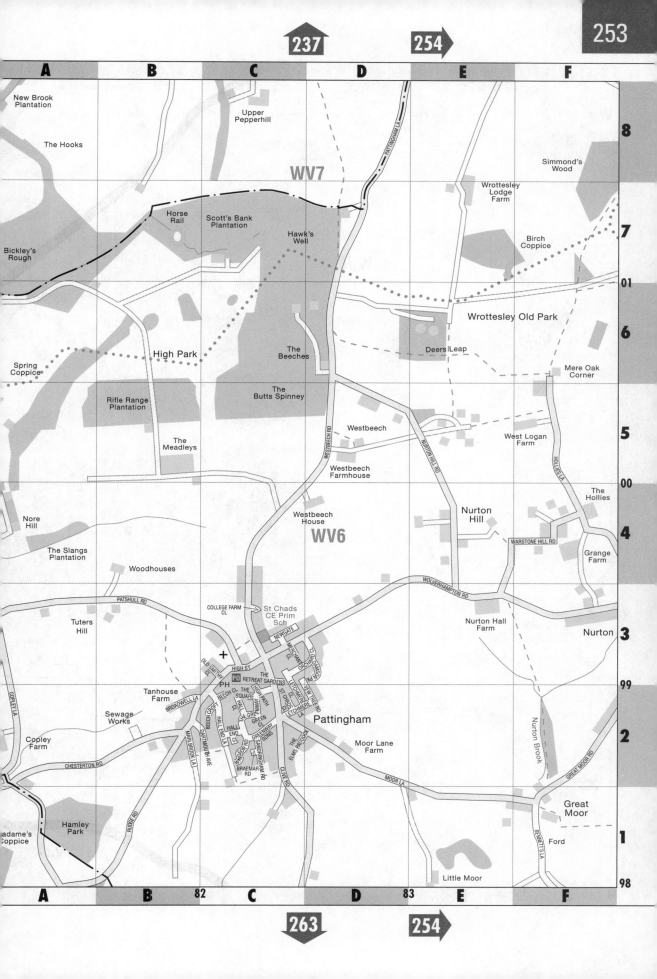

237
254

A B C D E F

8

New Brook
Plantation

The Hooks

Upper
Pepperhill

WV7

7

Horse
Rail

Scott's Bank
Plantation

Hawk's
Well

Bickley's
Rough

01

Wrottesley
Lodge
Farm

Simmond's
Wood

Birch
Coppice

Wrottesley Old Park

6

Spring
Coppice

High Park

The Beeches

Deers Leap

Mere Oak
Corner

Rifle Range
Plantation

The
Butts Spinney

WESTBEECH RD

Westbeech

NURTON HILL RD

West Logan
Farm

HOLLIES LA

5

The
Meadleys

Westbeech
Farmhouse

00

Nore
Hill

Westbeech
House

WV6

Nurton
Hill

The
Hollies

4

The Slangs
Plantation

Woodhouses

WARSTONE HILL RD

WOLVERHAMPTON RD

Grange
Farm

PATSHULL RD

Tuters
Hill

COLLEGE FARM
CL

St Chads
CE Prim
Sch

NEWGATE

Nurton Hall
Farm

Nurton

3

OLD SMITHY
CL

HIGH ST

PO

THE
RETREAT GARDENS

MEWMANS
CL

ORCHARD
YEW TREE RD

CLOSE
Rd

Tanhouse
Farm

BROADWELL LA

PH

HOBBS CROFT

BEECH CL

THE SQUARE

HIGH PATH

HALL
PL

THE GREEN

ST CHADS

LETCHMERE
LETCHMERE
LA

99

Sewage
Works

HALL END LA

HALL
END
CL

GREENWAY
GDNS

THE PATH

WYNN
CL

THE
ELMS PADDOCK

Pattingham

Copley
Farm

MARLBROOK LA

DARTMOUTH AVE

SANDRINGHAM RD

CLIVE RD

Moor Lane
Farm

MOOR LA

Nurton
Brook

GREAT MOOR RD

2

CHESTERTON RD

BRAEMAR
RD

Great
Moor

RUDGE RD

Hamley
Park

Madame's
Coppice

BENNETT'S LA

Ford

1

Little Moor

98

A B 82 C D 83 E F

254

253

238

WV7

Simmond's Wood

The Bradshaws

Wrottesley Hall

Bull Ride

WROTTESLEY CT

CH

Inland Pool

Wrottesley Park

WV8

HOLYHEAD RD

HEATHFIELDS

HEATH HOUSE LA

Heath House Farm

WERGS HALL RD

WERGS HALL

WERGS RD

River Penk

The Grange

WESTCROFT RD

Salt's Pool

Smith's Rough

Cranmoor

Cranmoor Lodge

HAWKSTONE CT

SUNNINGDALE AVE

SCAMPTON CL 1
HUDSON GR 2
TANGMERE CL 3
LIVINGSTONE AVE 4

BOWEN-COOKE AVE

FOWLER CL

DEAN RD

MERE OAK RD

WROTTESLEY RD W

Dippons Lane

HEPWORTH CL 1
LOWRY CL 2
MOORE CL 3
THIRLMERE GR 4
WASTWATER CT 5
BUTTERMERE CT 6
CHARTLEY CL 7
KENILWORTH RD 8

TURNBERRY GR

WENTWORTH GR

COLLET RD

BRUNEL WEBB

STEPHENSON AVE

EDWARD RD

ROYCOT CL

MERCIA DR

IDONIA RD

GANSBOROUGH RD

Perton

WROTTESLEY PARK RD

THE PASTURES

HOYLAKE RD

MOOR PK

ST ANDREWS DR

TROON CT

GLENEAGLES RD

FRANKLYN CL

SHANBURY CT

ANSON CL

COSFORD CT

GAYDON CL

BRANSDALE CT

MAESTONE CL

OTTAS DR

CORNWOOD

EGELWIN CL

ATHELSTAN GR

GUTHRUM CL

VINGTON CL

PENDA GR

Sch

SHACKLEY

DARWIN

WORDSWORTH

BROWNING

STANLEY CT

COOK CL

CABOT CL

MILTON CT

ELVERIDGE DR

SHADOWN DR

EPSOM CL

LINGFIELD

SEDGEFIELD GR

The Parkway

WV6

THE CLOVERFIELD

BELFRY

CULLWICK

BELL

KELSO GDNS

EDBURY

ELGIN CT

MELFORT CL

TINTERN CT

TAMAR GR

CHURCH RD

SPENSER AVE

AUDEN

INGFIELD

Sch

ENNERDALE DR

GRASMERE RD

RHOAL RD

RICHMOND

Liby

CUNNINGHAM RD

ANDERS SQ

WYE CL

THE PADDOCK 1
FALLOWFIELD 2
THE CARTWAY 3
THE WINDROW 4
THE SADDLESTONES 5
MEADOW CROFT 6
WORCESTER GR 7

COLVER GR

WELLS CL

WITERBURY RD

CHESHIRE GR

CROWLAND

SEVERN DR

TRENT DR

MALLORY RD

WHITNEY

GIBSON RD

HAMBLE GR

AVON RD

CASTER

RICHMOND DR

CHEPSTOW CL

ST MAWE

CORRE

STOKESAY

ELMLEY

KINNSWE

THE WHEATLANDS

OATLANDS

CORRIN

THE HEATHLANDS

LEASOWES

CHERITON AVE

BY RD

ADMIRAL GR

HOPTON CL

WARWICK AVE

CRANBROOK

STOURBRIDGE

NASH AVE

FOSTER

PAXTON

ROWTON AVE

ROCKINGHAM DR

BERKELEY CL

WREN AVE

HYDE CL

NEWHAM

RIP AVE

EDGE HILL DR

RODWAY

WINGAY RD

TURNHAM

The Greens

VANBRUGH

WYKEHAM GR

DR

BUTTERFIELD CL

Nurton

NURTON BANK

WOLVERHAMPTON RD

HOLLIES LA

GREAT MOOR RD

Perton Orchard

CH

Sling Wood

Old Perton

PATTINGHAM RD

Perton House

South Perton Farm

Freehold Wood

Middle Wood

JENNY WALKERS LA

Perton Court

WOLVERHAMPTON

Boundary Farm

BOUNDARY FARM

BOUNDARY WAY

PERTON RD

THE HIGHFIELDS

WALL MEADOW

QUAIL GREEN

ROOKWOOD DR

PERTON BROOK VALE

RAVENSHILL

TINACRE HILL

Wightwick Hall Sch

Wightwick

CHERRINGHAM

HEATH HILL RD

WIGHTWICK HALL RD

MAYSWOOD DR

BRIDGNORTH RD

P

Wightwick Manor

CASTLECROFT LA

WV3

A454

SABRINA RD

HEADL

A B C D E F

WV8

River Penk

Brookside
Farm

Palmers
Cross

Wergs
Plantation

The Waltons

CH

Wergs Farm

Keepers La

Chartsworth

Coppice La

Danescourt

CH

Stockwell
End

WV6

Tettenhall

WV8

WV9

Sewage
Works

Blakeley
Green

Aldersley

Claregate

St Joseph's
Convent Sch

Aldersley
Stadium

Dunstall Park
Race Course

New Park
Sch

Kingston
Ctr
Midpoint
Ctr

The
Gifford
RC Prim
Sch

St Andrews
CE Prim Sch

Wergs

Cemy

WERGS RD

Danescourt RD

The King's
CE Sch

Woodthorne
Prim Sch

Liby

Perton
Mid Sch

Christ
Church
Jun Sch

James
Beattie
Ho

Nuffield

Tettenhall
Wood

THE ROCK

St Michael's
CE Jun &
Inf Sch

The Drive Sch
(Tettenhall Coll)

Tettenhall
Coll

HENWOOD RD

Smestow Brook

Valley Park
Nature Reserve

Staffordshire and Worcestershire Canal

Newbridge Prep Sch

St Peter's
Collegiate
CE Sch

Newbridge

St Edmunds
RC Sch

New Hampton RD W

Wolverhampton
Girls' High Sch

St Jude's
CE Prim
Sch

A41 Wolverhampton

Tettenhall RD

Tettenhall
Wood

Univ of Wolverhampton
Compton Park Campus

The Cedars
Hort Unit

Compton

Wolverhampton Coll
Wulfrun Campus

Rean
Ctr

BRIDGNORTH RD

Hospice

Wightwick
Bridge

Smestow
Sch

COMPTON RD W A454

Finchfield Hill

WV3

Compton RD A454

Merridale

Wolverhampton
Gram Sch

Wolverhampton
Gram Sch

Graiseley Brook

Bantock House
Mus

Cemy

F3
1 ALBERT RD
2 BROMFORD DALE
3 SLADE HILL
4 ST JUDES'S CT
5 THE CEDARS

F4
1 BRIMFIELD PL
2 BALFOUR CT
3 NEWBRIDGE MEWS
4 GRAFTON CT

259
249

New House Farm

BANGLEY LA

A453

SUTTON RD

CANSTON CL

GAINSBOROUGH DR

KIRKLAND WAY

CRANWELL RISE

Bourne Bridge

Alder Wood

Bourne Brook

Bourne Brook Cut

Seventeen Acre Wood

Longwood House

Fazeley

YORKSAND RD

REINDEER RD

DAMA RD

MAYAMA RD

DRAYTON MANOR DR

SWISS LODGE DR

Works

Duck Decoy

Hill Farm

A453

Lodge Farm

Drayton Manor Park

DRAYTON MANOR DR

CH

Longwood Stables

COLESHILL RD

A4091

Heathley Farm

HEATHLEY LA

Bullocks End Farm

Edden's Wood

Drayton Bassett

OLD MANOR CL

MOAT DR

EDDENS WOOD CL

Manor Prim Sch

CHURCH CL

PEEL CL

NEW ROW

PO

SHIRRAL DR

Oak Farm Craft Ctr

Stone House

DRAYTON LA

Heart of England Way

RECTORY CL

Sewage Works

SALTS LA

Ashdene Farm

B78

PORTLEYS LA

Brook End Farm

Drayton Brick Bridge

Heart of England

Brook Farm

Birmingham and Fazeley Canal

Upper House Farm

Gallows Brook

COPPICE LA

Quarry

Mill Plantation

Middleton Park

Newhouse Farm

Middleton

CHURCH ROW

SIMMONS CL

Highfields Farm

CHURCH LA

Walker's Spinney

Park-gate Farm

Middleton Pool

PO

CRANBERRY LA

Sewage Works

A4091

The Green Man (PH)

VICARAGE HILL

Langley Brook

Middleton Hall

259

F6
7 LEISURE WLK
1 BAKERS WLK
2 CALLIS WLK
3 LINTHOUSE WLK
4 COTTAGE WLK
5 STONEHILL WLK
6 IVYHOUSE WLK

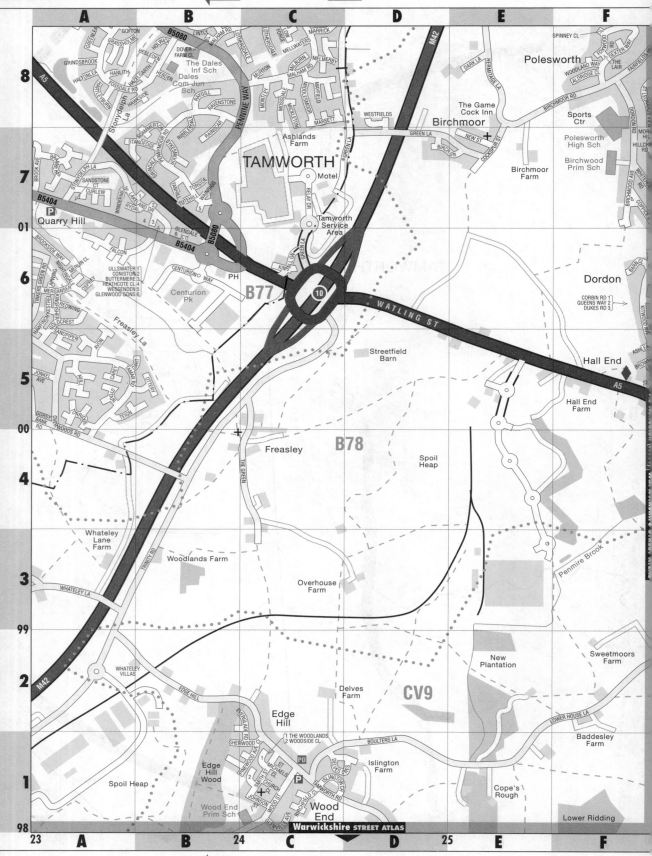

263
254

A B C D E F

8

JENNY WALKERS LA

A454

Sewage
Works

Perton Mill
Farm

CASTLECROFT
LA

POOL HA
CR

POOL HALL

CASTLECRO
RD

WV6

WV3

Monarch's Way

7

BRIDGNORTH RD

Trescott

Ford

SHOP LA

Pool
Hall

Mops Farm
Bridge

Staffordshire and Worcestershire Canal

BADNHOR LA

97

A454

6

Trescott Grange

Langlade
Farm

LANGLEY RD

Langley
Hall

Furnace
Grange

Twin Oaks
Farm

Valley Park

WV4

MARKET LA

Langley Hall

5

Staffordshire Way

DIMMINGSDALE RD

GREYHOUND LA

PH

Home
Farm

SPRING HILL LA

96

Old Smithy
Farm

EBSTREE RD

Holly Bush
(PH)

Pear Tree
Farm

Monarch's Way

DENE RD

Manor
Farm

Lowe
Penn

4

PENSTONE LA

The
Lindens

Orton
House

3

The Elms

WV5

TRYSULL HOLLOWAY

Orton

BLACKPIT LA

ORTON LA

SHOWELL

Orton
Hall
Farm

95

THE HOLLOWAY

BEECH HURST
GDNS

EBSTREE RD

EBSTREE MDW

POST OFFICE RD

Sand Pit

FLASH LA

2

Seisdon

Meadow
Cottage

The
Grotto

Awbridge
Farm

UNION LA

Awbridge
Bridge

CHURCH LA

Smestow Brook

1

The
Hall

SEISDON RD

CROCKINGTON LA

Manor
House

WHITE ROW

SCHOOL RD

BELL RD

THATCHERS
CT

Trysull

Monks
Path

Monkspath
Farm

TRYSULL RD

Clee
View

BEECHOUSE LA

PH

94

84 A B 85 C D 86 E F

263
269

255
266
270
266

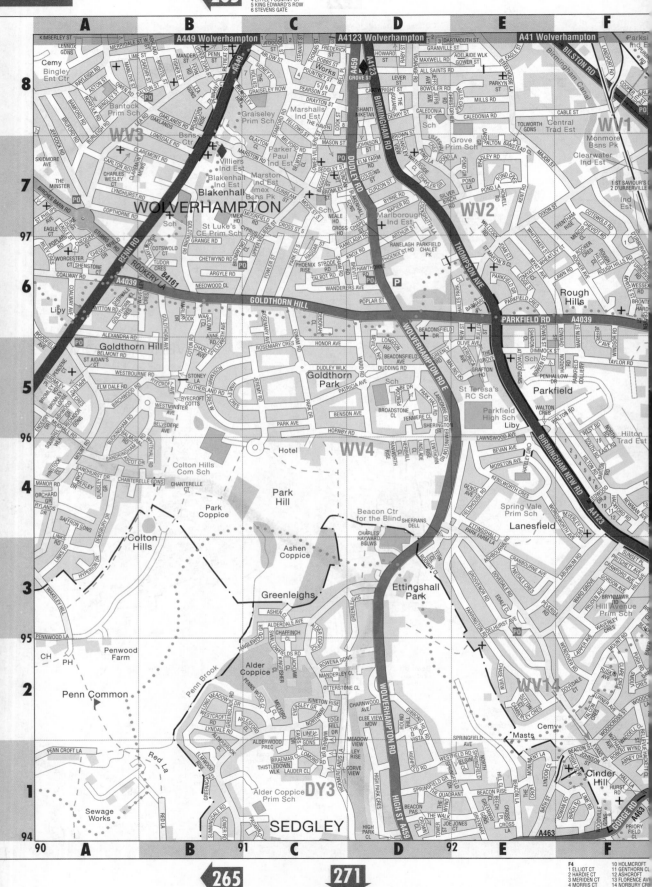

265

C8
1 PAUL ST
2 BLOOMSBURY ST
3 St Johns Ret Pk
4 LITTLE POUNTNEY ST
5 KING EDWARD'S ROW
6 STEVENS GATE

7 Hollies Ind Est
8 RAINBOW ST

D8
1 DARTMOUTH ST
2 GORDON ST
3 GRANVILLE CL

F4
1 ELLIOT CT
2 HARDIE CT
3 MERIDEN CT
4 MORRIS CT
5 WESLEY CT
6 WARWICK CT
7 RYLCROFT
8 AVONCROFT
9 FIRCROFT
10 HOLMCROFT
11 GENTHORN CL
12 ASHCROFT
13 FLORENCE AV
14 NORBURY CRE
15 CENTRAL AVE

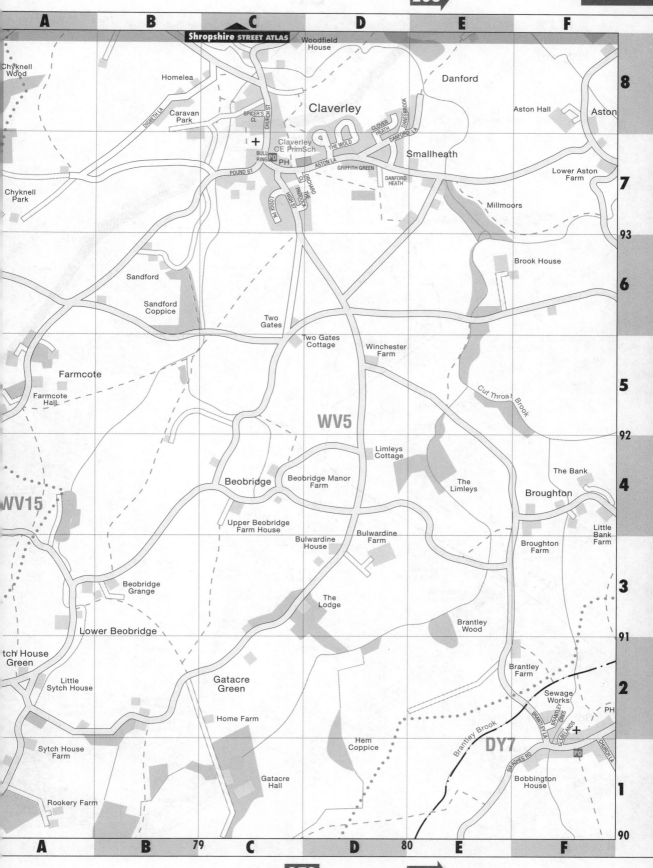

268

Shropshire STREET ATLAS

Woodfield House

Chyknell Wood

Danford

Homelea

Claverley

Aston Hall

Aston

Caravan Park

SPICER'S CL

Clover Heath

Lower Aston Farm

Chyknell Park

Claverley CE Prim Sch

Aston La

Smallheath

Griffith Green

Danford Heath

Millmoors

Pound St

Brook House

Sandford

Sandford Coppice

Two Gates

Two Gates Cottage

Winchester Farm

Cut Throat Brook

Farmcote

Farmcote Hall

WV5

Limleys Cottage

The Bank

Broughton

WV15

Beobridge

Beobridge Manor Farm

The Limleys

Upper Beobridge Farm House

Bulwardine House

Bulwardine Farm

Broughton Farm

Little Bank Farm

Beobridge Grange

The Lodge

Brantley Wood

Lower Beobridge

tch House Green

Brantley Farm

Little Sytch House

Gatacre Green

Sewage Works

PH

Home Farm

Brantley Brook

DY7

Sytch House Farm

Hem Coppice

Bobbington House

Rookery Farm

Gatacre Hall

267
263

| | A | B | C | D | E | F |

8

White House Farm

Long Common

The Wellings

Seisdon Common Rd

B4176

WV5

The Bungalow

Abbot's Castle Hill

Staffordshire Way

7

The Wellings

Shellfields Farm

The Dwellings

93

Gay Hills

Admoor Cottage

Upper Whittimere Cottage

Clan Park

Gorse La

6

Draycott

Whittimere

Vineyard

Sand Pit

Upper Whittimere Farm

The Eaves

Heathton

Old Gate Inn (PH)

Swan Cottage

Gayton

TOM LA

Staffordshire Way

War Stone

5

Heathton House

92

Cranmere

The Royal Oak (PH)

NEW RD

4

Halfpenny Green

Ferndale Farm

Blackhill Plantation

DY3

Blakelands

Gospel Ash

Manor Farm

White Cross Farmhouse

Blacklands Farm

DY7

3

SIX ASHES RD

Blacklands Plantation

Yew Tree Farm

GOSPEL ASH RD

Claire Hayes

91

White Cross

Saltershall Farm

Wolverhampton Bsns Airport

FOREST LA

Forest Cottage

2

Corbett Prim Sch

Bobbington

CRAB LA

Twin Oaks

Leaton Cottage

Crab Mill Farm

WATER LA

Forest Covert

Dogkennel Covert

CHURCH LA

Leaton Lodge

Gorse Covert

Staffordshire Way

DY3

1

Highgate Farm

P

Highgate Country Park

UTLEY LA

LEATON HALL

WHITE HOUSE LA

90

| 81 | A | 82 | B | C | 82 | D | 83 | E | | F |

PEAR TREE LA

267
273

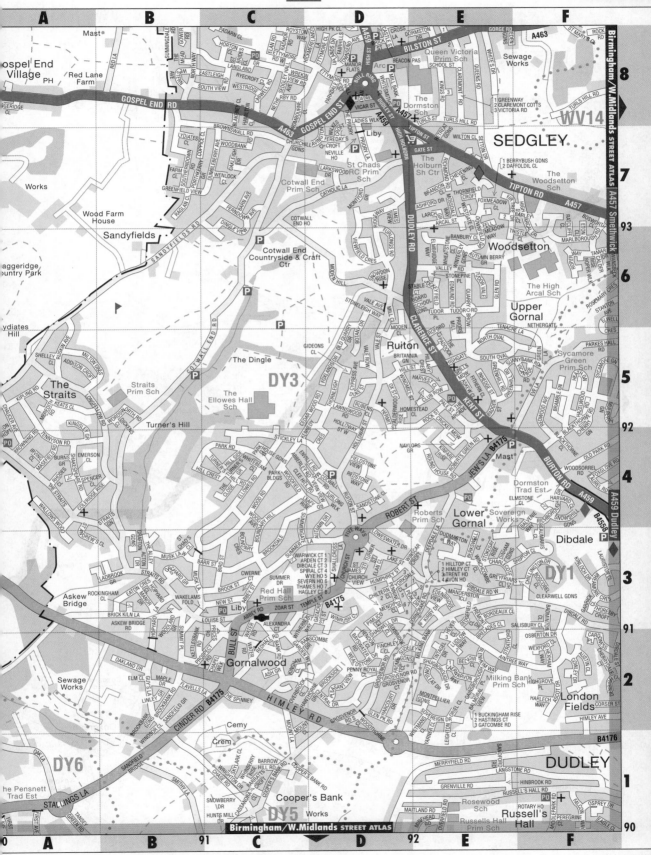

273
269

A B C D E F

8

Chasepool Farm

Hollow Mill Farm

Hinksfor

Highgate Common

DY3

Caravan Park

The Old Bush Inn (PH)

SWINDON RD

7

Greenforge Rough

CAMP HILL RD

Camp Farm

My Lady's Farm

MILE FLAT

89

Camp Cottages

Bank Farm

Greensforge Farm

6

Greensforge

PH

DY6

Ashwood Lodge Farm

ENVILLE COMMON RD

Lodge Plantation

Smestow Brook

5

Ashwood

DOCTORS LA

88

The Gorse

Old Mill Pond

P

Spittle Brook

WATERWORKS COTTS

P

Mill Farm

GREAT CHECKHILL RD

Monarch's Way

4

Windmill

Checkhill Farm

LITTLE CHECKHILL LA

MILL LA

Staffordshire and Worcestershire Canal

Holloway House Farm

3

Rumford Hill

DY7

GREENSFORGE LA

Gothersley Bridge

87

Radway Hill

The Million

GOTHERSLEY LA

Gothersley Rough

2

Gothersley Farm

Gothersley Hall

Prestwood Bridge

Prestwood

A449

1

PAVILION

LORDS LA

ONG

HEADINGLEY DR

WICKET

COVERS LA

BOUNDARY LA

Hampton Valley

Stourton Gorse

Nursing Home

86

84 A B 85 C D 86 E F

273
278

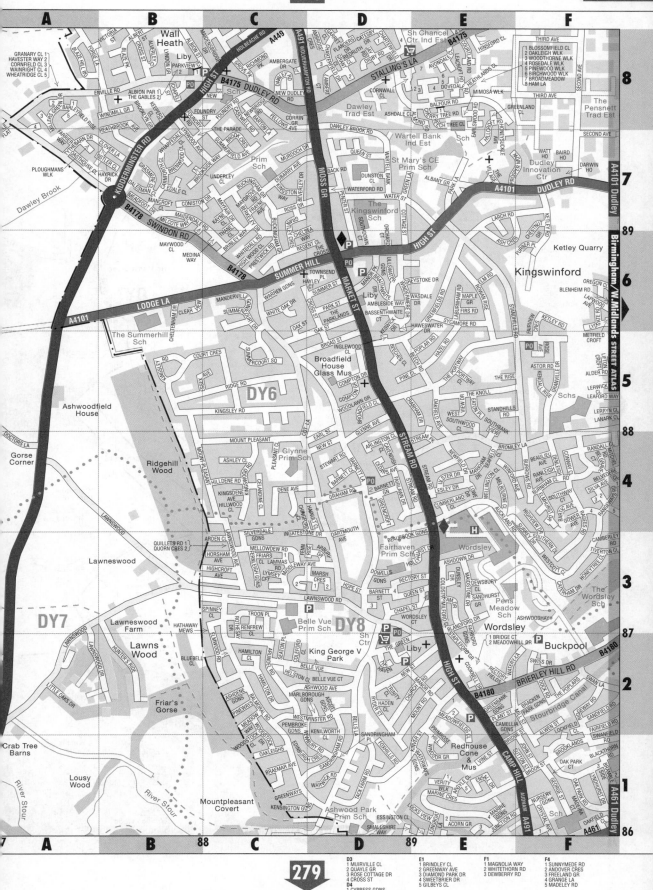

D3
1 MUIRVILLE CL
2 QUAYLE GR
3 ROSE COTTAGE DR
4 CROSS ST
D4
1 CYPRESS GDNS
2 THE SHOPS

E1
1 BRINDLEY CL
2 GREENWAY AVE
3 DIAMOND PARK DR
4 SWEETBRIER DR
5 GILBEYS CL

F1
1 MAGNOLIA WAY
2 WHITETHORN RD
3 DEWBERRY RD

F4
1 SUNNYMEDE RD
2 ANDOVER CRES
3 FREELAND GR
4 GRANGE LA
5 MADELEY RD

A442 Bridgnorth

Shropshire STREET ATLAS

Worcestershire STREET ATLAS

E8
1 THE JUNCTION
2 ALDRIDGE CL
3 LONGBOAT LA
4 STEWKINS CT

F8
1 CRYSTAL AVE
2 SURREY HO
3 WILTSHIRE HO
4 DEVON HO
5 LANCASTER HO
6 HANOVER HO

7 ALLAN CL
8 CORBETT HO
9 DENNIS HALL

KIDDERMINSTER

Worcestershire STREET ATLAS

DY7

Sugarloaf Farm

A451

COUNTY LA

OUNTY JOHN LA

Burys Hill

8

Mast

Crown Inn (PH)

Iverley

KIDDERMINSTER RD

SUGAR LOAF LA

CROWN LA

Birmingham /W. Midlands STREET ATLAS

7

Iverley House Farm

Iverley Hay Farm

The Birches

81

Highdown Cottages

North Worcestershire Path

Upper Brake Farm

Haybridge High Sch & Sixth Form

6

STOURBRIDGE RD

DY8

BRAKE LA

Hagley RC High Sch

THE BRAKE

Common Farm

Palmer's Hill

WOODLAND AVE

THE COPPICE

IVERLEY LA

Hagley

HOARSTONE

SWEETPOOL LA

HAYBRIDGE AVE

SUMMERVALE RD

5

Five Ways

Brakemill Plantation

THE CRESCENT

WILLOW CL

THE GREENWAY

THE OAKS

Pumping Station

Brakemill Farm

Sewage Works

80

THE SYCAMORES 1
THE HAZELS 2
THE SPRUCES 3
THE HAWTHORNS 4
THE BRIARS 5
THE GREEN 6
LONG CL 7
SPRING CL 8

CHESTNUT

MILESTONE DR

CAVENDISH DR

A456 Birmingham

4

STAKENBRIDGE LA

Stakenbridge Farm

BEECHES MEWS 9
PINEWOODS CT 10

PINEWOODS AVE

FALCON CROFT

PINEWOODS CL

A450

DY10

CHURCH FARM BARN & COTTS

Churchill

Bridge Farm

Stakenbridge

STONEY LA

A456

KIDDERMINSTER RD S

The Falconry Ctr

THICKNALL LA

WORCESTER RD

DY9

CHURCHILL LA

Churchill Farm

Harborough Hill

Harborough Farm

Nursery

3

WAGGON LA

Broome Mill

79

SOULTHORPE RD

THE CROFT

WHEATMILL CL

Birmingham Rd

Harborough Hall

Windmill Pool

Monarch's Way

BROOME LA

2

CH

MILL LA

MILL CL

LC

Blakedown

Broome Lodge Farm

BROOME LA

ELM DR

BROOKSIDE WAY

STATION DR

Blakedown

STOURBRIDGE RD

Wannerton House

Downs Plantation

WANNERTON RD

ROYALL CL

LYNWOOD DR

PO

Blakedown CE Fst Sch

Knoll Hill House

1

Sewage Works

SWAN CL

A456

B4188

FORGE LA

BELBROUGHTON RD

B4188

A450

Hackman's Gate

Hundred Acre Farm

Swan Pool

Forge Pool

New House Farm

78

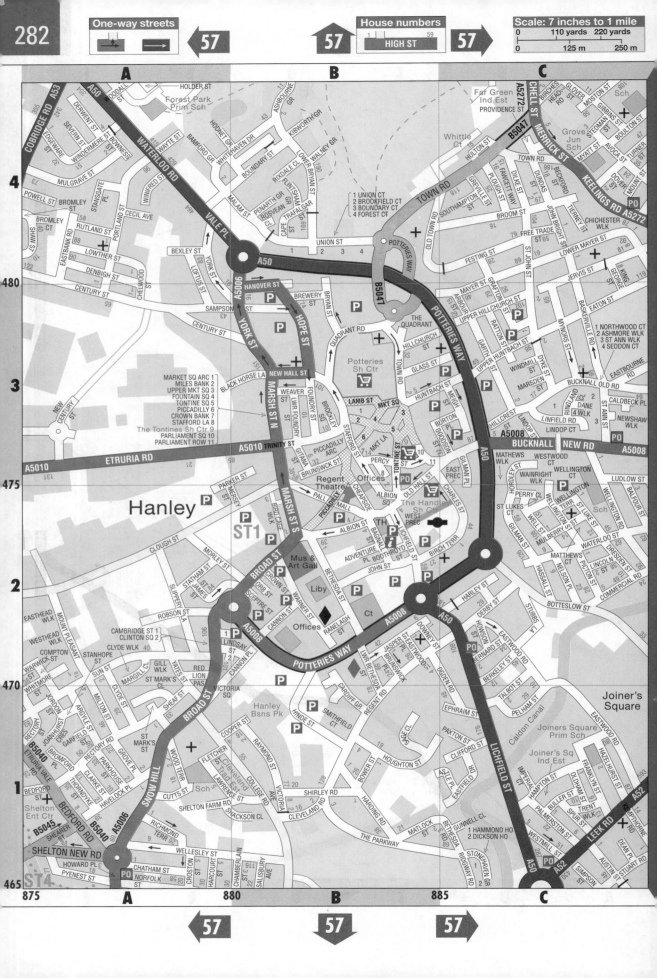

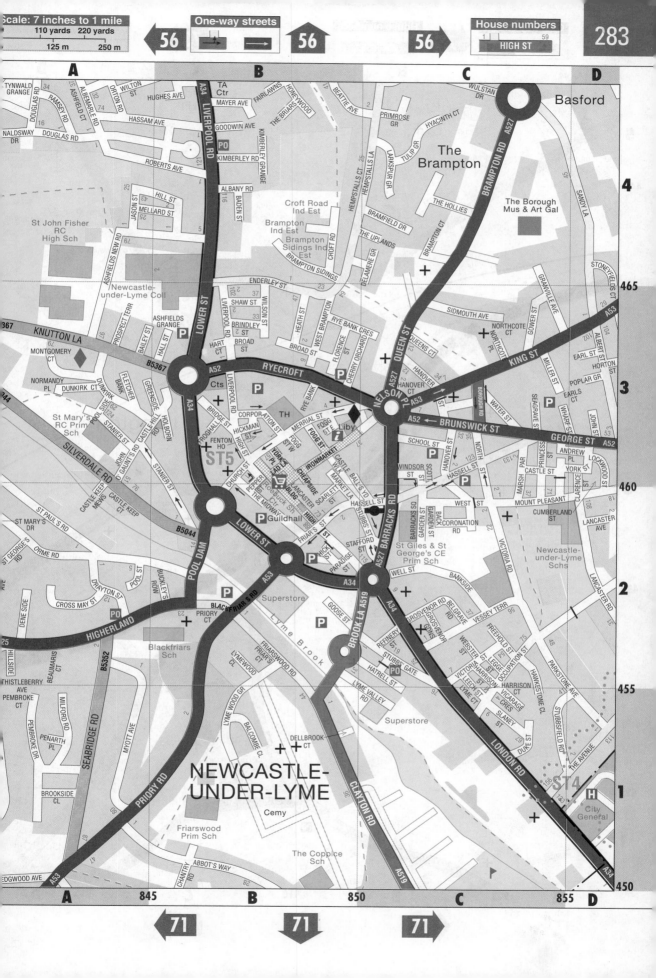

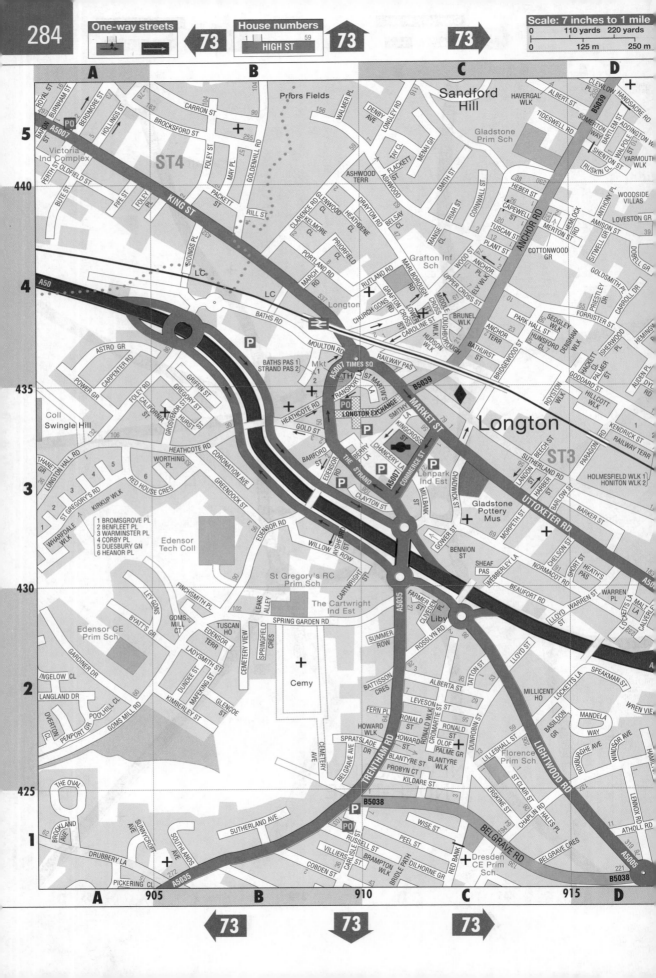

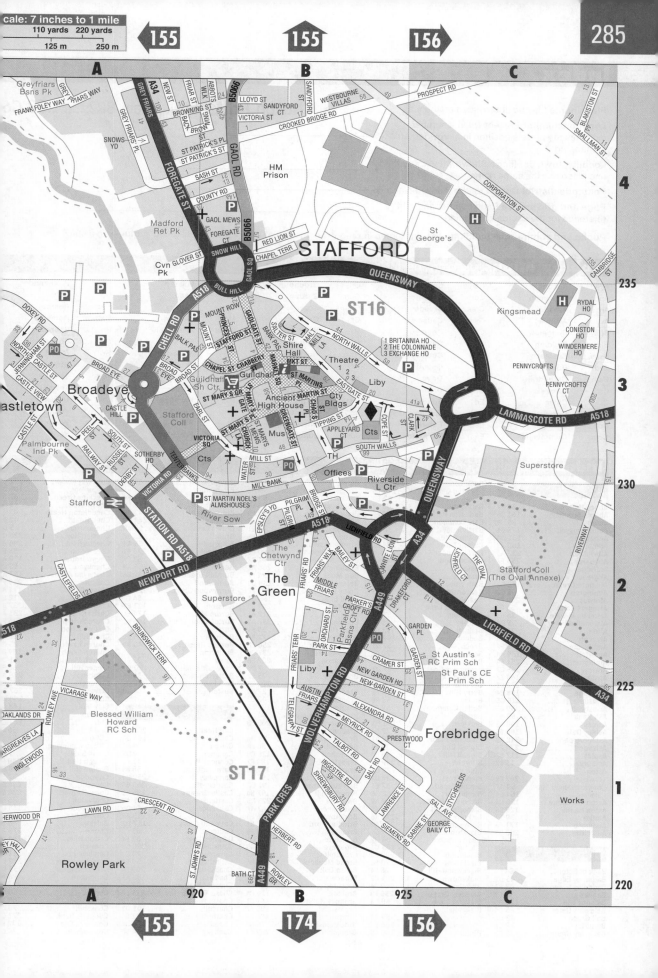

Index

Place name May be abbreviated on the map

Location number Present when a number indicates the place's position in a crowded area of mapping

Locality, town or village Shown when more than one place has the same name

Postcode district District for the indexed place

Page and grid square Page number and grid reference for the standard mapping

Church Rd **6** Beckenham BR2.........**53** C6

Public and commercial buildings are highlighted in magenta **Places of interest** are highlighted in blue with a star★

Abbreviations used in the index

Acad	Academy	Comm	Common	Gd	Ground	L	Leisure	Prom	Promenade
App	Approach	Cott	Cottage	Gdn	Garden	La	Lane	Rd	Road
Arc	Arcade	Cres	Crescent	Gn	Green	Liby	Library	Recn	Recreation
Ave	Avenue	Cswy	Causeway	Gr	Grove	Mdw	Meadow	Ret	Retail
Bglw	Bungalow	Ct	Court	H	Hall	Meml	Memorial	Sh	Shopping
Bldg	Building	Ctr	Centre	Ho	House	Mkt	Market	Sq	Square
Bsns, Bus	Business	Ctry	Country	Hospl	Hospital	Mus	Museum	St	Street
Bvd	Boulevard	Cty	County	HQ	Headquarters	Orch	Orchard	Sta	Station
Cath	Cathedral	Dr	Drive	Hts	Heights	Pal	Palace	Terr	Terrace
Cir	Circus	Dro	Drove	Ind	Industrial	Par	Parade	TH	Town Hall
Cl	Close	Ed	Education	Inst	Institute	Pas	Passage	Univ	University
Cnr	Corner	Emb	Embankment	Int	International	Pk	Park	Wk, Wlk	Walk
Coll	College	Est	Estate	Intc	Interchange	Pl	Place	Wr	Water
Com	Community	Ex	Exhibition	Junc	Junction	Prec	Precinct	Yd	Yard

Index of localities, towns and villages

A

Abbey Hulton 58 B7
Abbots Bromley 161 B6
Acton 86 C8
Acton Trussell 175 B1
Adbaston 131 D4
Admaston 160 A3
Albrighton 237 A6
Aldersley 255 F7
Aldridge 256 A6
Allgreave 1 C3
Allimore Green 172 D3
Almington 98 C2
Alrewas 200 F3
Alsagers Bank 54 F5
Alsop en le Dale 36 E3
Alstonefield 35 D4
Alton 78 F1
Alvecote 251 D6
Amblecote 279 F7
Amerton 139 A4
Amington 251 B4
Anslow 165 C7
Anslow Gate 164 E7
Apeton 172 C1
Armitage 198 B4
Armsdale 115 D5
Armshead 59 B5
Ash Bank 59 A3
Ashley 100 B5
Ashley Dale 100 B5
Ashmore park 242 A2
Ashwood 274 F5
Aspley 117 B7
Astbury 15 B7
Aston
  Claverley 267 F8
  Newcastle-under-Lyme . . 84 A7
  Stafford 154 E4
Aston-By-Stone 120 C4
Aston Heath 129 B6
Audley 39 E2
Audmore 171 F8
Austcliffe 280 B5

B

Back of Ecton 34 F8
Baddeley Edge 43 D1
Baddeley Green 43 B3
Bagnall 43 F2
Balance Hill 126 C5
Baldwins Gate 85 C4
Ball Green 42 D6
Balterley 38 C1
Balterley Green 38 C2

Bank Top

Draycott in the Clay 144 B6
Stoke-on-Trent 42 B4
Barlaston 88 F2
Barlaston Park 88 F4
Barr Common 256 C3
Barthomley 38 C5
Barton Gate 183 B3
Barton Turn 184 B1
Barton-under-
  Needwood 183 C2
Basford 283 D4
Baswich 156 D1
Bath Vale 6 B3
Beaconside 156 B5
Beamhurst 110 B6
Beamhurst Lane 110 C4
Bearstone 83 A4
Beasley 55 F7
Bednall 193 F8
Bednall Head 194 A8
Beech 87 C1
Beffcote 170 F2
Belgrave 250 E1
Bemersley Green 27 D1
Bentilee 58 D2
Beobridge 267 C4
Berry Hill 57 F1
Betley 53 A6
Betley Common 52 F6
Betton 98 A6
Bickford 191 D1
Biddulph 27 B7
Biddulph Moor 17 B1
Bignall End 39 F3
Bignall Hill 40 B2
Bilbrook 239 C4
Billington 173 D6
Birch Cross 127 C2
Birches Head 57 E6
Birchmoor 262 D8
Bishop's Offley 132 A8
Bishops Wood 221 F8
Bishton 178 A6
Bitterscote 250 A4
Blackbrook
  Baldwin's Gate 84 D2
  Tutbury 145 C1
Blackfords 209 E2
Blackshaw Moor 20 E4
Blackwood Hill 28 F4
Blakedown 281 C2
Blakeley 269 F4
Blakeley Green 255 F8
Blakeley Lane 60 C3
Blakenhall
  Chorlton 52 A4
  Wolverhampton 266 B7
Blithbury 180 A5

Blore

Loggerheads 99 A2
Swinscoe 65 F7
Bloreheath 98 E3
Blount's Green 126 A5
Blundies 273 E3
Blurton 72 E1
Blymhill 203 F5
Blymhill Lawn 204 B3
Blythe Bridge 90 E8
Blythe Marsh 91 B7
Bobbington 268 A2
Bog Moor 194 B7
Bolehall 250 D4
Boley Park 231 F7
Bond End 166 D1
Bonehill 249 E2
Boney Hay 212 A1
Boningale 237 A2
Boon Hill 39 F1
Boothen 72 B5
Borough Park 250 C8
Borrowcop Hill 231 C6
Boscomoor 207 E6
Bosley 7 D8
Boundary 75 E2
Bowers 102 B4
Braddocks Hay 27 C8
Bradeley 42 C3
Bradley 191 C8
Bradley in the Moors . . . 94 C7
Bradmore 265 E8
Bradnop 31 E3
Bradshaw 29 D4
Bradwell 56 B8
Bramshall 125 C8
Branston 184 F7
Brazenhill 172 F8
Brereton 197 B5
Brereton Cross 197 D3
Breretonhill 197 B4
Brewood 223 D5
Bridgemere 67 A7
Bridgtown 226 E6
Brindley Ford 27 B1
Brineton 203 F8
Brinsford 240 D7
Broadeye 285 A3
Broadhill 170 E3
Broad Meadow 55 E6
Broad Oak 272 A7
Broadwaters 280 A1
Brockton 117 B4
Brocton 176 C4
Bromley Hurst 161 B1
Bromstead 188 E7
Bromstead Heath 188 E7
Brookhouses 76 A3
Broomhill 209 E4

Broomyshaw 63 C8

Broughton

Claverley 267 F4
Loggerheads 115 C8
Brown Edge 43 A8
Brownhills 244 D8
Brown Lees 27 A5
Brund 23 E7
Bucknall 58 A4
Buckpool 275 F2
Buddileigh 52 F7
Buglawton 6 A4
Burnhill Green 252 B6
Burntwood 229 C5
Burntwood Green 229 D6
Burslem 56 F7
Burston 121 B1
Burton Manor 174 E6
Burton upon Trent 166 E1
Burybank 104 C4
Bushbury 240 E2
Butters Green 40 A2
Butterton
  Leek 33 F5
  Newcastle-under-Lyme . . 70 D1
Butterton Moor 33 B5
Butt Lane 25 D1
Buxton 4 D8

C

Calf Heath 225 A6
Callingwood 164 D4
Calton 49 E1
Cannock 209 D2
Cannock Wood 211 F5
Carmountside 58 B8
Carroway Head 259 C4
Castlecroft 265 B8
Castle Gresley 186 E1
Castletown 285 A3
Cats Edge 44 D6
Catshill 245 A6
Cat's Hill Cross 117 D2
Cauldon 63 F7
Cauldon Lowe 63 E4
Caunsall 280 C7
Caverswall 74 E2
Cellarhead 59 E4
Chadsmoor 209 F4
Chadwell 188 A1
Chapel Chorlton 102 B8
Chase Terrace 228 E8
Chasetown 228 F6
Chatcull 101 D2
Chatterley 41 B3
Cheadle 76 D4
Chebsey 134 E6

Checkley Madeley . . . . . 52 C
  Upper Tean . . . . 109 E
Checkley Green . . . . 67 E
Cheddleton . . . . 45 C
Cheddleton Heath . . . . . 45 E
Chell Heath . . . . 42 A
Chelmorton . . . . 5 D
Cheslyn Hay . . . . 226 G
Chesterfield 246
Chesterton . . . . 55 F
Cheswardine . . . . 130 A
Chetwynd . . . . 168 G
Chetwynd Aston . . . . . 187 A
Chilcote 219
Chipnall 114
Chorley 212
Chorlton 37
Christ Church 231
Churchbridge 226
Church Eaton 190
Churchill . . . . 281 G
Church Lawton . . . . 25 C
Church Leigh 109
Church Mayfield . . . . . . 81 C
Cinder Hill 266
Clanbrook 278
Claregate 255
Claverley . . . . 267 G
Clayhanger . . . . 244 D
Clay Mills 148
Clayton 71
Cliff 261
Cliff Vale 56
Clifton 81
Clifton Campville 218
Cloud Side 7
Clough Hall 40
Coalpit Hill 40
Cobridge 57
Codsall 238
Codsall Wood 238
Coldeaton 36
Coldmeece 118
Cold Well 212
Colshaw 3
Colton 179
Colton Hills 266
Colwich 177
Combridge . . . . 111 G
Compton Kinver 277
  Wolverhampton 255
Congleton 6
Congreve 207
Consall . . . . 60 C
Cookley 280
Cookshill . . . . 74 G
Cooper's Bank 271
Copmere End 132
Coppenhall 174

Cornhill . . . 42 D5
Cotes . . . 103 A2
Cotes Heath . . . 102 D4
Coton
  Gnosall . . . 171 B5
  Milwich . . . 122 D5
  Tamworth . . . 249 C6
Coton Clanford . . . 154 A4
Coton Green . . . 249 F8
Coton Hayes . . . 122 F6
Coton Hill . . . 122 F5
Coton in the Clay . . . 144 F7
Cotonwood . . . 170 E6
Cotton . . . 78 D8
Cotwalton . . . 105 F2
Coven . . . 224 A2
Coven Heath . . . 240 C6
Coven Lawn . . . 240 A8
Cowall Moor . . . 28 B4
Cowley . . . 171 D4
Coxgreen . . . 272 E2
Crackley . . . 55 E8
Cracow Moss . . . 53 B3
Craddocks Moss . . . 53 F5
Crakemarsh . . . 111 D5
Cranberry . . . 102 D5
Crateford . . . 224 B7
Craythorne . . . 147 D2
Creighton . . . 111 A5
Cresswell . . . 91 C3
Creswell . . . 155 A7
Creswell Green . . . 212 E1
Crossgate . . . 106 D7
Cross Green . . . 224 D1
Cross Heath . . . 56 A3
Crowborough . . . 28 B7
Crowdecote . . . 13 E7
Croxall . . . 216 F8
Croxden . . . 94 D4
Croxton . . . 116 B5
Croxtonbank . . . 116 B6
Curborough . . . 214 D5

D
Dagdale . . . 110 A1
Dales Green . . . 26 C5
Danebridge . . . 9 B7
Dane in Shaw . . . 16 C8
Danford . . . 267 E8
Dapple Heath . . . 140 F1
Darnford . . . 231 F6
Dayhills . . . 121 F6
Denford . . . 44 F8
Denstone . . . 95 D6
Derrington . . . 154 D1
Dibdale . . . 271 F3
Dilhorne . . . 75 D4
Dimsdale . . . 56 B5
Dods Leigh . . . 108 E2
Doley . . . 130 E8
Dordon . . . 262 F6
Dorrington . . . 83 C7
Dosthill . . . 261 C5
Dove Bank . . . 26 A2
Dove Head . . . 3 D6
Doveridge . . . 127 B7
Doxey . . . 155 B4
Draycott . . . 268 A6
Draycott in the Clay . . . 144 C6
Draycott in the Moors . . . 91 E5
Drayton Bassett . . . 260 D5
Drointon . . . 140 B2
Dudley . . . 271 F1
Duke Bank . . . 42 F4
Dunsley . . . 278 C4
Dunstal . . . 141 F1
Dunstall . . . 183 D6
Dunston . . . 192 F8
Dunston Heath . . . 192 C7
Dunwood . . . 29 D3

E
Earl Sterndale . . . 5 C3
Eaton . . . 6 A8
Eccleshall . . . 133 E6
Ecton . . . 23 D2
Edge Hill . . . 262 C2
Edgmond . . . 168 A3
Edial . . . 229 F6
Edingale . . . 217 D5
Egginton . . . 148 B5
Elford . . . 216 C2
Ellastone . . . 80 B3
Ellenhall . . . 134 A1
Elmhurst . . . 214 A5
Endon . . . 43 E7
Endon Bank . . . 43 E8
Englesea-brook . . . 38 A4
Enson . . . 137 C6
Enville . . . 273 D2
Essington . . . 241 F3
Etchinghill . . . 178 B1
Etruria . . . 56 F4
Ettingshall Park . . . 266 D3

F
Fairoak . . . 115 D6
Farewell . . . 213 A4
Far Hoarcross . . . 162 E2
Farley Park . . . 78 D5
Farmcote . . . 267 A5

Fauld . . . 145 C6
Fawfieldhead . . . 12 F3
Fazeley . . . 260 F8
Featherstone . . . 241 C7
Fegg Hayes . . . 42 B7
Fenton . . . 72 E5
Fenton Low . . . 72 E7
Festival Park . . . 57 A4
Finchfield . . . 265 D8
Finney Green . . . 54 C1
Fishley . . . 243 C4
Flash . . . 3 A3
Fole . . . 109 E7
Footherley . . . 246 E3
Ford Green . . . 42 E2
Fordhouses . . . 240 D2
Forebridge . . . 285 C1
Forsbrook . . . 91 B7
Forton . . . 169 A7
Foston . . . 129 D4
Four Ashes
  Coven . . . 224 C6
  Enville . . . 272 E3
Four Crosses . . . 225 F7
Four Oaks . . . 257 F3
Foxholes . . . 144 E4
Foxley . . . 39 D7
Foxt . . . 62 C6
Fradley . . . 215 E7
Fradswell . . . 123 A3
Freasley . . . 262 C4
Freehay . . . 93 A7
Froghall . . . 62 A4
Fulford . . . 106 D8

G
Gailey . . . 207 C1
Gailey Wharf . . . 207 C1
Garshall Green . . . 122 C8
Gateham . . . 35 B6
Gayton . . . 138 E6
Gentleshaw . . . 212 A4
Gerrard's Bromley . . . 101 A2
Giggetty . . . 269 E6
Gillow Heath . . . 16 C2
Gillway . . . 250 B8
Glascote Heath . . . 250 F2
Gnosall . . . 171 D6
Gnosall Heath . . . 171 D5
Goldenhill . . . 41 B7
Goldthorn Hill . . . 266 A5
Goldthorn Park . . . 266 C5
Goodleybrook . . . 75 D5
Goosemoor Green . . . 212 C4
Gornalwood . . . 271 C2
Gorstey Ley . . . 229 C7
Gorstyhill . . . 37 E2
Gorsty Hill . . . 142 D7
Gospel Ash . . . 268 D3
Gospel End Village . . . 271 A8
Gradbach . . . 10 A8
Gratwich . . . 124 C4
Great Bridgeford . . . 135 D3
Great Chatwell . . . 188 C1
Great Chell . . . 42 A6
Great Haywood . . . 158 C2
Great Moor . . . 253 F1
Great Saredon . . . 225 E5
Great Wyrley . . . 227 B3
Green Fields . . . 139 C1
Greenhead . . . 60 F2
Greenleighs . . . 266 C3
Greensforge . . . 274 D6
Grindley . . . 140 D7
Grindon . . . 34 B2
Groundslow Fields . . . 103 F8
Grub Street . . . 151 A7
Gunstone . . . 239 A6

H
Hackman's Gate . . . 281 F1
Hagley . . . 281 E5
Hagley Park . . . 196 D8
Hales . . . 113 F8
Halfpenny Green . . . 268 D4
Hall End . . . 262 F5
Hall Green . . . 25 E5
Halmer End . . . 54 D7
Hammerwich . . . 229 D4
Hamstall Ridware . . . 180 E3
Hanbury . . . 145 A5
Hanbury Woodend . . . 144 E2
Hanchurch . . . 87 B7
Handsacre . . . 198 C8
Hanford . . . 71 E1
Hangingbridge . . . 81 E8
Hanley . . . 282 A2
Hansley Cross . . . 78 C2
Hardings Booth . . . 12 D5
Harding's Wood . . . 25 E2
Hardwick . . . 256 E3
Harlaston . . . 217 D2
Harper's Gate . . . 29 E8
Harriseahead . . . 26 E4
Hartington . . . 24 D5
Hartley Green . . . 138 D8
Hartsgreen . . . 276 C4
Hartshill . . . 71 E7
Hartwell . . . 89 C2
Haselour . . . 217 B2
Hatherton . . . 208 E1
Hatton . . . 146 D8
Haughton . . . 172 F5

Haughtondale . . . 173 B7
Haunton . . . 218 B2
Hawks Green . . . 210 B1
Hazelslade . . . 211 B6
Hazles . . . 61 C5
Heath End . . . 244 A1
Heath Hayes . . . 210 F1
Heath Hill . . . 187 C1
Heathton . . . 268 A5
Heatley . . . 141 D3
Heaton . . . 8 E2
Hednesford . . . 210 D5
Heighley . . . 53 E3
Hem Heath . . . 88 D7
Heron Cross . . . 72 F4
Highbridge . . . 244 B6
High Carr . . . 40 F3
Highfields
  Burntwood . . . 228 F4
  Stafford . . . 174 C8
High Heath . . . 244 D2
Highlanes . . . 116 D6
High Offley . . . 132 B1
High Town . . . 210 A5
Highwood . . . 126 D4
Hilderstone . . . 106 D1
Hill . . . 258 A4
Hill Chorlton . . . 85 D3
Hill Hook . . . 257 E6
Hill Ridware . . . 198 A8
Hill Top . . . 210 C4
Hill Wood . . . 258 C5
Hilton
  Egginton . . . 147 E8
  Shenstone . . . 246 A8
Himley . . . 270 B3
Hinksford . . . 274 F1
Hints . . . 248 D3
Hints Hill . . . 248 D5
Hixon . . . 158 D8
Hixon Heath . . . 139 B1
Hobble End . . . 243 B7
Hockley . . . 261 E5
Hodgefield . . . 28 B2
Hollies Common . . . 171 B8
Hollington . . . 94 B2
Hollins
  Biddulph Moor . . . 28 F8
  Kidsgrove . . . 40 E8
  Kingsley . . . 61 A3
Hollinsclough . . . 4 C1
Holly Bank . . . 245 B3
Hollybush . . . 72 E3
Holly Wall . . . 41 B5
Holmcroft . . . 155 C7
Hookgate . . . 99 F3
Hope . . . 35 D3
Hopedale . . . 35 C2
Hopton . . . 137 D1
Hopton Heath . . . 137 E1
Hopwas . . . 249 B7
Horninglow . . . 166 C7
Horse Bridge . . . 45 A8
Horsebrook . . . 206 D2
Horton . . . 29 C7
Huddlesford . . . 232 C8
Hulme . . . 74 A8
Hulme End . . . 23 F3
Huntington . . . 209 D7
Huntley . . . 92 C7
Hyde Lea . . . 174 C5

I
Ilam . . . 50 E3
Ingestre . . . 157 E6
Ipstones . . . 62 A8
Ireland's Cross . . . 83 C7
Islington . . . 168 F5
Ismere . . . 280 F5
Iverley . . . 281 B7
Ivetsey Bank . . . 204 E3

J
Jack Hayes . . . 58 E8
Joiner's Square . . . 282 C1
Jugbank . . . 100 A4

K
Keele . . . 69 F7
Kerry Hill . . . 58 F7
Kettlebrook . . . 250 B3
Key Green . . . 6 E4
Kiddemore Green . . . 222 D6
Kidderminster . . . 280 B1
Kidsgrove . . . 26 B1
King's Bromley . . . 199 C6
Kingsley . . . 61 E3
Kingsley Holt . . . 62 A1
Kingsley Moor . . . 60 F1
Kingslow . . . 252 C2
Kingstone . . . 141 C8
Kingswinford . . . 275 F6
Kingswood . . . 237 E1
Kingswood Common . . . 238 B2
Kinver . . . 278 B3
Knightley . . . 152 A6
Knightley Dale . . . 152 B3
Knighton
  Adbaston . . . 130 F3
  Loggerheads . . . 83 C5
Knotbury . . . 2 F5
Knowl Bank . . . 53 E7

Knutton . . . 55 F2
Knypersley . . . 27 C5

L
Ladfordfield . . . 134 E1
Landywood . . . 243 A8
Lane Ends . . . 27 A2
Lane Green . . . 239 C7
Lanesfield . . . 266 E4
Laney Green . . . 226 A3
Langley . . . 206 B6
Lask Edge . . . 28 C7
Latherford . . . 225 B4
Lawnhead . . . 152 E6
Lawns Wood . . . 275 B2
Lawton-gate . . . 25 A4
Leadendale . . . 89 F3
Lea Heath . . . 159 B8
Leamonsley . . . 230 E7
Leek . . . 30 E6
Leekbrook . . . 45 F8
Leighswood . . . 256 A7
Levedale . . . 191 F6
Leycett . . . 54 C2
Leyfields . . . 249 F7
Ley Hill . . . 258 B1
Leys . . . 62 C3
Lichfield . . . 231 D5
Light Oaks . . . 43 E1
Lightwood
  Cheadle . . . 76 F3
  Longton . . . 89 E7
Limepits . . . 85 D8
Linton . . . 186 A1
Lipley . . . 114 E3
Little Aston . . . 257 B4
Little Bloxwich . . . 243 A5
Little Bridgeford . . . 135 B3
Little Burton . . . 166 D4
Little Chell . . . 41 F4
Little Drayton . . . 112 A8
Little Hay . . . 247 C1
Little Haywood . . . 177 C8
Little Madeley . . . 68 F8
Little Saredon . . . 225 E3
Little Sugnall . . . 116 F3
Littlewood . . . 226 E4
Littleworth
  Cannock . . . 210 E4
  Stafford . . . 156 A4
Little Wyrley . . . 243 E8
Loggerheads . . . 99 C5
London Fields . . . 271 F2
Long Common . . . 268 C8
Long Compton . . . 153 D2
Longdon . . . 197 F1
Longdon Green . . . 213 B7
Longford . . . 168 B1
Longnor . . . 13 A6
Longport . . . 56 D8
Longridge . . . 192 C4
Longsdon . . . 29 F2
Longton . . . 284 C3
Lower Beobridge . . . 267 A3
Lower Elkstone . . . 22 D1
Lower Ellastone . . . 80 C2
Lower Gornal . . . 271 E4
Lower Green . . . 224 A3
Lower Hatton . . . 102 D6
Lower Knightley . . . 152 A4
Lower Leigh . . . 108 F4
Lower Nobut . . . 109 F2
Lower Penn . . . 264 F4
Lower Stonnall . . . 246 A4
Lower Tean . . . 92 F2
Loxley Green . . . 125 C2
Loynton . . . 150 F5
Lullington . . . 218 E7
Lynn . . . 188 B4

M
Madeley . . . 68 E6
Madeley Heath . . . 69 B8
Maer . . . 85 C1
Mapleton . . . 64 F4
Marchington . . . 127 E2
Marchington
  Woodlands . . . 143 A6
Market Drayton . . . 97 B2
Marsh Green . . . 16 D3
Marston
  Stafford . . . 136 E4
  Wheaton Aston . . . 204 E8
Marston on Dove . . . 147 B8
Mavesyn Ridware . . . 198 A6
May Bank . . . 56 C3
Mayfield . . . 81 C8
Meaford . . . 104 D4
Meerbrook . . . 19 F7
Meir . . . 74 A1
Meir Heath . . . 90 A5
Mere Green . . . 258 B3
Meretown . . . 169 B6
Merridale . . . 255 C2
Merry Hill . . . 265 D7
Middle . . . 226 A4
Middle Madeley . . . 68 F7
Middle Mayfield . . . 81 B6
Middleport . . . 56 D7
Middleton . . . 260 A1
Middleton Green . . . 108 B3
Mile Oak . . . 249 D1
Miles Green . . . 54 E8
Milford . . . 176 B7

Milldale . . . 35 F2
Millend . . . 39 C5
Mill Green
  Aldridge . . . 256 F7
  Cannock . . . 226 F8
Millmeece . . . 117 F7
Milton . . . 43 A1
Milwich . . . 122 D5
Mitton . . . 191 C3
Mobberley . . . 92 D7
Moddershall . . . 105 F6
Moneystone . . . 63 A1
Moor Green . . . 91 A8
Moor Hall . . . 258 D1
Moreton
  Drayton in the Clay . . . 144 C8
  Newport . . . 188 D7
Morrey . . . 181 D2
Morrilow Heath . . . 107 E4
Mossgate . . . 106 D7
Mossley
  Congleton . . . 16 A8
  Rugeley . . . 196 F7
Moss Pit . . . 174 E5
Mount Pleasant
  Mow Cop . . . 26 B5
  Stoke-on-Trent . . . 72 C5
  Tamworth . . . 250 C1
  Uttoxeter . . . 126 B7
  Werrington . . . 60 B2
Mow Cop . . . 26 C7
Mucklestone . . . 99 B7
Muckley Corner . . . 230 A2

N
Napley . . . 98 F8
Napley Heath . . . 83 A1
Needwood . . . 164 B5
Netherland Green . . . 126 E2
Netherseal . . . 219 E7
Nether Stowe . . . 214 C3
Nethertown . . . 198 F8
Newborough . . . 162 E8
Newborough Brick Hill . . . 163 A5
Newbridge . . . 255 E3
Newcastle-under-Lyme . . . 283 B1
Newchapel . . . 26 E2
Newchurch . . . 163 B5
Newfield . . . 41 D5
Newhall . . . 186 F6
Newpool . . . 27 B6
Newport . . . 168 D4
Newstead . . . 88 E6
Newton . . . 159 D8
Newton Hurst . . . 141 A1
Newton Regis . . . 236 D4
Newton Solney . . . 167 E8
Newtown
  Biddulph . . . 17 B5
  Great Wyrley . . . 243 B6
  Longnor . . . 12 C3
New Town . . . 228 F2
No Man's Heath . . . 236 F6
Norbury
  Gnosall . . . 151 A3
  Roston . . . 80 D1
Norbury Junction . . . 151 D2
Northwood
  Hanley . . . 57 E4
  Newcastle-under-Lyme . . . 71 D2
Norton . . . 279 D2
Norton Bridge . . . 119 A1
Norton Canes . . . 227 F5
Norton East . . . 228 A6
Norton Green . . . 43 A5
Norton in Hales . . . 82 C1
Norton-in-the-Moors . . . 42 F4
Nurton . . . 253 F3
Nurton Hill . . . 253 E4

O
Oakamoor . . . 78 B7
Oaken . . . 238 D2
Oak Hill . . . 71 F5
Oakley . . . 98 C6
Oaks Green . . . 128 D7
Offleybrook . . . 132 A8
Offleyhay . . . 132 D7
Offleymarsh . . . 132 A7
Offleyrock . . . 132 B7
Oldfallow . . . 209 D3
Oldfurnace . . . 77 E4
Old Perton . . . 254 B2
Olive Green . . . 181 B2
Onecote . . . 32 F3
Onneley . . . 68 A3
Orgreave . . . 200 B5
Orslow . . . 188 E3
Orton . . . 264 F3
Otherton . . . 207 F6
Oulton
  Newport . . . 151 A1
  Stone . . . 105 C4
Oulton Heath . . . 105 B6
Ounsdale . . . 269 F6
Outlands . . . 115 E1
Outwoods
  Broadhill . . . 170 A1
  Burton upon Trent . . . 166 A4
Overley . . . 200 C4
Overmoor . . . 60 A3
Overton . . . 93 F1
Oxbarn . . . 265 E7
Oxford . . . 42 B8

P

Packmoor 26 F1
Palmer Moor 127 E7
Palmers Cross 255 D8
Park End 39 A4
Parkfield 266 E5
Parkgate 79 F5
Parkside 155 D8
Pasford 252 E3
Pattingham 253 D2
Pave Lane 187 B7
Peacock Hay 40 F4
Pelsall 244 B3
Pelsall Wood 243 F5
Pendeford 239 F2
Penkhull 71 E6
Penkridge 192 E2
Penn 265 E5
Penn Fields 265 F6
Perry Crofts 250 B7
Pershall 133 B8
Perton 254 D4
Piccadilly 261 F1
Pillaton 208 C7
Pipe Gate 83 D6
Pipehill 230 C5
Pipe Ridware 198 C8
Pitts Hill 41 F5
Plardiwick 171 B6
Podmore 101 A4
Polesworth 262 F8
Poolend 19 B1
Poolfold 16 F4
Porthill 56 C6
Potter's Cross 278 A5
Prestwood Denstone 79 E1
  Kinver 274 F1
Prospect Village 211 C4
Puleston 149 C1
Pye Green 194 F1

Q

Quarry Hill 262 A7
Queensville 175 B8
Quixhill 95 E7

R

Rake End 179 F1
Rakeway 93 A8
Ramshorn 79 B7
Rangemore 164 C3
Ranton 153 D5
Ranton Green 153 B3
Ravenhill 196 F6
Ravenscliffe 41 A5
Ravenshall 53 A4
Rawnsley 211 B5
Red Bull 98 D3
Redhill 133 F6
Red Street 40 E3
Rickerscote 174 F5
Ridgeway 42 E8
Rileyhill 199 B2
Rising Brook 174 E7
Robin Hill 28 A8
Rocester 96 A3
Rock End 27 F6
Rodbaston 207 E4
Rolleston on Dove 147 B4
Romsley 276 A2
Rosehill 112 A1
Roston 96 E7
Rough Close 89 F3
Roughcote 74 C6
Rough Hills 266 F6
Roughley 258 D3
Rowley Park 285 A1
Rownall 59 E8

S

Salt 137 F4
Salt Heath 137 E3
Sandborough 181 B3
Sandfields 231 A5
Sandon 137 D7
Sandonbank 137 C5
Sandyfields 271 B6
Sandyford
  Stoke-on-Trent 41 D6
  Swynnerton 103 E6
Saverley Green 91 A2
Scholar Green 25 E8
Scot Hay 54 E4
Scounslow Green 142 C8
Scropton 129 E1
Seabridge 70 F3
Seckington 236 A3
Sedgley 271 F7
Seighford 154 B7
Seisdon 263 F2
Shackerley 221 B1
Shaffalong 45 A5
Shallowford 135 B7
Shareshill 225 D2
Sharpley Heath 107 B3
Shawfield 22 C8
Shebdon 150 C8
Sheen 24 A7
Sheepwash 74 E7
Shelfield 244 C1
Shelton 57 B1
Shelton under Harley 86 B3
Shenstone 247 A5
Shenstone Woodend 247 A1
Shire Oak 245 A6
Shirleywich 157 F8
Shobnall 166 A4
Shraleybrook 39 A1
Shut Heath 172 E8
Shutlanehead 70 B2
Shutt Green 223 A8
Shuttington 251 F7
Sideway 72 B3
Silverdale 55 B1
Six Ashes 272 B6
Slade Heath 224 E1
Slindon 117 D5
Slitting Mill 196 C7
Smallrice 121 E4
Smallthorne 42 C2
Smestow 269 C4
Smith's Green 38 B7
Snelston 81 C3
Sneyd Green 57 D7
Somerford 223 F6
Soudley 130 B6
Spade Green 230 A8
Sparklow 14 C8
Spath 111 B3
Springfields 71 E5
Springhill 245 E8
Spring Hill 265 C4
Springwood 55 C8
Stableford 86 B2
Stafford 285 B4
Stakenbridge 281 E3
Stallington 90 C4
Standon 102 A2
Stanfield 42 A3
Stanhope Bretby 167 F1
Stanley 44 A5

S (cont.)

Rudge 263 A7
Rudyard 29 E8
Rugeley 196 E8
Ruiton 271 D5
Rumer Hill 226 F7
Rushton Spencer 8 B2
Russell's Hall 271 F1
Ryecroft Gate 18 C8
Rye Hills 39 E1

Stanley Moor 43 F4
Stanshope 35 D1
Stanton
  Mayfield 65 D1
  Swadlincote 186 C4
Stapenhill 185 F8
Stockton 187 D6
Stockton Brook 43 d5
Stockwell End 255 D6
Stockwell Heath 179 A8
Stoke 72 A7
Stoke-on-Trent 72 D7
Stone 120 B8
Stonefield 104 F2
Stone Heath 107 C3
Stonehouses 91 B6
Stonnall 245 E4
Stourbridge 279 D4
Stourton 278 F7
Stowe 214 C1
Stowe-by-Chartley 139 C3
Stowford 37 C8
Stramshall 111 A4
Streethay 215 A2
Streetley 257 D3
Streetly 257 D3
Stretton
  Brewood 206 C3
  Burton upon Trent 166 E8
Stubwood 95 D4
Sturbridge 117 E1
Sudbury 128 E4
Sugnall 116 D2
Sutton 150 D1
Sutton Coldfield 258 E1
Swadlincote 186 F4
Swindon 269 F2
Swinscoe 65 E5
Swynnerton 103 B4
Sytch House Green 267 A2

T

Tadgedale 99 C5
Talke 40 C7
Talke Pits 40 E5
Tamworth 250 B3
Tatenhill 165 A1
Tatenhill Common 164 F1
Teanford 92 D6
Tettenhall 255 D5
Tettenhall Wood 255 C3
The Bank 26 B7
The Blythe 140 F5
The Brampton 283 C4
The Bratch 269 E8
The Deanery 207 C7
The Four Alls 112 E4
The Green 285 B2
The Handfords 154 B1
The Leys 250 A5
The Lymes 70 C3
The Quarry 39 C2
The Rookery 26 C3
The Shruggs 121 C2
The Straits 271 A5
Thorncliffe 20 E2
Thornes 245 E3
Thorpe 51 C1
Thorpe Constantine 235 F6
Threapwood 77 E2
Thurvaston 96 F1
Tillington 155 C6
Timbersbrook 6 E2
Tittensor 88 B1
Tixall 157 D2
Tompkin 44 C3
Tong 220 D3
Tong Forge 220 A5
Tong Norton 220 D5
Totmonslow 92 B4
Townend 106 F8
Townhead 62 E7

U

Town Head 78 F1
Townsend 58 C3
Trentham 88 A6
Trent Vale 71 F3
Trescott 264 B7
Triangle 229 B4
Trinity Fields 155 B8
Trysull 264 C1
Tuckhill 272 B5
Tunstall
  Stoke-on-Trent 41 C3
  Woodseaves 131 E3
Tuppenhurst 198 D4
Turnhurst 41 F7
Tutbury 146 C5
Two Gates 261 D8

Ubberley 58 D1
Underhill 241 B2
Upper Aston 263 A1
Upper Cotton 63 B4
Upper Elkstone 22 A3
Upper Ellastone 80 B4
Upper Gornal 271 F6
Upper Hatton 102 D7
Upper Hulme 20 E7
Upper Landywood 242 E8
Upper Leigh 108 E5
Upper Longhorn 197 C2
Upper Mayfield 66 B1
Upper Nobut 109 E4
Upper Tean 92 D3
Uttoxeter 126 D7

V

Vauxhall 168 D2
Vigo 244 F2

W

Wain Lee 26 F4
Walford 117 B8
Walk Mill 132 D8
Wall 230 D2
Wallbridge Park 30 C4
Wall Heath 275 B8
Wallington Heath 243 B2
Walsall 243 B2
Walsall Wood 244 F4
Walton
  Eccleshall 134 E4
  Stone 119 E7
Walton Heath 119 E5
Walton-on-the-Hill 175 F7
Walton-on-Trent 184 E1
Warslow 23 B1
Warstone 242 C8
Warton 150 D2
Washerwall 59 A4
Water Eaton 207 A2
Waterhouses 49 A1
Weaverslake 181 F3
Wedges Mills 226 B6
Weeford 248 A4
Weeping Cross 175 D7
Wereton 39 C1
Wergs 255 A6
Werrington 59 D4
West Broughton 128 A6
West Chadsmoor 209 F5
Westcroft 241 B3
Western Downs 174 A8
West Heath 52 E8
West Hill 210 B6
Westlands 71 A6
Weston
  Crewe 37 C5
  Stafford 138 D3

Y

Weston Coyney 74 A5
Weston Jones 150 C5
Weston-under-Lizard 203 E3
Westwood 30 B6
Wetley Moor 58 F5
Wetley Rocks 60 B7
Wetmore 166 F5
Wetton 34 F4
Wetwood 115 F7
Whateley 261 F3
Wheaton Aston 205 B6
Whiston
  Cheadle 62 D3
  Penkridge 191 E1
Whitecross 172 F8
White Hill 26 B2
Whitehurst 75 D7
Whitemoor 16 D6
Whitfield 42 C7
Whitgreave 135 F5
Whitley Heath 133 A1
Whitmore 86 A6
Whittington
  Croxton 116 D8
  Kinver 278 C2
  Lichfield 232 B5
Whittington Heath 232 C4
Wigginton 234 B2
Wightwick 254 E1
Wildboarclough 1 C1
Wildwood 175 D6
Willoughbridge 84 A5
Willslock 125 F3
Wilnecote 261 F8
Wimblebury 210 F3
Wincle 9 A7
Winnington 83 B1
Winnothdale 93 C5
Winshill 167 B3
Withington 109 B3
Withystakes 59 E5
Wollaston
  Church Eaton 190 E4
  Stourbridge 279 D6
Wolstanton 56 D5
Wolverhampton 266 B7
Wombourne 269 E6
Woodcock Heath 141 A5
Woodcote 187 D3
Woodcroft 30 D5
Woodedge 144 A6
Woodend 145 B1
Wood End 262 C1
Woodgate 126 E5
Wood Gate 144 C5
Woodhouse Green 7 D2
Woodhouses 182 C3
Woodlane 182 D6
Wood Lane 40 E4
Woodmill 181 F7
Woodseaves
  Eccleshall 151 E8
  Market Drayton 112 E3
Woodsetton 271 E6
Woodshutts 25 F1
Woodwall Green 116 A4
Woore 67 B1
Wootton
  Eccleshall 133 D3
  Ellastone 79 E4
Wordsley 275 E3
Wrinehill 53 B3
Wychnor 201 B5

Yarlet 136 C6
Yarnfield 118 F7
Yoxall 182 A2

Index of streets, hospitals, industrial estates, railway stations, schools, shopping centres, universities and places of interest

A

Aarons Dr ST7 . . . . 39 F2
Abberley Rd DY3 . . . . . . 271 D4
Abberley B77 . . . . 251 C2
Abbey Arc DE14 . . . . 166 E2
Abbey Cl 8 Stafford ST17 175 A8
Penkridge ST19 . . . . 208 A8
Rocester ST14 . . . . 96 A3
Abbey Ct Bucknall ST2 . . . 58 B5
Newport TF10 . . . . 168 F2
Abbeydale Cl CW2 . . . . . . 37 C2
Abbey Dr Colwich ST18 . . . 177 D8
Walsall WS3 . . . . 244 A5
Abbeyfield Rd WV10 . . . . 240 F4
Abbeyfields ST18 . . . . . . 158 B2
Abbey Gdns ST18 . . . . . . 158 B2
Abbey Green Rd ST13 . . . . 30 D7
Abbey Hill Sch & Performing Arts Coll ST12 . . . . 58 C5
Abbey Hulton Prim Sch ST2 . . . . 58 A5
Abbey La ST2 . . . . 58 A5
Abbey Park Way CW2 . . . . 37 E3
Abbey Prim Sch WS3 . . . . 242 E2
Abbey Rd Bucknall ST2 . . . 58 B5
Dudley,Gornalwood DY3 . . 271 C3
Rocester ST14 . . . . 95 F3
Tamworth B77 . . . . 250 D3
Wetley Rocks ST9 . . . . . . 60 B6
Abbeyside ST18 . . . . 153 F5
Abbey Sq WS3 . . . . 242 E2
Abbey St Bucknall ST2 . . . 58 A6
Burton u T DE14 . . . . . . 166 D2
Cannock WS12 . . . . 210 B7
Dudley DY3 . . . . 271 C3
Newcastle-u-L ST5 . . . . . . 55 C1
Stone ST15 . . . . 120 A8
Abbey Way TF9 . . . . 97 D2
Abbey Wood Cl 1 ST13 . . 30 D7
Abbot Beyne Sch (Evershed Bldg) DE15 . . . . 167 B4
Abbot Beyne Sch (Linnell Bldg) 167 A3
Abbot Cl DE14 . . . . 166 A3
Abbots Bromley Hospl WS15 . . . . 160 F6
Abbots Bromley Rd DE13 . . . . 162 C4
Abbots Ct ST2 . . . . 58 B7
Abbots Field WS11 . . . . . 209 E5
Abbotsford Rd WS4 . . . . . 231 E7
Abbotsholme Sch ST14 . . . 96 B2
Abbots Pl ST2 . . . . 58 B6
Abbots Rd ST2 . . . . 58 B6
Abbot's Way ST5 . . . . 71 B6
Abbots Way WV3 . . . . . . 255 E1
Abbots Wlk Rugeley WS15 . . . . . . 197 B5
Stafford ST16 . . . . 155 E5
Abbott's Cl CW12 . . . . . . 16 B8
Abbotts Dr ST1 . . . . 57 E8
Abbotts Pl WS3 . . . . 243 D1
Abbott's Rd ST13 . . . . 31 A7
Abbotts St WS3 . . . . 243 D2
Abelia B77 . . . . 250 F4
Abercorn St ST4 . . . . 72 F5
Aberford St ST1 . . . . 57 F5
Abingdon Rd WS3 . . . . . . 242 F2
Abingdon Way Stoke-on-T ST4 . . . . 88 B7
Walsall WS3 . . . . 242 F2
Ablon Ct ST19 . . . . 207 F7
Ablow St WV2 . . . . 266 C8
Abnalls Croft WS13 . . . . . 213 F1
Abnalls Ct WS13 . . . . 213 F1
Abnalls La Lichfield WS13 213 D1
Lichfield WS13 . . . . 213 F1
Abney Dr WV14 . . . . 266 F1
Acacia Ave ST5 . . . . 55 E2
Acacia Cres WV8 . . . . 239 B4
Acacia Ct DY8 . . . . 279 E6
Acacia Gdns ST7 . . . . 26 C3
Acacia Gr Cannock WS12 . 210 F3
Newcastle-u-L ST5 . . . . . . 55 E2
Achilees Cl WS6 . . . . 226 F1
Achilles Way ST2 . . . . 57 F1
Ackleton Gdns WV3 . . . . 265 F7
Acorn Cl Burntwood WS7 . 212 A1
Cannock WS11 . . . . 210 C2
Great Wyrley WS6 . . . . . 227 A1
Loggerheads TF9 . . . . 99 D5
Acorn Gr Codsall WV8 . . 238 E2
Stourbridge DY8 . . . . . . 275 E1
Acorn La CW12 . . . . 6 E3
Acorn Rd WV11 . . . . 242 A1
Acorn Rise 89 E8
Acorn Starter Units WS7 . . . . 228 D2
Acorn View WS7 . . . . 229 C6
Acres Nook ST6 . . . . 41 A7
Acres Nook Rd ST6 . . . . . 41 A6
Acres The Newcastle-u-L ST5 . . . . . . 55 D1
Wolverhampton WV3 . . . 255 C1
Acreswood Rd ST6 . . . . . . 42 B2
Acton Ct ST18 . . . . 174 F2
Acton Dr DY3 . . . . 271 B3
Acton Hill Rd ST17 . . . . . 175 C7
Acton St ST1 . . . . 57 D6
Adam Ct WS11 . . . . 209 D1

Adams Ave ST6 . . . . 41 D5
Adams Cl TF10 . . . . 168 E2
Adams Cres TF10 . . . . . . 168 E2
Adams' Gram Sch TF10 . 168 E3
Adams Gr ST13 . . . . 30 C4
Adamson Cl WS11 . . . . . 209 B1
Adams Rd Brownhills WS8 245 B5
Wolverhampton WV3 . . . 265 C8
Adams St Newcastle-u-L ST5 . . . . . . 56 C4
Stoke-on-T ST2 . . . . 43 B1
Adamthwaite Cl ST11 . . . 90 D7
Adamthwaite Dr ST11 . . . 90 D7
Adderley Pl ST12 . . . . 88 F3
Adderley Rd Market Drayton TF9 . . . . . 97 B3
Stoke-on-T ST6 . . . . 42 E3
Adderley Road Ind Est 97 C2
Addie Rd DE13 . . . . 166 B6
Addington Way ST3 . . . . 284 D5
Addison Cl WS11 . . . . . . 209 E5
Addison Croft DY3 . . . . . 271 A5
Addison Gr WV11 . . . . . . 241 B3
Addison Rd WV3 . . . . . . 265 F8
Addison St ST1 . . . . 57 D6
Adelaide Cres DE15 . . . . 167 C2
Adelaide Dr WS12 . . . . . 210 F3
Adelaide St ST6 . . . . 57 A7
Adelaide Wlk WV2 . . . . . 266 E8
Adies Alley 7 ST15 . . . . 120 A8
Adkins St ST6 . . . . 57 C7
Admiral Parker Dr WS14 246 F5
Adonis Cl B79 . . . . 250 C7
Adrian St ST4 . . . . 72 E6
Advance Bsns Pk WS11 . 210 B3
Adventure Pl ST1 . . . . . . 282 B2
Adwalton Rd WV6 . . . . . 254 F2
Aegean Cl ST4 . . . . 88 C8
Aelfgar Ctr WS15 . . . . . . 178 E1
Aelfgar Ho WS15 . . . . . . 178 E1
Affleck Ave B78 . . . . 249 D1
Agenoria Dr DY8 . . . . . . 279 F5
Agger Hill ST9 . . . . 54 C1
Aiden Ct WS13 . . . . 231 C7
Ainsdale Cl 2 Longton ST3 73 D1
Stourbridge DY8 . . . . . . 279 F2
Ainsley Ct ST2 . . . . 58 B6
Ainsworth Ave ST10 . . . . 61 D3
Ainsworth Rd WV10 . . . . 240 E4
Ainsworth St ST4 . . . . . . 72 C5
Aintree Cl Burton u T DE14 . . . . . . 185 A7
Cannock WS12 . . . . 210 F6
Stoke-on-T ST4 . . . . 88 B7
Aintree Rd Upper Tean ST10 . . . . 92 E4
Wolverhampton WV10 . . 240 D4
Aintree Way DY1 . . . . . . 271 F2
Airdale Gr ST15 . . . . 105 B2
Airdale Rd ST15 . . . . 105 B2
Airdale Spinney ST15 . . . 105 B2
Airfield Ind Est ST18 . . . 153 E8
Aitken Cl B78 . . . . 250 A2
Aitken St ST6 . . . . 56 E8
Ajax Cl WS6 . . . . 226 F1
Ajax Way ST2 . . . . 57 F1
Akesmoor La Biddulph ST8. 27 A8
Mow Cop ST7 . . . . 26 F7
Alanbrook Gr ST3 . . . . . . 89 E8
Alandale Ave WS15 . . . . 198 C4
Alan Dale ST9 . . . . 59 B4
Alanley Cl ST6 . . . . 42 D1
Alan Rd ST2 . . . . 58 C3
Alastair Rd ST4 . . . . 71 F4
Albany Dr Cannock WS12 210 E3
Rugeley WS15 . . . . 178 D3
Albany Gr Kingswinford DY6 . . . . . 275 E7
Stoke-on-T ST4 . . . . 71 D8
Willenhall WV11 . . . . . . 242 C1
Albany Rd Newcastle-u-L ST5 . . . . . 283 B4
Stoke-on-T ST4 . . . . 71 D8
Albany St ST6 . . . . 41 C7
Albemarle Rd Newcastle-u-L ST5 . . . . . . 56 A3
Stourbridge DY8 . . . . . . 279 F2
Alberta St ST3 . . . . 284 C2
Albert Ave ST3 . . . . 73 E3
Albert Cl WV8 . . . . 238 E4
Albert Davie Dr WS12 . . 210 E4
Albert Dr DY3 . . . . 269 C2
Albert Pl ST3 . . . . 73 B1
Albert Rd Fazeley B78 . . 261 E4
Stoke-on-T ST4 . . . . 88 B6
Tamworth B79 . . . . 250 B5
Albert St 2 Leek ST13 . . 30 E6
Audley ST7 . . . . 39 F3
Biddulph ST8 . . . . 27 D8
Broomhill WS11 . . . . 209 E4
Burton u T DE14 . . . . . . 166 C4
Cannock WS12 . . . . 210 D5
Kingswinford DY6 . . . . . 275 B8
Longton ST3 . . . . 284 C5
Newcastle-u-L,Chesterton ST5 . . . . 55 E7
Newcastle-u-L,Silverdale ST5 . . . . 55 C2
Newcastle-u-L ST5 . . . . . 283 C3
Stone ST15 . . . . 105 A1
Stourbridge DY8 . . . . . . 279 F5

Albert Terr Newcastle-u-L ST5 . . . . . . 56 C5
Stafford ST16 . . . . 155 E5
Albion Par DY6 . . . . 275 B8
Albion Pl WS11 . . . . 209 E4
Albion Rd WS8 . . . . 244 B8
Albion Sq ST1 . . . . 282 B2
Albion St Hanley ST1 . . . 282 B2
Kingswinford DY6 . . . . . 275 B8
Leek ST13 . . . . 30 E5
Rugeley WS15 . . . . 178 F1
Tamworth B79 . . . . 250 C5
Albion Terr DE14 . . . . . . 166 E6
Albion Way WS7 . . . . . . 211 F1
Albrighton By Pass WV7 . 237 B6
Albrighton Jun & Inf Schs WV7 . . . . 237 A4
Albrighton Sta WV7 . . . . 237 B5
Albrighton Trust (for the disabled)★ WV7 . . . . . . 237 A7
Albutts Rd WS11 . . . . . . 228 B3
Alcester Cl ST6 . . . . 42 B6
Alcove The WS3 . . . . 243 D2
Aldbury Cl ST16 . . . . 136 D1
Aldbury Pl ST3 . . . . 72 E1
Aldeburgh Cl WS3 . . . . . 243 A3
Aldeburgh Dr ST5 . . . . . . 71 B2
Alden Hurst WS7 . . . . . . 228 B2
Alderbrook Cl Rolleston on D DE13 . . . . 147 C4
Sedgley DY3 . . . . 266 B1
Alder Cl Kidsgrove ST7 . . . 41 A8
Lichfield WS14 . . . . 231 F7
Loggerheads TF9 . . . . 99 E5
Alder Coppice Prim Sch DY3 . . . . 266 C1
Alder Coppice DY3 . . . . . 266 C1
Alderdale Ave DY3 . . . . . 266 C3
Alder Dale WV3 . . . . 255 E2
Alderflat Dr ST4 . . . . 88 D6
Alderford Cl WV8 . . . . . . 255 F8
Aldergate B79 . . . . 250 B5
Alder Gr Burton u T DE15 . 185 F7
Newcastle-u-L ST5 . . . . . . 55 D8
Stafford ST17 . . . . 174 B7
Alderhay La ST7 . . . . 26 C4
Alderhithe Gr B74 . . . . . 257 B3
Alderholme Dr 1 DE13 . 147 F1
Alderney Cl ST5 . . . . 70 E4
Alderney Cres ST3 . . . . . . 72 F3
Alder Rd Kingswinford DY6 . . . . . 275 F5
Market Drayton TF9 . . . . 112 A8
Aldersea Cl ST6 . . . . 41 C1
Aldershaw Cl ST16 . . . . . 136 C5
Alders La B79 . . . . 249 E6
Aldersleigh Dr ST17 . . . . 175 C5
Aldersley Ave WV6 . . . . 255 E7
Aldersley Cl WV6 . . . . . . 255 E7
Aldersley High Sch WV8. 239 E1
Aldersley Rd WV6 . . . . . 255 F6
Aldersley Stadium WV6 . 255 E7
Alderson Dr DE13 . . . . . 147 F1
Alders Rd ST8 . . . . 17 B1
Alders The DE13 . . . . . . 183 C1
Alderton Dr WV3 . . . . . . 265 E8
Alderton Gr ST3 . . . . 90 B6
Alder Way WS12 . . . . . . 211 A6
Alder Wlk ST4 . . . . 71 E4
Alderwood Prec DY3 . . . 266 C1
Alderwood Rise DY3 . . . 271 D5
Aldin Ct DE11 . . . . 249 E2
Aldridge By-Pass WS9 . . 256 A6
Aldridge Cl 2 Stourbridge DY8 . . . . 279 E8
Polesworth B78 . . . . 262 F8
Aldridge Rd Aldridge B74 256 D1
Little Aston B74,WS9 . . . 257 B6
Aldridge Sch WS9 . . . . . 256 A4
Aldrin Cl Meir ST3 . . . . . . 90 C7
Stafford ST16 . . . . 156 B5
Aldwych Cl WS9 . . . . . . 256 B8
Aldwyck Dr WV3 . . . . . . 265 A8
Alesmore Mdw WS13 . . . 230 F6
Alexander Cl WS13 . . . . . 215 D6
Alexander Patterson Sch The DY10 . . . . 280 C3
Alexander Rd WV8 . . . . . 239 C3
Alexander Trad Est ST4 . . 57 A2
Alexandra Cres ST14 . . . 126 B8
Alexandra Ct Burton u T DE15 . . . . . . 167 A3
Dudley DY3 . . . . 271 C3
Alexandra Dr DE13 . . . . 182 A3
Alexandra Inf Sch ST3 . . . 73 E2
Alexandra Jun Sch ST3 . . 73 F1
Alexandra Mews B79 . . . 250 C5
Alexandra Rd Burton u T DE15 . . . . . . 167 A3
Longton ST3 . . . . 73 E2
Market Drayton TF9 . . . . 97 B1
Newcastle-u-L ST5 . . . . . . 56 A4
Stafford ST16 . . . . 285 B1
Wolverhampton WV4 . . . 266 A6
Alexandra St 2 ST15 . . . 104 F1
Alexandra Way WS9 . . . . 256 E6
Alford Dr ST2 . . . . 59 A3
Alfred Lyons Cl WS15 . . . 160 F6
Alfred St Burton u T DE14 166 C2
Stoke-on-T ST4 . . . . 72 E7
Tamworth B79 . . . . 250 A5
Walsall WS3 . . . . 243 C1

Alfreton Rd ST4 . . . . 73 A6
Algar Rd ST4 . . . . 71 E6
Alicia Way ST2 . . . . 43 A2
Alison Dr WV8 . . . . 279 E3
Allan Cl 7 DY8 . . . . 279 F8
Allard B77 . . . . 250 C1
Allen Birt Wlk WS15 . . . . 178 D3
Allenby Cl ST5 . . . . 70 F3
Allenby Sq ST4 . . . . 71 E4
Allendale ST16 . . . . 155 B8
Allendale Wlk ST3 . . . . . 72 F1
Allen Gdns TF9 . . . . 112 B8
Allens Croft ST14 . . . . . . 127 E2
Allen's La ST14 . . . . 127 E2
Allens La WS3 . . . . 243 F2
Allensmead B77 . . . . 250 C2
Allensmore Ave ST4 . . . . 73 B5
Allen St Cheadle ST10 . . . 76 E2
Cheadle ST10 . . . . 76 E3
Stoke-on-T ST4 . . . . 71 E8
Tamworth B77 . . . . 250 C1
Allensway ST5 . . . . 70 E4
Allerdale Rd WS8 . . . . . . 244 E6
Allerton Rd ST4 . . . . 87 F7
Alleston Rd WV10 . . . . . 240 D1
Alleston Wlk WV10 . . . . 240 D2
Alleyne's High Sch ST15 105 A1
Alley's La ST20 . . . . 190 A8
Alley The DY3 . . . . 271 B3
Alliance St ST16 . . . . 155 D6
Allington Ave 5 WS13 . . 230 F6
Alliss Cl ST16 . . . . 156 C4
Allport Mews WS11 . . . . 209 E1
Allport Rd WS11 . . . . . . 209 E1
Allport St WS11 . . . . 209 E2
All Saints CE Fst Sch Church Leigh ST10 . . . . 109 A4
Denstone ST14 . . . . 95 E6
Leek ST13 . . . . 30 F4
Standon ST21 . . . . 102 C3
All Saints CE Inf Sch ST18 . . . . 153 C5
All Saints CE Prim Sch Alrewas DE13 . . . . 201 A2
Bednall ST17 . . . . 193 E8
Rangemore DE13 . . . . . . 164 C2
Trysull WV5 . . . . 269 C8
All Saints Croft DE14 . . . 185 C8
All Saints Dr B74 . . . . . . 258 A2
All Saints Rd Burton u T DE14 . . . . . . 185 C8
Stoke-on-T ST4 . . . . 72 A5
Wolverhampton WV2 . . . 266 D8
Allthorpe Pl ST5 . . . . 70 F3
Allton Ave B78 . . . . 249 D1
Allton Ct B77 . . . . 250 E3
Allways Cl ST18 . . . . 122 C5
All Ways ST18 . . . . 122 C5
Allways The ST18 . . . . . . 122 C5
Alma Cl ST7 . . . . 25 E7
Alma Rd DE13 . . . . 186 F6
Almar Pl ST6 . . . . 42 A5
Alma St Burton u T DE14 . 166 C2
Leek ST13 . . . . 30 D6
Stoke-on-T ST4 . . . . 72 D6
Stone ST15 . . . . 104 F3
Almond Cl Cannock WS11. 210 C2
Walsall WS3 . . . . 243 F1
Almond Ct DE13 . . . . . . 147 E1
Almond Gr Stoke-on-T ST4 . 72 E1
Swadlincote DE11 . . . . . 186 E5
Almond Pl ST5 . . . . 40 E1
Almond Rd Huntington WS12 . . . . . 209 D8
Kingswinford DY6 . . . . . 275 E6
Alms Hos TF11 . . . . 203 E2
Almshouse Croft ST18 . . 191 E4
Almshouses Biddulph ST8. 16 E3
Madeley CW3 . . . . 68 E5
Newton Solney DE15 . . . 167 E8
Penkridge ST19 . . . . 192 E1
Rugeley WS15 . . . . 178 E1
Wolverhampton WV4 . . . 265 F3
Alnwick Cl WS12 . . . . . . 210 E2
Alnwick Rd WS3 . . . . . . 243 A4
Alpha Way WS6 . . . . 243 A8
Alpine Dr WS12 . . . . 210 D4
Alpine Way WV3 . . . . . . 255 C2
Alrewas Rd DE13 . . . . . . 199 E6
Alsager Rd ST7 . . . . 39 D5
Alsop Crest ST17 . . . . . . 175 E5
Alsop Moor Cotts DE6 . . . 36 D5
Alsop St ST13 . . . . 30 E5
Alston Cl Cannock WS12 . 210 E2
Sutton Coldfield B74 . . . 258 A2
Alstone Cl ST16 . . . . 155 B7
Alstonefield Youth Hostel★ DE6 . . . . 35 F4
Alstone Rd La ST18 . . . . 172 F2
Althorp Way DE13 . . . . . 166 D8
Althrop Gr ST3 . . . . 73 D3
Altona ST15 . . . . 105 B2
Alton Cl Newcastle-u-L ST5 55 B1
Wolverhampton WV10 . . 240 E3
Alton Gr Bucknall ST2 . . . 73 D7
Cannock WS11 . . . . 209 B1
Newport TF10 . . . . 168 E1
Alton Rd ST14 . . . . 95 D6
Alton Towers Theme Pk★ ST10 . . . . 78 E4
Alvaston Cl WS3 . . . . . . 243 C3

Alvecote Cotts B79 . . . . . 251 D6
Alvecote Pools Nature Reserve★ B79 . . . . 251 E6
Alverley Cl DY6 . . . . 275 B8
Alverstoke Cl WV9 . . . . . 240 A2
Alverton Cl B77 . . . . 261 C4
Alvis Cl B79 . . . . 249 F7
Alwen St DY8 . . . . 275 F2
Alwyn Cl WS6 . . . . 227 A3
Alwyn Cres ST6 . . . . 57 D8
Alwyn Rd DE13 . . . . 182 A2
Alwyn B77 . . . . 261 E7
Amanda Ave WV4 . . . . . 265 D2
Amber Bsns Village B77 . 251 B3
Amber Cl B77 . . . . 251 B3
Amber Ct Stoke-on-T ST9 . 43 E5
Tamworth B77 . . . . 251 B3
Amberfield Cl ST3 . . . . . . 73 E4
Ambergate Cl WS3 . . . . . 243 C3
Ambergate Dr DY6 . . . . . 275 C8
Amber Gn WS11 . . . . . . 210 C2
Amber Gr WS11 . . . . 210 C2
Amberlands DE13 . . . . . . 147 F1
Amberley Way B74 . . . . . 256 E1
Amblecote Dr ST3 . . . . . . 73 E4
Amblecote Prim Sch DY8 . . . . 279 F8
Amblefield Way ST16 . . . 136 C5
Ambleside Cl ST15 . . . . . 120 D7
Ambleside Gr WV11 . . . . 242 B1
Ambleside Pl ST6 . . . . . . 42 A3
Ambleside Way DY6 . . . . 275 D6
Ambrose Cres DY6 . . . . . 275 D8
Ambrose Pl ST6 . . . . 41 F7
Amelia Cl ST2 . . . . 43 A2
America St ST6 . . . . 41 D3
Amerton Farm★ ST18 . . 139 A4
Amerton La Amerton ST18 . . . . 139 A3
Weston ST18 . . . . 138 F1
Amicable St ST6 . . . . 56 F7
Amicombe B77 . . . . 251 C1
Amington Cl B77 . . . . . . 258 D3
Amington Hall B79 . . . . . 251 A8
Amington Heath Com Sch B77 . . . . 251 A4
Amington Ind Est B77 . . 251 B3
Amington Pk B77 . . . . . . 251 A6
Amington Rd B77 . . . . . . 250 D4
Amison St ST3 . . . . 73 D4
Ampleforth Dr ST17 . . . . 156 F1
Ampthill Pl ST4 . . . . 71 F1
Amptronik Trad Est WV5 . . . . 269 D4
Ancaster St ST6 . . . . 41 D7
Anchor Cl B77 . . . . 250 E4
Anchor Ct B77 . . . . 250 E4
Anchor Par WS9 . . . . 256 B6
Anchor Pl ST3 . . . . 284 C4
Anchor Rd Aldridge WS9. 256 B6
Longton ST3 . . . . 284 C4
Anchor Terr ST3 . . . . 284 C4
Anchor Way ST20 . . . . . . 171 D7
Ancient High House★ ST16 . . . . 285 B3
Anderby Gdns DE11 . . . . 186 F2
Anderson Pl ST6 . . . . 42 E3
Anders Sq WV6 . . . . 254 E4
Anderstaff Ind Pk DE14. . 166 E5
Anders B79 . . . . 250 A6
Anderton View ST15 . . . . 104 E3
Andover Cl ST3 . . . . 73 C6
Andover Cres 2 DY6 . . . 275 C8
Andover Pl WS11 . . . . . . 210 A4
Andrew Mulligan Cl ST6. . 41 C5
Andrew Pl ST5 . . . . 283 D3
Andrews Ho WS13 . . . . . 231 A7
Andrews Rd WS9 . . . . . . 245 B4
Andrew St ST6 . . . . 41 C7
Aneurin Bevan Pl WS15 . 178 D2
Angel Croft WS7 . . . . . . 211 E1
Angelica B77 . . . . 250 F4
Anglesey Bsns Pk WS12 . 210 E4
Anglesey Cl WV7 . . . . . . 228 F4
Anglesey Cres Brownhills WS8 . . . . 228 F2
Cannock WS12 . . . . 210 C5
Anglesey Ct Burton u T DE14 . . . . . . 166 B1
Rugeley WS15 . . . . 197 B6
Anglesey Dr ST3 . . . . 73 A3
Anglesey Ho WS15 . . . . . 197 B6
Anglesey Mews WS12 . . 210 C5
Anglesey Prim Sch DE14 166 C1
Anglesey Rd Brownhills WS8 . . . . 228 F2
Burton u T DE14 . . . . . . 166 B1
Lichfield WS13 . . . . 214 B2
Anglesey St Burton u T DE14 . . . . . . 165 F4
Cannock WS12 . . . . 210 B5
Angle St 6 ST13 . . . . 30 D6
Anglia Dr DE11 . . . . 186 F1
Anglia Rd WS11 . . . . 209 D3
Angorfa Cl WS13 . . . . . . 230 F7
Angus Cl ST2 . . . . 58 C4
Anker Cl WS7 . . . . 229 D6
Ankerdrive B79 . . . . 250 B4
Ankermoor Ct B77 . . . . . 250 E5

Ankermoor Prim Sch
  B77 . . . . 250 E5
Ankerside Sh Ctr B79 . . 250 B4
Anker View B77. . . . . 250 C3
Annan Cl 🄰 CW12 . . . . 6 A1
Annandale ST2 . . . . 251 B1
Anna Wlk ST6 . . . . 56 F7
Ann Cres WS11 . . . . 209 E6
Anne Ct ST7 . . . . 40 D6
Annefield Cl TF9 . . . . 97 C2
Anne Rd WV4 . . . . 266 B6
Anne St ST4 . . . . 41 C7
Annette Rd ST4 . . . . 73 B6
Anslow Gdns WV11 . . . . 241 F1
Anslow La DE13 . . . . 147 A2
Anslow Rd DE13 . . . . . . 145 A2
Ansmede Gr ST4 . . . . 72 F1
Anson Ave WS13 . . . . . . 214 A1
Anson CE Prim Sch ST18 158 B2
Anson Ct Burntwood WS7 . 229 C5
  Great Wyrley WS6 . . . . . 226 F1
  Perton WV6 . . . . 254 E5
Anson Ct Burton u T DE14. 166 E3
  Fazeley B78 . . . . 261 B8
  Stafford ST18 . . . . 156 D5
Anson Dr ST17 . . . . 175 F6
Anson Mews WS15 . . . . . 178 F1
Anson Rd Alrewas DE13 . . 201 A2
  Great Wyrley WS6 . . . . . 226 F1
  Meir ST3 . . . . 90 A8
Anson's Row ST18 . . . . . 177 C8
Anson St WS15 . . . . 178 E1
Anstree Cl WS6 . . . . 226 D1
Ansty Dr WS12 . . . . 210 D1
Anthony Gr ST3 . . . . 89 F4
Anthony Pl ST3 . . . . 284 D4
Antler Dr WS15 . . . . 178 B2
Antom Ct ST16. . . . . 155 F7
Apedale Bsns Pk ST5 . . . 55 C7
Apedale Com Ctry Pk★
  ST5 . . . . 55 A6
Apedale Rd
  Audley,Wood Lane ST7 . . . 55 A8
  Newcastle-u-L ST5 . . . . . . 55 C6
Apex Bsns Pk WS11 . . . . 227 F4
Apex Rd WS8 . . . . 244 C7
Apley Pl ST4 . . . . 87 F8
Apley Rd DY8 . . . . 279 E7
Apollo Cl WS11 . . . . 210 A5
Apollo B79 . . . . 249 F6
Apollo Wlk ST6 . . . . 42 C1
Appian Cl B77 . . . . 261 D7
Appleby Gdns WV11 . . . 242 C2
Appleby Glade Ind Est
  DE11 . . . . 186 E2
Appleby Glade DE11. . . . 186 D2
Apple Croft CW3 . . . . 68 C7
Applecroft ST5 . . . . 40 E1
Applecross B74 . . . . 257 F1
Appledore Cl
  Cannock WS12 . . . . 210 E3
  Great Wyrley WS6 . . . . . 227 A3
  Stafford ST17 . . . . 175 E8
Appledore Gr ST6 . . . . . . 41 E7
Appleford Pl ST3 . . . . 72 C7
Applegarth Cl ST4 . . . . . . 73 B6
Apple Gr TF9 . . . . 97 A1
Appleton Cl Biddulph ST8 . . 27 E6
  Burton u T DE15 . . . . . . 185 E8
  Congleton CW12 . . . . 15 E8
  Swadlincote DE11 . . . . . 186 F6
Appleton Cres WV4 . . . . 266 A5
Appleton Dr ST5 . . . . 85 D5
Appletree Gr WS9 . . . . . 256 B5
Apple Wlk WS11 . . . . . . 210 C2
Applewood ST14 . . . . . . 111 A1
Applewood Cres ST3 . . . . 90 C8
Appleyard Ct ST16 . . . . . 285 B3
Appleyard The ST19 . . . . 223 C6
Apse Cl WV5. . . . . 269 F7
Apsley Gr ST2 . . . . 88 A1
Aqualate Cl TF10 . . . . . . 169 A4
Aqualate Ho ST17 . . . . . 174 E6
Aquaries Ct ST3 . . . . 73 E1
Aquinas St ST4 . . . . 72 B7
Arbor B77 . . . . 250 D3
Arborfield Rd ST14 . . . . . 143 F7
Arbor Gate WS9 . . . . 245 B4
Arbour Cl CW3 . . . . 68 E7
Arbourfield Dr ST2 . . . . . . 58 A2
Arbour Mews WS11 . . . . 227 F6
Arbour St Hanley ST1 . . . 282 C3
  Talke Pits ST7 . . . . 40 D5
Arbourtree Ct WV5. . . . . 270 B7
Arbury Dr DY8 . . . . 275 D3
Arcade The DY3 . . . . 271 E5
Arcadia Pk WS15. . . . . . . 197 B7
Arcal St DY3 . . . . 271 E7
Arch St ST4 . . . . 196 F4
Arclid Way ST2 . . . . 58 B2
Arctic Pl ST4 . . . . 88 B8
Arden Cl Leek ST13 . . . . . 31 B5
  Rugeley WS15 . . . . 178 C1
  Stourbridge DY8 . . . . . . 275 C3
  Stourbridge,Wordsley DY8 275 C3
  Tamworth B77 . . . . 250 E5
Arden Ct Congleton CW12. . 16 B7
  Dudley DY3 . . . . 271 D3
Arden Rd Barton-u-N DE13 201 E8
  Tamworth B77 . . . . 261 F5
Arden Wlk WS15 . . . . . . 198 C4
Ardgay Dr WS12 . . . . . . 209 F7
Ardingley Ave ST17 . . . . 156 B1
Argles Rd ST13 . . . . 31 A7
Argosy Cl ST3 . . . . 90 B7

Argyle Ave B77 . . . . 250 D4
Argyle Cl DY8 . . . . 275 E1
Argyle Rd WV2. . . . . 266 B6
Argyle St Hanley ST1 . . . 282 A1
  Tamworth B77 . . . . 250 E4
Argyll Cl ST11 . . . . 90 E6
Argyll Rd ST3 . . . . 73 D1
Ariane B79 . . . . 249 E7
Aries Cl ST6 . . . . 41 F6
Arion Cl B77 . . . . 250 D5
Arkall Cl B79 . . . . 250 C7
Arkle Cl ST14 . . . . 126 D7
Arkle B77 . . . . 261 D4
Arkwright Gr ST1 . . . . 57 F8
Arlescote Cl B75 . . . . . . 258 C2
Arley Dr DY8 . . . . 279 E3
Arley Gr WV4 . . . . 265 D5
Arlington Cl DY6 . . . . . . 275 D4
Arlington Way Meir ST3. . . 90 A7
  Stoke-on-T ST3 . . . . 89 F7
Armishaw Pl WS15 . . . . . 197 D5
Armitage Gdns WS15. . . 197 B6
Armitage Hill DE13 . . . . . 183 D1
Armitage Ho WS15 . . . . 214 E1
Armitage La WS15 . . . . . 197 D5
Armitage Rd WS15 . . . . . 197 A6
Armshead Rd ST9 . . . . . . 59 B5
Armside Cl WS3 . . . . 244 B4
Armstead Rd WV9 . . . . . 240 A3
Armstrong Ave ST4 . . . . 156 A4
Armstrong Gn ST6 . . . . . . 57 C7
Armstrong B79 . . . . 249 F6
Arnold Cl B79. . . . . 250 A6
Arnold Gr ST5 . . . . 56 B7
Arnotdale Dr WS12. . . . . 209 F7
Arnot Rd DE14 . . . . 185 A7
Arps Rd WV8 . . . . 238 F3
Arran Cl WS11 . . . . 210 A3
Arran Dr Stoke-on-T ST7 . . 41 F8
  Tamworth B77 . . . . 261 F7
Arrow Dr WV7 . . . . 237 A5
Arthur Cotton Ct ST6 . . . . 42 A1
Arthur Evans Cl WS15 . . 197 A5
Arthurs Ct DE13. . . . . . . 147 E2
Arthur St
  🄰 Stoke-on-T ST6 . . . . . 41 E3
  Burton u T DE14. . . . . . . 166 C5
  Cannock,Chadsmoor WS11 209 F4
  Cannock WS11 . . . . 210 F3
  Newcastle-u-L ST5 . . . . . . 55 F2
  Stone ST15 . . . . 105 A2
  Wolverhampton WV2. . . . 266 D7
Arthur Terry Sch The
  B74 . . . . 258 A3
Arthur Wood Pl WS15 . . 178 D2
Arundel Cl ST10 . . . . 76 F3
Arundel Gr WV6 . . . . 254 F3
Arundel Rd
  Stourbridge DY8 . . . . . . 275 C2
  Wolverhampton WV10 . . 240 B2
Arundel B77 . . . . 261 C7
Arundel Way ST3 . . . . . . 73 C6
Ascot Cl Burton u T DE15 . 167 A1
  Lichfield WS14. . . . . 231 D7
Ascot Dr Cannock WS11 . . 226 C8
  Dudley DY1 . . . . 271 F2
  Tamworth B77 . . . . 261 D4
  Wolverhampton WV4 . . . 266 A4
Ascot Gdns DY8 . . . . 275 D2
Ascot Rd ST17 . . . . 156 C1
Ash Bank Rd ST2,ST9 . . . . 59 B3
Ashbourne Dr WS11 . . . 210 A4
Ashbourne Dr
  Chorlton CW2 . . . . 37 C1
  Market Drayton TF9. . . . . . 97 C2
  Newcastle-u-L ST5. . . . . . 55 B1
  Swadlincote DE11 . . . . . 186 F1
Ashbourne Gr ST1 . . . . . 282 B4
Ashbourne La DE6 . . . . . . 35 A2
Ashbourne Rd
  Cheadle ST10. . . . . 76 F3
  Leek ST13 . . . . 31 B4
  Mayfield DE6 . . . . 81 C4
  Rocester ST14. . . . . 95 F4
  Uttoxeter,Spath ST14. . . . 111 B3
  Uttoxeter ST14 . . . . 111 B1
  Walsall WS3. . . . . 243 C3
  Wetton DE6 . . . . 35 B3
  Wolverhampton,Ettingshall Park
  WV4 . . . . 266 E3
Ashbrook Cl Gnosall ST20 171 D7
  Uttoxeter ST14 . . . . 126 C6
Ashbrook La WS15 . . . . . 161 C5
Ashburton St ST6 . . . . . . 57 B7
Ashby Cres ST3 . . . . 72 F1
Ashby Rd DE15 . . . . 167 B3
Ashby Rd E DE15 . . . . . . 167 C1
Ashby Rd B79 . . . . 250 C8
Ash Cl Cheadle ST10. . . . . 76 F2
  Codsall WV8. . . . . 239 A3
  Uttoxeter ST14 . . . . 126 A8
Ashcombe Gn ST3 . . . . . . 72 F1
Ashcombe Rd ST13 . . . . . 45 C4
Ashcombe Way ST13 . . . . 30 F4
Ashcott Wlk ST2 . . . . 58 C1
Ash Cres ST5 . . . . 275 E6
Ashcroft 🄱 WV4 . . . . . . 266 A4
Ashcroft Ave ST4 . . . . . . 71 E2
Ashcroft ST5 . . . . 56 A6
Ashcroft ST5 . . . . 56 B6
Ashcroft Inf Sch B79 . . . 250 C7
Ashcroft La
  Lichfield WS14. . . . . 230 E1
  Shenstone WS14 . . . . . . 246 E7
Ashcroft Oval ST5 . . . . . . 56 B6
Ashcroft ST5 . . . . 56 B6
Ashcroft Rd ST5 . . . . 56 A6

Ashdale Cl 🄰 Stone ST15. 120 A7
  Burton u T DE15 . . . . . . 186 A8
  Huntington WS12 . . . . . 209 D7
  Kingswinford DY6 . . . . . 275 D8
Ashdale Dr ST16 . . . . . . 155 D8
Ashdale Pk ST15 . . . . . . 118 F6
Ashdale Rd Leek ST13. . . . 31 B6
  Stoke-on-T ST4 . . . . 72 C5
  Tamworth B77 . . . . 250 D5
Ashdale Rise ST5 . . . . . . 71 B3
Ashdene Gdns DY8 . . . . . 275 C2
Ashdown Dr DY8 . . . . . . 275 E3
Ash Dr ST18 . . . . 172 F5
Ashen Cl DY3 . . . . 266 C3
Ashendene Gr
  Stoke-on-T ST4 . . . . 71 F1
  Trentham ST4 . . . . 87 F8
Ashenden Rise WV3. . . . 265 A8
Ashenhurst Way ST13 . . . 30 F4
Ashenough Rd ST7. . . . . . 40 D6
Ashe's La DE6 . . . . 144 D7
Ashfield Ct ST5 . . . . 283 A4
Ashfield Gr WV10 . . . . . 240 C3
Ashfield Rd
  Wolverhampton,Compton
  WV3 . . . . 255 D2
  Wolverhampton,Fordhouses
  WV10 . . . . 240 C3
Ashfields WV7 . . . . 237 A5
Ashfields Grange ST5 . . . 283 B3
Ashfields New Rd ST5. . . 283 A4
Ashfield Sq ST2 . . . . 58 A2
Ash Flats La ST17,ST18. . . 174 F4
Ashford Dr DY3 . . . . 271 E7
Ashford Gr ST15 . . . . . . 120 C7
Ashford Rd DE13 . . . . . . 166 A6
Ashford St ST4 . . . . 72 C8
Ash Gr Albrighton WV7. . . 237 A4
  Barlaston ST12 . . . . 88 D1
  Blythe Bridge ST11 . . . . . 90 C8
  Brewood ST19 . . . . 223 D6
  Cannock WS11. . . . . 209 F4
  Dudley DY3 . . . . 271 C2
Ash Green Cl ST4 . . . . 88 A7
Ash Green Prim Sch ST4 . 88 B7
Ash Gr Lichfield WS14 . . . 231 E8
  Newcastle-u-L ST5. . . . . . 55 B2
Ashgrove WS7 . . . . 228 F5
Ash Grove La DE65 . . . . . 148 C6
Ash Gr Stoke-on-T ST4. . . . 72 C2
  Tamworth B77 . . . . 261 F5
  Werrington ST2 . . . . 58 F3
  Wheaton Aston ST19 . . . 205 C6
Ash Hill WV3 . . . . 255 D2
Ash La WS6 . . . . 227 A3
Ashlands Ave ST4 . . . . . . 71 E8
Ashlands Cl B79 . . . . . . 250 D5
Ashlands Gr ST4 . . . . 71 E7
Ashlands ST18 . . . . 139 D1
Ashlands Rd ST4 . . . . 71 E7
Ashland St WV3 . . . . . . 266 B8
Ash La B79 . . . . 236 F6
Ashlar Cl B79 . . . . 42 A8
Ash La ST15 . . . . 118 E5
Ashlea Ct TF9 . . . . 97 E2
Ashlea B78 . . . . 262 F5
Ashlea Dr B6 . . . . 81 D7
Ashleigh Ave DE11 . . . . . 186 F5
Ashleigh Cres ST19 . . . . 205 C7
Ashleigh Dr
  Tamworth B77 . . . . 261 E8
  Uttoxeter ST14 . . . . 110 F1
Ashleigh Rd
  Rugeley WS15 . . . . 196 E7
  Upper Tean ST10 . . . . 92 E4
Ashley Cl Burton u T DE15 . 167 A3
  Kingswinford DY6 . . . . . 275 C4
  Stafford ST16 . . . . 155 A4
  Stourbridge DY8 . . . . . . 279 D2
Ashley Croft ST20 . . . . . 190 A8
Ashley Ct DE15 . . . . 167 A3
Ashley Gdns WV8 . . . . . 238 F4
Ashley Gr ST5 . . . . 56 C4
Ashley Mount WV6. . . . . 255 D5
Ashley Rd Burntwood WS7 211 E1
  Kidderminster DY10. . . . 280 B5
  Walsall WS3. . . . . 242 F1
  Wolverhampton WV4 . . . 265 E5
Ashley View TF9 . . . . 97 C1
Ashmall WS7 . . . . 229 D4
Ashman St ST6 . . . . 42 C2
Ashmead Rd WS7 . . . . . 229 A8
Ashmole Ave WS7 . . . . . 229 E8
Ashmole Cl WS14 . . . . . 231 E6
Ashmore Ave WV11 . . . . 242 A1
Ashmore Dr ST20 . . . . . 171 D7
Ashmore Wlk ST1 . . . . . 282 C3
Ashover Gr ST6 . . . . 41 E8
Ashover Rd DE11. . . . . . 186 E5
Ash Park Ind Est WS11 . . 210 B3
Ash Rd ST15 . . . . 120 B7
Ashridge Ave ST5 . . . . . . 71 B2
Ashridge Gr ST3 . . . . 73 D5
Ashridge Wlk ST16 . . . . 136 D1
Ash Rise ST17 . . . . 174 E4
Ash St Burton u T DE14. . 166 B1
  Walsall WS3. . . . . 243 D1
Ashton Cl CW12 . . . . 6 B1
Ashton Ct
  Newcastle-u-L ST5. . . . . . 71 C2
  Werrington ST9 . . . . 59 A3
Ashton Dr WV4 . . . . 244 C2
Ashtree Bank WS15 . . . . 197 B6
Ashtree Cl ST18. . . . . . . 177 D8
Ashtree Ct ST18 . . . . . . 209 D4
Ash Tree Hill ST10 . . . . . . 76 C2
Ash Tree La WS13. . . . . . 215 A1

Ash Tree Rd DE13 . . . . . . 183 D1
Ashtree Rd WS3 . . . . 244 A3
Ashurst Gr 🄲 ST3. . . . . . 90 B7
Ash View
  Huntington WS12. . . . . . 209 D8
  Kidsgrove ST7 . . . . 26 B2
Ash Way Newcastle-u-L ST5 71 A4
  Werrington ST2 . . . . 58 F3
Ashwell Rd ST4 . . . . 71 D8
Ashwood Ave DY8 . . . . . 275 D2
Ashwood Cl TF9 . . . . 97 A1
Ashwood Gr
  Blythe Bridge ST11 . . . . . 91 A6
  Wolverhampton WV4 . . . 266 A5
Ashwoodhay DY8 . . . . . . 275 F3
Ashwood DY8 . . . . 284 C4
Ashwood Park Prim Sch
  DY8 . . . . 275 D1
Ashwood Terr ST13 . . . . 284 C5
Ashworth Ave DE15 . . . . 167 C2
Ashworth Ho
  🄱 Lichfield WS13 . . . . . 231 B8
  Cannock WS11 . . . . 210 A4
Ashworth St ST4 . . . . 72 D6
Ashworth Way TF10. . . . 168 F2
Askerbank La SK11. . . . . . 8 A1
Askern Cl ST3 . . . . 73 E1
Askew Bridge Rd DY3 . . 271 B3
Askew Cl DY3 . . . . 271 E5
Aspen Cl
  🄱 Lichfield WS13 . . . . . 231 E8
  Harriseahead ST7. . . . . . . 26 E3
Aspen Croft ST17 . . . . . . 174 B8
Aspen Ct WS12 . . . . 211 A6
Aspen Gr WS7 . . . . 228 F8
Aspen Rd DE13 . . . . 201 D8
Aspen Way TF10 . . . . . . 168 F2
Asphodel B74 . . . . 257 F5
Aspley Cl WV10 . . . . 224 E5
Aspley La WV10. . . . . . . 224 D3
Asquith Ct ST3 . . . . 27 E8
Asquith Dr WS11 . . . . . . 210 C2
Astbury Cl Kidsgrove ST7 . . 26 C3
  Walsall WS3. . . . . 243 A4
Astbury Lane Ends CW12. 15 F8
Astbury St Mary's CE Prim
  Sch CW12 . . . . 15 B8
Aster Cl ST3 . . . . 74 B6
Aster Dr DE15 . . . . 166 F1
Astil St DE15 . . . . 166 F1
Astle Pl ST1 . . . . 282 C1
Astles Rock Wlk DY7. . . . 278 A3
Aston Bk ST16,ST18. . . . 154 F4
Aston Cl Colwich ST18. . . 177 D8
  Penkridge ST19 . . . . 208 A2
  Shenstone WS14 . . . . . . 246 F6
Aston Dr TF10 . . . . 168 E2
Aston La Aston TF9 . . . . . 83 F8
  Claverley WV5 . . . . 267 F3
  Stone ST15 . . . . 120 D3
  Sudbury DE6 . . . . 129 A5
Aston Lodge Parkway
  ST15 . . . . 120 D6
Aston Rd ST5 . . . . 40 D1
Aston St WV3 . . . . 266 B8
Aston Terr ST16 . . . . 155 E6
Astoria Cl WV12 . . . . . . 242 D1
Astoria Dr ST17 . . . . 174 F6
Astoria Gdns Newcastle-u-L WV12. . . . 242 D1
Astor Rd Aldridge B74 . . . 257 A1
  Kingswinford DY6 . . . . . 275 F5
Astro Gr ST3 . . . . 284 A4
Astron Bsns Pk DE11. . . . 186 F3
Athelney Ct WS3 . . . . . . 244 A4
Athelstan Cl ST19 . . . . . 208 A8
Athelstan Gr WV6 . . . . . 254 F5
Athelstan St 🄰 ST6 . . . . . 41 D3
Athelstan Way B79. . . . . 249 F7
Athena Rd ST1 . . . . 57 F5
Atherstone Rd ST4 . . . . . 88 A7
Atherstone St B77,B78.. 261 B8
Athelstan Way DE13. . . . 147 C1
Athlone St ST6. . . . . 42 D2
Atholl Rd ST3 . . . . 284 D1
Atkins Way ST14 . . . . 95 F3
Atlam Cl ST2 . . . . 58 A3
Atlantic Gr ST4 . . . . 88 B8
Atlas St ST4 . . . . 72 E5
Attingham Dr WS11 . . . . 210 B2
Attlee Cres Rugeley WS15 196 F7
  Stafford ST17 . . . . 174 D7
Attlee Gr WS11 . . . . 210 C2
Attlee Rd WS11 . . . . 76 D2
Attwell Pk WV3 . . . . 265 D7
Attwood Gdns WV4 . . . . 266 A4
Attwood Rd WS7 . . . . . . 228 C2
Attwood St ST7 . . . . 26 A2
Aubrey St ST6 . . . . 41 B7
Auchinleck Dr WS13 . . . 214 C1
Auckland Dr DY6 . . . . . . 275 E4
Auckland St ST6 . . . . 57 A8
Auden Ct WV6 . . . . 254 F5
Auden Pl ST3 . . . . 284 D4
Auden Way ST17 . . . . . . 174 C8
Audlem Rd CW3 . . . . 67 B2
Audley Ave TF10 . . . . . . 169 A2
Audley Avenue Bsns Pk
  TF10 . . . . 169 B2
Audley Avenue Ind Est
  TF10 . . . . 169 B2
Audley Cl DE13 . . . . 201 A3

Audley Ho TF10. . . . . . . 169 A2
Audley House Mews
  TF10. . . . . 169 A2
Audley Pl ST5. . . . . 71 B5
Audley Rd Audley ST7 . . . 39 D8
  Barthomley CW2 . . . . 38 E5
  Newcastle-u-L ST7,ST5. . . 40 B2
  Newport TF10 . . . . 168 F3
  Talke ST7 . . . . 40 B6
Audley St
  Newcastle-u-L ST5. . . . . . 55 E3
  Stoke-on-T ST6 . . . . 41 D3
Audmore Rd ST20. . . . . . 171 D7
Audnam DY8 . . . . 275 F1
Augustine Cl ST15 . . . . . 120 C7
Augustine Gr B74. . . . . . 257 F5
Augustines Wlk WS13 . . 214 A3
Aulton Rd B75 . . . . 258 E2
Aumbry Cl TF9. . . . . 97 A1
Austcliffe Dr DY10 . . . . . 280 C5
Austcliffe Pk DY10 . . . . . 280 B6
Austcliffe Rd DY10 . . . . . 280 B5
Austin Cl Cheadle ST10. . . 76 C2
  Dudley DY1 . . . . 271 F2
  Stone ST15 . . . . 120 A7
Austin Cote La WS14 . . . 231 F7
Austin Ct B74. . . . . 257 E3
Austin Friars ST17 . . . . . 285 B1
Austin St ST1 . . . . 282 C1
Austrey La
  Newton Regis B79 . . . . . 236 E3
  No Man's Heath B79 . . . . 236 F6
Austwick Gr ST4 . . . . 71 E5
Autumn Berry Gr DY3 . . 271 E6
Autumn Cl WS4. . . . . . . 244 C1
Autumn Dr Dudley DY3 . . 271 D4
  Lichfield WS13 . . . . 214 C3
  Walsall WS4. . . . . 244 C2
Avalon Ho 🄱 WS11 . . . . 209 F4
Aveling Gn ST1 . . . . 57 F8
Aveling Rd ST1 . . . . 57 F8
Avenue One CW1 . . . . . . 37 C8
Avenue Rd Cannock WS12 210 E2
  Newport TF10 . . . . 168 F2
Avenue Rd S TF10. . . . . . 168 F2
Avenue Rd Stoke-on-T ST4 . 57 C3
  Wolverhampton WV3. . . . 255 E2
Avenue The Bagnall ST9. . . 43 F4
  Blakedown DY10 . . . . . . 281 B2
  Blythe Bridge ST11 . . . . . 91 A7
  Cheadle ST10. . . . . 76 D2
  Cheddleton ST13 . . . . . . 45 C4
  Endon ST9 . . . . 43 E7
  Enville WV5 . . . . 273 D1
  Featherstone WV10 . . . . 241 C7
  Kidsgrove ST7 . . . . 25 F1
  Newcastle-u-L,Basford ST5 56 D2
  Newcastle-u-L ST4 . . . . . . 71 D8
  Stone ST15 . . . . 105 A2
  Stretton ST19 . . . . 206 D3
  Wolverhampton,Castlecroft
  WV3 . . . . 265 B8
  Wolverhampton,Penn WV4 265 E4
  Wootton DE6 . . . . 79 C5
Avenue Two CW1 . . . . . . 37 C8
Averill Dr WS15 . . . . 178 D2
Averill Rd ST17 . . . . 174 D8
Aviation La DE13 . . . . . . 165 C4
Avill B77 . . . . 262 A5
Avington Cl DY3 . . . . . . 271 D4
Avion Cl ST3. . . . . 90 C7
Avoca St ST1 . . . . 282 C4
Avon Bsns Pk WS11 . . . . 226 C7
Avon Cl Kidsgrove ST7. . . . 26 B2
  Newcastle-u-L ST5. . . . . . 71 B4
  Perton WV6 . . . . 254 F4
  Stafford ST16 . . . . 156 B3
Avon Cres WS3 . . . . 244 A4
Avoncroft 🄷 WV4 . . . . . 266 F4
Avondale Cl DY6 . . . . . . 275 D8
Avondale Rd WV6 . . . . . 255 F3
Avondale St ST6 . . . . 56 D4
Avon Gr Cheadle ST10 . . . 76 E1
  Loggerheads TF9 . . . . 99 C5
  Stone ST15 . . . . 120 B6
Avon Hill ST16 . . . . 156 C3
Avon Ho DY3 . . . . 271 E3
Avonlea Gdns WS15. . . . 178 C1
Avon Rd Burntwood WS7. . 228 C5
  Cannock WS11. . . . . 226 D8
  Stourbridge DY8 . . . . . . 279 C3
  Walsall WS3. . . . . 243 E1
Avon Rise ST16 . . . . 156 B4
Avonside Ave ST6. . . . . . 41 F4
Avon B77. . . . . 262 A5
Avon Way
  Burton u T DE15. . . . . . . 167 A1
  Hilton DE65 . . . . 147 D8
Avonwick Gr ST1. . . . . . . 58 A6
Axborough La DY10 . . . . 280 C6
Axbridge Wlk ST6 . . . . . . 42 C1
Axon Cres ST3 . . . . 74 B3
Aylesbury Rd ST2 . . . . . . 58 C2
Aylesford Cl DY3. . . . . . . 266 C2
Aylesford Dr B74. . . . . . . 257 E5
Aynsley Ave ST5 . . . . 71 B3
Aynsley Cl ST10. . . . . 76 D1
Aynsley Rd ST4 . . . . 57 B1
Aynsley's Dr ST11. . . . . . . 90 E7
Aynsley Specl Sch ST11 . . 90 E7
Ayreshire Gr ST3 . . . . 73 D1
Ayr Rd ST10 . . . . 76 E5
Ayrshire Way CW12 . . . . . 6 A1
Ayrton Cl WV6 . . . . 255 A4
Ayshford St ST3 . . . . 284 B3
Azalea Cl WV8 . . . . 239 B3

Babbacombe Ave ST17 . . **175** E8
Babbington Cl
  Tutbury DE13 . . . . **146** C5
  Whittington WS14 . . . . . . **232** E5
Babworth Cl WV9 . . . . **240** A2
Back Browning ST16 . . **285** A4
Backcester La WS13 . . . **231** B8
Backcrofts 3 WS11 . . . **209** H3
Back Cross La CW12 . . . . . **16** A8
Back Ford Green Rd ST6 . **42** D2
Back Garden St ST5 . . . . **283** C2
Back Heathcote St ST7 . . **26** A2
Back La Aldridge WS9 . . . . **256** F8
  Alstonefield DE6 . . . . **35** E3
  Alton ST10 . . . . **78** F1
  Ashley TF9 . . . . **100** A5
  Betley CW3 . . . . **53** B8
  Brown Edge,Hodgefield ST6 **28** B1
  Brown Edge ST6 . . . . **43** B7
  Colwich ST18 . . . . **177** D8
  Cotes Heath ST21 . . . . . . **102** D5
  Ellastone DE6 . . . . **80** A3
  Gnosall ST20 . . . . **171** C5
  Haughton ST18 . . . . **173** A5
  Hixon ST18 . . . . **139** C1
  Leek ST13 . . . . **30** F6
  Ranton ST18 . . . . **153** D4
  Shenstone WS14 . . . . **246** E1
  Sutton TF10 . . . . **150** D1
  Uttoxeter ST14 . . . . **126** C8
  Warslow SK17 . . . . **23** A2
  Waterhouses ST10 . . . . . . **49** E1
  Weston-Under-Lizard
    TF11 . . . . **203** D6
  Wheaton Aston ST19 . . . . **205** C5
  Whittington WS14 . . . . . . **232** E6
  Woodseaves ST20 . . . . . . **151** D8
  Wootton DE6 . . . . **79** F7
Back Radfords 2 ST15 . . **105** A1
Back Rd DY6 . . . . **275** D4
Back Westlands Rd ST14 **126** B6
Baddeley Green La ST2 . . **43** B3
Baddeley Hall Rd ST2 . . . **43** C2
Baddeley Rd ST2 . . . . **43** B1
Baddeley St Burslem ST6 . **41** F1
  Cheadle ST10 . . . . **76** E2
Baddely's Ct TF10 . . . . . **168** F2
Baden Powell Cl WS15 . . **211** F6
Baden Rd ST6 . . . . **42** C1
Baden St ST5 . . . . **283** B4
Bader Rd WV6 . . . . **254** E1
Badger Brow Rd TF9 . . . . **99** D5
Badger Cl WS12 . . . . **209** D6
Badger Gr ST3 . . . . **90** C7
Badger La TF9,ST5 . . . . . . **84** C3
Badgers Bank Rd B74 . . **257** F5
Badgers Brow ST1 . . . . . . **57** E3
Badgers Cl WS3 . . . . **244** A5
Badgers Croft
  Derrington ST18 . . . . **154** E2
  Ecclesham ST21 . . . . **133** F7
  Newcastle-u-L ST5 . . . . . . **40** E1
  Stafford ST17 . . . . **175** C6
Badger's End ST19 . . . . . **205** B6
Badgers Hollow ST10 . . . . **93** B1
Badgers Rise ST13 . . . . . . **30** E6
Badgers Sett ST13 . . . . . . **30** E6
Badger St DY3 . . . . **271** E5
Badgers Way WS12 . . . . . **210** D1
Badgery Cl ST14 . . . . **111** A2
Badminton Cl DY1 . . . . . **271** F3
Badnall Cl ST13 . . . . **30** E6
Badnall Rd ST13 . . . . **30** D6
Baggeridge Cl DY3 . . . . . **271** A8
Baggeridge Ctry Pk★
  DY3 . . . . **270** E6
Baggott Pl ST5 . . . . **70** F8
Baggott St WV2 . . . . **266** C7
Bag La Marchington ST14 . . **127** E2
  Newton WS15 . . . . **159** D4
  Roston DE6 . . . . **96** F7
Bagnall Rd ST2 . . . . **43** C1
Bagnall St ST1 . . . . **282** B2
Bagot Gr ST1 . . . . **57** F8
Bagots Oak ST17 . . . . . . **174** C7
Bagot St WS15 . . . . **160** F6
Bagots View
  Abbots Bromley WS15 . . . **161** A6
  Church Leigh ST10 . . . . . **109** A4
Bagridge Cl WV3 . . . . . . **265** B8
Bagridge Rd WV3 . . . . . . **265** B8
Bailey Ave B77 . . . . **261** F5
Bailey Cl Burntwood WS7 . **228** D8
  Cannock WS11 . . . . **210** A4
Bailey Cres CW12 . . . . **6** A4
Bailey Rd ST3 . . . . **72** E4
Bailey's Bank ST6 . . . . . . **16** D3
Bailey St Burton u T DE14 **166** D1
  Newcastle-u-L ST5 . . . . . **283** A3
  Stafford ST17 . . . . **285** B2
  Stoke-on-T ST4 . . . . **56** F1
Bailye Cl WS13 . . . . **214** F1
Bainbridge Rd ST4 . . . . . . **88** A7
Bains Dr WS13 . . . . **231** A6
Bains Gr ST5 . . . . **55** F8
Baird Ho DY6 . . . . **275** F7
Baker Ave WV14 . . . . **266** F2
Baker Cl WS13 . . . . **231** A6
Baker Cres N ST2 . . . . **43** C3
Baker Cres S ST2 . . . . **43** B3
Baker Cres ST2 . . . . **43** C3
Baker Dr WS13 . . . . **215** C7
Bakers Gdns WV8 . . . . . **238** E4

Baker's La
  5 Lichfield WS13 . . . . . . **231** B7
  Aldridge WS9 . . . . **256** B6
  Weston Jones TF10 . . . . . **150** C4
Baker St Burntwood WS7 . **228** F6
  Burton u T DE15 . . . . **185** E7
  Stoke-on-T ST4 . . . . **72** E6
Bakers Way
  Cannock WS12 . . . . **210** B5
  Codsall WV8 . . . . **238** F4
Bakers Wlk 1 B77 . . . . . **261** F6
Bakewell Cl
  Newcastle-u-L ST5 . . . . . . **55** B1
  Walsall WS3 . . . . **243** A5
Bakewell Dr ST15 . . . . . . **120** D5
Bakewell Gn DE11 . . . . . **186** E5
Bakewell St ST4 . . . . **71** F5
Balaam's La ST15 . . . . . . **106** D6
Bala Gr ST10 . . . . **76** F4
Bala Ho ST17 . . . . **174** E6
Balcombe Cl ST5 . . . . . . **283** B1
Baldwin Gr WS11 . . . . . . **210** C2
Baldwin's Gate CE Prim Sch
  ST5 . . . . **85** D5
Baldwin Way DY3 . . . . . . **269** E2
Balfour Cres WV6 . . . . . . **255** F4
Balfour Ct
  2 Wolverhampton WV6 . . **255** F4
  Sutton Coldfield B74 . . . . **258** A3
Balfour Gr Biddulph ST8 . . **27** C8
  Stafford ST16 . . . . **155** C8
Balfour Rd DY6 . . . . **275** E8
Balfour St
  Burton u T DE13 . . . . **166** C6
  Hanley ST1 . . . . **282** B2
Balfour B79 . . . . **250** A4
Balk Pas ST16 . . . . **285** B3
Balk The DE13 . . . . **146** D6
Ballam Mews WS15 . . . . **178** E1
Ballarat Wlk DY8 . . . . . . **279** F5
Ball Green Prim Sch ST6 . **42** D5
Ball Haye Gn ST13 . . . . . . **31** A7
Ball Haye Rd ST13 . . . . . . **30** F6
Ball Hayes Rd ST6 . . . . . . **42** C5
Ball Haye St ST13 . . . . . . **30** F6
Ball Haye Terr ST13 . . . . . **30** F6
Ballington Gdns ST13 . . . . **30** F5
Ballington View ST13 . . . . **30** F4
Ballinson Rd ST3 . . . . **72** F1
Balliol Bsns Pk WV9 . . . **239** E3
Balliol St ST4 . . . . **72** A7
Ball La Coven Heath WV10 **240** C6
  Leek ST13 . . . . **30** E6
  Stoke-on-T ST6 . . . . **43** B5
Balloon St ST4 . . . . **56** D1
Ball's Yd ST5 . . . . **283** B3
Balmain Cres WV11 . . . . **241** B1
Balmoral Cl
  Lichfield WS14 . . . . **231** D6
  Stoke-on-T ST4 . . . . **72** A2
  Stone ST15 . . . . **120** B6
Balmoral Ct WS11 . . . . . **210** A5
Balmoral Dr
  Cannock WS12 . . . . **209** F7
  Cheadle ST10 . . . . **76** B2
  Market Drayton TF9 . . . . . . **97** E2
  Wombourne WV5 . . . . . . **265** A1
Balmoral Rd
  Burton u T DE15 . . . . **167** A3
  Stafford ST17 . . . . **156** C1
  Stourbridge DY8 . . . . **275** C2
  Sutton Coldfield B74 . . . . **257** F5
  Wolverhampton WV4 . . . . **266** A5
Balmoral View DY1 . . . . **271** E2
Balmoral Way WS7 . . . . . **211** E1
Balterley Rd CW2 . . . . **53** C8
Baltic Cl Cannock WS11 . . **209** E2
  Stoke-on-T ST4 . . . . **88** B7
Balvenie Way DY1 . . . . . **271** F4
Bamber Cl WV3 . . . . **265** E8
Bamber Pl ST5 . . . . **55** F6
Bamber St ST4 . . . . **72** B8
Bamborough Cl DE13 . . . **166** D7
Bamburgh B77 . . . . **261** C7
Bambury St ST3 . . . . **73** C6
Bamford Cl WS3 . . . . **243** C3
Bamford Gr Hanley ST1 . . **282** A4
  Uttoxeter ST14 . . . . **110** F2
Bamford Ho WS3 . . . . . . **243** C3
Bamford Rd Walsall WS3 . **243** C3
  Wolverhampton WV3 . . . . **266** A8
Bamford St B77 . . . . **250** B8
Bampton Ave 4 WS7 . . . **229** A8
Bampton Ct ST5 . . . . **43** F8
Banbery Dr WV5 . . . . **269** F4
Banbury Cl DY3 . . . . **271** E6
Banbury Gr ST8 . . . . **27** C7
Banbury Rd WS11 . . . . . . **226** C8
Banbury St ST7 . . . . **25** D1
Bancroft La
  Blythe Bridge ST11 . . . . . . **90** F6
  Nethertown WS15 . . . . . . **199** A8
Bancroft B77 . . . . **250** E4
Bandridge La SK11 . . . . . **18** A8
Baneberry Dr WV10 . . . . **241** B1
Bangley La
  Drayton Bassett B78 . . . . **259** E6
  Mile Oak B78 . . . . **260** A8
Bangor Terr ST10 . . . . **63** E4
Bank Cl ST14 . . . . **126** C7
Bank Cres WS7 . . . . **228** F5
Bank Ct 5 ST7 . . . . **26** A2
Bank End ST6 . . . . **43** B7
Bankerwall La DE6 . . . . . . **80** C7
Bankfield Gr ST5 . . . . **54** E4

Bankfield Rd ST3 . . . . **89** F8
Bank Hall Rd ST6 . . . . **42** B2
Bank Ho ST10 . . . . **76** D3
Bankhouse Dr CW12 . . . . . **6** A5
Bank House Dr ST5 . . . . . **56** E2
Bankhouse Rd
  Forsbrook ST11 . . . . **91** B8
  Stoke-on-T ST4 . . . . **71** F1
  Trentham ST4 . . . . **87** F8
Bank Pas ST16 . . . . **285** B3
Bank Rd DY3 . . . . **271** C2
Bank Side SK17 . . . . **24** D6
Bankside Meaford ST15 . . **104** D4
  Newcastle-u-L ST5 . . . . . **283** C2
  Stanton DE6 . . . . **65** C1
Bank Side ST15 . . . . **119** F6
Bankside Way WS9 . . . . . **245** B2
Bankside WV5 . . . . **269** F7
Banks La ST10 . . . . **61** E4
Banksman Rd ST2 . . . . **73** D7
Bank St Cannock WS12 . . **210** E1
  Cheadle ST10 . . . . **76** D3
  Kidsgrove ST7 . . . . **26** C4
  Stoke-on-T ST6 . . . . **41** D4
Bank The ST7 . . . . **26** B7
Bank Top Ave ST6 . . . . **42** A3
Banktop Ct ST5 . . . . **56** C6
Bank Top La ST17 . . . . . . **175** B1
Banktop Rd DE6 . . . . **144** B6
Bank Top WS15 . . . . **178** D1
Bank View ST10 . . . . **62** A3
Bank Wlk DE13 . . . . **166** B8
Banky Brook Cl ST6 . . . . . **42** C3
Bannister Ct ST4 . . . . **72** B4
Bannut Tree La DY7 . . . . . **277** C5
Banstead Cl WV2 . . . . . . **266** E7
Bantock Ave WV3 . . . . . . **265** E1
Bantock Ct WV3 . . . . **265** E1
Bantock Gdns WV3 . . . . . **255** E1
Bantock House Mus★
  WV3 . . . . **255** F1
Bantock Prim Sch WV3 . . **266** A8
Baonal Way WS15 . . . . . . **118** B6
Baptist St 9 ST6 . . . . **57** A8
Barbara St B79 . . . . **250** A5
Barber Cl WS12 . . . . **210** E2
Barber Dr ST7 . . . . **25** E7
Barber Pl ST6 . . . . **41** F6
Barber Rd ST6 . . . . **41** F6
Barber's Sq ST5 . . . . **56** D4
Barbridge Rd ST5 . . . . **40** D1
Barbrook Ave ST3 . . . . **73** E4
Barclay Cl WV7 . . . . **237** B6
Barclay St ST3 . . . . **73** C5
Barcliff Ave B77 . . . . **250** E3
Bardell Cl WS13 . . . . **230** E6
Bardolph Cl DE11 . . . . . . **186** F3
Bardsey Wlk 1 ST3 . . . . . **73** A3
Bardwell Cl WV8 . . . . **255** F8
Bardy La Armitage WS15 . **197** B3
  Longdon WS15 . . . . **197** C1
Barford Rd ST5 . . . . **70** F3
Barford St ST3 . . . . **284** B3
Bargate La ST19 . . . . **223** C6
Bargate St ST19 . . . . **223** C6
Bargery Rd WV11 . . . . . . **242** A1
Bargrave Dr ST5 . . . . **56** B8
Bargrave St ST2 . . . . **58** D1
Bar Hill CW3 . . . . **68** C4
Barker Cl ST16 . . . . **155** C3
Barker Ho ST3 . . . . **88** F8
Barker St Longton ST3 . . . **284** B1
  Newcastle-u-L ST5 . . . . . . **55** F6
Barks Dr ST6 . . . . **42** C4
Bar La DE13 . . . . **183** A2
Barlaston CE Fst Sch
  ST12 . . . . **88** E1
Barlaston Cl ST16 . . . . . . **155** B4
Barlaston Hall★ ST12 . . . **88** E3
Barlaston Old Rd ST4 . . . . **88** B5
Barlaston Rd Barlaston ST3 **89** B5
  Stoke-on-T ST3 . . . . **88** F7
Barlaston Sta ST12 . . . . . **88** D1
Barley Cl Aldridge WS9 . . **256** E2
  Burton u T DE14 . . . . **166** E6
  Cannock WS12 . . . . **210** B5
  Dudley DY3 . . . . **271** F7
  Wolverhampton WV8 . . . . **239** E1
Barleycorn Cl DE15 . . . . . **167** A1
Barleycroft ST10 . . . . **76** E1
Barley Croft WS9 . . . . . . **254** D3
Barleycroft Terr ST7 . . . . . **25** F7
Barley Croft WS14 . . . . . **232** E6
Barley Field WV3 . . . . . . **191** A8
Barley Fields Audley ST7 . . **39** D2
  Stoke-on-T ST6 . . . . **42** C3
Barleyfields Audley ST7 . . . **39** D2
Barleyford Dr ST3 . . . . **73** D6
Barley Green La DE13 . . . **201** C1
Barley Orch ST20 . . . . . . **171** E6
Barley Rd ST10 . . . . **62** A8
Barlow Cl B77 . . . . **250** E4
Barlow St ST3 . . . . **284** C3
Barlstone Ave ST11 . . . . . **90** F6
Barmouth Cl ST6 . . . . **27** E6
Barmouth Gr ST8 . . . . **27** B2
Barnaby Sq WV10 . . . . . **240** F4
Barnard Pl WV2 . . . . **266** E4
Barnard Rd WV11 . . . . . . **241** F1
Barnard Way WS11 . . . . . **209** F2
Barn Ave DY3 . . . . **271** C5
Barn Bank La ST17,ST18 . **174** D5
Barnbridge B77 . . . . **250** C2
Barn Cl Dordon B78 . . . . . **262** F6
  Lichfield WS13 . . . . **214** B3

Barn Cl continued
  Rugeley WS15 . . . . **197** B5
  Stafford ST17 . . . . **174** E5
Barn Comm ST20 . . . . . . **151** D8
Barn Croft
  Burntwood WS7 . . . . **229** A4
  Great Wyrley WS6 . . . . . . **227** A3
Barncroft Rd ST5 . . . . **42** C6
Barn Ct ST5 . . . . **71** C3
Barn End Rd ST17 . . . . . . **193** B8
Barnescroft WS15 . . . . . . **106** D2
Barnes Rd
  Shenstone WS14 . . . . **247** A6
  Stafford ST17 . . . . **174** C7
Barnes Way ST3 . . . . **73** C1
Barnett Cl DY6 . . . . **275** D4
Barnett Gn DY6 . . . . **275** D4
Barnett Gr ST6 . . . . **41** F5
Barnett La DY6,DY8 . . . . . **275** D4
Barnetts La WS8 . . . . **228** F1
Barnett DY8 . . . . **275** D3
Barnfield Cl
  Lichfield WS13 . . . . **231** B6
  Stone ST15 . . . . **119** F7
Barnfield Pl ST13 . . . . **30** E4
Barnfield Rd Burslem ST6 . **57** A7
  Leek ST13 . . . . **30** D4
  Upper Tean ST10 . . . . **92** E4
Barnfields Cl ST13 . . . . . . **30** D3
Barnfields La ST13 . . . . . . **61** D2
Barnfields Prim Sch
  ST17 . . . . **175** C6
Barnfield ST4 . . . . **71** F6
Barnfield Way
  Cannock WS12 . . . . **211** A6
  Stafford ST17 . . . . **175** C6
Barngate St ST13 . . . . **30** D5
Barn Gn WV3 . . . . **265** D5
Barnhurst La WV8 . . . . . . **239** E2
Barn La Brewood ST19 . . . **223** C7
  Standon ST21 . . . . **101** C5
Barnlea Gr ST3 . . . . **90** A5
Barnmeadow Cl TF10 . . . **169** A3
Barnmeadow Rd TF10 . . . **169** A2
Barn Owl Dr WS3 . . . . . . **243** F4
Barn Rd WS15 . . . . **198** C4
Barns Cl WS9 . . . . **244** F4
Barns Croft B74 . . . . **257** B4
Barnsdale Cl ST4 . . . . **88** C5
Barnswood Cl WS11 . . . . **226** B8
Barnton Edge ST5 . . . . . **104** E3
Barnwell Cl ST14 . . . . . . **111** A4
Barnwell Gr ST4 . . . . **72** A1
Barnwood Rd WV8 . . . . . **239** E1
Baron Cl WS7 . . . . **211** E1
Baron St ST4 . . . . **284** A5
Baron's Way ST18 . . . . . . **158** C8
Barracks La WS9,WS14 . . **245** C8
Barracks Rd ST5 . . . . **283** C2
Barracks Sq ST5 . . . . **283** C2
Barracks Way 2 ST13 . . . . **30** D6
Barrage Rd ST8 . . . . **28** B7
Barrar Cl DY8 . . . . **279** E8
Barratt Gdns ST2 . . . . **58** B8
Barratts Croft DY5 . . . . . **271** C1
Barr Common Cl WS9 . . . **256** B3
Barr Common Rd WS9 . . **256** B3
Barrett Cres ST6 . . . . **57** A6
Barrett Dr ST5 . . . . **57** A6
Barrie Gdns ST7 . . . . **40** C8
Barrington Cl
  Albrighton WV7 . . . . **237** A5
  Stretton DE13 . . . . **147** C1
  Wolverhampton WV10 . . . **240** C1
Barrington Ct ST5 . . . . **56** E3
Barrow Cl WS9 . . . . **244** F4
Barrow Hill Rd DY5 . . . . . **271** C3
Barr St DY3 . . . . **271** C3
Barry Ave ST2 . . . . **58** A4
Bartholomew Rd ST3 . . . . **73** F1
Bartholmey Rd Audley ST7 **39** A2
  Balterley ST7 . . . . **38** F3
  Barthomley CW2 . . . . **38** B7
  Hanley ST1 . . . . **57** D6
Bartic Ave DY6 . . . . **275** F4
Bartlem St ST3 . . . . **284** D5
Bartlett Cl ST19 . . . . **207** F8
Barton Cottage Hospl
  DE13 . . . . **183** D1
Barton Cres ST6 . . . . **41** E1
Barton Gate DE13 . . . . . . **183** B2
Barton La Bradley ST18 . . **191** A8
  Kingswinford DY6 . . . . . . **275** C8
Barton Lodge DE13 . . . . . **183** D1
Barton Rd WV4 . . . . **266** F4
Barton's La TF9 . . . . **112** B8
Barton's Rd TF9 . . . . **112** B8
Barton St DE14 . . . . **185** C8
Barton Turn DE13 . . . . . . **184** A1
Bar Wlk WS9 . . . . **245** C1
Barwood Ave ST7 . . . . **25** A5
Basfordbridge La ST13 . . . **45** D4
Basfordbridge Terr ST13 . . **45** E8
Basford La ST13 . . . . **45** F8
Basford Lane Ind Est
  ST13 . . . . **45** F8
Basford Park Rd ST5 . . . . . **56** D3
Basford View ST13 . . . . . . **45** D6
Basford Villas ST5 . . . . . . **56** D2
Basil Cl ST17 . . . . **174** F5
Basildon Gr ST3 . . . . **284** C4
Basin La DY3 . . . . **250** D3
Baskerville Rd ST1 . . . . . **282** C3
Baskeyfield Cl WS14 . . . . **231** D7
Baskeyfield Pl ST6 . . . . . . **42** B5
Baslow Cl WS3 . . . . **243** C3

Baslow Gn DE11 . . . . **186** E5
Baslow Rd WS3 . . . . **243** B3
Basnett's Wood ST9 . . . . . **43** E6
Bass Cotts DE14 . . . . **166** E4
Bassenthwaite Ct DY6 . . **275** D6
Bassett Cl Cheadle ST10 . . **76** D3
  Wolverhampton WV4 . . . . **265** C6
Bassilow Rd ST4 . . . . **72** F7
Bass's Bldgs DE14 . . . . . **166** B3
Baswich Bsns Pk ST17 . . **156** D2
Baswich Crest ST17 . . . . **156** D1
Baswich House Dr ST17 . **175** D7
Baswich House Way
  ST17. . . . . **175** D7
Baswich La ST17,ST18 . . . **156** D2
Batchelor Cl DY8. . . . . . . **279** F8
Batch La DE6 . . . . **127** B7
Bateman Ave ST8 . . . . **27** B5
Batesmans Way ST14. . . . **126** C8
Bateswaw WS15 . . . . **197** C4
Batfield La DY7 . . . . **272** E2
Bath Ct ST17 . . . . **285** B1
Bath La DY7 . . . . **277** D5
Bath Mews DY8 . . . . **279** F5
Batholdi Way ST17 . . . . . **175** A8
Bath Rd Cannock WS11 . . **209** E5
  Newcastle-u-L ST5 . . . . . . **54** F2
  Stourbridge DY8 . . . . **279** F5
Baths La ST18 . . . . **158** C8
Baths Pas ST3 . . . . **284** B4
Baths Rd ST3 . . . . **284** B4
Bath St Leek ST13 . . . . **30** F6
  Meir ST3 . . . . **74** B5
  Sedgley DY3 . . . . **266** E1
  Stoke-on-T ST4 . . . . **72** A7
Bath Terr 9 ST4 . . . . **72** A7
Bathurst St ST3 . . . . **284** C4
Bath Vale Cotts CW12 . . . . **6** A3
Batkin Cl ST6 . . . . **42** B5
Batten Cl ST3 . . . . **90** A5
Batten Wlk ST15 . . . . **118** F6
Battison Cres ST3 . . . . . . **284** C2
Battlefield Hill WV5 . . . . **270** B7
Battlefield La WV5 . . . . . **270** B6
Battlefield Terr WV5 . . . . **270** B6
Battle Ridge ST18 . . . . . . **156** D8
Battlesteads ST10 . . . . **78** D1
Baulk La ST11 . . . . **106** E8
Baxter Gn ST16 . . . . **155** B4
Bayham Wlk ST2 . . . . **58** A4
Bayley Hills TF10 . . . . . . **168** A3
Baylie Ct DY8 . . . . **279** F5
Baylie St DY8 . . . . **279** F4
Bayliss Ct WV3 . . . . **255** E2
Bayston Ave WV3 . . . . . . **265** E8
Bayswater Rd
  Dudley DY3 . . . . **271** D2
  Rugeley WS15 . . . . **178** D1
Baytree Cl
  Birches Head ST1 . . . . **57** F6
  Walsall WS3 . . . . **243** A2
Baytree Rd WS3 . . . . **243** A2
Baytree Wlk WS14 . . . . . **232** E6
Baywood Cl ST17 . . . . . . **156** C1
Beach Ave WV14 . . . . . . **266** F3
Beachcroft Rd DY6 . . . . . **270** C1
Beachwood Ave DY6 . . . . **270** C1
Beacon Ctr for the Blind
  WV4 . . . . **266** D4
Beacon Dr DE13 . . . . **147** B3
Beaconfields 1 WS13 . . . **231** A8
Beacon Gdns WS13 . . . . **214** A1
Beacon Hill WS9 . . . . **256** C1
Beacon La Kinver DY7 . . . **277** B2
  Romsley DY11,DY12,WV15 **276** E1
  Sedgley DY3 . . . . **266** E1
Beacon Pas DY3 . . . . **266** D1
Beacon Pk ST19 . . . . **221** F7
Beacon Rd Aldridge WS9 . **256** B1
  Rolleston on D DE13 . . . . **147** B3
  Stone ST15 . . . . **120** A5
Beacon Rise
  Aldridge WS9 . . . . **256** B3
  Sedgley DY3 . . . . **266** E1
  Stone ST15 . . . . **120** A5
Beaconsfield Ave WV4 . . **266** D5
Beaconsfield Dr
  Stoke-on-T ST3 . . . . **72** E1
  Stoke-on-T ST3 . . . . **88** E8
  Wolverhampton WV4 . . . . **266** D6
Beaconsfield ST5 . . . . **56** C7
Beaconsfield Rd DE13 . . . **166** B7
Beaconside Cl ST16 . . . . . **156** A5
Beaconside Sports Ctr
  ST18 . . . . **156** D4
Beaconside
  Stafford,Beaconside
    ST16 . . . . **156** B5
  Stafford ST16 . . . . **136** D1
Beacon St Lichfield WS13 . **231** A8
  Wolverhampton WV14 . . . **266** F1
Beacon Trad Est WS9 . . . **256** A6
Beacon Way
  Brownhills WS9 . . . . **245** A3
  Cannock WS12 . . . . **210** F3
Beadnell Gr ST3 . . . . **73** C1
Beale St DY8 . . . . **279** F5
Bealeys Cl WS3 . . . . **243** A3
Bealeys La WS3 . . . . **243** A2
Beamhill Rd DE13 . . . . . . **165** F8
Beamish La WV7,WV8 . . . **237** C5
Beard Gr ST2 . . . . **58** B7
Bearnett Dr WV4 . . . . **265** C2
Bearnett La WV4 . . . . **265** B2

Bearstone Rd
Bearstone TF9 . . . . 83 A4
Knighton TF9 . . . . 83 C4
Norton in H TF9 . . . . 82 E3
Beasley Ave ST5 . . . . 55 F7
Beasley Pl ST5 . . . . 55 F7
Beata Rd ST5 . . . . 40 F1
Beat La Ryecroft Gate SK11 18 A8
Woodhouse Green ST8 . . . . 17 E8
Beaton Rd B74 . . . . 258 A3
Beatrice Cl ST4 . . . . 72 A2
Beatrice Ct DE14 . . . . . . 166 B4
Beatrice Rd ST5 . . . . 283 B4
Beattie Ave ST5 . . . . 283 B4
Beatty Dr CW12 . . . . 6 A4
Beatty Rd ST13 . . . . 31 A6
Beaubrook Gdns DY6 . . . 275 E3
Beauchamp Rd B77 . . . . 261 F5
Beauchamp Ind Pk B77 . 261 D8
Beau Ct WS11 . . . . 209 F1
Beaudesert WS7 . . . . . . 212 A1
Beaudesert View WS12 . 211 A5
Beaufighter Gr ST6 . . . . . 41 C5
Beaufort Ave ST9 . . . . . . 59 A3
Beaufort Ct ST3 . . . . 73 F1
Beaufort Rd
Burton u T DE15 . . . . 167 B1
Longton ST3 . . . . 284 C2
Beaufort Way WS9 . . . . . 256 B4
Beaulieu Ave DY6 . . . . . 275 F4
Beaulieu Cl ST9 . . . . 59 B3
Beaumaris Cl Dudley DY1 . 271 F4
Stoke-on-T ST4 . . . . 71 D8
Beaumaris Ct ST4 . . . . . 283 A2
Beaumaris Rd TF10 . . . . 168 E3
Beaumont Cl Biddulph ST8 16 D3
Great Wyrley WS6 . . . . . . 226 F2
Beaumont Ct ST5 . . . . . . 70 F3
Beaumont Gdns ST17 . . 174 B8
Beaumont Rd
Great Wyrley WS6 . . . . . . 226 F2
Stoke-on-T ST6 . . . . 41 E3
Beaumont Rise ST11 . . . . 90 D3
Beaumont Way WS11 . . 228 A4
Beauty Bank Cres DY8 . . 279 F6
Beauty Bank Prim Sch
DY8 . . . . 279 F6
Beaver Cl ST4 . . . . 71 E4
Beaver Dr ST10 . . . . 76 E2
Bebington Cl WV8 . . . . . 255 F8
Beckbury Ave WV4 . . . . 265 C5
Beckdale ST14 . . . . 126 A8
Beckenham Cl ST3 . . . . . 90 C8
Becket Cl Burton u T DE13 166 B6
Sutton Coldfield B74 . . . . 257 F6
Beckett Ave ST3 . . . . 74 B1
Becketts Ct ST3 . . . . 166 C7
Beckford St ST1 . . . . . . 282 C4
Beckfields Cl ST8 . . . . . . 17 B1
Beckminster Rd WV3 . . . 265 F7
Beck Rd CW3 . . . . 68 F7
Beck's La DE13 . . . . 162 F2
Beck The B79 . . . . 216 E2
Beckton Ave ST6 . . . . . . 41 E3
Bedale Pl ST3 . . . . 72 E1
Bedcroft ST12 . . . . 88 F2
Beddow Way ST6 . . . . . . 41 F6
Bedford Ave ST16 . . . . . 156 A3
Bedford Cres ST5 . . . . . . 71 C4
Bedford Pl WS12 . . . . . . 210 B4
Bedford Rd
Burton u T DE15 . . . . 185 D7
Hanley ST1 . . . . 282 A1
Kidsgrove ST7 . . . . 26 A3
Bedford St ST1 . . . . 57 A2
Bedford Way WS15 . . . . 196 D6
Bedingstone Dr ST19 . . . 208 A7
Bednall Barns ST17 . . . . 193 F8
Bednall Ct ST17 . . . . . . 193 F8
Bednall Rd ST17 . . . . . . 175 C1
Beecham Bsns Pk WS9 . 256 A8
Beecham Ct WS9 . . . . . . 256 A8
Beech Ave
Burton u T DE13 . . . . 166 F7
Cheddleton ST13 . . . . 45 C4
King's Bromley DE13 . . . . 199 C6
Tamworth B77 . . . . 250 E3
Beech Cl Armitage WS15 . 198 C4
Biddulph ST8 . . . . 17 B1
Cheadle ST10 . . . . 76 F2
Dunsley DY7 . . . . 278 B4
Haughton ST18 . . . . 172 F5
Beechcliff La ST4,ST12 . . 87 C2
Newport TF10 . . . . 168 F1
Pattingham WV6 . . . . 253 C2
Sedgley DY3 . . . . 266 E1
Sutton Coldfield B75 . . . . 258 A4
Tamworth B79 . . . . 250 A8
Uttoxeter ST14 . . . . 126 A8
Wheaton Aston ST19 . . . . 205 C6
Beech Cres WS7 . . . . . . 228 F6
Beechcroft Ave ST16 . . . 155 C1
Beechcroft Ct ST12 . . . . . 88 F2
Beechcroft Cres B74 . . . 256 D1
Beechcroft Ct B74 . . . . . 258 A1
Beechcroft Grange ST16 155 C1
Beech Croft Madeley CW3 . 68 E7
Pattingham WV6 . . . . 253 C2
Beech Ct Cannock WS12 . 210 B7
Great Wyrley WS6 . . . . . . 227 A4
Stone ST15 . . . . 120 B8
Beechdale La
Beech ST4,ST12 . . . . 87 D1

Beechdale La *continued*
Tittensor ST12 . . . . 103 E8
Beech Dr Burton u T DE13 166 F8
Talke ST7 . . . . 40 E8
Beechen Gr WS7 . . . . . . 228 F8
Beeches Cl DY6 . . . . 275 D5
Beeches Croft WS13 . . . 215 D7
Beeches Mews DY9 . . . . 281 F4
Beeches Rd WS15 . . . . . 197 A6
Beeches The
Newcastle-u-L ST5 . . . . . . 56 C7
Rugeley WS15 . . . . 178 D3
Sutton Coldfield,Little Aston
B74 . . . . 257 D4
Beechfield Dr ST17 . . . . 175 D5
Beechfield Rd ST4 . . . . . 88 B6
Beechfield Rise WS14 . . 231 D8
Beechfields ST12 . . . . . . 88 F2
Beechfields Way TF10 . . 168 F5
Beech Gate B74 . . . . 257 C5
Beech Gdns Codsall WV8 . 238 F2
Lichfield WS14 . . . . 231 C5
Beech Gr
Huntington WS12 . . . . . . 209 D8
Leek ST13 . . . . 30 C6
Loggerheads TF9 . . . . 99 E5
Newcastle-u-L ST5 . . . . . . 56 C4
Stoke-on-T ST4 . . . . 72 C5
Swadlincote DE11 . . . . . . 186 F7
Beech Ho B74 . . . . 257 B5
Beechhouse La WV5 . . . 264 A1
Beech Hurst Gdns WV5 . 264 A2
Beech La Burton u T DE13 166 E8
Coppenhall ST18 . . . . . . 174 C3
Stretton DE13 . . . . 147 E1
Beechlawn Dr DY7 . . . . 278 E7
Beechmere Rise WS15 . 178 B2
Beechmount Gr ST1 . . . . 57 F6
Beechmount Rise [9]
ST17 . . . . 175 C7
Beech Pine Cl WS12 . . . 210 A8
Beech Rd
Barton-u-N DE13 . . . . . . 183 D1
Eccleshall ST21 . . . . 133 E6
Kingswinford DY6 . . . . . . 275 E5
Stoke-on-T ST3 . . . . 72 F1
Stourbridge DY8 . . . . 279 F3
Tamworth B79 . . . . 250 A8
Wolverhampton WV10 . . . 240 B1
Beech St Burton u T DE14 166 B1
Longton ST3 . . . . 284 C2
Beech Tree Cl DY6 . . . . 275 E8
Beech Tree La WS11 . . . 226 D8
Beechtree La DY10 . . . . 280 E6
Beech Tree Rd WS9 . . . 244 F3
Beechway ST6 . . . . 155 D6
Beech Wlk WS15 . . . . . . 198 A1
Beechwood Bsns Pk
WS11 . . . . 210 B3
Beechwood Cl
Blythe Bridge ST11 . . . . . . 91 A6
Newcastle-u-L ST5 . . . . . . 71 D1
Walsall WS3 . . . . 243 B3
Beechwood Cres B77 . . 250 F5
Beechwood Croft B74 . . 257 D5
Beechwood Ct WV6 . . . . 255 C3
Beechwood Dr
Stone ST15 . . . . 120 A6
Wolverhampton WV6 . . . . 255 A2
Beechwood WS14 . . . . . 232 E5
Beecroft Ave WS13 . . . . 214 B1
Beecroft Ct WS11 . . . . . 209 E2
Beecroft Hill Sch WS11 . 209 E2
Beecroft Rd WS11 . . . . . 209 E1
Beekes Croft B78 . . . . . 261 A8
Bee La WV10 . . . . 240 D3
Beelow La ST10 . . . . 78 D6
Bees La WS5 . . . . 178 E1
Beeston Rd DY10 . . . . . . 280 B5
Beeston Ridge ST17 . . . 174 B7
Beeston St ST3 . . . . 73 C5
Beeston View ST7 . . . . . . 41 A4
Beffcote Rd ST20 . . . . . . 171 B4
Beggars Bush La WV5 . . 270 B5
Beggars La ST13 . . . . 30 C5
Beighterton Farm Barns
TF11 . . . . 203 F4
Beighterton La TF11 . . . 203 F3
Beighton Cl B74 . . . . . . 257 F6
Belbroughton Rd
Blakedown DY10 . . . . 281 D1
Stourbridge DY8 . . . . 279 E3
Belfast Cl ST6 . . . . 42 B2
Belfield Ave ST5 . . . . 56 C4
Belford Pl ST4 . . . . 56 F1
Belfort Way ST17 . . . . . . 175 A8
Belfry Cl WS3 . . . . 243 A3
Belfry Dr DY8 . . . . 279 E6
Belfry The Perton WV6 . . 254 D4
Stretton DE13 . . . . 147 C1
Belgrade Rd WV10 . . . . 240 B1
Belgrave Ave ST3 . . . . . 284 B2
Belgrave CE Prim Sch
ST3 . . . . 73 D1
Belgrave Cres ST3 . . . . 284 C1
Belgrave Ct DY6 . . . . . . 275 D5
Belgrave High Sch B77 . 250 E1
Belgrave Rd Longton ST3 284 C1
Newcastle-u-L ST5 . . . . . 283 C2
Tamworth B77 . . . . 261 E8
Belgrove Ho WS11 . . . . 209 D1
Bellamour La WS15,ST17 178 C6
Bellamour Way WS15 . . 178 F5
Bellapart Rd TF9 . . . . 82 A4
Bellassis St ST16 . . . . . . 155 E6
Bell Ave ST3 . . . . 73 D2
Bellbrook ST19 . . . . 192 F1
Bell Cl Lichfield WS13 . . . 213 F1

Bell Cl *continued*
Stafford ST16 . . . . 155 F5
Bell Cotts DE6 . . . . 127 D8
Bell Dr WS12 . . . . 210 C7
Bellfield View ST5 . . . . . . 56 C3
Bellencroft Gdns WV3 . 265 C7
Bellerton La ST6 . . . . 42 E2
Belle Vue Cl DY8 . . . . . . 275 D2
Belle Vue ST13 . . . . 30 D6
Belle Vue Rd ST13 . . . . . 30 D6
Belle Vue DY8 . . . . 275 D2
Belle Vue Prim Sch DY8 275 C3
Bellevue St WV14 . . . . . 266 F2
Bellflower Cl WV10 . . . . 241 A7
Bell Heather Rd WS8 . . . 244 D6
Bell Ho ST3 . . . . 88 F8
Bellhouse Rd DE13 . . . . 164 E6
Bellhurst La ST19 . . . . . 205 A5
Bellingham Gr ST1 . . . . . 57 D6
Bellingham B77 . . . . 251 D5
Bell La Barlaston ST12 . . . 88 E4
Barton-u-N DE13 . . . . . . 183 D1
Doveridge DE6 . . . . 127 C8
Walsall,Wallington Heath
WS3 . . . . 243 B1
Bellman's Yd TF10 . . . . 168 F2
Bell Orch TF9 . . . . 100 C5
Bell Pl WV2 . . . . 266 C8
Bell Rd WV5 . . . . 264 D1
Bellringer Cl ST3 . . . . . . 27 C7
Bellringer Rd ST4 . . . . . . 88 D7
Bells End Rd DE12 . . . . 184 D1
Bell's Hollow ST5 . . . . . . 40 E3
Bellsize Cl WS11 . . . . . . 227 F5
Bells La Burntwood WS7 . 211 F1
Stourbridge DY8 . . . . 275 D2
Bell St DY8 . . . . 279 F5
Bellwood Cl ST3 . . . . 90 A5
Belmont Ave WS11 . . . . 209 C2
Belmont Cl Aldridge WS9 256 A7
Great Wyrley WS11 . . . . . 227 A4
Belmont Rd Hanley ST1 . . 57 A3
Ipstones ST10 . . . . 61 D8
Tamworth B77 . . . . 261 C7
Wolverhampton WV4 . . . . 266 A5
Belmot Rd DE13 . . . . . . 145 F1
Belper Rd WV3 . . . . 243 C3
Belsay Cl ST3 . . . . 284 C4
Belsize B77 . . . . 250 E2
Belton Ave WV11 . . . . . 241 B1
Belt Rd WS12,WS11 . . . . 210 A5
Belvedere Ave WV4 . . . . 266 B5
Belvedere Cl
Burntwood WS7 . . . . 228 F5
Kingswinford DY6 . . . . . . 275 D5
Stafford ST17 . . . . 175 C8
Tamworth B79 . . . . 250 C7
Belvedere Gdns WV6 . . . 255 E7
Belvedere Jun Sch DE14 166 B5
Belvedere Rd
Burton u T DE13 . . . . 166 A6
Stoke-on-T ST4 . . . . 72 A1
Belvide Gdns WV8 . . . . 238 F4
Belvoir Ave ST4 . . . . 88 C5
Belvoir Cl Burton u T DE13 166 B5
Dudley DY1 . . . . 271 C2
Belvoir Rd DE13 . . . . . . 166 A5
Belvoir B77 . . . . 261 C7
Belwell Dr B74 . . . . 258 A2
Belwell La B74 . . . . 258 A2
Bemersley Rd
Chell Heath ST6 . . . . 27 C1
Stoke-on-T ST6 . . . . 42 E6
Benches Cl WS7 . . . . . . 228 D6
Bencroft WV8 . . . . 239 B4
Bend Oak Dr DE15 . . . . 167 C4
Bend Oak Jun Sch DE15 167 C3
Benedict Pl ST2 . . . . 58 A5
Benenden Cl ST17 . . . . 156 B1
Benfleet Pl ST3 . . . . 284 A3
Bengal Gr ST4 . . . . 88 C8
Bengry Rd ST3 . . . . 73 E2
Benion Rd WS11 . . . . . . 209 F5
Benjamins Way ST7 . . . . 39 F2
Ben Jones Ave TF10 . . . 169 A4
Bennett Pl ST5 . . . . 56 B7
Bennett Rd B74 . . . . 257 D3
Bennetts La Bosley SK11 . . 7 E6
Bramshall ST14 . . . . 125 C6
Bennett's La WV6 . . . . . 253 F1
Bennetts La WV6 . . . . . . 263 F7
Bennett St ST6 . . . . 56 E7
Bennick Trad Est WS11 . 226 E6
Bennion Gr ST14 . . . . . . 95 E5
Bennion St ST3 . . . . 284 C3
Benson Ave WV4 . . . . . . 266 D5
Benson Cl Lichfield WS13 214 D1
Perton WV6 . . . . 254 E5
Benson St ST6 . . . . 41 F5
Benson View B79 . . . . . 250 C8
Bentilee Prim Sch ST2 . . 73 D8
Bent La Astbury CW12 . . . 15 A8
Whitmore ST5 . . . . 86 A4
Bentley Ave ST5 . . . . 56 B4
Bentley Brook La WS12 . 211 A6
Bentley Cl ST15 . . . . 104 E3
Bentley Dr WV8 . . . . . . 238 F4
Bentley Rd Stoke-on-T ST6 42 C5
Uttoxeter ST14 . . . . 110 F1
Wolverhampton WV10 . . . 240 E2
Bentleys Rd TF9 . . . . . . 112 A8
Bentley Way B79 . . . . . 249 F7
Benton Cres WS3 . . . . . 243 D2
Benton's La WS6 . . . . . . 227 A1
Bents La ST10 . . . . 109 A3
Bentygrange La ST13 . . . 48 D3
Beowulf Covert DE13 . . . 147 B1
Berdmore St ST4 . . . . . . 284 A5

Beresford Cres ST5 . . . . . 71 A6
Beresford Dale
Madeley CW3 . . . . 68 D6
Swadlincote DE11 . . . . . . 186 F2
Beresford St ST4 . . . . 57 B1
Bergamot Dr ST3 . . . . . . 90 A6
Berkeley Cl Gnosall ST20 171 E7
Perton WV6 . . . . 254 F3
Berkeley Dr DY6 . . . . . . 275 C7
Berkeley St Hanley ST1 . . 282 C2
Stone ST15 . . . . 104 F2
Berkeley Way WS15 . . . 198 A1
Berkshire Gr ST5 . . . . . . 71 C5
Berkshire The WS3 . . . . 243 A3
Berkswell Cl Dudley DY1 . 271 E3
Sutton Coldfield B74 . . . . 257 E4
Berkswich CE Prim Sch
ST17 . . . . 175 F6
Bernard Cheadle Cl
ST15 . . . . 103 C4
Bernard Gr ST3 . . . . 89 F4
Bernard St ST1 . . . . 282 C2
Berne Ave ST5 . . . . 70 E6
Bernwall Cl DY8 . . . . . . 279 F4
Berrisford Cl TF9 . . . . 97 E1
Berrisford Rd TF9 . . . . . . 97 E1
Berrybush Gdns DY3 . . . 271 E7
Berryfield Gr ST3 . . . . . . 73 F4
Berryfields WS9 . . . . . . 245 E5
Berry Gdns DE15 . . . . . 167 C4
Berry Hedge La DE15 . . . 167 C4
Berry Hill WS12 . . . . 210 C4
Berry Hill High Sch ST2 . 58 A1
Berry Hill Rd ST4 . . . . . . 57 E1
Berry Hill Village ST2 . . . 58 A1
Berry La ST3 . . . . 284 B3
Berry Rd ST16 . . . . 155 B8
Berry St ST4 . . . . 72 B7
Bertelin Rd ST16 . . . . . . 155 F7
Bert Smith Way TF9 . . . . 97 C2
Berwick Dr WS11 . . . . . 226 B8
Berwick Rd ST1 . . . . 57 E8
Berwick Wlks ST5 . . . . . . 70 F7
Berwyn Gr WS6 . . . . . . 226 F3
Besom Way WS6 . . . . . 226 C2
Best Ave DE15 . . . . 167 B1
Best St ST4 . . . . 72 F5
Beswick Cl ST10 . . . . 76 D1
Beswick Rd ST6 . . . . 41 F6
Beswicks La TF9 . . . . 82 C2
Bethany Ct DE15 . . . . . 185 E7
Bethany Mews [4] WS11 . 209 F4
Bethell Rd ST1 . . . . 57 D7
Bethesda Rd ST1 . . . . . 282 C1
Bethesda St ST1 . . . . . . 282 B2
Betjeman Pl WV10 . . . . 241 A1
Betjeman Wlk ST17 . . . . 174 C2
Betley CE Prim Sch CW3 . 53 B6
Betley Hall Gdns CW3 . . 53 A6
Betley Pl ST5 . . . . 71 C6
Betlingspring La DE6 . . . 81 D3
Beton Way ST16 . . . . . . 155 D8
Betony Rd DE15 . . . . . . 167 C2
Bettany Glade WV10 . . . 240 E4
Bettany Rd ST6 . . . . 57 A7
Betton Rd TF9 . . . . 97 E2
Betty Hatch La ST16 . . . 155 C5
Betty's La WS11 . . . . . . 228 A4
Beulah Dr TF9 . . . . 97 B1
Bevan Ave Talke Pits ST7 . 40 E6
Wolverhampton WV4 . . . . 266 E4
Bevan Cl WS4 . . . . 244 C1
Bevandean Cl ST4 . . . . . 88 C5
Bevan Lee Rd WS11 . . . 209 D3
Bevan Pl CW3 . . . . 68 E7
Beveridge Cl ST3 . . . . . . 74 B2
Beverley Cl ST19 . . . . . . 207 F7
Beverley Cres
Forsbrook ST11 . . . . 91 A8
Wolverhampton WV6 . . . . 266 F4
Beverley Dr Bucknall ST2 . 58 D2
Kingswinford DY6 . . . . . . 275 C7
Stafford ST16 . . . . 155 C8
Beverley Hill WS12 . . . . 210 D6
Beverley Rd DE14 . . . . . 185 A7
Beverston Rd WV6 . . . . 255 A4
Beville St ST4 . . . . 72 E6
Bevin La ST2 . . . . 58 A3
Bewcastle Gr ST3 . . . . . . 90 A7
Bewick Ct WV6 . . . . 255 C2
Bew St ST5 . . . . 42 E5
Bexhill Gr ST1 . . . . 57 F6
Bexley St ST1 . . . . 282 A4
Bexmore Dr WS13 . . . . . 214 F1
Beyer Cl B77 . . . . 251 A2
Bhylls Acre Prim Sch
WV3 . . . . 265 B7
Bhylls Cres WV3 . . . . . . 265 C7
Bhylls La WV3 . . . . 265 C7
Bibbey's Gn WV10 . . . . 240 F4
Bickford Cl ST19 . . . . . . 206 A6
Bickford Rd ST19 . . . . . 206 B7
Bickley Ave B74 . . . . . . 257 E5
Bickley Ho B74 . . . . 257 E5
Bida La CW12 . . . . 16 B8
Biddles La ST21 . . . . . . 102 D4
Biddulph Common Rd
ST8 . . . . 17 A7
Biddulph Grange Ctry Pk★
ST8 . . . . 16 E3
Biddulph Grange Gdn★
ST8 . . . . 16 E3
Biddulph High Sch ST8 . . 27 D5
Biddulph Park Rd ST8 . . . 17 A5

Biddulph Rd
Congleton CW12 . . . . 16 B8
Mow Cop ST7 . . . . 26 F6
Stoke-on-T ST8 . . . . 42 B7
Biddulph St CW12 . . . . . 16 C7
Bideford Ave ST17 . . . . . 175 D8
Bideford Way WS11 . . . . 226 B8
Biggin Cl WV6 . . . . 254 E5
Bignall End Rd ST7 . . . . . 40 A4
Bigsbury Wlk [2] ST6 . . . . 56 F7
Bigwood La ST18 . . . . . 173 F4
Bilberry Bank WS11 . . . 209 E6
Bilberry Cres WS12 . . . . 209 C5
Bilberry Wlk WS15 . . . . 178 C1
Bilbrook CE Mid Sch
WV8 . . . . 239 B3
Bilbrook Ct WV8 . . . . . . 239 B3
Bilbrook Gr WV8 . . . . . . 239 B3
Bilbrook Rd WV8 . . . . . . 239 B4
Bilbrook Sta WV8 . . . . . 239 A2
Billinge St ST6 . . . . 56 E8
Billington Ave ST18 . . . . 158 D1
Billington Bank WS11 . . 173 D6
Billington La ST18 . . . . . 154 C2
Billy Buns La WV5 . . . . . 270 B8
Billy Wright Cl WV4 . . . . 265 D6
Bilston Rd WV2 . . . . 266 F8
Bilston St DY3 . . . . 271 E8
Bilton St ST4 . . . . 72 A6
Bingley Ent Ctr WV3 . . . 266 A8
Bingley St WV3 . . . . 266 A8
Birchall Ave ST6 . . . . 41 C5
Birchall Cl ST13 . . . . 30 F2
Birchall La ST13 . . . . 30 F2
Birchall Park Ave ST13 . . 30 F3
Bircham Wlk ST5 . . . . . . 71 B2
Birch Ave Biddulph ST8 . . 27 A6
Brownhills WS8 . . . . 244 E8
Burntwood WS7 . . . . 228 F6
Cannock WS11 . . . . 226 C8
Swadlincote DE11 . . . . . . 186 F7
Birchbrook Ind Pk WS14 . 246 E6
Birch Brook La WS14 . . . 246 E6
Birch Bsns Pk WS11 . . . 226 F6
Birch Cl Burton u T DE14 . 185 A8
Denstone ST14 . . . . 95 D6
Great Haywood ST18 . . . . 158 C2
Walton-on-t-H ST17 . . . . 175 F6
Birch Coppice WV5 . . . . 269 E6
Birch Croft WS9 . . . . . . 256 C8
Birch Dale CW3 . . . . 68 E6
Birchdown Ave ST6 . . . . 42 B3
Birch Dr Little Aston B74 . 257 D5
Stourbridge DY8 . . . . 279 E6
Birchendale Cl ST10 . . . . 92 F2
Birchenfields La ST10 . . . 75 F5
Birchenwood Rd ST6 . . . 26 E1
Birchenwood Way ST7 . . 26 C1
Birches Ave WV8 . . . . . . 239 C1
Birches Barn Ave WV3 . . 265 F7
Birches Barn Rd WV3 . . 265 F7
Birches Cl DE13 . . . . . . 166 F7
Birches Farm Mews CW3 . 68 F5
Birches Fst Sch WV8 . . . 239 B1
Birches Head High Sch
ST1 . . . . 57 F7
Birches Head Rd
Bucknall ST2 . . . . 58 A4
Hanley ST1 . . . . 57 E6
Birches Park Rd WV8 . . . 239 A2
Birches Rd WV8 . . . . . . 239 B2
Birches The ST10 . . . . . . 76 D2
**Birches Valley Forest Ctr &
Wlk**★ WS15 . . . . 195 D6
Birches Valley WS15 . . . 195 D6
Birches Way [7] ST7 . . . . 26 B2
Birchfield Ave WV6 . . . . 255 B6
Birchfield Cl CV9 . . . . . . 262 C1
Birchfield Rd Bucknall ST2 . 58 C6
Burton u T DE15 . . . . 185 C6
Birchfield Sch WV7 . . . . 237 D5
Birchfields Cl ST15 . . . . 119 F6
Birchfields Dr WS12 . . . 210 D1
Birchgate ST2 . . . . 58 C4
Birchgate Gr ST2 . . . . . . 58 C4
Birchglade WV3 . . . . . . 255 D1
Birch Gr B78 . . . . 262 D7
Birch Green Gr ST1 . . . . 57 E7
Birch Gr Forsbrook ST11 . . 91 A7
Lichfield WS14 . . . . 231 D8
Meir Heath ST3 . . . . 90 A4
Birch Hill Ave WV5 . . . . 269 F5
Birch Ho B74 . . . . 257 B5
Birch House La
Cotes ST15 . . . . 103 A1
Millmeece ST21 . . . . 117 F8
Birch House Rd
Coldmeece ST15 . . . . . . 118 A8
Newcastle-u-L ST5 . . . . . . 55 D8
Birch House Way WS15 . 118 A8
Birchill Pl WV5 . . . . 269 F5
Birch La WS9 . . . . 245 D1
Birchlands Rd ST1 . . . . . 57 F6
Birch La Rugeley WS15 . . 197 A5
Walsall WS4 . . . . 244 C1
Birchmoor La ST20 . . . . 189 D1
Birchmoor Rd B78 . . . . . 262 F8
Birchover Way ST6 . . . . . 42 A8
Birch Rd Audley ST7 . . . . 39 F1
Sedgley DY3 . . . . 266 F1
Stone ST15 . . . . 120 B8
Wolverhampton WV11 . . . 241 F1
Birch Rise TF9 . . . . 99 E3
Birch St ST1 . . . . 57 E5
Birch Terr
Burntwood WS7 . . . . 212 A1
Hanley ST1 . . . . 282 B2

Birchtree Dr ST13........45 C8
Birch Tree Gdns WS9...256 B5
Birchtree La WS15....196 E6
Birch Tree La
　The Bank ST7..........26 B8
　Whitmore ST5..........85 C7
Birch Valley Rd ST7....26 C1
Birchtree Rd ST3.......73 A1
Birchwood Ave B78....262 F7
Birchwood Cl WV11...242 A3
Birchwood Prim Sch
B78.................262 F7
Birchwood Rd
　Lichfield WS14.......231 F7
　Wolverhampton WV4...266 A5
Birchwood Rise WS15..161 B5
Birchwood Wlk DY6...275 E8
Bird Cage Wlk ST1....282 B2
Birdhope B77.........251 C1
Bird Rd ST3............74 B2
Bird's Barn La DY11...277 C2
Birds Bush Prim Sch
B77.................261 E8
Birds Bush Rd B77....261 F8
Birdsgrove La DE6......66 D3
Bird St Dudley DY3...271 D3
　Lichfield WS13.......231 B7
Birkdale Ave DE14....185 A6
Birkdale Cl DY8.......279 F2
Birkdale Dr Kidsgrove ST7..26 C3
　Stafford ST16........156 C3
Birkdale Rd WS3......243 A3
Birkholme Dr ST3......90 A5
Birks Dr TF9...........99 E5
Birks St ST4...........72 B5
Birmingham New Rd
WV4................266 E4
Birmingham Rd
　Aldridge WS9........256 A4
　Blakedown DY10.....281 C2
　Lichfield WS14.......231 A4
　Shenstone WS14.....247 A4
　Wolverhampton WV2..266 D7
Birrell St ST4..........72 F5
Biscay Gr ST4..........88 C8
Bishop Cl WS11.......209 D2
Bishop Ct ST2..........58 B5
Bishop Rawle CE Prim Sch
ST10.................76 D3
Bishop Rd ST6.........42 B5
Bishop's Cl ST7........40 D8
Bishops Ct ST21.......133 E7
Bishops Dr ST19......223 D7
Bishops Grange WS15..178 F2
Bishops La TF9.........97 B1
Bishops Mdw B75.....258 E3
Bishop Stamer CE Prim Sch
ST4..................72 B6
Bishop St ST4..........73 A5
Bishops Way B74.....257 F6
Bishton La ST17,ST18..178 A6
Bitham Cl ST19.......207 F8
Bitham Ct DE13.......147 C1
Bitham La DE13.......147 D1
Bittell Cl WV10........240 E4
Bitterne Pl ST2........73 D8
Bittern La ST10........76 E3
Bitterscote La B78....250 A2
Black Bank Rd ST13....44 D5
Blackbank Rd ST5......55 C4
Blackberry La
　Brownhills WS9......245 B4
　Stafford ST16........155 C4
　Sutton Coldfield B74..257 E4
Blackberry Way ST20..151 D8
Blackbird Cl ST14.....126 C6
Blackbird Way
■ Packmoor ST7........26 F1
　Biddulph ST8.........27 B8
　Stoke-on-T ST7.......41 F8
Blackbrook Ave ST5....55 D8
Blackbrook Way WV10.240 E4
Blackbrook Zoological Pk★
ST13.................48 A4
Blackburn Ave WV6...255 F7
Blackdown B77........251 C1
Black Dr ST18.........157 C6
Blackflats Rd ST15....103 C1
Blackfriars Cl B79....249 E5
Blackfriars F Ed Unit ST2..58 B5
Blackfriar's Rd ST5...283 B2
Blackfriars Sch ST5...283 B2
Blackhalve La WV11...241 D2
Blackheath Cl ST3......73 D3
Blackheath La ST18...156 E4
Blackhole La ST18....154 D2
Black Horse La ST1...282 B3
Blackie's La Stone ST15..120 D6
　Stone ST15..........120 D7
Blacklake Dr ST3......90 A4
Black La Sutton TF10..150 E1
　Whiston ST10.........62 D3
Blackmere Cl TF10...168 D2
Blackpit La
　Doveridge DE6.......127 B8
　Orton WV4...........264 E3
Blackpool St DE14....185 C8
Blackroot Cl WS7.....229 D4
Blackshaw Cl CW12.....6 B1
Blackshaw Grange Cvn Pk
ST13.................20 E4
Blackshaw Moor CE Prim
Sch ST13.............20 E5
Blacksmith Dr ■ ST5..258 E3
Blacksmiths La WS14..232 E5
Blacksmiths Cl DE12..219 F7
Blacksmith's La
　Eggington DE65......148 A6

Blacksmith's La continued
　Newton Solney DE15..167 E8
Blackthorn Ave WS12..228 F4
Blackthorn Cres WS12..211 A6
Blackthorn Cl DY1....271 F4
Blackthorne Rd
　Dudley DY1..........271 F5
　Lichfield WS14.......231 D7
Blackthorn Pl ST5......55 E8
Blackthorn Rd
　Burton u T DE15.....185 E6
　Stourbridge DY8.....275 F1
Blackwell's Row ST6....57 B6
Blackwood Pl ST3......73 E4
Blackwood Rd
　Aldridge B74.........256 E1
　Tamworth B77.......261 C7
Blackwood Sch B74...256 E1
Bladon Ave ST5........71 B3
Bladon Cl ST6..........42 A8
Bladon House Sch DE15..167 B6
Bladon St DE15.......167 C4
Bladon's Yd DE13.....147 B4
Bladon View
　Burton u T DE13.....148 A2
　Stretton DE13.......147 F2
Blaizefield Cl CW3.....67 C2
Blake Cl WS11........210 A5
Blakedown CE Fst Sch
DY10................281 C1
Blakedown Sta DY10..281 C2
Blakeley Ave WS6.....255 F7
Blakeley Heath Dr WV5..270 A5
Blakeley Heath Prim Sch
WV5................270 A5
Blakeley La ST11.......63 A2
Blakeley Rise WV6....255 F2
Blakelow La DE6.......65 B1
Blakelow Rd ST2.......58 B6
Blakemore Rd WS9....245 A3
Blakenall Heath WS3..243 D1
Blakeney Ave
　Newcastle-u-L ST5....71 B3
　Stourbridge DY8.....279 D6
Blakeney Cl DY3......271 C8
Blakenhall Gdns WV2..266 D7
Blakenhall Ind Est WV2..266 B7
Blake Cl ST6...........56 F8
Blake Street Sta B74..257 F6
Blake St B74..........257 F6
Blake Valley Tech Coll
WS12................209 F6
Blakeways Cl B79.....217 C5
Blakiston St ST16.....285 C4
Blanchard Cl ST3......90 C7
Blandford Dr DY8.....275 E3
Blandford Gdns WS7..229 C6
Blanefield WV8.......239 E2
Blanford Mere Prim Sch
DY6.................275 E8
Blantyre St ST3.......284 C2
Blantyre Wlk ST3.....284 C2
Blatchford Cl ST3......74 B2
Blaydon Ave B75......258 E2
Blaydon Rd WV9,WV10..240 A1
Blaze Hill Rd DY6.....275 A8
Blaze Pk DY6.........275 B8
Bleak Pl ■ ST5.........57 A7
Bleakridge Ave ST5....56 B8
Bleak St ST5...........56 D3
Bleeding Wolf La ST7..25 E5
Blencarn Gr ST9.......43 C4
Blenheim Cl
　Burton u T DE15.....167 D3
　Stafford ST18........156 D3
　Tamworth B77.......250 C4
Blenheim Ho DE14....184 F7
Blenheim Rd
　Burntwood WS7.....229 A8
　Kingswinford DY6....275 F6
　Norton Canes WS11..228 B4
Blenheim St ST4.......72 D5
Blenheim Way
　Dudley DY1..........271 E2
　Fradley WS13........215 C5
Bleriot Cl ST3..........90 C7
Blessed Mother Teresa's RC
　Prim Sch ST17.......174 C8
Blessed William Howard RC
　Sch ST17............285 A1
Bletchley Dr B77......261 C8
Blewitt St WS12.......210 B7
Blithbury Rd Colton WS13..179 B3
　Hamstall Ridware WS15..180 E3
Blithe View ST11.......90 F6
Blithfield Cl ST9.......59 A2
Blithfield Rd ST17....174 F6
Blithfield Pl WS11....210 B1
Blithfield Rd WS8....228 C2
Bloomfield Cl WS3....269 D6
Bloomfield Cres WS13..214 B2
Bloomfield Dr WV12..242 D1
Bloomfield Way B79..249 F8
Bloomsbury St ■ WV2..266 C8
Bloomsbury Way WS14..231 E7
Blore Rd TF9...........98 E1
Blossomfield Cl DY6..275 E8
Blount Cl ST19.......207 F7
Blount's Dr ST14......126 A6
Bloxwich CE Prim Sch
WS3.................243 B1
Bloxwich North Sta WS3..242 F2
Bloxwich Sta WS3....243 A1
Bluebell Cl Biddulph ST8..27 E7
　Cannock WS12.......210 B6
　Stourbridge DY8.....275 C2
　Tittensor ST12......103 E8

Bluebell Dr ST5........71 A4
Bluebell Hollow ST17..175 F7
Bluebell La WS6......227 A1
Bluebell Rd WS9.....245 B3
Bluebird Cl WS14....231 D8
Blue Cedars Dr DE15..167 D2
Blue Cedars DY8.....279 C6
Blue House Barns TF10..168 E4
Blue House La WV7...237 B7
Bluestone Ave ST6.....42 B2
Bluestone La DE15...186 A7
Bluestones Cl ST13....20 E4
Blundies La DY7......273 D3
Blunt's Hollow WS15,
DE13................162 A4
Blunt St ST3...........56 D4
Blurton Cotts ST3......72 E1
Blurton High Sch ST3..88 E8
Blurton Prim Sch ST3..72 E2
Blurton Priory ST3.....88 F8
Blurton Rd Barlaston ST12..89 A4
　Stoke-on-T ST3.......72 E2
Blymhill Lawn La TF11..204 C3
Blymhill Marsh TF11..203 F6
Blythe Ave ST3........90 A5
Blythebridge Bank ST14,
ST18................141 A7
Blythe Bridge High Sch
ST11.................90 F7
Blythe Bridge Rd
　Blythe Bridge ST11...90 F8
　Caverswall ST11......74 E1
Blythe Bridge Sta ST11..90 F7
Blythe Cl
　Blythe Bridge ST11...90 D7
　Burntwood WS7.....229 D6
Blythe Gdns WV8.....238 F4
Blythe Lodge ST11.....90 D7
Blythe Mount Pk ST11..91 A7
Blythe Pk ST11.........91 D3
Blythe Rd
　Blythe Bridge ST11...91 A7
　Stafford ST17........174 E6
Blythe St B77.........250 C4
Blythe View
　Hamstall Ridware WS15..180 E1
　Saverley Green ST11..91 A2
Blythfield DE14......166 E3
Boardman Cres ST16..155 C3
Boardman Ind Est DE11..186 E3
Boardman Rd DE11...186 E2
Boardmans Bank ST6...28 A1
Board School Gdns DY3..271 E6
Boathorse Rd
　Kidsgrove ST7........41 A8
　Stoke-on-T ST6.......41 B5
Boat House La WS15..198 A5
Boat La
　Muckley Corner WS14..229 F1
　Weston ST18.........138 C3
Boatman's La WS9....244 E2
Boatyard Cotts ST12..104 D8
Bode Bsns Pk ST13....31 A7
Bodiam Ct WV6.......255 A3
Bodicote Gr ST5......258 E3
Bodington Cl WS7....229 E7
Bodington Rd B75....258 B3
Bodmin Ave ST17.....175 D4
Bodmin Wlk ST16.....42 D1
Bognop Rd WV11.....241 D4
Bogs Cotts ST5.........70 B8
Bolberry Cl ST3.......73 E1
Bold St ST1............57 E5
Bolebridge Mews B79..250 B5
Bolebridge St B79....250 C4
Bolehall Ho B77......250 C4
Boley Cl WS14........231 D7
Boley Cottage La WS14..231 E7
Boley La WS14........231 D7
Boleyn Cl WS6........226 D2
Boley Park Ctr WS14..231 E7
Bolina Gr ST3..........73 B6
Bolney Gr ST9..........57 F5
Bolsover Cl ST6........42 A8
Bolton Pl ST3..........89 F8
Bolton Way WS3......242 F3
Boma Rd ST4...........87 F8
Bond Ct DE13.........182 A2
Bondfield La DE13....181 F2
Bondfield Way ST3.....74 B2
Bond St Burton u T DE14..166 D1
　Stoke-on-T ST4.......41 D4
Bondway WS12.......209 F2
Bonehill Ind Est B78..249 F1
Boney Hay Prim Sch
WS7.................211 F1
Boney Hay Rd WS7...229 B7
Boningale Way ST17..174 B8
Bonington Cres ST16..155 C2
Bonnard Cl ST3........90 C6
Bonner Cl ST4..........71 E4
Bonville Gdns WV10..240 E4
Boon Ave ST4..........72 A7
Boon Gr ST17.........174 E6
Boon Hill Rd ST7.......39 F1
Boons Ind Est ST18...154 E1
Booth Cl WS13.......214 A2
Boothen CE Prim Sch
ST4..................72 A5
Boothen Gn ST4........72 B5
Boothen Old Rd ST4...72 B5
Boothen Rd ST4........72 B6
Boothenwood Terr ST4..72 A5
Booth La ST18........140 E3
Boothroyd St ST1....282 B2

Booth St Audley ST7....39 D1
　Cannock WS12.......210 B6
Boothstone Gdns ST15..118 F6
Booth St ST4...........72 B6
Booton Ct DY10......280 A1
Bordeaux Cl DY1.....271 E3
Bordeaux Rd ST3......90 A8
Bordeaux Wlk ST5.....70 F3
Borden Cl
　Wheaton Aston ST19..205 C2
　Wolverhampton WV8..255 F8
Border Way ST17.....174 E6
Bore St WS13.........231 B7
Borman B79...........249 C3
Borough Cres DY3....279 E5
Borough La WS15.....212 D1
Borough Mus & Art Gal The★
ST5.................283 C4
Borough Rd
　Burton u T DE14.....166 C3
　Newcastle-u-L ST5...283 C3
　Tamworth B79.......250 C4
Borrowcop Ho WS14..231 C6
Borrowcop La WS14..231 C5
Borrowdale Rd ST6....42 E3
Boscobel Cl DY1......271 F3
Boscobel Gr ST19....223 C7
Boscobel Ho★ ST19...221 E5
Boscombe Gr ST4......88 C5
Boscomoor Cl ST19..207 E7
Boscomoor Ct ST19..207 E7
Boscomoor Ind Est ST19..207 E7
Boscomoor La ST19..207 E7
Boscomoor Sh Ctr ST19..207 E7
Bosinney Cl ST4........73 B5
Bosley Brook CW12....16 D5
Bosley Gr ST3..........41 C6
Bosley View CW12......6 B1
Boss Gate Cl WV5....270 A5
Bostock Cl ST15.....120 D5
Boston Cl Cannock WS12..210 E1
　Stoke-on-T ST6.......41 C4
Boston Ind Est WS15..178 E2
Bosty La WS9.........256 A4
Boswell Rd WS11.....209 D4
Boswell St ST4.........56 F1
Bosworth Cl DY3......271 F7
Bosworth Dr DE13...166 B7
Botany Bay Rd ST1.....57 E5
Botany Dr DY3........271 D6
Botesworth Gdns ST6..41 D1
Botfield Cl WV7......237 B6
Botham Dr ST3.........45 D5
Botteslow St ST1.....282 C2
Botterham La DY3,WV5..269 E4
Bottom La Ipstones ST10..47 C5
　Market Drayton TF9..112 A7
　Swynnerton ST15....103 B7
Boucher Rd ST13......45 C4
Boughey Rd Audley ST7..39 F2
　Newport TF10.......168 E2
　Stoke-on-T ST6.......72 C8
Boughey St ST4........72 A4
Boulevard The ST6.....41 E3
Boulters La CV9......262 D1
Boulton Cl WS7......229 C8
Boulton St Hanley ST1..282 C4
　Newcastle-u-L ST5....56 D6
Boundary Cl Leek ST13..30 C1
　Stone ST15..........119 F5
Boundary Cres DY3...271 C3
Boundary Ct ST1.....282 B4
Boundary Farm WV6..254 F2
Boundary Hill DY3...271 C4
Boundary Ind Est WV10..240 C5
Boundary La
　Congleton CW12......16 B8
　Kinver DY7..........274 E1
Boundary Rd
　Brownhills WS9......244 F3
　Eggington DE65......148 D8
Boundary St Hanley ST1..282 B4
　Newcastle-u-L ST5....56 D1
Boundary View ST10...76 B2
Boundary Way
　Wolverhampton,Penn
WV4................265 C5
　Wolverhampton WV6..254 F2
Bourne Ave Fazeley B78..249 E1
　Ranton ST18.........153 C5
Bourne Cl Cannock WS12..210 E2
　Tutbury DE13........146 B6
Bourne Pl ST13........30 C6
Bourne Rd ST7.........25 F2
Bournes Bank ST6......56 F8
Bournes Bank S ■ ST6..57 A8
Bourne St Mow Cop ST7..26 D7
　Stoke-on-T ST4.......72 E4
Bourne Vale WS9.....256 D3
Bouverie Par ST1......57 F7
Bowden St ST6.........42 B1
Bowdler Rd WV2......266 E8
Bowen-cooke Ave WV6..254 E6
Bowen St WV4........266 E5
Bower Cl WS13.......214 C2
Bower End La CW3.....68 C6
Bower La WS15.......178 C3
Bowers Bent ST21....102 C4
Bowers Cl ST15......120 D7
Bowers La Bowers ST21..102 B4
　Stone ST15..........120 C3
Bower St ST1.........282 B1
Bowes Dr WV11.....209 F4
Bowfell Gr ST3.........73 B6
Bowhill La Betley CW3..53 B6
　Knowl Bank ST7.......53 C6
Bowland Ave ST5......55 E2

Bowlers Cl ST6........57 A6
Bowlinggalley La DE6...96 D8
Bowling Alley or Vicarage La
ST17.................193 F8
Bowling Green Ave B77..261 F7
Bowling Green Rd DY8..279 E5
Bowman Gr ST3........42 B7
Bowman Ho ST3........89 F8
Bowmead Cl ST4.......88 C6
Bowmere Cl ST8.......16 C1
Bowness Gr WV11....242 B1
Bowness Rd ST1.....282 A4
Bowood Dr WV6......255 D6
Bowsey Wood Rd CW3..68 E8
Bowstead St ST4.......72 B7
Bow St WS15.........178 E1
Bowyer Ave ST6........42 E5
Boxer Cl WS15.......198 C3
Box La ST3.............73 F2
Boxwood Pl ST5........55 D8
Boxwood Rd ST10......92 E4
Boyden Cl Cannock WS11..209 B1
　Penkridge ST19......208 A7
Boyles Hall Rd ST7.....39 E2
Brabazon Cl ST3......90 C7
Bracebridge Ho B74..257 F2
Bracken Ave TF9.......99 E5
Brackenberry ST5......56 B3
Bracken Cl
　Burntwood WS7.....229 C7
　Cannock WS12.......210 D8
　Lichfield WS14.......231 E6
　Stafford ST16........155 B7
　Stoke-on-T ST3.......89 F5
　Tittensor ST12........88 A1
　Wolverhampton WV8..239 C1
Bracken Dale ST3......30 B4
Brackenfield Ave ST2..58 C1
Brackenfield Way ST16..155 D8
Brackenhill Rd WS7..229 A8
Bracken Park Gdns DY8..275 D4
Bracken Rd ST13......89 C5
Brackens Cl ST15....209 C5
Brackens The ST5......71 C2
Bracken St ST4........72 E4
Bracken View ST17..176 B3
Bracken Way
　Newport TF10.......168 F4
　Rugeley WS15.......178 C2
Brackenwood Mews CW2..37 D2
Brackenwood Rd DE15..185 E6
Bracklesham Way B77..251 A6
Brackley Gr ST6........42 B1
Bradbury Cl
　Brownhills WS8.....244 F5
　Stoke-on-T ST6.......42 E3
Bradbury Gdns CW12..15 F8
Bradbury La
　Cannock WS12.......210 B8
　Enville DY7..........272 E3
　King's Bromley DE13..199 C3
Bradbury Rise ST16...155 A4
Bradeley Village ST6...42 C3
Braden Rd WV4......265 D4
Bradford Rd WS8....244 E8
Bradford St
　Cannock WS11.......210 A5
　Tamworth B79.......249 F5
Bradford Terr ST1......57 E6
Bradgate Dr B74......257 E5
Bradley Dr ST21......117 F3
Bradley La ST18......173 B3
Bradley Lakes WS15..197 F2
Bradley St ST18......174 C5
Bradley Rd
　Stourbridge DY8.....279 D5
　Wolverhampton WV2..266 E7
Bradley St
　Burton u T DE15.....185 E7
　Uttoxeter ST14......126 C8
Bradmore Rd
　Burton u T DE13.....166 B5
　Wolverhampton WV3..265 F8
Bradshaw Way ST16..155 D8
Bradwell Croft B75...258 E3
Bradwell Grange ST5...56 B7
Bradwell Hospl ST5....56 A7
Bradwell La
　Cannock Wood WS15..211 F5
　Newcastle-u-L ST5....56 A7
Bradwell Prim Sch ST5..56 A7
Bradwell St ST6........56 B8
Braeburn Cl WS13....214 D1
Braemar Ave DY8.....275 C4
Braemar Cl Bucknall ST2..58 D3
　Sedgley DY3.........266 C1
Braemar Gdns WS12..209 F2
Braemar Rd
　Norton Canes WS11..228 B4
　Pattingham WV6.....253 C2
Braemore Rd ST2......58 B6
Braeside Way WS3....243 F3
Braham B79...........249 D6
Brailsford Ave DE11..186 E5
Brain St B77..........251 A2
Braithwaite Dr DY6..275 D6
Braithwell Dr ST2......43 A2
Brake La DY8.........281 D6
Brakespeare St ST6....41 C7
Brake The Hagley DY8..281 F6
　The Bank ST7.........26 B7
Brake Village ST7......26 B7
Bramall Cl ST6........155 C6
Bramall La ST16......155 C6
Bramber Dr WV5......269 F6

Bramber B77 . . . . .250 D1
Bramber Way DY8 . . . . . . .279 F2
Bramble Cl WS8 . . . . .244 E5
Bramble Ct DE15 . . . . .185 E6
Bramble Dr WS12 . . . . .210 A3
Bramble Gn DY1 . . . . .271 F5
Bramble La WS7 . . . . .229 B8
Brambles Ct ST8 . . . . .27 D7
Brambleside
⑩ Stafford ST17 . . . . .175 C5
Stourbridge DY8 . . . . .275 F1
Brambles The
Lichfield WS14 . . . . .231 D6
Newcastle-u-L ST5 . . . . . . .71 C2
Norton Canes WS11 . . . . . .228 A5
Bramble Way WS15 . . . . . . .178 C1
Bramblewood Dr WV3 . . . .265 E8
Bramblewood
Swadlincote DE11 . . . . . . .186 F6
Wombourne WV5 . . . . .270 A7
Brambling Cl ST14 . . . . . . .126 C6
Bramblings The ST17 . . . . .175 D5
Brambling B77 . . . . .262 A7
Bramdean Dr ST19 . . . . . . .192 F1
Bramdean Wlk WV4 . . . . . .265 C6
Bramell Cl DE14 . . . . .184 F7
Bramfield Dr ST5 . . . . .283 C4
Bramhall ST18 . . . . .154 B7
Bramley Cl ST10 . . . . .76 E2
Bramley Dale DE11 . . . . . . .186 F2
Bramley Pl ST14 . . . . .71 E2
Bramley Way WS14 . . . . . . .232 D5
Bramling Cross Rd DE14 . . .166 F6
Brammall Dr ST11 . . . . .90 E7
Brammer St ST6 . . . . .42 C3
Brampton Cl
Cookley DY10 . . . . .280 B4
Gorstyhill CW2 . . . . .37 E3
Stoke-on-T ST9 . . . . .43 F8
Brampton Ct ST5 . . . . .283 C4
Brampton Dr WS12 . . . . . .210 E2
Brampton Gdns ST5 . . . . . . .56 C3
Brampton Ind Est ST5 . . . . .283 B4
Brampton Rd ST5 . . . . .283 C4
Brampton Sidings Ind Est
ST5 . . . . .283 B4
Brampton Sidings ST5 . . . . .283 B4
Brampton Wlk ST3 . . . . . . .284 C1
Bramshall Ind Est ST14 . . . .125 A7
Bramshall Rd ST14 . . . . . . .125 E8
Bramshaws Acre ST10 . . . . . .76 E2
Bramstead Ave WV6 . . . . . .255 B2
Bramwell Dr WS6 . . . . .226 D1
Brancaster Cl ST7 . . . . .251 A5
Branchal Rd WS9 . . . . .245 C1
Sedgley DY3 . . . . .271 E7
Brandon Cl Aldridge WS9 . . .256 F3
Brandon Gr ST4 . . . . .87 F8
Brandon Pk WV3 . . . . .265 E7
Brandons The ST17 . . . . . . .174 F5
Bransdale Rd WS8 . . . . .244 E6
Branson Ave ST3 . . . . .73 E3
Branston Rd
Burton u T DE14 . . . . .185 C8
Tatenhill DE13,DE14 . . . . . .184 C8
Branston Water Pk★
DE14 . . . . .184 D6
Bransty Gr ST4 . . . . .88 C3
Brant Ave ST5 . . . . .56 A4
Brantley Ave WV3 . . . . .255 C1
Brantley Cres DY7 . . . . .267 F2
Brantley La
Bobbington DY7 . . . . .267 F2
Seisdon WV5,WV6 . . . . . . .263 A3
Branton Hill La WS9 . . . . . .256 C5
Brantwood Ave WS7 . . . . . .229 A5
Brassington St CW3 . . . . . . .53 A6
Brassington Terr CW3 . . . . . .52 F3
Brassington Way ST2 . . . . . . .58 C1
Bratch Common Rd
WV5 . . . . .269 E7
Bratch Hollow WV5 . . . . . .270 A8
Bratch La WV5 . . . . .269 F8
Bratch Pk WV5 . . . . .269 F8
Brattice Pl ST2 . . . . .73 D7
Braunton Ave ST17 . . . . . . .175 E7
Braystones Cl ST6 . . . . .41 E8
Brazenhill La ST18 . . . . .172 F7
Breach La Foston DE6 . . . . .129 C5
Upper Tean ST10 . . . . .92 C5
Breach Rd ST6 . . . . .43 C7
Breadmarket St WS13 . . . . .231 B8
Breamore Cres DY1 . . . . . . .271 F3
Bream B77 . . . . .261 D7
Bream Way ST6 . . . . .42 B3
Brean Rd ST17 . . . . .175 E6
Brecon Way ST2 . . . . .58 C2
Bredon Cl WV7 . . . . .237 A5
Bredon Ct B75 . . . . .258 A4
Breech Cl ST10 . . . . .48 F2
Breedon Cl ST5 . . . . .55 F3
Breedon Way WS4 . . . . .244 C1
Breeze Ave
Norton Canes WS11 . . . . . .228 B5
Stoke-on-T ST6 . . . . .41 E5
Brelades Cl DY1 . . . . .271 E3
Brempton Croft ST15 . . . . .106 D2
Brendale Cl ST4 . . . . .72 A1
Brendon Cl ST17 . . . . .175 D8
Brendon B77 . . . . .251 B1
Brent Cl ⑨ ST17 . . . . .175 A8
Brentmill Cl WV10 . . . . . . .240 F4
Brentnall Dr B75 . . . . .258 B3

Brentnor Cl ST3 . . . . .73 F3
Brenton Rd WV4 . . . . .265 F3
Brent B77 . . . . .261 E7
Brentwood Ct ST9 . . . . .59 B4
Brentwood Dr ST9 . . . . .59 B4
Brentwood Gr
Stoke-on-T ST9 . . . . .43 C3
Werrington ST9 . . . . .59 B4
Brenwood Cl DY6 . . . . .275 B7
Breretonhill La WS15 . . . . .197 C2
Brereton Hill WS15 . . . . . . .197 B5
Brereton Lodge WS17 . . . . .197 A6
Brereton Manor Ct
WS15 . . . . .197 B5
Brereton Pl ST6 . . . . .41 E1
Brereton Rd WS15 . . . . . . .196 F7
Bretby Bsns Pk DE15 . . . . . .186 F8
Bretby Fairways DE15 . . . . .167 F2
Bretby Hollow DE11 . . . . . .186 F7
Bretby Hts DE11 . . . . .186 F7
Bretby La DE15 . . . . .167 E3
Bretby Rd DE11 . . . . .186 F7
Bretby Stoneware Ind Est
DE11 . . . . .186 E8
Bretherton Pl ST6 . . . . .42 A6
Bretlands Way DE15 . . . . . .186 A6
Brettell La DY8 . . . . .279 F8
Brevitt Rd WV2 . . . . .266 D6
Brewers Dr WS3 . . . . .244 A1
Brewers Terr WS3 . . . . .244 A2
Brewery La Hanley ST1 . . . . .282 B3
Brewery St Hanley ST1 . . . . .282 B3
Rugeley WS15 . . . . .196 F8
Brewster Rd ST2 . . . . .57 F3
Brewhouse Ct WS13 . . . . . .213 F1
Brewhouse The ST4 . . . . . . .166 D2
Brewood CE Mid Sch
ST19 . . . . .223 C6
Brewood Park Cotts
WV9 . . . . .224 A3
Brewood Rd
Coven,Cross Green WV9 . . .224 C1
Coven WV9 . . . . .224 B3
Brewster Cl ST6 . . . . .57 C7
Brianson Ave ST6 . . . . .57 C7
Briar Ave B74 . . . . .257 A1
Briarbank Cl ST4 . . . . .71 F1
Briar Cl Cannock WS12 . . . .210 A8
Rugeley WS15 . . . . .178 C1
Swadlincote DE11 . . . . . . .186 F5
Walton-on-T-H ST17 . . . . . .175 F6
Briar Gr ST15 . . . . .118 E5
Briarsleigh ST17 . . . . .175 C7
Briars The Aldridge WS9 . .256 A7
Hagley DY9 . . . . .281 F4
Newcastle-u-L ST5 . . . . . . .283 B4
Briars Way WS12 . . . . .211 D4
Briarswood Biddulph ST8 . . .16 C1
Kidsgrove ST7 . . . . .26 B1
Briar B77 . . . . .251 A3
Briar Way ST21 . . . . .102 E2
Briarwood Pl ST3 . . . . .74 B2
Brickbridge La WV5 . . . . . .269 E5
Brickfield Pl ST18 . . . . .139 D1
Brickfield Pl ST3 . . . . .73 C6
Brickhill La DE13 . . . . .163 A6
Brickhouse La B79 . . . . .176 E5
Brick House St ⑥ ST6 . . . . . .56 F8
Brickin St WS8 . . . . .244 F7
Brick Kiln La
Brocton ST17 . . . . .175 F3
Codsall Wood ST19 . . . . . .222 C2
Dudley DY3 . . . . .271 B3
Hopton ST18 . . . . .137 D1
Brick-Kiln La
Newcastle-u-L ST5 . . . . .55 B8
Rolleston on D DE13 . . . . . .147 A3
Brick Kiln La
Stoke-on-T ST4 . . . . .56 E1
Weston ST18 . . . . .137 F2
Wheaton Aston ST19 . . . . .205 A5
Brick Kiln Way WS15 . . . . . .196 F5
Brick St DY3 . . . . .271 D8
Brickworks Rd WS12 . . . . . .210 A2
Brickyard Rd
Aldridge,Leighswood
WS9 . . . . .256 A7
Aldridge,Leighswood WS9 . .256 A8
Aldridge,Vigo WS9 . . . . . . .244 F1
Bridestowe Cl ④ ST3 . . . . . .90 A7
Bridge Ave WS6 . . . . .226 E4
Bridge Cl Audley ST7 . . . . . . .39 F2
Brownhills WS8 . . . . .244 E6
Weston ST18 . . . . .138 C3
Bridge Cres ST15 . . . . .120 A7
Bridge Croft ST6 . . . . .42 B6
Bridge Cross Rd WS7 . . . . .229 A4
Bridge Ct
Blythe Bridge ST11 . . . . . . .90 F6
Stoke-on-T ST4 . . . . .71 E3
Stourbridge DY8 . . . . .275 E2
Uttoxeter ST14 . . . . .126 D7
Woodseaves ST20 . . . . . . .151 D7
Bridge End ST13 . . . . .30 C7
Bridge Farm DE13 . . . . . . .147 E1
Bridgefoot Wlk WV8 . . . . . .239 F1
Bridge Ho ST5 . . . . .55 C2
Bridge Ind Est ST6 . . . . .57 B7
Bridge La ST18 . . . . .139 B3
Bridgeman Ct TF11 . . . . . . .203 F2
Bridgemary Cl WV10 . . . . . .240 E4
Bridgemere Garden World★
CW5 . . . . .67 A3
Bridge Rd Armitage WS15 . .198 C4
Cookley DY10 . . . . .280 A6
Market Drayton TF9 . . . . . . .97 A1
Stoke-on-T ST4 . . . . .71 E3
Uttoxeter ST14 . . . . .126 D7

Bridge Rd continued
Walsall WS4 . . . . .244 B1
Bridges Cres WS11 . . . . . . .227 F5
Bridgeside DE13 . . . . .147 E1
Bridgeside Trad Est B77 . . . .250 C3
Bridges Rd WS11 . . . . .227 F5
Bridge St Brindley Ford ST8 . .27 B2
Brownhills WS8 . . . . .244 E6
Burton u T DE14 . . . . .166 F3
Cannock WS11 . . . . .226 E5
Newcastle-u-L,Silverdale
ST5 . . . . .55 C2
Newcastle-u-L ST5 . . . . . . .283 B3
Bridge Street Ind Units
ST14 . . . . .126 C7
Bridge St Stafford ST16 . . . .285 B2
Stretton DE13 . . . . .147 E1
Tamworth B77 . . . . .250 E5
Tutbury DE13 . . . . .146 C7
Uttoxeter ST14 . . . . .126 C7
Bridge Terr Newport TF10 . .168 E3
Upper Hulme ST13 . . . . .20 E6
Bridge The ST10 . . . . .92 D6
Bridgett Cl ST4 . . . . .71 E5
Bridge View DE6 . . . . .81 D8
Bridgewater Cl
Congleton CW12 . . . . .6 B1
Penkridge ST19 . . . . .207 F8
Bridgewater Dr WV5 . . . . . .269 F7
Bridgewater Rd WS15 . . . . .196 F8
Bridgewater St
Burslem ST6 . . . . .56 D8
Tamworth B77 . . . . .250 D5
Bridge Way WS8 . . . . .244 D5
Bridgwood St ST3 . . . . .284 C4
Bridgford Ave DE14 . . . . . . .184 D4
Bridgnorth Ave WS9 . . . . . .269 F5
Bridgnorth Gr ST5 . . . . .40 E2
Bridgnorth Rd
Enville DY7 . . . . .273 D2
Himley DY3 . . . . .270 B3
Kinver DY7 . . . . .278 C7
Seisdon WV6 . . . . .263 E5
Stourbridge DY7,DY8 . . . . .279 C6
Trescott WV6 . . . . .264 C3
Wolverhampton WV6 . . . . .255 B2
Wombourne WV5 . . . . .269 D5
Bridgtown Bsns Ctr
WS11 . . . . .226 E6
Bridgtown Prim Sch
WS11 . . . . .226 E6
Bridgwater Cl WS9 . . . . . . .244 F3
Bridgwood Rd ST11 . . . . . . .91 A7
Bridle La Ellenhall ST20 . . . .153 D8
Stanton DE15 . . . . .186 A5
Bridle Path The
Madeley CW3 . . . . .68 D7
Newcastle-u-L ST5 . . . . . . .70 F3
Bridle Path ST2 . . . . .59 A3
Bridle Rd Stafford ST17 . . . .175 D6
Stourbridge DY8 . . . . .279 D6
Bridleway The TF9 . . . . .97 B1
Bridle Wlk WS15 . . . . .178 B3
Brierley Hill Rd DY8 . . . . . . .275 F2
Brierley Lodge ST5 . . . . .70 F8
Brierley St ST6 . . . . .42 C1
Brierley Rd CW12 . . . . .6 B1
Brierlow Bar SK17 . . . . .5 B8
Brier Sch The DY6 . . . . .275 F5
Briertey Hill La WS11 . . . . . .212 B4
Brieryhurst Cl ST2 . . . . .58 C5
Brieryhurst Rd ST7 . . . . .26 B3
Bright Cres B77 . . . . .250 C2
Brightgreen St ST3 . . . . .73 D6
Brighton St ② ST4 . . . . .72 A7
Brighton The ST5 . . . . .55 B2
Brights Ave ⑥ ST5 . . . . .26 B2
Bright St ST3 . . . . .74 A1
Brightstone Cl WV10 . . . . . .240 F4
Bright St DY8 . . . . .279 D6
Brimfield Pl ① WV6 . . . . . .255 F4
Brindewell Gr ST4 . . . . .88 C6
Brindley Ave WV11 . . . . . . .242 A1
Brindley Bank Rd WS15 . . . .178 E3
Brindley Brae DY7 . . . . .278 C5
Brindley Cl
① Stourbridge DY8 . . . . . .275 E1
Albrighton WV7 . . . . .237 A6
Kidsgrove ST7 . . . . .25 E1
Penkridge ST19 . . . . .208 A7
Stafford ST16 . . . . .155 F8
Stone ST15 . . . . .104 E2
Talke ST7 . . . . .40 E8
Wombourne WV5 . . . . .269 D6
Brindley Cres
Cannock WS12 . . . . .210 C8
Cheddleton ST13 . . . . .45 C4
Brindley Heath Jun Sch
DY7 . . . . .278 A5
Brindley Heath Rd WS12 . . .195 C2
Brindley La ST2,ST9 . . . . . . .43 C3
Brindley Mill Mus The★
ST13 . . . . .30 D7
Brindley Pl ST6 . . . . .42 C6
Brindley Rd WS12 . . . . .195 A3
Brindleys Bsns Pk WS11 . . .210 B3
Brindley St ST5 . . . . .283 B3
Brindleys Way ST7 . . . . .39 F2
Brindley Way CW12 . . . . .6 B1
Brindon Cl ST3 . . . . .74 B3
Brinley Way DY6 . . . . .275 C6
Brinscall Gn ST6 . . . . .42 A7
Brinsford La WV10 . . . . .240 D7
Brinsford Rd WV10 . . . . . . .240 C3
Brinsley Ave ST4 . . . . .88 A6

Brisbane Rd ST16 . . . . .155 B7
Brisbane Way WS12 . . . . . .210 E3
Brisley Hill ST4 . . . . .71 F6
Bristol Cl WS11 . . . . .210 B1
Bristol St
Newcastle-u-L ST5 . . . . .56 D5
Wolverhampton WV3 . . . . .266 B8
Britannia Dr
Burton u T DE13 . . . . .166 D8
Stretton DE13 . . . . .147 D1
Britannia Gn DY3 . . . . .271 E5
Britannia Ho
Burton u T DE14 . . . . .166 D2
Stafford ST16 . . . . .285 B3
Britannia Park Ind Est
ST6 . . . . .57 B7
Britannia St ⑥ ST13 . . . . . . .30 E6
Britannia Stadium (Stoke City
FC) ST4 . . . . .72 C2
Britannia Way WS13 . . . . . .231 F8
Britch La ST20 . . . . .204 E8
Brittain Ave ST5 . . . . .55 F7
Brittain Rd ST13 . . . . .45 D5
Brittle Pl ST6 . . . . .42 D2
Britton St ST4 . . . . .56 F1
Brixham Cl ST2 . . . . .57 F1
Brizlincote La DE15 . . . . . . .167 D1
Brizlincote St DE15 . . . . . . .166 F1
Broadacres WV9 . . . . .224 B3
Broadbent Cl ❶ WS13 . . . . .230 F6
Broad Eye ST16 . . . . .285 A3
Broadfield Cl DY6 . . . . .275 D5
Broadfield House Glass
Mus★ DY6 . . . . .275 D5
Broadfield Rd ST6 . . . . .41 C7
Broadholes La ST19 . . . . . . .205 A6
Broadhurst Cl WS12 . . . . . .194 D3
Broadhurst Gn WS12 . . . . . .194 F2
Broadhurst Green Rd ST19,
WS12 . . . . .194 D2
Broadhurst St ST6 . . . . .42 B1
Broad La Burntwood WS7 . .230 B5
Church Eaton ST20 . . . . . . .171 C1
Lichfield WS14 . . . . .231 D6
Broadlands DE13 . . . . .166 D8
Broadlands Rise WS14 . . . . .231 D8
Broadlands WV10 . . . . .240 D5
Broad Lane Gdns WS3 . . . . .243 A2
Broad La
Stoke-on-T ST6,ST9 . . . . . . .43 C8
Walsall,Essington WS3 . . . .242 E4
Walsall WS4 . . . . .244 C2
Whittington WS13 . . . . . . .215 E1
Broadlawns Dr ST3 . . . . .73 B6
Broad La WV3 . . . . .265 E8
Broadlee B77 . . . . .251 C1
Broad Mdw WS9 . . . . .256 B8
Broad Meadow Croft
ST16 . . . . .155 A4
Broad Meadow Ct ST5 . . . . . .55 E6
Broadmeadow DY6 . . . . . . .275 E8
Broad Meadow La ST4 . . . . . .72 F6
Broadmine St ST4 . . . . .72 F6
Broadoaks Cl WS11 . . . . . . .227 F6
Broad Oaks ST17 . . . . .174 E5
Broadoak Way ST3 . . . . .72 E1
Broadsmeath B77 . . . . .250 C1
Broad St Cannock WS11 . . .226 E6
Hanley ST1 . . . . .282 A1
Kingswinford DY6 . . . . .275 D5
Leek ST13 . . . . .30 E5
Newcastle-u-L ST5 . . . . . . .283 B3
Broadstone Cl WV4 . . . . . . .266 D5
Broad St ST6 . . . . .285 A3
Broadway Cannock WS12 . .209 F6
Codsall WV8 . . . . .238 E3
Broadway Ct ❶ ST3 . . . . . . .73 F1
Broadway Gdns WV10 . . . . .240 E2
Broadway La ST10 . . . . .49 A4
Broadway Longton ST3 . . . . .73 F2
Newport TF10 . . . . .169 A3
Broadway Pl ❶ ST3 . . . . . . .73 F2
Broadway St DE14 . . . . .166 C1
Broadway The
Stourbridge DY8 . . . . .279 D3
Wombourne WV5 . . . . .270 A5
Broad Way WS4 . . . . .244 C1
Broadway
Wolverhampton,Bushbury
WV10 . . . . .240 E2
Wolverhampton,Compton
WV3 . . . . .255 C2
Broadwell La WV6 . . . . .253 B2
Broc Cl ST19 . . . . .208 A8
Brockbank Pl ST6 . . . . .42 B5
Brockeridge Cl WV12 . . . . . .242 C1
Brockhill TF9 . . . . .99 D5
Brockhurst La
Blymhill Lawn TF11 . . . . . . .204 B4
Blymhill TF11 . . . . .203 F5
Weeford B75 . . . . .259 B7
Brockhurst Rd
Blymhill TF11 . . . . .204 C6
Sutton Coldfield B75 . . . . . .258 D1
Brocklehurst Way ST1 . . . . . .57 E8
Brockley Sq ST1 . . . . .282 B3
Brockley's Wlk DY7 . . . . . . .278 C3
Brocksford St ST4 . . . . .284 D5
Brockton La ST21 . . . . .117 C3
Brockton Wlk ST3 . . . . .72 E1
Brock Way ST5 . . . . .55 E2
Brocton Cres ST17 . . . . .175 F3
Brocton Hts ST17 . . . . .176 C3
Brocton La ST17 . . . . .175 F6
Brocton Rd ST17 . . . . .176 C6
Brogan St ST4 . . . . .72 F6
Bromfield Ct Stone ST15 . . .105 A1

Bromfield Ct continued
Wolverhampton WV6 . . . . .255 B3
Bromford Dale ② WV6 . . . .255 F3
Bromford Pl ST1 . . . . .282 A1
Bromford Rise WV3 . . . . . . .266 B8
Bromley Cl WS12 . . . . .210 C7
Bromley Ct ST1 . . . . .282 A4
Bromley Gdns WV8 . . . . . . .239 A4
Bromleyhedge La ST13 . . . . .48 C1
Bromley Hills Prim Sch
DY6 . . . . .275 F5
Bromley Hough ST4 . . . . . . .71 F5
Bromley Ho WV4 . . . . .266 A5
Bromley La DY6 . . . . .275 E4
Bromley Lodge WV4 . . . . . .266 A5
Bromley Pl WV4 . . . . .266 A5
Bromley St Hanley ST1 . . . . .282 A4
Wolverhampton WV2 . . . . .266 C7
Bromley Wood WS15 . . . . . .161 E5
Brompton Dr ST2 . . . . .43 B3
Brompton Lawns WV6 . . . . .255 A3
Bromsberrow Way ST3 . . . . .90 A7
Bromsgrove Pl ST3 . . . . .284 A3
Bromstead Cres ST16 . . . . .155 B6
Bromwich Dr WS13 . . . . . . .215 D8
Bromwynd Cl WV2 . . . . .266 B6
Bronant Wlk ④ ST6 . . . . . . .57 A7
Bronte Cl DE14 . . . . .166 D7
Bronte Ct B79 . . . . .250 A6
Bronte Dr WS11 . . . . .210 C2
Bronte Gr ST2 . . . . .43 B4
Bronte Rd WV2 . . . . .266 F6
Brookbank Gdns DY3 . . . . . .271 B2
Brookbank Rd DY3 . . . . .271 B2
Brook Cl
Blythe Bridge ST11 . . . . . . .91 A7
Brownhills WS9 . . . . .245 A3
Coven WV9 . . . . .224 B3
Doveridge DE6 . . . . .127 C3
Endon ST9 . . . . .44 A8
Lichfield WS13 . . . . .214 A1
Penkridge ST19 . . . . .207 E7
Brook Cres DY6 . . . . .275 C7
Brookdale Dr WV4 . . . . .265 E6
Brookdale ST3 . . . . .271 C3
Brook End
Burntwood WS7 . . . . .229 A4
Fazeley B78 . . . . .261 B8
Haughton ST18 . . . . .172 F6
Longdon WS15 . . . . .198 A1
Brooke Rd WS12 . . . . .209 F6
Brookes Ct ST4 . . . . .72 E6
Brookfield Ave ST9 . . . . .43 E7
Brookfield Cl
Aldridge WS9 . . . . .245 A1
Whiston ST10 . . . . .62 D3
Brookfield Ct Hanley ST1 . . .282 B4
Haughton ST18 . . . . .172 E6
Stone ST15 . . . . .120 C6
Brookfield Dr WS11 . . . . . . .226 E7
Brookfield TF9 . . . . .99 D5
Brookfield Rd
Aldridge WS9 . . . . .245 A4
Codsall WV8 . . . . .239 B3
Stoke-on-T,Baddeley Green
ST2 . . . . .59 C8
Stoke-on-T,Springfields ST4 .71 E5
Brookfields Rd ST10 . . . . . . .62 A8
Brookgate ST1 . . . . .91 B8
Brook Gdns ST8 . . . . .16 D1
Brook Glen Rd ST17 . . . . . . .174 E7
Brook Gr WV8 . . . . .239 B2
Brookhay La WS13 . . . . .215 E3
Brookhill Cl WV12 . . . . .242 D1
Brookhill Way WV12 . . . . . .242 D1
Brook Ho TF10 . . . . .168 E3
Brookhouse Cl WV10 . . . . . .241 B6
Brookhouse Ct ST14 . . . . . .126 F1
Brookhouse Dr ST12 . . . . . . .88 D2
Brookhouse La
Bucknall ST2 . . . . .58 E4
Cheddleton ST13 . . . . .45 A3
Congleton CW12 . . . . .6 C2
Featherstone WV10 . . . . . .241 B7
Wolverhampton WV10 . . . .240 F6
Brookhouse Rd
Cheadle ST10 . . . . .76 B3
Gnosall ST20 . . . . .171 D7
Meir ST3 . . . . .74 B2
Newcastle-u-L ST5 . . . . .55 F8
Brookhouses Ind Est ST10 . .76 B2
Brookhouse Way
Cheadle ST10 . . . . .76 B2
Gnosall ST20 . . . . .171 D6
Brook La Brocton ST17 . . . . .176 C4
Brownhills WS9 . . . . .244 F3
Church Leigh ST10 . . . . . . .108 F6
Great Wyrley WS6 . . . . .227 A3
Brookland Ave ST3 . . . . .284 C4
Brookland Gr WS9 . . . . .244 F3
Brookland Rd
Brownhills WS9 . . . . .244 F3
Stoke-on-T ST6 . . . . .41 C6
Brooklands Ave WS6 . . . . . .226 F4
Brooklands Cl ST14 . . . . . . .126 B6
Brooklands Rd
Albrighton WV7 . . . . .237 B6
Cannock WS11 . . . . .210 A4
Brooklands Sch ST16 . . . . . .155 C6
Brooklands DY8 . . . . .275 F1
Brooklands The DY3 . . . . . . .269 C4
Brooklands Way
Cheddleton ST13 . . . . .46 A8
Leek ST13 . . . . .45 F8
Brook La
Newcastle-u-L ST5 . . . . . . .283 B3
Ranton ST18 . . . . .153 C3

Brook La continued
Stoke-on-T ST9 . . . . 43 F8
Brooklime Gdns
Featherstone WV10. . . . . 241 B7
Stafford ST16 . . . . 155 A5
Brooklyn Gr DY6 . . . . 275 B8
Brooklyn Gr
Burntwood WS7. . . . . . . 229 A4
Cannock WS12. . . . . 210 D1
Brook Mdws WV8 . . . . . . 239 B4
Brookmead Gr ST3. . . . . . 73 B6
Brookmead Ind Est ST16 155 F8
Brook Path ST15 . . . . 119 F8
Brook Pl Newcastle-u-L ST5 71 C5
Stoke-on-T ST4 . . . . 56 F1
Brook Prim Sch DY8 . . . . 275 F1
Brook Rd
Cheslyn Hay WS6. . . . . . 226 E4
Stoke-on-T ST4 . . . . 88 A7
Wombourne WV5. . . . . . 269 F6
Brookside Ave TF10 . . . . 168 E1
Brookside Bsns Ctr ST15 118 B5
Brookside Bsns Pk ST16 126 D7
Burton u T DE15. . . . . . . 167 B5
Brookside Cl
Newcastle-u-L ST5. . . . . 283 A1
Wombourne WV5. . . . . . 269 F6
Brookside Cotts DE6 . . . . 81 C3
Brookside Ct ST10 . . . . . . 76 B3
Brookside Cvn Site WV9. 224 B2
Brookside Dr Endon ST9. . . 44 A8
Stoke-on-T ST3 . . . . 72 E2
Brookside Dudley DY3. . . 271 D2
Enville DY7. . . . . 273 D3
Brookside Gdns ST19 . . . 221 E8
Brookside Ind Est ST6. . . 56 D8
Brookside ST10 . . . . 62 A3
Brookside La ST15 . . . . . . 119 F7
Brookside
Marchington ST14 . . . . . 127 A2
Ranton ST18 . . . . 153 D5
Brookside Rd
Barton-u-N DE13. . . . . . 183 C1
Tamworth B79 . . . . 249 D1
Uttoxeter ST14 . . . . 126 D7
Brook Side DE13 . . . . 147 B4
Brookside Way
Blakedown DY10 . . . . . . 281 B2
Kingswinford DY6 . . . . . 275 C4
Tamworth B77 . . . . 262 A6
Brook Sq 1 WS15 . . . . . . 196 E8
Brook St Biddulph ST8. . . 27 A5
Burton u T DE14. . . . . . . 166 D4
Dudley,Gornalwood DY3 . 271 C3
Kingswinford DY6 . . . . . 270 B1
Leek ST13 . . . . 30 E5
Newcastle-u-L ST5. . . . . . 55 C2
Stoke-on-T ST4 . . . . 72 B7
Stourbridge,Amblecote
DY8. . . . . 275 F1
Stourbridge DY8 . . . . . . 279 E5
Swadlincote DE11 . . . . . 186 E6
Brook Vale WS11 . . . . . . 226 E8
Brookview Dr ST3. . . . . . . 73 F4
Brookweed B77. . . . . 251 A3
Brookwillows 5 ST17. . . 175 C7
Brookwood Cl ST5 . . . . . . 71 B3
Brookwood Dr ST3. . . . . . 74 B2
Broom Covert Rd WS14 . 247 D5
Broome Cl DE13 . . . . 199 C6
Broome Hill ST9 . . . . 71 C1
Broome La DY9 . . . . 281 F2
Broome Wlk WS15 . . . . . 198 C4
Broomfield Ave B78. . . . 261 A8
Broomfield Cl
Newport TF10 . . . . 168 D3
Stone ST15 . . . . 120 B6
Broomfield La ST14 . . . . . 79 F2
Broomfield Pl TF10 . . . . 168 D3
Broomfield Pl N ST1 . . . . 57 A3
Broomfield Pl S ST1 . . . . 57 A3
Broomfield Rd
Newport TF10 . . . . 168 D3
Stoke-on-T ST6 . . . . 42 E6
Broomfields ST8. . . . . 17 B1
Broomhill Bank WS11 . . 209 E3
Broomhill Cl WS11. . . . . 209 E4
Broomhills The DE12. . . 219 E7
Broomhill St ST1 . . . . 41 D4
Broom Hollow TF9. . . . . . 99 E5
Broom Lea TF9 . . . . 99 D4
Broom's La DE6. . . . . 129 B2
Brooms Park Cvn Pk
ST15. . . . . 120 B5
Brooms Rd ST15 . . . . 120 B5
Broom St ST1. . . . . 282 C4
Broomyclose La ST14 . . . 111 A4
Brough Cl Leek ST13. . . . . 30 E6
Wolverhampton WV4,
WV11 . . . . 266 F3
Brough La ST4. . . . . 88 B7
Brough Rd DE15 . . . . 167 C3
Broughton Cl ST16. . . . . 155 C7
Broughton Cres ST12 . . . . 88 E1
Broughton WV6. . . . . 255 A3
Broughton Rd Bucknall ST2 57 F3
Newcastle-u-L ST5. . . . . . 56 D2
Wolverhampton WV3. . . 255 C1
Brow Hill TF13. . . . . 30 E6
Brown Ave
Lawton-gate ST7 . . . . 25 A5
Tamworth B77 . . . . 261 C8
Brownhill Rd ST3. . . . . . . 74 A2
Brownhill Rd ST6. . . . . . . 43 B8
Brownhills Bsns Pk ST6. . 41 D2
Brownhills Com Tech Coll
WS8 . . . . 228 F1

Brownhills High Sch ST6 . 41 E1
Brownhills Rd
Brownhills WS8. . . . . . . 245 A4
Norton Canes WS11 . . . . 228 B4
Stoke-on-T ST6 . . . . 41 D2
Brownhills West Prim Sch
WS8 . . . . 228 C2
Brownhills West Sta★
WS7 . . . . 228 C3
Browning Cl Cheadle ST10. 76 C2
Tamworth B79 . . . . 249 F8
Browning Cres WV10. . . . 240 C2
Browning Gr Perton WV6. 254 E4
Talke ST7. . . . . 40 C8
Browning Rd
Burntwood WS7. . . . . . . 229 C7
Dudley DY3. . . . . 271 A4
Stoke-on-T ST6 . . . . 72 F2
Browning St ST16 . . . . . . 285 A4
Brown La SK17. . . . . 3 B3
Brown Lees Ind Est ST8 . . 27 B4
Brown Lees Rd
Biddulph ST8 . . . . 27 A5
Biddulph ST8 . . . . 27 B4
Harriseahead ST8 . . . . . . 26 F4
Brownley Rd ST6 . . . . 42 D1
Brownsea Pl ST3. . . . . 72 E4
Brownsfield Rd WS13 . . . 214 D1
Brownshill Bsns Pk WS8. 244 F5
Brownshore La WV11 . . . 242 A3
Brown's La B78. . . . . 262 F5
Brown's Lake DY7 . . . . . . 273 D3
Brown's La Tamworth B79 250 C8
Yoxall DE13 . . . . 182 A2
Brown St Burslem ST6. . . . 57 A8
Wolverhampton WV2. . . 266 D7
Brownswall Rd DY3 . . . . . 271 A4
Browns Wlk WS15 . . . . . 178 D1
Browsholme B79. . . . . . . 249 D6
Broxwood Pk WV6 . . . . . 255 B3
Bruford Rd WV3 . . . . 266 A8
Brund La ST13 . . . . 45 A3
Brundall Oval ST2. . . . . . . 58 D2
Brundle Ave ST16 . . . . . . 155 B3
Brunel Cl Burntwood WS7. 229 B8
Stafford ST16 . . . . 155 F1
Tamworth B79 . . . . 250 B6
Brunel Ct
Four Ashes WV10 . . . . . . 224 D5
Wombourne WV5. . . . . . 270 A7
Brunel Gr WV6. . . . . 254 E5
Brunel Way DE11 . . . . . . 186 E1
Brunel Wlk ST3 . . . . 284 C4
Brunslow Cl WV10 . . . . . . 240 C1
Brunswick Mill 5 ST13. . . 30 E6
Brunswick Pl ST1. . . . . . . 282 B2
Brunswick Rd WS11. . . . . 209 E2
Brunswick St 3 Leek ST13 30 F6
Hanley ST1. . . . . 282 B3
Newcastle-u-L ST5. . . . . 283 C3
Brunswick Terr ST16. . . . 285 A2
Brunt St ST6. . . . . 56 D7
Brutus Rd ST5 . . . . 55 D6
Bryan Ave WV4 . . . . 265 D4
Bryans La WS15. . . . . 178 F1
Bryan St ST1. . . . . 282 B3
Bryans Way WS12. . . . . . 210 F4
Bryant Rd ST2 . . . . 58 B5
Brymbo Rd ST3. . . . . 55 F5
Brynmawr Rd WV14. . . . 266 F3
Bryony Burton u T DE14. . 185 B8
Sutton Coldfield B74 . . . 257 F5
Buccleuch Rd ST3 . . . . . . 73 D2
Buckden B77 . . . . 251 C1
Buckingham Cl
6 Burton u T DE13. . . . 166 D8
Stafford ST17 . . . . 156 C3
Buckingham Cres ST4. . . 72 A1
Buckingham Ct DE15. . . . 167 C3
Buckingham Gdns WS14 231 B6
Buckingham Gr DY6. . . . 275 C2
Buckingham Pl 3 WS12. 210 C1
Buckingham Rd
Tamworth B79 . . . . 249 E7
Wolverhampton WV4. . . 266 A5
Buckingham Rise DY1. . . 271 D2
Buckland Cl WS12 . . . . . 210 D1
Buckland Gr ST4. . . . . 88 C5
Buckland Rd ST16. . . . . . 136 D1
Buckland Wlk TF10 . . . . . 168 F5
Buckley Cl ST14. . . . . 125 C7
Buckley Rd Stoke-on-T ST6. 42 D5
Wolverhampton WV4. . . 265 D5
Buckley's Row ST5. . . . . 283 B2
Buckmaster Ave ST5 . . . . 71 C6
Bucknall Hospl ST2 . . . . . 58 C4
Bucknall New Rd ST1 . . . 282 C3
Bucknall Old Rd ST1 . . . 282 C3
Bucknall Rd Hanley ST1. . 57 F3
Wolverhampton WV11. . 242 B1
Buckthorn Cl WS12 . . . . 209 F8
Buckton Cl B75 . . . . 258 E2
Bude Dr ST17. . . . . 156 E1
Buds Rd
Cannock Wood WS15. . . 211 F5
Gentleshaw WS15. . . . . 212 A5
Buglawton Hall Specl Sch
CW12 . . . . 6 D5
Buglawton Prim Sch CW12 6 A4
Buildwas Cl WS3. . . . . . . 242 F2
Bulldog La WS13. . . . . . . 214 B1
Buller St Hanley ST1. . . . 282 C1
Wolverhampton WV4. . . 266 E6
Bullgap La DE6 . . . . 65 C4
Bull Hill ST16 . . . . 285 B3
Bull La Packmoor ST8. . . . 27 A2
Wombourne WV5. . . . . . 270 B7
Bullmeadow La WV5 . . . 270 A8

Bullmoor La
Muckley Corner WS14. . . 230 A1
Muckley Corner WS14. . . 230 B1
Bullocks House Rd ST7. . . 26 E3
Bullows Rd WS8 . . . . 244 C6
Bull Ring Claverley WV5 . 267 C7
Sedgley DY3. . . . . 271 D8
Bull Ring The ST18. . . . . 138 C1
Bullrushes Cl
6 Hanley ST1. . . . . 56 F2
Stoke-on-T ST1 . . . . 57 A2
Bull St DY3 . . . . 271 C2
Bulrush Cl WS8. . . . . 244 E7
Bulstrode St 3 ST1. . . . . 56 F1
Bumblehole Mdws WV5. 269 F7
Bungalows The
Adbaston ST20. . . . . 131 D4
Chipnall TF9. . . . . 114 A3
Leek ST13 . . . . 31 A5
Bungham La ST19. . . . . . 207 D8
Bun La Blymhill TF10. . . . 188 C1
Great Chatwell TF10. . . . 203 C8
Bunny Hill ST5. . . . . 71 C5
Bunting Cl ST14. . . . . 126 B6
Buntingsdale Rd TF9. . . . 112 A7
Bunting The Kingsley ST10 61 D3
Wetley Rocks ST9 . . . . . . 60 A7
Bunt's La ST9. . . . . 43 D4
Bunyan Pl ST5. . . . . 209 E4
Burcham Cl ST16 . . . . . . 155 B7
Burcot Cl DY4 . . . . 257 F2
Burdock Cl WS11 . . . . . . 210 B3
Burford Ave ST5 . . . . 40 D1
Burford Rd Stafford ST17 156 D1
Wheaton Aston ST19. . . . 205 B6
Burford Way ST2. . . . . 58 A1
Burgage Cl TF9. . . . . 97 C1
Burgage Gr TF10 . . . . . . 168 F2
Burgage The
Eccleshall ST21 . . . . 133 F7
Market Drayton TF9. . . . . 97 C1
Burgesses The DY7 . . . . 278 B3
Burgess St ST6 . . . . 56 F7
Burgis Cl ST13 . . . . 45 D4
Burgoyne St WS11. . . . . 210 A5
Burgundy Gr 3 WS11 . . . 90 A7
Burland Ave WV6 . . . . . . 255 E6
Burland Rd ST5 . . . . 40 D1
Burleigh Cl WS12 . . . . . . 210 A8
Burleigh Croft WS7 . . . . 229 A4
Burleigh Gr ST5. . . . . 56 D3
Burleigh Rd WV3 . . . . . . 266 A8
Burlidge Rd ST6. . . . . 42 A6
Burlington Ave ST5 . . . . . 56 D3
Burlington Ct B78. . . . . . 261 B8
Burlington Dr ST17 . . . . . 174 B8
Burmarsh Wlk
4 Burslem ST6. . . . . 56 F7
Wolverhampton WV8. . . 255 F7
Burnaby Rd ST6. . . . . 41 C6
Burnell Gdns WV3 . . . . . 265 B8
Burnett Ct ST15. . . . . 155 A5
Burnett Pl ST6. . . . . 42 D4
Burnett Rd B74. . . . . 257 B2
Burnfield Dr WS15. . . . . 178 D1
Burnfields Way WS9 . . . . 256 A7
Burnham Ave 1 ST17 . . . 175 D6
Burnham Cl DY6 . . . . 275 F4
Burnham Gn WS11 . . . . . 226 B8
Burnham St ST4 . . . . 284 A5
Burnhays Rd ST6. . . . . . . 41 F2
Burnley St ST1. . . . . 57 D6
Burnsall Rd WV9 . . . . . . 240 A3
Burns Ave Stafford ST17. 174 B8
Wolverhampton WV10. . 240 D2
Burns Cl Kidsgrove ST7. . . 41 A8
Lichfield WS14. . . . . 231 B6
Burns Dr WS7 . . . . 229 C4
Burns Gr DY3 . . . . 271 A4
Burnside Cl ST5 . . . . 90 A4
Burnside DE13 . . . . 147 B4
Burns Rd Congleton CW12. . 6 A2
Tamworth B79 . . . . 250 A6
Burns Row ST3 . . . . 74 B2
Burns St WS11. . . . . 210 A3
Burnthill La WS15. . . . . . 196 E8
Burntwood Bsns Pk
WS7 . . . . 228 D7
Burntwood Rd
Hammerwich WS7. . . . . 229 D4
Norton Canes WS11 . . . . 228 A7
Burntwood Town Sh Ctr
WS7 . . . . 228 F7
Burntwood View TF9. . . . 99 E4
Burnwood Com Prim Sch
ST6. . . . . 42 B5
Burnwood Ct ST6. . . . . . . 42 D2
Burnwood Gr ST7 . . . . . . 26 B2
Burnwood Pl ST6 . . . . . . 42 B5
Burrington Dr ST4 . . . . . . 88 C6
Burrows Rd DY6. . . . . 275 F4
Burrows The DE11 . . . . . 186 F5
Burslem Cl WS3 . . . . 243 A3
Burslem Ent Ctr ST6 . . . . 57 A8
Bursley Cl ST17. . . . . 174 D6
Bursley Prim Sch ST5. . . 56 B8
Bursley Rd ST6 . . . . 57 A7
Bursley Way ST5. . . . . . . 56 A8
Bursnips Rd WV11 . . . . . 242 C4
Burton Bank La
Stafford,Moss Pit ST17 . . 174 E5
Stafford ST17,ST18. . . . 174 D5
Burton Borough Sch The
TF10 . . . . 169 A2
Burton Cl ST4. . . . . 250 C7
Burton Coll (Town Campus)
DE14. . . . . 166 E2

Burton Cres
Kingsley Holt ST10. . . . . 76 F8
Stoke-on-T ST1 . . . . 57 E7
Burton Ct ST17 . . . . 174 E7
Burton Ent Pk DE14 . . . . 166 E5
Burton House Gdns
ST17. . . . . 174 E7
Burton Manor Prim Sch
ST17. . . . . 174 E7
Burton Manor Rd ST17 . . 174 D6
Burton Mews ST14 . . . . . 110 F1
Burton Old Rd E WS14. . . 231 E8
Burton Old Rd
Lichfield,Boley Park
WS14 . . . . 231 F8
Lichfield,Streethay WS13. 214 F1
Burton Old Rd W WS14. . 231 D8
Burton-on-Trent Sta
DE14. . . . . 166 C3
Burton Pl ST1. . . . . 282 C2
Burton Rd Alrewas DE13. 201 B3
Burton u T DE14. . . . . . . 185 B7
Dudley DY1. . . . . 271 F4
Egginton DE65 . . . . 148 A3
Elford DE79 . . . . 216 E1
Lichfield WS13. . . . . 214 F1
Newton Solney DE15,DE65 148 F7
Swadlincote DE11 . . . . . 186 D2
Tutbury DE13 . . . . 146 D4
Whittington WS14 . . . . . 232 E7
Burton Sq ST17 . . . . 174 E7
Burton St Leek ST13 . . . . . 30 D5
Tutbury DE13 . . . . 146 C6
Burton Terr ST14 . . . . . . 126 C8
Burt St ST3 . . . . 74 B3
Burwaye Cl WS13 . . . . . . 231 A6
Burway Mdw DE13 . . . . . 201 A2
Bury Ring ST18 . . . . 173 D6
Bushberry Cl ST15 . . . . . 119 F6
Bushbury Hill Prim Sch
WV10 . . . . 240 F1
Bushbury La WV10 . . . . . 240 E2
Bush Cl WV7. . . . . 237 A5
Bush Dr WS15 . . . . 178 C1
Bushey Cl B74 . . . . 256 F2
Bushfield Rd WV7. . . . . . 237 A5
Bush Gr WS3 . . . . 244 A2
Bushton La DE13. . . . . . . 146 B2
Bustomley La ST10. . . . . 108 A5
Bute St ST4. . . . . 284 A4
Butler Ct DE14. . . . . 166 B3
Butlers Lane Sta B74. . . . 258 A3
Butlers La B74. . . . . 258 A3
Butler St ST4 . . . . 72 B6
Butter Bk ST18. . . . . 154 B3
Butterbank La ST18. . . . . 154 B2
Buttercross The 2 TF9. . . 97 C1
Butterfield Cl WV6. . . . . . 254 D3
Butterfield Pl 3 ST6. . . . . 41 E3
Butterhill Bank WS15. . . 121 A2
Butterhill La ST15. . . . . . 121 F5
Buttermere Cl
Burslem ST6 . . . . 56 E8
Cannock WS11. . . . . 210 A3
Wolverhampton WV6. . . 255 D8
Buttermere Dr WV6 . . . . 254 F4
Buttermere Dr WV11 . . . 242 A2
Buttermere Gr WV11 . . . 242 B1
Buttermere B77 . . . . 262 B7
Butterton La ST5. . . . . 70 D2
Butthouse La ST21. . . . . . 102 C5
Butt La Ranton ST18. . . . . 153 C1
Talke ST7. . . . . 40 E8
Buttons Farm Rd WV4. . . 265 D3
Butts Cl ST15 . . . . 227 E4
Butts Croft DE13 . . . . . . 200 F3
Butts Gn ST2 . . . . 58 C6
Butt's La ST10 . . . . 63 F8
Butts La
Norton Canes WS11 . . . . 227 E4
Warslow SK17 . . . . 23 C2
Butts Rd
Market Drayton TF9. . . . . 97 B1
Wolverhampton WV4. . . 265 F4
Butts The Betley ST7. . . . . 53 A5
Lichfield WS14. . . . . 230 D7
Newcastle-u-L ST5. . . . . . 55 A2
Buxton Ave Fazeley B78. . 261 B8
Newcastle-u-L ST5. . . . . . 55 A2
Buxton Old Rd CW12 . . . . 6 A4
Buxton Rd Congleton CW12. 6 C6
Leek ST13 . . . . 31 B7
Longnor SK17 . . . . 13 B7
Walsall WS3. . . . . 243 C3
Wetton DE6 . . . . 35 B5
Buxton St ST1. . . . . 57 D7
Byatt's Gr ST3. . . . . 284 A2
Bycars Farm Croft WS13 215 E8
Bycars La ST6. . . . . 42 A1
Bycars Rd ST6. . . . . 41 F1
Byland Pl ST5. . . . . 71 A5
Byland B77 . . . . 250 D3
Byland Way WS3. . . . . . . 242 F1
By Pass Rd B77 . . . . 251 A5
Byrd's Cl ST14 . . . . 125 F8
Byrd's La ST14 . . . . 126 A8
Byrkley Park Ctr★ DE13. 164 A3
Byrkley St DE14. . . . . 166 B4
Byrne Rd WV2 . . . . 266 D7
Byrom St 9 ST13. . . . . . . 30 D6
Byron Cl Burntwood WS7. 211 C1
Cheadle ST10. . . . . 76 B2
Market Drayton TF9. . . . 112 A7
Stafford ST16 . . . . 156 A5

Bro – Cam 295

Byron Croft Dudley DY3. . 271 A5
Sutton Coldfield B74 . . . 257 F6
Byron Ct Kidsgrove ST7. . . 41 A8
Sutton Coldfield B74 . . . 258 A5
Byron Pl Cannock WS11 . . 209 F5
Rugeley WS15 . . . . 178 C2
Byron Rd Tamworth B79 . 250 A7
Wolverhampton WV10. . 241 A1
Byron St ST4 . . . . 56 D1
Bywater Gr 3 ST3. . . . . . . 73 D6
Byways WS3 . . . . 243 C3

C

Cable St WV2. . . . . 266 F8
Cabot Gr WV6 . . . . 254 E4
Cacklehill La DE6 . . . . 81 C2
Cadeby Gr ST2. . . . . 43 B2
Cadley Hill Ind Est DE11 186 D2
Cadley Hill Rd DE11. . . . . 186 E3
Cadman Cres ST6 . . . . . . 42 E3
Cadman's La WS6,WS3 . . 243 D6
Cadogan Rd B77 . . . . 261 D5
Caernarvon Ave ST15 . . . 120 C6
Caernarvon Cl
Burton u T DE13. . . . . . . 166 E8
Market Drayton TF9. . . . . 97 E2
Caernarvon Way DY1. . . 271 C2
Cairn Cl ST2. . . . . 58 D3
Cairns Cl DE15. . . . . 167 C3
Cairns Dr ST16. . . . . 156 B5
Caister B77 . . . . 251 A6
Caistor Cl Mile Oak B78. . 260 D8
Stoke-on-T ST2 . . . . 43 A1
Calais Rd DE13. . . . . 166 B6
Calcot Dr WV6. . . . . 255 E7
Caldbeck Pl ST1 . . . . 282 C3
Caldercrofts TF10 . . . . . . 168 F4
Calder Rise DY3 . . . . 271 F6
Calder B77 . . . . 251 B2
Caldervale Dr 4 ST17. . . 175 D6
Caldew Gr ST15 . . . . 88 C5
Caldon Way ST15 . . . . . . 104 E3
Cale Cl B77. . . . . 250 C2
Caledonian B77 . . . . 250 F2
Caledonia Rd Hanley ST4. . 57 B1
Wolverhampton WV2. . . 266 E8
Calgary Cres DE15 . . . . . 167 D3
Calibre Ind Est WV10. . . . 224 D5
Californian Gr WS7 . . . . . 228 E8
California St ST3. . . . . . . 284 A3
Callaghan Gr 3 WS11 . . 210 C2
Callender Pl ST6. . . . . 57 A8
Callingwood La DE13. . . 164 F3
Callister Way DE14. . . . . 165 F3
Callis Wlk 2 B77 . . . . . . 261 F6
Callow Hill La ST10 . . . . . 75 D3
Calrofold Dr ST5. . . . . 40 D1
Calvary Cres ST2. . . . . 73 D8
Calveley Cl ST15 . . . . 118 F6
Calverley St ST3 . . . . 284 D2
Calver St 5 ST6. . . . . 41 D3
Calvert Gr ST5 . . . . 56 B7
Calvin Cl
Wolverhampton WV10. . 240 D3
Wombourne WV5. . . . . . 269 F5
Calving Hill WS11 . . . . . . 209 E2
Camberley Cres WV4. . . . 266 E2
Camberley Dr WV4. . . . . 266 A4
Camberley Rd DY6 . . . . . 275 F3
Camberwell Gr ST4 . . . . . 88 C6
Camborne
Congleton CW12 . . . . . . 15 E8
Stafford ST17 . . . . 175 C8
Camborne Cres ST5. . . . . 70 F5
Cambrian La WS15. . . . . 178 C3
Cambrian B77 . . . . 251 A2
Cambrian Way ST2. . . . . . 58 C4
Cambria St WS11 . . . . . . 209 D4
Cambridge Cl
Aldridge WS9. . . . . 256 B8
Biddulph ST8. . . . . 16 C1
Cambridge Ct ST5 . . . . . . 71 D4
Cambridge Dr ST5 . . . . . . 71 D4
Cambridge St
Burton u T DE14. . . . . . . 166 B1
Hanley ST1. . . . . 282 A2
Stafford ST16 . . . . 156 A4
Camden Dr B77. . . . . 250 E3
Camden St
Brownhills WS9. . . . . . . 244 F4
Stoke-on-T ST4 . . . . 72 E4
Camden Way DY6 . . . . . . 270 D1
Camelford Ct ST17 . . . . . 175 E8
Camellia Cl ST14. . . . . . . 54 E1
Camellia Gdns
Stourbridge DY8 . . . . . . 275 E2
Wolverhampton WV9. . . 239 F3
Camelot Cl Cannock WS11 209 F4
Stoke-on-T ST4 . . . . 88 C4
Stretton DE13 . . . . 147 E2
Cameo Dr DY8 . . . . 279 F8
Cameo Way ST16 . . . . . . 155 B7
Cameron Cl DE15 . . . . . . 167 C3
Cameron Wharf WS15 . . 104 F1
Camhouses B77 . . . . 251 B1
Camillus Rd ST5 . . . . 55 F2
Camoys Ct 8 ST6. . . . . . . 57 A7
Camoys Rd ST6 . . . . 57 A7
Campbell Ave ST13 . . . . . 30 C4
Campbell Cl
Congleton CW12 . . . . . . 6 A4
Rugeley WS15 . . . . 178 D2
Tamworth B79 . . . . 249 F8

Campbell Pl ST4 . . . . **72** B7
Campbell Rd
  Market Drayton TF9 . . . . . . **97** D2
  Stoke-on-T ST4 . . . . **72** B5
Campbell Terr ST1 . . . . **57** E6
Camp Hill Rd DY7 . . . . **273** F8
Camp Hill
  Stourbridge DY8 . . . . **275** E1
  Whitmore ST5 . . . . **85** A5
Campian's Ave WS6 . . . . . **226** D2
Campian Way ST6 . . . . **42** E2
Campion Ave ST5 . . . . **56** D3
Campion Cl
  Eccleshall ST21 . . . . **133** D6
  Wombourne WV5 . . . . **269** E6
Campion Dr
  Featherstone WV10 . . . . . **241** A7
  Tamworth B77 . . . . **250** C3
Campion B74 . . . . **257** F5
Camp Rd
  Cannock ST17,WS12 . . . . **194** D6
  Shenstone B75 . . . . **258** D6
  Stoke-on-T ST6 . . . . **42** C1
Camrose Gdns WV9 . . . . . **240** A3
Camsey La
  Burntwood WS7 . . . . **229** E8
  Creswell Green WS13 . . . . **212** F1
Canal Cotts ST20 . . . . **151** C2
Canal La ST6 . . . . **41** D2
Canal Mews The ST4 . . . . . **88** C6
Canal Rd CW12 . . . . **15** F8
Canal Side ST12 . . . . **88** D1
Canalside Cl
  Penkridge ST19 . . . . **207** F7
  Walsall WS3 . . . . **243** F1
Canalside Rd ST15 . . . . . . **104** C2
Canal St Burslem ST6 . . . . **56** D8
  Burton u T DE14 . . . . . . **166** C2
  Stourbridge DY8 . . . . **279** F6
Canal View Bsns Pk
  WS15 . . . . **197** B6
Canary Rd ST2 . . . . **73** D7
Canaway Wlk WS15 . . . . . **178** C2
Canberra Cres ST3 . . . . . . **90** C6
Canberra Dr ST16 . . . . . . **156** B4
Candle La CW3 . . . . **67** B2
Canford Cres WV8 . . . . . . **238** E3
Cannel Rd WS7 . . . . **228** D6
Canning Rd B77 . . . . **250** F4
Canning St ST4 . . . . **72** F5
Cannock Chase Ctry Pk
  Brocton ST17 . . . . **176** D2
  Cannock WS12 . . . . **195** A3
Cannock Chase Ent Ctr
  WS12 . . . . **195** D1
Cannock Chase High Sch
  WS11 . . . . **209** E2
Cannock Chase Tech Coll
  WS11 . . . . **209** D1
Cannock Com Hospl
  WS11 . . . . **209** E2
Cannock Ind Ctr WS11 . . **226** D5
Cannock Motor Village
  WS11 . . . . **210** B3
Cannock Rd Brocton ST17 **176** A3
  Burntwood,Chase Terrace
  WS7 . . . . **228** D7
  Burntwood,Gorstey Ley
  WS7 . . . . **229** B7
  Cannock,Heath Hayes
  WS12 . . . . **227** C8
  Cannock WS12,WS11 . . . . **210** A5
  Featherstone WV10 . . . . . **241** C7
  Huntington ST19 . . . . **208** B8
  Penkridge ST19 . . . . **192** F1
  Stafford ST17 . . . . **175** D5
Cannock Sh Ctr WS11 . . . . **209** E1
Cannock Sta WS11 . . . . . . **226** F8
Cannock Wood Ind Est
  WS12 . . . . **211** C6
Cannock Wood Rd WS12 . **211** B5
Cannock Wood St WS12 . **211** A6
Cannon Pl ST1 . . . . **282** B2
Cannon Rd WV5 . . . . **270** A6
Cannon St ST1 . . . . **282** B2
Canons Cl ST15 . . . . **120** A6
Canterbury Cl
  Lichfield WS13 . . . . **214** C3
  Tamworth B77 . . . . **250** D3
  Walsall WS3 . . . . **244** A4
Canterbury Dr
  Burntwood WS7 . . . . **229** E7
  Perton WV6 . . . . **254** E4
  Rugeley WS15 . . . . **196** D6
  Stoke-on-T ST6 . . . . **42** C4
Canterbury Rd
  Burton u T DE15 . . . . . . **167** C3
  Wolverhampton WV4 . . . . **265** E5
Canterbury Way WS12 . . . **210** B1
Canvey Gr ST3 . . . . **90** B7
Canwell Dr B75 . . . . **259** B5
Canwell Gate B75 . . . . . . **258** E4
Cape Ave ST17 . . . . **174** B7
Cape Cl WS8 . . . . **245** A6
Cape St ST1 . . . . **282** B4
Capesthorne Cl ST9 . . . . . **59** B3
Capewell St ST3 . . . . **284** C4
Capper Cl ST7 . . . . **26** A2
Cappers La WS13,WS14 . . **231** F8
Capper's La WS14 . . . . . . **232** A7
Capper St 5 ST6 . . . . **41** E3
Capricorn Way ST6 . . . . . **41** F6
Captain's Cl WV3 . . . . . . **255** D2

Captain's La DE13 . . . . . . **201** D8
Caradoc B77 . . . . **251** A2
Caraway Dr DE14 . . . . . . **185** A8
Caraway Pl ST3 . . . . **90** A6
Carberry Way ST3 . . . . . . **74** A4
Carder Ave ST16 . . . . **155** B7
Carder Gn SK17 . . . . **13** B6
Cardiff Gr ST1 . . . . **282** B1
Cardiff St WV3 . . . . **266** B8
Cardigan Ave WS15 . . . . **196** D6
Cardigan Gr ST4 . . . . **88** C6
Cardigan Ho WS12 . . . . . **210** C5
Cardigan Pl WS12 . . . . . . **210** C5
Cardinal Griffin RC High Sch
  WS11 . . . . **209** D2
Cardinal Way WS11 . . . . . **209** D2
Cardington Cl ST5 . . . . . . **71** A4
Cardoness Pl DY1 . . . . . . **271** F2
Card St ST6 . . . . **57** A7
Cardway ST5 . . . . **56** B7
Cardwell St ST1 . . . . **57** E5
Carey B77 . . . . **262** A5
Carfax WS11 . . . . **226** E8
Carina Gdns ST6 . . . . **42** D1
Carisbrooke Dr
  2 Stretton DE13 . . . . . . **147** E1
  Stafford ST17 . . . . **174** B7
Carisbrooke Gdns WV10 . **240** E3
Carisbrooke Rd
  Perton WV6 . . . . **255** A3
  Wolverhampton WV10 . . . **240** E3
Carisbrooke B77 . . . . **251** A2
Carisbrooke Way ST4 . . . **88** C5
Carlcroft B77 . . . . **251** B2
Carling Cl ST16 . . . . **155** B5
Carling Gr ST4 . . . . **73** A5
Carlisle Rd WS11 . . . . **226** B7
Carlisle St ST3 . . . . **284** B1
Carlos Cl ST10 . . . . **76** D3
Carlos Pl ST5 . . . . **41** B1
Carlow Ho WS15 . . . . **197** B6
Carlton Ave Aldridge B74 . **257** A2
  Brown Edge ST6 . . . . **43** B6
  Newcastle-u-L ST5 . . . . . . **71** B3
  Stoke-on-T ST6 . . . . **42** A4
Carlton Cl Brown Edge ST6 . **43** B6
  Cannock WS12 . . . . **210** D1
  Cheadle ST10 . . . . **76** D1
Carlton Cres
  Burntwood WS7 . . . . **229** A8
  Tamworth B79 . . . . **249** F8
Carlton Croft B74 . . . . . . **257** A2
Carlton Ct DE14 . . . . **166** B3
Carlton Ho B75 . . . . **258** B2
Carlton Rd Stoke-on-T ST4 . **72** C8
  Wolverhampton WV3 . . . . **266** A7
Carlton Sq ST17 . . . . **174** B8
Carlton St DE13 . . . . **166** B6
Carlton Terr ST13 . . . . . . **31** A6
Carlyon Pl ST1 . . . . **57** D8
Carmel Cl WS12 . . . . **210** C5
Carmichael Cl WS14 . . . . **231** D7
Carmount Rd ST2 . . . . . . **58** B7
Carmountside Prim Sch
  ST2 . . . . **58** B7
Carnation Cl ST3 . . . . . . **74** B6
Carnforth Cl DY6 . . . . . . **275** B7
Carnforth Gr ST6 . . . . . . **41** E8
Carnoustie Cl WS3 . . . . . **243** A3
Carnoustie B77 . . . . **251** C5
Carol Gdns DY8 . . . . **279** F8
Caroline Cl ST9 . . . . **59** B4
Caroline Cres ST6 . . . . . **43** B6
Caroline St ST3 . . . . **284** C4
Caroline Terr DE14 . . . . **166** C2
Carousels The DE14 . . . . **166** C5
Carpenter Cl DE15 . . . . . **167** C1
Carpenter Rd ST3 . . . . . **284** A4
Carr Bank ST10 . . . . **78** B7
Carriage Dr ST8 . . . . **16** E1
Carrick Cl WS3 . . . . **244** A5
Carrick Pl ST4 . . . . **72** A1
Carriers Fold WV5 . . . . . **270** B7
Carriers Rd DE65 . . . . . . **148** D6
Carr La Audley ST7 . . . . . **39** A1
  Wetton ST3,DE6 . . . . **34** F2
Carroll Dr ST3 . . . . **284** D4
Carron St ST4 . . . . **284** B5
Carroway Head Hill B78 . **259** D4
Carr St ST7 . . . . **26** F1
Carryer Pl ST4 . . . . **70** F7
Carshalton Gr WV2 . . . . **266** E7
Carson Rd ST6 . . . . **41** F3
Carson Way ST14 . . . . . **155** C3
Carter Ave WV8 . . . . **239** B3
Carters Croft ST10 . . . . . **92** F3
Cartersfield La WS9 . . . . **245** E6
Carter St ST14 . . . . **126** C7
Cartlich St ST6 . . . . **41** D5
Cartlidge St ST1 . . . . . . **56** D1
Cartmel Pl ST6 . . . . **42** B3
Cartway The WV6 . . . . . **254** D4
Cartwright Dr ST20 . . . . **171** D7
Cartwright Ho WS3 . . . . **243** B1
Cartwright Ind Est The
  ST3 . . . . **284** B2
Cartwright Rd B75 . . . . . **258** C3
Cartwright St
  Longton ST3 . . . . **284** B3
  Wolverhampton WV2 . . . . **266** D8
Carver Gdns DY8 . . . . . . **279** E2
Carver Rd
  Burton u T DE13 . . . . . . **166** C4
  Stafford ST16 . . . . **155** E6
Casa Mia Ct WS12 . . . . . **210** C5
Casewell Rd
  Kingswinford DY6 . . . . . . **275** C8
  Stoke-on-T ST6 . . . . **57** C7

Casey La Burton u T DE14 . **166** B4
  Weston CW2 . . . . **37** A5
Casey The ST13 . . . . **48** A1
Cash La ST21 . . . . **132** E4
Caslon Cres DY8 . . . . . . **279** D4
Caspian Gr ST4 . . . . **88** B7
Caspian Way ST19 . . . . . **205** C6
Cassandra Cl DY5 . . . . . . **271** C1
Castel Cl ST5 . . . . **70** E3
Castle Acre ST4 . . . . **174** B7
Castle Bank ST16,ST17 . . **174** A8
Castle Barns DY10 . . . . . **280** B3
Castlechurch Prim Sch
  ST17 . . . . **174** B8
Castle Cl Brownhills WS8 . **228** F2
  Tamworth B77 . . . . **250** E4
Castlecroft Ave WV3 . . . **265** A8
Castlecroft Gdns WV3 . . **265** C8
Castlecroft Ho WV3 . . . . **265** A8
Castlecroft La WV6 . . . . **254** F1
Castlecroft Prim Sch
  WV3 . . . . **265** B8
Castlecroft Rd WV3 . . . . **265** B8
Castle Ct Stone ST15 . . . . **120** C6
  Tutbury DE13 . . . . **146** C7
Castledene Dr ST16 . . . . **155** C1
Castledine Gr ST3 . . . . . **73** E4
Castle Dyke 6 WS13 . . . . **231** B7
Castlefields ST16 . . . . . . **285** A2
Castlefield St ST4 . . . . . . **57** A2
Castlefort Jun Mix Inf Sch
  WS9 . . . . **245** A4
Castlefort Rd WS9 . . . . . **245** A3
Castle Gr ST2 . . . . **58** B5
Castlehall B77 . . . . **251** A2
Castle Hayes La DE13 . . . **146** A5
Castle Hill Rd ST10 . . . . . **78** E1
Castlehill Rd ST5 . . . . . . **283** A4
Castle Hill Rd ST5 . . . . . **283** A3
Castle Hill Stafford ST16 . **285** A3
  Tutbury DE13 . . . . **146** B7
Castle Ho ST7 . . . . **26** C3
Castle House Dr ST17 . . . **155** B1
Castle House Sch TF10 . . **168** F4
Castle Inn Rd CW12 . . . . **16** C7
Castle Keep Ct ST5 . . . . . **283** A2
Castle Keep Mews ST5 . . **283** A2
Castle La CW3 . . . . **68** F5
Castle Mount ST5 . . . . . . **55** E6
Castle Park Inf Sch DE13 **166** B8
Castle Park Rd DE13 . . . . **166** B8
Castle Prim Sch ST7 . . . . **26** D6
Castle Rd Brownhills WS9 . **245** A3
  Cookley DY10 . . . . **280** A4
  Mow Cop ST7 . . . . **26** D7
  Swadlincote DE11 . . . . . . **186** F1
  Tamworth B77 . . . . **261** F5
Castle Ridge ST5 . . . . . . **70** F8
Castle Ring Fort WS15 . . **211** B6
Castleton Rd
  Stoke-on-T ST3 . . . . **89** E8
  Walsall WS3 . . . . **243** C3
Castle View Biddulph ST8 . **27** C5
  Derrington ST18 . . . . **154** E2
Castle View Est ST18 . . . **154** E1
Castleview Gr ST6 . . . . . **41** F7
Castle View DE65 . . . . . **146** C8
Castleview Rd ST7 . . . . . **26** B3
Castle View Stafford ST16 **285** A3
  Tamworth B77 . . . . **250** C3
Castle Way The DE65 . . . **148** F5
Castle Way ST16 . . . . . . **155** C2
Castle Wlk ST5 . . . . **283** B3
Castrum ST14 . . . . **96** A3
Caswell Rd DY3 . . . . **271** C8
Catalan Cl 4 ST17 . . . . . **175** A8
Catalina Pl ST3 . . . . **90** C6
Cat And Kittens La
  WV10 . . . . **240** E6
Caterbanck Way 2
  WS13 . . . . **230** F6
Caterham Dr DY6 . . . . . . **275** F3
Caterham Pl ST3 . . . . . . **90** B6
Catesby Dr DY6 . . . . **275** D8
Catharine Rd ST6 . . . . . . **42** C6
Cathcart Rd DY8 . . . . . . **279** E5
Cathedral Cl 4 WS13 . . . **231** B8
Cathedral Rise WS13 . . . **231** A8
Catherine Ho 1 ST4 . . . . **71** F8
Catherine St ST5 . . . . . . **56** D4
Catholic La DY3 . . . . **271** D7
Catholme La DE13 . . . . . **201** F5
Catisfield Cres WV8 . . . . **239** F1
Catkin Wlk WS15 . . . . . . **178** C2
Catmeadow La WS15 . . . **197** D1
Caton Cres ST4 . . . . **42** F1
Catsbridge La WS11 . . . . **225** E7
Catshill Rd WS8 . . . . **245** A7
Cauldon Ave
  Cheddleton ST13 . . . . . . **45** D5
  Newcastle-u-L ST5 . . . . . . **56** A7
Cauldon Cl ST13 . . . . . . **30** F4
Cauldon Ct ST4 . . . . **57** B1
Cauldon Pl ST4 . . . . **57** B1
Cauldon Rd ST4 . . . . **57** C1
Caulton St ST6 . . . . **41** F1
Caunsall Rd DY11 . . . . . **280** B6
Causeley Gdns ST2 . . . . **58** B3

Causeley Rd ST2 . . . . . . **58** B3
Causeway Pl ST13 . . . . . **33** F6
Cavalier Circus WV10 . . **240** E4
Cavan's Cl WS11 . . . . . . **209** E4
Cavens Wood Park Home Est
  WS12 . . . . **209** D5
Cavell Ct ST11 . . . . **90** D3
Cavell Rd WS7 . . . . **229** E8
Cavendish Cl DY6 . . . . . **275** D4
Cavendish Dr DY9 . . . . . **281** F4
Cavendish Gr ST5 . . . . . **71** B3
Cavendish Rd ST10 . . . . **92** E5
Cavendish St ST1 . . . . . . **57** A3
Cavendish B79 . . . . **249** E7
Cavendish Way WS9 . . . . **256** B5
Caverswall La ST3 . . . . . **90** C8
Caverswall Old Rd ST11 . **90** F8
Caverswall Rd
  Blythe Bridge ST11 . . . . . **90** F8
  Dilhorne ST11 . . . . **75** B3
  Meir ST3 . . . . **74** C4
Caverswall Road Sta★
  ST11 . . . . **74** F1
Cavour St ST1 . . . . **56** F3
Cawdry Bldgs 2 ST13 . . . **30** F6
Caxton Ct
  4 Cannock WS11 . . . . . **226** E8
  Burton u T DE14 . . . . . . **166** D1
Caxton St WS11 . . . . **226** E8
Cayley Ct ST3 . . . . **90** C6
Cecil Ave ST1 . . . . **282** A4
Cecilly St ST10 . . . . **76** E4
Cecilly Terr ST10 . . . . . . **76** E4
Cecil Payton Cl WS15 . . **160** F6
Cecil Rd Biddulph ST8 . . . **16** C2
  Swadlincote DE11 . . . . . . **186** F5
Cecil St Cannock WS11 . . **209** E4
  Stourbridge DY8 . . . . **279** F5
Cedar Ave
  Blythe Bridge ST11 . . . . . **91** A6
  Brownhills WS8 . . . . **245** A8
  Kidsgrove ST7 . . . . **25** D1
Cedar Cl Burntwood WS7 . **229** A6
  Cannock WS12 . . . . **195** A4
  Cheadle ST10 . . . . **76** F2
  Lichfield WS14 . . . . **231** F7
  Market Drayton TF9 . . . . . **97** A1
  Stourbridge DY8 . . . . **279** D2
  Uttoxeter ST14 . . . . **110** F1
Cedar Cres Audley ST7 . . **39** F1
  Endon ST9 . . . . **43** E6
  Rugeley WS15 . . . . **197** A5
Cedar Ct Congleton CW12 . **15** F8
  Tamworth B77 . . . . **261** E6
Cedar Dr Albrighton WV7 . **237** A5
  Aldridge B74 . . . . **256** E1
  Stramshall ST14 . . . . **110** F4
  Tamworth B79 . . . . **250** A8
Cedar Gdns DY7 . . . . **277** F6
Cedar Gr Biddulph ST8 . . . **17** B1
  Codsall WV8 . . . . **239** B3
  Great Wyrley WS6 . . . . . . **227** B4
  Stoke-on-T ST3 . . . . **72** E3
  Wolverhampton WV3 . . . . **265** F7
Cedarhill Dr ST10 . . . . . . **78** D1
Cedarhill Dr WS11 . . . . . **209** F3
Cedar Ho B74 . . . . **257** B5
Cedar Park Rd WV12 . . . . **242** C1
Cedar Pk ST15 . . . . **120** B8
Cedar Rd
  Barton-u-N DE13 . . . . . . **183** D1
  Burntwood WS7 . . . . **229** A7
  Newcastle-u-L ST5 . . . . . . **40** C1
Cedars Ave
  Kingswinford DY6 . . . . . . **275** D4
  Wombourne WV5 . . . . **270** A5
Cedars Bsns Ctr The
  WS11 . . . . **226** C7
Cedars Dr ST15 . . . . **120** B5
Cedars Hort Unit The
  WV3 . . . . **255** D2
Cedars The
  5 Wolverhampton,Newbridge
  WV6 . . . . **255** F3
  Wolverhampton,Tettenhall
  WV6 . . . . **255** D5
Cedartree Gr ST1 . . . . . . **57** E8
Cedar Way ST17 . . . . **175** F6
Cedarwood Cl WV9 . . . . **224** B3
Cedar Wood Rd DY3 . . . . **271** D5
Celandine Cl
  Burton u T DE15 . . . . . . **167** C2
  Kingswinford DY6 . . . . . . **275** C4
  Stoke-on-T ST3 . . . . **43** B1
Celandines The WV5 . . . **269** E6
Celandine
  Sutton Coldfield B74 . . . . **257** F5
  Tamworth B77 . . . . **250** C3
Celebration Cl ST6 . . . . . **42** C3
Cellarhead Rd ST9 . . . . . **59** E4
Celtic Ave ST7 . . . . **41** F8
Celtic Rd WS11 . . . . **209** E3
Cemetery Ave ST3 . . . . . **284** B2
Cemetery Rd
  Cannock WS11 . . . . **209** E4
  Hanley ST1 . . . . **57** B1
  Market Drayton TF9 . . . . . **97** B1
  Newcastle-u-L,Knutton ST5 . **55** B3
  Newcastle-u-L,Silverdale
  ST5 . . . . **55** E7
  Weston CW2 . . . . **37** B5
Cemetery St WS6 . . . . . . **226** C2
Cemetery View
  Longton ST3 . . . . **284** B2
  Newcastle-u-L ST5 . . . . . . **55** B3
Cemetery Way WS3 . . . . **243** B1
Cemlyn Ave ST3 . . . . . . **72** E3

Central Ave
  15 Wolverhampton WV4 . **266** F4
  Bucknall ST2 . . . . **58** B4
  Cannock WS11 . . . . **209** F5
  Coldmeece ST15 . . . . **118** B8
Central Ave S ST15 . . . . . **118** B7
Central Cl WS3 . . . . **243** A1
Central Dr
  Dudley,Gornalwood DY3 . . **271** D2
  Stoke-on-T ST3 . . . . **72** E3
  Walsall WS3 . . . . **243** A1
Central Sq ST10 . . . . **49** A1
Central St ST7 . . . . **26** B6
Central Trad Est WV2 . . . **266** E8
Central Way DE13 . . . . . **166** B7
Centre Rd ST15 . . . . **104** C2
Centrum East Ret Pk
  DE14 . . . . **184** E8
Centurion Pk B77 . . . . . . **262** B6
Centurion Way B77 . . . . . **262** B6
Century St ST5 . . . . **40** F2
Century St ST1 . . . . **282** B3
Ceramica★ ST6 . . . . **56** F8
Chadsfield Rd WS15 . . . . **178** E2
Chadsmead Prim Sch
  WS13 . . . . **214** A1
Chadsmoor CE Jun Sch
  WS11 . . . . **210** A3
Chadsmoor Inf Sch
  WS11 . . . . **210** A4
Chadswell Hts WS13 . . . . **214** D2
Chadwell Gdns WV8 . . . . **238** F4
Chadwell Way ST2 . . . . . **58** D1
Chadwick Cl WV4 . . . . . . **265** D6
Chadwick Cres WS15 . . . **198** A8
Chadwick Ct 4 WS15 . . . **196** F8
Chadwick St ST4 . . . . . . **284** C3
Chadwyn Dr ST2 . . . . . . **43** B2
Chaffinch Cl
  Cannock WS12 . . . . **210** B4
  Sedgley DY3 . . . . **271** D2
Chaffinch Dr Biddulph ST8 . **27** E8
  Uttoxeter ST14 . . . . **126** C6
Chaff La DE6 . . . . **65** D3
Chain La ST17 . . . . **174** E4
Chain St ST6 . . . . **42** C2
Chalcot Dr WS12 . . . . . . **210** A7
Chaldon Cl WV9 . . . . **240** A4
Chalfield B79 . . . . **249** D6
Chalfont Ave WS11 . . . . **226** C7
Chalfont Cres CW2 . . . . . **37** B2
Chalfont Ct WS11 . . . . . . **226** C7
Chalfont Gn ST2 . . . . . . **58** B2
Challenge Cl ST6 . . . . . . **42** C3
Challinor Ave ST4 . . . . . **72** A4
Chamberlain Ave ST4 . . . **72** A4
Chamberlain Cl DE13 . . . **199** D6
Chamberlain Ct CW3 . . . **53** A6
Chamberlain's La WV4 . . **265** C1
Chamberlain St ST1 . . . . **282** B1
Chamberlain Way ST8 . . . **27** E8
Chambley Gn WV9 . . . . . **224** B3
Chance Hall La ST7 . . . . . **25** B8
Chancel Dr TF9 . . . . **97** A2
Chancel Ind Est DY6 . . . . **270** E1
Chancel Inf Sch WS15 . . . **178** E2
Chancery Dr WS12 . . . . . **210** C2
Chancery La ST3 . . . . . . **284** C3
Chandler Ave DY7 . . . . . **277** F5
Chandler Dr WV4 . . . . . . **265** D3
Chandlers Cl WV9 . . . . . **240** A3
Chandlers Dr B77 . . . . . . **251** B5
Chandlers Keep WS8 . . . **245** A6
Chanterelle Ct WV4 . . . . **266** B4
Chanterelle Gdns WV4 . . **266** B4
Chantry Rd
  Newcastle-u-L ST5 . . . . . . **283** B1
  Stourbridge DY7 . . . . **279** C2
Chapel Ave WS8 . . . . **228** E2
Chapel Bank
  Kidsgrove ST7 . . . . **26** D6
  Wheaton Aston ST19 . . . . **205** C6
Chapel Cl
  Mount Pleasant ST7 . . . . . **26** B6
  Wombourne WV5 . . . . **269** F6
Chapel Ct Barlaston ST12 . . **88** C1
  Gnosall ST20 . . . . **171** C6
  Kidderminster DY10 . . . . . **280** A1
  Newcastle-u-L ST5 . . . . . . **55** C2
Chapel Dr Brownhills WS8 . **228** E2
  Mile Oak B78 . . . . **249** C1
Chapel Gn DE6 . . . . **127** C8
Chapel Hill DY10 . . . . . . **280** A1
Chapel La Anslow DE13 . . **165** A3
  Ashley TF9 . . . . **100** B6
  Audley ST7 . . . . **39** D2
  Biddulph ST8 . . . . **17** A1
  Bradley ST18 . . . . **191** B6
  Brown Edge ST6 . . . . **28** B3
  Burslem ST6 . . . . **57** A8
  Cannock Wood WS15 . . . . **211** E6
  Cheadle ST10 . . . . **77** D2
  Clifton DE6 . . . . **81** F6
  Codsall WV8 . . . . **238** F3
  Gentleshaw WS15 . . . . . . **212** A4
  Gratton ST9 . . . . **29** A4
  Hanbury DE13 . . . . **144** F2
  Harriseahead ST7 . . . . . . **26** E4
  Kingsley Holt ST10 . . . . . **62** A3
  Knighton TF9 . . . . **83** C5
  Lichfield WS14 . . . . **231** B6
  Loggerheads TF9 . . . . . . **99** E3
  Newborough DE13 . . . . . **162** F7
  Norton in H TF9 . . . . **82** C2
  Rangemore DE13 . . . . . . **164** C2
  Rolleston on D DE13 . . . . **147** B6
  Smestow DY3 . . . . **269** C2
  Whittington WS14 . . . . . . **232** E1

Chapel Mews B77 251 A5
Chapel Mus Mow Cop★ ST7 26 D7
Chapelon B77 251 A2
Chapel Rd WS15 197 F5
Chapelside WS15 178 D2
Chapel Sq WS6 226 D3
Chapel St Audley ST7 39 E3
Brownhills WS8 228 E2
Bucknall ST2 58 B4
Burntwood WS7 228 E8
Cannock WS12 210 E1
Cheadle ST10 76 D3
Forsbrook ST11 91 A8
Kidsgrove ST7 25 D2
Kingsley ST10 61 D3
Kingswinford DY6 275 B8
Longnor SK17 13 B6
Mount Pleasant ST7 26 B6
Newcastle-u-L,Knutton ST5 55 E3
Newcastle-u-L,May Bank ST5 56 D4
Newcastle-u-L,Silverdale ST5 55 C2
Norton Canes WS11 227 F5
Stafford ST16 285 B3
Stourbridge,Wordsley DY8 275 D3
Swadlincote DE11 186 F6
Walsall WS3 244 A3
Wolverhampton WV2 266 D7
Wombourne WV5 269 F5
Chapel Terr ST16 285 B4
Chapel Wlk DY3 271 C2
Chaplain Rd WS12 210 E2
Chaplin Rd ST3 284 C1
Chapter Wlk ST2 58 A5
Charlecote Dr DY1 271 E3
Charlemonte Cl WS12 210 D3
Charles Ave
Essington WV11 241 F4
Kidderminster DY10 280 A1
Wolverhampton WV4 266 B5
Charles Cl WS6 226 D1
Charles Cotton Dr CW3 68 D6
Charles Cotton St ST16 155 C6
Charles Cres WS3 244 A5
Charlesdale Dr WS9 256 B4
Charles Hayward Bglws WV4 266 D3
Charles Rd DY8 279 E4
Charles St Biddulph ST8 27 D7
Cheadle ST10 76 D3
Hanley ST1 282 C2
Newcastle-u-L ST5 56 D3
Charlestown Gr ST3 90 A7
Charlesway TF9 112 B8
Charles Wesley Ct WV3 266 A7
Charlock Gr WS11 210 C3
Charlotte Cl ST18 177 D8
Charlotte Ct DE14 185 C8
Charlotte St ST6 41 C7
Charlton St ST4 72 B8
Charminster Rd ST3 90 B7
Charmouth Cl ST1 58 A6
Charnes Rd TF9 100 C5
Charnley Dr B75 258 E2
Charnley Rd ST16 155 F6
Charnock Pl ST6 42 A7
Charnsford La TF9 100 B4
Charnwood 11 ST7 26 B1
Charnwood Ave DY3 266 D2
Charnwood Cl
Cannock WS12 210 C3
Leek ST13 30 C4
Lichfield WS13 214 C1
Rugeley WS15 178 C1
Charnwood Ho WS13 214 B2
Charnwood Prim Sch WS13 214 C2
Charnwood Rd
Burton u T DE13 166 B7
Longton ST3 73 F1
Charolais Cres ST3 89 D8
Charsley Pl ST3 72 F1
Charter Cl WS11 227 E4
Charter Ct TF9 97 D2
Charterfield Dr
Cannock WS12 210 C1
Kingswinford DY6 275 D8
Charterfields Sh Ctr DY6 275 D8
Charterhouse Dr ST17 156 B1
Charter Rd ST5 56 A3
Charters Ave WV8 239 B1
Charters The WS13 214 B1
Chartley Cl
Blythe Bridge ST11 90 E6
Perton WV6 254 F4
Stafford ST16 155 C8
Chartley Cotts ST18 139 D5
Chartley Ct ST14 126 C7
Chartley Gate Cl ST14 126 A6
Chartway The WS3 244 B4
Chartwell Cl ST9 59 A3
Chartwell Dr
Sutton Coldfield B74 257 D4
Wolverhampton WV10 240 E1
Wombourne WV5 269 F5
Chartwell Rd ST17 175 C8
Chartwell B79 249 D7
Chartwood TF9 99 E5
Chase Acad WS11 226 E8
Chase Ave WS6 226 E3
Chase Cres ST17 176 A3
Chaselands WS7 228 D7
Chase La ST15 103 F6
Chase L Ctr WS11 209 D2
Chaseley Ave WS11 209 C2
Chaseley Cl WS15 178 B1
Chaseley Croft WS11 209 C2
Chaseley Gdns
Burntwood WS7 229 C7
Rugeley WS15 178 B1
Chaseley Rd WS15 178 B1
Chase Park Ind Est WS7 228 D7
Chasepool Rd DY3 274 C8
Chase Rd Brocton ST17 176 D2
Brownhills WS8 229 A1
Burntwood WS7 229 B6
Dudley DY3,DY5 271 C1
Chaseside Dr WS11 210 B3
Chaseside Ind Est WS11 210 B3
Chase Side Rd WS15 196 D8
Chase Terrace Prim Sch WS7 228 F7
Chase Terrace Tech Coll WS7 229 A7
Chasetown Com Sch WS7 228 E5
Chasetown Ind Est WS7 228 E7
Chasetown Specialist Sports Coll WS7 228 E4
Chasetown Sta★ WS7 228 D5
Chase Vale WS7 228 E6
Chase View WS15 198 A4
Chase View Com Prim Sch WS15 196 E7
Chase View La ST18 174 C3
Chaseview Rd DE13 200 F2
Chase View WV4 266 E2
Chasewater★ WS7 228 C4
Chasewater Country Pk★ WS7 228 C5
Chasewater Gr ST10 76 F4
Chasewater Heaths Sta★ WS7 228 D6
Chasewater Rly★ WS11 228 B5
Chasewater Way WS11 227 F5
Chase Wlk Cannock WS12 209 C4
Stoke-on-T ST3 89 F7
Chasewood Park Bsns Ctr WS12 210 E1
Chatcull La ST21 101 F1
Chatfield Cl DE15 167 C1
Chatfield Pl ST3 73 D2
Chatham St ST1 282 A1
Chatsworth Dr
Cannock WS11 210 A4
Ford Green ST6 42 F5
Tutbury DE13 146 C6
Werrington ST9 59 B3
Chatsworth Gdns WV6 255 A7
Chatsworth Ho DE14 184 F7
Chatsworth Mews ST21 133 E7
Chatsworth Park Ave ST4 72 A1
Chatsworth Pl Longton ST3 73 F1
Newcastle-u-L ST5 55 F7
Chatsworth B79 249 C7
Chatteris Cl ST3 90 B6
Chatterley Cl ST5 56 B8
Chatterley Dr ST7 41 B8
Chatterley Rd ST6 41 C4
Chatterley St ST6 41 F2
Chatterton Ave WS13 230 E6
Chatterton Pl ST3 73 D3
Chatwell La Blymhill TF10 188 D1
Great Chatwell TF10,TF11 203 B7
Chaucer Ave DY3 271 A5
Chaucer Cl
Burton u T DE14 166 D6
Lichfield WS14 231 B6
Tamworth B79 250 A6
Chaucer Dr WS7 212 A1
Chaucer Rd ST17 174 C8
Chaulden Rd ST16 136 D1
Chawner Cl WS7 211 E1
Cheadle Cl ST19 207 F7
Cheadle High Sch ST10 76 D2
Cheadle Hospl ST10 76 D3
Cheadle Prim Sch ST10 76 D2
Cheadle Rd Alton ST10 78 E1
Blythe Bridge ST11 91 A7
Cheddleton ST13 45 C3
Draycott in t M ST11 91 F6
Kingsley ST10 61 D2
Leek ST13 45 E8
Upper Tean ST10 92 D5
Uttoxeter ST14 111 B1
Warslow SK17 23 B2
Wetley Rocks ST9 60 B7
Cheadle Sh Ctr ST10 76 D3
Cheam Gdns WV6 255 E8
Cheapside Hanley ST1 282 B2
Newcastle-u-L ST5 283 B3
Cheatle Ct B77 261 D5
Chebsey Cl ST2 58 C4
Chebsey Dr ST16 155 A6
Checkley Dr ST8 16 D1
Checkley Gr 6 ST3 73 D6
Checkley La CW5 52 E1
Checkley Rd ST5 40 C1
Checkley Row CW5 67 C8
Cheddar Dr ST5 54 F2
Cheddleton Flint Mill Mus★ ST13 45 C6
Cheddleton Heath Rd ST13 45 E7
Cheddleton Park Ave ST13 45 D5
Cheddleton Rd ST13 30 F4
Cheddleton Sta ST13 45 E5
Cheedale Cl DE15 167 B5
Chelford Cl ST19 193 A1
Chell Cl ST19 207 F7
Chell Green Ave ST6 42 A6
Chell Green Ct ST6 42 A6
Chell Gr ST5 56 A7
Chell Heath Rd
Stoke-on-T ST6 42 B5
Stoke-on-T ST6 42 C4
Chell Rd ST16 285 A3
Chell St ST1 57 D6
Chelmarsh Ave WV3 265 B8
Chelmorton Dr ST3 73 E1
Chelmsford Dr ST2 58 D1
Chelmsford Rd ST5 56 C5
Chelsea Cl ST8 16 C1
Chelsea Dr B74 257 F4
Chelsea Way
Kingswinford DY6 275 C6
Stafford ST16 155 C1
Chelson St ST3 284 C3
Chelston Dr WV6 255 E4
Cheltenham Ave ST10 76 E5
Cheltenham Dr
Kingswinford DY6 275 B6
Stafford ST17 175 C7
Cheltenham Gr
Birches Head ST1 57 F5
Newcastle-u-L ST5 54 F2
Chelwood St ST1 282 A4
Chemical La ST6 41 C1
Chenet Way WS11 209 E2
Chepstow Cl Biddulph ST8 16 C1
Perton WV6 254 F4
Chepstow Dr ST17 175 C7
Chepstow Pl ST3 73 C6
Chepstow Rd
Walsall WS3 242 F1
Wolverhampton WV10 240 D5
Chepstow Way WS3 242 F1
Chequerfield Dr WV4 266 A6
Chequers Ave WV5 265 A1
Chequers Ct WS11 228 A5
Chequers The 3 WS13 231 C8
Chequer St WV3 266 A4
Cheriton Gn ST2 58 D1
Cheriton Gr WV6 254 E3
Cherrington Dr WS6 226 F4
Cherrington Gdns WV6 255 B2
Cherry Bank WS12 210 C6
Cherrybrook Dr ST19 193 A1
Cherry Cl Burntwood WS7 228 F8
Fulford ST11 106 E8
Newcastle-u-L ST5 40 D1
Cherry Ct DE14 184 F8
Cherrydale Ct DY1 271 F2
Cherry Gn DY1 271 F4
Cherry Gr Stoke-on-T ST3 72 E3
Stourbridge DY8 279 E4
Cherry Hill Ave ST3 74 A2
Cherry Hill La ST5 55 E2
Cherry Hill CW3 68 E6
Cherry La Cheadle ST10 77 A5
Congleton CW12 16 E8
Gayton ST18 138 E5
Great Bridgeford ST18 135 C3
Himley DY3 270 C3
Cherry Leys DE15 167 C4
Cherryl Ho B74 257 E3
Cherry Orch
Lichfield WS14 231 C7
Newcastle-u-L ST5 283 B3
Stone ST15 120 C7
Cherry St Stourbridge DY8 279 E4
Tamworth B79 250 B5
Cherry Tree Ave ST7 25 A5
Cherry Tree Cl
Eccleshall ST21 133 E7
Stoke-on-T ST4 88 A7
Stone ST15 119 F5
Swadlincote DE11 186 F6
Cherrytree Cres ST18 135 B3
Cherry Tree Gdns WV8 239 B3
Cherry Tree Ho WS15 196 F6
Cherry Tree La
Biddulph ST8 17 B1
Codsall WV8 239 B3
Woore CW3 67 C2
Cherry Tree Rd ST7 39 F1
Cherrytree Rd DE15 185 F6
Cherry Tree Rd
Huntington WS12 209 D8
Kingswinford DY6 275 E8
Newcastle-u-L ST5 40 E1
Norton Canes WS11 228 B5
Rugeley WS15 196 F6
Cherry Trees Sch WV5 269 F6
Cherry Tree Wlk B79 250 A8
Cherry Way TF9 97 D2
Cherrywood Cl 1 ST17 175 C6
Cherrywood Gr ST3 89 F6
Cherrywood Rd B74 256 D1
Cherrywood Way B74 257 D4
Chertsey Pl ST1 57 D8
Chervil Cl ST3 90 A6
Cherwell Dr WS8 228 C2
Cherwell B77 250 D1
Chesham Gr ST3 90 A6
Chesham Rd ST16 155 F6
Cheshire Cl
Burntwood WS7 229 F8
Stourbridge DY8 279 D8
Cheshire Dr ST19 223 D6
Cheshire Gdns TF9 97 C2
Cheshire Gr WV6 254 E4
Cheshire St TF9 97 C2
Cheslyn Dr WS6 226 D2
Cheslyn Hay High Sch WS6 226 C3
Cheslyn Hay Prim Sch WS6 226 C3
Chessington Cres ST4 88 C7
Chestall Rd WS15 211 F5
Chester Ave WV6 255 F7
Chester Cl Cannock WS11 210 B1
Lichfield WS13 214 C3
Talke ST7 40 E7
Chester Cres ST5 71 B5
Chesterfield Ave DE11 186 E6
Chesterfield Ct WS9 244 F4
Chesterfield Rd WS14 231 A5
Chester Rd Aldridge B74 256 E4
Audley ST7 39 D2
Chetwynd TF10 168 C8
Eccleshall ST21 133 C7
Enville DY7 273 F2
Kinver DY7 277 F7
Rugeley WS15 196 D6
Stonnall WS9 245 D3
Talke ST7 40 D7
Weston-Under-Lizard TF11 203 B4
Whittington WS14 232 C3
Chester Road N WS8 228 D1
Chesterton Com High Sch ST5 55 E7
Chesterton Prim Sch ST5 55 F7
Chesterton Rd
Burton u T DE14 166 D7
Pattingham WV6 253 A2
Chesterton Stadium ST5 55 D5
Chesterton Way
Gorstyhill CW2 37 E3
Tamworth B79 250 A7
Chester Wood WS9 256 F2
Chesterwood Rd ST6 42 B3
Chestnut Ave B79 250 B7
Chestnut Cl Aldridge B74 257 A3
Armitage WS15 198 C3
Cannock WS11 210 C2
Codsall WV8 238 F2
Derrington ST18 154 E2
Gnosall ST20 171 D7
Stourbridge DY8 279 D3
Upper Tean ST10 92 F3
Chestnut Cres ST11 91 A6
Chestnut Ct
1 Stone ST15 104 F2
Burntwood WS7 228 F4
Cotes Heath ST21 102 D2
Rugeley WS15 196 E8
Chestnut Dr
Cheslyn Hay WS6 226 D3
Great Wyrley WS6 226 F3
Hagley DY9 281 F4
Shenstone WS14 246 F5
Stafford ST17 174 E5
Wombourne WV5 270 A5
Yarnfield ST15 118 E6
Chestnut Gr
Kingswinford DY6 275 F6
Kinver DY7 277 F5
Newcastle-u-L ST5 40 E1
Penkridge ST19 207 E8
Stone ST15 104 F2
Tamworth B77 250 C3
Chestnut La B79 218 F2
Chestnut Rd
Brown Edge ST6 43 C7
Burton u T DE15 185 F7
Loggerheads TF9 99 E5
Market Drayton TF9 112 A8
Chestnut Way WV3 265 D8
Cheswardine Prim Sch TF9 130 A8
Cheswardine Rd ST5 56 B8
Cheswell Cl WV6 255 B2
Chetney Cl ST16 155 B4
Chetton Gn WV10 240 B3
Chetwode Cl TF9 83 C5
Chetwynd Ave
Stoke-on-T ST6 42 E5
Werrington ST2 59 A3
Chetwynd Cl
Penkridge ST19 207 F7
Rugeley WS15 196 E6
Chetwynd Ctr The ST16 285 B2
Chetwynd End TF10 168 E3
Chetwynd Gdns WS11 209 D3
Chetwynd Gr TF10 168 F4
Chetwynd Pk
Cannock WS12 211 B5
Chetwynd TF10 168 D8
Chetwynd Rd
Chetwynd TF10 168 C6
Newcastle-u-L ST5 56 B6
Newport TF10 168 E4
Wolverhampton WV2 266 B6
Chetwynd St
Newcastle-u-L ST5 56 D5
Stoke-on-T ST6 42 D1
Chevening Cl DY3 271 E7
Chevin The DE13 147 C1
Cheviot Cl ST5 55 E3
Cheviot Ct B75 258 A4
Cheviot Dr Rugeley WS15 178 C3
Stoke-on-T ST6 42 C2
Cheviot Rd WV2 266 F7
Cheviot Rise WS12 210 C5
Cheviot B77 251 C1
Chichester Cl WS15 196 D6
Chichester Dr WS12 210 C1
Chichester Wlk ST1 282 C4
Chieveley Cl WS15 178 C1
Childerplay Rd ST8 27 C3
Chilgrove Cl ST1 57 F5
Chilgrove Gdns WV6 255 C5
Chillingham B77 261 C7
Chillington Cl WS6 226 F1
Chillington Dr
Codsall WV8 238 F4
Dudley DY1 271 F3
Chillington Hall★ WV8 222 E2
Chillington Ho WV6 255 E5
Chillington La WV8 238 D6
Chillington St
Codsall Wood WV8 222 F2
Coven WV9 223 A2
Chillington Way ST6 42 E1
Chiltern Cl
Cheslyn Hay WS6 226 D1
Chorlton CW2 37 B1
Dudley DY3 271 D3
Chiltern Ct B75 258 A4
Chiltern La ST21 133 F6
Chiltern Pl ST5 55 E3
Chiltern Rd
Swadlincote DE11 186 F3
Tamworth B77 251 C1
Chilton Ct DE13 147 E1
Chilton St ST4 72 E5
Chilwell Ave ST18 177 E7
Chilworth Gr ST3 72 F1
China St ST4 72 F5
Chingford Cl DY8 275 C4
Chivelstone Gr ST4 88 C6
Cholerton Cl ST4 72 E5
Chorley Ave ST6 42 A6
Chorley Rd WS7 212 A2
Chorley St ST13 30 E5
Chorlton La CW2 37 B2
Chorlton Moss ST5 85 D4
Chorlton Rd ST1 57 D6
Chorlton Terr ST14 111 C1
Christ Church CE Fst Sch ST15 105 A1
Christ Church CE Inf Sch WV6 255 B3
Christ Church CE Jun Sch WV6 255 C4
Christ Church CE Mid Sch ST15 105 A2
Christ Church CE Prim Sch
Lichfield WS13 230 F7
Stoke-on-T ST4 72 E6
Christ Church Gdns WS13 230 F7
Christ Church Inf Sch DE14 166 C2
Christchurch La WS13 230 F7
Christ Church La TF9 112 A7
Christchurch St ST4 72 E5
Christchurch Way ST15 105 A1
Christie Ave ST16 155 C3
Christie Pl ST3 73 F5
Christine St ST2 58 A3
Christopher Rd WV2 266 E8
Christopher Sq ST4 72 F5
Christopher Terr ST17 156 A2
Christopher Wlk WS13 214 A3
Chubb Way ST4 71 E4
Chub B77 261 D7
Chumleigh Gr ST6 42 A2
Church Ave Grindon ST13 34 B1
Hatton DE65 146 D8
Stoke-on-T ST2 43 B2
Church Bank Audley ST7 39 D2
Cauldon ST10 63 F7
Keele ST5 69 F7
Oakamoor ST10 78 A6
Churchbridge Pk WS11 226 E5
Church Cl Biddulph ST8 27 D6
Burton u T DE15 167 B3
Drayton Bassett B78 260 E5
Dunston ST18 192 F8
Gnosall ST20 171 E6
Haughton ST18 172 E6
Kingstone ST14 141 C8
Marchington ST14 127 F2
Ranton ST18 153 D5
Rugeley WS15 196 B7
Shenstone WS14 247 A5
Stafford ST17 174 F6
Stoke-on-T ST3 89 F5
Stone ST15 120 B8
Wood End CV9 262 C1
Church Cotts
Biddulph Moor ST8 17 B1
Coppenhall ST18 174 B3
Penkridge ST19 192 E1
Rangemore DE13 164 C2
Church Cres WV11 241 F3
Church Croft ST14 125 C7
Churchcroft Gdns WS15 178 E2
Church Dr B78 249 B7
Church Eaton Prim Sch ST20 190 A8
Church Eaton Rd TF10 188 E6
Church Farm TF9 100 C5
Church Farm Barn & Cotts DY10 281 B3
Church Farm Cl ST19 192 E1
Church Farm Mews DE13 199 C7
Church Farm ST14 110 F4
Churchfield Ave ST3 73 C1
Churchfield Cl
Coven WV9 224 C2
Stafford ST17 156 C1
Churchfield Ct ST10 46 F1
Churchfield Rd ST21 133 D6
Churchfields CE Jun Sch WS15 196 E8
Church Fields Keele ST5 69 F7
Norton in H TF9 82 C2
Churchfields Prim Sch ST5 55 F6

Churchfields DE13 . . . . . . 182 A2
Church Gdns ST3 . . . . 284 C4
Church Gr ST21 . . . . 133 D7
Church Hill
  Cannock WS12 . . . . 210 D4
  Codsall WV8 . . . . 238 F5
Church Hill Dr WV6 . . . . . 255 E5
Church Hill Kinver DY7 . . . 278 E2
  Longdon WS15 . . . . 213 A8
Church Hill Rd WV6 . . . . . 255 D5
Church Hill St DE15 . . . . . 167 B3
Church Hill WV4 . . . . 265 E4
Church Hollow B79 . . . . . 217 C5
Churchill Ave
  Cheddleton ST13 . . . . 45 D5
  Trentham ST4 . . . . 87 F7
Churchill Cl
  Blythe Bridge ST11 . . . . . . 90 E6
  Uttoxeter ST14 . . . . 126 C5
Churchill Cres DE13 . . . . . 200 F2
Churchill Gdns DY3 . . . . . 271 C7
Churchill La DY10 . . . . . . 281 B3
Churchill Rd Cheadle ST10 . 76 E4
  Shenstone WS14 . . . . 247 A5
  Stone ST15 . . . . 119 F7
Churchill Way
  Stafford ST17 . . . . 174 E6
  Trentham ST4 . . . . 87 F7
Church La
  Albrighton WV7 . . . . 237 A2
  Armitage WS15 . . . . 197 F5
  Barton-u-N DE13 . . . . . . 183 D1
  Betley CW3 . . . . 53 C5
  Biddulph ST8 . . . . 17 B1
  Bobbington DY7 . . . . 268 A1
  Bradley ST18 . . . . 173 C1
  Bramshall ST14 . . . . 125 C2
  Cannock WS11 . . . . 208 F1
  Cauldon ST10 . . . . 63 F7
  Checkley ST10 . . . . 109 B8
  Cheslyn Hay WS11 . . . . . . 225 F8
  Chilcote DE12 . . . . 219 E3
  Codsall WV8 . . . . 238 F4
  Coven WV9 . . . . 224 C2
  Croxton ST21 . . . . 116 A6
  Derrington ST18 . . . . 154 A2
  Draycott in t M ST11 . . . . . 91 E5
  Edingale B79 . . . . 217 D3
  Ellastone DE6 . . . . 80 B4
  Endon ST9 . . . . 43 F8
  Fradley WS13 . . . . 215 E8
  Gayton ST18 . . . . 138 D5
  Gnosall TF10 . . . . 188 D8
  Hammerwich WS7 . . . . . . 229 D3
  Hanbury DE13 . . . . 145 A4
  Hill Ridware WS15 . . . . . . 198 A4
  Hixon ST18 . . . . 158 C8
  Ipstones ST10 . . . . 46 E1
  King's Bromley DE13 . . . . 199 C6
  Kingstone ST14 . . . . 141 C7
  Lapley ST19 . . . . 206 A6
  Lawton-gate ST7 . . . . 25 C4
  Leek ST13 . . . . 30 E6
  Marchington ST14 . . . . . . 127 F2
  Mayfield DE6 . . . . 81 C6
  Middleton B78 . . . . 260 C1
  Mow Cop ST7 . . . . 26 E7
  Newcastle-u-L,Knutton ST5 . 55 E2
  Newcastle-u-L,Wolstanton
    ST5 . . . . 56 D4
  Newton Solney DE15 . . . . 167 B8
  Oulton ST15 . . . . 105 C3
  Rocester ST14 . . . . 96 A3
  Rugeley WS15 . . . . 178 B2
  Scholar Green ST7 . . . . . . 25 C7
  Seisdon WV5 . . . . 264 B2
  Shuttington B79 . . . . 251 E7
  Stafford ST16 . . . . 285 B3
  Standon ST21 . . . . 102 B3
  Stoke-on-T ST4 . . . . 71 F2
  Stonnall WS9 . . . . 245 E4
  Tamworth B79 . . . . 250 B5
  Thorpe DE6 . . . . 51 D1
Church Lawton Prim Sch
  ST7 . . . . 25 A5
  Norton in H TF9 . . . . 82 C2
Church Mdw Ipstones ST10 46 F1
Church Mews DE65 . . . . . 146 D8
Church Moat WS3 . . . . . . 243 B1
Church of the Ascension CE
  Prim Sch DY6 . . . . 275 C8
Church Plantation ST5 . . . 70 A5
Church Rd Alrewas DE13 . . 200 F3
  Ashley TF9 . . . . 100 C6
  Biddulph ST8 . . . . 27 D6
  Brewood ST19 . . . . 223 C6
  Brown Edge ST6 . . . . 43 B8
  Brownhills WS8 . . . . 244 F7
  Burntwood WS7 . . . . 229 D7
  Burton u T DE14 . . . . 184 E7
  Codsall WV8 . . . . 238 F4
  Egginton DE65 . . . . 148 B4
  Elford B79 . . . . 216 D1
  Hixon ST18 . . . . 139 C1
  Huntington WS11 . . . . . . 209 A2
  Kinver DY7 . . . . 278 A2
  Norton Canes WS11 . . . . . 227 E4
  Penkridge ST19 . . . . 192 E1
  Perton WV6 . . . . 254 E4
  Rolleston on D DE13 . . . . 147 A4
  Shareshill WV10 . . . . 225 D2
  Shenstone WS14 . . . . 246 F5
  Snelston DE6 . . . . 81 C3
  Stoke-on-T ST3 . . . . 88 F8
  Stonnall WS9 . . . . 245 E3

Church Rd continued
  Stourbridge DY8 . . . . 275 E2
  Stretton DE13 . . . . 147 F2
  Swindon DY3 . . . . 269 D2
  Tamworth B77 . . . . 261 C4
  Walsall WS3 . . . . 244 A3
  Wolverhampton,Bradmore
    WV3 . . . . 265 F7
  Wolverhampton,Oxley
    WV10 . . . . 240 C1
  Wolverhampton,Tettenhall Wood
    WV6 . . . . 255 B3
  Wolverhampton,Tettenhall
    WV6 . . . . 255 C5
  Wombourne WV5 . . . . . . 270 B7
Church Row B78 . . . . 260 B1
Churchside B79 . . . . 217 C2
Churchside Way WS9 . . . . 245 B2
Church Sq ST6 . . . . 56 E8
Church St Alstonefield DE6 . 35 E3
  Audley,Bignall End ST7 . . . 39 D2
  Audley,Wood Lane ST7 . . . 40 A1
  Brownhills WS8 . . . . 244 E6
  Burntwood WS7 . . . . 228 E5
  Cannock,Bridgtown WS11 226 D6
  Cannock,Chadsmoor
    WS11 . . . . 210 A4
  Cannock WS11 . . . . 209 E1
  Cheadle ST10 . . . . 76 D3
  Claverley WV5 . . . . 267 C7
  Clifton Campville B79 . . . . 218 E2
  Dudley,Gornalwood DY3 . . 271 D3
  Eccles101 ST21 . . . . 133 D7
  Hartington SK17 . . . . 24 D5
  Kidsgrove,Butt Lane ST7 . . 25 D1
  Kidsgrove ST7 . . . . 26 C4
  Kingsley ST10 . . . . 61 E2
  Leek ST13 . . . . 30 E6
  Lichfield WS13,WS14 . . . . 231 C8
  Longnor SK17 . . . . 13 B6
  Market Drayton TF9 . . . . . 97 D1
  Mow Cop ST7 . . . . 26 C6
  Nethersea l DE12 . . . . . . 219 F6
  Newcastle-u-L,Chesterton
    ST5 . . . . 55 E7
  Newcastle-u-L,Silverdale
    ST5 . . . . 55 B2
  Newcastle-u-L ST5 . . . . . 283 B3
  Rugeley WS15 . . . . 178 E1
  Stoke-on-T ST4 . . . . 72 B7
  Stone ST15 . . . . 120 B8
  Tamworth B79 . . . . 250 B5
  Tutbury DE13 . . . . 146 C7
  Uttoxeter ST14 . . . . 126 C8
  Whittington WS14 . . . . . . 232 B5
Church Terr Burslem ST6 . . 57 B6
  Sutton Coldfield B75 . . . . 258 C3
  Warslow SK17 . . . . 23 B2
Church Vale WS11 . . . . . . 227 E4
Church View
  Adbaston ST20 . . . . 131 C4
  Aldridge WS9 . . . . 256 B6
  Brownhills WS9 . . . . 244 F3
  Burton u T DE13 . . . . 166 C7
  Clifton DE6 . . . . 81 F6
  Cotes Heath ST21 . . . . . . 102 E2
  Dudley DY3 . . . . 271 D3
Church View Gdns DY7 . . 278 A4
Church View
  Great Haywood ST18 . . . . 158 B2
  Newcastle-u-L ST5 . . . . . . 55 E2
  Rugeley WS15 . . . . 197 A5
  Scot Hay ST5 . . . . 54 E4
  Tamworth B77 . . . . 261 F7
Churchward Dr DE13 . . . . 147 F1
Churchward Gr WV5 . . . . 270 A8
Church Way
  Longdon WS15 . . . . 198 A1
  Walsall WS4 . . . . 244 C2
Churchwell Ct WV5 . . . . . 270 A6
Church Wlk Edingale B79 . 217 C5
  Newcastle-u-L ST5 . . . . . . 55 E7
Church Wlks TF9 . . . . 82 C2
Church Wlk
  Wolverhampton,Penn
    WV3 . . . . 265 F7
  Wolverhampton,Tettenhall
    WV6 . . . . 255 E5
Churnet Cl
  Cheddleton ST13 . . . . 45 B4
  Mayfield DE6 . . . . 81 C7
Churnet Ct
  Burton u T DE14 . . . . 166 E3
  Cheddleton ST13 . . . . 45 D6
Churnet Gr WV6 . . . . 254 F4
Churnet Rd
  Blythe Bridge ST11 . . . . . 91 A7
  Cheadle ST10 . . . . 76 E1
  Hilton DE65 . . . . 147 D8
Churnet Row ST14 . . . . . . 95 F3
Churnetside Bsns Pk
  ST13 . . . . 45 D6
Churnet Valley Railway★
  ST13 . . . . 45 E4
Churnet Valley Rd ST10 . . 62 A2
Churnet Valley Rly Ctr★
  ST13 . . . . 45 E5
Churnet Valley Wildlife
  Sanctuary★ ST10 . . . . . . 61 E4
Churnet View ST13 . . . . . 31 A8
Churnet View Mid Sch
  ST13 . . . . 31 A8
Churnet View Rd ST10 . . . 78 A7
Churn Hill Rd WS9 . . . . . 256 B4
Churns Hill La DY3 . . . . . 270 B3
Churston Cl
  Newcastle-u-L ST5 . . . . . . 71 B2
  Walsall WS3 . . . . 243 A3

Churston Pl ST1 . . . . 57 D8
Cicely Haughton Sch
  ST13 . . . . 44 F2
Cinderhill Ind Est ST3 . . . 73 E4
Cinder Hill La WV9 . . . . . 224 B3
Cinderhill La ST3 . . . . 73 D3
Cinder-Hill La ST7 . . . . . . 25 F7
Cinder Rd
  Burntwood WS7 . . . . 228 E7
  Dudley DY3 . . . . 271 B2
Cinder Rock Way ST7 . . . . 26 C1
Circular Rd WV7 . . . . 220 E1
City Arc ❶ WS13 . . . . 231 B7
City Bank ST8 . . . . 16 C2
City La ST9 . . . . 30 A3
City of Stoke-on-Trent Sixth
  Form Coll ST4 . . . . 72 D7
City Rd ST4 . . . . 72 D6
Clamgoose La ST10 . . . . . 76 C7
Clanbrook Rd DY7 . . . . . . 278 C3
Clandon Ave ST6 . . . . 41 E4
Clanford Cl ST17 . . . . 174 F5
Clanford La ST18 . . . . 154 A5
Clanford Rd ST18 . . . . . . 154 A7
Clanway St ST6 . . . . 41 E5
Clap Gate Gr WV5 . . . . . . 269 E6
Clap Gate Rd WV5 . . . . . . 269 E7
Clare Ave
  Newcastle-u-L ST5 . . . . . . 56 B6
  Wolverhampton WV11 . . . 241 F1
Clare Cres WV14 . . . . 266 F2
Claregate Prim Sch WV6 . 255 F7
Claremont Cl
  Newcastle-u-L ST5 . . . . . . 56 C7
  Stone ST15 . . . . 120 B8
Claremont Cotts DY3 . . . . 271 E8
Claremont Gr ST17 . . . . . 174 B8
Claremont Mews WV3 . . . 266 A7
Claremont Rd
  Eccles101 ST21 . . . . 133 E6
  Sedgley DY3 . . . . 271 E8
  Tamworth B79 . . . . 250 A8
  Wolverhampton WV3 . . . . 266 B7
Clarence Gdns B74 . . . . . 257 F3
Clarence Rd Longton ST3 . 284 B4
  Sutton Coldfield B74 . . . . 257 F4
Clarence St
  Burton u T DE14 . . . . 166 C1
  Dudley DY3 . . . . 271 E5
  Newcastle-u-L,Porthill ST5 . 56 B5
  Stoke-on-T ST4 . . . . 72 C6
Clarendon Dr ST17 . . . . . 174 B8
Clarendon Pl WS3 . . . . . . 243 F3
Clarendon Rd
  Sutton Coldfield B75 . . . . 258 C3
  Walsall WS4 . . . . 244 C2
Clarendon St
  Stoke-on-T ST4 . . . . 72 C6
  Walsall WS3 . . . . 243 B1
Clare Rd ST16 . . . . 155 C7
Clare St Harriseahead ST7 . 26 C4
  Mow Cop ST7 . . . . 26 C6
  Stoke-on-T ST4 . . . . 56 D1
Claridge Rd ST4 . . . . 56 E1
Clarion Way WS11 . . . . . . 209 E5
Clarke Ho WS3 . . . . 243 A1
Clarke Ind Est DE14 . . . . 166 E4
Clarke's Ave WS12 . . . . . . 195 A1
Clarkes Cl ST14 . . . . 111 B1
Clarke St ST1 . . . . 282 A1
Clark Rd WV3 . . . . 255 F2
Clark's Cres WS15 . . . . . . 161 A6
Clark St Stafford ST16 . . . . 285 C3
  Stourbridge DY8 . . . . 279 E4
Claud St ST4 . . . . 72 D4
Claverdon Cl WS8 . . . . . . 245 A8
Claverdon Dr B74 . . . . . . 257 B4
Claverhouse Rd DE15 . . . 167 A2
Claverley CE Prim Sch
  WV5 . . . . 267 C7
Claverley Dr WV4 . . . . . . 265 D5
Clayalders Bank ST1 . . . . 101 C6
Claydon Cres ST5 . . . . 71 B2
Claydon Rd DY6 . . . . 270 C1
Clayfield Gr ST3 . . . . 73 C6
Clayfield Gr W ST3 . . . . . . 73 C6
Claygate Rd WS12 . . . . . . 210 E3
Clay Gates Rd ST19 . . . . . 207 A1
Claygates Rd ST19 . . . . . . 223 F8
Clayhanger Cl ST5 . . . . . . 56 B8
Clayhanger La WS8 . . . . . 244 D6
Clayhanger Rd WS8 . . . . . 244 F6
Clayhanger St ❺ ST6 . . . . 56 F8
Clay Hills ST6 . . . . 41 D3
Clay Lake ST9 . . . . 43 E7
Claymills Rd
  Burton u T DE13 . . . . 148 A2
  Stretton DE13 . . . . 147 F2
Claymore B77 . . . . 261 E7
Clay Pit La WS14 . . . . 230 F3
Clay St E DE15 . . . . 167 A1
Clay's La DE14 . . . . 184 F8
Clay St Burton u T DE15 . . 166 F1
  Penkridge ST19 . . . . 192 E1
Clayton Ave CW12 . . . . 6 A5
Clayton Cl WV2 . . . . 266 C7
Clayton Hall Bsns &
  Language Coll ST5 . . . . . 71 C3
Clayton La
  Newcastle-u-L ST5 . . . . . . 71 C4
  Stoke-on-T SY4,ST5 . . . . . 71 D5
Clayton Rd ST5 . . . . 71 C4
Clayton St ST3 . . . . 284 C4
Claytonwood Rd ST4 . . . . 71 E3
Cleadon Pl ST2 . . . . 58 B6
Clear View DY6 . . . . 275 B6
Clearwater Ind Est WV2 . . 266 F7
Clearwell Gdns DY1 . . . . . 271 F3

Cleasby B77 . . . . 251 C1
Cleaveland Mews ❷
  WS13 . . . . 214 A1
Cleave Rd DE14 . . . . 185 A8
Clee Hill Dr WV3 . . . . 255 A1
Clee Hill Rd DY3 . . . . 271 D4
Clee Rd DY10 . . . . 280 B5
Cleeton St WS12 . . . . 210 D1
Cleeve Dr B74 . . . . 257 F6
Cleeve Rd WS3 . . . . 242 F3
Cleeve B77 . . . . 250 D3
Cleeve Way WS3 . . . . 242 F3
Clee View Mdw DY3 . . . . 266 D2
Clee View Rd WV5 . . . . . 269 E5
Clegg Rd WS7 . . . . 229 E7
Clematis Ave ST11 . . . . . . 90 F6
Clematis Cl ST18 . . . . . . 135 B2
Clematis Cres DE15 . . . . 186 A8
Clematis Dr WV9 . . . . . . 239 F3
Clematis B77 . . . . 250 F3
Clement Cl ST16 . . . . 155 F5
Clement Pl ST6 . . . . 42 A3
Clement Rd ST6 . . . . 42 A6
Clent View Rd DY8 . . . . . 279 C2
Clerk Bank ST13 . . . . 30 E6
Clermont Ave ST4 . . . . . . 72 A2
Clevedon Ave ST17 . . . . . 175 C7
Cleveland Cl WV11 . . . . . 241 F1
Cleveland Ct DE15 . . . . . 167 B3
Cleveland Dr WS11 . . . . . 210 B4
Cleveland Rd Hanley ST1 . 282 B5
  Newcastle-u-L ST5 . . . . . . 55 E3
Cleveland St
  ❶❺ Burslem ST6 . . . . 56 F8
  Stourbridge DY8 . . . . 279 E4
Cleveland Trad Est ST1 . . 282 A1
Cleveland Wlk ST17 . . . . . 174 B8
Cleves Cres WS6 . . . . 226 D1
Clewley Dr WV9 . . . . 240 B3
Clewley Rd DE14 . . . . . . 184 F8
Clewlow Pl ST3 . . . . 284 D5
Clewlows Bank ST9 . . . . . . 43 F3
Clews St ST6 . . . . 56 E7
Clews Wlk ST5 . . . . 56 C5
Cley Gr ST5 . . . . 71 B2
Cliffdon Ho DE65 . . . . . . 146 D8
Cliffe Pl ST6 . . . . 42 A3
Cliff Hall La B78 . . . . 261 C1
Clifford Ave ST6 . . . . 42 F5
Clifford Cl B77 . . . . 250 F3
Clifford Rd TF9 . . . . 112 B8
Clifford St Hanley ST1 . . . 282 C1
  Tamworth B77 . . . . 250 E3
Cliff Rd ST18 . . . . 158 C1
Cliffs La TF10 . . . . 150 E1
Cliff St ST6 . . . . 42 C1
Cliff Vale Pl ST4 . . . . 56 F1
Clifton Ave Aldridge WS9 . 245 C1
  Brownhills WS8 . . . . 244 D7
  Cannock WS11 . . . . 226 C7
  Tamworth B79 . . . . 250 A7
Clifton CE Prim Sch DE6 . 81 F6
Clifton Cl Stafford ST16 . . 156 B3
  Stoke-on-T ST4 . . . . 72 E5
  Swadlincote DE11 . . . . . . 186 F2
Clifton Dr ST16 . . . . 156 B3
Clifton Gdns WV8 . . . . . . 239 C3
Clifton La B79 . . . . 235 B3
Clifton Rd Clifton DE6 . . . . 81 F7
  Kidderminster DY10 . . . . 280 C3
  Netherseal DE12 . . . . . . 219 D6
  Wolverhampton WV6 . . . . 255 D5
Clifton St
  Newcastle-u-L ST5 . . . . . . 56 D4
  Sedgley WV14 . . . . 266 E1
  Stoke-on-T ST4 . . . . 72 E5
  Stourbridge DY8 . . . . 279 E4
Clifton Way DE15 . . . . . . 167 B2
Clinton Cres WS7 . . . . . . 229 B8
Clinton Gdns ❹ ST15 . . . 120 A7
Clinton Sq ST1 . . . . 282 A2
Clive Ave ST2 . . . . 43 B3
Clive Cl ST5 . . . . 258 D2
Cliveden Ave WS9 . . . . . . 245 D1
Cliveden Coppice B74 . . . 257 F1
Cliveden Pl ST3 . . . . 284 C2
Cliveden Rd ST2 . . . . 58 B5
Clive Gdns TF9 . . . . 97 C1
Clive Ho DE15 . . . . 167 C3
Clive Rd Burntwood WS7 . . 229 A7
  Market Drayton TF9 . . . . . 97 C1
  Newcastle-u-L ST5 . . . . . . 56 D6
  Pattingham WV6 . . . . . . 263 C7
Clive St ST6 . . . . 41 E4
Clockmill Ave WS3 . . . . . 243 F3
Clockmill Pl WS3 . . . . . . 243 F3
Clockmill Rd WS3 . . . . . . 243 F3
Cloister Rd ST4 . . . . 72 A5
Cloisters The
  Burton u T DE15 . . . . 166 F1
  Gnosall ST20 . . . . 171 E6
Cloister Wlk Bucknall ST2 . 58 A5
  Whittington WS14 . . . . . . 232 E5
Close Bank DE13 . . . . . . 146 C6
Close La ST7 . . . . 26 D7
Close The Dudley DY3 . . . 271 C4
  Enville DY7 . . . . 273 D2
  Lichfield WS13 . . . . 231 B8
  Madeley CW3 . . . . 68 E7
  Meir ST3 . . . . 74 B5
  Newton Solney DE15 . . . . 167 B6
  Stafford,Moss Pit ST17 . . 174 B1
  Stafford,Rowley Park ST16 155 C1
  Stoke-on-T ST9 . . . . 43 F7
  Swindon DY3 . . . . 269 C2
  Tutbury DE13 . . . . 146 B6
Cloud The★ CW12 . . . . . . 7 A4
Cloud View CW12 . . . . 6 A2

Clough Hall Dr ST7 . . . . . 40 E6
Clough Hall Rd ST7 . . . . . 40 F8
Clough Hall Tech Sch ST7 25 F1
Clough La ST9 . . . . 59 A2
Clough St ST1 . . . . 282 A2
Cloughwood Way ST6 . . . . 41 D1
Clovelly Wlk ❷ ST6 . . . . . 56 E7
Clover Ct DE14 . . . . 184 E6
Cloverdale
  ❻ Stafford ST17 . . . . . . 175 C7
  Perton WV6 . . . . 254 D4
Cloverdale Pl ST3 . . . . 73 F3
Cloverdale Rd ST5 . . . . . . 56 B3
Clover Heath WV5 . . . . . . 267 D7
Clover La DY6 . . . . 275 B7
Clover Mdws WS12 . . . . . 210 C1
Clover Rd ST5 . . . . 56 D6
Clover Ridge WS6 . . . . . . 226 C3
Clowes Rd ST2 . . . . 58 A3
Club Cotts WV10 . . . . . . 240 C6
Club La WV10 . . . . 240 C6
Club Row DY3 . . . . 271 E5
Club St ST4 . . . . 72 A6
Clumber Ave ST5 . . . . 71 C6
Clumber Gr ST5 . . . . 71 C5
Cluny Pl ST2 . . . . 58 A5
Clyde Ave ST8 . . . . 16 E1
Clyde Pl ST5 . . . . 71 A4
Clyde Rd ST6 . . . . 57 A7
Clydesdale Rd WS8 . . . . . 244 E6
Clyde St ST1 . . . . 282 A1
Clyde Wlk ST1 . . . . 282 A2
Clynes Way ST3 . . . . 74 B3
Coach Gdns ST19 . . . . . . 205 C5
Coach Ho The ST7 . . . . . . 25 C4
Coach House La WS15 . . 178 E1
Coach House Rise B77 . . . 261 F7
Coachmans Cl ST16 . . . . 155 C8
Coachman's Wlk ST15 . . 178 F5
Coalbourn La DY8 . . . . . . 279 C7
Coal Haulage Rd WS12 . . 227 F8
Coalmeadow Cl WS3 . . . . 242 F3
Coalpitford La ST13 . . . . . 44 E4
Coalpit Hill ST7 . . . . 40 D8
Coalpit La WS15 . . . . 197 A5
Coalport Cl ST10 . . . . 76 D1
Coalport Dr ST15 . . . . . . 119 D2
Coalville ST13 . . . . 74 B5
Coalway Ave WV3 . . . . . . 266 A6
Coalway Gdns WV3 . . . . . 265 D7
Coalway Rd
  Rugeley WS15 . . . . 197 B6
  Walsall WS3 . . . . 243 B1
  Wolverhampton WV3 . . . . 265 E6
Coates Pl ST6 . . . . 42 B8
Coatsgate Wlk WV8 . . . . . 239 F1
Cobbett Rd WS7 . . . . 228 D7
Cobbles The ST19 . . . . . . 205 C6
Cobden Cl WS12 . . . . 210 C7
Cobden St Longton ST3 . . 284 B1
  Newcastle-u-L ST5 . . . . . . 56 D6
  Stourbridge DY8 . . . . 279 E5
Cobham Cl ST15 . . . . 118 F6
Cobham Pl ST3 . . . . 90 A8
Cobia B77 . . . . 261 D7
Cob Moor Rd ST7 . . . . 26 A4
Cobridge Ind Est ST6 . . . . 57 B7
Cobridge Rd ST1 . . . . 57 A5
Coburn Dr B75 . . . . 258 D2
Cocketts Nook WS15 . . . . 178 C3
Cock La ST17 . . . . 193 E7
Cocknage Rd Longton ST3 . 73 B1
  Meir Heath ST3 . . . . 89 D6
Cockshut Ind Est ST4 . . . . 56 F1
Cockshutts La WV2 . . . . . 266 D7
Cocks La Stoke-on-T ST9 . . 43 C3
  Stoke-on-T ST9 . . . . 43 C4
Cocksparrow La WS12,
  WS19 . . . . 209 B5
Cockspur St B78 . . . . 262 E7
Cockster Brook La ST4 . . . 72 C3
Cockster Rd ST3 . . . . 72 F3
Cocton Cl WV6 . . . . 254 E6
Codsall Com High Sch
  WV8 . . . . 239 A4
Codsall Gdns WV8 . . . . . 238 E4
Codsall Ho WV8 . . . . 238 E4
Codsall Mid Sch WV8 . . . 239 A3
Codsall Rd Codsall WV8 . . 239 C1
  Wolverhampton WV6 . . . . 255 D7
Codsall Sta WV8 . . . . 238 E3
Coghlan Cl ST17 . . . . 174 C8
Colbourne Rd B78 . . . . . . 250 A2
Colbrook B77 . . . . 250 D1
Colclough Ave ST5 . . . . . . 56 A8
Colclough La ST6 . . . . 41 D7
Colclough Rd ST3 . . . . . . 74 B1
Cold Meece Ind Est
  ST15 . . . . 118 B6
Cold Norton Cotts ST15 . 119 C5
Coldridge Cl WV8 . . . . . . 239 F1
Coldstream Dr DY8 . . . . . 275 E3
Cole Dr ST16 . . . . 155 C2
Coleford Cl DY8 . . . . 275 C2
Colehill B79 . . . . 250 B5
Coleman St WV6 . . . . 255 F4
Colenso Way ST5 . . . . 56 B8
Coleridge Cl
  Market Drayton TF9 . . . . . 112 A3
  Tamworth B79 . . . . 250 A6
  Walsall WS3 . . . . 244 A5
Coleridge Ct DE14 . . . . . 166 C6
Coleridge Dr Cheadle ST10 76 C2
  Perton WV6 . . . . 254 E4
  Stafford ST17 . . . . 174 C8
Coleridge Rd ST3 . . . . . . 73 A2

Coleridge Rise DY3 . . . . . **271** A4
Colesden Wlk WV4 . . . . . **265** C6
Coleshill Rd B78 . . . . . **261** A7
Coleshill St B78 . . . . . **261** A8
Cole St ST8 . . . . **27** C7
Coley Gr ST18 . . . . . **177** D8
Coley La ST18 . . . . . **158** D1
Colin Cres ST3 . . . . . **74** B4
Colindene Gr ST4 . . . . . **72** A6
Colinwood Cl WS6 . . . . . **226** F1
Collard Ave ST5 . . . . . **56** B3
College Cl CW3 . . . . . **68** E8
College Cl WV6 . . . . . **255** D4
College Farm Cl WV6 . . . . . **253** C3
College Fields ST15 . . . . . **118** F6
College La B79 . . . . . **250** B5
College Rd Denstone ST14 . . . . . **95** D6
Hanley ST1,ST4 . . . . . **57** C1
Wolverhampton WV6 . . . . . **255** D4
College View WV6 . . . . . **255** D3
Collet Rd WV6 . . . . . **254** E5
Collets Brook B75 . . . . . **259** A2
Collett B77 . . . . . **251** A1
Colley Rd ST6 . . . . . **41** F6
Collier Cl
  Cheslyn Hay WS6 . . . . . **226** D2
  Walsall WS8 . . . . . **244** C7
Colliers Way ST8 . . . . . **27** C7
Colliery Dr WS3 . . . . . **242** F3
Colliery Rd WS15 . . . . . **196** F4
Collinbourne Cl ST4 . . . . . **88** B6
Collindale Ct DY6 . . . . . **270** D1
Collingwood Ct ST15 . . . . . **120** B8
Collingwood Gr ST4 . . . . . **71** E8
Collingwood Rd WV10 . . . . . **240** E2
Collin Rd ST4 . . . . . **71** F5
Collins Dr **3** WS13 . . . . . **230** F6
Collins Hill WS13 . . . . . **214** A2
Collinson Rd
  Barton-u-N DE13 . . . . . **183** D1
  Stoke-on-T ST6 . . . . . **41** D7
Collins Rd WS8 . . . . . **245** A5
Collin St ST14 . . . . . **126** B7
Collis St DY8 . . . . . **279** F8
Colonnade The ST16 . . . . . **285** B3
Colshaw Rd DY8 . . . . . **279** E4
Coltman Cl WS14 . . . . . **231** D7
Colton Hills Com Sch
  WV4 . . . . . **266** B4
Colton Rd WS15 . . . . . **178** E4
Coltsfoot View WS6 . . . . . **226** E2
Columbian Cres WS7 . . . . . **228** F8
Columbian Dr WS11 . . . . . **209** F3
Columbian Way ST11 . . . . . **209** F3
Columbine Wlk **11** ST6 . . . . . **41** D3
Colville Cl DE12 . . . . . **218** D7
Colville St ST4 . . . . . **72** F6
Colwall Rd DY3 . . . . . **271** D4
Colwich CE Prim Sch
  ST17 . . . . . **177** E7
Colwich Cres ST16 . . . . . **156** C3
Colwyn Dr ST8 . . . . . **27** D5
Combe Dr ST3 . . . . . **90** A5
Comberford La B79 . . . . . **234** A2
Comberford Rd B79 . . . . . **250** A7
Comber Gr DY7 . . . . . **278** A3
Combermere TF9 . . . . . **97** D2
Comber Rd DY7 . . . . . **278** A3
Combine B75 . . . . . **258** D4
Comfrey Cl ST3 . . . . . **90** A6
Commerce Dr ST19 . . . . . **207** E7
Commerce St ST3 . . . . . **284** C3
Commercial Rd ST1 . . . . . **282** C2
Commercial St ST4 . . . . . **57** A7
Common Barn La Bednall ST17 . . . . . **194** A8
  Betley CW3 . . . . . **52** F6
  Cannock WS11 . . . . . **210** A3
  Fradley WS13 . . . . . **215** D7
  Gratwich ST14 . . . . . **124** C2
  Stoke-on-T ST3 . . . . . **89** F4
  Stone ST15 . . . . . **119** D4
  Tamworth B79 . . . . . **250** B4
  Upper Hatton ST21 . . . . . **102** F1
  Waterhouses ST10 . . . . . **64** F7
  Whitmore ST5 . . . . . **85** D4
  Whittington WS14 . . . . . **232** D4
Common Rd
  Stafford ST16 . . . . . **155** E7
  Wombourne WV5 . . . . . **270** A6
Common Road Ind Est
  ST16 . . . . . **155** E7
Commonside
  Brownhills WS8 . . . . . **245** A6
  Burntwood WS15 . . . . . **212** A1
Commonside Cl ST16 . . . . . **155** D6
Commonside Enville DY7 . . . . . **273** A3
  Walsall WS3 . . . . . **244** A2
Common The ST10 . . . . . **75** D3
Common View
  Burntwood WS7 . . . . . **212** A1
  Cannock WS12 . . . . . **210** B8
Community Dr ST6 . . . . . **42** D1
Como The DY7 . . . . . **278** A3
Compa The DY7 . . . . . **278** A3
Compton Cl Kinver DY7 . . . . . **277** F4
  Stafford ST17 . . . . . **156** A1
Compton Ct B74 . . . . . **257** F3
Compton Dr DY6 . . . . . **275** D5
Compton Flats ST13 . . . . . **30** E5
Compton Gdns DY7 . . . . . **277** F4
Compton Gr DY6 . . . . . **275** D5
Compton Hill Dr WV3 . . . . . **255** D2
Compton Ho **6** ST13 . . . . . **30** E5
Compton ST13 . . . . . **30** E5

Compton Mews ST13 . . . . . **30** F5
Compton Pk WV6 . . . . . **255** E3
Compton Rd Kinver DY7 . . . . . **277** D4
  Stafford ST17 . . . . . **156** D1
  Tamworth B79 . . . . . **249** F7
  Wolverhampton WV3 . . . . . **255** F5
Compton Rd W WV3 . . . . . **255** D2
Comptons The TF9 . . . . . **130** A8
Compton St ST1 . . . . . **282** A2
Condlyffe Rd ST13 . . . . . **30** E4
Condor Gr WS12 . . . . . **210** C1
Conduit Rd WS11 . . . . . **228** A4
Conduit St WS13 . . . . . **231** B8
Conewood Pl ST3 . . . . . **72** E1
Coney Gr ST3 . . . . . **74** A3
Congleton Edge Rd CW12 . . . . . **16** B6
Congleton Rd
  Biddulph,Braddocks Hay
    ST8 . . . . . **27** D8
  Biddulph,Marsh Green ST8 . . . . . **16** D2
  Kidsgrove ST7 . . . . . **25** D1
  Mow Cop ST7 . . . . . **26** E8
Congleton Rd N ST7 . . . . . **25** E6
Congleton Rd S ST7 . . . . . **25** D2
Congleton Sta CW12 . . . . . **6** A1
Congreve Cl ST17 . . . . . **175** F7
Congreve Rd ST3 . . . . . **72** F2
Conifer Cl WS12 . . . . . **210** A8
Conifer Gr Stafford ST17 . . . . . **174** B7
  Stoke-on-T ST3 . . . . . **72** F2
Coniston Cl ST15 . . . . . **120** D7
Coniston Dr Cheadle ST10 . . . . . **76** F4
  Kingswinford DY6 . . . . . **275** B7
Coniston Gr ST5 . . . . . **71** B4
Coniston Rd ST16 . . . . . **285** C3
Coniston Pl ST4 . . . . . **87** F7
Coniston Rd Aldridge B74 . . . . . **256** F3
  Wolverhampton WV6 . . . . . **255** D8
Coniston B77 . . . . . **262** B6
Coniston Way WS11 . . . . . **209** L1
Conners La TF10 . . . . . **168** A3
Conrad Cl ST3 . . . . . **73** D3
Consall Gr ST4 . . . . . **88** C6
Consall La ST9 . . . . . **60** D6
Consall Nature Pk* ST9 . . . . . **61** A5
Consall Station ST9 . . . . . **61** B6
Consett Rd ST3 . . . . . **88** F8
Consort Pl B79 . . . . . **250** C5
Consort St ST4 . . . . . **72** B7
Constable Ave ST5 . . . . . **55** E6
Constable Cl ST3 . . . . . **90** B7
Constance Ave ST4 . . . . . **88** B8
Convent Cl
  Burton u T DE15 . . . . . **185** F8
  Cannock WS11 . . . . . **226** D8
  Colwich ST18 . . . . . **177** D7
  Stoke-on-T ST4 . . . . . **72** A8
Convent Ct ST4 . . . . . **72** A8
Convent La ST15 . . . . . **105** B4
Conway Cl
  5 Burton u T DE13 . . . . . **166** D8
  Kingswinford DY6 . . . . . **275** F4
Conway Gr ST10 . . . . . **76** E1
Conway Rd Biddulph ST8 . . . . . **27** C6
  Cannock WS11 . . . . . **226** B8
  Perton WV6 . . . . . **254** F3
  Stafford ST16 . . . . . **155** A4
Conway St ST4 . . . . . **72** C8
Congyree La DE6 . . . . . **81** D7
Cook Cl WV6 . . . . . **254** C4
Cooke Cl ST19 . . . . . **192** E2
Cooke St WV2 . . . . . **266** C8
Cookley La DY7 . . . . . **278** B1
Cookley Sebright Fst Sch
  DY10 . . . . . **280** A5
Cooknell Dr DY8 . . . . . **275** E2
Cook Rd WS3 . . . . . **243** D2
Cook's Bank ST11 . . . . . **175** B1
Cook's Hollow WS13 . . . . . **47** A8
Cook's La ST13 . . . . . **32** A1
Cookson Ave ST3 . . . . . **73** C1
Coolidge St **18** ST6 . . . . . **41** D3
Coombe Croft WV9 . . . . . **240** A3
Coombe Park Rd ST15 . . . . . **119** F5
Coombesdale ST5 . . . . . **85** F2
Coombes Valley Nature
  Reserve* ST10 . . . . . **46** D6
Co-Operative La ST7 . . . . . **54** D7
Co-operative St ST16 . . . . . **155** D6
Cooper Ave ST5 . . . . . **56** E2
Cooper Cl ST15 . . . . . **120** D7
Cooper & Jordan CE Prim
  Sch WS9 . . . . . **256** C6
Cooper Perry Prim Sch
  ST18 . . . . . **154** C6
Cooper's Bank Rd DY5 . . . . . **271** C1
Coopers Cl ST13 . . . . . **30** C5
Cooper's Sq DY4 . . . . . **166** D2
Cooper St Hanley ST1 . . . . . **282** A2
  Newcastle-u-L ST5 . . . . . **55** E6
  Wolverhampton WV2 . . . . . **266** F5
Coopers Way ST8 . . . . . **27** B8
Coors Visitor Ctr* DE14 . . . . . **166** D3
Copeland Ave
  Newcastle-u-L ST5 . . . . . **71** B3
  Tittensor ST12 . . . . . **88** A1
Copeland Cl ST10 . . . . . **76** D1
Copeland Dr ST15 . . . . . **120** D5
Copelands The DY7 . . . . . **278** A3
Copeland St ST4 . . . . . **72** B7
Cope's Ave ST6 . . . . . **41** E3

Cope's Dr B79 . . . . . **250** B7
Cope St Stafford ST16 . . . . . **285** B3
  Stoke-on-T ST2 . . . . . **43** A1
Copes Way ST14 . . . . . **111** A1
Copley La WV6 . . . . . **253** A2
Coplow Ave ST10 . . . . . **92** C4
Coplow La ST15 . . . . . **129** D5
Copperas Rd DE11 . . . . . **186** D5
Copper Beech Dr
  Kingswinford DY6 . . . . . **270** D1
  Wombourne WV5 . . . . . **270** B6
Copperfields WS14 . . . . . **231** B3
Copper Glade ST16 . . . . . **156** B3
Copperhill Rd CW12 . . . . . **16** B7
Copperkins Rd WS12 . . . . . **210** E4
Coppermill Cl WS12 . . . . . **209** F7
Coppice Ave ST5 . . . . . **55** A1
Coppice Brook ST17 . . . . . **176** C4
Coppice Cl Biddulph ST8 . . . . . **27** B5
  Burntwood WS7 . . . . . **228** F8
  Cheslyn Hay WS6 . . . . . **226** D4
  Sedgley DY3 . . . . . **271** C6
  Stone ST15 . . . . . **105** A1
  Wolverhampton WV11 . . . . . **242** A1
Coppice Cres ST5 . . . . . **244** D7
Coppice Ct WS11 . . . . . **226** B3
Coppice Dr Newport TF10 . . . . . **168** E5
  Polesworth B78 . . . . . **262** F7
Coppice Farm Way
  WV11 . . . . . **242** B1
Coppice Gdns ST15 . . . . . **105** B1
Coppice Gr
  Lichfield WS14 . . . . . **231** F7
  Meir ST3 . . . . . **74** A3
Coppice Ho ST7 . . . . . **40** C8
Coppice La Aldridge WS9 . . . . . **244** F1
  Brownhills WS8 . . . . . **244** D6
  Cheslyn Hay WS6 . . . . . **226** D4
  Clifton Campville B79 . . . . . **218** F1
  Middleton B78 . . . . . **259** D2
  Muckley Corner WS7,
    WS14 . . . . . **230** A3
  Wolverhampton WV8 . . . . . **255** B6
Coppice Prim Sch B75 . . . . . **258** B1
Coppice Rd
  Brownhills WS8,WS9 . . . . . **244** F4
  Rugeley WS15 . . . . . **196** E6
  Stone ST15 . . . . . **105** A1
  Talke ST7 . . . . . **40** C8
  Wolverhampton WV3 . . . . . **265** D8
Coppice Sch The ST5 . . . . . **283** B1
Coppice Side WS8 . . . . . **244** D7
Coppice Side Ind Est
  WS8 . . . . . **244** C8
Coppice The
  Cannock WS12 . . . . . **210** E1
  Hagley DY8 . . . . . **281** F5
  Market Drayton TF9 . . . . . **97** B1
  Stoke-on-T ST6 . . . . . **57** C7
Coppice View ST5 . . . . . **56** A4
Coppice Way ST16 . . . . . **155** C8
Coppins The
  2 Stafford ST17 . . . . . **175** C7
  Leek ST13 . . . . . **30** C5
Copp La ST6 . . . . . **41** C2
Copplestone Gr ST3 . . . . . **73** E3
Coppull Pl ST3 . . . . . **42** A7
Coppy Hall Gr WS9 . . . . . **245** B1
Coppy Nook La WS7 . . . . . **229** C5
Copse Cres WS3 . . . . . **244** A4
Copse Dr WS15 . . . . . **198** B4
Copse The B74 . . . . . **257** F1
Copsy Dale ST21 . . . . . **115** C6
Copthorne Ave WS7 . . . . . **228** F4
Copthorne Rd WV3 . . . . . **266** A7
Coracle Gr ST8 . . . . . **27** E6
Coral Gr ST4 . . . . . **88** B7
Corbet Ct **4** ST4 . . . . . **97** C1
Corbett Ho **8** DY8 . . . . . **279** F4
Corbett Hospl DY8 . . . . . **279** F7
Corbett Prim Sch DY7 . . . . . **268** A2
Corbett Wlk **13** ST6 . . . . . **41** D3
Corbin Rd B78 . . . . . **262** F6
Corby Pl ST3 . . . . . **284** A3
Corden Ave DE13 . . . . . **166** F8
Cordy La WV7 . . . . . **237** C7
Corfe Cl WV6 . . . . . **254** F3
Corfe Gn ST3 . . . . . **73** C6
Corfield Pl ST4 . . . . . **42** D5
Corfton Dr WV6 . . . . . **255** C3
Corina Way ST3 . . . . . **73** D4
Corinth Way **1** ST6 . . . . . **41** D3
Cormie Cl ST6 . . . . . **42** B5
Corncrake Rd DY1,DY3 . . . . . **271** E3
Cornelious St **3** ST3 . . . . . **74** A1
Cornel B77 . . . . . **250** F4
Corner Ways ST18 . . . . . **154** E2
Cornes St ST1 . . . . . **57** D1
Corneville Rd ST2 . . . . . **58** C3
Corn Exchange The **5**
  WS13 . . . . . **231** B8
Cornfield Cl DY6 . . . . . **275** A8
Cornfield Dr WS14 . . . . . **231** E7
Cornfield Rd ST8 . . . . . **27** E7
Cornfield WV8 . . . . . **239** F2
Cornflower Cl WV10 . . . . . **241** A7
Cornflower Rd WS8 . . . . . **244** D6
Cornhill WS11 . . . . . **209** E5
Cornhill Cl ST5 . . . . . **40** D1
Cornhill Gdns ST13 . . . . . **30** E4
Cornhill Rd ST6 . . . . . **42** C5
Cornhill St **10** ST6 . . . . . **30** E5
Cornmell Lea TF10 . . . . . **168** F3
Cornmill Gr WV6 . . . . . **254** D3
Corn Mill La DE13 . . . . . **146** E6
Cornovian Cl WV6 . . . . . **254** E5
Corns Gr WV5 . . . . . **269** F5

Cornwall Ave
  Newcastle-u-L ST5 . . . . . **71** D4
  Tamworth B78 . . . . . **250** A1
Cornwall Cl
  4 Congleton CW12 . . . . . **6** A1
  Aldridge WS9 . . . . . **245** A1
  Kingswinford DY6 . . . . . **275** D8
Cornwall Ct ST4 . . . . . **72** B6
Cornwall Dr ST17 . . . . . **156** D1
Cornwallis St ST4 . . . . . **72** B6
Cornwall Rd
  Burton u T DE15 . . . . . **185** E6
  Cannock WS12 . . . . . **210** B5
  Stourbridge DY8 . . . . . **279** D8
  Wolverhampton WV6 . . . . . **255** D8
Cornwall St ST4 . . . . . **284** C4
Cornwood Gr ST3 . . . . . **89** E8
Coronation Ave
  Biddulph ST8 . . . . . **27** B5
  Longton ST3 . . . . . **284** B3
  Mile Oak B78 . . . . . **249** D1
Coronation Cotts DE13 . . . . . **184** A8
Coronation Cres
  Kidsgrove ST7 . . . . . **25** E1
  Rocester ST14 . . . . . **96** A4
  Shuttington B79 . . . . . **251** C7
Coronation Rd
  Brownhills WS9 . . . . . **245** A3
  Newcastle-u-L ST5 . . . . . **283** C2
  Stafford ST16 . . . . . **156** A6
  Stoke-on-T,Hartshill ST4 . . . . . **71** E8
  Walsall WS4 . . . . . **244** B2
Coronation St
  Cheadle ST10 . . . . . **76** D3
  Stoke-on-T ST6 . . . . . **41** E4
  Tamworth B79 . . . . . **250** A5
Corporation St
  Newcastle-u-L ST5 . . . . . **283** B3
  Stafford ST16 . . . . . **285** C4
  Stoke-on-T ST4 . . . . . **72** B6
  Tamworth B79 . . . . . **250** B5
Corran Rd ST17 . . . . . **174** D6
Correen B77 . . . . . **251** C1
Corrie Roy Cotts B78 . . . . . **250** A4
Corrin Gr DY6 . . . . . **275** C8
Corser St DY1 . . . . . **271** F2
Corsham St ST14 . . . . . **143** F7
Corsican Cl WS7 . . . . . **229** A8
Corsican Dr WS12 . . . . . **210** A8
Cort Dr WS7 . . . . . **229** B8
Corve Gdns WV6 . . . . . **255** E5
Corve View DY3 . . . . . **266** C1
Coseley St ST6 . . . . . **42** C2
Cosford Ct WS5 . . . . . **254** E5
Cosgrove Wlk WV8 . . . . . **239** F1
Cotehill Rd ST9 . . . . . **59** B4
Cote La DY7 . . . . . **273** C1
Cotesheath St ST1 . . . . . **57** D1
Cotes La
  Cotes Heath ST21 . . . . . **102** F2
  Swynnerton ST15 . . . . . **103** B2
Cot La DY6,DY8 . . . . . **275** C5
Coton Ave ST16 . . . . . **156** A4
Coton Green Prec
  B79 . . . . . **249** F7
Coton Green Prim Sch
  B79 . . . . . **249** F8
Coton La
  Coton Clanford ST18 . . . . . **154** A3
  Ranton ST18 . . . . . **153** E4
  Tamworth B79 . . . . . **249** E4
Coton Pk DE12 . . . . . **186** C1
Coton Rd
  Walton-On-Trent DE12 . . . . . **202** E6
  Wolverhampton WV4 . . . . . **266** B5
Coton Rise ST12 . . . . . **88** E1
Cotsdale Rd WV4 . . . . . **265** E3
Cotswold Ave
  Great Wyrley WS6 . . . . . **226** F3
  Newcastle-u-L ST5 . . . . . **55** E3
Cotswold Cl
  Aldridge WS9 . . . . . **245** C1
  Cannock WS12 . . . . . **210** A8
Cotswold Cres ST4 . . . . . **43** A1
Cotswold Dr
  Sutton Coldfield B75 . . . . . **258** A4
  Wolverhampton WV3 . . . . . **266** B6
Cotswold Gr WV7 . . . . . **237** B5
Cotswold Gr WV12 . . . . . **242** B1
Cotswold Rd
  Burton u T DE14 . . . . . **184** F8
  Cannock WS12 . . . . . **210** A8
  Wolverhampton WV2 . . . . . **266** F7
Cottage Cl
  Burntwood WS7 . . . . . **228** F5
  Cannock WS12 . . . . . **210** D5
  Longton ST3 . . . . . **73** E1
Cottage Ct WS7 . . . . . **228** F5
Cottage Farm Rd B77 . . . . . **261** D7
Cottage La
  Biddulph Moor ST8 . . . . . **28** A8
  Burntwood WS7 . . . . . **228** F5
  Wolverhampton WV10 . . . . . **240** D3
Cottage Mews WS9 . . . . . **256** C4
Cottage View DY3 . . . . . **239** B4
Cottage Wlk **4** B77 . . . . . **261** F6
Cotterill Dr ST5 . . . . . **56** B8
Cotterill Gr ST5 . . . . . **56** F7
Cotters Hill Cl ST18 . . . . . **177** D8
Cottesmore Dr DE15 . . . . . **167** A1
Cotton Cl DE13 . . . . . **200** A1
Cotton Gr WS12 . . . . . **195** A1
Cotton La ST10 . . . . . **63** B2
Cotton Lane Cotts ST10 . . . . . **63** B3
Cotton Rd ST6 . . . . . **41** C6
Cotton Way WS7 . . . . . **211** F1

Cottonwood Gr
  Harriseahead ST7 . . . . . **26** E4
  Longton ST3 . . . . . **284** C4
Cottrell Cl WS15 . . . . . **160** F6
Cotts The ST3 . . . . . **74** A8
Cotwall End Countryside &
  Craft Ctr* DY3 . . . . . **271** C7
Cotwall End Ho DY3 . . . . . **271** C7
Cotwall End Prim Sch
  DY3 . . . . . **271** D7
Cotwall End Rd DY3 . . . . . **271** C5
Coulson Cl WS7 . . . . . **211** D1
Coulter Gr WV6 . . . . . **254** D4
Coulter La WS7 . . . . . **229** A1
Coulthwaite Way WS15 . . . . . **196** F6
Council Hos
  Bramshall ST14 . . . . . **125** C7
  Chetwynd Aston TF10 . . . . . **187** A7
  Church Leigh ST10 . . . . . **109** A4
  Kingstone ST14 . . . . . **125** C1
  Kingstone,The Blythe ST18 . . . . . **140** E5
Council Hos The ST21 . . . . . **116** B4
Country Park View ST5 . . . . . **55** A8
County Dr B78 . . . . . **250** A2
County La
  Codsall WV7,WV8 . . . . . **237** C3
  Iverley DY8 . . . . . **281** D8
County Rd ST16 . . . . . **285** B4
Coupe Dr ST3 . . . . . **74** A5
Court Cres DY6 . . . . . **275** C5
Court Dr WS14 . . . . . **246** F4
Court Farm La DE14 . . . . . **184** E7
Courtland Mews ST16 . . . . . **155** F5
Courtland Rd DY6 . . . . . **275** E8
Courtlands The WV6 . . . . . **255** E4
Court La ST5 . . . . . **56** B4
Courtney Pl ST3 . . . . . **89** E8
Court No 1 ST3 . . . . . **73** E1
Court Par WS9 . . . . . **256** B6
Court Rd WV6 . . . . . **255** F4
Courts The WV7 . . . . . **237** A4
Courtway Dr ST1 . . . . . **57** D8
Court Wlk CW3 . . . . . **53** A5
Cousins St WV2 . . . . . **266** D7
Covan Farm Mobile Home Pk
  WV9 . . . . . **224** C1
Coven Cl WS3 . . . . . **244** A5
Coven Mill Cl WV9 . . . . . **224** C1
Coven Rd WV9 . . . . . **223** D4
Coventry Ct ST16 . . . . . **155** A5
Coverdale Cl ST3 . . . . . **90** A7
Coverley Pl ST4 . . . . . **71** F6
Covers La DY7 . . . . . **274** E1
Covert Cl ST18 . . . . . **158** B2
Covert Gdns ST7 . . . . . **40** D8
Covert La DY8 . . . . . **279** D2
Covert The Keele ST5 . . . . . **70** B7
  Newcastle-u-L ST5 . . . . . **71** C2
  Wolverhampton WV8 . . . . . **239** E1
Covey Cl WS13 . . . . . **214** D1
Cowallmoor La WS13 . . . . . **28** B5
Cowan Dr ST16 . . . . . **156** A4
Cowen St ST6 . . . . . **42** E6
Cowhill La WS3 . . . . . **200** E1
Cowhouse La ST10 . . . . . **109** B3
Cow La Cauldon ST10 . . . . . **63** F7
  Whateley B78 . . . . . **261** F3
Cowley Cl Penkridge ST19 . . . . . **207** F7
  Stafford ST17 . . . . . **174** C8
Cowley Dr DY1 . . . . . **271** F2
Cowley Gn WS12 . . . . . **209** F8
Cowley La ST20 . . . . . **171** D5
Cowley B77 . . . . . **250** E2
Cowley Way ST2 . . . . . **73** E7
Cowlishaw Cl ST8 . . . . . **27** B5
Cowlishaw Rd ST6 . . . . . **42** C6
Cowlishaw Way WS15 . . . . . **196** F6
Cowlow La SK17 . . . . . **23** D3
Cowper St ST4 . . . . . **72** F6
Coxmoor Cl WV3 . . . . . **242** F3
Coyney Gr ST3 . . . . . **74** A3
Crabbery St ST16 . . . . . **285** B3
Crab La Bobbington DY7 . . . . . **268** C2
  Cannock WS11 . . . . . **210** A3
  Stafford ST16 . . . . . **155** B8
  Willenhall WV12 . . . . . **242** D1
Crabtree Ave ST8 . . . . . **27** C7
Crabtree Cl ST4 . . . . . **72** F8
Crabtree Way WS5 . . . . . **178** C2
Cracklehill La DE6 . . . . . **81** C3
Crackley Bank ST5 . . . . . **40** E1
Crackley Bank Prim Sch
  ST5 . . . . . **40** E1
Crackley La ST5 . . . . . **54** E3
Cracow Moss CW3 . . . . . **53** A3
Craddock Rd WS15 . . . . . **155** C7
Craftdown Cl ST17 . . . . . **174** F4
Craigside **5** ST8 . . . . . **27** C8
Cramer St ST17 . . . . . **285** B2
Cranberry Ave ST10 . . . . . **93** B1
Cranberry Cl ST16 . . . . . **155** A6
Cranberry St ST5 . . . . . **40** D1
Cranberry Marsh ST21 . . . . . **102** D3
Cranborne Ave ST2 . . . . . **43** B2
Cranbourne Ave WV4 . . . . . **266** C4
Cranbrook Cl ST4 . . . . . **88** A7
Cranbrook Gr WV6 . . . . . **254** F3
Cranbrooks ST19 . . . . . **205** C7
Cranbrook Wlk ST17 . . . . . **174** B8
Cranebrook Hill B78 . . . . . **259** E5
Cranebrook La
  Stonnall WS14 . . . . . **245** F7
  Wall WS14 . . . . . **246** A8
Crane Dr WS7 . . . . . **229** A4
Crane Field WS13 . . . . . **214** B1

Crane Hollow WV5...... 269 E5
Cranesbill Cl WV10.....241 C7
Crane St ST1.............57 B6
Crane Terr WV6.........255 E5
Cranfield Pl ST2...........58 B2
Cranfield Rd WS7..........229 A7
Cranford Pl WS11........209 F1
Cranford Rd WV3.........265 D8
Cranford Way ST2.........58 D3
Cranham Dr DY6.........275 C6
Cranleigh Ave ST1........57 D8
Cranleigh Cl
  Aldridge WS9............256 B5
  Willenhall WV12.........242 E1
Cranleigh Way WS14.....231 E7
Cranley Dr WV8..........238 F4
Cranmer Cl WS6.........226 D1
Cranmere Ave WV6......255 A6
Cranmere Ct WV6........255 A6
Cranmer Gr B74..........257 F6
Cranmer St ST4...........72 B7
Cranmore Gr ST15.......120 C7
Cranmore Rd WV3........255 F3
Cranswick Gr ST2.........58 D1
Crantock Cl WV11........242 C1
Cranwell Gn WV5.........269 F5
Cranwell Pl ST3...........89 F8
Cranwell Rise B78.........249 C1
Cranwood Rd ST12........88 A1
Cranworth Gr ST3.........89 E8
Crateford La ST19........224 B7
Crathorne Ave WV10......240 C1
Crauford Rd CW12..........6 A8
Craven Cl ST4............88 A8
Craven St Burton u T DE13 166 C6
  Wolverhampton WV2......266 F6
Craven B77...............251 B1
Crawford Ave WV4.......266 F3
Crawfurd St ST4..........72 D5
Crawley La DE13.........199 C5
Crayford Ave ST15.......120 C7
Craythorne Rd DE13......147 D3
Crediton Ave ST6.........42 C4
Creighton La ST14........111 A5
Cremorne Dr ST17.......175 D7
Cremorne Rd B75........258 B2
Cremorne Wlk B75........258 B2
Crescent Gr ST4..........56 E1
Crescent Prim Sch ST3...74 C1
Crescent Rd ST17.........285 A1
Crescent The Ashley TF9 100 C5
  Burntwood WS7..........211 F1
  Cookley DY10............280 B4
  Eccleshall ST21.........133 D6
  Great Wyrley WS6........227 A4
  Hagley DY8..............281 F5
  Leek ST13................31 A7
  Mayfield ST14............81 D7
  Newcastle-u-L,Silverdale
    ST5....................55 B2
  Newcastle-u-L ST5.......71 A6
  Rudyard ST13.............18 C1
  Stafford,Doxey ST16.....155 B4
  Stoke-on-T ST4...........71 E4
  Stone ST15..............105 A1
  Swadlincote DE11........186 E6
  Walton-on-t-H ST17......175 F7
  Wolverhampton WV6......255 B3
Cressington Dr B74.......258 A1
Cresswell Ave ST5.........40 D1
Cresswell Cres WS3.......242 F2
Cresswell Ct WV10........240 A3
Cresswell La
  Brewood ST19...........223 D1
  Cresswell ST11...........91 D4
Cresswell Old Rd ST11....91 E3
Cresswell Rd Hanley ST1..57 E3
  Hilderstone ST15........106 C3
Cressy Cl ST15...........104 E3
Crestbrook Rd ST2.........58 C6
Crestfield Rd ST3..........89 F8
Crestway Rd ST2..........43 C2
Crestwood Cl DE13........166 D8
Crestwood Dr ST15.......119 F6
Crestwood Glen WV6.....255 E7
Crestwood Pk ST19.......223 D7
Crestwood Rise WS15....178 C3
Crestwood Sch The DY6.275 F5
Crestwood B77...........251 A5
Creswell Dr ST18.........154 F8
Creswell Farm Dr ST16...155 B7
Creswell Gr
  Creswell ST18...........154 F8
  Stafford ST18...........155 A8
Crewe Gates Ind Est CW1 37 A8
Crewe Hall Ent Pk CW1....37 D8
Crichton Ave DE13.......166 D7
Cricket Cl ST6...........167 E8
Cricketers Cl DE15.......185 A6
Cricketers Mews ST5.....56 C5
Cricketers The DE13.....200 F2
Cricket La WS14.........231 C5
Cricket Mdw Dudley DY1.271 E5
  Wolverhampton WV10....240 D4
Crick Rd ST1.............57 E2
Crigdon B77..............251 C1
Crinan Gr ST17...........174 D6
Cringlebrook B77.........250 D1
Crispin Cl ST16..........155 C8
Critchlow Gr ST3..........73 A1
Critchlows Ct ST3.........72 F1
Crockett The ST11........74 E3
Crockford Dr B75.........258 B3

Crockington Cl WV5......263 F2
Crockington La WV5......264 A1
Crocus Cres WV9........240 A3
Croft Ave Cannock WS12. 195 A1
  Newcastle-u-L ST5........56 B6
  Tamworth B79...........250 B6
Croft Cl Elford B79.......216 E2
  Netherseal DE12.........219 F7
  Rolleston on D DE13.....147 B4
Croft Cres
  Brownhills WS8...........244 D7
  Stoke-on-T ST4...........72 A6
Croft Ct ST6..............42 C1
Crofter Cl ST8............27 B8
Crofters Ct ST5...........40 D3
Crofters La B75...........258 E3
Crofters The TF10........188 D6
Crofters Wlk WV8.........239 E1
Croftfield St ST2..........73 D8
Croft Gdns WS7...........229 A8
Croft Gr ST14............111 C1
Croft Leys The WS15.....198 C4
Croft Par WS9...........256 C6
Croft Prim Sch WS15.....197 F5
Croft Rd Cheadle ST10....76 D3
  Newcastle-u-L ST5.......283 B4
  Stone ST15..............119 F6
Croft Road Ind Est ST5...283 B4
Croft St ST6..............56 F8
Croftstead Ave ST14......95 D6
Croft St B79.............250 B6
Croft The
  Blakedown DY10.........281 C2
  Burton u T DE15.........166 F1
  Cheadle ST10............76 E6
  Cheddleton ST13.........45 C4
  Cheslyn Hay WS6........226 E2
  Hixon ST18..............158 C8
  King's Bromley DE13.....199 D6
  Longdon WS15...........197 F1
  Maer ST5................84 C2
  Norton in H TF9...........82 B3
  Sedgley DY3.............266 E1
  Stoke-on-T ST4...........71 F5
  Swadlincote DE11........186 E6
  Wombourne WV5.........269 D5
Croft Way TF9.............97 B1
Cromartie St ST3.........284 C2
Cromdale B77............251 C1
Cromer Cres ST1..........57 E4
Cromer Gdns WV6........255 F5
Cromer Rd ST1............57 F4
Cromer St ST5............56 D4
Crompton Cl
  Colwich ST18............177 E8
  Congleton CW12...........6 A6
Crompton Ct WV8.........239 B4
Crompton Gr ST4..........88 C5
Crompton Rd ST15.......120 B7
Cromwell Cl Hopton ST18 137 D1
  Tutbury DE13............146 C5
Cromwell Ct WS6.........227 A1
Cromwell Rd
  Cannock WS12...........210 E1
  Tamworth B79...........249 E8
  Wolverhampton WV10....240 E4
Cromwells Mdw WS14....231 D5
Cromwell St Biddulph ST8 27 C8
  Hanley ST1...............57 D6
Cromwell Terr ST13.......30 F5
Crony Cl ST13.............45 C4
Crooked Bridge Rd ST16 285 B4
Crook La WS9............256 B1
Crosby Cl WV6............255 F5
Crosby Rd ST4.............71 E3
Cross Butts ST21.........133 C5
Crossdale Ave ST2.........43 A2
Cross Edge ST6............43 B7
Crossfield B77............251 B1
Crossfield Ave
  Biddulph ST8.............27 C6
  Blythe Bridge ST11.......90 F6
Crossfield Rd Ind Est
  WS13...................231 B8
Crossfield Rd WS13.......231 B8
Crosshill Bank ST18.......122 F5
Crossings The ST8........231 A6
Cross In Hand La
  Lichfield,Farewell WS13 213 C3
  Lichfield WS13...........213 F1
Crossland Cres WV6......255 F7
Crossland Pl E ST3........90 A8
Crossland Pl W ST3.......74 A1
Crosslands CW12...........6 A1
Cross La Oulton ST15.....105 C4
  Rolleston on D DE13.....147 B2
  Sedgley DY3.............266 E1
  Waterhouses ST10........48 E3
Crossley Rd ST6...........42 A3
Crossley Stone WS15.....178 E1
Crosslow La DE6...........36 E5
Crossman St ST14.........166 A3
Cross May St ST5.........283 A2
Crossmead Gr ST1.........57 F6
Cross of the Hand WS15. 161 B2
Cross Pl DY3.............266 E1
Cross Rd Albrighton WV7.237 A5
  Rugeley WS15...........196 C5
  Uttoxeter ST14..........111 B1

Crossington Cl ST3........90 C6
Cross St S WV2..........266 C7
Cross Side DE6............81 F7
Cross St
  ▲ Stourbridge,Wordsley
    DY6....................275 D3
  ▼ Leek ST13..............30 F5
  Biddulph ST8.............27 C8
  Burntwood WS7..........228 E8
  Burton u T DE14.........166 C3
  Cannock,Bridgtown WS11 226 E5
  Cannock WS12...........210 E1
  Cheadle ST10.............76 E1
  Cheslyn Hay WS6........226 D2
  Gnosall ST20............171 C5
  Kingsley ST10............61 D3
  Kingswinford DY6........275 D6
  Kingswinford,Wall Heath
    DY6....................275 B8
  Market Drayton TF9.......97 D1
  Meir ST3.................74 B5
  Newcastle-u-L ST5.......55 E8
  Stafford ST16...........155 D5
  Stone ST15.............105 A1
  Stourbridge DY8.........279 E5
  Tamworth B79...........250 B5
  Tamworth,Kettlebrook
    B77...................250 C3
  Tunstall ST6..............56 C8
  Walsall WS3.............244 A1
Cross The DY6...........275 D6
Crossway Rd ST6..........57 C7
Crossways Biddulph ST8...16 E1
  Pipe Gate TF9.............83 D7
Crossways Rd ST7.........25 A4
Crossway ST16...........156 A3
Crossway The ST5.........56 C3
Croston St ST1...........282 A1
Crotia Ave CW2............37 B5
Crouch Ave ST5...........42 A4
Crouch La CW12............6 D4
Crowberry Cl WS8........244 D6
Crowberry La DE13.......183 D2
Crowborough Rd ST8,
  ST13....................28 B6
Crowcrofts Rd ST4........88 E7
Crowden Rd B77..........251 A1
Crowfoot La DE65........129 E8
Crowland Ave WV6.......254 E4
Crown Bank WS15........161 A6
Crown Bank Cres ST7.....40 D6
Crown Bank Hanley ST1...282 B3
  Talke Pits ST7............40 C6
Crown Bridge ST19.......192 E1
Crown Cl DY3............266 D1
Crown Ct B74............257 E2
Crowndale Pl ST6..........41 E8
Crown Gdns ST4...........40 D6
Crown Ind Est DE14.......166 B1
Crown La Iverley DY8......281 C7
  Stourbridge DY8.........279 F5
  Sutton Coldfield B74.....257 E3
Crown Specl Sch DE13...147 D1
Crown St Hanley ST1......282 B2
  Newcastle-u-L ST5.......55 C2
  Stone ST15.............120 A8
Crowther Gr WV6.........255 F7
Crowther Rd WV6........255 F5
Crowther St ST4...........72 C8
Crowtrees Farm Ind Est
  ST10.....................48 F2
Croxall Rd Alrewas DE13.201 B2
  Edingale B79............217 C5
  Edingale B79,WS13......217 B6
Croxden Abbey ✝ ST14...94 C4
Croxden Ave WS3.........243 A1
Croxden Rd ST2...........58 B6
Croxley Dr WV2..........210 C3
Croxstalls Cl WS3.........243 A1
Croyde Pl ST3.............90 B6
Croydon Dr ST19.........207 F8
Cruso St ST13.............30 E5
Crutchley Ave B78........250 A2
Crystal Ave DY8..........275 F1
Crystal Gdns DY7.........278 A3
Crystal St ST6.............57 B6
Cubley La DE6............96 E2
Cuckoo Cage La DE13....164 F1
Cuckoo Cl WS11..........210 C2
Cullamore La ST14........126 B4
Culland Rd DE14.........185 B7
Cull Ave ST16...........156 A3
Cumberbatch Ave ST6....42 B7
Cumberland Cl
  Kingswinford DY6........275 E4
  Talke ST7.................40 E7
Cumberland Cres WS7....229 A8
Cumberland Dr B78.......250 A1
Cumberland Rd
  Burton u T DE15.........185 D6
  Cannock WS11...........210 A4
Cumberland St
  Newcastle-u-L ST5.......283 C3
  Stoke-on-T ST4...........72 E6
Cumberledge Hill WS15. 211 E5
Cumbers The ST18........154 E6
Cumbria Ho ST5...........71 C5
Cumming St ST4...........71 E8
Cunningham Rd WV6.....254 E4
Curborough Rd WS13.....214 B2
Curland Pl ST3............73 F2
Curlew Cl Lichfield WS14. 231 E7
  Uttoxeter ST14..........126 C6
Curlew Dr WV8...........238 E4
Curlew Hill WS11.........210 A3
Curlew Rd ST7.............26 E1
Curlew B77..............262 A7
Curtis Cl DE13...........166 C7

Curtiss Pl ST3............90 C6
Curtis Way DE14.........166 B4
Curzon Pl WS15..........196 E7
Curzon Rd ST6............42 A2
Curzon Rise ST13..........30 B5
Curzon St W DE14........166 B3
Curzon St
  Burton u T DE14.........166 C3
  Newcastle-u-L ST5.......56 D2
  Wolverhampton WV2.....266 D7
Cushman Ave WS5........269 E7
Cuttlestone Ho ST19.....192 E1
Cutts St ST1.............282 A1
Cwerne Ct DY3...........271 C3
Cyclamen Cl DE14.......185 A8
Cygnet Cl Cannock WS12. 210 C7
  Madeley Heath CW3.......69 A8
  Wolverhampton WV2.....266 D7
Cygnet Dr Brownhills WS8 244 E7
  Tamworth B79...........249 F5
Cynthia Gr ST6............42 A2
Cypress Ave DY3.........271 D5
Cypress Cl
  Market Drayton TF9.......97 A1
  Stafford ST17...........156 C1
Cypress Gdns ▲ DY6.....275 D4
Cypress Gr
  Blythe Bridge ST11.......91 A6
  Newcastle-u-L ST5.......55 D8
Cypress Rise WS12.......211 A6
Cyprus St WV2...........266 C6

D

Dace Gr ST6..............42 B3
Daffodil Cl DY3..........271 E7
Daffodil Wlk WS15.......178 C2
Dag La DE12.............218 E2
Dahlia Cl ST3.............74 B6
Daimler Cl ▲ ST17.......175 A8
Dain Pl ST4...............56 B6
Dain St ST6...............56 E7
Daintry Cl ST13...........30 E5
Daintry Dr B78...........249 E7
Daintry St Leek ST13......30 E5
  Stoke-on-T ST4...........71 F4
Dairy Cl Leek ST13.........31 A6
  Market Drayton TF9.......97 D1
Dairyfields Way ST1.......57 D7
Dairyhouse La
  Dilhorne ST10............60 B2
  Overmoor ST10...........60 E1
Dairylands Rd ST7.........25 A4
Daisy Bank Cl ST2........209 F8
Daisy Bank WS3.........244 A1
Daisy Bank ST13..........30 E6
Daisy La Alrewas DE13....200 F2
  Alrewas DE13...........200 F2
Daisy Pl ST4..............72 E4
Daisy Wlk WV9...........240 A3
Dakota Gr ST6............41 E4
Dalbeg Cl WV8...........255 E8
Dale Ave ST4.............42 E6
Dalebrook Rd DE15.......167 B5
Dale Cl Cheadle ST10......76 E2
  Whitmore ST5............85 C5
Dalecot Gn ST2............73 D8
Dale Cres CW12............6 A2
Dale Dr WV7.............229 B7
Dalegarth Gr ST3..........89 E8
Dalehall Gdns ▲ ST6......56 E8
Dalehead Ct ST3..........89 F8
Dalehouse Rd ST13........45 C4
Daleian Ct ST5............55 C1
Dale La ST18.............173 A7
Dalelands Est TF9........112 B8
Dalelands W TF9.........112 B7
Dale La DE6...............64 F4
Dale Rd DY8.............279 F2
Dales Cl Biddulph Moor ST8. 28 B8
  Swadlincote DE11........186 E5
Dales Com Jun Sch B77..262 B8
Dales Green Rd ST7.......26 C5
Daleside ST6.............167 B1
Dales Inf Sch The B77....262 B8
Dalesman Cl DY6.........275 B7
Dale St Burslem ST6.......56 E8
  Burton u T DE14.........166 C2
Dale The Ashley TF9......100 B5
  Warslow DE6,SK17........23 C2
Dale View Ct ST11.........90 E1
Daleview Dr ST5...........55 C1
Dale View
  Earl Sterndale SK17.......5 B3
  Meir ST3.................74 B3
  Mow Cop ST7.............26 C5
Dalewood Rd ST5..........55 F5
Dallow Cl DE14..........166 C5
Dallow Cres DE14........166 C5
Dallow St DE14..........166 C5
Dalton Ave DE15.........167 B1
Dalton Cl WV5...........269 E7
Dalton Gr ST2.............58 D1
Dalton St WV3...........266 B8
Daltry Way CW3...........68 F7
Daly Cres ST5.............55 B1
Dama Rd B78.............260 F8
Dame Paulet Wlk DE14...166 D2
Dam La Alsop en le D DE6..36 E3
  Biddulph ST8.............17 B2
Dampier St ST13..........30 E5
Damson Pk WV6.........253 D3
Dams The ST11............74 D2
Dam St WS13............231 B8
Danbury Gdns WV10.....240 C2

Danby Crest ST17........174 A8
Danby Dr WS12..........211 D4
Dandillion Ave ST10.......92 D8
Danebower Rd ST4........88 C6
Danebridge Gr ST1........57 F5
Dane Dr ST8..............16 E1
Dane Gdns ST7............26 C2
Dane Gr ST10.............76 E1
Danehill Gr ST4...........71 F1
Danehill Wlk WV8.........255 F8
Danelagh Cl B79..........249 F7
Danemead Cl ST3..........90 A7
Danesbrook WV5.........267 D8
Danes Cl WV11...........241 F4
Danescourt Rd WV6......255 C6
Danes Croft ST4...........88 B7
Danesmore Park Jun & Inf
  Sch WV11...............242 A1
Daneswood Dr WS9......244 F3
Dane Wlk ST1...........282 C3
Danford Heath WV5......267 D3
Danford La WV5.........267 D7
Daniels Cross TF10.......169 B4
Daniels La WS9.........256 C5
Danilo Rd WS11.........209 D1
Danta Way ST17.........156 C1
Darby Ave WS14.........232 E6
Darelyn Cvn Site WV9....224 B2
Darges La WS6..........226 F4
Darius Cl ST5.............56 B8
Dark La Alrewas DE13....201 A3
  Birchmoor B78..........262 D6
  Brinsford WV10.........240 D8
  Featherstone WV10......241 D7
  Great Wyrley WS6.......227 C1
  Kinver DY7..............278 B3
  Lichfield WS13..........213 B1
  Longdon WS15..........212 D7
  Newborough DE13.......162 D7
  Newport TF10...........168 E1
Darley Cl DE15..........167 C1
Darley Dale DE11........186 F2
Darley Gr ST10............76 E1
Darlings La WS15........212 A5
Darnbrook B77...........251 C1
Darnel Hurst Rd B75.....258 D3
Darnford Cl ST16.........155 C6
Darnford La
  Lichfield WS14..........231 F6
  Whittington WS14.......232 B5
Darnford Moors WS14...231 E6
Darnford View WS13.....214 F1
Darnley St ST4............72 C8
Darrall Gdns ST4..........71 E3
Darsham Gdns ST5.......71 C2
Dart Ave Stafford ST17...174 B8
  Stoke-on-T ST6...........42 A4
Dart Cl ST8...............16 D1
Dartford Pl ST6...........42 C4
Dartford Rd WS3.........242 F1
Dart Gr ST10.............76 E1
Dartmouth Ave
  Cannock WS11...........226 C8
  Newcastle-u-L ST5.......71 A5
  Pattingham WV6.........253 C2
  Stourbridge DY8.........275 D3
Dartmouth Dr WS9.......256 A5
Dartmouth Pl ST3.........89 F8
Dartmouth Rd WS11.....209 C1
Dartmouth St
  ▲ Wolverhampton WV2. 266 D8
  Stafford ST16...........156 A3
  Stoke-on-T ST6...........42 B1
  Wolverhampton WV2.....266 E8
Dart Pl ST5...............71 A4
Dart B77.................262 A5
Darwell Pk B77..........251 B2
Darwin Dr Burntwood WS7 229 B7
  Burton u T DE15.........167 C1
  Cannock WS11...........210 E2
  Lichfield WS13..........231 A8
  Stafford ST16...........156 C4
  Stone ST15.............104 E2
Darwin Ct WV6..........254 E4
Darwin Ho DY6...........275 F7
Dash Gr ST6..............42 C1
Datteln Rd WS11.........210 A4
Daurada Dr ST17.........175 A8
Davenport Cl ST13........30 B4
Davenport Rd WV6.......255 B5
Davenport St ST6..........41 E1
Davenport Way ST5.......70 F3
Daventry Cl ST2...........57 F2
Davey Cl WS7...........228 F4
David Garrick Gdns
  WS13...................214 B2
David Rd ST3.............73 F1
Davidson Ave CW12........6 A5
Davidson Rd WS14.......231 B7
Davies Dr ST14..........110 F1
Davies Ho WS3..........243 B1
Davis Cl ST16...........156 A4
Davison St ST6...........57 A7
Davis Rd B77............250 F4
Davis St ST4..............57 A2
Davy Cl ST2..............58 A3
Davy Pl WS15...........196 F6
Dawes La WS8..........229 A1
Dawley Brook Prim Sch
  DY6....................275 D7
Dawley Brook Rd DY6....275 D7
Dawley Rd DY6...........275 D8
Dawley Trad Est DY6.....275 D8
Dawlish Ave ST17.........175 D7
Dawlish Dr Bucknall ST2...58 C1
  Bucknall ST2.............73 D8
Dawn Ave ST6............42 A4

Dawney Dr B75 . . . . 258 A4
Dawn View ST3 . . . . 74 B3
Dawson Ave WV14 . . . 266 F2
Dayson Pl ST5 . . . . . . 56 A7
Dayton Dr WS15 . . . . . . 178 C3
Daywell Rise WS15 . . . . 178 C3
Deacons Way WS15 . . . 178 F2
Deakin Ave WS8 . . . . . 228 F1
Deakin Gr ST5 . . . . 71 C5
Deakin Rd ST6 . . . . 42 B5
Deal Ave WS7 . . . . . . 229 A1
Dean Cl TF9 . . . . 97 A1
Dean Ct WV6 . . . . 254 E6
Deanery Cl Rugeley WS15 178 F2
Shareshill WV10 . . . . . 225 C2
Dean Hollow ST7 . . . . . 39 D2
Dean Pl ST1 . . . . 282 C1
Dean Rd WV5 . . . . 269 F5
Deansberry Cl ST4 . . . . 88 A8
Deans Croft WS14 . . . . 231 C8
Deanscroft Way ST3 . . . 73 E4
Deansfield Cl ST19 . . . 223 C8
Deansfield Rd ST19 . . . 223 C8
Deansfield Rd ST19 . . . 223 C8
Deansgate ◆ ST13 . . . . 30 F6
Deanshill Cl ST16 . . . . 155 C2
Deans La CW2 . . . . 38 C4
Dean's La ST5 . . . . 40 D2
Dean's Slade Dr WS14 . 231 A5
Dean St Brewood ST19 . 223 C6
Bucknall 58 C4
Sedgley DY3 . . . . 271 D8
Deansway ST4 . . . . 88 B6
Dean View ST7 . . . . 39 D1
Dearnsdale Cl ST16 . . . 155 B7
Deavall Way WS11 . . . . 210 B2
Deaville Rd ST2 . . . . . . 58 C3
Debenham Cres ST2 . . . 58 A2
Deborah Cl WV4 . . . . . 266 C6
Decade Cl ST5 . . . . 40 F2
Deebank Ave ST13 . . . . 31 B6
Dee Cl Biddulph ST8 . . . 16 E1
Talke ST7 . . . . 40 E7
Dee Gr WS11 . . . . 226 D8
Dee La ST5 . . . . 71 B4
Deeley ST7 . . . . 251 A1
Deep Cut Rd DE6 . . . . 144 A7
Deepdale
Burton u T DE15 . . . . . 167 B5
Stoke-on-T ST6 . . . . . . 42 F2
Deepdale La Dudley DY3 271 B5
Snelston DE6 . . . . 81 A2
Deepdales Stafford ST17 175 C6
Wombourne WV5 . . . . . 269 E6
Deepdale ST7 . . . . 251 D2
Deep Hayes Ctry Pk★
ST13 . . . . 45 A7
Deepmore Cl
Alrewas DE13 . . . . 201 A2
Four Ashes WV10 . . . . 224 D5
Norton Canes WS11 . . . 228 B7
Walsall WS3 . . . . 243 C1
Dee Rd WS3 . . . . 243 E1
Deerfold Cres WS7 . . . 229 B7
Deer Hill ST17 . . . . . . 176 C4
Deerhill B77 . . . . 251 E1
Deerhurst Rise WS12 . . 210 F6
Deerleap Way WS15 . . 178 C1
Deer Park Dr TF10 . . . 168 F5
Deer Park Rd B78 . . . . 249 E1
Deer Pk ST20 . . . . 171 E7
Deer Wlk WV8 . . . . . . 239 F2
De Ferrers Croft DE13 . 166 D8
De Ferrers Specialist Tech
Coll (Dove Campus)
DE13 . . . . 166 B8
De Ferrers Specialist Tech
Coll (Trent Campus)
DE13 . . . . 166 C8
Defford Ave WS4 . . . . 244 C1
Defoe Dr ST3 . . . . 73 E4
De Havilland Dr ST15 . 118 F6
Delafield Way WS15 . . 178 C2
Delamere Cl CW2 . . . . 37 C4
Delamere Gr
Newcastle-u-L ST5 . . . 283 C4
Stoke-on-T ST4 . . . . . . 88 A7
Delamere La ST17 . . . . 174 A8
Delaney Dr ST3 . . . . . . 73 F4
Delhi Cl DE15 . . . . 167 C3
Delhurst Ave WV4 . . . 266 E3
Delius Gr ST1 . . . . 57 F5
Dellbrook Cl ST5 . . . . 283 B1
Dell Cl ST16 . . . . 155 B8
Dell The Cannock WS12 . 210 F4
Lichfield WS13 . . . . . . 230 F7
Newcastle-u-L ST5 . . . . 55 C1
Stourbridge DY8 . . . . . 279 E6
Tamworth B79 . . . . . . 250 B6
Dellway Ct DY8 . . . . . 279 E5
Dellwood Gr ◆ ST3 . . . 73 D6
Delphouse Rd
Boundary ST10 . . . . . . 75 F2
Cheadle ST10 . . . . 76 A2
Delphside ST7 . . . . 39 F2
Delph Wlk ST4 . . . . 72 F6
Delta Way Bsns Ctr
WS11 . . . . 226 D6
Delta Way WS11 . . . . . 226 D7
Deltic ST5 . . . . 251 A1
Delves Cres CV9 . . . . . 262 C1
Delves Pl ST5 . . . . 71 B5
Demontort Way ST14 . . 126 C6
Denbigh Cl Biddulph ST8 . 27 C4
Burton u T DE13 . . . . . 166 D7
Dudley DY1 . . . . 271 F2

Denbigh Cl continued
Newcastle-u-L ST5 . . . . 71 D4
Denbigh St ST1 . . . . . 282 C4
Denbury Cl WS12 . . . . 210 D1
Denby Ave ST3 . . . . . . 284 C5
Dency Gr ST6 . . . . 42 A3
Dene Ave DY6 . . . . . . 275 C4
Dene Cl ST19 . . . . 207 F8
Dene Croft WS3 . . . . . 243 A4
Denefield ST19 . . . . . 207 F8
Denehurst Cl ◆ ST3 . . . 74 A2
Dene Rd Lower Penn WV4 264 F4
Stourbridge DY8 . . . . . 279 F3
Dene Side ST5 . . . . . . 283 A2
Denewood Pl ST3 . . . . 74 B1
Denford St ST6 . . . . . . 44 F8
Denham Sq ST3 . . . . . . 72 E1
Den La CW3 . . . . 52 D4
Denleigh Rd DY6 . . . . 275 F4
Denmark Rise WS12 . . 210 D7
Denmark Villas WS3 . . 230 C5
Dennfield Dr WS6 . . . . 226 A1
Dennington Cres ST3 . . 72 E1
Dennis Barsby Cl DE11 . 186 E3
Dennis Hall ◙ DY8 . . . . 279 F4
Dennis St Stoke-on-T ST4 . 72 F5
Stourbridge DY8 . . . . . 279 F3
Dennis B77 . . . . 250 C5
Dennis Viollet Ave ST4 . 72 C3
Denry Cres ST5 . . . . . . 56 B8
Denshaw Wlk ST3 . . . . 284 C4
Denston Ct B74 . . . . . 257 F2
Denstone Ave ST17 . . . 156 B1
Denstone Cres ST3 . . . 72 F2
Denstone Coll ST14 . . . 95 B5
Denstone Gdns WV10 . 240 F3
Denstone La ST14 . . . . 95 C7
Dentdale Cl ST3 . . . . . 90 A7
Denton Cl ST5 . . . . 71 C3
Denton Gr ST3 . . . . . . 73 E3
Denton Rd DE14 . . . . . 166 A6
Denton Rise DE13 . . . . 166 A7
Dent St B79 . . . . 250 C5
Denver Fold ST17 . . . . 174 A4
Denyer Ct WS13 . . . . . 215 C6
Denzil Gn ST17 . . . . . . 174 A8
Derby Ave WV6 . . . . . 255 F7
Derby Mews ST14 . . . . 110 F1
Derby Pl ST5 . . . . 71 C4
Derby Rd
Burton u T DE13,DE14 . 166 E7
Doveridge DE6 . . . . . . 127 C8
Egginton DE15 . . . . . . 148 C4
Stretton DE15 . . . . . . 148 A1
Talke ST7 . . . . 40 D7
Uttoxeter ST14 . . . . . . 111 D1
Whittington WS14 . . . . 232 D3
Derby St E DE14 . . . . . 166 C4
Derby St Burton u T DE14 . 166 C4
Hanley ST1 . . . . 282 C2
Leek ST13 . . . . 30 F5
Stafford ST16 . . . . 285 A3
Derby Turn DE14 . . . . 166 D5
Dereham Way ST2 . . . . 58 D1
Dereton Hill WS15 . . . 197 B5
Derrington La
Bradley ST18 . . . . 173 E8
Derrington ST18 . . . . . 154 E1
Derry St Stoke-on-T ST4 . 72 F4
Wolverhampton WV2 . . 266 D8
Derwent Ave ST15 . . . 120 D7
Derwent Cl Aldridge WS9 256 F3
Burton u T DE14 . . . . . 166 E3
Derwent Cres ST7 . . . . 26 C2
Derwent Dr
◪ Congleton CW12 . . . . 6 A1
Biddulph ST8 . . . . 16 E1
Cheadle ST10 . . . . 76 E1
Loggerheads TF9 . . . . . 99 E5
Derwent Gr
Burntwood WS7 . . . . . 229 D6
Cannock WS11 . . . . . . 226 D8
Derwent Ho ST17 . . . . 174 E6
Derwent Pk DE14 . . . . 166 E5
Derwent Pl ST5 . . . . . . 56 A3
Derwent Rd
Burton u T DE15 . . . . . 167 A1
Wolverhampton WV6 . . 255 E8
Derwent St ST1 . . . . . 282 A4
Derwent B77 . . . . 250 D1
Devall Cl WS15 . . . . . 196 E7
Devana Wlk ST3 . . . . . 74 C2
Devereux Ho B79 . . . . 250 A4
Devereux Rd B75 . . . . 258 C1
Deveron Cl DE13 . . . . 147 C1
Devil's La ST9,ST13 . . . 29 E5
Devon Cl Burton u T DE15 . 185 E6
Newcastle-u-L ST5 . . . . 71 C4
Devon Cres WS9 . . . . . 245 A1
Devon Cl WS11 . . . . . 226 C8
Devon Gn WS11 . . . . . 226 F8
Devon Gr ST8 . . . . 16 C1
Devon Ho ◪ DY4 . . . . 279 F8
Devonport Cl ◆ ST13 . . 30 E6
Devon Rd Cannock WS11 . 226 B7
Kinver DY6 . . . . 274 F5
Stourbridge DY8 . . . . . 279 E7
Devonshire Ct B74 . . . 258 A2
Devonshire Dr
Rugeley WS15 . . . . . . 196 D6
Tamworth B78 . . . . . . 250 A1
Devonshire Sq ST2 . . . 58 C1
Devon Way ST17 . . . . . 174 D6
Dewberry Rd ◎ DY8 . . 275 D5
Dewick Ind Est ST17 . . 175 F3
De-Wint Rd ST15 . . . . 120 B7
Dewsbury Cl DY8 . . . . 275 E3

Dewsbury Dr
Burntwood WS7 . . . . . 229 C6
Wolverhampton WV4 . . 266 A4
Dewsbury Rd ST4 . . . . 72 E8
Dexter Way B78 . . . . . 262 F8
Dexton Rise ST17 . . . . 174 A8
Deykin Rd WS13 . . . . . 231 A6
Dial La Biddulph CW12,SK11 . 7 B1
Stourbridge DY8 . . . . . 279 E8
Diamond Ave ◙ ST7 . . . 26 B2
Diamond Cl
Barlaston ST12 . . . . . 104 C8
Biddulph ST8 . . . . 27 C8
Meir Heath ST3 . . . . . . 90 A4
Diamond Gr WS11 . . . 210 C3
Diamond Jubilee Cotts
DE6 . . . . 81 E8
Diamond Park Dr ◙
DY8 . . . . 275 E1
Diamond Ridge ST12 . . 104 C8
Diamond Way WS15 . . 120 B5
Diana Cl WS9 . . . . 245 B3
Diana Rd ST1 . . . . 57 F6
Diarmid Rd ST4 . . . . . 71 F1
Dibble Rd DE14 . . . . . 185 A4
Dibdale Ct DY3 . . . . . 271 D3
Dibdale Rd DY1 . . . . . 271 F3
Dibdale Rd W DY1 . . . 271 E3
Dibdale St DY1 . . . . . 271 F2
Dibden Ct ◙ ST4 . . . . . 72 A7
Dickens Cl
Burton u T DE14 . . . . . 166 D6
Dudley DY3 . . . . 271 B5
Dickenson Rd E ST6 . . . 57 C7
Dickenson Rd W ST6 . . 57 C7
Dickens Rd WV10 . . . . 241 A1
Dickinson Rd WV5 . . . 270 A4
Dickson Ho ST1 . . . . . 282 C1
Dickson Rd ST16 . . . . 156 A5
Dicky's La ST20 . . . . . 151 E7
Didcot Ct DE14 . . . . . 143 F7
Digbeth La WV5 . . . . . 267 B8
Digby Rd DY6 . . . . . . 275 D8
Diglake Cl ST5 . . . . . . 40 C6
Diglake St ST7 . . . . . . 39 F3
Digmire La DE6 . . . . . 51 D1
Dig St SK17 . . . . 24 D6
Dilhorne Endowed Prim Sch
ST10 . . . . 75 D5
Dilhorne Gr ST3 . . . . . 284 C1
Dilhorne La
Caverswall ST10 . . . . . 74 F3
Dilhorne ST10 . . . . . . 75 B2
Dilhorne Rd Cheadle ST10 . 76 B3
Forsbrook ST11 . . . . . . 75 B2
Dilke St ST1 . . . . 282 C4
Dill Gr ST3 . . . . 90 B6
Dimble La DE6 . . . . . . 94 E8
Dimbles Hill WS13 . . . 214 B1
Dimbles La WS13 . . . . 214 A2
Dimmelow St ST3 . . . . 74 B5
Dimmingsdale Rd WV4 . 264 E5
Dimmingsdale YH★ ST10 . 78 A4
Dimmock St WV4 . . . . 266 E5
Dimsdale Par E ST5 . . . 56 C5
Dimsdale Par W ST5 . . 56 A6
Dimsdale St ST6 . . . . . 56 E7
Dimsdale View E ST5 . . 56 B6
Dimsdale View ST5 . . . 55 F6
Dimsdale View W ST5 . . 56 B6
Dingle Dr DE13 . . . . . 165 E4
Dingle La Bridgemere CW5 . 67 A5
Hilderstone ST15 . . . . 106 D2
Woodhouse Green ST8 . . 17 E7
Dingle Rd Brownhills WS8 244 E6
Wombourne WV5 . . . . 269 F6
Dingle The Brown Edge ST6 43 B7
Burton u T DE15 . . . . . 185 E8
Wolverhampton WV3 . . 255 D1
Dingle View DY3 . . . . 271 C7
Dinham Gdns DY1 . . . 271 E3
Dippons Dr WV6 . . . . 255 A3
Dippons Ho WV6 . . . . 255 A3
Dippons Mill Cl WV6 . . 255 A3
Dirtyfoot La WV4 . . . . 265 A5
District Ctr WS12 . . . . 210 C2
Ditch Cotts SK17 . . . . . 5 F8
Ditch The SK17 . . . . . . 5 F8
Dividy Rd ST2 . . . . . . 58 B2
Dixon Cl ST15 . . . . . . 104 E2
Dixon Rd CW12 . . . . . 6 A5
Dixon's Row ST5 . . . . . 55 C7
Dixon St WV2 . . . . . . 266 E7
Dobbinhorse La DE6 . . 81 F5
Dobbs St WV2 . . . . . . 266 E8
Dobell Gr ST4 . . . . . . 284 D4
Dobree Cl ST17 . . . . . 177 E7
Dobson St ST6 . . . . . . 57 C7
Dock Rd DY8 . . . . 275 F2
Doctor's Bank TF9 . . . 100 C5
Doctors Cl ST8 . . . . . . 27 C8
Doctors La
Kingswinford DY6 . . . . 275 A4
Kinver DY6 . . . . 274 F5
Shenstone WS14 . . . . 247 A6
Doddington Pl ST5 . . . 71 B6
Doddlespool Barns CW3 . 52 F7
Dodds La Astbury CW12 . 15 C6
Chorley WS13 . . . . . . 212 C3
Dodslow Ave DE13 . . . 147 B3
Dogcroft Rd ST6 . . . . . 42 C5
Dog Kennel La TF9 . . . 112 D8
Dog La Butterton ST13 . . 33 E7
Calton ST10 . . . . 50 A1
Leek ST13 . . . . 30 E5

Doglands Rd ST18 . . . 123 A1
Dog La Netherseal DE12 219 F6
Ranton ST18 . . . . 153 D4
Stableford ST4,ST5 . . . 86 C3
Tamworth B77 . . . . . . 251 B6
Weeford WS14 . . . . . . 248 A4
Dogmoor La ST10 . . . . 64 F8
Dogshead La DE13 . . . 201 C7
Dolefoot La DE13 . . . . 162 F4
Doles La DE6 . . . . 81 F7
Dolespring ST11 . . . . . 91 A8
Doley Cl ST20 . . . . . . 171 D6
Dolly's La ST6 . . . . . . 42 A2
Dolphin Cl Stafford ST17 156 C1
Walsall WS3 . . . . 243 F1
Dominic St ◙ Stone ST15 104 F1
Donald Bates Ho ST4 . . 71 F6
Donald Rd ST1 . . . . . . 57 E6
Doncaster La ST4 . . . . 71 F7
Don Gr WS11 . . . . 226 D7
Donington La WV7 . . . 237 B8
Donithorne Ct DE13 . . 166 C2
Donkey La ST10 . . . . . 76 E5
Dorado B77 . . . . 261 D7
Dorcas Dr ST3 . . . . . . 72 F4
Dorchester Cl ST7 . . . . 26 A2
Dorchester Rd
Cannock WS11 . . . . . . 209 B1
Willenhall WV12 . . . . . 242 C1
Dorchester Wlk ST2 . . . 58 C2
Dordon Rd B78 . . . . . 262 F8
Doreen Ave CW12 . . . . 16 B8
Dorian Way ST9 . . . . . 43 F7
Doris Robinson Ct ST4 . 89 F7
Dorking Cl ST2 . . . . . . 57 F2
Dorlan Cl ST9 . . . . 43 C3
Dormer Ave ST7 . . . . . 250 D5
Dormston Dr DY3 . . . . 271 E8
Dormston Sch The DY3 . 271 E8
Dormston Trad Est DY1 . 271 F4
Dorothy Clive Garden The★
TF9 . . . . 84 A4
Dorridge Gr ST5 . . . . . 56 E4
Dorrington Cl ST2 . . . . 43 A1
Dorrington Dr ST16 . . . 155 E6
Dorrington Gr ST5 . . . . 56 C6
Dorrington Ind Pk ST16 . 155 E6
Dorrington La CW3 . . . 83 B7
Dorset Cl Bucknall ST2 . 58 C3
Burton u T DE15 . . . . . 185 E6
Tamworth B78 . . . . . . 250 A1
Dorset Dr Aldridge WS9 . 245 B1
Biddulph ST8 . . . . 27 B8
Dorset Pl Kidsgrove ST7 . 26 A2
Newcastle-u-L ST5 . . . . 40 D2
Dorset Rd Cannock WS12 210 E1
Stourbridge DY8 . . . . . 279 D8
Dosthill Prim Sch B77 . 261 D5
Dosthill Rd (Two Gates)
B77 . . . . 261 D7
Double Gates TF9 . . . . 112 B8
Douglas Ave Biddulph ST8 . 27 D7
Stoke-on-T ST4 . . . . . . 71 F5
Douglas Pl ST5 . . . . . . 57 E2
Douglas Rd
Newcastle-u-L ST5 . . . . 56 A3
Stafford ST16 . . . . 156 A5
Douglas Rd W ST16 . . . 156 A5
Douglas St ST1 . . . . . . 57 B6
Doulton Cl Cheadle ST10 . 76 D1
Stone ST15 . . . . 119 E6
Doulton Dr ST5 . . . . . . 56 B7
Doulton Rd ST16 . . . . 156 B8
Doulton St ◙ ST6 . . . . 57 A8
Douse La ST10 . . . . . . 32 D4
Doval Gdns ST10 . . . . 92 A6
Dovebank Gr ST5 . . . . 90 A6
Dove Bank Prim Sch ST7 26 A2
Dove Bank ST14 . . . . . 126 C8
Dove Cl Burntwood WS7 . 229 D6
Fradley WS13 . . . . 215 B5
Dovecliff Cres DE13 . . 147 F2
Dovecliff Rd DE13 . . . 147 F3
Dove Ct ST17 . . . . 174 F5
Dovecote Cl WV6 . . . . 255 C4
Dovecote Pl ST5 . . . . . 89 E8
Dovecotes Prim Sch
WV8 . . . . 239 F1
Dovecotes The B75 . . . 258 B3
Dovedale Ave WS3 . . . 244 B5
Dovedale Cl WS11 . . . 210 A5
Dovedale Cl
Burton u T DE15 . . . . . 167 B5
Cheadle ST10 . . . . 76 E6
Congleton CW12 . . . . . 6 A4
Stoke-on-T ST6 . . . . . . 41 B7
Dovedale Ct WV4 . . . . 266 F2
Dovedale Pl ST5 . . . . . 55 A1
Dovedale Rd Kingsley ST10 61 E2
Kingswinford DY6 . . . . 275 E8
Wolverhampton WV4 . . 266 E3
Dovefields ST14 . . . . . 95 F3
Dove Fields ST14 . . . . 126 D8
Dove Fst Sch ST14 . . . 96 A3
Dove Gr Biddulph ST8 . . 16 D1
Egginton DE65 . . . . . 148 A5
Dove Hollow
Cannock WS12 . . . . . . 210 E4
Great Wyrley WS6 . . . . 226 F1
Dovehouse Fields WS14 231 B6
Dove La ST14 . . . . 96 A4
Dove Lea DE13 . . . . . . 147 B4
Dove Pl ST5 . . . . 71 A4
Dover Ct DE13 . . . . . . 166 C2
Dove Rd ST11 . . . . 91 A7

Dove Ridge SK17 . . . . . 13 C6
Doveridge Prim Sch
DE6 . . . . 127 C8
Doveridge Rd DE15 . . 167 B1
Dover Rd DE13 . . . . . 166 B7
Dover St ST1 . . . . 282 C4
Dove Side DE65 . . . . . 146 D8
Doveside DE6 . . . . 81 D7
Dove St DE6 . . . . 80 B2
Dovestone B77 . . . . . 251 D1
Dove View DE13 . . . . . 146 C6
Dove Way The ST14 . . 111 C2
Dove Way ST10 . . . . . 48 F2
Dove Wlk ST14 . . . . . 126 D8
Dowells Gdns DY8 . . . 275 D3
Dower Rd B75 . . . . . . 258 B1
Downderry Cl ST17 . . . 174 A8
Downend Cl WV10 . . . 240 F4
Downesway WS11 . . . 209 C2
Downey St ST1 . . . . . . 282 B2
Downfield Cl WS3 . . . . 243 A4
Downfield Dr DY3 . . . . 271 E6
Downfield Gr ST16 . . . 155 D8
Downfield Pl ST2 . . . . 42 F1
Downfields TF10 . . . . 168 F5
Downford Ct ST19 . . . 205 C6
Downford La ST19 . . . 205 C6
Downham Pl WV3 . . . . 265 F8
Downham Rd ST5 . . . . 55 E2
Downie Rd WV8 . . . . . 239 C3
Downing Ave ST5 . . . . 56 E3
Downing Dr B79 . . . . 249 E5
Downing Gdns ◙ ST15 . 120 A7
Downs The Aldridge WS9 . 256 C6
Stafford ST17 . . . . . . 175 C7
Downsview Gr ST3 . . . 72 F4
Dowty Way WV9 . . . . . 240 A3
Doxey Fields ST16 . . . 154 F4
Doxey Ho ST16 . . . . . 155 A4
Doxey Prim Sch ST16 . 155 B4
Doxey ST16 . . . . 155 B4
Dragon Sq ST5 . . . . . 55 E8
Drake Ave ST19 . . . . . 207 F6
Drake Cl Berry Hill ST2 . 57 F1
Walsall WS3 . . . . 243 B1
Drake Croft ◪ WS13 . . 231 C8
Drake Ct WS3 . . . . . . 243 B1
Drakeford Ct
Stafford ST16 . . . . . . 285 B2
Stoke-on-T ST6 . . . . . . 42 E4
Drakeford Dr ST6 . . . . 42 E4
Drake Rd WS3 . . . . . . 243 C1
Drakes Hill Cl DY8 . . . 279 C4
Draw-Well La ST9 . . . . 59 C4
Draycott Cliff DE6 . . . 144 C5
Draycott Cl WV4 . . . . 265 C5
Draycott Cres B77 . . . 250 D1
Draycott Cross Rd
Cheadle ST10 . . . . 76 A1
Draycott in t M ST10 . . 91 F8
Draycott Dr Cheadle ST10 . 76 D1
Newcastle-u-L ST5 . . . . 40 D2
Draycott Manor Prim Sch
ST11 . . . . 91 D5
Draycott Old Rd ST11 . 91 F8
Draycott Rd ST10 . . . . 92 C4
Drayton Cl B75 . . . . . 258 B3
Drayton Gn ST2 . . . . . 58 A2
Drayton Gr TF9 . . . . . . 97 C1
Drayton La B78 . . . . . 260 C5
Drayton Manor Dr
Drayton Bassett B78 . . 260 F7
Fazeley B78 . . . . 260 F8
Drayton Manor Pk B78 . 260 F7
Drayton Mill Ct TF9 . . . 97 C1
Drayton Rd Hanchurch ST4 . 87 B5
Longton ST3 . . . . 284 C1
Drayton St
Newcastle-u-L ST5 . . . 283 A2
Wolverhampton WV2 . . 266 C8
Dreieich Cl ST16 . . . . 155 F5
Drenfell Rd ST7 . . . . . 25 F7
Dresden CE Prim Sch
ST3 . . . . 284 C1
Dresden St ST1 . . . . . 282 C2
Dreys The ST4 . . . . . . 88 B7
Driffield Cl ST2 . . . . . 58 C1
Drive Fields WV4 . . . . 265 B6
Drive Sch (Tettenhall Coll)
The WV6 . . . . 255 D4
Drive The
Alsagers Bank ST7 . . . . 54 F6
Burton u T DE13 . . . . . 166 C2
Codsall WV8 . . . . 238 F3
Rudyard ST13 . . . . 29 E8
Shenstone WS14 . . . . 247 E8
Stafford ST16 . . . . 155 B4
Walsall,Pelsall WS3 . . . 243 E2
Walsall WS3 . . . . 244 C1
Wolverhampton WV6 . . 255 C5
Droitton La ST18 . . . . 139 D3
Droitwich Cl ST1 . . . . 54 F2
Drovers Way TF10 . . . 169 A4
Droveway The WV9 . . . 239 F2
Droxford Wlk WV8 . . . 239 E1
Drubbery La ST3 . . . . 284 A1
Druid Park Rd WV12 . . 242 C1
Druids Ave WS9 . . . . . 256 C8
Druids Way ST19 . . . . 207 F7
Druids Wlk WS9 . . . . . 245 A3
Drumart Ho DY10 . . . . 280 A5
Drumber La ST7 . . . . . 26 B8
Drumburn Cl ST5 . . . . 41 F7
Drummond Cl WV11 . . 242 A2
Drummond Rd ST16 . . 155 E6

Drummond St ST6 . . . . 41 D7
Drury La WV8 . . . . 238 F4
Dryburgh Cl ST17 . . . . 174 B7
Dryburg Wlk ST2 . . . . 58 A4
Dryden Cres ST17 . . . . 155 C1
Dryden Rd Burslem ST6 . . . . 57 A6
  Tamworth B79 . . . . 250 A6
  Wolverhampton WV10 . . . . . 240 F1
Dryden Way ST10 . . . . 76 C2
Dual Way WS12 . . . . 209 D8
Dubarry Ave DY6 . . . . 275 C7
Duchy Cl DE13 . . . . 166 E8
Duchy Rd CW1 . . . . 37 A8
Duck La WV8 . . . . 239 B3
Duck St DE65 . . . . 148 B5
Duddell Rd ST6 . . . . 42 C2
Dudding Rd WV4 . . . . 266 D5
Dudley Innovation Ctr
  DY6 . . . . 275 F7
Dudley Pl ST3 . . . . 90 A8
Dudley Rd Dudley DY3 . . . . 271 E6
  Himley DY3 . . . . 270 D3
  Kingswinford DY6 . . . . 275 F7
  Kingswinford,Wall Heath
  DY6 . . . . 275 C8
  Wolverhampton WV2 . . . . . 266 D7
Dudley St DY3 . . . . 271 D8
Dudley Wlk WV4 . . . . 266 C5
Dudmaston Way DY1 . . . . . 271 E3
Duffield Cl WV8 . . . . 239 F1
Duesbury Gn ST3 . . . . 284 A3
Dugdale Cl WS12 . . . . 210 F3
Dugdale Cres B75 . . . . 258 C4
Duke Bank Terr ST6 . . . . 42 F4
Duke Pl ST5 . . . . 55 C1
Duke Rd WS7 . . . . 211 E1
Dukes La ST13,ST10 . . . . 63 D7
Dukes Rd B78 . . . . 262 F6
Duke St Biddulph ST8 . . . . . . 27 D7
  Burton u T DE14 . . . . 166 C2
  Dudley DY3 . . . . 271 D5
  Leek ST13 . . . . 30 F5
  Newcastle-u-L ST5 . . . . . . 283 C1
  Stoke-on-T ST4 . . . . 72 E4
  Stoke-on-T ST4 . . . . 72 F5
  Tutbury DE13 . . . . 146 C4
  Wolverhampton,Penn Fields
  WV3 . . . . 266 A7
Dulverton Ave ST5 . . . . 71 A5
Dumbill Ho ST7 . . . . 40 C8
Dumbleberry Ave DY3 . . . . 271 C8
Dumolo's La B77 . . . . 250 F3
Dumore Hay La WS13 . . . . . 215 F8
Duncalfe Dr B75 . . . . 258 B3
Duncalf St ST6 . . . . 56 B7
Duncalf St ST6 . . . . 56 F8
Duncan St Stoke-on-T ST4 . . 72 E6
  Wolverhampton WV2 . . . . . 266 C7
Duncombe St DY8 . . . . 279 D5
Dundalk La WS6 . . . . 226 D2
Dundas St ST2 . . . . 282 C4
Dundee St ST3 . . . . 284 B2
Dundee Rd ST1 . . . . 57 A3
Dunedin Cres DE15 . . . . . . 167 C2
Dunedin B77 . . . . 251 A1
Dungarven Dr TF10 . . . . . . 168 D2
Dunhampton Dr DY10 . . . . 280 B1
Dunkirk ST7 . . . . 40 A6
Dunkirk Ct ST5 . . . . 283 A3
Dunkirk ST5 . . . . 283 A3
Dunlin Dr WV10 . . . . 241 B7
Dunnerdale Rd WS8 . . . . . . 244 D6
Dunning St ST6 . . . . 41 D3
Dunnington Ave DY10 . . . . 280 A1
Dunnock Cl ST14 . . . . 126 C6
Dunnock Way ST8 . . . . 27 E8
Dunrobin St ST3 . . . . 284 C2
Dunsany Gr ST1 . . . . 57 E6
Dunsford Ave ST2 . . . . 43 A2
Dunsley Dr Dunsley DY7 . . 278 C4
  Stourbridge DY8 . . . . 275 C3
Dunsley Gr WV4 . . . . 266 A4
Dunsley Rd Dunsley DY7 . . 278 C4
  Stourbridge DY8 . . . . 279 C4
Dunstall Brook DE15 . . . . . 167 A1
Dunstall Cross DE15 . . . . . 183 A6
Dunstall Hill DE13 . . . . 183 B6
Dunstall La B78 . . . . 249 D4
Dunstall Rd
  Barton-u-N DE13 . . . . 183 E3
  Tatenhill DE13 . . . . 184 A7
Dunster Cl ST17 . . . . 174 B7
Dunster Gr WV6 . . . . 254 F3
Dunster Rd ST3 . . . . 73 C5
Dunster B77 . . . . 261 C7
Dunston Cl
  Great Wyrley WS6 . . . . . . 242 E8
  Kingswinford DY6 . . . . . . 275 D7
Dunston Dr WS7 . . . . 229 A8
Dunton Rd B75 . . . . 258 A4
Dunwood Dr ST6 . . . . 42 A3
Dunwood La ST9,ST13 . . . . . 29 D4
Durban Cl DE15 . . . . 167 C3
Durber Cl Audley ST7 . . . . . 39 D1
  Stoke-on-T ST4 . . . . 71 E4
D'Urberville Cl WV2 . . . . . 266 F6
D'Urberville Rd WV2 . . . . . 266 F6
D'Urberville Wlk 1
  WS11 . . . . 210 A2
Durfield La DE13 . . . . 163 B7
Durham Dr B78 . . . . 250 A2
Durham Dr Rugeley WS15 . 196 D6
  Stoke-on-T ST3 . . . . 89 C8
Durham Gr ST5 . . . . 71 D4

Durham Rd DY8 . . . . 279 D8
Durlston Cl B77 . . . . 250 F5
Durose Ct ST14 . . . . 125 C7
Dursley Dr WS11 . . . . 209 B2
Dursley Rd WS7 . . . . 229 A7
Durston Pl ST3 . . . . 73 E3
Dutton's La B75 . . . . 258 E4
Duttons The ST18 . . . . 123 B3
Dutton Way ST15 . . . . 119 F5
Dyke Rd WS15 . . . . 198 A4
Dykes La TF10 . . . . 188 D8
Dyke St ST1 . . . . 282 C3
Dylan Rd Biddulph ST8 . . . . . 27 E6
  Longton ST3 . . . . 73 D3
Dyott Ave WS14 . . . . 232 E6
Dyott Cl WS13 . . . . 215 A1
Dyson Ct ST18 . . . . 156 C5
Dyson Way ST18 . . . . 156 C5

E

Eagle Cl Cheslyn Hay WS6 . 226 D2
  Dudley DY1 . . . . 271 F1
  Uttoxeter ST14 . . . . 126 B6
Eagle Cres ST21 . . . . 133 D6
Eagle Ct
  Wolverhampton,Pendeford
  WV10 . . . . 240 B3
  Wolverhampton,Penn Fields
  WV3 . . . . 266 A4
Eagle Dr B77 . . . . 251 A4
Eagle Gr WS12 . . . . 210 C1
Eagle Hts DE15 . . . . 167 D3
Eagle Mill 1 ST13 . . . . 30 F5
Eagle St Hanley ST1 . . . . . . 57 E3
  Wolverhampton,Monmore Green
  WV2 . . . . 266 E8
  Wolverhampton,Penn Fields
  WV3 . . . . 266 A7
Ealand St DE13 . . . . 147 D4
Ealingham B77 . . . . 251 B1
Eamont Ave ST14 . . . . 42 A4
Eardleyend Rd ST7 . . . . 39 F7
Eardley St ST4 . . . . 71 F6
Earl Dr WS7 . . . . 211 E1
Earlsbrook Dr ST4 . . . . 88 C7
Earls Ct Burton u T DE13 . . 166 B8
  Newcastle-u-L ST5 . . . . . . 283 D3
Earl's Dr ST5 . . . . 71 B7
Earls Rd ST4 . . . . 88 B7
Earl Sterndale CE Prim Sch
  SK17 . . . . 5 C3
Earl St Kingswinford DY6 . . 275 D4
  Leek ST13 . . . . 30 F6
  Newcastle-u-L,Silverdale
  ST5 . . . . 55 C1
  Newcastle-u-L ST5 . . . . . . 283 D3
  Stafford ST16 . . . . 285 B3
Earls Way ST18 . . . . 158 C2
Earlsway ST10 . . . . 64 B8
Earlswood Cres WV9 . . . . . 240 A3
Earlswood Rd Bucknall ST1 . 58 A6
  Kingswinford DY6 . . . . . . 275 D5
Early La ST15 . . . . 103 C4
Easby Cl ST17 . . . . 174 B7
Easby Way WS3 . . . . 242 F2
Easdale Pl ST5 . . . . 71 B5
Easedale Ct ST14 . . . . 43 A2
Easing La ST13 . . . . 31 E8
East Ave CW2 . . . . 37 C5
Eastbank Rd ST1 . . . . 282 A4
East Bank Ride ST11 . . . . . . 91 B8
East Beeches WV9 . . . . . . 224 B2
Eastbourne Cl ST13 . . . . . . 30 D6
Eastbourne Rd ST1 . . . . 57 E4
Eastbridge Ave ST1 . . . . . . 57 D8
East Butts Rd WS15 . . . . . 178 B1
East Cannock Rd WS12 . . 210 C4
East Cl ST15 . . . . 119 F7
Eastcote Cres WS7 . . . . . . 229 A5
East Cres
  Newcastle-u-L ST5 . . . . . . 56 D3
  Stoke-on-T ST1 . . . . 57 E8
East Croft Rd WV4 . . . . . . 265 C5
Eastdean Ave ST2 . . . . 58 A2
East Dr Biddulph ST8 . . . . . 27 D8
  Cheddleton ST13 . . . . 45 D7
Eastern Ave
  Burton u T DE13 . . . . 166 F8
  Lichfield WS13 . . . . 214 C2
Eastern Way WS11 . . . . . . 210 A2
Easters Gr ST2 . . . . 43 B1
Eastfield Cl Aldridge WS9 . 256 A6
  Stoke-on-T ST3 . . . . 88 B8
Eastfield Dr ST4 . . . . 282 C1
Eastfields Rd ST14 . . . . . . 126 C8
Eastgate Brewood ST19 . . 223 D7
  Cannock WS12 . . . . 211 A5
Eastgate Ct WS14 . . . . 231 C6
Eastgate St
  Burntwood WS7 . . . . 228 E8
  Stafford ST16 . . . . 285 B3
East Gn WV4 . . . . 265 D6
East Gr ST3 . . . . 74 A1
Easthall St ST19 . . . . 223 B8
Easthead Wlk ST1 . . . . 282 A2
Eastholme ST15 . . . . 106 D1
Eastlands Cl ST17 . . . . 174 E8
Eastlands Gr ST17 . . . . . . 174 E8
Eastlands ST17 . . . . 174 E8
East Lawns CW3 . . . . 53 A6
Eastleigh DY3 . . . . 271 C8
Eastmoor Dr ST4 . . . . 257 B2
Eastney Cres WV8 . . . . . . 255 F8
East Prec ST1 . . . . 282 C3
East Rd
  Featherstone WV10 . . . . . 241 A7

East Rd continued
  Wolverhampton WV4 . . . . . 266 F4
Eastridge Croft WS14 . . . . 247 A5
East St Burton u T DE15 . . . 167 C3
  Cannock WS11 . . . . 226 E6
  Dudley,Gornalwood DY3 . . 271 D3
  Leek ST13 . . . . 31 A6
  Meir ST3 . . . . 74 B6
  Tamworth B77 . . . . 261 D5
East Terr ST6 . . . . 42 B6
East View Burslem ST6 . . . . 56 F7
  Mayfield DE6 . . . . 81 D7
  Shuttington B79 . . . . 251 F7
  Tamworth B77 . . . . 261 D5
Eastward Glen WV8 . . . . . 239 C1
Eastwick Cres ST4 . . . . 88 A8
Eastwood Ave
  Burntwood WS7 . . . . 229 A8
  Stoke-on-T ST6 . . . . 42 A4
Eastwood Pl ST1 . . . . 282 B2
Eastwood Rd ST1 . . . . 282 C1
Eastwood Rise ST5 . . . . . . 85 A7
Eaton Cres DY3 . . . . 271 B3
Eaton Dr WS15 . . . . 178 E2
Eaton Park Prim Sch ST2 . . 58 A2
Eaton Pl DY6 . . . . 275 C5
Eaton Rd ST14 . . . . 95 F3
Eaton St ST1 . . . . 282 C3
Eaves Court Dr ST3 . . . . . 266 C1
Eaves La Bucknall ST2 . . . . 58 C6
  Cheadle ST10 . . . . 76 E1
  Oakamoor ST10 . . . . 78 A4
  Whiston ST10 . . . . 62 F1
Eaveswood Rd ST2 . . . . 58 C6
Ebenezer St WS12 . . . . . . 210 A7
Ebony Cl ST16 . . . . 155 C4
Ebstree Mdw WV5 . . . . . . 264 A3
Ebstree Rd Seisdon WV5 . . 264 A2
  Seisdon WV5 . . . . 264 C4
Ebury Gr ST3 . . . . 73 F1
Ecclesfield Rd
  Great Bridgeford ST18 . . . 135 D2
  Loggerheads,Hookgate TF9 . 99 E3
  Loggerheads,Tadgedale TF9 99 B6
  Stafford ST16 . . . . 155 C5
  Stone ST15 . . . . 119 E6
Eccleston Pl ST6 . . . . 42 A6
Edale Cl Kingswinford DY6 275 B7
  Newcastle-u-L ST5 . . . . . . 55 B1
  Stoke-on-T ST6 . . . . 41 B7
  Wolverhampton WV4 . . . . 266 C5
Edale B77 . . . . 251 B1
Eddens Wood Cl B78 . . . . 260 E5
Eddies La B79 . . . . 216 E1
Eddisbury Dr ST5 . . . . 40 C2
Edenbridge Cl CW2 . . . . . . 37 B2
Edenbridge View DY1 . . . . 271 E3
Eden Cl Biddulph ST8 . . . . . 16 E1
  Cannock WS12 . . . . 210 E2
  Hilton DE65 . . . . 147 C8
  Kidsgrove ST7 . . . . 26 B2
Eden Ct WV10 . . . . 240 F8
Edenfield Pl B77 . . . . 251 B1
Eden Gdns DY3 . . . . 271 E8
Eden Gr Cheadle ST10 . . . . 76 E1
  Loggerheads TF9 . . . . 99 E5
  Longton ST3 . . . . 73 F1
Edenhurst Ave ST3 . . . . . . 90 C8
Edenhurst Prep Sch ST5 . . 70 F7
Edensor CE Prim Sch
  ST3 . . . . 284 A2
Edensor Ct ST5 . . . . 55 E7
Edensor Rd ST3 . . . . 284 B3
Edensor St ST5 . . . . 55 E7
Edensor Tech Coll ST3 . . . 284 B3
Edensor Terr ST3 . . . . 284 B2
Edes Farm Dr ST14 . . . . . . 95 F4
Edgar Cl B79 . . . . 249 F7
Edgar Pl ST3 . . . . 73 C6
Edgbaston Dr ST4 . . . . 88 D7
Edge Ave ST6 . . . . 42 A6
Edgecliff High Sch DY7 . . 278 A4
Edgefield La ST6,ST9 . . . . . 43 C5
Edgefield Rd ST5 . . . . 73 C5
Edge Hill Ave WV10 . . . . . 241 B1
Edge Hill Dr Perton WV6 . . 254 C3
  Sedgley DY3 . . . . 266 C2
Edge Hill Jun Sch DE15 . . 185 F7
Edge Hill Rd DY1 . . . . 277 F4
Edgehill Rd ST13 . . . . 30 C5
Edge Hill Rd B74 . . . . 257 E4
Edge Hill CV9 . . . . 262 B2
Edge La ST19 . . . . 43 D7
Edgeley Rd ST8 . . . . 27 D7
Edgemoor Mdw WS12 . . . 210 C1
Edge St ST6 . . . . 41 F2
Edge View Cl Kinver DY7 . . 277 F5
  Stoke-on-T ST2 . . . . 43 C2
Edge View Ct ST8 . . . . 27 C7
Edgeview Rd CW12 . . . . . . 16 B7
Edge View Rd ST2 . . . . 43 C2
Edge View Wlk DY7 . . . . . 277 F5
Edgeware Rd ST1 . . . . 282 A4
Edgeworth Ho WS13 . . . . . 214 A2
Edgmond Rd TF10 . . . . . . 168 A3
Edinburgh Cres DY8 . . . . . 275 C1
Edinburgh Rd CW12 . . . . . . 6 A2
Edinburgh Way DE13 . . . . 166 D8
Edison Cl WS12 . . . . 210 C7
Edison Rd ST16 . . . . 155 F5
Edison St ST4 . . . . 72 D6
Edmonton Cl WS11 . . . . . . 210 B2
Edmonton Gr ST2 . . . . 42 F1
Edmonton Pl DE15 . . . . . . 167 C3
Edmund Ave ST17 . . . . . . 174 B8
Edmund Rd DY3 . . . . 271 E6

Ednam Pl ST3 . . . . 74 A1
Ednam Rd WV4 . . . . 266 C5
Edwal Rd ST3 . . . . 74 A4
Edward Ave Aldridge WS9 256 A7
  Cannock WS11 . . . . 209 E4
  Stoke-on-T ST4 . . . . 88 B7
Edward Ct B77 . . . . 250 F4
Edward Davies Rd ST6 . . . 42 C2
Edward Rd WV6 . . . . 254 E5
Edwards Dr ST16 . . . . 155 C3
Edwards Farm Rd WS13 . . 215 E8
Edwards Rd
  Burntwood WS7 . . . . 228 F5
  Sutton Coldfield B75 . . . . 258 D3
Edward St 6 Stone ST15 . 105 A1
  Audley ST7 . . . . 39 F3
  Burton u T DE14 . . . . 166 C4
  Cannock WS11 . . . . 209 E4
  Newcastle-u-L ST5 . . . . . . 56 D4
  Stoke-on-T ST4 . . . . 72 E7
  Tamworth B79 . . . . 250 A5
  Wolverhampton WV4 . . . . 266 F5
Edwin Cl Penkridge ST19 . 207 F8
  Stafford ST17 . . . . 155 B1
Efflinch La DE13 . . . . 201 E7
Egelwin Cl WV6 . . . . 254 E5
Egerton Cl ST11 . . . . 91 A6
Egerton Rd Aldridge B74 . . 256 F1
  Stoke-on-T ST4 . . . . 71 E8
  Wolverhampton WV10 . . . 240 E3
Egerton St ST1 . . . . 57 D1
Eggington Dr ST19 . . . . . . 207 F7
Eggington Rd Hilton DE65 147 F8
  Stourbridge DY8 . . . . 279 D6
Egginton Prim Sch DE65 148 B5
Egginton Rd DE65 . . . . . . 148 B8
Egg La ST18 . . . . 158 E7
Eighth Ave DE14 . . . . 184 F8
Eights Croft WS7 . . . . 228 D8
Elaine Ave ST6 . . . . 42 B1
Elan Cl Cookley DY10 . . . . 280 B4
  Dudley DY3 . . . . 271 D3
Elan Rd DY3 . . . . 271 C8
Elburton Rd ST4 . . . . 73 A6
Elderberry Cl DY8 . . . . 279 C3
Elder Cl Cannock WS11 . . 210 C2
  Uttoxeter ST14 . . . . 126 B6
Elder Gr WV5 . . . . 269 F6
Elder La WS7 . . . . 229 C7
Elder Pl ST6 . . . . 57 B6
Elder Rd ST6 . . . . 57 B6
Elderside Cl WS8 . . . . 244 F8
Eldertree La TF9 . . . . 100 C6
Eldon St Burton u T DE15 . 167 B3
  Hanley ST1 . . . . 57 D6
Eldridge Cl WV9 . . . . 239 F2
Eleanor Cres ST5 . . . . 71 A6
Eleanor Harrison Dr
  DY10 . . . . 280 B5
Eleanor Pl ST5 . . . . 71 A6
Eleanor View ST5 . . . . 71 B6
Electric Ind Est DE14 . . . . 166 E5
Electric St DE14 . . . . 166 E5
Elenora St ST4 . . . . 72 B7
Elers Gr ST6 . . . . 56 E7
Elford Cl Aldridge B74 . . . 257 A2
  Stafford ST16 . . . . 155 C8
Elford Heath ST21 . . . . . . 133 C6
Elgar Cl Cannock WS11 . . 209 E5
  Lichfield WS13 . . . . 214 B3
Elgar Cres ST11 . . . . 58 A5
Elgin Cl DY3 . . . . 266 E1
Elgin Ct WV6 . . . . 254 E4
Elgin Rd WS3 . . . . 243 A4
Elgin St ST4 . . . . 57 B1
Elgood La ST6 . . . . 41 C7
Elias Cl WS14 . . . . 231 E6
Eliases La ST1 . . . . 17 B2
Eliot Cl Armitage WS15 . . 198 B4
  Tamworth B79 . . . . 250 A7
Eliot Way ST17 . . . . 155 C1
Elisabeth Ct B74 . . . . 258 B3
Elizabethan Way WS15 . . 196 D7
Elizabeth Ave
  Rolleston on D DE13 . . . . 147 B3
  Wolverhampton WV4 . . . . 266 B5
Elizabeth Bache Cnr
  DY10 . . . . 280 A5
Elizabeth Ct
  Burton u T DE15 . . . . 167 C3
  Market Drayton TF9 . . . . . 112 C8
  Stoke-on-T ST4 . . . . 71 F8
  Talke Pits ST7 . . . . 40 D5
Elizabeth Dr
  Newcastle-u-L ST5 . . . . . . 55 E7
  Tamworth B79 . . . . 250 A6
Elizabeth Rd WS11 . . . . . . 209 E6
Elizabeth St ST1 . . . . 57 E4
Elkes Gr ST14 . . . . 110 F2
Elkington Cl TF10 . . . . 168 E2
Elkington Rise CW3 . . . . . . 68 F7
Elkstone Cl ST6 . . . . 41 E4
Ellam's Pl ST3 . . . . 55 E1
Ellastone Gr ST4 . . . . 71 F6
Ellastone Rd ST10 . . . . 63 C5
Elldawn Ave ST6 . . . . 42 F2
Ellerbeck B77 . . . . 251 B1
Ellesmere Ct TF10 . . . . . . 168 E2
Ellesmere Gr 3 TF9 . . . . 112 A8
Ellesmere Rd WS11 . . . . . 226 B8
Elgreave St ST6 . . . . 56 E8
Ellington Ave ST16 . . . . . . 156 B5
Ellington Cl ST2 . . . . 58 A2
Elliot Ct 1 WV4 . . . . 266 F4
Elliot Dr ST9 . . . . 59 B4
Elliott Cl WS11 . . . . 209 F5
Elliott Rd ST4 . . . . 72 F6

Elliotts La WV8 . . . . 239 A3
Elliott St ST5 . . . . 56 D1
Ellison Prim Sch ST5 . . . . 56 D5
Ellison St ST5 . . . . 56 D5
Ellis St ST6 . . . . 57 C7
Ellis Wlk WS11 . . . . 226 F8
Ellowes Hall Sch The
  DY3 . . . . 271 C5
Ellowes Rd DY3 . . . . 271 C4
Ellsmore Mdw WS13 . . . . 231 A6
Elm Ave ST17 . . . . 175 F6
Elmbridge Way DY3 . . . . . 271 E6
Elmbrook Cl ST3 . . . . 89 E8
Elm Cl Burton u T DE14 . . 184 F8
  Cookley DY10 . . . . 280 B4
  Doveridge DE6 . . . . 127 C8
  Dudley DY3 . . . . 271 B2
  Great Haywood ST18 . . . . 158 B2
  Kidsgrove ST7 . . . . 41 B8
  Leek ST13 . . . . 30 C5
  Newport TF10 . . . . 168 F1
  Stourbridge DY8 . . . . 279 D2
Elm Cres ST18 . . . . 158 C8
Elmcroft Gdns WV10 . . . . 240 E3
Elmcroft Rd ST2 . . . . 58 B6
Elm Ct ST18 . . . . 174 C5
Elmdale Dr WS9 . . . . 256 C8
Elm Dale Rd WV4 . . . . 266 A5
Elmdon Cl
  Penkridge ST19 . . . . 208 A8
  Wolverhampton WV10 . . . 240 A1
Elmdon Pl ST3 . . . . 90 B7
Elmdon Rd WV10 . . . . 240 A1
Elm Dr Blakedown DY10 . . 281 B2
  Bradley ST18 . . . . 191 C8
  Cheadle ST10 . . . . 76 F2
  Market Drayton TF9 . . . . . 112 A8
Elm Farm Rd WV2 . . . . . . 266 D7
Elm Gdns WS14 . . . . 231 C7
Elm Gr Codsall WV8 . . . . . 239 A3
  Huntington WS12 . . . . . . 209 D8
  Kinver DY7 . . . . 277 E8
Elmhurst Cl Berry Hill ST2 . 57 F2
  Coven WV9 . . . . 224 B3
  Stafford ST16 . . . . 155 C8
Elmhurst Dr
  Burntwood WS7 . . . . 229 A4
  Kingswinford DY6 . . . . . . 275 C4
Elmhurst Eggington DE65 . 148 A5
  Newcastle-u-L ST5 . . . . . . 70 A4
Elmley Gr WV6 . . . . 254 F3
Elmore Ct 4 WS15 . . . . . 196 E8
Elmore Green Prim Sch
  WS3 . . . . 243 B1
Elmore Green Rd WS3 . . . 243 B1
Elmore Ho WS15 . . . . 178 E1
Elmore La WS15 . . . . 178 E1
Elmore Row WS3 . . . . 243 B1
Elm Pl Cookley DY10 . . . . 280 B4
  Stoke-on-T ST3 . . . . 72 F7
Elm Rd Kingswinford DY6 . 275 E6
  Norton Canes WS11 . . . . 228 B5
  Stone ST15 . . . . 120 C8
Elms Cl WV10 . . . . 225 C1
Elmsdale WV6 . . . . 255 A2
Elms St WS11 . . . . 209 C1
Elms La WV10 . . . . 225 C1
Elmsmere Rd ST2 . . . . 73 A1
Elmsmere Rd ST2 . . . . 58 C1
Elms Paddock The WV6 . . 253 C2
Elms Rd DE15 . . . . 166 F2
Elm St ST6 . . . . 57 A7
Elmstead Ct ST4 . . . . 71 F1
Elms The ST5 . . . . 56 C7
Elm St ST5 . . . . 56 B3
Elmstone Cl
  3 Stafford ST17 . . . . 175 D5
  Dudley DY3 . . . . 271 F4
Elms Way ST3 . . . . 74 A2
Elm Tree Cl WV5 . . . . 269 F5
Elm Tree Dr ST7 . . . . 39 F1
Elmtree Rd B74 . . . . 256 D1
Elm Tree Wlk B79 . . . . . . 249 E6
Elm View ST14 . . . . 95 E6
Elm Wlk ST19 . . . . 207 E8
Elmwood Ave WV11 . . . . . 242 A3
Elmwood Cl
  Blythe Bridge ST11 . . . . . . 91 A6
  Cannock WS11 . . . . 210 A3
  Gnosall ST20 . . . . 171 D7
  Lawton-gate ST7 . . . . 25 A4
Elmwood Dr ST11 . . . . 91 A6
Elmwood Gr ST14 . . . . . . 110 F1
Elmwood Rd DY8 . . . . 275 C2
Elmwood Rise DY3 . . . . . . 266 B1
Elphinstone Rd ST4 . . . . . 71 F3
Elsby Pl ST6 . . . . 42 A6
Elsdon Rd ST18 . . . . 174 C6
Elsing St ST4 . . . . 72 D6
Elston Hall La WV10 . . . . 240 D2
Elston Hall Prim Sch
  WV10 . . . . 240 D2
Elstree Cl ST3 . . . . 73 F2
Elstree Gr ST1 . . . . 58 A6
Elswick Rd ST4 . . . . 72 E8
Eltham Gdns ST5 . . . . 56 D3
Elton Cl Newborough DE13 162 F8
  Wolverhampton WV10 . . . 240 F4
Elton La DE13 . . . . 162 F8
Elton Terr ST6 . . . . 41 D7
Elton Way ST20 . . . . 171 D2
Elunda Gr WS7 . . . . 228 E5
Elviron Dr WV6 . . . . 255 B5
Elwell Cres DY1 . . . . 271 F6
Elworth Cl ST16 . . . . 156 A5
Elwyn Cl DE13 . . . . 147 D3
Ely Cl WS11 . . . . 210 B3
Ely Wlk ST3 . . . . 284 C4

Emanuals La SK17 . . . . 23 B2
Embers Way ST9 . . . . 44 A8
Emberton St
  Newcastle-u-L,Chesterton
   ST5 . . . . 55 E6
  Newcastle-u-L,Wolstanton
   ST5 . . . . 56 C5
Emberton Way B77 . . . . . . 250 E5
Embleton Wlk **1** ST6 . . . 56 E7
Embry Ave ST16 . . . . 156 A5
Emerald Way ST15 . . . . . . 120 B4
Emerson Cl DY3 . . . . 271 A4
Emerson Rd Burslem ST6. . . 57 A6
  Wolverhampton WV10. . . 240 F1
Emery Ave
  Newcastle-u-L ST5. . . . . . 71 A7
  Stoke-on-T ST1 . . . . 57 E8
Emery St ST6 . . . . 57 B6
Emmanuel Rd WS7 . . . . . . 229 B7
Empire Ind Est WS9 . . . . . 244 F1
Empire Pas ST4. . . . . 72 A6
Empire Rd DE15 . . . . 167 D3
Empire St ST4. . . . . 72 A6
Emsworth Cres WV9 . . . . . 240 A2
Emsworth Rd ST3. . . . . 88 E8
Encounter Pl ST1 . . . . 57 E5
Enderby Dr WV4 . . . . 266 A5
Enderby Rise DE13 . . . . . . 166 B7
Enderley Cl WS3. . . . . 243 B3
Enderley Dr WS3 . . . . 243 B3
Enderley St ST5 . . . . 283 B4
End Hall Rd WV6. . . . . 255 A3
Endon Dr ST8. . . . . 27 D7
Endon Hall Prim Sch ST9. . . 43 F8
Endon High Sch ST9 . . . . . 43 E6
Endon Rd ST6 . . . . 42 F5
End The DE15. . . . . 167 E8
Endwood Dr B74. . . . . 257 C4
Engine La Tamworth B77 . . 251 A2
  Walsall WS3. . . . . 244 C8
Englesea Ave ST3. . . . . 74 A5
Englesea Brook La CW2 . . 38 A3
Englesea Brook Mus of
  Primitive Methodism★
  CW2 . . . . 38 A3
Engleton La ST19 . . . . 223 D7
Engleton Mill La ST19. . . 223 D8
English Martyrs RC Prim Sch
  ST8 . . . . 27 D7
Ennerdale Cl
  1 Burslem ST6. . . . . 56 E8
  Brownhills WS8. . . . . 244 E7
Ennerdale Dr WV6 . . . . . . 254 F4
Ennerdale Rd WV6. . . . . . 255 D8
Enoch St ST6 . . . . 56 F7
Ensall Dr DY8. . . . . 275 E1
Ensford Cl B74. . . . . 257 E5
Enson La Marston ST18. . . 137 B7
  Stone ST15 . . . . 120 D1
Ensor Dr B78 . . . . 251 F1
Enstone Cl ST3 . . . . 88 F8
Enstone Ct ST5 . . . . 71 B3
Enterprise Dr WV10 . . . . . 224 E5
Enterprise St WS3 . . . . . . 244 B5
Enterprise Ind Pk WS13 . . 231 F8
Enville Cl WS3 . . . . 243 B3
Enville Common Rd
  Enville DY7. . . . . 273 F5
  Kinver DY7. . . . . 274 A3
Enville Pl DY8 . . . . 279 E5
Enville Rd Dudley DY3. . . . 271 D4
  Kingswinford DY6 . . . . . . 275 B8
  Kinver DY7. . . . . 278 A5
  Wolverhampton WV4. . . . 265 C4
Enville St DY8 . . . . 279 F5
Ephraim St ST1 . . . . 282 C1
Epping Rd ST4. . . . . 71 E3
Epsley's Yd ST5 . . . . 285 B2
Epsom Cl Burton u T DE14. 184 F7
  Cheadle ST10. . . . . 76 E5
  Lichfield WS14. . . . . 231 D7
  Perton WV6. . . . . 254 F4
  Tamworth B77 . . . . 261 C4
Epsom Dr **8** ST17. . . . . 175 C7
Epworth Ho DE15 . . . . . . 167 D3
Epworth St ST4 . . . . 72 A7
Erasmus Way WS13 . . . . . 231 A8
Erdington Rd WS9 . . . . . . 256 C3
Eremon Cl WS15 . . . . 196 F6
Eringden B77. . . . . 251 E1
Ermington Rd WV4. . . . . . 266 D4
Ernald Gdns **5** ST15 . . 120 D4
Ernest Edgerton Cl ST6. . . 41 C5
Eros Cres ST1 . . . . 57 E6
Errill Cl ST4 . . . . 72 D6
Erskine St ST3 . . . . 284 C1
Eskdale Pl
  Newcastle-u-L ST5. . . . . . 71 B5
  Stoke-on-T ST4 . . . . 88 F4
Eskrett St WS12. . . . . 210 C5
Esk Way ST5. . . . . 71 B4
Esperanto Way ST6 . . . . . . 57 C8
Esselie Ave TF9 . . . . 100 F8
Essex Ave DY6 . . . . 275 B5
Essex Dr Biddulph ST8. . . . 16 D2
  Cannock WS12. . . . . 210 B4
  Castle Gresley DE11 . . . . 186 E1
  Great Haywood ST18. . . . 158 B3
  Kidsgrove ST7 . . . . 25 F2
  Rugeley WS15 . . . . 196 D6
  Stone ST15 . . . . 119 F5
Essex Gdns DY8. . . . . 279 D7
Essex Pl ST5. . . . . 71 A6
Essex Rd Burntwood WS7. . 229 C6
  Sutton Coldfield B75 . . . . 258 D2
Essington Cl
  Alrewas DE13 . . . . 201 A3
  Lichfield WS14. . . . . 231 A5

Essington Cl continued
  Shenstone WS14 . . . . 247 A7
  Stourbridge DY8 . . . . 275 E1
Essington Ind Est WV11 . 241 F4
Essington Rd WV12 . . . . . 242 B1
Estridge La WS6 . . . . 227 A2
Etchell Rd B78. . . . . 249 F3
Etching Hill CE Prim Sch
  WS15 . . . . 178 C2
Etching Hill Rd WS15. . . . 178 A2
Ethelfleda Rd B77. . . . . . 261 F5
Ethelred Cl B74. . . . . 258 A3
Eton Ave ST5 . . . . 70 F4
Eton Cl Burton u T DE14. . 166 E6
  Dudley DY3. . . . . 271 F6
  Stafford ST17 . . . . 156 B1
Eton Ct Lichfield WS14. . . 231 B6
  Sutton Coldfield B74 . . . . 257 F2
Eton Park Jun Sch DE14 . 166 D7
Eton Pk DE14 . . . . 166 E6
Eton Rd DE14 . . . . 166 D6
Etruria Industrial Mus★
  ST4 . . . . 57 A2
Etruria Locks ST5. . . . . . . 57 A2
Etruria Old Rd ST1 . . . . . . 56 F3
Etruria Rd
  Hanley,Etruria ST5. . . . . . 56 F3
  Hanley ST1. . . . . 282 A3
Etruria Vale Rd ST1 . . . . . 57 A3
Etruria Way ST5 . . . . 56 E2
Etruscan Prim Sch ST1. . . 57 A3
Etruscan St ST1. . . . . 56 F2
Etruscan Way ST12. . . . . . 88 F4
Ettingshall Park Farm La
  WV4. . . . . 266 C4
Ettymore Cl DY3. . . . . . . 271 D8
Ettymore Rd DY3. . . . . . . 271 D8
Ettymore Rd W DY3 . . . . . 271 C8
Etwall Rd DE65. . . . . 148 B7
Europa Way WS13 . . . . . . 231 F8
Eva Gr ST5 . . . . 87 D8
Evans Croft B78. . . . . 250 A1
Evans St Burslem ST6. . . . . 41 F1
  Wolverhampton,Cinder Hill WV4,
   WV14. . . . . 266 F1
Eve La DY1 . . . . 271 F5
Evelyn St ST4 . . . . 72 E5
Everest Rd ST7 . . . . 26 C3
Everglade Rd CV9. . . . . . . 262 C1
Evergreen Hts WS12 . . . . 210 A8
Evergreens The DE13 . . . 166 F8
Evershed Way DE14 . . . . . 166 C2
Eversley Ave ST13. . . . . . . 30 E5
Eversley Gr DY3. . . . . 266 C2
Eversley Rd ST3 . . . . 73 E2
Evesham Cres WS3 . . . . . 242 F3
Evesham Way ST3 . . . . 73 E2
Eveson Rd ST3 . . . . 279 E2
Ewe Dale La DE6. . . . . 35 A3
Exbury Cl WV9. . . . . 239 F2
Excelsior Gr WS3 . . . . . . 244 B5
Exchange Ho ST16 . . . . . 285 B3
Exchange Ind Est The
  WS11 . . . . 226 E5
Exchange Rd DE13 . . . . . 201 A3
Exchange The WS3 . . . . . 243 B1
Exeter Dr B79. . . . . 249 E5
Exeter Gn ST2 . . . . 58 C2
Exeter Rd WS11. . . . . 226 B8
Exeter St ST17 . . . . 174 F8
Exley B77. . . . . 250 D1
Exmouth Gr ST6 . . . . 57 A7
Exonbury St WS11 . . . . . . 209 F2
Eyam Cl DE15. . . . . 167 B2
Eynsham Ct WV6. . . . . . . 255 E6
Eyre St ST6. . . . . 56 E7
Eyrie The DE15 . . . . 167 C3

F

Faber RC Prim Sch The
  ST10 . . . . 78 C8
Faceby St ST4 . . . . 90 C7
Fairbank Ave ST4 . . . . 71 F5
Fairbanks Wlk ST15 . . . . . 103 B4
Fairburn Cres WS3. . . . . . 244 B5
Fairclough Pl ST6. . . . . 42 A3
Fairfax Rd WV10 . . . . 240 E3
Fairfax St ST1 . . . . 57 D6
Fairfield Ave
  Brown Edge ST6. . . . . 43 B7
  Newcastle-u-L ST5. . . . . . 56 C4
  Rolleston on D DE13. . . . 147 D4
  Stoke-on-T ST3 . . . . 89 C8
Fairfield Cl WS12. . . . . . . 210 D1
Fairfield Cres DE11. . . . . . 186 E5
Fairfield Ct ST16. . . . . . . 155 F6
Fairfield Dr Codsall WV8. . 238 E4
  Kinver DY7. . . . . 278 A3
  Penkridge ST19 . . . . 207 F6
  Walsall WS3. . . . . 244 A4
Fairfield Rd
  Stourbridge DY8 . . . . 275 F2
  Uttoxeter ST14 . . . . 126 B8
Fairfield Rise DY8. . . . . . . 279 D5
Fairfields ST7 . . . . 39 F2
Fairfields Hill B78. . . . . . . 262 F8
Fairfields Rd ST8 . . . . 17 B1
Fairford Gdns
  Burntwood WS7. . . . . . . 229 C6
  Stourbridge DY8 . . . . 275 E3
Fairgreen Rd ST5. . . . . 85 D5
Fairgreen Way B74 . . . . . 257 A1
Fairham Rd DE13 . . . . . . 147 F1
Fairhaven Cl. 37 B1
Fairhaven Gr ST1 . . . . 57 E6
Fairhaven Prim Sch DY8 275 D3

Fairhills DY3. . . . . 271 D8
Fair Lady Dr WS7 . . . . . . 228 D8
Fair Lawn WV7 . . . . 237 A5
Fairlawn Cl Stoke-on-T ST3. 89 E8
  Willenhall WV12 . . . . 242 C1
Fairlawn Ct WV7. . . . . . . 237 B5
Fairlawn Dr DY6 . . . . 275 D4
Fairlawns ST5 . . . . 283 B4
Fairlawns Cl WV12. . . . . . 242 C1
Fairlight Gr ST3. . . . . 90 A7
Fair Mdws WS5 . . . . 179 A7
Fairmead Cl ST17 . . . . . . 175 C6
Fairmeadows Prim Sch
  DE11. . . . . 186 E5
Fairmount Dr **5** WS11 . 226 E8
Fairmount Way WS15 . . . 178 C1
Fairoak Ave ST16 . . . . . . 155 C8
Fairoak Bank ST21. . . . . . 115 D6
Fairoak Dr WV6. . . . . 255 B3
Fair Oak Pk WV6. . . . . . . 255 B3
Fair Oak Prim Sch WS6 . . . 70 F4
Fair Oak Rd TF10 . . . . . . 168 F4
Fair Oak St 40 D1
Fair Oaks Bsn & Ent Coll
  WS15 . . . . 196 D8
Fair Oaks Dr WS6 . . . . . . 243 A8
Fair Oaks WS15 . . . . 196 B6
Fair View WS15 . . . . 198 C4
Fairview Cl
  Cheslyn Hay WS6. . . . . . . 226 D2
  Tamworth B77 . . . . 250 F5
Fairview Cres DY6 . . . . . . 275 F6
Fair View Rd ST13 . . . . 31 A4
Fairview Rd WV4. . . . . . . 265 C5
Fairview Villas ST5. . . . . . 85 C5
Fairview Way ST17 . . . . . 156 C1
Fairway Burton u T DE14 . 185 B6
  Cannock WS11. . . . . 226 D6
Fairway Ct B77 . . . . 251 B3
Fairway Rd ST6. . . . . 42 A3
Fairways Ave DY8 . . . . . . 279 E2
Fairways Cl DY8 . . . . 279 E2
Fairways ST16,ST17. . . . . 156 A2
Fairways The DE6. . . . . . . 81 F6
Fairway B77 . . . . 261 E5
Fairway The
  3 Rugeley WS15 . . . . . 196 E8
  Swadlincote DE11 . . . . . . 186 E5
Fairway Trentham ST4. . . . 87 E8
  Walsall WS4. . . . . 244 D1
Falcon Bsns Ctr DE14 . . . 166 E5
Falcon Cl Burton u T DE14. 166 F4
  Cannock WS11. . . . . 209 C2
  Cheslyn Hay WS6. . . . . . . 226 C2
Falcon Cres WV14 . . . . . . 266 F2
Falcondale Rd WV12 . . . . 242 C1
Falcon Dr ST4. . . . . 232 E5
Falcon Pk B77. . . . . 261 E7
Falcon Rd ST3 . . . . 90 A6
Falcon Rise DY8 . . . . 279 C6
Falconry Ctr The★ DY9 . . 281 F3
Falcon B77 . . . . 262 A6
Falcon Way DY1 . . . . 271 F1
Faldo Cl DE14. . . . . 185 B6
Falkirk Grange ST5 . . . . . . 70 F7
Falklands Cl DY3. . . . . . . 269 E2
Fallow Deer Lawn TF10 . . 168 F5
Fallow Field WS11 . . . . . . 209 E3
Fallowfield Cl
  Penkridge ST19 . . . . 207 E8
  Stone ST15 . . . . 120 C6
Fallowfield Dr DE13 . . . . 183 C2
Fallow Field
  Lichfield WS13 . . . . 214 C3
  Little Aston B74. . . . . . . 257 B3
Fallow Rd DE13 . . . . 249 F1
Falmouth Ave ST17 . . . . . 175 E8
Falmouth Ct ST17 . . . . . . 175 E8
Falmouth Ct ST5. . . . . 71 C5
Falmouth Dr B77 . . . . . . 250 F5
Falmouth Rd CW12. . . . . . 15 E3
Falna Cres B79. . . . . 249 F7
Fancourt Rd WV4 . . . . . . 265 D4
Fancy Wlk ST16. . . . . 155 D5
Fane Rd ST1. . . . . 242 B2
Fanlizard La ST20 . . . . . . 171 D3
Faraday Ct DE14 . . . . 184 E7
Faraday Pl ST4 . . . . 71 E7
Faraday Rd ST16. . . . . . . 155 F5
Farcroft Ave ST5 . . . . 55 F6
Farcroft Dr TF9 . . . . 97 A1
Fareham Cres WV4 . . . . . 265 C6
Fareham Gr ST3 . . . . 89 E7
Farewell La WS7 . . . . 229 E6
Far Green Ind Est ST1. . . . 57 D6
Farifields Rd TF9 . . . . 97 D2
Faringdon Pl ST6. . . . . 42 A6
Farington Pl ST6. . . . . 42 A6
Farland Gr ST6 . . . . 42 A6
Far Lane Ind Est ST10. . . . 62 A7
Farleigh Dr WV3 . . . . 265 A8
Farleigh Gr ST2. . . . . 58 C1
Farleigh Rd WV6. . . . . . . 255 A3
Farley La ST10. . . . . 78 D3
Farley Rd ST10. . . . . 78 B5
Farmadine ST4 . . . . 88 B7
Farman Cl ST3. . . . . 90 C7
Farmbrook Ave WV10 . . . 240 D3
Farm Cl Burton u T DE13. . 166 B7
  Cannock WS12. . . . . 210 A4
  Codsall WV8. . . . . 239 B2
  Market Drayton TF9 . . . . . 97 A1
  Rugeley WS15 . . . . 178 C2

Farm Cl continued
  Sedgley DY3. . . . . 271 B7
  Tamworth B79. . . . . 250 C7
Farm Ct DE15. . . . . 166 C7
Farmdown Rd ST17. . . . . 156 C1
Farmers Bank ST5 . . . . . . 55 C1
Farmer St ST3 . . . . 284 C2
Farmfields Rise CW3. . . . . 67 C1
Farm Gr TF10. . . . . 168 D3
Farm Hollow ST7 . . . . 40 A2
Farm House La **6** B75 . 258 E3
Farm La DE15. . . . . 167 E7
Farm Lea
  Hilderstone ST15. . . . . . . 106 D2
  Stoke-on-T ST15 . . . . 42 E6
Farmoor Way WV10 . . . . 240 E4
Farm Rd
  Burnhill Green WV6. . . . . 252 D7
  Burton u T DE13. . . . . . . 166 C7
  Wolverhampton WV3. . . . 265 C8
Farmside Gn WV9. . . . . . 239 F2
Farmside La ST8. . . . . 17 B1
Farm Side DE11. . . . . 186 F5
Farm View ST15 . . . . 106 D2
Farm Wood Cl ST3 . . . . . . 74 B1
Farnborough Ct B75 . . . . 258 C2
Farnborough Dr ST3 . . . . . 90 C7
Farncote Dr B74. . . . . 257 F3
Farndale St **3** ST6. . . . . 41 D3
Farne Ct ST3 . . . . 73 A3
Farnham Dr ST8 . . . . 27 B6
Farnworth Cl ST8 . . . . 27 B6
Farnworth Rd ST3 . . . . . . 73 E3
Far Ridding ST20 . . . . 171 C5
Farrier Cl ST15 . . . . 120 D7
Farriers Gn TF10 . . . . 169 B3
Farriers Mill WS3. . . . . . . 243 E4
Farrier Way DY6 . . . . 275 A7
Farrington Cl ST16. . . . . . . 42 E3
Farrington Rd WV4 . . . . . 266 E3
Farthings The WS14. . . . . 246 F5
Farwall La ST10. . . . . 49 E2
Farway Gdns WV8. . . . . . 238 F2
Fasson Cl B77 . . . . 261 C8
Fauld Ind Pk DE13 . . . . . . 145 E6
Fauld La Tutbury DE13. . . . 146 A6
  Tutbury,Fauld DE13. . . . . 145 D7
Faulkner Cl DY8 . . . . 279 F4
Faulkner Pl ST3. . . . . 73 F4
Faversham Cl WV8. . . . . . 255 E8
Faversham Rd DE13 . . . . 166 A6
Fawcett Way ST1 . . . . 282 C4
Fawfield Dr ST6 . . . . 41 C6
Fawn Cl Huntington WS12. 209 D5
  Meir ST3 . . . . 90 A8
Fazeley Rd Tamworth B78 . 250 A4
  Tamworth,Fazeley B78. . . 250 B2
Fearns Ave ST5 . . . . 41 B1
Fearon Gn ST6. . . . . 42 E3
Featherbed La
  Hixon ST18. . . . . 158 C8
  Lichfield WS13 . . . . 213 E3
Featherstone Gr ST4. . . . . 72 E4
Featherstone La
  Featherstone WV10. . . . . 241 B8
  Shareshill WV10 . . . . 225 B1
Featherstone Rd B74. . . . 257 A2
Fecknam Way WS13. . . . . 214 C1
Federation Rd ST6 . . . . . . 41 F1
Fegg Hayes Rd ST6 . . . . . . 42 A6
Feiashill Cl WV5 . . . . 269 B7
Feiashill Rd WV5. . . . . . . 269 B7
Felcourt Gdns ST1. . . . . . 57 E5
Felden Cl ST16. . . . . 136 C1
Fellbrook Cl ST2. . . . . 58 A4
Fellbrook La ST2. . . . . 58 A4
Fellfield Way ST16. . . . . . 155 D8
Fellmeadow Way DY3 . . . 271 E7
Fellows Ave DY6 . . . . 275 C8
Fellows St WV2 . . . . 266 C8
Fell St ST6 . . . . 42 C1
Felspar Rd B77 . . . . 251 B3
Felstead Cl B77. . . . . 261 C4
Felsted St ST2 . . . . 43 B3
Felthouse La ST13 . . . . . . 45 B2
Femwork Ind Est DE14. . . 166 E5
Fence La CW12 . . . . 15 D4
Fenlow Ave ST3 . . . . 57 F2
Fenmere Cl WV4. . . . . . . 266 D5
Fennel Cl
  Cheslyn Hay WS6. . . . . . . 226 D3
  Uttoxeter ST14. . . . . 126 B3
Fennel Dr ST17 . . . . 174 F5
Fennel Gr ST3 . . . . 90 B6
Fenn Rise DY8. . . . . 275 D3
Fenn St B77 . . . . 250 E1
Fenpark Ind Est ST4 . . . . . 73 A5
Fenpark Rd ST4. . . . . 73 A6
Fenton Cl CW12. . . . . 6 A1
Fenton Ho ST5. . . . . 283 B3
Fenton House La ST19. . . 205 B6
Fenton Ind Est ST4. . . . . . 72 E8
Fenton Pk ST4 . . . . 73 A6
Fenton Pk Berry Hill ST2. . 57 F2
  Bucknall ST2 . . . . 58 A3
Fereday Rd WS9 . . . . 245 B3
Fereday's Croft DY3. . . . . 271 D7
Ferguson St WV11 . . . . . 242 A1
Fermain Cl ST5 . . . . 70 F3
Ferncombe Dr WS15 . . . . 178 C2
Fern Cres CW12. . . . . 6 A3
Ferncroft Cl ST4 . . . . 88 B7

Fern Croft WS13 . . . . 213 F1
Ferndale Cl
  Blythe Bridge ST11. . . . . . 90 F6
  Burntwood WS7. . . . . . . 229 B6
  Werrington ST9 . . . . 59 A4
  Weston CW2 . . . . 37 B5
Ferndale Gdns ST7. . . . . . 26 E3
Ferndale Rd
  Essington WV11. . . . . . . 242 B3
  Lichfield WS13. . . . . 213 F1
Fern Dell Cl WS11. . . . . . 209 C2
Fern Dene CW3. . . . . 68 D7
Ferndown Ave DY3. . . . . . 271 C7
Ferndown Cl Longton ST3. 73 D1
  Walsall WS3. . . . . 243 B4
Ferndown Dr ST5 . . . . 71 C2
Ferndown Dr S ST5 . . . . . 71 C1
Ferndown Way CW2. . . . . 52 C8
Fern Dr Great Wyrley WS6 227 A4
  Stafford ST16 . . . . 155 A5
Ferney Pl ST6 . . . . 41 C6
Fernhill Rd TF10 . . . . 150 C1
Fernhurst Cl ST15 . . . . . . 120 C7
Fernhurst Gr ST3 . . . . 89 E8
Fernie Cl ST15. . . . . 120 C6
Fernlea Cres ST9 . . . . 43 F8
Fernleigh Ave WS7. . . . . . 229 A8
Fernleigh Gdns
  Stafford ST16 . . . . 155 A5
  Stourbridge DY8 . . . . 275 C3
Fern Leys WV3 . . . . 255 D1
Fern Pl ST3. . . . . 284 C2
Fern Rd Huntington WS12. 209 D5
  Wolverhampton WV3. . . . 266 B8
Fernwood Croft ST13 . . . . 30 C4
Fernwood Ctr The WS15. . 178 C2
Fernwood Dr Leek ST13. . . 30 C4
  Rugeley WS15 . . . . 178 C2
Fernwood Gn ST4. . . . . . . 88 C7
Fernwood St16. . . . . 155 D7
Ferrand Cl ST4 . . . . 72 A2
Ferrers Ave DE13 . . . . . . 146 B5
Ferrers Cl B75. . . . . 258 D2
Ferrers Rd Tamworth B77 . 250 D4
  Weston ST18 . . . . 138 C2
  Yoxall DE13 . . . . 182 A2
Ferrie Gr WS8 . . . . 244 E8
Ferry Farm Dr **11** ST17. 175 A8
Ferry St DE15 . . . . 185 E8
Ferry Vale Cl DE15 . . . . . 185 E8
Festing St ST1 . . . . 282 C4
Festival Cl ST6. . . . . 57 A5
Festival Ct Cannock WS11. 209 E5
  Lichfield WS13. . . . . 231 A7
Festival Heights Ret Pk
  ST1 . . . . 57 A5
Festival Mews WS12 . . . . 209 F6
Festival Rd DE14 . . . . . . 184 E7
Festival Way ST1. . . . . . . 56 F5
Fiddlers Bank ST6 . . . . . . 43 B8
Fiddler's La ST13 . . . . . . 146 F4
Field Ave Hatton DE65. . . 146 C8
  Stoke-on-T ST2 . . . . 43 B2
Field Cl Blythe Bridge ST11. 90 E6
  Burton u T DE13. . . . . . . 166 A7
  Walsall WS4. . . . . 244 B2
  Whitmore ST5. . . . . 85 C5
Field Cotts ST18 . . . . 175 A1
Field Cres ST18 . . . . 154 E2
Field Ct WS4 . . . . 244 B2
Field Dr DE13 . . . . 147 B4
Fielden Cl ST6. . . . . 42 F2
Field End Cl ST4 . . . . 88 F4
Fieldfare WS7 . . . . 229 D5
Field Farm Dr B79 . . . . . . 217 C5
Field Farm Rd B77 . . . . . 250 D1
Field Head WV6 . . . . 255 B4
Field House Ct WS15 . . . 104 F2
Fieldhouse Rd
  Burntwood WS7. . . . . . . 229 A7
  Cannock WS12. . . . . 209 F7
  Wolverhampton WV4. . . . 266 E4
Fielding St ST4 . . . . 72 B5
Field La Burton u T DE13 . 166 A7
  Church Leigh ST10. . . . . . 109 B1
  Great Wyrley WS6 . . . . . . 226 F3
  Stanton DE6. . . . . 80 C8
  Walsall WS4. . . . . 244 B2
Field Pl Longton ST3 . . . . 73 C5
  Rugeley WS15 . . . . 196 B7
  Stafford ST16 . . . . 155 A5
Field Rd Lichfield WS13. . . 214 B3
  Walsall WS3. . . . . 243 C1
Field Rise DE13 . . . . 166 B7
Field Rise Rd ST12. . . . . . 103 E8
Fieldside Stafford ST17. . . 175 D5
  Yarnfield ST15 . . . . 118 E6
Fields Rd CW12. . . . . 15 F8
Field St WS11. . . . . 209 F3
Fields The WV8 . . . . 239 B4
Field St ST13 . . . . 30 E5
Fieldstone View DY3 . . . . 271 D4
Fieldsway Rd ST5 . . . . . . 119 E8
Field Terr ST15 . . . . 105 A1
Field View Biddulph ST8. . 16 D1
  Meir ST3 . . . . 74 B4
Fieldway
  Blythe Bridge ST11. . . . . . 90 D7
  Stoke-on-T ST3 . . . . 72 E3
Field Way DE11. . . . . 186 F5
Fieldway Trentham ST4. . . 87 E7
  Werrington ST2. . . . . 58 F3
Field Wlk WS9 . . . . 256 B7

Fife St ST4 . . . . 284 A4
Fifth Ave ST7 . . . . 25 E1
Filance Cl ST19 . . . . 207 F7
Filance La ST19 . . . . 207 F8
Filey Cl Bucknall ST2 . . . . . . 58 D2
Cannock ST11 . . . . 226 C8
Filey Rd WV10 . . . . 240 B2
Filey B77 . . . . 250 F6
Fillybrooks Cl ST15 . . . . . . 119 E8
Fillybrooks The ST15 . . . . . 119 F8
Filton Ave WS7 . . . . 229 A8
Fincham Cl WV9 . . . . 240 A3
Finchdean Cl ST3 . . . . 90 A7
Finchdene Gr WV3 . . . . 255 D1
Finches Hill WS15 . . . . 178 C3
Finchfield Cl DY8 . . . . 279 C4
Finchfield Gdns WV3 . . . . . 255 C1
Finchfield Hill WV3 . . . . . . 255 C1
Finchfield La WV3 . . . . 265 C8
Finchfield Rd WV3 . . . . 255 C1
Finchfield Rd W WV3 . . . . . 255 D1
Finchley Cl DY3 . . . . 271 D2
Finch Pl ST7 . . . . 27 B2
Finchsmith Pl ST3 . . . . 284 B2
Finch St ST8 . . . . 27 B1
Finch Way WS13 . . . . 215 E6
Fine La WS13 . . . . 215 E6
Finger Post Dr WS3 . . . . . . 244 A5
Finney Gn ST2 . . . . 58 A3
Finstock Ave ST3 . . . . 88 E8
Firbank Pl ST3 . . . . 73 F4
Firbank Way WS3 . . . . 243 F2
Firbeck Gdns ST17 . . . . . . 175 C7
Firbob La ST10 . . . . 93 F3
Fir Cl WS12 . . . . 209 D8
Fircroft [9] WV4 . . . . 266 F4
Fircroft Cl [3] WS11 . . . . . . 210 A3
Firecrest WS11 . . . . 210 C2
Fir Gr DY6 . . . . 279 D6
Firmstone Ct DY8 . . . . 279 E7
Firmstone St DY8 . . . . 279 E7
Firs Cl The ST17 . . . . 175 D7
Firs Mobile Home Pk The [4]
WS11 . . . . 210 A4
Firs Rd DY6 . . . . 275 E6
First Ave Brownhills WS8 . . 245 A8
Bucknall ST2 . . . . 58 D3
Burton u T DE14 . . . . 184 E8
Kidsgrove ST7 . . . . 25 F1
Kingswinford DY6 . . . . 271 A4
Newcastle-u-L ST5 . . . . . . 56 C7
Stafford ST16 . . . . 155 C7
Firs The WS15 . . . . 211 F5
Fir St DY3 . . . . 270 F7
Firsway The ST19 . . . . 221 E8
Firsway WV6 . . . . 255 A2
Firtree Cl ST18 . . . . 174 C3
Fir Tree Cl B79 . . . . 249 E7
Fir Tree Cotts CW2 . . . . . . 38 C5
Fir Tree Dr DY3 . . . . 271 E7
Fir Tree Pl ST5 . . . . 55 E8
Fir Tree Rd Stoke-on-T ST3 . . 89 E8
Wolverhampton WV3 . . . . . 265 D8
Firwood Rd ST8 . . . . 16 F1
Fisher Rd WS3 . . . . 242 F2
Fishers Lock TF10 . . . . 168 F4
Fisher St Brindley Ford ST8 . . 27 B2
Cannock WS12 . . . . 209 F8
Wolverhampton WV3 . . . . . 266 B8
Fisherwick Cl ST14 . . . . . . 232 F6
Fisherwick Rd WS14 . . . . . 232 F5
Fishley Cl WS3 . . . . 243 C4
Fishley La WS3 . . . . 243 D5
Fishpond La
Egginton DE65 . . . . 148 A5
Tutbury DE13 . . . . 146 C6
Fishpond Way ST2 . . . . 58 A4
Fistral Cl ST3 . . . . 73 D4
Fistral Gdns WV3 . . . . 265 F7
Fitchet's Bank WS7 . . . . . . 229 F6
Fithern Cl DY3 . . . . 271 E5
Fitzgerald Pl ST3 . . . . 74 B4
Fitzherbert Cl ST15 . . . . . . 103 B4
Fitzherbert Rd ST1 . . . . . . 57 E8
Five Lands Rd DE15 . . . . . . 185 F8
Five Lanes End ST20 . . . . . 153 D7
Five Oaks Cl ST5 . . . . 70 E3
Fives Gr WS7 . . . . 228 C8
Five Ways Dudley DY3 . . . . 271 D3
Iverley DY10 . . . . 281 A5
Five Ways Prim Sch
WS12 . . . . 210 D2
Five Ways WV3 . . . . 265 C7
Flackets La DE6 . . . . 128 B7
Flackett St ST3 . . . . 284 C5
Flamborough Gr ST6 . . . . . 56 E7
Flanders Dr DY6 . . . . 275 D8
Flashbrook Cross Roads
TF10 . . . . 149 D5
Flash CE Prim Sch SK17 . . . . 3 B3
Flashes The ST20 . . . . 171 E7
Flash La Blore TF9 . . . . 98 F1
Orton WV4 . . . . 264 E2
Stoke-on-T,Baddeley Edge
ST2 . . . . 43 C2
Stoke-on-T,Trent Vale ST4 . . 71 E3
Flash Ley Prim Sch ST17 . . 174 F4
Flash The CW12 . . . . 15 E6
Flather La DE6 . . . . 65 D1
Flats La WS14 . . . . 248 A6
Flatts Cl DE13 . . . . 166 B6
Flatts Rd ST6 . . . . 42 E5
Flavells La DY3 . . . . 271 D2
Flaxcroft Ct ST12 . . . . 88 C2
Flax Croft ST15 . . . . 120 B7

Flax Hill Jun Sch B79 . . . 250 B7
Flaxley Rd WS15 . . . . 196 D6
Flaxman Cl ST12 . . . . 88 F4
Flax Ovens The ST19 . . . . 192 E2
Flax St ST4 . . . . 72 B6
Fleckney Ave ST3 . . . . 73 E3
Fleets La ST13 . . . . 49 B8
Fleet St DE14 . . . . 166 D1
Fleming Rd ST4 . . . . 72 B7
Flemmynge Cl WV8 . . . . . 238 E4
Fletcher Bank ST5 . . . . . . 283 A3
Fletcher Cres ST2 . . . . 43 B2
Fletcher Dr WV13 . . . . . . 215 C6
Fletcher Rd Stoke-on-T ST4 72 A5
Walsall WV12 . . . . 242 D1
Fletcher St ST1 . . . . 282 A1
Fletches The DE14 . . . . . . 147 B1
Fleur Gr ST4 . . . . 73 B6
Flinn Cl WS14 . . . . 231 D7
Flints Cnr WS12 . . . . 195 B4
Flintsham Gr ST1 . . . . 282 B4
Flint St ST3 . . . . 74 B5
Flora Cl B79 . . . . 250 C7
Florence St [13] WV4 . . . . 266 F4
Florence Dr DE6 . . . . 127 C8
Florence Prim Sch ST3 . . . 284 C2
Florence Rd Codsall WV8 . . 239 C3
Trentham ST4 . . . . 71 F1
Florence St
Cannock WS12 . . . . 210 B7
Newcastle-u-L ST5 . . . . . . 283 B3
Florence Terr ST9 . . . . 29 A1
Florendine Com Prim Sch
B77 . . . . 250 F5
Florendine St B77 . . . . . . 250 F5
Florida Cl ST6 . . . . 57 B8
Floyd St ST4 . . . . 72 B8
Flynn Row ST4 . . . . 72 F8
Foden Ave ST7 . . . . 25 A3
Foden Cl ST14 . . . . 246 F6
Foden St ST4 . . . . 72 A5
Fog Cotts Rugeley WS15 . . 178 F7
Wrinehill CW3 . . . . 52 E4
Fogg St E ST5 . . . . 283 B3
Fogg St W ST5 . . . . 283 B3
Fogg St ST5 . . . . 283 B3
Fold La ST8 . . . . 16 E4
Fold Terr ST13 . . . . 45 C5
Fold The Oaken WV8 . . . . 238 D2
Oulton ST15 . . . . 105 C3
Wolverhampton WV4 . . . . 265 F4
Folebank Barns ST14 . . . . 109 F8
Fole La ST14 . . . . 109 F8
Foley Ave WV6 . . . . 255 C3
Foley Church Cl B74 . . . . . 257 A2
Foley Ct B74 . . . . 256 F1
Foley Dr WV6 . . . . 255 C3
Foley Gr WV5 . . . . 269 E5
Foley Inf Sch DY7 . . . . . . 278 A3
Foley Pl ST4 . . . . 284 A4
Foley Rd E B74 . . . . 257 A2
Foley Rd ST3 . . . . 284 A3
Foley Rd W B74 . . . . 256 E1
Foley St Dunsley DY7 . . . . 278 B4
Longton ST4 . . . . 284 B5
Foley Wood Cl B74 . . . . . . 256 E1
Folly Fields ST13 . . . . 45 B2
Folly La ST9 . . . . 60 C7
Folly View TF9 . . . . 99 D5
Fontaine Pl ST4 . . . . 72 A4
Fontenaye Rd B79 . . . . . . 249 F7
Fonthill Wlk ST2 . . . . 58 A4
Fonthil Rd ST16 . . . . 155 F6
Fontwell Rd
Burton u T DE14 . . . . . . 184 F7
Wolverhampton WV10 . . . 240 D4
Footherley La WS14 . . . . . 246 C4
Footherley Rd WS14 . . . . . 246 F5
Forber Rd ST4 . . . . 71 F4
Ford Ave ST6 . . . . 42 B5
Ford Brook La WS3 . . . . . 244 B2
Ford Cl ST15 . . . . 120 A7
Ford Dr ST15 . . . . 118 E6
Ford Green Hall (Mus)★
ST6 . . . . 42 D2
Ford Green Rd ST6 . . . . . . 42 D2
Fordham Gr WV9 . . . . 240 A3
Ford Hayes La
Bucknall ST2 . . . . 73 D8
Bucknall ST3 . . . . 58 F1
Werrington ST3 . . . . 59 A1
Fordhouse Rd Ind Est
WV10 . . . . 240 D1
Fordhouse Rd WV10 . . . . . 240 D1
Ford La
Creswell Green WS13 . . . . 212 F2
Longdon WS15 . . . . 198 A2
Ford Rd TF10 . . . . 168 L1
Fordrough The B74 . . . . . 258 A1
Fords La ST7 . . . . 26 D6
Ford St Burton u T DE15 . . 185 E7
Leek ST13 . . . . 30 F6
Newcastle-u-L ST5 . . . . . . 55 B2
Stoke-on-T ST4 . . . . 56 E1
Ford Way WS15 . . . . 198 B5
Foregate St ST16 . . . . 285 B4
Foregate St ST16 . . . . 285 A4
Forest Cl Colwich ST18 . . . 177 D8
Newcastle-u-L ST5 . . . . . . 70 E4
Forest Ct ST1 . . . . 282 B4
Forest Dr DY7 . . . . 277 F4
Forest Edge ST6 . . . . 57 C6
Forest Edge Way DE13 . . . 166 A8
Forest Glade WS6 . . . . . . 226 F2
Forest La DY7 . . . . 268 E2
Forest Lawns B74 . . . . . . 257 C3
Forest Park Prim Sch
ST1 . . . . 282 A4

Forest Rd Burton u T DE13 165 E4
Draycott in t C DE6 . . . . . 144 B4
Dunstall DE13 . . . . 183 B5
Market Drayton TF9 . . . . 112 A8
Stoke-on-T ST3 . . . . 89 F7
Forest School St DE13 . . 147 C4
Forestside ST4 . . . . 72 A2
Forest Way WS6 . . . . 227 A1
Forge Cl
Hammerwich WS7 . . . . . . 229 D5
Wolverhampton WV8 . . . . 239 E1
Forge La
Aldridge,Leighswood
WS9 . . . . 256 A5
Aldridge,Mill Green WS9 . . 256 A7
Blakedown DY10 . . . . 281 B1
Burntwood WS7 . . . . 229 F6
Burton u T DE13 . . . . . . 148 A2
Hanley ST1 . . . . 56 F4
Kingswinford DY6 . . . . . . 275 A8
Lichfield WS13 . . . . 214 A1
Norton in H TF9 . . . . 82 C1
Shenstone B74,WS14 . . . 257 C7
Stretton DE13 . . . . 147 F2
Forge Leys WV5 . . . . 269 E6
Forge Mews WS15 . . . . . 178 F1
Forge Rd Rugeley WS15 . . 178 F1
Stourbridge DY8 . . . . 279 F6
Walsall WS3 . . . . 243 F5
Forge Rise ST18 . . . . 191 C8
Forge Row WV15 . . . . . . 196 B6
Forge Side ST9 . . . . 44 A8
Forge St WS12 . . . . 210 C4
Forge Valley Way WV5 . . . 269 E6
Forge Way ST8 . . . . 27 B4
Formby Ave WV6 . . . . 254 D4
Formby Way WS3 . . . . . . 243 A3
Forrest Ave
Cannock WS11 . . . . 226 E8
Essington WV11 . . . . 242 A4
Forrest Ct [9] WS13 . . . . 231 B7
Forrester Cl
[3] Biddulph ST8 . . . . . . 27 C8
Fradley WS13 . . . . 215 D6
Forrester Rd ST15 . . . . . . 120 B7
Forresters Bank ST2,ST9 . . 43 C3
Forrister St ST3 . . . . 73 D4
Forsbrook CE Prim Sch
ST11 . . . . 91 A7
Forster St ST6 . . . . 41 D3
Forsyte Rd ST3 . . . . 73 C6
Forsyth Cl ST4 . . . . 71 E8
Forsythia Gr WV8 . . . . . . 239 A3
Fort Cres ST9 . . . . 245 A3
Fortescue La WS15 . . . . . 178 E2
Forties B77 . . . . 261 E2
Forton Cl WV6 . . . . 255 B2
Forton Glade TF10 . . . . . . 168 F5
Forton Rd TF10 . . . . 168 F5
Forty Acre Cl TF9 . . . . 99 E5
Forum The [5] WS11 . . . . 209 L1
Forum The ST5 . . . . 55 D5
Fosbrooke Pl ST4 . . . . 71 D8
Fossdale Rd B77 . . . . 262 A8
Fosseway La WS13,WS14 . . 230 E4
Fosseway WS14 . . . . 231 A5
Foster Ave WS12 . . . . 209 F6
Foster Cres DY7 . . . . 278 A4
Foster Ct ST3 . . . . 72 F3
Foster Gn WV6 . . . . 254 E3
Foster Pl DY8 . . . . 279 E6
Foster Rd CW12 . . . . 6 A5
Foster St DY7 . . . . 278 A4
Foston Ave DE13 . . . . 166 B6
Foston Cl DE65 . . . . 146 C7
Fotherley Brook Rd WS9 . 256 F5
Foundry La Bucknall ST2 . . 58 A3
Scholar Green ST7 . . . . . . 25 F7
Walsall WS3 . . . . 243 E3
Foundry Rd DY6 . . . . 275 C8
Foundry Sq ST6 . . . . 43 A5
Foundry St Hanley ST1 . . . 282 B3
Kingswinford DY6 . . . . . . 275 C8
Fountain Ct
[10] Burslem ST6 . . . . . . 56 F8
Biddulph ST8 . . . . 16 D1
Fountain Fold ST20 . . . . . 171 C3
Fountain Pl [9] ST6 . . . . . 56 F8
Fountain Rd DE6 . . . . 144 D6
Fountains Ave ST5 . . . . . . 71 B5
Fountains Sq ST1 . . . . . . 282 B3
Fountains Rd WS3 . . . . . . 242 E2
Fountain St Leek ST13 . . . 30 F6
Stoke-on-T ST4 . . . . 72 B6
Fountains Way ST3 . . . . . 242 E2
Four Ashes Ind Est
WV10 . . . . 224 D6
Four Ashes Rd ST19 . . . . . 223 E7
Four Crosses La WS11 . . . 225 E7
Four Crosses Rd WS4 . . . . 242 F1
Fourlane Ends ST20,ST21 . 131 E8
Four Lane Ends
Eccleshall ST21 . . . . 134 A5
Milwich ST18 . . . . 122 B8
Four Lanes End
Gorstyhill CW2 . . . . 37 F2
Haughton ST18 . . . . 173 A5
Seighford ST18 . . . . 153 E8
Uttoxeter ST14 . . . . 126 C4
Four Oaks Common Rd
B74 . . . . 257 F3
Four Oaks Ct B74 . . . . . . 258 B1
Four Oaks Inf Sch B74 . . . 257 E4
Four Oaks Jun Sch B74 . . . 257 E4
Four Oaks Rd B74 . . . . . . 258 A1
Fourth Ave
Brownhills WS8 . . . . 229 A1
Bucknall ST2 . . . . 58 E4

Fourth Ave continued
Kidsgrove ST7 . . . . 25 F1
Fourways CW2 . . . . 37 B5
Fowlchurch Rd ST13 . . . . 30 F7
Fowler Cl WV6 . . . . 254 E6
Fowler's La ST21 . . . . 43 D1
Fowler St WV2 . . . . 266 C6
Fox Cl Burton u T DE14 . . 185 B8
Seisdon WV5 . . . . 263 F2
Tamworth B77 . . . . 261 C8
Foxcote Cl ST17 . . . . 175 E5
Fox Covert DY8 . . . . 279 E5
Foxcroft Cl WV7 . . . . 229 B5
Fox Ct DE13 . . . . 199 C6
Foxes La ST19 . . . . 222 C6
Foxes Rake WS11 . . . . . . 209 E3
Foxfield Cl ST10 . . . . 76 E6
Foxfield Steam Railway★
ST10,ST11 . . . . 75 B5
Foxfield Steam Rly★
ST11 . . . . 90 E8
Foxfields Way ST12 . . . . . 209 C7
Foxfield Way ST3 . . . . 88 F8
Fox Gdns ST7 . . . . 40 D8
Foxglove Ave
Burton u T DE15 . . . . . . 186 A8
Uttoxeter ST14 . . . . 126 B6
Foxglove Cl
Featherstone WV10 . . . . . 241 B7
Lichfield WS14 . . . . 231 A5
Meir ST3 . . . . 74 B5
Rugeley WS15 . . . . 178 C1
Walsall WS3 . . . . 244 A5
Foxglove La ST5 . . . . 71 C2
Foxglove Rd DY1 . . . . 271 F4
Foxgloves Ave ST18 . . . . . 177 E7
Foxglove B77 . . . . 251 A4
Foxglove Wlk WS12 . . . . . 210 C7
Fox Gr ST5 . . . . 71 C2
Foxhill Cl WS12 . . . . 210 D2
Fox Hill Rd B75 . . . . 258 F2
Foxhill's Cl WS7 . . . . 229 A5
Foxhills Rd
Stourbridge DY8 . . . . 275 D1
Wolverhampton WV4 . . . . 265 C4
Fox Hollow
Eccleshall ST21 . . . . 133 F6
Loggerheads TF9 . . . . . . 99 D5
Wolverhampton WV6 . . . . 255 C2
Fox La Alrewas DE13 . . . . 200 F2
Lichfield WS13 . . . . 214 A5
Foxland Ave WS6 . . . . . . 227 A3
Foxlands Ave WV4 . . . . . . 265 D3
Foxlands Cl ST2 . . . . 58 D3
Foxlands Cres WV4 . . . . . 265 C3
Foxlands Dr Dudley DY3 . . 271 D5
Wombourne WV4 . . . . . . 265 D3
Fox Leigh Mdws WS15 . . 198 B4
Foxley La ST2 . . . . 43 A3
Foxmeadow Cl DY3 . . . . . 271 E2
Fox Rd WV5,WV6 . . . . . . 263 E3
Foxtail Way WS12 . . . . . . 210 E4
Foxton Cl DE13 . . . . 201 A2
Foxton Man B74 . . . . 258 A1
Fox Wlk WS9 . . . . 245 B3
Foxwood Cl ST15 . . . . . . 119 E6
Foxwood Rd B78 . . . . 262 F8
Fradgley Ct ST14 . . . . 125 C7
Fradgley Gr ST14 . . . . . . 110 F2
Fradley La WS13 . . . . 215 E7
Fradswell La ST18 . . . . . . 123 A2
Framlingham Gr WV6 . . . . 255 A3
Frampton Gr ST6 . . . . 41 E6
Frances Dr WS3 . . . . 243 B2
Francis Cl
[1] Kingswinford DY6 . . . 275 D8
Penkridge ST19 . . . . 208 A8
Francis Green La ST19 . . . 207 F8
Francis Rd Lichfield WS13 . 214 A2
Stourbridge DY8 . . . . 279 C5
Francis St ST6 . . . . 41 F5
Frank Foley Way ST16 . . . 285 A4
Frank Gee Cl WS15 . . . . . 178 D1
Franklin Cl DE15 . . . . 167 B1
Franklin Dr WS7 . . . . 229 B7
Franklin Rd ST4 . . . . 71 F7
Franklyn Cl WV6 . . . . 254 E5
Franklyn St ST1 . . . . 282 C1
Frank Rogers Wlk WS15 . . 178 D2
Frank St ST4 . . . . 72 A6
Fraser Cl ST15 . . . . 119 F5
Fraser St ST6 . . . . 57 B7
Frayne Ave DY6 . . . . 275 C7
Frazer Ho [5] ST3 . . . . . . 89 F8
Freckleton Pl ST3 . . . . . . 90 C7
Fred Brewer Way DE13 . . 165 E4
Frederick Ave ST4 . . . . . . 72 A7
Frederick Ct B77 . . . . 250 B3
Frederick Rd ST19 . . . . . . 192 F1
Fredericks Cl DY8 . . . . . . 279 E4
Frederick St
Burton u T DE15 . . . . . . 185 E8
Stoke-on-T ST4 . . . . 72 E6
Wolverhampton WV2 . . . . 266 C8
Freebridge Cl ST3 . . . . . . 73 E4
Freedom Dr ST7 . . . . 26 C3
Freedom Wlk ST6 . . . . . . 42 C3
Freeford Gdns WS14 . . . . 231 D5
Freehold St ST6 . . . . 283 C2
Freeland Gr [3] DY6 . . . . 275 D5
Freemen St ST16 . . . . . . 155 E5
Freer Dr WS7 . . . . 229 B5
Freeth Rd WS8 . . . . 229 A1
Free Trade St ST1 . . . . . . 282 C4
Fremantle Dr WS12 . . . . . 210 E2
Fremantle Rd ST4 . . . . . . 71 F4
Fremont Dr DY1 . . . . 271 E5
French Ave B78 . . . . 249 C1

Frenchmore Gr ST3 . . . . . 73 E1
Frensham Cl WS6 . . . . . . 226 E4
Freshwater Dr
Chorlton CW2 . . . . 37 B1
Weston CW2 . . . . 52 C8
Freshwater Gr ST2 . . . . . 57 F3
Freville Cl B79 . . . . 250 A5
Frew Cl ST16 . . . . 156 A4
Friar's Alley WS13 . . . . . . 231 B7
Friars Ave ST15 . . . . 120 A7
Friars Cl Cheadle ST10 . . . 76 D4
Stourbridge DY8 . . . . 275 C3
Friar's Ct ST5 . . . . 283 B2
Friars Gorse DY7 . . . . 279 C8
Friar's La TF11 . . . . 220 D4
Friars Pl ST2 . . . . 58 B7
Friars Rd ST2 . . . . 58 B7
Friars' Rd ST17 . . . . 285 B2
Friar's St ST5 . . . . 283 B2
Friars' Terr ST17 . . . . 285 B2
Friar St Longton ST3 . . . . 284 C4
Stafford ST16 . . . . 155 D5
Friars' Wlk
Newcastle-u-L ST5 . . . . . . 71 B6
Stafford ST17 . . . . 285 B2
Friars Wlk B77 . . . . 250 C5
Friarswood Prim Sch
ST5 . . . . 283 B1
Friarswood Rd ST5 . . . . . 283 B2
Friary Ave
Abbots Bromley WS15 . . . 160 F5
Lichfield WS13 . . . . 231 A6
Friary Dr B74 . . . . 257 F3
Friary Gdns WS13 . . . . . . 231 A7
Friary Grange Sports Ctr
WS13 . . . . 213 F2
Friary Ho WS13 . . . . 213 F1
Friary Rd WS13 . . . . 231 A7
Friary Sch The WS13 . . . . 213 E2
Friary The WS13 . . . . 231 A7
Friday Acre WS13 . . . . . . 214 A2
Friendly Ave ST5 . . . . 56 B8
Friesian Gdns ST5 . . . . . . 40 C2
Friezland La WS8 . . . . . . 245 A5
Friezland Way WS8 . . . . . 245 A5
Frinton Cl ST16 . . . . 155 F5
Frith St ST13 . . . . 30 C6
Frobisher Cl WS6 . . . . . . 226 F1
Frobisher Dr ST15 . . . . . . 103 B4
Frobisher St ST6 . . . . 43 A5
Frodingham Rd ST2 . . . . . 58 L1
Froghall ST5 . . . . 283 B3
Froghall Rd Cheadle ST10 . 76 E6
Ipstones ST10 . . . . 62 A6
Froghall Wharf★ ST10 . . . 62 E6
Frog La Lichfield WS13 . . . 231 B7
Market Drayton TF9 . . . . 97 C1
Wheaton Aston ST19 . . . . 205 C6
Frogmore Cl TF9 . . . . 97 C1
Frogmore Pl TF9 . . . . 97 C1
Frogmore Rd TF9 . . . . . . 97 C1
Frome Cl DY3 . . . . 271 D2
Frome Wlk ST6 . . . . 42 A4
Froyle Cl WV6 . . . . 255 C5
Fuchsia Dr WV9 . . . . 239 F3
Fulfen Prim Sch WS7 . . . 229 A1
Fulford Prim Sch ST11 . . 106 E8
Fulford Rd ST11 . . . . 106 E8
Fullbrook Ave DE13 . . . . . 201 E8
Fullelove Rd WS8 . . . . . . 245 A4
Fuller St ST4 . . . . 41 E4
Fullerton Cl WV8 . . . . . . 239 E1
Fullmore Cl ST19 . . . . . . 207 F7
Fullwood Wlk ST2 . . . . . . 58 C1
Fulmar Pl ST3 . . . . 90 B7
Furber Pl DY6 . . . . 275 F6
Furlong Ave ST10 . . . . . . 92 F3
Furlong Cl Alrewas DE13 . . 201 A2
Upper Tean ST10 . . . . . . 92 L3
Weston ST18 . . . . 138 C2
Furlong Dr ST10 . . . . 92 L3
Furlong Ind Est ST6 . . . . . 56 E7
Furlong La Alrewas DE13 . . 201 A2
Bradley ST18 . . . . 173 C2
Burslem ST6 . . . . 56 E7
Hope DE6 . . . . 35 C4
Furlong Par [12] ST6 . . . . 56 F8
Furlong Pas [11] ST6 . . . . 56 F8
Furlong Rd ST6 . . . . 41 E4
Furlongs Rd DY3 . . . . 271 D6
Furlong The ST15 . . . . . . 118 F6
Furlong Wlk DY3 . . . . 271 D4
Furmston Pl ST13 . . . . . . 31 A7
Furnace Cl WV5 . . . . 269 E6
Furnace La CW3 . . . . 68 E7
Furnace Rd ST3 . . . . 73 D2
Furness Cl WS3 . . . . 242 F4
Furness Gr ST17 . . . . 174 B7
Furness B77 . . . . 250 D3
Furnivall Cres WS13 . . . . 214 D1
Furnival St ST6 . . . . 57 B6
Furrows Dr DE13 . . . . . . 166 A8
Furst St WS8 . . . . 245 A4
Fyfield Rd DE15 . . . . 185 E6
Fynney Fields ST13 . . . . . 45 F8
Fynney St ST13 . . . . 30 F5

G

Gable Cotts ST11 . . . . . . 74 E2
Gable Croft WS14 . . . . . . 231 F6
Gables The
Kingswinford DY6 . . . . . . 275 B8
Swadlincote DE11 . . . . . . 186 E5
Gable St ST4 . . . . 72 B6
Gaelic Rd WS11 . . . . 209 D4
Gagarin B79 . . . . 249 F5

Gag La DE6 . . . . 51 D6
Gaiafields Rd WS13 . . . . 214 B1
Gaia La WS13 . . . . 231 B8
Gaialands Cres WS13 . . . 214 B1
Gaia Stowe WS13 . . . . . 214 B1
Gail Cl WS9 . . . . 245 B4
Gailey Lea La ST19 . . . . 208 B2
Gailey Pottery★ ST19 . . 207 C2
Gail Pk WV3 . . . . 265 D7
Gainford Cl WV8 . . . . . . 239 F1
Gainsborough Dr
  Mile Oak B78 . . . . . . 260 B8
  Perton WV6 . . . . 255 A4
Gainsborough Hill DY8 . . 279 D6
Gainsborough Pl DY1 . . . 271 E2
Gainsborough Rd
  Newcastle-u-L ST5 . . . 55 C6
  Stoke-on-T ST3 . . . . . 88 B8
Gainsborough Way ST15 167 B3
Gainsbrook Cres WS11 . . 227 F5
Gains La WS3,WS11 . . . . 227 D2
Gairloch Rd WV11 . . . . . 242 B1
Galahad Dr DE13 . . . . . 147 D2
Galena B77 . . . . 251 B2
Galleys Bank ST7 . . . . . 26 B3
Galliers Cl B77 . . . . 261 F5
Gallimore Cl ST6 . . . . . . 41 E1
Gallimore Ho ST7 . . . . . 40 D8
Galloway Rd ST2 . . . . . . 73 B8
Gallows Hill DY7 . . . . . . 277 F6
Gallowstree La
  Mayfield DE6 . . . . 81 C8
  Newcastle-u-L ST5 . . . . 70 E7
Galsworthy Rd ST3 . . . . 73 B6
Galveston Gr ST4 . . . . . 72 F5
Galway Rd WS7 . . . . . . 229 A7
Gamesfield Gn WV3 . . . 255 F1
Ganton Rd WS3 . . . . . . 243 A3
Ganton Wlk WV8 . . . . . 255 F8
Gaol Butts ST21 . . . . . . 133 D6
Gaolgate St ST16 . . . . . 285 B3
Gaol Mews ST16 . . . . . 285 B4
Gaol Rd ST16 . . . . 285 B4
Gaol Sq ST16 . . . . 285 B4
Garage Cl B77 . . . . 250 D5
Garbett St ST6 . . . . 41 D7
Garden Cotts ST20 . . . . 171 C5
Garden Cres WS3 . . . . . 243 F3
Garden Croft WS9 . . . . . 256 B7
Garden Dr WS15 . . . . . . 197 A7
Gardeners Cl ST8 . . . . . 27 B5
Gardeners Way WV5 . . . 269 F5
Gardenholm Cl ST3 . . . . 89 F8
Garden La ST19 . . . . . . 206 D4
Garden Pl Stafford ST17 . 285 C2
  Stoke-on-T ST4 . . . . . 71 E8
Gardens The Elford B79 . 216 D2
  Lawton-gate ST7 . . . . . 25 C4
Garden St Leek ST13 . . . 30 D6
  Newcastle-u-L ST5 . . . 283 C2
  Stafford ST17 . . . . . . 285 C2
  Stoke-on-T ST4 . . . . . 71 F6
Garden View WS15 . . . . 178 D1
Garden Village ST10 . . . 92 C4
Garden Wlk DY3 . . . . . . 271 C2
Gardiner Dr ST3 . . . . . . 284 A2
Gardner Pl ST14 . . . . . . 111 A1
Garfield Ave ST4 . . . . . . 71 F1
Garfield Cres ST4 . . . . . 71 F1
Garfield Ct ST4 . . . . 71 F1
Garfield St ST1 . . . . 282 A1
Garibaldi St ST1 . . . . . . 56 F3
Garlick St ST6 . . . . 42 B1
Garner St ST4 . . . . 56 F4
Garners Wlk CW3 . . . . . 68 E7
Garnet St ST1 . . . . 57 A3
Garnett Rd E ST5 . . . . . 56 B5
Garnett Rd W ST5 . . . . . 56 B6
Garret Cl DY6 . . . . 275 D8
Garrett Sq DE13 . . . . . . 147 C4
Garrick Cl Dudley DY1 . . 271 F3
  Lichfield WS13 . . . . . 213 F2
Garrick Ct WS13 . . . . . 213 F2
Garrick Rd Cannock WS11 209 D4
  Lichfield WS13 . . . . . 213 F2
Garrick Rise
  Burntwood WS7 . . . . . 229 B7
  Rugeley WS15 . . . . . 197 B6
Garridge Cl WV7 . . . . . 237 A4
Garrigill B77 . . . . 251 B1
Garrod Sq ST16 . . . . . . 156 B5
Garsdale Cres ST3 . . . . 88 F8
Gartan Rd DE14 . . . . . . 185 A8
Garth Cl ST17 . . . . 174 E5
Garth Rd ST17 . . . . 174 F5
Garth St ST1 . . . . 282 C3
Garth The WS13 . . . . . . 214 B2
Gaskell Rd ST2 . . . . 58 D3
Gas St ST14 . . . . 111 C1
Gas Works Ind Est ST7 . . 25 E2
Gatacre St DY3 . . . . . . 271 D3
Gatcombe Cl
  Stretton DE13 . . . . . 147 D1
  Wolverhampton WV10 . 240 F1
Gatcombe Rd DY1 . . . . 271 C2
Gatehouse Trad Est WS8 . 229 B1
Gate St Meir ST3 . . . . . . 74 B5
  Sedgley DY3 . . . . . . 271 E7
Gateway Ave ST5 . . . . . 85 C5
Gateway St ST5 . . . . . . 40 D2
Gatherwynd La TF11 . . . 203 E6
Gatley Gr ST3 . . . . 90 B6
Gauledge La SK17 . . . . . 13 B6
Gaunt St B ST13 . . . . . 30 D6
Gawain Gr DE13 . . . . . . 147 E2
Gawbutts The ST10 . . . . 76 C2
Gawsworth Cl ST3 . . . . . 73 C6

Gawsworth B79 . . . . . . 249 D7
Gaydon Cl WV6 . . . . . . 254 E5
Gaydon Rd WS9 . . . . . . 256 A4
Gay La ST20 . . . . 204 F8
Gayle B77 . . . . 251 A1
Gaymore Rd DY10 . . . . 280 B5
Gayton Ave ST2 . . . . . . 43 B2
Geary La DE15 . . . . 167 F2
Geen St ST4 . . . . 72 B7
Gemini Dr WS11 . . . . . . 226 F6
Gemini Gr ST6 . . . . 41 F6
Geneshall Cl ST20 . . . . 171 D7
Geneva Dr
  Birches Head ST1 . . . . 57 F6
  Newcastle-u-L ST5 . . . 70 E6
Genge Ave WV4 . . . . . . 266 E4
Genista Cl DE15 . . . . . . 186 A8
Genthorn Cl II WV4 . . . . 266 F4
Gentian B74 . . . . 257 F5
Gentleshaw Prim Sch
  WS15 . . . . 212 A5
Gentleshaw Wildlife Ctr★
  ST21 . . . . 134 A7
Geoffrey Ave ST13 . . . . 30 D5
Geoffrey St ST3 . . . . . . 74 A4
George Ave Meir ST3 . . . 74 B1
  Mile Oak B78 . . . . . . 249 C1
George Baily Ct ST17 . . . 285 C1
George Brealey Cl WS15 . 196 F7
George Eardley Ct ST4 . . 41 C5
George Eastham Ave ST4 . 72 D3
George Elliott Cl ST14 . . 126 C6
George Hill Ct B ST16 . . 155 F5
George La Lichfield WS13 . 231 C8
  Stone ST15 . . . . 120 D7
George St Audley ST7 . . . 39 D1
  Burton u T DE14 . . . . 166 B3
  Cannock WS12 . . . . . 210 C4
  Newcastle-u-L,Chesterton
    ST5 . . . . 55 E7
  Newcastle-u-L,Porthill ST5 . 56 D6
  Newcastle-u-L,Silverdale
    ST5 . . . . 55 B1
  Newcastle-u-L ST5 . . . 283 C1
  Stafford ST16 . . . . . 155 D5
  Stoke-on-T ST4 . . . . . 72 E7
  Stourbridge DY8 . . . . 275 F1
  Tamworth B79 . . . . . 250 B4
Georges Way ST7 . . . . . 39 F2
George Walker Ct DE14 . 166 C5
Georgian Pl WS11 . . . . . 209 C2
Gerald Rd DY8 . . . . 279 E7
Gerards Way TF9 . . . . . 100 C5
Gerard St B77 . . . . 249 E2
Gerrard St ST4 . . . . 72 A8
Germander B74 . . . . . . 257 F5
Gerrard St ST4 . . . . 72 A8
Gettings Cl WS7 . . . . . . 229 F7
Gibbet La Kinver DY7 . . . 278 F4
  Stourbridge DY7 . . . . 279 B4
Gibbins St ST1 . . . . 282 C4
Gibb La DE6 . . . . 128 E5
Gibbons Gr WV6 . . . . . . 255 F5
Gibbons Hill Rd DY3 . . . 266 D2
Gibbons Rd
  Sutton Coldfield B75 . 258 B3
  Wolverhampton WV6 . 255 F4
Gibraltar DY7 . . . . 278 C4
Gibson Cl ST16 . . . . . . 155 F5
Gibson Gr ST5 . . . . 55 D8
Gibson Pl ST3 . . . . 74 A2
Gibson Rd WV6 . . . . . . 254 E3
Gibson St ST6 . . . . 41 E2
Giddywell La WS15 . . . . 197 F1
Gideons Cl DY3 . . . . . . 271 D5
Giffard Cl ST19 . . . . . . 223 D6
Giffard RC Prim Sch The
  WV6 . . . . 255 F5
Giffard Pl ST14 . . . . 71 F6
Giffords Croft WS13 . . . 214 A1
Giggetty La WV5 . . . . . 269 F6
Gig Mill Prim Sch DY8 . . 279 E4
Gigmill Way DY8 . . . . . . 279 E4
Gilbanks Rd DY8 . . . . . 279 D7
Gilbern Dr ST8 . . . . 27 B5
Gilbert Cl B Kidsgrove ST7 . 26 A2
  Newport TF10 . . . . . . 168 D2
Gilbert La WV5 . . . . 270 B7
Gilbert Pl WS13 . . . . . . 214 C2
Gilbert St ST6 . . . . 41 C7
Gilbert Wlk WS13 . . . . . 214 C2
Gilbeys Cl B DY8 . . . . . . 275 E1
Gilchrist Ct ST6 . . . . . . 57 B6
Giles Cl ST10 . . . . 76 D3
Giles Ho ST13 . . . . 45 C8
Giles Rd WS13 . . . . 214 A3
Giles Wlk ST1 . . . . 57 E5
Gill Bank Rd Kidsgrove ST7 . 41 B8
  Stoke-on-T ST6 . . . . . 41 B7
Gillespie Cl WS13 . . . . . 215 D6
Gillette Cl ST18 . . . . . . 156 C5
Gilliard's Croft DE13 . . . 199 C6
Gilliat Wlk ST2 . . . . 58 C1
Gillingham Cres ST16 . . 155 B2
Gillway B79 . . . . 250 B8
Gill Wlk ST2 . . . . 282 A2
Gillyflower Cl ST6 . . . . . 42 D2
Gilman Ave ST2 . . . . . . 43 B2
Gilman Pl ST1 . . . . 282 C3
Gilman St ST1 . . . . 282 C2
Gilmour Cl DE13 . . . . . . 183 E1
Gilpin Cres WS3 . . . . . . 244 A4
Gilpins Croft WS6 . . . . . 226 D1
Gilwell Rd WS15 . . . . . . 211 F5
Gimson St ST4 . . . . 72 E6
Ginger Hill ST20 . . . . . . 171 D5
Ginger La ST21 . . . . . . 116 B3

Gipsy La Alstonefield DE6 . . 35 F4
  Cookley DY7,DY11 . . . . 280 A8
Girsby Cl ST4 . . . . 88 C5
Girton Rd WS11 . . . . . . 226 F8
Gisborne Cl DE13 . . . . . 182 A3
Gitana St ST1 . . . . 282 B3
Glades The WS9 . . . . . . 256 B7
Glade The Aldridge B74 . 256 E1
  Cannock WS11 . . . . . 209 C2
  Newcastle-u-L ST5 . . . 71 B2
  Stafford ST17 . . . . . . 175 B8
  Wolverhampton WV8 . 239 E1
Gladman Bsns Quarter
  WV9 . . . . 239 F3
Gladstone Dr DY8 . . . . . 279 D6
Gladstone Gr
  B Kingswinford DY6 . . 275 D8
  Biddulph ST8 . . . . . . 27 A5
Gladstone Pl ST4 . . . . . 71 F5
Gladstone Pottery Mus★
  ST3 . . . . 284 C3
Gladstone Prim Sch
  Longton ST3 . . . . . . 284 C5
  Stoke-on-T ST3 . . . . . 73 D5
Gladstone Rd
  Cannock WS12 . . . . . 210 E1
  Stourbridge DY8 . . . . 279 D6
Gladstone St Leek ST13 . 30 E5
  Stoke-on-T ST4 . . . . . 56 E1
Gladstone Terr ST10 . . . 94 E8
Gladstone Way ST18 . . . 156 C5
Gladwyn St ST2 . . . . . . 58 C4
Glaisher Dr ST3 . . . . . . 90 C7
Glamis Cl DE13 . . . . . . 166 D8
Glamis Dr ST5 . . . . 120 C5
Glamorgan Way DE11 . . 186 F1
Glandore Rd ST3 . . . . . . 73 F4
Glanville Dr B75 . . . . . . 258 A4
Glascote Ct B77 . . . . . . 250 E4
Glascote Heath Prim Sch
  B77 . . . . 251 A2
Glascote La B77 . . . . . . 261 F8
Glascote Rd
  Tamworth B77 . . . . . 251 B2
  Tamworth,Glascote Heath
    B77 . . . . 250 E3
Glasscroft Cotts WS7 . . 229 A5
Glassford Dr WV6 . . . . . 255 E6
Glasshouse Coll DY8 . . . 279 F7
Glass La WS15 . . . . 161 E2
Glass St ST1 . . . . 282 B3
Glastonbury Cl
  Stafford ST17 . . . . . . 175 D6
  Stoke-on-T ST9 . . . . . 43 D3
Glastonbury Cres WS3 . . 242 E2
Glastonbury Way WS3 . . 242 E1
Glebe Ave ST15 . . . . . . 155 D6
Glebe Cl Blythe Bridge ST11 . 91 A6
  Cheswardine TF9 . . . . 130 A8
  Doveridge DE6 . . . . . 127 B8
  Rolleston on D DE13 . . 147 A4
  Stoke-on-T ST4 . . . . . 72 C7
Glebedale Ct ST4 . . . . . 72 E5
Glebedale Rd ST4 . . . . . 72 E5
Glebefields ST20 . . . . . 151 D7
Glebe Gdns ST10 . . . . . 76 C2
Glebe La ST20 . . . . 171 E7
Glebelands
  Bobbington DY7 . . . . . 267 F2
  Stafford ST17 . . . . . . 174 F6
Glebe La DY8 . . . . 279 E4
Glebe Prim Sch ST4 . . . 72 F6
Glebe Rd Armitage WS15 . 198 C5
  Cheadle ST10 . . . . . . 76 C2
  Kingsley ST10 . . . . . . 61 E2
  Stoke-on-T ST4 . . . . . 72 B7
Glebe The
  Albrighton WV7 . . . . . 237 A5
  Norton Bridge ST15 . . 135 A8
Glebeville ST13 . . . . . . 30 E4
Gledhill Pk WS14 . . . . . 231 C5
Glencastle Way WS4 . . . 88 C5
Glen Cl WS11 . . . . 209 E5
Glencoe Dr WS11 . . . . . 210 A4
Glencoe St ST3 . . . . . . 284 B2
Glencroft Cl DE14 . . . . . 185 B7
Glen Ct Codsall WV8 . . . 239 A4
  Wolverhampton WV6 . 255 F5
Glendale Cl WV3 . . . . . 265 C8
Glendale Ct
  Newcastle-u-L ST5 . . . 71 C2
  Tamworth B77 . . . . . 262 D6
Glendale Dr WV5 . . . . . 270 A6
Glendale Gdns WS11 . . . 210 A4
Glendale St ST6 . . . . . . 57 A7
Glendawn Cl II WS11 . . . 210 A3
Glendene Rd WS12 . . . . 210 D6
Glendon Ct B TF9 . . . . . 112 A8
Glendower Cl ST20 . . . . 171 C6
Glendower Rd WS9 . . . . 245 B1
Glendue Gr ST4 . . . . . . 88 C6
Gleneagles Cres ST1 . . . 57 E6
Gleneagles Dr
  Stafford ST16 . . . . . . 156 C3
  Stretton DE13 . . . . . 147 C1
Gleneagles Rd
  Perton WV6 . . . . 254 D5
  Walsall WS3 . . . . 242 F3
Gleneagles B79 . . . . . . 251 B5
Glenfield Rise DE13 . . . 166 B7
Glenfield B77 . . . . 250 C1
Glenfield Way ST2 . . . . 73 E7
Glenfield WV8 . . . . 239 E2
Glengarry Gdns WV3 . . . 255 F1
Glenhaven WS15 . . . . . 178 C2

Glenmore Ave WS7 . . . . 229 A6
Glenmore Cl WV3 . . . . . 265 E7
Glen Park Rd DY3 . . . . . 271 D2
Glen Rd Dudley DY3 . . . 271 E6
  Stourbridge DY8 . . . . 279 F3
Glen Rise DE13 . . . . . . 166 A7
Glenroyd Ave ST2 . . . . . 58 A1
Glenroyd Wlk ST2 . . . . . 58 C1
Glensyl Way DE14 . . . . 166 E4
Glen The B ST15 . . . . . 120 A7
Glenthorne Cl ST17 . . . 175 D5
Glenthorne Dr WS6 . . . . 226 E3
Glenthorne Ho WS6 . . . 226 D2
Glenthorne Prim Sch
  WS6 . . . . 226 E3
Glenville Ave CV9 . . . . . 262 C1
Glenwood Cl Longton ST3 . 284 B4
  Newcastle-u-L ST5 . . . 55 C3
Glenwood Gdns ST7 . . . 262 B6
Glenwood Rise WS9 . . . 245 D3
Globe Ave ST17 . . . . . . 174 F6
Globe St ST6 . . . . 56 E8
Gloucester Cl WS13 . . . 214 B3
Gloucester Grange ST5 . . 71 C5
Gloucester Rd ST7 . . . . 26 A3
Gloucester Way
  Burton u T DE15 . . . . 167 B1
  Cannock WS11 . . . . . 210 B1
Glovers Cl WS12 . . . . . . 210 F3
Glover St Cannock WS12 . 210 F3
  Hanley ST1 . . . . 282 C4
  Stafford ST16 . . . . . 285 A4
Glyme Dr WV6 . . . . 255 E5
Glyndebourne B79 . . . . 249 D7
Glynne Ave DY6 . . . . . . 275 D5
Glynne Prim Sch DY6 . . 275 D5
Glyn Pl ST6 . . . . 41 F3
Gnosall Rd
  Gnosall,Knightley Dale
    ST20 . . . . 152 B3
  Gnosall TF10 . . . . . 170 D2
Goddard St ST3 . . . . . . 284 D4
Godfrey Rd ST2 . . . . . . 58 B3
Godleybarn La ST10 . . . 75 E6
Godley La ST10 . . . . . . 75 D5
Godolphin B79 . . . . 249 D7
Gofton B77 . . . . 262 A8
Golborn Ave ST3 . . . . . . 90 A4
Golborn Cl ST3 . . . . 90 B4
Goldcrest B77 . . . . 262 A6
Goldcrest Way ST8 . . . . 27 E8
Golden Cl WS15 . . . . . . 196 D7
Golden Hill CW2 . . . . . . 37 E3
Goldenhill Prim Sch ST6 . 41 C7
Goldenhill Rd ST4 . . . . . 284 B5
Goldenhill St Joseph's RC
  Prim Sch ST6 . . . . . . 41 D7
Goldfinch Rd B ST7 . . . . 26 E1
Goldfinch View TF9 . . . . 99 C3
Goldhurst DR ST10 . . . . 92 F2
Golding Cres DE14 . . . . 166 F6
Goldsborough B77 . . . . 251 A1
Goldsmith Pl
  Longton ST3 . . . . . . 284 D4
  Tamworth B79 . . . . . 250 A7
Gold St ST3 . . . . 284 B3
Goldthorn Ave WV4 . . . . 266 B6
Goldthorn Cres WV4 . . . 266 A6
Goldthorne Ave WS11 . . 209 C6
Goldthorn Hill WV2,WV4 . 266 C6
Goldthorn Park Prim Sch
  WV4 . . . . 266 D5
Goldthorn Rd WV2,WV3 . 266 B6
Golf Links Cl ST6 . . . . . . 41 C7
Goms Mill Ct ST3 . . . . . 284 B2
Goms Mill Rd ST3 . . . . . 284 A2
Goodfellow St ST6 . . . . 41 D4
Goodill Cl ST15 . . . . . . 119 F5
Goodman St ST1 . . . . . . 282 C3
Goodrich Ave WV6 . . . . 255 A3
Goodson St ST1 . . . . . . 282 C3
Goods Station La ST19 . . 192 E2
Goodwick Cl ST4 . . . . . . 88 C5
Goodwin Ave ST5 . . . . . 283 B4
Goodwin Rd ST3 . . . . . . 74 B2
Goodwood Ave ST10 . . . 76 F3
Goodwood Cl
  Cannock WS12 . . . . . 211 A5
  Lichfield WS14 . . . . . 231 D7
  Stretton DE13 . . . . . 147 C1
Goodwood Pl ST4 . . . . . 88 B7
Goosefield Cl TF9 . . . . . 97 B1
Goose La WS15 . . . . . . 160 F5
Goosemoor Gr B ST3 . . . 90 A7
Goose St ST5 . . . . 283 B2
Goostry Cl B77 . . . . 250 D5
Goostry Rd B77 . . . . . . 250 D5
Gordale Cl CW12 . . . . . . 6 A5
Gordon Ave Cheadle ST10 . 76 B3
  Stafford ST16 . . . . . 155 C7
  Stoke-on-T ST6 . . . . . 57 C7
  Wolverhampton WV4 . 266 D8
Gordon Banks Dr ST4 . . 72 C3
Gordon Cl DE13 . . . . . . 30 C4
Gordon Cres ST1 . . . . . . 57 E7
Gordon Ct ST5 . . . . 55 E3
Gordon Rd ST6 . . . . 41 C6
Gordon St
  B Wolverhampton WV2 . 266 D8
  Burton u T DE14 . . . . 166 C4
  Newcastle-u-L ST5 . . . 55 E3
  Stoke-on-T ST4 . . . . . 42 B1

Gorse La Astbury CW12 . . 15 D5
  Church Eaton ST19 . . 190 E2
  Fradley WS13 . . . . . . 215 A7
  Gnosall ST20,ST21 . . 152 A7
  Lichfield WS14 . . . . . 231 E6
  Rugeley WS15 . . . . . 196 C5
  Wombourne WV5 . . . 269 B6
Gorsemoor Prim Sch
  WS12 . . . . 210 D1
Gorsemoor Rd WS12 . . . 210 D1
Gorsemoor Way WV11 . . 242 B3
Gorse Rd WS15 . . . . . . 196 F6
Gorse Rd ST4 . . . . 72 E4
Gorseway ST7 . . . . 229 B5
Gorse Way WS12 . . . . . 210 C8
Gorsey Bank ST6 . . . . . 42 E6
Gorsey La Cannock WS11 . 209 C6
  Great Wyrley WS6 . . . 226 F1
  Netherseal DE12 . . . 219 F8
  Norton Canes WS3 . . 227 E1
Gorsley Dale ST17 . . . . 175 C6
Gorstey Lea WS7 . . . . . 229 C7
Gorsty Bank WS14 . . . . 231 E8
Gorsty Hayes WV8 . . . . 238 F3
Gorsty Hill Cl CW2 . . . . 37 F2
Gorsty Hill Rd ST10 . . . . 92 E5
Gorsty La ST18 . . . . . . 154 B3
Gorsy Bank Rd B77 . . . . 261 F5
Gorsy La
  Cotes Heath ST21 . . . 102 C5
  Weston Jones TF10 . . 150 A3
Gort Rd ST5 . . . . 55 F4
Gosberryhole La CW12 . . . 7 A2
Goscote Ind Est WS3 . . 243 E1
Goscote Rd WS3 . . . . . . 243 E1
Goscote Rd WS3 . . . . . . 244 A1
Gosforth Gr ST3 . . . . . . 90 C7
Gospel Ash Rd DY7 . . . . 268 D2
Gospel End Rd DY3 . . . . 271 B8
Gospel End St DY3 . . . . 271 D8
Gothersley La DY7 . . . . . 274 D2
Gough Cl ST16 . . . . 155 C8
Gough Side DE14 . . . . . 166 D2
Gould Firm La WS9 . . . . 256 E6
Govan Rd ST4 . . . . 72 F8
Gowan Ave ST6 . . . . . . 42 A4
Gower Ave DY6 . . . . . . 275 F4
Gower Rd Sedgley DY3 . . 271 B8
  Stone ST15 . . . . 120 B7
Gower St Longton ST3 . . 284 C3
  Newcastle-u-L ST5 . . . 283 C3
  Wolverhampton WV2 . 266 E8
Gowland Dr WS11 . . . . . 209 B1
Goya ST WS11 . . . . 210 D2
Grace Moore Ct WS11 . . 209 F4
Grace St ST13 . . . . 30 C6
Gradbach Mill★ SK17 . . . 2 A1
Graffam Gr ST10 . . . . . 76 F4
Grafton Ave ST6 . . . . . . 42 B1
Grafton Ct B WV6 . . . . . 255 F4
Grafton Gdns DY3 . . . . . 271 B3
Grafton Ho WV4 . . . . . . 266 E5
Grafton Inf Sch ST3 . . . 284 C4
Grafton Rd
  Burton u T DE15 . . . . 167 B1
  Longton ST3 . . . . . . 284 C4
Grafton St ST1 . . . . 282 C3
Graham Cl DE14 . . . . . . 185 C7
Graham Ho B74 . . . . . . 256 F2
Graham Rd DY6,DY8 . . . 275 D4
Graham St ST2 . . . . 58 A3
Grainger St ST1 . . . . . . 209 D2
Graiseley Hill WV2 . . . . 266 C8
Graiseley Prim Sch WV2 . 266 C8
Graiseley Row WV2 . . . . 266 C8
Granary Cl Cannock WS12 . 210 B5
  Kingswinford DY6 . . . 275 D8
Granary Rd WV8 . . . . . . 239 E1
Granary The WS9 . . . . . 256 B6
Granby Wlk ST4 . . . . . . 71 F6
Granchester Cl ST3 . . . . 90 B6
Grange Ave Aldridge WS9 . 245 A3
  Burntwood WS7 . . . . 229 B7
  Penkridge ST19 . . . . 207 C2
  Sutton Coldfield B75 . 258 C3
Grange Cl
  Burton u T DE14 . . . . 166 B4
  Ellenhall ST21 . . . . . 134 A1
  Gorstyhill CW2 . . . . . 37 F3
  Tamworth B77 . . . . . 261 C8
Grange Cotts ST19 . . . . 207 D7
Grange Court TF10 . . . . 158 C8
Grange Cres ST19 . . . . 207 D7
Grange Ct Biddulph ST8 . 16 D2
  Burslem ST6 . . . . . . 57 A7
  Egginton DE65 . . . . . 148 B5
  Newcastle-u-L ST5 . . . 56 D5
Grange Dr WS11 . . . . . . 209 D2
Grangefield Cl
  Cheddleton ST13 . . . . 45 D4
  Wolverhampton WV8 . 239 F1
Grangefields ST8 . . . . . 16 E3
Grange Gdns WS15 . . . . 197 C2
Grange Hill ST8 . . . . . . 16 E3
Grange Inf Sch DE14 . . . 166 B4
Grange La
  B Kingswinford DY6 . . 275 F4
  Lichfield WS13 . . . . . 213 F2
  Newcastle-u-L ST5 . . . 56 D4
  Sutton Coldfield B75 . 258 C3
Grange Park Dr ST8 . . . . 16 E3
Grange Prim Sch ST3 . . 90 A7
Grange Rd Biddulph ST8 . 16 E4
  Burntwood WS7 . . . . 229 A5
  Cheddleton ST13 . . . . 45 C4

Grange Rd *continued*
Meir ST3 90 A6
Norton Canes WS11 228 B6
Penkridge ST19 207 E8
Stone ST15 120 C7
Swadlincote DE11 186 E5
Uttoxeter ST14 111 A1
Wolverhampton,Blakenhall WV2 266 B6
Wolverhampton,Tettenhall WV6 255 C4
Woodseaves ST20 151 F5
Grange St Burslem ST6 57 B6
Burton u T DE14 166 B3
Grange The
Burton u T DE14 166 B3
King's Bromley DE13 199 D6
Longdon WS15 197 C2
Meir ST3 74 A2
Stafford ST18 174 C5
Wombourne WV5 270 A7
Grangewood Ave ST3 89 F6
Grangewood Rd ST3 74 A1
Granstone Cl ST6 42 A7
Grant Cl DY6 275 D8
Grantham Pl ST2 58 A6
Grantley Cl ST3 73 A1
Grantley Cres DY6 275 C7
Grantown Gr WS3 243 A4
Grant St ST4 72 C7
Grants Yd DE14 166 C3
Granville Ave
Newcastle-u-L ST5 283 C3
Newport TF10 168 F2
Stoke-on-T ST1 57 D7
Granville Cl
3 Wolverhampton WV2 266 D8
Newport TF10 168 F2
Granville Dr DY6 275 F5
Granville Rd Bucknall ST2 58 B5
Newport TF10 168 F2
Granville Sq 3 ST15 105 A1
Granville St WV2 266 D8
Granville B77 250 F1
Granville Terr ST15 105 A1
Granville Villas TF10 168 F2
Grasmere Ave
Aldridge B74 257 A2
Newcastle-u-L ST5 71 B4
Perton WV6 254 F4
Grasmere Cl
Burton u T DE15 167 B1
Kingswinford DY6 275 B7
Wolverhampton,Tettenhall WV6 255 E8
Grasmere Pl WS11 209 E5
Grasmere Terr ST6 42 A3
Grassholme B77 262 A8
Grassmere Ct WS6 226 D3
Grassmere Dr DY8 279 F3
Grassmere Hollow ST16 154 F5
Grassygreen La ST7 39 E1
Grassy La WV10,WV11 241 B1
Gratley Croft WS12 209 C4
Gratton La ST9 29 A3
Gratton Rd ST2 58 D3
Gravel Hill WV5 270 B6
Gravel La
Huntington WS12 209 C5
Stafford ST17 174 F4
Gravelly Bank ST3 89 F7
Gravelly Dr TF10 168 E2
Gravelly Hill TF9 100 A5
Gravelly La WS9 245 F3
Gravenhunger La CW3 83 D8
Graycar Bsns Pk DE13 184 B1
Grayling Gr ST6 42 B3
Grayling B77 261 D6
Grayling Willows CW3 68 E6
Gray Rd WS12 209 F6
Gray's Cl ST7 26 B7
Grayshott Rd ST6 41 E5
Grayston Ave B77 250 E4
Gray Wlk ST17 174 C7
Grazier Ave B77 261 C8
Grazings The DY7 278 C3
Greasley Rd ST2 58 B6
Greatbatch Ave ST4 71 F7
Great Charles St WS8 244 F8
Great Checkhill Rd DY7 274 C4
Great Fenton Bsns Pk ST4 72 D4
Great Furlong DE13 201 A2
Great Hales St TF9 97 D1
Greatmead B77 250 C1
Great Moor Rd
Nurton WV6 254 A3
Pattingham WV6 253 F2
Greatoak Rd ST7 39 F4
Great Wood Com Prim Sch ST10 92 E3
Great Wood Rd ST10 92 E4
Great Wyrley High Sch WS6 226 F3
Greaves La DE6,DE13 144 E4
Greenacre Cl B77 251 B5
Greenacre Dr WV8 239 B2
Greenacre ST18 139 D1
Greenacres Ave
Blythe Bridge ST11 90 C8
Wolverhampton WV10 241 B2
Greenacres Cl WS9 256 E2
Greenacres WV9 224 B3
Greenacres Dr ST14 111 A2
Greenacres Prim Sch B77 251 B5
Greenacres
Rugeley WS15 196 E7
Sedgley DY3 266 B1
Greenacres Way TF10 168 D3
Greenacres WV6 255 B5
Green Acres WV5 269 F5
Greenacre The DE6 81 F7
Greenaway Ct WV10 241 C7
Greenbank Gdns DY8 275 E2
Greenbank Rd
Newcastle-u-L ST5 56 C3
Stoke-on-T ST6 42 A3
Green Barn Ct ST18 138 D2
Green Barns La WS14 258 C8
Greenbirches Ind Est ST6 41 D4
Green Brook Ct ST5 56 B3
Green Cl Barlaston ST12 88 D1
Blythe Bridge ST11 90 D7
Pattingham WV6 253 C2
Stone ST15 119 F7
Greencroft
Kingswinford DY6 275 D4
Lichfield WS13 214 A2
Green Croft ST15 118 F6
Green Ct 8 WS13 231 B7
Greendale Cotts ST10 77 E4
Greendale Dr ST5 40 D1
Greendale La ST10 77 D4
Greendock St ST3 284 B3
Greenfield Ave
Armitage WS15 198 A4
Brown Edge ST6 43 C7
Stourbridge DY8 279 F5
Greenfield ST8 27 D6
Greenfield Bldgs WV5 270 A7
Greenfield Cl ST6 43 C7
Greenfield Cres ST10 76 E4
Greenfield Dr ST14 126 A8
Greenfield La WV10 240 E5
Greenfield Pl ST6 43 C7
Greenfield Prim Sch DY8 279 F5
Greenfield Rd Endon ST9 43 E8
Stafford ST17 175 D5
Stoke-on-T ST6 41 E5
Greenfields Aldridge WS9 256 B7
Cannock WS11 209 E2
Denstone ST14 95 D6
Greenfields Dr WS15 178 D1
Greenfields ST20 171 E7
Greenfields La TF9 97 B2
Greenfields Rd
Hixon ST18 139 C1
Kingswinford DY6 275 E6
Kinver DY7 277 C3
Walsall WS4 244 D2
Wombourne WV5 270 A5
Greenfield View DY3 271 B7
Greenfinch Cl ST14 126 C6
Greengates St ST6 41 E4
Greengate St ST16 285 B3
Green Gore La ST17 175 F7
Greenhall Com Specl Sch ST16 155 B7
Greenhead St ST6 56 F8
Greenheart B77 251 A4
Green Heath Rd WS12 210 A7
Greenhill Cl B77 261 C5
Greenhill Ct WV5 270 B5
Greenhill Gdns WV5 270 B5
Greenhill La ST19 205 C7
Greenhill WS13 231 C8
Greenhill Mews WS13 231 C8
Greenhill Rd Dudley DY3 271 E5
Stoke-on-T ST6 42 E6
Greenhill Way WS9 245 B1
Greenhill WV5 270 B6
Greenhough Rd WS13 231 A8
Green La Aldridge WS9 256 E5
Alsop en le D DE6 36 C2
Ashley TF9 100 D5
Birchmoor B77,B78 262 D7
Blythe Bridge ST11 91 A6
Brownhills WS8 229 B2
Burntwood WS7 212 D1
Burton u T DE13 166 B7
Cannock WS11 226 E6
Chorley WS13 212 C3
Clifton Campville DE12 218 B7
Clifton DE6 81 E7
Dudley DY3 271 F5
Eccleshall ST21 133 E6
Hamstall Ridware WS15 181 B3
Kingswinford DY6 275 D7
Lichfield WS14 230 D2
Marchington ST14 128 A2
Greenland Cl DY6 275 E8
Greenlands WV5 269 F7
Green Lane Venture Ctr WS11 226 E6
Green La Newport TF10 168 E4
Roston DE6 96 F8
Rudyard ST13 18 F2
Rugeley WS15 178 D1
Stafford ST18 174 C4
Sutton TF10 150 E1
Tamworth B77 262 C6
Tutbury DE13 146 C5
Walsall,High Heath WS4, WS9 244 D3
Walsall,Pelsall WS3 244 A4
Waterhouses DE6 65 A7
Whitgreave ST18 135 F7
Wolverhampton WV6 255 F7
Greenlea Cl ST4 88 C5
Green Lea Fst Sch ST18 122 D4
Greenlea B77 262 A8
Greenleighs DY3 266 D3
Greenline Bsns Pk DE14 166 B3
Greenly Rd WV4 266 D5
Green Mdws 2 WS12 210 C1
Green Meadow Cl WV5 269 E5
Greenmeadow Gr ST9 43 E6
Greenmeadows Rd CW3 68 E7
Greenmoor Ave ST6 42 A8
Green Oak Rd WV8 239 B2
Greenock Cl ST5 70 F7
Green Pk Checkley ST10 109 C8
Eccleshall ST21 133 F6
Fulford ST11 90 E1
Green Rd Stoke-on-T ST4 71 E3
Weston ST18 138 D2
Green Rock La WS3 243 D1
Green Rock Prim Sch WS3 243 E1
Greensforge La
Kinver DY7 274 E3
Stourton DY7 278 D8
Greenside Ave ST9 43 C3
Greenside Cl ST7 41 A7
Greenside
Newcastle-u-L ST5 283 A3
Yarnfield ST15 118 F6
Greens Ind Est WS12 210 C7
Green Slade Gr WS12 210 C7
Greenslade Rd DY3 266 B2
Green's La ST2 58 E3
Greensleeves B74 257 F1
Greensmith Cl DE15 167 C3
Greensome Cl ST16 155 A4
Greensome Cres ST16 155 A5
Greensome Ct ST16 155 A4
Greensome La ST16 155 A5
Green St DE14 166 D1
Greens The WV6 254 E3
Green St DY8 279 F5
Green The Aldridge WS9 256 C6
Armitage WS15 198 C5
Barton-u-N DE13 183 C1
Brocton,Milford ST17 176 C7
Brocton ST17 176 B3
Brown Edge ST6 43 B7
Caverswall ST11 74 D3
Cheadle ST10 76 B2
Chebsey ST21 134 E6
Fazeley B78 249 E2
Fulford ST11 90 E1
Hagley DY9 281 F4
Kingsley ST10 61 D2
Lawton-gate ST7 25 A4
Newcastle-u-L ST5 71 C3
Rugeley WS15 197 A6
Seckington B79 236 A3
Stourbridge DY8 275 D2
Stretton DE13 147 E1
Tamworth B77 251 B5
Walsall WS3 243 B1
Weston ST18 138 D2
Whittington WS14 232 E5
Wood End B78 262 C4
Woodseaves ST20 151 C8
Greenvale Cl DE15 185 F8
Green Valley Dr DE13 166 A8
Green View TF11 203 F8
Green Way WS9 245 B2
Greenway Ave
2 Stourbridge DY8 275 E1
Stoke-on-T ST6 42 B2
Stone ST15 120 B6
Greenway Bank ST8 27 D3
Greenway Bank Ctry Pk★ ST8 27 E3
Greenway Bank ST2 43 C2
Greenway
Burton u T DE15 167 A4
Eccleshall ST21 133 E6
Greenway Gdns
Pattingham WV6 253 C2
Sedgley DY3 266 E1
Greenway Hall Rd ST2, ST9 43 D3
Greenway Pl ST2 58 B7
Greenway Rd ST8 16 E2
Greenways Audley ST7 39 F2
Chorley WS13 212 E3
Greenways Dr ST10 76 D4
Greenway DY3 266 E1
Greenways ST19 208 A8
Greenways Prim Sch ST9 43 C4
Greenways Stafford ST18 174 C5
Stourbridge DY8 275 C1
Greenway ST16 156 A3
Greenways The 1 ST2 43 C3
Greenway ST3 72 E3
Greenway The
Hagley DY9 281 F5
Newcastle-u-L ST5 56 C3
Pattingham WV6 253 C2
Greenway ST4 87 E7
Green Way ST14 126 B8
Greenwich Ave DE11 186 E1
Greenwood Ave ST4 71 E2
Greenwood Dr WS14 231 B6
Greenwood Gr ST17 174 C7
Greenwood Pk
Aldridge WS9 245 C2
Cannock WS12 210 B8
Greenwood Rd
Aldridge WS9 245 B2
Burton u T DE15 185 E8
Forsbrook ST11 91 A8
Greenwoods The DY8 279 E5
Gregory La ST20 150 D6
Gregory Rd
Burntwood WS7 229 E7
Stourbridge DY8 279 D5
Gregorys Gn WV9 224 B3
Gregory St ST3 284 B3
Gregson Cl 5 ST3 73 A3
Greig Ct WS11 210 C2
Grenadier Cl ST4 88 C4
Grendon Gdns WV3 265 D6
Grendon Gn ST2 58 C2
Grenfell Rd WS3 243 D3
Grenville Cl ST14 110 F1
Grenville Rd DY1 271 E1
Gresham Rd WS11 209 F3
Gresley Cl B74 258 A4
Gresley Row WS13 231 C8
Gresley B77 250 F1
Gresley Way ST7 39 F2
Gresley Wood Rd DE11 186 F2
Gresty St ST4 72 A7
Gretton Ave DE13 147 E1
Greville Cl ST19 207 F8
Greville St ST1 282 C4
Greyfriars Bsns Pk ST16 285 A4
Greyfriars Cl DY1 271 E3
Greyfriars Ct 2 ST16 155 D5
Greyfriars Dr B79 249 E6
Grey Friars' Pl ST16 285 A4
Greyfriars Rd ST2 58 A5
Grey Friars ST16 155 D5
Grey Friars Way ST16 155 D5
Greyhound Ct CW3 68 E6
Greyhound La
Lower Penn WV4 264 E5
Stourbridge DY8 279 D2
Greyhound Way ST1,ST6 57 A5
Greylarch La ST17 175 C7
Greysan Ave ST7 41 F8
Greysbrooke Prim Sch WS14 247 A6
Greysbrooke WS14 247 A5
Greystoke Dr DY6 275 D6
Greyswood Rd ST4 71 E3
Grice Rd ST4 71 E8
Griffin Cl Burntwood WS7 228 E8
Norton in H TF9 82 C2
Griffin St ST3 284 B3
Griffithgreen WV5 267 D7
Griffiths Dr
Wolverhampton WV11 242 A1
Wombourne WV5 270 A5
Griffiths Way ST15 120 D6
Grimley Way WS11 209 F4
Grindcobbe Gr WS15 178 D3
Grindley Hill Ct ST4 71 E6
Grindley La
Kingstone ST18 140 E6
Meir ST3,ST11 90 B6
Grindley Pl ST4 71 F6
Grindsbrook B77 262 A8
Grisedale Cl 5 ST3 90 A7
Grissom Cl ST16 156 A5
Gristhorpe Way ST2 58 D1
Gritton St ST6 41 D2
Grizedale Cl DE15 167 B1
Grocott Cl ST19 192 E2
Grosvenor Ave
Aldridge B74 256 F1
Stoke-on-T ST4 71 F4
Grosvenor Cl
Lichfield WS14 231 D6
Penkridge ST19 192 F1
Stoke-on-T ST9 43 F8
Sutton Coldfield B75 258 C1
Wolverhampton WV10 240 D2
Grosvenor Cres WV10 240 D2
Grosvenor Ct Dudley DY3 271 D2
Shenstone WS14 246 F6
Wolverhampton,Tettenhall WV6 255 A3
Grosvenor Gdns ST5 283 C2
Grosvenor Pk WV4 265 F5
Grosvenor Pl
Newcastle-u-L ST5 56 C5
Stoke-on-T ST6 41 D4
Grosvenor Rd
Dudley DY3 271 D2
Longton ST3 73 F1
Market Drayton TF9 97 D2
Newcastle-u-L ST5 283 C2
Wolverhampton,Bushbury WV10 240 D2
Wolverhampton,Ettingshall Park WV4 266 E3
Grosvenor Road S DY3 271 D2
Grosvenor St Leek ST13 30 F5
Longton ST3 284 B3
Grosvenor Way ST17 175 F6
Grotto La WV6 255 E5
Grotto Rd TF9 112 B8
Groundhollow ST10 94 A3
Grounds Dr B74 257 F3
Grounds Rd B74 257 F3
Grove Ave Kidsgrove ST7 25 E1
Lawton-gate ST7 25 A4
Stoke-on-T ST4 72 E4
Talke ST7 40 E8
Grovebank Rd ST4 71 E3
Grove Cl WS11 227 F5
Grove Cres Walsall WS3 243 F3
Woore CW3 83 C8
Grove Gdns TF9 97 D1
Grove Jun Sch ST1 282 C4
Grove La DE6 127 E8
Grovelands Cres WV10 240 D3
Grove La
Norton Canes WS3 227 E1
Wolverhampton WV6 255 B2
Grovenor Ct TF9 97 D2
Grove Park Ave ST7 25 A4
Grove Pk DY6 275 C8
Grove Pl ST1 282 A1
Grove Prim Sch The ST17 174 D8
Grove Prim Sch WV2 266 E8
Grove Rd Stoke-on-T ST4 72 D4
Stone ST15 119 F8
Grove Road Ind Est ST4 72 D4
Grove Sch The TF9 97 D1
Groveside Way WS3 244 A5
Grove St Burslem ST6 57 A6
Leek ST13 30 D6
Newcastle-u-L ST5 55 E3
Wolverhampton WV2 266 D8
Grove Terr 11 ST13 30 D6
Grove The
Blythe Bridge ST11 90 E6
Burntwood WS7 228 D8
Lawton-gate ST7 25 A4
Little Aston B74 257 D6
Newcastle-u-L ST5 71 B6
Stoke-on-T ST6 42 B2
Stone ST15 120 C3
Tatenhill DE13 184 A8
Wolverhampton,Lanesfield WV4 266 E5
Grub St ST20 151 A6
Grunmore Dr DE13 147 E2
Guernsey Cl CW12 6 A1
Guernsey Dr ST5 70 E3
Guernsey Wlk 2 ST3 73 A3
Guildford St ST4 72 C8
Guildhall Sh Ctr ST16 285 B3
Guild La TF10 169 F8
Guild St DE14 166 D3
Guinevere Ave DE13 147 E2
Gullet The B78 251 F1
Gullick Way WS7 228 D8
Gun Battery La ST8 28 A8
Gunby Hill DE12 219 F8
Gunnell Cl Hanley ST1 282 C1
Stafford ST16 155 C2
Gunn St ST8 27 C8
Gunstone La WV8 238 F5
Gurnard Cl WV12 242 B1
Gurnard B77 261 D6
Guthrum Cl WV6 254 F5
Guy's Almshouses B79 250 B5
Guys Cl B79 249 F7
Guy's La DY3 271 B2
Guy St ST2 58 B4
Gwendoline Way WS9 245 B4
Gwenys Cres ST3 72 E4
Gwyn Ave ST8 27 D5
Gypsum Way DE6 144 D6

H

Hackett Cl Longton ST3 284 D4
Wolverhampton WV14 266 F1
Hackford Rd WV4 266 F4
Hackwood Cl ST12 88 F4
Hadden Cl ST9 59 B2
Haddon Gr ST5 55 F6
Haddon La ST5 85 E1
Haddon Pl Bucknall ST2 58 C5
Stone ST15 120 D7
Haden Cl DY8 275 D2
Hadfield Gn ST6 42 D2
Hadleigh Cl ST5 71 B2
Hadleigh Rd ST2 58 B6
Hadley Dr CW2 37 E4
Hadley End DE13 181 E5
Hadley Park Sports Coll WS15 196 D8
Hadley St DE13 181 F3
Hadrians Cl B77 261 D8
Hadrian Way ST5 55 D5
Haggar St WV2 266 C6
Hagley Ct DY3 271 D3
Hagley Dr WS15 178 D1
Hagley Park Gdns WS15 196 D7
Hagley RC High Sch DY8 281 F6
Hagley Rd WS15 178 D1
Haig Cl WS11 210 A5
Haigh Cl ST13 45 D5
Haig Rd ST13 31 A7
Haig St ST3 73 D2
Hailes Park Cl WV2 266 E6
Hailsham Cl ST6 41 F5
Hainer Cl 6 ST17 175 A8
Hainult Cl DY8 275 D4
Halcyon Way DE14 166 B4
Hales Hall Rd ST10 76 F4
Hales Pl ST3 284 C1
Halesworth Cres ST5 71 B2
Halesworth Rd WV9 239 F2
Halford St B79 250 A5
Halfpenny Green Vineyard★ DY7 268 D6
Halfshire La DY10 281 B1
Halfway Pl ST5 55 E1
Halifax Cl ST3 90 C7
Halifax Rd WV7 220 F1
Haliford Ave ST1 57 D7
Haling Cl ST19 207 F8
Haling Rd ST19 192 F1
Hallahan Cl ST15 120 C6
Hallahan Gr ST4 72 A8
Hallam Rd ST14 110 F1
Hallams Row DE14 166 C4
Hallam St ST4 72 E6
Hall Ave ST13 31 A7
Hall Bank SK17 24 E5
Hallbridge Cl WS3 243 F2

Hall Cl Pattingham WV6... 253 C2
Stafford ST17 ....175 A7
Hallcourt Cl **3** WS11.. 226 E8
Hallcourt Cres **2** WS11. 226 E8
Hallcourt La WS11.... 226 E8
Hallcroft Cl TF10...... 168 E3
Hallcroft Gdns TF10.... 168 E3
Hallcroft Way WS9.... 256 C5
Halldearn Ave ST11.... 74 D3
Hall Dr Enville DY7 .... 273 C5
  Hanbury DE13 .... 145 A4
  Meir ST3 ....74 B4
Hall End Cl CV6 ...... 253 C2
Hall End La WV6 ....253 C2
Hallfarm Cl ST19...... 223 D6
Hall Farm Cl ST15 .... 139 C1
Hall Farm Cres ST18 .. 137 F4
Hallfarm Rd ST19 ..... 223 D6
Hallfield Gr ST6........ 41 E5
Hallfields Rd DE15 .... 186 C4
Hall Gdns ST14 .... 127 C2
Hall Green Ave DE13 .. 147 F2
Hall Grounds DE13 .... 147 A4
Hall Hill Dr ST2 .... 73 D8
Hallhill La WS15 ...... 161 A5
Hall La Brownhills WS9 . 244 A5
  Cotes Heath ST21 .... 102 D3
  Doveridge DE6 .... 127 B8
  Great Wyrley WS6 .... 227 A3
  Hammerwich WS7 .... 229 D4
  Hilderstone ST15 .... 106 F3
  Muckley Corner WS7,
    WS14 .... 229 F2
  Stanton DE6 .... 80 A7
  Swynnerton ST15..... 103 F3
  Walsall WS3........... 243 F3
  Wolverhampton WV14.. 266 F1
  Wootton DE6 .... 79 F7
Hall Mdw WS11 ...... 226 B6
Hall Orch Bramshall ST14. 125 C7
  Cheadle ST10.......... 76 D3
Hall Pl ST5 .... 56 D5
Hall Rd Armitage WS15 . 198 C5
  Marchington ST14 .... 127 E2
  Rolleston on D DE13 .. 146 F4
  Rolleston on D DE13 .. 147 A4
  Uttoxeter ST14 ...... 126 A8
Halls Rd Biddulph ST8 .. 16 C1
  Mow Cop ST7.......... 26 C7
Hall St Audley ST7 ..... 39 D2
  Burslem ST6 .... 56 F8
  Newcastle-u-L ST5..... 283 B3
  Sedgley DY3.......... 271 D8
Hall Yd ST10.......... 92 E4
Halston Rd WS7 ...... 229 B8
Halton Gn ST3 .... 88 E8
Haltonlea B77 .... 262 A8
Hambledon Cl WV9 ... 240 A2
Hamble Gr WV6...... 254 E4
Hamble Rd WV4 ...... 265 C6
Hamble B77 .... 250 D2
Hambleton Pl ST8..... 27 B5
Hamble Way ST2....... 58 D1
Hambridge Cl ST17 ... 174 D7
Hambro ST6 .... 42 B7
Hamelin St WS11 ..... 209 E3
Hames La B79 .... 236 D3
Hamil Dr ST13 .... 30 D6
Hamil Rd ST6.......... 42 A1
Hamilton Ave DY8.... 279 D6
Hamilton Cl
  Cannock WS12........ 210 F4
  Sedgley DY3........... 271 C8
  Stourbridge DY8 ..... 275 C2
Hamilton Ct ST5....... 71 C2
Hamilton Dr DY8...... 275 C2
Hamilton Fields DE15 . 167 A2
Hamilton Gdns WV10. 240 F3
Hamilton Ho WS3..... 243 C1
Hamilton Inf Sch ST1 .. 57 D6
Hamilton Lea WS11 ... 228 A6
Hamilton Rd
  Burton u T DE15...... 167 A2
  Longton ST3.......... 284 D2
Hamilton Rise ST2..... 43 B2
Hamilton St
  Stoke-on-T ST4 ...... 72 C5
  Walsall WS3........... 243 C1
Ham La DY6 .... 270 E1
Hamlet The WS11 .... 227 E5
Hamlett Pl ST6 .... 42 E3
Hammersley Hayes Rd
  ST10................. 76 E6
Hammersley St ST1 ... 57 E6
Hammerwich Ave ST2 . 57 F2
Hammerwich Hospl
  WS7 .... 229 B5
Hammerwich La WS7... 229 F3
Hammerwich Rd WS7.. 229 D5
Hammond Ave ST6.... 43 B7
Hammond Ho ST1 .... 282 C1
Hammond Rd ST5..... 55 E8
Hammonds Croft ST18. 158 C8
Hammoor Gr ST2...... 58 B2
Hamner Gn ST2....... 73 D8
Hampden Ho DE15.... 185 E6
Hamps Cl WS7........ 229 D7
Hampshire Cl
  Stoke-on-T ST9 ...... 43 F7
  Tamworth B78 .... 249 F2
Hampshire Cres ST3 .. 89 C8
Hampson Cl ST5 ..... 120 B8
Hampstead Gr ST4.... 88 C4
Hamps Valley Rd ST10. 48 F2
Hampton Cl
  Newport TF10 .... 169 A3
  Tamworth B79 .... 250 C7
Hampton Ct Leek ST13 ... 30 D5

Hampton Ct continued
  Rugeley WS15 .... 178 D3
  Wolverhampton WV10.. 241 B2
Hampton Dr
  Market Drayton TF9.... 97 B2
  Newport TF10 .... 169 A3
Hampton Gdns ST18 .. 156 D3
Hampton Gn WS11.... 226 E7
Hampton Gr Dunsley DY7. 278 C4
  Walsall WS3........... 244 A4
Hampton Rd WV10 ... 240 B1
Hampton St
  Cannock WS11........ 226 D7
  Hanley ST1.......... 282 C1
Hams Cl ST8........... 27 C7
Hanbridge Ave ST5 ... 56 A7
Hanbury Cres WV4.... 265 E6
Hanbury Hill DE13 ... 145 A5
Hanbury Rd
  Brownhills WS8 ...... 228 F2
  Norton Canes WS11... 227 F5
  Tamworth B77 .... 250 F4
Hanbury's Farm Com Prim
  Sch B77................ 250 D1
Hanchurch Cl ST15 ... 167 A4
Hanchurch Crossroad
  ST5................... 87 C8
Hanchurch Hills Circular
  Wlks★ ST4 .... 86 F4
Hanchurch La ST4 ..... 87 B7
Hancock St ST4........ 72 C7
Handel Ct WS11 ...... 210 C2
Handel Gr ST1........ 58 A6
Handel Wlk WS13 .... 214 C2
Hand La TF11 .... 187 D1
Handley Banks ST11 .. 74 E4
Handley Dr ST8 .... 27 B2
Handley Rd DE14..... 165 F3
Handley Sh Ctr The ST1. 282 B2
Handley St ST7 .... 27 A2
Handsacre Cl DE11.... 186 F3
Handsacre Cres WS15.. 198 C3
Handsacre Rd ST3 .... 284 D5
Hand St ST6............ 41 D4
Hangmans La B79 .... 236 A2
Hankins Heys La CW3 . 82 B8
Hanley Bsns Pk ST1... 282 B1
Hanley Rd ST6,ST1.... 57 D8
Hanlith B77............ 262 A8
Hannaford Way WS11. 209 F2
Hanover Ct
  Newcastle-u-L ST5..... 283 C3
  Tamworth B79 .... 249 E7
  Wolverhampton WV6... 255 C4
Hanover Ho
  6 Stourbridge DY8.... 279 F8
  Longton ST4.......... 73 B5
Hanover Pl WS11 ..... 209 E2
Hanover St Hanley ST1. 282 B3
  Newcastle-u-L ST5..... 283 C3
Hanson Man B74...... 258 A1
Hanyards La ST18 .... 156 F4
Harald Cl WV6........ 254 E5
Harber St ST3 .... 284 C3
Harbin Rd DE12...... 184 D1
Harborne Cres ST10... 76 E4
Harborne Rd ST10 ... 76 E4
Harborough Ct B74... 258 A2
Harborough Dr WS9 .. 256 B5
Harbourne Ct ST10... 76 E4
Harbury St DE13 ..... 166 A6
Harcourt Ave ST3 .... 73 F1
Harcourt Dr Dudley DY3. 271 D2
  Newport TF10 .... 169 A4
  Sutton Coldfield B74.. 257 F4
Harcourt Ho B79...... 250 A4
Harcourt Rd DE14.... 184 F8
Harcourt St ST1 ...... 282 A1
Harcourt Way ST16 ... 155 B7
Hardewick Cl ST9..... 59 B3
Hardie Ave WS15 .... 196 F1
Hardie Ct **2** WV4..... 266 F4
Hardie Gn WS11 ..... 209 F3
Hardinge St ST4 ...... 72 D6
Hardings Mdw ST1.... 25 F2
Hardingswood Rd ST7. 25 E2
Harding Terr ST4...... 72 A6
Hardman St ST2 ...... 43 A1
Hardon Rd WV4...... 266 F5
Hardwick Cl ST4 ..... 88 C4
Hardwick Ct Aldridge B74. 256 F2
  Tamworth B79 .... 250 C5
Hardwick Rd B74..... 257 A2
Hardy Cl Barton-u-N DE13. 201 E7
  Cheadle ST10.......... 76 C2
Hardy Rd ST17....... 174 B8
Hardy Sq WV2 .... 266 F6
Hardy St ST6 .... 41 D4
Harebell Cl
  Cannock WS12........ 210 D2
  Featherstone WV10... 241 A7
Harebell Gr ST7....... 26 F1
Harebell Rd B77 ..... 251 A4
Harecastle Ave ST7 .. 25 E1
Harecastle Bank ST15. 104 E3
Harecastle Ct ST7..... 40 E6
Haredene La
  Burton u T DE13...... 166 B8
  Stretton DE13 .... 147 B1
Hareshaw Gr ST6 ..... 42 A8
Hares La ST10......... 77 C3
Harewell Dr ST5...... 258 C1
Harewood Cl ST10 ... 76 D4
Harewood Est ST10... 76 B5

Harewood St ST6...... 41 D2
Hargate Rd DE15..... 167 C1
Hargreave Cl ST3 ..... 90 C7
Hargreaves Ct **5** ST13. 30 E5
Hargreaves La ST17.... 285 A1
Harington Dr ST3 ..... 73 E5
Harland Cl ST18 ..... 177 D8
Harland Rd B74....... 258 A3
Harlaxton St DE13.... 166 A6
Harlech Ave ST3 ...... 73 E1
Harlech Dr ST8 .... 27 C6
Harlech Way
  Burton u T DE13...... 166 D8
  Dudley DY1 .... 271 F2
Harlequin Dr ST6 ..... 42 C2
Harlestones Ho DY8.. 279 F7
Harley Cl Brownhills WS8. 245 A6
  Rugeley WS15 .... 196 F6
Harley La
  Abbots Bromley WS15.. 160 F7
  Beech ST4 .... 87 C1
Harley St ST1.......... 282 C2
Harley Thorn La ST4 ... 87 B3
Harman Dr WS13 .... 230 F6
Harmon Rd DY8...... 279 C5
Harmony Gn ST17..... 174 B8
Harney St WS15 ...... 178 D3
Harold St ST6.......... 42 C1
Harper Ave
  Burton u T DE13...... 166 C7
  Newcastle-u-L ST5..... 56 B4
Harper Ct DE13 ...... 166 C7
Harper St ST6 .... 56 E7
Harpfield Prim Sch ST4. 71 D8
Harpfield Rd ST4 ..... 71 E5
Harplands Hospl ST4... 71 D6
Harplow La ST4 .... 76 B1
Harptree Wlk ST4 .... 71 F2
Harpur-Crewe Cotts DE6. 35 D3
Harrier Cl ST3 .... 90 A6
Harringay Dr DY8 .... 279 E3
Harrington Ct ST13.... 30 E3
Harrington Rd WS13 .. 213 F1
Harriotts Hayes Rd WV7. 237 F6
Harriseahead La ST7... 26 D4
Harrison Cl
  Burton u T DE14...... 185 B8
  Cheslyn Hay WS6..... 226 D1
  Halmer End ST7....... 54 D7
  Walsall WS3........... 243 C1
Harrison Ct ST5........ 283 C1
Harrison Rd
  Cannock WS11........ 226 E7
  Stoke-on-T ST6 ...... 42 C3
  Sutton Coldfield B74.. 257 E5
  Walsall WS4........... 244 C2
Harrisons La ST19..... 207 E1
Harrison St
  Newcastle-u-L ST5..... 283 C2
  Walsall WS3........... 243 C1
Harrison Way ST13.... 45 D5
Harrison & Woodburn Cotts
  ST5................... 54 C3
Harris Rd ST16........ 156 B4
Harris St ST4 .... 72 A8
Harrogate Gr ST5 .... 54 F2
Harrop St ST1 .... 57 D6
Harrop Way DY8 ..... 279 E8
Harrots La SK17...... 24 D6
Harrowby Ct WV10... 240 B3
Harrowby Dr ST5 .... 70 F4
Harrowby Rd Meir ST3. 90 A8
  Wolverhampton WV10.. 240 C2
Harrowby St ST16..... 156 A3
Harrow Ct B74......... 257 F2
Harrow Dr DE14 ..... 185 C8
Harrow Pl ST15 ...... 120 D7
Harrow Rd DY6 ...... 270 D1
Harrows Mobile Home Pk
  The WV9.............. 224 C4
Hart Ct ST5.......... 283 B3
Hartill Rd WV4....... 265 D3
Hartill St ST4 .... 72 C8
Hartington CE Prim Sch
  SK17................. 24 D5
Hartington Hall Youth
  Hostel★ SK17........ 24 E5
Hartington Dr Leek ST13. 30 E5
  Newcastle-u-L ST5..... 56 B5
Hartland Ave
  Stafford ST17 .... 175 E8
  Stoke-on-T ST6 ...... 42 C3
Hartlands Rd ST21.... 133 E4
Hartlebury Cl WS11 .. 210 C2
Hartleyburn B77 ..... 262 A8
Hartley Dr Aldridge WS9. 256 B4
  Stone ST15 .... 104 F1
Hartley Gdns CW12 .. 16 B8
Hartsbourne Way ST17. 175 C7
Hartshill Rd ST4...... 71 F8
Hartslade WS14....... 231 E6
Hartwell Gr ST16..... 155 A7
Hartwell La
  Great Wyrley WS6 .... 227 A3
  Hartwell ST15 .... 89 C2
Hartwell St ST5 ...... 70 F4
Hartwell Rd ST3 ..... 90 A8
Hartwood Cl TF10.... 168 E5
Hartwood Cres WV3 .. 265 F5
Harvard Cl DY1 ...... 271 F4
Harvest Cl DY3........ 271 C5
Harvesters Ct WS9 ... 256 E2
Harvesters Wlk WV8 . 239 E1
Harvest Fields Way
  Sutton Coldfield B75.. 258 A4
  Sutton Coldfield B75.. 258 E3
Harvey Dr B75........ 258 C2

Harvey Pl ST14 ...... 111 B1
Harvey Rd Armitage WS15. 198 C4
  Burton u T DE14...... 185 A8
  Congleton CW12 ..... 6 A5
  Meir ST3 .... 74 B2
Harvine Wlk DY8..... 279 E3
Harwell Cl B79........ 250 C7
Harwin Cl WV6 ...... 255 F7
Harwood Ave DE14... 184 F8
Harwood Dr B77 ..... 261 D4
Harwood Rd WS13 .. 214 B3
Haslemere Ave ST2 .. 43 B1
Haslington Cl ST5.... 40 D1
Hassall St ST1 .... 282 C2
Hassam Ave ST5 ..... 283 A4
Hassam Par ST5...... 56 B5
Hassell St ST5 .... 283 C3
Haste Hill Ave ST10 .. 61 F2
Hastings Cl B77....... 261 F6
Hastings La B79 ..... 217 C5
Hatchett La B79 ..... 217 C5
Hatch Heath Cl WV5 . 269 F7
Hatch La TF11 .... 203 D4
Hateley Dr WV4...... 266 E4
Hatfield Cres ST3 .... 88 E8
Hathaway Mews DY8. 275 C3
Hathaway Rd B74.... 258 A4
Hathersage Cl ST3 ... 73 C5
Hatherton Cl ST5 .... 40 D2
Hatherton Croft WS11. 209 C1
Hatherton Gdns WV10. 240 E2
Hatherton Pl WS9.... 256 A7
Hatherton Rd
  Cannock WS11........ 209 C1
  Penkridge ST19 ..... 192 F1
Hatherton St
  Cheslyn Hay WS6..... 226 C2
  Stafford ST16........ 156 A3
Hatrell St ST5........ 283 C4
Hatton Rd Cannock WS11. 209 A1
  Wolverhampton WV6... 255 F3
Hattons Gr WV8...... 239 B2
Hatton Waterworks Cotts
  ST21................. 102 D7
Haughton St Giles CE Prim
  Sch ST18............. 172 F5
Haunton Rd B79 ..... 217 D3
Havannah La CW12... 6 A5
Havannah Prim Sch CW12. 6 A5
Havefield Ave WS14... 231 E7
Havelet Dr ST5 ...... 70 F3
Havelock Cl WV3 .... 265 F8
Havelock Gr ST8 ..... 27 C7
Havelock Pl ST1 ..... 282 A1
Haven Ave ST6........ 57 D8
Haven Cres ST9 ..... 59 B4
Haven Cvn Site DE14. 185 C8
Haven Gr ST5........ 56 C7
Havensfield Dr ST10 . 92 E5
Haven The
  Stourbridge DY8 ..... 275 D2
  Wolverhampton WV2... 266 C8
Havergal CE Prim Sch
  WV10................. 225 D2
Havergal Pl WV10.... 225 D1
Havergal Wlk ST3.... 73 C5
Haverhill Cr Chorlton CW2. 37 B3
Havisham Ct TF10.... 168 E3
Hawcroft WS15 ...... 197 F2
Hawes St ST6........ 41 D4
Haweswater Dr DY6.. 275 D6
Hawfield La
  Burton u T DE15...... 167 C3
  Burton u T DE15...... 167 D4
Hawfinch Rd ST10 ... 76 E3
Hawfinch B77 .... 262 A6
Hawk Cl ST3.......... 90 A7
Hawke Rd ST16....... 155 C7
Hawkesford Cl B74... 258 B1
Hawkesmoor Dr WS14. 231 D8
Hawkesmore Dr ST18. 177 D7
Hawkestone Cl ST5 .. 283 C2
Hawkesville Dr **7** WS11. 209 F2
Hawkeswell Dr **6** DY6. 275 D8
Hawkhurst Dr WS15... 197 F5
Hawkins Cl WS13 .... 214 B2
Hawkins Dr WS11 ... 226 C4
Hawkins Rd
  Burton u T DE14...... 166 E5
  Fradswell ST18 ...... 122 F2
Hawkins Lane Ind Est
  DE14................. 166 E5
Hawkins St ST4 ...... 72 D6
Hawks Cl WS6........ 226 D1
Hawksdale Cl ST3.... 90 A7
Hawk's Dr DE15....... 167 D3
Hawks Green La WS11. 210 A1
Hawkside B77 .... 262 B8
Hawksley Dr DE13 ... 147 B4
Hawksmoor Cl ST3... 89 E7
Hawksmoor Rd ST7.. 174 E2
Hawkstone Ave TF10.. 168 E2
Hawkstone Cl WS6... 254 D5
Hawkswell Ave WV5 . 270 A5
Hawksworth Dr ST13.. 30 D4
Hawksworth Cl ST13 . 30 D4
Hawksworth B77..... 250 F2
Hawkyard Ct WS11... 210 A4
Hawley Cl ST15 ...... 120 D5
Haworth Ave CW12... 6 A5
Hawthorn Ave
  Great Wyrley WS6 .... 227 A1
  Netherseal DE12 ..... 219 F4
  Stone ST15 .... 119 F5
Hawthorn Cl
  Denstone ST14 .... 95 E6

Hawthorn Cl continued
  Gnosall ST20 .... 171 E7
  Great Bridgeford ST18. 135 B2
  Haughton ST18 ...... 172 E6
  Lichfield WS14 ...... 231 D8
Hawthorn Cres DE15.. 185 F7
Hawthornden Ave ST14. 126 A8
Hawthornden Cl ST14. 126 A8
Hawthornden Gdns ST14. 125 F8
Hawthornden Manor Mews
  ST14................. 126 A8
Hawthornden Manor
  ST14................. 126 A8
Hawthorne Ave Audley ST7. 39 F1
  Stoke-on-T ST4 ...... 71 E5
  Tamworth B79 .... 250 B8
Hawthorne Cl ST10... 92 F3
Hawthorne Cres WS7. 229 A6
Hawthorne Dr ST19 .. 205 C6
Hawthorne Gr DY3 ... 271 D2
Hawthorne La WV8 .. 238 F2
Hawthorne Rd
  Cannock WS12........ 210 F3
  Cheslyn Hay WS6..... 226 A4
  Essington WV11...... 242 A3
  Huntington WS12..... 209 D8
  Wheaton Aston ST19.. 205 C6
  Wolverhampton WV2... 266 D6
Hawthorne Terr ST13 .. 30 F6
Hawthorn Gdns ST7... 40 D8
Hawthorn Gr ST8 ..... 27 E7
Hawthorn Mews ST14. 126 C8
Hawthorn Pl **2** ST3... 89 F8
Hawthorn Rd
  Aldridge B74......... 257 A1
  Newcastle-u-L ST5..... 40 E1
  Walsall WS4........... 244 B1
Hawthorn Rise DE11.. 186 F7
Hawthorn St ST6..... 57 B6
Hawthorns The
  Hagley DY9 .... 281 F4
  Keele ST5............. 69 C5
Hawthorn Way
  Market Drayton TF9... 97 D2
  Rugeley WS15 .... 178 D2
  Stafford ST17 .... 156 A1
Haybank La ST10..... 78 E5
Hay Barns The ST10.. 103 B4
Haybarn The ST16 ... 155 F7
Haybridge Ave DY8 . 281 F5
Haybridge High Sch & Sixth
  Form ST9............. 281 F6
Haycroft Dr B74...... 258 A4
Haydock Cl
  Burton u T DE14...... 185 A7
  Cheadle ST10.......... 76 E5
  Tamworth B77 .... 261 D4
Haydock Ct ST5....... 55 C1
Haydon Ct ST4........ 56 E2
Haydon St ST4........ 56 E1
Hay End La WS13 .... 215 C8
Hayes Cl ST13 .... 30 F7
Hayes Meadow Prim Sch
  WS15................. 198 C4
Hayes St ST6 .... 42 C2
Hayes The TF9........ 112 A7
Hayes View Dr WS6.. 226 E4
Hayes View Rd WS13 . 213 F1
Hayes Way WS12..... 210 C1
Hayeswood La ST4.... 54 E6
Hayfield Cres ST4.... 72 E7
Hayfield Hill WS15 ... 211 F4
Hayfield Rd ST5...... 55 B1
Hay Gr WS8 .... 244 F8
Hayhead Cl ST4 ..... 26 B2
Hay La Ellastone DE6... 79 E4
  Foston DE65 .... 129 E5
  Longdon WS15....... 213 A7
Hayle Cl ST17........ 156 E1
Hayle B77 .... 250 D2
Hayley Ct DY6........ 275 D6
Hayley Gr WV2....... 266 B6
Hayling Gr WV2...... 266 B6
Hayling Pl ST3........ 72 F3
Haymaker Way WS12. 210 F4
Haymarket **3** ST6 .... 41 D3
Haymarket The WV8 . 239 E1
Haymoor WS14 ...... 231 E7
Hayner Gr ST3........ 74 B4
Hayrick Dr DY6 ..... 275 B7
Hays La ST10......... 48 F4
Haywain Cl WV9 ..... 239 F2
Haywards Cl WS3..... 243 F3
Haywood Ct CW3 .... 68 E5
Haywood Dr WV6.... 255 C4
Haywood Grange ST18. 177 D7
Haywood High Sch ST6. 42 A2
Haywood Hospl ST6.. 42 A3
Haywood Hts ST18... 177 D8
Haywood La TF9...... 113 C1
Haywood Rd ST6..... 42 A2
Haywood St Leek ST13. 30 F5
  Stoke-on-T ST4 ...... 57 B1
Hayworth Cl B79..... 249 F8
Hayworth Rd WS13... 214 C2
Hazel Cl Kidsgrove ST7. 26 B3
  Stoke-on-T ST4 ...... 71 F5
  Uttoxeter ST14 ...... 126 B6
Hazeldene ST18...... 158 C2
Hazeldene Rd ST4 ... 88 E8
Hazel Dr Armitage WS15. 198 B4
  Cannock WS12........ 211 A6
Hazelgarth B77....... 262 B8
Hazel Gdns WV8 ..... 239 A4

Hazel Gr 2 Longton ST3... **73** F2
Biddulph ST8............**17** B1
Lawton-gate ST7........**25** A2
Leek ST13.............**30** C5
Lichfield WS14.........**231** C7
Stafford ST16..........**155** C8
Stourbridge DY8........**279** C3
Wombourne WV5........**270** A7
Hazelhurst Dr ST13....**45** D4
Hazelhurst Rd ST6......**41** F6
Hazelhurst St ST1......**282** C1
Hazel La WS6........**227** B2
Hazelmere Dr
Burntwood WS7........**228** F4
Wolverhampton WV3....**255** A1
Hazel Rd
Kingswinford DY6......**275** E5
Newcastle-u-L ST5......**55** D8
Wolverhampton WV3....**265** E7
Hazel Slade Com Prim Sch
WS12................**211** A6
Hazelslade Ho WS12....**210** F6
Hazelslade Nature Reserve★
WS12................**211** B6
Hazels The DY9........**281** F5
Hazelwood Cl
Cheslyn Hay WS6........**226** D2
Hanley ST6............**57** C6
Hazelwood Gr WS11....**226** C8
Hazelwood Rd
Aldridge B74..........**256** D1
Burton u T DE15........**185** E6
Dudley DY1............**271** F5
Endon ST9............**43** E6
Hazlemere Dr B74......**258** B1
Hazlemere Gr WS11....**226** B8
Hazlescross Rd ST10....**61** D3
Hazlestrine La ST17....**175** C5
Hazleton Gn ST17......**174** D6
Hazlitt Way ST3........**73** E5
HCM Ind Est DE14......**166** E4
Headborough Wlk WS9..**245** B1
Headingley Dr DY7......**274** F1
Headingley Gr ST4......**88** D7
Headland Rd WV3......**255** A1
Headlands The B74......**257** C3
Headland Way ST10......**78** F1
Headway Rd WV10......**240** C3
Heakley Ave ST6........**42** F4
Healey B77............**250** E2
Healey Ave ST8........**27** B5
Heanor Pl ST3.........**284** A3
Heantun Row WV11....**242** B2
Hearn Ct ST17........**174** D7
Hearthcote Rd DE11...._**186** F3
Heart Of The Country Ctr★
WS14................**247** E8
Heath Ave
Newcastle-u-L ST5......**56** B3
Werrington ST9........**59** E4
Whittington WS14......**232** C3
Heathbank Dr WS12....**209** C6
Heathbrook Ave DY6....**275** B7
Heath Cl WS14........**245** E5
Heathcote Ave TF9......**99** F3
Heathcote Cl 1 ST3....**73** D5
Heathcote Ct B78......**249** C1
Heathcote Rd
Halmer End ST7........**54** E7
Longton ST3..........**284** B3
Heathcote Rise ST3......**74** B5
Heathcote St
Kidsgrove ST7.........**26** A2
Longton ST3..........**73** C5
Newcastle-u-L ST5......**55** E8
Heath Croft Rd B75....**258** D1
Heath Cross ST14......**126** A8
Heath Cvn Pk WV10....**240** C6
Heathdene Cl ST3......**284** B4
Heath Dr
Kidderminster DY10....**280** B1
Stafford ST16..........**155** B7
Heather Cl Brocton ST17..**176** C4
Burton u T DE14........**185** A8
Great Bridgeford ST18...**135** C2
Lichfield WS13........**214** D1
Rugeley WS15.........**196** F6
Werrington ST9........**59** A4
Heather Cres ST3.......**90** A4
Heather Dr
Huntington WS12......**209** D5
Kinver DY7............**277** F4
Heather Glade CW3....**68** D7
Heather Hill ST17......**176** C4
Heather Hills WV3......**43** D5
Heatherlands Cl ST3....**89** F5
Heatherleigh Gr ST1....**57** F6
Heather Mews ST10....**210** A8
Heather Rd WV3.......**210** A8
Heatherside ST7........**26** C6
Heather Valley WS12....**210** D6
Heather View ST6......**42** E6
Heath Farm Rd
Codsall WV8..........**239** B2
Stourbridge DY8........**279** E3
Heathfield Ave WS15....**120** A7
Heathfield Ct ST6......**41** C7
Heathfield Dr
Newcastle-u-L ST5......**40** D1
Walsall WS3...........**243** B4
Heathfield Gdns DY8....**279** F4
Heathfield Gr ST3......**89** F6
Heathfield Rd
Stoke-on-T ST6........**42** C5

Heathfield Rd continued
Sutton Coldfield B74....**257** F3
Uttoxeter ST14........**126** B8
Heathfields WV8......**238** E1
Heathfields Inf Sch B77..**261** F6
Heathfield Specl Sch ST6..**42** C5
Heath Gap WS13......**215** D7
Heath Gap Rd WS11....**209** F1
Heath Gdns ST15......**119** F6
Heath Gr DY1........**271** F5
Heath Gr Codsall WV8..**239** B3
Loggerheads ST7......**99** D4
Meir Heath ST3........**90** A5
Heath Hayes Prim Sch
WS12................**210** F2
Heath Hill Rd WV6....**254** E1
Heath House Dr WV5....**269** D5
Heath House La
Bucknall ST2..........**58** A4
Codsall WV8..........**238** E1
Lower Tean ST10......**93** A3
Rudyard ST13..........**18** C1
Heathland Cl WS12....**210** D2
Heathlands Cl DY6......**275** E6
Heathlands Dr ST14....**111** B1
Heathlands Grange
DE15................**185** E7
Heathlands The WV5....**269** D5
Heath La Newton WS15..**140** D1
Stourbridge DY8........**279** F4
Heathley La B78........**260** E5
Heathley Mews DE14....**185** C8
Heathmill La WV5......**269** D4
Heathmill Ent Ctr WV5..**269** D3
Heath Mill Rd WV5......**269** D4
Heath Pl ST5..........**56** C3
Heath Rd Burton u T DE15..**185** E7
Gnosall TF10..........**188** E7
Rugeley WS15.........**196** F6
Uttoxeter ST14........**111** F6
Whitmore ST5.........**85** D7
Willenhall WV12......**242** D1
Heath Row ST4........**69** B8
Heathside Dr WS3......**244** A4
Heathside La ST6......**41** C7
Heath's Pas ST3........**284** D3
Heath St Biddulph ST8....**27** C7
Cannock WS12.........**210** B7
Newcastle-u-L,Broad Meadow
ST5................**55** F6
Newcastle-u-L ST5......**283** B3
Stoke-on-T ST6........**41** C7
Tamworth B79.........**250** C5
Heath Top TF9........**99** F4
Heath View
Burntwood WS7........**212** A1
Cannock WS12.........**227** E8
Heathview ST13........**45** E7
Heath View CW2.......**37** B5
Heath Way WS11......**210** B3
Heathway Colton WS15..**179** A7
Gnosall ST20.........**171** C5
Heath Way DE65......**146** C8
Heathway Rd TF10......**168** D2
Heatley Back La WS15....**141** C3
Heatley La ST20........**141** C2
Heaton Cl WV10........**240** E5
Heaton Terr
Endon Bank ST9........**29** A1
Newcastle-u-L ST5......**56** B6
Heaton Villas ST6......**43** C7
Heaton Way CW2......**37** E4
Hebden Gr WV11......**242** B1
Hebden B77..........**262** B8
Heber St ST3..........**284** C4
Hedgerow Cl WS12......**209** F7
Hedgerow Dr DY6......**270** D2
Hedgerows The
Lichfield WS14........**231** B5
Tamworth B77.........**261** F8
Hedgerow Wlk WV8....**239** E1
Hedges The WV5......**269** E6
Hedging Lane Ind Est
B77................**261** E5
Hedging La B77........**261** E5
Hedley Pl ST5........**70** F8
Hednesford Hills Common
Nature Reserve★
WS12................**210** E5
Hednesford Rd
Brownhills WS8........**228** C2
Cannock,Blackfords WS11.**209** F2
Cannock WS12.........**210** A1
Norton Canes WS11.....**227** F6
Rugeley WS15.........**196** F6
Hednesford Sta WS12....**210** B5
Hednesford St WS11....**209** F1
Heenan Gr Lichfield WS13.**213** F2
Stafford ST17........**174** C5
Heighley Castle Way CW3 **68** E8
Heighley Ct CW3......**53** A6
Heighley La CW3......**53** F3
Heights The ST13......**30** B2
Helen Sharman Dr ST16..**156** B5
Helford Gr ST17......**174** B8
Heligan Pl WS12......**210** E2
Hellaby Ho B74........**257** F3
Hellier Dr WV5........**269** E2
Hellier Rd WV10......**240** E2
Helmingham B79......**249** D7
Helston Ave ST3......**73** E3
Helston Cl Stafford ST17..**156** C1
Stourbridge DY8........**275** C2
Tamworth B79.........**250** C8
Heming Pl ST2........**58** A4
Hemingway Rd ST3......**73** D4
Hemlock Bsns Ctr WS11..**210** B2
Hemlock Pk WS11......**210** B2

Hemlock Rd ST3......**284** D4
Hemlock Way WS11....**210** B3
Hemmings Cl DY8......**279** F5
Hempbutts The ST15....**120** B8
Hempits Gr ST17......**175** B1
Hemplands Rd DY8......**279** F5
Hempstalls Ct ST5......**283** B4
Hempstalls Gr ST5......**56** B3
Hempstalls La ST5......**283** C4
Hempstalls Prim Sch ST5 **56** B3
Hemsby Way ST5......**71** B2
Hencroft ST13........**30** E6
Henderson Cl WS14....**231** D7
Henderson Gr ST3......**74** B2
Hendon Cl DY3........**271** D2
Henhurst Farm DE13....**165** D5
Henhurst Hill DE13....**165** C4
Henhurst Ridge DE13....**165** C4
Hen La ST10..........**108** D6
Henley Ave ST8........**27** A6
Henley Cl Barlaston ST12..**88** E4
Burntwood WS7........**229** B5
Tamworth B79.........**250** C6
Walsall WS3...........**243** A5
Henley Ct WS14........**231** B6
Henley Dr Newport TF10..**169** A4
Sutton Coldfield B74....**258** A3
Henley Grange WS15....**178** A1
Henley Rd Chorlton CW2..**37** B1
Wolverhampton WV10...**240** B1
Henney Cl ST19........**207** F7
Henry Chadwick Prim Sch
WS15................**198** A8
Henry Prince CE Fst Sch The
DE6................**81** D7
Henry St Stafford ST16...**155** F5
Stoke-on-T ST6........**41** F4
Hensel Dr WV3........**265** C8
Henshall Hall Dr CW12...._**6** B1
Henshall Pl ST6........**41** D6
Henshall Rd ST5......**55** E8
Henshaw Way ST15....**119** A6
Henwood Cl WV6......**255** C3
Henwood Rd WV6......**255** C3
Hepburn Cl WS9......**256** A4
Hepworth Cl WV6......**254** A4
Herbert Rd 2 Longton ST3 **73** D2
Aldridge WS9.........**245** A1
Stafford ST17........**285** A1
Herbert St
Burton u T DE15........**167** B3
Stoke-on-T ST6........**72** D6
Herbhill Cl WV4......**266** C2
Herd St ST6..........**41** F1
Hereford Ave ST5......**71** C4
Hereford Cl WS9......**256** A8
Hereford Gr ST2......**58** D2
Hereford Rd WS12......**210** B4
Hereford Way
Rugeley WS15.........**196** D6
Tamworth B79.........**250** A2
Heritage Ct WS14......**231** B6
Heritage Way DE15....**167** A1
Herm Cl ST5..........**70** E4
Hermes Cl ST3........**90** C7
Hermes Ct B74........**257** F3
Hermes Rd WS13......**214** D1
Hermitage Cl B78......**251** F1
Coven WV9............**224** B2
Madeley CW3..........**68** F7
Stoke-on-T ST7........**41** F8
Hermitage Gdns 1 ST14 **111** A4
Hermitage La Mayfield DE6 **81** B6
Polesworth B78........**251** E1
Hermit St DY3........**271** D5
Heron Cl Brownhills WS8..**244** E1
Heron Cross Prim Sch
ST4................**72** D4
Heron Ct DE13........**201** A4
Herondale WS12......**210** B4
Herondale Cres DY8....**279** C4
Herondale Rd DY8......**279** C4
Heron Dr Penkridge ST19..**208** A6
Uttoxeter ST14........**126** A6
Heron Mill WS3........**243** E3
Heronry The WV6......**254** F2
Herons Cl ST17........**175** C7
Herons Gate Rd DY7....**277** B4
Heron St Rugeley WS15...**196** F8
Stoke-on-T ST4........**72** E5
Heronswood ST17......**175** C7
Heron Way TF10........**168** F5
Hertford Gr ST5......**71** D4
Hertford St ST4........**72** E4
Hesketh Ave ST6......**42** D6
Hesketh Rd ST17......**174** E6
Heskin Way ST6......**42** A6
Hesleden B77..........**262** B8
Hester Cl ST3........**73** C6
Hethersett Wlk ST2....**58** D2
Hever Cl DY1..........**271** E3
Hewell Cl DY6........**270** D1
Hewitt Cl WS13........**214** A2
Hewitt Cres ST9......**59** B3
Hewitt St ST6........**41** F6
Hewston Croft WS12....**210** D4
Hexham Way DY1......**271** F2
Hextall La ST18........**153** D6
Heybridge Cl ST10......**92** F2
Heyburn Cres ST6......**56** E8
Heyfields Cotts ST12....**104** B8
Heygate Way WS9......**245** B1
Heysham Cl ST3........**74** B4
Hickman St ST5........**283** B4
Hickmerelands La DY3..**266** C1
Hickory Ct WS11......**210** C2
Hick St ST5..........**283** B2

Hidden Hills CW3........**68** E8
Hide La Hartington SK17...**24** E7
Sparklow SK17........**14** F1
Hide Pl ST4..........**72** B7
Hide St ST4..........**72** B7
Higginson Cl CW12......**16** C8
Higgins Rd DE11......**186** F6
Higgott Cl DE14......**185** B8
Higgs Rd WV11........**242** A1
High Arcal Dr DY3......**271** F7
High Arcal Rd DY3......**270** F4
High Arcal Sch The DY3 **271** F6
High Bank WS11......**226** E8
High Bank Pl ST6......**42** B1
High Bank Rd DE15....**167** B3
Highbrook Cl WV5......**240** A2
High Broome Ct B78....**250** A3
Highbury Rd
Sutton Coldfield B74....**257** C3
Werrington ST9........**59** C4
High Carr Bsns Pk ST5...._**40** F2
High Carr Network Ctr
ST5................**40** F2
High Chase Ho ST18....**177** D8
High Chase Rise ST18...._**177** D8
Highcliffe Rd B77......**261** D8
High Croft WS9........**245** B2
Highcroft Ave DY8......**275** C3
High Croft Cres WS14...._**231** C7
Highcroft Dr
Burton u T DE14........**165** F4
Sutton Coldfield B74....**257** E3
Highcroft Rd WS3......**244** B6
Highcroft Wlk ST6......**42** B2
High Cross SK17........**24** F5
Higher Ash Rd ST7......**40** D8
Higherland ST5........**283** A2
Higher Woodcroft ST13..**30** D4
Higher Works Cotts SK11...._**7** C6
Highfield Ave
Burntwood WS7........**229** B7
Cheadle ST10..........**76** D4
Kidsgrove ST7........**26** B2
Longton ST3..........**73** F1
Tamworth B77.........**251** A5
Wolverhampton WV10...**241** A2
Highfield Cl
Acton Trussell ST17....**193** B8
Blythe Bridge ST11....**90** D7
Burntwood WS7........**229** B7
Burton u T DE13........**166** F3
Highfield Cres ST10....**76** D4
Highfield Ct
Cannock WS11.........**210** B5
Newcastle-u-L ST5......**71** C6
Highfield Dr
Burton u T DE15........**166** F3
Colwich ST18..........**177** D8
Stoke-on-T ST3........**72** E3
Highfield Gdns WS14....**231** B6
Highfield Grange ST5....**56** E4
Highfield Gr ST17......**174** D8
Highfield La SK17......**24** F5
Highfield Rd
Burntwood WS7........**229** C7
Cannock WS12.........**210** E1
Cookley DY10.........**280** A5
Highfield Rd E ST8......**27** D8
Highfield Rd N WS3......**243** F5
Highfield Rd Sedgley DY3 **266** D1
Walsall WS3...........**244** A4
Highfield Rd W ST8......**27** D8
Highfield Rise ST4......**87** F8
Highfields Ave WS15....**198** C4
Highfields WS7........**229** B7
Highfields Ct WV4......**265** D6
Highfields Dr WV5......**270** A3
Highfields Grange WS6..**226** D1
Highfields TF9........**112** B8
Highfields Pk WS6......**226** D1
Highfields Prim Sch
WS7................**229** C7
Highfields Rd WS7......**228** F4
Highfields Science Specialist
Sch WV4............**265** C5
Highfields The
Croxton ST21.........**116** B5
Wolverhampton WV6....**255** A3
Highfield Way WS9......**245** B1
Highgate B74..........**257** A1
Highgate Ave WV4......**265** D6
Highgate Cl ST6........**42** E4
Highgate Country Pk★
DY3................**269** A1
Highgate ST3..........**271** E5
Highgate Rd DY7......**273** F7
High Gn Brewood ST19...._**223** C6
Cannock WS11.........**209** D1
High Grange
Cannock WS11.........**210** A5
Lichfield WS13........**213** F1
High Green Ct WS11....**209** D1
Highgrove Cl
Stretton DE13.........**147** D1
Tamworth B79.........**250** B7
Highgrove Ct DY10......**280** A1
Highgrove Pl DY1......**271** F2
Highgrove Rd ST14......**71** F3
Highgrove Stone ST15...._**120** C5
Wolverhampton WV6....**255** C3
High Hill WV11........**242** A2
High Holborn DY3......**271** D7
High House La WV7......**237** D4
High La Alsagers Bank ST7 **55** A5

High La continued
Brown Edge ST6......**43** B6
Leek ST13............**45** E7
Highland Cl
Biddulph Moor ST8......**28** B8
Blythe Bridge ST11....**90** E7
Highland Dr Longton ST3..**73** D1
Stoke-on-T ST3........**89** D8
High Land Rd WS9......**245** B3
Highland Rd
Cannock WS12.........**209** C4
Newport TF10.........**168** E2
Highlands Dr DE15......**167** A4
Highlands Rd WV3......**265** B8
Highlands Stafford ST17..**174** D8
Stone ST15...........**119** F5
Highland Way WS15....**178** A5
Highlanes ST21........**116** E5
High La ST6..........**42** A3
High Lowe Ave CW12...._**6** A4
High Lows La ST5......**118** F6
High Mdw
Cannock Wood WS15...._**211** F5
Norbury ST20.........**151** B3
High Mdws Newport TF10.._**169** A3
Wolverhampton WV6....**255** C3
Wombourne WV5........**270** B6
High Mount St WS12....**210** B6
High Offley Rd ST20....**151** D8
Highover Dr B75........**258** A4
Highpark Ave DY8......**279** D5
High Park Cl DY3......**271** D8
High Park Cres DY3......**266** D1
High Path WV6........**253** C2
High Pk ST16..........**155** C1
High Ridge WS15......**178** C3
High St (May Bank) ST5..**56** D4
High St (Sandyford) ST6..**41** D5
High St
Abbots Bromley WS15...._**161** A5
Albrighton WV7........**237** A5
Aldridge WS9.........**256** B6
Alsagers Bank ST7......**54** E6
Alton ST10............**78** E1
Audley ST7............**40** A3
Biddulph ST8..........**27** C8
Brownhills,Clayhanger
WS8................**244** E6
Brownhills,Vigo WS9....**244** F3
Brownhills WS8........**244** F8
Burntwood,Chasetown
WS7................**228** F6
Burntwood WS7........**211** E1
Burton u T DE14........**166** E2
Caverswall ST11......**74** E3
Cheadle ST10.........**76** D3
Cheslyn Hay WS6......**226** D2
Cheswardine TF9......**130** A8
Church Eaton ST20......**190** B8
Claverley WV5.........**267** C7
Colton ST15...........**179** A6
Dilhorne ST10.........**75** C4
Ecclesshall ST21......**133** E7
Edgmond TF10.........**168** A3
Gnosall ST20..........**171** D6
Harriseahead ST7......**26** E5
Hixon ST18...........**158** C8
Ipstones ST10.........**47** A1
Kidsgrove,The Rookery ST7.**26** C4
Kingsley ST10.........**61** E2
Kingswinford DY6......**275** E6
Kingswinford,Wall Heath
DY6................**275** C8
Kinver DY7............**278** B3
Leek ST13............**30** E6
Longdon WS15.........**197** F2
Longnor SK17.........**13** C6
Marchington ST14......**127** E2
Market Drayton TF9......**97** D3
Mow Cop ST7.........**26** D7
Newcastle-u-L,Chesterton
ST5................**55** E7
Newcastle-u-L,Knutton ST5 **55** E3
Newcastle-u-L,Silverdale
ST5................**55** B1
Newcastle-u-L ST5......**283** B2
Newcastle-u-L,Wolstanton
ST5................**56** C5
Newchapel ST7........**26** E2
Newport TF10.........**168** E3
Norton Canes WS11.....**228** B5
Pattingham WV6........**253** C3
Rocester ST14.........**95** F3
Sedgley DY3..........**271** D8
Stoke-on-T,Golden Hill ST6 **41** D7
Stoke-on-T,Newfield ST6..**41** D4
Stoke-on-T,Tunstall ST6..**41** E3
Stone ST15...........**120** A8
Stourbridge,Amblecote
DY8................**279** F7
Stourbridge,Wollaston
DY8................**279** F5
Stourbridge,Wordsley DY8 **275** E2
Swadlincote DE11......**186** F6
Swindon DY3..........**269** E2
Talke Pits ST7.........**40** D6
Tamworth B77.........**261** C6
Tutbury DE13.........**146** C6
Upper Tean ST10......**92** D4
Uttoxeter ST14........**126** C8
Walsall,Wallington Heath
WS3................**243** B1
Walsall WS3...........**244** A4
Wheaton Aston ST19....**205** B6
Wolverhampton WV6....**255** C3
Wombourne WV5........**270** B2
Highton Ct ST2........**43** C1
Highton St ST2........**43** C1

Highup Rd ST13. . . . . 19 C1
Highview Dr DY6. . . . . . 275 F4
High View Meir Heath ST3 . 90 A5
 Mount Pleasant ST7 . . . . 26 B5
Highview Rd ST11. . . . . . 106 E8
 Stoke-on-T ST9 . . . . 43 F8
High View Rd Leek ST13 . . 31 B5
 Stoke-on-T ST9 . . . . 43 F8
Highway La ST5. . . . . 69 E7
High Wood Cl DY6 . . . . . 275 C6
Highwood Ct ST14 . . . . . 126 C6
Highwood Rd ST14. . . . . . 126 D5
Higson Ave ST4. . . . . 72 A8
Hilary Dr Aldridge WS9 . . 256 A5
 Wolverhampton WV3 . . . 265 D7
Hilcote Gdns ST21 . . . . . 134 B8
Hilcote Hollow ST16 . . . . 155 B6
Hilderstone Rd
 Hilderstone ST15. . . . . . 106 D5
 Meir Heath ST3,ST15. . . . 90 A2
Hillary Ave CW12 . . . . 6 A2
Hillary Crest Dudley DY3 . 271 E5
 Rugeley WS15 . . . . 196 E6
Hillary Rd CW3. . . . . 67 F4
Hillary St ST6. . . . . 57 B6
Hill Avenue Prim Sch
 WV4 . . . . 266 F3
Hill Ave WV4 . . . . 266 F3
Hillberry Cl ST2. . . . . 58 A2
Hillboro Rise DY7. . . . . . . 278 A5
Hillchurch St ST1. . . . . . . 282 B3
Hill Cl Sedgley DY3 . . . . . 266 E1
 Uttoxeter ST14 . . . . 110 F1
Hillcott Wlk ST3 . . . . 284 D3
Hill Cres Alsagers Bank ST7 . 54 F6
 Stone ST15 . . . . 120 A6
Hillcrest Ave
 Burton u T DE15. . . . . . . 167 A4
 Kingsley Holt ST10. . . . . . 62 A2
 Wolverhampton WV10 . . . 240 E1
Hillcrest ST19 . . . . 223 D7
Hillcrest Cl
 Kingsley Holt ST10. . . . . . 62 A2
 Tamworth B79 . . . . 250 B6
Hill Crest Dr WS13 . . . . . 214 A1
Hill Crest DY3 . . . . 271 C4
Hillcrest Rd B78 . . . . 262 F7
Hillcrest Rise WS7 . . . . . . 229 B4
Hill Crest ST17. . . . . 174 C8
Hillcrest St ST1. . . . . 282 C3
Hillcrest DE13 . . . . 146 B5
Hillcroft Ave ST17. . . . . . 175 E7
Hill Croft ST18. . . . . 158 C8
Hillcroft Rd DY6 . . . . 275 E7
Hilldene Rd DY6 . . . . 275 C4
Hill Dr ST15 . . . . 120 A6
Hill End ST15 . . . . 105 C5
Hillfarm Cl ST17 . . . . 174 F5
Hillfield Ave ST4. . . . . 71 E4
Hillfield La DE13 . . . . 147 F1
Hillgreen Rd ST3. . . . . 73 D5
Hill Hook Ho B74. . . . . . . 257 E5
Hill Hook Rd B74 . . . . 257 F5
Hill La Burntwood WS7. . . 211 E1
 Church Leigh ST10. . . . . 108 B3
 Middleton B75. . . . . 259 B2
Hillman St ST2. . . . . 43 B1
Hillman B77. . . . . 250 E2
Hillmorton Rd B74. . . . . . 257 F4
Hillmorton B74. . . . . 257 F3
Hill Pk WS9. . . . . 245 A4
Hill Pl WV11 . . . . 242 A1
Hillport Ave ST5. . . . . 56 B7
Hillrise ST10. . . . . 94 E8
Hill Rise ST18. . . . . 137 F4
Hillsdale La ST13 . . . . 33 F3
Hillsdale Rd DE15. . . . . . . 167 B5
Hillside WS15. . . . . 161 B5
Hillside Ave
 Forsbrook ST11. . . . . 91 A8
 Kidsgrove ST7 . . . . 41 A8
 Longton ST3. . . . . 73 F1
 Stoke-on-T ST9 . . . . 43 F8
Hillside WS8. . . . . 245 A6
Hillside Cl Biddulph ST8 . . 17 B1
 Brownhills WS8. . . . . . . 245 A6
 Burntwood WS7. . . . . . . 228 E5
 Cannock WS12. . . . . . . 210 A7
 Fulford ST11. . . . . 106 E8
 Gorstyhill CW2. . . . . 37 E3
 Kidsgrove ST7 . . . . 26 D7
 Rugeley WS15 . . . . 197 B5
 Stoke-on-T ST2 . . . . 43 C3
Hillside Cres WS3 . . . . . . 243 F3
Hillside Dr Colwich ST18. . 177 D8
 Leek ST13 . . . . 30 C4
Hillside ST21 . . . . 133 E6
Hillside Gdns DE11. . . . . . 186 F2
Hillside Gr DY10 . . . . 280 C3
Hillside Lichfield WS13 . . . 231 D6
 Market Drayton TF9. . . . . 112 E4
 Newcastle-u-L ST5. . . . . 283 A2
Hillside Prim Sch ST2. . . . . 43 C2
Hillside Rd
 Cheddleton ST13. . . . . . . 45 C4
 Stoke-on-T ST2 . . . . 43 C3
 Sutton Coldfield B74 . . . . 258 A4
 Werrington ST9. . . . . 59 B4
Hillside DE13. . . . . 146 C6
Hillside Wlk ST4. . . . . 71 D8
Hillside WV5. . . . . 269 E8
Hill St Burntwood WS7. . . 228 E5
 Burton u T DE15. . . . . . . 185 E8
 Cannock WS12. . . . . . . 210 C3
 Cheslyn Hay WS6. . . . . . 226 C2

Hill St continued
 Dudley,Upper Gornal DY3 .271 D5
 Essington WV11. . . . . . . 241 F3
 Newcastle-u-L ST5. . . . . 283 B4
 Norton Canes WS11 . . . . 227 F6
 Rugeley WS15 . . . . 196 E8
 Stoke-on-T ST4 . . . . 72 B7
Hill Terr ST7. . . . . 39 D2
Hilltop ST5. . . . . 56 E2
Hill Top Ave B79 . . . . 250 B8
Hill Top Cl ST6 . . . . 28 B2
Hill Top ST6 . . . . 28 B1
Hilltop Com Prim Sch
 ST7 . . . . 40 D7
Hill Top Cres ST3 . . . . 90 A5
Hilltop Ct DY3 . . . . 271 C4
Hilltop WS15 . . . . 196 F7
Hill Top View WS15 . . . . . 198 C3
Hill Top Wlk WS9 . . . . 245 C1
Hill View WS9 . . . . 245 B2
Hillview Cres ST5 . . . . 85 C5
Hill View Leek ST13 . . . . . 31 A5
 Stoke-on-T ST2 . . . . 43 B3
Hill Village Rd
 Sutton Coldfield B75 . . . . 258 A4
 Werrington ST9 . . . . 59 C4
Hillway Cl ST5 . . . . 178 D1
Hill West Prim Sch B74 . 257 F4
Hillwood Cl DY6 . . . . 275 C4
Hillwood Common Rd
 B75 . . . . 258 B6
Hillwood Rd
 Madeley Heath CW3 . . . . 69 A8
 Sutton Coldfield B75 . . . . 258 C5
Hill Wood WS3 . . . . 243 F2
Hilmore Way B77 . . . . 261 E8
Hilsea Cl WV8 . . . . 239 F1
Hilsea Cres ST14 . . . . 143 F7
Hilston Ave WV4 . . . . 265 C4
Hilton Cl WS3 . . . . 243 A2
Hilton Cross Bsns Pk
 WV10 . . . . 241 B5
Hilton Cross WV10 . . . . . 241 B5
Hilton Dr ST21 . . . . 117 F3
Hilton La
 Featherstone WV10,
   WV11 . . . . 241 E8
 Great Wyley,Warstone
   WV11 . . . . 242 B7
 Great Wyrley WS6 . . . . . 227 A2
Hilton Main Ind Est
 WV11 . . . . 241 C5
Hilton Park Service Area
 WV11 . . . . 242 B7
Hilton Rd Burntwood WS7 . 228 C8
 Egginton DE65 . . . . 148 B7
 Featherstone WV10 . . . . 241 C7
 Stoke-on-T ST4 . . . . 71 E7
 Willenhall WV12 . . . . . . 242 C1
 Wolverhampton WV4 . . . 266 F4
Hilton Trad Est WV4 . . . . 266 F4
Himley Ave DY1 . . . . 271 F2
Himley Cres WV4 . . . . . . 266 B5
Himley Ct DY3 . . . . 271 E3
Himley Gdns DY3 . . . . . . 270 D4
Himley Hall* DY3. . . . . . . 270 D4
Himley La DY3 . . . . 269 F2
Himley Rd DY1,DY3 . . . . . 271 C2
Hinbrook Rd DY1 . . . . . . 271 C1
Hinchco Pl ST6 . . . . 42 E4
Hinckes Rd WV6 . . . . 255 B5
Hinckley Gr ST4 . . . . 88 E5
Hinde St ST1 . . . . 282 B1
Hines St ST4. . . . . 72 E5
Hingley Croft WS9 . . . . . . 256 F3
Hinksford Cl WS3 . . . . . . 269 E1
Hinksford La DY3,DY6 . . . 269 F1
Hinsford Cl DY6 . . . . 275 E8
Hinsley Mill La TF9 . . . . . 97 E2
Hinstock Cl WV4 . . . . 266 A4
Hinton Cl Stafford ST17 . . 174 F4
 Stoke-on-T ST3 . . . . 88 F8
Hints Ct B78 . . . . 248 D2
Hints La Hopwas B78 . . . . 249 B5
 Weeford B78 . . . . 248 F4
Hints Rd Hopwas B78 . . . . 249 B6
 Mile Oak B78 . . . . 249 C2
Hislop Rd WS15 . . . . 196 E6
Histons Dr WV8 . . . . 238 F2
Histons Hill WV8 . . . . 238 F2
Hitchman St ST4 . . . . 72 E6
Hixon Airfield Est (Ind Est)
 ST18 . . . . 139 B1
Hixon Ind Est ST18. . . . . . 158 B7
HM Young Offender Inst
 (Swinfen Hall) WS14 . . . 231 E1
Hoarstone DY8 . . . . 281 F5
Hobart Cl DE15 . . . . 167 C2
Hobart Ct B74 . . . . 258 A3
Hobart Rd WS12 . . . . 210 E2
Hobart St ST6 . . . . 57 A7
Hobb La ST14 . . . . 142 A7
Hobble End La WS6 . . . . . 243 B7
Hobfield La WS15 . . . . . . 161 B8
Hobby Cl ST3 . . . . 90 A7
Hob Hill CE Methodist Prim
 Sch WS15 . . . . 197 B5
Hobnock Rd WV11 . . . . . . 242 B5
Hobs Hole La WS9 . . . . . . 256 D7
Hobson St ST6. . . . . 57 A8

Hob's Rd WS13 . . . . 214 E1
Hobstone Hill La WS13 . . 212 F1
Hockley Rd
 Tamworth B77 . . . . 261 F5
 Uttoxeter ST14 . . . . 126 B7
Hodge La
 Marchington ST14. . . . . . 127 A1
 Tamworth B77 . . . . 251 B6
Hodgkins Cl WS8. . . . . . . 245 A6
Hodgkinson St ST5. . . . . . 55 F6
Hodnet Gr ST1. . . . . 282 A4
Hodnet Pl WS11 . . . . 210 B2
Hodson Way WS11 . . . . . . 210 B2
Hogan Way ST10 . . . . 156 C4
Hogarth Pl ST5 . . . . 55 E6
Holbeach St ST2 . . . . 58 A2
Holbeache La DY6 . . . . . . 270 D1
Holbeache Rd DY6. . . . . . 275 C8
Holbeach Way ST16 . . . . . 155 B4
Holborn ST5. . . . . 283 B3
Holborn Row ST10. . . . . . 92 E4
Holborn Sh Ctr The DY3 . 271 D7
Holborn The CW3 . . . . 68 E5
Holbrook Wlk ST2 . . . . 58 C1
Holbury Cl WV9. . . . . 240 A2
Holcroft Rd DY6 . . . . 270 C1
Holdcroft Rd ST2 . . . . 58 C5
Holden Ave ST5. . . . . 56 D3
Holden Ave N ST6. . . . . . . 57 D8
Holden Ave S ST6. . . . . . . 57 D8
Holden Lane High Sch
 ST1. . . . . 57 F8
Holden Lane Prim Sch
 ST1. . . . . 57 F7
Holden Rd WV4 . . . . 265 D3
Holder Dr WS11. . . . . 209 B2
Holder St ST1. . . . . 57 B6
Holdiford Rd
 Brocton ST18. . . . . 176 C8
 Tixall ST18. . . . . 157 D1
Holding Cres ST7 . . . . 54 D7
Holdings La CW3 . . . . 67 F4
Holditch Ind Est ST5 . . . . . 56 A4
Holditch Rd ST5 . . . . 55 F5
Holecroft St ST6 . . . . 57 A8
Holehouse La
 Endon ST6,ST9. . . . . 28 D2
 Scholar Green ST7. . . . . . 25 D8
Holehouse Rd ST2 . . . . 58 C6
Holendene Way WV5. . . . . 269 E7
Holland Cl WS13. . . . . 215 A1
Holland Ct B79 . . . . 217 D5
Holland Pk DE13 . . . . 183 E2
Holland Pl WS3 . . . . 243 D1
Hollands Rd WS3 . . . . 243 D1
Hollands The ST8. . . . . 17 C3
Holland's Way WS3 . . . . . 243 F4
Hollies Ave WS11 . . . . 209 F1
Hollies Brook Cl ST20 . . . 171 D7
Hollies Cl Clifton DE6. . . . . 81 F6
 Newton Solney DE15. . . . 167 E8
Hollies Ct WS11. . . . . 209 F1
Hollies Dr ST3 . . . . 90 A8
Hollies Ind Est [7] WV2 . . . 266 C8
 Nurton WV6. . . . . 254 A4
 Pattingham WV6 . . . . . . 253 D1
Hollies Park Rd WS11 . . . 209 F1
Hollies The
 Newcastle-u-L ST5. . . . . 283 C4
 Wolverhampton WV2 . . . 266 C8
Hollings St ST4. . . . . 284 A5
Hollington Dr ST6. . . . . . . 42 B8
Hollington La ST14. . . . . . 110 F5
Hollins Bsns Ctr [4] ST16 155 D5
Hollinsclough CE Prim Sch
 SK17. . . . . 4 D2
Hollinsclough Rake SK17. . . 4 D2
Hollins Cres ST1 . . . . 25 E1
Hollins Grange ST7 . . . . . . 40 D8
Hollinscroft Ct ST10. . . . . . 92 E3
Hollinshead Ave ST5. . . . . 56 B4
Hollinshead Cl ST7. . . . . . . 25 F7
Hollins La ST10 . . . . 61 B4
Hollinwell Cl WS3. . . . . . . 243 A3
Hollinwood Cl ST7 . . . . . . 40 E8
Hollinwood Rd ST7 . . . . . . 40 E8
Hollis La ST14 . . . . 95 B6
Holloway Dr WV5 . . . . 269 E5
Holloway La ST5. . . . . 84 C6
Holloway St W DY3 . . . . . 271 D4
Holloway St DY3 . . . . 271 D4
Holloway B79. . . . . 250 D4
Holloway The
 Seisdon WV5. . . . . 264 A3
 Stourbridge DY8 . . . . . . 279 F7
 Swindon DY3 . . . . 269 D2
 Wolverhampton WV6. . . . 255 C2
Hollow Cres ST5. . . . . 167 C4
Hollow La
 Burton u T DE15. . . . . . . 167 C4
 Cheddleton ST13 . . . . . . 45 C5
 Colton WS15 . . . . 179 A5
 Draycott in t C DE6 . . . . 144 D6
 Mayfield DE6. . . . . 66 C1
Hollowood Pl ST6. . . . . . . 42 E5
Hollowood Wlk ST6. . . . . . 42 D5
Hollows The ST16. . . . . . . 166 F1
Hollow The
 Caverswall ST11 . . . . 74 C3
 Mount Pleasant ST7 . . . . 26 B5
 Roston DE6 . . . . 96 E7
 Uttoxeter ST14 . . . . 126 C6
Holly Ave WS15. . . . . 45 C4
Hollybank Ave WV11 . . . . 242 A3
Hollybank Cl WS3. . . . . . . 243 A2

Hollybank Cres ST4 . . . . . 72 A5
Holly Bank St ST4 . . . . 87 E7
Holly Bank View WS15 . . . 197 B5
Holly Bush Cl DE12 . . . . . 219 F7
Holly Bush Cotts ST13 . . . 44 F8
Hollybush Cres ST3 . . . . . 72 E3
Hollybush La WV8 . . . . . . 238 E2
Holly Bush La ST5. . . . . . . 85 B4
Hollybush La
 Stourbridge DY8 . . . . . . 279 F7
 Wolverhampton WV4 . . . 265 D4
Holly Bush Rd DE13 . . . . . 143 F7
Hollybush Rd ST3 . . . . 72 E3
Holly Cl Kinver DY7 . . . . . 277 F5
 Market Drayton TF9 . . . . 112 A8
 Tamworth B79 . . . . 250 B7
Hollycroft Gdns WV6 . . . . 255 B6
Holly Dr Fradley WS13 . . . 215 D8
 Walton-on-t-H ST17 . . . . 175 F6
 Werrington ST2 . . . . 59 A3
Holly Fields ST15 . . . . 118 E6
Holly Gn DE15 . . . . 185 F8
Holly Grove La WS7 . . . . . 211 E1
Holly Grove Prim Sch
 WS7 . . . . 211 E1
Holly Gr Stone ST15 . . . . . 120 B7
 Stourbridge DY8 . . . . . . 279 F5
 Wolverhampton WV3 . . . 265 F7
Holly Hill WS6 . . . . 242 E8
Hollyhill La WS14 . . . . . . 246 E5
Holly Hill Rd
 Cannock Wood WS15 . . . 211 E6
 Shenstone WS14 . . . . . . 246 F5
Hollyhock Way DE14 . . . . 184 B6
Hollyhurst Dr DY6 . . . . . . 275 E3
Hollyhurst La ST18 . . . . . 140 F5
Hollyhurst Rd ST17 . . . . . 175 D5
Holly La Aldridge WS9 . . . 256 F6
 Bradley WS14 . . . . 173 C1
 Brownhills WS9 . . . . 245 A4
 Great Wyrley WS6 . . . . . 242 F8
 Harriseahead ST7 . . . . . . 26 F5
 Huntington WS12 . . . . . . 209 C2
 Ranton ST18 . . . . 153 E1
 Sutton Coldfield B74 . . . . 258 A3
 Uttoxeter ST14 . . . . 125 D1
Holly Mdw ST10 . . . . 109 C3
Holly Mews ST6 . . . . 69 F7
Hollyoak Way WS11 . . . . . 209 F1
Holly Pl ST4 . . . . 72 E4
Holly Rd Barton-u-N DE13 . 183 D1
 Newcastle-u-L ST5. . . . . . 40 D1
 Uttoxeter ST14 . . . . 111 B1
Hollys Rd DE13 . . . . 182 B1
Holly St [2] Burton u T DE15 . 185 F8
 Cannock WS12. . . . . 209 F6
Holly Tree Dr ST8 . . . . 16 C2
Holly View WV11 . . . . 242 A3
Hollywall La ST5. . . . . 41 C5
Hollywall Prim Sch ST6 . . 41 C6
Hollywood La ST5. . . . . . . 54 D1
Holmbridge Gr WS4 . . . . . 244 D2
Holm Cl ST4. . . . . 72 B5
Holmcroft [10] ST6. . . . . . 266 F4
Holmcroft Rd ST16 . . . . . 155 F4
Holme Bank DE6 . . . . 81 D7
Holme Farm Ave DE15 . . . 185 F8
Holme Mill WV10 . . . . 240 D4
Holme Rise ST19 . . . . 193 A1
Holmes Cl ST16 . . . . 155 B2
Holmesfield Wlk ST3 . . . . 284 D3
Holmes Way ST6 . . . . 42 A8
Holm Oak Dr CW3 . . . . . . 68 C2
Holm Rd ST10 . . . . 78 C2
Holmroyd Gdns WV9 . . . . 224 C2
Holm View WS14 . . . . 246 F6
Holst Dr ST1 . . . . 58 A4
Holston Cl WS12 . . . . 210 F1
Holsworth Cl B77 . . . . . . 250 D1
Holt Cres WS11 . . . . 210 B2
Holte Dr B75 . . . . 258 D2
Holt La ST10 . . . . 61 F2
Holt's La DE13 . . . . 164 F1
Holwick B77 . . . . 262 B8
Holy Austin Rock* DY7 . . . 277 F3
Holyhead Cres ST4 . . . . . . 74 C4
Holyhead Rd
 Albrighton WV7 . . . . 237 C3
 Codsall WV8. . . . . 238 C1
Holyoake Pl WS15 . . . . . . 178 D3
Holyrood Cl
 Stafford ST18 . . . . 156 C2
 Stone ST15 . . . . 120 C6
Holy Rosary RC Prim Sch
 DE15 . . . . 167 A3
Holy Trinity CE Prim Sch
 Brownhills WS8 . . . . 244 A6
 Burton u T DE14 . . . . . . 166 A4
Holywell Cl ST8 . . . . 27 E6
Holywell Rise WS14 . . . . . 231 D6
Home Farm Cotts SK17 . . . 5 C2
Home Farm Ct
 Castle Gresley DE11 . . . . 186 D1
 Ingestre ST18 . . . . 157 D6
Home Farm Rd WV6 . . . . . 252 C7
Home Farm ST21 . . . . 116 D2
Homefield Rd WV8. . . . . . 239 C3
Homelands Park The
 WV10 . . . . 240 C6
Homelodge Ho [7] WS13 . . 231 B7
Homer Pl ST6. . . . . 42 B5
Homer Rd B75 . . . . 258 D2
Homer St ST1. . . . . 57 E4
Homestead Cl DY3 . . . . . . 271 E5
Homestead Cotts ST2 . . . . 43 C3
Homestead Ct ST16 . . . . . 155 E7

Homestead Dr B75. . . . . . 258 C3
Homestead St ST2 . . . . . . 73 D8
Homestead The ST9 . . . . . 43 D3
Honesty Cl WS8. . . . . 244 D6
Honeybourne Cres WV5 . . 269 E5
Honeybourne B77. . . . . . . 250 D2
Honeysuckle Ave
 Blythe Bridge ST11 . . . . . 90 F6
 Kingswinford DY6 . . . . . 275 E7
Honeysuckle Cl ST10 . . . . 92 F3
Honeysuckle Dr WV10 . . . 241 C7
Honeysuckle La ST9 . . . . . 29 E2
Honeysuckle Rise ST17 . . 175 F7
Honeysuckle View DE15 . . 186 A8
Honeysuckle Way WS6 . . . 227 B4
Honeytree Cl DY6 . . . . . . 275 C3
Honeywall Ho [4] ST4. . . . . 72 A7
Honeywall La
 Madeley Heath CW3 . . . . 69 B7
 Stanton DE6. . . . . 80 E8
Honeywall ST4. . . . . 72 A7
Honeywood ST5 . . . . 283 B4
Honiton Cl ST17 . . . . 175 D8
Honiton Wlk ST3. . . . . . . 284 D3
Honor Ave WV4 . . . . 266 C5
Hood La Armitage WS15 . . 198 A4
 Longdon WS15 . . . . 197 F2
Hook Dr B74. . . . . 257 F4
Hook La Shenstone WS14 . 246 C3
 Stramshall ST14 . . . . . . 111 B6
Hook La The WV7 . . . . . . 237 B1
Hoo La DY7. . . . . 273 C4
Hoomill La ST18 . . . . 158 B5
Hoon Ave ST5 . . . . 56 B4
Hoon Rd DE65 . . . . 146 D8
Hoover St ST6 . . . . 41 D3
Hopedale Cl Longton ST4 . 73 B6
 Newcastle-u-L ST5. . . . . . 71 B3
Hope St Audley ST7 . . . . . 39 F3
 Hanley ST1 . . . . 282 B3
 Stourbridge DY8 . . . . . . 275 D3
Hopley Rd DE13 . . . . 165 B5
Hopleys Cl B77 . . . . 250 E2
Hopmeadow Way DE15 . . 167 A1
Hopshort TF9. . . . . 130 B5
Hopstone Gdns WV4 . . . . 265 F4
Hopton Bank ST18 . . . . . . 137 C5
Hopton Cl WV6 . . . . 254 F3
Hopton Cres ST18 . . . . . . 155 D5
Hoptonhall La ST18 . . . . . 137 D1
Hopton La ST18 . . . . 137 C1
Hopton Mdw WS12 . . . . . 210 C1
Hopton St ST6 . . . . 155 F6
Hopton Way ST6 . . . . 42 A8
Hopwas Hill B78 . . . . 249 A6
Hopwood La DE14 . . . . . . 166 F4
Hopwood Pl ST2 . . . . 58 B3
Horatius Rd ST5 . . . . 55 D6
Hordern Cl WV6 . . . . 255 F5
Hordern Gr WV6 . . . . 255 F5
Hordern Rd WV6 . . . . 255 F5
Hordley St ST1. . . . . 282 C3
Hornbeam Cres WS12 . . . 211 A6
Hornbeams The [2] ST14 . . 111 A1
Hornbeam B77 . . . . 251 A4
Hornbrook Cl DE13 . . . . . 166 B8
Hornbrook Rd DE13 . . . . . 166 B7
Hornby Rd WV4 . . . . 266 C5
Hornby Row ST4 . . . . 72 A7
Horner Ave WS13 . . . . . . 215 C5
Horninglow Croft DE13 . . 166 C6
Horninglow Inf Sch
 DE13 . . . . 166 C6
Horninglow Rd DE14 . . . . 166 C6
Horninglow Road N
 DE13 . . . . 166 C7
Horninglow St DE14 . . . . 166 D3
Horns Croft WS15 . . . . . . 196 B7
Hornton Cl B74 . . . . 257 D5
Hornton Rd DE13 . . . . . . 166 B7
Horse Bridge La DY7 . . . . 278 D2
Horsebrook Hall La
 ST19 . . . . 206 D1
Horsebrook La ST19 . . . . . 223 C8
Horsecroft Cres ST13 . . . . 31 A7
Horsecroft Gr ST13 . . . . . 31 B7
Horse Fair
 Eccleshall ST21 . . . . 133 E7
 Rugeley WS15 . . . . 196 E8
Horsehills Dr WV3 . . . . . . 255 E2
Horse Rd ST10 . . . . 78 E1
Horseshoe Dr
 Cannock WS12 . . . . 210 F4
 Rugeley WS15 . . . . 178 D2
Horsey La WS15 . . . . 212 C8
Horsham Ave DY8 . . . . . . 275 C3
Horsley Gr ST3 . . . . 88 E8
Horsley La
 Eccleshall ST21 . . . . 132 F5
 Shenstone WS14 . . . . . . 246 D8
Horsley Rd
 Coldmeece ST15 . . . . . . 118 C8
 Little Aston B74. . . . . . . 257 F3
Horsley Way ST15 . . . . . . 118 C7
Horton Ave DE13 . . . . . . 166 F7
Horton Cl
 [3] Cannock WS11 . . . . . 209 C4
 Sedgley DY3. . . . . 271 C8
Horton Dr ST3 . . . . 74 A5
Horton Lodge Com Specl Sch
 ST13 . . . . 18 D2
Horton Rd DY7. . . . . 277 F5
Horton St Leek ST13 . . . . . 30 F6

Horton St continued
Newcastle-u-L ST4......**56** D1
Horwood Gdns ST6......**42** C1
Horwood ST5......**70** C6
Hose St ST6......**41** D3
Hoskings Cl ST15......**120** C7
Hoskins Rd ST6......**41** E5
Hospital La
Cheslyn Hay WS6......**226** B2
Market Drayton TF9......**112** A8
Hospital Rd WS7......**229** B5
Hospital St B79......**250** B5
Hotel Bldgs WS14......**230** A2
Hothill La ST10......**109** C1
Hot La Biddulph ST8......**17** C2
Burslem ST6......**57** B8
Hot Lane Ind Est ST6......**57** B8
Hougher Wall Rd ST7......**39** D1
Hough Hill ST6......**43** B8
Houghton St ST1......**282** B1
Houghwood La ST9......**43** D4
Houlbrooke Ho 1 WS14.**231** C8
Houldsworth Dr ST6......**42** B7
Housefield Rd ST2......**73** D8
Houseman Dr ST3......**73** F4
Houston Ave ST9......**43** E8
Houting B77......**261** D5
Houx The DY8......**279** E8
Hoveringham Dr
Berry Hill ST2......**57** F1
Bucknall ST2......**58** A1
Howard Cl Leek ST13......**30** C4
Werrington ST9......**59** B4
Howard Cres
Cannock WS12......**210** C7
Hanley ST1......**57** E2
Howard Gr ST5......**71** A6
Howard Pl Hanley ST1...**282** A1
Newcastle-u-L ST5......**71** A6
Howard Prim Sch B79..**216** D2
Howard St Longton ST3...**284** C2
Wolverhampton WV2...**266** C4
Howard Wlk ST3......**284** C2
Howdle's La WS8......**228** F2
Howe Gr ST5......**55** E2
Howell Rd WV2......**266** E2
Howitt Cres ST14......**111** B2
Howitt House Sch DE13.**144** E3
Howland Cl WV9......**239** F2
Howson St ST1......**282** C2
Hoylake Cl WS3......**243** B4
Hoylake Rd WV6......**254** D5
Hoylake B77......**251** B4
Hubbal La TF11......**220** D3
Huddlesford La WS14...**232** D7
Huddlestone Cl WV10...**241** B6
Huddocks View WS3...**243** F5
Hudson Cl Cannock WS11.**210** B2
Gnosall ST20......**171** E8
Hudson Dr WS7......**229** C6
Hudson Gr WV6......**254** E5
Hudson Wlk WV3......**284** C4
Hugh Bourne Pl ST8...**27** B2
Hughes Ave
Newcastle-u-L ST5......**283** B4
Wolverhampton WV3...**265** F8
Hughes St ST6......**57** A7
Hugh Porter Way WV6..**255** F6
Hughson Gr ST6......**42** E3
Hugo Meynell CE Prim Sch
TF9......**99** E4
Hugo St ST13......**30** E5
Hugo Way TF9......**99** E4
Hulland Cl ST5......**55** B1
Hullock's Pool Rd ST7..**39** E5
Hulme Cl ST5......**55** B1
Hulme La ST3,ST9......**59** A2
Hulme St ST4......**71** E8
Hulme St ST4......**73** B6
Hulse Cl CW12......**6** B1
Hulton Rd ST2......**58** B6
Hulton St ST1......**282** C4
Humber Dr ST8......**27** E8
Humbert Rd ST1......**56** F3
Humber Way ST1......**71** B3
Humphrey St DY3......**271** D3
Humphries Ho WS8......**244** F7
Hungerford La CW3......**68** F5
Hungerford Pl CW2......**38** D5
Hungerford Rd DY8......**279** E2
Hungry La WS14......**247** F5
Hunsford Cl ST3......**284** C4
Hunslet Rd WS7......**229** B8
Huntbach St ST1......**282** B3
Hunter Ave WS7......**229** B7
Hunter Cl WS14......**231** D6
Hunter Rd WS11......**226** E8
Hunters Cl ST8......**27** C8
Hunters Cl ST18......**137** F4
Hunters Dr ST4......**71** F6
Hunter's Point TF9......**99** D5
Hunters Ride ST17......**174** E4
Hunter's Ride DY7......**275** B2
Hunter St DE14......**166** D6
Hunters Way
Stoke-on-T ST4......**72** A6
Talke Pits ST7......**40** D8
Huntilee Rd ST6......**41** F3
Huntingdon Cl B78......**249** F2
Huntingdon Pl ST1......**57** F6
Huntingdon Rd DE15...**185** D7
Huntington Ind Est
WS12......**209** B6

Huntington Prim Sch
WS12......**209** C8
Huntington Terrace Rd
WS11......**209** F4
Huntley Ave ST4......**72** A6
Huntley Cl ST10......**76** D1
Huntley La ST10......**92** C8
Huntley Rd ST13......**44** E7
Huntsbank Dr ST5......**40** D1
Hunts La DE12......**219** E7
Huntsmans Dr DY7......**277** F5
Huntsmans Gate WS7..**229** B8
Huntsman's Hill WS15..**197** C2
Huntsmans Rise WS12.**209** C8
Huntsmans Wlk
Kinver DY7......**277** F6
Rugeley WS15......**178** D1
Hunts Mill Dr DY5......**271** C1
Hunt St 2 ST6......**41** E3
Hurlingham Rd ST16...**155** C7
Huron Cl WS11......**210** B2
Huron Gr ST4......**88** A8
Hurricane Cl ST16......**136** B1
Hurricane Gr ST16......**41** C4
Hurstbourne Cl WS15..**178** C2
Hurst Cl ST7......**40** D6
Hurst Dr DE13......**147** E1
Hurstmead Dr ST17...**175** C5
Hurstons La ST10......**78** E1
Hurstons The ST10......**78** E1
Hurst Rd Biddulph ST8...**17** A3
Sedgley WV14......**266** F1
Hurst St ST3......**284** B3
Hurst Yd ST10......**76** D3
Husphins La WV8......**238** B5
Hussey Cl ST19......**207** F7
Hussey Rd
Brownhills WS8......**244** E8
Norton Canes WS11...**227** F5
Hutchinson Cl WS15...**178** B2
Hutchinson Meml CE Fst Sch
ST10......**109** B8
Hutchinson Wlk 6 ST3..**73** A3
Hut Hill La WS6......**227** A4
Hutton Dr CW12......**6** A2
Hutton Way ST2......**58** D2
Huxley Cl WV9......**240** A3
Huxley Pl ST3......**73** D4
Hyacinth Ct ST5......**283** C4
Hyacinth Rd ST4......**56** E1
Hyde Cl DY7......**278** A5
Hyde Ct ST17......**174** D7
Hyde La DY7......**278** A6
Hyde Lea Bank ST18...**174** C5
Hyde Mill Croft ST19...**223** C5
Hyde Mill La ST19......**223** C5
Hylton Cl DE14......**185** A7
Hyndley Cl ST2......**58** A3
Hyperion Dr WV4......**266** A3
Hyperion Rd DY7......**279** C7
Hyssop Cl WS11......**210** B3
Hyssop Pl ST6......**42** D2**

I

Ian Rd ST7......**26** D3
Ibsen Rd ST3......**74** A4
Ibstock St DE13......**166** B6
Icknield Cl B74......**257** A1
Idonia Rd WV6......**254** F5
Ikins Dr ST7......**39** F2
Ilam CE Prim Sch DE6..**50** E2
Ilam Cl ST5......**55** B1
Ilam Ctry Pk★ DE6......**50** E2
Ilam-Moor La DE6......**50** E6
Ilford Side ST3......**88** E8
Ilkley Pl ST5......**54** F2
Illshaw WV9......**240** A3
Image Bsns Pk WS11...**210** B3
Imandra Cl ST4......**88** A8
Imex Bsns Pk DE14......**166** B3
I-Mex Bsns Pk ST4......**72** F5
Imex Bsns Pk WV2......**266** C7
Imex Ho WV2......**266** B7
Imex Tech Pk ST4......**88** D7
Imogen Cl ST4......**73** B6
Imperial Ct ST1......**282** C1
Impstones ST20......**171** C5
Ingatestone Dr DY8...**275** C3
Inge Dr DE13......**201** A2
Ingelow Cl ST3......**73** A8
Ingestre Cl Cannock WS11.**210** B1
Newport TF10......**168** D2
Walsall WS3......**242** F3
Ingestre Ho ST4......**39** F2
Ingestre Rd Stafford ST17.**285** B1
Wolverhampton WV10...**240** C1
Ingestre Sq ST1......**88** F8
Ingleborough Pl ST2...**43** D1
Ingleby Cl DE11......**186** F3
Ingleby Rd ST3......**88** E8
Inglefield Ave ST6......**42** B1
Inglemere Dr ST17......**175** C6
Ingleside WS15......**178** C1
Ingleton Gr ST3......**90** A7
Inglewood Ave WV3...**265** F8
Inglewood Cl DY6......**275** D5
Inglewood Dr ST5......**56** D6
Inglewood Gr
Aldridge B74......**256** F2
Newcastle-u-L ST5......**56** C6
Inglewood ST17......**285** A1
Inglis St ST4......**72** C8
Ingram Pit La B77......**251** A5
Ingram Pl WS3......**243** D1
Ingram Rd ST3......**243** D1
Inhedge St DY3......**271** E5

Intake La ST20......**190** A8
Intake Rd ST6......**42** E4
Intakes La ST10......**108** E4
Inworth WV9......**240** B3
Iona Pl ST3......**72** F3
Irene Ave
Newcastle-u-L ST5......**56** D2
Stoke-on-T ST6......**41** F4
Ireton Rd WV10......**240** E3
Iris Cl Meir ST11......**74** C5
Tamworth B79......**250** C6
Irnham Rd B74......**258** B1
Ironbridge Dr ST5......**55** F1
Ironmarket ST5......**283** B3
Ironstone La WS13......**215** E5
Ironstone Rd
Burntwood WS7......**228** E8
Prospect Village WS12.**211** D4
Ironwalls La DE13......**146** C5
Irvine Rd ST9......**59** C4
Irving Cl Dudley DY3...**271** A4
Lichfield WS13......**213** E2
Irwell B77......**250** E2
Isabel Cl ST17......**174** B8
Isherwood Pl ST3......**284** D4
Island Gn ST17......**175** D6
Island The Mile Oak B78..**249** C1
Oakamoor ST10......**78** A6
Upper Tean ST10......**92** D4
Islay Wlk 3 ST3......**73** A3
Islington Cl TF10......**168** F4
Islington Cres CV9......**262** C1
Ismere Way DY10......**280** A1
Itchen Gr WV6......**254** E4
Ivanhoe Rd WS14......**231** B6
Ivatt B77......**250** F2
Iverley La DY10,DY8.....**281** C5
Ivetsey Bank Rd ST19..**221** F8
Ivetsey Cl ST19......**205** B5
Ivetsey Rd
Ivetsey Bank ST19......**204** F3
Wheaton Aston ST19...**205** A5
Ivy Cl Acton Trussell ST17..**175** B1
Cannock WS11......**226** D8
Uttoxeter ST14......**126** A8
Ivy Cottage Mobile Home Pk
ST18......**137** C2
Ivy Cotts ST13......**20** A6
Ivycourt ST17......**175** B1
Ivy Croft WV9......**239** F3
Ivy Ct Acton Trussell ST17..**175** B1
Eggington DE65......**148** A5
Hixon ST18......**158** B8
Ivy Gdns WS11......**228** A5
Ivy Gr Brownhills WS8...**245** A4
Burton u T DE13......**166** C7
Trentham ST4......**87** F8
Ivy Ho WS9......**245** A4
Ivy House Dr ST12......**88** E4
Ivy House La ST5......**206** E1
Ivy House Rd Biddulph ST8.**16** C2
Hanley ST1......**57** E3
Ivyhouse Wlk 6 B77...**261** F6
Ivy La WS5......**211** F5
Ivy Lodge Cl DE15......**185** E7
Izaac Walton Way CW3.**68** E5
Izaak Walton Cl ST16...**155** D6
Izaak Walton's Cottage &
Mus★ ST15......**135** D2
Izaak Walton St ST16...**155** D5**

J

Jack Ashley Ct ST4......**72** E6
Jackdaw Cl DY3......**266** C2
Jackfield Inf Sch ST6...**42** B1
Jackfield St ST6......**42** B1
Jack Haye La Bagnall ST2..**58** E8
Stoke-on-T ST2......**43** D1
Jack La CW2......**37** D6
Jacklin Cl DE14......**185** A6
Jackman Cl WS13......**215** D6
Jackman Rd WS13......**215** D6
Jacks La ST14......**127** E2
Jackson Ave DE13......**166** F7
Jackson Cl
Featherstone WV10......**241** A6
Norton Canes WS11......**227** C2
Jackson Rd WS13......**214** B3
Jackson St 2 ST6......**57** A8
Jacobean St ST5......**167** C4
Jacobs Croft ST16......**155** C7
Jacob's Hall La WS6...**227** B1
Jacqueline St ST6......**41** D4
Jade Cl ST3......**73** D4
Jade Gr WS11......**210** C2
Jaguar B77......**250** E2
Jamage Rd
Newcastle-u-L ST7......**40** D4
Talke Pits ST7......**40** D5
James Beattie Ho WV6..**255** F4
James Brindley Cl ST1...**57** A2
James Brindley High Sch
ST6......**41** F6
James Brindley Way
DE13......**166** F8
James Cres ST9......**59** C4
James Ct ST1......**166** C1
James Greenway WS13..**214** A4
James Hutchens Ct ST7..**228** F5
James St Burton u T DE14..**166** C2
Cannock WS11......**209** F5
Kinver DY7......**278** A4
Leek ST13......**30** D5
Newcastle-u-L ST5......**56** B6
Stoke-on-T ST4......**72** A5

James St continued
Uttoxeter ST14......**126** B8
James Warner Cl WS15..**178** D1
James Way ST8......**27** A6
Janet Pl ST1......**57** E4
Janson St ST4......**71** F1
Jardines La ST14......**95** D4
Jasmine Cl
Blythe Bridge ST11......**90** F6
Burton u T DE15......**186** A7
Wolverhampton WV9...**240** A3
Jasmine Cres ST7......**26** D2
Jasmine Gr WV8......**239** B3
Jasmine Rd
Great Bridgeford ST18...**135** C2
Tamworth B79......**251** A4
Jasmin Way ST7......**27** A2
Jason Cl B77......**250** D5
Jason St ST5......**283** A4
Jasper Cl Barlaston ST12..**88** F4
Newcastle-u-L ST5......**56** B7
Jasper St ST1......**282** B2
Java Cres ST4......**88** B7
Jaycean Ave ST6......**41** E4
Jay Rd DY6......**275** D8
Jean Cl ST6......**42** A2
Jedburgh Ave WV6......**254** E4
Jeddo St WV2......**266** C8
Jeffcock Rd WV3......**266** A7
Jefferson St ST6......**41** D4
Jeffery Cl WS15......**178** D3
Jeffrey Ave WV4......**266** F5
Jeffs Ave WV5......**266** D8
Jenkinson Cl ST5......**70** F8
Jenkins St 2 ST6......**56** F8
Jenkinstown Rd WS12...**211** A6
Jenks Ave DY7......**277** F5
Jenks Rd WV5......**269** F5
Jennings Way DE14......**166** A3
Jenny Walkers La WV6..**254** D1
Jensen B77......**250** E2
Jephson Rd DE14......**185** B7
Jerbourg Cl ST5......**70** E4
Jeremy Cl ST4......**71** F6
Jeremy Rd WV4......**266** C5
Jerningham St ST16......**285** A3
Jerome Ct B74......**256** F1
Jerome Dr WS11......**228** A5
Jerome Prim Sch WS11..**227** F5
Jerome Rd WS11......**228** A5
Jerome Way WS7......**229** C7
Jerry's La WS14......**217** A4
Jersey Cl Congleton CW12..**6** A2
Newcastle-u-L ST5......**70** E4
Jersey Cres ST3......**73** D1
Jervis Cres B74......**257** D3
Jervis La ST15......**104** C3
Jervison St ST3......**73** D6
Jervis Pk B74......**257** C4
Jervis Rd Stone ST15......**120** B7
Tamworth B77......**261** F5
Jervis St ST1......**282** C4
Jesmond Cl WS12......**211** A6
Jesmond Gr ST3......**88** E8
Jessie Rd WS9......**245** B1
Jessop Dr B77......**250** E5
Jew's La DY3......**271** E4
Jinny Cl DE65......**146** C8
Joan Eaton's Cross ST20.**189** E7
Joanhurst Cres ST1......**282** A1
Joan St WV2......**266** E6
Jockey Field DY3......**271** E6
Jodrell View ST7......**41** B8
Joe Jones Ct DY3......**266** D1
Joeys La WV8......**239** C3
John Amery Dr ST17......**174** D6
John Ball Cl WS15......**178** D3
John Bamford Prim Sch
WS15......**178** C1
John Baskeyfield CE Prim Sch
Burslem ST6......**41** E1
Burslem ST6......**56** F8
John Bright St ST1......**282** C4
John Donne St ST16......**155** D6
Johndoro B77......**261** D6
John Offley Rd CW3......**68** E6
John of Rolleston Prim Sch
DE13......**147** C3
John O' Gaunt's Rd ST5.**283** A3
John Pershall Ct ST21...**133** D7
John Rhodes Way ST6...**41** D5
Johns Ave WS15......**198** C4
Johnsgate ST19......**223** D7
Johns La WS6......**227** A3
Johnson Ave ST5......**56** A4
Johnson Cl Congleton CW12..**6** B1
Lichfield WS13......**214** C1
Ranton ST18......**153** C5
Rugeley WS15......**178** D2
Johnson Cres ST10......**61** D2
Johnson Gr ST15......**120** D2
Johnson Pl ST6......**42** B6
Johnson Rd
Burntwood WS7......**228** B8
Cannock WS11......**209** D4
Uttoxeter ST14......**111** B1
Johnson St
Newcastle-u-L ST5......**55** D7
Wolverhampton,Cinder Hill
WV14......**266** F1
Wolverhampton WV2...**266** D7
Wood End CV9......**262** C1
John St Biddulph ST8......**27** C8
Cannock,Chadsmoor
WS11......**210** A4
Cannock,Wimblebury
WS12......**210** F3

John St continued
Hanley ST1......**282** B2
Leek ST13......**30** E5
Newcastle-u-L,Knutton ST5..**55** E2
Newcastle-u-L ST5......**283** D3
Johnstone Ave ST9......**59** C4
John St Stafford ST16......**156** A4
Stourbridge DY8......**275** F1
Swadlincote DE11......**186** E6
Tamworth B77......**250** E4
Uttoxeter ST14......**126** B8
John Taylor High Sch
DE13......**183** E2
John Till Cl WS15......**178** E1
John Wheeldon Prim Sch
ST16......**155** E5
Joiner's Square Ind Est
ST1......**282** C1
Joiner's Square Prim Sch
ST1......**282** C1
Jolley St ST6......**42** C1
Jolliffe St 11 ST13......**30** E5
Jolpool La ST18......**121** C4
Jolt La ST18......**172** E5
Jolyon Cl ST4......**73** B6
Jonathan Rd ST4......**88** C5
Jones Cl Fradley WS13......**215** E8
Stafford ST17......**174** D7
Jones La Burntwood WS7..**229** F7
Great Wyrley WS6......**227** B1
Rugeley WS15......**196** C8
Jones Rd WV12......**242** D1
Jonkel Ave B77......**262** A5
Jordan Ave DE13......**147** F2
Jordan Cl
3 Lichfield WS13......**231** A8
Fradley WS13......**215** D6
Sutton Coldfield B75......**258** B1
Jordan Croft WS13......**215** D7
Jordan Rd B75......**258** C2
Jordan Way Aldridge WS9.**245** B1
Stone ST15......**120** B7
Jordon St ST1......**282** A1
Joseph Dewsbury Cl
WS7......**228** F8
Joseph Dix Dr WS15......**178** D2
Joseph St 6 ST6......**56** F8
Josiah Wedgwood St ST1.**57** A3
Joules Dr ST15......**104** E3
Jowett B77......**250** E2
Joyce Ave ST6......**42** B2
Joyce's La ST17......**194** A8
Jubilee Ave ST1......**57** A3
Jubilee Cl Biddulph ST8...**27** D8
Great Wyrley WS6......**226** F2
Jubilee Ct Stafford ST16...**155** F5
Uttoxeter ST14......**126** B8
Jubilee Dr ST10......**62** D3
Jubilee Gr TF11......**203** F5
Jubilee Rd
Newcastle-u-L ST5......**56** D3
Trentham ST4......**87** F8
Jubilee Rise DE15......**167** C3
Jubilee Sq DE6......**81** D7
Jubilee St WS15......**178** D1
Jubilee Terr 12 ST13......**30** D6
Judes Wlk WS13......**213** F2
Judgefield La ST6......**28** A2
Judith Gr ST4......**72** C5
Jug Bank Ashley TF9......**100** B4
Burslem ST6......**57** B6
Julian Cl WS6......**227** A3
Junction Rd Leek ST13......**30** E4
Stourbridge,Amblecote
DY8......**275** D2
Junction The 1 DY8...**279** E8
June Cres DE15......**250** E5
June Rd ST4......**73** B6
Juniper Cl
Burntwood WS7......**229** C6
Cannock WS12......**211** A6
Meir ST3......**90** A6
Newcastle-u-L ST5......**40** E1
Juniper Row TF10......**168** F1
Juniper B77......**251** A4
Jupiter Bsns Pk ST18...**139** B2
Jupiter St ST6......**42** C1
Jupiter Way 10 ST17...**175** A8
Justin Cl ST5......**56** C5**

K

Kamienna Cl ST17......**174** E4
Kara Pl ST4......**88** B8
Kaydor Cl ST9......**59** B4
Kay Dr DE11......**186** F5
Kayne Cl DY6......**275** C7
Kean Cl WS13......**213** E2
Kearsley Way ST3......**88** E8
Keary St ST4......**72** B6
Keates St 7 ST6......**56** F8
Keating Gdns B75......**258** A4
Keats Ave Cannock WS11..**209** E5
Stafford ST17......**174** C8
Keats Cl Dudley DY3......**271** A5
Sutton Coldfield B74......**257** F6
Tamworth B79......**249** F8
Keats Gdns ST7......**41** A8
Keats Rd WV10......**241** A1
Keble Cl Burntwood WS7..**229** C7
Burton u T DE15......**167** C2
Cannock WS11......**226** E8
Keble Way ST3......**73** A2
Keble Wlk B79......**250** A6
Kedleston Cl
Stretton DE13......**147** C1
Walsall WS3......**243** A3**

Kedleston Rd ST6 42 A2
Keele Rd Keele ST5 70 A7
Madeley Heath CW3 69 B8
Newcastle-u-L ST5 70 D8
Keele Science Pk ST5 70 B7
Keele Service Area ST5 69 F4
Keele St ST6 41 D4
Keele Univ ST5 70 B7
Keeling Dr WS11 209 B1
Keeling Rd ST10 76 E3
Keelings Dr ST4 71 F4
Keelings Rd ST1 57 E5
Keeling St ST5 56 C6
Keene Cl ST6 42 E3
Keepers Cl WS9 244 F3
Keeper's Cl WS7 229 A6
Keepers Cl
Kingswinford DY6 275 B8
Lichfield WS14 231 E7
Keepers La Codsall WV8 239 A1
Wolverhampton WV6,WV8 255 A7
Keepers Rd B74 257 C5
Keep The ST17 174 C8
Keir Pl DY8 279 E8
Keld Ave ST17 174 A8
Keldy Cl WV6 255 F5
Kelham Rd ST4 73 A6
Kelly Ave WS15 196 F6
Kelly Gn ST6 42 B6
Kelmore Cl ST3 284 B4
Kelsall St ST6 42 B1
Kelsall Way ST7 39 D1
Kelso Gdns WV6 254 D4
Kelvedon Way WS15 178 C1
Kelvestone Ho WS11 209 D1
Kelvin Ave ST1 57 D7
Kelvin Dr WS11 210 A3
Kelvin St ST5 56 D4
Kemball Ave ST4 72 D4
Kemball Specl Sch ST4 72 F5
Kemberton Cl WV3 255 C1
Kemberton Rd WV3 255 C1
Kemnay Ave ST6 42 B8
Kempson Rd ST19 192 F1
Kempthorne Ave WV10 240 E1
Kempthorne Gdns WS3 243 A2
Kempthorne Rd ST1 282 C1
Kempton Cl WS12 211 A6
Kempton Dr
Great Wyrley WS6 226 F2
Tamworth B77 261 D4
Kempton Gr ST10 76 E5
Kempton Rd DE15 167 A3
Kempton Way DY8 279 E3
Kendal Cl Stafford ST17 174 B7
Wolverhampton WV6 255 F6
Kendal Ct Brownhills WS9 244 F4
Cannock WS11 226 B8
Kendal Gr ST2 58 D2
Kendall Rise DY6 275 F5
Kendal Pl ST5 71 B6
Kendal Rise WV6 255 F6
Kendal Way CW2 37 C1
Kenderdine Cl ST17 193 F8
Kendlewood Rd DY10 280 B1
Kendrick St ST3 73 D3
Kenelyn Cres ST3 72 E4
Kenilworth Ave DE13 166 D7
Kenilworth Cl
Market Drayton TF9 97 E2
Penkridge ST19 208 A8
Stourbridge DY8 275 D2
Kenilworth Cres WV4 266 E4
Kenilworth Ct 2 WS11 209 E1
Kenilworth Dr WS11 209 D4
Kenilworth Gr
2 Longton ST3 73 F1
Newcastle-u-L ST5 56 E3
Kenilworth Rd
Lichfield WS14 231 B6
Perton WV6 254 F4
Tamworth B77 250 E4
Kenilworth Wlk ST10 76 B2
Kenley Ave ST9 43 F8
Kenmore Ave WS12 209 F7
Kennedy Cl B77 250 C1
Kennedy Cres DY3 271 D4
Kennedy Ct DY8 279 F5
Kennedy Pl ST21 133 D6
Kennedy Rd ST4 88 B6
Kennedy Way ST16 155 B8
Kennedy Wlk ST9 59 B4
Kennermont Rd ST2 58 C6
Kennet Cl Brownhills WS8 228 C2
Newcastle-u-L ST5 71 B3
Kennet B77 250 D1
Kennington Oval ST4 88 D8
Kenrick Cl CW3 67 C1
Kenrose Mill DY7 278 B3
Kensington Cl ST15 120 C5
Kensington Ct
Stoke-on-T,Trent Vale ST4 71 E3
Stoke-on-T,Tunstall ST6 41 E4
Kensington Dr
Stafford ST18 156 C3
Sutton Coldfield B74 257 F5
Tamworth B79 250 B7
Kensington Gdns
Cannock WS11 209 C2
Stourbridge DY8 275 C1
Kensington Pl WS12 227 C8
Kensington Rd
Burton u T DE15 167 A3
Stoke-on-T ST4 72 A4
Kensworth Cl ST5 71 A3
Kent Ave B78 249 F2
Kent Cl WS9 245 B1
Kent Dr ST9 43 E6
Kent Gr Newcastle-u-L ST5 55 E8
Stone ST15 104 F2
Kent Ho ST7 40 D6
Kentish Cl ST17 174 A8
Kentmere Cl Longton ST4 73 B5
Penkridge ST19 193 A1
Stafford ST17 174 A8
Kentmere Pl ST5 71 B6
Kenton Ave WV6 255 F4
Kent Pl Cannock WS12 210 F1
Stoke-on-T ST4 72 E6
Kent Rd Burton u T DE15 185 E6
Stourbridge DY8 279 D7
Wolverhampton WV2 266 E7
Kents Row ST12 88 E2
Kent St DY3 271 E5
Kent Way ST17 175 B8
Kentwell B79 249 D7
Kenworthy Rd ST16 155 E6
Kenworthy St ST6 41 E4
Kepler B79 249 E7
Kerria Ctr B77 251 A4
Kerria Rd B77 251 B4
Kerridge Cl WV9 240 A2
Kerry La ST21 133 C6
Kersbrook Cl ST4 88 C6
Kervis Gr ST3 90 B6
Kesterton Rd B74 257 E5
Kesteven Wlk ST2 58 B3
Kestrel Ave ST3 90 C7
Kestrel Cl Biddulph ST8 27 B6
Newport TF10 169 A5
Stafford ST17 156 C1
Uttoxeter ST14 126 B6
Whittington WS14 232 F5
Kestrel Ct WS7 229 F8
Kestrel Dr
Loggerheads TF9 99 D4
Sutton Coldfield B74 257 F5
Kestrel Gr WS12 210 C1
Kestrel La ST10 76 E3
Kestrel Rise WV6 255 F7
Kestrel B77 262 A6
Kestrel Way
Burton u T DE15 167 D3
Cheslyn Hay WS6 226 C2
Keswick Dr DY6 275 D6
Keswick Gr Aldridge B74 256 F2
Stafford ST17 174 A8
Keswick Pl ST5 71 B6
Ketley Rd
Kingswinford DY6 275 F6
Kingswinford DY6 275 F7
Kettering Dr Berry Hill ST2 57 F1
Bucknall ST2 58 A1
Kettlebrook Rd B77 250 C3
Kettlesbank Rd DY3 271 B2
Ketton Cl ST6 42 B8
Kewstoke Cl WV12 242 B1
Kewstoke Rd WV12 242 C1
Keyes Dr DY6 270 D1
Keynsham Wlk ST6 42 D2
Keys Cl WS12 210 C3
Keys Park Rd WS12 210 E3
Keystone La WS15 196 F8
Keystone Mews 3 WS15 196 F8
Keystone Rd WS15 196 F8
Keyworth Wlk ST2 58 A2
Kibblestone Rd ST15 105 C5
Kibworth Gr ST1 282 B4
Kidbrooke Pl ST3 88 E8
Kiddemore Green Rd
Brewood ST19 223 A6
Kiddemore Green ST19 222 D6
Kidderminster Rd
Iverley DY8 281 C7
Kingswinford DY6 275 B7
Kidderminster Rd S DY9 281 F3
Kidsgrove Bank ST7 41 B8
Kidsgrove Rd ST6 41 C8
Kidsgrove Sta ST7 25 F1
Kidson Eventide Homes
WV6 255 F5
Kielder Cl WS12 210 E2
Kilburn Dr DY6 270 E1
Kilburn Pl ST2 57 F2
Kilburn Way DE11 186 F5
Kilbye Cl B77 261 F5
Kildare St ST3 284 C2
Kilmorie Rd WS11 209 C2
Kiln Bank Cres TF9 112 C8
Kiln Bank Rd TF9 112 C8
Kiln Croft ST10 92 D4
Kilndown Cl ST1 57 A2
Kiln La ST13 30 C6
Kiln Way B78 251 F1
Kilsby Gr ST2 43 B2
Kimberlee Ave DY10 280 B4
Kimberley Cl B74 257 A2
Kimberley Dr
Burton u T DE15 167 C3
Uttoxeter ST14 110 F1
Kimberley Grange ST5 283 B4
Kimberley Rd Hanley ST1 57 A3
Newcastle-u-L ST5 283 B4
Kimberley St Longton ST3 284 B2
Wolverhampton WV3 266 A8
Kimberley B77 261 F7
Kimberley Way
Rugeley WS15 196 F5
Stafford ST17 174 A8
Kinder Pl ST5 55 B1
Kineton Rise DY3 266 C2
Kinfare Dr WV6 255 B4
Kinfare Rise DY3 271 E4
King Charles Cl ST3 90 A7
Kingcross St ST3 284 C3
Kingcup Rd ST17 174 E5
King Edward Pl DE14 166 B3
King Edward's Row 5
WV2 266 C8
King Edward St ST10 76 E4
King Edward VI High Sch
ST17 155 C1
King Edward VI Sch
WS14 231 C6
Kingfisher Cl
Brownhills WS8 244 E7
Madeley CW3 68 F7
Newport TF10 168 F5
Sedgley DY3 266 C2
Kingfisher Cres
Cheadle ST10 76 F3
Fulford ST11 106 E8
Kingfisher Ct WS7 229 F8
Kingfisher Dr
Cannock WS12 210 C5
Colwich ST18 177 E8
Stourbridge DY8 279 C4
Kingfisher Gr ST6 42 C3
Kingfisher B77 262 A6
Kingfisher Way ST14 126 C6
Kingfisher Wlk ST19 207 F8
King George St ST1 282 C4
Kingham Cl DY3 271 C2
King Ho ST7 40 D5
Kings Ave Cannock WS12 210 C4
Market Drayton TF9 112 A8
King's Ave
Newcastle-u-L ST5 56 C5
Stone ST15 105 A1
Kingsbridge Ave ST5 71 B5
Kings Bridge WV9 224 A3
King's Bromley La WS15 198 D6
Kings Bromley Rd DE13 200 F2
Kingsbury Cl DE15 167 A4
Kingsbury Gr ST1 57 F6
King's CE Sch The WV6 255 B5
Kingsclere Gr ST1 57 E7
Kingsclere Wlk WV4 265 C6
Kings Croft WS12 210 E4
Kingscroft ST18 158 D1
King's Croft ST4 56 D1
Kings Ct Stourbridge DY8 279 E5
Sutton Coldfield B75 258 B3
Kingsdale Cl ST3 90 A7
Kingsdale Croft DE13 166 D8
Kingsdene Ave DY6 275 C4
Kingsdown Cl CW2 37 C1
Kingsdown Mews ST5 71 C4
Kingsdown Rd WS7 211 E1
Kings Dr ST18 156 D8
Kingsfield Cres ST8 27 D8
Kingsfield Fst Sch ST8 27 C8
Kingsfield Oval ST4 56 D1
Kingsfield Rd Biddulph ST8 27 D8
Stoke-on-T ST4 56 D1
Kingsford Country Park★
DY11 277 D1
Kingsford La DY7,DY11 277 D2
Kingsford Pl ST3 90 A8
Kingshayes Rd WS9 245 B1
Kings Head Pk TF10 168 E4
King's Hill Rd WS14 231 C6
Kingside Gr ST4 88 C5
Kingsland Ave ST4 71 F4
Kingsland CE Prim Sch
ST2 58 C4
Kingsland Cl ST15 120 C7
Kingsland Ct ST15 120 C7
Kingsland Rd ST15 120 C7
King's La B79 236 C5
Kingsleigh Croft B75 258 B2
Kingsley Ave
Cannock WS12 210 C7
Wolverhampton WV6 255 B4
Kingsley Cl Stafford ST17 174 E8
Talke Pits ST7 40 D6
Tamworth B79 250 A6
Kingsley & Froghall Sta★
ST10 62 B3
Kingsley Gdns WV8 238 E3
Kingsley Gr DY3 271 A5
Kingsley Rd
Burton u T DE14 166 D6
Congleton CW12 6 A3
Kingswinford DY6 275 C5
Overmoor ST9 60 B3
Stafford ST17 174 E8
Talke Pits ST7 40 D6
Werrington ST9 59 F3
Kingsley St ST3 74 A1
Kingsley View ST13 45 D5
Kingsley Wood Rd WS15 195 D7
Kingslow Ave WV4 265 D6
Kingsmead DE13 166 E8
Kingsmead Hospl ST16 285 C3
Kingsmead Rd ST3 89 F7
Kingsmead Tech Coll
WS12 210 C4
Kings Mews WS14 231 B5
Kingsnorth Pl ST3 90 B6
Kings Pl ST4 56 D2
Kings Rd Sedgley DY3 271 E8
Shareshill WV10 225 A6
Stoke-on-T ST4 72 A1
King St Audley ST7 39 D1
Biddulph ST8 27 C8
Blymhill TF10,TF11 189 A1
Brownhills WS9 244 F2
Burntwood WS7 228 F5
Burton u T DE14 166 C1
Kings Terr ST4 56 D1
King St Kidsgrove ST7 26 A2
Leek ST13 30 E5
Longton ST3,ST4 284 B4
King St *continued*
Newcastle-u-L,Chesterton
ST5 55 E7
Newcastle-u-L,Cross Heath
ST5 56 A3
Newcastle-u-L ST5 283 C3
Kingston Arc WS11 209 E1
Kingston Ave
Stafford ST16 156 B4
Stoke-on-T ST1 57 E7
Kingston Cl B79 250 C7
Kingston Ctr WV6 255 F5
Kingston Dr ST15 120 B6
Kingston Hill Ct ST16 156 C3
Kingston Pl Biddulph ST8 16 E2
Stoke-on-T ST6 42 E3
Kingston Rd DE15 167 C2
Kingston Row ST16 156 A3
Kingston Way DY6 275 C7
King St Rugeley WS15 196 F8
Stourbridge DY8 279 E6
Talke Pits ST7 40 D5
Tamworth B79 250 B5
Yoxall DE13 182 A3
Kingsway Burton u T DE14 185 B8
Cannock WS11 210 A4
Kingsway E ST5 71 B6
Kingsway Essington WV11 242 A4
Stafford ST16 155 C2
Stoke-on-T ST4 72 B7
Stourbridge DY8 279 E8
Kingsway W ST5 71 A6
Kingswear Ave WV6 254 F3
Kingswell Rd ST4 56 D1
Kingswinford Pl ST4 57 D7
Kingswinford Sch The
DY6 275 D7
Kings Wlk DE13 199 B6
Kingswood Ave
Cannock WS11 226 C7
Chorlton CW2 37 B3
Kingswood Bsns Pk WV7 237 F1
Kingswood Colliery Cvn Site
WS6 227 A4
Kingswood Ctr WV7 237 F2
Kingswood Dr
Great Wyrley WS6 227 A4
Norton Canes WS11 227 F5
Kingswood Gdns WV4 265 F6
Kingswood ST7 26 B1
Kingswood Mobile Homes
WV7 237 E1
Kingswood Rd
Albrighton WV7 237 C4
Albrighton WV7 237 D3
Kingswinford DY6 275 C4
King William St
Stoke-on-T ST6 41 E3
Stourbridge DY8 279 F8
Kinlet Cl WV3 265 A8
Kinloch Dr DY1 271 F3
Kinnersley Ave ST7 40 F8
Kinnersley St 1 ST7 26 A2
Kinross Ave WS12 209 F7
Kinsall Gn B77 262 C6
Kinsey St ST5 55 B2
Kinver Cl DE6 81 C8
Kinver Cres WS9 245 C1
Kinver Dr WV4 265 C5
Kinver Edge★ DY7 277 E2
Kinver La DY11 280 B7
Kinver Mt DY7 278 A3
Kinver Rd
Burton u T DE15 167 A4
Kinver DY7 277 E8
Kinver St Stoke-on-T ST6 42 C1
Stourbridge DY8 275 E1
Kiplass La ST18 121 C4
Kipling Ave WS7 212 A1
Kipling Rd Dudley DY3 271 A5
Wolverhampton WV10 240 D2
Kipling Rise B79 249 F8
Kipling Way ST2 58 D1
Kirby Dr DY1 271 E3
Kirby St ST6 57 A6
Kirkbride Cl ST3 73 D4
Kirkham St ST4 72 A6
Kirkland La ST4 72 A6
Kirkland Way B78 260 B8
Kirkside Gr WS8 244 F7
Kirkstall Ave ST17 174 B7
Kirkstall Cl WS3 242 F2
Kirkstall Cres WS3 242 F2
Kirkstall Pl ST5 71 B5
Kirkstone Cres WV5 269 F6
Kirk St ST6 42 C1
Kirkup Wlk ST3 284 A3
Kirkwall Gr ST2 43 B2
Kirstead Gdns WV6 255 B3
Kirtley B77 250 E2
Kirton Gr WV6 255 C4
Kitchen La WV11 241 F1
Kite Gr Kidsgrove ST7 26 D3
Meir ST3 90 A6
Kitling Greaves La DE13 166 A7
Kitlings La ST17 175 F7
Kittoe Rd B74 258 A3
Kitwood Ave B78 262 F6
Knarsdale Cl 2 ST3 73 D5
Knaves Castle Ave WS8 228 F2
Knebworth Ct CW12 16 B8
Knenhall La
Moddershall ST3,ST15 89 F1
Stone ST15 89 F1
Knenhall ST15 105 E7
Knight Ave ST16 156 A4
Knight La ST10 78 E1
Knightley Cl ST20 171 D6
Knightley CW3 68 F5
Knightley Rd ST20 171 D8
Knightley Way ST20 171 D7
Knighton Cl B74 257 F3
Knighton Dr B74 257 F3
Knighton Rd
Cannock WS12 210 E3
Sutton Coldfield B74 257 D5
Knight Rd WS7 211 E1
Knights Ave WV6 255 E6
Knightsbridge Cl B74 257 F4
Knightsbridge Way
12 Stoke-on-T ST6 41 D3
Burton u T DE13 166 D7
Knights Cl ST19 207 F7
Knights Cres WV6 255 E7
Knights Croft ST5 69 F7
Knights Ct
Norton Canes WS11 228 A4
Stretton DE13 147 E2
Knightsfield Rd DE13 144 E2
Knights Hill WS9 256 B3
Knight St ST6 41 D4
Kniveden La ST13 31 B5
Knoll Cl WS7 229 A5
Knoll Croft WS9 245 C1
Knoll The DY6 275 E5
Knotty La CW12 17 A8
Knowlbank Rd ST7 53 F7
Knowle La WS14 231 B3
Knowle Rd Biddulph ST8 27 C7
Stafford ST17 175 D7
Knowles Hill DE13 147 B3
Knowle St ST4 72 A8
Knowle Wood View ST3 72 F3
Knowsley La Kidsgrove ST7 26 A4
Lawton-gate ST7 25 F4
Knowsley Rd ST9 44 D3
Knox Rd WV2 266 D6
Knox's Grave La WS14,
B78 248 D7
Knoyle Ct 1 DY8 279 F6
Knutsford Rd ST7 25 A6
Knutton La ST5 55 F2
Knutton Rd ST5 56 C5
Knutton St Mary's Prim Sch
ST5 55 E2
Knype Cl ST5 56 A7
Knypersley Fst Sch ST8 27 B6
Knypersley Rd ST6 42 E4
Knype Way Biddulph ST8 27 B6
Newcastle-u-L ST5 56 A7
Kohima Dr DY8 279 E5
Kurtus B77 261 D6
Kyffin Rd ST2 58 B6
Kyle Cl WV10 240 B1
Kyle Rd DE65 147 D8
Kynaston Cres WV8 239 B2
Kynnersley Croft ST14 111 B1

L

Laburnam Cl ST7 40 E7
Laburnham Ct WS14 231 C5
Laburnham Rd DY6 275 E6
Laburnum Ave
Cannock WS11 226 E7
Tamworth B79 250 B8
Laburnum Cl
Blythe Bridge ST11 91 A6
Cannock WS11 226 E7
Great Bridgeford ST18 135 B2
Kinver DY7 277 F5
Market Drayton TF9 97 D2
Stourbridge DY8 279 E7
Walsall WS3 244 A2
Laburnum Gr
Burntwood WS7 228 F6
Stoke-on-T ST3 72 E3
Laburnum Ho WS4 244 D1
Laburnum Pl
1 Stoke-on-T ST3 89 F8
Newcastle-u-L ST5 40 D1
Laburnum Rd
Brownhills WS9 245 A3
Burton u T DE15 185 F6
Swadlincote DE11 186 F6
Wolverhampton WV4 266 F3
Laburnum St DY8 279 E7
Laches Cl WV10 224 D5
Laches La WV10 224 E2
Ladbrook Gr DY3 271 B3
Ladderedge Ctry Pk★
ST13 30 B4
Ladderedge ST13 30 C2
Ladford Covert Ind Pk
ST18 134 E1
Ladfordfields Ind Est
ST18 134 D1
Ladfordfields Ind Pk
ST18 153 D8
Ladford Trad Pk ST18 134 E1
Ladies Wlk DY3 271 D8
Lad La ST5 283 B3
Ladle End La DE12 184 D1
Ladybank Gr ST3 88 E8
Lady Bank B79 250 B4
Ladydale Cl ST13 30 F4
Ladyfields Way DE11 186 F6
Ladygates CW3 53 B6
Lady Grey's Wlk DY8 279 D5
Lady Hill Terr WS15 196 B7
Lady Meadow Cl
Denstone ST14 95 E5

Lady Meadow Cl *continued*
  Tamworth B78 . . . . 250 A3
Ladymoor La ST6 . . . . 28 B3
Ladysmith Rd ST1 . . . . 57 A3
Ladysmith St ST3 . . . . 284 B2
Ladywell Cl Stretton DE13 147 E1
  Wombourne WV5 . . . . 270 A8
Ladywell Rd ST6 . . . . 41 D3
Lagonda Cl ST8 . . . . 27 B6
Lagonda B77 . . . . 250 E3
Lagrange B79 . . . . 249 E6
Lair The B78 . . . . 262 F8
Lakeland Dr B77 . . . . 262 B7
Lakenheath B79 . . . . 250 C7
Lake Rd ST13 . . . . 18 E1
Lakesedge Betley CW3 . . . . 53 A6
  Bosley SK11 . . . . 7 D8
Lakeside Cl ◼ Hanley ST1 . 56 F2
  Whitmore ST5 . . . . 85 C4
Lakeside Dr WS11 . . . . 228 B6
Lakeside B74 . . . . 257 B5
Lakeside Pk B78 . . . . 249 F1
Lakeside Prim Sch B77 . . 250 E2
Lakeside View WS15 . . . . . 198 B4
Lake St DY3 . . . . 271 D3
Lakewood Dr ST12 . . . . 88 E4
Lakewood Gr ST1 . . . . 57 A3
Lally Pl ST8 . . . . 27 B2
Lamb Cres WV5 . . . . 269 F6
Lambert Ct DY6 . . . . 275 D8
Lambert Dr WS7 . . . . 229 A8
Lambert Rd ST4 . . . . 110 F1
Lambert's La CW12 . . . . 15 E4
Lambert St ST6 . . . . 41 E3
Lamb La ST15 . . . . 119 F7
Lambourn Cl WS3 . . . . 243 C2
Lambourne Cl
  ◪ Lichfield WS14 . . . . . . 231 E8
  Great Wyrley WS6 . . . . . . 226 A7
Lambourne Dr ST2 . . . . 43 C1
Lambourne Way WS11 . . . . 228 A5
Lambourn Pl ST3 . . . . 88 C2
Lamb Shutt Flats TF9 . . . . 97 D1
  Kidsgrove ST7 . . . . 26 A2
Lamb St Hanley ST1 . . . . . . 282 B3
Lamerton Gr ST3 . . . . 73 F2
Lammascote Rd ST16 . . . . 285 C3
Lammas Rd DY8 . . . . 275 C3
Lamorna Cl WV3 . . . . 265 B8
Lamotte Cl ST4 . . . . 73 B5
Lamprey B77 . . . . 261 D6
Lanark Cl DY6 . . . . 275 F5
Lanark Wlks ST5 . . . . 70 F7
Lancaster Ave
  Aldridge WS9 . . . . 256 B8
  Fulford ST11 . . . . 90 E1
  Leek ST13 . . . . 30 F7
  Newcastle-u-L ST5 . . . . . . 283 D2
Lancaster Bldg ST5 . . . . . 283 B2
Lancaster Cres ST4 . . . . . . 71 D8
Lancaster Dr
  Stoke-on-T DE13 . . . . 42 F4
  Tutbury DE13 . . . . 146 B5
Lancaster Gdns WV4 . . . . . 265 E5
Lancaster Ho
  ◾ Stourbridge DY8 . . . . . 279 F8
  Cannock WS12 . . . . 210 D1
Lancaster Pl WS3 . . . . 243 C2
Lancaster Rd
  Fradley WS13 . . . . 215 C5
  Newcastle-u-L ST5 . . . . . . 283 D2
  Stafford ST17 . . . . 175 A8
Lance Dr WS7 . . . . 211 F1
Lancelot Dr DE13 . . . . 147 E2
Lanchester Cl Biddulph ST8 27 B6
  Tamworth B79 . . . . 249 E7
Lancia Cl ST8 . . . . 27 B5
Lancing Ave ST17 . . . . 175 B8
Lander Cl ST15 . . . . 120 D7
Lander Pl ST6 . . . . 42 B6
Landon St ST3 . . . . 284 C3
Landor Cres WS15 . . . . 196 F2
Landor Way ST17 . . . . 174 B8
Landport Rd WV2 . . . . 266 E4
Landrake Gr ST6 . . . . 41 F7
Landsberg B79 . . . . 249 E6
Landseer ST15 . . . . 55 E6
Landstone Rd ◾ ST17 . . . . 175 A8
Landywood Ent Pk WS6 . 242 F8
Landywood Gn WS6 . . . . . . 226 E2
Landywood La WS6 . . . . . . 226 E2
Landywood Prim Sch
  WS6 . . . . 242 F8
Landywood Sta WS6 . . . . . 226 F2
Lane End SK17 . . . . 23 D7
Lane Farm Gr ST1 . . . . 57 E7
Lane Green Ave WV8 . . . . . 239 C1
Lane Green Ct WV8 . . . . . . 239 B3
Lane Green Fst Sch WV8 239 B4
Lane Green Rd WV8 . . . . . . 239 C2
Lane Green Rd Maisonettes
  WV8 . . . . 239 B3
Lane Green Sth Par WV8 . 239 B3
Lane Head SK17 . . . . 13 B7
Lanehead Rd ST1 . . . . 56 F3
Lanehead Wlk WS15 . . . . . 178 C2
Lanes Cl
  King's Bromley DE13 . . . . 199 C6
  Wombourne WV5 . . . . 269 C6
Lane The ST18 . . . . 174 C3
Langdale Cl WS8 . . . . 244 E6
Langdale Cres ST1 . . . . 57 D7
Langdale Ct B77 . . . . 251 A6
Langdale Dr WS11 . . . . 226 C7

Langdale Gn WS11 . . . . . . 226 C7
Langdale Jun & Inf Schs
  ST5 . . . . 71 B5
Langdale Rd ST5 . . . . 71 B5
Langer Cl DE14 . . . . 185 B6
Langford Rd Bucknall ST2 . 58 C3
  Newcastle-u-L ST5 . . . . . . 71 A4
Langford St ST13 . . . . 30 D5
Langham Gn B74 . . . . 256 F1
Langham Rd ST4 . . . . 43 A1
Langholm Dr ST12 . . . . 210 E2
Langland Dr Longton ST3 . 73 A2
  Sedgley DY3 . . . . 271 C8
Langley Cl
  Brownhills WS9 . . . . 245 A3
  Newcastle-u-L ST5 . . . . . . 40 D2
Langley Gdns WV3 . . . . . . 265 D7
Langley Rd WV3,WV4 . . . . . 265 B7
Langley St ST4 . . . . 56 D1
Langot La ST21 . . . . 115 D4
Langstone Rd DY1 . . . . 271 F1
Langton Cres WS14 . . . . . . 232 E6
Langton Ct
  ◼ Lichfield WS13 . . . . . . 214 A1
  Werrington ST9 . . . . 59 A4
Langtree Cl WS12 . . . . 210 D1
Lanrick Gdns WS15 . . . . . . 178 E2
Lansbury Cl ST17 . . . . 174 E8
Lansbury Dr WS11 . . . . 209 E4
Lansbury Gr ST3 . . . . 74 B3
Lansbury Rd WS15 . . . . . . 196 E6
Lansdell Ave ST5 . . . . 56 B6
Lansdowne Ave WV8 . . . . . 238 F2
Lansdowne Cl Leek ST13 . 30 C5
  Stone ST15 . . . . 119 F5
Lansdowne Cres
  Tamworth B77 . . . . 261 D8
  Werrington ST9 . . . . 59 B4
Lansdowne Inf Sch
  DE14 . . . . 166 D5
Lansdowne Rd
  Burton u T DE14 . . . . 184 F7
  Stoke-on-T ST5 . . . . 56 E1
Lansdowne St ST3 . . . . 73 B1
Lansdowne Terr DE14 . . . . 166 D5
Lansdowne Way
  Rugeley WS15 . . . . 178 C2
  Stafford ST17 . . . . 175 D6
Lant Cl DE13 . . . . 199 D6
Lanthorn Cl WS13 . . . . 231 A4
Lapley Ave ST16 . . . . 155 A7
Lapley Dr DE13 . . . . 166 E8
Lapley Hall Mews ST19 . . 206 A6
Lapley La ST19 . . . . 206 C4
Lapley Rd ST19 . . . . 205 D7
Lapper Ave WV4 . . . . 266 F2
Lapwing Cl
  ◾ Packmoor ST7 . . . . 26 F1
  Brownhills WS8 . . . . 244 E7
  Cheslyn Hay WS6 . . . . 226 C1
Lapwing Rd ST7 . . . . 26 D3
Lapwing B77 . . . . 262 A6
Lapwood Ave DY6 . . . . 275 F6
Lapworth Way TF10 . . . . . . 169 A3
Lara Cl ST16 . . . . 155 B3
Larch Cl Kidsgrove ST7 . . . 41 A8
  Kinver DY7 . . . . 278 C3
  Lichfield WS14 . . . . 231 C7
Larch Ct ◾ ST6 . . . . 57 A7
Larches The ◾ ST6 . . . . 57 A7
Larches The TF10 . . . . 168 E4
Larchfields ST15 . . . . 120 B6
Larch Gr Sedgley DY3 . . . . 271 C8
  Stoke-on-T ST3 . . . . 72 C2
Larch Ho DY8 . . . . 279 C6
Larchmere Dr WV11 . . . . . . 242 B3
Larchmont Cl ST4 . . . . 88 B7
Larch Pl ST15 . . . . 55 E8
Larch Rd
  Kingswinford DY6 . . . . . . 275 E7
  Rugeley WS15 . . . . 196 F6
  Swadlincote DE11 . . . . . . 186 F6
Larchwood Dr WS11 . . . . . 210 A4
Larchwood Keele ST5 . . . . 70 A6
  Stafford ST17 . . . . 175 C5
Larcombe Dr WV4 . . . . 266 D5
Lark Ave ST7 . . . . 26 D3
Larkfield ST7 . . . . 26 B1
Lark Hall Com Inf Sch
  B79 . . . . 250 A8
Larkhill La TF9 . . . . 100 A4
Larkhill Rd DY8 . . . . 279 C4
Larkholme Cl WS15 . . . . . . 178 A1
Larkin Ave ST3 . . . . 73 D4
Larkin Cl Stafford ST17 . . . 174 C7
  Wolverhampton WV10 . . . 241 A1
Lark Rise ST14 . . . . 126 B6
Larksfield Rd ST6 . . . . 42 D1
Larksmeadow Vale ST17 . 175 D6
Larkspur Ave WS7 . . . . 229 A5
Larkspur Dr WV10 . . . . 241 B7
Larkspur Gr ST5 . . . . 283 C4
Larkspur B77 . . . . 261 D4
Larkspur Way WS8 . . . . . . 244 D6
Larkstone La ST13,DE6 . . . 34 E1
Larkswood Dr
  Sedgley DY3 . . . . 271 D7
  Wolverhampton WV4 . . . . 265 C3
Lascelles St ST6 . . . . 41 D2
Lask Edge Rd ST9,ST13 . . 28 D7
Laski Cres ST3 . . . . 74 B2
Latebrook Cl ST6 . . . . 41 C7
Latham Cl DE15 . . . . 167 C2
Latham Gr ST6 . . . . 42 B7
Latherford Cl WV10 . . . . . . 224 C5
Latham Rd WV10 . . . . 225 B4
Lathkill Dale DE11 . . . . 186 F2
Latimer Way ST2 . . . . 58 C2

Lauder Cl DY3 . . . . 266 C1
Lauderdale Cl WS8 . . . . . . 244 E6
Lauderdale Gdns WV10 . . 240 E3
Lauder Gr ST18 . . . . 158 C8
Lauder Pl N ST2 . . . . 73 E8
Lauder Pl S ST2 . . . . 73 E8
Launceston Cl B77 . . . . . . 250 D2
Laureates Wlk B74 . . . . . . 258 A1
Laurel Bank B79 . . . . 250 B6
Laurel Cl WS14 . . . . 231 D8
Laurel Cres ST9 . . . . 59 A3
Laurel Dr Burntwood WS7 . 229 C7
  Cannock WS12 . . . . 210 E4
  Harriseahead ST7 . . . . 26 E3
  Newport TF10 . . . . 168 F3
Laurel Gr Burton u T DE15 . 185 E5
  Stafford ST17 . . . . 174 F7
  Stoke-on-T ST3 . . . . 72 D2
  Wolverhampton WV4 . . . . 265 E2
Laurel Rd DY1 . . . . 271 F4
Laurels The WS15 . . . . 196 F5
Laurence Gr WV6 . . . . 255 F2
Lauren Cl ST4 . . . . 72 E6
Lauriston Cl DY1 . . . . 271 F3
Lavender Ave ST11 . . . . 90 F5
Lavender Cl
  Burton u T DE14 . . . . 185 A8
  Great Bridgeford ST18 . . . 135 C2
  Meir ST3 . . . . 74 C5
  Wolverhampton WV9 . . . . 239 F3
Lavender La DY8 . . . . 279 D3
Lavender Lodge ST17 . . . . 177 E7
Lavender Rd B77 . . . . 250 F4
Laverock Gr CW3 . . . . 68 E6
Lawford Ave WS14 . . . . 231 E7
Lawford Cotts ST17 . . . . . . 174 F4
Lawley Cl WS4 . . . . 244 B5
Lawley St ST3 . . . . 73 D3
Lawn Ave DY8 . . . . 279 E4
Lawn Farm Cres ST2 . . . . . 73 D7
Lawn La Cheswardine TF9 . 113 F1
  Coven Heath WV9 . . . . . . 240 A7
Lawnoaks Cl WS8 . . . . 228 C5
Lawn Rd Stafford ST17 . . . 285 A1
  Wolverhampton WV2 . . . . 266 F6
Lawnsfield Wlk ST16 . . . . 136 C1
Lawns The
  Market Drayton TF9 . . . . . 97 D1
  Rolleston on D DE13 . . . . 147 A4
  Uttoxeter ST14 . . . . 111 A3
Lawn St ST7 . . . . 279 E4
Lawnswood Ave
  Burntwood WS7 . . . . 228 F5
  Stourbridge DY8 . . . . 275 C3
  Wolverhampton,Parkfield
  WV4 . . . . 266 E4
  Wolverhampton,Tettenhall
  WV6 . . . . 255 E8
Lawnswood Cl ◼ WS12 . . . 210 D1
Lawnswood Dr
  Brownhills WS9 . . . . 245 A3
  Stourbridge DY7 . . . . 275 A2
Lawnswood Rd
  Dudley DY3 . . . . 271 D5
  Stourbridge DY8 . . . . 275 A2
Lawnswood Rise WV6 . . . . 255 F8
Lawnswood DY7 . . . . 275 A2
Lawn The ST17 . . . . 174 E5
Lawrence Ct B79 . . . . 250 A6
Lawrence Dr ST15 . . . . 103 B4
Lawrence St Hanley ST1 . . 282 A1
  Stafford ST17 . . . . 285 A1
Lawrence Way WS13 . . . . . 230 F5
Lawson Cl WS9 . . . . 256 B4
Lawson Terr
  Newcastle-u-L,Knutton
  ST5 . . . . 55 E2
  Newcastle-u-L,Porthill ST5 56 C6
Lawton Ave ST7 . . . . 25 D3
Lawton Coppice ST7 . . . . . 25 E4
Lawton Cres ST8 . . . . 27 D8
Lawtongate Est ST7 . . . . . . 25 A5
Lawton Hall ST7 . . . . 25 C4
Lawton St Biddulph ST8 . . 27 D8
  Kidsgrove ST7 . . . . 26 C4
  Stoke-on-T ST6 . . . . 42 A2
Laxey Rd ST5 . . . . 56 A3
Laxton Gr ST4 . . . . 88 C4
Lazar La ST17 . . . . 176 B6
Lazy Hill Rd WS9 . . . . 245 D1
Lazy Hill WS9 . . . . 245 D2
Lea Castle Dr DY10 . . . . . . 280 C5
Lea Castle Hospl DY10 . . . 280 C3
Leacliffe Way WS9 . . . . 256 F3
Lea Cl ST5 . . . . 85 D5
Leacote Dr WV6 . . . . 255 C4
Lea Cres ST17 . . . . 174 D7
Leacroft Ave WV10 . . . . . . 240 F1
Leacroft Cl WS9 . . . . 245 B1
Leacroft WS15 . . . . 179 A1
Leacroft La WS11 . . . . 226 C5
Leacroft Rd
  Kingswinford DY6 . . . . . . 275 D6
  Meir ST3 . . . . 90 A8
  Penkridge ST19 . . . . 193 A1
Leacroft ST15 . . . . 120 D7
Leadbeater Ave ST4 . . . . . . 71 F5
Leadendale La ST3 . . . . 89 F3
Leadendale Mews ST3 . . . 89 F8
Leafdown Cl WS12 . . . . 210 D3
Leafenden Ave WS7 . . . . . . 229 A6
Leaford Way DY6 . . . . 275 F5
Leaford Wlk ST7 . . . . 57 F2
Leafy Glade B74 . . . . 257 A3
Leafy Rise DY3 . . . . 271 D5
Lea Gdns WV3 . . . . 266 B8
Lea Gn ST16 . . . . 155 C8
Lea Hall Dr WS7 . . . . 211 D1

Lea Hall Ent Pk WS15 . . . 197 B6
Lea Hall La WS15 . . . . 197 B5
Leahurst Cl ◪ ST17 . . . . . . 175 C6
Leaks Alley ST9 . . . . 284 B2
Lea La Admaston WS15 . . . 159 F2
  Cookley DY10 . . . . 280 A5
  Great Wyrley WS6 . . . . . . 227 A3
Lea Manor Dr WV4 . . . . 265 E4
Leam Dr WS7 . . . . 229 D7
Leamington Cl WS11 . . . . . 226 C7
Leamington Gdns ST5 . . . 56 E3
Leamington Rd DE14 . . . . 184 E7
Leander Cl
  Burntwood WS7 . . . . 211 E1
  Great Wyrley WS6 . . . . . . 226 F1
Leander Rise DE15 . . . . . . 186 A8
Lea Pl ST3 . . . . 74 B2
Lea Rd Hixon ST18 . . . . . . 139 E1
  Stone ST15 . . . . 119 F6
  Wolverhampton WV3 . . . . 266 B8
Lear Rd WV5 . . . . 270 B8
Leasawe Cl ST18 . . . . 158 C2
Leaside Ave WS15 . . . . 198 C5
Leaside Rd ST4 . . . . 71 E5
Leason Rd ST3 . . . . 74 B2
Leason St ST4 . . . . 72 B7
Leasowe Rd WS15 . . . . 197 A5
Leasowes Dr Perton WV6 . 254 D4
  Wolverhampton WV4 . . . . 265 D6
Leasowes Jun & Inf Schs
  ST17 . . . . 175 D8
Leasowe The WS13 . . . . . . 214 A1
Leas The Ecclesshall ST21 134 A8
  Featherstone WV10 . . . . . 241 C7
Leaswood Cl ST5 . . . . 71 C2
Leaswood Pl ST5 . . . . 71 C2
Leathermill La WS15 . . . . . 178 F1
Leathersley La DE6,DE65 . 129 C2
Lea The ST4 . . . . 88 B7
Leaton Hall DY7 . . . . 268 B1
Lea Vale Rd DY8 . . . . 279 F3
Leawood Rd ST4 . . . . 71 E3
Lebanon Gr WS7 . . . . 228 F8
Ledbury Cl WS9 . . . . 245 C1
Ledbury Cres ST1 . . . . 57 E4
Ledstone Way ST3 . . . . 73 E4
Leech Ave ST5 . . . . 55 F6
Leech St ST5 . . . . 283 C1
Lee Ct WS9 . . . . 244 F3
Leedham Ave B77 . . . . 250 D5
Leedhams Croft DE12 . . . . 202 D8
Leeds St ST4 . . . . 72 F5
Lee Gr ST5 . . . . 71 B4
Leekbrook Ind Est ST13 . . 45 E8
Leekbrook Way ST13 . . . . . 30 F1
Leek Coll of F Ed & Sch of
  Art ST13 . . . . 30 F6
Leek Fst Sch ST13 . . . . 31 A5
Leek High Sch ST13 . . . . . 31 A6
Leek La ST8 . . . . 28 B8
Leek Morlands Hospl
  ST13 . . . . 31 A5
Leek New Rd ST1,ST2,ST6 . 42 F1
  Cheadle ST10 . . . . 76 C5
Leek Old Rd ST9 . . . . 29 E1
Leek Rd Brown Edge ST6 . . 43 C7
  Bucknall ST2 . . . . 58 A6
  Cheadle ST10 . . . . 60 C3
  Cheddleton,Cheddleton Heath
  ST13 . . . . 45 D7
  Cheddleton ST9,ST10 . . . . 60 C3
  Congleton CW12 . . . . 16 A8
  Endon ST9 . . . . 43 E6
  Hanley ST1 . . . . 57 E2
  Longnor SK17 . . . . 13 B6
  Longsdon ST2 . . . . 43 B1
  Stoke-on-T ST6 . . . . 42 F4
  Warslow SK17 . . . . 23 A2
  Werrington ST9 . . . . 59 F3
  Wetley Rocks ST9 . . . . 60 A6
  Wetton DE6 . . . . 34 D3
Leek Road Ind Est SK17 . . 23 A2
Lees Cl WS15 . . . . 197 B5
Leese La
  Acton Trussell ST17 . . . . . 175 B1
  Moddershall ST15 . . . . . . 105 F6
Leese St ST4 . . . . 72 B7
Lees La ST10 . . . . 108 E2
Leet Ct WS15 . . . . 198 B4
Lee Wlk WS11 . . . . 210 B4
Legge La WS18 . . . . 139 D1
Legge St
  Newcastle-u-L ST5 . . . . . . 283 C2
  Wolverhampton WV2 . . . . 266 E6
Legion Cl WS11 . . . . 228 A6
Legs La WV10 . . . . 240 F3
Leicester Ct ST5 . . . . 71 C5
Leicester St ST14 . . . . 110 F1
Leicester Pl ST2 . . . . 58 C2
Leicester St DE14 . . . . 185 C8
Leigh Ave WS7 . . . . 229 B7
Leigh Bank ST10 . . . . 108 F8
Leigh Cl ST17 . . . . 174 F5
Leigh La Bramshall ST14 . . 125 B8
  Church Leigh ST10 . . . . . . 108 D5
  Lower Tean ST10 . . . . 92 F1
  Stoke-on-T ST6 . . . . 41 C1
Leigh Rd Congleton CW12 . .6 B5
  Newport TF10 . . . . 168 E2
Leighs Cl WS4 . . . . 244 C1
Leighs Rd WS4 . . . . 244 C1
Leigh St ST6 . . . . 42 B2
Leighswood ◼ ST17 . . . . . . 175 C7
Leighswood Ave WS9 . . . . 256 B7
Leighswood Cl WS11 . . . . . 227 B7
Leighswood Ct WS9 . . . . . 256 B6
Leighswood Gr WS9 . . . . . 256 A7
Leighswood Ind Est
  WS9 . . . . 256 A8

Leighswood Rd WS9 . . . . 256 A6
Leighswood Sch WS9 . . . 256 B8
Leighton Cl Dudley DY1 . . 271 E2
  Stoke-on-T ST9 . . . . 43 C4
  Uttoxeter ST14 . . . . 126 C6
Leighton Rd
  Uttoxeter ST14 . . . . 126 C6
  Wolverhampton WV4 . . . . 265 F6
Leisure La SK17 . . . . 24 E5
Leisure Wlk ◪ B77 . . . . 261 F6
Lema Way ST16 . . . . 156 C3
Le More B74 . . . . 258 A2
Lennox Gdns WV3 . . . . 266 A8
Lennox Rd ST3 . . . . 284 D1
Lenpark Ind Est ST3 . . . . . 284 C3
Lenthall Ave CW12 . . . . 15 F8
Leofric Cl DE13 . . . . 199 C6
Leomansley Cl WS13 . . . . 230 F7
Leomansley Ct WS13 . . . . 230 E7
Leomansley Rd WS13 . . . . 230 F7
Leomansley View WS13 . 230 E7
Leonard Ave
  Kidderminster DY10 . . . . 280 A1
  Stoke-on-T ST2 . . . . 43 B3
Leonard Dr ST6 . . . . 43 B7
Leonard Rd DY8 . . . . 279 C5
Leonard St Leek ST13 . . . . 30 F5
  Stoke-on-T ST6 . . . . 42 B1
Leonora St ST4 . . . . 56 F7
Leopold St ST4 . . . . 72 E7
Lerridge La ST20 . . . . 131 E6
Lerryn Cl DY6 . . . . 275 F5
Lerwick Cl DY6 . . . . 275 F5
Lesley Dr DY6 . . . . 275 E4
Leslie Rd B74 . . . . 257 B2
Lesscroft Cl WV9 . . . . 240 A3
Lessways Cl ST5 . . . . 56 A8
Lessways Wlk ◼ ST6 . . . . . 56 F7
Lester Gr WS9 . . . . 256 C2
Letchmere Cl WS3 . . . . 253 C2
Letchmere La WV6 . . . . . . 253 C2
Letheridge Gdns ST17 . . . 174 A8
Levedale Cl ST16 . . . . 155 A7
Levedale Rd Bradley ST18 191 C8
  Penkridge ST18,ST19 . . . . 192 C3
Levels The WS15 . . . . 196 F5
Leven Dr WV11 . . . . 242 B1
Lever St WV2 . . . . 266 D8
Leveson Ave WS6 . . . . 226 E2
Leveson Rd Trentham ST4 . 71 F1
  Wolverhampton WV11 . . . 241 F1
Leveson St ST3 . . . . 284 C1
Levett Rd Tamworth B77 . . 251 B5
  Whittington WS14 . . . . . . 232 C1
Levetts Fields WS14 . . . . . 231 C7
Levetts Hollow WS12 . . . . 210 D3
Levetts Sq ◪ WS13 . . . . . . 231 B7
Levington Cl WV6 . . . . 254 F5
Levita Rd ST4 . . . . 71 F4
Lewis Cl WS14 . . . . 231 E7
Lewis Dr DE13 . . . . 166 B7
Lewisham Dr ST6 . . . . 41 C7
Lewisham Rd WV10 . . . . . . 240 B2
Lewis's La DE13 . . . . 199 B6
Lewis St ST4 . . . . 72 B8
Lewthorn Rise WV4 . . . . . . 266 D4
Lexham Pl ST3 . . . . 73 E2
Lexington Gn ST17 . . . . . . 174 A8
Leybourne Cres WV9 . . . . 239 F2
Leycett La ST5 . . . . 54 C2
Leycett Rd ST5 . . . . 54 E4
Leyfield Rd ST4 . . . . 88 B6
Leyfields Farm Mews
  DE13 . . . . 165 C7
Leyfields WS13 . . . . 214 B2
Ley Gdns ST3 . . . . 284 A2
Ley Hill Rd B75 . . . . 258 C1
Leyland Ave WV3 . . . . 255 F1
Leyland Croft WS3 . . . . 243 F4
Leyland Dr WS15 . . . . 178 E2
Leyland Gn ST6 . . . . 42 A6
Leyland Rd B77 . . . . 250 E3
Ley Rise DY3 . . . . 266 C3
Leys Dr ST5 . . . . 70 F2
Leys La ST2 . . . . 43 C2
Leys The DE11 . . . . 186 E6
Liberty Ct WS6 . . . . 226 D3
Liberty La ST6 . . . . 42 C3
Liberty Pk ST17 . . . . 174 A8
Liberty Rd B77 . . . . 261 F5
Libra Cl B79 . . . . 249 F7
Libra Pl ST6 . . . . 41 F6
Lichen Cl WS12 . . . . 209 C6
Lichfield Bsns Ctr WS13 . 214 D1
Lichfield Cathedral Sch
  WS13 . . . . 231 B8
Lichfield Cath ★ WS13 . . . 231 B8
Lichfield City Sta WS14 . . 231 B7
Lichfield Cl ST5 . . . . 55 D2
Lichfield Cres B78 . . . . 249 B7
Lichfield Ct ST17 . . . . 285 C2
Lichfield Dr
  Blymhill Lawn TF11 . . . . . 204 B1
  Great Haywood ST18 . . . . 158 B1
Lichfield Rd
  Abbots Bromley WS15 . . . 161 B3
  Armitage WS15 . . . . 178 B8
  Brownhills,Shireoak Hill WS8,
  WS9 . . . . 245 B5
  Brownhills WS8,WS14 . . . 245 A8
  Burntwood WS7 . . . . 229 C6
  Burton u T DE13,DE14 . . . 184 C4
  Cannock WS11 . . . . 227 B8
  Hamstall Ridware WS15 . . 180 F7
  King's Bromley DE13 . . . . 199 C6
  Lichfield ST7,WS13 . . . . . 230 B6
  Sandon ST18 . . . . 137 D8
  Stafford ST17 . . . . 285 B4

Lichfield Rd continued
Stafford ST17 . . . . .285 C2
Stone ST15 . . . . .120 C7
Sutton Coldfield B74 . . . . .258 A3
Talke ST7 . . . . .40 D7
Tamworth B78,B79 . . . . . .249 E6
Walsall,Highbridge WS3 . .244 B5
Walsall,New Invention WS3,WS4,
 WS8,WS9 . . . . .242 E1
Walsall,Shelfield WS4 . . . .244 C1
Walsall,Wallington Heath
 WS3 . . . . .243 C2
Lichfield Road Ind Est
B79 . . . . .249 E6
Lichfield St
Burton u T DE14 . . . . . . .166 D2
Fazeley B78 . . . . .249 F1
Hanley ST1 . . . . .282 C1
Rugeley WS15 . . . . .196 F8
Stone ST15 . . . . .120 A8
Tamworth B79 . . . . .250 A5
Lichfield Trent Valley Sta
WS13 . . . . .231 F8
Liddiard Ct DY8 . . . . .279 E6
Liddle St ST4 . . . . .72 A6
Lidgate Gr ST3 . . . . .72 F2
Lidgate Wlk ST5 . . . . .71 B2
Lid La Cheadle ST10 . . . . .76 C3
Roston DE6 . . . . .96 E7
Liffs Rd DE6,SK17 . . . . . . .36 C7
Lifton Ct DY6 . . . . .275 F5
Light Ash Cl WV9 . . . . . . .224 C3
Light Ash WV9 . . . . .224 C3
Light Ash La WV9 . . . . . . .224 C3
Lightfoot St ST4 . . . . .110 F1
Light Oaks Ave ST2 . . . . . .43 D1
Light Oaks Cl DE14 . . . . . .166 E6
Lightoaks ST10 . . . . .77 F5
Lightwater Gr ST2 . . . . . . .42 F1
Lightwood Rd
Longton ST3 . . . . .284 C2
Newcastle-u-L ST5 . . . . . .40 D1
Stoke-on-T ST4 . . . . .89 F6
Yoxall DE13 . . . . .181 F2
Lilac Ave WS11 . . . . .226 D7
Lilac Cl
Great Bridgeford ST18 . . . .135 C2
Meir ST3 . . . . .74 C5
Newcastle-u-L ST5 . . . . . .40 D1
Uttoxeter ST14 . . . . .126 B6
Lilac Gr DY5 . . . . .269 F6
Lilac Gr Burntwood WS7 . .228 F2
Burton u T DE15 . . . . . . .185 F6
Stafford ST17 . . . . .174 F2
Stoke-on-T ST3 . . . . .72 E3
Lilac Ho WS4 . . . . .244 D1
Lilac La WS6 . . . . .243 A8
Lilac Rd B79 . . . . .250 A8
Lilleshall Cres WV2 . . . . . .266 D7
**Lilleshall Hall National
 Sports Ctr** TF10 . . . . . . .187 A2
Lilleshall Rd ST5 . . . . .71 D5
Lilleshall St ST3 . . . . .284 C2
Lilleshall Way ST17 . . . . . .174 B7
Lillington Cl [2] WS13 . . . .231 A8
Lillydale Rd ST2 . . . . .58 B3
Lily St ST5 . . . . .56 D5
Limbrick Rd ST7 . . . . .39 A1
Lime Cl Church Leigh ST10 .109 A4
Doveridge DE6 . . . . .127 B8
Great Wyrley WS6 . . . . . . .226 F4
Meir ST3 . . . . .74 C5
Lime Ct Burton u T DE15 . .185 E7
Market Drayton TF9 . . . . . .97 D1
Limedale Ct [8] ST15 . . . . .104 F1
Lime Gr Barlaston ST12 . . . .88 F4
Burntwood WS7 . . . . .229 C6
Burton u T DE15 . . . . . . .185 E5
Kinver DY7 . . . . .278 C3
Lichfield WS14 . . . . .231 D8
Waterhouses ST10 . . . . . . .48 F3
Limeheath PI ST6 . . . . . . .41 E5
Limehurst Ave WV3 . . . . . .255 C1
Lime Kiln La Alton ST10 . . .78 E1
Kidsgrove ST7 . . . . .25 E2
Lime La
Norton Canes WS3 . . . . . .228 A1
Walsall WS3 . . . . .244 A7
Limepit La WS11,WS12 . . .209 D6
Lime Rd Huntington WS12 .209 D8
Sedgley DY3 . . . . .266 F1
Limes Ave ST9 . . . . .30 A1
Limes Ct Stoke-on-T ST4 . . .71 E8
Wolverhampton WV6 . . . . .255 D5
Limes Rd WV6 . . . . .255 D4
Limes The
Albrighton WV7 . . . . .237 A4
Himley DY3 . . . . .270 B3
Newcastle-u-L ST5 . . . . . .56 C7
Lime St Stoke-on-T ST4 . . .72 B6
Wolverhampton WV3 . . . . .266 B8
Limes View DY3 . . . . .271 D7
Limetree Ave ST16 . . . . . .155 D5
Lime Tree Ave WV6 . . . . . .255 A3
Lime Tree Gdns WV8 . . . . .239 B4
Limetree Rd B74 . . . . .256 D1
Lime Tree Rd WV8 . . . . . . .239 B4
Lime Wlk ST19 . . . . .207 E8
Limewood Cl ST11 . . . . . . .91 A6
Linacre Rd ST21 . . . . .133 C6
Linacre Way ST3 . . . . .73 E5
Lincoln Ave
Newcastle-u-L ST5 . . . . . .71 C5
Tamworth B79 . . . . .249 E6
Lincoln Cl WS13 . . . . .214 C1
Lincoln Croft WS14 . . . . . .246 F6
Lincoln Ct ST14 . . . . .110 F1
Lincoln Dr WS11 . . . . .226 F8

Lincoln Gn WV10 . . . . . . .240 D2
Lincoln Gr ST5 . . . . .71 C5
Lincoln Mdw ST17 . . . . . .174 A8
Lincoln Rd Burslem ST6 . . .57 A7
Burton u T DE15 . . . . . . .185 D7
Kidsgrove ST7 . . . . .25 F2
Lincoln St ST1 . . . . .282 C2
Lindale Cl CW12 . . . . .6 A5
Lindale Dr WV5 . . . . .269 F6
Lindale Gr [3] ST3 . . . . . . .90 B7
Linda Rd ST6 . . . . .41 E5
Linden Ave WS7 . . . . .229 B5
Lindenbrook Vale ST17 . . .175 C7
Linden Cl Congleton CW12 . .16 A8
Newcastle-u-L ST5 . . . . . .56 B3
Stafford ST17 . . . . .174 A8
Tamworth B77 . . . . .250 F4
Linden Dr ST8 . . . . .16 C1
Linden Gr Biddulph ST8 . . .16 C1
Newcastle-u-L ST5 . . . . . .56 B3
Linden Lea WV3 . . . . .255 D1
Linden PI ST3 . . . . .72 F1
Linden Rd DE13 . . . . .183 C5
Lindens The Stone ST15 . . .120 B5
Wolverhampton WV6 . . . . .255 B3
Linden View WS12 . . . . . .210 B4
Linden Way TF9 . . . . .97 D2
Lindera B77 . . . . .251 A4
Lindisfarne B77 . . . . .250 D3
Lindley PI ST3 . . . . .90 A4
Lindley St ST6 . . . . .57 B7
Lindon Cl WS8 . . . . .245 A6
Lindon Dr WS8 . . . . .244 F7
Lindon Rd WS8 . . . . .244 F5
Lindon View WS8 . . . . . . .245 A5
Lindop Ct ST1 . . . . .282 A5
Lindop St ST1 . . . . .282 C3
Lindrick Cl WS3 . . . . .242 F3
Lindrosa Rd B74 . . . . .256 F3
Lindsay St ST1 . . . . .282 A2
Lindum Ave ST4 . . . . .88 C7
Line Houses Cvn Site ST6 . .41 A6
Lineker Cl ST16 . . . . .155 B3
Linet Gr ST7 . . . . .26 E1
Linfield Gdns DY3 . . . . . . .266 C1
Linfield St ST1 . . . . .282 C3
Linford Cl WS15 . . . . .198 C4
Lingard St ST4 . . . . .57 A8
Lingfield Ave
Stoke-on-T ST6 . . . . .43 A8
Wolverhampton WV10 . . . .240 D5
Lingfield Dr WS6 . . . . .226 F2
Lingfield Dr WS6 . . . . .226 F2
Lingfield Gr WV6 . . . . .254 F4
Lingfield Rd
Burton u T DE14 . . . . . . .184 F7
Norton Canes WS11 . . . . .228 A5
Lingmoor Gr WS9 . . . . . . .256 A7
Ling Rd WS12 . . . . .209 C5
Linhope Gr [1] ST3 . . . . . .90 B7
Linkend Cl ST1 . . . . .57 F5
Link Rd Brownhills WS9 . . .245 A5
Wombourne WV5 . . . . . . .270 A7
Links Ave
Newcastle-u-L ST5 . . . . . .56 B4
Wolverhampton WV6 . . . . .255 D7
Links Dr DY8 . . . . .279 E2
Linksfield Rd ST16 . . . . . .155 D8
Links Rd WV4 . . . . .266 A3
Links Side Way WS9 . . . . .256 C8
Links View B74 . . . . .257 B1
Linksway CW12 . . . . .15 E8
Linksway CW12 . . . . .15 E8
Linkway Ret Pk WS12 . . . .226 B6
Linkwood Ind Est DY8 . . . .279 F6
Linley Dr WV10 . . . . .240 E1
Linley Dr Dudley DY3 . . . . .271 B2
Lawton-gate ST7 . . . . .25 A3
Linley La ST7 . . . . .25 A2
Linley Rd Lawton-gate ST7 . .25 A2
Stoke-on-T ST4 . . . . .71 E8
Talke ST7 . . . . .40 C8
Linley Trad Est
Kidsgrove ST7 . . . . .25 C1
Talke ST7 . . . . .40 C8
Linnburn Rd ST3 . . . . .73 E4
Linnet Cl WS12 . . . . .209 D7
Linnet Way ST8 . . . . .27 E8
Linslade Cl WV4 . . . . .266 D4
Lintake Dr WS11 . . . . .160 F6
Linthouse Wlk [3] B77 . . . .261 F6
Lintly B77 . . . . .251 B1
Linton Rd WV4 . . . . .265 E5
Linwood Dr WS12 . . . . . . .209 F7
Linwood Way ST6 . . . . . . .41 E5
Lionel Gr ST4 . . . . .71 E6
Lionfields Cl DY10 . . . . . . .280 A5
Lionfields Rd DY10 . . . . . .280 B5
Lion Gr ST5 . . . . .55 E8
Lion Ind Est WS9 . . . . . . .256 A8
Lion Pas ST9 . . . . .279 F5
Lion's Den WS7,WS14 . . . .229 E2
Lion St Rugeley WS15 . . . .178 E1
Stoke-on-T ST4 . . . . .72 A7
Stourbridge DY8 . . . . .279 F5
Lion Way ST17 . . . . .175 A8
Lisbon PI ST5 . . . . .70 F7
Liskeard Cl ST2 . . . . .58 A1
Lister Gr ST11 . . . . .90 D3
Lister Rd ST16 . . . . .155 F5
Litley Dr ST10 . . . . .92 D8
Little Aston Hall Dr B74 . . .257 B5
Little Aston Hall B74 . . . . .257 B5
Little Aston Hospl B74 . . . .257 B5
Little Aston La B74 . . . . . .257 D6
Little Aston Park Rd B74 . .257 A4

Little Aston Prim Sch
B74 . . . . .257 C6
Little Aston Rd WS9 . . . . .256 D6
Little Barrow Wlk [3]
 WS13 . . . . .214 A1
Little Birches WV3 . . . . . . .265 F8
Little Bloxwich CE Prim Sch
 WS3 . . . . .243 D3
Little Burton E DE14 . . . . .166 D4
Little Burton W DE14 . . . . .166 D4
Little Checkhill La DY7 . . . .274 D4
Little Chell La ST6 . . . . . . .41 F5
Little Church La B79 . . . . .250 B5
Little Cliffe Rd ST3 . . . . . .72 E4
Little Comm WS3 . . . . .244 A4
Littlecote B79 . . . . .249 D7
Little Eaves La ST2 . . . . . .58 C6
Littlefield La Ellastone DE6 .80 A2
Snelston DE6 . . . . .81 B4
Little-Field ST4 . . . . .71 E4
Little Grange WS13 . . . . . .213 F1
Littlehales Rd TF10 . . . . . .187 A6
Little Hardwick Rd WS9 . . .256 C1
Little Hay La WS14 . . . . . .231 D3
Little Johnson's La WS9 . . .256 B1
Little Lakes CW2 . . . . .37 D2
Little Lawns Cl WS9 . . . . .245 A4
Little Marsh Gr ST19 . . . . .192 F1
Little Marsh Pk ST19 . . . . .193 A1
Little Moss Cl ST5 . . . . . . .25 E5
Little Moss La ST5 . . . . . . .25 E5
Little Oaks Dr DY7 . . . . . .275 A2
Little Onn Rd ST20 . . . . . .190 A7
Little Orch WS15 . . . . . . .178 E2
Little Pipe La
Creswell Green WS13 . . . .212 F1
Lichfield WS13 . . . . .213 A1
Little Pountney St [4]
 WV2 . . . . .266 C8
Little Row
 [5] Kidsgrove ST7 . . . . . .26 B2
Stoke-on-T ST4 . . . . .72 F8
Little Sutton La B75 . . . . .258 C1
Little Sutton Prim Sch
 B75 . . . . .258 D3
Little Sutton Rd B75 . . . . .258 D2
Little Tixall La ST18 . . . . . .158 C2
Littleton Bsns Pk WS12 . . .209 D4
Littleton Cl ST16 . . . . .156 A3
Littleton Cres ST19 . . . . . .192 F1
Littleton Dr WS12 . . . . . . .209 C7
Littleton Way WS7 . . . . . . .211 D1
Littlewood La WS6 . . . . . . .226 E4
Littlewood Rd WS6 . . . . . . .226 E4
Littleworth Hill WS12 . . . . .210 D4
Littleworth Rd WS12 . . . . .210 C4
Littondale Cl CW12 . . . . . .6 A5
Litton B77 . . . . .251 C1
Littywood La ST18 . . . . . . .173 C2
Liverpool Rd E ST7 . . . . . .25 C2
Liverpool Rd
Kidsgrove ST7 . . . . .26 A1
Newcastle-u-L,Cross Heath
 ST5 . . . . .56 A3
Newcastle-u-L,Red Street
 ST5 . . . . .40 D2
Newcastle-u-L ST5 . . . . . .283 B3
Stoke-on-T ST4 . . . . .72 B7
Liverpool Rd W ST7 . . . . . .25 B4
Livingstone Ave WV6 . . . . .254 E5
Livingstone Rd WS3 . . . . . .243 E2
Livingstone St Leek ST13 . . .30 F5
Stoke-on-T ST4 . . . . .42 C2
Lizard La TF11 . . . . .220 A6
Llewellyn Roberts Way
 TF9 . . . . .97 D2
Lloyd Dr WV4 . . . . .265 C2
Lloyd George Gr WS11 . . . .210 C2
Lloyd Hill WV4 . . . . .265 C3
Lloyd Rd WV6 . . . . .255 D5
Lloyd Roberts Bldgs
 WV4 . . . . .265 F1
Lloyd St Cannock WS11 . . .209 D1
Longton ST3 . . . . .284 C2
Stafford ST16 . . . . .285 B4
Wolverhampton WV6 . . . . .255 F4
Lloyd The TF9 . . . . .113 F7
Lochalsh Gr WV11 . . . . . .242 B1
Lochsong Cl WS11 . . . . . .261 D4
Lockerbie Cl ST13 . . . . . . .31 B5
Locketts La WS11 . . . . . . .209 F5
Locketts Ct WS11 . . . . . . .209 F5
Lockett St ST1 . . . . .57 D6
Locke Way ST16 . . . . .156 B3
Lockfield Cl DY8 . . . . .275 D4
Lockhart Dr B75 . . . . .258 C1
Lockington Ave ST2 . . . . . .58 D1
Lock Keepers Cl WS11 . . . .227 F4
Lockley St ST1 . . . . .57 E5
Lock Rd ST19 . . . . .207 F8
Lockside Dr DY7 . . . . .278 B4
Lockside View WS15 . . . . .196 F8
Lockside WV5 . . . . .269 E7
Locks View DY8 . . . . .275 D4
Lockwood Cl
Newcastle-u-L ST5 . . . . . .283 D3
Stoke-on-T ST2 . . . . .43 B3
Lode La DE6 . . . . .35 B4
Lodge Barn Rd ST8 . . . . . .27 F6
Lodgefield Mobile Home Pk
 ST17 . . . . .156 D2
Lodge Gr Aldridge WS9 . . .256 A5
Newcastle-u-L ST5 . . . . . .56 C6
Lodge Hill DE13 . . . . .146 E3

Lodge La
Cheslyn Hay WS11 . . . . . .226 C5
Chorley WS15 . . . . .212 D3
Fairoak ST21 . . . . .115 F5
Hope DE6 . . . . .35 B3
Ilam DE6 . . . . .50 D3
Kingswinford DY6 . . . . . . .275 B6
Woodseaves ST20 . . . . . .151 E6
Yoxall DE13 . . . . .182 B8
Lodge Pk WV5 . . . . .267 C7
Lodge Rd Burntwood WS7 . .56 C8
Netherseal DE12 . . . . . . .219 E8
Rugeley WS15 . . . . .197 A6
Stoke-on-T ST4 . . . . .71 E7
Talke Pits ST7 . . . . .40 D6
Walsall WS4 . . . . .244 B1
Lodges TF11 . . . . .203 F2
Lodge View WS6 . . . . .226 C3
Loftus Ct WS7 . . . . .229 A5
Loftus St ST4 . . . . .282 A4
Loganbeck Gr ST3 . . . . . . .73 E5
Lohengrin Ct DE13 . . . . . .147 E2
Lomas St ST4 . . . . .57 A2
Lomax Cl WS13 . . . . .214 A1
Lomax Rd WS12 . . . . .210 B7
Lombard Gdns [1] WS13 . .231 B8
Lombard St WS13 . . . . . . .231 B8
Lombardy Gr
Burntwood WS7 . . . . .228 F8
Meir ST3 . . . . .74 A2
Lomita Cres B77 . . . . .261 D8
Lomond Gr ST3 . . . . .73 E5
Lomond Gr ST10 . . . . .76 F5
Lomond Rd DY3 . . . . .266 C1
Lomond Wlk ST3 . . . . .88 F7
London Rd
Bridgemere CW5 . . . . . . .67 A5
Knighton CW3,TF9 . . . . . .83 C6
Lichfield WS14 . . . . .231 C5
Newcastle-u-L,Chesterton
 ST5 . . . . .55 E7
Newcastle-u-L,City General Hospl
 ST5 . . . . .283 C1
Shenstone B75,WS14 . . . .258 A6
Stoke-on-T ST4 . . . . .72 A6
Sutton Coldfield B75 . . . . .259 A4
Weeford WS14 . . . . .247 F3
Weston ST18 . . . . .138 D2
London St ST13 . . . . .30 F5
Long Acre WV8 . . . . .238 F2
Longacres Cannock WS12 .210 F5
Little Aston B74 . . . . .257 C5
Longboat La DY8 . . . . .275 E1
Longbow Cl DE13 . . . . . . .147 C1
Longbow Gr DE13 . . . . . . .147 C1
Longbridge Hayes Rd ST5 . .56 C8
Long Bridge Rd WS14 . . . .231 C5
Longbrook Ave ST3 . . . . . .72 F2
Longclough Rd ST5 . . . . . .40 D2
Long Croft
Albrighton WV7 . . . . .237 B5
Cannock WS12 . . . . .209 C4
Longcroft La DE13 . . . . . . .182 B4
Longdoles ST3 . . . . .73 F3
Longdon Ave WV4 . . . . . . .266 D5
Longdon Dr B74 . . . . .257 E4
Longfellow Cl DE14 . . . . . .166 D7
Longfellow PI WS11 . . . . .209 E4
Longfellow Rd
Burntwood WS7 . . . . .212 A1
Dudley DY3 . . . . .271 B5
Longfellow Wlk B79 . . . . . .249 F8
Longfield Ave WS15 . . . . . .119 F7
Longfield Cl B77 . . . . .250 E4
Longfield Dr B74 . . . . .257 D4
Longfield Rd ST4 . . . . .71 E8
Longford Cl
Burton u T DE15 . . . . . . .167 B2
Wombourne WV5 . . . . . . .269 D5
Longford Ct WS11 . . . . . . .226 B8
Longford Gn WS11 . . . . . .226 C8
Longford Ind Est WS11 . . .226 D6
Longford Pk TF10 . . . . . . .168 B1
Longford Prim Sch
 WS11 . . . . .226 C8
Longford Rd
Cannock WS11 . . . . .226 D7
Newport TF10 . . . . .168 C2
Longford Wlk ST2 . . . . . . .58 A2
Long Furrow WV8 . . . . . . .239 E1
Longhedge La DE13 . . . . . .146 F1
Longhope Dr ST15 . . . . . . .119 F6
Longhurst ST16 . . . . .156 C4
Long La Alrewas WS13 . . . .200 E1
Derrington ST18 . . . . .154 C2
Great Wyrley WS6 . . . . . . .242 E6
Harriseahead ST7 . . . . . . .26 E4
Longlake Ave WV6 . . . . . . .255 B3
Longlands Dr B77 . . . . . . .250 F4
Longlands PI WS15 . . . . . .160 F6
Longlands Prim Sch TF9 . . .97 D2
Longlands The WV5 . . . . . .270 A6
Longleat Dr DY1 . . . . .271 E2
Longleat Rd WS9 . . . . . . .245 A1
Longleat B79 . . . . .249 D7
Longley Rd ST3 . . . . .73 C5
Long Mdw
Newcastle-u-L ST5 . . . . . .71 C3
Stafford ST17 . . . . .174 E5
Long Meadow Dr DY3 . . . .266 B2
Longmead Rd DE13 . . . . . .166 C6
Longmoor Ho B74 . . . . . . .257 F2
Long Mynd Cl WV11 . . . . .242 B1
Longnor Craft Ctr* SK17 . .13 B6
Longnor PI ST2 . . . . .58 A2
Longport Rd ST6 . . . . .56 D7

Longport Sta ST6 . . . . . . .56 D7
Long Row Caverswall ST11 .74 D3
Kidsgrove ST7 . . . . .26 A1
Longsdon Cl ST5 . . . . .40 C1
Longsdon Gr ST3 . . . . .73 E4
Longshaw Ave ST5 . . . . . .56 B7
Longshaw La Alton ST10 . . .78 E5
Oakamoor ST10 . . . . .78 E7
Longshaw St ST6 . . . . .56 D8
Longshore Cl ST18 . . . . . .174 C6
Longslow Cl TF9 . . . . .97 B1
Longslow Rd TF9 . . . . .97 A1
Longstaff Ave WS12 . . . . .211 C4
Longstaff Croft WS13 . . . . .213 F2
Long St Burton u T DE15 . .185 E7
Wheaton Aston ST19 . . . . .205 C6
Longton Exchange ST3 . . . .284 C3
Longton Hall Rd ST3 . . . . .72 F2
Longton High Sch ST3 . . . .73 F2
Longton Hospl ST3 . . . . . .73 D1
Longton Rd Barlaston ST12 .88 F2
Oulton ST15 . . . . .105 D4
Stoke-on-T ST4 . . . . .88 B6
Longton Sta ST3 . . . . .284 C2
Longus Ind Est ST6 . . . . . .41 D4
Long Valley Rd ST8 . . . . . .16 C2
Longview Cl ST3 . . . . .73 D5
Longwood Path B78 . . . . . .249 D1
Longwood Prim Sch
 B78 . . . . .249 D1
Longwood Rd WS9 . . . . . .256 B2
Lonsdale CE Prim Sch
 ST21 . . . . .133 D6
Lonsdale Ct
Eccleshall ST21 . . . . .133 D7
Market Drayton TF9 . . . . . .97 D1
Lonsdale Rd
Burton u T DE14 . . . . . . .185 B8
Wolverhampton WV3 . . . . .266 B7
Lonsdale St ST4 . . . . .72 B6
Loomer Rd ST5 . . . . .55 E6
Loomer Road Ind Est ST5 . .55 E5
Loop Rd ST5 . . . . .118 C7
Lord Cromwell Ct WS11 . . .210 A5
Lords St ST4 . . . . .88 D7
Lordship La ST4 . . . . .72 D7
Lords La DY7 . . . . .274 E1
Lordsley La TF9 . . . . .100 A7
Lord St Biddulph ST8 . . . . .27 D7
Stoke-on-T ST6 . . . . .42 C1
Lordswell Rd DE14 . . . . . .165 F4
Lordswood Rd ST4 . . . . . . .88 D7
Lorien Cl ST13 . . . . .30 C4
Lorien Ct ST4 . . . . .72 A8
Loring Rd ST5 . . . . .56 B6
Loring Terr S ST5 . . . . . . .56 B6
Lorne St Burntwood WS7 . .228 E8
Stoke-on-T ST6 . . . . .42 A1
Lorraine St ST7 . . . . .26 F1
Lorton B79 . . . . .249 D7
Lothersdale B77 . . . . .262 C8
Lothians Rd Walsall WS3 . .244 A5
Wolverhampton WV6 . . . . .255 E6
Lotus Ave ST8 . . . . .27 B6
Lotus Ct ST15 . . . . .105 A2
Lotus Dr WS11 . . . . .209 E5
Lotus B77 . . . . .250 E3
Lotus Way ST16 . . . . .155 F5
Loughborough Wlk ST3 . . .284 C4
Loughshaw B77 . . . . .251 C1
Louise Dr ST3 . . . . .72 F3
Louise St Dudley DY3 . . . . .271 C3
Stoke-on-T ST6 . . . . .42 A2
Lount La DE13 . . . . .146 E1
Louvain Ave ST1 . . . . .57 D7
Lovage Gr ST2 . . . . .58 A3
Lovatt Ave ST5 . . . . .56 A4
Lovatt Cl DE13 . . . . .147 F2
Lovatt PI WS11 . . . . .209 E5
Lovatt St Stafford ST16 . . .155 D5
Stoke-on-T ST4 . . . . .72 B7
Lovelace Cl ST17 . . . . .174 C8
Love La Great Wyrley WS6 .227 B3
Rugeley WS15 . . . . .178 F1
Wolverhampton WV6 . . . . .255 D6
Lovell Dr ST16 . . . . .156 B5
Lovell Rd DE13 . . . . .182 A2
Lovell B79 . . . . .249 F6
Loveridge Cl WV8 . . . . . . .238 F3
Lovers La ST9 . . . . .99 F4
Loveston Gr ST3 . . . . .284 D4
Lovett Ct WS15 . . . . .178 D2
Lowdham B77 . . . . .251 C1
Lowe Dr DY6 . . . . .275 E4
Lowell Dr ST3 . . . . .73 F4
Lower Ash Rd ST7 . . . . . . .25 E1
Lower Bar TF10 . . . . .168 E3
Lower Bedford St ST4 . . . . .57 A2
Lower Bethesda St ST1 . . .282 B2
Lower Birches Way
 WS15 . . . . .196 D7
Lower Brook St WS15 . . . .178 E1
Lower Bryan St ST1 . . . . . .282 B4
Lower Cres ST4 . . . . .71 E8
Lowercroft Way ST4 . . . . . .257 E6
Lower Cross St ST3 . . . . . .284 C4
Lower Farm Prim Sch
 WS3 . . . . .243 C3
Lower Farm WS9 . . . . .245 E4
Lower Foundry St ST1 . . . .282 B3
Lower Gn WV6 . . . . .255 D5
Lower Gungate B79 . . . . . .250 B5
Lower Hadderidge [13] ST6 .56 F8

Lower High St
Mow Cop ST7................26 D7
Stourbridge DY8.........279 F6
Tutbury DE13............146 C7
Lower House La CV9....262 F2
Lower Keys Bsns Pk
WS12....................210 D3
Lower La Chorley WS13....212 D3
Hopton ST18.............156 D8
Lower Lodge Residential Mobile Home Pk WS15 197 E5
Lower Mayer St ST1.....282 C4
Lower Milehouse La ST5 . 55 F3
Lower Outwoods Rd
DE13....................165 F6
Lower Oxford Rd ST5....56 E2
Lowerpark B77...........250 C1
Lower Penkridge Rd
ST17....................175 B1
Lower Rd Ashley TF9.....100 B4
Cannock WS12...........210 C3
Gnosall ST20............152 B5
Lower Rookery Rd ST15 . 118 C6
Lower Sandford St
WS13....................231 A7
Lower Spring Rd 3 ST3 . 73 D2
Lower St 1 Burslem ST6 . 57 A7
Doveridge DE6...........127 B8
Newcastle-u-L ST5.......283 B3
Wolverhampton WV6.....255 E5
Lower Villiers St WV2...266 C7
Lower Way WS15........197 C1
Lowe St ST4................72 B7
Loweswater Dr DY3......271 D3
Lowfield Dr ST5.............56 E5
Lowfield La ST20........171 C5
Lowforce B77............251 C1
Lowhurst Dr ST6...........42 A7
Lowland Rd WS12.......209 C5
Lowlands Ave WV6......255 E6
Lowlands Ct WV6........255 E6
Lowlands Rd ST6..........41 B4
Lowndes Cl ST4............71 F6
Lowndes Rd DY8........279 E6
Lowry Cl WV6...........254 F4
Low St WS6..............226 D3
Lowther Pl ST13...........31 A5
Lowther St ST1..........282 A4
Lowthorpe Way ST2......58 E1
Loxley Hall Sch ST14...125 C5
Loxley La ST14...........125 C5
Loxley Pl ST3..............89 F7
Loxley Rd B75...........258 D3
Loxton Cl B74...........257 D5
Loynton Cl ST16.........155 B7
Loynton Sands ST20.....151 A5
Lucas St ST6...............56 E8
Lucepool La DE13.......182 C3
Lucerne Pl ST5.............70 E7
Ludbrook Rd ST4..........73 B5
Ludford Cl ST5.............40 D2
Ludgate St DE13........146 C6
Ludgate B79.............250 A5
Ludgrove Way ST17.....175 B8
Lud La ST5...............250 A5
Ludlow Cl WS11.........210 C2
Ludlow St ST1...........282 C1
Ludlow Way DY1.........271 E2
Ludstone Ave WV4......265 D5
Ludwall Rd ST3............73 E1
Lugano Ct ST1.............70 F6
Lukesland Ave ST4.......71 E6
Luke St ST6................56 E7
Lukes Wlk WS13.........214 A2
Lullington Rd
Clifton Campville B79...218 C3
Edingale B79............217 D5
Lulworth Gr ST6...........41 E6
Lulworth Rd WS7........229 A7
Lulworth Wlk WV4......265 C6
Lundy Rd ST3..............72 F3
Lune Cl 1 CW12...........6 A1
Lunns Croft WS13.......231 C8
Lunts Moss ST7...........25 C7
Lutley Cl WV3...........265 E7
Lutley La DY7...........273 B8
Luttrell Rd B74..........258 A1
Lychgate Cl ST4...........72 A5
Lydford Pl ST3.............73 F3
Lydford Rd WS3.........243 B3
Lydgate Rd DY6.........275 F6
Lydia Croft B74..........257 E6
Lydia Dr ST1...............57 F6
Lydiates Cl DY3.........271 B7
Lyme Brook Pl ST4........71 E3
Lyme Ct ST5..............283 C1
Lymedale Small Firms Ctr
ST5......................55 F5
Lyme Dr ST4..............71 D5
Lyme Gr ST5..............56 C3
Lyme Rd ST3..............74 B1
Lymer Rd WV10.........240 C1
Lymer's La ST18.........123 A1
Lymes Rd ST3.............70 B4
Lymevale Rd ST4..........71 E4
Lyme Valley Rd ST5.....283 C1
Lymewood Cl ST5.......283 B2
Lyme Wood Gr ST5......283 B1
Lymington Rd
Burntwood WS7.........211 F1
Stafford ST16...........156 C4

Lyn Ave WS13...........213 F1
Lynch The B78...........251 F1
Lyncroft WV7............237 A5
Lyndale B77..............261 F6
Lyndale Rd DY3.........266 B2
Lyndhurst Ave DE15....166 F1
Lyndhurst Dr Biddulph ST8 . 27 A6
Stourbridge DY8........275 F1
Lyndhurst Gr ST15.....120 D6
Lyndhurst Rd
Cannock WS12..........210 E1
Wolverhampton WV3...266 E1
Lyndhurst St ST6..........56 E8
Lyndon Cl DY3..........266 E1
Lyndon Gr DY6..........275 B8
Lyne Ct DE14............166 A3
Lyne Hill Ind Est ST19 . 207 E7
Lyneham Cl B79.........250 C8
Lyneside Rd ST8..........27 B5
Lynfield Rd WS13.......213 F1
Lynmouth Cl
Aldridge WS9...........256 A5
Biddulph ST8.............27 C6
Lynmouth Gr ST6.........41 F7
Lynn Ave ST7..............40 C8
Lynn La WS14...........246 D6
Lynn St ST3...............74 B5
Lynsey Cl ST7.............54 E7
Lynton Ave Stafford ST17 175 D8
Wolverhampton WV6...255 F6
Lynton Gr ST3.............89 E8
Lynton Rd ST5.............70 F5
Lynwood Ave DY6......275 B7
Lynwood Cl
Burton u T DE14........184 F7
Walsall WV12...........242 F1
Lynwood Dr DY10.......281 C2
Lynwood Rd DE14......184 E8
Lyric Cl ST17...........174 F6
Lysander Rd ST3..........90 B7
Lysander Way WS11....209 E3
Lysways St WS13,WS15 . 213 C8
Lytham Cl DY8..........279 F2
Lytham Dr ST16.........156 C3
Lytham Gr WS3..........243 A4
Lytham Rd WV6........254 D4
Lytham B77.............251 C5
Lyttelton Rd DY8.......279 D5
Lytton Ave WV4.........265 E4
Lytton St ST4.............72 C7

M

Macadam Cl WS7.......229 B8
McAdam Cl DE15.......167 B3
McBean Rd WV6........255 F4
Macbeth Ho ST7..........40 C8
Macclesfield Rd
Congleton CW12..........6 A8
Leek ST13................30 C7
Macclesfield St ST6......42 B1
Macdonald Cres ST3.....74 A3
Mace St ST4................71 F4
McGeough Wlk WS11...210 B5
McGhie St WS12.........210 B6
McGough St 8 ST6......41 D3
McGowan Ho ST7.........40 D8
Macgregor Cres B77....250 F3
Macgregor Tithe B79....250 B5
Machin Cres ST5..........56 B7
Machin St ST6.............41 E4
Macintyre St ST6..........57 A7
Mackay Rd WS3.........243 D2
McKellin Cl ST7...........39 E2
Mackenzie Cres ST10....76 E1
McKie Way WS15.......196 F6
McKinley St ST6..........41 D3
Maclagan St ST4..........72 B6
McLean Rd WV10.......240 C1
Macrome Rd WV6.......255 E8
Madden Cl WS15........196 F6
Madeira Ave WV8......239 A2
Madeira Ct DY8.........275 F1
Madeira Pl ST3............41 D3
Madeley High Sch CW3 . 68 C3
Madeley Rd 5 DY6......275 F4
Madeley St N ST5........55 B2
Madeley St
Newcastle-u-L ST5.......55 B1
Stoke-on-T ST6..........41 D4
Madford Ret Pk ST16...285 A4
Madison St ST6............41 D4
Madox Cl ST9............89 E8
Madras Rd DE15........167 C3
Madrona B77............251 B4
Maer La TF9...............97 D2
Maer Lane Ind Est TF9 . 97 D2
Maer La ST21...........101 E5
Maerway La ST5..........84 C5
Mafeking St ST4.........284 B2
Magazine La ST19......205 C7
Magdalen Rd ST3.........88 E8
Magdalen Wlk ST3.......88 E7
Magenta Dr ST5..........55 E2
Magna Cl WS6..........226 E3
Magnolia Cl ST18.......135 E3
Magnolia Dr ST6..........42 F2
Magnolia Gr WV8......239 B3
Magnolia B77............251 A4
Magnolia Way 1 DY8 . 275 F1
Magnus St ST6............56 F7
Magnus B77.............261 E6
Magpie Cres 9 ST7......26 B2

Mahogany Dr ST16.....155 C4
Maidendale Rd DY6.....275 B7
Maidensbridge Dr DY6 . 275 C8
Maidensbridge Gdns
DY6....................270 B1
Maidensbridge Prim Sch
DY6....................270 B1
Maidensbridge Rd DY6 . 270 B1
Maidstone Dr
Burntwood WS7.........229 D6
Stourbridge DY8........275 D3
Maidstone Gr ST2........58 C2
Main Rd Abbaston ST21 . 131 D6
Anslow DE13............165 C7
Armitage WS15.........197 C4
Betley CW3..............53 A5
Main Rd Brereton WS15 . 197 A6
Main Rd Cauldon Lowe ST10 63 E4
Coldmeece ST15........118 B7
Colwich ST18...........177 D7
Draycott in t C DE6.....144 D7
Edingale B79............217 D5
Harlaston B79...........217 D1
Harlaston B79...........217 E3
Mayfield DE6.............81 D8
Newton Regis B79......236 C2
Norton in H TF9..........82 C1
Stafford ST17...........176 B7
Sudbury,Aston Heath DE6 . 129 A4
Sudbury DE6............128 E5
Tamworth B79..........250 B8
Weston CW2..............37 C6
Wetley Rocks ST9........60 B7
Wigginton B79..........234 B2
Main Road Brereton
WS15....................197 A6
Main St Alrewas DE13...201 A3
Barton-u-N DE13........183 C2
Burton u T DE14........184 F7
Burton u T,Stapenhill DE15 185 E8
Clifton Campville B79...218 F2
Egginton DE65...........148 B5
Meir ST3.................74 B5
Netherseal DE12........219 F7
Newton Solney DE15....167 E8
Shenstone WS14........246 F6
Stonnall WS9............245 D4
Stretton DE13...........147 E1
Swadlincote DE12......186 E6
Tatenhill DE13...........165 B1
Walton-on-T DE12......184 D1
Whittington WS14......232 E5
Yoxall DE13.............182 A2
Mainwaring Dr B75...258 E2
Maitland Gr ST4..........88 B6
Maitland Rd DY1.........271 E1
Maitland B77.............250 F2
Majors Barn ST10.........76 C2
Major St WV2............266 E7
Maker La DE13..........162 D2
Malam St ST1...........282 A4
Malcolm Cl ST2...........43 B2
Malcolm Ct ST5..........58 C5
Malcolm Dr ST2..........58 C5
Malcolm Rd ST17.......174 D6
Maldale B77.............251 C1
Malhamdale Rd CW12....6 A5
Malham Rd
Newcastle-u-L ST5.......55 E2
Tamworth B77..........262 C8
Malins Rd WV4..........266 E5
Malkin Way ST6..........56 E6
Mallard Ave ST17.......175 A7
Mallard Cl Uttoxeter ST14 126 C6
Walsall WS3.............244 A5
Mallard Croft 5 WS13 . 231 C8
Mallard Way
Penkridge ST19.........208 A6
Stoke-on-T ST6..........42 D3
Mallens Croft ST14.....125 C7
Mallicot Cl WS13.......214 D1
Mallorie Rd ST6..........42 D4
Mallory Cl ST15........120 B6
Mallory Cres WS3......243 D2
Mallory Rd WV6........254 E3
Mallory Way ST10.......76 F3
Mallow Cl ST21.........133 E5
Mallowdale Cl ST4.......88 C6
Malloy Ho ST13..........45 D7
Malpass Gdns WV8....238 E4
Malpas Wlk ST6..........41 C7
Malstone Ave ST2........43 C2
Malthouse La
Barlaston ST12...........88 F2
Bradley ST18............173 C1
Caverswall ST3..........74 C8
Malt House La
Church Eaton ST20......190 A7
Shareshill WV10........225 C6
Malthouse La
Wheaton Aston ST19...205 A6
Wolverhampton WV6...255 E6
Malthouse Rd Alton ST10 . 78 L1
Bucknall ST2.............58 B3
Malt House Rd WS15...212 B5
Malt Houses WV10....225 D6
Malthouse The DE14....166 E3
Maltings Ind Est DE14 . 166 E6
Maltings The
Aldridge WS9...........256 C6
Burton u T,Stapenhill DE15 167 A1
Burton u T,Wetmore DE14 . 166 E5
Coven WV9..............224 B2
Uttoxeter ST14..........126 C8
Malt La ST3.............284 D2
Malt Mill La ST16.......285 B3
Malton Gr ST6............41 D5

Malvern Ave
Burton u T DE15........167 A1
Newcastle-u-L ST5.......54 F2
Malvern Cl Stafford ST17 . 156 F1
Stoke-on-T ST4...........88 A7
Malvern Ct B74..........257 F2
Malvern Dr Aldridge WS9 . 256 C8
Rugeley WS15...........178 C8
Malvern St DE15.........166 F1
Malvern View Rd DY3...271 D4
Mamble Rd DY8.........279 E5
Manchester Ct ST14....110 F1
Mancroft Cl DY6.........275 B7
Mancroft Gdns WV6...255 C5
Mancroft Rd WV6......255 C5
Mandela Way ST3.......284 D2
Manderley Cl DY3......266 C2
Manderston Cl DY1.....271 E3
Mander St WV3.........266 B8
Mandeville Gdns DY6...275 C6
Mandeville Cl ST6........42 C3
Manifold CE Prim Sch
SK17....................23 A2
Manifold Cl
Burntwood WS7.........229 D6
Newcastle-u-L ST5.......55 B1
Waterhouses ST10.......48 F2
Manifold Dr ST10.........76 E1
Manifold Rd ST11........90 F8
Manifold Valley Visitor Ctr
SK17....................23 E3
Manifold Wlk ST2.........58 C1
Manley Rd WS13........214 D1
Manlove St WV3........266 A8
Mannin Cl ST3............74 A4
Mann St ST3...............74 C3
Manor Ave
Cannock WS11..........209 D1
Great Wyrley WS6......227 A4
Manor Cl Codsall WV8...239 B4
Congleton CW12..........6 A1
Draycott in t M ST11.....91 C6
Great Haywood ST18...158 B2
Harlaston B79...........217 D2
Market Drayton TF9......97 C1
Stanton DE15...........186 A6
Uttoxeter ST14..........126 B8
Weston ST18............138 D2
Wolverhampton WV4...265 F4
Manor Cotts WS14......230 D2
Manor Court Dr WS15 . 198 B4
Manor Cres DE15.......186 A6
Manor Croft
Burton u T DE14........166 D2
Tatenhill DE13...........184 A8
Uttoxeter ST14..........126 C8
Manor Ct
Barton-u-N DE13........183 D2
Stone ST15..............119 F6
Manor Ct St ST4..........71 F6
Manor Dr Burton u T DE14 . 166 E2
Dudley DY3.............271 B3
Netherseal DE12........219 F6
Shareshill WV10........225 D2
Swindon DY3...........269 E2
Manor Farm Cres ST17 . 174 E5
Manor Farm Rd ST18....177 D8
Manorfield Cl ST19.....207 E8
Manor Fields DE13.....200 F3
Manor Flats DY3........271 D8
Manor Fold WV8.......238 D2
Manor Gdns
Albrighton WV7.........237 A5
Market Drayton TF9......97 C1
Wombourne WV5.......270 B7
Manor Glade ST5.........85 A7
Manor Gn ST17.........174 D7
Manor Hill Fst Sch ST15 . 119 E7
Manor Ho WV8.........239 A4
Manor Ho ST6...........255 D5
Manorial Rd B75........258 E3
Manor La Harlaston B79 . 217 D2
Stourbridge DY8........279 D3
Wigginton B79..........233 E3
Manor Pk DY6..........275 D6
Manor Prim Sch
Aldridge WS14..........257 A1
Drayton Bassett B78....260 E5
Manor Rd Aldridge B74 . 257 A1
Edgmond TF10..........168 A3
Gnosall ST20...........171 E7
King's Bromley DE13...199 C5
Madeley CW3............68 E3
Mile Oak B78............249 D1
Stanton DE15...........186 A6
Stourbridge DY8........275 A6
Tamworth B77..........250 D4
Uttoxeter ST14..........126 B8
Whitmore ST5............85 A7
Wolverhampton,Penn WV4 265 F4
Manor Rise
Burntwood WS7.........229 A5
Lichfield WS14..........231 C7
Stone ST15..............119 F7
Manor Sq ST17.........174 D7
Manor St Stoke-on-T ST4 . 72 E7
Wolverhampton WV6...255 D5
Manor Trad Est DE14...166 E4
Manor Way ST5........179 A6
Manor Wlk DE13........199 B6
Mansard Cl WV3........265 F8
Manse Cl ST3...........284 C4
Mansell Cl ST16........155 C2
Mansfield Cl
Newcastle-u-L ST5.......71 C2
Tamworth B79..........249 E6
Mansfield Dr ST8.........27 A5

Mansion Cl ST10..........76 E2
Mansion Ct WV5........269 D5
Mansion Dr WS7........229 D4
Manson Ct WV4........265 D5
Manston Dr WV6........254 E5
Manston Hill ST19......207 E7
Manston View B79......250 C8
Manta Rd B77...........261 D6
Manton Cl
2 Stretton DE13.........147 F1
Swadlincote DE11......186 F6
Maple Ave
Newcastle-u-L ST5.......40 E1
Talke ST7.................40 D8
Maple Cl Burntwood WS7 228 F7
Cheadle ST10.............76 F2
Kinver DY7...............278 A5
Stoke-on-T ST6..........43 A5
Stourbridge DY8........279 D2
Yarnfield ST15..........118 F5
Maple Cres
Blythe Bridge ST11.......91 A6
Cannock WS11..........209 C5
Maple Ct Lichfield WS14 . 231 C5
Stafford ST15...........155 C5
Mapledene Cl 1 ST17...175 D5
Maple Dr Derrington ST18 156 F1
Dudley DY3.............271 B2
Huntington WS12.......209 D8
Loggerheads TF9.........99 D5
Maple Gdns ST15.......120 A6
Maple Gr Burton u T DE15 185 E3
Cheddleton ST13.........45 C7
Kingswinford DY6......275 E6
Lichfield WS14..........231 F7
Stafford ST17...........174 E7
Wolverhampton WV3...255 C2
Maple Hayes Hall Sch
WS13....................230 D8
Maple Ho Little Aston B74 . 257 B5
Walsall WS4..............244 F5
Maplehurst Cl ST6.......57 B8
Maple Pl ST3..............74 B2
Maple Rd Walsall WS3...243 F2
Wolverhampton WV3...265 E8
Maple Rise B77..........251 A4
Maple St WS3...........243 D2
Maple Way DE14........184 F8
Maple Wood ST17.....175 C5
Marcel Cl ST4.............72 A2
Marchant Rd WV6......255 F2
March Banks WS15......178 D1
March Cl WS6...........226 E1
Marchington Ind Est
ST14....................143 F8
March La Overmoor ST9....60 A3
Whitgreave ST18........135 C4
March Rd ST3...........284 B4
March Way WS9........245 C2
Marchwood Ct ST14......71 E6
Marcia Rice Ct WS15...161 A5
Marconi Gate ST18......156 C5
Marconi Pl WS12.......210 C7
Marcus Ind Est ST1......57 F3
Mardale Cl CW12.........6 A5
Maree Gr WV11........242 B1
Margam Cres WS3......242 F2
Margam Terr WS3......242 F2
Margam Way WS3......242 F2
Margaret Ave ST4........87 F8
Margaret Dr WS11......209 E6
Margaret St
6 Stone ST15..........104 F1
Hanley ST1................57 E4
Margery Ave ST7.........25 E7
Margill Cl ST1...........282 A2
Marholm Cl WV9.......239 F2
Maries Way ST5...........55 D1
Marigold Cl WS11......210 D3
Marina Cres WS12......210 A5
Marina Dr ST5............56 C3
Marina Rd ST4............71 F3
Marina Way ST1..........57 A4
Marine Cres DY8........275 E1
Marine Gdns DY8.......275 E1
Mariner B79.............249 E6
Market Drayton Cottage
Hospl TF9................112 C8
Market Drayton Inf Sch
TF9......................97 C1
Market Drayton Jun Sch
TF9......................112 B8
Market Drayton Rd TF9. . 99 D3
Marketfields ST21......133 E7
Market Hall St WS11...209 E1
Market La Hanley ST1...282 B3
Lichfield WS14..........230 E2
Lower Penn WV4........264 F5
Newcastle-u-L ST5.......283 B3
Market Mews TF10.....168 F3
Market Pl 10 Leek ST13 . 30 E6
Market Pl
4 Cannock WS11......209 E1
4 Stone ST15...........120 A8
Abbots Bromley WS15 . 161 A6
Brewood ST19..........223 C6
Burslem ST6..............56 F8
Burton u T DE14........166 E2
Cheadle ST10.............76 D3
Hartington SK17.........24 D5
Longnor SK17............13 B6
Penkridge ST19.........192 E1
Tamworth B79..........250 B4
Uttoxeter ST14..........126 C7
Walsall WS3.............243 B1
Market Sq Arc ST1.....282 B2
Market Sq Hanley ST1...282 B3
Rugeley WS15...........178 E1
Stafford ST16...........285 B2

Market St Cannock WS12 . **210** C5
Kidsgrove ST7 . . . . **26** A1
Kingswinford DY6 . . . . **275** D6
Leek ST13 . . . . **30** F6
Lichfield WS13 . . . . **231** B8
Longton ST3. . . . . **284** C3
Penkridge ST19 . . . . **192** E1
Rugeley WS15 . . . . **178** F1
Stafford ST16 . . . . **285** B3
Tamworth B79 . . . . **250** B4
Uttoxeter ST14 . . . . **126** C7
Markham Croft WV9 . . . . **240** A2
Markham Dr DY6 . . . . **275** E4
Marklew Cl WS8 . . . . **245** A5
Marklin Ave WV10 . . . . . . **240** D1
Marks Wlk WS13 . . . . **214** A1
Marlborough Ave ST16 . . **156** C4
Marlborough Cl
Great Haywood ST18. . . . . **158** C2
Sutton Coldfield B74 . . . . . **257** E6
Marlborough Cres
Burton u T DE15. . . . . **186** A8
Endon ST9 . . . . **43** E8
Marlborough Ct
Lichfield WS13 . . . . **231** B7
Sutton Coldfield,Four Oaks
B74 . . . . **257** F2
Marlborough Gdns
Stourbridge DY8 . . . . **275** D2
Wolverhampton WV6 . . . . . **255** E4
Marlborough Ind Est
WV2 . . . . **266** D7
Marlborough Rd
Dudley DY3 . . . . **271** F6
Longton ST3. . . . . **284** C4
Stone ST15 . . . . **119** F5
Marlborough St
Stoke-on-T ST4 . . . . **72** D5
Walsall WS3. . . . . **243** B1
Marlborough Way
Stoke-on-T ST6 . . . . **41** C5
Tamworth B77 . . . . **250** F2
Uttoxeter ST14 . . . . **110** F1
Marlbrook Dr WV4 . . . . . . **266** B6
Marlbrook La WV6 . . . . . . **253** B2
Marldon Pl ST6 . . . . **41** D6
Marley Mount Cres TF9 . . **97** C2
Marlin B77 . . . . **261** D6
Marlow Cl ST3 . . . . **73** D5
Marlow Dr DE14 . . . . **185** A4
Marlowe Rd ST17 . . . . **174** B8
Marlow Rd Longton ST3 . . **73** D5
Tamworth B77 . . . . **250** D5
Marlpit La Denstone ST14. . **95** D6
Ellastone DE6 . . . . **80** A3
Moddershall ST15 . . . . **105** F5
Sutton Coldfield B75 . . . . . **258** D3
Marlpit Rise ◼**1** B75 . . . . . . **258** E3
Marlpool Dr WS3 . . . . **244** A1
Marmion Pk B79 . . . . **250** B6
Marmion St B79 . . . . **250** B5
Marnel Dr WV3 . . . . **265** E7
Marney Wlk ST6 . . . . **42** B2
Marquis Dr ST6 . . . . **73** A5
Marquis Dr WS12,WS15. . **195** D3
Marquis Drive Visitor Ctr★
WS15 . . . . **195** C3
Marquis's Dr WS15. . . . . . **196** B2
Marrick B77 . . . . **251** C1
Marriott St ST4 . . . . **73** A5
Marsden St ST1 . . . . **282** C3
Marsett B77 . . . . **262** C8
Marshall Ave ST6 . . . . **43** B7
Marshall Cl WS9 . . . . **256** B4
Marshall Gr CW12. . . . . . . **16** B8
Marshall St Burslem ST6. . **41** F1
Tamworth B77 . . . . **250** E5
Marsh Ave
Newcastle-u-L ST5. . . . . . . **56** C5
Newchapel ST7 . . . . **26** E2
Stoke-on-T ST6 . . . . **42** B2
Marshbrook Fst Sch
ST19 . . . . **192** F1
Marsh Cl ST9 . . . . **59** A4
Marsh Cres DY8. . . . . **275** D3
Marsh Ct ST16. . . . . **155** D5
Marshfield La ST8 . . . . **16** C3
Marsh Gr ST8 . . . . **16** C3
Marsh Green Cl ST8. . . . . . **16** D2
Marshgreen Rd ST8 . . . . . **16** D3
Marsh Gr DY3. . . . . **269** E2
Marsh La
Cheswardine TF9 . . . . **130** A8
Ellenhall ST21 . . . . **134** B1
Lichfield WS14 . . . . **231** C5
Marshland Gr ST6. . . . . **42** A8
Marshlands ST17 . . . . **175** C6
Marsh Lane Par WV10. . . . **240** C2
Marsh La Penkridge ST19 . **192** F1
Stanton DE6 . . . . **80** D8
Whittington WS14 . . . . **232** B5
Wolverhampton WV10. . . . **240** B2
Marsh Mdws ST20 . . . . . . **131** C4
Marsh Par ST5. . . . . **283** C3
Marsh Prim Sch ST11 . . . . **91** A6
Marsh St N ST1 . . . . **282** B3
Marsh St S ST1 . . . . **282** B2
Marsh St ST16 . . . . **155** D5
Marsh View ST3 . . . . **90** A5
Marsh Way ST5 . . . . **56** C5
Marshwood Cl ◼**2** WS11 . . **210** A2
Marsland Cl ST16 . . . . **155** A4
Marsland Rd ST16. . . . . . . **155** A4
Mars St ST6 . . . . **42** C1
Marston Cl
Stourbridge DY8 . . . . **279** D4
Wheaton Aston ST19. . . . . **205** C6

Marston Croft ST19 . . . . . . **205** C6
Marston Ct ST16 . . . . **155** D5
Marston Dr ST16. . . . . **155** E5
Marston Gr Stafford ST16. . **155** E5
Stoke-on-T ST1 . . . . **57** D8
Marston Ind Est WV2. . . . . **266** C7
Marston La Hatton DE65. . **146** D8
Marston ST18 . . . . **136** E3
Rolleston on D DE13 . . . . . **147** A4
Marston Old La DE65. . . . . **146** D8
Marston Pk B78. . . . . **249** F4
Marston Rd
Cannock WS12. . . . . **209** F6
Marston-On-Dove DE65. . . **147** B8
Stafford ST16 . . . . **155** E5
Wheaton Aston ST19. . . . . **205** B7
Wolverhampton WV2. . . . . **266** C7
Marston Rise DE15 . . . . . . **185** F8
Marsworth Way ST16. . . . . **136** D1
Martham Dr WV6 . . . . **255** B2
Martin Croft WS13 . . . . . . **214** A1
Martindale
◼**6** Stafford ST17. . . . . **175** D6
Cannock WS11 . . . . **210** A2
Martindale Cl ST3. . . . . **89** F8
Martindale Trad Est
WS11 . . . . **210** A2
Martin Dr ST16 . . . . **155** C3
Martin Dale TF9 . . . . **99** D5
Martin's La DE13 . . . . **145** A4
Martinslow La ST10,ST11,ST . **48** A4
Martins Mill CW12 . . . . **16** C8
Martin St Burslem ST6. . . . **57** B7
Stafford ST16 . . . . **285** B3
Wolverhampton WV4. . . . . **266** F5
Martins Way ST18. . . . . . . **158** C8
Martley Rd WS4 . . . . **244** C2
Martlin La WS15 . . . . **179** A5
Marton Ave WS7. . . . . **229** A8
Marwood Croft B74 . . . . . . **257** A2
Marychurch Rd ST2. . . . . . **58** B3
Maryfield Wlk ST4 . . . . **71** E7
Maryhill Cl ST7 . . . . **26** A3
Maryhill High Sch ST7 . . . . **26** A3
Maryhill Prim Sch ST7 . . . . **26** A3
Mary Howard CE Prim Sch
B79 . . . . **217** C5
Mary Rand Cl ST17 . . . . . . **174** D8
Mary Rose Cl Bucknall ST2. **58** B3
Cheslyn Hay WS6. . . . . **226** D1
Marysgate ST19 . . . . **223** D7
Mary St ST12 . . . . **210** B7
Maryvale ST2 WS14. . . . . . **231** D7
Masefield Cl
Burntwood WS7. . . . . **212** A1
Cheadle ST10. . . . . **76** D5
Lichfield WS14 . . . . **231** B6
Market Drayton TF9. . . . . . **112** A7
Masefield Cres DE14 . . . . . **166** D7
Masefield Dr
Stafford ST17 . . . . **155** C1
Tamworth B79 . . . . **250** A7
Masefield Gr WS11 . . . . . . **209** E4
Masefield Mews WV10 . . . **241** A1
Masefield Rd Dudley DY3. . **271** A4
Longton ST3. . . . . **73** A4
Wolverhampton WV10. . . . **241** A1
Mason Cres WV4. . . . . **265** C5
Mason Dr ST8 . . . . **27** B8
Masons Lawn ST20. . . . . . **171** C5
Masons Pl TF10 . . . . **168** E4
Mason's Pl TF10 . . . . **168** E5
Mason St Stoke-on-T ST4 . **72** F5
Wolverhampton WV2. . . . . **266** C7
Masterson St ST4. . . . . **72** D6
Mathews Wlk ST2 . . . . **282** C3
Matlock Cl WS3. . . . . **243** C3
Matlock Dr WS11 . . . . **210** A4
Matlock Pl ST5 . . . . **55** A4
Matlock Rd WS3 . . . . **243** C3
Matlock St ST1. . . . . **282** B1
Matthews Ct ST1. . . . . **282** C2
Matthews Pl CW12 . . . . . . **6** A2
Matthews Rd ST17 . . . . . . **174** C7
Matthews Wlk WS13 . . . . . **214** A2
Maud St ST4. . . . . **72** E7
Maunders Rd ST2 . . . . **43** A1
Maureen Ave ST6 . . . . **41** D6
Maureen Gr ST5 . . . . **56** C3
Mavesyn Cl WS15 . . . . **198** A8
Mavis Rd WS12 . . . . **210** B7
Mavor Ave WS7 . . . . **211** D1
Mawdesley St ST6 . . . . **57** B6
Mawgan Dr WS4. . . . . **231** D6
Mawson Gr ST4. . . . . **57** D1
Maxstoke Cl
Tamworth B77 . . . . **261** C4
Walsall WS3. . . . . **243** A3
Maxtock Ave WS13. . . . . . **231** A6
Maxton Way ST3. . . . . **74** B2
Maxwell Cl WS14 . . . . **231** C7
Maxwell Pl ST4 . . . . **71** E7
Maxwell Rd
Congleton CW12 . . . . **16** A8
Wolverhampton WV2. . . . . **266** D8
Mayall Dr B75. . . . . **258** D4
Mayama Rd B78 . . . . **260** F8
May Ave Newcastle-u-L ST5. **56** D3
Stoke-on-T ST6 . . . . **41** F3
Maybank WS14 . . . . **231** E8
May Bank Inf Sch ST5. . . . **56** D3
Maybank WS5. . . . . **196** E2
Maybrook Ind Est WS8 . . . **244** F5
Maybrook Rd WS8 . . . . **244** F5
Maybury Cl WV8 . . . . **238** E4
Maybury Way ST2. . . . . . . **43** A1

Maybush Gdns WV10. . . . . **240** C1
May Cl WS7 . . . . **211** F1
Maycroft Cl WS12. . . . . **209** F7
Mayer Ave ST5. . . . . **283** B4
Mayer Bank ◼**6** ST6. . . . . . **57** A8
Mayers Ct ◼**3** ST13 . . . . . . **30** E5
Mayer St ST1 . . . . **282** C3
Mayfair Ave ST10 . . . . **62** A8
Mayfair Dr WV7 . . . . **237** A5
Mayfair Dr Fazeley B78. . . . **261** A7
Kingswinford DY6 . . . . **275** C7
Mayfair Gdns
◼**14** Stoke-on-T ST6. . . . . . **41** D3
Wolverhampton WV3. . . . . **255** D2
Mayfair Gr ST9 . . . . **43** E8
Mayfair DE11 . . . . **186** E6
Mayfield Ave Hanley ST1. . **57** E5
Mayfields DE6. . . . . **81** C7
Newcastle-u-L ST5. . . . . . . **283** C5
Penkridge ST19 . . . . **207** E8
Mayfield Cl ST13 . . . . **30** B5
Mayfield Cres ST1 . . . . **57** E4
Mayfield Dr
Blythe Bridge ST11 . . . . . . **90** D8
Burton u T DE15. . . . . **186** A8
Mayfield Pl E ST4 . . . . **71** E5
Mayfield Pl ST5. . . . . **56** C4
Mayfield Pl W ST4 . . . . **71** E5
Mayfield Rd
Albrighton WV7 . . . . **237** A5
Biddulph ST8 . . . . **27** D6
Burton u T DE15. . . . . **167** A3
Hangingbridge DE6 . . . . . . **81** F8
Stafford ST17 . . . . **156** C1
Mayfields Dr WS8. . . . . **228** B2
Mayfield Terr DE6 . . . . **81** D6
Mayflower Dr WV15. . . . . . **178** C1
Maygrove Rd DY6 . . . . **275** C7
Maylea Cres ST5. . . . . **54** C7
Maynard Ave DY8 . . . . **279** D3
Maynards Croft TF10 . . . . **169** A4
Mayneford Pl ST4. . . . . **71** F1
Mayne St ST4. . . . . **71** F1
Mayock Cres ST16 . . . . **155** B2
Mayole Ct WS3. . . . . **244** A4
Maypole Cl WV5 . . . . **270** A6
Maypole Dr DY8 . . . . **279** E5
Maypole St WV5 . . . . **270** B7
May St Newcastle-u-L ST5. . **55** C1
Stoke-on-T ST6 . . . . **42** B1
Mays Wlk DE13 . . . . **200** F3
Mayswood Dr WV6 . . . . . . **254** F1
Maythorne Rd ST3. . . . . . . **73** A1
Maythorn Gdns
Codsall WV8. . . . . **239** A4
Wolverhampton WV6 . . . . . **255** C3
Maywood Dr DY6. . . . . **275** B6
Mead Ave ST7 . . . . **25** E7
Mead Cl WS9 . . . . **256** B6
Mead Cres DE15 . . . . **186** A6
Meadfoot Dr DY6 . . . . **275** B7
Meadlands The WV5 . . . . . **269** E6
Meadow Ave Longton ST3 . **73** C1
Newcastle-u-L ST5. . . . . . . **56** A4
Weston CW2 . . . . **37** B5
Wetley Rocks ST9 . . . . **60** B6
Meadowbank Ave ST18. . . **138** C3
Meadowbank Grange
WS6. . . . . **226** E4
Meadow Bank B78 . . . . . . **250** B1
Meadow Bank Wlk ST16 . . **155** C8
Meadowbrook Ct ST15 . . . **120** D6
Meadowbrook Gdns
WV8. . . . . **239** B4
Meadowbrook Rd WS13 . . **214** B3
Meadow Cl Aldridge B74.. . **256** F2
Blythe Bridge ST11 . . . . . . **90** E6
Eccleshall ST21 . . . . **133** E7
Forsbrook ST11 . . . . **91** B8
Gnosall ST20 . . . . **171** E4
Leek ST13 . . . . **31** A5
Market Drayton TF9. . . . . . **97** A1
Penkridge ST19 . . . . **207** D5
Wheaton Aston ST19. . . . . **205** B6
Meadowcroft Ave ST3. . . . **90** C8
Meadow Croft WS12 . . . . . **209** C4
Meadowcroft Gdns ST19 . **205** C6
Meadow Croft
Hagley DY9 . . . . **281** F4
Perton WV6 . . . . **254** D3
Streethay WS13 . . . . **215** A1
Meadow Ct Barlaston ST12. **88** C2
Burton u T DE14. . . . . **166** F3
Newchapel ST7 . . . . **26** E2
Norton Bridge ST15. . . . . . **135** A8
Stafford ST17 . . . . **175** A8
Meadow Dr Cheadle ST10. . **76** D3
Haughton ST18 . . . . **172** E6
Stoke-on-T ST3 . . . . **89** A8
Meadowfields Cl DY8 . . . . . **275** E2
Meadow Glade ST18 . . . . . **158** C8
Meadow Hill Dr ◼**5**
WS11 . . . . **210** A3
Meadowhill Dr DY8 . . . . . . **275** D5
Meadow La
Acton Trussell ST17. . . . . . **193** B8
Burton u T DE13. . . . . **167** A8
Colwich ST18. . . . . **177** C7
Coven Heath WV10 . . . . . . **240** C6
Derrington ST18 . . . . **154** E2
Fulford ST11 . . . . **106** E8
Millmeece ST17. . . . . **117** E7
Meadowlands Dr WS4. . . . **244** A1
Meadow La ST5. . . . . **56** A4

Meadow Lark Cl WS12 . . **210** B4
Meadow La Roston DE6. . . **96** C7
Stoke-on-T ST4 . . . . **88** C7
Swadlincote DE11 . . . . **186** F5
Wombourne WV5. . . . . **270** B8
Yoxall DE13 . . . . **200** B7
Meadowpark Rd DY8 . . . . . **279** D8
Meadow Pk B79 . . . . **249** F5
Meadow Pl ST3 . . . . **74** B1
Meadow Rd
Albrighton WV7 . . . . **237** B5
Aldridge WS9. . . . . **256** A6
Barlaston ST12 . . . . **88** D1
Brown Edge ST6 . . . . **43** B6
Coldmeece ST15 . . . . **118** A6
Newport TF10 . . . . **169** A3
Stafford ST17 . . . . **174** F8
Stoke-on-T ST6 . . . . **42** C5
Tamworth B78 . . . . **249** C5
Wolverhampton WV3. . . . . **265** D8
Meadow Ridge ST17 . . . . . **175** C8
Meadows Gr WV8 . . . . **239** A4
Meadow Rise DE13. . . . . . **183** E1
Meadows Rd ST7 . . . . **25** C7
Meadow Side ST8. . . . . **27** B6
Meadow Side DE14 . . . . . . **166** E3
Meadowside La ST7. . . . . . **26** B7
Meadowside
Loggerheads TF9 . . . . **99** E5
Mayfield DE6 . . . . **81** D6
Meadowside Rd B74 . . . . . **257** F3
Meadowside
Saverley Green ST11. . . . . . **91** B2
Stoke-on-T ST4 . . . . **88** C7
Meadows Prim Sch CW3 . **69** A8
Meadows Rd ST7 . . . . **25** D5
Meadows The
Brewood ST19 . . . . **223** D6
Hilderstone ST15. . . . . **106** D2
Kingstone ST14 . . . . **141** C8
Rugeley WS15 . . . . **197** B6
Salt ST18 . . . . **137** F4
Stoke-on-T ST9 . . . . **43** F7
Uttoxeter ST14 . . . . **111** A2
Wrinehill CW3 . . . . **53** A3
Meadow Stile Home Park
Cvn Site ST8 . . . . **27** A4
Meadow St
Newcastle-u-L ST5. . . . . . . **55** F6
Stoke-on-T ST2 . . . . **43** B1
Tamworth B77 . . . . **250** C6
Meadow Sweet ST6 . . . . . . **42** E2
Meadowsweet Dr ST17. . . **175** F7
Meadowsweet Way
WS12 . . . . **210** E4
Meadow Vale WV8 . . . . **239** B2
Meadow View WS7. . . . . . . **229** D6
Meadow View Cl TF10. . . . **169** A3
Meadow View Cvn Pk
WV10. . . . . **240** C6
Meadow View DE6 . . . . . . **127** C8
Meadow View Rd
Newport TF10 . . . . **169** A3
Swadlincote DE11 . . . . **186** F5
Meadow View
Meir Heath ST3. . . . . **90** A4
Sedgley DY3. . . . . **266** C1
Meadowview ST6 . . . . **42** E3
Meadow View Terr WV6. . . **255** B4
Meadowview WS15 . . . . . . **118** E6
Meadow Way
Armitage WS15 . . . . **198** B4
Cannock WS12. . . . . **210** C1
Codsall WV8. . . . . **238** E2
Lawton-gate ST7 . . . . **25** A5
Stone ST15 . . . . **119** F6
Stourbridge DY8 . . . . **275** C2
Upper Tean ST10 . . . . **92** D3
Whitmore ST5 . . . . **85** D5
Mead The Sedgley DY3. . . . **271** D8
Stoke-on-T ST4 . . . . **88** B7
Meadway Cl WS12 . . . . **210** C3
Meadway Dr ST17. . . . . **175** C6
Meadway Rd WS8. . . . . **228** C2
Meadway The WV6. . . . . . . **255** A5
Mead Wlk DE15 . . . . **186** A6
Meaford Ave ST15 . . . . **104** F3
Meaford Dr ST3 . . . . **72** E3
Meaford Rd ST12,ST15. . . **104** D6
Meakin Ave ST5 . . . . **71** B3
Meakin Cl Cheadle ST10 . . **76** C1
Congleton CW12 . . . . **6** B1
Stone ST15 . . . . **120** C6
Meakin Gr ST16. . . . . **155** B6
Meakin Ho ST15. . . . . **104** F1
Mear Greaves La DE15 . . . **167** B4
Mear's La WS15 . . . . **198** F8
Mease Ave WS7 . . . . **229** C6
Mease La B79 . . . . **218** B2
Mease The DE65. . . . . **147** E8
Meddins Cl DY7 . . . . **278** A4
Meddins La DY7 . . . . **277** F4
Meddins Rise DY7. . . . . **277** F4
Media Way ST1 . . . . **56** F4
Medina Cl WV10 . . . . **240** F4
Medina B77 . . . . **262** B6
Medina Way Kidsgrove ST7 . **26** B2
Kingswinford DY6 . . . . **275** C6
Medway Dr ST8. . . . . **16** D1
Medway Pl ST5 . . . . **71** B4
Medway Rd WS8 . . . . **228** C2
Medway B77. . . . . **250** E1
Medway Wlk
Brownhills WS8 . . . . **228** C2
Stoke-on-T ST6 . . . . **42** A4
Meece Ave ST15 . . . . **118** D7
Meece Rd ST15 . . . . **118** D6

Meerash La WS7 . . . . **229** C3
Meerbrook Cl ST4 . . . . **88** B5
Meerbrook Rd ST13 . . . . . **19** D1
Meerbrook Youth Hostel★
ST13 . . . . **19** F6
Meere Cl ST6 . . . . **42** E3
Meeson Cl WV7 . . . . **237** E5
Megacre ST7 . . . . **40** A1
Meg La WS7 . . . . **212** B1
Meigh Rd ST2,ST9 . . . . . . **59** A4
Meigh St ST1 . . . . **282** C3
Meiklejohn Pl ST6 . . . . **42** A6
Meirhay Rd ST3. . . . . **73** D2
Meir Heath Prim Sch ST3 . **90** A4
Meir Prim Sch ST3. . . . . . . **74** B1
Meir Rd ST3 . . . . **73** E1
Meir St ST6. . . . . **41** E4
Meir View ST3 . . . . **74** A1
Melbourne Ave DE15 . . . . **167** C3
Melbourne Cl ST6 . . . . **275** E4
Melbourne Cres
Cannock WS12. . . . . **210** F2
Stafford ST16 . . . . **156** B5
Melbourne Rd WS12 . . . . . **210** F2
Melbourne St ST3. . . . . **73** D5
Melbury Way ◼**1** WS11. . . . **209** F2
Melchester Gr ST3 . . . . **73** E1
Melchester Wlk ◼**2** WS11 **209** F2
Melfont St ST6. . . . . **41** E3
Melford Cl DY3 . . . . **266** C2
Melford Grange WV7. . . . . **211** E1
Melford Rise WS7. . . . . **211** E1
Melford B79 . . . . **249** E6
Meliden Way ST4 . . . . **71** F6
Mellard St Audley ST7. . . . **39** D1
Newcastle-u-L ST5. . . . . . . **283** C5
Mellor Dr Alrewas DE13 . . **200** F2
Sutton Coldfield B74 . . . . . **257** E3
Uttoxeter ST14 . . . . **111** B1
Mellor Rd DE14 . . . . **185** B7
Mellors Bank ST7. . . . . **26** D6
Mellor St ST7 . . . . **26** F2
Mellowdew Rd DY8 . . . . . . **275** C3
Mellow La ST10,ST13 . . . . **47** E3
Mellwaters B77. . . . . **262** C6
Melmerby B77 . . . . **262** C8
Melrose Ave
Meir Heath ST3 . . . . **90** A4
Newcastle-u-L ST5. . . . . . . **71** A5
Stafford ST17 . . . . **174** C8
Stoke-on-T ST1 . . . . **57** D7
Stone ST15 . . . . **120** C5
Stourbridge DY8 . . . . **279** F2
Melrose Cres TF9 . . . . **112** B8
Melrose Dr
Cannock WS12. . . . . **209** F7
Perton WV6 . . . . **254** E4
Melrose Pl ST13 . . . . **30** B5
Melstone Ave ST6. . . . . **41** F3
Melville Ct ST5 . . . . **71** C1
Melville Rd ST3 . . . . **73** E2
Melville St ST1 . . . . **57** E3
Melvyn Cres ST6 . . . . **56** C7
Menai Dr ST8. . . . . **27** D6
Menai Gr ST3. . . . . **284** C3
Mendip Ave ST7 . . . . **175** E6
Mendip Cl Dudley DY3. . . . **271** D3
Wolverhampton WV2. . . . . **266** F7
Mendip Gn ST2 . . . . **43** A1
Mendip Pl ST5. . . . . **55** E3
Mendip Rd ST4. . . . . **195** A1
Mendip Way B77. . . . . **251** C1
Mentone Cres TF10 . . . . . . **168** B4
Menzies Ho
◼**4** Stoke-on-T ST3. . . . . . **89** F8
Cheddleton ST13 . . . . **45** C7
Meon Gr WV6. . . . . **254** F4
Mercer Ave WS15. . . . . **120** C7
Mercer St ST3 . . . . **73** B1
Merchant Cl WV6 . . . . **253** C3
Merchants Pk WS9. . . . . . . **256** A7
Merchants Way ST5 . . . . . **256** A7
Mercia Cl Hatton DE65. . . . **146** D8
Tamworth B79 . . . . **249** E7
Mercia Cres ST6 . . . . **57** A6
Mercia Dr WV6 . . . . **254** E5
Mercian Ct
Lichfield WS14 . . . . **231** C7
Market Drayton TF9. . . . . . **97** C1
Mercian Pk B77. . . . . **251** A3
Mercian Way Lapley ST19 **206** B3
Tamworth B77 . . . . **251** B3
Mercury Pk B77 . . . . **251** B3
Mercury Pl ST6 . . . . **42** C1
Mercury Rd WS11 . . . . **210** A5
Mere Cl TF10 . . . . **168** C4
Mere Croft WS11 . . . . **227** C4
Mere Ct CW2 . . . . **37** B5
Meredith Cl DE14 . . . . **166** D6
Meredith Rd DY3 . . . . **271** A5
Mere Dr B75. . . . . **258** B2
Mere Green Cl B75. . . . . . . **258** C2
Mere Green Comb Sch
B75. . . . . **258** B2
Mere Green Rd B75. . . . . . **258** C2
Mere La DY7. . . . . **273** C6
Merelake Rd ST7 . . . . **40** B8
Meremore Dr ST5. . . . . **40** D2
Mere Oak Rd WV6. . . . . . . **254** E5
Mere Pool Rd B75 . . . . **258** E2
Mere Rd Stourbridge DY8 . **279** F2
Weston CW2 . . . . **37** B5
Mere Rise ST21 . . . . **132** D7
Mere Side Cl ◼**5** ST1. . . . . **56** F2
Merevale Ave ST2. . . . . **58** A2

Merganser B77 . . . . 262 A6
Meriden Ave DY8 . . . . . . 279 D6
Meriden Cl
  Cannock WS11 . . . . 226 B8
  Stourbridge DY8 . . . . 279 D6
Meriden Ct **3** WV4 . . . 266 F4
Meriden Rd
  Newcastle-u-L ST5 . . . . . . 71 C2
  Wolverhampton WV10 . . . . 240 B1
Merino Cl ST3 . . . . 89 C8
Merlin Cl Cannock WS11 . 209 C2
  Stoke-on-T ST6 . . . . 42 A8
  Tamworth B77 . . . . 262 A6
  Uttoxeter ST14 . . . . 126 C6
Merlin Cres DE14 . . . . . . 184 F8
Merlin Ct WS7 . . . . 229 F8
Merlin Gn WS7 . . . . 68 E6
Merlin Way Kidsgrove ST7 . 26 D3
  Whittington WS14 . . . . . . 232 F5
Merrial St ST5 . . . . 283 B3
Merrick St ST1 . . . . 282 C4
Merridale Ave WV3 . . . . . 255 F2
Merridale Ct WV3 . . . . . . 255 F1
Merridale Gr WV3 . . . . . . 255 E1
Merridale St W WV3 . . . . 266 A8
Merrill Cl WS6 . . . . 226 E2
Merrion Dr ST6 . . . . 42 B3
Merrivale Rd ST17 . . . . . . 174 E7
Merrydale B77 . . . . 262 C8
Merryfield Rd DY1 . . . . . . 271 E1
Merryfields St ST5 . . . . . . 56 B4
Merry Rd ST17 . . . . 174 E7
Mersey Cl WS15 . . . . 178 E3
Mersey Rd
  Newcastle-u-L ST5 . . . . . . 71 A4
  Walsall WS3 . . . . 243 E1
Mersey St ST1 . . . . 282 A2
Merthyr Gr ST8 . . . . 27 E6
Merton Ct WS7 . . . . 228 F5
Merton St ST3 . . . . 284 C4
Mervyn Rd DE15 . . . . . . 167 A3
Mesnes Gn WS14 . . . . . . 231 C7
Metcalf Cl WS7 . . . . 229 C8
Metcalfe Cl WS12 . . . . . . 210 C6
Metcalfe Rd ST6 . . . . 42 A3
Metfield Cl B79 . . . . 250 C8
Metfield Croft DY6 . . . . . 275 F6
Mewies Cl DE12 . . . . 184 D1
Mews Cl ST2 . . . . 58 A2
Mews The Cannock WS11 . 209 D1
  Newcastle-u-L ST5 . . . . . . 56 D4
Meynell Cl DE15 . . . . 167 B1
Meynell Field TF9 . . . . 99 E4
Meyrick Rd ST17 . . . . 285 E1
Mica Cl B77 . . . . 251 B2
Michael Cl ST3 . . . . 74 B3
Michaels Cl ST5 . . . . 56 C7
Michael's La DE6 . . . . 80 C5
Micklea La ST9 . . . . 29 F1
Micklehome Dr DE13 . . . 201 B3
Micklegate ST19 . . . . 223 D7
Micklehome Dr DE13 . . . 201 B3
Mickleton B77 . . . . 262 C8
Micklewood Cl ST19 . . . . 207 F7
Micklewood La ST19 . . . . 208 B4
Middle Cross St ST3 . . . . 284 C4
Middle Entry B79 . . . . . . 250 B4
Middlefield ST20 . . . . . . 171 E7
Middlefield Rd ST2 . . . . . . 73 D8
Middlefield WV8 . . . . 239 E2
Middle Friars ST17 . . . . . 285 B2
Middlehurst Specl Sch
  ST7 . . . . 41 F7
Middle La Codsall WV8 . . 238 C2
  Congleton CW12 . . . . 6 D4
  Wolverhampton WV9 . . . . 240 A5
Middlemore La WS9 . . . . 256 A6
Middlepark Rd DY1 . . . . . 271 F1
Middlesmoor B77 . . . . . . 262 C8
Middleton Cl
  Hammerwich WS7 . . . . . . 229 D4
  Stoke-on-T ST6 . . . . 42 E3
Middleton Hall★ B78 . . . 260 E1
Middleton Rd
  Aldridge B74 . . . . 257 A1
  Brownhills WS8 . . . . 229 A4
  Whittington WS14 . . . . . . 232 E6
Midfield Cl ST18 . . . . 16 C2
Midgley Ct TF10 . . . . 168 F8
Midgley Dr B74 . . . . 258 A2
Midhurst Cl ST7 . . . . 41 F8
Midhurst Dr WS12 . . . . . 210 C7
Midhurst Gr WV6 . . . . . . 255 C5
Midland Rd WS12 . . . . . . 209 C5
Midpoint Ctr WV6 . . . . . . 255 F5
Midway Dr ST11 . . . . 90 E6
Midway The ST5 . . . . 283 B2
Midwinter Ct ST6 . . . . 56 E6
Milan Dr ST5 . . . . 70 E6
Milan Gr ST3 . . . . 73 E4
Milborne Dr ST5 . . . . 71 C5
Milburn Rd ST6 . . . . 57 B6
Milburn B77 . . . . 262 C8
Milcote Way DY6 . . . . . . 275 F7
Mildenhall B79 . . . . 250 C8
Mile Ct ST5 . . . . 55 F3
Mile Flat
  Kingswinford DY6 . . . . . . 275 A7
  Kinver DY7 . . . . 274 C7
Milehouse La ST5 . . . . 56 B4

Mile Oak Cross Rds B78 . 249 C2
Miles Bank ST1 . . . . 282 B3
Miles Green Rd ST7 . . . . . . 54 E8
Milestone Ct WV6 . . . . . . 255 A3
Milestone Dr DV9 . . . . . . 281 F4
Milford Ave ST9 . . . . 59 B4
Milford Cl DY8 . . . . 275 E3
Milford Rd
  Newcastle-u-L ST5 . . . . . . 283 A1
  Walton-on-t-H ST17 . . . . . 175 F7
  Wolverhampton WV2 . . . . 266 C7
Milford St ST4 . . . . 72 F5
Milgreen Ave ST1 . . . . 57 D7
Milking Bank DY1 . . . . . . 271 E2
Milking Bank Prim Sch
  DY1 . . . . 271 E2
Milk St ST13 . . . . 30 F7
Mill Bank Dr ST14 . . . . 96 A3
Millbank Pl ST5 . . . . 55 F1
Mill Bank Sedgley DY3 . . . 271 D8
  Stafford ST16 . . . . 285 B3
Millbank St Longton ST3 . . 284 C3
  Wolverhampton WV11 . . . 241 F1
Millbeck Cl CW2 . . . . 37 B5
Millbridge Cl ST3 . . . . 90 B6
Millbrook Cl **4** WS11 . . 209 F2
Millbrook Dr WS14 . . . . . 246 F6
Millbrook Gdns ST11 . . . . 90 F7
Millbrook Gr ST2 . . . . 43 A1
Millbrook Way ST10 . . . . . 76 D2
Mill Cl Blakedown DY10 . . 281 B2
  Caverswall ST3 . . . . 74 C3
  Dudley DY3 . . . . 271 D6
  Newton Solney DE15 . . . . 167 E8
  Stowe-by-Chartley ST18 . . 139 C5
Millcourt ST4 . . . . 87 F7
Mill Cres Barton-u-N DE13 201 E8
  Cannock WS11 . . . . 210 B2
Millcroft Way WS15 . . . . . 198 C4
Mill Ct
  Great Haywood ST18 . . . . 158 B2
  Shenstone WS14 . . . . 247 A6
Milldale Cres WV10 . . . . . 240 D3
Milldale Rd WV10 . . . . . . 240 D4
Mill End La DE13 . . . . 200 F4
Millend La ST7 . . . . 39 C5
Millenium Way ST5 . . . . . . 40 F2
Millennium Cl WS3 . . . . . 244 A4
Millennium Way
  Codsall WV8 . . . . 239 B4
  Stone ST15 . . . . 104 A4
Miller Cl WS13 . . . . 214 B2
Millersdale Cl DE15 . . . . . 167 B5
Millers Gate **2** ST15 . . 120 A8
Millers Gn WV7 . . . . 237 A5
Millers Green Dr DY6 . . . 275 A8
Millers La
  Burton u T DE14 . . . . 166 C3
  Stoke-on-T ST2 . . . . 43 A1
Miller St ST5 . . . . 283 C3
Millers Vale
  Cannock WS12 . . . . 210 D1
  Wombourne WV5 . . . . . . 269 D5
Millers View Cheadle ST10 . 76 F2
  Kidsgrove ST7 . . . . 26 A1
Millers Wharf B78 . . . . . . 251 F1
Millers Wlk WS3 . . . . 243 E3
Millett Rd ST7 . . . . 58 A3
Mill Farm Ct ST21 . . . . . . 134 D6
Millfield Ave
  Walsall,Little Bloxwich
  WS3 . . . . 243 D3
  Walsall WS4 . . . . 244 B1
Millfield Cres ST2 . . . . 43 A1
Millfield Dr TF9 . . . . 97 F2
Millfield Prim Sch
  Brownhills WS8 . . . . 245 A7
  Fazeley B78 . . . . 261 A8
Millfield Rd WS8 . . . . 245 A7
Mill Fields DY7 . . . . 278 B3
Millfields Way WV5 . . . . . 269 E5
Mill Gn WV10 . . . . 240 D4
Mill Gr Cheadle ST10 . . . . . 76 E2
  Codsall WV8 . . . . 239 C3
Mill Green Nature Pk★
  WS11 . . . . 209 F1
Mill Gr ST7 . . . . 25 D1
Mill Hayes Rd
  Biddulph ST8 . . . . 27 C4
  Burslem ST6 . . . . 41 E1
Mill Hill Cres ST5 . . . . 42 A4
Mill Hill Dr DE15 . . . . . . 167 B4
Mill Hill La DE15 . . . . . . 167 B4
Mill Hill Prim Sch ST6 . . . 41 F4
Mill Ho DY7 . . . . 278 B3
Millhouse Dr ST10 . . . . . . 76 E1
Millhouse Gdns ST10 . . . 192 F1
Millicent Cl WS12 . . . . . . 210 B6
Millicent Ho ST3 . . . . 284 C2
Millicent St ST4 . . . . 72 E6
Millington St WS15 . . . . . 178 F2
Mill La
  Acton Trussell ST17 . . . . . 175 A2
  Albrighton WV7 . . . . 220 F1
  Aldridge WS9 . . . . 256 F7
  Barthomley CW2 . . . . 38 C7
  Barton-u-N DE13 . . . . 201 E8
  Blakedown DY10 . . . . 281 B2
  Blakenhall CW5 . . . . 52 B4
  Codsall WV8 . . . . 238 F5
  Congleton CW12 . . . . 16 C8
  Doveridge DE6 . . . . 127 A8
  Edingale DE6 . . . . 80 A7
  Ellastone DE6 . . . . 80 D2
  Fazeley B78 . . . . 261 A8
  Foston DE65 . . . . 129 D7
  Gnosall ST20 . . . . 171 C5

Mill La continued
  Gratwich ST14 . . . . 124 E3
  Great Haywood ST18 . . . . 158 B2
  Hammerwich WS7 . . . . . . 229 D3
  Hartington SK17 . . . . 24 D5
  Kinver,Blundies DY7 . . . . . 274 A4
  Kinver DY7 . . . . 278 B3
  Little Aston WS9 . . . . 257 A7
  Lower Tean ST10 . . . . 92 F2
  Madeley CW3 . . . . 68 F7
  Milwich ST18 . . . . 122 D4
  Moddershall ST15 . . . . . . 105 E6
  Roston DE6 . . . . 96 D7
  Rugeley WS15 . . . . 178 F1
  Scropton DE65 . . . . 129 F1
  Shenstone WS14 . . . . 247 A6
  Standon ST21 . . . . 102 C3
  Stonnall WS9,WS14 . . . . . 246 A4
  Sudbury DE6 . . . . 128 E1
  Tamworth B79 . . . . 250 C5
  Tettenhall Wood WV6 . . . . 255 A3
  The Bank ST7 . . . . 26 A7
  Weston CW2 . . . . 37 B6
  Weston-u-L TF11 . . . . 220 D7
  Weston-Under-Lizard
  TF11 . . . . 203 D1
  Wetley Rocks ST9 . . . . 59 F7
  Wheaton Aston ST19 . . . . 205 C5
  Wombourne WV5 . . . . . . 270 B6
Mill Mdw DE13 . . . . 162 F8
Mill Meece Marsh ST21 . . 102 C3
Mill Meece Pumping
  Station★ ST21 . . . . 117 E8
Millmoor Ave WS5 . . . . . 198 A4
Mill Park Ind Est WS11 . . 210 A1
Mill Pk WS11 . . . . 210 A2
Mill Pond The WS13 . . . . 214 C2
Mill Pool Cl WV5 . . . . 269 D5
Mill Pool Rd WS12 . . . . . 210 B6
Millpool The WV5 . . . . . . 263 F2
Mill Rd Brownhills WS8 . . 245 A7
  Cheadle ST10 . . . . 76 E2
  Coldmeece ST15 . . . . 118 B6
  Oakamoor ST10 . . . . 78 A6
  Walsall WS4 . . . . 244 C1
Mill Rise ST7 . . . . 26 A1
Millrise Rd ST2 . . . . 43 A1
Mills Cres WV2 . . . . 266 E8
Millside Rugeley WS15 . . . 196 B7
  Wombourne WV5 . . . . . . 269 E5
Mills Rd WV2 . . . . 266 E8
Mill St Cannock WS11 . . . 209 E1
  Leek ST13 . . . . 30 D6
  Newcastle-u-L ST5 . . . . . . 55 D1
Millstone Ave ST7 . . . . 25 E1
Millstone Edge ST13 . . . . . 45 B1
Mill St ST19 . . . . 192 F1
Millstream Cl ST10 . . . . . . 76 E2
Mill St Rocester ST14 . . . . . 96 A3
  Stafford ST16 . . . . 285 B3
  Stone ST15 . . . . 120 A8
  Stourbridge DY8 . . . . 275 F2
Mill The ST7 . . . . 26 C5
Milltown Way ST13 . . . . . . 31 A4
Mill View ST6 . . . . 42 D6
Millwalk Ave WS15 . . . . . 120 C7
Millwalk Dr WV9 . . . . 240 A3
Millward Rd ST2 . . . . 58 C3
Mill Waters ST10 . . . . 76 E1
Millway La DE6 . . . . 35 F3
Mill Way WS15 . . . . 198 A1
Mill Way The ST15 . . . . . . 103 B4
Milne Ave WS13 . . . . 215 D6
Milner Dr B79 . . . . 251 E7
Milner Terr ST13 . . . . 31 A7
Milnes Cl ST13 . . . . 73 A2
Milo Cres B78 . . . . 250 A2
Milton Ave B79 . . . . 250 A7
Milton Cres Dudley DY3 . . 271 A5
  Talke ST7 . . . . 40 C8
Milton Ct WV6 . . . . 254 E4
Milton Dr TF9 . . . . 97 C2
Milton Gr ST17 . . . . 174 B8
Milton Ho DE14 . . . . 166 D3
Milton Prim Sch ST2 . . . . . 43 B1
Milton Rd Cannock WS11 . 209 E4
  Stoke-on-T ST1 . . . . 42 F1
  Stoke-on-T ST1 . . . . 57 E8
Milton St Burton u T DE14 . 166 C3
  Hanley ST1 . . . . 282 A1
Milvale St ST6 . . . . 56 E7
Milverton Dr ST14 . . . . . . 110 F1
Milverton Pl **4** ST3 . . . . 73 A3
Milward Rd ST2 . . . . 89 F6
Mimosa Wlk DY6 . . . . . . 275 E8
Minard Gr ST3 . . . . 74 A4
Minden Gr ST6 . . . . 57 D8
Mineal Rd ST2 . . . . 73 D7
Minehead Rd Dudley DY1 . 271 E1
  Wolverhampton WV10 . . . 240 B2
Miners Way WS7 . . . . 228 C7
Miners Wlk ST7 . . . . 26 A1
Minerva Cl Biddulph ST8 . . 27 B5
  Tamworth B77 . . . . 250 D5
Minerva Rd ST4 . . . . 72 F6
Minewood Cl WS3 . . . . . . 242 F3
Minfield Cl ST7 . . . . 41 A8
Minn-End-La SK11 . . . . 8 B6
Minnie St ST7 . . . . 54 E7
Minors Hill WS14 . . . . . . 231 D6
Minshall Ct ST4 . . . . 72 C5
Minshall St ST4 . . . . 72 C5
Minsterley WV3 . . . . 265 E8
Minster St ST5 . . . . 42 B1
Minster The WV3 . . . . . . 266 A1
Minstrel Ct ST8 . . . . 27 D7

Minton Cl Cheadle ST10 . . . 76 D1
  Congleton CW12 . . . . 6 B1
Minton Pl ST5 . . . . 56 D5
Minton St
  Newcastle-u-L ST5 . . . . . . 56 D5
  Stoke-on-T ST4 . . . . 71 E8
Miranda Gr ST6 . . . . 42 D1
Miras Bsns Est WS12 . . . . 210 D3
Mires Brook La WS15 . . . 160 F6
Mires The DE6 . . . . 35 A3
Mirfield Cl WV9 . . . . 240 A3
Miss Pickerings Field
  ST17 . . . . 175 B1
Mistley Wlk ST6 . . . . 41 C7
Mitcham Cl WS12 . . . . . . 209 F7
Mitchell Ave ST7 . . . . 25 C1
Mitchell Cl WS13 . . . . . . 215 C6
Mitchell Dr ST7 . . . . 25 C1
Mitchell High Sch ST2 . . . . 58 C3
Mitchell Rise ST15 . . . . . . 118 F6
Mitchell's Ct B79 . . . . 250 B5
Mitchell St ST6 . . . . 41 F1
Mitchel Rd DY6 . . . . 275 F4
Mitre Cl WV11 . . . . 242 A3
Mitre Rd WS6 . . . . 226 D2
Mitton Rd ST18 . . . . 191 C7
Moat Bank DE15 . . . . 167 D2
Moat Brook Ave WV8 . . . 238 E4
Moatbrook La WV8 . . . . . 238 D4
Moat Dr B78 . . . . 260 E5
Moat Farm Way WS3 . . . . 244 A5
Moat Hall Prim Sch WS6 . 226 F3
Moathouse Cl ST17 . . . . . 193 B8
Moat House Dr ST18 . . . . 172 E6
Moat La Audley ST7 . . . . . . 39 B3
  Great Wyrley WS6 . . . . . . 227 A2
  Newborough DE13 . . . . . 162 F6
Moatside Cl WS3 . . . . 244 A5
Moat The ST3 . . . . 74 B4
Moat Way WS15 . . . . 198 B4
Mobberley Rd ST6 . . . . 41 C7
Mob La WS4 . . . . 244 C4
Moccasin Way ST16 . . . . . 155 F5
Moddershall Oaks ST3,
  ST15 . . . . 90 A1
Moden Cl DY3 . . . . 271 D6
Moden Hill DY3 . . . . 271 D6
Modular Ct WV10 . . . . . . 224 D5
Moffat Gr ST2 . . . . 73 E7
Moffatt Way ST5 . . . . 55 A2
Moises Hall Rd WV5 . . . . 270 B7
Moisty La
  Marchington ST14 . . . . . . 127 C3
  Uttoxeter ST14 . . . . 126 F4
Mollatts Cl ST13 . . . . 30 B2
Mollatts Wood Rd ST13 . . . 30 B1
Mollison Rd ST3 . . . . 90 A8
Monaco ST5 . . . . 70 E7
Monarch Cl DE13 . . . . . . 166 D8
Monarchy Cl WS15 . . . . . 196 D7
Mona Rd DE13 . . . . 166 B6
Moncreiff Dr DE13 . . . . . 148 A1
Moneystone Cotts ST10 . . . 63 A1
Monkhouse ST10 . . . . 76 D3
Monkleigh Cl ST4 . . . . 88 B5
Monks Cl
  Newcastle-u-L ST5 . . . . . . 71 C4
  Wombourne WV5 . . . . . . 269 E6
Monksfield TF9 . . . . 97 A1
Monk St DE13 . . . . 146 C7
Monks Way
  Swynnerton ST15 . . . . . . 103 B4
  Tamworth B77 . . . . 250 F5
Monks Wlk ST20 . . . . 171 C5
Monkton Cl ST3 . . . . 73 A1
Monmore Bsns Pk WV2 . . 266 F7
Monmouth Pl ST5 . . . . 71 D4
Monsaldale Cl
  Brownhills WS8 . . . . 244 D7
  Burton u T DE15 . . . . 167 B4
Monsal Gr ST1 . . . . 57 F5
Monteagle Dr DY6 . . . . . . 270 D1
Montford Gr DY3 . . . . 271 D7
Montfort Pl ST5 . . . . 71 B6
Montgomery Ct ST5 . . . . . 283 A3
Montgomery Pl ST3 . . . . . . 74 B2
Montley B79 . . . . 262 C8
Montpelier Cl DE14 . . . . . 185 A7
Montpellier Gdns DY1 . . . 271 E2
Montrose Cl WS11 . . . . . . 209 F5
Montrose Dr ST4 . . . . 72 F5
Montville Dr ST17 . . . . . . 155 B1
Monty Pl ST4 . . . . 73 B6
Monument Cl ST12 . . . . . . 88 A2
Monument Dr WV10 . . . . 241 C8
Monument La
  Sedgley DY3 . . . . 266 E1
  Tittensor ST12 . . . . 88 A2
Monument Rd ST7 . . . . 40 D6
Monument View ST7 . . . . . 39 F2
Monyash Cl ST3 . . . . 90 C7
Monyash Dr ST13 . . . . 31 A5
Moon's La WS6 . . . . 226 D1
Moor Cl
  Acton Trussell ST17 . . . . . 175 B1
  Biddulph ST8 . . . . 16 E1
  Burntwood WS7 . . . . 229 B7
Moorcroft Ave ST5 . . . . . . 71 B3
Moorcroft Cl ST10 . . . . . . 76 C1
Moor Croft WS15 . . . . . . 179 A6
Moorcroft Mus★ ST6 . . . . 57 B7

Moorfield Ct TF10 . . . . . . 168 E2
Moorfield La TF10 . . . . . . 168 E1
Moorfield Prim Sch
  TF10 . . . . 168 E1
Moorfield Rd WV2 . . . . . . 266 C7
Moorfields Cl
  Aldridge WS9 . . . . 256 A7
  Cauldon Lowe ST10 . . . . . 63 E4
Moorfields Ind Est ST21 . . 102 F3
Moorfields Leek ST13 . . . . 30 F5
  Stafford ST16 . . . . 155 D7
Moor Fst Sch ST8 . . . . 17 B1
Moor Furlong DE13 . . . . . 147 F1
Moorgate Com Prim Sch
  B79 . . . . 250 A5
Moorgate B79 . . . . 250 A5
Moor Gr ST14 . . . . 126 A8
Moor Hall Dr B75 . . . . . . 258 D1
Moor Hall La ST19 . . . . . . 208 A7
Moor Hall Prim Sch B75 . . 258 D2
Moorhead Dr ST9 . . . . 43 F4
Moorhen Cl WS8 . . . . 244 E7
Moorhen Way ST6 . . . . 41 E8
Moorhill Prim Sch
  Cannock WS11 . . . . 209 E5
  Cannock WS11 . . . . 209 E5
Moorhouse St ST15 . . . . . 119 A6
Moorhouse St ST13 . . . . . . 30 F5
Moorings The
  3 Stone ST15 . . . . 120 A8
  Alrewas DE13 . . . . 200 F3
  Colwich ST17 . . . . 177 E7
  Wolverhampton WV9 . . . . 239 F2
Moor La Cheadle ST10 . . . . 76 F3
  Church Leigh ST10 . . . . . 108 E5
  Colton WS15 . . . . 179 A8
  Gayton ST18 . . . . 138 F6
Moorland Ave ST9 . . . . 59 C4
Moorland Cl
  Rugeley WS15 . . . . 178 C1
  Werrington ST9 . . . . 59 B4
Moorland Rd Biddulph ST8 . 27 D8
  Burslem ST6 . . . . 57 A8
  Cannock WS11 . . . . 209 E5
  Cheddleton ST13 . . . . 45 C5
  Leek ST13 . . . . 31 B5
  Mow Cop ST7 . . . . 26 D7
  Newport TF10 . . . . 168 E2
  Stoke-on-T ST6 . . . . 57 A8
Moorlands Dr DE6 . . . . . . 81 C7
Moorlands Farm Pk The★
  ST10 . . . . 47 D3
Moorlands Sixth Form Ctr
  ST10 . . . . 76 D1
Moorland View ST6 . . . . . 42 C3
Moorland Wlk ST10 . . . . . 76 D3
Moor La Pattingham WV6 . 253 C2
  Seighford ST18 . . . . 154 D7
  Shenstone WS14 . . . . 246 E2
  Tamworth,Amington B79 . . 251 A6
  Tamworth,Bolehall B77 . . . 250 D5
Moorleys La ST18 . . . . . . 139 A5
Moorpark Jun Sch ST6 . . . 42 A1
Moor Pk Perton WV6 . . . . 254 D5
  Walsall WS3 . . . . 243 B3
Moor St S WV2 . . . . 266 C7
Moors Dr WV9 . . . . 224 B2
Moors Hill Cotts DE13 . . . 183 F8
Moorside High Sch ST6 . . . 59 E4
Moorside Rd ST9 . . . . 59 D4
Moorson Ave ST7 . . . . 25 F8
Moor St Burton u T DE14 . 166 C2
  Tamworth B79 . . . . 250 A5
Moorsyde Rd ST4 . . . . 71 E5
Moor The WS13 . . . . 215 B5
Moorthorne Cres ST5 . . . . 56 A6
Moor View WS7 . . . . 212 B2
Moorview Gdns ST7 . . . . . 26 E6
Moran Gr ST6 . . . . 56 E7
Moran Rd ST5 . . . . 55 F2
Mordaunt Dr B75 . . . . . . 258 E2
Mordern Mobile Home Pk
  WV10 . . . . 240 C6
Moresby Cl ST2 . . . . 43 B1
Moreton Ave
  Hanchurch ST5 . . . . 87 B4
  Kingsley ST10 . . . . 61 D2
  Wolverhampton WV4 . . . . 266 E4
Moreton Cl Kidsgrove ST7 . 41 B8
  Werrington ST9 . . . . 59 B2
Moreton Com Sch WV10 . 240 F1
Moreton Ho ST7 . . . . 56 D4
Moreton La
  Draycott in t C DE6 . . . . . 144 C3
  Great Haywood ST18 . . . . 158 E4
Moreton Par ST5 . . . . 56 D4
Moreton Pl ST7 . . . . 25 C9
Moreton Rd WV10 . . . . . . 240 D1
Moreton St WS11 . . . . . . 209 F4
Morfe Hall La DY7 . . . . . . 273 D4
Morfe La DY7 . . . . 273 C4
Morford Rd WS9 . . . . 256 A7
Morgan Rd B78 . . . . 250 A2
Morgan Way ST6 . . . . 42 B6
Morland Cl ST15 . . . . 120 B5
Morley Cl DE15 . . . . 167 B2
Morley Dr CW12 . . . . 6 A1
Morley Rd WS7 . . . . 229 B7
Morley Road Sh Ctr WS7 . 229 B7
Morley's Hill DE13 . . . . . 166 B7
Morley St Hanley ST1 . . . . 282 A4
  Leek ST13 . . . . 30 D5
Morlings Dr WS7 . . . . 229 B8
Morning Pines DY8 . . . . . 279 E4
Mornington Rd ST1 . . . . . 57 E8
Morpeth ST3 . . . . 284 C3
Morpeth B77 . . . . 261 C7

Morridge Side ST13 . . . . . . 32 A1
Morridge View ST13 . . . . . 45 C4
Morris Ct 4 WV4 . . . . 266 F4
Morris Dr ST16 . . . . 156 C3
Morris Hill B78 . . . . 262 F7
Morris Sq ST5 . . . . 56 D5
Morston Dr ST5 . . . . 71 B2
Morston B77 . . . . 261 D4
Mortimer Pl ST3 . . . . 73 F4
Morton Rd ST17 . . . . 174 D6
Morton St ST6 . . . . 56 E7
Morville Cl ST4 . . . . 72 E7
Moscow La ST20 . . . . 151 D7
Mosedale Ave ST3 . . . . . . 89 E8
Moseley Ct WV11 . . . . . . 241 F3
Moseley Old Hall★
. . . . 241 A5
Moseley Old Hall La
WV10 . . . . 241 A5
Moseley Rd WV10 . . . . . . 241 A4
Moseley Row ST18 . . . . . 137 C1
Mosley Dr ST14 . . . . 111 A1
Mosley Mews DE13 . . . . . 147 A4
Mosley Prim Sch DE13 . . 165 C7
Mosley St ST14 . . . . 166 C3
Mossbank Ave WS7 . . . . . 229 A6
Moss Cl Aldridge WS9 . . . 256 A5
Werrington ST9 . . . . 59 B4
Moss Cres WS12 . . . . 209 C5
Mossdale WV3 . . . . 271 E2
Mossdale Way DY3 . . . . . 271 E7
Mossfield TF9 . . . . 130 A6
Mossfield Cres 4 ST7 . . . 26 B2
Mossfield Dr ST8 . . . . 27 E7
Mossfield Rd ST3 . . . . 73 C6
Moss Gn WS15 . . . . 178 C2
Moss Green Rd ST2 . . . . . 73 D7
Moss Gr Kingswinford DY6 275 D7
Newcastle-u-L ST5 . . . . . 40 D3
Moss Hill WS3 . . . . 43 D5
Moss La Betton TF9 . . . . . 97 F6
Chipnall TF9 . . . . 114 C3
Hilderstone ST15 . . . . . 106 E6
Lawton-gate ST7 . . . . . . 25 F4
Madeley CW3 . . . . 68 D6
Maer ST5 . . . . 84 F1
Mossland Rd ST3 . . . . 73 C5
Moss La Whitmore ST5 . . 85 C5
Woodseaves ST20,ST21 . 151 F8
Yarnfield ST15 . . . . 119 A7
Mossley CE Prim Sch
CW12 . . . . 16 B8
Mossley Cl WS3 . . . . 242 F1
Mossley Ct CW12 . . . . . . 15 F8
Mossley Garth Cl 5 CW12 6 A1
Mossley La WS3 . . . . 242 F2
Mossley Prim Sch WS3 . . 242 F2
Moss Park Ave ST9 . . . . . 59 B4
Mosspit ST17 . . . . 174 F4
Moss Pl ST7 . . . . 26 B3
Moss Rd Cannock WS11 . . 210 A3
Congleton CW12 . . . . . . 15 E7
Moss Rise ST5 . . . . 71 C1
Moss Side ST1 . . . . 57 E8
Moss St Cannock WS11 . . 210 A4
Stoke-on-T ST6 . . . . 42 C5
Mossvale Gr ST16 . . . . . . 155 A5
Mosswood St WS11 . . . . 226 D7
Moston St ST1 . . . . 57 D6
Mostyn Cl ST8 . . . . 27 E6
Mott Pl ST6 . . . . 56 D8
Moulton Rd ST3 . . . . 284 B4
Mounfield Pl ST4 . . . . 72 D6
Mountain Ash Rd WS8 . . 244 E5
Mountain Pine Cl ST4 . . . 210 A8
Mount Ave Cannock WS12 210 B7
Stoke-on-T ST4 . . . . 71 F7
Stone ST15 . . . . 104 F2
Mountbatten Cl
1 Burton u T DE13 . . . . 166 D8
Burntwood WS7 . . . . . . 211 F1
Mount Cl
Cheslyn Hay WS6 . . . . . 226 E2
Dudley DY3 . . . . 271 C2
Stone ST15 . . . . 120 C6
Werrington ST9 . . . . 59 C4
Wombourne WV5 . . . . . 270 A7
Mount Cotts ST20 . . . . . . 131 B4
Mount Cres ST15 . . . . . . 104 F2
Mount Ct WV6 . . . . 255 B2
Mount Dr WV5 . . . . 270 A7
Mount Edge ST18 . . . . . . 137 B1
Mount Fields ST10 . . . . . . 94 B2
Mountford Cres WS9 . . . . 256 C8
Mountford St ST6 . . . . 41 F1
Mount Gdns WV8 . . . . . . 238 F4
Mount Ind Est ST15 . . . . 104 F2
Mount La Dudley DY3 . . . 271 C2
Market Drayton TF9 . . . . 112 C8
Mount Pleasant Ave
WV5 . . . . 269 F7
Mount Pleasant Cl ST15 . 120 D6
Mount Pleasant
Derrington ST18 . . . . . . 154 E2
Hanley ST1 . . . . 282 A2
Ipstones ST10 . . . . 62 A8
Kidsgrove ST7 . . . . 26 A1
Kingswinford DY6 . . . . . 275 C4
Leek ST13 . . . . 30 D1
Loggerheads TF9 . . . . . . 99 F5
Mount Pleasant Mobile
Home Pk B77 . . . . 250 C1
Mount Pleasant
Newcastle-u-L,Chesterton
ST5 . . . . 55 C4
Newcastle-u-L ST5 . . . . . 283 C2

Mount Pleasant Rd ST7 . . 26 B7
Mount Pleasant B77 . . . . 261 C8
Mount Pl ST11 . . . . 91 A7
Mount Rd
Blythe Bridge ST11 . . . . . 91 A7
Burntwood WS7 . . . . . . 229 B6
Castle Gresley DE11 . . . . 186 D1
Kidsgrove ST7 . . . . 26 B1
Leek ST13 . . . . 31 B5
Rugeley WS15 . . . . 178 B2
Stone ST15 . . . . 104 F2
Stourbridge,Wordsley DY8 275 E2
Walsall WS3 . . . . 244 A4
Wolverhampton,Goldthorn Hill
WV4 . . . . 266 A4
Wolverhampton,Lanesfield
WV4 . . . . 266 F2
Wolverhampton,Tettenhall Wood
WV6 . . . . 255 A3
Wombourne WV5 . . . . . 270 A7
Mount Road Ind Est
WS7 . . . . 229 B6
Mount Row ST16 . . . . . . 285 B3
Mount St Georges The
ST5 . . . . 56 C6
Mountside Gdns ST13 . . . 31 B6
Mount Side St ST10 . . . . . 210 C7
Mountsorrel Cl ST4 . . . . . 88 C6
Mount St Burton u T DE15 . 167 A3
Cannock WS11 . . . . 210 B7
Hanley ST1 . . . . 57 E5
Newcastle-u-L ST5 . . . . . 55 E6
Stafford ST16 . . . . 285 B3
Stone ST15 . . . . 105 A2
Mount The Creswell ST18 . 154 E5
Kidsgrove ST7 . . . . 26 A1
Newcastle-u-L ST5 . . . . . 55 E6
Scholar Green ST7 . . . . . 25 E7
Mountwood Covert WV6 . 255 B3
Mouse Hill WS3 . . . . 243 F3
Mousley St ST6 . . . . 56 E8
Mowbray Croft WS7 . . . . 211 E1
Mowbray Wlk ST1 . . . . . . 57 F8
Mow Cop Rd ST7 . . . . 26 D6
Mow La Biddulph ST7,ST8 . 16 B2
Mount Pleasant ST7 . . . . 26 B5
Mow Cop ST7 . . . . 15 F4
Moxhull Cl WV12 . . . . . . 242 C1
Moxhull Gdns WV12 . . . . 242 C1
Moxley Ave ST5 . . . . 57 D7
Mozart Ct WS11 . . . . 210 C2
Muchall Rd WV4 . . . . 266 A5
Mucklestone Rd
Loggerheads TF9 . . . . . . 99 D5
Norton in H TF9 . . . . 82 D2
Mucklestone Wood La
TF9 . . . . 99 E6
Muirfield Cl WS3 . . . . 243 A3
Muirfield B77 . . . . 251 C5
Muirville Cl 1 DY8 . . . . . 275 D3
Mulberry Cl TF10 . . . . . . 168 F1
Mulberry Dr 3 WS13 . . . 231 E8
Mulberry Gn DY1 . . . . . . 271 F5
Mulberry Pl
Newcastle-u-L ST5 . . . . . 55 E8
Walsall WS3 . . . . 242 F1
Mulberry Rd
Cannock WS11 . . . . 209 E3
Walsall WS3 . . . . 243 A1
Mulberry St ST1 . . . . 282 C2
Mulberry Way ST13 . . . . . 31 A4
Muldoon Cl WS11 . . . . . . 210 B4
Mulgrave St ST1 . . . . 282 A4
Mullein B74 . . . . 257 F5
Mulliner Cl ST2 . . . . 58 D3
Munro St ST4 . . . . 72 A5
Munster Terr ST4 . . . . 71 F5
Murdoch Dr DY6 . . . . 275 C7
Murhall St ST6 . . . . 56 E8
Murray St ST6 . . . . 41 C7
Murton B77 . . . . 262 C8
Muse La DE6 . . . . 129 B7
Musk La DY3 . . . . 271 C8
Musk La W DY3 . . . . 271 C8
Mus of Cannock Chase★
WS12 . . . . 210 A2
Mustang Cl ST6 . . . . 41 C4
Mustang Dr ST16 . . . . . . 155 B8
Muxloe Cl WS3 . . . . 243 A3
Myatt Ave
Burntwood WS7 . . . . . . 229 A7
Wolverhampton WV2 . . . 266 E6
Myatt St WV2 . . . . 266 E6
Myatt St ST1 . . . . 282 C4
Myatt Way WS15 . . . . . . 196 D6
Mynors St Hanley ST1 . . . 282 C3
Stafford ST16 . . . . 156 A3
Myott Ave ST5 . . . . 283 A1
Myrtle Ave ST3 . . . . 74 B3
Myrtle Gr Brewood ST19 . 223 D6
Wolverhampton WV3 . . . 265 E6
Myrtle St WV2 . . . . 266 F6

N

Nabb La Alton ST10 . . . . . 94 F7
Denstone ST14 . . . . 95 A4
Nabbs Cl ST7 . . . . 26 B2
Nabbswood Rd ST7 . . . . . 26 B2
Nab Hill Ave ST13 . . . . . . 30 D6
Nab Hill Ct ST13 . . . . 30 C6
Naden Ho WS12 . . . . 209 C5
Naesby Rd WS4 . . . . 254 F3
Nagington Dr ST19 . . . . . 207 F3
Nailers Dr WS7 . . . . 229 D6
Nairn Rd WS3 . . . . 243 A4
Nancy Talbot Cl WS15 . . 161 B5

Nankirk La DE13 . . . . 165 A6
Nanny Goat La ST15 . . . . 105 A1
Nantwich Rd Audley ST7 . 39 B1
Balterley ST7 . . . . 38 F1
Woore CW3 . . . . 67 B1
Naomi Way WS9 . . . . 245 B4
Napier Gdns 3 ST7 . . . . 26 A2
Napier Rd WV2 . . . . 266 D7
Napier St Burton u T DE14 166 C1
Stoke-on-T 72 D6
Napier B77 . . . . 250 E3
Naples Cl ST3 . . . . 73 E4
Naples Dr ST5 . . . . 70 F6
Napley Dr ST7 . . . . 82 C2
Napley Rd TF9 . . . . 82 D1
Narlow La DE6 . . . . 51 F2
Narrow La
Brownhills WS8 . . . . 244 F8
Colton WS15 . . . . 179 B7
Denstone ST14 . . . . 95 D6
Milwich ST15 . . . . 121 C7
Narvik Cres ST6 . . . . 42 C2
Nash Ave Perton WV6 . . . 254 E3
Stafford ST16 . . . . 155 B6
Nashe Dr ST3 . . . . 73 A2
Nash La
Acton Trussell ST17 . . . . 193 B8
Lichfield WS13 . . . . 214 A5
Nash Peake St ST6 . . . . . 41 D3
Nash St ST5 . . . . 55 E2
Natham Cl ST11 . . . . 74 D3
Nathan St WS15 . . . . 196 F5
Nathans Mdw CW12 . . . . 16 C7
National Meml Arboretum
The★ DE13 . . . . 201 D3
Nave Rd ST4 . . . . 72 A5
Navigation Loop ST15 . . . 104 C2
Navigation Rd ST6 . . . . . . 56 F7
Navigation St ST6 . . . . . . 56 F7
Navigation Way WS11 . . . 210 A2
Naylors Gr DY3 . . . . 271 E4
Naylor St ST6 . . . . 41 F5
Naylor Yd 1 ST13 . . . . . . 30 E6
Neachless Ave WV5 . . . . . 270 A5
Neachley La TF11 . . . . . . 220 A2
Neal Croft WS14 . . . . 232 E6
Neale Ho WV2 . . . . 266 C7
Neale Pl ST2 . . . . 58 B5
Neander B79 . . . . 249 F6
Near Ridding ST20 . . . . . 171 D5
Neath Cl ST3 . . . . 73 D3
Neath Pl 2 ST3 . . . . 73 C6
Neath Rd WS3 . . . . 242 F6
Neath Way WS3 . . . . 242 F2
Needwood Ave DE13 . . . 147 C4
Needwood CE Prim Sch
DE13 . . . . 162 F7
Needwood Cl WV2 . . . . . 266 B6
Needwood Cl DE13 . . . . . 146 C4
Needwood Dr WV4 . . . . . 266 F4
Needwood Grange
WS15 . . . . 161 A5
Needwood Hill WS13 . . . 214 A4
Needwood Pk DE13 . . . . 183 D1
Needwood St DE14 . . . . 166 B4
Nellan Cres ST6 . . . . 42 D1
Nelson Bank ST6,ST7 . . . 41 A7
Nelson Bldgs ST7 . . . . . . 26 A1
Nelson Cres ST21 . . . . . . 102 E2
Nelson Dr WS12 . . . . 210 F4
Nelson Ind Est ST7 . . . . . 25 C1
Nelson Pl Hanley ST1 . . . 282 C2
Newcastle-u-L ST5 . . . . . 283 C3
Nelson Rd ST4 . . . . 71 E8
Nelson St Burton u T DE15 167 C4
Leek ST13 . . . . 30 F7
Newcastle-u-L ST5 . . . . . 56 C5
Stoke-on-T ST4 . . . . 72 D6
Nelson Way ST17 . . . . . . 174 E6
Nemesia B77 . . . . 251 B4
Nene Cl DE13 . . . . 147 C1
Nene Way DE65 . . . . 147 D8
Nephew St ST6 . . . . 56 E8
Neptune Gr ST1 . . . . 57 F6
Ness Gr ST1 . . . . 76 E5
Nest Comm WS3 . . . . . . 243 F5
Nether Beacon WS13 . . . 214 A1
Netherbridge Ave WS14 . 231 F4
Netherby Rd DY3 . . . . . . 271 C8
Nethercote Pl ST2 . . . . . . 73 D8
Nethergate DY3 . . . . 271 F5
Nether La WS3 . . . . 229 D8
Netherseal Rd
Chilcote DE12 . . . . 219 F4
Clifton Campville B79 . . . 218 F2
Netherset Hey La CW3 . . 68 F4
Netherstone Gr B74 . . . . 257 F5
Nether Stowe High Sch
WS13 . . . . 214 B1
Netherstowe La WS13 . . . 214 D2
Netherstowe WS13 . . . . . 214 C2
Netherton Gr ST2 . . . . . . 43 C2
Nethy Dr WV6 . . . . 255 B5
Netley Pl ST3 . . . . 88 E7
Netley Rd WS3 . . . . 242 E2
Netley Way WS3 . . . . 242 E2
Nevada La ST6 . . . . 57 B8
Neve Ave WV10 . . . . 240 F1
Neville Ave WV4 . . . . 266 D5
Neville Cl DE13 . . . . 147 B3
Neville Ho DY3 . . . . 271 D7
Neville St Stoke-on-T ST4 . 71 F4
Tamworth B77 . . . . 250 E3
Nevill St B79 . . . . 251 C5
Nevin Ave ST8 . . . . 27 D5
Nevis Ct WV6 . . . . 255 E2
Nevis Gr WV12 . . . . 242 B1
Newall Ave ST16 . . . . 156 B5

Newark Gr ST6 . . . . 41 C7
New Ave ST11 . . . . 91 C6
New Barns La WS14 . . . . 246 B3
New Bldgs Barlaston ST12 . 88 D1
Biddulph ST8 . . . . 27 C3
Newbold Cl WS13 . . . . . . 231 A5
Newborough CI ST1 . . . . 57 F6
Newbridge Ave WV6 . . . . 255 E3
Newbridge Cres WV6 . . . 255 E4
Newbridge Dr WV6 . . . . . 255 E4
Newbridge Gdns WV6 . . . 255 E4
Newbridge Mews 3
WV6 . . . . 255 F4
Newbridge Prep Sch
WV6 . . . . 255 E4
Newbridge Rd DY6 . . . . . 275 C8
Newbridge St WV6 . . . . . 255 F4
Newburn Gr ST4 . . . . 88 B8
Newbury Cl
Great Wyrley WS6 . . . . . 226 F2
Stafford ST17 . . . . 175 C7
Newbury Dr DE13 . . . . . . 147 C1
Newbury Gr ST3 . . . . 88 E7
Newbury Rd
Norton Canes WS11 . . . 228 A5
Stourbridge DY8 . . . . . . 275 D1
Wolverhampton WV10 . . 240 C2
Newby Cl DE15 . . . . 167 B1
Newcastle Com High Sch
ST5 . . . . 70 F7
Newcastle Ent Ctr ST5 . . 55 E2
Newcastle La ST4 . . . . . . 71 E6
Newcastle Rd Ashley TF9 . 100 B3
Astbury CW12 . . . . 15 A7
Cotes Heath ST21 . . . . . 102 B3
Eccleshall ST21 . . . . 133 E8
Leek ST13 . . . . 30 D4
Loggerheads TF9 . . . . . . 99 E5
Madeley CW3 . . . . 68 F7
Market Drayton TF9 . . . . 97 F2
Newcastle-u-L ST5 . . . . . 71 C1
Stoke-on-T ST4 . . . . 71 E5
Stone ST15 . . . . 104 E1
Talke ST7 . . . . 40 E7
Woore CW3 . . . . 67 E1
Newcastle St Burslem ST6 . 56 E8
Newcastle-u-L ST5 . . . . . 55 D2
Stone ST15 . . . . 104 F1
Newcastle-under-Lyme Coll
ST5 . . . . 283 A3
Newcastle-under-Lyme Schs
ST5 . . . . 283 C2
New Century St ST1 . . . . 282 A3
New Chapel St ST6 . . . . . 41 A1
Newchapel Observatory★
ST7 . . . . 26 E2
Newchapel Rd ST7 . . . . . 26 C3
New Close St ST11 . . . . . 91 B8
Newcomen Cl WS7 . . . . . 229 C8
Newcomen Dr ST2 . . . . . 73 D7
New Cott DE6 . . . . 36 E3
Newcott Cl WV9 . . . . 239 F7
New Cotts Foxt ST10 . . . . 62 C5
Oaken WV8 . . . . 238 D2
Six Ashes WV15 . . . . . . 272 C6
Stourton DY7 . . . . 278 F8
New Council Hos TF9 . . . 98 C2
Newcroft St ST5 . . . . 56 C5
Newcrofts Wlk ST6 . . . . . 42 D6
New Dudley Rd DY6 . . . . 275 C8
Newfield Dr DY6 . . . . 275 E4
Newfield Rd DE15 . . . . . . 167 B4
Newfield St ST6 . . . . 41 D4
Newfold Cres ST6 . . . . . . 43 B8
Newford Cres ST2 . . . . . . 42 F1
New Ford Prim Sch ST6 . . 42 D1
New Garden Ho ST7 . . . . 285 B2
New Garden St ST17 . . . . 285 B1
Newgate WV6 . . . . 253 C5
Newgate St WS7 . . . . 229 A5
New Gdns WS7 . . . . 228 F5
New Haden Rd ST10 . . . . 76 B1
Newhall Com Jun Sch
DE11 . . . . 186 E6
Newhall Gdns WS11 . . . . 209 F2
Newhall Inf Sch DE11 . . . 186 F7
New Hall Rd ST3 . . . . 73 E2
Newhall St WS11 . . . . . . 209 D1
New Hall St ST1 . . . . 282 B3
Newhall St ST10 . . . . 61 D3
New Hampton Rd W
WV6 . . . . 255 F4
Newhaven Gr ST4 . . . . . . 88 B5
New Hayes Rd
Prospect Village WS12 . . 211 C4
Stoke-on-T ST6 . . . . 41 E4
Newhay DE13 . . . . 147 F1
New Homage Gdns WV9 . 224 B2
New Horse Rd WS6 . . . . . 226 E3
New Hos TF11 . . . . 203 F5
Newhouse Ct ST2 . . . . . . 58 B5
Newhouse La WV7 . . . . . 237 A3
Newhouse Rd ST2 . . . . . . 58 B5
Newick Ave B74 . . . . 257 B3
Newington Gr ST4 . . . . . . 88 C5
New Inn Bank ST21 . . . . 131 D8
New Inn La ST4 . . . . 88 A7
New Inn Row ST17 . . . . . 175 F3
New King St ST7 . . . . 39 C1
New Kingsway ST3 . . . . . 74 A4
New La ST6 . . . . 28 B1
Newland Ave ST16 . . . . . 155 D7
Newland Cl WV4 . . . . 244 C2
Newlands Cl
Newcastle-u-L ST5 . . . . . 71 B5
Penkridge ST19 . . . . 207 F7
Stone ST15 . . . . 119 F6

Newlands Ct WS12 . . . . . 227 E8
Newlands La
Colton WS15 . . . . 179 D7
Norton Canes WS15 . . . 227 D8
Newlands St ST4 . . . . 57 B1
New Landywood La WS6 . 242 E7
Newleigh St ST2 . . . . 43 B1
Newlyn Ave CW12 . . . . . . 15 F8
Newlyn Cl WS14 . . . . 231 D7
Newman Ave WV4 . . . . . 266 F4
Newman Cl ST15 . . . . . . 120 C7
Newman Dr DE14 . . . . . . 185 B8
Newman Gr WS15 . . . . . 196 F7
Newman Rd WV10 . . . . . 241 A1
Newmarket Rd WS11 . . . 228 B4
Newmarket Way ST10 . . . 76 B5
New Mill La B78 . . . . 261 A7
Newmill St ST7 . . . . 43 B1
Newmount Rd ST4 . . . . . 73 B5
New Park Gdns ST4 . . . . 88 C5
New Park Sch WV6 . . . . . 255 F5
New Penkridge Rd
WS11 . . . . 209 C1
New Plant La WS7 . . . . . 228 C8
New Pool Cotts ST8 . . . . . 27 B5
Newpool Rd ST8 . . . . 27 B6
Newpool Terr ST8 . . . . . . 27 B5
Newport CE Jun Sch
TF10 . . . . 168 F2
Newport Cl DE14 . . . . . . 166 E2
Newport Girls' High Sch
TF10 . . . . 168 E1
Newport Gr ST5 . . . . 40 F7
Newport Inf Sch TF10 . . . 168 F2
Newport La ST6 . . . . 56 E7
Newport Rd
Albrighton TF11,WV7 . . . 220 D1
Codsall WV7 . . . . 237 F2
Eccleshall ST21 . . . . 133 E6
Edgmond TF10 . . . . 168 C4
Gnosall ST20 . . . . 171 B5
Great Bridgeford ST18 . . 135 C2
Market Drayton TF9 . . . . 112 C6
Stafford ST16 . . . . 285 B3
Tong TF11 . . . . 220 D3
Woodseaves ST20 . . . . . 151 D7
Newport St
Brewood ST19 . . . . 223 C6
Burslem ST6 . . . . 56 E8
Newport B77 . . . . 250 F5
Newquay Ave ST17 . . . . . 175 D4
Newquay Cl ST12 . . . . . . 15 E8
New Rd Aldridge WS9 . . . 256 A5
Alton ST10 . . . . 78 E1
Armitage WS15 . . . . 198 B5
Astbury CW12 . . . . 15 B4
Audley ST7 . . . . 39 E3
Brownhills WS8 . . . . 244 F7
Burntwood WS7 . . . . . . 229 B6
Checkley ST10 . . . . 109 B8
Cookley DY11 . . . . 280 B7
Dilhorne ST10 . . . . 75 C4
New Rd Est (Ind Est)
ST18 . . . . 139 B1
New Rd Flash SK17 . . . . . 3 A3
Hales TF9 . . . . 113 F8
Halfpenny Green DY3 . . . 268 F4
Hixon ST18 . . . . 158 A8
Kidderminster DY10 . . . . 280 C3
Madeley CW3 . . . . 68 E7
Penkridge ST19 . . . . . . 192 E1
Shenstone WS14 . . . . . . 246 F6
Shuttington B79 . . . . . . 251 E8
Slade Heath WV10 . . . . 224 F1
Smestow DY3 . . . . 269 B3
Swadlincote DE11 . . . . . 186 E6
Tamworth B77 . . . . 261 F7
Upper Tean ST10 . . . . . . 92 D4
Uttoxeter ST14 . . . . 111 A1
Werrington ST9 . . . . 58 F3
Wolverhampton,Newbridge
WV6 . . . . 255 E4
New Row
Drayton Bassett B78 . . . 260 E5
Madeley Heath CW3 . . . . 69 A8
Stafford ST18 . . . . 174 C5
Tatenhill DE13 . . . . 165 A1
Newshaw Wlk ST1 . . . . . 282 C3
New Sreet Cotts CW12 . . 6 A6
New St
6 Cannock,Mill Green
WS11 . . . . 226 E8
Biddulph Moor ST8 . . . . 28 A8
Biddulph ST8 . . . . 27 F7
Birchmoor B78 . . . . 262 E7
Burntwood,Chase Terrace
WS7 . . . . 228 E8
Burntwood,Chasetown
WS7 . . . . 228 E5
Burslem ST6 . . . . 56 E8
Burton u T DE14 . . . . . . 166 C1
Cannock,Bridgtown WS11 226 D6
Cannock WS12 . . . . 210 C4
Dudley,Gornalwood DY3 . 271 C3
Essington WV11 . . . . . . 242 A3
Fazeley B78 . . . . 261 B8
Great Wyrley WS6 . . . . . 227 A1
Kingswinford DY6 . . . . . 275 D4
Kingswinford,Wall Heath
DY6 . . . . 275 C8

New St continued
Leek ST13 . . . . 30 F6
Newcastle-u-L ST5 . . . . 56 D5
Newport TF10 . . . . 168 E3
Norton Bridge ST15 . . . . . 135 A8
Stafford ST16 . . . . 155 D5
Stourbridge DY8 . . . . 279 F5
Stourbridge,Wordsley DY8 275 D2
Tamworth,Bolehall B77 . . . 250 E4
Tamworth,Mount Pleasant
  B77 . . . . 250 C1
Uttoxeter ST14 . . . . 126 B7
Walsall,Wallington Heath
  WS3 . . . . 243 B1
Walsall WS4 . . . . 244 D1
Wolverhampton,Merry Hill
  WV3 . . . . 265 D7
Wolverhampton,Parkfield
  WV4 . . . . 266 E6
Newton Cl DE15 . . . . 167 E8
Newton Ct ST9 . . . . 59 A4
Newton La
Newton Regis CV9 . . . . . . 236 F2
Newton Solney DE15 . . . . 167 F7
Seckington B79 . . . . 236 B3
Newton Leys DE15 . . . . . . 167 C4
Newton Mews DE15 . . . . . 166 F3
Newton Rd Lichfield WS13 213 F2
Newcastle-u-L ST5 . . . . . . 56 B5
Newton Solney DE15 . . . . 167 B6
Stafford ST16 . . . . 155 F5
Newton Regis CE Prim Sch
  B79 . . . . 236 C3
Newton's Coll WS13 . . . . . 231 B8
Newton Solney CE Inf Sch
  DE15 . . . . 167 E8
Newton St ST4 . . . . 56 E2
Newtown
Market Drayton TF9 . . . . . 112 D8
Newchapel ST7 . . . . 26 E2
Newport TF10 . . . . 168 E1
New Wood Cl DY7 . . . . . . 279 C8
New Wood Gr WS9 . . . . . . 245 A3
Niall Rd ST4 . . . . 71 F1
Nicholas St ST13 . . . . 30 B5
Nicholas St [3] ST4 . . . . . . 56 F8
Nicholl's La ST15 . . . . 105 B3
Nicholls St ST4 . . . . 72 B5
Nicholls Way WS12 . . . . . . 210 F1
Nicholson Way
Burton u T DE14 . . . . 166 A1
Leek ST13 . . . . 30 D6
Nicklaus Cl DE14 . . . . 185 A7
Nidderdale Cl CW12 . . . . . . 6 A5
Nightingale Cl
Huntington WS12 . . . . . . 209 C7
Lower Tean ST10 . . . . 92 F1
Nightingale Ct WS7 . . . . . 229 F8
Nightingale B77 . . . . 262 A6
Nightingale Wlk WS7 . . . . 229 F8
Nile St ST6 . . . . 57 A8
Nimbus B77 . . . . 261 D4
Ninefoot La
Tamworth,Belgrave B77 . . 261 C1
Tamworth,Wilnecote B77 . 261 F7
Ninian Pk B77 . . . . 261 D6
Ninian Way B77 . . . . 261 E6
Nirvana Cl WS11 . . . . 209 C2
Noblett Rd ST1 . . . . 57 E7
Nocke Rd WV11 . . . . 241 F1
Noddington Ave WS14 . . . 232 E6
Noddington La WS14 . . . . 232 E6
Noddy Park Rd WS9 . . . . . 256 B7
Noddy Pk WS9 . . . . 256 B7
No Man's Green La DY7 . . 276 B6
No Man's Heath Rd DE12 219 F3
No Name Rd WS7 . . . . 228 C7
Nook The WS6 . . . . 226 C1
Noon Croft DE13 . . . . 200 F2
Norbroom Ct TF10 . . . . . . 169 A4
Norbroom Dr TF10 . . . . . . 169 A4
Norbury Ave
Stoke-on-T ST2 . . . . 43 B1
Walsall WS3 . . . . 244 A3
Norbury CE Prim Sch DE6 96 E2
Norbury Cl ST20 . . . . 171 D6
Norbury Cres [14] WV4 . . . 266 F4
Norbury Ct ST15 . . . . 120 A8
Norbury Hollow DE6 . . . . . 80 D1
Norbury Rd ST20 . . . . 171 A7
Norfolk Cl ST5 . . . . 71 B2
Norfolk Cres WS9 . . . . . . 256 B8
Norfolk Dr B78 . . . . 250 A1
Norfolk Gr Biddulph ST8 . . 16 C1
Great Wyrley WS6 . . . . . . 226 F1
Norfolk Ho ST7 . . . . 40 D6
Norfolk Rd
Burton u T DE15 . . . . 185 D7
Kidsgrove ST7 . . . . 25 F2
Stourbridge DY8 . . . . 279 D8
Wolverhampton WV3 . . . . 266 A8
Norfolk St ST1 . . . . 282 A1
Norfolk Way ST17 . . . . 174 C7
Normacot Grange Rd ST3 90 A7
Normacot Rd ST3 . . . . 284 C3
Norman Ave ST6 . . . . 41 F3
Normanbrook Ct TF9 . . . . . 97 C1
Norman Cl B79 . . . . 249 E7
Normandy Gr ST2 . . . . 43 A4
Normandy Pl ST5 . . . . 283 A3
Norman Gr ST5 . . . . 56 D2
Norman Keep DE13 . . . . . . 146 C6
Norman Rd
Penkridge ST19 . . . . 208 A8

Norman Rd continued
Tutbury DE13 . . . . 146 C6
Normanton Gr ST3 . . . . 73 D6
Norris Cl TF9 . . . . 100 C5
Norris Rd ST6 . . . . 41 F3
Northam Rd ST1 . . . . 57 D6
North Ave Leek ST13 . . . . . 30 D5
Stafford ST16 . . . . 155 D7
North Castle St ST16 . . . . 285 A3
Northcliffe [4] ST13 . . . . . . 30 D6
Northcote Ave ST4 . . . . . . 72 A8
Northcote Cl ST18 . . . . . . 177 E8
Northcote Ct ST5 . . . . 283 C3
Northcote Pl ST5 . . . . 283 C3
Northcote Pl ST4 . . . . 57 B1
North Cres WV10 . . . . 241 C7
Northdale WV6 . . . . 255 B4
North Dr ST20 . . . . 171 C5
Northesk Pl ST5 . . . . 71 A5
Northesk St [4] ST5 . . . . . . 105 A1
Northfield ST14 . . . . 96 A4
Northfield Cl ST14 . . . . . . 111 A2
Northfield Dr ST8 . . . . 16 E2
Northfield Gr WV3 . . . . . . 265 C7
Northfield Rd DE13 . . . . . 166 C7
Northfields Way WS8 . . . . 244 D7
Northfleet St ST2 . . . . 58 A3
Northgate WS9 . . . . 256 A7
Northgate Cl ST4 . . . . 71 F1
Northgate Way WS9 . . . . . 256 A8
North Gn WV4 . . . . 265 D6
Northicote Recn Ctr
  WV10 . . . . 240 E3
Northicote Sch The
  WV10 . . . . 240 E3
Northlands CW3 . . . . 67 C1
North Oval DY3 . . . . 271 C6
Northover Cl WV11 . . . . . . 240 A2
North Pl Bucknall ST2 . . . . 58 B6
Stafford ST16 . . . . 155 D5
North Prim Sch ST6 . . . . . 57 B7
North Rd Burslem ST6 . . . . 57 B7
Wolverhampton,Parkfield
  WV4 . . . . 266 F5
North Springfield DY3 . . . 266 E1
North Staffordshire Hospl
Ctr (Outpatients Dept)
  ST4 . . . . 71 E8
North Staffordshire Medical
Inst ST4 . . . . 71 E8
North Staffordshire Nuffield
Hospl The ST5 . . . . 71 C3
North Staffordshire Royal
Infmy ST4 . . . . 71 F7
North St Burntwood WS7 . 211 F1
Burton u T DE15 . . . . 167 B3
Cannock WS11 . . . . 226 E6
Leek ST13 . . . . 30 D6
Mount Pleasant ST7 . . . . . 26 B6
Newcastle-u-L ST5 . . . . . 283 C3
North Street ST4 . . . . 72 A8
North St ST4 . . . . 72 A8
North Terr ST1 . . . . 57 E4
Northumberland Cl B78 . . 250 A1
Northumberland Rd
  DE15 . . . . 185 D7
North Walls ST16 . . . . 285 B3
Northway DY3 . . . . 266 C2
North West Terr ST6 . . . . . 42 C1
North Wlk ST3 . . . . 74 B1
Northwood Cl ST5 . . . . 71 D2
Northwood Gn ST1 . . . . . . 57 E4
Northwood Cl ST1 . . . . . . 282 C3
Northwood Inf Sch ST1 . . 57 E4
Northwood La
Ellastone DE6 . . . . 80 C5
Newcastle-u-L ST5 . . . . . . 71 D2
Northwood Park Cl
  WV10 . . . . 240 E3
Northwood Park Prim Sch
  WV10 . . . . 240 E3
Northwood Park Rd
Hanley ST1 . . . . 57 E4
Wolverhampton WV10 . . . 240 E3
Northycote Farm & Ctry Pk ★
  WV10 . . . . 240 F4
Northycote La WV10 . . . . 240 F4
Norton Ave ST6 . . . . 42 A3
Norton Bridge Sta ST15 . . 135 A8
Norton Canes High Sch
  WS11 . . . . 228 A7
Norton Canes Prim Sch
  WS11 . . . . 228 A6
Norton Cl Tamworth B79 . . 250 C7
Wolverhampton WV4 . . . . 265 C3
Norton Cres ST6 . . . . 57 D8
Norton Dr ST6 . . . . 57 D8
Norton East Rd WS11 . . . . 228 B6
Norton Ind Est ST4 . . . . . . 42 E2
Norton in Hales CE Prim Sch
  TF9 . . . . 82 C2
Norton La
Burntwood WS7 . . . . 229 C6
Great Wyrley WS6 . . . . . . 227 A4
Norton Lakeside Sta ★
  WS11 . . . . 228 C6
Norton La
Norton Canes WS12 . . . . . 227 B7
Stoke-on-T ST6 . . . . 42 F3
Norton Prim Sch ST6 . . . . 42 F3
Norton Rd
Burton u T DE13 . . . . 166 A6

Norton Rd continued
Norton Canes WS11,WS12 227 F8
Stourbridge DY8 . . . . 279 E2
Walsall WS3 . . . . 244 A5
Norton Springs WS11 . . . . 227 F5
Norton St ST2 . . . . 43 B1
Norton Terr WS11 . . . . 227 F6
Norwich Cl WS13 . . . . 214 C3
Norwich Pl ST5 . . . . 71 C5
Norwich Rd ST2 . . . . 58 D2
Norwood Ho WS15 . . . . . . 178 B1
Nottingham Ct ST14 . . . . . 110 F1
Nottingham Rd WS14 . . . . 232 D3
Novi La ST13 . . . . 31 A7
Nuffield Hospl WV6 . . . . . 255 C4
Nunn's Cl ST5 . . . . 74 C5
Nunn St ST13 . . . . 30 D6
Nuns La WS15 . . . . 180 B6
Nurseries The WV9 . . . . . 224 B2
Nursery Ave
Aldridge WS9 . . . . 256 B5
Stoke-on-T ST9 . . . . 43 C4
Nursery Cl Bradley ST18 . . 191 C8
Brown Edge ST6 . . . . 43 B7
Cheadle ST10 . . . . 76 C3
Kidsgrove ST7 . . . . 25 D1
Nursery Croft WS13 . . . . . 213 F1
Nursery Dr Biddulph ST8 . . 16 C2
Penkridge ST19 . . . . 192 E2
Wombourne WV5 . . . . 269 F4
Nursery Gdns
Codsall WV8 . . . . 238 F4
Stourbridge DY8 . . . . 275 F1
Nursery La Hopwas B78 . . 249 B6
Stafford ST16 . . . . 155 D5
Stoke-on-T ST9 . . . . 43 C3
Sutton Coldfield B74 . . . . 258 A2
Nursery Rd Rugeley WS15 197 A5
Scholar Green ST7 . . . . . . 25 E5
Nursery St ST4 . . . . 72 A5
Nursery View Cl WS9 . . . . 256 E2
Nursery Way ST18 . . . . . . 158 B3
Nursery Wlk WV6 . . . . 255 D4
Nurton Bank WV6 . . . . . . 254 A3
Nurton Hill Rd WV6 . . . . . 253 E5
Nutbrook Ave ST4 . . . . 72 C4
Nuthurst Dr WS11 . . . . . . 226 F4
Nyewood Ave ST4 . . . . 73 D5
Nymet B77 . . . . 261 E8

O

Oadby Rise DE13 . . . . 166 A6
Oakamoor Rd ST10 . . . . . . 77 C4
Oakapple Cl ST19 . . . . 221 D6
Oak Ave Cheddleton ST13 . 45 C4
Great Wyrley WS6 . . . . . . 227 A1
Huntington WS12 . . . . . . 209 D8
Newport TF10 . . . . 168 F1
Walton-on-t-H ST17 . . . . . 175 F6
Oak Cl Church Eaton ST20 190 B7
Great Haywood ST18 . . . . 158 C1
Kinver DY7 . . . . 278 C3
Uttoxeter ST14 . . . . 110 F1
Oak Ct B74 . . . . 257 E5
Oakdale Rd ST4 . . . . 257 A1
Oakdale Cl CW2 . . . . 37 B3
Oakdale ST5 . . . . 71 C3
Oakdale Trad Est DY6 . . . . 270 E1
Oakden Cl ST14 . . . . 125 C7
Oakdene Ave ST5 . . . . 56 A6
Oakdene Cl
Cheslyn Hay WS6 . . . . . . 226 D2
Forsbrook ST11 . . . . 91 B6
Newcastle-u-L ST5 . . . . . . 56 A6
Oakdene Gr ST5 . . . . 56 A6
Oakdene Rd WS7 . . . . 229 A6
Oakdene Way ST8 . . . . 27 D7
Oak Dr Mile Oak B78 . . . . . 249 C1
Scholar Green ST7 . . . . . . 25 E6
Seisdon WV5 . . . . 263 F2
Wheaton Aston ST19 . . . . 205 C6
Oaken Covert WV8 . . . . . . 238 E2
Oaken Dr WV8 . . . . 238 E3
Oakenfield WS13 . . . . 214 A2
Oaken Gdns WS7 . . . . 229 A8
Oaken Grange WS6 . . . . . 226 F1
Oaken Gr WV8 . . . . 238 E2
Oakenhayes Cres WS8 . . . 228 F1
Oakenhayes Dr WS8 . . . . . 228 F1
Oaken La WV8 . . . . 238 C3
Oaken Lanes WV8 . . . . . . 238 E2
Oaken Pk WV8 . . . . 239 A2
Oak Farm Craft Ctr ★
  B78 . . . . 260 B5
Oakfield Ave DY6 . . . . 275 D6
Oakfield Cl Rugeley WS15 178 A2
Stourbridge DY8 . . . . 275 D5
Oakfield Dr WS3 . . . . 244 B5
Oakfield Gr ST3 . . . . 27 E7
Oakfield Rd
Alrewas DE13 . . . . 201 A2
Codsall WV8 . . . . 239 C2
Market Drayton TF9 . . . . . 97 B1
Oakfields DE13 . . . . 145 A4
Oak Gdns ST18 . . . . 172 F5
Oak Gn WV6 . . . . 255 B3
Oakham Way ST2 . . . . 58 C2
Oakhill Ave ST4 . . . . 71 F4
Oakhill Cl ST10 . . . . 92 C4
Oakhill Prim Sch
Stoke-on-T ST4 . . . . 71 F3
Tamworth B77 . . . . 250 F2
Oakhill Rd WS11 . . . . 209 F2
Oak Hill WV3 . . . . 265 F7
Oak Ho Great Wyrley WS6 . 227 A1
Little Aston B74 . . . . 257 B5

Oakhurst Cres ST3 . . . . . . 90 A6
Oakhurst Rd WS14 . . . . . . 231 C7
Oakhurst Pk WS15 . . . . . . 196 F5
Oak Ind Pk The DY6 . . . . . 270 E1
Oak La Astbury CW12 . . . . . 15 B4
Bradley ST18 . . . . 191 C7
Burntwood WS7 . . . . 212 A1
Cheslyn Hay WV10 . . . . . 225 C7
Kingswinford DY6 . . . . . . 271 A1
Oakland Ct B79 . . . . 250 A5
Oakland Dr DY3 . . . . 271 B2
Oakland Ho B74 . . . . 258 A4
Oaklands Ave ST5 . . . . 56 C6
Oaklands Cl
Fradley WS13 . . . . 215 D6
Hill Ridware WS15 . . . . . . 198 A8
Huntington WS12 . . . . . . 209 C6
Wetley Rocks ST9 . . . . . . 60 A6
Oaklands Dr ST17 . . . . 285 A1
Oaklands Ind Est WS12 . . 210 B3
Oaklands Rd WV3 . . . . 266 B8
Oaklands The
Church Eaton ST20 . . . . . 190 A7
Rugeley WS15 . . . . 178 C1
Oaklands WV3 . . . . 266 B8
Oak Lea ST13 . . . . 30 B4
Oakleigh Ave DE11 . . . . . . 186 F5
Oakleigh Ct ST5 . . . . 120 D6
Oakleigh Dr Codsall WV8 . 239 A3
Rugeley WS15 . . . . 197 B6
Sedgley DY3 . . . . 271 C7
Oakleighs DY8 . . . . 275 C1
Oakleigh Wlk DY6 . . . . . . 275 E8
Oakley Ave WS9 . . . . 256 A5
Oakley Cl Lichfield WS13 . . 214 B2
Penkridge ST19 . . . . 193 C1
Oakley Copse WS15 . . . . . 196 B7
Oakley Folly TF9 . . . . 99 A4
Oakley Gr WV4 . . . . 265 D5
Oakley La TF9 . . . . 98 A6
Oakley Pl ST5 . . . . 42 A7
Oakley Rd WV4 . . . . 265 D5
Oakleys ST19 . . . . 223 D6
Oak Leys WS9 . . . . 255 C1
Oakmoor Pl WS9 . . . . 256 F2
Oakmount Cl ST3 . . . . 243 F3
Oak Mount Rd ST9 . . . . . . 59 C4
Oakover Cl ST14 . . . . 126 C6
Oak Park Ct
Stourbridge DY8 . . . . 275 F1
Sutton Coldfield B74 . . . . 257 E3
Oak Park Rd DY8 . . . . 275 F1
Oak Pl ST3 . . . . 73 F2
Oak Rd Barton-u-N DE13 . . 201 D8
Brewood ST19 . . . . 223 D6
Brownhills WS9 . . . . 245 D5
Denstone ST14 . . . . 95 D5
Eccleshall ST21 . . . . 133 D6
Oak Rd Flats ST5 . . . . 120 B6
Oak Rd Newcastle-u-L ST5 . 55 D2
Stone ST15 . . . . 120 B8
Walsall,Pelsall Wood WS3 . 243 F5
Walsall WS4 . . . . 244 C1
Oakridge Cl ST17 . . . . 175 E5
Oakridge Dr WS6 . . . . 226 E2
Oakridge Prim Sch ST17 . 175 E6
Oakridge Way ST17 . . . . . 175 E5
Oaks Dr Cannock WV10 . . 209 C1
Featherstone WV10 . . . . . 240 F8
Wombourne WV5 . . . . 270 A5
Oakshaw Cl WV9 . . . . 224 B3
Oakshaw Gr ST4 . . . . 88 B8
Oaksmoor Cl ST19 . . . . . . 205 C6
Oak Sq DE11 . . . . 186 F2
Oak St Burton u T DE14 . . 166 C1
Cheadle ST10 . . . . 76 D3
Hanley ST1 . . . . 57 A3
Oaks The Loggerheads TF9 . 99 F4
Walsall WS3 . . . . 243 A1
Walton-on-t-H ST17 . . . . . 175 F7
Oak St Kingswinford DY6 . . 275 D6
Newcastle-u-L ST5 . . . . . . 56 D3
Oak Tree Cl ST17 . . . . 174 B8
Oaktree La ST7 . . . . 40 D5
Oaktree Rd Rugeley WS15 196 F5
Stoke-on-T ST4 . . . . 88 B6
Oak Tree Rise WV8 . . . . . . 238 E4
Oak Tree Wlk B79 . . . . 249 F7
Oakville Ave ST6 . . . . 42 B2
Oakwell Cl ST3 . . . . 73 C1
Oakwell Gr ST3 . . . . 73 C1
Oakwood Cl
Brownhills WS9 . . . . 244 E4
Essington WV11 . . . . 242 B3
Hatton DE65 . . . . 146 C8
Shenstone WS14 . . . . 247 A6
Oakwood Pl ST5 . . . . 55 E8
Oakwood Rd Leek ST13 . . . 30 C6
Stoke-on-T ST4 . . . . 72 F2
Oakwood WS15 . . . . 178 B1
Oakwoods WS11 . . . . 226 D8
Oakwood Sch WS9 . . . . . . 245 A3
Oasis The DY9 . . . . 281 F5
Oasthouse Cl DY6 . . . . 275 A7
Oatfield Cl WS7 . . . . 229 A4
Oatlands Way WV6 . . . . . . 254 D3
Oban Cl ST5 . . . . 70 F8
Oberon Cl ST6 . . . . 42 D1
Occupation Rd WS8 . . . . . 245 A4
Occupation St ST5 . . . . . . 283 C2
Octagon Ctr The DE14 . . . 166 D2
Octagon Sh Pk The ST1 . . 57 A4
Odell Gr ST6 . . . . 41 E1
Odger Cl ST3 . . . . 74 B2
Odiham Cl B79 . . . . 250 C7
Odin Cl WS11 . . . . 210 A5
Offadrive B79 . . . . 250 B5

Offa's Dr WV6 . . . . 254 E5
Offa St B79 . . . . 250 B5
Offoxey Rd TF11,ST19 . . . 221 C5
Ogden Rd ST3 . . . . 282 C2
Ogley Cres WS8 . . . . 245 A7
Ogley Hay Rd
Burntwood,Boney Hay
  WS7 . . . . 229 B8
Burntwood,Triangle WS7,
  WS8 . . . . 229 A3
Ogley Rd WS8 . . . . 245 A7
Ogley Vale WS7 . . . . 229 B8
Ogmore Gr ST3 . . . . 90 A8
O'Hare Pl ST13 . . . . 31 B7
Ohio Gr ST6 . . . . 57 B8
Oldacre La ST17 . . . . 176 B3
Oldacres Rd ST4 . . . . 88 C5
Old Armoury The TF9 . . . . 112 C8
Old Bank DE6 . . . . 81 D8
Old Barn Cl ST20 . . . . 171 E8
Old Barn House Mews
  WS15 . . . . 198 C1
Oldbury Ct B79 . . . . 250 B5
Old Butt La ST7 . . . . 25 D2
Old Cannock Rd WV10 . . . 225 D1
Oldcastle Ave ST5 . . . . 56 A6
Old Castle Gr WS8 . . . . . . 228 F2
Old Chancel Rd WS15 . . . 178 E2
Old Chapel Cl ST5 . . . . 69 E8
Old Coach La ST17 . . . . . . 176 B4
Old Coach Rd ST19 . . . . . 221 F7
Old Coalpit La SK17 . . . . 5 E8
Old Colehurst Manor ★
  TF9 . . . . 112 A3
Old Cottage Hospl The [4]
  ST13 . . . . 30 F6
Oldcott Cres ST7 . . . . 41 C8
Oldcott Dr ST7 . . . . 41 C8
Oldcourt St ST6 . . . . 41 D3
Old Croft Rd ST17 . . . . . . 175 E6
Old Dalelands TF9 . . . . . . 112 B8
Old Eaton Rd WS15 . . . . . 178 E3
Olde Hall La WS6 . . . . 226 F3
Olde Hall Rd WV10 . . . . . . 241 C2
Oldershaws La ST20 . . . . . 150 F7
Old Fallings La WV10 . . . . 240 F1
Old Fallow Ave WS11 . . . . 209 E3
Old Fallow Rd WS11 . . . . . 209 E3
Old Falls Cl WS6 . . . . 226 D3
Old Farm Dr WV8 . . . . 239 A4
Old Farm Mdw WV3 . . . . . 265 C8
Old Fdr ST15 . . . . 105 B3
Oldfield Ave ST6 . . . . 42 D5
Oldfield Dr ST15 . . . . 120 C6
Oldfield Ind Est ST4 . . . . . . 72 F5
Oldfields Cres ST18 . . . . . 158 C3
Oldfields Hall Mid Sch
  ST14 . . . . 126 A4
Oldfields Rd ST14 . . . . 126 B7
Oldfield St ST4 . . . . 73 A5
Oldford La ST18 . . . . 154 B4
Old Forge Cl DE65 . . . . . . 148 A5
Old Forge The ST18 . . . . . 158 B2
Old Hall Ct B79 . . . . 236 D3
Old Hall Dr Elford B79 . . . . 216 C2
Newcastle-u-L ST5 . . . . . . 56 A8
Old Hall La Fradley WS13 . 215 D8
Millmeece ST21 . . . . 117 F7
Norton Canes WS11,WS12 227 B7
Old Hall St ST1 . . . . 282 B3
Oldham Cotts WS15 . . . . . 179 A5
Old Hampton La WV11 . . . 241 C2
Oldham St ST1 . . . . 282 C1
Old Hedging La B77 . . . . . 261 C6
Old Hednesford Rd
  WS11 . . . . 210 A3
Oldhill Cl ST7 . . . . 40 E5
Oldhill La ST18 . . . . 157 F1
Old Hill WV6 . . . . 255 D5
Oldicote La DE15 . . . . 167 E3
Old Knotty Way ST14 . . . . 126 C7
Old La Beech ST4 . . . . 87 B1
Brown Edge ST6 . . . . 28 A1
Checkley ST10 . . . . 109 D8
Featherstone WV10 . . . . . 241 C7
Old Landywood La WS6 . . 242 D7
Old La WV6 . . . . 254 F2
Old Lodge Hill Cctry Pk ★
  WS15 . . . . 211 B3
Old London Rd WS14 . . . . 231 C1
Old Man of Mow ★ ST7 . . . 26 D8
Old Manor Cl B78 . . . . 260 B5
Old Manor Flats WV6 . . . . 255 D5
Old Mill Gdns WS4 . . . . . . 244 C2
Old Mill House Cl WS4 . . . 244 B1
Old Mill La Bagnall ST9 . . . 44 A3
Bagnall,Tompkin ST9 . . . . 44 C3
Oldmill St ST4 . . . . 72 C7
Old Mill The [9] ST13 . . . . . 30 E6
Old Oak Cl WS9 . . . . 256 B8
Old Park Rd
Cannock WS12 . . . . 211 A5
Dudley DY1 . . . . 271 F4
Stowford CW1 . . . . 37 C7
Stowford CW1 . . . . 37 B3
Old Penkridge Mews
  WS11 . . . . 209 C2
Old Penkridge Rd WS11 . . 209 C2
Old Quarry Dr DY3 . . . . . . 271 D5
Old Rd Armitage WS15 . . . 198 B5
Audley ST7 . . . . 39 E3
Burton u T DE14 . . . . 184 E7
Old Rd Cl ST15 . . . . 105 A1
Old Rd Oulton ST15 . . . . . . 105 B5
Stoke-on-T ST4,ST12 . . . . 88 C3
Upper Tean ST10 . . . . 92 D4
Weston ST18 . . . . 138 D2

Old Rd continued
Wrenhill CW3 . . . . 53 A3
Old Rectory Gdns WS9 . 256 C6
Old Rectory Rd ST15 . . 120 B8
Old Rickerscote La ST17. 175 A5
Old Saddler's Yd ST14. . 126 C7
Old School Cl
 Kidsgrove ST7 . . . . . . 26 A1
 Weston ST18 . . . . 138 D3
Old School Ct ST19 . . 205 C6
Old School Dr ST16 . . 155 C8
Old School Pl ⑧ ST13. . 30 E5
Old School Wlk B79. . 250 B6
Old School Yd The B77. 251 A5
Old Shackerley La WV7. 221 B1
Old Smithy Cl WV6 . . . 253 C3
Old Stafford Rd
 Brinsford WV10 . . . . . 240 C8
 Slade Heath WV10 . . . 224 D2
Old Town La WS3 . . . 243 F3
Old Town Rd ST1 . . . 282 B4
Old Tramway ST4 . . . 72 F5
Old Vicarage Cl
 Walsall WS3. . . . . 244 A2
 Wombourne WV5. . . . 270 B7
Old Warstone La WV11 . 242 A3
Oldway Pl ST3 . . . . . . 73 C5
Old Weston Rd ST19 . . 221 F8
Old Wharf Pl ST1 . . . 57 E2
Old Wharf Rd DY8. . . . 279 F6
Old Whieldon Rd ST4 . . 72 C6
Olive Ave WV4 . . . . 266 E5
Olive Gr ST5 . . . . 40 C1
Oliver Lodge Ho ⑧ ST4. 72 A7
Oliver Rd ST4. . . . . 71 E7
Ollison Dr B74. . . . . . . 256 F2
Olof Palme Gr ST3 . . 284 C2
Omega Way ST4 . . . . . . 88 A8
One Oak Rise ST17. . . 174 F5
Onsetter Rd ST2 . . . . 73 D7
Onslow Dr ST5. . . . . 56 B8
Ontario Cl ST4. . . . . . . 88 A8
Opal Bsns Ctr ST15 . . . . 120 A5
Opal Rd ST4. . . . . 72 E5
Opal Way ST15. . . . . . . 120 A5
Oram's La ST19 . . . . . 223 D2
Orange La WS15 . . . . . 161 C1
Orbital Way WS11 . . . . 226 F6
Orb St ST1. . . . . 282 B2
Orchard Ave WS11 . . . . 209 C2
Orchard Cl Ashley TF9 . . 100 C5
 Cheslyn Hay WS6. . . . 226 E3
 Claverley WV5. . . . . . 267 C7
 Coven WV9 . . . . 224 B2
 Lichfield WS13. . . . . . 213 F1
 Oulton ST15. . . . . 105 C4
 Pattingham WV6 . . . . 253 D3
 Penkridge ST19. . . . . 192 F1
 Rugeley WS15 . . . . . . 178 E3
 Stone ST15 . . . . 119 F7
 Sudbury DE6 . . . . 128 E5
 Tamworth B77 . . . . . 261 C5
 Uttoxeter ST14. . . . . 111 B1
 Walton-on-T DE12. . . 184 D1
Orchard Cotts WS15 . . 198 B5
Orchard Cres
 Kidsgrove ST7 . . . . . . 25 D1
 Penkridge ST19. . . . . 192 F1
 Wolverhampton WV3. . 265 B7
Orchard Ct
 Kingswinford DY6 . . . 275 D6
 Leek ST13 . . . . 30 C6
 Wolverhampton WV3. . 265 B7
Orchard Gdns
 Cannock WS12. . . . . . 209 F6
 Leek ST13 . . . . 30 C6
Orchard Gr Aldridge WS9. 256 B4
 Cookley WV8. . . . . . . 280 A6
 Dudley DY3 . . . . 271 B3
 Dunsley DY7. . . . . . . 278 B4
 Sutton Coldfield B74 . 257 C5
 Wolverhampton WV4. . 266 A4
Orchard La Codsall WV8. 239 B3
 Shareshill WV10 . . . . 225 C3
 Stafford ST18 . . . . . 174 C5
Orchard Mobile Home Pk
 ST18. . . . . 137 C2
Orchard Pk DE14. . . . 166 D2
Orchard Pl ST12 . . . . 88 D1
Orchard Rd DY10 . . . . 280 C3
Orchard Rise
 Blythe Bridge ST11 . . 90 E7
 Market Drayton TF9 . . 112 A8
Orchard St DE14. . . . . 166 D2
Orchards The
 Armitage WS15 . . . . . 198 C4
 Stoke-on-T ST3 . . . . 72 E4
Orchard The
 Albrighton WV7 . . . . . 237 A5
 Brewood ST19 . . . . . . 223 C6
 Burntwood WS7. . . . . 229 B8
 Colwich WS15 . . . . . . 177 D8
 Newcastle-u-L ST5. . 55 D8
 Stoke-on-T ST6 . . . . 43 A8
 Stramshall ST14 . . . . 111 A4
 Swynnerton ST15. . . . 103 B4
 Walsall WS3. . . . . 243 D2
 Wolverhampton WV6. . 255 E6
Orchid Cl DE15 . . . . . 186 A8
Orchid Gr ST4 . . . . . 56 E1
Ordish Ct DE14. . . . . . 166 D2

Ordish St DE14. . . . . 166 D2
Ordley La DE6 . . . . 65 F1
Oregon Cl DY6 . . . . . 275 F6
Oregon Gdns WS7 . . . . 228 F8
Orford Rd ST9 . . . . . . 43 F7
Orford St ST5. . . . . 56 D7
Orford Way ST3 . . . . . 88 E8
Orgreaves Cl ST5 . . . . 56 B8
Orgreave St ST6 . . . . . 57 A7
Oriel Cl Cannock WS11 . . 226 E8
 Dudley DY1 . . . . 271 E2
Oriel Dr WV10 . . . . . . 240 D3
Oriel St ST4 . . . . 72 A7
Oriole Cl ST14 . . . . . 126 C6
Orion Cl WS6 . . . . 226 F1
Orion Cl ST5. . . . . 70 F8
Orion St ST6. . . . . 42 C1
Orkney Ave WV11 . . . . 209 F5
Orkney Dr B77 . . . . . . 261 F7
Orlestone Pl ST6. . . . . 42 B7
Orme Rd Biddulph ST8. . 27 D5
 Newcastle-u-L ST5. . 283 A2
 Newcastle-u-L ST5. . 55 F1
Ormes La WV6. . . . . . . 255 C3
Orme St ST6 . . . . 56 E8
Ormonde St ST4 . . . . 72 F5
Ormonds Cl WS13. . . . 230 E6
Orpheus Gr ST1. . . . . 57 F6
Orton Gr WV4 . . . . . . 265 F4
Orton La WV4,WV5. . . . 265 A2
Orton Rd ST5. . . . . 283 A4
Orwell Cl DY8. . . . . . 279 D4
Orwell Dr Longton ST3. . 73 F5
 Stafford ST17. . . . . 174 B8
Orwell Pl ST5. . . . . . 71 B4
Osberton Dr DY1. . . . . 271 F2
Osborne Cres ST17. . . 175 C8
Osborne Ct DE13. . . . 166 B6
Osborne Ho ST10 . . . 76 D4
Osborne Rd Stoke-on-T ST4 71 E8
 Wolverhampton WV4. . 265 F5
Osborne St
 Burton u T DE15. . . 167 A3
 Leek ST13 . . . . 31 A6
Osborne B79 . . . . 249 D5
Osbourne Gdns DE15. . 167 A3
Oslo Gr ST1. . . . . 57 F6
Osmaston Rd DY8. . . . 279 F2
Osprey Ave ST3 . . . . 90 A7
Osprey Cl
 Burton u T DE15. . . 167 D4
 Whittington WS14. . 232 E5
Osprey Ct WS7. . . . . . 229 F8
Osprey Dr DY1. . . . . . 271 F1
Osprey Gr WS12 . . . . 210 C1
Osprey B77 . . . . 262 A6
Osprey View ST7. . . . 26 D3
Ostend Pl ST5 . . . . . 70 F7
Ostler Cl DY6 . . . . . 275 B7
Ostlers La ST13 . . . . 45 B4
Oswald Ave ST3. . . . 74 B5
Otherton Cl ST19. . . . 207 B8
Otherton La ST19 . . . 207 F6
Otterburn Cl
 ❸ Stafford ST17. . . 175 D6
 Cannock WS12. . . . . 210 A2
Otterstone Cl DY3. . . . 266 C2
Ottery B77. . . . . 262 B5
Oulton CE Fst Sch ST15. 105 C4
Oulton La TF10,ST10 . . 170 A8
Oulton Mews ST15. . . 105 A1
Oulton Rd Cheadle ST10. . 76 F3
 Stoke-on-T ST6 . . . 42 B7
 Stone ST15. . . . . 105 B2
Oulton Way ST16. . . . 155 B6
Oundle B74. . . . . 257 F2
Ounsdale Cres WV5. . . 270 A7
Ounsdale High Sch WV5. 269 F7
Ounsdale Rd WV5. . . . . 269 E6
Our Lady & St Benedict RC
 Prim Sch ST2. . . . . . 58 A5
Our Lady & St Werburgh's RC
 Prim Sch ST5. . . . . . 71 B4
Our Lady's RC Prim Sch
 ST4. . . . . 72 D6
Our Lady's RC Prim Sch
 ST15. . . . . 103 B3
Ousley La DE6 . . . . . 80 C5
Outclough Rd ST8 . . . 27 B1
Outfield Rd DE15. . . . 185 F8
Outlook The ST6. . . . . 42 C3
Outwoods Cl
 Burton u T DE13. . . 166 A6
 Weston ST18. . . . . . . 138 D2
Outwoods Gn ST18. . . 138 D2
Outwoods La
 Anslow DE13 . . . . . . 165 C7
 Burton u T DE13. . . 165 E7
Outwoods St DE14. . . 166 B5
Oval Bglws The TF10. . 169 A3
Ovaldene Way ST4. . . 88 D7
Oval The Longton ST3. . 284 A2
 Market Drayton TF9. . 112 C8
 Stafford ST17. . . . . 285 C2
 Werrington ST9 . . . 59 E4
Overbrook Cl DY3. . . . 271 C2
Overcroft ST14 . . . . 125 C7
Overdale Pl ST13. . . . 30 B5
Overfield Rd DY1 . . . 271 E1
Overhill Rd
 Burntwood WS7. . . . 229 B5
 Stafford ST17. . . . . 175 D6
Overhouse St ST6. . . . 41 F1
Overland Cl WS11. . . . 197 A6
Overland Dr ST6. . . . . 43 A8
Overpool Cl WS15. . . . 196 D8
Oversetts Ct DE11. . . . 186 F6

Oversetts Rd DE11. . . . 186 E5
Oversley Rd ST6 . . . . . 42 B7
Overstrand WV9 . . . . . 239 F3
Over The Hill ST8. . . . . 17 A2
Overton Bank ⑧ ST13. . 30 E6
Overton Cl ST3 . . . . . 284 A2
Overton La WS7 . . . . . 229 C4
Overton Rd ST8. . . . . . 16 F6
Overton Wlk WV4 . . . . 265 C6
Overwood Pl ST6. . . . . 41 F7
Overwoods Rd B77. . . . 262 A4
Owen Gr ❸ ST6. . . . . . 57 A4
Owen Rd WV3 . . . . . . 266 A8
Owen's Bank DE13 . . . 146 B6
Owens Cl WS15 . . . . . 178 E1
Owen Wlk ST17 . . . . . 174 C7
Oxbarn Ave WV3 . . . . 265 E6
Oxbarn Rd ST17. . . . . . 174 D6
Oxbridge Way B79 . . . 249 E6
Oxclose La DE6 . . . . . 36 C2
Oxford Ave ST1 . . . . . 57 D7
Oxford Cl WS6 . . . . . . 226 F3
Oxford Cres ST4 . . . . 72 A7
Oxford Dr DY8 . . . . . . 279 F4
Oxford Gdns ST16. . . . 155 F5
Oxford Gn WS11 . . . . 226 F8
Oxford Rd Cannock WS11. 226 F8
 Newcastle-u-L ST5. . 56 D3
Oxford St Burton u T DE14. 166 B1
 Stoke-on-T ST4 . . . 72 A7
 Stoke-on-T ST4 . . . 72 A8
Oxhay Ct ST5 . . . . 56 C3
Oxhay View ST5. . . . . . 56 C3
Ox-Hey Cres ST8. . . . . 16 D1
Ox-Hey Dr ST8. . . . . . . 16 D1
Oxhey Fst Sch ST8 . . . 16 E1
Oxleathers Ct ST17. . . 174 B7
Oxley Cl WS6 . . . . 226 F1
Oxley Moor Rd
 Wolverhampton,Blakeley Green
  WV9. . . . . 255 F8
 Wolverhampton,Oxley WV9,
  WV10. . . . . 240 B1
Oxley Rd DE15 . . . . . 167 A3
Oxmead DE6. . . . . 81 D7
Ox Pasture ST13 . . . . 45 C5
Ox St DY3. . . . . 271 D5
Oyster Cl DE14. . . . . . 185 B7

P

Pacific Rd ST4. . . . . . . 88 B7
Packett St ST4. . . . . . . 284 B4
Pack Horse La ST5 . . . 56 F8
Packington Ct B74. . . . 257 E4
Packington La B74. . . . 248 F5
Packmoor Prim Sch ST7. 26 E1
Padarn Cl DY3. . . . . . 266 C1
Padbury La WS7 . . . . 212 D1
Padbury WV9. . . . . . . 240 B3
Paddock Cl ST16. . . . 155 C8
Paddock Cotts ST4. . . . 88 A6
Paddock La Aldridge WS9 256 A6
 Great Wyrley WS6 . . 227 A3
Paddock Rise ST4. . . . 88 A6
Paddocks Cl B78. . . . . 251 F1
Paddocks Gn CW12 . . 15 F8
Paddocks The
 Market Drayton TF9. . 97 B1
 Swadlincote DE11 . . 186 F5
 Yarnfield ST15. . . . . 118 F6
Paddock The
 Burton u T DE15. . . 167 B4
 Cheadle ST10. . . . . . 76 D2
 Claverley WV5. . . . . 267 C7
 Codsall WV8. . . . . . . 238 F2
 Coven WV9 . . . . 224 B2
 Dudley DY3 . . . . 271 E5
 Lichfield WS14. . . . . 231 C5
 Perton WV6. . . . . . . 254 D4
 Seighford ST18 . . . . 154 C6
 Wombourne WV5. . . . 269 E6
Padstow Dr ST17. . . . . 156 E1
Padstow B77. . . . . 250 F5
Padstow Way ST4. . . . 88 C5
Padworth St ST3. . . . . 74 A3
Paget Cl Colwich ST18. . 177 E8
 Lichfield WS13. . . . . 214 D3
 Penkridge ST19. . . . 208 A7
Paget Dr ST1 . . . . 211 E1
Paget High Sch DE14. . 185 A7
Paget Rd WV3,WV6. . . 255 F3
Paget Rise WS15. . . . 160 F6
Pagets Chase WS12. . 211 C4
Paget St DE14. . . . . . 166 C2
Pagham Cl WV9 . . . . 239 F2
Painsley RC High Sch
 ST10. . . . . 76 D2
Paisley Pl ST2. . . . . . . 73 E8
Paladin Ave ST3 . . . 74 B4
Palatine ST5. . . . . 55 D6
Pale St DY3. . . . . 271 E5
Palfrey Rd DY8. . . . . . 279 D5
Palisadings ST19. . . . 192 E1
Pall Mall ST1. . . . . . . 282 B2
Palmbourne Ind Pk
 ST16. . . . . 285 A3
Palmer Cl
 Barton-u-N DE13. . . 183 D2
 Burton u T DE14. . . 185 B8
 Stafford ST17. . . . . 156 B4
 Wolverhampton WV11. 241 F1
Palmers St ST6. . . . . . 239 C1
Palmers Cross Prim Sch
 WV6. . . . . 255 D8

Palmers Gn ST4. . . . . . 71 D8
Palmer St ST3 . . . . . . 284 D4
Palmerston Ave B77. . 261 C6
Palmerston Ct B77. . . 261 F6
Palmerston St
 ❷ Newcastle-u-L ST5. . 56 C5
 Hanley ST1. . . . . 282 C1
Palmerston Way ST8. . 16 D1
Palmers Way
 Codsall WV8. . . . . . . 239 C1
 Newcastle-u-L ST5. . 71 D8
Palomino Cl ST3. . . . . 89 C8
Pandora Gr ST1. . . . . . 57 F6
Panton Cl ST16 . . . . . 156 B4
Pantulf Cl ST17. . . . . 155 B1
Panturner Rd ST2. . . . 73 D7
Parade The
 Brownhills WS8 . . . . 228 C1
 Coven WV9 . . . . 224 B2
 Kingswinford DY6 . . 275 B7
 Newcastle-u-L ST5. . 55 C1
Parade View WS8 . . . . 244 E8
Paradise Gr WV3 . . . . 243 F3
Paradise La
 Slade Heath WV10 . . 224 D2
 Walsall WS3. . . . . . . 243 F3
 Wolverhampton WV10. 240 E8
Paradise St
 ❻ Stoke-on-T ST6. . 41 D3
 Newcastle-u-L ST5. . 283 B2
Paragon Ave ST5 . . . 71 B3
Paragon Cl ST10 . . . . 76 C1
Paragon Rd ST3 . . . . 284 D3
Paramount Bsns Pk ST6. 57 A8
Parbury B77. . . . . 261 D5
Parchments The WS13. 214 B5
Pargeter St DY8 . . . . 279 F4
Paris Ave ST5 . . . . . . 70 E6
Park Ave Burntwood WS7. 229 B8
 Cheadle ST10. . . . . . 76 E2
 Meir ST3 . . . . 74 A5
 Newcastle-u-L ST5. . 56 C5
 Norton Canes WS11. 228 A5
 Stafford ST17. . . . . 174 D8
 Stone ST15 . . . . 119 E8
 Talke ST7. . . . . 40 E8
 Uttoxeter ST14. . . . 111 B2
 Werrington ST9 . . . 59 D4
Park Ave W ST5. . . . . 56 B5
Park Ave
 Wolverhampton,Goldthorn Park
  WV4. . . . . 266 C5
 Wombourne WV5. . . . 269 F5
Park Bldgs DY3 . . . . . 271 D8
Park Cl Barton-u-N DE13. . 183 C1
 Brownhills WS8 . . . . 244 F8
 Cheslyn Hay WS6. . . 226 E3
 Madeley CW3. . . . . . . 68 E8
Park Cres ST17. . . . . . 285 B1
Park Croft WS7 . . . . . 228 C8
Park Ct ST5. . . . . 55 E7
Parkdale DY3. . . . . . . 271 D8
Park Dr Barlaston ST12. . 104 D8
 Cheadle ST10. . . . . . 76 D4
 Little Aston B74. . . . 257 C4
 Sutton Coldfield B74. 257 F2
 Trentham ST4 . . . . 87 F7
 Werrington ST9 . . . 59 C4
 Wolverhampton WV4. . 266 C5
Parkend ST11. . . . . . . 91 B8
Park End Lichfield WS14. . 231 E7
 Newport TF10 . . . . . 168 F5
Parker Bowles Dr ❶
 TF9. . . . . 112 A8
Parker-Jervis Rd ST3. 73 F4
Parker Paul Ind Est WV2 266 C7
Parker Rd WV11 . . . . 241 F1
Parkers Cl ST10 . . . . 190 A7
Parker's Croft Rd ST17. 285 B2
Parkers Ct WV9. . . . . 224 C1
Parker St Burton u T DE14 166 D5
 Hanley ST1. . . . . 282 A3
 Leek ST13 . . . . 31 A5
 Walsall WS3. . . . . . . 243 A1
Parkes Ave ST3 . . . . 239 B2
Parkes Hall Rd DY1. . 271 F5
Park Farm Rd B77 . . . 250 C1
Park Farm View ST6. . 41 D7
Parkfield Ave B77 . . . 250 C1
Parkfield Bsns Ctr ST17. 285 B1
Parkfield Chalet Pk
 WV2. . . . . 266 D6
Parkfield Cl B77. . . . . 261 C8
Parkfield Colliery WV4. . 266 E6
Parkfield Cres
 Tamworth B77 . . . . 261 C8
 Wolverhampton WV2. . 266 E6
Parkfield Gr WV2 . . . 266 E6
Parkfield High Sch WV4. 266 E6
Parkfield La DE6. . . . 81 D4
Parkfield Prim Sch WV4. 266 E6
Parkfield Rd Longton ST3. 73 C1
 Wolverhampton WV2,WV4. 266 E6
Parkfields Cl
 Barlaston ST12 . . . . 88 C1
 Newcastle-u-L ST5. . 55 A2
Parkfields Farm ST12. . 88 C1
Parkfields Stafford ST17. 174 D8
 Stoke-on-T ST9 . . . 43 F7
Parkgate La DE6 . . . 79 C7
Park Gate Rd
 Cannock Wood WS15. 211 F5
 Kidderminster DY10. 280 B2
Park Hall Ave ST3 . . . 74 A4
Park Hall Bsns Village
 ST3. . . . . 73 E5
Park Hall Cl WS15. . . 178 D3
Park Hall Cres ST3. . . 74 A4

Parkhall Ctry Pk★ ST3. 74 A6
Parkhall Ctry Pk★ ST3. 73 F6
Park Hall Ind Est ST6. . 41 E2
Parkhall La ST10. . . . . . 109 B5
Park Hall Prim Sch ST3. 74 A4
Park Hall Rd Longton ST3. 73 E5
 Meir ST3 . . . . 74 A4
 Wolverhampton WV4. . 266 D5
Park Hall St ST3. . . . . 284 C4
Parkhead Cres ST3. . . 74 A3
Parkhead Dr ST3. . . . . 74 A3
Parkhead Gr ST3. . . . . 74 A4
Parkhill Rd WS7 . . . . 229 A8
Park Ho WV11 . . . . . 242 A3
Park House Dr ST3. . . 120 C7
Parkhouse Gdns DY3. . 271 C4
Parkhouse Ind Est E ST5. 56 A8
Parkhouse Ind Est ST5. . 40 F1
Parkhouse Ind Est W ST5. 55 F1
Parkhouse Rd E ST5 . . 40 E1
Parkhouse Rd W ST5. . 40 E1
Parkhouse St ST1. . . . 282 A1
Park La Ashley TF9 . . . 100 B8
 Audley ST7. . . . . 39 B4
 Biddulph ST8. . . . . . 27 D6
 Blore TF9. . . . . 99 B1
 Brewood WV9 . . . . . 223 C2
 Brocton ST17. . . . . . 176 B4
 Cheadle ST10. . . . . . 76 C3
 Cheddleton ST13. . . 45 B6
 Colton WS15 . . . . . . 179 B8
 Congleton CW12 . . . 6 A1
 Endon ST9 . . . . 44 B7
 Fazeley B78. . . . . . . 249 E2
 Great Wyrley WS6. . 227 A3
 Haughton ST18. . . . . 172 E5
 High Offley ST20. . . 132 B1
 Ipstones ST10 . . . . . 47 B1
 Kingswinford DY6 . . 275 E7
Parklands ST8. . . . . . . 17 B1
 Congleton CW12 . . . 6 A2
Parklands Dr CW2 . . 37 E3
Parklands ST7. . . . . . . 26 B1
Parklands Rd ST10. . . 92 E4
Parklands The
 Congleton CW12 . . . 6 A2
 Kingswinford DY6 . . 275 D6
 Wolverhampton WV3. . 255 D1
Park Lane Cl ST10 . . . 76 C3
Park Lane Shenstone WS14. 247 B4
 Stoke-on-T ST4 . . . 72 F5
 Stretton ST19 . . . . . 206 A6
 Tutbury DE13. . . . . . 146 B6
 Whittington WS13. . 232 D8
Park Mid Sch ST8. . . . 27 C6
Park Pale The DE13. . 146 C5
Park Pl Stoke-on-T ST4 . . 72 F6
 Uttoxeter ST14. . . . 126 C8
Park Rd Alrewas DE13. . 201 A3
 Barton-u-N DE13. . . 183 C2
 Burntwood,Chase Terrace
  WS7. . . . . 228 F8
 Burntwood,Triangle WS7. 229 B5
 Cannock WS11. . . . . 209 D1
 Dudley,Lower Gornal DY3. 271 D2
 Featherstone WV10. . 241 D8
 Leek ST13 . . . . 30 E7
 Newcastle-u-L,Butterton
  ST5. . . . . 70 E2
 Newcastle-u-L,Silverdale
  ST5. . . . . 70 D8
 Newcastle-u-L ST5. . 55 C1
 Norton Canes WS11. 228 A5
 Stoke-on-T ST6 . . . 42 B1
 Stourbridge DY8 . . . 279 D5
 Swadlincote DE15,DE11. 186 D5
 Tamworth B77 . . . . 261 C5
 Walsall,Wallington Heath
  WS3. . . . . 243 B1
 Werrington ST9 . . . 59 C4
Park Rd W DY8 . . . . . 279 D5
Park Rise WV3 . . . . . 255 E2
Park St S WV2 . . . . . 266 C6
Park St B79. . . . . 250 A7
Parks Cres WV11. . . . 242 A3
Parkside Ave ST16. . . 155 D8
Parkside Cres ST9 . . 43 F8
Parkside Dr ST5 . . . . 56 D3
Parkside Gr ST5 . . . . 56 D3
Parkside Ind Est WV1 . . 266 D6
Parkside La Gayton ST18. 139 A7
 Huntington WS11. . . 209 D2
Parkside Prim Sch ST16 155 D8
Parkside Stoke-on-T ST4. 88 B7
 Tamworth B77 . . . . 250 E1
Parkside Way B74 . . . 257 A1
Park St Burton u T DE14. 166 C2
 Cannock WS11. . . . . 226 E6
 Cheslyn Hay WS6. . . 226 E3
 Stafford ST17. . . . . 285 B2
 Stoke-on-T ST4 . . . 72 F6
 Stourbridge DY8 . . . 279 F8
 Tamworth B79 . . . . 250 A5
 Uttoxeter ST14. . . . 111 C1
Park Terr ST6. . . . . . . 41 E3
Park The DE6. . . . . . . 81 C8
Park Venture Ctr WS11. 226 E6
Park View
 Blythe Bridge ST11 . . 90 E6
 Burntwood WS7. . . . 228 E8
Parkview Cl ST3 . . . . 72 E2
Park View Ct WS11. . 209 D1

Parkview Ct DY6........275 B8
Park View Ct ST3........73 B1
Parkview Dr WS8........228 F2
Park View Dr ST2........43 C2
Park View Rd
 Kidsgrove ST7........26 B3
 Sutton Coldfield B74....257 D3
Park View ST15........103 B3
Park View Terr WS15....178 D1
Parkway DE14........165 F1
Park Way ST11........91 A8
Parkway ST15........120 C7
Parkway The Hanley ST1. 282 B1
 Perton WV6........254 F4
Parkway ST4........87 E7
Park Way WV11........242 A1
Parkwood Ave ST4........87 F8
Parkwood Cl WS8........245 A5
Park Wood Ct B74........257 F2
Park Wood Dr ST5........85 A7
Parkyn St WV2........266 C8
Parliament Row ST1....282 B3
Parliament Sq ST1....282 B3
Parliament St DE11....186 F6
Parma Gr ST3........73 E4
Parnell Ave WS13....231 A6
Parnell Sq CW12........6 A2
Parsonage St ST6........41 D4
Parsons Cl SK17........24 D5
Parsons Dr ST20........171 E6
Parsons Dr ST2........37 D3
Parsons Hollow B77....261 E7
Parsons La ST13........33 D3
Parson St B77........261 E7
Parson's Wlk B79........218 F2
Parton Gr ST3........74 A3
Partridge Cl 7 Meir ST3. 90 A7
 Cannock WS11........210 A1
 Huntington WS12........209 D1
Partridge Croft WS13....231 C8
Partridge Dr ST14....126 C6
Partridge Mill WS3....243 E3
Partridge Rd DY8........279 C4
Partridge Ride TF9........99 D4
Parva Ct ST14........110 F1
Parville Ho ST6........57 A6
Paskin Cl WS13........215 D8
Pass Ave WS14........232 E6
Passfield Ave WS12....210 C7
Pastoral Cl CW3........68 F5
Pasture Cl ST5........85 D5
Pasturefields Ent Pk
 ST18........158 B6
Pasturefields ST18....158 A7
Pasturefields Ind Est
 ST18........158 B7
Pasturefields La ST18.. 158 B7
Pasture Gate WS11....209 C2
Pasture La DE6........35 E1
Pastures Dr CW2........37 D3
Pastures The
 Perton WV6........254 D4
 Swadlincote DE11....186 F5
Pasture View WS3....243 F2
Patch Cl DE13........166 B6
Patch Meadow Rd ST10.. 76 B3
Paterson Ave ST21....117 F3
Paterson Pl WS8........245 D5
Patricia Ave WV4........266 D5
Patrick Ho 2 WS11....210 A3
Patrick Mews WS13....213 F1
Patrick Pl ST7........27 B2
Patshull Ave WV10....240 A4
Patshull Ct WV10........240 B3
Patshull Gr WV10........240 B3
Patshull Ho WV6........255 E5
Patshull Rd WV6........253 D8
Patterdale Rd WS11....210 A4
Patterdale St ST6........42 A3
Pattingham La WV7....253 D8
Pattingham Rd WV6....254 C2
Paulet High Sch DE15.. 185 F7
Pauls Coppice WS8....245 A5
Paul St 1 WV2........266 C8
Pauls Wlk WS13........214 A3
Pavement The ST19....223 D6
Pavilion Cl WS13........213 F1
Pavilion Dr ST1........57 A5
Pavilion End DY7........274 E1
Pavilions Garden Village
 The★ WV6........263 F5
Pavilion The B77........251 B3
Pavillion Cl WS9........256 C7
Pavior's Rd WS7........228 E4
Paxton Ave WV6........254 E3
Paxton St ST1........282 C1
Paynter St ST4........72 F5
Peace Cl WS6........226 E3
Peacehaven Gr ST4....88 C5
Peach Ave ST17........174 F7
Peacock Hay Rd ST7.... 40 F4
Peacock La ST4,ST5....87 A8
Peacock Rd ST5........55 F5
Peacock View ST4........57 F1
Peak Cl WS5........198 B4
Peak Dale Ave ST6........41 C7
Peak Dr DY3........271 E3
Peake Cres WS8........244 F5
Peake Rd WS8........245 A5
Peakes Rd WS15........178 B1
Peake St ST5........55 E3
 Peaks L Ctr B79........250 B3
Peak View ST13........31 A5
Pearis Dr ST10........94 E8
Pearl Gr ST3........90 A8

Pear Pl ST2........73 D7
Pearson Dr ST15........120 C7
Pearson St WV2........266 C8
Peartree Cl ST12........88 D1
Pear Tree Ave DE11....186 F7
Pear Tree Cl
 Gnosall ST20........171 E6
 Huntington WS12........209 C7
 Shuttington B79........251 E7
Pear Tree Dr CW3........68 D7
Peartree La WS15....180 B6
Pear Tree La
 Bobbington WV5........268 A4
 Brownhills WS8........228 C2
 Newcastle-u-L ST5.... 55 D8
 Wolverhampton WV11....241 B1
Pear Tree Rd ST7........39 F1
Peascroft Rd ST6........42 D4
Pebble Cl B77........251 B3
Pebble Mill Cl WS11....209 F2
Pebble Mill Dr WS11....210 A2
Pebble Mill St ST1........56 F4
Peckforton View ST7.... 41 A7
Peck Mill La ST8........27 C1
Pedley Cl ST3........88 F8
Pedley Gr ST6........42 D1
Pedley La CW12........6 F4
Peebles Gn ST2........58 C2
Peebles Rd ST5........54 F2
Peel Cl B78........260 E5
Peel Ct 4 Kidsgrove ST7.. 26 A2
 Fazeley B78........261 B8
 Tamworth B77........261 F6
Peel Dr Astbury CW12....15 B7
 Cannock WS12........209 F8
 Tamworth B77........261 F6
Peelers Way B77........250 C1
Peel Hollow WS7........39 A2
Peel Ho B79........250 A4
Peel La CW12........15 D7
Peel St Burton u T DE14.. 166 C1
 Longton ST3........284 C1
 Newcastle-u-L ST5.... 56 C5
 Stafford ST16........285 A3
 Tunstall ST6........56 C8
Peel Terr ST16........155 E5
Pegasus Ct B74........258 A3
Pegasus Gr ST6........42 D1
Pegasus Wlk B79........249 F7
Peggs La ST7........150 E8
Peggy's Bank ST7........54 F8
Pegroy Gr ST6........42 D2
Pelham St ST1........282 C1
Pellfield Ct ST18........138 D2
Pelsall La
 Walsall,Little Bloxwich
 WS3........243 D3
 Walsall WS3,WS4........244 A1
Pelsall Rd WS8........244 D7
Pelsall Village Sch WS3. 243 F4
Pemberton Cres DY10.. 280 C3
Pemberton Dr ST3........90 A5
Pembridge Rd ST3........88 E7
Pembroke Cl B79........249 D6
Pembroke Ct ST5........283 A1
Pembroke Dr
 Newcastle-u-L ST5....283 A2
 Stone ST15........120 C3
Pembroke Gdns DY8....275 C2
Pembroke Rd ST2........43 B1
Penarth Gr ST1........282 B4
Penarth Pl ST5........283 A1
Pencombe Dr WV4....266 D5
Penda Gr WV6........254 F5
Pendeford Ave WV6....255 E5
Pendeford Bsns Pk WV9. 239 F3
Pendeford Cl WV6........255 E8
Pendeford Hall La WV9.. 239 D5
Pendeford High Sch
 WV10........240 B2
Pendeford La WV10....240 A3
Pendeford Mill La WV8.. 239 C3
Pendeford Mill Nature
 Reserve★ WV9........239 E4
Pendene Ct WV4........266 A5
Penderell Cl WV10....241 A6
Penderel St WS3........243 C1
Pendinas Dr WV8........239 B3
Pendle Gr ST4........73 B6
Pendle Hill WS12........210 C4
Pendrel Cl WS6........242 F8
Pendrell Ho WS3........239 A3
Pendrill Rd WV10....240 E3
Pendryl Ct ST19........223 C7
Penfleet Ave ST3........74 A1
Pengrove Cl ST6........41 E8
Penhallow Dr WV4....266 E5
Penk Dr WS7........229 D6
Penk Dr N WS15........178 C2
Penk Dr S WS15........178 C2
Penkhull Ct 6 ST4........72 A7
Penkhull Ed Ctr ST4.... 72 A7
Penkhull New Rd ST4.. 72 A6
Penkhull Terr ST4........72 A6
Penk Rd ST11........91 A7

Penleigh Gdns WV5....269 F7
Penmark Gr ST3........89 E8
Penmere Dr
 Newcastle-u-L ST5........71 C1
 Werrington ST9........59 A3
Pennant Ct WV3........266 B8
Penn Bridge SK11........7 E6
Penn Cl WS3........243 C1
Penn Common Rd WV4.. 265 F1
Penn Croft ST18........177 D8
Penn Croft La WV4....266 A1
Penncroft WV4........265 E4
Pennell St ST2........58 B4
Penn Fields Sch WV3.. 265 F7
Penn Hall Sch WV4....265 E3
Penn Hospl WV4........265 E4
Pennhouse Ave WV4.. 265 F5
Pennine Dr
 Cannock WS11........209 E2
 Dudley DY3........271 D3
Pennine Way Biddulph ST8. 16 E1
 Newcastle-u-L ST5........55 E3
 Tamworth B77........262 C8
Pennington Cl ST3........74 C2
Penn Rd Sedgley DY3.. 270 F8
 Wolverhampton WV2,WV3,
 WV4........266 A6
Penn St WV3........266 B8
Penns Wood Cl DY3....266 C2
Pennwood Ct WV4....265 D6
Pennwood La WV4....265 F3
Penny Bank Cl WS15.. 178 E1
Penny Bank Ho 6 ST13.. 30 F1
Pennycress Gdns WV10. 241 C7
Pennycroft La ST14....111 C1
Pennycroft Rd ST14....111 A1
Pennycrofts Ct ST16.. 285 C3
Pennycrofts ST16....285 C3
Penny Ct WS6........242 F8
Penny Farthing Arc DY3. 271 D8
Pennyfields Ave ST6.... 41 D1
Pennyfields Rd ST7........26 D2
Penny La ST10........76 D3
Pennymoor Rd B77....262 B7
Pennymore Cl ST4........88 B8
Penny Royal Cl DY3....271 D2
Pennys Croft WS13....214 E1
Penport Gr ST3........284 A2
Penrhyn Ave ST6........42 B1
Penrhyn Cl ST4........88 C6
Penrith Cl ST5........71 B6
Pensett Trad Est The
 DY6........271 A1
Pensford Gr ST1........57 F5
Pensgreave Rd DE13.. 166 B6
Penshaw Cl WV9........240 A2
Pens Meadow Sch DY8.. 275 E3
Pensnett Trad Est The
 DY6........275 F8
Penstone La WV4........264 E4
Pentire Rd WS14........231 D6
Pentland Gdns WV6....255 E2
Pentland Gr ST5........55 E3
Penton Pl ST3........88 E7
Penton Wlk ST3........88 E7
Pen-Y-Bont Wlk ST8.... 27 E6
Pen-Y-Bryn Way TF10.. 168 F2
Penzance Way ST17....156 F1
Penzer St DY6........275 D7
Peolsford Rd WS3........244 A4
Peover La CW12........6 F6
Pepper St
 Newcastle-u-L,Silverdale
 ST5........54 F1
 Newcastle-u-L ST5....283 B2
Perceval St ST1........57 E5
Percival St ST9........43 C3
Percy St ST1........282 B3
Peregrine Cl
 Burton u T DE15........167 D3
 Dudley DY1........271 F1
 Whittington WS14....232 F5
Peregrine Gr ST3........90 A6
Perivale Ct ST1........58 A6
Periwinkle Cl WS8....244 D6
Perkins St ST6........41 C7
Perks Rd WV11........242 A1
Perle Brook ST21........133 D7
Perott Dr B75........258 D2
Perrin Cl ST17........174 F6
Perry Cl Hanley ST1....282 C2
 Tamworth B79........250 B6
Perrycrofts Cres B79.. 250 C7
Perrymount Ct ST4........71 F6
Pershore Cl WS3........242 F2
Pershore Dr DE14....185 A8
Pershore Rd WS3........242 F2
Pershore Way WS3....242 F2
Persia Wlk 16 ST6........41 D3
Perth Cl DE15........167 C2
Perth St ST4........284 A5
Perthy Gr ST4........87 F7
Perton Brook Vale WV6. 254 F5
Perton Fst Sch WV6.... 254 E5
Perton Gr WV6........254 F4
Perton Mid Sch WV6.. 255 A5
Perton Rd WV6........254 F2
Perton Sandown Fst Sch
 WV6........254 E4
Perton Wood View ST3.. 72 F4
Pessall Farm Holding
 B79........217 C8
Pessall La B79........217 C6
Petard Cl B77........261 C8
Peterborough Dr WS12.. 210 C1
Peterdale Dr WV4........265 F3
Peterhead B77........250 F5

Peter James Ct ST16.... 155 E6
Petersfield WS11........209 F4
Petersfield Rd ST6........42 A7
Petersfield Way CW2.... 37 D4
Petershouse Dr B74.... 257 F5
Peter's La WS7........230 A5
Peterson Ho 3 ST3........89 F8
Peters Wlk ST13........214 A2
Pethills La ST13........48 C5
Petrel Gr ST3........90 B7
Pettiford Gr WS13....215 D6
Pevensey Ct ST3........73 C6
Peverill Rd Perton WV6.. 254 F4
 Wolverhampton WV4....266 E3
Pezenas Dr TF9........97 B1
Pheasant Way WS11.. 210 A1
Pheasant Wlk TF9....99 D3
Philip Gr WS11........209 E6
Philip La ST9........59 B4
Philip St ST4........72 E6
Phillips Ave WV11....241 F1
Phillips Cl WS15........120 C7
Phillipson Way ST3.... 57 D8
Phoenix Bank TF9........97 D1
Phoenix Cl Kidsgrove ST7.. 26 C2
 Rugeley WS15........178 C1
Phoenix Ctr WS11....226 E6
Phoenix Rd WS11....210 A1
Phoenix Rise WV2....266 C6
Phoenix St
 4 Stoke-on-T ST1........41 D3
 Wolverhampton WV2....266 D6
Picasso Cl WS11........210 D2
Picasso Rise ST3........90 B7
Piccadilly Arc ST1....282 B3
Piccadilly Cres B78....261 F1
Piccadilly ST1........282 B2
Piccadilly La DE6........66 C1
Piccadilly B78........261 F1
Piccadilly 7 ST6........41 D3
Pickering Cl ST3........284 A1
Pickford Pl 8 ST3........74 A1
Pickleys La DE13........127 C8
Pickmere Cl ST2........43 B3
Picknal La ST14........126 C8
Picknalls Fst Sch ST14.. 126 B7
Picknalls ST14........126 B7
Pickstock TF10........149 B2
Pickwick Pl ST7........25 D2
Pickwood Ave WS13.. 31 A5
Pickwood Cl WS13.... 31 A5
Picton St Hanley ST1.. 282 C2
 Leek ST13........30 D5
Piddocks Rd DE15....186 B5
Pidduck St ST6........56 E7
Pierce St ST6........41 D3
Pier St WS8........244 F7
Pigeonhay La ST14....110 C2
Piggott St ST2........58 A3
Pike Cl ST16........156 A5
Pike La WS15........198 A4
Pikelow La ST10........49 B3
Pilgrim Pl ST16........285 B2
Pilgrim St ST16........285 B2
Pilkington Ave ST5........71 A6
Pillar Cl ST2........73 D7
Pillaton Cl ST19........207 F7
Pillaton Dr WS12........209 C6
Pillaton Hall Farm ST19.. 208 C7
Pilsbury Gr ST5........56 D6
Pilsden Pl ST3........90 C7
Pilstones Rd ST15....103 B1
Pilstones Way WS15.. 103 C1
Pimlico Ct DY3........271 D3
Pinch The DE6........36 B2
Pine Cl Burton u T DE14.. 185 A8
 Great Wyrley WS6....226 F4
 Kingswinford DY6....275 D5
 Kinver DY7........278 C3
 Market Drayton TF9.... 97 B1
 Talke ST7........40 D7
 Tamworth B79........250 B8
Pine Cres ST17........175 F6
Pine Ct Blythe Bridge ST11.. 90 D8
 Loggerheads TF9........99 E4
Pine Gr Burntwood WS7.. 228 F5
 Swadlincote DE11....186 F6
Pine Leigh B74........258 B1
Pine Rd ST4........72 C4
Pineside Ave WS15.. 211 F5
Pines Park Home Est The
 WS12........209 D5
Pines The Lichfield WS14. 231 F7
 Wolverhampton WV3.. 255 D7
Pine St WS3........243 D2
Pine Tree Cl WS12....195 A1
Pinetree Dr Aldridge B74. 256 D1
 Blythe Bridge ST11.... 90 D7
Pinetrees La TF9........99 F5
Pinetrees WS15........196 F4
Pine View Rugeley WS15. 178 C3
 Smestow DY3........269 D3
Pineways Dr WV6........255 E4
Pineways Stourbridge DY8. 275 C2
 Sutton Coldfield B74.. 257 C3
Pine Wlk Codsall WV8.. 238 F2
 Uttoxeter ST14........125 F8
Pinewood Ave
 Cannock WS11........209 D4
 Wood End CV9........262 C6
Pinewood Cl
 Brownhills WS8........228 E2
 Wolverhampton WV3.. 265 A8
 Wombourne WV5....270 A6
Pinewood Cres ST3....74 C1
Pinewood Dr
 Colwich ST18........177 D8

Pinewood Dr continued
 Loggerheads TF9........99 E4
Pinewood Gr
 Blythe Bridge ST11....91 A6
 Newcastle-u-L ST5.... 40 E1
Pinewood Rd
 Burton u T DE15........185 F6
 Loggerheads TF9........99 F5
Pinewoods Ave DY9.. 281 F4
Pinewoods Cl DY9....281 F4
Pinewoods Ct DY9....281 F4
Pinewoods TF10........168 E1
Pinewood Wlk DY6.. 275 E8
Pinfold Ave ST6........42 D4
 Wheaton Aston ST19.. 205 B6
Pinfold Cl Tutbury DE13. 146 C5
 Wheaton Aston ST19.. 205 B6
Pinfold Cres WV4........265 D6
Pinfold Dr WS15........198 C5
Pinfold Gr WV4........265 D6
Pinfold Hill WS14....246 F6
Pinfold La
 Abbots Bromley WS15.. 161 C3
 Blore TF9........98 C2
 Cheslyn Hay WS6....226 C2
 Norbury ST20........151 B4
 Norton Canes WS11.. 227 E4
 Penkridge ST19........192 D1
 Wheaton Aston ST19.. 205 B6
 Wolverhampton WV4.. 265 E5
Pinfold Rd WS13........213 F1
Pinfold St ST14........126 C7
Pingle Farm Rd DE11.. 186 F5
Pingle La
 Hammerwich WS7....229 D5
 Stone ST15........120 B7
Pingle The WS15........196 B7
Pinhoe Pl ST3........73 E3
Pinnox St ST6........41 E2
Pintail Cl ST17........175 A7
Pioneer Pl ST6........42 C3
Pioneer Way ST17....175 A7
Pipe Hall Farm Nature
 Reserve★ WS13........230 A8
Pipe Hay La DE6........144 D5
Pipe La WS15........198 B8
Piper Cl WV6........254 F4
Piper Pl DY8........279 F8
Piper Rd WV3........265 C8
Pipers Croft WS13....214 A2
Piper's La TF10........168 A3
Piper's Lodge TF10.. 168 A3
Pipe Wood La WS15.. 180 B4
Pippins The
 Newcastle-u-L ST5........71 C3
 Stafford ST17........174 E5
Pireford Pl ST5........41 A1
Pirehill La ST15........119 F5
Pirehill Prim Sch ST15.. 119 F6
Pirehill Rd ST5........41 B1
Pirie Cl CW12........6 A4
Pirie Rd CW12........6 A4
Pitchcroft La TF10....187 A5
Pitcher La ST5........31 B5
Pitfield Ave ST5........56 D3
Pitgreen La ST5........56 D6
Pit La ST7........40 C6
Pitlea Pl 1 ST3........73 C6
Pitsford St ST3........73 E2
Pitstone Cl ST16........136 C1
Pitt St E ST6........57 A8
Pitt St W ST6........57 A8
Pitts Hill Bank ST6........41 D8
Pitt St Kidderminster DY10. 280 A1
 Stafford ST16........155 C6
Plainfield St ST2........73 D8
Plainview Cl WS9........256 E2
Plaisaunce The ST5.... 71 B6
Plane Gr ST5........40 E1
Planks La WV5........269 C8
Plantation La Himley DY3. 270 B3
 Hopwas B78........249 B4
Plantation Pk ST5........70 C6
Plantation Rd
 Cannock WS12........195 A1
 Stoke-on-T ST4........88 D7
Plant Cres ST17........174 F7
Plant La WS7........228 E7
Plants Cl WS6........243 A8
Plant St Cheadle ST10.. 76 E2
 Longton ST3........284 C4
 Stourbridge DY8........275 E2
Plant Way WS3........243 F4
Plardiwick Rd ST20.. 171 B6
Platts Ave ST9........43 E6
Platts Cres DY8........279 E8
Platts Dr DY8........279 F8
Platts Rd DY8........279 E8
Platt St WS11........210 A5
Playdale TF10........168 B4
Pleasant Cl DY6........275 C4
Pleasant St ST6........56 F7
Pleasant View DY3....271 D2
Plex St ST6........41 D3
Pleydell St ST1........57 F7
Plough Bank
 Weston-Under-Lizard
 TF11........203 A6
 Wetley Rocks ST9........60 B7
Plough La TF10........168 B4
Ploughmans Croft TF10. 169 A4
Ploughmans Pl B75.. 258 C4
Ploughmans Wlk
 Kingswinford DY6....275 A7
 Lichfield WS13........214 C3
 Wolverhampton WV8.. 239 F1
Plough Mews DY7....278 A3
Plough St ST1........282 C4

Plover Cl
Featherstone WV10......241 B7
Meir ST3..........90 A7
Plover Dr ST8..........27 E8
Plover Field CW3......68 D6
Plovers Rise WS15......178 D2
Plummer Rd DE11......186 F6
Plumtree Gr ST1........57 F6
Plymouth Gr ST5........55 F7
Pochard Cl ST6........42 C2
Podmore Ave ST7......54 F6
Podmore La ST7........54 E6
Podmore St ST6........57 A7
Pointon Gr ST6........43 A5
Polesworth High Sch
B78..........262 F7
Police Dr TF9..........112 C8
Polperro Way 9 ST3....90 A7
Pomona Rise ST1........57 D8
Pond Cres WV2......266 E7
Pond Gr WV2..........266 E7
Pond La WV2..........266 D7
Ponesfield Rd WS13....214 B2
Ponesgreen WS13......214 B2
Pool Ave WS11........228 B5
Pool Cl WV10..........225 D1
Pool Dam ST5..........283 B2
Poole Ave ST2..........43 B2
Poole Cres WS8........228 D2
Pooles Rd ST8..........17 B1
Poole St DY8..........279 E4
Poole's Way WS7......229 C2
Pooley La Gnosall TF10..188 C7
Polesworth B78........251 F2
Poolfield Ave ST5......70 F8
Poolfield Ave N ST5......71 A8
Poolfield Rd WS13......230 E6
Poolfields ST6..........43 C7
Poolfields Cl ST5......70 F8
Pool La WS9..........256 A5
Pool Green Terr WS9....256 A5
Pool Hall Cres WV3....265 A8
Pool Hall Rd WV3......265 A8
Poolhill Cl ST3..........284 A2
Pool House Rd WV5....269 D6
Pool La ST17..........176 C4
Pool Mdw WS6........226 D1
Pool Meadow WS15....196 D1
Pool Rd Brownhills WS7..228 S3
Burntwood WS8........228 E4
Poolside Cotts ST18....121 A1
Poolside CW3..........68 E6
Pool Side
Newcastle-u-L ST5......283 A3
Scholar Green ST7......25 A3
Poolside ST3..........88 F8
Pool St Longton ST4......73 B6
Newcastle-u-L ST5......283 A2
Wolverhampton WV2....266 C8
Pool View WS6........227 A4
Pope Gdns ST17......174 C7
Pope Gr WS12..........209 F6
Pope Rd WV10........241 B1
Popes La WV6..........255 A6
Poplar Ave
Brownhills WS8........245 A8
Burntwood WS7........228 F6
Cannock WS11........209 E4
Newcastle-u-L ST5......56 A3
Poplar Cl
Blythe Bridge ST11......91 A6
Eccleshall ST21........133 E6
Haughton ST18........172 A6
Newcastle-u-L ST5......56 A3
Stone ST15..........119 F1
Uttoxeter ST14........110 F1
Wombourne WV5......270 B6
Poplar Cres DY8......279 D3
Poplar Ct ST5..........56 A3
Poplar Dr Kidsgrove ST7..26 A1
Stoke-on-T ST3........72 F2
Poplar Gr Longton ST3....73 A1
Newcastle-u-L ST5......283 D3
Poplar La Bearstone TF9..82 F5
Cannock WS11........209 B1
Poplar Rd Brownhills WS8..245 A8
Great Wyrley WS6......227 A4
Kingswinford DY6......275 E5
Stourbridge DY8......279 E3
Wolverhampton WV3....266 A6
Poplar Rise B74......257 D6
Poplars Dr WV8........238 F2
Poplars Farm Way WV9..224 B2
Poplars Park Cvn Pk
DE6..........144 A7
Poplars Rd
Armitage WS15........198 C4
Burton u T DE13........166 C7
Poplars The
Cannock WS11........209 E4
Stourbridge DY8......275 F2
Poplar St
Norton Canes WS11......228 A6
Wolverhampton WV2....266 D6
Poplar Way ST17......174 E6
Poppit's La ST14......110 F4
Poppy Gdns DE13......201 A4
Porchester Cl WS9....245 A2
Porlock Ave ST17......175 D8
Porlock Gr ST4........88 B6
Portal Rd ST16..........156 B5
Porters Farm Ct ST14..127 E2
Porters La ST13..........31 F3
Porthill Bank ST5......56 C6
Porthill ST6..........56 D7
Porthill Gn ST5........56 C6
Porthill Grange ST5....56 C6
Porthill Rd ST6........56 D7

Porthkerry Gr DY3......271 B7
Port La
Abbots Bromley WS15..160 E5
Brewood WV9..........223 B3
Portland Ave
Aldridge WS9..........256 B5
Burton u T DE14........185 A4
Tamworth B79..........249 F8
Portland Ct ST11......90 D7
Portland Ct WS9......256 B6
Portland Dr Biddulph ST8..16 D2
Forsbrook ST11........91 B8
Market Drayton TF9....97 A1
Scholar Green ST7......25 E6
Portland Gr ST5........71 B3
Portland Mews ST5....56 B6
Portland Pl Barlaston ST12..88 F4
Cannock WS11........226 C7
Waterhouses ST10......48 F2
Portland Rd Aldridge WS9..256 B6
Longton ST3..........284 B4
Portland St N ST13......30 F6
Portland St S ST13......30 F6
Portland St Hanley ST1..282 A4
Leek ST13..........30 F6
Portleven Cl ST17......175 E7
Portleys La B78........260 D4
Portobello WS15......178 E2
Portrush Rd WV6......254 D4
Port St ST6..........56 F7
Portswood Cl WV9....239 F1
Port Vale St ST6........42 A1
Port Vale St ST6........56 E8
Portway Cl DY6........275 E5
Portway Dr DE13......146 C5
Portway La B79........234 C7
Portway Pl DY10......280 A5
Portway The DY6......275 E5
Postern Rd DE13......165 B3
Post La ST9..........43 F6
Post Office La
Gnosall TF10..........188 D6
Gorstyhill CW2..........37 F1
Rugeley WS15........196 B7
Post Office Rd
Alrewas DE13..........201 A3
Seisdon WV5..........263 F3
Post Office Row ST17..193 B8
Post Office Sq CW3....68 E5
Pothooks La ST13......33 F4
Potsmans La ST18......122 D7
Potteries Mus & Art Gall
The★ ST1..........282 B2
Potteries Sh Ctr ST1....282 B3
Potteries Way ST3......282 C3
Potters Ave ST15......118 F6
Potters Croft B79......218 E2
Potters End ST8........16 C1
Potts La ST14..........141 E8
Pouk La WS14..........245 F7
Poulson St ST4........72 B7
Pound Gdns ST6........42 D4
Poundsgate Gr ST4....88 B8
Pound St WV5..........267 C2
Pountney St WV2......266 C8
Pourbaix Ho WS13......231 B6
Povey Pl ST6..........41 B1
Powderham Cl ST6....41 E8
Powell Pl TF10........168 F3
Powell St ST1........282 A4
Power Gr ST3..........284 A1
Power Station Rd WS15..178 F1
Power Station Road Ind Est
WS15..........178 F1
Power Wash Ind Est ST8..27 B4
Pown St SK17..........23 F6
Powy Dr ST7..........26 B2
Poxon Rd WV9........245 A3
Poynings The WV6....255 C5
Precinct The B79......250 B5
Preedys Cl WS15......160 F5
Prescott Ave ST16......156 A4
Prescott Dr ST19......193 A1
Prestbury Ave ST5......71 B8
Preston St ST6........57 C8
Preston Vale La ST19..192 C1
Prestwick Rd DY6......275 C6
Prestwood Ct ST17....285 B1
Prestwood Dr
Stourbridge DY7......279 A7
Stourton DY7..........278 F8
Prestwood La ST14......79 E1
Prestwood Rd DY7....278 E6
Pretoria Rd ST1........57 A3
Priam Cl ST5..........41 B1
Priam Gr WS3..........244 B5
Price Ave B78..........249 D1
Price Cl TF9..........99 D5
Price Ct Burton u T DE14..165 F4
Burton u T DE14........166 A4
Prices Rd DY3..........271 C3
Price St Burslem ST6....56 F4
Cannock WS11........209 E1
Priestley Dr ST3......284 B1
Prime St ST1..........57 E5
Primitive St ST7........26 C2
Primley Ave B77........261 F5
Primrose Ave WV10....240 D3
Primrose Cl Walsall WS3..244 A5
Wheaton Aston ST19..205 C7
Primrose Dell CW3......68 D6
Primrose Dr
Burton u T DE14........185 A8
Newport TF10..........168 F1
Primrose Gdns
Codsall WV8..........239 A3
Featherstone WV10....241 B7
Primrose Gr ST5......283 C4

Primrose Hill
Stoke-on-T ST4........72 A2
Stourbridge DY8......275 E1
Primrose Mdw 1 WS11..210 C2
Primrose Way ST14....126 B8
Prince Albert Terr ST15..135 A8
Prince Ave ST18........172 F5
Prince Charles Ave ST13..31 B7
Princefield Ave ST1....207 F8
Princefield Fst Sch ST19..207 F8
Prince George St ST10..76 D3
Prince Rupert Mews
WS13..........231 A8
Prince Rupert's Way
WS13..........231 A8
Princes Dr WV8........239 A2
Princes Gdns WV8....239 A2
Princes Rd Stoke-on-T ST4..71 F8
Stourbridge DY8......279 D3
Princess Ave Audley ST7..39 D1
Leek ST13..........31 B8
Princess Cl WS7......228 E7
Princess Ct ST7........40 D5
Princess Dr ST3........74 B4
Princess Gdns TF10....168 F1
Princess Pl ST16......155 E5
Princes Sq ST6........56 D8
Princess Rd ST14......111 A1
Princess St Biddulph ST8..27 D7
Burntwood WS7......228 E8
Burton u T DE14........166 C4
Cannock WS11........209 F5
Newcastle-u-L ST5......283 C3
Talke Pits ST7........40 D5
Princes St ST16........285 B3
Prince's St ST5........105 A2
Princess Way WS13....166 E7
Prince St Brownhills WS9..244 F2
Cannock WS11........209 E6
Leek ST13..........31 A6
Princeton Gdns WV9..239 F2
Princetown Cl ST3......90 A7
Priorfield Cl ST3........284 B4
Priors La TF9..........97 A1
Priors Mill DY3........271 E5
Prior's Pl ST19..........206 A6
Priory Ave ST13........31 A8
Priory CE Prim Sch ST4..87 E8
Priory Cl Congleton CW12..16 B7
Tamworth B79..........249 F7
Tutbury DE15..........146 B5
Priory Ct Brownhills WS9..245 A4
Market Drayton TF9....97 A1
Newcastle-u-L ST5......283 B2
Priory Dr ST18........177 D8
Priory Field Cl WV14..266 F1
Priory Green Prim Sch
WV9..........240 A2
Priory Lands DE13......147 A3
Priory La DY3..........271 D7
Priory Pl ST7..........26 A3
Priory Rd Bucknall ST2..58 B6
Cannock WS12........210 D4
Newcastle-u-L ST5......283 D4
Rugeley WS15........197 B5
Stone ST15..........120 B7
Priory The Endon ST9....44 A8
Pritchett Ave WV4......266 F1
Probert Rd WV10......240 B1
Probyn Ct ST3..........284 C2
Proctors Rd WS15......198 C4
Proffitt Cl WS8........245 A5
Progress Dr WS11......226 F6
Progress Ind Ctr WS11..226 F7
Prospect Dr WS13......231 F8
Prospect Manor Ct
WS12..........210 C3
Prospect Pk WS11......226 D9
Prospect Pl 9 Leek ST13..30 E5
Prospect Rd
Burntwood WS7......229 B6
Dudley DY3..........271 C4
Leek ST13..........31 A5
Market Drayton TF9....97 B1
Stafford ST17..........155 F5
Prospect St Burslem ST6..56 E7
Tamworth B79..........250 A5
Prospect Terr ST5......283 A3
Prosper Mdw DY6......275 F7
Providence St ST1......282 C4
Provost Pl ST13........31 A7
Pruden Ave WV4......266 F3
Puddle Bank La CW12..15 F5
Puddle Hill ST18........139 D1
Puddy La ST9..........44 A5
Pudsey Dr B75..........258 C3
Pugh Rd WV4,WV14....266 F1
Pugin Cl WV6..........254 D3
Pullman Cl B77........251 A2
Pullman Ct ST10........76 D2
Pulteney Dr TF16......155 B6
Pump Bank ST5........69 F7
Pump Ct ST7..........39 E2
Pump La Doveridge DE6..127 B8
Rugeley WS15........178 C3
Pump St Leek ST13......31 A7
Stoke-on-T ST4........72 A7
Purbeck St ST6........57 B7
Purbrook Rd WV1......266 F8
Purbrook B77..........261 E8
Purcell Ave WS13......214 C2
Purser Cres ST6........56 B5
Pyebirch La ST21......134 B5
Pye Green Rd WS11....209 E4
Pye Green Valley Prim Sch
WS12..........210 A7

Pyenest St ST1........282 A1
Pyrus Gr WS15........196 D6

Q

Quabbs La ST11........91 C8
Quadrangle The ST9....43 F7
Quadrant Rd ST1........282 B3
Quadrant The Hanley ST1..282 B3
Sedgley DY3..........266 D1
Quadrille Lawns WV9..239 F2
Quail Gn WV6..........254 F2
Quail Gr ST3..........90 A7
Quantico Cl 12 ST17....175 A8
Quantock Cl WS8......245 A4
Quarry Ave ST4........71 F8
Quarry Bank
Hollington ST10......94 A4
Keele ST5..........69 F8
Quarry Bank Rd Keele ST5..69 F8
Market Drayton TF9....112 B7
Quarry Berry La DE12..235 D2
Quarry Brow DY3......271 E6
Quarry Cl
Cheslyn Hay WS6......226 E3
Rugeley WS15........196 B8
Stoke-on-T ST9........43 C3
Werrington ST9........59 B4
Quarry Hills La WS14..231 D6
Quarry House La TF9..112 A7
Quarry La ST20........171 C4
Quarry Lodge WS14....231 D5
Quarry Pl TF9..........112 B7
Quarry Rd Hollington ST10..94 A3
Stoke-on-T ST4........71 F8
Quarry Terr ST7........26 A1
Quarter La SK17........23 B2
Quayle Gr 2 DY8......275 D3
Quee La ST14..........126 B1
Queen Anne St ST4....72 D8
Queen Elizabeth II Ct ST4..72 D6
Queen Elizabeth's Mercian
Sch B79..........250 C6
Queen Margaret's Rd TF9..99 D5
Queen Mary Rd ST4....72 F1
Queen Mary's Dr ST12..88 E3
Queen's Ave ST6........41 F3
Queensberry Rd ST3....73 D2
Queens Cotts ST19....206 B7
Queen's Croft Com Sch
WS13..........231 B7
Queens Ct
Burton u T DE14........185 B8
Caverswall ST11........74 D3
Longton ST3..........73 B1
Newcastle-u-L ST5......283 C3
Queen's Dr ST8........27 D6
Queens Dr
Burntwood WS7......228 F5
Leek ST13..........31 B8
Newport TF10..........168 F1
Queens Gdns
Codsall WV8..........238 F3
Talke Pits ST7........40 D5
Queen's Hospl DE13....166 A6
Queensland Cres DE15..167 C2
Queensmead Rd ST3....89 F7
Queens Park Ave ST3..73 B1
Queen's Prim Sch ST4..73 A5
Queens Rd Sedgley DY3..271 E8
Shareshill WV10......225 B6
Queen's Rd Stoke-on-T ST4..71 F7
Stourbridge DY8......279 F6
Queens Rise DE13......146 C6
Queen's Row ST12......88 F2
Queen's Sq 3 ST15....105 A2
Queens Sq WS11......209 E6
Queen St Audley ST7....39 C1
Brownhills WS9......244 F2
Burntwood WS7......228 F5
Burslem ST6..........56 F8
Burton u T DE14........166 C1
Cannock,Blackfords WS11..209 D7
Cannock WS11........210 A5
Cheadle ST10........76 E4
Cheslyn Hay WS6......226 D3
Queens Terr ST1........57 E4
Queen St Kidsgrove ST7..26 A2
Kingswinford DY6......275 D7
Leek ST13..........30 F6
Lichfield WS13........231 A7
Longnor SK17..........13 B6
Market Drayton TF9....97 C1
Newcastle-u-L,Chesterton
ST5..........55 E7
Newcastle-u-L,Porthill ST5..56 B6
Newcastle-u-L ST5......283 C3
Rugeley WS15........196 F8
Stourbridge DY8......279 F6
Uttoxeter ST14........126 C7
Queensville Ave ST17..156 A1
Queensville Bridge ST17..156 A1
Queensville Ret Pk ST17..175 A8
Queensville Stafford ST17..156 A1
Stafford ST17........175 B8
Queensway Ct 7 ST3....74 A1
Queensway Ind Est ST6..56 C8
Queensway
Newcastle-u-L ST5......71 B6
Rugeley WS15........196 E7
Stafford ST16........285 B5
Stoke-on-T ST4........72 C6
Tamworth B79..........250 A8
Queens Wlk ST3........74 B4

Pyenest St...Queens Wlk
Plo – Ran   321

Queenswood Rd B75..258 B1
Queen Victoria Prim Sch
DY3..........271 E8
Quendale WV5..........269 E6
Quillets Rd DY8........275 C3
Quince B77..........251 B3
Quince Tree Sch B77..251 A3
Quinton Ave WS6......226 F3
Quinton Gr ST5........56 B4
Quinton Pl WS11......228 A4
Quinton Wlk ST6......42 C2
Quixhill Bank ST14......95 F8
Quixhill La ST14........95 E8
Quonians La WS13....231 B8
Quorn Cl DE15........167 A1
Quorn Cres DY8......275 C3

R

Rabbit La WV10........241 A8
Raby St WV2..........266 D8
Racecourse La DY8....279 F1
Race Course ST5........55 C1
Racecourse Rd ST4....72 A4
Rachel Gr ST4..........73 B6
Raddle La B79..........217 E5
Radford Bank ST17....175 C8
Radford Cl ST15........105 A1
Radford Dr WS4........244 C2
Radford La WV3,WV4..264 F7
Radford Rd ST4........56 F1
Radford Rise ST17......175 C8
Radford ST15..........105 A1
Radhurst Rise DE13..183 C2
Radley Way ST9........59 B3
Radmore Cl WS7......228 D8
Radmore La
Abbots Bromley WS15..161 C7
Gnosall TF10,ST20......170 D7
Radnor Cl WS9........244 F4
Radnor Rd DY3........271 C8
Radnor Rise WS12......210 B4
Radstock Cl ST17......175 E6
Radstock Rd WV12....242 C1
Radstone Rise ST5......71 B3
Radway Green Rd
Barthomley CW2......38 D6
Barthomley CW2......38 E8
Ragees Rd DY6........275 F4
Raglan Ave WV6........254 F3
Raglan Cl
8 Burton u T DE13....166 D8
Aldridge WS9..........256 A5
Sedgley DY3..........271 B7
Raglan St ST4..........72 D6
Raglan Wlk ST4........72 D6
Ragley Cl WS3..........243 A1
Raikes La WS14........246 C7
Railswood Dr WS3......244 B3
Railton Ave ST3........73 A1
Railway Cotts
Colwich ST17..........177 D7
Congleton CW12........6 A1
Cotes Heath ST21......102 D3
Cresswell ST11........91 D3
Egginton DE65........148 B7
Leek ST13..........30 E1
Leek ST13..........45 E8
Norton Bridge ST15....135 A8
Rugeley WS15........197 A5
Railway Ct ST9........43 F7
Railway Ent Ctr ST4....57 A1
Railway La WS7........211 E1
Railway Pas ST3........284 C4
Railway Rd ST3........73 C2
Railway St Cannock WS11..226 E8
Norton Canes WS11....228 A5
Stafford ST16........285 A3
Stoke-on-T ST6........41 E2
Railway Terr
Brocton ST17..........176 C7
Kingsley Holt ST10......62 A3
Longton ST3..........284 D3
Rainbow St 8 WV2....266 C8
Rainford Cl ST7........26 F1
Rainham Gr ST6........42 A8
Rainscar B77..........262 B7
Rake End Ct WS15......179 F1
Rakegate Prim Sch
WV10..........240 B1
Rake Hill WS7..........229 B8
Rakes La DE6..........51 F6
Rakeway Rd ST10......76 D7
Raleigh Hall Ind Est
ST21..........117 E2
Ralph Ct ST17..........174 B8
Ralph Dr ST17..........57 F7
Ralston Cl WS3........243 A4
Ramage Gr ST3........176 D6
Rambleford Way ST16..155 D8
Ramillies Cres WS6....226 F1
Ramsay Cl ST12........88 E4
Ramsey Rd ST5........283 A4
Ramsey St ST4........72 C5
Ramshaw Gr 5 ST3....73 D6
Ramshaw View ST1....31 B8
Ramshorn Rd ST10......78 E8
Randall Cl DY6........275 F4
Randle Dr B75..........258 C3
Randles La ST9..........60 B6
Randle's View CW12....16 C8
Ranelagh Ho WV2....266 D7
Ranelagh Rd WV2....266 D6
Ranelagh St ST1........282 B2

Rangeley View ST15. . . . . . 104 E2
Rangemoor La DE6 . . . . . 80 D6
Rangemoor Hall Mews
DE13 . . . . 164 B1
Rangemore Hill DE13 . . . 183 B7
Rangemore St DE14. . . . . 166 B3
Rangemore Terr ST5. . . . . 56 D3
Ranger's Wlk WS15 . . . . . 178 B1
Rangeways Rd DY6 . . . . . 275 F4
Rangifer Rd B78 . . . . 249 F1
Rank The ST20. . . . . 171 C5
Ranleigh Ave DY6. . . . . . 275 F4
Ranscombe Dr DY3 . . . . . 271 D2
Ransome Pl ST3 . . . . 73 E4
Ranton Park Area 3
WS11 . . . . 210 A2
Ranworth Cl ST5. . . . . 71 B2
Ranworth Rise WV4. . . . . 266 D4
Ratcliffe Ave DE14 . . . . . 185 B8
Ratcliffe Cl DY3 . . . . 271 F6
Rathbone Ave ST5 . . . . . . 56 C5
Rathbone St 4 ST6 . . . . . 41 E3
Rathlin Cl WV9 . . . . 240 A3
Rathmore Cl DY8 . . . . . . 279 E2
Rathwell Cl WV9 . . . . 240 A1
Rattigan Dr ST3. . . . . 73 F4
Ratton St ST1. . . . . 282 C3
Raven Cl Cannock WS12 . . 210 E4
 Cheslyn Hay WS6. . . . . . 226 D2
 Huntington WS12. . . . . . 209 C7
Raven Ct
 Market Drayton TF9 . . . . . 97 C1
 Wolverhampton WV10. . . 240 B3
Ravenhill Cl WS15 . . . . . 196 F6
Ravenhill Dr WV8 . . . . . . 239 A4
Ravenhill Terr WS15 . . . . 196 F7
Ravenna Way ST3. . . . . . . 73 E4
Raven Rd DE13 . . . . 182 A2
Ravensbank Mobile Home Pk
 ST18. . . . . 137 D2
Ravens Cl ST7 . . . . 39 E3
Ravenscliffe Rd ST7. . . . . 41 A8
Ravenscroft DY8 . . . . . . 279 C6
Ravens Ct WS8 . . . . 244 F7
Ravensholme WV6 . . . . . 254 F5
Raven's La ST7 . . . . 39 F3
Ravenslea Rd WS15 . . . . 196 F6
Ravensmead Com Prim Sch
 ST7 . . . . 39 E3
Ravenstone B77 . . . . 262 B8
Ravens Way DE14 . . . . . . 166 B4
Ravenswood Cl ST5 . . . . . 71 B3
Ravenswood Crest 4
 ST17. . . . . 175 C7
Rawle Cl ST10 . . . . 76 C3
Rawlett Sch
 Tamworth B79 . . . . 250 A8
 Wigginton B79 . . . . 234 A1
Rawlins St ST1. . . . . 57 E5
Rawnsley Rd WS12 . . . . . 210 E6
Ray Ct B74 . . . . 257 F3
Raygill B77 . . . . 262 B8
Rayleigh Rd WV3 . . . . . . 266 A4
Rayleigh Way ST2. . . . . . . 58 D1
Raymond Ave ST1. . . . . . . 57 D7
Raymond St ST1. . . . . . . 282 B1
Reacliffe Rd SK11,ST13 . . 18 B4
Read Ave ST16. . . . . 155 F5
Reade's La CW12 . . . . 16 D8
Reading Way ST2 . . . . 58 D2
Reads Rd ST4. . . . . 72 F8
Reapers Wlk WV8 . . . . . . 239 F1
Reason Rd ST17 . . . . 174 F5
Rebecca Gdns WV4 . . . . . 265 F4
Rebecca St ST1. . . . . 72 B8
Recorder Gr ST6. . . . . 42 B6
Recreation Rd ST3 . . . . . . 73 E2
Rectory Cl
 Church Leigh ST10. . . . . 109 A5
 Drayton Bassett B78. . . . 260 E5
Rectory Dr TF11 . . . . 203 F2
Rectory Fields DY8. . . . . 275 E2
Rectory Gdns
 Armitage WS15 . . . . 198 A4
 Talke Pits ST7 . . . . 40 D6
Rectory La
 Armitage WS15 . . . . 197 F4
 Haughton ST18 . . . . 172 F5
Rectory Mews
 Egginton DE65 . . . . 148 B4
 Mucklestone TF9 . . . . . . 99 A7
Rectory Rd Hanley ST1. . . 282 A1
 Hollington ST10. . . . . . . 94 C2
Rectory St Hanley ST1. . . 282 A1
 Stourbridge DY8 . . . . . . 275 E3
Rectory View ST7 . . . . . . 40 D6
Redacres WV6. . . . . 255 C6
Red Bank La TF9 . . . . 112 B8
Red Bank Longton ST3. . . 73 C1
 Market Drayton TF9. . . . 112 B8
Redbourne Dr CW2 . . . . . 37 D1
Redbourn Rd WS3 . . . . . . 243 A4
Redbridge Cl ST4. . . . . . . 71 F1
Redbrook Cl WS12 . . . . . 210 D2
Redbrook La WS15 . . . . . 196 F5
Redcar Rd Stoke-on-T ST4 . 88 B7
 Wolverhampton WV10. . . 240 D4
Redcliffe Dr WV5 . . . . . . 270 A6
Redcliff B77 . . . . 250 F5
Redfern Dr WS7 . . . . 229 B5
Redfern Rd Stone ST15. . . 119 F5
 Uttoxeter ST14 . . . . 111 A1
Redford Dr WV7 . . . . 237 B5
Redgrave Dr ST16. . . . . . 155 C2
Red Hall La ST7 . . . . 54 C5

Red Hall Prim Sch DY3 . . 271 C3
Redhall Rd DY3 . . . . 271 C2
Redheath Cl ST5 . . . . 55 A2
Redhill Ave WV5 . . . . 270 A6
Redhill Cl B79 . . . . 250 A7
Redhill Dr ST10 . . . . 92 E5
Redhill Gdns WS15 . . . . . 120 B8
Redhill Gorse ST16. . . . . 155 C5
Red Hill WV7 . . . . 277 E4
Redhill La DE13 . . . . 146 B5
Redhill Prim Sch WS11. . . 209 F4
Red Hill Rd Cannock WS11. 209 F4
 Stone ST15. . . . . 105 C1
Redhills ST21 . . . . 133 E6
Redhills Rd Bucknall ST2. . 58 A7
 Stoke-on-T ST2 . . . . 57 F8
Red Hill ST16. . . . . 155 C5
Red Ho The
 Albrighton WV7 . . . . 237 A5
 Market Drayton TF9. . . . . 97 C1
Redhouse Cone & Mus★
 DY8. . . . . 275 E1
Red House Mews ST3 . . . 284 A3
Red House Ind Est WS9 . . 256 A6
Redhouse Rd WV6 . . . . . 255 B5
Redhurst Dr WV10 . . . . . 240 B3
Red La WV11 . . . . 242 C3
Redlake B77 . . . . 261 E8
Redland Dr ST5. . . . . 58 D3
Redlands The ST15. . . . . 120 C7
Redlands Way B74 . . . . . 257 A1
Red La Sedgley DY3 . . . . . 271 B8
 Stoke-on-T ST2 . . . . 43 C2
Red Lion Ave WS11 . . . . . 228 A4
Red Lion Cl ST7. . . . . 40 D7
Red Lion Cres WS11. . . . . 228 A4
Red Lion La WS11. . . . . . 228 B4
Red Lion Pas ST1 . . . . . . 282 A2
Red Lion St ST16. . . . . . . 285 B4
Redlock Field WS14. . . . . 231 A5
Redman Gr ST6. . . . . 57 C7
Redmine Cl ST5. . . . . 56 A4
Redmond Cl WS15 . . . . . 178 C2
Redmoor Cl DE15 . . . . . . 167 B3
Redmoor Gdns WV4 . . . . 266 A5
Redmoor Rd WS15 . . . . . 211 F4
Rednall Dr B75 . . . . 258 C3
Redrock Cres ST7. . . . . . . 26 C1
Redrock Dr WV8 . . . . 238 F2
Redruth Cl DY6 . . . . 275 D8
Redruth Dr ST17 . . . . 156 D1
Redstone Way DY3. . . . . . 271 D4
Redwell Cl B77 . . . . 250 D5
Redwing Cl
 3 Packmoor ST7 . . . . . . 26 F1
 Hammerwich WS7 . . . . . 229 D5
Redwing Dr Biddulph ST8. . 27 E8
 Huntington WS12. . . . . . 209 C7
Redwing B77 . . . . 262 A6
Redwood Ave Dudley DY1 271 F5
 Stone ST15. . . . . 120 B5
Redwood Cl B74 . . . . 256 F2
Redwood Dr
 Burntwood WS7 . . . . 228 F8
 Burton u T DE15. . . . . . . 186 A8
 Cannock WS11. . . . . 210 A3
Redwood Pl ST3 . . . . 73 F1
Redwood Rd DY7 . . . . . . 278 C3
Reedbed Gr ST6. . . . . 42 C3
Reedham Gdns WV4 . . . . 265 D5
Reedham Way ST2. . . . . . 58 D2
Reedly Rd WV12 . . . . 242 C1
Reedmace B77 . . . . 250 C2
Rees Dr WV5 . . . . 270 B7
Reeve Cl WS15. . . . . 198 B4
Reeve La WS13 . . . . 231 B8
Reeves Ave
 Newcastle-u-L ST5. . . . . . 56 B3
 Stoke-on-T ST6 . . . . 42 A3
Reeves Gdns WV8. . . . . . 239 A4
Refinery St ST5 . . . . 283 C2
Regal Cl B77 . . . . 261 C8
Regency Cl ST7 . . . . 40 D5
Regency Ct WS15 . . . . . . 197 B6
Regency Dr ST9. . . . . 43 C4
Regency Way DE13. . . . . 166 D8
Regency Wlk B74 . . . . . . 257 D5
Regent Ave ST6. . . . . 41 F3
Regent Cl DY6 . . . . 275 C6
Regent Coll ST4 . . . . 57 A2
Regent Ct Ipstones ST10. . 62 A8
 Newcastle-u-L ST5. . . . . . 56 B6
Regent Rd Hanley ST1. . . 282 B1
 Wolverhampton WV4. . . . 265 C5
Regents Ho DE14 . . . . . . 184 F7
Regent St Leek ST13 . . . . 30 F6
 Stoke-on-T ST4 . . . . 72 A5
 Stone ST15 . . . . 104 F1
Regent Theatre★ ST1 . . . 282 B2
Regina Cres ST6 . . . . 255 B4
Reginald Mitchell Prim Sch
 The ST7 . . . . 25 D1
Reginald Mitchell Way
 ST6. . . . . 41 C5
Reginald St 5 ST6. . . . . . 57 A8
Regina St ST6 . . . . 42 D2
Regis Beeches WV6. . . . . 255 C5
Regis Rd WV6 . . . . 255 C5
Registry St ST4 . . . . 72 B8
Reid Cl WS7 . . . . 229 F7
Reid St ST6. . . . . 56 E8
Reindeer Rd B78. . . . . . . 249 E1
Relay Dr B77 . . . . 262 C7
Remer St ST6. . . . . 57 B6

Remington Dr WS11 . . . . 226 F8
Renard Way ST3 . . . . 90 B7
Rendel Gr ST15 . . . . 104 E2
Rendermore Cl ST19 . . . . 207 E7
Rene Rd B77. . . . . 250 E5
Renfrew Cl
 Newcastle-u-L ST5. . . . . . 70 F8
 Stourbridge DY8 . . . . . . 275 C3
Renfrew Pl ST4 . . . . 72 A1
Rennie Cres ST13 . . . . . . 45 D5
Rennison Dr WV5 . . . . . . 270 A6
Renown Cl ST2 . . . . 57 F1
Renshaw Dr DE11 . . . . . . 186 F5
Renshaw Wood La WV8 . . 222 E1
Renton Gr WV10 . . . . 240 A1
Renton Rd WV10 . . . . 240 A1
Repington Rd N B77. . . . . 251 A5
Repington Rd S B77 . . . . . 251 A5
Repington Rd ST1. . . . . . . 57 F8
Repton Ave WV6 . . . . 254 E3
Repton Cl Cannock WS11 . 226 B8
 Stafford ST17 . . . . 156 B1
Repton Dr ST5. . . . . 70 F5
Repton Rd DE15. . . . . . . 167 E8
Reservoir Rd
 Burton u T DE14. . . . . . . 165 F4
 Cannock WS12. . . . . 210 D4
 Longton ST3. . . . . 73 E2
Retreat Gdns DY3 . . . . . . 271 D7
Retreat Gdns The WV6 . . . 253 C3
Retreat St WV3 . . . . 266 B8
Reva Rd ST17 . . . . 174 E8
Revival St WS3 . . . . 243 B1
Reynards La SK17 . . . . . . 24 E4
Reynards Rise TF9 . . . . . . 99 D5
Reynolds Ave ST5. . . . . . . 55 E6
Reynolds Cl
 Lichfield WS13 . . . . 214 B2
 Swindon DY3. . . . . 269 C2
Reynolds Gr WV6 . . . . . . 254 F5
Reynolds Rd ST6. . . . . . . 42 A3
Rhein Way 2 ST17 . . . . . 175 A8
Rhodes Cl DY3. . . . . 271 A4
Rhodes Ct ST5. . . . . 56 C7
Rhodes Ho DE15 . . . . . . 167 C3
Rhodes St ST1. . . . . 57 D6
Rhondda Ave ST6 . . . . . . 57 C7
Rialto Pl ST6 . . . . 41 D3
Ribble Cl Hilton DE65 . . . 147 D8
 Newcastle-u-L ST5. . . . . . 71 B4
Ribble Dr ST8. . . . . 16 E1
Ribble Ind Est ST6 . . . . . . 56 F6
Ribblesdale Ave CW12 . . . 6 A5
Ribblesdale B77 . . . . 262 B7
Ricardo St ST3. . . . . 73 C1
Riceyman Rd ST5. . . . . . . 56 B8
Richard Clarke Fst Sch
 WS15 . . . . 161 A6
Richard Cooper Rd
 WS14. . . . . 246 F5
Richard Crosse CE Prim Sch
 DE13. . . . . 199 C6
Richard Heathcote Com Prim
 Sch The ST7 . . . . 54 E6
Richards Ave
 Stafford ST16 . . . . 156 A4
 Stoke-on-T ST6 . . . . 41 F3
Richards Ct WS11 . . . . . . 227 F6
Richardson Ct WS7 . . . . . 228 E8
Richardson Dr DY8. . . . . . 279 E8
Richardson Pl ST6. . . . . . 42 B6
Richardson Way WS15 . . . 178 D3
Richard Wakefield CE Prim
 Sch DE13. . . . . 146 C6
Richborough Dr DY1 . . . . 271 F4
Riches St WV6. . . . . 255 F5
Richfield La ST17 . . . . . . 193 F8
Richmere Ct WV6 . . . . . . 255 B3
Richmond Ave
 Stoke-on-T ST1 . . . . 57 D8
 Wolverhampton WV3. . . . 255 F1
Richmond Cl
 Cannock WS11 . . . . 210 A5
 Chorlton CW2 . . . . 37 D1
 Newport TF10 . . . . 168 F1
 Stafford ST17 . . . . 174 F1
 Tamworth B79 . . . . 250 A5
Richmond Dr
 Lichfield WS14 . . . . 231 D7
 Perton WV6 . . . . 254 F3
 Wolverhampton WV3. . . . 255 E1
Richmond Gdns
 Stourbridge DY8 . . . . . . 279 F7
 Wombourne WV5. . . . . . 270 A5
Richmond Grove ST5. . . . . 56 D3
Richmond Gr DY8 . . . . . . 279 E8
Richmond Pk
 Kingswinford DY6 . . . . . 275 C8
 Rugeley WS15 . . . . 196 F5
Richmond Rd
 Sedgley DY3. . . . . 271 E7
 Stoke-on-T ST4 . . . . 72 A1
 Wolverhampton WV3. . . . 255 E1
Richmond St
 Burton u T DE14. . . . . . . 166 C4
 Stoke-on-T ST4 . . . . 72 A7
Richmond Terr ST1. . . . . . 282 A1
Rickerscote Ave ST17 . . . 175 A6
Rickerscote Hall La
 ST17. . . . . 175 A5
Rickerscote Rd ST17 . . . . 174 F6
Ridding Bank WS14. . . . . 87 B7
Ridding La Denstone ST14 . 79 E2
 Gratwich ST14 . . . . 124 C3
Riddings Cres WS3. . . . . . 243 F4
Riddings La DE6. . . . . . . 144 D6
Riddings The B77 . . . . . . 250 E5
Rider's Way WS15 . . . . . . 178 B1

Ridge Cl ST12. . . . . 104 C8
Ridge Cres ST3 . . . . 89 F6
Ridge Croft ST15. . . . . . . 120 C7
Ridgefields ST8. . . . . 17 B1
Ridge Hill Dr CW3. . . . . . 69 B7
Ridge Ho 57 A4
Ridgehouse Dr ST1 . . . . . 57 A4
Ridgemont Ct ST15 . . . . . 120 C7
Ridge Prim Sch The DY8 279 C5
Ridge Rd
 Kingswinford DY6 . . . . . 275 C5
 Stoke-on-T ST6 . . . . 41 D6
Ridge St DY8 . . . . 279 C6
Ridge The DE15. . . . . . . 167 B6
Ridget La WS13 . . . . 201 B1
Ridge Way WS9. . . . . 256 B4
Ridgeway Cl Hopton ST18 156 B8
 Stafford ST16 . . . . 174 C5
Ridgeway Dr WV4. . . . . . 265 F3
Ridgeway ST18 . . . . 158 D8
Ridgeway Prim Sch WS7 229 A5
Ridgeway Rd
 Burton u T DE14. . . . . . . 185 E6
 Stourbridge DY8 . . . . . . 275 F2
Ridgeway Ridgeway ST6 . . 42 E8
 Sedgley DY3. . . . . 271 D7
Ridgeway The
 Burntwood WS7. . . . . . . 229 A4
 Stafford ST16 . . . . 155 A5
Ridge Wlk ST3 . . . . 89 F7
Ridgewood Ave DY8. . . . . 279 C7
Ridgewood Dr B75. . . . . . 258 B1
Ridgewood High Sch
 DY8. . . . . 279 C5
Ridgewood Rise B77 . . . . 251 A5
Ridgmont Rd ST5 . . . . . . 70 F4
Ridgway Dr ST11. . . . . . . 90 D7
Ridgway Pl ST5 . . . . 56 D3
Ridgway Rd ST1,ST4. . . . . 57 D1
Ridings Brook Dr 3
 WS11 . . . . 210 A2
Ridings Cl TF9 . . . . 97 B1
Ridings Park Trad Est
 WS11 . . . . 210 A3
Ridings The
 Brewood ST19 . . . . 223 C7
 Cannock WS11. . . . . . . 226 F8
Ridley St ST4 . . . . 72 C5
Ridley Wlk ST4 . . . . 72 C5
Ridware Ho WS13 . . . . . 214 E1
Ridware Rd WS15 . . . . . 198 B7
Rifle Range Cnr WS15 . . . 195 B6
Rigby Dr WV11 . . . . 209 F4
Rigby Rd D77 . . . . 26 B3
Righton Ho B77 . . . . 250 D1
Riley Ave ST6. . . . . 42 B2
Riley Cres WV4 . . . . 266 A6
Riley La ST20 . . . . 151 F7
Riley St N ST6. . . . . 56 E8
Riley St S ST6. . . . . 56 F8
Rileys Way ST7 . . . . 39 F2
Riley B77. . . . . 250 E3
Rill St ST4 . . . . 284 B4
Rimbach Dr ST18 . . . . . . 177 D8
Rimini Cl ST3. . . . . 73 E5
Rindleford Ave WV4. . . . . 265 C6
Rindle The ST10 . . . . 76 B3
Ringhills Rd WV8 . . . . . . 239 B2
Ringland Cl ST1. . . . . . . 282 C3
Ring Rd WS7 . . . . 228 E7
Ring The ST18 . . . . 158 C1
Ringway WS11. . . . . 209 E1
Ringway Ind Est WS13 . . . 214 C3
Ringwood Ave WV9 . . . . . 256 B5
Ringwood Rd WV10 . . . . . 240 A1
Ripon Ave WS5. . . . . 55 E7
Ripon Dr ST17 . . . . 175 C7
Ripon Rd ST3 . . . . 88 F8
Riseley Rd ST4. . . . . 71 D8
Rise The
 Kingswinford DY6 . . . . . 275 E5
 Lichfield WS13 . . . . 230 F7
 Rugeley WS15 . . . . 196 F6
 Stafford ST17 . . . . 175 C7
 Swadlincote DE11 . . . . . 186 F5
Rishworth Ave WS15 . . . . 178 E2
Rising Brook High Sch
 ST17. . . . . 174 E6
Rising Brook
 Stafford ST17 . . . . 174 E7
 Wolverhampton WV6. . . . 255 B4
Rivendell Gdns WV6 . . . . 255 B5
Rivendell La ST13. . . . . . . 30 F2
Rivercroft Cl ST14 . . . . . . 96 A3
Riverdale DE15. . . . . 167 B3
Riverdale Dr ST6. . . . . . . 41 E8
Riverdrive B78,B79. . . . . 250 B3
Riverfield Gr B77 . . . . . . 250 D5
Riverhead Cl ST6 . . . . . . 42 F5
River Lea Mews CW3 . . . . 68 E6
Riversfield Dr ST14 . . . . . 95 F3
Riverside Ct Bucknall ST1. . 57 F4
 Dunsley DY7. . . . . 278 B4
Riverside Dr DE14. . . . . . 184 F7
Riverside Gdns
 Burton u T DE14. . . . . . . 166 F6
 Codsall WV8. . . . . 239 B5
Riverside Gr 7 DE15 . . . . 104 F1
Riverside Ho ST19 . . . . . 192 E1
Riverside Ind Est B78 . . . 250 B3
Riverside L Ctr ST16 . . . . 285 B3
Riverside Pk DE14 . . . . . 166 F6
Riverside Rd
 Stoke-on-T ST4 . . . . 71 E2
 Upper Tean ST10 . . . . . . 92 D4
Riverside Rugeley WS15 . . 178 F2
 Walton-on-T DE12 . . . . . 184 C1
Riverside WV9 . . . . 224 B2

Riversleigh Dr DY8. . . . . . 279 E8
Riversmeade Way ST16. . . 155 A5
Riversmead ST5 . . . . 71 B4
River View SK17 . . . . 13 B6
Riverway ST17 . . . . 285 C2
River Way ST15 . . . . 120 A7
Rivington Cl WV3 . . . . . . 279 E4
Rivington Cres ST6. . . . . . 42 A6
Rixdale Cl ST1. . . . . 282 B4
Roaches Sch ST8 . . . . 27 C6
Roaches The★ ST13 . . . . . 10 C2
Roach B77 . . . . 261 D6
Road One CW1. . . . . 37 D8
Road Two CW1 . . . . 37 C8
Robert Cl B79 . . . . 249 F7
Robert Heath St ST6 . . . . 42 C2
Roberts Ave ST5 . . . . . . 283 B4
Roberts Cl
 Alsagers Bank ST7 . . . . . 54 F6
 Brownhills WS9 . . . . . . 244 F7
Roberts Green Rd DY3 . . . 271 E4
Robertson Dr ST5 . . . . . . 55 F3
Robertson Sq ST4. . . . . . 71 E4
Roberts Prim Sch DY3 . . . 271 D4
Robert St Dudley DY3 . . . 271 D4
 Stoke-on-T ST6 . . . . 41 D4
Robert Sutton RC Sch
 DE15. . . . . 186 A7
Robertville Rd ST2. . . . . . 58 B3
Robey's La B78 . . . . 251 D3
Robina Dr ST10 . . . . 76 E3
Robin Cl Huntington WS12 209 C7
 Stoke-on-T ST7 . . . . 41 F8
 Tamworth B77 . . . . 261 C8
 Uttoxeter ST14 . . . . 126 B6
Robin Croft 14 ST6 . . . . . 56 F8
Robin Hill ST8 . . . . 28 A7
Robin Hill Gr ST4 . . . . . . 73 B5
Robinia B77 . . . . 251 A4
Robin La TF10 . . . . 168 A4
Robins Cl WS6. . . . . 226 D1
Robins Croft WS11 . . . . . 210 A1
Robinson Ave ST6. . . . . . . 57 D8
Robinson Cl B79 . . . . . . 249 E7
Robinson Ct ST3 . . . . 88 F8
Robinson Rd
 Burntwood WS7. . . . . . . 228 F8
 Swadlincote DE11 . . . . . 186 F6
 Trentham ST4 . . . . 87 F8
Robins Rd WS7 . . . . 228 E7
Robins The TF9 . . . . 99 D4
Robinswood ST17. . . . . . 175 C6
Robson Cl WS8 . . . . 244 F5
Robson St ST1. . . . . 282 A2
Rocester La ST10 . . . . . . 49 A2
Roche Ave ST13. . . . . 31 A8
Roche Rd WS3. . . . . 242 F1
Rochester Ave WS7 . . . . . 229 A7
Rochester Rd ST3. . . . . . . 73 C5
Rochester Way WS12. . . . 210 C1
Roche The
 Burntwood WS13. . . . . . 230 A8
 Cheddleton ST13 . . . . . . 45 C4
 Creswell Green WS13 . . . 212 F1
Roche Way WS3 . . . . 242 F1
Rochford Cl ST13 . . . . . . 30 C5
Rochford Gr WV4 . . . . . . 265 D5
Rochford Way ST2 . . . . . . 58 D1
Rock Cres ST15 . . . . 105 C4
Rock End Dr ST13. . . . . . . 45 B1
Rockeries The ST17 . . . . . 175 A6
Rock Farm Rd WS14 . . . . 232 E6
Rockfield Ave ST3. . . . . . . 43 D1
Rock Hill B78,WS14. . . . . 248 C4
Rock House Dr ST12 . . . . 88 D1
Rockhouse Dr ST18 . . . . . 158 B2
Rockhouse La ST7 . . . . . . 40 C7
Rockingham Cl
 Dudley DY3. . . . . 271 C3
 Walsall WS3. . . . . 243 B1
Rockingham Dr
 Cheadle ST10. . . . . 76 F3
 Perton WV6 . . . . 254 F3
Rock La Ashley TF9 . . . . . 100 C8
 Mucklestone TF9 . . . . . . 99 C2
Rocklands Cres WS13 . . . 214 C5
Rocklands ST5. . . . . 56 C7
Rocklands Sch WS13 . . . . 231 D8
Rock La ST21 . . . . 102 B1
Rockmount Gdns DY7. . . 278 B3
Rock Rd WV14. . . . . 271 F8
Rockrose Gdns WV10 . . . 241 A7
Rockside ST7. . . . . 26 C6
Rock St DY3 . . . . 271 C3
Rocks The Brown Edge ST6. 43 B8
 Standon ST21 . . . . 102 C2
Rock The WV6. . . . . 255 B4
Rocky Wall DY7. . . . . 277 E4
Rodbaston Coll ST19 . . . . 207 E3
Rodbaston Dr ST19 . . . . . 207 E3
Roddam Ct TF10 . . . . 168 E2
Roddige La WS13 . . . . . . 216 A8
Rode Hall★ ST7 . . . . 25 D4
Rodenhurst House Flats 3
 TF9 . . . . 97 C1
Rodger Ave CW3. . . . . . . 53 A6
Rodgers St ST6. . . . . 41 C7
Rodway Cl WV4. . . . . . . 266 D3
Roebuck Cl ST15. . . . . . . 106 C2
Roebuck Sh Ctr ST5. . . . . 283 B2
Roebuck St ST4. . . . . 72 C7
Roedean Ave ST17 . . . . . 175 B8
Roe Deer Gn TF10 . . . . . 168 C5
Roe La ST5 . . . . 71 A4
Roe Pk ST7. . . . . 15 E1
Roford Ct DY3 . . . . 271 C5
Rogate Cl ST4 . . . . 73 B6
Rogers Ave ST5. . . . . 55 F3

Rogers Cl WV11.........242 A2
Rogerson Rd WS13......215 D6
Rogerstone Ave ST4.....71 E6
Rokewood Cl DY6.......270 D1
Rokholt Cres WS11.....209 C1
Rolfe Cl ST4............72 A2
Rolleston La DE13.....146 D5
Rolleston Rd DE13.....166 C8
Rolling Mill Rd WS11...227 F4
Rolt Cl ST15...........104 E3
Roma ST3...............89 D8
Roman Cl WS8..........228 E2
Roman Ct Cannock WS11.226 E5
  Tamworth B77........261 E7
Roman Dr ST5..........55 D5
Roman La B74.........257 B4
Roman Pk B74.........257 B4
Roman Pl B74.........257 B2
Roman Rd Coven WV9...224 A3
  Little Aston B74.....257 C4
Roman Rd (Sandy La)
  DY8................279 C3
Romans Grange B74....257 C4
Roman View WS11......226 F5
Roman Way
  Lichfield WS14......231 D7
  Tamworth B79........249 E7
Roman Wlk WS14.......230 D2
Romany Way DY8.......279 C3
Romer Side ST2........73 C8
Romesco Way
  [7] Stafford ST17.....175 A8
  Stafford ST17.......175 A8
Romford Mdw ST21....133 D6
Romford Pl ST3........90 B7
Romford Rd ST16......155 E6
Romilly Cl Lichfield WS14.231 E7
  Stourbridge DY8.....279 E6
Romney Ave ST5.......55 E6
Romney Dr ST16.......155 B4
Romney Gr ST3.........89 C8
Romney B77...........261 F8
Romsey Cl ST2.........73 D8
Romsey Gr WV10......240 C3
Romsey Rd WV10......240 C3
Romsey Way WS3......242 F3
Romsley Cl WS4.......244 C2
Romsley La WV15......276 A2
Ronald St ST3.........284 C2
Ronaldsway Dr ST5....283 A4
Ronald Wlk ST3.......284 C2
Ronson Ave ST4........71 E4
Rooker Ave WV2.......266 F6
Rooker Cres WV2......266 F6
Rookery Ave ST3.......73 A1
Rookery Cl
  Armitage WS15......198 C5
  Yoxall DE13.........182 A2
Rookery Cotts ST21...115 E6
Rookery Cres ST11....91 C2
Rookery Ct
  Lichfield WS13......230 E7
  Stoke-on-T ST4......71 E3
Rookery La Aldridge WS9.256 B6
  Stoke-on-T ST4......71 F3
  Weeford B75,B78.....248 C2
  Wolverhampton WV2..266 B6
Rookery Par WS9......256 B6
Rookery Rd
  Coldmeece ST15......118 C7
  Kidsgrove ST7.......26 C3
  Wombourne WV5......270 B6
Rookery Rise WV5.....270 B6
Rookery The
  Newcastle-u-L ST5...55 C1
  Stoke-on-T ST4......71 E3
Rookswood Copse [2]
  ST17...............175 C6
Rookwood Dr WV6.....254 E4
Roper Way DY3........271 F6
Roper Wlk DY3........271 F6
Rope St ST4...........56 D1
Ropewalk The DE14....166 C1
Roseacre Gr ST3.......89 F6
Roseacre La ST11......90 F6
Roseacre ST5..........70 F7
Rose Ave Burton u T DE13.148 A2
  Kingswinford DY6....275 D5
Rose Bank Cres ST10...78 B6
Rose Bank St ST13.....30 E6
Rose Bank Terr ST13...30 E6
Rose Bay Mdw [2] WS11.210 C2
Roseberry Dr CW3......68 E2
Roseberry Gdns DY10..280 C3
Rosebery Cl ST8.......27 E8
Rosebery Rd B77......261 D4
Rosebery St ST4.......41 F5
Rosebury Gr WV5......269 E6
Rose Cottage Dr [3] DY8.275 D3
Rose Cottage Gdns
  DE14...............166 D1
Rose Cotts TF11......203 F8
Rosedale Wlk DY6.....275 E8
Rose Dr WS8..........244 E5
Rosehill WS12........209 F8
Rosehill Cl ST2.......43 B1
Rose Hill ST16.......155 C3
Rose La WS7..........229 C7
Roseland Cres ST2.....43 B1
Roseleigh Cres DE11..186 F6
Rosemary Ave
  Cheslyn Hay WS6....226 D3
  Stafford ST17.......174 F5
  Wolverhampton WV4..266 C6
Rosemary Cl WS8.....244 D6
Rosemary Cres
  Dudley DY1.........271 F6
  Wolverhampton WV4..266 C5

Rosemary Cres W WV4..266 B5
Rosemary Ct B74......257 D4
Rosemary Dr
  Huntington WS12.....209 D5
  Little Aston B74.....257 C3
  Uttoxeter ST14......126 B6
Rosemary Ednam ST14..71 E8
Rosemary Hill Rd B74.257 D5
Rosemary La DY8......279 D3
Rosemary Nook B74....257 D5
Rosemary Pl ST1.......57 E7
Rosemary Rd
  Cheslyn Hay WS6....226 D3
  Tamworth B77.......250 F4
Rosemary St ST5......55 E1
Rose Mill TF9.........99 E5
Rosemount Rd DE15...166 F3
Rosemount WV6......255 D5
Rosendale Ave ST5....55 F6
Rosendale Rd ST5.....56 A5
Roseneath Pl ST2.....43 B1
Rose St ST1...........57 E5
Rose Tree Ave ST4....71 E4
Rose Tree La DE11....186 F7
Rosevale Bsns Pk ST5..55 F8
Rosevale Cl ST5......55 E8
Rosevale St ST5......55 E8
Rosevale St ST2......43 B1
Roseville Dr CW12
Roseville Gdns WV8...239 A4
Rose Way WS15.......178 C2
Rosewood Ave ST9.....43 C4
Rosewood Cl
  Little Aston B74.....257 D5
  Tamworth B77.......250 D4
Rosewood Ct B77.....250 D4
Rosewood Gdns
  Essington WV11.....242 B3
  Stafford ST16.......155 D5
Rosewood Pk WS6.....226 D2
Rosewood Rd DE15....185 D4
Rosewood Sch DY1....271 E1
Rosliston Rd DE15....185 E7
Rosliston Rd S DE15..185 E5
Rosliston Rd
  Swadlincote DE15....185 D3
  Walton-On-Trent DE12.202 E8
Rossall Ave ST5.......70 F5
Ross Cl Longton ST3...74 A4
  Wolverhampton WV6..255 F2
Ross Dr DY5..........275 C7
Rossett Gr ST6.......41 F8
Rosslyn Rd ST3.......284 C2
Rossmore Cl ST10.....62 C2
Rosvean Cl ST1.......282 B4
Rosy Bank ST9........43 C3
Rosy Cross B79.......250 B5
Rotary Ho DY1.......271 F1
Rothbury Gn WS12....210 E2
Rother Wlk ST6.......42 A4
Rotherwood Dr ST17..285 A1
Rothesay Ave ST5.....70 F7
Rothesay Ct Longton ST3.73 D2
  Newcastle-u-L ST5...70 F7
Rothesay Dr DY8.....275 C3
Rothesay Rd ST3......73 D2
Rothley Gn ST3........88 F7
Rothsay Ave ST1......57 D8
Rothwell St ST4.......71 F6
Rotten Row WS14.....231 C7
Rotterdam ST5........55 F1
Rotterdam Rd ST5.....55 F1
Rough Bank CW12......16 E8
Roughcote La ST11....74 C5
Rough Hills Cl WV2...266 F6
Rough Hills Rd WV2...266 F6
Roughley Dr B75.....258 C2
Roughley Farm Rd B75.258 E3
Roughlow La DE6......80 D1
Roundfields ST9.......43 C3
Round Hill DY3.......266 D2
Roundhill Way WS8...229 A2
Round House Rd DY3...271 E4
Roundway Down WV6..254 F3
Roundway ST3.........72 D2
Roundwell St ST6.....41 D3
Rouse Cl ST16........155 C7
Rowallan Rd B75.....258 D2
Rowanburn Cl ST3.....73 D5
Rowan Cl
  Biddulph Moor ST8...28 B8
  Kidsgrove ST7......41 A8
  Lichfield WS14......231 D8
  Stone ST15.........120 B6
Rowan Cres WV3......265 E7
Rowan Ct ST14........95 E4
Rowan Dr Armitage WS15.198 C3
  Essington WV11.....242 B3
  Newport TF10.......168 F1
Rowan Glade ST17....175 C6
  Burntwood WS7......228 F7
  Stoke-on-T ST4......72 E3
Rowan La TF9.........99 F5
Rowan Pl ST5.........55 D8
Rowan Rd Cannock WS11.209 C2
  Market Drayton TF9..97 C2
  Sedgley DY3........266 F1
Rowan Rise DY6......275 E6
Rowbury Dr DE15.....167 B2
Rowena Gdns DY3.....266 C2
Rowhurst Cl ST5......55 D7
Rowhurst Pl ST6......42 C5
Rowland St ST3.......73 B1
Rowley Ave
  Newcastle-u-L ST5...55 F7
  Stafford ST17.......285 A1

Rowley Bank Gdns ST17.174 E8
Rowley Bank Ho ST17..174 E8
Rowley Bank ST17.....174 E8
Rowley Cl Cannock WS12.210 B8
  Edingale B79........217 C5
  Rugeley WS15.......197 A6
Rowley Hall Cl ST17...174 C8
Rowley Hall Dr ST17...174 C8
Rowley Hall Hospl ST17.174 D8
Rowleyhill Dr ST19...206 F4
Rowley St ST16.......155 D5
Row Moor Way ST6.....42 E2
Rownall Pl [2] ST3....74 A2
Rownall Rd Meir ST3..74 A1
  Werrington ST9......59 D5
Rownall View ST13....30 C4
Rowney Cl ST1........57 F6
Rownton Cl B74......257 D4
Row The ST18........137 F4
Rowton Ave WV6.....254 E4
Rowton St DE13......166 C6
Roxall Cl DY10.......281 C2
Roxburghe Ave ST3...284 C2
Royal Cl Rugeley WS15.196 D7
  Stoke-on-T ST2......43 A3
Royal Oak Dr ST19...221 E8
Royal St ST4.........284 A5
Royal Way ST2........43 B3
Royal Wlk ST10.......76 D3
Royal Wolverhampton Sch
  The WV3...........266 B7
Royce Ave ST8........27 B5
Roycroft Cl ST5......56 B8
Royden Ave ST1......57 F4
Royds Cl ST18.......172 E6
Roylance St ST6......41 D3
Royston Chase B74...257 A3
Royston Way DY3....271 C8
Royston Wlk ST3.....284 C3
Royville Pl ST6.......57 F8
Rozel Ave DY10......280 B1
Ruabon Cl ST8........27 E6
Rubens Cl DY3.......271 D5
Rubens Way ST3.......90 B7
Rubian St ST4.........72 F6
Rudge Dale Rd TF9...100 A4
Rudge Rd WV6.......263 B7
Rudyard Cl Stone ST15.104 E2
  Wolverhampton WV10.240 E4
Rudyard Gr ST5.......56 C4
Rudyard Ho ST13......18 E3
Rudyard Lake Steam Rly★
  ST13...............18 E2
Rudyard Lake Visitors Ctr★
  ST13...............18 E1
Rudyard Rd Biddulph ST8.17 C1
  Poolend ST13.......19 A1
  Rudyard ST13.......29 E8
Rudyard Vale Cvn Pk
  ST13...............18 D2
Rudyard Way ST10.....76 F4
Ruelow Mdw ST10.....62 A7
Ruffin Ct ST15.......120 C7
Rufford B79.........249 E6
Rugby Cl Burton u T DE14.185 D4
  Newcastle-u-L ST5...70 F4
Rugby Dr ST3.........73 C1
Rugby Rd DY8........279 D7
Rugeley Rd
  Armitage WS15......197 D5
  Burntwood,Chase Terrace
    WS7.............211 F2
  Burntwood,Gorstey Ley
    WS7.............229 C7
  Cannock WS12.......211 B7
  King's Bromley DE13.199 A5
  Rugeley WS15.......196 D1
Rugeley Town Sta SW15.196 E6
Rugeley Trent Valley Sta
  WS15..............178 F3
Ruiton St DY3........271 D4
Rumbold Ave ST10....215 D6
Rumer Hill Bsns Est
  WS11..............226 E7
Rumer Hill Rd WS11..226 F8
Running Hills WS15..197 F4
Runnymede Cl ST2....58 B3
Runnymede ST15......120 A6
Rupert St [1] ST8.....27 C8
Rushall Cl DY8.......279 E8
Rushall JMI Sch WS4..244 B1
Rushall Rd WV10.....240 C1
Rushbrook WS8......244 D6
Rushcliffe Dr ST5.....90 B7
Rushes Mill WS3.....243 E3
Rushey La WV7.......252 D8
Rushford Ave WV5...270 A6
Rush La
  Market Drayton TF9..97 A2
  Tamworth B77,B78...261 D4
Rushmoor Gr [4] ST3..90 B7
Rushton Ave ST15....120 D7
Rushton Cl ST6.......61 D2
Rushton CE Prim Sch SK11.8 B2
Rushton Cl Brown Edge ST6.43 B7
  Tutbury DE13.......146 C6
Rushton Gr [1] ST6...57 A7
Rushton Mews WS12..211 C4
Rushton ST5..........70 F4
Rushton Rd ST6.......57 A7
Rushtons La ST15....105 F6
Rushton Way ST11....91 A8
Rushwater Cl WV5...269 E6
Ruskin Ave Dudley DY3..271 A1
  Wolverhampton WV4..266 F2
Ruskin Cl ST3........284 D5
Ruskin Dr ST18.......154 E7
Ruskin Glass Ctr★ DY8.279 F7

Ruskin Pl DE14.......166 D6
Ruskin Rd WV10.....241 A1
Rusper Cl ST1........57 F6
Russell Bank Rd B74..257 E4
Russell Cl Congleton CW12.16 A8
  Tamworth B77.......261 E6
  Uttoxeter ST14......126 D8
  Wolverhampton WV11.241 F1
Russell Ct ST4.......257 D3
Russell Gr ST9........59 B4
Russell Ho B77......250 F2
Russell Pl ST6.......41 D6
Russell Rd ST6.......41 D6
Russells Hall Prim Sch
  DY1...............271 E1
Russell's Hall Rd DY1.271 F1
Russell St
  Burton u T DE14.....166 D2
  Leek ST13..........30 E5
  Longton ST3........284 B1
  Newcastle-u-L ST5...56 C5
Russel St ST16.......285 A3
Russet Cl [2] ST3.....90 A7
Russett Cl WS7......229 A6
Russetts The ST17...174 F6
Russet Wlk WV8.....239 E1
Rustington Ave ST3...73 E3
Ruston Ave ST6.......42 B6
Rutherford Ave ST5...71 B3
Rutherford Ct ST18..156 C5
Rutherford Ct ST4....71 E7
Rutherglen Cl WS15..178 C1
Ruthin Gr ST8........27 E6
Ruthin Rd ST2.......58 D2
Rutland Ave
  Rugeley WS15.......196 D6
  Wolverhampton WV4..265 D4
Rutland Cl DE15......185 D6
Rutland Cres WS9....245 B1
Rutland Dr B78......250 A1
Rutland Pl
  Newcastle-u-L ST5...71 C4
  Stourbridge DY8....279 D8
Rutland Rd
  Cannock WS12.......210 C1
  Kidsgrove ST7......26 A2
  Longton ST3........284 C4
Rutland St ST1.......282 A4
Ruxley Cl ST2........57 F3
Ruxley Rd ST2.......58 A3
Ryandra Bsns Pk ST10..76 B2
Ryburn Cl CW2
Rycroft CE Mid Sch ST14.95 E4
Rydal Aldridge B74...256 F2
  Cannock WS12.......210 A8
Rydal Dr WV6........254 F4
Rydal Est WS15......178 F3
Rydal Ho ST16.......285 C3
Rydal B77...........262 A7
Rydal Way ST5.......71 B4
Rydal Way ST3.......284 C3
Ryder Cl DE11.......186 C2
Ryder Rd ST3........90 A8
Ryders Hayes Com Sch
  WS3...............244 A5
Ryders Hayes La WS3..244 B4
Ryder St DY8........275 C3
Rye Bank Cres ST5...283 B3
Rye Bank ST5........283 B3
Ryebrook Gr ST6.....41 F6
Ryecroft Ave WV4...266 B5
Ryecroft Sedgley DY3.271 C8
  Upper Tean ST10....92 F3
Ryecroft Cotts WV4..266 B5
Ryecroft Ct [3] WS7..229 A8
Ryecroft ST5.........283 B3
Ryecroft Sh Ctr WS7.229 A8
Rye Ct ST15.........155 A5
Ryedale Way CW12....16 C8
Ryefield WV8........239 E1
Ryehills ST7.........39 E1
Ryeland Cl ST3.......89 C8
Ryhope Wlk WV9.....240 A3
Ryknild St WS13.....215 E7
Ryknild Cl B74......257 F6
Ryknild St Alrewas DE13.201 A2
  Lichfield WS14.....231 E6
Ryknild Trad Est DE14.166 E6
Rylands Dr WV4.....266 A4
Rylcroft [7] WV4.....266 F4
Rylestone Cl ST3.....90 B7
Ryle St WS3.........243 D1
Ryton B77..........261 F8
Ryton Way DE65.....147 D8

S
Sabine St ST17.......285 C1
Sabrina Rd WV6.....254 E1
Sackville St ST4.....56 E1
Saddler Ave ST15....120 D7
Saddlers Cl WS14....231 E8
Saddlestones The WV6.254 D4
Saddleworth Rd WS3..243 A4
Sadler Ctr WS8......245 A8
Sadler Rd WS8.......245 A8
Sadlers Mill WS8....245 A7
Saffron Cl
  Barton-u-N DE13....183 C1
  Meir ST3...........90 A6
Saffron Gdns WV4...266 A4
Saffron B77.........251 B4
Sage Cl ST1.........282 B4
St Aidan's Cl DE13...166 C8
St Aidan's Cl WV4...266 A5
St Aidan's Rd WS11..209 E5

St Aidan's St ST6......41 D4
St Albans Cl WV11....242 A1
St Albans Ct DE13....166 C7
St Albans Rd ST16....155 E7
St Andrew Cl WS12...211 A5
St Andrews Ave WS3..244 B4
St Andrew's CE Prim Sch
  B79................218 E1
St Andrews CE Prim Sch
  Weston ST18........138 D2
  Wolverhampton WV6..255 F4
St Andrew's Cl
  Clifton Campville B79.218 F2
  Dudley DY3.........271 A3
St Andrews Cl DY3....279 F2
St Andrews Cres ST1..57 D7
St Andrews Dr DE13..166 C8
St Andrews Dr ST7....26 C3
St Andrew's Dr ST5...70 F8
St Andrews Dr WV6...254 D5
St Andrews Rd WS17..174 C7
St Andrew's Sq [3] ST4.72 A7
St Andrews B77......251 B4
St Andrews Way TF10.168 E1
St Anne's CE Prim Sch
  ST6................28 E1
St Anne's Cl WS7....228 E4
St Anne's RC Prim Sch
  ST17..............175 D7
St Annes Rd WS13....214 B3
St Anne's Rd WV10..240 B1
St Anne's Vale ST6...43 B8
St Ann St ST1........282 C3
St Ann Wlk ST1......282 C3
St Anthonys Cl WS15.196 F8
St Anthonys Cl ST4..72 B5
St Anthony's Dr ST5..71 A7
St Anthonys Dr ST3..244 B5
St Anthony's RC Prim Sch
  WV10..............240 D3
St Augustine's CE Fst Sch
  DE6...............144 D5
St Augustines Dr CW2.37 D4
St Augustine's RC Prim Sch
  ST3...............89 F8
St Augustine's Rd WS15.196 E6
St Austell Cl
  Stafford ST17.......175 D8
  Tamworth B79.......250 A6
St Austin's RC Prim Sch
  ST17..............285 C2
St Barbara Ho WS15..178 E1
St Barbara's Rd WS15.178 E1
St Bartholomew's CE Prim
  Sch SK17...........13 B7
St Bartholomew's CE Prim
  Sch WV4...........265 E3
St Bartholomews ST6..42 E4
St Bede's Sch WS15..178 A6
St Benedict Bishop CE Prim
  Sch WV3...........270 B7
St Benedict's Dr ST18.177 D8
St Benedict's Rd WS7.229 B6
St Benedicts Rd WS5.270 A6
St Bernadette's RC Prim Sch
  WS8...............244 F8
St Bernadettes RC Prim Sch
  WV5...............269 F6
St Bernard Pl ST2....58 A5
St Bernard's Cl WS12.211 D4
St Bernard's Rd ST5..55 F2
St Bertelin Cl ST16..155 C6
St Blaise Rd B75.....258 D3
St Brides Cl Sedgley DY3.271 C8
  Wombourne WV5....269 F6
St Catherines Cl ST14.126 D8
St Catherine's Cres WV4.265 F4
St Catherines Rd WS13.214 B3
St Catherine's Rd DE11.186 F5
St Chad Ct B77......250 F2
St Chad's CE Prim Sch
  Lichfield WS13.....231 C8
  Newcastle-u-L ST5..40 D2
St Chads CE Prim Sch
  WV6...............253 C3
St Chads Cl ST19....223 D6
St Chad's Cl
  Burton u T DE13.....166 C8
  Cannock WS11......210 A4
St Chads Cl ST18....177 D7
St Chad's Cl
  Denstone ST14......95 D6
  Dudley DY3.........271 B3
St Chads Cl
  Lichfield WS13.....214 B1
  Pattingham WV6....253 C2
St Chad's Cl ST15...120 C7
St Chad's Cl [3] WS13.231 B8
St Chad's Pl ST6.....285 B3
St Chads RC Prim Sch
  DY3...............271 D7
St Chad's Rd DE13..166 C7
St Chad's Rd ST21..133 D6
St Chad's Rd WS13..214 C1
St Chads Rd ST6.....41 E3
St Chads Way TF9....82 C2
St Christopher Cl WS12.211 A5
St Christopher's Cl ST4.72 B5
St Christopher's Dr B77.250 C1
St Christophers RC Prim Sch
  WV8...............239 A3
St Clair St ST3......284 C2
St Clements Cl CW2..37 B1
St David Cl WS12....211 A6
St Davids Cl WS3....244 B5

St David's Dr DE13 . . . . . 166 D8
St Davids Pl WS3 . . . . . 243 D2
St Davids Rd
　Clifton Campville B79 . . . . 218 F2
　Stafford ST17 . . . . 174 D7
St Davids Way ST8 . . . . . . 27 E6
St Dominics Ct ST4 . . . . . 72 A8
St Dominics Ind Jun Sch
　ST4 . . . . 71 F8
St Dominic's Priory Sch
　ST15 . . . . 104 F1
St Dominic's RC Prim Sch
　ST15 . . . . 105 A1
St Dominic's Sch ST19 . . 223 C7
St Editha's Cl B79 . . . . . 250 B5
St Editha's Ct
　Church Eaton ST20 . . . . . 190 B8
　Tamworth B79 . . . . 250 B7
St Edmund's Ave ST5 . . . . 56 D6
St Edmund's Cl WV6 . . . . 255 F3
St Edmunds RC Sch
　WV3 . . . . 255 E3
St Edward's CE Fst Sch
　ST13 . . . . 45 B5
St Edwards CE Mid Sch
　ST13 . . . . 30 C5
St Edwards Ct DE11 . . . . 186 F5
St Edwards Gn WS15 . . . . 196 E7
St Edward's Hall ST13 . . . 45 C7
St Edward's Rd ST13 . . . . 45 C4
St Edward St ST13 . . . . . 30 E5
Sainte Foy Ave WS13 . . . 231 A6
St Elizabeth's RC Prim Sch
　B79 . . . . 249 F8
St Filumena's RC Prim Sch
　ST11 . . . . 74 E2
St Foy Ave WS13 . . . . . . 230 F5
St Francis Cl
　Burton u T DE13 . . . . . . 166 D8
　Cannock WS12 . . . . 211 A5
　Walsall WS3 . . . . 244 B5
St Francis of Assisi RC Sch
　WS9 . . . . 256 C6
St Francis RC Prim Sch
　WS4 . . . . 244 C1
St Gabriel's RC Prim Sch
　B77 . . . . 250 E1
St George Dr WS12 . . . . 211 A5
St George & St Martin's RC
　Prim Sch ST1 . . . . . . 282 C4
St Georges Ave ST9 . . . . 43 E6
St George's Ave N ST5 . . . 56 B5
St George's Ave S ST5 . . . 56 B5
St Georges Ave ST6 . . . . 42 B4
St George's Ave W ST5 . . . 56 B5
St George's Cres ST4 . . . . 72 A1
St Georges Ct B74 . . . . . 257 E5
St Georges Hospl ST16 . . 285 C4
St George's Rd
　Burton u T DE13 . . . . . . 165 F5
　Newcastle-u-L ST5 . . . . 283 A2
　Stafford ST17 . . . . 156 A2
　Stone ST15 . . . . 120 B8
　Stourbridge DY8 . . . . . . 279 D2
St George's St 4 ST13 . . . 30 E4
St George's Way B77 . . . 250 F4
St Giles Gr ST18 . . . . . . 172 F6
St Giles' RC Prim Sch
　ST10 . . . . 76 D3
St Giles Rd WS7 . . . . . . 229 B6
St Gile's Rd ST5 . . . . . . 55 F2
St Giles & St George's CE
　Prim Sch ST5 . . . . . . 283 C4
St Gregory's RC Prim Sch
　ST3 . . . . 284 B3
St Gregory's Rd ST3 . . . . 284 A3
St Helens Rd WS13 . . . . 214 B3
St Helier Cl ST5 . . . . 70 F3
St Hilda's Ave ST13 . . . . . 45 C4
St Ives Cl Stafford ST17 . . 175 B8
　Tamworth B79 . . . . 250 B6
St James CE Prim Sch
　Longdon WS15 . . . . . . 198 A2
　Stourbridge DY8 . . . . . . 279 D7
St James Cl
　Longdon WS15 . . . . . . 198 A1
　Walsall WS3 . . . . 244 B5
St James Cres ST17 . . . . 193 B8
St James Ct Audley ST7 . . 39 D2
　Barton-u-N DE13 . . . . . 183 D2
St James' Ct ST8 . . . . . . 16 E3
St James Gdns WS8 . . . . 244 F7
St James Gn ST21 . . . . . 102 E3
St James Pl ST4 . . . . 72 A1
St James Prim Sch WS8 . . 244 F8
St James' Rd DE13 . . . . . 183 D1
St James Rd
　Cannock WS11 . . . . . . 209 C1
　Norton Canes WS11 . . . . 228 B5
　Sutton Coldfield B75 . . . 258 C2
St James' St DY3 . . . . . . 271 D3
St James St ST1 . . . . . . 282 A2
St James Wlk WS8 . . . . . 244 F7
St John Cl B75 . . . . 258 D4
St John Fisher RC High Sch
　ST5 . . . . 283 A4
St John's Ave
　Newcastle-u-L ST5 . . . . . 56 C7
　Oulton ST15 . . . . 105 C3
　Stoke-on-T ST4 . . . . 71 E4
St John's CE Fst Sch
　ST19 . . . . 221 E7
St Johns CE Prim Sch
　WS9 . . . . 245 A3

St John's CE Prim Sch
　Cheddleton ST9 . . . . 60 A7
　Essington WV11 . . . . . . 242 A4
　Keele ST5 . . . . 69 F7
　Stafford ST16 . . . . 156 B4
St Johns Cl WS9 . . . . . . 244 F3
St Johns Cl WS7 . . . . . . 211 E1
St John's Cl
　Cannock WS11 . . . . . . 226 D8
　Lichfield WS13 . . . . . . 231 B6
St Johns Cl
　Rugeley WS15 . . . . 196 C8
　Stowe-by-Chartley ST18 . . 139 C3
St John's Cl DY3 . . . . . . 269 D2
St John's Ct
　Burton u T DE13 . . . . . . 166 C7
　Cannock WS12 . . . . . . 210 E1
　Walsall WS3 . . . . 243 B1
St John's Dr
　Shenstone WS14 . . . . . 246 F5
　Swadlincote DE11 . . . . . 186 C5
St John's Hill WS14 . . . . 246 F5
St Johns Ho B74 . . . . . . 257 E3
St Johns Pl ST8 . . . . 27 D7
St John's Pl Biddulph ST8 . 27 D7
　Newcastle-u-L ST5 . . . . . 55 F2
St John's Prep Sch
　WS15 . . . . 213 A8
St John's Prim Sch DY3 . . 269 E2
St John's Rd
　ST10 . . . . 78 E1
　ST18 . . . . 158 B2
St Johns Rd TF9 . . . . . . 100 C5
St Johns Rd ST8 . . . . 27 D7
St Johns Rd WS8 . . . . . 245 A5
St John's Rd
　Burton u T DE13 . . . . . . 166 C7
　Cannock WS13 . . . . . . 226 E7
　Congleton CW12 . . . . . . 6 A5
St Johns Rd
　Essington WV11 . . . . . . 242 A3
　Stafford ST17 . . . . 174 D8
St John's Rd ST17 . . . . . 174 D8
St Johns Rd WS3 . . . . . 244 B5
St Johns Ret Pk 3 WV2 . . 266 C8
St Johns Sch WS13 . . . . 231 B7
St John's Sq
　8 Burslem ST6 . . . . . . 56 F8
　Uttoxeter ST14 . . . . . . 110 F1
St John's St B79 . . . . . . 250 B5
St John St Hanley ST1 . . . 282 C4
　Lichfield WS13 . . . . . . 231 B7
St Johns Way TF9 . . . . . 100 C5
St John's Wlk ST16 . . . . 156 A3
St Johns Wood ST5 . . . . . 25 F1
St Johns Wood WS14 . . . 247 A5
St John The Evangelist RC
　Prim Sch (Annexe) ST7 . 25 F1
St Joseph & St Theresa RC
　Prim Sch WS7 . . . . . 228 E6
St Josephs Cl WS3 . . . . 244 A4
St Joseph's Coll ST4 . . . . 71 F3
St Joseph's Convent Sch
　WV6 . . . . 255 E6
St Josephs Ct WV4 . . . . 265 D6
St Joseph's RC Prim Sch
　Cannock WS12 . . . . . . 210 C4
　Lichfield WS14 . . . . . . 231 C7
　Rugeley WS15 . . . . 196 F7
　Uttoxeter ST14 . . . . . . 126 B8
St Joseph St ST4 . . . . . . 41 D7
St Jude's CE Prim Sch
　WV3 . . . . 255 F3
St Jude's Ct 4 WV6 . . . . 255 F3
St Jude's Rd WV6 . . . . . 255 F3
St Jude's Rd W WV6 . . . . 255 F3
St Jude's Way DE13 . . . . 166 C8
St Lawrence CE Prim Sch
　ST20 . . . . 171 E6
St Lawrence Rd WS11 . . . 210 B2
St Lawrence View SK17 . . 23 B2
St Lawrence Way ST20 . . 171 D7
St Leonard's Ave
　Ipstones ST10 . . . . 62 A8
　Stafford ST17 . . . . 156 A1
St Leonard's CE Fst Sch
　Dunston ST18 . . . . 192 F8
　Ipstones ST10 . . . . 62 A8
St Leonard's CE Prim Sch
　B79 . . . . 234 C1
St Leonard's Ct
　ST17 . . . . 156 A1
St Leonards View ST8 . . . 262 F8
St Leonard's Way CW3 . . 67 C1
St Lucy's Dr ST5 . . . . . . 56 C7
St Lukes CE Prim Sch
　ST9 . . . . 43 E7
St Luke's CE Prim Sch
　Hanley ST1 . . . . 282 C2
　Newcastle-u-L ST5 . . . . . 55 A2
St Luke's CE Prim Sch
　WV2 . . . . 266 B7
St Luke's Cl
　Cannock WS11 . . . . . . 226 D8
　Newcastle-u-L ST5 . . . . . 55 B2
St Lukes Cl ST15 . . . . . . 135 A8
St Lukes Cl ST1 . . . . . . 282 C2
St Lukes Prim Sch (Inf Site)
　WV2 . . . . 266 C7
St Luke's Rd
　Barton-u-N DE13 . . . . . 183 D1
　Burntwood WS7 . . . . . . 229 C6
　Burton u T DE13 . . . . . . 166 C8
St Luke St ST1 . . . . 282 C2
St Luke's Wlk WS15 . . . . 198 C4
St Margarets DE13 . . . . 165 F5

St Margaret's CE Jun Sch
　ST5 . . . . 56 D4
St Margaret's Ct CW3 . . . 53 B6
St Margaret's Ct
　Draycott in t M ST11 . . . . 91 E5
　Newcastle-u-L ST5 . . . . . 56 D5
St Margaret's Dr ST1 . . . . 57 E8
St Margarets Gr ST3 . . . . 72 E3
St Margarets Rd WS13 . . 214 B3
St Margaret's Rd B79 . . . 250 B7
St Margarets Rd WS3 . . . 244 A4
St Margaret's B74 . . . . . 257 C3
St Margaret Ward RC Sch &
　Arts Coll ST16 . . . . . . 41 F5
St Maria Goreti RC Prim Sch
　ST2 . . . . 58 C2
St Mark's CE Prim Sch
　ST1 . . . . 282 A1
St Marks Cl WS6 . . . . . . 226 F4
St Mark's Cl ST1 . . . . . . 282 A2
St Marks Rd WS8 . . . . . 245 A5
St Mark's Rd
　Burntwood WS7 . . . . . . 229 C6
　Burton u T DE13 . . . . . . 166 C8
St Marks Rd WS3 . . . . . 244 A4
St Mark's St ST1 . . . . . . 282 A1
St Martin Noel's Almshouses
　ST16 . . . . 285 B3
St Martin's Cl
　Burton u T DE13 . . . . . . 166 C8
　Wolverhampton WV2 . . . 266 E6
St Martin's La ST3 . . . . . 284 C4
St Martin's Pl ST16 . . . . 285 B3
St Martin's Rd
　Newcastle-u-L ST5 . . . . . 70 F8
　Talke Pits ST7 . . . . 40 E6
St Mary of the Angels RC
　Prim Sch WS9 . . . . . 256 B5
St Mary & St Chad CE Fst
　Sch ST19 . . . . 223 C6
St Mary's CE Fst Sch
　Uttoxeter ST14 . . . . . . 111 B1
　Wheaton Aston ST19 . . . 205 C7
St Marys CE Prim Sch
　WV7 . . . . 237 B5
St Mary's CE Prim Sch
　Bosley SK11 . . . . 7 D8
　Colton ST10 . . . . 178 F6
　Kingswinford DY6 . . . . . 275 D7
　Mucklestone TF9 . . . . . . 99 A7
　Stoke-on-T ST6 . . . . 41 D3
St Mary's Cl WV7 . . . . . 237 A5
St Marys Cl ST18 . . . . . 173 C1
St Mary's Cl
　Checkley ST10 . . . . 109 B8
　Newton Solney DE15 . . . 167 E8
　Sedgley DY3 . . . . 271 F8
St Marys Cl WV10 . . . . . 225 C2
St Mary's Cres ST14 . . . . 111 B1
St Mary's Ct 7 ST13 . . . . 30 E5
St Mary's Dr
　Burton u T DE13 . . . . . . 166 C8
　Newcastle-u-L ST5 . . . . . 71 A8
　Stretton DE13 . . . . 147 F2
St Mary's Gate ST16 . . . . 285 B3
St Mary's Gr ST13 . . . . . 30 E5
St Marys Gr B79 . . . . . . 236 D3
St Marys Mews ST16 . . . 285 B3
St Mary's Pl ST16 . . . . . 285 B3
St Marys RC Prim Sch
　ST19 . . . . 223 B6
St Mary's RC Prim Sch
　WS11 . . . . 226 E8
St Mary's RC Prim Sch
　Leek ST13 . . . . 30 E5
　Newcastle-u-L ST5 . . . . 283 A3
　Stoke-on-T ST6 . . . . 42 A3
St Mary's Rd
　Colwich ST18 . . . . 177 D8
　Lichfield WS13 . . . . . . 214 B3
　Loggerheads TF9 . . . . . . 99 D5
　Longton ST3 . . . . 73 D5
　Newcastle-u-L ST5 . . . . . 56 D5
St Mary's & St John's RC Sch
　WV2 . . . . 266 D8
St Mary's St
　Market Drayton TF9 . . . . 97 D1
　Newport TF10 . . . . 168 F3
St Mary's Way
　Aldridge WS9 . . . . 256 B5
　Tamworth B77 . . . . 250 E4
St Matthew Cl WS12 . . . . 211 A5
St Matthew's Ave WS7 . . 229 A5
St Matthews CE Prim Sch
　ST3 . . . . 89 E4
St Matthews Cl WS3 . . . . 244 B5
St Matthews Ct ST4 . . . . 72 F6
St Matthews Dr ST18 . . . 154 D2
St Matthew's Rd WS7 . . . 229 F7
St Matthew St ST4 . . . . . 72 F6
St Mawes Cl ST17 . . . . . 175 D8
St Mawes Rd WV6 . . . . . 255 A3
St Michael Rd WS13 . . . . 231 C8
St Michaels CE Fst Sch
　ST19 . . . . 192 E1
St Michael's CE Fst Sch
　Rudyard ST13 . . . . 18 C2
　Stone ST15 . . . . 120 C6
St Michael's CE Jun & Inf Sch
　WV6 . . . . 255 E5
St Michaels CE Prim Sch
　Annexe WS3 . . . . 244 A3
St Michael's CE Prim Sch
　Lichfield WS14 . . . . . . 231 C7
　Lichfield WS14 . . . . . . 231 C8
St Michaels CE Prim Sch
　WS3 . . . . 243 F2

St Michael's Cl
　Adbaston ST20 . . . . . . 131 C4
　Penkridge ST19 . . . . . . 207 E8
　Stafford ST17 . . . . 175 E8
St Michaels Cl ST15 . . . . 120 B8
St Michael's Cl WS3 . . . . 244 A2
St Michaels Cl CV9 . . . . 262 C1
St Michaels Ct 5 ST15 . . 120 A8
St Michael's Dr WV6 . . . 255 E5
St Michael's Dr WS12 . . . 211 A6
St Michael's Dr WS15 . . . 197 A5
St Michael's Hospl
　WS13 . . . . 231 D8
St Michaels Mount ST15 . 120 C6
St Michael's RC Prim Sch
　WV3 . . . . 265 D7
St Michaels Rd
　Burton u T DE13 . . . . . . 166 D8
　Dudley DY3 . . . . 270 F5
St Michael's Rd
　Newcastle-u-L ST5 . . . . . 56 B3
　Penkridge ST19 . . . . . . 207 E8
　Rugeley WS15 . . . . 197 A5
　Stoke-on-T ST6 . . . . 41 F5
　Stramshall ST14 . . . . . . 110 F4
St Michael's Sq ST19 . . . 192 E1
St Mildred's CE Prim Sch
　ST10 . . . . 62 D3
St Modwen Way ST19 . . . 207 F7
St Modwen's Cl DE13 . . . 166 C7
St Modwen's RC Prim Sch
　DE13 . . . . 166 B5
St Modwen's Wlk DE14 . . 166 E2
St Nicholas Ave ST6 . . . . 42 E4
St Nicholas CE Fst Sch
　WV8 . . . . 238 F4
St Nicholas Cl WS3 . . . . 244 A4
St Nicholas Way WS15 . . 160 F6
St Oswald's CE Fst Sch
　DY10 . . . . 280 A1
St Patrick Cl WS12 . . . . 211 A6
St Patrick's Dr ST5 . . . . . 70 F8
St Patrick's Pl ST16 . . . . 285 B3
St Patrick's RC Prim Sch
　ST16 . . . . 285 B4
St Patricks Rd 3 DE13 . . 166 D8
St Patricks's Pl ST16 . . . 285 B4
St Patrick's St ST16 . . . . 285 B4
St Paul's CE Fst Sch
　WV9 . . . . 224 B3
St Paul's CE Prim Sch
　ST17 . . . . 285 C2
St Pauls CE Prim Sch
　WV9 . . . . 240 A2
St Paul's Cl
　Cannock WS11 . . . . . . 210 B1
　Coven WV9 . . . . 224 C2
St Pauls Cres WS3 . . . . 244 B5
St Paul's Ct
　Burton u T DE14 . . . . . . 166 B3
　Stoke-on-T ST3 . . . . 72 C2
　Tamworth B77 . . . . 261 C4
St Paul's Mews 2 WS15 . 196 F8
St Pauls Rd 1 WS15 . . . 196 F8
St Paul's Rd
　Burntwood WS7 . . . . . . 229 C6
　Cannock WS11 . . . . . . 210 F3
　Newcastle-u-L ST5 . . . . 283 A2
St Paul's St W DE14 . . . . 166 B4
St Paul's Sq ST16 . . . . . 166 B3
St Paul St ST6 . . . . 56 E8
St Peter & St Paul RC Prim
　Sch
　Lichfield WS13 . . . . . . 214 B1
　Newport TF10 . . . . 168 E3
St Peter's Bridge DE14 . . 166 E1
St Peter's CE Fst Sch
　Alton ST10 . . . . 78 E1
　Marchington ST14 . . . . . 127 F2
St Peter's CE High Sch &
　International Language Coll
　ST4 . . . . 71 F7
St Peter's CE Prim Sch
　WS12 . . . . 210 D4
St Peter's CE Prim Sch
　Caverswall ST11 . . . . . . 74 D2
　Edgmond TF10 . . . . . . 168 A1
St Peter's CE Prim Sch
　ST18 . . . . 158 B7
St Peter's Cl ST17 . . . . . 174 F6
St Peters Cl
　Stonnall WS9 . . . . 245 E4
　Tamworth B77 . . . . 250 D1
St Peter's Collegiate CE Sch
　WV3 . . . . 255 E3
St Peters Ct
　Burton u T DE15 . . . . . . 166 F1
　Lichfield WS13 . . . . . . 214 B2
St Peter's Ct ST20 . . . . . 151 A4
St Peters Ct WS3 . . . . . 243 B1
St Peters Dr WS3 . . . . . 244 A4
St Peters Gdns ST17 . . . 174 F5
St Peters La ST11 . . . . . 91 A7
St Peter's Rd
　Burntwood WS7 . . . . . . 229 C6
　Cannock WS12 . . . . . . 210 D4
St Peter's St DE15 . . . . . 166 F1
St Peter's Wlk ST6 . . . . . 57 A6
St Phillip's Ave WV3 . . . . 265 F7
St Phillips Ave WV3 . . . . 265 F8
St Phillip's Gr WV3 . . . . 265 F7

St Michael's Cl
St Saviour's CE Prim Sch
　ST7 . . . . 25 D1
St Saviour's Cl WV2 . . . 266 F6
St Saviour's St ST7 . . . . . 25 D1
St Stephens Ct
　Burton u T DE13 . . . . . . 166 C7
　Cannock WS12 . . . . . . 210 C4
　Great Haywood ST18 . . . 158 B2
St Stephen's Prim Sch
　WS13 . . . . 215 D7
St Stephen's Rd WS7 . . . 229 C6
St Teresa's RC Prim Sch
　ST4 . . . . 71 F2
St Teresa's RC Prim Sch
　WV4 . . . . 266 C5
St Thomas Aquinas RC Prim
　Sch ST4 . . . . 56 F1
St Thomas CE Prim Sch
　ST7 . . . . 26 A1
St Thomas' Cl WS9 . . . . 245 B1
St Thomas Dr WS12 . . . 211 A5
St Thomas La ST18 . . . . 156 D3
St Thomas More RC Coll
　ST3 . . . . 73 A3
St Thomas More RC Prim
　Sch WS6 . . . . 227 A4
St Thomas Pl ST4 . . . . . 71 F7
St Thomas' RC Prim Sch
　ST10 . . . . 92 E4
St Thomas's Rd ST10 . . . 92 E4
St Thomas St Mow Cop ST7 26 E7
　Stafford ST16 . . . . 156 A3
St Vincent Mews WS15 . . 104 D4
St Vincent Pl ST5 . . . . . 55 F2
St Vincent Rd ST15 . . . . 119 F7
St Werburgh's CE Prim Sch
　Hanbury DE13 . . . . . . 145 A4
　Kingsley ST10 . . . . 61 E2
St Wilfrid's RC Prim Sch
　ST6 . . . . 41 F3
St Wulstan's RC Prim Sch
　ST5 . . . . 56 D4
Salcombe Ave ST17 . . . . 175 D8
Salcombe Cl WS11 . . . . 226 C2
Salcombe Pl ST1 . . . . . . 57 D7
Sale La DE13 . . . . 200 C1
Salem St ST1 . . . . 56 F3
Sales La DE15 . . . . 167 C4
Salisbury Ave
　Burton u T DE15 . . . . . . 167 D3
　Hanley ST1 . . . . 282 B1
Salisbury Cl Dudley DY1 . 271 F3
　Lichfield WS13 . . . . . . 214 C3
　Madeley CW3 . . . . 68 F7
　Rugeley WS15 . . . . 196 C6
Salisbury Dr
　Cannock WS12 . . . . . . 210 B1
　Stafford ST16 . . . . 156 B4
Salisbury Hill View TF9 . . 112 B7
Salisbury Rd
　Market Drayton TF9 . . . . 112 B8
　Stafford ST16 . . . . 156 B4
Salisbury St Leek ST13 . . . 30 E6
　Stoke-on-T ST6 . . . . 41 E3
Salkeld Pl ST6 . . . . 42 B5
Sallow Gr WS8 . . . . 229 A1
Sallyfield La DE6 . . . . . . 65 E1
Sally Ward Dr WS9 . . . . 245 A4
Salmond Ave ST16 . . . . 156 B5
Salop Dr WS11 . . . . . . 226 F3
Salop Gr ST5 . . . . 71 C4
Salop Pl ST7 . . . . 26 A3
Salt Ave ST17 . . . . 285 C2
Salt Banks ST18 . . . . . . 137 C3
Saltbrook La DE6 . . . . . 144 F8
Saltdean Cl ST3 . . . . . . 73 E2
Salters Cl ST9 . . . . 59 B3
Salter's Ct TF10 . . . . . . 168 E3
Saltersford La ST10 . . . . 94 F8
Saltersford Rise ST15 . . . 104 E3
Salters Grange WS15 . . . 160 F6
Salters Green Way DE13 . 201 B3
Salter's La TF10 . . . . . . 168 E3
Salters La Tamworth B79 . 250 B6
　Werrington ST9 . . . . . . 59 B2
Salter's Mews TF10 . . . . 168 E3
Salter's Rd WS9 . . . . . . 245 A3
Salter St ST16 . . . . 285 B3
Salthealth La ST18 . . . . 137 E3
Saltings Mobile Home Pk
　The ST18 . . . . 156 D2
Salt La ST18 . . . . 137 D5
Salt Rd Salt ST18 . . . . . 137 E4
　Stafford ST17 . . . . 285 B1
Salts La B78 . . . . 260 E5
Salt Works La ST18 . . . . 138 D2
Sambar Rd B78 . . . . . . 249 F1
Sambrook Cres TF9 . . . . 97 E2
Sampson St ST1 . . . . . . 282 A3
Samuel Cl WS13 . . . . . . 214 C2
Samuel Ho WS3 . . . . . . 243 B1
Samuel Johnson's Birthplace
　Mus ★ WS13 . . . . . . 231 B8
Samuel St Packmoor ST7 . 26 F1
　Walsall WS3 . . . . 243 B1
Sancton Gn 2 ST6 . . . . . 56 E8
Sandalwood Dr ST16 . . . 155 F5
Sandalwood Rd DE15 . . . 185 E6
Sandbach Rd ST6 . . . . . 57 B7
Sand Bank WS3 . . . . . . 243 A1
Sandcrest Pl ST3 . . . . . 73 F1
Sandcrest Wlk ST3 . . . . 73 F1
Sanderling Cl WV10 . . . . 241 B7
Sanderling Rise WS7 . . . 229 B6
Sandfield Bridge DY5 . . . 271 B1
Sandfield Gr DY3 . . . . . 271 B2
Sandfield Mdw WS13 . . . 231 A6

Sandfield Rd DY8 .... 275 F2
Sandford Cl WS15.... 198 A8
Sandford Cres CW2 .... 37 D1
Sandford Hill Prim Sch ST3 .... 73 C6
Sandford Ho WS13.... 231 A7
Sandford Rd DY1 .... 271 E1
Sandford Rise WV6 .... 255 E6
Sandford St
  Lichfield WS13.... 231 B7
  Longton ST3.... 73 C5
  Newcastle-u-L ST5.... 55 E8
Sandgate St ST3 .... 73 D3
Sandhill St WS3 .... 243 A1
Sandhurst Ave 4 ST3.... 73 F1
Sandhurst Cl ST5.... 56 C4
Sandhurst Dr WV4 .... 266 A4
Sandhurst Gr DY8 .... 275 E3
Sandhurst Pl ST3 .... 89 F8
Sandhurst Rd B74.... 257 F5
Sandiford Cres TF10 .... 168 E2
Sandiway DE13 .... 201 E8
Sandiway Pl ST1.... 57 E6
Sandmere Rise WV10 .... 240 E1
Sandon Ave ST5 .... 71 A5
Sandon Cl ST11.... 91 C2
Sandon Ct ST3.... 89 F7
Sandon High Sch ST3.... 89 F8
Sandon Ho WV6 .... 255 C5
Sandon La ST18.... 122 C5
Sandon Mews ST16 .... 155 F6
Sandon Old Rd ST3 .... 89 F7
Sandon Rd Cresswell ST11. 91 C3
  Hilderstone ST15.... 106 D1
  Hopton ST18.... 137 C2
  Stafford ST16,ST18.... 155 F6
  Stoke-on-T ST3.... 89 F7
  Wolverhampton WV10 .... 240 B2
Sandon St Hanley ST1.... 57 A3
  Leek ST13.... 30 E3
Sandown Ave WS6 .... 226 E3
Sandown Cl
  Burntwood WS7.... 211 F1
  Burton u T DE14.... 185 A7
  Cannock WS12.... 211 A6
  Cheadle ST10.... 76 E5
Sandown Dr WV6 .... 254 F4
Sandown Pl ST2 .... 43 C2
Sandown Rd ST7.... 250 F5
Sandpiper Cl WS12.... 210 C7
Sandpiper Ct ST7 .... 26 C2
Sandpiper Dr ST14.... 126 B6
Sandpiper B77.... 262 A5
Sandra Cl Aldridge WS9 . 256 B5
  Stoke-on-T ST6.... 42 A2
Sand Rd DE13.... 164 C7
Sandringham Ave DE15. 167 A1
Sandringham Cl
  Burntwood WS7.... 211 E1
  Market Drayton TF9.... 97 C2
  Stafford ST17.... 175 C8
Sandringham Cres ST5.. 72 A1
Sandringham Dr WS9 .. 245 B1
Sandringham Pl DY8 .... 275 D1
Sandringham Rd
  Pattingham WV6.... 253 C2
  Stafford ST17.... 175 C8
  Stourbridge DY8.... 275 D1
  Wolverhampton WV4.... 266 A4
  Wombourne WV5.... 269 F6
Sandsdown Cl ST8.... 16 C1
Sands La ST6.... 28 B2
Sandstone Cl DY3.... 271 D4
Sandstone Ct B77.... 262 A7
Sandwell Pl ST3 .... 89 E8
Sandwell Rd WV10.... 240 B1
Sandwick Cres ST1 .... 57 F6
Sandwood Cres ST3.... 73 C5
Sandy Bank ST21 .... 102 C4
Sandybrook Cl ST13.... 30 F3
Sandybrook La ST13.... 30 F2
Sandy Cres WV11 .... 242 A1
Sandy Croft TF10.... 168 F3
Sandyfield Cl ST8.... 16 C1
Sandyfield Rd ST1.... 57 E6
Sandyfields Rd DY3.... 271 B6
Sandyfields ST5.... 85 C5
Sandyford Ct ST16.... 285 B4
Sandyford St ST16.... 155 E5
Sandy Gr WS8 .... 228 F1
Sandy Hill ST9.... 59 C4
Sandy Hollow WV6.... 255 C2
Sandy La Ashley TF9 .... 100 B7
  Blore TF9.... 98 C3
  Brewood ST19.... 223 C6
  Brown Edge ST6.... 43 B7
  Cannock WS11.... 209 B1
  Chapel Chorlton ST5 .... 85 C4
  Codsall WV8.... 238 F4
  Copmere End ST21 .... 132 D7
  Cotes Heath ST21.... 102 D4
  Hollington ST10.... 93 E7
  Kinver DY7,DY11.... 277 F1
  Linton DE12.... 186 A1
  Longsdon ST9.... 44 F8
  Market Drayton TF9.... 112 D6
  Newcastle-u-L ST5.... 283 D4
  Newton Regis B79.... 236 D6
  Rugeley WS15.... 196 E8
  Stoke-on-T ST2.... 43 C2
  Weston ST18.... 138 C4
  Whittington WS14.... 232 D4
  Wolverhampton,Bushbury WV10.... 240 E1
  Wolverhampton,Tettenhall WV6.... 255 E6
Sandy Mount WV5.... 270 B7

Sandy Rd Biddulph ST8 .... 16 C2
  Stoke-on-T ST6.... 41 D6
  Stourbridge DY8.... 279 D1
Sandy Way B77.... 251 B3
Sangster La ST6.... 42 D2
Sankey Cres WS15.... 196 E7
Sankey Rd WS11.... 209 F3
Sankey's Cnr WS7.... 228 F7
Sanstone Cl WS3.... 243 C3
Sanstone Rd WS3.... 243 C3
Sant St ST6.... 56 E8
Sapling Rise ST10.... 92 E3
Saplings Cl ST19.... 192 F1
Saplings The
  Newcastle-u-L ST5.... 71 C3
  Penkridge ST19.... 192 F1
  Stafford ST17.... 156 A1
Sapperton La DE65.... 129 F8
Sapphire Dr WS11.... 210 C3
Saracen Way 10 ST3 .... 74 A1
Sara Cl B74.... 258 A3
Sarah Challinor Cl 6 WS15.... 196 E8
Sarah Siddons Ho 2 WS13.... 231 B7
Saredon Cl WS3.... 244 A1
Saredon Rd
  Shareshill WV10.... 225 D2
  Wedges Mills WS6,WS11, WV10.... 226 B3
Sargeant Ave ST6.... 42 A6
Sark Cl ST5.... 70 E4
Sark Pl 1 ST3.... 73 D6
Sarraine Ind Pk ST10.... 76 B2
Sarver La ST10.... 75 D4
Sash St ST16.... 285 B4
Saturn Rd Cannock WS11. 210 A5
  Stoke-on-T ST6.... 42 C1
Saul Ct ST14.... 126 B7
Saunders Cl WS12.... 211 A6
Saunders Rd ST5.... 56 B4
Saverley Green Rd ST11. 106 E8
Savey La ST13.... 181 F2
Savoureuse Dr ST17.... 175 A8
Savoy Rd CW1.... 37 A8
Sawpit La ST17.... 176 A3
Sawyer Dr ST8.... 16 C1
Saxifrage Dr ST15.... 120 C6
Saxon Cl Burton u T DE15. 185 F7
  Great Wyrley WS6.... 227 A2
  Polesworth B78.... 251 F1
  Tamworth B77.... 261 D6
Saxoncourt WV6.... 255 C5
Saxon Ct WS13.... 230 E7
Saxondrive B79.... 250 C5
Saxonfields WV6.... 255 C5
Saxon Hill Sch WS14.... 231 C6
Saxon Mill La B79.... 250 C4
Saxon Rd ST19.... 207 F8
Saxon St DE15.... 185 F7
Saxon Wlk WS13.... 230 E7
Saxton Dr B74.... 257 F6
Sayers Rd ST16.... 155 C7
Scalpcliffe Cl DE15.... 166 F3
Scalpcliffe Rd DE15.... 166 F3
Scammerton B77.... 262 B7
Scamnell La ST21.... 134 E7
Scampton Cl WV6.... 254 E5
Scampton Way B79.... 250 C8
Scarecrow La B75.... 258 A4
Scarlett St ST5.... 283 B2
Scarratt Cl ST11.... 91 B8
Scarratt Dr ST11.... 91 B8
Sceptre St ST1.... 282 B2
Schofield La B79.... 217 D5
Sch of St Mary & St Anne WS15.... 161 A6
Scholar Green Prim Sch ST7.... 25 E6
Scholars Gate
  Burntwood WS7.... 229 D7
  Rugeley WS15.... 197 A5
Schoolacre Rise B74.... 256 E1
School Ave WS8.... 244 B8
School Bank ST10.... 94 B2
School Cl Audley ST7.... 40 A1
  Burntwood WS7.... 228 D8
  Codsall WV8.... 239 A4
  Dilhorne ST10.... 75 D4
  Leek ST13.... 30 C4
  Norton Canes WS11.... 228 B6
  Trysull WV5.... 269 C8
  Wolverhampton WV3.... 265 B2
School Cres WS11.... 228 A6
School Ct WS12.... 210 C6
School Dr Oakamoor ST10 . 78 A7
  Stourbridge DY8.... 279 D7
Schoolfields Rd WS14... 247 A5
Schoolgate Cl WS4.... 244 D1
School Ground La TF10.. 169 A3
School Ho Rd WS7.... 229 D7
School House La WS15.. 161 A6
School La
  Admaston WS15.... 159 F3
  Ashley TF9.... 100 B6
  Astbury CW12.... 15 B8
  Biddulph ST8.... 17 B1
  Bradnop ST13.... 31 E3
  Burntwood WS7.... 228 D8
  Caverswall ST3,ST11.... 74 D2
  Colton ST18.... 178 F6
  Coven WV9.... 224 B3
  Dunston ST18.... 192 D7
  Edingale B79.... 217 C5
  Gentleshaw WS15.... 212 A5
  Great Haywood ST18.... 158 B2
  Hill Ridware WS15.... 198 A8
  Hopwas B78.... 249 B7

School La continued
  Longsdon ST9.... 30 A2
  Maer TF9.... 84 A7
  Market Drayton TF9.... 112 A8
School Lane Cl ST17.... 174 F5
School La
  Norton Canes WS3.... 227 E2
  Onneley CW3.... 68 A1
  Rolleston on D DE13.... 147 B4
  Sandon ST18.... 137 E7
  Shareshill WV10.... 225 D2
  Shuttington B79.... 251 F7
  Stafford,Rickerscote ST17. 174 F5
  Stoke-on-T ST3.... 89 A8
  Stretton ST19.... 206 C3
  Sudbury DE6.... 128 E4
  Tamworth B77.... 261 D6
  Walsall WS3.... 243 F4
  Walton-on-t-H ST17.... 175 F6
  Warslow SK17.... 23 B1
  Weeford B78.... 248 D2
  Weston-Under-Lizard TF11 203 E2
  Wolverhampton WV10.... 240 E2
School Pl ST16.... 155 E5
School Rd Bagnall ST9 .... 43 F2
  Brewood ST19.... 223 C6
  Bucknall ST2.... 58 A5
  Eccleshall ST21.... 133 C4
  Edgmond TF10.... 168 A3
  Himley DY3.... 270 B3
  Norton Canes WS11.... 228 A6
  Rugeley WS15.... 178 D2
  Trysull WV5.... 269 C8
  Uttoxeter ST14.... 110 F1
  Wheaton Aston ST19.... 205 C5
  Wolverhampton,Tettenhall WV6.... 255 B3
  Wombourne WV5.... 270 B7
School St 3 Leek ST13.... 30 E6
  Newcastle-u-L,Broad Meadow ST5.... 55 F6
  Newcastle-u-L ST5.... 283 C3
  Sedgley ST3.... 271 E8
  Stoke-on-T ST4.... 71 E3
  Stourbridge DY8.... 279 F6
  Tamworth B77.... 250 B4
  Walsall WS4.... 244 D1
School View ST14.... 141 D4
School Wlk
  Burntwood WS7.... 228 D8
  Tamworth B79.... 250 B6
Scimitar Cl B79.... 249 E7
Scotch Orchard Prim Sch WS13.... 214 D1
Scotch Orch WS13.... 214 D1
Scot Hay Rd
  Alsagers Bank ST7.... 54 E5
  Newcastle-u-L ST5.... 54 F3
Scotia Bsns Pk ST6.... 41 E2
Scotia Rd Burslem ST6.... 41 F1
  Cannock WS11.... 209 D3
Scott Ave WV4.... 265 E4
Scott Cl WS14.... 231 B6
Scott Lidgett Ind Est ST6. 56 D8
Scott Lidgett Rd ST6.... 56 D7
Scott Rd Stoke-on-T ST6 .... 41 F4
  Tamworth B77.... 250 E4
Scotts Ho 1 ST16.... 155 D5
Scott's Rd DY8.... 279 F6
Scott St Cannock WS12.... 210 F3
  Newcastle-u-L ST5.... 283 C3
Scott Way WS7.... 211 F1
Scragg St ST7.... 41 F8
Scrimshaw Dr ST6.... 42 C3
Scrivener Rd ST4.... 56 F1
Scropton Old Rd DE65.... 146 C8
Scropton Rd Hatton DE65. 146 B8
  Scropton DE65.... 129 F1
Sculthorpe Rd DY10.... 281 B2
Seabridge Jun & Inf Schs ST5.... 71 A4
Seabridge La ST5.... 71 B4
Seabridge Rd ST5.... 283 A1
Seabrooke Rd WS15.... 197 A5
Seafield Cl DY6.... 275 E4
Seaford St ST4.... 57 B1
Seaforth Gr WV11.... 242 B1
Seagram Way ST14.... 126 D7
Seagrave Pl ST5.... 71 A6
Seagrave St ST5.... 283 C3
Searchlight La ST21.... 134 E7
Searle Ave ST16.... 155 C2
Seaton Ave ST17.... 175 E8
Seaton Cl ST3.... 89 E8
Seaton Pl DY8.... 275 E4
Seaton B77.... 261 F8
Sebring Ave ST3.... 89 E8
Seckham Rd 4 WS13.... 231 A8
Seckington La B79.... 236 C3
Second Ave
  Branston DE14.... 165 E1
  Brownhills WS8.... 229 A1
  Bucknall ST2.... 58 D4
  Kidsgrove ST7.... 25 E1
  Kingswinford,Wall Heath DY6.... 275 F8
  Newcastle-u-L ST5.... 56 C7
  Stafford ST17.... 155 C7
Sedbergh Cl ST5.... 70 F4
Seddon Ct ST1.... 282 C3
Seddon Rd ST3.... 89 F8
Sedgefield Cl DY1.... 271 E3
Sedgefield Gr ST4.... 72 A5
Sedgefield Rd DE14.... 184 F7
Sedgemoor Rd WS7.... 229 B5
Sedgefield Way WS11.... 228 B4
Sedgley Hall Ave DY3.... 271 C8

Sedgley Rd WV4.... 265 F2
Sedgley St WV2.... 266 C7
Sedgley Wlk ST3.... 284 C1
Seedcroft La WS15.... 160 F4
Seedfields Rd ST3.... 72 E3
Seeds La WS8.... 244 F8
Seedymill La WS13.... 213 E7
Seesall The ST20.... 171 E7
Sefton Ave Congleton CW12. 6 A1
  Stoke-on-T ST1.... 57 E7
Sefton Cl DE15.... 167 B1
Sefton Rd Longton ST3 .... 73 E2
  Tamworth B77.... 261 D4
Sefton St ST1.... 57 A3
Seighford Rd ST18.... 154 D5
Seisdon Rd WV5.... 264 A1
Selborne Rd ST13.... 30 E4
Selbourne Dr ST6.... 41 F7
Selby Cl ST5.... 71 A5
Selby St ST3.... 74 B5
Selby Way WS3.... 242 E2
Selby Wlk ST3.... 88 E7
Selker Dr B77.... 250 F5
Sellman St ST20.... 171 E6
Selmans Hill WS3.... 243 C2
Selman's Par WS3.... 243 C2
Selsdon Rd WS3.... 242 F3
Selwood Cl ST3.... 73 D1
Selworthy Dr ST17.... 175 E6
Selworthy Rd ST6.... 43 A5
Selwyn Cl Alrewas DE13 .. 201 A3
  Wolverhampton WV2.... 266 C7
Selwyn Ct ST21.... 133 E7
Selwyn Rd WS7.... 229 F8
Selwyn St ST4.... 72 B6
Selwyn Wlk B77.... 257 C4
Semper Cl CW12.... 6 A4
Senior Cl WV11.... 242 A3
Serin Cl ST14.... 126 C6
Seton Ho B74.... 257 E7
Setterfield Way WS15.... 196 F2
Settle Gr ST3.... 90 A7
Setton Dr ST3.... 271 E7
Seven Acres WS9.... 256 B5
Seven Arches Way ST4 .. 72 C7
Sevenoaks Gr ST3.... 90 B6
Seven Springs Nature Trail★ ST17.... 177 C5
Sevens Rd ST12.... 211 D3
Severn Cl Biddulph ST8 .. 16 E1
  Congleton CW12.... 6 A1
  Stretton DE13.... 147 C1
  Uttoxeter ST14.... 126 C6
Severn Dr
  Burntwood WS7.... 229 D6
  Burton u T DE14.... 166 E3
  Hilton DE65.... 147 D8
  Newcastle-u-L ST5.... 71 B4
  Perton WV6.... 254 E4
Severn Ho DY3.... 271 D3
Severn St ST1.... 282 A4
Seward Cl WS14.... 231 D6
Seymour Ave DE14.... 166 E2
Seymour Cl WS6.... 226 D1
Seymour Gdns B74.... 257 E3
Seymour St ST1.... 57 E3
Shackerley La WV7.... 221 B1
Shackleton Dr
  Perton WV6.... 254 E5
  Stoke-on-T ST6.... 41 C7
Shackleton Rd WS3.... 243 D4
Shackleton Way WS16... 136 B1
Shackson Cl ST1.... 282 B1
Shadwell Dr ST3.... 271 D3
Shaffalong La ST13.... 45 A5
Shaftesbury Ave ST6.... 42 A2
Shaftesbury Dr WS12.... 210 C2
Shaftesbury Rd WS15.... 196 E6
Shakespeare Ave WS14 . 231 B6
Shakespeare Cl
  Kidsgrove ST7.... 41 A8
  Stoke-on-T ST2.... 43 A2
  Tamworth B79.... 250 A6
Shakespeare Ct ST8.... 27 C7
Shakespeare Gr WS11... 209 D4
Shakespeare Rd
  Burntwood WS7.... 228 F8
  Burton u T DE14.... 166 D6
  Dudley DY3.... 271 A4
  Stafford ST17.... 174 C8
Shaldon Ave ST9.... 43 C4
Shales The WV5.... 269 C5
Shallcross La DY3.... 271 D3
Shallowford Ct ST1.... 57 A3
Shallowford Mews ST16. 155 D5
Shanklin Cl WS6.... 227 A3
Shannon App DE14.... 166 D2
Shannon Dr
  Brownhills WS8.... 228 C2
  Stoke-on-T ST6.... 41 C7
Shannon Rd ST17.... 174 C6
Shannon's Mill B79.... 250 A5
Shannon B77.... 261 B8
Shannon Wlk WS8.... 228 C2
Shanti Niketan WV2.... 266 D7
Shardlow Cl Longton ST4 . 73 A6
  Stone ST15.... 120 C6
Sharman Cl ST4.... 71 F7
Sharmon Way ST20.... 171 E7
Sharnbrook Dr WS15.... 178 C2
Sharnbrook Gr ST17.... 175 C6
Sharon Cl WV4.... 266 C5
Sharon Way WS12.... 210 D3

Sharpe St B77.... 251 A5
Sharplands TF9.... 99 D5
Sharrat Field B75.... 258 D2
Sharron Dr ST13.... 31 B5
Shaver's La WS15.... 197 B1
Shawbury Gr WV6.... 254 E5
Shaw Cl WS13.... 215 D8
Shaw Ct WS11.... 228 A5
Shaw Dr Burntwood WS7.. 212 A1
  Fradley WS13.... 215 C6
Shawe Park Rd ST10.... 76 E8
Shaw Gdns ST17.... 174 C7
Shaw Hall La WV9 .... 240 C7
Shaw La Albrighton WV7.. 237 B5
  Armitage WS15.... 198 F2
  Gentleshaw WS15.... 212 A4
  King's Bromley WS13.... 199 A4
  Lichfield WS13.... 231 A8
  Tong TF11.... 220 D5
  Wolverhampton WV6.... 255 B3
Shawmans La ST18.... 172 E8
Shawms Crest ST17.... 175 C8
Shawm s The ST17.... 175 C8
Shaw Pl ST13.... 31 A6
Shawport Ave ST5.... 56 A8
Shaw Rd WV4.... 266 C6
Shaws La ST21.... 133 C6
Shaw's La WS6.... 227 A2
Shaw St Biddulph ST8 .... 27 C7
  Hanley ST1.... 282 A4
  Newcastle-u-L ST5.... 283 B3
Shaw-Wall La ST10.... 62 F7
Shay La Foxt ST10 .... 62 C6
  Weston Jones TF10.... 150 A4
Shayler Gr WV2.... 266 C7
Sheaf Pas ST3.... 284 C3
Sheaf St ST1.... 282 A1
Shearers Pl 4 B75.... 258 E3
Shearer St ST1.... 282 A1
Shearwater Ct WV10.... 240 B3
Shebdon Cl ST16.... 155 B7
Sheepcote La B77.... 250 F4
Sheep Fair WS15.... 178 E1
Sheep Market ST13.... 30 E6
Sheepwalks La DY7.... 277 B7
Sheepwash La DY11.... 277 C2
Sheffield Cl ST14.... 110 F1
Sheffield St DE14.... 166 C1
Shefford Rd ST5.... 70 F3
Shelburne St ST4.... 72 A5
Sheldon Ave CW12.... 6 A1
Sheldon Gr ST5.... 55 F6
Sheldon Rd WV10.... 240 A1
Sheldrake Gr ST4.... 73 B6
Shelfield Sports & Com Coll WS4.... 244 C3
Shelford Rd ST3.... 41 D6
Shelley Ave DE14.... 166 D6
Shelley Cl Armitage WS15 198 B4
  Burton u T DE14.... 166 D6
  Colwich ST18.... 177 D8
  Dudley DY3.... 271 A5
  Kidsgrove ST7.... 41 A8
  Stafford ST16.... 156 A5
Shelley Dr Cheadle ST10... 76 C2
  Sutton Coldfield B74.... 257 F6
Shelley Rd Bucknall ST2... 58 B6
  Burntwood WS7.... 212 A1
  Cannock WS11.... 209 E5
  Tamworth B79.... 250 A7
  Wolverhampton WV10.... 240 D2
Shelmore Cl ST16.... 155 B8
Shelmore Way ST20.... 171 D7
Shelsley Cl ST19.... 193 A1
Shelsley Rd ST10.... 76 F4
Shelton Ent Ctr ST1.... 282 A4
Shelton Farm Rd ST1.... 282 A1
Shelton New Rd ST4.... 56 E1
Shelton Old Rd ST4.... 72 B8
Shelton St B77.... 261 F7
Shemilt Cres ST6.... 42 C3
Shendon Ct ST5.... 56 A7
Shenfield Gn ST2.... 58 C2
Shenley Gr ST17.... 174 D6
Shenstone Ave DY8.... 279 D3
Shenstone Cl B74.... 257 E6
Shenstone Ct WV3.... 266 A6
Shenstone Dr WS9.... 256 A8
Shenstone Ho WS13.... 214 E1
Shenstone Lodge Sch WS14.... 247 A3
Shenstone Sta WS14.... 246 F6
Shenton St ST3.... 284 D5
Shephard Cl ST18.... 158 B3
Shepherd Cl WS13.... 214 C3
Shepherds Bush St ST16. 155 E5
Shepherds Ct TF10.... 169 A3
Shepherds Fold ST17.... 175 C6
Shepherds Pool Rd B75. 258 E2
Shepherd St ST8.... 27 C7
Shepherds Wlk WV8.... 239 F2
Shepley Cl ST15.... 120 C7
Shepley Gr ST3.... 88 E7
Sheppard St ST4.... 72 A6
Shepwell Gdns WV10.... 241 D7
Sheraton Cl Aldridge WS9 256 B6
  Cannock WS11.... 210 A7
Sheraton Grange DY8.... 279 F2
Sherborne Cl ST3.... 88 E7
Sherborne Ct WV10.... 240 E1
Sherborne Dr ST5.... 71 A5
Sherborne Gdns WV8.... 239 A3
Sherborne Rd WV10.... 240 D1
Sherbourne Ave WS12.... 210 E4
Sherbourne Dr DE14.... 185 A7

Sherbrook Cl ST17 . . . . . . 176 A3
Sherbrooke Ave B77 . . . . 261 E6
Sherbrook Rd WS11. . . . 209 C1
Sheridan Gdns
  Dudley DY3 . . . . 270 F5
  Stoke-on-T ST3 . . . . 72 F2
Sheridan St ST16 . . . . . . 156 A4
Sheridan Way ST15 . . . . 120 D7
Sheriden Way ST5 . . . . . . 55 E2
Sheriffs Cl WS14 . . . . . . 231 E6
Sheriffs Way ST21 . . . . . 133 D7
Sherifoot La B75 . . . . . . 258 B4
Sheringham Covert
  ST16 . . . . 156 C4
Sheringham Dr WV15 . . 178 B2
Sheringham Pl ST5 . . . . . 56 D4
Sherracop La WS15 . . . . 160 A1
Sherrans Dell WV4 . . . . 266 D4
Sherratt St ST6 . . . . 42 C3
Sherringham Dr WV11 . . 242 C1
Shervale Cl WV4 . . . . . . 266 A6
Sherwin Rd ST6. . . . . 41 F3
Sherwood Ave ST17 . . . . 174 E8
Sherwood Cl CV9 . . . . . . 262 C1
Sherwood Dr WS11 . . . . 210 A3
Sherwood Rd
  Stoke-on-T ST3 . . . . 89 F7
  Stourbridge DY8 . . . . . . 279 E2
Shetland Ave B77 . . . . . 261 F7
Shetland Rd ST3 . . . . 72 F3
Shillingford Dr ST4 . . . . 88 B8
Shilton Cl ST4 . . . . 71 F5
Shinwell Gr ST3 . . . . 90 A8
Shipley Cl DE14. . . . . . . 185 B8
Shipley Pl ST6. . . . . 42 C2
Shippy La ST18 . . . . 172 C8
Shipston Rd ST17 . . . . . 156 D1
Shipton Cl DY1 . . . . 271 F3
Shipton Dr ST14 . . . . . . 110 F1
Shirburn Rd ST13 . . . . . . 31 A6
Shirebrook Cl ST3 . . . . . . 88 E7
Shirehall Pl WS11 . . . . . 210 B2
Shire Lea WS8 . . . . 245 B6
Shirelea Cl WS7 . . . . . . 229 B8
Shire Oak Sch WS9 . . . . 245 A5
Shireoaks Dr ■ ST17 . . . 175 C6
Shire Ridge WS9. . . . . . 245 B4
Shires Ind Est WS14 . . . 231 A6
Shireview Gdns WS3 . . . 244 B4
Shireview Rd WS3 . . . . . 244 B4
Shirewood WS11 . . . . . . 209 B2
Shirley Ave ST9. . . . . 59 B4
Shirley Dr ST10 . . . . 94 E8
Shirley Rd ST1. . . . . 282 B1
Shirley St Burslem ST6 . . 56 D8
  Leek ST13 . . . . 30 D5
Shirleywich ST18 . . . . . 138 E1
Shirley Wlk B79. . . . . . . 249 F7
Shirrall Dr B78 . . . . 259 E4
Shoal Hill Cl WS11 . . . . 209 B2
Shobnall Cl DE14 . . . . . 166 B4
Shobnall Ct DE14 . . . . . 166 B3
Shobnall Prim Sch DE14 165 F4
Shobnall Rd DE14 . . . . . 166 A3
Shobnall St DE14 . . . . . 166 B4
Sholing Cl WV8 . . . . 239 F1
Shoobridge St ST13 . . . . 30 F5
Shooting Butts Rd WS15 . 196 A8
Shop La Brewood ST19 . . 223 C6
  Oaken WV8 . . . . 238 D2
  Trescott WV6. . . . . 264 B7
Shops The ■ DY6 . . . . . 275 D4
Short Bambury St ST3. . . 73 D6
Shortbutts La ST17 . . . . 231 E5
Short La Barton-u-N DE13 183 D1
  Cheslyn Hay WS6. . . . . . 226 E3
  Gratwich ST14. . . . . 124 D3
Shortlands La WS3. . . . . 243 F3
Short Rd WV10 . . . . 240 E1
Short St Brownhills WS8 . 244 F7
  Burton u T DE15. . . . . . . 185 E7
  Cannock WS11. . . . . 209 F3
  Longton ST3. . . . . 284 D3
Short Street Com Inf Sch
  DE15 . . . . 185 E7
Short St Stourbridge DY8. 279 F5
  Uttoxeter ST14 . . . . 126 C8
Shorwell Gr ST6 . . . . 41 E8
Shotsfield Pl ST2 . . . . . . 43 A1
Shotsfield St ST2 . . . . . . 43 A1
Shotwood Cl DE13 . . . . 147 A4
Shotwoodhill La DE13 . . 147 A5
Showan Ave ST5 . . . . 56 D3
Showell La WV4 . . . . . . 265 B3
Shraleybrook Rd ST7. . . . 54 B7
Shredicote La ST18 . . . . 191 B7
Shrewsbury Cl WS3 . . . . 242 F1
Shrewsbury Dr
  Newcastle-u-L ST5. . . . . . 40 E2
  Weston-Under-Lizard TF11 203 E2
Shrewsbury Mall WS15. . 178 F1
Shrewsbury Rd
  Edgmond TF10 . . . . 168 A4
  Market Drayton TF9. . . . . 112 B8
  Stafford ST17 . . . . 285 B1
  Stretton DE13 . . . . 147 F2
Shrewsbury Way TF10. . . 168 E2
Shropshire Brook Rd
  WS15 . . . . 198 B4
Shropshire St TF9 . . . . . . 97 C1
Shrubbery Cl DY10 . . . . 280 A5
Shrubbery Hill DY10 . . . 280 A5
Shrubbery The
  Elford B79 . . . . 216 E1

Shrubbery The continued
  Rugeley WS15 . . . . 197 B6
Shruggs La ST18. . . . . . . 121 C1
Shugborough Cl WS3 . . . 243 B1
Shugborough Cotts
  ST18. . . . . 177 C8
Shugborough Dr DY1 . . . 271 E2
Shugborough Farm Mus★
  ST17 . . . . 177 A8
Shugborough Hall★
  ST17 . . . . 158 A1
Shugborough Rd WS15. . 178 C3
Shugborough Way
  WS11. . . . . 210 C1
Shughborough Cl ST9. . . 59 A2
Shuker's Cl TF10 . . . . . . 169 A2
Shut La ST21 . . . . 116 B6
Shutt Green La
  Brewood ST19 . . . . 223 B8
  Kiddemore Green ST19 . . 222 E8
Shuttington Rd B77,B79 . 251 B6
Sich La DE13 . . . . 182 D4
Sidcot Pl ST11 . . . . 57 D8
Siddalls St DE15 . . . . . . 167 B3
Siddons Cl WS13. . . . . . 213 F2
Sides La DE6 . . . . 81 B5
Sidestrand WV9 . . . . . . 239 F3
Sideway Rd ST4. . . . . 72 B5
Sidings Ind Est DE14 . . 166 E4
Sidings Pl ST3,ST4. . . . . 284 E4
Sidings The
  Cannock WS12. . . . . 210 C7
  Cheadle ST10. . . . . 76 D2
  Stone ST15 . . . . 120 B8
Sidmouth Ave
  Newcastle-u-L ST5. . . . . 283 C3
  Stafford ST17 . . . . 156 D1
Sidney Ave ST17 . . . . . . 174 E7
Sidney Dr ST10 . . . . 62 A2
Sidney St WV2. . . . . 266 C8
Sidon Hill Way WS11 . . . 210 C2
Siemens Rd ST17 . . . . . . 285 B1
Signal Gr WS3 . . . . 243 A1
Signal Wlk B77 . . . . 251 A2
Silica Rd B77 . . . . 251 B2
Silk Mill La DE13 . . . . . 146 C6
Silkmore Cres ST17 . . . . 175 A7
Silkmore La ST17 . . . . . 175 A8
Silkmore Prim Sch ST17 . 174 F7
Silk St ST13 . . . . 30 E6
Sill Gn B79 . . . . 234 C1
Sillitoe Pl ST4 . . . . 72 A6
Silsden Gr ST3 . . . . 74 C2
Silva Ave DY6. . . . . 275 F4
Silver Birch Coppice
  B74 . . . . 257 D5
Silver Birch Dr
  Kinver DY7. . . . . 277 F5
  Uttoxeter ST14 . . . . 126 B6
Silver Birch Rd
  Aldridge B74 . . . . 256 F1
  Huntington WS12. . . . . . 209 D8
  Norton Canes WS11 . . . . 228 B5
  Wolverhampton WV2. . . . 266 E7
Silver Cl ST8. . . . . 27 C8
Silver Court Gdns WS8 . . 244 F7
Silver Ct WS8. . . . . 244 F7
Silverdale Cl Chorlton CW2 37 C2
  Newport TF10 . . . . 168 C1
Silverdale Dr WS7 . . . . . 228 D7
Silverdale TF10 . . . . 168 A4
Silverdale Gdns DY8. . . . 275 C3
Silverdale Prim Sch ST5. . 55 C1
Silverdale Rd
  Newcastle-u-L,Knutton
  ST5. . . . . 55 E1
  Newcastle-u-L,Wolstanton
  ST5. . . . . 56 C5
Silverdale St ST5 . . . . . . 55 E1
Silver Fir Cl WS12. . . . . 210 A8
Silverhill Cl DE13 . . . . . 166 C8
Silver La ST14 . . . . 127 F1
Silver Link Rd B77 . . . . . 250 F1
Silvermine Cl ■ ST7 . . . . 26 B2
Silver Poplars Mobile Homes
  Pk WV7 . . . . 237 C4
Silver Ridge ST12 . . . . . 104 D8
Shuker's Cl WS3 . . . . . . 243 F4
Silver St Brownhills WS8. . 244 F7
  Cheadle ST10. . . . . 76 C6
Silverstone Ave ST10. . . . 76 E3
Silverstone Cres ST10 . . . 76 E3
Silver St Stoke-on-T ST6 . 42 E4
  Tamworth B79 . . . . 250 B5
  Uttoxeter ST14 . . . . 126 C8
Silverthorn Way ST17 . . 175 C7
Silverton Cl ST15 . . . . . . 56 A8
Silvertrees Cvn Pk WS15 195 E7
Silverwood ST7. . . . . 26 B1
Silvester Way ST17. . . . . 175 E6
Simcox St WS12 . . . . . . 210 D4
Simeon Way ST15. . . . . . 120 C6
Simister Ct ⑩ ST5 . . . . . 41 D3
Simmonds Cl WS3 . . . . . 243 D3
Simmonds Rd WS3. . . . . 243 D3
Simmonds Way WS8 . . . 245 A6
Simmons Cl B78 . . . . . . 260 B1
Simmons Rd WV11. . . . . 242 B1
Simmonburn Ave ST4. . . 71 E6
Simon Pl ST4. . . . . 57 B1
Simpkins Cl WS9. . . . . . 245 A3
Simpson Cl ST16 . . . . . . 155 B7
Simpson Rd WS13 . . . . . 214 B2
Simpson St Hanley ST1. . 282 C1
  Newcastle-u-L ST5. . . . . . 56 B5

Sinai Cl DE13 . . . . 165 E4
Sion Ave DY10 . . . . 280 A1
Sion Hill Mid Sch DY10. . 280 A1
Sir Graham Balfour High Sch
  ST16 . . . . 155 D8
Sir John Offley CE Prim Sch
  CW3 . . . . 68 E5
Sir Robert Peel Hospl
  B78 . . . . 249 D2
Sir Thomas Boughey High
  Sch ST7 . . . . 54 D7
Siskin Cl WS7. . . . . 229 D5
Siskin Pl ST3 . . . . 90 B7
Sister Dora Ave WS7 . . . 229 F7
Sitwell Gr ST3 . . . . 284 D4
Six Ashes Rd
  Bobbington DY7. . . . . . . 267 F1
  Halfpenny Green DY7 . . . 268 B3
  Six Ashes WV15. . . . . . . 272 D7
Six Roads End DE6 . . . . 144 C4
Skeath La ST18 . . . . 137 C4
Skidmore Ave
  Tamworth B77 . . . . 261 C5
  Wolverhampton WV3. . . . 265 F8
Skipacre Ave ST6 . . . . . . 42 D1
Skipness B77 . . . . 250 E5
Skipton Pl WS11. . . . . . . 226 B7
Skye Cl Longton ST3 . . . . 73 E3
  Tamworth B77 . . . . 261 F7
Skylark Cl Dudley DY5. . . 271 C1
  Huntington WS12. . . . . . 209 C7
  Uttoxeter ST14 . . . . 126 C6
Slab La ST9,ST20 . . . . . . 190 B2
Slacken La ST7 . . . . 25 D2
Slack La Mayfield DE6 . . . 81 C8
  Mayfield,Middle Mayfield
  DE6. . . . . 81 B7
Slacky La WS3 . . . . 243 F1
Slade Ave WS7 . . . . 229 A8
Slade Fields ST14 . . . . . 111 B1
Slade Gdns WV3 . . . . . . 239 A4
Slade Hill ■ WV6 . . . . . . 255 F3
Sladehollow La DE6. . . . . 65 C1
Slade La
  Sutton Coldfield B75 . . . 259 A3
  Tamworth B77 . . . . 261 C4
  Waterhouses ST10 . . . . . 49 A5
Slade Rd
  Sutton Coldfield B75 . . . 258 E3
  Wolverhampton WV10 . . . 240 C3
Slade View Rise WS12. . . 211 A6
Slaidburn Gr
  Birches Head ST1. . . . . . . 57 F5
  Stafford ST17 . . . . 175 C7
Slaney St ST5. . . . . 283 C1
Slang La WS15 . . . . 211 F5
Slapton Cl ST2. . . . . 57 F1
Slate La WV8 . . . . 238 D5
Slater St Biddulph ST8. . . 27 C7
  Burslem ST6 . . . . 56 E7
Sleeve The ST13 . . . . 30 C4
Sleigh Gr ST13. . . . . 30 E5
Slessor Rd ST16 . . . . . . 156 A5
Slindon Cl ST5. . . . . 40 D1
Sling La ST19 . . . . 206 B4
Slingsby B77 . . . . 261 C7
Slippery La ST1. . . . . . . 282 A2
Slitting Mill Rd WS15. . . 196 B7
Sloane Way ST4 . . . . 73 B6
Smallbrook La WV5 . . . . 270 B7
Smallcross Cl ST14. . . . . 126 C5
Smalley Cl WS11. . . . . . 210 A5
Small La ST21 . . . . 133 C7
Smallman St ST16 . . . . . 285 C4
Small Mdws DE13. . . . . . 183 E2
Smallridge WS13 . . . . . . 213 F2
Smallshire Way DY8 . . . 279 E8
Smallthorne Prim Sch
  ST6 . . . . 42 D2
Smallwood Cl ST5 . . . . . 40 D1
Smallwood Gr ST1. . . . . . 57 F6
Smallwood Rd WV8 . . . . 239 E2
Smarts Ave WS14 . . . . . 258 A4
Smedley Ct DE65. . . . . . 148 B5
Smestow Bridge Ind Est
  WV5 . . . . 269 C6
Smestow La DY3 . . . . . . 269 C5
Smestow Mews WV5. . . . 269 D4
Smestow Sch WV3 . . . . . 255 B1
Smillie Pl WS11. . . . . . . 209 F3
Smith Child St ST6. . . . . . 41 D4
Smith Ho WS3 . . . . 243 C3
Smithpool Rd ST4. . . . . . 72 D5
Smiths Bldgs ▣ ST3 . . . . 74 A1
Smith's Cl WS7 . . . . 228 D6
Smiths Pas ST4 . . . . 73 A5
Smith St Longton ST3 . . . 284 C5
  Wood End CV9. . . . . 262 C1
Smithy Bank ST10. . . . . . 78 E1
Smithy Croft ST20. . . . . . 190 B7
Smithy Dr WS3. . . . . 244 A4
Smithyfield Rd ST6 . . . . . 42 D4
Smithy La Barthomley CW2. 38 C6
  Barthomley CW2. . . . . . . 38 D7
  Bednall ST17 . . . . 193 F8
  Biddulph ST8. . . . . 16 D7

Smithy La continued
  Bosley SK11. . . . . 7 E6
  Bradley ST18. . . . . 191 C8
  Cheadle ST10. . . . . 92 D8
  Clifton Campville B79 . . . 218 E2
  Dudley DY5 . . . . 271 B1
  Eccleshall ST21 . . . . 117 B2
  Hixon ST18. . . . . 158 C8
  Knighton TF9 . . . . 83 B5
  Lichfield WS13 . . . . 214 A1
  Longdon WS15. . . . . 212 F8
  Longton ST3. . . . . 284 C3
  Norton Bridge ST15. . . . . 118 F1
  Seighford ST18 . . . . 154 B7
  Tamworth B77 . . . . 261 F7
  Weston CW2 . . . . 37 C5
  Whitmore ST5. . . . . 85 F6
Smokies Way ST8. . . . . . 16 C1
Smout Cres WV14 . . . . . 266 F2
Snape Hall Cl ST5. . . . . . 85 D6
Snape Hall Rd ST5 . . . . . 85 C5
Snape Hollow CW2. . . . . 37 F4
Snape La CW2 . . . . 37 E4
Snape Rd WV11 . . . . . . 242 B1
Snapes La B81 . . . . 81 B1
Snead Cl ST16 . . . . 156 C4
Sneyd Ave Leek ST13 . . . 30 E5
  Newcastle-u-L ST5. . . . . . 70 F7
Sneyd Cl ST13 . . . . 45 C4
Sneyd Com Sch WS3 . . . 242 E2
Sneyd Cres ST5 . . . . 70 F7
Sneyd Green Prim Sch
  ST6 . . . . 57 C7
Sneyd Hall Rd WS3. . . . . 243 A1
Sneyd Hill ST6. . . . . 57 C7
Sneyd Hill Ind Est ST6. . . 57 B8
Sneyd Ho WS3 . . . . 242 F1
Sneyd Ind Est ST6. . . . . . 57 B8
Sneydlands WS15 . . . . . 178 C1
Sneyd La Walsall WS3. . . 242 F1
  Willenhall WV11 . . . . . . 242 C1
Sneyd Pl ST6 . . . . 41 C6
Sneyd St Hanley ST6,ST1. . 57 C6
  Leek ST13 . . . . 30 E5
Sneyd Terr ST5 . . . . 55 B2
Sneyd Wood View ST6 . . 57 C7
Snipe Cl WV10 . . . . 241 B7
Snowberry Dr DY5 . . . . . 271 C1
Snowden Way ST3 . . . . . 74 B2
Snowdon Rd
  Burnhill Green WV6. . . . . 252 B6
  Cannock WS11. . . . . 209 E6
Snowdon Rise DY3 . . . . . 271 C6
Snowdon Way WV12 . . . 242 B1
Snowdrop Cl WS8 . . . . . 244 D6
Snow Hill Hanley ST1 . . . 282 A1
  Stafford ST16 . . . . 285 B4
Snows Ct TF10 . . . . 168 F2
Snowshill Gdns DY1. . . . 271 F4
Snows Yd ST16. . . . . 285 A4
Soames Cres ST3 . . . . . . 73 C6
Solent Cl WV9 . . . . 239 F2
Solney Cl DE11 . . . . 186 F3
Solway Cl B79 . . . . 250 A7
Solway Gr ST3 . . . . 73 E4
Somerfield Cl WS4. . . . . 244 C1
Somerford Cl Coven WV9. 224 B2
  Great Wyrley WS6 . . . . . 226 E1
Somerford Gdns WV10 . . 240 E2
Somerford La ST19. . . . . 223 F5
Somerley Rd ST1 . . . . . . 57 F6
Somerset Ave
  Kidsgrove ST7 . . . . 25 F2
  Rugeley WS15. . . . . 196 D6
Somerset Cl B78 . . . . . . 250 A1
Somerset Dr DY8. . . . . . 279 D2
Somerset Pl WS11 . . . . . 209 F3
Somerset Rd
  Burton u T DE15. . . . . . . 185 D6
  Hanley ST1. . . . . 57 E4
  Stafford ST17 . . . . 174 C7
Somerton Rd ST9 . . . . . . 59 A3
Somerton Way ST3 . . . . 284 D5
Somervale ST17 . . . . . . 175 C6
Somerville Ave ST5 . . . . 56 D3
Somerville Cl B79. . . . . . 249 D6
Somerville Rd DE13 . . . . 201 A2
Somerville Sq ST17 . . . . 174 F6
Sonning Dr WV9 . . . . . . 239 F2
Sophia Way ST5 . . . . 56 B8
Sopwith Cl ST15 . . . . . . 118 F6
Sorbus B77. . . . . 251 B4
Sorrel Ave ST10. . . . . 92 F3
Sorrel Cl Bucknall ST2. . . 58 A3
  Featherstone WV10. . . . . 241 B7
  Lichfield WS13 . . . . 230 E6
  Uttoxeter ST14 . . . . 126 B6
Sorrel B77. . . . . 251 B5
Sotherby Rd ST16. . . . . . 285 A3
Souldern Way ST3 . . . . . 73 D4
Southall Way ST17 . . . . . 58 A1
Southampton St ST1 . . . 282 C4
South Ave DY8 . . . . 279 F4
Southbank St ST13 . . . . . 30 F5
Southbank View DY6. . . . 275 E4
Southborough Cres ST6. . 42 C4
Southbourne Pl WS11. . . 209 D2
Southbourne Rd WV10 . . 240 C3
South Broadway St
  DE14. . . . . 185 C8
South Cl WS11 . . . . 226 C8
South Cres WV10 . . . . . 241 C6
Southdown Cl ST3. . . . . . 89 C4
Southdown Ct DY6. . . . . 275 D6
South Dr DE11. . . . . 186 F5
Southern Cl DY6 . . . . . . 275 F3

Southern Cross WS14 . . . 231 C7
Southern Ct ■ ST4 . . . . . 72 A7
Southerndown Rd DY3 . . 271 B7
Southern Way ST6 . . . . . 42 D1
Southfield Cl WS9 . . . . . 256 A6
Southfield Gr WV3 . . . . . 265 C9
Southfields Cl ST17 . . . . 174 D5
Southfields Rd ST17. . . . 174 D6
Southfield Way WS6 . . . 226 F2
Southgate Ave ST4. . . . . . 88 C2
Southgate Brewood ST19 . 223 D7
  Cannock WS11. . . . . 226 B7
Southgate End WS11. . . . 226 B7
South Gn WV4 . . . . 265 D5
South Hill DE13 . . . . 147 D4
Southlands Ave
  Longton ST3. . . . . 284 B1
  Newcastle-u-L ST5. . . . . . 56 C5
Southlands Cl ST13 . . . . 30 C5
Southlands Ct ST21 . . . . 133 E7
Southlands Rd CW12 . . . 16 A4
Southlowe Ave ST9 . . . . . 59 E4
Southlowe Rd ST9 . . . . . 59 E4
South Oak St DE14 . . . . 185 B8
South Oval DY3 . . . . 271 E5
South Pl ST6 . . . . 42 E6
South Rd Bucknall ST2. . . 58 B5
  Coldmeece ST15 . . . . . . 118 D6
  Stourbridge DY8. . . . . . . 279 E4
  Wolverhampton WV4. . . . 266 F4
South Staffordshire Bsns Pk
  WS11 . . . . 226 C4
South St
  Mount Pleasant ST7 . . . . . 26 B6
  Stafford ST16 . . . . 285 A3
  Stoke-on-T ST6 . . . . 42 D6
South Terr
  Newcastle-u-L ST5. . . . . . 56 C5
  Stoke-on-T ST4 . . . . 72 A5
South Uxbridge St DE14. 185 B8
South View ▣ ST8 . . . . . 27 C8
South View Cl
  Codsall WV8. . . . . 239 B2
  Featherstone WV10. . . . . 241 B6
South View DE6. . . . . 81 D6
South View Rd DY3 . . . . 271 C8
South View ST14. . . . . . 126 B7
South View Wlk ST14 . . . 95 F3
South Walls ST16 . . . . . . 285 B3
Southwark Cl WS13 . . . . 214 C3
Southway Ct DY6 . . . . . . 275 F4
Southwell Est ST21 . . . . 133 E6
South Wlk ST3 . . . . 74 B1
South Wolfe St ST4 . . . . . 72 B7
Southwood Cl DY6 . . . . . 275 E5
South Wood ST5 . . . . 48 B4
Sovereign Bsns Pk DE14 166 C2
Sovereign Dr
  Burton u T DE14. . . . . . . 185 B8
  Dudley DY1 . . . . 271 E2
Sovereign La TF9 . . . . . . 100 C5
Sovereign Works DY1 . . . 271 E4
Sowdley Gn ST19 . . . . . . 205 B5
Sowdley La ST19 . . . . . . 205 B4
Sowers Ct B75. . . . . 258 D4
Spalding Pl ST2. . . . . 73 E8
Sparch Ave ST5. . . . . 56 C4
Sparch Gr ST5 . . . . 56 C4
Sparch Hollow ST5. . . . . 56 C4
Spark St ST4 . . . . 72 A7
Spark Terr ST4 . . . . 72 A7
Sparrowbutts Gr ST7. . . . 26 C2
Sparrow Cl ST18 . . . . . . 177 D8
Sparrows End La ST19. . . 223 D6
Sparrow St ST6. . . . . 42 D2
Sparrow Terr ST5. . . . . . . 56 B6
Spa St ST6 . . . . 57 C7
Speakman St ST4 . . . . . 284 D2
Spearhill WS14 . . . . 231 E8
Spedding Rd ST4 . . . . . . 72 F8
Spedding Way ST8. . . . . . 27 E8
Speechly Dr WS15 . . . . . 178 D2
Speedwall St ST3 . . . . . . 73 C5
Speedwell Cl WS9 . . . . . 256 A5
Speedwell Gdns WV10 . . 241 B8
Speedwell Rd ST5 . . . . . . 40 F1
Speedwell Rise ST16 . . . 155 A5
Speedy Cl WS11 . . . . . . 209 E5
Spencer Ave Endon ST9 . . 43 E6
  Leek ST13 . . . . 30 E5
Spencer Cl Dudley DY3. . . 271 A4
  Stretton DE13 . . . . 147 C5
  Uttoxeter ST14 . . . . 126 C5
  Weston ST18. . . . . 138 C2
Spencer Dr WS7 . . . . . . 228 E8
Spencer Pl ST5 . . . . 55 E6
Spencer Rd
  Lichfield WS14 . . . . 231 B6
  Stoke-on-T ST4 . . . . 72 C5
Spencroft Rd ST5 . . . . . . 56 A5
Spend La Mapleton DE6. . 66 F7
  Thorpe DE6 . . . . 51 E2
Spenser Ave WV6. . . . . . 254 F4
Spenser Cl Stafford ST17 . 174 C8
  Tamworth B79 . . . . 250 A6
Spens St ST6 . . . . 56 F8
Sperry Cl ST3 . . . . 90 B7
Spey Dr ST7 . . . . 26 C2
Spiceal Mews ST14 . . . . 126 C7
Spicer's Cl WV5. . . . . . . 267 C8
Spills Mdw DY3 . . . . 271 E5
Spindlewood Cl ■
  WS12. . . . . 210 D1
Spinney Cl
  Burntwood WS7 . . . . . . 212 A1
  Endon ST9 . . . . 43 E8
  Norton Canes WS11 . . . . 227 F5

Spinney Cl *continued*
Polesworth B78 . . . . **262** F8
Stourbridge DY8 . . . . **275** C3
Walsall WS3 . . . . **244** A5
Spinney Dr CW2 . . . . . . **37** B5
Spinney Farm Rd WS11 . . **226** B7
Spinneyfields 2 ST17 . . **175** D5
Spinney La WS7 . . . . **211** F1
Spinney Lodge DE13 . . **145** E6
Spinney Rd DE14 . . . . . . **184** F6
Spinney The Biddulph ST8 . **27** C6
Dudley DY3 . . . . **271** C2
Lawton-gate ST7 . . . . **25** E4
Little Aston B74 . . . . **257** B6
Madeley Heath CW3 . . . . **69** A8
Newcastle-u-L ST5 . . . . . **71** C2
Wolverhampton WV3 . . . **255** D1
Spinning School La B79 . **250** B5
Spiral Ct DY3 . . . . **271** D3
Spire Cl ST6 . . . . **42** E3
Spires Croft WV10 . . . . . **225** D1
Spires The WS14 . . . . . . **231** E6
Spitfire Cl ST16 . . . . **136** B1
Spitfire Way ST6 . . . . . . **41** C4
Splash La WS12 . . . . **210** C3
Spode Ave
Armitage WS15 . . . . **198** C4
Hopton ST18 . . . . **156** B8
Spode Cl Cheadle ST10 . . **76** E2
Stone ST15 . . . . **119** E5
Spode Gr ST5 . . . . **71** B3
Spode Mus★ ST4 . . . . . . **72** B7
Spode Pl WS11 . . . . **210** B2
Spode St ST4 . . . . **72** B5
Spoutfield Rd ST4 . . . . . . **56** F1
Spout La ST2 . . . . **43** C1
Spragg House La ST6 . . . **42** E3
Spratslade Dr ST3 . . . . . **284** B2
Spreadoaks Dr ST17 . . . . **175** D5
Sprengers Cl ST19 . . . . . **193** A1
Springbank Ave ST9 . . . . **43** E6
Spring Bank Flats ST16 . . **155** D6
Spring Bank ST7 . . . . **26** A7
Spring Cl Hagley DY9 . . . **281** F4
Kinver DY7 . . . . **277** F5
Swadlincote DE11 . . . . . . **186** F1
Walsall WS4 . . . . **244** C2
Spring Cres ST6 . . . . **43** C7
Springcroft ST11 . . . . **90** F6
Springcroft Prim Sch
ST11 . . . . **90** E7
Springdale Jun & Inf Schs
WV4 . . . . **265** D5
Springfarm Rd DE15 . . . . **167** A1
Springfield Ave
Newport TF10 . . . . **168** E1
Rugeley WS15 . . . . **196** F7
Sedgley DY3 . . . . **266** E1
Springfield ST11 . . . . **90** E8
Springfield Cl Leek ST13 . . **31** A5
Newcastle-u-L ST5 . . . . . **55** F6
Springfield Com Specl Sch
ST13 . . . . **31** A5
Springfield Cres ST3 . . . . **284** B2
Springfield Ct Leek ST13 . . **31** A6
Stafford ST17 . . . . **174** E5
Wolverhampton WV10 . . **240** D4
Springfield Dr
Forsbrook ST11 . . . . **91** A8
Leek ST13 . . . . **31** A6
Stafford ST17 . . . . **174** E5
Talke ST7 . . . . **40** E8
Wheaton Aston ST19 . . . **205** C7
Springfield Gn DY3 . . . . . **266** E1
Springfield Gr
Biddulph ST8 . . . . **27** D7
Sedgley DY3 . . . . **266** E1
Springfield La WV10 . . . . **240** D4
Springfield TF9 . . . . **99** E5
Springfield Mobile Home Pk
4 TF9 . . . . **112** A8
Springfield Prim Sch ST4 . **71** E6
Springfield Rd
Biddulph ST8 . . . . **27** D7
Leek ST13 . . . . **31** A6
Tamworth B77 . . . . **261** D8
Uttoxeter ST14 . . . . **126** B8
Springfield Rise WS12 . . . **210** C6
Springfields Fst Sch
ST15 . . . . **118** F6
Springfields Ind Est
TF10 . . . . **168** F1
Springfields TF10 . . . . . . **168** F1
Springfields Rd
Rugeley WS15 . . . . **178** D3
Stoke-on-T ST4 . . . . **71** E6
Springfield Terr DE15 . . . **167** A1
Spring Garden Rd ST3 . . . **284** B2
Spring Gdns
Forsbrook ST11 . . . . **91** B8
Leek ST13 . . . . **30** D5
Stone ST15 . . . . **120** A5
Springhead Cl ST7 . . . . . **40** D6
Springhead Prim Sch ST7 **40** D6
Springhill Ave WV4 . . . . . **265** C4
Springhill Cl WS4 . . . . . . **244** D1
Springhill Gr WV4 . . . . . . **265** C4
Springhill La WV4 . . . . . . **265** B4
Springhill Pk WV4 . . . . . . **265** B3
Springhill Prim Sch
WS7 . . . . **229** B6
Springhill Rd
Brownhills WS8 . . . . **245** A7
Burntwood WS7 . . . . **229** A6
Springhill Terr WS15 . . . . **196** F7
Spring Hollow ST21 . . . . . **133** E6
Spring La
Bishops Wood ST19 . . . . **221** E8

Spring La *continued*
Walsall WS4 . . . . **244** C2
Whittington WS14 . . . . . **232** B6
Spring Leasow ST20 . . . . **151** A4
Springle Styche La WS7 . **212** C1
Spring Mdw WS6 . . . . . . **226** D1
Spring Meadows Cl WV8 . **239** B4
Springpool ST5 . . . . **70** C6
Spring Rd Lichfield WS13 . **214** D2
Longton ST3 . . . . **73** E2
Walsall WS4 . . . . **244** D1
Springs Bank ST9 . . . . . . **44** A2
Springside Pl ST3 . . . . . . **88** E7
Spring St Cannock WS11 . **226** E8
Stoke-on-T ST5 . . . . **56** D1
Spring Terrace Rd DE15 . **166** F1
Spring Terr WS7 . . . . **228** E5
Springvale Prim Sch
WS11 . . . . **226** E8
Spring Vale Prim Sch
WV4 . . . . **266** E4
Springvale Rise ST16 . . . **155** D8
Spring View ST16 . . . . . . **43** C7
Springwater Dr CW2 . . . . **37** C1
Springwood Dr ST15 . . . . **120** D7
Springwood Rd ST5 . . . . **55** C8
Sprinkbank Rd ST6 . . . . . **42** A5
Sprink La CW12 . . . . **6** D5
Sprinkswoods La DE6 . . . **81** E5
Sprinkwood Gr ST3 . . . . . **74** A3
Sproston Rd ST6 . . . . **41** F4
Spruce Rd WS12 . . . . **194** F1
Spruces The DY9 . . . . . . **281** F4
Spruce B77 . . . . **251** B4
Spruce Way
Stafford ST16 . . . . **155** C3
Wolverhampton WV3 . . . **255** D1
Spruce Wlk WS15 . . . . . . **178** C3
Spur Lea ST18 . . . . **173** C1
Spur St ST1 . . . . **282** C1
Spur Tree Ave WV3 . . . . . **255** A1
Square The Aldridge WS9 . **256** B6
Caverswall ST11 . . . . **74** C2
Checkley ST14 . . . . **109** E7
Codsall WV8 . . . . **238** F4
Derrington ST18 . . . . **154** D2
Elford B79 . . . . **216** D2
Fazeley B78 . . . . **261** A8
Great Haywood ST18 . . . **158** B2
Marchington ST14 . . . . . **127** E2
Meir ST3 . . . . **74** B2
Newcastle-u-L ST5 . . . . . **71** B6
Newport TF10 . . . . **168** F3
Oakamoor ST10 . . . . **78** A6
Pattingham WV6 . . . . **253** C2
Whiston ST10 . . . . **62** D3
Wolverhampton WV2 . . . **266** D4
Woore CW3 . . . . **67** C1
Squires Gate WS7 . . . . . . **229** C8
Squires View ST4 . . . . . . **72** C7
Squirrel Cl
Cannock WS12 . . . . **210** D2
Huntington WS12 . . . . . . **209** C6
Squirrel Hayes Ave ST8 . . **27** E6
Squirrel Hayes Cotts ST7 . **27** E6
Squirrel Hayes Fst Sch
ST8 . . . . **27** D7
Squirrels Cnr DE13 . . . . . **162** E7
Squirrels Hollow WS7 . . . **212** A2
Squirrels The
Lichfield WS14 . . . . **231** C7
Newcastle-u-L ST5 . . . . . **71** C3
Squirrel Wlk
Little Aston B74 . . . . **257** C5
Stafford ST17 . . . . **174** E4
Wolverhampton WV4 . . . **266** A5
Stable Ct DY3 . . . . **271** E4
Stableford Bank ST5 . . . . **86** A1
Stableford Cvn Pk ST5 . . . **86** B2
Stable La
Market Drayton TF9 . . . . **97** B1
Shareshill WV10 . . . . **225** A4
Wetton DE6 . . . . **35** B1
Stables The
Great Haywood ST18 . . . **158** B2
Lawton-gate ST7 . . . . **25** C4
Stacey Cl SK17 . . . . **23** B2
Stackhouse Cl WS9 . . . . . **245** A4
Stackhouse Dr WS3 . . . . . **244** A4
Stackyard La TF10 . . . . . **168** A4
Stadium Ct ST6 . . . . **57** A6
Stadmorslow La
Harriseahead ST7 . . . . . **26** F4
Packmoor ST6,ST7 . . . . . **27** A3
Stafford Ave ST5 . . . . . . **71** C5
Stafford Brook Rd WS15 . **195** F8
Stafford Castle★ ST16 . . **155** A4
Stafford Cl Stone ST15 . . **120** A7
Walsall WS3 . . . . **243** B4
Stafford Coll ST16 . . . . . . **285** A3
Stafford Cres
Newcastle-u-L ST5 . . . . . **71** C4
Whittington WS14 . . . . . **232** D3
Stafford Ct WV10 . . . . . . **240** C5
Stafford Gram Sch ST18 . **174** C6
Stafford La
Cannock WS12 . . . . **210** B5
Codsall WV8 . . . . **238** E1
Hanley ST1 . . . . **282** B3
Stafford Rd
Brewood WV10 . . . . **224** C5
Cannock WS11 . . . . **209** D1
Coven Heath WV10 . . . . **240** D4
Eccleshall ST21 . . . . **133** F6
Gnosall ST20 . . . . **171** E6
Huntington WS11,WS12 . **209** C5
Lichfield WS13 . . . . **213** E2
Newport TF10 . . . . **169** A3

Stafford Rd *continued*
Penkridge ST19 . . . . **192** E2
Stone ST15 . . . . **120** A6
Stone ST15 . . . . **120** A7
Uttoxeter ST14 . . . . **126** A6
Walsall WS3 . . . . **243** B4
Weston ST18 . . . . **156** F1
Staffordshire Ct ST18 . . . **156** D4
Staffordshire Enamels★
ST3 . . . . **73** F3
Staffordshire General Hospl
ST16 . . . . **156** A4
Staffordshire Regiment Mus
The★ WS14 . . . . **232** C2
Staffordshire Tech Pk
ST18 . . . . **156** C5
Staffordshire Univ WS13 . **231** B7
**Staffordshire Univ (Stafford
Campus)** ST18 . . . . **156** C5
**Staffordshire Univ (Stoke
Campus)** ST4 . . . . **72** C8
**Staffordshire Yeomanry
Mus★** ST16 . . . . **285** B3
Stafford Sta ST16 . . . . . . **285** A2
Stafford St Brewood ST19 . **223** C6
Burton u T DE14 . . . . . . **166** D5
Cannock WS11 . . . . **210** E1
Eccleshall ST21 . . . . **133** E7
Hanley ST1 . . . . **282** B3
Market Drayton TF9 . . . . **97** D1
Newcastle-u-L ST5 . . . . . **283** C2
Newport TF10 . . . . **168** F3
Stafford ST16 . . . . **285** B3
Stagborough Way WS12 . **210** B4
Stag Cl WS15 . . . . **178** B1
Stag Cres WS11 . . . . **228** A6
Stag Dr WS12 . . . . **209** C6
Staines St ST15 . . . . **120** C7
Staite Dr DY10 . . . . **280** B5
Staite Terr DY10 . . . . **280** A5
Stakenbridge La DY10 . . . **281** D4
Staley Croft WS12 . . . . . . **209** C4
Stalling's La DY6 . . . . **275** D8
Stallington Cl ST11 . . . . . **90** D4
Stallington Gdns ST11 . . . **90** F6
Stallington Rd ST11 . . . . . **90** C3
Stamer St ST4 . . . . **72** B6
Stamford Cres WS7 . . . . . **229** A8
Stamford St ST4 . . . . **279** F7
Stamford Way WS9 . . . . . **245** C1
Stamps DE15 . . . . **167** C3
Standard St ST4 . . . . **72** B6
Standege B77 . . . . **262** B7
Standersfoot PI ST6 . . . . . **42** B6
Standhills Rd DY6 . . . . . . **275** E6
Standing Butts Cl DE12 . . **202** D8
Standon Ct ST21 . . . . **101** F4
Stanfield Rd ST6 . . . . **42** A1
Stanfield St 4 ST3 . . . . . **73** D6
Stanford Cl ST19 . . . . **192** E1
Stanford Rd WV2 . . . . **266** C8
Stanhope Gn DE15 . . . . . **167** F1
Stanhope Ho B79 . . . . . . **250** A4
Stanhope St
Burton u T DE15 . . . . . . **167** B3
Hanley ST1 . . . . **282** A1
Stanier St
Newcastle-u-L ST5 . . . . . **283** B3
Stoke-on-T ST4 . . . . **72** E6
Stanley Bank ST9 . . . . . . **44** A5
Stanley Cl DE12 . . . . **219** F7
Stanley Cres ST14 . . . . . . **111** A2
Stanley Ct WV6 . . . . **254** E4
Stanley Dr
Newcastle-u-L ST5 . . . . . **40** D1
Swindon DY3 . . . . **269** E2
Stanley Gr
Newcastle-u-L ST5 . . . . . **56** D2
Stoke-on-T ST2 . . . . **43** B2
Stanley Matthews Sports Ctr
ST4 . . . . **72** C8
Stanley Matthews Way
Stoke-on-T,Hem Heath
ST4 . . . . **88** D7
Stoke-on-T,Hollybush ST4 . **72** C3
Stanley Moss La ST9 . . . . **43** E5
Stanley Moss Rd ST9 . . . . **43** F5
Stanley Rd Biddulph ST8 . . **16** C2
Cannock WS12 . . . . **210** A6
Newcastle-u-L ST5 . . . . . **56** E2
Stoke-on-T,Hartshill ST4 . . **71** E8
Stoke-on-T,Stanley Moor
ST9 . . . . **43** E4
Stourbridge DY8 . . . . **279** F3
Wolverhampton WV10 . . **240** D1
Stanley St Biddulph ST8 . . **27** C8
Burton u T DE14 . . . . . . **166** C2
Leek ST13 . . . . **30** E5
Stoke-on-T ST6 . . . . **41** E4
Walsall WS3 . . . . **243** D1
Stanmore Rd ST3 . . . . . . **74** B2
Stanstow Ave DY1 . . . . . . **271** F6
Stanton Ave DY1 . . . . **271** F6
Stanton Cl ST5 . . . . **55** F2
Stanton La Ellastone DE6 . . **80** C4
Upper Mayfield DE6 . . . . **66** A2
Stanton Prim Sch DE15 . . **186** B5
Stanton Rd
Burton u T DE15 . . . . . . **185** F7
Meir ST3 . . . . **74** A1
Stanway Ave ST6 . . . . . . **57** C7
Stanway Cl ST14 . . . . **126** A6
Stanway Rd ST16 . . . . . . **155** F5
Stanways La ST8 . . . . **17** B2
Stapenhill Rd DE15 . . . . . **166** F2
Stapleford Gdns WS7 . . . **229** D6

Stapleford Gr DY8 . . . . . . **275** E2
Stapleton Cres ST3 . . . . . **73** A1
Star And Garter Rd ST3 . . **89** E8
Star Bank Cotton ST10 . . . **63** E1
Oakamoor ST10 . . . . **78** C7
Star Cvn Site The WV9 . . . **224** B1
Starkey's La ST19 . . . . . . **205** D7
Starling Cl ST7 . . . . **26** D3
Starling Ct WV10 . . . . **240** B3
Star St WV3 . . . . **265** E8
Startley La WS5 . . . . **196** F1
Starwood Rd ST3 . . . . . . **89** C8
Starwood Terr ST10 . . . . . **78** A6
Statfold La Alrewas DE13 . **200** F3
Fradley WS13 . . . . **215** D8
Statham St ST1 . . . . **282** A2
Station App
Lichfield WS13 . . . . **231** F8
Stone ST15 . . . . **104** F1
Sutton Coldfield,Hill Hook
B74 . . . . **257** F6
Station Bridge Rd ST4 . . . **72** E5
Station Cl WV8 . . . . **238** F7
Station Cotts
Sudbury DE6 . . . . **128** C3
Whitmore ST5 . . . . **85** D5
Station Cres ST6 . . . . **42** D2
Station Ct Cannock WS11 . **226** F8
Newport TF10 . . . . **169** A1
Station Dr Armitage WS15 . **198** B4
Blakedown DY10 . . . . . . **281** C2
Four Ashes WV10 . . . . . . **224** C5
Keele ST5 . . . . **69** D8
Stationfields Park Homes
B79 . . . . **250** C5
Station Gr ST2 . . . . **43** A1
Station Ind Est ST1 . . . . . **57** F3
Station La
Rushton Spencer SK11 . . . **8** B2
Walton-on-T DE12 . . . . . **184** D1
Station Rd
Albrighton WV7 . . . . **237** B5
Aldridge WS9 . . . . **256** A5
Alton ST10 . . . . **78** E1
Barlaston ST12 . . . . **88** D1
Barton-u-N DE13 . . . . . . **183** E2
Biddulph ST8 . . . . **16** C1
Biddulph ST8 . . . . **27** C8
Cannock WS12 . . . . **210** C6
Cheadle ST10 . . . . **76** D2
Cheddleton ST13 . . . . . . **45** D6
Codsall WV8 . . . . **238** E3
Coldmeece ST15 . . . . . . **118** C6
Cotes Heath ST21 . . . . . **102** D3
Draycott in t C DE6 . . . . . **144** D8
Four Ashes WV10 . . . . . . **224** D5
Gnosall ST20 . . . . **171** D6
Great Wyrley WS6 . . . . . **226** F4
Halmer End ST7 . . . . **54** D7
Hammerwich WS7 . . . . . **229** E3
Hatton DE65 . . . . **146** D8
Haughton ST18 . . . . **172** E7
Keele ST5 . . . . **69** E8
Kidsgrove ST7 . . . . **25** F1
Lichfield WS13 . . . . **231** C7
Madeley CW3 . . . . **68** E5
Madeley Heath ST5 . . . . **69** D8
Mow Cop ST7 . . . . **26** C8
Newcastle-u-L ST5 . . . . . **55** B2
Newchapel ST7 . . . . **26** E2
Newport TF10 . . . . **168** F1
Norton Bridge ST15 . . . . **118** F1
Onneley CW3 . . . . **68** B2
Penkridge ST19 . . . . **192** E1
Rolleston on D DE13 . . . . **147** C4
Rugeley WS15 . . . . **178** F2
Scholar Green ST7 . . . . . **26** A8
Shenstone WS14 . . . . . . **246** F6
Stafford ST16 . . . . **285** A4
Stoke-on-T,Endon ST9 . . . **43** F7
Stoke-on-T ST4 . . . . **72** B8
Stone ST15 . . . . **104** F1
Stowe-by-Chartley ST18 . **139** C4
The Bank ST7 . . . . **26** A8
Uttoxeter ST14 . . . . **126** D7
Walsall WS3 . . . . **244** A3
Wombourne WV5 . . . . . . **270** A8
Station St Burslem ST6 . . **56** B8
Burton u T DE14 . . . . . . **166** D3
Cheslyn Hay WS6 . . . . . . **226** B3
Leek ST13 . . . . **30** D5
Station View ST3 . . . . . . **74** A1
Station Wlks ST7 . . . . **54** D7
Station Yd ST13 . . . . **201** B2
Staunton Rd WS3 . . . . . . **243** A3
Staveley Cl ST2 . . . . **58** A3
Staveley Pl ST5 . . . . **55** A1
Steadman Cres ST17 . . . . **174** E6
Stedman St ST1 . . . . **282** C1
Steele Ave ST6 . . . . **42** B2
Steele Cl ST13 . . . . **45** D5
Steenwood La WS15 . . . . **160** A2
Steeple Way ST4 . . . . **72** A5
Steere Ave B79 . . . . **250** C7
Stellar St ST6 . . . . **42** C1
Stenbury Cl WV10 . . . . . . **240** F1
Stephanie Gr B77 . . . . . . **251** A6
Stephen Ave ST10 . . . . . . **61** D7
Stephenson Cl B77 . . . . . **251** A2
Stephenson Dr WV6 . . . . **254** E5
Stephenson Way WS12 . . **210** B5
Stephens Rd DE14 . . . . . . **185** B8
Stephens Way ST7 . . . . . . **39** F2
Stephens Wlk WS13 . . . . **214** A2
Stepping Stones
4 Leek ST13 . . . . **30** E5

Stepping Stones *continued*
Rugeley WS15 . . . . **178** D1
Step Row 12 ST13 . . . . . . **30** E5
Steps Gdns ST18 . . . . . . **172** E6
Sterling Pk B77 . . . . **261** E7
Sterndale Dr Longton ST4 . **73** B6
Newcastle-u-L ST5 . . . . . **71** B3
Sterndale Moor SK17 . . . . **5** E6
Sterrymere Gdns DY7 . . . **278** B4
Stevens Dr WS12 . . . . . . **210** D6
Stevens Gate 6 WV2 . . . **266** C8
Stevenson Dr ST17 . . . . . **174** C7
Stevenson Rd Bucknall ST2 **58** A4
Doveridge DE6 . . . . **127** B8
Tamworth B79 . . . . **250** A6
Stevenson Wlk WS14 . . . **231** B6
Steventon Pl 16 ST6 . . . . **56** F8
Stewart Cl DE14 . . . . **185** A6
Stewart Ct ST2 . . . . **58** D1
Stewart Rd
Brownhills WS9 . . . . **245** A3
Kingswinford DY6 . . . . . . **275** D4
Wolverhampton WV2 . . . **266** C8
Stewart St Stoke-on-T ST4 . **72** D6
Stewkins Ct 4 DY8 . . . . . **279** E8
Stewkins DY8 . . . . **279** E8
Stewponey The DY7 . . . . **278** E6
Stickley La DY3 . . . . **271** C4
Stile Cl Biddulph ST8 . . . . **27** B5
Rugeley WS15 . . . . **196** F6
Stile Cop Rd WS15 . . . . . **196** D4
Stile House La ST13 . . . . **31** E6
Stirling Cl Bucknall ST2 . . **73** E7
Castle Gresley DE11 . . . . **186** F1
Stirling Pl WS11 . . . . **226** B8
Stirling Rise 7 DE13 . . . . **166** D8
Stirling St 8 ST4 . . . . . . **57** A8
Stitchings The DE6 . . . . . **65** C1
Stockbridge Cl WV6 . . . . **254** F2
Stockfield Rd ST3 . . . . . . **89** F7
Stockford La WS13 . . . . . **216** A3
Stockhay La WS7 . . . . . . **229** D5
Stockholm Gr ST1 . . . . . . **57** E7
Stocking-Gate La ST18 . . **153** B7
Stocking La ST18 . . . . . . **153** B5
Stockings La
Longdon WS15 . . . . **197** C6
Wheaton Aston ST19 . . . **205** D5
Stock La ST14 . . . . **143** B8
Stocks La ST14 . . . . **125** C7
Stockton La ST17 . . . . . . **175** C7
Stockwell End WV6 . . . . . **255** D6
Stockwell Gr ST3 . . . . . . **73** D3
Stockwell Rd WV6 . . . . . . **255** D5
Stockwell St ST13 . . . . . . **30** F6
Stockwood Rd ST5 . . . . . **71** A3
Stoke Bsns Pk ST4 . . . . . **72** B6
Stoke Old Rd ST4 . . . . . . **56** E1
**Stoke-on-Trent Coll
(Burslem Campus)**
Burslem ST6 . . . . **57** B8
Stoke-on-T ST6 . . . . **42** B1
**Stoke-on-Trent Coll
(Cauldon Campus)** ST4 . **57** B1
Stoke-on-Trent Sta ST4 . **72** B8
Stoke Rd ST4 . . . . **57** B1
Stoke Recn Ctr ST4 . . . . . **72** B6
Stokesay Ave WV6 . . . . . **254** F3
Stokesay Dr ST10 . . . . . . **76** F3
Stokesay Gr ST4 . . . . **57** A7
Stokesay Rise DY1 . . . . . **271** E3
Stoke Ski Ctr ST6 . . . . . . **56** F5
Stoke's La WS11 . . . . **227** F1
Stoneacre Cl WV3 . . . . . . **255** A1
Stone Bank Rd ST7 . . . . . **41** B8
Stonebridge Rd ST19 . . . **223** D6
Stone Bsns Pk ST15 . . . . **120** B4
Stone Chair La ST7 . . . . . **25** E7
Stone Cotts Clifton DE6 . . **81** E8
Congleton CW12 . . . . . . **6** E2
Weston-Under-Lizard
TF11 . . . . **203** C4
Stonecrop Cl WS8 . . . . . . **244** D6
Stone Cross ST19 . . . . . . **192** E1
Stone Ent Ctr ST15 . . . . . **120** B4
Stonefield Cl 2 ST15 . . . . **104** F2
Stonefield Sq ST15 . . . . . **105** A1
Stonehaven Gr ST1 . . . . . **282** C1
Stonehaven B77 . . . . **250** F5
Stonehill Wlk 5 B77 . . . . **261** F6
Stonehouse Cres ST9 . . . **59** B3
Stonehouse Dr B74 . . . . . **257** C4
Stonehouse Rd
Rugeley WS15 . . . . **178** A1
Werrington ST9 . . . . **59** B3
Stonelea WS9 . . . . **256** B5
Stoneleigh Ct ST18 . . . . . **174** C5
Stoneleigh Gdns WV8 . . . **238** F4
Stoneleigh Rd ST6 . . . . . **42** A5
Stoneleigh Way DY3 . . . . **271** D6
Stone Pine Cl WS12 . . . . **209** F8
Stonepine Pl DY3 . . . . . . **271** E6
Stonepit B77 . . . . **250** C1
Stone Rd Eccleshall ST21 . **134** B7
Stafford,Parkside ST16 . . **155** C3
Stafford ST16 . . . . **155** D5
Stoke-on-T,Hanford ST4 . . **71** F3
Stoke-on-T,Trent Vale ST4 . **71** F1
Tittensor ST4,ST12 . . . . . **88** A3
Trentham ST4 . . . . **87** F7
Uttoxeter ST14 . . . . **126** B8
Yarlet ST16,ST18 . . . . . . **136** B2

Stone Sta ST15. . . . . . . 104 F2
Stone St ST4 . . . . 72 A7
Stonewall Ind Est ST5. . . . 55 D2
Stonewall PI ST5. . . . . . . 55 D2
Stonewood CI ST4 . . . . . . 71 E3
Stoney Brook Leys WV5 . 269 E5
Stoney Croft WS11. . . . . 209 F1
Stoneycroft ST2 . . . . 43 B2
Stoneydale CI DE11 . . . . 186 F5
Stoney Dale ST10. . . . . . . 77 E4
Stoneydelph Prim Sch
B77 . . . . 251 A1
Stoneyfields Ave ST2. . . . . 43 B2
Stoneyfields St. 28 B8
Stoneyfields CI 3 WS11. 209 F2
Stoneyfields Ct ST5 . . . . 283 D4
Stoneyfold La SK17 . . . . . 22 D3
Stoneyford Terr ST14 . . . 126 C6
Stoney La Cauldon ST10 . . 63 D6
Endon ST9 . . . . 43 E7
Gratwich ST14. . . . . . . 124 B3
Stakenbridge DY10. . . . 281 D3
Stretton ST19 . . . . 206 D3
Walsall WS3. . . . . 243 D3
Wolverhampton WV4. . . 266 B5
Stoney Lea Rd WS11 . . . . 209 F1
Stoneywell La WS13. . . . . 213 A6
Stonall Gate WS9. . . . . . 256 C8
Stonall Rd WS9. . . . . . . 256 C8
Stonor St ST6. . . . . 57 A6
Stonydelph La B77. . . . . 262 A7
Stonyford La WS15. . . . . 179 E4
Stony La ST10 . . . . 49 D1
Stormont CI ST6. . . . . . . 42 C2
Stourbridge Coll (Longlands
Ctr) DY8. . . . . 279 E5
Stourbridge Rd
Hackman's Gate DY9 . . 281 F1
Kidderminster DY10. . . 280 D2
Wombourne WV5,DY3 . . 270 B5
Stour CI Burntwood WS7 . 229 D5
Hilton DE65 . . . . 147 E8
Stour B77. . . . . 262 A5
Stourton Cres DY7 . . . . . 278 F7
Stourton Dr WV4 . . . . . . 265 C5
Stowecroft WS13 . . . . . . 214 C2
Stowe Hill Gdns WS13. . . 214 C1
Stowe La ST18 . . . . 139 C2
Stowe Rd WS13. . . . . . . 231 C8
Stowe St WS13 . . . . 231 C8
Stowford Gr ST4. . . . . . . 88 C8
Stradbroke Dr ST3. . . . . . 73 A1
Straight Mile WV10 . . . . . 225 B6
Straits Gn DY3. . . . . 271 B4
Straits Prim Sch DY3. . . . 271 B5
Straits Rd DY3 . . . . 271 B3
Straits The DY3. . . . . . . 271 A4
Strand CI ST2. . . . . 58 A2
Strand Pas ST3 . . . . 284 B3
Strand The ST3. . . . . . . 284 B3
Strangman St ST13. . . . . . 30 E5
Stranraer CI ST3 . . . . 74 C4
Stratford Ave ST5. . . . . . . 56 D3
Stratford Dr Dudley DY1 . 271 E2
Forsbrook ST11. . . . . . . 91 A8
Stoke-on-T ST6 . . . . . . 42 F1
Stratford Dr WS4 . . . . . 256 C8
Stratford Way WS11. . . . 209 F5
Stratheden Rd ST6. . . . . . 42 B2
Strathfield Wlk WV3,
WV4. . . . . 265 C6
Strathmore Cres WV5. . . 265 A1
Strathmore PI 6 WS11. . 209 F2
Strawberry La WS6 . . . . . 242 E8
Strawmoor La WV8 . . . . . 238 C3
Stream Mdw WS4. . . . . . 244 D1
Stream Pk DY6 . . . . 275 E4
Stream Rd DY6,DY8. . . . 275 D4
Streamside CI ST19 . . . . 207 F8
Streather Rd WS75 . . . . . 258 C2
Streetly Cres B74 . . . . . 257 D3
Streetly Dr B74 . . . . . . 257 D3
Streetly La B74 . . . . . . 257 D3
Streetly Wood B74. . . . . 257 A2
Streets Corner Gdns
WS9. . . . . 245 A4
Streets La WS6 . . . . 226 F1
Street The ST20. . . . . . . 150 F5
Streetway Rd WS14 . . . . 247 B7
Stretton Ave
Newport TF10 . . . . 168 E2
Stafford ST17 . . . . 155 B6
Stretton Brook Sch
DE13. . . . . 147 C1
Stretton Gdns WV8. . . . . 238 F4
Stretton Rd Lapley ST19 . 206 A6
Newcastle-u-L ST5. . . . . 54 F7
Willenhall WV12 . . . . . 242 D1
Stretton St B77 . . . . 250 E3
Strine Way TF10 . . . . . . 168 F4
Stringer CI B75 . . . . 258 A4
Stringer Ct 17 ST6 . . . . . 41 D3
Stringers Hill WS12 . . . . 210 D7
Stringer's La DE13. . . . . 182 C2
Stringer's St 2 ST8. . . . . 27 C8
Strode Ho B79. . . . . 250 A1
Strode Rd WV2 . . . . 266 C6
Stroma CI 3 ST6 . . . . . . 56 F7
Stross Ave ST4. . . . . 41 F5
Stroud CI ST3. . . . . 90 B7
Stuart Ave
Draycott in t M ST11. . . . 91 C6

Stuart Ave continued
Stoke-on-T ST4 . . . . 88 A7
Stuart CI N ST15. . . . . . 119 F6
Stuart CI ST15 . . . . 119 F5
Stuart Gr ST5. . . . . 56 C4
Stuart Rd ST1. . . . . 57 E2
Stuart Way TF9 . . . . 97 B2
Stubbers Green Rd WS9. 256 F1
Stubbs Dr ST15 . . . . . . 120 D7
Stubbsfield Rd ST5. . . . . 283 C1
Stubbs' Gate ST5 . . . . . 283 C2
Stubbs La Hanley ST1. . . 282 D7
Stanton DE6. . . . . 65 C2
Stubbs Rd WV3 . . . . . . 266 E8
Stubbs St ST6. . . . . 56 E8
Stubbs' St ST5. . . . . . . 283 C2
Stubby La DE6. . . . . . . 144 B6
Stubwood Hollow ST14. . . 95 D5
Stubwood La ST14 . . . . . 95 A4
Stud Farm Cotts B78 . . . 249 E2
Studley Gate DY8 . . . . . 279 D5
Studley Rd WV3. . . . . . . 265 C8
Sturgeon's Hill ST14. . . . 231 C7
Sturgess St ST4. . . . . 72 A6
Stychbrook Gdns WS13. . 214 B2
Stychfields ST17. . . . . . 285 C1
Suckling Green La WV8 . 238 F2
Sudbourne CI ST6. . . . . . 41 E8
Sudbury Hall & Mus of
Childhood★ DE6. . . . . 128 D5
Sudbury Pk DE6 . . . . . . 128 D7
Sudbury PI ST5 . . . . 71 B2
Sudbury Prim Sch DE6. . 128 E4
Sudbury Rd DE13 . . . . . 182 A4
Sudeley Gdns DY1 . . . . 271 D2
Sudlow St ST6. . . . . 57 B7
Sudgrove PI ST3. . . . . . . 90 B7
Sudlow St ST6 . . . . 57 B7
Suffolk CI ST5 . . . . 71 D4
Suffolk Dr WS9 . . . . 256 B8
Suffolk Rd
Burton u T DE15. . . . . . 185 D7
Stoke-on-T ST3 . . . . 89 C8
Suffolk Way B78 . . . . . . 250 A1
Sugar Loaf La DY10 . . . . 281 B7
Sugar St SK11. . . . . 8 C2
Sugnall Bsns Ctr ST21. . . 116 D2
Sullivan Way WS13. . . . . 214 C2
Sullivan Wlk WS13. . . . . 214 C2
Summerbank Prim Sch
ST6. . . . . 41 D4
Summerbank Rd ST6. . . . 41 D4
Summercourt Dr DY6. . . 275 C6
Summercourt Sq DY6 . . 275 C5
Summer Dr DY3. . . . . . . 271 C2
Summerfield Arc 6
ST15. . . . . 120 A8
Summerfield Ave DY6. . . 275 C7
Summerfield CI B77. . . . 250 D4
Summerfield Dr ST14 . . . 126 A8
Summerfield ST7 . . . . . . 26 B1
Summerfield Rd
Burntwood WS7. . . . . . 229 A5
Tamworth B77. . . . . . . 250 D4
Summerfields ST15 . . . . 118 E6
Summergate DY3. . . . . . 271 C4
Summer Gr WS13 . . . . . 214 D2
Summerhill Dr ST5. . . . . . 40 D1
Summerhill Gdns TF9 . . . 112 C8
Summer Hill DY6 . . . . . . 275 C6
Summerhill La ST18. . . . 135 E5
Summerhill Sch The
DY6. . . . . 275 B6
Summerhill WS14. . . . . . 245 A8
Summerhouse Gr TF10 . . 168 F4
Summerhouse La ST3 . . . 212 E3
Summer La Dudley DY3 . . 271 C2
Walsall WS4. . . . . 244 C2
Summer Row ST3. . . . . . 284 C2
Summerside Ave WS12. . 211 C4
Summer St
Kingswinford DY6 . . . . 275 D6
Stoke-on-T ST4 . . . . . . 72 A5
Stourbridge DY8 . . . . . 279 F8
Summerville Rd ST4 . . . . 71 E3
Summit PI DY3. . . . . . . 271 B2
Sunbeam Dr WS6 . . . . . 226 F3
Sunbeam St WV2 . . . . . 266 C7
Sunbeam B77. . . . . 250 E3
Sunbury Ave WS14 . . . . 231 E7
Sunbury CI ST4 . . . . 88 C6
Sundorne PI ST2. . . . . . . 58 B2
Sundour Cres WV11 . . . . 241 B1
Sundown Dr ST17. . . . . 174 B7
Sundridge Wlk WV4. . . . 265 C6
Sunfield Rd WS11. . . . . 209 B1
Suningdale CI DE13 . . . . 147 C1
Sunley Dr WS12. . . . . . 210 D7
Sunningdale Ave WV6. . . 254 D5
Sunningdale CI
Stoke-on-T ST6 . . . . . . 42 B3
Stourbridge DY8 . . . . . 279 F2
Sunningdale Gr ST5. . . . . 55 D8
Sunningdale Rd DY3 . . . 266 B3
Sunningdale Stone ST15 . 120 A7
Tamworth B77. . . . . . . 251 C5
Sunningdale View ST3 . . . 89 C3
Sunningdale Way WS3 . . 243 A3
Sunny Bank ST6 . . . . 56 E6
Sunnybank CI WS9. . . . . 256 E2
Sunnybank Ct ST6 . . . . . 42 A3
Sunnybank Cvn Pk ST19. 205 E7
Sunny Bank DE6. . . . . . . 81 C7
Sunnybank Rd DY3. . . . . 271 F5
Sunnycroft Ave ST6 . . . . 284 A1
Sunny Gdns TF10 . . . . . 168 F5

Sunny Hill CI WV5. . . . . 270 B6
Sunnyhills Rd ST13. . . . . 30 D3
Sunny Hollow ST5. . . . . . 56 C3
Sunnymead Rd 1 WS7. 229 A8
Sunnymede Rd 1 DY6 . 275 F4
Sunnyside Ave ST6. . . . . 41 F4
Sunnyside WS9 . . . . . . 245 A2
Sunnyside CI DE11. . . . . 186 F7
Sunny Side ST10. . . . . . . 61 D3
Sunnyside ST14. . . . . . 111 B1
Sunnyside DE11. . . . . . 186 E7
Sunridge Ave WV5. . . . . 270 A7
Sunridge CI ST4. . . . . . . 43 B2
Sunrise Hill WS12. . . . . 210 B6
Sunset CI Coven WV9 . . . 224 B3
Great Wyrley WS6 . . . . 226 F3
Tamworth B79. . . . . . . 250 A5
Sunset PI WV4. . . . . . . 266 F3
Sun St Cheadle ST10 . . . . 76 E3
Hanley ST1. . . . . 282 A2
Sunwell Gdns ST10. . . . . 76 E3
Surrey CI Cannock WS11. 226 F8
Rugeley WS15. . . . . . . 196 D6
Surrey Dr
Kingswinford DY6 . . . . 275 F3
Tamworth B78. . . . . . . 250 A1
Wolverhampton WV3. . . 255 C1
Surrey Ho 2 DY8 . . . . . 279 F8
Surrey Rd Kidsgrove ST7. . 26 A2
Stafford ST17 . . . . 174 C8
Surrey Wlk WS9 . . . . . . 245 A1
Surtees Gr ST4 . . . . 73 B5
Sussex Ave WS9 . . . . . . 256 A8
Sussex Dr Cannock WS12. 210 B5
Kidsgrove ST7 . . . . 25 F2
Wolverhampton WV3. . . 255 C1
Sussex PI ST3. . . . . 73 D1
Sussex Rd DE15. . . . . . 185 E6
Sutherland Ave
Longton ST3. . . . . 284 B1
Wolverhampton WV2. . . 266 F8
Sutherland Cres ST11. . . . 90 E6
Sutherland Dr
Newcastle-u-L ST5. . . . . 70 F5
Wombourne WV5. . . . . 265 A1
Sutherland Gr WV6 . . . . 254 F4
Sutherland Prim Sch ST3 . 72 F1
Sutherland Rd
Cheslyn Hay WS6. . . . . 226 C2
Longsdon ST9 . . . . 30 A1
Longton ST3. . . . . 284 C3
Stone ST15 . . . . 120 C7
Tittensor ST12. . . . . 88 A1
Wolverhampton WV4. . . 266 B5
Sutherland St ST4. . . . . . 72 C6
Sutton Ave B78 . . . . 250 A2
Sutton CI WS15 . . . . . . 196 F6
Sutton CI Forton TF10. . . 169 C8
Wolverhampton WV4. . . 266 C2
Sutton Dr Stafford ST16 . 155 A4
Stoke-on-T ST4 . . . . . . 71 F4
Stoke-on-T ST4 . . . . . . 71 F5
Sutton La TF9. . . . . 112 C4
Sutton PI ST6. . . . . 42 B5
Sutton Rd Aldridge WS9 . 256 A1
Mile Oak B78 . . . . 260 A7
Tamworth B78 . . . . 249 C1
Sutton St
Newcastle-u-L ST5. . . . . 55 E6
Stourbridge DY8 . . . . . 275 F1
Sutton Way TF9. . . . . . . 112 B7
Swadlincote La DE11. . . 186 E2
Swaffham Way ST12 . . . . 58 D2
Swaffield Pk WS11. . . . . 210 B3
Swainsfield Rd DE13 . . . 182 A2
Swainsley CI 3 ST6. . . . . 57 A7
Swaledale Ave CW12. . . . 6 A5
Swallow CI
1 Kidsgrove ST7 . . . . . . 26 B2
Huntington WS12. . . . . 209 C7
Meir ST3 . . . . 90 A7
Rugeley WS15. . . . . . . 178 D2
Uttoxeter ST14 . . . . . . 126 B6
Swallow Croft Leek ST13. . 30 C3
Lichfield WS13 . . . . . . 214 A1
Swallow Ct Alrewas DE13. 201 A2
Wolverhampton WV10. . 240 B3
Swallowdale
5 Stafford ST17 . . . . . 175 D6
Brownhills WS9 . . . . . . 245 B4
Wolverhampton WV6. . . 254 F2
Swallowfall Ave DY8 . . . 279 C4
Swallowfields Dr WS12. . 210 B3
Swallowfields Rd DY3 . . 266 C2
Swallowfield B79 . . . . . 249 E6
Swallowmore View ST7 . . 40 C8
Swallow Rd 4 ST7. . . . . 26 F1
Swallows CI WS3 . . . . . 244 A5
Swallowsreach WS13 . . . 213 F1
Swallow Wlk ST8 . . . . . . 27 D7
Swanage CI ST3 . . . . 90 B7
Swancote Dr WV4. . . . . 265 C6
Swan Cotts WS14 . . . . . 232 E6
Swan Ct Burton u T DE14.. 166 F7
Church Eaton ST20. . . . 190 B8
Swan Dr WS8. . . . . 244 E7
Swan Farm La CW3 . . . . 67 B1
Swanfield Rd DY8. . . . . . 275 F1

Swanfields WS7 . . . . . . 229 C6
Swan Gr ST6. . . . . 41 D1
Swanholme Way ST5. . . . 85 C4
Swan La WS15 . . . . 161 A6
Swanland Gr ST3 . . . . . . 73 D4
Swan La Penkridge ST18 . 192 F6
Shareshill WV10 . . . . . 225 C1
Stoke-on-T ST4 . . . . . . 71 E3
Stourbridge DY8 . . . . . 275 F2
Swanmere TF10. . . . . . 168 F5
Swan Mews WS13. . . . . 231 A8
Swanmote B79 . . . . 249 F5
Swannington St DE13. . . 166 B6
Swan Pas ST11 . . . . 90 F7
Swan Pk B77. . . . . 250 C3
Swan Pool Gr WS4. . . . . 244 D1
Swan Rd
Draycott in t C DE6. . . . 144 D6
Lichfield WS13 . . . . . . 231 A7
Whittington WS14 . . . . 232 B6
Swansmoor Dr ST18 . . . 139 D1
Swan Sq ST6 . . . . 56 F8
Swan St Stoke-on-T ST4. . 72 B8
Stourbridge DY8 . . . . . 279 E5
Swanton PI ST4. . . . . . . 87 F7
Swan Wlk DE14 . . . . . . 166 D2
Swarbourn CI DE13 . . . . 182 A2
Swaythling Gr ST2 . . . . . 58 D1
Sweetbriar Way
Cannock WS12. . . . . . 210 D2
Stafford ST17 . . . . 175 C6
Sweetbrier Dr 4 DY8 . . 275 E1
Sweetman St WV6 . . . . . 255 F4
Sweetplace La ST20. . . . 189 E2
Sweetpool La DY8 . . . . . 281 F5
Swift CI Kidsgrove ST7. . . 26 B2
Uttoxeter ST14 . . . . . . 126 B6
Swift Dr ST8. . . . . 27 E8
Swift PI ST3 . . . . 73 F5
Swift B77. . . . . 250 E3
Swinburne CI
Stafford ST17 . . . . 174 C8
Stoke-on-T ST3 . . . . . . 72 F2
Swindale. 262 B7
Swindon Rd DY6. . . . . . 275 B6
Swinfen Broun Rd WS13. 231 A4
Swinford Leys WV5 . . . . 269 D5
Swin Forge Way DY3 . . . 269 E2
Swingle Hill Rd ST3 . . . . 72 F3
Swinscoe Hill DE6 . . . . . 66 B2
Swinson CI ST14 . . . . . . 96 A3
Swiss Dr DY8 . . . . 275 F2
Swiss Lodge Dr B78. . . . 260 F8
Swithin Dr ST4 . . . . 73 B6
Swynnerton Dr WV11 . . . 241 F4
Sycamore CI Biddulph ST8. 16 E2
Burton u T DE15. . . . . . 185 E5
Meir Heath ST3 . . . . . . 90 A5
Stourbridge DY8 . . . . . 279 D2
Talke ST7. . . . . 40 E8
Uttoxeter ST14 . . . . . . 125 F8
Sycamore Cres WS15 . . . 197 A6
Sycamore Dr Hixon ST18. 158 C8
Wolverhampton WV5. . . 255 D1
Sycamore Gdns ST6. . . . . 56 D8
Sycamore Gn
Cannock WS11. . . . . . 209 E6
Dudley DY1 . . . . 271 F5
Sycamore Green Prim Sch
DY1 . . . . 271 F5
Sycamore Gr
Newcastle-u-L ST5. . . . . 56 D3
Stoke-on-T ST3 . . . . . . 72 E3
Sycamore Hill WS15 . . . 211 F5
Sycamore La ST17 . . . . . 174 B8
Sycamore PI WS7 . . . . . 228 F7
Sycamore Rd
Burntwood WS7. . . . . . 228 F7
Burton u T DE15. . . . . . 185 F6
Cannock WS12. . . . . . 210 F4
Kingswinford DY6 . . . . 275 E6
Mayfield DE6. . . . . 81 C7
Stone ST15 . . . . 120 B8
Sycamores The
Hagley DY9 . . . . 281 F5
Lichfield WS13 . . . . . . 231 B5
Sutton Coldfield B74 . . . 257 F4
Sycamore B77. . . . . . . 261 E7
Sycamore Way
Huntington WS12. . . . . 209 D8
Market Drayton TF9. . . . 97 D2
Sydenham PI ST2 . . . . . . 73 D8
Sydnall La WV6 . . . . . . 112 F1
Sydney St
Burton u T DE14. . . . . . 166 D6
Newcastle-u-L ST5. . . . . 56 D2
Syerscote La
Clifton Campville B79 . . 218 B1
Wigginton B79 . . . . . . 234 C2
Sykesmoor B77. . . . . . . 262 B7
Sylvan Gr ST4. . . . . 71 E3
Sylvan Way ST17 . . . . . 175 C5
Sylvester St ST6. . . . . . . 57 A8
Sytch La WV5. . . . . 270 A5
Sytch Rd ST6 . . . . 43 B7

T

Tack Farm Rd DY8 . . . . . 275 D1
Tadgedale Ave TF9. . . . . 99 D5
Tagg La DE45. . . . . 14 D5
Tag La Cheswardine TF9 . 113 F3
Chipnall TF9 . . . . 114 A3
Talaton CI WV9 . . . . . . 240 A2
Talbot Ave B74 . . . . 257 B3
Talbot CI TF10 . . . . 168 D1

Talbot Fst Sch ST14. . . . 141 C8
Talbot Rd Rugeley WS15. . 196 F6
Stafford ST17 . . . . 285 B1
Wolverhampton WV2. . . 266 C2
Talbotshill La DY10. . . . . 280 C4
Talbot St 5 Leek ST13. . . 30 F5
Hanley ST1. . . . . 282 C1
Rugeley WS15. . . . . . . 196 F6
Talbot B77. . . . . 250 E3
Talbot Way TF9 . . . . 97 C2
Talke Rd
Newcastle-u-L,Red Street
ST7. . . . . 40 D4
Newcastle-u-L ST5. . . . . 55 E8
Talland Ave B77. . . . . . 250 E5
Tall Ash Ave CW12 . . . . . 6 A4
Tallis Gr ST1. . . . . 57 F5
Tallpines ST17 . . . . 175 C7
Tall Trees CI B74. . . . . . 257 D4
Tally CI ST2 . . . . 73 D7
Talsarn Gr ST4. . . . . 88 C6
Tamar CI WS8 . . . . 228 C2
Tamar Dr DY3. . . . . 271 F6
Tamar Gr Cheadle ST10. . 76 E1
Perton WV6. . . . . 254 E4
Stafford ST17 . . . . 174 B8
Tamar Rd Kidsgrove ST7. . 26 B2
Tamworth B77. . . . . . . 262 A5
Tame Ave WS7. . . . . . . 229 D6
Tame CI ST8. . . . . 16 D1
Tame Ct Fazeley B78 . . . 261 B8
Tamworth B79. . . . . . . 250 A5
Tamedrive B78,B79. . . . 250 A4
Tame Dr WS3. . . . . 244 A1
Tame Gr WS11. . . . . . . 226 D8
Tame St 2 ST6. . . . . . . 57 A5
Tame St B77. . . . . 250 D1
Tame Valley Bsns Pk
B77. . . . . 261 E6
Tame Valley Ind Est B77. 261 E6
Tame Wlk ST3 . . . . 73 A4
Tamworth Bsns Ctr B77 . 251 B3
Tamworth Bsns Pk B77. . 251 B3
Tamworth Castle Mus★
B79 . . . . 250 B4
Tamworth Castle★ B79. . 250 B4
Tamworth CI WS8. . . . . 228 F2
Tamworth & Lichfield Coll
(Tamworth Campus)
B79 . . . . 250 B6
Tamworth Rd (Amington)
B77 . . . . 250 F5
Tamworth Rd B78. . . . . 261 C2
Tamworth Rd (Dosthill)
B77 . . . . 261 C6
Tamworth Rd Elford B79. 233 E8
Lichfield WS14. . . . . . 231 E5
Polesworth B78. . . . . . 251 E1
Sutton Coldfield B75 . . 259 A2
Tamworth,Mount Pleasant
B77 . . . . 250 F7
Tamworth,Two Gates B77. 261 D8
Whittington WS14 . . . . 232 B3
Wood End CV9. . . . . . 262 C1
Tamworth Sta B79. . . . . 250 C5
Tamworth St WS13. . . . . 231 B8
Tan Bank TF10. . . . . . . 168 F3
Tanfield CI WV6 . . . . . . 255 B3
Tanglewood Gr DY3. . . . 266 C2
Tangmere CI WV6. . . . . 254 E5
Tanhill B77. . . . . 262 B7
Tanners Rd ST2. . . . . . . 58 B7
Tannery CI WS15. . . . . . 178 F1
Tansey CI ST2. . . . . 58 A3
Tansey Green Rd DY6 . . 271 A1
Tansley View WV2 . . . . . 266 D7
Tansy Sutton Coldfield B74. 257 F4
Tamworth B77. . . . . . . 250 C3
Tanyard WS13 . . . . 231 C8
Tape St ST10 . . . . 76 D5
Taplin CI ST16 . . . . 155 D7
Taplow PI WS11. . . . . . 209 F4
Tapton CI WS3. . . . . . . 243 C3
Tara Gr ST2 . . . . 43 A3
Targate Ct WS15 . . . . . 198 A5
Target CI ST7. . . . . 40 E6
Tarleton Rd ST1. . . . . . . 57 E4
Tarporley Gr ST4 . . . . . . 71 E5
Tarquin CI DE13 . . . . . . 147 E2
Tarragona Dr ST17. . . . . 175 A8
Tarragon Dr ST3. . . . . . . 90 A6
Tarrant B77. . . . . 261 F8
Tarvin Gr ST6. . . . . 41 F6
Tasman Dr ST18 . . . . . . 156 C5
Tasman Gr WV6 . . . . . . 254 E5
Tasman Sq ST1. . . . . . . 57 E5
Tatenhill Comm DE13 . . 164 E1
Tatenhill La
Burton u T DE13. . . . . . 184 D7
Rangemore DE13. . . . . 164 C2
Tatenhill DE13. . . . . . . 184 A8
Tatlowfold La ST10. . . . . 48 F4
Tatton CI ST13. . . . . . . 30 B5
Tatton St ST3. . . . . 284 C2
Taunton Ave WV10 . . . . 240 D4
Taunton PI ST5 . . . . 55 F7
Taunton Way ST2 . . . . . 58 D2
Taurus Gr ST6. . . . . 41 F6
Taverners CI WV12 . . . . 242 C1
Taverners Dr ST15 . . . . 120 D6
Tavistock Ave ST17 . . . . 156 D1
Tavistock CI B79. . . . . . 250 C7
Tavistock Cres ST5. . . . . 71 A5
Tavistock PI ST4. . . . . . . 56 E1
Tawney CI ST7. . . . . 26 B2
Tawney Cres ST3 . . . . . . 74 B2
Tay CI Biddulph ST8 . . . . 16 E1
Cheadle ST10. . . . . . . 76 E5
Longton ST3. . . . . 284 C5

Taylor Ave ST5 . . . . 56 C4
Taylor Rd Bucknall ST2 . . . . 58 B6
 Wolverhampton WV4 . . . 266 F5
Taylors La ST14 . . . . 95 D4
Taylor's La WS15 . . . . 178 E1
Taylor St
 Newcastle-u-L ST5 . . . . . . 56 C4
 Stoke-on-T ST6 . . . . 41 C7
Taylor Wlk ST17 . . . . 174 C7
Taynton Cl ST6 . . . . 42 B8
Teal Cl ST5 . . . . 85 C5
Teal View ST6 . . . . 42 D2
Tean Cl Burntwood WS7 . . 229 D6
 Burton u T DE15 . . . . . . 167 A1
Teanhurst Cl ST10 . . . . 92 F2
Teanhurst Rd ST10 . . . . . . 92 F2
Tean Rd ST10 . . . . 76 D1
Teasel Gr WV10 . . . . 241 B7
Tebworth Cl WV9 . . . . 239 F2
Tedder Rd ST16 . . . . 156 B5
Teddesley Ct WS11 . . . . . . 209 E3
Teddesley Rd
 Acton Trussell ST19 . . . . 193 B6
 Penkridge ST19 . . . . 192 F2
 Stafford ST17 . . . . 175 D1
Teddesley Way WS12 . . . . 209 C6
Teign B77 . . . . 262 A5
Telegraph St ST17 . . . . . . 285 B1
Telford Ave
 Albrighton WV7 . . . . 237 B6
 Great Wyrley WS6 . . . . . 226 F3
Telford Cl
 Burntwood WS7 . . . . 229 C8
 Congleton CW12 . . . . 6 C2
 Stone ST15 . . . . 120 C6
 Talke ST7 . . . . 40 C8
Telford Dr ST16 . . . . 155 F8
Telford Gdns
 Brewood ST19 . . . . 223 C7
 Wolverhampton WV3 . . . 265 D7
Telford Gr WS12 . . . . 210 B7
Telford La ST20 . . . . 171 C5
Telford Rd B79 . . . . 249 F8
Telford Way ST6 . . . . 42 A4
Tellright Gr ST5 . . . . 56 B7
Tellwright St ST6 . . . . 42 A1
Telmah Cl DE13 . . . . 147 D1
Teme Rd DY8 . . . . 279 F3
Temperance Pl ST6 . . . . . . 41 D7
Tempest St B79 . . . . 250 A5
Templar Cres ST5 . . . . 56 B6
Templars Way ST19 . . . . . 207 F8
Templar Terr ST5 . . . . 56 B6
Temple Cl DE14 . . . . 166 E7
Temple St Dudley DY3 . . . 271 D3
 Stoke-on-T ST4 . . . . 72 D6
Templeton Ave ST2 . . . . . . 73 C8
Tenacre La DY3 . . . . 271 E6
Tenbury Cl WS9 . . . . 256 C8
Tenbury Ct WV4 . . . . 265 D5
Tenbury Gdns WV4 . . . . . 265 D5
Tengam Gr ST2 . . . . 58 C1
Ten Butts Cres ST17 . . . . 174 F5
Tenby Dr ST16 . . . . 155 F6
Tenby Gr ST5 . . . . 55 F7
Tenford La ST10 . . . . 92 E5
Tennant St ST5 . . . . 56 B7
Tennscore Ave WS6 . . . . . 226 E3
Tennyson Ave
 Burntwood WS7 . . . . 212 A1
 Kidsgrove ST7 . . . . 41 A8
 Sutton Coldfield B74 . . . 257 F6
 Tamworth B79 . . . . 250 A6
Tennyson Cl Cheadle ST10 . . 76 B2
 Market Drayton TF9 . . . . 112 A4
Tennyson Gdns ST3 . . . . . . 72 F2
Tennyson Rd
 Burton u T DE14 . . . . . . 166 D7
 Dudley DY3 . . . . 271 A4
 Stafford ST17 . . . . 174 C8
 Wolverhampton WV10 . . 241 A1
Tenterbanks ST16 . . . . . . 285 A3
Tercel Gr ST3 . . . . 90 A7
Terence Wlk ST8 . . . . 27 B2
Tern Ave ST7 . . . . 26 C2
Tern Cl Biddulph ST8 . . . . . 27 E8
 Wolverhampton WV4 . . . 266 D3
Tern Gr TF9 . . . . 99 E5
Tern Ridge TF9 . . . . 97 D1
Tern View TF9 . . . . 112 B7
Terrace The Cheadle ST10 . . 76 D3
 Wolverhampton WV3 . . . 255 C1
Terrington Dr ST5 . . . . 71 B2
Terry Cl Lichfield WS13 . . . 213 F2
 Meir ST3 . . . . 74 B3
Terson Way ST4 . . . . 73 F4
Tettenhall Arc WV6 . . . . . 255 D5
Tettenhall Coll WV6 . . . . . 255 D4
Tettenhall Rd WV1,WV3,
 WV6 . . . . 255 F4
Tettenhall Wood Sch
 WV6 . . . . 255 B3
Teveray Dr ST19 . . . . 207 F7
Teviot Gdns WV8 . . . . 239 A5
Tewe WS13 . . . . 231 A6
Tewkesbury Gr ST2 . . . . . . 58 A4
Tewkesbury Rd WS3 . . . . 242 E2
Tewnals La WS13 . . . . 213 C5
Tewson Gr ST6 . . . . 57 C7
Thackeray Dr Longton ST3 . . 73 A2
 Tamworth B79 . . . . 250 A7
Thackeray Wlk ST17 . . . . 174 C7
Thames Dr Biddulph ST8 . . . 27 E8
 Cheadle ST10 . . . . 76 E1
Thames Ho DY3 . . . . 271 D3
Thames Rd
 Newcastle-u-L ST5 . . . . . . 71 B4
 Walsall WS3 . . . . 243 E1

Thames Way ST17 . . . . . . 174 B8
Thanet Cl DY6 . . . . 275 C7
Thanet Gr ST3 . . . . 284 A3
Thatcham Gr ST3 . . . . 88 F7
Thatcher Gr ST8 . . . . 27 B8
Thatchers Ct WV5 . . . . . . 264 C1
Thatchmoor La DE13 . . . . 182 C7
Thelma Ave ST6 . . . . 43 B7
Theodore Rd ST2 . . . . 58 B3
Theresa Cl ST4 . . . . 72 A2
Third Ave Branston DE14 . . 165 F1
 Brownhills WS8 . . . . 229 A1
 Bucknall ST2 . . . . 58 D4
 Kidsgrove ST7 . . . . 25 F1
 Kingswinford DY6 . . . . . 275 F8
Thirlmere Cl
 Cannock WS11 . . . . 209 E1
 Wolverhampton WV6 . . . 255 D8
Thirlmere Dr WV11 . . . . . 242 A2
Thirlmere Gr Longton ST3 . . 73 E3
 Perton WV6 . . . . 254 F4
Thirlmere Pl ST5 . . . . 71 B5
Thirlmere Rd WV6 . . . . . . 255 D8
Thirlmere Way ST17 . . . . 174 E7
Thirsk Pl ST5 . . . . 55 A2
Thistleberry Ave ST5 . . . . . 70 F7
Thistle Cl Dudley DY3 . . . 271 F6
 Rugeley WS15 . . . . 178 C2
Thistle Down Cl B74 . . . . 257 A2
Thistledown Dr
 3 Cannock WS12 . . . . 210 D1
 Featherstone WV10 . . . . 241 A7
Thistledown Wlk DY3 . . . 266 C1
Thistles The ST5 . . . . 70 F7
Thistley Hough High Sch
 ST4 . . . . 71 E6
Thistley Hough ST4 . . . . . . 71 F6
Thistley Nook WS13 . . . . 214 A1
Thomas Alleyne's High Sch
 ST14 . . . . 126 C8
Thomas Ave
 Newcastle-u-L ST5 . . . . . . 56 A4
 Stafford ST16 . . . . 155 B3
 Stone ST15 . . . . 120 C8
Thomas Barnes Prim Sch
 B78 . . . . 249 B7
Thomas Greenway
 WS13 . . . . 214 A2
Thomas Hardy Ct B79 . . . 250 A7
Thomas Ho WS3 . . . . 243 D3
Thomas Russell Inf Sch
 DE13 . . . . 183 E1
Thomas Russell Jun Sch
 DE13 . . . . 183 E1
Thomas St Biddulph ST8 . . . 16 D1
 Leek ST13 . . . . 30 D6
 Packmoor ST7 . . . . 26 F1
 Talke ST7 . . . . 40 D8
 Tamworth B77 . . . . 250 D4
 Wolverhampton WV2 . . . 266 C6
Thompson Ave WV2 . . . . . 266 E6
Thompson Cl ST17 . . . . . . 174 C7
Thompson Rd WS15 . . . . 197 B6
Thompstone Ave ST5 . . . . . 55 F3
Thor Cl WS11 . . . . 210 A5
Thoresby Croft DY1 . . . . . 271 F3
Thoresby B79 . . . . 249 E6
Thorley's Hill WS15 . . . . . 212 C6
Thornbridge Gr WS9 . . . . 244 F3
Thornburrow Dr ST4 . . . . . 71 E8
Thornbury Ct WV6 . . . . . . 255 A3
Thornby Ave B77 . . . . 261 B6
Thorncliffe View WS13 . . . 31 B8
Thorncliff Gr ST5 . . . . 57 F5
Thorncliff Rd ST13 . . . . 31 C7
Thorn Cl WS15 . . . . 197 A7
Thorndyke St ST1 . . . . . . 282 A1
Thorne Pl ST5 . . . . 74 B3
Thornescroft Gdns DE14 . 185 B6
Thornes Croft WS9 . . . . . 245 E4
Thornewill Dr DE13 . . . . . 147 F1
Thorneycroft Ave ST6 . . . . 42 B2
Thorneyfields La
 Stafford ST17 . . . . 174 A8
 Stafford ST17 . . . . 174 A7
Thorney Lanes
 Gorsty Hill DE13 . . . . . . 143 B2
 Newborough DE13 . . . . . 162 D6
Thorney Rd B74 . . . . 256 F1
Thornfield Ave ST13 . . . . . 31 B5
Thornfield Cres WS7 . . . . 229 A8
Thornfield Croft DY3 . . . . 271 E7
Thornham Cl ST5 . . . . 71 B2
Thornham Gn ST2 . . . . 58 C1
Thornhill Cl DE13 . . . . 183 C1
Thornhill Dr CW3 . . . . 68 E7
Thornhill Rd Bucknall ST2 . . 73 E8
 Cannock WS12 . . . . 209 F7
 Leek ST13 . . . . 30 C4
 Little Aston B74 . . . . 257 B1
Thornleigh DY3 . . . . 271 D5
Thornley Cl WV11 . . . . . . 241 F1
Thornley Croft WS6 . . . . . 226 D1
Thornley Rd
 Stoke-on-T ST6 . . . . 42 A3
 Wolverhampton WV11 . . 241 F1
Thornley St DE14 . . . . 166 D5
Thornton Rd ST4 . . . . 72 C8
Thornton Way B77 . . . . . . 261 C8
Thorn Tree La DE11 . . . . . 186 F8
Thornyedge Rd
 Bagnall ST9 . . . . 44 A1
 Bagnall,Tompkin ST9 . . . 44 C1
Thornyhurst La WS14 . . . 246 A6
Thorny Rd WS15 . . . . 118 B6
Thorpe Ave WS7 . . . . 228 D8

Thorpe Cl
 Burntwood WS7 . . . . 228 D8
 Burton u T DE15 . . . . . . 167 C2
Thorpe Dr WS13 . . . . 215 E8
Thorpe Gn ST3 . . . . 88 F7
Thorpe Rise ST10 . . . . 76 E6
Thorpe St WS7 . . . . 228 D8
Three Mile La ST5 . . . . 69 F4
Three Spires Sh Ctr
 WS13 . . . . 231 B7
Three Tuns La WV10 . . . . 240 D1
Three Tuns Par WV10 . . . 240 D1
Thrift Rd DE14 . . . . 185 B8
Thurlstone Dr WV4 . . . . . 265 F4
Thurlstone Rd WS3 . . . . . 243 B3
Thurlwood Dr ST6 . . . . 42 F2
Thurne B77 . . . . 261 F8
Thursfield Ave ST7 . . . . . . 26 C3
Thursfield Pl ST6 . . . . 42 D4
Thursfield Prim Sch ST7 . . 26 E3
Thursfield Wlk ST6 . . . . . . 42 D5
Thurso B77 . . . . 250 E5
Thurston Way ST2 . . . . 73 C8
Thurvaston Rd DE6 . . . . . . 96 F1
Thyme Gr ST3 . . . . 90 B6
Tibberton Dr WV3 . . . . . . 265 D7
Tibb St ST7 . . . . 39 F2
Tiber Dr ST5 . . . . 55 E5
Tickhill La ST10,ST11 . . . . 74 F5
Tidebrook Pl ST6 . . . . 41 E7
Tideswell Gn DE11 . . . . . . 186 E5
Tideswell Rd ST3 . . . . 284 C5
Tierney St ST1 . . . . 282 C4
Tiffany La WV9 . . . . 239 F2
Tilbrook Cl ST2 . . . . 73 C8
Tilbury Cl WV3 . . . . 265 A8
Tilcon Ave ST18 . . . . 156 D2
Tildesley Ct ST19 . . . . 207 E8
Tildesley Rd ST19 . . . . . . 207 E8
Tilehurst Pl ST3 . . . . 72 E1
Tilery La ST3 . . . . 88 D8
Tilewright Cl ST7 . . . . 26 B2
Tilia Rd B77 . . . . 251 B5
Tiller Gr B75 . . . . 258 D4
Tillett Gn ST3 . . . . 74 B3
Tilling Dr ST5 . . . . 120 A6
Tillington Manor Prim Sch
 ST16 . . . . 155 C6
Tillington St ST16 . . . . . . 155 D5
Till Wlk ST3 . . . . 73 D6
Tilson Ave ST4 . . . . 71 F7
Tilstone Cl ST7 . . . . 41 A8
Timberfields Rd ST16 . . . 155 C5
Timberfields ST15 . . . . . . 118 E6
Timber Gr ST19 . . . . 223 D6
Timber La ST14 . . . . 126 B6
Timber Pit La ST19 . . . . . 205 B4
Timble Cl ST2 . . . . 73 C8
Times Sq ST3 . . . . 284 B4
Timmis Cl ST6 . . . . 42 A4
Timmis St ST1 . . . . 57 A3
Timor Gr ST4 . . . . 88 B8
Timothy Cl ST3 . . . . 73 C6
Tinacre Hill WV6 . . . . 254 E2
Tinker's Castle Rd WV5 . . 263 D1
Tinkers Green Rd B77 . . . 261 F6
Tinkers La Ashley TF9 . . . 100 A4
 Brewood ST19 . . . . 223 E6
Tinker's La ST14 . . . . 143 A7
Tinsell Brook DE65 . . . . . 147 E8
Tintagel Cl Perton WV6 . . 254 F3
 Stretton ST19 . . . . 147 E2
Tintagel Dr DY1 . . . . 271 E2
Tintern Cres WS3 . . . . . . 242 F2
Tintern Cl WV6 . . . . 254 E4
Tintern Pl ST5 . . . . 55 F7
Tintern St ST1 . . . . 57 E3
Tintern Way WS3 . . . . . . 242 F2
Tipping Ave ST3 . . . . 74 B1
Tipping St ST16 . . . . 285 B3
Tipton Rd DY3 . . . . 271 F7
Tipton St DY3 . . . . 271 E7
Tirley St ST4 . . . . 72 E5
Tissington Pl ST3 . . . . 90 C7
Titan Way WS13 . . . . 231 F8
Titchfield Cl WV10 . . . . . 240 E4
Tithe Barn Ct ST16 . . . . . 156 A4
Tithe Barn La WS13,
 WS15 . . . . 212 C5
Tithebarn Rd WS15 . . . . . 178 E2
Tithe Barn Rd ST16 . . . . . 156 A4
Tittensor CE Fst Sch ST12 . 88 A1
Tittensor Rd
 Barlaston ST12 . . . . 104 B8
 Newcastle-u-L ST5 . . . . . . 71 C5
Titterton La ST13 . . . . 33 B4
Titterton St ST4 . . . . 72 C6
Tittesworth Ave ST13 . . . . 31 A7
Tittesworth Rest ST13 . . . . 20 E4
Tiverton Ave ST17 . . . . . . 175 D4
Tiverton Cl DY8 . . . . 275 F3
Tiverton Rd ST2 . . . . 73 C8
Tixall Ct ST18 . . . . 157 E3
Tixall Mews ST18 . . . . . . 157 D3
Tixall Rd Stafford ST18 . . 156 D3
 Tixall ST18 . . . . 157 B2
Toby's Hill DE6 . . . . 144 C7
Toft End Rd ST6 . . . . 41 B1
Tolkien Way ST4 . . . . 72 A8
Toll Bar Rd ST9 . . . . 59 D4
Tolldish La ST18 . . . . 158 C2
Tollgate Ave ST5 . . . . 85 D5
Tollgate Cl ST7 . . . . 40 C8
Tollgate Cotts DE6 . . . . . . 81 E8
Tollgate Dr ST16 . . . . 155 F8
Tollgate Ind Est ST16 . . . 155 F8
Tollgate La B79 . . . . 233 E3

Tollgate Rd ST13 . . . . 29 C6
Tollhouse Way WV5 . . . . . 269 E7
Tolman Dr B77 . . . . 250 D3
Tolson Ave B78 . . . . 261 B8
Tolson Cl B77 . . . . 261 D5
Tolworth Gdns WV2 . . . . 266 F2
Tom Fields ST7 . . . . 39 F1
Tomkinson Cl TF10 . . . . . 169 A4
Tom La DY7 . . . . 268 E5
Tomlinson Bsns Pk DE65 129 F4
Tomlinson St ST6 . . . . 56 D8
Tommy's La CW12 . . . . 6 A4
Tompkin Rd ST9 . . . . 44 B4
Tom Williams Way B77 . . 261 C8
Tonadine Cl WV11 . . . . . . 242 A1
Tonbridge Ave B78 . . . . . . 42 B4
Toney Pl ST2 . . . . 57 F3
Tong Cl ST9 . . . . 221 E8
Tong Dr TF11 . . . . 203 F1
Tong Rd ST19 . . . . 221 F7
Tongue Ave B78 . . . . 261 A8
Tongue La ST6 . . . . 27 F1
Tontine Sq ST1 . . . . 282 B3
Tontines Sh Ctr The ST1 . 282 B3
Tontine St ST1 . . . . 282 B3
Tony Waddington Pl ST4 . . 72 D4
Toothill Rd ST14 . . . . 126 C4
Top Chapel La ST6 . . . . . . 28 B1
Topham Pl ST2 . . . . 57 F3
Top Heath Row ST6 . . . . . . 43 B8
Top La Beech ST4 . . . . . . 103 C8
 Beech ST4 . . . . 87 C1
Top Rd
 Acton Trussell ST17 . . . . 175 B1
 Biddulph ST8 . . . . 17 D3
Top Station Rd ST7 . . . . . . 26 D7
Torbay B77 . . . . 250 E5
Torc Ave ST7 . . . . 250 E4
Torc High Sch B77 . . . . . 250 F1
Torfield WV8 . . . . 239 E2
Torrance Cl DE14 . . . . . . 185 A6
Torrance Gr ST14 . . . . . . 110 F2
Torres Wlk ST1 . . . . 57 E5
Torridge Dr ST17 . . . . . . 174 B8
Torridge B77 . . . . 262 A5
Torridon Cl ST4 . . . . 88 C6
Torridon Rd WV11 . . . . . 242 B1
Torrington Ave ST17 . . . . 175 E8
Torside B77 . . . . 262 B7
Tor St ST1 . . . . 57 D7
Torvale Rd WV6 . . . . 255 A2
Torville Dr ST8 . . . . 27 E8
Tor Way WS3 . . . . 243 F3
Totnes Cl DE13 . . . . 166 D7
Tower Bsns Pk WS15 . . . 197 B5
Tower Cl Biddulph ST8 . . . 27 B6
 Market Drayton TF9 . . . . 97 B1
Tower Crane Dr ST10 . . . . 76 B1
Tower Hill Rd
 Biddulph ST8 . . . . 27 A6
 Mow Cop ST7 . . . . 26 F7
Tower Rd Burton u T DE15 167 B2
 Cannock WS12 . . . . 194 F1
 Loggerheads TF9 . . . . . . 99 F4
 Sutton Coldfield B75 . . . 258 B3
Tower Sq ST6 . . . . 41 D3
Tower St DY3 . . . . 266 D3
Tower View Prim Sch
 DE15 . . . . 167 C3
Tower View Rd WS6 . . . . 242 F8
Town End ST10 . . . . 76 C3
Townend ST11 . . . . 106 E8
Townend La Swinscoe DE6 . 65 E5
 Waterhouses ST10 . . . . . 48 F4
Townfield Cl ST7 . . . . 25 D2
Townfields WS13 . . . . . . 231 A7
Townfold WS3 . . . . 244 A4
Town Head ST10 . . . . 78 F1
Town Head Farm ST10 . . . 78 F1
Town Hill DE13 . . . . 182 B2
Town Meadows Way
 ST14 . . . . 126 C8
Town Rd ST1 . . . . 282 B4
Townsend Ave DY3 . . . . . 271 D8
Townsend Cl B79 . . . . 236 D4
Townsend Ho B79 . . . . . . 250 A4
Townsend La ST7 . . . . 25 A8
Townsend Pl Bucknall ST2 . 58 B3
 Kingswinford DY6 . . . . . 275 D6
Town Wells Mews TF10 . . 168 F1
Town Yard Ind Est ST13 . . 30 D5
Toy Cl WS15 . . . . 178 D1
Trade St ST4 . . . . 72 B7
Trafalgar Cl WS12 . . . . . . 210 E4
Trafalgar Ct **6** ST6 . . . . . 57 A7
Trafalgar Ho WS12 . . . . . 210 E4
Trafalgar Rd ST4 . . . . 71 E4
Trafalgar St ST1 . . . . 282 B4
Trafford Cl ST13 . . . . 31 B5
Tramway The DE11 . . . . . 186 F7
Transport La ST3 . . . . 284 B3
Tranter Cres WS11 . . . . . 210 B3
Tranter Rd ST2 . . . . 58 B6
Tranwell Cl WV9 . . . . 239 F2
Travellers Cl WS7 . . . . . . 229 A5
Travers Ct ST4 . . . . 72 D6
Travers St ST6 . . . . 56 E7
Treasure Cl B77 . . . . 250 E4
Trecastle Gr ST3 . . . . 73 E1
Tregaron Rd ST2 . . . . 59 A3
Tregenna Cl **8** ST3 . . . . . 90 A7
Tregew Pl ST5 . . . . 55 D2
Tregony Rise WS14 . . . . . 231 D6
Tregowan St ST6 . . . . 42 B3
Trenance Cl WS14 . . . . . . 231 D7

Trenchard Ave ST16 . . . . 156 A5
Trent Bridge Cl ST4 . . . . . 88 D7
Trent Bridge Ho DE14 . . . 166 F3
Trent Cl Burntwood WS7 . 229 D6
 Cheadle ST10 . . . . 76 E1
 Great Haywood ST18 . . . 158 B2
 Perton WV6 . . . . 254 E4
 Stafford ST17 . . . . 174 F6
 Stone ST15 . . . . 119 F8
Trent Ct ST15 . . . . 119 F8
Trentfield La ST18 . . . . . . 137 D5
Trentfields Rd ST2 . . . . . . 43 B2
Trent Gr Biddulph ST8 . . . . 27 D6
 Newcastle-u-L ST5 . . . . . 71 A3
Trentham Bsns Ctr ST4 . . 88 D7
Trentham Cl WS11 . . . . . 210 B1
Trentham Ct ST4 . . . . 88 A1
Trentham Gardens Cl ST4 87 F7
Trentham Gdns★ ST4 . . . . 87 F7
Trentham Gr ST5 . . . . 56 C4
Trentham High Sch ST4 . . 87 F8
Trentham Rd
 Hanchurch ST5 . . . . 86 E8
 Newcastle-u-L ST5 . . . . . 71 A1
 Stoke-on-T ST4,ST3 . . . . 88 E7
Trentham Rise WV2 . . . . . 266 F7
Trent Ho Cannock WS11 . 210 C5
 Dudley DY3 . . . . 271 E3
Trent Ind Est DE14 . . . . . 166 E4
Trent La
 Great Haywood ST18 . . . 158 B2
 Hixon ST18 . . . . 157 E8
 Newton Solney DE15 . . . 167 D8
Trentley Dr ST8 . . . . 28 B8
Trentley Rd ST4 . . . . 88 A7
Trentmill Rd ST1 . . . . 57 E2
Trent Rd
 Blythe Bridge ST11 . . . . . 91 A7
 Cannock WS11 . . . . 209 E6
 Stone ST15 . . . . 104 E1
 Walsall WS3 . . . . 244 A1
Trentside Rd ST6 . . . . 43 A5
Trent St Bucknall ST2 . . . . 57 F3
 Burton u T DE14 . . . . . . 166 C1
Trent Terr
 Burton u T ST4 . . . . 166 C3
 Stoke-on-T ST6 . . . . 43 A5
Trent Vale CE Prim Sch
 ST4 . . . . 71 E3
Trent Valley Cotts WS13 . 214 F1
Trent Valley Rd
 Lichfield WS13,WS14 . . . 231 D3
 Stoke-on-T ST4 . . . . 71 F5
Trent Valley Trad Est
 WS15 . . . . 178 D2
Trent View Cl WS15 . . . . 197 A7
Trentway Cl ST2 . . . . 58 A3
Trent Wlk Hanley ST1 . . . 282 C1
 Ingestre ST18 . . . . 157 E7
Tresham Rd **2** DY6 . . . . 275 D8
Trevelyan's Cl ST16 . . . . . 155 C8
Trevelyn Cl DE15 . . . . . . 167 C2
Trevithick Cl Bucknall ST2 . 73 D7
 Burntwood WS7 . . . . 229 C8
Trevitt Pl ST19 . . . . 205 C6
Trevor Ave WS6 . . . . 227 A3
Trevor Dr ST11 . . . . 74 D3
Trevor Rd WS3 . . . . 243 F5
Trevose Cl WS3 . . . . 242 F3
Trimley Way ST2 . . . . 58 A2
Trimpley Gdns WV4 . . . . 265 E3
Trimpos ST1 . . . . 76 A4
Triner Pl ST6 . . . . 42 E4
Tring Cl ST2 . . . . 73 C8
Tring Ct WV6 . . . . 255 F4
Trinity Cl Cannock WS11 . 226 E8
 Shenstone WS14 . . . . . . 246 F6
 Stourbridge DY8 . . . . . . 275 D2
Trinity Ct Congleton CW12 . 6 B1
 Newcastle-u-L ST5 . . . . . 55 F7
Trinity Dr Stone ST15 . . . 104 F1
 Tamworth B79 . . . . 249 D6
Trinity Gorse ST16 . . . . . 155 B8
Trinity Pl Bucknall ST2 . . . 58 B3
 Congleton CW12 . . . . . . 16 B8
Trinity Rd Eccleshall ST21 133 D6
 Sutton Coldfield B75 . . . 258 C1
 Uttoxeter ST14 . . . . 126 C7
 Wood End B78,CV9 . . . . 262 B3
Trinity Rise ST16 . . . . 155 B8
Trinity Sq ST14 . . . . 126 C7
Trinity St ST1 . . . . 282 B3
Trinity Wlk ST14 . . . . 126 C7
Tristram Gr DE13 . . . . . . 147 E2
Triton Cl WS6 . . . . 226 F1
Triton Wlk ST6 . . . . 42 D1
Triumph B77 . . . . 250 E3
Trojan B77 . . . . 250 E3
Troon Cl Stretton DE13 . . 147 C1
 Walsall WS3 . . . . 243 A3
Troon Ct WV6 . . . . 254 D5
Troon Pl DY8 . . . . 275 C3
Troon B77 . . . . 251 C4
Troutdale Cl ST4 . . . . 73 B6
Trowbridge Cres ST2 . . . . 58 C3
Trubshaw Cl ST18 . . . . . . 177 E8
Trubshaw Cross ST6 . . . . 56 D8
Trubshaw Ct ST7 . . . . 26 B3
Trubshawe Cl ST6 . . . . . . 56 D8
Trubshaw Pl ST7 . . . . 26 B3
Truro Cl Congleton CW12 . 15 E8
 Lichfield WS13 . . . . 214 B3
 Rugeley WS15 . . . . 196 D6
Truro Pl Bucknall ST2 . . . . 58 B2
 Cannock WS12 . . . . 227 C8

Truro Way ST17 . . . . .156 D1
Trussel Grange ST17 . . . . .175 B1
Trussell Cl ST17 . . . . .175 A1
Trustley Cl DE14 . . . . .185 B7
Trysull Gdns WV3 . . . . . .265 D2
Trysull Holloway WV5 . . . .264 C3
Trysull Rd Orton WV5 . . . .264 E1
Wolverhampton WV3 . . . . . .265 D2
Wombourne WV5 . . . . .269 E8
Tuckers Pl TF10 . . . . .168 E3
Tudor Cl Burntwood WS7 .229 C6
Cheslyn Hay WS6 . . . . . . .226 E3
Lichfield WS14 . . . . .231 F6
Market Drayton TF9 . . . . . . .97 B2
Newport TF10 . . . . .169 A4
Stoke-on-T ST4 . . . . .72 A6
Stone ST15 . . . . .119 F6
Tudor Cres Tamworth B77 .250 C4
Wolverhampton WV2 . . . . .266 B6
Tudor Ct Essington WV11 .241 F4
Fulford ST11 . . . . .90 C1
Newcastle-u-L ST5 . . . . . . .56 B6
Sutton Coldfield B74 . . . . .258 A4
Tudor Gdns DY8 . . . . .279 E5
Tudor Gr ST5 . . . . .56 C4
Tudor Hollow
2 Burton u T DE13 . . . .166 D8
Fulford ST11 . . . . .90 E1
Tudor Park Ct B74 . . . . . .257 F3
Tudor Park Gdns WS7 . . . .229 C6
Tudor Pl DY3 . . . . .271 E6
Tudor Rd Burntwood WS7 .229 C6
Cannock WS12 . . . . .209 F8
Dudley DY3 . . . . .271 E6
Tudor Rise
Clifton Campville B79 . . . . .218 E2
Stafford ST16 . . . . .155 C8
Tudor Rose Ct ST6 . . . . . . .42 E2
Tudor Rose Way ST6 . . . . . .42 E2
Tudor Row **3** WS13 . . . . .231 B1
Tudors The ST6 . . . . .41 E4
Tudor Vale DY3 . . . . .271 E6
Tudor Way
Cheslyn Hay WS6 . . . . . . .226 D1
Stafford ST17 . . . . .155 B1
Tuke Pl WS13 . . . . .213 F1
Tulip Gr ST5 . . . . .283 C4
Tulley Pl ST2 . . . . .58 A3
Tullis Cl ST16 . . . . .155 C2
Tulsa Cl ST2 . . . . .58 A1
Tunbridge Dr ST5 . . . . .54 F2
Tunley St ST15 . . . . .104 F1
Tunnicliffe Cl ST3 . . . . .73 E3
Tunnicliffe Dr WS15 . . . . .178 D1
Tunnicliffe Way ST14 . . . . .110 F2
Tunstall La ST20 . . . . .131 F2
Tunstall Rd Biddulph ST8 . .27 C5
Bosley CW12,SK11 . . . . .7 F2
Congleton CW12 . . . . .6 F2
Tunstall Road Ind Est ST8 .27 B4
Tuppenhurst La WS15 . . . .198 D3
Turf Cl WS11 . . . . .228 A4
Turf Cotts WV4 . . . . .265 F2
Turf Pitts La B75 . . . . .258 F4
Turin Cl ST3 . . . . .73 E4
Turin Dr ST5 . . . . .70 E6
Turls Hill Rd Sedgley DY3 .271 F8
Sedgley WV14 . . . . .271 F8
Turls St DY3 . . . . .271 E8
Turnberry Dr ST4 . . . . .88 A8
Turnberry Gr WV6 . . . . . . .254 D5
Turnberry Rd WS3 . . . . . . .243 A4
Turnberry B77 . . . . .251 C5
Turnbull Rd WS13 . . . . . . .215 C6
Turnbury Cl DE14 . . . . . . .185 A7
Turner Ave Audley ST7 . . . .40 A1
Wolverhampton WV4,
WV14 . . . . .266 F2
Turner Cl WS11 . . . . .210 D2
Turner Cres ST5 . . . . .55 E6
Turner Croft WS13 . . . . . . .215 D8
Turner Gr WV6 . . . . .255 A4
Turner's Gr DY3 . . . . .271 C4
Turner's Hill Rd DY3 . . . . .271 C4
Turners La TF10 . . . . .168 A3
Turner St
Dudley,Gornalwood DY3 . .271 D3
Hanley ST1 . . . . .57 E5
Turney Gr ST17 . . . . .174 C8
Turney Rd DY8 . . . . .279 F6
Turnham Gn WV6 . . . . . . .254 E3
Turnhill Cl ST18 . . . . .174 C6
Turnhill Gr ST5 . . . . .56 B7
Turnhurst Rd ST7 . . . . .41 F7
Turnlea Cl ST8 . . . . .27 B6
Turnock St ST2 . . . . .58 C4
Turnpike Way WV9 . . . . . .224 C1
Turnstone Dr WV10 . . . . . .241 B2
Turquoise Gr WS11 . . . . . .210 C3
Turton Cl Alrewas DE13 . . .201 A2
Walsall WS3 . . . . .243 A4
Tuscan Cl ST10 . . . . .76 D1
Tuscan Ho ST3 . . . . .284 B2
Tuscan St ST3 . . . . .284 C4
Tuscan Way ST5 . . . . .55 D6
Tutbury Ave WV6 . . . . . . .255 A3
Tutbury Castle ★ DE13 . .146 B7
Tutbury Cl WS11 . . . . .210 C3
Tutbury Gr ST3 . . . . .73 D4
Tutbury & Hatton Sta
DE65 . . . . .146 D8
Tutbury Rd
Burton u T DE13 . . . . .166 B8
Stretton DE13 . . . . .147 A1
Tutbury B77 . . . . .261 C7

Tutehill B77 . . . . .262 B7
Twayblade DE14 . . . . .185 B8
Tweed Gr ST5 . . . . .71 A4
Tweed St ST4 . . . . .72 E4
Twemlow Cl ST18 . . . . . . .154 D2
Twemlow St ST1 . . . . .57 A3
Twentylands ST3 . . . . .147 D4
Twickenham Ct DY8 . . . . .279 C7
Twigg St ST2 . . . . .58 B2
Twizles La B79 . . . . .218 A1
Two Gates Com Prim Sch
Tamworth B77 . . . . .261 C8
Tamworth,Mount Pleasant
B77 . . . . .250 C1
Two Gates Ind Est B77 . . .261 D7
Two Oaks Ave WS14 . . . . .228 D8
Two Trees Cl B78 . . . . .249 B6
Twyford Cl Aldridge WS9 . .256 B5
Swadlincote DE11 . . . . . . .186 F2
Twyning Gn ST3 . . . . .88 F7
Tylecote Cres ST18 . . . . . .158 B2
Tyler Gr **5** Burslem ST6 . . .56 E8
Stone ST15 . . . . .119 E7
Tyndall Pl ST4 . . . . .71 E7
Tyne Cl WS8 . . . . .228 C2
Tynedale Cres WV4 . . . . . .266 E3
Tyneham Gr ST2 . . . . .43 A2
Tyne Way ST5 . . . . .71 B4
Tyning Cl WV9 . . . . .240 A2
Tyninghame Ave WV6 . . . .255 D7
Tynings La WS9 . . . . .256 A5
Tynsel Parkes CE Fst Sch
ST14 . . . . .110 F1
Tynwald Grange ST5 . . . . . .56 A3
Tyrell Gr ST1 . . . . .57 F8
Tyria Way **3** ST17 . . . . . .175 A8
Tyrley Cl WV6 . . . . .255 B2
Tyrley Rd TF9 . . . . .112 F5
Tyrol Cl DY8 . . . . .279 D6
Tyson Gn ST2 . . . . .73 D8
Tythebarn Dr DY6 . . . . . . .275 A7

U

Ubberley Gn ST2 . . . . .58 C2
Ubberley Rd ST2 . . . . .58 C1
Uffington Par ST2 . . . . .73 C8
Ufton Cl ST3 . . . . .88 F7
Ullswater Ave ST6 . . . . .56 E7
Ullswater Dr Cheadle ST10 .76 E4
Stone ST15 . . . . .120 D7
Ullswater Gdns DY6 . . . . .275 D6
Ullswater Ho ST6 . . . . .57 C4
Ullswater Pl WS11 . . . . . . .209 E1
Ullswater Rd WV11 . . . . . .242 B1
Ullswater B77 . . . . .262 B7
Ulster Cl WS11 . . . . .210 A3
Ulster Dr DY6 . . . . .275 E4
Ulster Terr ST4 . . . . .72 A5
Ulverston Rd ST3 . . . . .88 F7
Umberleigh Rd ST3 . . . . . . .88 F7
Underhill Cl TF10 . . . . .168 F3
Underhill La WV10 . . . . . . .241 A2
Underhill Prim Sch
WV10 . . . . .241 B1
Underhill Wlk DE14 . . . . . .166 D2
Underley Cl DY6 . . . . .275 B7
Under Rainow Rd CW12 . . . .6 E1
Under the Hill ST8 . . . . .17 A2
Undertown La DE6 . . . . .96 D6
Underwood Cl ST16 . . . . . .155 D8
Underwood Rd ST5 . . . . . . .55 A1
Unicorn Ind Est ST6 . . . . . .56 D8
Unicorn Pl ST6 . . . . .41 F5
Union Ct ST1 . . . . .282 B4
Union La WV5 . . . . .264 D2
Union St Burntwood WS7 . .228 E5
Burton u T DE14 . . . . .166 C1
Cannock WS11 . . . . .226 C6
Hanley ST1 . . . . .282 B4
Leek ST13 . . . . .30 F6
Unity Ave ST1 . . . . .57 D7
Unity Way ST7 . . . . .40 D8
University Ct ST18 . . . . . . .156 C5
University Way CW1 . . . . . .37 A8
Univ of Sheffield SK17 . . . . .4 B8
Univ of Wolverhampton
Compton Park Campus
WV6 . . . . .255 E2
Unwin Cres DY8 . . . . .279 E5
Unwin St ST6 . . . . .42 B3
Upfield Cotts WS7 . . . . . . .229 E7
Upfield Way WS15 . . . . . . .178 C2
Uplands Ave
Stoke-on-T ST6 . . . . .41 F6
Werrington ST9 . . . . .59 B3
Wolverhampton WV3 . . . . .265 D8
Uplands Cl
Cannock Wood WS15 . . . . .211 F5
Penkridge ST19 . . . . .192 B3
Uplands Croft ST9 . . . . .59 A4
Uplands Dr Sedgley DY3 . .271 E6
Werrington ST9 . . . . .59 A3
Wolverhampton WV3 . . . . .265 E8
Wombourne WV5 . . . . .270 A6
Uplands Gn WS11 . . . . . . .196 D6
Uplands Jun Sch WV3 . . . .265 D8
Uplands Rd Bucknall ST2 . . .58 B7
Stafford ST17 . . . . .174 D6
Uplands The Biddulph ST8 .16 E2
Great Haywood ST18 . . . . .158 B2
Newcastle-u-L ST5 . . . . . .283 C4
Upmeadows Dr ST16 . . . . .155 B1
Upper Ave
Codsall Wood ST19 . . . . . .222 F2
Coven WV9 . . . . .223 B3
Upper Bar TF10 . . . . .168 F2

Upper Belgrave Rd ST3 . . .73 D1
Upper Brook St **2** WS15 .196 E8
Upper Cres ST4 . . . . .71 E8
Upper Cross Rd WS15 . . . .196 E7
Upper Cross St ST3 . . . . . .284 C4
Upper Furlong ST4 . . . . . . .72 D6
Upper Gn WV6 . . . . .255 D5
Upper Gungate B79 . . . . . .250 B6
Upper Hattons Cotts
WV9 . . . . .239 D5
Upper Hillchurch St ST1 . .282 C3
Upper Huntbach St ST1 . . .282 C3
Upper Keys Bsns Pk
WS12 . . . . .210 E3
Upper Landywood La
Cheslyn Hay WS6 . . . . . . .226 D1
Great Wyrley WS6 . . . . . . .242 D8
Upper Lodge Rd WS15 . . . .197 F4
Upper Market Sq ST1 . . . . .282 B3
Upper Marsh ST5 . . . . .56 D3
Upper Normacot Rd **1**
ST3 . . . . .73 D2
Upper St John St WS14 . . .231 B6
Upper Sneyd Rd WV11 . . . .242 B2
Upper St WV6 . . . . .255 D5
Upper Villiers St WV2 . . . .266 C6
Upper Way WS15 . . . . .197 B2
Upper Zoar St WV3 . . . . . .266 B8
Upton Ct TF9 . . . . .97 D1
Upton Pl WS15 . . . . .178 D2
Urmston Pl ST3 . . . . .88 F7
Usam Trad Est WV10 . . . . .240 D2
Usulwall Cl ST21 . . . . .133 D6
Utterby Side ST2 . . . . .73 C8
Uttoxeter Heritage Ctr ★
ST14 . . . . .126 C7
Uttoxeter Race Course ★
ST14 . . . . .126 E6
Uttoxeter Rd
Abbots Bromley WS15 . . . .160 E6
Alton ST10 . . . . .94 E8
Armitage WS15 . . . . .198 C4
Blithbury WS15 . . . . .180 A5
Blythe Bridge ST11 . . . . . . .90 E7
Checkley ST10,ST14 . . . . .109 D8
Foston DE65 . . . . .129 E4
Foston,HM Detention Ctr
DE65 . . . . .129 C4
Fradswell ST18 . . . . .123 B6
Hilderstone ST15 . . . . .121 D7
Hill Ridware WS15 . . . . . . .198 A8
Longton ST3 . . . . .284 C3
Meir ST3 . . . . .74 A1
Milwich ST18 . . . . .122 D5
Scropton DE65 . . . . .129 F3
Stone ST15 . . . . .120 E7
Uttoxeter Sta ST14 . . . . . .126 D7
Uxbridge Cl DY3 . . . . .271 D2
Uxbridge Ct
Burntwood WS7 . . . . .228 F5
Cannock WS12 . . . . .210 C5
Uxbridge St
Burton u T DE14 . . . . .166 C1
Cannock WS12 . . . . .210 C4

V

Vale Ave Aldridge WS9 . . .256 D3
Dudley DY3 . . . . .271 D6
Vale Cl WS13 . . . . .214 B1
Vale Gdns ST19 . . . . .207 E8
Vale Head Dr WV6 . . . . . . .255 A2
Valentine Rd ST7 . . . . .26 A1
Vale Park (Port Vale FC) ★
ST6 . . . . .42 A1
Vale Pleasant ST5 . . . . .55 C2
Vale Pl ST1 . . . . .282 A4
Valerian B74 . . . . .257 F4
Valerian Way ST3 . . . . .90 A6
Vale Rise ST19 . . . . .207 F8
Vale Row DY3 . . . . .271 D5
Vale St Dudley DY3 . . . . . .271 D5
Newcastle-u-L,Chesterton
ST5 . . . . .55 E8
Newcastle-u-L,Silverdale
ST5 . . . . .55 B2
Stoke-on-T ST4 . . . . .72 B7
Vale View Aldridge WS9 . . .256 B4
Cheddleton ST13 . . . . .45 D5
Newcastle-u-L ST5 . . . . . . .56 D7
Valley Dr ST13 . . . . .30 B5
Valley Gn WS6 . . . . .226 E2
Valley Heritage Ctr ★
WS12 . . . . .210 D6
Valley La Lichfield WS13 . . .231 D8
Tamworth B77 . . . . .261 E7
Valley Park Nature Reserve ★
WV6 . . . . .255 D5
Valley Park Way ST3 . . . . . .72 F3
Valley Prim Sch ST10 . . . . .78 A4
Valley Rd
Cannock,Hazelslade
WS12 . . . . .211 A6
Cannock,Hednesford
WS12 . . . . .210 D6
Coldmeece ST15 . . . . .118 B7
Dudley DY3 . . . . .271 E6
Meir ST3 . . . . .74 B3
Stone ST15 . . . . .120 B6
Walsall WS3 . . . . .243 D1
Valley Side WS3 . . . . .243 F2
Valley The WS7 . . . . .228 D8
Valley View
Brownhills WS8 . . . . .245 A7
Market Drayton TF9 . . . . . .112 A7
Valley View Wlk ST14 . . . . .96 A3
Vanbrugh Ct WV6 . . . . . . .254 E3

Vancouver Dr DE15 . . . . .167 C3
Van Diemans Rd WV5 . . . .269 F5
Van Gogh Cl WS11 . . . . . .210 D2
Vanguard B77 . . . . .261 D6
Vanity Cl ST15 . . . . .105 C4
Vanity La ST15 . . . . .105 C4
Varden Ct WS15 . . . . .178 E1
Vardon Cl ST16 . . . . .156 C3
Vaudrey Cres CW12 . . . . . .6 A3
Vaughan Cl B74 . . . . .257 F6
Vaughan Gdns WV8 . . . . . .238 F4
Vaughan's La ST15 . . . . . .159 C6
Vaughan Way ST17 . . . . . .155 C1
Vauxhall Cres TF10 . . . . . .168 E2
Vauxhall Terr TF10 . . . . . .168 E3
Venice Ct ST5 . . . . .70 E7
Venn Pl ST1 . . . . .57 E2
Ventnor Gr ST3 . . . . .88 F6
Venton Cl ST6 . . . . .42 E4
Ventura Park Rd B78 . . . . .249 F3
Ventura Pk Rd B78 . . . . . .250 A3
Ventura Pk B78 . . . . .250 A3
Venture Way ST6 . . . . .42 C3
Vercourt B74 . . . . .257 B3
Verdi Ct WS13 . . . . .214 C2
Verdon Ct ST19 . . . . .208 A7
Verity Wlk DY8 . . . . .275 E1
Vermont Gn **4** WS11 . . . .210 A3
Verney Cl ST14 . . . . .125 C7
Verney Way ST3 . . . . .88 F7
Vernon Ave Audley ST7 . . . .39 D2
Brownhills WS8 . . . . .245 A8
Congleton CW12 . . . . .15 F8
Vernon Cl Audley ST7 . . . . .39 D2
Essington WV11 . . . . .241 F4
Sutton Coldfield B74 . . . . .257 E5
Vernon Ho ST14 . . . . .126 C7
Vernon Lodge Prep Sch
ST19 . . . . .206 C3
Vernon Rd ST14 . . . . .72 B8
Vernons Pl WV10 . . . . . . .225 D1
Vernon Terr DE14 . . . . . . .166 C4
Vernon Way WS3 . . . . .242 E1
Verona Gr ST3 . . . . .73 E5
Veronica Ave WV4 . . . . . . .266 E5
Verulam Ct ST16 . . . . .155 E7
Verulam Rd ST16 . . . . .155 E7
Verwood Cl ST16 . . . . .156 C4
Vesey Cl B74 . . . . .257 F2
Vessey Terr ST5 . . . . .283 C2
Vestry Ct DY8 . . . . .279 E6
Vicarage Bank ST18 . . . . .138 E6
Vicarage Cl
Brownhills WS8 . . . . .245 A7
Burton u T DE15 . . . . .167 B4
Dordon B78 . . . . .262 F5
Eccleshall ST21 . . . . .133 D7
Vicarage Cres
Caverswall ST11 . . . . .74 D3
Newcastle-u-L ST5 . . . . . .283 C1
Tittensor ST12 . . . . .88 A1
Upper Tean ST10 . . . . .92 E3
Vicarage Croft DE13 . . . . .199 D6
Vicarage Ct
Burntwood WS7 . . . . .228 F6
Kinver DY7 . . . . .278 A3
Stramshall ST14 . . . . .110 F4
Vicarage Dr Kinver DY7 . . .278 A3
Vicarage Field DE15 . . . . .166 F1
Vicarage Hill B78 . . . . .260 B1
Vicarage La Barlaston ST12 .88 F2
King's Bromley DE13 . . . . .199 D6
Madeley CW3 . . . . .68 E5
Stoke-on-T ST4 . . . . .71 E4
Vicarage Rd
Brewood ST19 . . . . .223 D6
Brownhills WS8 . . . . .245 A7
Dudley,Woodsetton DY3 . .271 F5
Four Ashes WV10 . . . . . . .224 F6
Leek ST13 . . . . .30 F6
Stoke-on-T ST4 . . . . .71 F8
Stourbridge DY8 . . . . .279 D7
Upper Tean ST10 . . . . .92 E3
Walsall WS3 . . . . .244 B2
Wolverhampton,Blakenhall
WV2 . . . . .266 D8
Wolverhampton,Penn WV4 .265 E3
Vicarage Row ST6 . . . . .78 E1
Vicarage Way Hixon ST18 .139 C1
Stafford ST17 . . . . .285 E7
Vicar's Cl Lichfield WS13 . .231 A8
Oulton ST15 . . . . .105 C4
Vicar St DY3 . . . . .271 D8
Vichy Cl ST5 . . . . .70 E7
Vickers Rd ST6 . . . . .42 A3
Victoria Ave
Halmer End ST7 . . . . .54 E7
Hanley ST1 . . . . .282 B1
Kidsgrove ST7 . . . . .25 F2
Walsall,Wallington Heath
WS3 . . . . .243 C1
Victoria Cl ST15 . . . . .55 C1
Victoria Com Sch DE14. . .166 C4
Victoria Cotts DE14 . . . . . .61 A2
Victoria Cres DE14 . . . . . .166 C5
Victoria Ct
8 Kidsgrove ST7 . . . . . .26 A2
Biddulph ST8 . . . . .27 B4
Leek ST13 . . . . .30 D5
Market Drayton TF9 . . . . . .112 B8
Newcastle-u-L ST5 . . . . . . .56 C3
Norton Canes WS11 . . . . .228 B5
Stoke-on-T ST6 . . . . .72 E6
Victoria Dr B78 . . . . .261 B8
Victoria Gdns WS13 . . . . .230 F6
Victoria Gr WV5 . . . . .270 A8
Victoria Ho **2** ST4 . . . . . . .71 F8

Victoria Hospl WS13 . . . .231 A6
Victoria Ind Complex
ST4 . . . . .284 A5
Victoria Mdw DE13 . . . . . .199 D6
Victoria Park Rd ST6 . . . . . .41 E4
Victoria Pk TF10 . . . . .168 F3
Victoria Pl
Newcastle-u-L,Chesterton
ST5 . . . . .55 E7
Newcastle-u-L,Wolstanton
ST5 . . . . .56 D5
Stoke-on-T ST4 . . . . .72 E6
Victoria Rd
Burton u T DE14 . . . . .166 C4
Market Drayton TF9 . . . . . . .97 B1
Newcastle-u-L ST5 . . . . . .283 C2
Sedgley DY3 . . . . .271 E8
Stafford ST16 . . . . .285 A3
Stoke-on-T ST4 . . . . .72 E7
Tamworth B79 . . . . .250 C5
Walsall WS3 . . . . .244 A8
Wolverhampton,Penn WV3 .265 D3
Wolverhampton,Tettenhall
WV6 . . . . .255 E5
Victoria Row ST8 . . . . .27 C4
Victoria Sq Hanley ST1 . . .282 A1
Stafford ST16 . . . . .285 B3
Victoria St
Broomhill WS11 . . . . .209 E4
Burton u T DE14 . . . . .166 C4
Cannock,Bridgtown WS11 .226 D8
Cannock WS12 . . . . .210 C6
Cheadle ST10 . . . . .76 E3
Kingswinford DY6 . . . . . . .270 B1
Leek ST13 . . . . .31 A6
Newcastle-u-L,Chesterton
ST5 . . . . .55 E7
Newcastle-u-L,Silverdale
ST5 . . . . .55 C2
Newcastle-u-L ST5 . . . . . .283 C2
Stafford ST16 . . . . .285 B4
Stoke-on-T ST4 . . . . .56 D1
Stone ST15 . . . . .105 A1
Yoxall DE13 . . . . .182 A3
Victoria Terr ST16 . . . . . . .155 E5
Victoria Way ST17 . . . . . . .175 E5
Victor St Stone ST15 . . . . .104 F1
Walsall WS3 . . . . .244 A4
Victory Ave WS7 . . . . .228 F7
Victory Cl WS12 . . . . .210 F4
Victory Cres ST10 . . . . .76 E4
Victory Terr B78 . . . . .261 B8
Vienna Pl ST5 . . . . .70 F6
Vienna Way ST3 . . . . .73 E5
Viewfield Ave WS12 . . . . . .209 F8
Viewfield Cres DY3 . . . . . .271 D6
Viewlands Dr WV6 . . . . . . .255 A8
View St WS12 . . . . .209 F6
Viggars Pl ST5 . . . . .55 F2
Vigo Cl WS9 . . . . .244 F2
Vigo Pl WS9 . . . . .256 A8
Vigo Rd WS9 . . . . .244 E1
Vigo Terr WS9 . . . . .244 F2
Viking B77 . . . . .261 D7
Villa Cl Biddulph ST8 . . . . . .27 C7
Shareshill WV10 . . . . .225 D1
Village Gdns ST17 . . . . . . .175 F7
Village Mews The WV6 . . .255 C5
Village The Astbury CW12 .15 B8
Endon Bank ST9 . . . . .29 A1
Keele ST5 . . . . .69 F7
Kingswinford DY6 . . . . . . .275 D7
Walton-on-t-H ST17 . . . . . .175 D6
Villa Melita ST11 . . . . .90 D7
Villa Rd ST13 . . . . .45 C8
Villas The Foxt ST10 . . . . . .62 C5
Stoke-on-T ST4 . . . . .72 A5
Villa St ST4 . . . . .72 A5
Villiers Ind Est WV2 . . . . . .266 B7
Villiers St ST3 . . . . .284 B1
Vincent St ST1 . . . . .57 E5
Vine Bank Rd ST7 . . . . .26 A1
Vinebank St ST4 . . . . .72 A6
Vine Cl Hixon ST18 . . . . . .158 B8
Wolverhampton WV10 . . . .240 D3
Vinegar Hill ST21 . . . . .132 C2
Vine La WS11 . . . . .226 D5
Vine Row ST4. . . . . .72 A6
Vine St DY8 . . . . .275 E1
Vineyard Dr TF10 . . . . .168 F3
Vineyard Rd TF10 . . . . . . .168 F3
Violet Cl DE15 . . . . .185 F8
Violet La DE15 . . . . .185 F8
Violet Lane Inf Sch DE15 .185 F8
Violet Way ST15 . . . . .186 A8
Virginia Ave ST17 . . . . . . .175 A8
Virginia Dr WV4 . . . . .265 F4
Virginsalley La DE6 . . . . . . .81 D2
Viscount Rd WS7 . . . . .211 E1
Viscount Wlk **6** ST3 . . . . . .90 A7
Vista The DY3 . . . . .266 D2
Vivian Rd ST4. . . . . .72 F6
Vowchurch Way ST2 . . . . . .58 C1
Voyager Dr WS11 . . . . . . .226 F6
Vulcan Cl WS13 . . . . .214 E1

W

Waddell Cl WV14 . . . . .266 F2
Wadden La ST18 . . . . .138 E4
Wade Ave ST5 . . . . .55 D6
Wadebridge Rd ST2. . . . . . .58 B1
Wade Cl Cheadle ST10. . . . .76 D1
Hill Ridware WS15 . . . . . . .197 F8
Wade Croft WS15 . . . . . . .179 F1
Wade Ct ST7 . . . . .26 A1
Wade La WS15 . . . . .197 E8
Wadesmill Lawns WV10 . .240 E4

Wade St Lichfield WS13... 231 B7
Stoke-on-T ST6 .... 42 B1
Wadham St ST4.......... 72 A7
Waggon Cotts ST7 ...... 38 E1
Waggoner's La B78 ...... 259 E8
Waggon La DY10........ 281 A3
Wain Ave
Newcastle-u-L ST5...... 70 F8
Stoke-on-T ST6 .... 42 E5
Wain Dr ST4............ 71 E5
Wainrigg B77............ 262 B7
Wain St ST6............. 41 F1
Wainwood Rise ST4...... 71 F5
Wainwright Cl DY6...... 275 A8
Wainwright Wlk ST1..... 282 C3
Wakefield Ave DE13.... 146 B6
Wakefield Rd ST4....... 71 F4
Wakelams Fold DY3..... 271 C3
Wakeley Hill WV4....... 265 F4
Wakeman Ct WV11..... 241 F3
Walcot Cl B75 .... 258 B3
Walcot Gr ST2 .... 58 A2
Waldale Cl WV11........ 242 C1
Walden Ave ST16....... 155 D6
Walden Gdns WV4...... 265 E6
Wales La DE13......... 183 D1
Walford Ave WV3....... 265 F8
Walford Back La ST21... 117 C8
Walford Rd DE13....... 147 D3
Walhouse CE Jun Sch
WS11 .... 209 C1
Walhouse Dr ST19...... 207 F7
Walhouse St WS11..... 226 E8
Walker Dr DY10........ 280 A1
Walker Rd ST6.......... 41 F4
Walkers Croft WS4..... 214 C2
Walkersgreen Rd ST5.... 40 D2
Walkers Rise WS12 ..... 210 D8
Walker St Burton u T DE14. 166 B1
Stoke-on-T ST6 .... 41 D2
Walkfield Rd DE13 ..... 200 F2
Walklate Ave ST5 .... 56 D3
Walk La WV5 .... 270 A6
Walkley Bank TF10...... 169 C4
Walkmill Bsns Pk
Cannock WS11......... 226 D5
Market Drayton TF9..... 112 C7
Walkmill Dr TF9 .... 112 D8
Walkmill La WS11...... 226 D5
Walkmill Marsh Nature
Reserve ★ TF9 .... 112 C7
Walkmill Rd TF9....... 112 C8
Walkmill Way WS11.... 226 D5
Walks The ST13........ 30 D5
Wallace Ct WS11....... 227 F5
Wallace Ct WS6....... 226 C1
Wallace Rd WS8....... 244 E8
Walland Gr ST16....... 155 B4
Wallash DE6............ 81 C7
Wallbridge Cl ST13..... 30 D4
Wallbridge Dr ST13..... 30 C4
Wallbridge Prec ST13... 30 C4
Wallbrook Rd ST18..... 122 F3
Wall Croft WS9 .... 256 B7
Wall Ditch DE6......... 35 B2
Wall Dr B74............ 257 F4
Walley Dr ST6.......... 41 D6
Walley Pl ST6.......... 57 A7
Walley's Dr ST5......... 56 D2
Walley St Biddulph ST8... 27 C8
Burslem ST6........... 57 A7
Wallfield Cl ST10...... 92 D4
Wallheath Cres WS14... 245 E5
Wallheath La WS14..... 245 F5
Wallhill Ct ST13........ 30 E3
Wallington Cl WS3..... 243 B4
Wallington Heath WS3.. 243 B2
Wallis Pl ST2.......... 58 B5
Wallis St ST4........... 72 F6
Wallis Way ST2 .... 43 B2
Wall Lane Terr ST13.... 45 C6
Wall La WS13,WS14.... 230 D3
Wall (Letocetvm) Roman Site
(Town) ★ WS14...... 230 E2
Walnut Wlk WS13..... 230 F6
Wallows Wood DY3.... 271 A4
Wall Rd DE14......... 185 A7
Wall Roman Site (Letocetvm)
Mus ★ WS14......... 230 D2
Wallshead Way TF10... 168 F1
Walls Wood ST5........ 85 B7
Walmer Mdw WS9..... 256 B7
Walmer Pl ST4......... 284 B5
Walmers The WS9..... 256 B7
Walmsley Ct DY7....... 278 B3
Walney Gr ST1......... 282 B4
Walnut Ave WV8....... 239 B3
Walnut Cl Cannock WS11. 209 F3
Newport TF10......... 168 F1
Walnut Crest ST18..... 158 C8
Walnut Ct WS15....... 197 A6
Walnut Dr Cannock WS11. 209 F3
Wolverhampton WV3... 255 D1
Walnut Gr Lichfield WS14. 231 F7
Newcastle-u-L ST5..... 55 D8
Walnut Tree La TF10... 188 B7
Walpole St ST3......... 284 D5
Walrand Cl B79........ 234 B1
Walsall Acad WS3..... 243 C2
Walsall Rd Aldridge WS9. 256 A5
Brownhills WS9....... 244 E2
Cannock WS11........ 226 E7
Great Wyrley WS6..... 227 A2
Leamonsley WS13..... 230 E6
Lichfield,Christ Church
WS13 .... 231 A7

Walsall Rd continued
Lichfield,Pipehill WS13,
WS14 .... 230 C5
Norton Canes WS11 ... 227 F4
Stonnall WS14 .... 245 E8
Sutton Coldfield B74 ... 257 D4
Walsall WS3........... 244 A1
Walsall Wood Rd WS9... 256 B7
Walsall Wood Sch WS8.. 245 A4
Walsingham Gdns ST5 .. 71 B2
Walter St WS3......... 244 A1
Waltonbury Cl ST17.... 175 F6
Walton Cres
Stoke-on-T ST4 .... 72 C6
Wolverhampton WV4... 266 C5
Walton Cross 120 A7
Walton Gdns WV8..... 238 F4
Walton Grange ST15... 120 A7
Walton Gr ST7........ 40 C8
Walton Hall ST21..... 134 B5
Walton Hall Sch ST21.. 134 B5
Walton Heath WS3.... 242 F3
Walton High Sch ST17.. 175 E6
Waltonhurst La ST21... 134 C4
Walton Ind Est WS15... 120 A6
Walton La ST17........ 176 B5
Walton Lodge ST17.... 175 F6
Walton Mead Cl ST17.. 175 F7
Walton-on-Trent CE Prim
Sch DE12........... 202 B2
Walton Pl ST5 .... 55 F6
Walton Priory Mid Sch
ST15 .... 119 F6
Walton Rd Aldridge WS9. 245 A1
Stoke-on-T ST4 .... 71 F3
Swadlincote DE15 ..... 185 D5
Wolverhampton WV4... 266 F5
Walton Way ST7....... 40 C8
Wanderers Ave WV2 ... 266 C6
Wandsbeck B77....... 261 E8
Wannerton Rd DY10... 281 B1
Wansbeck Wlk DY3... 271 F6
Warburton Ct 10 ST6... 57 A7
Warburton St 7 ST6.... 57 A7
Ward Cl WS13........ 215 C6
Ward Gr WV4......... 266 F3
Wardle Cl B75 .... 258 A4
Wardle Cres ST13..... 30 E4
Wardle La ST2........ 43 C1
Wardle Pl WS11...... 209 C5
Wardles La WS6...... 226 F2
Wardle St Stoke-on-T ST6. 41 E3
Tamworth B79......... 250 A5
Wardlow Cl WV4....... 266 B6
Ward Pl ST6........... 42 B5
Ward Rd Codsall WV8... 238 F3
Wolverhampton WV4... 266 D5
Wards La CW12....... 16 C5
Ward St WS12......... 209 F6
Warings The WV5..... 269 F4
Warm Croft ST15...... 120 C7
Warminster Pl ST3.... 284 A3
Warmson Cl ST3...... 73 C6
Warner Rd WV8....... 238 F3
Warner St ST1......... 282 B2
Warnford Wlk WV4.... 265 C6
Warren Cl Cannock WS12. 211 A5
Lichfield WS14....... 231 E7
Stretton DE13........ 147 E1
Warren Croft WS15... 198 C4
Warren Ct 5 TF9..... 97 C1
Warren Dr DY3....... 266 C1
Warren Gdns DY6..... 275 C6
Warren Hill DE11..... 186 E5
Warren La DE14...... 184 F7
Warren Pl
Brownhills WS8....... 245 A7
Longton ST3.......... 284 D2
Warren Rd
Burntwood WS7...... 229 A5
Stoke-on-T ST6 .... 42 B6
Warrens La ST16..... 155 B6
Warren St ST3........ 284 D2
Warrilow Cl 1 ST3.... 90 A7
Warrilow Heath Rd ST5. 40 C1
Warrington Dr ST13... 30 C5
Warrington Rd ST1... 57 D1
Warrington St ST4.... 72 F6
Warsill Gr ST3........ 73 D4
Warstone Hill Rd WV6.. 253 F4
Warstone Rd WS6.... 242 C7
Warstones Cres WV4.. 265 D5
Warstones Dr WV4.... 265 C6
Warstones Gdns WV4.. 265 C6
Warstones Jun & Inf Sch
WV4 .... 265 B6
Warstones Rd WV4.... 265 D5
Wartell Bank Ind Est
DY6 .... 275 C7
Wartell Bank DY6..... 275 D7
Warwick Ave
3 Longton ST3......... 73 F1
Cheadle ST10......... 76 C2
Newcastle-u-L ST5.... 71 C4
Perton WV6.......... 254 F4
Warwick Cl
Burton u T DE14...... 184 F8
Cannock WS11....... 226 F8
Kidsgrove ST7....... 26 A3
Market Drayton TF9... 97 D2
Warwick Ct
6 Wolverhampton WV4. 266 F4
Dudley DY3.......... 271 D3
Warwick Dr WV8...... 238 E3
Warwick Gr ST5 ...... 56 C3
Warwick Rd
Stafford ST17........ 175 B8

Warwick Rd continued
Stourbridge DY8....... 275 D1
Tamworth B77......... 250 E4
Warwick St Biddulph ST8.. 27 C7
Burton u T DE13....... 166 C6
Hanley ST1........... 57 A3
Newcastle-u-L ST5.... 55 E7
Warwick Way WS9..... 245 A1
Wasdale Dr DY6...... 275 E6
Wasdale Rd WS8..... 244 D6
Washbrook La
Norton Canes WS11 ... 227 D5
Thorpe DE6.......... 51 F4
Wash Dale La ST15... 105 A6
Washerwall La ST9.... 59 A4
Washerwall St ST2.... 73 D8
Washford Rd DE65.... 147 E8
Washington Cl ST8.... 16 C2
Washington Dr WV3.. 255 D1
Washington Dr ST17... 175 A8
Washington St ST6.... 41 E2
Waste La DE6.......... 79 D4
Wastwater Ct WV6.... 254 F4
Watchfield Cl ST3..... 73 F1
Waterbeck Gr ST4.... 88 C5
Waterbridge La WV5... 269 E7
Waterbrook Cl ST19... 207 E7
Waterbrook Way WS11. 226 E6
Waterdale Gr ST3..... 73 E3
Waterdale WV3....... 255 E2
Waterdale WV5....... 269 E5
Water Dale WV3..... 255 E2
Water Eaton La ST19.. 207 B5
Waterfall La ST10...... 48 F2
Waterford Dr TF10.... 168 E1
Waterford Rd DY6.... 275 D7
Watergate St ST6..... 41 D3
Water Glades Cl 2 ST1. 56 F2
Waterhead Cl WV10... 241 A2
Waterhead Dr WV10... 241 B2
Waterhead Grange WS8. 244 E7
Waterhead Rd ST3.... 73 F1
Waterhouses CE Prim Sch
ST10 .... 48 C2
Watering Cl ST5...... 85 C4
Watering Trough Bank
CW3 .... 69 B8
Water La Bobbington DY7. 268 D2
Newport TF10........ 168 F3
Waterlily Cl WS12.... 210 E3
Water Lily Gr WS8.... 244 E7
Waterloo Bvd WS12... 210 E4
Waterloo Ct ST13.... 30 D5
Waterloo Gr ST7..... 26 A2
Waterloo Ho WS15... 197 B6
Waterloo Rd
Burslem ST6,ST1..... 57 A6
Edgmond TF10....... 168 A6
Waterloo St
Burton u T DE14...... 166 C4
Hanley ST1.......... 282 C2
Leek ST13........... 30 D5
Watermeadow Dr WS4.. 244 D1
Watermeadow Gr 3 ST1. 56 F2
Watermeet St ST1.... 56 F3
Watermill Cl WV10... 240 D3
Watermint Cl WS12... 210 E4
Waterpark Rd DE6.... 127 B8
Water Rd DY3........ 271 C2
Waters Dr B74....... 257 D3
Waters Edge WS15... 198 C5
Watersedge Gr 4 ST1.. 56 F2
Waterside Bsns Pk
WS15 .... 197 A7
Waterside DE15...... 185 D5
Waterside Cl Madeley CW3. 68 E6
Slade Heath WV10.... 224 E2
Wolverhampton WV2... 266 D7
Waterside Com Jun Sch
DE15 .... 185 D7
Waterside Ct
Branston DE14....... 165 F1
Gnosall ST20......... 171 C5
Tamworth B77........ 250 F5
Waterside Dr
Market Drayton TF9... 97 E2
Stoke-on-T ST3 .... 88 E7
Waterside Mews TF10... 168 E3
Waterside Rd DE15.... 185 D7
Waterside WS15...... 196 F6
Waterside Way
Brownhills WS8....... 228 D2
Wolverhampton WV9... 240 A3
Watersmead Cl WS12.. 210 F4
Watersmeet St ST15.. 120 C6
Watersmeet Ho B78... 261 B8
Waters Rd WS15..... 160 F3
Water St Burntwood WS7. 228 B8
Kingswinford DY6..... 275 D7
Newcastle-u-L,Red Street
ST5 .... 40 D2
Newcastle-u-L ST5.... 283 C3
Stafford ST16 .... 285 B3
Stoke-on-T ST4 ...... 72 A5
Waters View WS3..... 244 B5
Waterton Cl DE13.... 148 A1
Waterways Gdns DY8.. 275 D1
Waterworks Cotts DY6.. 274 F4
Watery La
Abbots Bromley WS15. 160 D4
Astbury CW12........ 15 C4
Clifton DE6.......... 81 E7
Codsall WV8......... 239 A5
Ellastone DE6........ 80 B4
Gentleshaw B77,WS15... 212 B3
Hangingbridge DE6.... 81 F8
Haughton ST18....... 172 F5
Kingstone ST14...... 125 B2
Lichfield WS13....... 214 C4

Watery La continued
Longton ST3.......... 73 D1
Scropton DE65........ 129 E2
Stourbridge DY8...... 275 E2
Swadlincote DE11..... 186 D5
Uttoxeter ST14....... 110 C6
Watford Gap Rd WS14.. 258 A6
Watford Gap WS14.... 258 A7
Watford St ST4........ 72 C8
Wathan Ave WV14.... 266 F1
Watkin St ST4......... 72 D6
Watkiss Dr WS15...... 178 D1
Watlands Ave ST5..... 56 C6
Watlands Rd ST7...... 39 E2
Watlands View ST5.... 56 B6
Watling St
Blymhill Lawn TF11... 204 C2
Brownhills WS8....... 228 D1
Cannock WS11....... 226 D6
Dordon B77,B78...... 262 D6
Hints B78............ 248 D3
Norton Canes WS11 .. 227 D3
Watling Street Bsns Pk
WS11 .... 228 A2
Watling Street Prim Sch
WS8 .... 228 E1
Watling St
Tamworth,Bonehill B78... 249 E1
Tamworth,Two Gates B77. 261 D7
Tamworth,Wilnecote B77,
B78 .... 261 D7
Watson Cl Fradley WS13. 215 E8
Rugeley WS15........ 178 D3
Watson Rd Stoke-on-T ST4. 71 F4
Wolverhampton,Lanesfield
WV14 .... 266 F2
Wolverhampton,Pendeford
WV10 .... 240 B2
Watson St
Burton u T DE14...... 166 D1
Stoke-on-T ST4 ...... 72 A8
Wattfield Cl WS15.... 197 A5
Wattles La ST17...... 175 B2
Watt Pl ST10.......... 76 D3
Watts Cl ST17........ 174 B8
Wat Tyler Cl WS15.... 178 D3
Waveney Ave WV6.... 254 E4
Waveney Ct ST5...... 71 B4
Waveney Gr
Cannock WS11....... 209 B1
Newcastle-u-L ST5.... 71 C4
Waveney Gr 261 E8
Waveney Wlk N ST6.. 42 A4
Waveney Wlk S ST6.. 42 A4
Wavenham Ct B74.... 257 E5
Waverley Cres
Wolverhampton,Goldthorn Hill
WV4 .... 266 B6
Wolverhampton,Lanesfield
WV4 .... 266 F3
Waverley Gdns
Rugeley WS15........ 178 B2
Wombourne WV5..... 270 B7
Waverley La DE14.... 166 B4
Waverley Pl ST5...... 71 B5
Waverley Rd ST3..... 242 F2
Waverley Wlk WS14... 231 B6
Waverton Rd ST2.... 73 E7
Wavertree Ave ST7... 25 E7
Waybutt La CW2...... 52 D8
Wayfield Dr ST16.... 155 D8
Wayfield Rd ST4..... 71 D8
Wayford Dr B74..... 257 C3
Wayside Acres WV8.. 238 F2
Wayside Ave ST5.... 56 C4
Wayside Dr B74...... 257 C3
Wayside WV8........ 239 F2
Wayte St ST4......... 282 A4
Wealden Hatch WV10.. 240 E4
Wealdstone Dr DY3... 271 D2
Weatheroaks WS9.... 245 B4
Weathercock La CW12.. 6 E3
Weaver Cl Biddulph ST8. 16 D1
Cheadle ST10........ 76 E5
Weaver Ct 8 B75..... 258 E3
Weaver Dr ST17...... 174 B8
Weaverlake Dr DE13.. 181 F3
Weaver Pl ST5....... 71 B4
Weaver Rd ST14..... 111 B2
Weavers La ST15..... 120 C7
Weavers St ST1...... 282 B3
Weavers The ST14... 95 D6
Weavers Wlk ST15.. 103 C4
Weaving Gdns 1 WS11. 209 E1
Webb Ave WV6...... 254 E5
Webb Cl WS13....... 215 C6
Webberley La ST3.... 284 C3
Webb St ST3......... 74 B3
Webley Rise WV10... 240 F4
Webster Ave ST3.... 73 E5
Webster St ST5...... 283 C1
Webster Wlk WS11.. 210 A4
Wedgewood Ave WS15. 119 E6
Wedgwood Cl
Burntwood WS7..... 229 C7
Burton u T DE15..... 167 B1
Wedgwood Ct WS4... 244 C1
Wedgwood Ave
Audley ST7.......... 40 A1
Newcastle-u-L ST5.... 71 C4
Wedgwood Cl WV5... 269 F7
Wedgwood Ct ST1... 57 D3
Wedgwood Dr ST12... 88 E4
Wedgwood Halt ST12.. 88 D3
Wedgwood La
Barlaston ST12...... 88 E4
Biddulph ST8....... 16 C2
Biddulph ST8....... 16 C3

Wedgwood Pl 1 ST6... 56 F8
Wedgwood Rd
Cheadle ST10......... 76 D1
Hopton ST18......... 156 B8
Stoke-on-T ST4....... 72 F6
Talke ST7............ 40 D7
Wedgwood St
4 Burslem ST6........ 56 F8
Newcastle-u-L ST5.... 56 D5
Wedgwood Story The ★
ST12 .... 88 D4
Weeford Dell 2 B75... 258 E3
Weeford Rd B75..... 258 F3
Weeping Cross ST17... 175 D7
Weetman St ST6...... 41 C7
Weighton Gr ST2..... 58 E1
Weir Bank DE15...... 185 E6
Weir Gr ST7.......... 26 B2
Weirside DE6......... 81 D7
Welbeck Pl ST2...... 58 C5
Welbury Gdns WV6.. 255 F5
Welby St ST6......... 72 D5
Welch St ST4......... 72 B7
Weldon Ave ST3..... 74 B4
Welford Gr B74...... 257 F3
Welford Rd B77...... 261 C5
Welford Rise DE13... 166 A6
Welland Cl DE15..... 167 A5
Welland Gr ST5...... 71 A3
Welland Rd DE65.... 147 D8
Wellbury Cl ST4..... 88 C5
Wellcroft Grange DE6... 65 D1
Weller Cl ST11....... 90 D3
Weller Ct WV3....... 255 D1
Weller St ST4........ 71 E8
Wellesbourne Cl WV3.. 265 B8
Wellesbourne B79.... 250 C8
Wellesley St ST1..... 282 A1
Wellfield Cl WS11.... 226 B7
Wellfield Rd
Aldridge WS9........ 256 B8
Alrewas DE13....... 201 A2
Bucknall ST2........ 58 C1
Wellington Ave WV3.. 265 F7
Wellington Cl
Kingswinford DY6.... 275 E4
Stafford ST16....... 155 E5
Wellington Cres WS13.. 215 B4
Wellington Ct
2 Leek ST13.......... 30 E5
Hanley ST1.......... 282 C3
Wellington Dr
Cannock WS11....... 226 B8
Rugeley WS15....... 196 E8
Wellington Mill 1 ST13.. 30 E5
Wellington Rd
Albrighton WV7....... 220 F1
Burton u T,Branston DE14. 184 E8
Burton u T DE14..... 166 A2
Hanley ST1.......... 282 C2
Kidsgrove ST7....... 26 A2
Newport TF10....... 168 E1
Wellington St W DE14.. 166 B3
Wellington St
1 Newcastle-u-L ST5... 56 C5
Burton u T DE14..... 166 B3
Hanley ST1.......... 282 C2
Leek ST13........... 30 E6
Wellington Terr ST1... 282 C2
Well La Biddulph ST8.. 16 D3
Great Wyrley WS6.... 227 A1
Walsall WS3......... 243 E1
Warslow SK17....... 22 B2
Weston Jones TF10... 150 C4
Wells Cl Biddulph ST8.. 27 D8
Cannock WS11....... 209 E6
Perton WV6.......... 254 D4
Rugeley WS15....... 196 C6
Wells Dr ST17....... 175 E7
Wells La ST18........ 191 C8
Wells Rd WV4....... 265 F5
Well St Biddulph ST8.. 27 D7
Cheadle ST10........ 76 E3
Forsbrook ST11...... 91 A8
Hanley ST1.......... 282 C2
Leek ST13........... 30 F5
Mow Cop ST7....... 26 D7
Newcastle-u-L ST5.... 283 C2
Wellyards Cl ST18.... 138 D2
Welney Gdns WV9.... 240 A3
Welsh Cl ST3........ 89 D8
Wembley La WS7.... 228 D8
Wembury B77....... 250 E5
Wem Gr ST5......... 40 E2
Wendell Crest WV10... 240 F4
Wendling Cl ST2..... 58 D1
Wendover Gr ST2.... 58 C1
Wendover Rd WV4... 266 F2
Wendy Cl ST2....... 58 B1
Wenger Cres ST4.... 88 A7
Wenham Dr ST3..... 90 B7
Wenlock Ave WV3... 265 E8
Wenlock Cl
Newcastle-u-L ST5.... 40 E2
Sedgley DY3......... 271 C7
Stoke-on-T ST6 ..... 42 B8
Wenlock Dr TF10.... 168 E2
Wenlock Rd B77..... 250 D3
Wensleydale Ave CW12.. 6 A5
Wensleydale Cl ST1... 57 D7
Wentlows Ave ST10... 92 D5
Wentlows Rd ST10... 92 D5
Wentworth Cl WS7... 229 C7
Wentworth Ct B75... 258 B1

Wentworth Dr
Kidsgrove ST7 . . . . 26 C3
Lichfield WS14 . . . . 231 D5
Stafford ST16 . . . . 156 C3
Stretton DE13 . . . . 147 D1
Wentworth Gr
Perton WV6 . . . . 254 D5
Stoke-on-T ST1 . . . . 57 F8
Wentworth Rd
Stourbridge DY8 . . . . 279 E7
Walsall WS3 . . . . 242 F3
Wolverhampton WV10 . . . . 240 F3
Werburgh Dr ST4 . . . . 88 A7
Wereton Rd ST7 . . . . 39 D1
Wergs Dr WV6 . . . . 255 A7
Wergs Hall WV8 . . . . 254 F7
Wergs Hall Rd
Codsall WV8 . . . . 254 F8
Wolverhampton WV6,WV8 255 A7
Wergs Rd Codsall WV8 . . . . 254 F7
Wolverhampton WV6 . . . . . 255 B6
Werneth Gr WS3 . . . . 243 A4
Werrington Prim Sch ST9 59 B3
Werrington Rd ST2 . . . . 58 B4
Wesker Pl ST3 . . . . 73 F4
Wesleyan Ct 5 ST13 . . . . . . 30 D6
Wesleyan Rd TF9 . . . . 100 A6
Wesley Ave
Cheslyn Hay WS6 . . . . 226 D3
Codsall WV8 . . . . 239 B2
Wesley Cl Burntwood WS7 211 F1
Wombourne WV5 . . . . 269 F5
Wesley Ct
5 Wolverhampton WV4 . 266 F4
Betley CW3 . . . . 53 A6
Cannock WS11 . . . . 209 E6
Wesley Dr ST15 . . . . 120 C6
Wesley Gdns 7 ST7 . . . . . . 26 A2
Wesley Pl Cannock WS12 . . 210 C7
Halmer End ST7 . . . . 54 D7
Newcastle-u-L ST5 . . . . 70 F8
Wesley Rd WV8 . . . . 239 B2
Wesley St Audley ST7 . . . . . 40 A1
Blythe Bridge ST11 . . . . 91 A7
Stoke-on-T ST6 . . . . 41 D3
Wesley Way B77 . . . . 250 F4
Wessenden B77 . . . . 262 B2
Wessex Cl WS8 . . . . 244 F7
Wessex Ct B79 . . . . 251 F7
Wessex Dr Cannock WS11 . 209 F2
Stoke-on-T ST4 . . . . 88 A8
Wessex Rd WV2 . . . . 266 F6
Westacre ST1 . . . . 57 F3
Westacre Cres WV3 . . . . . . 255 C1
Westacre Dr DE11 . . . . 186 F2
Westacre Inf Sch WV3 . . . . 255 C1
West Acres ST14 . . . . 141 C8
West Ave Kidsgrove ST7 . . . . 25 C1
Newcastle-u-L ST5 . . . . 56 D2
Stoke-on-T ST4 . . . . 71 F8
Weston CW2 . . . . 37 B5
West Bank ST4 . . . . 72 A6
West Beeches WV9 . . . . . . 224 B4
Westbeech Rd WV4 . . . . . . 253 D5
Westbook Way WV5 . . . . . . 269 F5
Westbourne Ave
Cannock WS11 . . . . 209 D3
Cheslyn Hay WS6 . . . . 226 E3
Westbourne Cl ST13 . . . . . . 30 C6
Westbourne Cres WS7 . . . . 229 B7
Westbourne Dr ST6 . . . . . . 41 E5
Westbourne Rd WV4 . . . . . 266 A5
Westbourne Villas ST16 . . 285 B4
West Brampton ST5 . . . . . . 283 B3
Westbrook Ave WV9 . . . . . 256 A5
Westbury Cl ST1 . . . . 57 F5
Westbury Hayes ST17 . . . . 174 A8
Westbury Rd ST5 . . . . 71 B3
West Butts Rd WS15 . . . . . 178 B1
West Cannock Way
WS12 . . . . 195 D1
Westcliffe 3 ST13 . . . . 30 D6
Westcliffe Ave ST5 . . . . 71 A3
Westcliffe Hospl ST6 . . . . . 41 F7
West Cl Stafford ST16 . . . . . 156 A3
Stone ST15 . . . . 119 F7
West Coppice Rd WS8 . . . . 244 C8
Westcott Cl DY6 . . . . 275 F3
Westcott La TF9 . . . . 130 A7
West Cres ST1 . . . . 57 E8
Westcroft Ave WV10 . . . . . 241 A1
Westcroft Rd
Sedgley DY3 . . . . 266 B2
Wolverhampton WV6 . . . . . 254 F6
Westcroft Sch WV10 . . . . . 241 B2
West Dr Cheddleton ST13 . . . 45 C7
Fazeley B78 . . . . 249 E2
West End Ave ST13 . . . . 30 D5
Westerby Dr ST9 . . . . 59 A3
Westerham Cl ST17 . . . . 87 F7
Westering Parkway
WV10 . . . . 240 F4
Western Ave DY3 . . . . 271 B8
Western By Pass WS13 . . . 213 C1
Western By-Pass WS13 . . . 230 F8
Western Rd
Cannock WS12 . . . . 210 B6
Stourbridge DY8 . . . . 279 F4
Western Springs Prim Sch
WS15 . . . . 178 D2
Western Springs Rd
WS15 . . . . 178 D2
Westfield Ave ST7 . . . . 39 C2
Westfield Dr
Aldridge WS9 . . . . 256 A6

Westfield Dr continued
Wombourne WV5 . . . . 269 F7
Westfield Gr WV3 . . . . 265 C8
Westfield Manor B75 . . . . . 258 A4
Westfield Prim Sch WV5 269 F7
Burton u T DE13 . . . . 166 B6
Mow Cop ST7 . . . . 26 C7
Sedgley DY3 . . . . 266 E1
Westfields
Cauldon Lowe ST10 . . . . . . 63 E4
Leek ST13 . . . . 30 F5
Westfields Rd WS15 . . . . . 197 F4
Westfields Rise CW3 . . . . . 67 C1
Westfields B78 . . . . 262 D8
Westgate Brewood ST19 . . 223 D7
Cannock WS12 . . . . 210 F6
Westgate Cl DY3 . . . . 271 E7
West Gn WV4 . . . . 265 C5
Westhall Cl ST19 . . . . 223 D6
Westhall Gate WS3 . . . . . . 243 B2
Westhead Ave ST16 . . . . . . 156 A4
Westhead Rd DY10 . . . . . . 280 A4
Westhead Rd N DY10 . . . . . 280 A4
Westhead Wlk ST1 . . . . 282 A2
West Hill Ave WS12 . . . . . . 210 B6
West Hill Prim Sch
WS12 . . . . 210 B6
West Hill ST14 . . . . 126 C6
Westhill WV3 . . . . 255 C2
Westhouse La ST14 . . . . 79 F3
Westland Ave WV3 . . . . . . 255 F2
Westland Gdns DY8 . . . . . 279 F7
Westland Rd
Market Drayton TF9 . . . . . . 97 B1
Wolverhampton WV6 . . . . . 255 F2
Westlands ST7 . . . . 39 F2
Westlands Ave ST5 . . . . 70 F7
Westlands Prim Sch ST5 . 70 F6
Westlands Rd ST14 . . . . . . 126 B6
Westlands The ST14 . . . . . . 95 D6
Westland St ST4 . . . . 72 A7
Westlands CW3 . . . . 83 B7
Westleigh Dr WV5 . . . . 269 F5
Westley Cl DY10 . . . . 280 C5
Westmarsh Gr ST6 . . . . 42 A4
Westmead Rd DE13 . . . . . . 183 C1
Westmere Cl CW2 . . . . 37 B5
Westmill St ST1 . . . . 282 C1
Westminster Ave WV4 . . . . 266 B5
Westminster Cl ST17 . . . . . 175 C8
Westminster Dr
4 Burton u T DE13 . . . . . . 166 D8
Market Drayton TF9 . . . . . . 112 A7
Westminster Pl ST4 . . . . 72 A1
Westminster Rd
Cannock WS11 . . . . 209 E6
Leek ST13 . . . . 31 A7
Stourbridge DY8 . . . . 275 D2
Westmoreland Ave ST7 . . . . 40 F7
Westmorland Cl
Stoke-on-T ST6 . . . . 42 A8
Tamworth B79 . . . . 250 A1
Weston Bank Cl TF11 . . . . . 203 E2
Weston Bank
Thurvaston DE6 . . . . 96 F1
Weston ST18 . . . . 138 A2
Weston-Under-Lizard TF11 203 E2
Weston Cl
Bishops Wood ST19 . . . . . . 221 E8
Cannock WS11 . . . . 210 C1
Newcastle-u-L ST5 . . . . 55 F3
Werrington ST2 . . . . 59 A4
Weston Coyney Inf Sch
ST3 . . . . 74 B5
Weston Coyney Jun Sch
ST3 . . . . 74 A3
Weston Coyney Rd
Longton ST3 . . . . 73 E3
Meir ST3 . . . . 74 A4
Weston Cres WS9 . . . . 256 B4
Weston Ct ST3 . . . . 74 A4
Weston Dr
Great Wyrley WS6 . . . . 226 F1
Meir ST3 . . . . 74 A4
Westonfields Dr ST3 . . . . . . 73 E3
Weston Ho WV6 . . . . 255 E5
Weston La Bowers ST21 . . . 102 A4
Standon ST21 . . . . 101 F6
Weston CW2 . . . . 37 A5
Weston Park Ave DE14 . . . . 166 D7
Weston Park TF11 . . . . 203 F1
Weston Rd
Albrighton WV7 . . . . 237 B5
Hopton ST16,ST18 . . . . . . 156 C4
Lichfield WS13 . . . . 214 A2
Meir ST3 . . . . 74 A3
Stowford ST17 . . . . 37 B8
Weston Road High Sch
ST18 . . . . 156 D5
Weston St Leek ST13 . . . . . . 31 A4
Longton ST3 . . . . 73 D6
Westonview Ave ST3 . . . . . . 73 D5
Weston Village Prim Sch
CW2 . . . . 37 C5
Westover Dr ST15 . . . . 120 C7
West Par ST4 . . . . 72 C5
Westport Lake Rd ST6 . . . . . 41 D1
Westport Rd ST6 . . . . 41 E1
West Prec ST1 . . . . 282 B2
West Rd WV4 . . . . 266 F5
Westridge DY3 . . . . 271 C8
West St Biddulph ST8 . . . . . . 27 C7
Burton u T DE15 . . . . 167 B3
Cannock WS11 . . . . 226 E6
Leek ST13 . . . . 30 E6
Meir ST3 . . . . 74 B5

West St continued
Mount Pleasant ST7 . . . . . . 26 B6
Newcastle-u-L,Porthill ST5 . 56 D7
Newcastle-u-L,Silverdale
ST5 . . . . 55 B1
Newcastle-u-L ST5 . . . . . . 283 C2
Stourbridge DY8 . . . . 279 F5
Tamworth B79 . . . . 250 C5
Tamworth,Kettlebrook B77 250 C3
West Terr ST6 . . . . 42 B6
West View ST14 . . . . 125 C7
West View Dr DY6 . . . . 275 E5
West View Mayfield DE6 . . . 81 D6
Newcastle-u-L ST5 . . . . 56 B5
Rocester ST14 . . . . 96 A3
Stoke-on-T ST3 . . . . 89 F4
Westward Cl ST14 . . . . 111 B1
West Way Gn ST17 . . . . . . 155 C1
Westway Ho WS4 . . . . 244 B1
West Way Stafford ST17 . . . 174 C8
Uttoxeter ST14 . . . . 110 F1
Walsall WS4 . . . . 244 B2
West Winds WV10 . . . . 241 C7
Westwood Ave DY8 . . . . . . 279 D3
Westwood Cl
Cheddleton ST13 . . . . 45 C4
Chorlton CW2 . . . . 37 B1
Westwood Ct
13 Leek ST13 . . . . 30 D6
Hanley ST1 . . . . 282 C3
Westwood Fst Sch ST13 . . 30 C5
Westwood Gr 10 ST13 . . . . 30 D6
Westwood Heath Rd ST13 30 C6
Westwood High Sch ST13 30 B5
Westwood Holdings
WS12 . . . . 209 B6
Westwood Park Ave ST13 30 B6
Westwood Park Dr ST13 . . . 30 B5
Westwood Pk DE11 . . . . . . 186 F5
Westwood Rd Leek ST13 . . . 30 D5
Meir ST3 . . . . 74 A2
Newcastle-u-L ST5 . . . . 56 D6
Westwoods Hollow WS7 . . 229 B8
Westwood Terr 7 ST13 . . . 30 D6
Westwood View ST13 . . . . . 30 D6
Wetherall Cl WS15 . . . . . . 178 C2
Wetherby Cl Cheadle ST10 . 76 E5
Newcastle-u-L ST5 . . . . 55 E7
Wolverhampton WV10 . . . . 240 D5
Wetherby Dr DE14 . . . . 184 F7
Wetherby Rd
Stoke-on-T ST4 . . . . 88 B7
Walsall WS3 . . . . 243 A4
Wetherel Rd DE15 . . . . 167 C2
Wetley Ave ST9 . . . . 59 F4
Wetley La ST13 . . . . 33 A2
Wetmore La DE14 . . . . 166 F6
Wetmore Rd
Burton u T DE14 . . . . 166 E5
Burton u T DE14 . . . . 166 E6
Wettenhall Dr ST13 . . . . . . 30 B4
Wetton Rd ST13 . . . . 34 B5
Wexford Cl ST1 . . . . 271 F2
Weybourne Ave ST2 . . . . . . 43 B3
Weyhill Cl WV9 . . . . 239 F2
Weymouth Dr B74 . . . . 257 F4
Weymouth Rd B79 . . . . 250 B5
Whalley Ave ST4 . . . . 71 E6
Wharf Cl WS14 . . . . 231 C7
Wharfe Cl ST14 . . . . 126 C8
Wharfedale Cl DY6 . . . . . . 275 B7
Wharfedale Rd CW12 . . . . . . 6 A5
Wharfedale Wlk ST3 . . . . . 284 A3
Wharf Hos DE13 . . . . 184 A1
Wharf La Astbury CW12 . . . . 15 B3
Burntwood WS8 . . . . 228 F3
Wharf Pl ST4 . . . . 72 C7
Wharf Rd Biddulph ST8 . . . . 27 C8
Burton u T DE14 . . . . 166 E5
Gnosall ST20 . . . . 171 C5
Rugeley WS15 . . . . 196 F7
Wharf Road Ind Est
DE14 . . . . 166 E5
Wharf St ST5 . . . . 283 D3
Wharf Terr ST4 . . . . 69 B8
Wharmadine La
Ashley TF9 . . . . 100 E7
Maer TF9 . . . . 84 F1
Wharwell La WS6 . . . . 227 A1
Whateley La B77,B78 . . . . . 261 F4
Whateley Villas CV9 . . . . . 262 A4
Whatmore St ST6 . . . . 42 C1
Wheat Breach Cl DE13 . . . . 166 B6
Wheatcroft Cl
3 Sutton Coldfield B75 . . 258 E3
Burntwood WS7 . . . . 229 A5
Penkridge ST19 . . . . 207 F8
Wheatfields ST6 . . . . 42 C3
Wheathill Cl WV4 . . . . 265 E3
Wheatland Gr WS9 . . . . . . 256 B4
Wheatlands Cl 1 WS12 . . 210 C1
Wheatlands Rd DE15 . . . . . 185 E7
Wheatlands The WV6 . . . . 254 D3
Wheatley Ave ST4 . . . . 71 E6
Wheatley Cl B75 . . . . 258 C3
Wheatley Gr WS6 . . . . 227 A2
Wheatley La DE15 . . . . 167 C4
Wheatley St WV2 . . . . 266 F6
Wheatmill Cl DY10 . . . . . . 281 B2
Wheatridge Cl DY6 . . . . . . 275 A8
Wheatsheaf Cl B75 . . . . . . 258 E4
Wheatsheaf Rd WV8 . . . . . 239 E1
Wheatstone Cl DY3 . . . . . . 271 E6
Wheel Ave WV8 . . . . 238 F3
Wheel Ct The WV8 . . . . . . 238 F3
Wheeler Cl WV8 . . . . 238 F4

Wheeler St DY8 . . . . 279 F5
Wheelfield WV8 . . . . 238 F3
Wheelhouse Rd WS5 . . . . . 197 B6
Wheel La WS13 . . . . 213 F1
Wheelock Way 2 ST7 . . . . 26 B2
Wheelwrights La ST21 . . . . 134 D7
Whetstone Field Prim Sch
WS9 . . . . 256 B4
Whetstone Gn WV10 . . . . . 240 D1
Whetstone La WS9 . . . . . . 256 B4
Whetstone Rd ST8 . . . . 16 C2
Whieldon Cres ST4 . . . . . . 72 C5
Whieldon Ind Est ST4 . . . . 72 C6
Whieldon Rd ST4 . . . . 72 C6
Whilmot Cl WV10 . . . . 241 B6
Whimple Side ST2 . . . . 58 B1
Whimster Sq ST17 . . . . . . 174 A8
Whinberry Rise DY5 . . . . . 271 C1
Whinyates Rise WS11 . . . . 226 F8
Whisper La ST4,ST5 . . . . . . 86 E7
Whiston Cl WV7 . . . . 237 A5
Whiston Eaves La ST10 . . . . 62 D2
Whitacre La WS14 . . . . 245 E7
Whitaker Rd ST3 . . . . 72 F3
Whitbread Dr ST8 . . . . 27 E8
Whitburn Cl WV9 . . . . 240 A2
Whitby Cl Stafford ST17 . . . 174 C7
Walsall WS3 . . . . 242 F3
Whitby Way WS11 . . . . 226 C8
Whitchurch Gr ST5 . . . . 40 E2
Whitcliffe Pl ST3 . . . . 72 F3
Whitcombe Rd ST3 . . . . 74 A2
White Bark Cl WS12 . . . . . 210 A8
Whitebeam Cl
Brownhills WS8 . . . . 244 E6
Dudley DY3 . . . . 271 C4
Newcastle-u-L ST5 . . . . 40 D1
Whitebridge Ind Est
ST15 . . . . 104 F2
Whitebridge La ST15 . . . . . 104 E2
Whitebridge Way ST15 . . . 104 F2
White Farm Rd B74 . . . . . . 257 E4
Whitefield Cl WV8 . . . . 239 B2
Whitefields La ST10 . . . . . . 49 B2
Whitegates CW12 . . . . 16 D4
Whitehall Ave ST7 . . . . 25 F2
Whitehall Cl ST14 . . . . 141 C8
Whitehall Ct WV3 . . . . 265 F6
Whitehall Rd
Kingswinford DY6 . . . . 275 C6
Wolverhampton WV4 . . . . . 266 B4
White Haven Cvn Pk DY7 . 278 A3
Whitehaven Dr ST1 . . . . . . 282 A4
Whitehead Rd ST6 . . . . 42 B8
Whiteheart Mews DE13 . . . 201 A2
White Hill DY7 . . . . 277 F5
Whitehill Rd ST7 . . . . 26 E2
White Hollies WS3 . . . . . . 243 F4
White Horse Rd WS8 . . . . . 228 E2
Whitehouse Ave WV3 . . . . 265 D8
Whitehouse Cres
Burntwood WS7 . . . . 229 B7
Wolverhampton WV11 . . . . 241 F1
Whitehouse Dr WS13 . . . . . 230 F6
White House La DY7 . . . . . 268 F1
Whitehouse La
Codsall WV8 . . . . 238 D7
Sandon ST15 . . . . 121 B7
White House La DY7,DY3 . . 269 B1
Whitehouse Rd
Bucknall ST2 . . . . 58 B5
Newcastle-u-L ST5 . . . . 56 B3
Whitehouse Rd N ST5 . . . . . 56 B4
Whitehouse Rd B78 . . . . . . 262 F7
White Houses La WV10 . . . 241 B6
Whitehurst La ST10 . . . . 75 D6
White Ladies Priory *
TF11 . . . . 221 D4
White Lion St ST17 . . . . . . 285 B2
Whitemill La ST14 . . . . 115 F7
White Oak Dr
Kingswinford DY6 . . . . 275 C6
Wolverhampton WV3 . . . . . 255 C1
Whiteoaks Dr ST19 . . . . . . 221 E8
White Oaks ST17 . . . . 175 D5
Whiteridge Rd ST7 . . . . 26 B2
White Row WV5 . . . . 264 C1
Whitesands Cl B77 . . . . . . 250 E5
Whitesands Gr ST3 . . . . 90 B7
White's Dr DY3 . . . . 271 E8
Whites La CW2 . . . . 37 B6
White's Mdw ST18 . . . . . . 153 D4
Whitesmiths Cl DY3 . . . . . . 271 D8
Whitestone Rd ST3 . . . . 90 B6
Whites Wood WV5 . . . . . . 270 A5
Whitesytch La ST15 . . . . . . 121 B8
Whitethorn Ave ST12 . . . . . 88 D1
Whitethorn Cl WS12 . . . . . 210 A8
Whitethorn Cres B74 . . . . . 256 D1
Whitethorn Rd 2 DY8 . . . . 275 F1
Whitethorn Way ST5 . . . . . 40 F1
Whitfield Ave ST5 . . . . 283 A1
Whitfield Rd
Cannock WS12 . . . . 210 C7
Kidsgrove ST7 . . . . 26 E2
Stoke-on-T ST6 . . . . 42 D6
Whitfield St ST14 . . . . 30 E4
Whitfield Valley Prim Sch
ST6 . . . . 42 B7
Whitgreave Ave WV10 . . . . 241 B7
Whitgreave Ct
Featherstone WV10 . . . . . . 241 B6
Stafford ST16 . . . . 155 D5
Whitgreave La
Great Bridgeford ST18 . . . . 135 D3
Rugeley WS15 . . . . 196 E6
Whitgreave ST18 . . . . 136 A4

Whitgreave Prim Sch
WV10 . . . . 241 B7
Whiting B77 . . . . 261 D7
Whitley Ave B77 . . . . 250 E5
Whitley Cl WV6 . . . . 255 B7
Whitley Rd ST6 . . . . 42 D*
Whitmore Ave ST9 . . . . 59 B4
Whitmore Rd
Hanchurch ST4 . . . . 87 D4
Newcastle-u-L ST5 . . . . 70 D4
Stourbridge DY8 . . . . 279 D3
Whitmore ST5 . . . . 86 B1
Whitmore St ST1 . . . . 57 A2
Whitney Ave DY8 . . . . 279 D6
Whitridge Gr ST2 . . . . 73 D8
Whittaker Mews ST14 . . . . 95 F3
Whittaker St WV2 . . . . 266 E6
Whittingham Dr ST7 . . . . . 174 B6
Whittington Common Rd
WS14 . . . . 232 B5
Whittington Hall La
Kinver DY7 . . . . 278 E2
Stourbridge DY7 . . . . 279 B3
Whittington Ho WS13 . . . . 214 E1
Whittington Prim Sch
WS14 . . . . 232 E4
Whittington Rd DY8 . . . . . . 279 E3
Whittle Ct ST1 . . . . 282 C4
Whittle Rd ST3 . . . . 90 B1
Whitty La
Blackshaw Moor ST13 . . . . 20 C6
Upper Hulme ST13 . . . . . . 20 D6
Whitworth La WS15 . . . . . . 178 B3
Whygate Gr ST1 . . . . 57 F6
Whytmore The WS13 . . . . 230 F5
Wickenlow La SK17 . . . . 3 C1
Wickenstones Ct ST8 . . . . . 27 D7
Wicket La DY7 . . . . 274 E1
Wickets The DE15 . . . . 185 F8
Wickstead Row CW3 . . . . . 53 A6
Widecombe Ave ST17 . . . . 175 E2
Widecombe Rd ST1 . . . . 57 F5
Widgeon Gr WV10 . . . . . . 241 B7
Widney Ave WS9 . . . . 245 B1
Wigford Rd B77 . . . . 261 C5
Wiggin Ho WS3 . . . . 243 C3
Wigginton Rd B79 . . . . 250 B7
Wightman Cl WS14 . . . . . . 231 E6
Wightwick Bank WV6 . . . . 255 A2
Wightwick Cl WS3 . . . . 243 B1
Wightwick Ct WV6 . . . . . . 255 A2
Wightwick Gr WV6 . . . . . . 255 A2
Wightwick Hall Rd WV6 . . 254 E1
Wightwick Hall Sch
WV6 . . . . 254 E2
Wightwick Manor * WV6 254 F1
Wigley Bank Rd WV6 . . . . . 277 D6
Wigmore Pl ST3 . . . . 73 C6
Wignall Rd ST6 . . . . 41 D6
Wilbraham's Wlk ST7 . . . . . 39 D2
Wilcox Ave WS12 . . . . 210 B7
Wildacres DY8 . . . . 279 C6
Wildfowl Wlk ST5 . . . . 85 C4
Wild Goose Ave ST7 . . . . . . 26 D3
Wildhay La Stanton DE6 . . . 80 C7
Wootton DE6 . . . . 80 A7
Wilding Rd ST6 . . . . 42 D6
Wildtree Ave WV10 . . . . . . 241 A2
Wildwood Dr
Stafford ST17 . . . . 175 D7
Stafford ST17 . . . . 175 C7
Wildwood Gate 2 ST17 . . . 175 D6
Wildwood Lawns ST17 . . . 175 C7
Wildwood Sh Ctr ST17 . . . 175 D6
Wileman Pl ST4 . . . . 72 E6
Wileman St ST4 . . . . 72 F6
Wilfred Owen Cl TF9 . . . . . 112 A7
Wilfred Pl ST4 . . . . 71 F8
Wilkes Cl WS3 . . . . 243 E3
Wilkes Croft DY3 . . . . 271 D7
Wilkes Rd WV8 . . . . 238 F3
Wilke's Wood ST18 . . . . . . 154 F8
Wilkin Rd WS8 . . . . 228 C2
Wilkins Croft DE13 . . . . . . 200 F2
Wilkins Ho WS3 . . . . 243 A1
Wilkinson Cl WS7 . . . . 229 B8
Wilkinson St ST6 . . . . 41 D2
Wilkinson Wlk 1 TF9 . . . . . 97 C1
Wilks St ST6 . . . . 41 E4
Willatt Pl ST2 . . . . 43 A1
Willcock Rd
Burton u T DE14 . . . . 185 A7
Wolverhampton WV2 . . . . . 266 F2
Willdale Gr ST1 . . . . 57 F5
Willerby Fold WV10 . . . . . . 240 F4
Willeton St ST2 . . . . 58 A3
Willett Ave WS7 . . . . 228 E5
Willey La ST20 . . . . 171 C6
Willfield La ST6,ST9 . . . . . . 43 C6
William Allitt Sch DE11 . . 186 E1
William Ave Biddulph ST8 . . 27 D7
Meir ST3 . . . . 90 C4
William Baxter Sch
WS12 . . . . 210 A6
William Birch Ct ST2 . . . . . 58 A1
William Birch Rd ST2 . . . . . 58 A1
William Cl ST11 . . . . 91 B7
William Clowes St ST6 . . . . 56 F8
William Coltman Way
ST6 . . . . 41 C5
William Fiske Ct ST4 . . . . . 71 F4
William Hutson Jun Sch
DE13 . . . . 166 D4
William IV Rd ST3 . . . . 201 A3
William Lunn's Homes 2
WS14 . . . . 231 C6
William MacGregor Prim Sch
B77 . . . . 250 D4

William Mews WV10 .... 225 C2
William Morris Ct WS15 178 D3
William Morris Gr WS11. 209 E4
William Nadin Way DE11 186 E3
William Newton Cl DE65. 148 B5
William Rd ST7 .... 26 A2
William Ruston Rd ST6 ... 42 D2
Williams Ave WS13 ...... 215 C6
Williams Cl ST16......... 155 B3
Williams Ct ST16......... 155 F5
William Shrewsbury Prim
Sch DE13............... 147 F2
Williamson Ave
Prospect Village WS12 .. 211 C4
Stoke-on-T ST6 .... 42 E6
Williamson St ST6 .... 41 E2
William St
Burton u T DE14........ 166 C5
Congleton CW12 .... 6 A4
Stoke-on-T ST7 .... 72 E6
Williams Wlk ST15 ...... 103 C4
William Terr ST6......... 42 B6
William Tolson's Ind Est
B78................... 261 A8
William Wiggin Ave
WS3................... 243 B2
Willington Rd B79 ...... 250 B7
Williscroft Pl WS15 ..... 179 A6
Willmer Cres ST7 .... 26 B6
Willmott Rd B75......... 258 D3
Willmott Rd B75......... 258 D3
Willots Hill Rd ST5 ...... 40 D1
Willoughby Cl ST19 ..... 207 F7
Willoughby Cl ST14 ..... 125 C1
Willoughby Rd B79...... 249 E2
Willoughby St ST6 .... 41 D7
Willow Ave WS7 .... 229 C6
Willowbank B78 .... 250 B1
Willow Bank WV3....... 255 C1
Willow Bottom La B79 .. 234 B7
Willowbrook ST18 ...... 154 C4
Willowbrook Dr ST6 ..... 42 E1
Willow Cl Coven WV9 ... 224 B3
Fradley WS13 .... 215 E8
Hagley DY9 .... 281 F5
Kidsgrove ST7 .... 41 A7
Newcastle-u-L ST5........ 40 D1
Penkridge ST19 .... 207 F6
Upper Tean ST10 .... 92 D5
Walton-on-t-H ST17...... 175 F6
Willowcroft Rise ST11.... 90 D7
Willowcroft ST20 .... 151 E7
Willow Ct WS14......... 231 C1
Willowdale Ave ST4...... 72 C5
Willowdale Grange WV6. 255 E5
Willow Dale ST15 .... 120 C3
Willow Dr Cheddleton ST13. 45 C8
Codsall WV8............. 239 B3
Swadlincote DE11 .... 186 F7
Willowfield Ct ST4....... 88 C7
Willowfield Dr ST4....... 88 C7
Willow Gr
Essington WV11.......... 242 B3
Stoke-on-T ST3 .... 72 C5
Willowherb Cl WS11..... 210 C2
Willow Ho WS4 .... 244 D1
Willow La ST3 .... 90 A3
Willowmoor ST17 .... 174 E5
Willow Pl Biddulph ST8 ... 17 B1
Burton u T DE15........ 185 C7
Willow Rd
Barton-u-N DE13........ 183 D1
Kinver DY7............. 278 C3
Stone ST15 .... 120 B7
Wolverhampton WV3..... 265 D8
Willow Row WS3 .... 284 B3
Willows Dr ST3 .... 90 A4
Willowsmere Dr WS4 .... 231 F7
Willows Prim Sch WS13. 214 B2
Willows Prim Sch The
ST4................... 71 F7
Willows The
Burton u T DE14........ 166 D2
Cannock WS11........... 209 C1
Leek ST13 .... 30 C5
Rugeley WS15 .... 197 A5
Stone ST15 .... 120 B6
Sutton Coldfield,Streetly
B74................... 257 F2
Wombourne WV5.......... 269 F5
Wrinehill CW3 .... 53 A3
Yarnfield ST15 .... 118 E6
Willowtree Cl WS13..... 214 B2
Willow Tree Gr ST4 ...... 72 E4
Willow Way ST11 .... 91 A8
Willow Wlk WS12 ...... 209 D8
Willridding La DE6....... 80 C7
Willsford St ST4......... 126 D7
Wilmcote Dr B75........ 258 B3
Wilmore Ct ST18........ 137 D1
Wilmore Hill La ST18.... 137 D1
Wilmore La DE13........ 164 B3
Wilmot Cl ST5 .... 55 F3
Wilmot Dr ST5........... 55 F3
Wilmot Gr ST4........... 73 C6
Wilmott Cl WS13........ 231 A5
Wilnecote High Sch B77 261 F6
Wilnecote Jun Sch B77 .. 261 F7
Wilnecote La B77........ 250 D2
Wilnecote Sta B77....... 261 D7
Wilner's View WS3...... 243 F5
Wilson Gr WS11......... 210 C2
Wilson Keys Ct WS15... 178 F2
Wilson Rd ST4........... 71 F1
Wilson St
Newcastle-u-L ST5........ 283 B3

Wilson St continued
Stoke-on-T ST6 .... 42 B2
Wilson Way ST6 .... 41 C6
Wilstell Rd Ind Est WS14 231 B7
Wiltell Rd WS14 .... 231 B6
Wilton Ave ST9 .... 59 F4
Wilton Cl DY3........... 271 E7
Wilton St ST5........... 283 A4
Wiltshire Gr ST5 .... 71 C4
Wiltshire Ho 3 DY8..... 279 F8
Wimberry Dr ST5 .... 40 D1
Wimblebury Rd WS12 ... 210 F2
Wimborne Ave ST3 ...... 88 F7
Wimshurst Mdw WV10 .. 240 F4
Winceby Rd WV6 .... 254 F3
Winchcombe Cl DY1 .... 271 E3
Winchcombe Dr DE15... 167 B1
Winchcombe Dr WS22 .. 58 D1
Winchester Cl
Armitage WS15 .... 198 B4
Lichfield WS13 .... 214 C3
Winchester Ct
Stafford ST17 .... 175 D6
Sutton Coldfield B74 .... 257 F2
Winchester Dr
Burton u T DE14........ 185 C8
Newcastle-u-L ST5....... 70 F4
Winchester Mews WS9.. 256 B4
Winchester Rd
Cannock WS11.......... 210 A3
Tamworth B78 .... 249 F3
Wolverhampton WV10 .. 240 C3
Wincote Dr WV6........ 255 C4
Wincote La ST21........ 133 C3
Windemere Way ST10 ... 76 F4
Windermere Dr
Aldridge B74 .... 256 F3
Kingswinford DY6 ...... 275 D6
Windermere Ho ST16 ... 285 C3
Windermere Pl WS11 ... 209 E1
Windermere Rd
Newcastle-u-L ST5....... 71 B4
Wolverhampton WV6..... 255 D8
Windermere St ST1 ..... 282 A4
Windermere B77......... 262 A7
Windings The WS13..... 214 A1
Windmill Ave ST7 .... 41 A8
Windmill Bank
Gentleshaw WS15 ...... 212 B5
Wombourne WV5........ 270 A7
Windmill Cl
4 Uttoxeter ST14....... 111 B1
Lichfield WS13 .... 214 A2
Stoke-on-T ST3 .... 89 F4
Tamworth B79 .... 250 A8
Windmill Cres WV3 ..... 255 A1
Windmill Dr ST14 ...... 127 E3
Windmill Dr DY6........ 275 B8
Windmillhill La ST14 ... 232 C8
Windmill Hill ST14 ..... 89 F4
Windmill La Croxton ST21 116 A4
Gentleshaw WS15 ...... 212 A4
Lichfield WS13 .... 214 A2
Snelston DE6........... 81 E2
Wolverhampton WV3..... 255 A1
Windmill St
Dudley,Gornalwood DY3 271 D5
Hanley ST1............. 282 C3
Windmill View ST6 ...... 59 C4
Windrow The WV6...... 254 D4
Windrush Cl
Stoke-on-T ST4 .... 88 C5
Walsall WS3........... 244 A1
Windrush Rd
Cannock WS11.......... 209 E6
Hilton DE65............ 147 D8
Windsmoor St ST4....... 72 B5
Windsor Ave
Cannock WS12.......... 210 B6
Longton ST3............ 284 D2
Wolverhampton WV4..... 265 E6
Windsor Cl
Burntwood WS7........ 211 E1
Dudley DY3............ 271 B2
Rugeley WS15 .... 196 D7
Stone ST15 .... 119 F5
Tamworth B79 .... 250 C7
Windsor Cres DY7 ...... 277 F4
Windsor Ct
Cannock WS12.......... 210 B6
Lichfield WS14......... 231 B6
Windsor Dr
Burton u T DE15........ 166 F1
Leek ST13 .... 31 B7
Market Drayton TF9..... 97 E2
Windsor Gdns
Codsall WV8............ 238 F3
Wolverhampton WV3..... 265 A8
Windsor Gr
Stourbridge DY8 .... 275 E1
Walsall WS4............ 244 C2
Windsor Holloway DY7.. 278 C1
Windsor Ho ST7 .... 40 D6
Windsor Ind Est DE14.. 166 C4
Windsor Park CE Mid Sch
ST14................. 126 B8
Windsor Rd
Albrighton WV7......... 237 A6
Cheslyn Hay WS6........ 226 E4
Pattingham WV6........ 253 C2
Stafford ST17 .... 175 B8
Stoke-on-T ST4 .... 72 A1
Stourbridge DY8 .... 279 E3
Uttoxeter ST14......... 111 A1
Wolverhampton WV4..... 266 C4
Wombourne WV5........ 269 F6
Windsor St ST3......... 283 C3
Windy Arbour ST10 ..... 76 E4

Windy Arbour La WV10.. 225 E4
Windycote La ST10...... 60 B2
Windyridge SK17 .... 13 B6
Winford Ave DY6........ 275 E4
Wingate Ct B74......... 257 E4
Wingate Wlk ST3 .... 88 F7
Winghay Cl ST6......... 56 C8
Winghay Pl ST6......... 42 B5
Winghay Rd ST7 .... 26 B2
Winghouse La ST15..... 103 E7
Wingrove 1 ST3........ 73 D1
Winifred Gdns ST3...... 88 E8
Winifred St ST1......... 282 A4
Winnipeg Cl ST4........ 88 B8
Winpenny Rd ST5....... 55 F8
Winrush Cl DY3......... 271 D3
Winscar Croft DY3...... 271 D3
Winsford Ave ST3....... 73 E2
Winsford Cres ST17..... 175 E6
Winslow Dr WV6........ 255 E4
Winslow Gn ST2........ 58 C1
Winsor Ave WS12....... 210 B6
Winstanley Cl WS15..... 178 D2
Winstanley Pl WS15..... 178 D2
Winster Gn DE11........ 186 E5
Winston Pl ST2.......... 58 A3
Winston Rd Cookley DY11. 280 A6
Swindon DY3 .... 269 E2
Winston Terr ST5 .... 56 C6
Winterbourne Gr ST3 ... 73 E3
Winter Cl WS13......... 214 D2
Wintercroft La DE6...... 51 E1
Winterfield La ST3...... 74 B7
Winterley Gdns DY3..... 271 D1
Winterside Cl ST5....... 40 D1
Wintonfield St ST4...... 72 C7
Winton Sq ST4.......... 72 C8
Winwood DY3 .... 279 F4
Wiscombe Ave ST19..... 193 A1
Wise St ST3............ 284 C1
Wissage Ct WS13....... 214 D1
Wissage La WS13....... 214 D1
Wissage Rd WS13....... 231 D8
Wisteria Dr WV8....... 228 C2
Wistmans Cl DY1 .... 271 E2
Wistwood Hayes WV10.. 240 F4
Witchford Cl ST3........ 88 F7
Witham Way ST8........ 16 E1
Withern Way DY3....... 271 D3
Withers Rd WV8 .... 239 B3
Withies Rd ST14 .... 71 E4
Within La ST18 .... 137 D1
Withington Rd ST6...... 42 A6
Withnell Gn ST6........ 42 A6
Withymere La WV5...... 270 C6
Withystakes Rd ST9..... 59 D4
Withywood Cl WV12..... 242 C1
Witley Dr 1 WS13...... 231 E8
Witney Cl B79.......... 249 F7
Witney Gr WV10........ 240 B3
Witney Rd ST17........ 156 D1
Witney Wlk ST3......... 88 F7
Witton Rd WV4......... 266 A6
Witton St DY8.......... 279 F4
Wobaston Ct WV10..... 240 B3
Wobaston Rd
Codsall WV9............ 239 E4
Wolverhampton WV9,
WV10................. 240 B4
Woburn Cl ST4......... 88 C5
Woburn Dr CW12 ...... 16 B8
Woburn B77............ 250 D3
Wodehouse Cl WV5..... 269 F5
Wodehouse Cotts WV5.. 270 D8
Woden Cl WV5.......... 269 F7
Wogan St WS16........ 155 E5
Wold The WV5.......... 267 D7
Wolfe St ST4........... 72 B6
Wolfscote Dale DE11.... 186 F2
Wolgarston High Sch
ST19................. 208 A8
Wolgarston Way ST19... 207 F2
Wollaston Ct DY8....... 279 C6
Wollaston Rd
Stourbridge DY8 .... 279 E8
Stourton DY7........... 279 C7
Wollery La TF11 .... 204 C2
Wolmer Rd WV11 ...... 242 A2
Wolmore La WV5....... 263 B2
Wolseley Cl ST17 ...... 177 E7
Wolseley Ctr The★ ST17 178 A5
Wolseley Ct
Rugeley WS15 .... 197 B6
Stafford ST18 .... 156 D5
Wolseley Gdns
Newcastle-u-L ST5....... 56 B5
Rugeley,Cannock Chase Ctry Pk
WS15................ 177 E1
Rugeley WS15 .... 178 E2
Stafford ST16 .... 156 C3
Stoke-on-T ST4 .... 71 F4
Wolseley B77........... 250 F7
Wolsey Rd WS13........ 213 F2
Wolstanton High Sch ST5 56 C4
Wolstanton Rd ST5...... 55 F6
Wolstanton Ret Pk ST5.. 56 A4
Wolstern Rd ST3........ 73 D5
Wolverhampton Bsns Airport
DY7................. 268 C2
Wolverhampton Coll Wulfrun
Campus WV6........... 255 C4
Wolverhampton Girls' High
Sch WV6.............. 255 F3
Wolverhampton Gram Sch
WV3................. 255 D4
Wolverhampton Rd
Cannock WS11.......... 226 D8

Wolverhampton Rd continued
Cheslyn Hay WV10,WS6.. 226 B2
Codsall WV8............ 239 A3
Cookley DY10........... 280 B3
Essington WV11......... 242 A3
Wolverhampton Rd E
WV4................. 266 D5
Wolverhampton Rd
Kingswinford DY6 ...... 270 C1
Nurton WV6............ 254 A3
Pattingham WV6........ 253 E3
Penkridge WS11 .... 207 E8
Sedgley DY3........... 266 D2
Stafford ST17 .... 285 B1
Stourton DY7........... 278 F7
Walsall,Pelsall WS3...... 243 F3
Walsall,Wallington Heath
WS3................. 243 B1
Wedges Mills WS11...... 226 B6
Wolverley Ave
Stourbridge DY8 .... 279 C6
Wolverhampton WV4..... 265 C5
Wolverley Ct WV7....... 237 A5
Wolverley Rd DY10...... 280 A2
Wolverson Rd WS9...... 245 A4
Wombourne Cl DY3..... 271 C8
Wombourne Ent Pk
WV5................. 269 D5
Wombourne Pk WV5.... 269 F3
Wombourne Rd DY3,WV5 269 F3
Wombrook Dale WV5.... 269 E3
Wombrook Ind Est WV5. 269 E6
Woodall St ST1......... 57 B6
Wood Ave Coven WV9... 224 B3
Dudley DY3 .... 271 C4
Kingsley ST10.......... 61 D2
Wood Bank La ST19..... 193 B6
Woodbank Rd DY3....... 271 C2
Wood Bank Rd WV3..... 265 A8
Woodbank St ST6........ 56 F8
Woodberry Ave ST4..... 71 F5
Woodberry Cl
Stafford ST17 .... 174 F4
Stoke-on-T ST6 .... 71 E5
Woodbine Cl DE14...... 184 E6
Woodbridge Cl
Walsall,Wallington Heath
WS3................. 243 A3
Walsall WS4............ 244 D1
Woodbridge Rd ST5..... 71 E5
Woodburn Rd ST6 ...... 42 E2
Woodcock Gdns WV10.. 241 B7
Woodcock La ST7....... 26 C6
Woodcock Rd WS15..... 178 C1
Woodcocks' Well CE Prim
Sch ST7.............. 26 C6
Wood Common Grange
WS3................. 243 F4
Woodcote Rd WV6...... 255 C4
Woodcote The 3 ST17.. 175 C7
Wood Cres Stafford ST16. 155 B6
Stone ST15 .... 119 F5
Woodcroft ST7 .... 40 A1
Woodcroft Ave Leek ST13. 30 B4
Tamworth B79 .... 250 D6
Woodcroft Fst Sch ST13. 30 C4
Woodcroft Rd ST13 ..... 30 D4
Woodcross La WV14..... 266 F2
Woodcross St WV14..... 266 F2
Wood Ct DE14.......... 166 C1
Wooddisse La ST13 ..... 33 E2
Wood Eaton Rd ST20.... 190 A4
Woodedge St ST14...... 143 F6
Wood End La
Fradley WS13 .... 215 A5
Lichfield WS13......... 214 D7
Woodend Pl WV6....... 255 B4
Wood End Prim Sch CV9 262 C1
Wood End Rd WV11..... 241 C1
Woodend St ST4........ 72 F6
Wood End Way WS9..... 245 B1
Woodfield Ave WV4..... 265 F6
Woodfield Cl WS11...... 227 F7
Woodfield Ct ST13 ..... 31 A6
Woodfield Dr WS11..... 227 F7
Woodfield Ho WS3...... 244 B3
Woodfield Hts WV6..... 255 D4
Woodfield Jun & Inf Schs
WV4................. 265 F6
Woodfield Rd DY3....... 271 C4
Woodfields Dr WS14.... 231 E5
Woodfold Croft WS9.... 256 B7
Woodford Cl WV9....... 239 F2
Woodford Cres WS7..... 229 B7
Woodford End 1 WS11. 209 F4
Woodford La WV5....... 269 D8
Woodford Way
Cannock WS12.......... 210 D1
Wombourne WV5........ 269 D6
Woodgate Ave ST7...... 25 A5
Woodgate St ST3 .... 74 A1
Woodgreen WS6........ 226 E5
Woodhall Pl ST5........ 54 F7
Woodhall Rd
Kidsgrove ST7 .... 26 C3
Wolverhampton WV4..... 265 E5
Woodhaven Walsall WS4. 244 D1
Wedges Mills WS11...... 226 B5
Woodseaves ST20 ...... 151 E7
Wood Hayes Croft WV10. 241 D6
Wood Hayes Rd WV11... 241 C6
Woodhead Rd ST2....... 58 C8
Woodhead Yd ST10...... 76 E5
Woodheyes Lawns
WS15................ 178 C1
Woodhill Cl WV5........ 269 F6
Wood Hill Dr WV5...... 269 F5

Woodhouse High Sch
B77................. 250 F4
Woodhouse La
Albrighton WV7......... 237 C2
Biddulph Moor ST8 ..... 17 A1
Biddulph ST8 .... 16 F2
Brown Edge ST6........ 42 F6
Foston DE65........... 129 F7
Haughton ST18......... 172 D8
Norton in H CW3....... 82 A7
Tamworth B77.......... 251 A5
Woodhouse Mid Sch ST8. 16 E2
Woodhouse Rd N WV6.. 255 B4
Woodhouse Rd WV6 .... 255 B4
Woodhouses La WS7..... 229 F6
Woodhouses Rd WS7.... 230 A7
Woodhouse St ST4...... 72 B6
Woodhurst Cl B77....... 250 F5
Woodingdean 3 ST3... 73 D5
Woodkirk Cl ST6........ 42 A8
Wood La Aldridge B74... 256 E2
Cannock WS12.......... 210 C4
Cheslyn Hay WS11...... 225 F6
Gratwich ST14.......... 124 D2
Hanbury DE13.......... 144 F3
Maer ST5.............. 84 D3
Woodland Ave
Cheddleton ST13........ 45 B1
Hagley DY8............ 281 F5
Newcastle-u-L ST5....... 56 C5
Stoke-on-T ST6 .... 42 F4
Wolverhampton WV6..... 255 B3
Woodland Cl
Albrighton WV7......... 237 A6
Cannock WS12.......... 210 B8
Leek ST13 .... 30 F2
Woodland Cres WV3 .... 265 D7
Woodland Ct
Cannock WS12.......... 209 C4
Shenstone WS14....... 258 A7
Woodland Dr
Cheslyn Hay WS6........ 226 E4
Foston DE65........... 129 D4
Rocester ST14.......... 95 F3
Woodland Gr Dudley DY3. 271 B3
Kidderminster DY10..... 280 C3
Stoke-on-T ST6 .... 42 B2
Woodland Hills CW3 .... 68 E8
Woodland Rd
Stanton DE6........... 186 B4
Tamworth B77.......... 251 A4
Wolverhampton WV3..... 265 D7
Woodlands Ave
Kidsgrove ST7 .... 25 D1
Stone ST15 .... 119 F8
Woodlands Cl
Stafford ST16 .... 155 C7
Stone ST15 .... 119 E8
Thorpe DE6........... 51 D1
Woodlands Com Prim Sch
The B77.............. 250 E4
Woodlands Cotts WV4.. 265 F4
Woodlands Cres WS3 .. 243 F5
Woodlands Dr
Chorlton CW2 .... 37 C3
Coven WV9............ 224 B3
Stone WV9............. 120 C3
Woodlands Gr ST3...... 90 A4
Woodlands La
Cheslyn Hay WS11...... 225 B8
Forsbrook ST11......... 91 B6
Woodlands Paddock
WV4................. 265 E4
Woodlands Rd
Cookley DY10........... 280 A4
Stafford ST16 .... 155 B7
Stoke-on-T ST4 .... 71 E4
Wombourne WV5........ 270 A5
Woodlands Rise DE6.... 144 A7
Woodland St ST8 ...... 27 D6
Woodlands The
Coldmeece ST15........ 118 C6
Kidsgrove ST7 .... 25 E3
Lichfield WS13......... 231 D8
Stoke-on-T ST4 .... 71 E4
Tatenhill DE13......... 184 A8
Wood End CV9.......... 262 C1
Woodland St ST6........ 41 E3
Woodlands Way WS15... 198 C4
Woodland View DE12 ... 219 F3
Woodland View ST14.... 127 E2
Woodland View DY3..... 269 C4
Woodland Way
Burntwood WS7........ 229 A6
Polesworth B78......... 262 E8
Wood Lane Prim Sch ST7. 40 A1
Wood La Shenstone WS14. 246 B2
Stone ST15 .... 119 F5
Stretton ST19 .... 206 C4
Swadlincote DE11 ...... 186 F7
Uttoxeter ST14......... 126 E6
Walsall WS3............ 243 F4
Wedges Mills WS11...... 226 A6
Woodlawn Gr DY6...... 275 D5
Wood La
Wolverhampton WV10 .. 240 D2
Yoxall DE13............ 182 A6
Woodleighton Gr ST14 .. 126 C6
Woodleighton Rd ST14.. 126 C6
Woodleyes Cres ST17 ... 175 D6
Woodman Gr 5 B75 ... 258 E3
Woodman La ST15...... 226 E4
Woodman St ST2 .... 43 B1
Woodmill La WS15...... 161 B2
Woodpark La ST3....... 89 D7

Woodpecker Dr
Packmoor ST7 . . . . **26** E1
Stoke-on-T ST7 . . . . **41** E8
Woodpecker View TF9 . . . **99** C3
Woodpecker Way WS11 . **210** C3
Wood Pl ST3 . . . . **74** B2
Wood Rd Codsall WV8 . . . **238** E4
Dudley DY3 . . . . **271** C4
Longsdon ST9 . . . . **45** A8
Wolverhampton WV6 . . . **255** C3
Wombourne WV5 . . . . . . **270** B7
Woodridge Cl TF10 . . . . . **168** A4
Wood Ridings WS13 . . . . **214** A1
Woodroffe's Cliff ST14 . **143** C5
Woodrow Way
Ashley TF9 . . . . **100** C5
Newcastle-u-L ST5 . . . . . **40** F1
Woodruff Cl ST7 . . . . **27** A1
Woods Croft WS13 . . . . . **214** A1
Woodseat Gr ST14 . . . . . **96** A4
Woodseaves CE Prim Sch
ST20 . . . . **151** E7
Woodsetton Sch The
DY3 . . . . **271** F7
Woodshot Ave WS15 . . . **198** C4
Woodshutt's St ST7 . . . . **25** E1
Woodside Ave
Brown Edge ST6 . . . . . . **43** B6
Kidsgrove ST7 . . . . **26** A1
Woodside ST5 . . . . **85** C3
Woodside Cl
Colwich ST18 . . . . **177** D8
Wood End CV9 . . . . **262** C1
Woodside Cotts ST10 . . . **77** F7
Woodside Cres ST5 . . . . . **71** C2
Woodside Dr
Little Aston B74 . . . . . . **257** C5
Meir Heath ST3 . . . . **90** A4
Woodside Gr WV8 . . . . . **239** B2
Woodside La ST13 . . . . . **30** C2
Woodside Lawton-gate ST7 . **25** E4
Madeley CW3 . . . . **68** E7
Woodside Pl
Cannock WS11 . . . . **209** E5
Stoke-on-T ST2 . . . . **43** B1
Woodside B74 . . . . **257** E2
Woodside Villas ST3 . . . **284** D4
Woodside Way WS9 . . . . **256** B5
Woods La
Burton u T DE15 . . . . . . **167** A1
Burton u T DE15 . . . . . . **167** B1
Woodsorrel Rd DY1 . . . . **271** E4
Wood St Audley ST7 . . . . **39** E3
Burton u T DE14 . . . . . . **166** C1
Woodstile Cl B75 . . . . . . **258** D3
Wood St Leek ST13 . . . . . **30** F5
Longton ST3 . . . . **284** C4
Mow Cop ST7 . . . . **26** D7
Woodstock Cl
Newcastle-u-L ST5 . . . . . **56** C3
Stourbridge DY8 . . . . . . **275** C1
Woodstock Dr
Huntington WS12 . . . . . **209** C7
Stourbridge DY8 . . . . . . **275** C2
Sutton Coldfield B74 . . . **257** D4
Woodstock Rd
Kidsgrove ST6 . . . . **41** A7
Stafford ST17 . . . . **156** D1
Woodstock St ST6 . . . . . **41** C8

Woodstone Ave ST9 . . . . **43** E6
Wood St Stourbridge DY8 . **279** D6
Wood End CV9 . . . . **262** C1
Wood Terr ST1 . . . . **282** A1
Wood The ST3 . . . . **74** C2
Woodtherne Cl ST19 . . . **207** F7
Woodthorne Cl
Dudley DY1 . . . . **271** D2
Rugeley WS15 . . . . **178** C2
Woodthorne Prim Sch
WV6 . . . . **255** B4
Woodthorne Rd S WV6 . . **255** A5
Woodthorne Rd WV6 . . . **255** A6
Woodthorne Wlk DY6 . . . **275** E8
Woodvale Cres ST9 . . . . . **43** E8
Wood View ST7 . . . . **40** A1
Woodview Rd DE11 . . . . **186** E5
Wood View WS15 . . . . . **196** F6
Woodville Gdns DY3 . . . **266** F1
Woodville Pl ST3 . . . . **74** A2
Woodville Rd ST3 . . . . . . **74** A2
Woodville Terr ST3 . . . . . **74** B2
Woodward St ST1 . . . . . . **57** D6
Woodyard Dr B79 . . . . . . **217** C5
Woodyard La DE65 . . . . **129** F5
Woody Bank WS6 . . . . . . **226** E2
Woolliscroft Ave ST5 . . . **56** D3
Woolliscroft Rd ST2 . . . . **58** B3
Woolrich St ST6 . . . . **56** E7
Woolridge Ct ST6 . . . . . . **42** D1
Woolston Ave CW12 . . . . . **6** A2
Woore Prim Sch CW3 . . . . **67** C1
Woosnam Cl DE14 . . . . . **185** A6
Wootton Cl WS11 . . . . . . **210** B3
Wootton Dr ST16 . . . . . **155** A7
Wootton La
Eccleshall ST21 . . . . . . **133** E3
Oakamoor ST10 . . . . **78** E4
Wootton Rd WV3 . . . . . . **265** D8
Woottons Ct WS11 . . . . . **209** F1
Worcester Cl
Cannock WS11 . . . . **226** F8
Lichfield WS13 . . . . **214** C3
Rugeley WS15 . . . . **196** C6
Sutton Coldfield B75 . . . **258** D3
Talke ST7 . . . . **40** D7
Worcester Ct WV3 . . . . . **266** A6
Worcester Gr WV6 . . . . . **254** D4
Worcester La B75 . . . . . **258** D4
Worcester Pl ST2 . . . . . . **58** D2
Worcester Rd
Burton u T DE15 . . . . . . **185** E6
Hagley DY9 . . . . **281** F3
Whittington WS14 . . . . . **232** C3
Wordsley Ct DY8 . . . . . . **275** E3
Wordsley Green Sh Ctr
DY8 . . . . **275** D2
Wordsley Hospl DY8 . . . . **275** E3
Wordsley Sch The DY8 . . **275** F3
Wordsworth Ave
Stafford ST17 . . . . **174** C8
Tamworth B79 . . . . **250** A6
Wolverhampton WV4 . . . **266** F4
Wordsworth Cl
Armitage WS15 . . . . . . **198** A4
Burton u T DE14 . . . . . . **166** D6
Cannock WS11 . . . . **209** D4
Cheadle ST10 . . . . **76** C2
Lichfield WS14 . . . . **231** B5
Wordsworth Ct WV6 . . . **254** E4
Wordsworth Dr TF9 . . . . **112** A7
Wordsworth Rd

Burntwood WS7 . . . . . . **229** A8
Dudley DY3 . . . . **271** B5
Worfield Gdns WV3 . . . . **265** F6
Worsley Dr CW12 . . . . **6** B1
Worston La ST15,ST18 . . **135** B5
Worth Cl ST3 . . . . **73** D4
Worthing Pl ST3 . . . . . . **284** B3
Worthington Rd WS13 . . **215** D6
Worthington Way DE14 . . **166** D3
Wragby Cl WV9 . . . . **240** B3
Wraggs La ST8 . . . . **17** B1
Wrekin Ave TF10 . . . . . . **168** E2
Wrekin Cl B74 . . . . **257** F2
Wrekin Dr
Wolverhampton,Penn
WV3 . . . . **265** E8
Wolverhampton,Tettenhall
WV6 . . . . **255** A5
Wrekin Gr WV11 . . . . . . **242** B1
Wrekin La WV6 . . . . **255** A5
Wrekin View
Brownhills WS8 . . . . . . **245** A5
Huntington WS12 . . . . . **209** C7
Wrekin View Rd DY3 . . . **271** C8
Wren Ave WV6 . . . . **254** D3
Wrenbury Cl ST5 . . . . . . **40** D1
Wrenbury Cres ST2 . . . . . **58** B1
Wren Cl ST8 . . . . **27** E8
Wrens Croft WS11 . . . . . **210** B1
Wrenswood ST17 . . . . . **175** C6
Wren View
Loggerheads TF9 . . . . . . **99** C4
Longton ST3 . . . . **284** D2
Wrexham Cl ST8 . . . . **16** D1
Wright Ave ST5 . . . . **55** F7
Wrighton Cl ST2 . . . . **57** F2
Wrighton Dr DY5 . . . . . . **271** C1
Wrighton Gr B78 . . . . . . **261** A8
Wright's Ave WS11 . . . . **209** F5
Wright St Kidsgrove ST7 . . **25** D1
Stafford ST16 . . . . **155** E5
Wrinehill Rd CW5 . . . . . . **52** A6
Wrottesley Ct WV8 . . . . **254** C8
Wrottesley Park Rd WV6,
WV8 . . . . **254** D5
Wrottesley Rd WV6 . . . . **255** B5
Wrottesley Rd W
Perton WV6 . . . . **254** F6
Wolverhampton WV6 . . . **255** A6
Wroxham Way ST5 . . . . . **71** B2
Wulfad Ct ST15 . . . . **120** C7
Wulfric Cl ST19 . . . . **208** A8
Wulfruna Gdns WV3 . . . **255** F1
Wulstan Dr ST5 . . . . **56** C3
Wulstan Rd ST6 . . . . **57** A6
Wyatt St ST6 . . . . **41** C7
Wychall Dr WV10 . . . . . **240** E4
Wychbold Cl WV12 . . . . **242** D1
Wychbold Way WV12 . . . **242** D1
Wychbury Rd WV3 . . . . . **265** C7
Wych Elm Rd WS8 . . . . . **244** E5
Wycherwood Gdns ST17 . **175** D5
Wychwood Pk
Chorlton CW2 . . . . **37** B2
Gorstyhill CW2 . . . . **37** E2
Wycliffe Rd ST6 . . . . **56** F8
Wye Cl Cheadle ST10 . . . . **76** E1
Hilton DE65 . . . . **147** D8
Perton WV6 . . . . **254** F4
Wye Dale DE11 . . . . **186** F2
Wye Ho DY3 . . . . **271** D3
Wye Rd Newcastle-u-L ST5 . **71** A3

Walsall WS3 . . . . **243** E1
Wyggeston St DE13 . . . . **166** C6
Wykeham Gr WV6 . . . . . **254** D3
Wyllie Mews DE14 . . . . . **166** D3
Wymondley Gr ST4 . . . . . **88** B6
Wynbank Cl ST7 . . . . **54** E8
Wynchcombe Ave WV4 . . **265** D4
Wyndham Cres DE15 . . . **167** C3
Wyndham Rd ST3 . . . . . . **88** F7
Wyndham Wood Cl
WS13 . . . . **215** D7
Wyndley Cl B74 . . . . **257** F6
Wyndley Manor B74 . . . **258** A6
Wynd The DY3 . . . . **266** D1
Wynford Pl ST2 . . . . **58** B1
Wynne Cres WV4 . . . . . **265** C3
Wynn Rd WV4 . . . . **265** F5
Wynstay Ave ST9 . . . . . . **59** A3
Wynstay Ct ST5 . . . . **71** C1
Wynyates B79 . . . . **249** E6
Wyre Cl WS9 . . . . **244** F4
Wyre Rd DY8 . . . . **279** E7
Wyrley Wlk ST3 . . . . **88** F6
Wyrley Brook Pk WS11 . . **226** D5
Wyrley Brook Ret Pk
WS11 . . . . **226** D6
Wyrley Cl Burntwood WS8 . **228** F3
Lichfield WS14 . . . . **231** A5
Wyrley La WS3 . . . . **243** E8
Wyrley Rd B75 . . . . **258** D1
Wyvern Gr WS12 . . . . . . **210** A5
Wyvern B77 . . . . **250** F3
Wyvis Cl WV6 . . . . **255** E2

Y

Yale St ST6 . . . . **56** E7
Yardley Pl ST3 . . . . **88** F6
Yardley St ST6 . . . . **42** F5
Yardley Wlk ST3 . . . . **88** F6
Yarlet Croft ST16 . . . . . **155** D6
Yarlet La ST18 . . . . **136** D5
Yarlet Sch ST18 . . . . . . **136** C7
Yarmouth Wlk ST3 . . . . **284** D5
Yarnbrook Gr ST6 . . . . . . **42** D3
Yarner Cl DY1 . . . . **271** E2
Yarnfield Cl ST3 . . . . **74** A2
Yarnfield La ST15 . . . . . **119** B8
Yarrow Cl
Burton u T DE15 . . . . . . **167** B2
Walsall WS3 . . . . **244** A5
Yateley Cl ST2 . . . . **58** B2
Yates Croft B74 . . . . . . **257** F6
Yates Ind Est WS3 . . . . . **227** F2
Yates St ST1 . . . . **282** A2
Yaxley Ct ST5 . . . . **71** B2
Yaxley Pl ST3 . . . . **88** F6
Yeadon Gdns WV3 . . . . . **265** D8
Yeager Ct ST15 . . . . **118** F6
Yeaman St ST4 . . . . **72** B6
Yeatsall Rd WS15 . . . . . **160** E5
Yeldham Pl ST3 . . . . **88** F6
Yelt La DE6 . . . . **127** D8
Yelverton Ave ST17 . . . . **175** D8
Yelverton Cl WS3 . . . . . **243** B4
Yemscroft WS6 . . . . **243** A8
Yenton Cl B78 . . . . **250** A1
Yeoman Ind Est DE14 . . . **166** E5
Yeoman Way WS15 . . . . **198** A4
Yeovil Pl ST3 . . . . **88** F6
Yeovilton B79 . . . . **250** C8
Yerley Hill DE6 . . . . **66** C5

Yew Cl WS15 . . . . **198** B4
Yew Pl ST5 . . . . **55** D8
Yew Tree Ave
Lichfield WS14 . . . . **231** E8
Stoke-on-T ST3 . . . . **72** E2
Yew Tree Cl
Derrington ST18 . . . . . . **154** E2
Norton Canes WS11 . . . . **228** A5
Stoke-on-T ST2 . . . . **43** D1
Yewtree Cres DE15 . . . . **185** F7
Yew Tree Ct ST17 . . . . . **174** E4
Yew Tree Dr ST19 . . . . . **205** C6
Yew Tree Gdns WV8 . . . **239** A4
Yew Tree La Astbury CW12 . **15** C3
Bridgemere CW5 . . . . . . **67** A6
Wolverhampton WV6 . . . **255** A5
Yew Tree Pl WS3 . . . . . . **243** D3
Yew Tree Rd
Pattingham WV6 . . . . . . **253** D2
Rugeley WS15 . . . . **196** F6
Yewtree Rd DE11 . . . . . **186** F7
Yew Tree Rd WS4 . . . . . **244** B1
Yew Tree Terr ST7 . . . . . **41** A8
York Ave Fulford ST11 . . . **90** E1
Wolverhampton WV3 . . . **255** E1
York Cl Biddulph ST8 . . . . **16** C2
Forsbrook ST11 . . . . **91** B8
Lichfield WS13 . . . . **214** C3
Rugeley WS15 . . . . **196** D6
Talke ST7 . . . . **40** D7
York Cres
Stourbridge DY8 . . . . . . **279** D7
Wolverhampton WV3 . . . **255** E1
Yorkdale Cl DY3 . . . . . . **271** D3
York Gdns WV3 . . . . **255** E1
York Pl ST5 . . . . **283** B3
York Rd Cannock WS11 . . . **226** F7
Meir ST3 . . . . **74** B3
Stafford ST17 . . . . **175** B8
Wolverhampton WV3 . . . **265** B6
Yorksand Rd B78 . . . . . . **260** F8
Yorkshire Way WS7 . . . . **229** F8
York St Burton u T DE14 . . **166** C4
Hanley ST1 . . . . **282** B3
Leek ST13 . . . . **30** F6
Newcastle-u-L ST5 . . . . **283** D1
Stone ST15 . . . . **105** A2
Youlgreave Ave ST2 . . . . **58** B2
Youlton Pl ST2 . . . . **58** B2
Young Ave ST16 . . . . . . **155** C6
Younger St ST4 . . . . **72** D6
Young St Cheadle ST10 . . . **76** E3
Stoke-on-T ST6 . . . . **41** F6
Yoxall Ave ST4 . . . . **71** F8
Yoxall Rd
King's Bromley DE13 . . . **199** D7
Newborough DE13 . . . . **162** E7

Z

Zamenhof Gr ST6 . . . . . . **42** C1
Zennor Gr ST2 . . . . **58** B2
Zetland Pl ST3 . . . . **88** F6
Zetland Wlk ST3 . . . . **88** F6
Zion Cl WS6 . . . . **226** D3
Zion St ST6 . . . . **57** A8
Zoar St DY3 . . . . **271** C3
Zodiac Dr ST6 . . . . **41** E6
Zouche Cl DY8 . . . . **279** E8